CORPORATIONS AND BUSINESS ASSOCIATIONS

Statutes, Rules, Materials, and Forms

1997 Edition

Selected and edited by

MELVIN ARON EISENBERG
Koret Professor of Law,
University of California at Berkeley

Westbury, New York
THE FOUNDATION PRESS, INC.
1997

TEXT IS PRINTED ON 10% POST CONSUMER RECYCLED PAPER

PREFACE

This Supplement is designed to provide students with the essential statutory provisions, rules, materials and forms needed in courses in Corporations and Business Associations, and to give students a hand's-on grasp of the tools with which the profession works in these areas.

This Supplement is comprised of state and federal statutes and rules; extensive excerpts from Restatement (Second) of Agency; the virtually complete text of the ALI's Principles of Corporate Governance together with selected Comments; selected forms; and other materials.

In general, the federal materials have been edited much more heavily than the state materials, because much of the federal material is more relevant to courses in Securities Regulation than to courses in Corporations and Business Associations. The aim of the editing of the federal materials has been to preserve the substance and the flow of the material, but to winnow out details that are unnecessary for the study of corporation law.

The following conventions have been used in the preparation of this Supplement:

(1) Omissions within a statutory section, rule, form, official comment, instruction, note, or other material are indicated by ellipses (. . .). The omission of an entire statutory section, rule, form, official comment, instruction, or note is not so indicated. However, in the case of the Delaware statute, the Revised Model Business Corporation Act, the Uniform Partnership Act, the Revised Uniform Partnership Act (1995), the Uniform Limited Partnership Act, the Securities Act, and the Securities Exchange Act, the Delaware Limited Liablity Company Act, and the Uniform Limited Liability Company Act, the omission of an entire section is indicated in the Table of Contents by an asterisk following the title of the omitted section.

(2) Editorial insertions in the text are indicated by brackets. In some cases, an official text itself includes bracketed material, but the context usually makes clear whether bracketed material consists of editorial insertions or original text.

(3) Sections of the securities acts have been numbered serially, beginning with Section 1, rather than with the number-and-letter combinations used in the United States Code. Rules and forms under those acts have been numbered without the prefatory Part numbers that appear in the Code of Federal Regulations.

_____

I thank the authors, publishers and copyrightholders who permitted me to reprint all or portions of the following works:

PREFACE

American Bar Association, Section of Business Law, Committee on Corporate Laws, Revised Model Business Corporation Act.

American Bar Foundation, Commentaries on Model Debenture and Indenture Provisions (1971).

American Law Institute, Restatement (Second) of Agency and Principles of Corporate Governance: Analysis and Recommendations.

Aspen Law & Business, Model Business Corporation Act Annotated.

R. F. Balotti and J. Finkelstein, The Delaware Law of Corporations and Business Organizations (2d ed. 1990).

Robert R. Keatinge, Form of Operating Agreement of Limited Liability Company.

National Conference of Commissioners on Uniform State Laws, Uniform Limited Liability Company Act (1995), Uniform Partnership Act, Revised Uniform Limited Partnership Act (1995), and Revised Uniform Limited Partnership Act.

MELVIN A. EISENBERG

May, 1997

iv

TABLE OF CONTENTS

TABLE OF CONTENTS

CORPORATIONS AND BUSINESS ASSOCIATIONS

Statutes, Rules, Materials, and Forms

*

RESTATEMENT (SECOND) OF AGENCY

(Selected Sections)

Chapter 1

INTRODUCTORY MATTERS

TOPIC 1. DEFINITIONS

TOPIC 3. ESSENTIAL CHARACTERISTICS OF RELATION

TOPIC 4. AGENCY DISTINGUISHED FROM OTHER RELATIONS

Chapter 2

CREATION OF RELATION

TOPIC 1. MUTUAL CONSENT AND CONSIDERATION

TOPIC 3. CAPACITY OF PARTIES TO RELATION

Chapter 3

CREATION AND INTERPRETATION OF AUTHORITY AND APPARENT AUTHORITY

TOPIC 1. METHODS OF MANIFESTING CONSENT

Chapter 7

LIABILITY OF PRINCIPAL TO THIRD PERSON; TORTS

TOPIC 2. LIABILITY FOR AUTHORIZED CONDUCT OR CONDUCT INCIDENTAL THERETO

TITLE B. TORTS OF SERVANTS

Who is a servant

Scope of employment

TITLE C. AGENTS' TORTS—LIABILITY NOT DEPENDENT UPON RELATION OF MASTER AND SERVANT

In general

Chapter 10

LIABILITY OF THIRD PERSON TO PRINCIPAL

TOPIC 1. CONTRACTS; DISCLOSED AGENCY

TOPIC 2. CONTRACTS; UNDISCLOSED AGENCY

TOPIC 5. EFFECT OF RATIFICATION

Chapter 11

LIABILITY OF AGENT TO THIRD PERSONS

TOPIC 1. CONTRACTS AND CONVEYANCES

TITLE A. AGENT A PARTY TO A TRANSACTION CONDUCTED BY HIMSELF

TITLE B. AGENT NOT PARTY TO TRANSACTION CONDUCTED BY HIMSELF

TITLE C. DEFENSES AND EFFECTS OF SUBSEQUENT EVENTS

Chapter 13

DUTIES AND LIABILITIES OF AGENT TO PRINCIPAL

TOPIC 1. DUTIES

TITLE B. DUTIES OF SERVICE AND OBEDIENCE

TITLE C. DUTIES OF LOYALTY

TOPIC 2. LIABILITIES

Chapter 14

DUTIES AND LIABILITIES OF PRINCIPAL TO AGENT

TOPIC 1. CONTRACTUAL AND RESTITUTIONAL DUTIES AND LIABILITIES

TITLE A. INTERPRETATION OF CONTRACTS AND LIABILITIES THEREUNDER

Chapter 1

INTRODUCTORY MATTERS

TOPIC 1. DEFINITIONS

§ 1. Agency; Principal; Agent

(1) Agency is the fiduciary relation which results from the manifestation of consent by one person to another that the other shall act on his behalf and subject to his control, and consent by the other so to act.

(2) The one for whom action is to be taken is the principal.

(3) The one who is to act is the agent.

§ 2. Master; Servant; Independent Contractor

(1) A master is a principal who employs an agent to perform service in his affairs and who controls or has the right to control the physical conduct of the other in the performance of the service.

(2) A servant is an agent employed by a master to perform service in his affairs whose physical conduct in the performance of the service is controlled or is subject to the right to control by the master.

(3) An independent contractor is a person who contracts with another to do something for him but who is not controlled by the other nor subject to the other's right to control with respect to his physical conduct in the performance of the undertaking. He may or may not be an agent.

Comment:

a. Servants and non-servant agents. A master is a species of principal, and a servant is a species of agent....

b. Servant contrasted with independent contractor. The word "servant" is used in contrast with "independent contractor". The latter term includes all persons who contract to do something for another but who are not servants in doing the work undertaken.

6

An agent who is not a servant is, therefore, an independent contractor when he contracts to act on account of the principal. Thus, a broker who contracts to sell goods for his principal is an independent contractor as distinguished from a servant. Although, under some circumstances, the principal is bound by the broker's unauthorized contracts and representations, the principal is not liable to third persons for tangible harm resulting from his unauthorized physical conduct within the scope of the employment, as the principal would be for similar conduct by a servant; nor does the principal have the duties or immunities of a master towards the broker. Although an agent who contracts to act and who is not a servant is therefore an independent contractor, not all independent contractors are agents. Thus, one who contracts for a stipulated price to build a house for another and who reserves no direction over the conduct of the work is an independent contractor; but he is not an agent, since he is not a fiduciary, has no power to make the one employing him a party to a transaction, and is subject to no control over his conduct.
. . .

   c. *Servants not necessarily menials.* As stated more fully in Section 220, the term servant does not denote menial or manual service. Many servants perform exacting work requiring intelligence rather than muscle. Thus the officers of a corporation or a ship, the interne in a hospital, all of whom give their time to their employers, are servants equally with the janitor and others performing manual labor. . . .

§ 3. General Agent; Special Agent

(1) A general agent is an agent authorized to conduct a series of transactions involving a continuity of service.

(2) A special agent is an agent authorized to conduct a single transaction or a series of transactions not involving continuity of service.

§ 4. Disclosed Principal; Partially Disclosed Principal; Undisclosed Principal

(1) If, at the time of a transaction conducted by an agent, the other party thereto has notice that the agent is acting for a principal and of the principal's identity, the principal is a disclosed principal.

(2) If the other party has notice that the agent is or may be acting for a principal but has no notice of the principal's identity, the principal for whom the agent is acting is a partially disclosed principal.

(3) If the other party has no notice that the agent is acting for a principal, the one for whom he acts is an undisclosed principal.

§ 7. Authority

Authority is the power of the agent to affect the legal relations of the principal by acts done in accordance with the principal's manifestations of consent to him.

§ 8. Apparent Authority

Apparent authority is the power to affect the legal relations of another person by transactions with third persons, professedly as agent for the other, arising from and in accordance with the other's manifestations to such third persons.

§ 8A. Inherent Agency Power

Inherent agency power is a term used in the restatement of this subject to indicate the power of an agent which is derived not from authority, apparent authority or estoppel, but solely from the agency relation and exists for the protection of persons harmed by or dealing with a servant or other agent.

§ 8B. Estoppel; Change of Position

(1) A person who is not otherwise liable as a party to a transaction purported to be done on his account, is nevertheless subject to liability to persons who have changed their positions because of their belief that the transaction was entered into by or for him, if

    (a) he intentionally or carelessly caused such belief, or

    (b) knowing of such belief and that others might change their positions because of it, he did not take reasonable steps to notify them of the facts.

(2) An owner of property who represents to third persons that another is the owner of the property or who permits the other so to represent, or who realizes that third persons believe that another is the owner of the property, and that he could easily inform the third persons of the facts, is subject to the loss of the property if the other disposes of it to third persons who, in ignorance of the facts, purchase the property or otherwise change their position with reference to it.

(3) Change of position, as the phrase is used in the restatement of this subject, indicates payment of money, expenditure of labor, suffering a loss or subjection to legal liability.

TOPIC 3. ESSENTIAL CHARACTERISTICS OF RELATION

§ 13. Agent as a Fiduciary

An agent is a fiduciary with respect to matters within the scope of his agency.

§ 14. Control by Principal

A principal has the right to control the conduct of the agent with respect to matters entrusted to him.

TOPIC 4. AGENCY DISTINGUISHED FROM OTHER RELATIONS

§ 14H. Agents or Holders of a Power Given for Their Benefit

One who holds a power created in the form of an agency authority, but given for the benefit of the power holder or of a third person, is not an agent of the one creating the power.

§ 14O. Security Holder Becoming a Principal

A creditor who assumes control of his debtor's business for the mutual benefit of himself and his debtor, may become a principal, with liability for the acts and transactions of the debtor in connection with the business.

Chapter 2

CREATION OF RELATION

TOPIC 1. MUTUAL CONSENT AND CONSIDERATION

§ 15. Manifestations of Consent

An agency relation exists only if there has been a manifestation by the principal to the agent that the agent may act on his account, and consent by the agent so to act.

TOPIC 3. CAPACITY OF PARTIES TO RELATION

§ 23. Agent Having Interests Adverse to Principal

One whose interests are adverse to those of another can be authorized to act on behalf of the other; it is a breach of duty for him so to act without revealing the existence and extent of such adverse interests.

Chapter 3

CREATION AND INTERPRETATION OF AUTHORITY AND APPARENT AUTHORITY

TOPIC 1.   METHODS OF MANIFESTING CONSENT

§ 26.   Creation of Authority: General Rule

Except for the execution of instruments under seal or for the performance of transactions required by statute to be authorized in a particular way, authority to do an act can be created by written or spoken words or other conduct of the principal which, reasonably interpreted, causes the agent to believe that the principal desires him so to act on the principal's account.

§ 27.   Creation of Apparent Authority: General Rule

Except for the execution of instruments under seal or for the conduct of transactions required by statute to be authorized in a particular way, apparent authority to do an act is created as to a third person by written or spoken words or any other conduct of the principal which, reasonably interpreted, causes the third person to believe that the principal consents to have the act done on his behalf by the person purporting to act for him.

TOPIC 2.   INTERPRETATION OF AUTHORITY AND APPARENT AUTHORITY

TITLE A.   AUTHORITY

§ 32.   Applicability of Rules for Interpretation of Agreements

Except to the extent that the fiduciary relation between principal and agent requires special rules, the rules for the interpretation of contracts apply to the interpretation of authority.

§ 33.   General Principle of Interpretation

An agent is authorized to do, and to do only, what it is reasonable for him to infer that the principal desires him to do in the light of the principal's manifestations and the facts as he knows or should know them at the time he acts.

Comment:

a. Authority an ambulatory power. The agency relation is normally the result of a contract and is always the result of an agreement between the parties. For the purpose of interpreting the words used, the effect of customs and all similar matters, the normal rules for the interpretation of contracts are applicable, as stated in Section 32. Nevertheless, an agreement creating an agency relation has elements different from those of other contracts. The implicit, basic understanding of the parties to the agency relation is that the agent is to act only in accordance with the principal's desires as manifested to him.... Whatever the original agreement or authority may have been, he is authorized at any given moment to do, and to do only, what he reasonably believes the principal desires him to do, in the light of what he knows or should know of the principal's purpose and the existing circumstances....

Illustrations:

1. P, a mill owner, directs A, his purchasing agent, to purchase a large quantity of raw material, to be used in executing an order for goods. The following day the order for goods is rescinded, as A learns. Without inquiry as to whether or not P still wishes the material, A has no authority to purchase the raw material.

2. P, the owner of a factory running on half time for lack of orders, before leaving for his vacation, directs his purchasing agent to "put in our usual monthly coal supply of 1000 tons." The following day a large order comes in which will immediately put the factory on full running time. It may be found that A is authorized to purchase sufficient coal to keep the factory running, this depending upon whether or not P can easily be reached, the amount of discretion usually given to A, the condition of P's bank balance, and other factors.

3. Same facts as in Illustration 2, except that P is present when the large order is received. A has no authority to order more than 1000 tons.

b. Authority distinct from contract of agency. An agent is a fiduciary under a duty to obey the will of the principal as he knows it or should know it. This will may change, either with or without a change in events. Whatever it is at any given time, if the agent has reason to know it, his duty is not to act contrary to it. The fact that in changing his mind the principal is violating his contract with the agent does not diminish the agent's duty of obedience to it. Hence the rule applicable to the interpretation of authority must be as flexible as the will of the principal may be. Thus, whether or not the agent is authorized to do a particular act at a particular time depends, not only on what the principal told the agent, but upon a great variety of other factors, including changes in the situation after the instructions were given. The interpretation of authority, therefore, differs in this respect from the interpretation of a contract, even the contract of agency.

The agent's authority may therefore be increased, diminished, become dormant or be destroyed, not only by further manifestations by the principal but also by the happening of events, dependent, in many situations, upon what the agent knows or should know as to the principal's purposes. This does not mean that the agent can do anything merely because he believes it to be of advantage to the principal. Nor does it mean that the agent is authorized to act if he believes the principal would authorize him to act if he knew the facts. The agent's scope of authority is limited to the authorized subject matter and the kind of transaction contemplated. An agent of a dealer in property, whose function is limited to selling, is not authorized to buy property even if he reasonably believes the principal would authorize its purchase if he knew of the opportunity. The ordinary store manager, in the absence of an emergency, is not authorized to borrow, even though he knows the principal would welcome the opportunity.

It is in accordance with this continuous comparison between the communication to the agent and the circumstances under which he acts, that his authority may broaden ... or may be diminished, suspended or terminated ..., however irrevocable the terms in which the authority is expressed. Whether or not the principal is liable for a breach of contract for revoking the authority, nevertheless he can do so.... Further, because the agent is under a duty to protect the principal's interests within the authorized field, if the circumstances are or become ambiguous, either intrinsically or because of extrinsic facts, and he cannot communicate with the principal, the agent is authorized to act reasonably in accordance with the facts as he knows or should know them....

§ 35. When Incidental Authority Is Inferred

Unless otherwise agreed, authority to conduct a transaction includes authority to do acts which are incidental to it, usually accompany it, or are reasonably necessary to accomplish it.

§ 39. Inference That Agent Is to Act Only for Principal's Benefit

Unless otherwise agreed, authority to act as agent includes only authority to act for the benefit of the principal.

§ 43. Acquiescence by Principal in Agent's Conduct

(1) Acquiescence by the principal in conduct of an agent whose previously conferred authorization reasonably might include it, indicates

that the conduct was authorized; if clearly not included in the authorization, acquiescence in it indicates affirmance.

(2) Acquiescence by the principal in a series of acts by the agent indicates authorization to perform similar acts in the future.

TITLE B. APPARENT AUTHORITY

§ 49. Interpretation of Apparent Authority Compared with Interpretation of Authority

The rules applicable to the interpretation of authority are applicable to the interpretation of apparent authority except that:

(a) manifestations of the principal to the other party to the transaction are interpreted in light of what the other party knows or should know instead of what the agent knows or should know . . . .

. . .

Chapter 4

RATIFICATION

TOPIC 1. DEFINITIONS

§ 82. Ratification

Ratification is the affirmance by a person of a prior act which did not bind him but which was done or professedly done on his account, whereby the act, as to some or all persons, is given effect as if originally authorized by him.

§ 83. Affirmance

Affirmance is either

(a) a manifestation of an election by one on whose account an unauthorized act has been done to treat the act as authorized, or

(b) conduct by him justifiable only if there were such an election.

TOPIC 2. WHEN AFFIRMANCE RESULTS IN RATIFICATION

§ 84. What Acts Can Be Ratified

(1) An act which, when done, could have been authorized by a purported principal, or if an act of service by an intended principal, can be ratified if, at the time of affirmance, he could authorize such an act.

(2) An act which, when done, the purported or intended principal could not have authorized, he cannot ratify, except an act affirmed by a

legal representative whose appointment relates back to or before the time of such act.

§ 85. Purporting to Act as Agent as a Requisite for Ratification

(1) Ratification does not result from the affirmance of a transaction with a third person unless the one acting purported to be acting for the ratifier.

(2) An act of service not involving a transaction with a third person is subject to ratification if, but only if, the one doing the act intends or purports to perform it as the servant of another.

§ 87. Who Can Affirm

To become effective as ratification, the affirmance must be by the person identified as the principal at the time of the original act or, if no person was then identified, by the one for whom the agent intended to act.

§ 88. Affirmance After Withdrawal of Other Party or Other Termination of Original Transaction

To constitute ratification, the affirmance of a transaction must occur before the other party has manifested his withdrawal from it either to the purported principal or to the agent, and before the offer or agreement has otherwise terminated or been discharged.

§ 89. Affirmance After Change of Circumstances

If the affirmance of a transaction occurs at a time when the situation has so materially changed that it would be inequitable to subject the other party to liability thereon, the other party has an election to avoid liability.

§ 90. Affirmance After Rights Have Crystallized

If an act to be effective in creating a right against another or to deprive him of a right must be performed before a specific time, an affirmance is not effective against the other unless made before such time.

TOPIC 3. WHAT CONSTITUTES AFFIRMANCE

§ 93. Methods and Formalities of Affirmance

(1) Except as stated in Subsection (2), affirmance can be established by any conduct of the purported principal manifesting that he consents to be a party to the transaction, or by conduct justifiable only if there is ratification.

(2) Where formalities are requisite for the authorization of an act, its affirmance must be by the same formalities in order to constitute a ratification.

(3) The affirmance can be made by an agent authorized so to do.

§ 94. Failure to Act as Affirmance

An affirmance of an unauthorized transaction can be inferred from a failure to repudiate it.

§ 97. Bringing Suit or Basing Defense as Affirmance

There is affirmance if the purported principal, with knowledge of the facts, in an action in which the third person or the purported agent is an adverse party:

(a) brings suit to enforce promises which were part of the unauthorized transaction or to secure interests which were the fruit of such transaction and to which he would be entitled only if the act had been authorized; or

(b) bases a defense upon the unauthorized transaction as though it were authorized; or

(c) continues to maintain such suit or base such defense.

§ 98. Receipt of Benefits as Affirmance

The receipt by a purported principal, with knowledge of the facts, of something to which he would not be entitled unless an act purported to be done for him were affirmed, and to which he makes no claim except through such act, constitutes an affirmance unless at the time of such receipt he repudiates the act. If he repudiates the act, his receipt of benefits constitutes an affirmance at the election of the other party to the transaction.

§ 99. Retention of Benefits as Affirmance

The retention by a purported principal, with knowledge of the facts and before he has changed his position, of something which he is not entitled to retain unless an act purported to be done on his account is affirmed, and to which he makes no claim except through such act, constitutes an affirmance unless at the time of such retention he repudiates the act. Even if he repudiates the act, his retention constitutes an affirmance at the election of the other party to the transaction.

TOPIC 4. LIABILITIES

§ 100. Effect of Ratification; In General

[T]he liabilities resulting from ratification are the same as those resulting from authorization if, between the time when the original act was performed and when it was affirmed, there has been no change in the capacity of the principal or third person or in the legality of authorizing or performing the original act.

§ 100A. Relation Back in Time and Place

The liabilities of the parties to a ratified act or contract are determined in accordance with the law governing the act or contract at the time and place it was done or made. Whether the conduct of the purported principal is an affirmance depends upon the law at the time and place when and where the principal consents or acts.

Chapter 5

TERMINATION OF AGENCY POWERS

TOPIC 1. TERMINATION OF AUTHORITY

TITLE B. TERMINATION BY MUTUAL CONSENT, REVOCATION, OR RENUNCIATION

§ 118. Revocation or Renunciation

Authority terminates if the principal or the agent manifests to the other dissent to its continuance.

Comment:

a. Such termination by act of the principal is revocation; by act of the agent, it is renunciation.

b. *Power to revoke or renounce.* The principal has power to revoke and the agent has power to renounce, although doing so is in violation of a contract between the parties and although the authority is expressed to be irrevocable. A statement in a contract that the authority cannot be terminated by either party is effective only to create liability for its wrongful termination.

Illustrations:

1. In consideration of A's agreement to advertise and give his best energies to the sale of Blackacre, its owner, P, grants to A "a power of attorney, irrevocable for one year" to sell it. A advertises and spends time trying to sell Blackacre. At the end of three months P informs A that he revokes. A's authority is terminated.

2. In consideration of $1000 and A's promise to endeavor to sell, P grants to A for a period of one year a power of attorney to sell property, with compensation at 25 per cent. of the selling price, the power of attorney ending with this phrase: "Hereby intending and agreeing that this power shall be irrevocable during one year, and that during this period A shall have a power coupled with an interest which shall not be affected by

my death or other circumstances.'' At the end of three months P informs A that he revokes. A's authority is terminated.

Comment:

    c. Liabilities. If there is a contract between principal and agent that the authority shall not be revoked or renounced, a party who revokes or renounces, unless privileged by the conduct of the other or by supervening circumstances, is subject to liability to the other. . . .

    d. Non-agency powers. A power in the form of an agency authority given for the protection of a person described as an agent, but who is not one, is not an agency authority and cannot be revoked by the power giver; if such a power is held for the benefit of a third person, it can be terminated neither by revocation nor renunciation. See § 139. . . .

. . .

TOPIC 5.   TERMINATION OF POWERS GIVEN AS SECURITY

§ 138.   Definition

    A power given as security is a power to affect the legal relations of another, created in the form of an agency authority, but held for the benefit of the power holder or a third person and given to secure the performance of a duty or to protect a title, either legal or equitable, such power being given when the duty or title is created or given for consideration.

Comment:

    a. A power given as security arises when a person manifests consent that the one to whom it is given can properly act to create liability against him, or to dispose of some of his interests, or to perfect or otherwise protect a title already in the power holder or in the person for whom he is to act. If the power is given as security for the performance of a duty, it must be supported by consideration, but consideration is not necessary if the power is in aid of and accompanies a transfer of a title to the power holder.

    b. Distinguished from authority. A power given as security is one held for the benefit of a person other than the power giver. . . .

. . .

§ 139.   Termination of Powers Given as Security

    (1) Unless otherwise agreed, a power given as security is not terminated by:

        (a) revocation by the creator of the power;

(b) surrender by the holder of the power, if he holds for the benefit of another;

(c) the loss of capacity during the lifetime of either the creator of the power or the holder of the power; or

(d) the death of the holder of the power, or, if the power is given as security for a duty which does not terminate at the death of the creator of the power, by his death.

(2) A power given as security is terminated by its surrender by the beneficiary, if of full capacity; or by the happening of events which, by its terms, discharges the obligations secured by it, or which makes its execution illegal or impossible.

Chapter 6

LIABILITY OF PRINCIPAL TO THIRD PERSONS; CONTRACTS AND CONVEYANCES

TOPIC 1.   GENERAL PRINCIPLES

§ 140.   Liability Based Upon Agency Principles

The liability of the principal to a third person upon a transaction conducted by an agent, or the transfer of his interests by an agent, may be based upon the fact that:

(a) the agent was authorized;

(b) the agent was apparently authorized; or

(c) the agent had a power arising from the agency relation and not dependent upon authority or apparent authority.

§ 143.   Effect of Ratification

Upon ratification with knowledge of the material facts, the principal becomes responsible for contracts and conveyances made for him by one purporting to act on his account as if the transaction had been authorized, if there has been no supervening loss of capacity by the principal or change in the law which would render illegal the authorization or performance of such a transaction.

TOPIC 2.   DISCLOSED OR PARTIALLY DISCLOSED PRINCIPAL

TITLE A.   CREATION OF LIABILITY BY AUTHORIZED ACTS

§ 144.   General Rule

A disclosed or partially disclosed principal is subject to liability upon contracts made by an agent acting within his authority if made in proper form and with the understanding that the principal is a party.

TITLE C.   CREATION OF LIABILITY BY UNAUTHORIZED ACTS

§ 159. Apparent Authority

A disclosed or partially disclosed principal is subject to liability upon contracts made by an agent acting within his apparent authority if made in proper form and with the understanding that the apparent principal is a party. The rules as to the liability of a principal for authorized acts, are applicable to unauthorized acts which are apparently authorized.

§ 160. Violation of Secret Instructions

A disclosed or partially disclosed principal authorizing an agent to make a contract, but imposing upon him limitations as to incidental terms intended not to be revealed, is subject to liability upon a contract made in violation of such limitations with a third person who has no notice of them.

§ 161. Unauthorized Acts of General Agent

A general agent for a disclosed or partially disclosed principal subjects his principal to liability for acts done on his account which usually accompany or are incidental to transactions which the agent is authorized to conduct if, although they are forbidden by the principal, the other party reasonably believes that the agent is authorized to do them and has no notice that he is not so authorized.

§ 161A. Unauthorized Acts of Special Agents

A special agent for a disclosed or partly disclosed principal has no power to bind his principal by contracts or conveyances which he is not authorized or apparently authorized to make, unless the principal is estopped, or unless:

> (a) the agent's only departure from his authority or apparent authority is
>
>> i.   in naming or disclosing the principal, or
>>
>> ii.   in having an improper motive, or
>>
>> iii.   in being negligent in determining the facts upon which his authority is based, or
>>
>> iv.   in making misrepresentations; or
>
> (b) the agent is given possession of goods or commercial documents with authority to deal with them.

TITLE D.   DEFENSES AND LIABILITY AFFECTED BY SUBSEQUENT EVENTS

§ 179.   Rights Between Third Person and Agent

Unless otherwise agreed, the liability of a disclosed or partially disclosed principal is not affected by any rights or liabilities existing between the other party and the agent at the time the contract is made.

§ 180.   Defenses of Principal—In General

A disclosed or partially disclosed principal is entitled to all defenses arising out of a transaction between his agent and a third person. He is not entitled to defenses which are personal to the agent.

TOPIC 3.   UNDISCLOSED PRINCIPAL

TITLE A.   CREATION OF LIABILITY BY AUTHORIZED ACTS

§ 186.   General Rule

An undisclosed principal is bound by contracts and conveyances made on his account by an agent acting within his authority, except that the principal is not bound by a contract which is under seal or which is negotiable, or upon a contract which excludes him.

TITLE B.   CREATION OF LIABILITY BY UNAUTHORIZED ACTS

§ 194.   Acts of General Agents

A general agent for an undisclosed principal authorized to conduct transactions subjects his principal to liability for acts done on his account, if usual or necessary in such transactions, although forbidden by the principal to do them.

§ 195.   Acts of Manager Appearing to Be Owner

An undisclosed principal who entrusts an agent with the management of his business is subject to liability to third persons with whom the agent enters into transactions usual in such businesses and on the principal's account, although contrary to the directions of the principal.

§ 195A.   Unauthorized Acts of Special Agents

A special agent for an undisclosed principal has no power to bind his principal by contracts or conveyances which he is not authorized to make unless:

    (a) the agent's only departure from his authority is

        (i) in not disclosing his principal, or

        (ii) in having an improper motive, or

(iii) in being negligent in determining the facts upon which his authority is based, or

(iv) in making misrepresentations; or

(b) the agent is given possession of goods or commercial documents with authority to deal with them.

TITLE C. DEFENSES AND LIABILITY AFFECTED BY SUBSEQUENT EVENTS

§ 203. Defenses of Undisclosed Principal—In General

An undisclosed principal is entitled to all defenses arising out of a transaction with an agent, but not defenses which are personal to the agent.

§ 205. Power of Agent to Modify Contract Before Disclosure of Principal

Until the existence of the principal is disclosed, an agent who has made a contract for an undisclosed principal has power to cancel the contract and to modify it with binding effect upon the principal if the contract or conveyance, as modified, is authorized or is within the inherent power of the agent to make.

Chapter 7

LIABILITY OF PRINCIPAL TO THIRD PERSON; TORTS

TOPIC 2. LIABILITY FOR AUTHORIZED CONDUCT OR CONDUCT INCIDENTAL THERETO

TITLE B. TORTS OF SERVANTS

§ 219. When Master is Liable for Torts of His Servants

(1) A master is subject to liability for the torts of his servants committed while acting in the scope of their employment.

(2) A master is not subject to liability for the torts of his servants acting outside the scope of their employment, unless:

(a) the master intended the conduct or the consequences, or

(b) the master was negligent or reckless, or

(c) the conduct violated a non-delegable duty of the master, or

(d) the servant purported to act or to speak on behalf of the principal and there was reliance upon apparent authority, or he was aided in accomplishing the tort by the existence of the agency relation.

WHO IS A SERVANT

§ 220.   Definition of Servant

(1) A servant is a person employed to perform services in the affairs of another and who with respect to the physical conduct in the performance of the services is subject to the other's control or right to control.

(2) In determining whether one acting for another is a servant or an independent contractor, the following matters of fact, among others, are considered:

(a) the extent of control which, by the agreement, the master may exercise over the details of the work;

(b) whether or not the one employed is engaged in a distinct occupation or business;

(c) the kind of occupation, with reference to whether, in the locality, the work is usually done under the direction of the employer or by a specialist without supervision;

(d) the skill required in the particular occupation;

(e) whether the employer or the workman supplies the instrumentalities, tools, and the place of work for the person doing the work;

(f) the length of time for which the person is employed;

(g) the method of payment, whether by the time or by the job;

(h) whether or not the work is a part of the regular business of the employer;

(i) whether or not the parties believe they are creating the relation of master and servant; and

(j) whether the principal is or is not in business.

SCOPE OF EMPLOYMENT

§ 228.   General Statement

(1) Conduct of a servant is within the scope of employment if, but only if:

(a) it is of the kind he is employed to perform;

(b) it occurs substantially within the authorized time and space limits;

(c) it is actuated, at least in part, by a purpose to serve the master, and

(d) if force is intentionally used by the servant against another, the use of force is not unexpectable by the master.

(2) Conduct of a servant is not within the scope of employment if it is different in kind from that authorized, far beyond the authorized time or space limits, or too little actuated by a purpose to serve the master.

§ 229. Kind of Conduct Within Scope of Employment

(1) To be within the scope of the employment, conduct must be of the same general nature as that authorized, or incidental to the conduct authorized.

(2) In determining whether or not the conduct, although not authorized, is nevertheless so similar to or incidental to the conduct authorized as to be within the scope of employment, the following matters of fact are to be considered:

    (a) whether or not the act is one commonly done by such servants;

    (b) the time, place and purpose of the act;

    (c) the previous relations between the master and the servant;

    (d) the extent to which the business of the master is apportioned between different servants;

    (e) whether or not the act is outside the enterprise of the master or, if within the enterprise, has not been entrusted to any servant;

    (f) whether or not the master has reason to expect that such an act will be done;

    (g) the similarity in quality of the act done to the act authorized;

    (h) whether or not the instrumentality by which the harm is done has been furnished by the master to the servant;

    (i) the extent of departure from the normal method of accomplishing an authorized result; and

    (j) whether or not the act is seriously criminal.

§ 230. Forbidden Acts

An act, although forbidden, or done in a forbidden manner, may be within the scope of employment.

§ 231. Criminal or Tortious Acts

An act may be within the scope of employment although consciously criminal or tortious.

TITLE C. AGENTS' TORTS—LIABILITY NOT DEPENDENT UPON RELATION OF MASTER AND SERVANT

IN GENERAL

§ 250. Non-liability for Physical Harm by Non-servant Agents

A principal is not liable for physical harm caused by the negligent physical conduct of a non-servant agent during the performance of the principal's business, if he neither intended nor authorized the result nor the manner of performance, unless he was under a duty to have the act performed with due care.

Chapter 10

LIABILITY OF THIRD PERSON TO PRINCIPAL

TOPIC 1. CONTRACTS; DISCLOSED AGENCY

§ 292. General Rule

The other party to a contract made by an agent for a disclosed or partially disclosed principal, acting within his authority, apparent authority or other agency power, is liable to the principal as if he had contracted directly with the principal, unless the principal is excluded as a party by the form or terms of the contract.

§ 298. Defenses of Other Party

The other party to a contract made by an agent on behalf of a disclosed or partially disclosed principal has all the defenses which he would have had against the principal if the principal had made the contract under the same circumstances.

§ 299. Rights Between Other Party and Agent

Unless otherwise agreed, the liability of the other party to a disclosed or partially disclosed principal upon a contract made by an agent is not affected by any rights or liabilities then existing between the other party and the agent.

TOPIC 2. CONTRACTS; UNDISCLOSED AGENCY

§ 302. General Rule

A person who makes a contract with an agent of an undisclosed principal, intended by the agent to be on account of his principal and within the power of such agent to bind his principal, is liable to the principal as if the principal himself had made the contract with him, unless he is excluded by the form or terms of the contract, unless his existence is fraudulently concealed or unless there is set-off or a similar defense against the agent.

§ 303. Principal Excluded From Transaction

A person with whom an agent makes a contract on account of an undisclosed principal is not liable in an action at law brought upon the contract by such principal:

(a) if the contract is in the form of a sealed or negotiable instrument; or

(b) if the terms of the contract exclude liability to any undisclosed principal or to the particular principal.

§ 306. Rights Between Other Party and Agent

(1) If the agent has been authorized to conceal the existence of the principal, the liability to an undisclosed principal of a person dealing with the agent within his power to bind the principal is diminished by any claim which such person may have against the agent at the time of making the contract and until the existence of the principal becomes known to him, if he could set off such claim in an action against the agent.

(2) If the agent is authorized only to contract in the principal's name, the other party does not have set-off for a claim due him from the agent unless the agent has been entrusted with the possession of chattels which he disposes of as directed or unless the principal has otherwise misled the third person into extending credit to the agent.

§ 308. Defenses of Other Party

In an action by an undisclosed principal against the other party to a contract, the other party has all the defenses, except those of a purely procedural nature:

(a) which he would have had against the principal if the principal had made the contract under the same circumstances,

(b) which he had against the agent until the discovery of the principal, unless the agent was authorized to contract only in the principal's name.

TOPIC 5.   EFFECT OF RATIFICATION

§ 319.   General Rule

Where a purported servant or other agent has entered into a transaction with a third person, its ratification by the purported master or other principal has the same effect upon the liabilities of the third person to the principal as an original authorization.

Chapter 11

LIABILITY OF AGENT TO THIRD PERSONS

TOPIC 1. CONTRACTS AND CONVEYANCES

TITLE A. AGENT A PARTY TO A TRANSACTION CONDUCTED BY HIMSELF

§ 320. Principal Disclosed

Unless otherwise agreed, a person making or purporting to make a contract with another as agent for a disclosed principal does not become a party to the contract.

§ 321. Principal Partially Disclosed

Unless otherwise agreed, a person purporting to make a contract with another for a partially disclosed principal is a party to the contract.

§ 322. Principal Undisclosed

An agent purporting to act upon his own account, but in fact making a contract on account of an undisclosed principal, is a party to the contract.

§ 326. Principal Known to Be Nonexistent or Incompetent

Unless otherwise agreed, a person who, in dealing with another, purports to act as agent for a principal whom both know to be nonexistent or wholly incompetent, becomes a party to such a contract.

Comment:

. . .

b. Promoters. The classic illustration of the rule stated in this Section is the promoter. When a promoter makes an agreement with another on behalf of a corporation to be formed, the following alternatives may represent the intent of the parties:

(1) They may understand that the other party is making a revocable offer to the nonexistent corporation which will result in a contract if the corporation is formed and accepts the offer prior to withdrawal. This is the normal understanding.

(2) They may understand that the other party is making an irrevocable offer for a limited time. Consideration to support the promise to keep the offer open can be found in an express or limited promise by the promoter to organize the corporation and use his best efforts to cause it to accept the offer.

(3) They may agree to a present contract by which the promoter is bound, but with an agreement that his liability terminates if the corporation is formed and manifests its willingness to become a party. There can be no ratification by the newly formed corporation, since it was not in existence when the agreement was made....

(4) They may agree to a present contract on which, even though the corporation becomes a party, the promoter remains liable either primarily or as surety for the performance of the corporation's obligation.

Which one of these possible alternatives, or variants thereof, is intended is a matter of interpretation on the facts of the individual case.

TITLE B.   AGENT NOT PARTY TO TRANSACTION CONDUCTED BY HIMSELF

§ 328. Liability of Authorized Agent for Performance of Contract

An agent, by making a contract only on behalf of a competent disclosed or partially disclosed principal whom he has power so to bind, does not thereby become liable for its nonperformance.

§ 329. Agent Who Warrants Authority

A person who purports to make a contract, conveyance or representation on behalf of another who has full capacity but whom he has no power to bind, thereby becomes subject to liability to the other party thereto upon an implied warranty of authority, unless he has manifested that he does not make such warranty or the other party knows that the agent is not so authorized.

§ 330. Liability for Misrepresentation of Authority

A person who tortiously misrepresents to another that he has authority to make a contract, conveyance, or representation on behalf of a principal whom he has no power to bind, is subject to liability to the other in an action of tort for loss caused by reliance upon such misrepresentation.

TITLE C.   DEFENSES AND EFFECTS OF SUBSEQUENT EVENTS

§ 333. Rights Between Other Party and Principal

Unless otherwise agreed, the liability of an agent upon a contract between a third person and the principal to which the agent is a party is not affected by any rights or liabilities existing between the third person and the principal not arising from the transaction, except that, with the consent of the principal, the agent can set off a claim which the principal would have in an action brought against him.

§ 334. Defenses of Agent—In General

In an action against an agent upon a contract between a third person and the principal to which the agent is a party, the agent has all the defenses which arise out of the transaction itself and also those which he has personally against the third person; defenses which are personal to the principal are not available to the agent.

§ 335. Agent Surety for Principal

In an action brought against an agent upon a contract to which the agent is a party but under which the primary duty of performance rests upon the principal, the agent has the defenses available to a surety.

§ 336. Election by Other Party to Hold Principal; Agency Disclosed

Unless otherwise agreed, the agent of a disclosed or partially disclosed principal who is a party to a contract made by another with such principal is not relieved from liability upon the contract by the determination of the other party to look to the principal alone, nor, unless the agent and the principal are joint contractors, by the fact that the other gets a judgment against the principal. He is relieved from liability to the extent that he is prejudiced thereby if he changes his position in justifiable reliance upon a manifestation of the other that he will look solely to the principal for performance.

§ 337. Election by Other Party to Hold Principal; Agency Undisclosed

An agent who has made a contract on behalf of an undisclosed principal is not relieved from liability by the determination of the other party thereto to look to the principal alone for the performance of the contract. He is discharged from liability if the other obtains a judgment against the principal, or, to the extent that he is prejudiced thereby, if he changes his position in justifiable reliance upon the other's manifestation that he will look solely to the principal for payment.

Chapter 13

DUTIES AND LIABILITIES OF AGENT TO PRINCIPAL

TOPIC 1. DUTIES

TITLE B. DUTIES OF SERVICE AND OBEDIENCE

§ 377. Contractual Duties

A person who makes a contract with another to perform services as an agent for him is subject to a duty to act in accordance with his promise.

§ 379. Duty of Care and Skill

(1) Unless otherwise agreed, a paid agent is subject to a duty to the principal to act with standard care and with the skill which is standard in the locality for the kind of work which he is employed to perform and, in addition, to exercise any special skill that he has.

(2) Unless otherwise agreed, a gratuitous agent is under a duty to the principal to act with the care and skill which is required of persons not agents performing similar gratuitous undertakings for others.

TITLE C. DUTIES OF LOYALTY

§ 387. General Principle

Unless otherwise agreed, an agent is subject to a duty to his principal to act solely for the benefit of the principal in all matters connected with his agency.

§ 388. Duty to Account for Profits Arising Out of Employment

Unless otherwise agreed, an agent who makes a profit in connection with transactions conducted by him on behalf of the principal is under a duty to give such profit to the principal.

Comment:

a. Ordinarily, the agent's primary function is to make profits for the principal, and his duty to account includes accounting for any unexpected and incidental accretions whether or not received in violation of duty. Thus, an agent who, without the knowledge of the principal, receives something in connection with, or because of, a transaction conducted for the principal, has a duty to pay this to the principal even though otherwise he has acted with perfect fairness to the principal and violates no duty of loyalty in receiving the amount. . . .

Illustrations:

1. A, a real estate broker acting for P, the seller, in order to assure himself of his commission, makes a contract with T, a purchaser, by which, if T cancels the contract with P, as he is given the right to do, T is to pay A the amount of A's commission. T repudiates the contract with P but pays A. A holds his commission as a constructive trustee for P.

2. P authorizes A to sell land held in A's name for a fixed sum. A makes a contract to sell the land to T, who makes a deposit which is to be forfeited if the transaction is not carried out. T forfeits the amount. A sells the land to another person at the price fixed by P. A is under a duty to account to P for the amount received from T. . . .

Comment:

b. Gratuities to agent. An agent can properly retain gratuities received on account of the principal's business if, because of custom or otherwise, an agreement to this effect is found. Except in such a case, the receipt and retention of a gratuity by an agent from a party with interests adverse to those of the principal is evidence that the agent is committing a breach of duty to the principal by not acting in his interests.

Illustrations:

4. A, the purchasing agent for the P railroad, purchases honestly and for a fair price fifty trucks from T, who is going out of business. In gratitude for A's favorable action and without ulterior motive or agreement, T makes A a gift of a car. A holds the automobile as a constructive trustee for P, although A is not otherwise liable to P. . . .

Comment:

c. Use of confidential information. An agent who acquires confidential information in the course of his employment or in violation of his duties has a duty not to use it to the disadvantage of the principal. . . . He also has a duty to account for any profits made by the use of such information, although this does not harm the principal. Thus, where a corporation has decided to operate an enterprise at a place where land values will be increased because of such operation, a corporate officer who takes advantage of his special knowledge to buy land in the vicinity is accountable for the profits he makes, even though such purchases have no adverse effect upon the enterprise. So, if he has "inside" information that the corporation is about to purchase or sell securities, or to declare or to pass a dividend, profits made by him in stock transactions undertaken because of his knowledge are held in constructive trust for the principal. He is also liable for profits made by selling confidential information to third persons, even though the principal is not adversely affected.

§ 389. Acting as Adverse Party Without Principal's Consent

Unless otherwise agreed, an agent is subject to a duty not to deal with his principal as an adverse party in a transaction connected with his agency without the principal's knowledge.

Comment:

a. The rule stated in this Section applies to transactions which the agent conducts for his principal, dealing therein with himself, and also to transactions in which the agent deals with his principal, who acts in person or through another agent; it is applicable to transactions in which the agent is acting entirely for himself and to those in which he has such a substantial interest that it reasonably might affect his judgment. Thus, an agent who is appointed to sell or to give advice concerning sales violates his duty if, without the principal's knowledge, he sells to himself or purchases from the principal through the medium of a "straw," or induces his principal to sell to a corporation in which he has a large concealed interest. . . .

. . .

c. Where no harm to principal. The rule stated in this Section is not based upon the existence of harm to the principal in the particular case. It exists to prevent a conflict of opposing interests in the minds of agents whose duty it is to act solely for the benefit of their principals. The rule applies, therefore, even though the transaction between the principal and the agent is beneficial to the principal. Thus, in the absence of a known custom or an agreement, an agent employed to sell at the market price cannot, without disclosure to the principal, properly buy the goods on his own account, even though he pays a higher price for them than the principal could obtain elsewhere. The rule applies also although the transaction is a public sale and the price received is above that stated by the principal to be adequate. Likewise, ordinarily, an agent appointed to buy or to sell at a fixed price violates his duty to the principal if, without the principal's acquiescence, he buys from or sells the specified article to himself at the specified price, even though it is impossible to obtain more or as much. However, if a broker is employed to sell property with an agreement that he is to retain all above a specified price, it may be inferred that the transaction gives him an option to purchase at that price without notice to the principal that he is acting for himself. . . .

. . .

§ 390. Acting as Adverse Party With Principal's Consent

An agent who, to the knowledge of the principal, acts on his own account in a transaction in which he is employed has a duty to deal fairly with the principal and to disclose to him all facts which the agent knows or should know would reasonably affect the principal's judgment, unless the principal has manifested that he knows such facts or that he does not care to know them.

Comment:

    a. Facts to be disclosed. One employed as agent violates no duty to the principal by acting for his own benefit if he makes a full disclosure of the facts to an acquiescent principal and takes no unfair advantage of him. Before dealing with the principal on his own account, however, an agent has a duty, not only to make no misstatements of fact, but also to disclose to the principal all relevant facts fully and completely. A fact is relevant if it is one which the agent should realize would be likely to affect the judgment of the principal in giving his consent to the agent to enter into the particular transaction on the specified terms. Hence, the disclosure must include not only the fact that the agent is acting on his own account (see § 389), but also all other facts which he should realize have or are likely to have a bearing upon the desirability of the transaction from the viewpoint of the principal. This includes, in the case of sales to him by the principal, not only the price which can be obtained, but also all facts affecting the desirability of sale, such as the likelihood of a higher price being obtained later, the possibilities of dealing with the property in another way, and all other matters which a disinterested and skillful agent advising the principal would think reasonably relevant.

    If the principal has limited business experience, an agent cannot properly fail to give such information merely because the principal says he does not care for it; the agent's duty of fair dealing is satisfied only if he reasonably believes that the principal understands the implications of the transaction.

Illustrations:

    1. P employs A to sell Blackacre for $1,000. A, having sought a customer, is unable to find one and reports such fact to P. He then states that he is willing to pay $1,000, telling P truthfully that he believes that a better sale might be made later in view of the chance that the locality will develop. A pays

P $1,000. A month later, A sells the land for $1,500. In the absence of other facts, A has violated no duty to P.

2. P employs A to purchase a suitable manufacturing site for him. A owns one which is suitable and sells it to P at the fair price of $25,000, telling P all relevant facts except that, a short time previously, he purchased the land for $15,000. The transaction can be rescinded by P . . . .

Comment:

c. Fairness. The agent must not take advantage of his position to persuade the principal into making a hard or improvident bargain. If the agent is one upon whom the principal naturally would rely for advice, the fact that the agent discloses that he is acting as an adverse party does not relieve him from the duty of giving the principal impartial advice based upon a carefully formed judgment as to the principal's interests. If he cannot or does not wish to do so, he has a duty to see that the principal secures the advice of a competent and disinterested third person. An agent who is in a close confidential relation to the principal, such as a family attorney, has the burden of proving that a substantial gift to him was not the result of undue influence. Even though an agent employed to sell is not in such a position, payment of less than the reasonable market value for property he buys from the principal is evidence that the bargain was unfair. If the principal is not in a dependent position, however, and the agent fully performs his duties of disclosure, a transaction of purchase and sale between them is not voidable merely because the principal receives an inadequate price or pays too great a price.

Illustrations:

4. P, a young physician with some inherited wealth and no business experience, places his property in charge of A to manage. Desiring a particular piece of land which represents a large share of P's assets, A waits until there is a slump in the price of land and, believing correctly that the slump is only temporary, suggests to P that it be sold, offering as an incentive that P's income from his profession will increase and that, although the price to be obtained is low, P can well afford to get more enjoyment from the proceeds now than from a larger amount later. P thereupon agrees to sell to A at a price which is as much as could be obtained at that time for the property. It may be found that A violated his duty of dealing fairly with P.

5. Same facts as in Illustration 4, except that A provides P with an independent experienced adviser, who gives disinterest-

ed advice, setting out the possibilities of accretion in values. It may be found that A has satisfied his duty of loyalty....

. . .

e. *Agreements for compensation.* A person is not ordinarily subject to a fiduciary duty in making terms as to compensation with a prospective principal....

. . .

§ 391. Acting for Adverse Party Without Principal's Consent

Unless otherwise agreed, an agent is subject to a duty to his principal not to act on behalf of an adverse party in a transaction connected with his agency without the principal's knowledge.

§ 392. Acting for Adverse Party With Principal's Consent

An agent who, to the knowledge of two principals, acts for both of them in a transaction between them, has a duty to act with fairness to each and to disclose to each all facts which he knows or should know would reasonably affect the judgment of each in permitting such dual agency, except as to a principal who has manifested that he knows such facts or does not care to know them.

§ 393. Competition as to Subject Matter of Agency

Unless otherwise agreed, an agent is subject to a duty not to compete with the principal concerning the subject matter of his agency.

§ 394. Acting for One With Conflicting Interests

Unless otherwise agreed, an agent is subject to a duty not to act or to agree to act during the period of his agency for persons whose interests conflict with those of the principal in matters in which the agent is employed.

§ 395. Using or Disclosing Confidential Information

Unless otherwise agreed, an agent is subject to a duty to the principal not to use or to communicate information confidentially given him by the principal or acquired by him during the course of or on account of his agency or in violation of his duties as agent, in competition with or to the injury of the principal, on his own account or on behalf of another, although such information does not relate to the transaction in which he is then employed, unless the information is a matter of general knowledge.

§ 396. Using Confidential Information After Termination of Agency

Unless otherwise agreed, after the termination of the agency, the agent:

(a) has no duty not to compete with the principal;

(b) has a duty to the principal not to use or to disclose to third persons, on his own account or on account of others, in competition with the principal or to his injury, trade secrets, written lists of names, or other similar confidential matters given to him only for the principal's use or acquired by the agent in violation of duty. The agent is entitled to use general information concerning the method of business of the principal and the names of the customers retained in his memory, if not acquired in violation of his duty as agent;

(c) has a duty to account for profits made by the sale or use of trade secrets and other confidential information, whether or not in competition with the principal;

(d) has a duty to the principal not to take advantage of a still subsisting confidential relation created during the prior agency relation.

TOPIC 2. LIABILITIES

§ 401. Liability for Loss Caused

An agent is subject to liability for loss caused to the principal by any breach of duty.

§ 403. Liability for Things Received in Violation of Duty of Loyalty

If an agent receives anything as a result of his violation of a duty of loyalty to the principal, he is subject to a liability to deliver it, its value, or its proceeds, to the principal.

§ 404. Liability for Use of Principal's Assets

An agent who, in violation of duty to his principal, uses for his own purposes or those of a third person assets of the principal's business is subject to liability to the principal for the value of the use. If the use predominates in producing a profit he is subject to liability, at the principal's election, for such profit; he is not, however, liable for profits made by him merely by the use of time which he has contracted to devote to the principal unless he violates his duty not to act adversely or in competition with the principal.

Comment:

a. The rule stated in this Section applies whether or not the agent uses the principal's facilities or other assets in competition with him. It applies irrespective of any harm done to the things used and irrespective of the use which the principal would have made of them.

Illustration:

> 1. P employs A to take care of the horses which P uses for driving purposes. P does not use them for a month and, during this period, without P's consent, A rents the horses to various persons who benefit the horses by the exercise thereby given them. A is subject to liability to P for the amount which he has received as rental.

Comment:

b. What are assets of the principal. The agent is subject to liability not only for the use of tangible things but also for the use of trade secrets, good-will, credit, and other intangible assets of the principal. Thus, an agent is subject to liability if, in selling his own goods, he uses the principal's trade-mark in territory in which the trade-mark is known but in which the principal does not sell and does not intend to sell similar goods.

Although the right to the services of an agent is a business asset of the principal, the agent's liability for profits made by his use of the principal's assets does not include a liability for profits made by him during hours which he should have devoted to the principal's service, unless he has thereby violated a fiduciary duty owed by him to the principal.

Illustration:

> 2. P employs A to give his full time to P as a bookkeeper. A uses portions of the time which he should have devoted to P's service in keeping the books for another employer, deriving thereby a greater salary than he receives from P. P cannot recover from A the amount of salary which A receives from the other employer.

c. Whether use of principal's assets predominates. Whether or not the use of assets of the principal predominates in producing a profit is a question of fact. Where an agent conducts a business upon the principal's premises, the location and facilities of the principal or the services of the agent may predominate in the creation of profits. If a ship captain uses the ship to carry heavy packages of his own, by selling which he makes a substantial profit, the owner is entitled to it; if the captain carries a box of trinkets for personal sale at ports of call, the ivory he thereby obtains does not necessarily go to the shipowner.

Illustration:

   3. A soldier uses his official uniform and position to smuggle forbidden goods into a friendly country and thereby makes large profits. The country by which he is employed is entitled to the profits.

Comment:

   d. *Other remedies of principal.* In addition to the rights which the principal has under the rule stated in this Section, the principal may have a cause of action for breach of contract or for a tort by the agent, or he may be entitled to a decree declaring a constructive trust in the specific proceeds of the use of an asset. These rights may be in the alternative or they may be cumulative, in accordance with the rules stated in Section 407. Thus, if the agent improperly uses the principal's chattels, the principal is entitled to recover their value, plus any damages caused to the business by their use, if the use amounts to a conversion; or he can recover the chattels in specie together with any profit which the agent has made from them, plus any damage to them or to the business caused by their use.

§ 407. Principal's Choice of Remedies

   (1) If an agent has received a benefit as a result of violating his duty of loyalty, the principal is entitled to recover from him what he has so received, its value, or its proceeds, and also the amount of damage thereby caused; except that, if the violation consists of the wrongful disposal of the principal's property, the principal cannot recover its value and also what the agent received in exchange therefor.

   (2) A principal who has recovered damages from a third person because of an agent's violation of his duty of loyalty is entitled nevertheless to obtain from the agent any profit which the agent improperly received as a result of the transaction.

Chapter 14

DUTIES AND LIABILITIES OF PRINCIPAL TO AGENT

TOPIC 1. CONTRACTUAL AND RESTITUTIONAL DUTIES AND LIABILITIES

TITLE A. INTERPRETATION OF CONTRACTS AND LIABILITIES THEREUNDER

§ 438. Duty of Indemnity; The Principle

   (1) A principal is under a duty to indemnify the agent in accordance with the terms of the agreement with him.

(2) In the absence of terms to the contrary in the agreement of employment, the principal has a duty to indemnify the agent where the agent

(a) makes a payment authorized or made necessary in executing the principal's affairs or, unless he is officious, one beneficial to the principal, or

(b) suffers a loss which, because of their relation, it is fair that the principal should bear.

§ 439. When Duty of Indemnity Exists

Unless otherwise agreed, a principal is subject to a duty to exonerate an agent who is not barred by the illegality of his conduct to indemnify him for:

(a) authorized payments made by the agent on behalf of the principal;

(b) payments upon contracts upon which the agent is authorized to make himself liable, and upon obligations arising from the possession or ownership of things which he is authorized to hold on account of the principal;

(c) payments of damages to third persons which he is required to make on account of the authorized performance of an act which constitutes a tort or a breach of contract;

(d) expenses of defending actions by third persons brought because of the agent's authorized conduct, such actions being unfounded but not brought in bad faith; and

(e) payments resulting in benefit to the principal, made by the agent under such circumstances that it would be inequitable for indemnity not to be made.

§ 440. When No Duty of Indemnity

Unless otherwise agreed, the principal is not subject to a duty to indemnify an agent:

(a) for pecuniary loss or other harm, not of benefit to the principal, arising from the performance of unauthorized acts or resulting solely from the agent's negligence or other fault; or

(b) if the principal has otherwise performed his duties to the agent, for physical harm caused by the performance of authorized acts, for harm suffered as a result of torts, other than the tortious institution of suits, committed upon the agent by third persons because of his employment, or for harm suffered by the refusal of third persons to deal with him; or

(c) if the agent's loss resulted from an enterprise which he knew to be illegal.

§ 442. Period of Employment

Unless otherwise agreed, mutual promises by principal and agent to employ and to serve create obligations to employ and to serve which are terminable upon notice by either party; if neither party terminates the employment, it may terminate by lapse of time or by supervening events.

UNIFORM PARTNERSHIP ACT

PART I. PRELIMINARY PROVISIONS

PART II. NATURE OF PARTNERSHIP

PART III. RELATIONS OF PARTNERS TO PERSONS DEALING WITH THE PARTNERSHIP

PART IV. RELATIONS OF PARTNERS TO ONE ANOTHER

PART V. PROPERTY RIGHTS OF A PARTNER

PART VI. DISSOLUTION AND WINDING UP

PART VII. MISCELLANEOUS PROVISIONS

PART I

PRELIMINARY PROVISIONS

§ 1. Name of Act

This act may be cited as Uniform Partnership Act.

§ 2. Definition of Terms

In this act, "Court" includes every court and judge having jurisdiction in the case.

"Business" includes every trade, occupation, or profession.

"Person" includes individuals, partnerships, corporations, and other associations.

"Bankrupt" includes bankrupt under the Federal Bankruptcy Act or insolvent under any state insolvent act.

"Conveyance" includes every assignment, lease, mortgage, or encumbrance.

"Real property" includes land and any interest or estate in land.

§ 3. Interpretation of Knowledge and Notice

(1) A person has "knowledge" of a fact within the meaning of this act not only when he has actual knowledge thereof, but also when he has knowledge of such other facts as in the circumstances shows bad faith.

* Omitted.

(2) A person has "notice" of a fact within the meaning of this act when the person who claims the benefit of the notice:

(a) States the fact to such person, or

(b) Delivers through the mail, or by other means of communication, a written statement of the fact to such person or to a proper person at his place of business or residence.

§ 4. Rules of Construction

(1) The rule that statutes in derogation of the common law are to be strictly construed shall have no application to this act.

(2) The law of estoppel shall apply under this act.

(3) The law of agency shall apply under this act.

(4) This act shall be so interpreted and construed as to effect its general purpose to make uniform the law of those states which enact it.

(5) This act shall not be construed so as to impair the obligations of any contract existing when the act goes into effect, nor to affect any action or proceedings begun or right accrued before this act takes effect.

§ 5. Rules for Cases Not Provided for in This Act

In any case not provided for in this act the rules of law and equity, including the law merchant, shall govern.

PART II

NATURE OF PARTNERSHIP

§ 6. Partnership Defined

(1) A partnership is an association of two or more persons to carry on as co-owners a business for profit.

(2) But any association formed under any other statute of this state, or any statute adopted by authority, other than the authority of this state, is not a partnership under this act, unless such association would have been a partnership in this state prior to the adoption of this act; but this act shall apply to limited partnerships except in so far as the statutes relating to such partnerships are inconsistent herewith.

§ 7. Rules for Determining the Existence of a Partnership

In determining whether a partnership exists, these rules shall apply:

(1) Except as provided by section 16 persons who are not partners as to each other are not partners as to third persons.

(2) Joint tenancy, tenancy in common, tenancy by the entireties, joint property, common property, or part ownership does not of itself

establish a partnership, whether such co-owners do or do not share any profits made by the use of the property.

(3) The sharing of gross returns does not of itself establish a partnership, whether or not the persons sharing them have a joint or common right or interest in any property from which the returns are derived.

(4) The receipt by a person of a share of the profits of a business is prima facie evidence that he is a partner in the business, but no such inference shall be drawn if such profits were received in payment:

(a) As a debt by installments or otherwise,

(b) As wages of an employee or rent to a landlord,

(c) As an annuity to a widow or representative of a deceased partner,

(d) As interest on a loan, though the amount of payment vary with the profits of the business,

(e) As the consideration for the sale of a good-will of a business or other property by installments or otherwise.

§ 8. Partnership Property

(1) All property originally brought into the partnership stock or subsequently acquired by purchase or otherwise, on account of the partnership, is partnership property.

(2) Unless the contrary intention appears, property acquired with partnership funds is partnership property.

(3) Any estate in real property may be acquired in the partnership name. Title so acquired can be conveyed only in the partnership name.

(4) A conveyance to a partnership in the partnership name, though without words of inheritance, passes the entire estate of the grantor unless a contrary intent appears.

PART III

RELATIONS OF PARTNERS TO PERSONS DEALING WITH THE PARTNERSHIP

§ 9. Partner Agent of Partnership as to Partnership Business

(1) Every partner is an agent of the partnership for the purpose of its business, and the act of every partner, including the execution in the partnership name of any instrument, for apparently carrying on in the usual way the business of the partnership of which he is a member binds the partnership, unless the partner so acting has in fact no authority to act for the partnership in the particular matter, and the person with

whom he is dealing has knowledge of the fact that he has no such authority.

(2) An act of a partner which is not apparently for the carrying on of the business of the partnership in the usual way does not bind the partnership unless authorized by the other partners.

(3) Unless authorized by the other partners or unless they have abandoned the business, one or more but less than all the partners have no authority to:

(a) Assign the partnership property in trust for creditors or on the assignee's promise to pay the debts of the partnership,

(b) Dispose of the good-will of the business,

(c) Do any other act which would make it impossible to carry on the ordinary business of a partnership,

(d) Confess a judgment,

(e) Submit a partnership claim or liability to arbitration or reference.

(4) No act of a partner in contravention of a restriction on authority shall bind the partnership to persons having knowledge of the restriction.

§ 10. Conveyance of Real Property of the Partnership

(1) Where title to real property is in the partnership name, any partner may convey title to such property by a conveyance executed in the partnership name; but the partnership may recover such property unless the partner's act binds the partnership under the provisions of paragraph (1) of section 9, or unless such property has been conveyed by the grantee or a person claiming through such grantee to a holder for value without knowledge that the partner, in making the conveyance, has exceeded his authority.

(2) Where title to real property is in the name of the partnership, a conveyance executed by a partner, in his own name, passes the equitable interest of the partnership, provided the act is one within the authority of the partner under the provisions of paragraph (1) of section 9.

(3) Where title to real property is in the name of one or more but not all the partners, and the record does not disclose the right of the partnership, the partners in whose name the title stands may convey title to such property, but the partnership may recover such property if the partners' act does not bind the partnership under the provisions of paragraph (1) of section 9, unless the purchaser or his assignee, is a holder for value, without knowledge.

(4) Where the title to real property is in the name of one or more or all the partners, or in a third person in trust for the partnership, a conveyance executed by a partner in the partnership name, or in his own name, passes the equitable interest of the partnership, provided the act is one within the authority of the partner under the provisions of paragraph (1) of section 9.

(5) Where the title to real property is in the names of all the partners a conveyance executed by all the partners passes all their rights in such property.

§ 11. Partnership Bound by Admission of Partner

An admission or representation made by any partner concerning partnership affairs within the scope of his authority as conferred by this act is evidence against the partnership.

§ 12. Partnership Charged With Knowledge of or Notice to Partner

Notice to any partner of any matter relating to partnership affairs, and the knowledge of the partner acting in the particular matter, acquired while a partner or then present to his mind, and the knowledge of any other partner who reasonably could and should have communicated it to the acting partner, operate as notice to or knowledge of the partnership, except in the case of a fraud on the partnership committed by or with the consent of that partner.

§ 13. Partnership Bound by Partner's Wrongful Act

Where, by any wrongful act or omission of any partner acting in the ordinary course of the business of the partnership or with the authority of his co-partners, loss or injury is caused to any person, not being a partner in the partnership, or any penalty is incurred, the partnership is liable therefor to the same extent as the partner so acting or omitting to act.

§ 14. Partnership Bound by Partner's Breach of Trust

The partnership is bound to make good the loss:

(a) Where one partner acting within the scope of his apparent authority receives money or property of a third person and misapplies it; and

(b) Where the partnership in the course of its business receives money or property of a third person and the money or property so received is misapplied by any partner while it is in the custody of the partnership.

§ 15. Nature of Partner's Liability

All partners are liable

(a) Jointly and severally for everything chargeable to the partnership under sections 13 and 14.

(b) Jointly for all other debts and obligations of the partnership; but any partner may enter into a separate obligation to perform a partnership contract.

§ 16. Partner by Estoppel

(1) When a person, by words spoken or written or by conduct, represents himself, or consents to another representing him to any one, as a partner in an existing partnership or with one or more persons not actual partners, he is liable to any such person to whom such representation has been made, who has, on the faith of such representation, given credit to the actual or apparent partnership, and if he has made such representation or consented to its being made in a public manner he is liable to such person, whether the representation has or has not been made or communicated to such person so giving credit by or with the knowledge of the apparent partner making the representation or consenting to its being made.

(a) When a partnership liability results, he is liable as though he were an actual member of the partnership.

(b) When no partnership liability results, he is liable jointly with the other persons, if any, so consenting to the contract or representation as to incur liability, otherwise separately.

(2) When a person has been thus represented to be a partner in an existing partnership, or with one or more persons not actual partners, he is an agent of the persons consenting to such representation to bind them to the same extent and in the same manner as though he were a partner in fact, with respect to persons who rely upon the representation. Where all the members of the existing partnership consent to the representation, a partnership act or obligation results; but in all other cases it is the joint act or obligation of the person acting and the persons consenting to the representation.

§ 17. Liability of Incoming Partner

A person admitted as a partner into an existing partnership is liable for all the obligations of the partnership arising before his admission as though he had been a partner when such obligations were incurred, except that this liability shall be satisfied only out of partnership property.

PART IV

RELATIONS OF PARTNERS TO ONE ANOTHER

§ 18. Rules Determining Rights and Duties of Partners

The rights and duties of the partners in relation to the partnership shall be determined, subject to any agreement between them, by the following rules:

(a) Each partner shall be repaid his contributions, whether by way of capital or advances to the partnership property and share equally in the profits and surplus remaining after all liabilities, including those to partners, are satisfied; and must contribute towards the losses, whether of capital or otherwise, sustained by the partnership according to his share in the profits.

(b) The partnership must indemnify every partner in respect of payments made and personal liabilities reasonably incurred by him in the ordinary and proper conduct of its business, or for the preservation of its business or property.

(c) A partner, who in aid of the partnership makes any payment or advance beyond the amount of capital which he agreed to contribute, shall be paid interest from the date of the payment or advance.

(d) A partner shall receive interest on the capital contributed by him only from the date when repayment should be made.

(e) All partners have equal rights in the management and conduct of the partnership business.

(f) No partner is entitled to remuneration for acting in the partnership business, except that a surviving partner is entitled to reasonable compensation for his services in winding up the partnership affairs.

(g) No person can become a member of a partnership without the consent of all the partners.

(h) Any difference arising as to ordinary matters connected with the partnership business may be decided by a majority of the partners; but no act in contravention of any agreement between the partners may be done rightfully without the consent of all the partners.

§ 19. Partnership Books

The partnership books shall be kept, subject to any agreement between the partners, at the principal place of business of the partnership, and every partner shall at all times have access to and may inspect and copy any of them.

§ 20. Duty of Partners to Render Information

Partners shall render on demand true and full information of all things affecting the partnership to any partner or the legal representative of any deceased partner or partner under legal disability.

§ 21. Partner Accountable as a Fiduciary

(1) Every partner must account to the partnership for any benefit, and hold as trustee for it any profits derived by him without the consent of the other partners from any transaction connected with the formation, conduct, or liquidation of the partnership or from any use by him of its property.

(2) This section applies also to the representatives of a deceased partner engaged in the liquidation of the affairs of the partnership as the personal representatives of the last surviving partner.

§ 22. Right to an Account

Any partner shall have the right to a formal account as to partnership affairs:

(a) If he is wrongfully excluded from the partnership business or possession of its property by his co-partners,

(b) If the right exists under the terms of any agreement,

(c) As provided by section 21,

(d) Whenever other circumstances render it just and reasonable.

§ 23. Continuation of Partnership Beyond Fixed Term

(1) When a partnership for a fixed term or particular undertaking is continued after the termination of such term or particular undertaking without any express agreement, the rights and duties of the partners remain the same as they were at such termination, so far as is consistent with a partnership at will.

(2) A continuation of the business by the partners or such of them as habitually acted therein during the term, without any settlement or liquidation of the partnership affairs, is prima facie evidence of a continuation of the partnership.

PART V

PROPERTY RIGHTS OF A PARTNER

§ 24. Extent of Property Rights of a Partner

The property rights of a partner are (1) his rights in specific partnership property, (2) his interest in the partnership, and (3) his right to participate in the management.

§ 25. Nature of a Partner's Right in Specific Partnership Property

(1) A partner is co-owner with his partners of specific partnership property holding as a tenant in partnership.

(2) The incidents of this tenancy are such that:

(a) A partner, subject to the provisions of this act and to any agreement between the partners, has an equal right with his partners to possess specific partnership property for partnership purposes; but he has no right to possess such property for any other purpose without the consent of his partners.

(b) A partner's right in specific partnership property is not assignable except in connection with the assignment of rights of all the partners in the same property.

(c) A partner's right in specific partnership property is not subject to attachment or execution, except on a claim against the partnership. When partnership property is attached for a partnership debt the partners, or any of them, or the representatives of a deceased partner, cannot claim any right under the homestead or exemption laws.

(d) On the death of a partner his right in specific partnership property vests in the surviving partner or partners, except where the deceased was the last surviving partner, when his right in such property vests in his legal representative. Such surviving partner or partners, or the legal representative of the last surviving partner, has no right to possess the partnership property for any but a partnership purpose.

(e) A partner's right in specific partnership property is not subject to dower, curtesy, or allowances to widows, heirs, or next of kin.

§ 26. Nature of Partner's Interest in the Partnership

A partner's interest in the partnership is his share of the profits and surplus, and the same is personal property.

§ 27. Assignment of Partner's Interest

(1) A conveyance by a partner of his interest in the partnership does not of itself dissolve the partnership, nor, as against the other partners in the absence of agreement, entitle the assignee, during the continuance of the partnership, to interfere in the management or administration of the partnership business or affairs, or to require any information or account of partnership transactions, or to inspect the partnership books; but it merely entitles the assignee to receive in accordance with his contract the profits to which the assigning partner would otherwise be entitled.

(2) In case of a dissolution of the partnership, the assignee is entitled to receive his assignor's interest and may require an account from the date only of the last account agreed to by all the partners.

§ 28. Partner's Interest Subject to Charging Order

(1) On due application to a competent court by any judgment creditor of a partner, the court which entered the judgment, order, or decree, or any other court, may charge the interest of the debtor partner with payment of the unsatisfied amount of such judgment debt with interest thereon; and may then or later appoint a receiver of his share of the profits, and of any other money due or to fall due to him in respect of the partnership, and make all other orders, directions, accounts and inquiries which the debtor partner might have made, or which the circumstances of the case may require.

(2) The interest charged may be redeemed at any time before foreclosure, or in case of a sale being directed by the court may be purchased without thereby causing a dissolution:

(a) With separate property, by any one or more of the partners, or

(b) With partnership property, by any one or more of the partners with the consent of all the partners whose interests are not so charged or sold.

(3) Nothing in this act shall be held to deprive a partner of his right, if any, under the exemption laws, as regards his interest in the partnership.

PART VI

DISSOLUTION AND WINDING UP

§ 29. Dissolution Defined

The dissolution of a partnership is the change in the relation of the partners caused by any partner ceasing to be associated in the carrying on as distinguished from the winding up of the business.

Official Comment

... In this act dissolution designates the point in time when the partners cease to carry on the business together; termination is the point in time when all the partnership affairs are wound up; winding up, the process of settling partnership affairs after dissolution.

§ 30. Partnership Not Terminated by Dissolution

On dissolution the partnership is not terminated, but continues until the winding up of partnership affairs is completed.

§ 31. Causes of Dissolution

Dissolution is caused:

(1) Without violation of the agreement between the partners,

(a) By the termination of the definite term or particular undertaking specified in the agreement,

(b) By the express will of any partner when no definite term or particular undertaking is specified,

(c) By the express will of all the partners who have not assigned their interests or suffered them to be charged for their separate debts, either before or after the termination of any specified term or particular undertaking,

(d) By the expulsion of any partner from the business bona fide in accordance with such a power conferred by the agreement between the partners;

(2) In contravention of the agreement between the partners, where the circumstances do not permit a dissolution under any other provision of this section, by the express will of any partner at any time;

(3) By any event which makes it unlawful for the business of the partnership to be carried on or for the members to carry it on in partnership;

(4) By the death of any partner;

(5) By the bankruptcy of any partner or the partnership;

(6) By decree of court under section 32.

Official Comment

Paragraph (2) will settle a matter on which at present considerable confusion and uncertainty exists. The paragraph as drawn allows a partner to dissolve a partnership in contravention of the agreement between the partners. . . .

The relation of partners is one of agency. The agency is such a personal one that equity cannot enforce it even where the agreement provides that the partnership shall continue for a definite time. The power of any partner to terminate the relation, even though in doing so he breaks a contract, should, it is submitted, be recognized.

The rights of the parties upon a dissolution in contravention of the agreement are safeguarded by section 38(2), infra.

§ 32. Dissolution by Decree of Court

(1) On application by or for a partner the court shall decree a dissolution whenever:

(a) A partner has been declared a lunatic in any judicial proceeding or is shown to be of unsound mind,

(b) A partner becomes in any other way incapable of performing his part of the partnership contract,

(c) A partner has been guilty of such conduct as tends to affect prejudicially the carrying on of the business,

(d) A partner wilfully or persistently commits a breach of the partnership agreement, or otherwise so conducts himself in matters relating to the partnership business that it is not reasonably practicable to carry on the business in partnership with him,

(e) The business of the partnership can only be carried on at a loss,

(f) Other circumstances render a dissolution equitable.

(2) On the application of the purchaser of a partner's interest under sections 28 or 29: [1]

(a) After the termination of the specified term or particular undertaking,

(b) At any time if the partnership was a partnership at will when the interest was assigned or when the charging order was issued.

§ 33.   General Effect of Dissolution on Authority of Partner

Except so far as may be necessary to wind up partnership affairs or to complete transactions begun but not then finished, dissolution terminates all authority of any partner to act for the partnership,

(1) With respect to the partners,

(a) When the dissolution is not by the act, bankruptcy or death of a partner; or

(b) When the dissolution is by such act, bankruptcy or death of a partner, in cases where section 34 so requires.

(2) With respect to persons not partners, as declared in section 35.

§ 34.   Right of Partner to Contribution From Co-partners After Dissolution

Where the dissolution is caused by the act, death or bankruptcy of a partner, each partner is liable to his co-partners for his share of any liability created by any partner acting for the partnership as if the partnership had not been dissolved unless

(a) The dissolution being by act of any partner, the partner acting for the partnership had knowledge of the dissolution, or

(b) The dissolution being by the death or bankruptcy of a partner, the partner acting for the partnership had knowledge or notice of the death or bankruptcy.

---

1. So in original. Probably should read "sections 27 or 28."

§ 35. Power of Partner to Bind Partnership to Third Persons After Dissolution

(1) After dissolution a partner can bind the partnership except as provided in Paragraph (3)

(a) By any act appropriate for winding up partnership affairs or completing transactions unfinished at dissolution;

(b) By any transaction which would bind the partnership if dissolution had not taken place, provided the other party to the transaction

(I) Had extended credit to the partnership prior to dissolution and had no knowledge or notice of the dissolution; or

(II) Though he had not so extended credit, had nevertheless known of the partnership prior to dissolution, and, having no knowledge or notice of dissolution, the fact of dissolution had not been advertised in a newspaper of general circulation in the place (or in each place if more than one) at which the partnership business was regularly carried on.

(2) The liability of a partner under Paragraph (1b) shall be satisfied out of partnership assets alone when such partner had been prior to dissolution

(a) Unknown as a partner to the person with whom the contract is made; and

(b) So far unknown and inactive in partnership affairs that the business reputation of the partnership could not be said to have been in any degree due to his connection with it.

(3) The partnership is in no case bound by any act of a partner after dissolution

(a) Where the partnership is dissolved because it is unlawful to carry on the business, unless the act is appropriate for winding up partnership affairs; or

(b) Where the partner has become bankrupt; or

(c) Where the partner has no authority to wind up partnership affairs; except by a transaction with one who

(I) Had extended credit to the partnership prior to dissolution and had no knowledge or notice of his want of authority; or

(II) Had not extended credit to the partnership prior to dissolution, and, having no knowledge or notice of his want of authority, the fact of his want of authority has not been advertised in the manner provided for advertising the fact of dissolution in Paragraph (1bII).

(4) Nothing in this section shall affect the liability under Section 16 of any person who after dissolution represents himself or consents to another representing him as a partner in a partnership engaged in carrying on business.

§ 36. Effect of Dissolution on Partner's Existing Liability

(1) The dissolution of the partnership does not of itself discharge the existing liability of any partner.

(2) A partner is discharged from any existing liability upon dissolution of the partnership by an agreement to that effect between himself, the partnership creditor and the person or partnership continuing the business; and such agreement may be inferred from the course of dealing between the creditor having knowledge of the dissolution and the person or partnership continuing the business.

(3) Where a person agrees to assume the existing obligations of a dissolved partnership, the partners whose obligations have been assumed shall be discharged from any liability to any creditor of the partnership who, knowing of the agreement, consents to a material alteration in the nature or time of payment of such obligations.

(4) The individual property of a deceased partner shall be liable for all obligations of the partnership incurred while he was a partner but subject to the prior payment of his separate debts.

§ 37. Right to Wind Up

Unless otherwise agreed the partners who have not wrongfully dissolved the partnership or the legal representative of the last surviving partner, not bankrupt, has the right to wind up the partnership affairs; provided, however, that any partner, his legal representative or his assignee, upon cause shown, may obtain winding up by the court.

§ 38. Rights of Partners to Application of Partnership Property

(1) When dissolution is caused in any way, except in contravention of the partnership agreement, each partner, as against his co-partners and all persons claiming through them in respect of their interests in the partnership, unless otherwise agreed, may have the partnership property applied to discharge its liabilities, and the surplus applied to pay in cash the net amount owing to the respective partners. But if dissolution is caused by expulsion of a partner, bona fide under the partnership agreement and if the expelled partner is discharged from all partnership liabilities, either by payment or agreement under section 36(2), he shall receive in cash only the net amount due him from the partnership.

(2) When dissolution is caused in contravention of the partnership agreement the rights of the partners shall be as follows:

(a) Each partner who has not caused dissolution wrongfully shall have,

I. All the rights specified in paragraph (1) of this section, and

II. The right, as against each partner who has caused the dissolution wrongfully, to damages for breach of the agreement.

(b) The partners who have not caused the dissolution wrongfully, if they all desire to continue the business in the same name, either by themselves or jointly with others, may do so, during the agreed term for the partnership and for that purpose may possess the partnership property, provided they secure the payment by bond approved by the court, or pay to any partner who has caused the dissolution wrongfully, the value of his interest in the partnership at the dissolution, less any damages recoverable under clause (2aII) of this section, and in like manner indemnify him against all present or future partnership liabilities.

(c) A partner who has caused the dissolution wrongfully shall have:

I. If the business is not continued under the provisions of paragraph (2b) all the rights of a partner under paragraph (1), subject to clause (2aII), of this section,

II. If the business is continued under paragraph (2b) of this section the right as against his co-partners and all claiming through them in respect of their interests in the partnership, to have the value of his interest in the partnership, less any damages caused to his co-partners by the dissolution, ascertained and paid to him in cash, or the payment secured by bond approved by the court, and to be released from all existing liabilities of the partnership; but in ascertaining the value of the partner's interest the value of the good-will of the business shall not be considered.

Official Comment

The right given to each partner, where no agreement to the contrary has been made, to have his share of the surplus paid to him in cash makes certain an existing uncertainty. At present it is not certain whether a partner may or may not insist on a physical partition of the property remaining after third persons have been paid.

§ 39. Rights Where Partnership Is Dissolved for Fraud or Misrepresentation

Where a partnership contract is rescinded on the ground of the fraud or misrepresentation of one of the parties thereto, the party entitled to rescind is, without prejudice to any other right, entitled,

(a) To a lien on, or a right of retention of, the surplus of the partnership property after satisfying the partnership liabilities to third persons for any sum of money paid by him for the purchase of an interest in the partnership and for any capital or advances contributed by him; and

(b) To stand, after all liabilities to third persons have been satisfied, in the place of the creditors of the partnership for any payments made by him in respect of the partnership liabilities; and

(c) To be indemnified by the person guilty of the fraud or making the representation against all debts and liabilities of the partnership.

§ 40. Rules for Distribution

In settling accounts between the partners after dissolution, the following rules shall be observed, subject to any agreement to the contrary:

(a) The assets of the partnership are:

I. The partnership property,

II. The contributions of the partners necessary for the payment of all the liabilities specified in clause (b) of this paragraph.

(b) The liabilities of the partnership shall rank in order of payment, as follows:

I. Those owing to creditors other than partners,

II. Those owing to partners other than for capital and profits,

III. Those owing to partners in respect of capital,

IV. Those owing to partners in respect of profits.

(c) The assets shall be applied in order of their declaration in clause (a) of this paragraph to the satisfaction of the liabilities.

(d) The partners shall contribute, as provided by section 18(a) the amount necessary to satisfy the liabilities; but if any, but not all, of the partners are insolvent, or, not being subject to process, refuse to contribute, the other partners shall contribute their share of the liabilities, and, in the relative proportions in which they share the profits, the additional amount necessary to pay the liabilities.

(e) An assignee for the benefit of creditors or any person appointed by the court shall have the right to enforce the contributions specified in clause (d) of this paragraph.

(f) Any partner or his legal representative shall have the right to enforce the contributions specified in clause (d) of this paragraph, to the extent of the amount which he has paid in excess of his share of the liability.

(g) The individual property of a deceased partner shall be liable for the contributions specified in clause (d) of this paragraph.

(h) When partnership property and the individual properties of the partners are in possession of a court for distribution, partnership creditors shall have priority on partnership property and separate creditors on individual property, saving the rights of lien or secured creditors as heretofore.

(i) Where a partner has become bankrupt or his estate is insolvent the claims against his separate property shall rank in the following order:

I.   Those owing to separate creditors,

II. Those owing to partnership creditors,

III. Those owing to partners by way of contribution.

§ 41.   Liability of Persons Continuing the Business in Certain Cases

(1) When any new partner is admitted into an existing partnership, or when any partner retires and assigns (or the representative of the deceased partner assigns) his rights in partnership property to two or more of the partners, or to one or more of the partners and one or more third persons, if the business is continued without liquidation of the partnership affairs, creditors of the first or dissolved partnership are also creditors of the partnership so continuing the business.

(2) When all but one partner retire and assign (or the representative of a deceased partner assigns) their rights in partnership property to the remaining partner, who continues the business without liquidation of partnership affairs, either alone or with others, creditors of the dissolved partnership are also creditors of the person or partnership so continuing the business.

(3) When any partner retires or dies and the business of the dissolved partnership is continued as set forth in paragraphs (1) and (2) of this section, with the consent of the retired partners or the representative of the deceased partner, but without any assignment of his right in partnership property, rights of creditors of the dissolved partnership and of the creditors of the person or partnership continuing the business shall be as if such assignment had been made.

(4) When all the partners or their representatives assign their rights in partnership property to one or more third persons who promise to pay the debts and who continue the business of the dissolved partnership, creditors of the dissolved partnership are also creditors of the person or partnership continuing the business.

(5) When any partner wrongfully causes a dissolution and the remaining partners continue the business under the provisions of section 38(2b), either alone or with others, and without liquidation of the partnership affairs, creditors of the dissolved partnership are also creditors of the person or partnership continuing the business.

(6) When a partner is expelled and the remaining partners continue the business either alone or with others, without liquidation of the partnership affairs, creditors of the dissolved partnership are also creditors of the person or partnership continuing the business.

(7) The liability of a third person becoming a partner in the partnership continuing the business, under this section, to the creditors of the dissolved partnership shall be satisfied out of partnership property only.

(8) When the business of a partnership after dissolution is continued under any conditions set forth in this section the creditors of the dissolved partnership, as against the separate creditors of the retiring or deceased partner or the representative of the deceased partner, have a prior right to any claim of the retired partner or the representative of the deceased partner against the person or partnership continuing the business, on account of the retired or deceased partner's interest in the dissolved partnership or on account of any consideration promised for such interest or for his right in partnership property.

(9) Nothing in this section shall be held to modify any right of creditors to set aside any assignment on the ground of fraud.

(10) The use by the person or partnership continuing the business of the partnership name, or the name of a deceased partner as part thereof, shall not of itself make the individual property of the deceased partner liable for any debts contracted by such person or partnership.

§ 42. Rights of Retiring or Estate of Deceased Partner When the Business Is Continued

When any partner retires or dies, and the business is continued under any of the conditions set forth in section 41(1, 2, 3, 5, 6), or section 38(2b) without any settlement of accounts as between him or his estate and the person or partnership continuing the business, unless otherwise agreed, he or his legal representative as against such persons or partnership may have the value of his interest at the date of dissolution ascertained, and shall receive as an ordinary creditor an amount equal to the value of his interest in the dissolved partnership with interest, or, at his option or at the option of his legal representative, in lieu of interest, the profits attributable to the use of his right in the property of the dissolved partnership; provided that the creditors of the dissolved partnership as against the separate creditors, or the representative of the retired or deceased partner, shall have priority on any claim arising under this section, as provided by section 41(8) of this act.

§ 43. Accrual of Actions

The right to an account of his interest shall accrue to any partner, or his legal representative, as against the winding up partners or the surviving partners or the person or partnership continuing the business, at the date of dissolution, in the absence of any agreement to the contrary.

REVISED UNIFORM PARTNERSHIP ACT (1994)

ARTICLE 1. GENERAL PROVISIONS

ARTICLE 2. NATURE OF PARTNERSHIP

ARTICLE 3. RELATIONS OF PARTNERS TO PERSONS DEALING WITH PARTNERSHIP

ARTICLE 4. RELATIONS OF PARTNERS TO EACH OTHER AND TO PARTNERSHIP

ARTICLE 5. TRANSFEREES AND CREDITORS OF PARTNER

ARTICLE 1

GENERAL PROVISIONS

Section 101.   Definitions.
Section 102.   Knowledge and Notice.
Section 103.   Effect of Partnership Agreement;   Nonwaivable Provisions.
Section 104.   Supplemental Principles of Law.
Section 105.   Execution, Filing, and Recording of Statements.
Section 106.   Governing Law.
Section 107.   Partnership Subject to Amendment or Repeal of [Act].

SECTION 101.   DEFINITIONS.

In this [Act]:

(1) "Business" includes every trade, occupation, and profession.

(2) "Debtor in bankruptcy" means a person who is the subject of:

(i) an order for relief under Title 11 of the United States Code or a comparable order under a successor statute of general application; or

(ii) a comparable order under federal, state, or foreign law governing insolvency.

(3) "Distribution" means a transfer of money or other property from a partnership to a partner in the partner's capacity as a partner or to the partner's transferee.

(4) "Foreign limited liability partnership" means a partnership that:

(i) is formed under laws other than the laws of this State; and

(ii) has the status of a limited liability partnership under those laws.

(5) "Limited liability partnership" means a partnership that has filed a statement of qualification under Section 1001 and does not have a similar statement in effect in any other jurisdiction.

61

(6) "Partnership" means an association of two or more persons to carry on as co-owners a business for profit formed under Section 202, predecessor law, or comparable law of another jurisdiction.

(7) "Partnership agreement" means the agreement, whether written, oral, or implied, among the partners concerning the partnership, including amendments to the partnership agreement.

(8) "Partnership at will" means a partnership in which the partners have not agreed to remain partners until the expiration of a definite term or the completion of a particular undertaking.

(9) "Partnership interest" or "partner's interest in the partnership" means all of a partner's interests in the partnership, including the partner's transferable interest and all management and other rights.

(10) "Person" means an individual, corporation, business trust, estate, trust, partnership, association, joint venture, government, governmental subdivision, agency, or instrumentality, or any other legal or commercial entity.

(11) "Property" means all property, real, personal, or mixed, tangible or intangible, or any interest therein.

(12) "State" means a State of the United States, the District of Columbia, the Commonwealth of Puerto Rico, or any territory or insular possession subject to the jurisdiction of the United States.

(13) "Statement" means a statement of partnership authority under Section 303, a statement of denial under Section 304, a statement of dissociation under Section 704, a statement of dissolution under Section 805, a statement of merger under Section 907, a statement of qualification under Section 1001, a statement of foreign qualification under Section 1102, or an amendment or cancellation of any of the foregoing.

(14) "Transfer" includes an assignment, conveyance, lease, mortgage, deed, and encumbrance.

Comment: ...

The definition of a "foreign limited liability partnership" includes a partnership formed under the laws of another state, foreign country, or other jurisdiction provided it has the status of a limited liability partnership in the other jurisdiction. Since the scope and nature of foreign limited liability partnership liability shields may vary in different jurisdictions, the definition avoids reference to similar or comparable laws. Rather, the definition incorporates the concept of a limited liability partnership in the foreign jurisdiction, however defined in that jurisdiction. The reference to formation "under laws other than the laws of this State" makes clear that the definition includes partnerships formed in foreign countries as well as in another state.

The definition of a "limited liability partnership" makes clear that a partnership may adopt the special liability shield characteristics of a limited liability partnership simply by filing a statement of qualification under Section 1001. A partnership may file the statement in this State regardless of where formed. When coupled with the governing law provisions of Section 106(b), this definition simplifies the choice of law issues applicable to partnerships with multistate activities and contacts. Once a statement of qualification is filed, a partnership's internal affairs and the liability of its partners are determined by the law of the State where the statement is filed. See Section 106(b). The partnership may not vary this particular requirement. See Section 103(b)(9).

The reference to a "partnership" in the definition of a limited liability partnership makes clear that the RUPA definition of the term rather than the UPA concept controls for purposes of a limited liability partnership. Section 101(6) defines a "partnership" as "an association of two or more persons to carry on as co-owners a business for profit formed under Section 202, predecessor law, or comparable law of another jurisdiction." Section 202(b) further provides that "an association formed under a statute other than this [Act], a predecessor statute, or a comparable statute of another jurisdiction is not a partnership under this [Act]." This language was intended to clarify that a limited partnership is not a RUPA general partnership. It was not intended to preclude the application of any RUPA general partnership rules to limited partnerships where limited partnership law otherwise adopts the RUPA rules. See Comments to Section 202(b) and Prefatory Note.

The effect of these definitions leaves the scope and applicability of RUPA to limited partnerships to limited partnership law, not to sever the linkage between the two Acts in all cases. Certain provisions of RUPA will continue to govern limited partnerships by virtue of Revised Uniform Limited Partnership Act (RULPA) Section 1105 which provides that "in any case not provided for in this [Act] the provisions of the Uniform Partnership Act govern." The RUPA partnership definition includes partnerships formed under the UPA. Therefore, the limited liability partnership rules will govern limited partnerships "in any case not provided for" in RULPA. Since RULPA does not provide for any rules applicable to a limited partnership becoming a limited liability partnership, the limited liability partnership rules should apply to limited partnerships that file a statement of qualification.

Partner liability deserves special mention. RULPA Section 403(b) provides that a general partner of a limited partnership "has the liabilities of a partner in a partnership without limited partners." Thus limited partnership law expressly references general partnership law for general partner liability and does not separately consider the liability of such partners. The liability of a general partner of a limited partnership that becomes a LLLP would therefore be the liability of a general partner in an LLP and would be governed by Section 306. The liability of a limited partner in a LLLP is a more complicated matter. RULPA Section 303(a) separately considers the liability of a limited partner. Unless also a general partner, a limited partner is not liable for the obligations of a limited partnership unless the partner participates in the control of the business and then only to persons reasonably believing the limited partner is a general partner. Therefore, arguably limited partners in a LLLP will have the specific RULPA Section 303(c) liability shield while general partners will have a superior Section 306(c) liability shield. In order to clarify limited partner liability and other linkage issues, states that have adopted RUPA, these limited liability partnership rules, and RULPA may wish to consider an amendment to RULPA. A suggested form of such an amendment is:

SECTION 1107. LIMITED LIABILITY LIMITED PARTNERSHIP.

(a) A limited partnership may become a limited liability partnership by:

(1) obtaining approval of the terms and conditions of the limited partnership becoming a limited liability limited partnership by the vote necessary to amend the limited partnership agreement except, in the case of a limited partnership agreement that expressly considers contribution obligations, the vote necessary to amend those provisions;

(2) filing a statement of qualification under Section 1001(c) of the Uniform Partnership Act (1994); and

(3) complying with the name requirements of Section 1002 of the Uniform Partnership Act (1994).

(b) A limited liability limited partnership continues to be the same entity that existed before the filing of a statement of qualification under Section 1001(c) of the Uniform Partnership Act (1994).

(c) Sections 306(c) and 307(f) of the Uniform Partnership Act (1994) apply to both general and limited partners of a limited liability limited partnership. . . .

The definition of "partnership agreement" is adapted from Section 101(9) of RULPA. The RUPA definition is intended to include the agreement among the partners, including amendments, concerning either the affairs of the partnership or the conduct of its business. It does not include other agreements between some or all of the partners, such as a lease or loan agreement. The partnership agreement need not be written; it may be oral or inferred from the conduct of the parties.

Any partnership in which the partners have not agreed to remain partners until the expiration of a definite term or the completion of a particular undertaking is a "partnership at will." The distinction between an "at-will" partnership and a partnership for "a definite term or the completion of a particular undertaking" is important in determining the rights of dissociating and continuing partners following the dissociation of a partner. See Sections 601, 602, 701(b), 801(a), 802(b), and 803.

It is sometimes difficult to determine whether a partnership is at will or is for a definite term or the completion of a particular undertaking. Presumptively, every partnership is an at-will partnership. See, e.g., Stone v. Stone, 292 So.2d 686 (La.1974); Frey v. Hauke, 171 Neb. 852, 108 N.W.2d 228 (1961). To constitute a partnership for a term or a particular undertaking, the partners must agree (i) that the partnership will continue for a definite term or until a particular undertaking is completed *and* (ii) that they will remain partners until the expiration of the term or the completion of the undertaking. Both are necessary for a term partnership; if the partners have the unrestricted right, as distinguished from the power, to withdraw from a partnership formed for a term or particular undertaking, the partnership is one at will, rather than a term partnership.

To find that the partnership is formed for a definite term or a particular undertaking, there must be clear evidence of an agreement among the partners that the partnership (i) has a minimum or maximum duration or (ii) terminates at the conclusion of a particular venture whose time is indefinite but certain to occur. See, e.g., Stainton v. Tarantino, 637 F.Supp. 1051 (E.D.Pa.1986) (partnership to dissolve no later than December 30, 2020); Abel v. American Art Analog, Inc., 838 F.2d 691 (3d Cir.1988) (partnership purpose to market an art book); 68th Street Apts., Inc. v. Lauricella, 362 A.2d 78 (N.J.Super.Ct.1976) (partnership purpose to construct an apartment building). A partnership to conduct a business which may last indefinitely, however, is an at-will partnership, even though there may be an obligation of the partnership, such as a mortgage, which must be repaid by a certain date, absent a specific agreement that no partner can rightfully withdraw until the obligation is repaid. See, e.g., Page v. Page, 55 Cal.2d 192, 359 P.2d 41 (1961) (partnership purpose to operate a linen supply business); Frey v. Hauke, supra (partnership purpose to contract and operate a bowling alley); Girard Bank v. Haley, 460 Pa. 237, 332 A.2d 443 (1975) (partnership purpose to maintain and lease buildings).

"Partnership interest" or "partner's interest in the partnership" is defined to mean all of a partner's interests in the partnership, including the partner's transferable interest and all management and other rights. A partner's "transferable interest" is a more limited concept and means only his share of the profits and losses and right to receive distributions, that is, the partner's economic interests. See Section 502 and Comment....

SECTION 102. KNOWLEDGE AND NOTICE.

(a) A person knows a fact if the person has actual knowledge of it.

(b) A person has notice of a fact if the person:

(1) knows of it;

(2) has received a notification of it; or

(3) has reason to know it exists from all of the facts known to the person at the time in question.

(c) A person notifies or gives a notification to another by taking steps reasonably required to inform the other person in ordinary course, whether or not the other person learns of it.

(d) A person receives a notification when the notification:

(1) comes to the person's attention; or

(2) is duly delivered at the person's place of business or at any other place held out by the person as a place for receiving communications.

(e) Except as otherwise provided in subsection (f), a person other than an individual knows, has notice, or receives a notification of a fact for purposes of a particular transaction when the individual conducting the transaction knows, has notice, or receives a notification of the fact, or in any event when the fact would have been brought to the individual's attention if the person had exercised reasonable diligence. The person exercises reasonable diligence if it maintains reasonable routines for communicating significant information to the individual conducting the transaction and there is reasonable compliance with the routines. Reasonable diligence does not require an individual acting for the person to communicate information unless the communication is part of the individual's regular duties or the individual has reason to know of the transaction and that the transaction would be materially affected by the information.

(f) A partner's knowledge, notice, or receipt of a notification of a fact relating to the partnership is effective immediately as knowledge by, notice to, or receipt of a notification by the partnership, except in the case of a fraud on the partnership committed by or with the consent of that partner.

Comment: ...

A person "knows" a fact only if that person has actual knowledge of it. Knowledge is cognitive awareness. That is solely an issue of fact. This is a change from the UPA Section 3(1) definition of "knowledge" which included the concept of "bad faith" knowledge arising from other known facts.

"Notice" is a lesser degree of awareness than "knows" and is based on a person's: (i) actual knowledge; (ii) receipt of a notification; or (iii) reason to know based on actual knowledge of other facts and the circumstances at the time. The latter is the traditional concept of inquiry notice.

Generally, under RUPA, statements filed pursuant to Section 105 [Execution, Filing, and Recording of Documents] do not constitute constructive knowledge or notice, except as expressly provided in the Act. See Section 301(1) (generally requiring knowledge of limitations on partner's apparent authority). Properly recorded statements of limitation on a partner's authority, on the other hand, generally constitute constructive knowledge with respect to the transfer of real property held in the partnership name. See Sections 303(d)(1), 303(e), 704(b), and 805(b)....

A notification is not required to be in writing. That is a change from UPA Section 3(2)(b). As under the UCC, the time and circumstances under which a notification may cease to be effective are not determined by RUPA....

SECTION 103. EFFECT OF PARTNERSHIP AGREEMENT; NONWAIVABLE PROVISIONS.

(a) Except as otherwise provided in subsection (b), relations among the partners and between the partners and the partnership are governed by the partnership agreement. To the extent the partnership agreement does not otherwise provide, this [Act] governs relations among the partners and between the partners and the partnership.

(b) The partnership agreement may not:

(1) vary the rights and duties under Section 105 except to eliminate the duty to provide copies of statements to all of the partners;

(2) unreasonably restrict the right of access to books and records under Section 403(b);

(3) eliminate the duty of loyalty under Section 404(b) or 603(b)(3), but:

(i) the partnership agreement may identify specific types or categories of activities that do not violate the duty of loyalty, if not manifestly unreasonable; or

(ii) all of the partners or a number or percentage specified in the partnership agreement may authorize or ratify, after full disclosure of all material facts, a specific act or transaction that otherwise would violate the duty of loyalty;

(4) unreasonably reduce the duty of care under Section 404(c) or 603(b)(3);

(5) eliminate the obligation of good faith and fair dealing under Section 404(d), but the partnership agreement may prescribe the standards by which the performance of the obligation is to be measured, if the standards are not manifestly unreasonable;

(6) vary the power to dissociate as a partner under Section 602(a), except to require the notice under Section 601(1) to be in writing;

(7) vary the right of a court to expel a partner in the events specified in Section 601(5);

(8) vary the requirement to wind up the partnership business in cases specified in Section 801(4), (5), or (6);

(9) vary the law applicable to a limited liability partnership under Section 106(b); or

(10) restrict rights of third parties under this [Act].

Comment:

1. The general rule under Section 103(a) is that relations among the partners and between the partners and the partnership are governed by the partnership agreement. See Section 101(5). To the extent that the partners fail to agree upon a contrary rule, RUPA provides the default rule. Only the rights and duties listed in Section 103(b), and implicitly the corresponding liabilities and remedies under Section 405, are mandatory and cannot be waived or varied by agreement beyond what is authorized. Those are the only exceptions to the general principle that the provisions of RUPA with respect to the rights of the partners *inter se* are merely default rules, subject to modification by the partners. All modifications must also, of course, satisfy the general standards of contract validity. See Section 104.

2. Under subsection (b)(1), the partnership agreement may not vary the requirements for executing, filing, and recording statements under Section 105, except the duty to provide copies to all the partners. A statement that is not executed, filed, and recorded in accordance with the statutory requirements will not be accorded the effect prescribed in the Act, except as provided in Section 303(d).

3. Subsection (b)(2) provides that the partnership agreement may not unreasonably restrict a partner or former partner's access rights to books and records under Section 403(b). It is left to the courts to determine what restrictions are reasonable. See Comment 2 to Section 403. Other information rights in Section 403 can be varied or even eliminated by agreement.

4. Subsection[s] (b)(3) through (5) are intended to ensure a fundamental core of fiduciary responsibility. Neither the fiduciary duties of loyalty or care, nor the obligation of good faith and fair dealing, may be eliminated entirely. However, the statutory requirements of each can be modified by agreement, subject to the limitation[s] stated in subsection[s] (b)(3) through (5).

There has always been a tension regarding the extent to which a partner's fiduciary duty of loyalty can be varied by agreement, as contrasted with the other partners' consent to a particular and known breach of duty. On the one hand, courts have been loathe to enforce agreements broadly "waiving" in advance a partner's fiduciary duty of loyalty, especially where there is unequal bargaining power, information, or sophistication. For this reason, a very broad provision in a partnership agreement in effect negating any duty of loyalty, such as a provision giving a managing partner complete discretion to manage the business with no liability except for acts and omissions that constitute wilful misconduct, will not likely be enforced. See, e.g., Labovitz v. Dolan, 189 Ill.App.3d 403, 136 Ill.Dec. 780, 545 N.E.2d 304 (1989). On the other hand, it is clear that the remaining partners can "consent" to a particular conflicting interest transaction or other breach of duty, after the fact, provided there is full disclosure.

RUPA attempts to provide a standard that partners can rely upon in drafting exculpatory agreements. It is not necessary that the agreement be restricted to a particular transaction. That would require bargaining over every transaction or opportunity, which would be excessively burdensome. The agreement may be drafted in terms of types or categories of activities or transactions, but it should be reasonably specific.

A provision in a real estate partnership agreement authorizing a partner who is a real estate agent to retain commissions on partnership property bought and sold by that partner would be an example of a "type or category" of activity that is not manifestly unreasonable and thus should be enforceable under the Act. Likewise, a provision authorizing that partner to buy or sell real property for his own account without prior disclosure to the other partners or without first offering it to the partnership would be enforceable as a valid category of partnership activity.

Ultimately, the courts must decide the outer limits of validity of such agreements, and context may be significant. It is intended that the risk of judicial refusal to enforce manifestly unreasonable exculpatory clauses will discourage sharp practices while accommodating the legitimate needs of the parties in structuring their relationship.

5. Subsection (b)(3)(i) permits the partners, in their partnership agreement, to identify specific types or categories of partnership activities that do not violate the duty of loyalty. A modification of the statutory standard must not, however, be manifestly unreasonable. This is intended to discourage overreaching by a partner with superior bargaining power since the courts may refuse to enforce an overly broad exculpatory clause. See, e.g., Vlases v. Montgomery Ward & Co., 377 F.2d 846, 850 (3d Cir.1967) (limitation prohibits unconscionable agreements); PPG Industries, Inc. v. Shell Oil Co., 919 F.2d 17, 19 (5th Cir.1990) (apply limitation deferentially to agreements of sophisticated parties).

Subsection (b)(3)(ii) is intended to clarify the right of partners, recognized under general law, to consent to a known past or anticipated violation of duty and to waive their legal remedies for redress of that violation. This is intended to cover situations where the conduct in question is not specifically authorized by the partnership agreement. It can also be used to validate conduct that might otherwise not satisfy the "manifestly unreasonable" standard. Clause (ii) provides that, after full disclosure of all material facts regarding a specific act or transaction that otherwise would violate the duty of loyalty, it may be authorized or ratified by the partners. That authorization or ratification must be unanimous unless a lesser number or percentage is specified for this purpose in the partnership agreement.

6. Under subsection (b)(4), the partners' duty of care may not be unreasonably reduced below the statutory standard set forth in Section 404(d), that is, to refrain from engaging in grossly negligent or reckless conduct, intentional misconduct, or a knowing violation of law.

For example, partnership agreements frequently contain provisions releasing a partner from liability for actions taken in good faith and in the honest belief that the actions are in the best interests of the partnership and indemnifying the partner against any liability incurred in connection with the business of the partnership if the partner acts in a good faith belief that he has authority to act. Many partnership agreements reach this same result by listing various activities and stating that the performance of these activities is deemed not to constitute gross negligence or wilful misconduct. These types of provisions are intended to come within the modifications authorized by subsection (b)(4). On the other hand, absolving partners of intentional misconduct is probably unreasonable. As with contractual standards of loyalty, determining the outer limit in reducing the standard of care is left to the courts.

The standard may, of course, be increased by agreement to one of ordinary care or an even higher standard of care.

70

7. Subsection (b)(5) authorizes the partners to determine the standards by which the performance of the obligation of good faith and fair dealing is to be measured. The language of subsection (b)(5) is based on UCC Section 1–102(3). The partners can negotiate and draft specific contract provisions tailored to their particular needs (e.g., five days notice of a partners' meeting is adequate notice), but blanket waivers of the obligation are unenforceable....

8. Section 602(a) continues the traditional UPA Section 31(2) rule that every partner has the power to withdraw from the partnership at any time, which power can not be bargained away. Section 103(b)(6) provides that the partnership agreement may not vary the power to dissociate as a partner under Section 602(a), except to require that the notice of withdrawal under Section 601(1) be in writing....

9. Under subsection (b)(7), the right of a partner to seek court expulsion of another partner under Section 601(5) can not be waived or varied (e.g., requiring a 90–day notice) by agreement. Section 601(5) refers to judicial expulsion on such grounds as misconduct, breach of duty, or impracticability.

10. Under subsection (b)(8), the partnership agreement may not vary the right of partners to have the partnership dissolved and its business wound up under Section 801(4), (5), or (6). Section 801(4) provides that the partnership must be wound up if its business is unlawful. Section 801(5) provides for judicial winding up in such circumstances as frustration of the firm's economic purpose, partner misconduct, or impracticability. Section 801(6) accords standing to transferees of an interest in the partnership to seek judicial dissolution of the partnership in specified circumstances.

11. Subsection (b)(9) makes clear that a limited liability partnership may not designate the law of a State other than the State where it filed its statement of qualification to govern its internal affairs and the liability of its partners. See Sections 101(5), 106(b), and 202(a). Therefore, the selection of a state within which to file a statement of qualification has important choice of law ramifications, particularly where the partnership was formed in another state. See Comments to Section 106(b)....

SECTION 104. SUPPLEMENTAL PRINCIPLES OF LAW.

(a) Unless displaced by particular provisions of this [Act], the principles of law and equity supplement this [Act].

(b) If an obligation to pay interest arises under this [Act] and the rate is not specified, the rate is that specified in [applicable statute].

Comment:

The principles of law and equity supplement RUPA unless displaced by a particular provision of the Act.... These supplementary principles encompass not only the law of agency and estoppel and the law merchant mentioned in the UPA, but all of the other principles listed in UCC Section 1–103: the law relative to capacity to contract, fraud, misrepresentation, duress, coercion, mistake, bankruptcy, and other common law validating or invalidating causes, such as unconscionability. No substantive change from either the UPA or the UCC is intended....

SECTION 105. EXECUTION, FILING, AND RECORDING OF STATEMENTS.

(a) A statement may be filed in the office of [the Secretary of State]. A certified copy of a statement that is filed in an office in another State may be filed in the office of [the Secretary of State]. Either filing has the effect provided in this [Act] with respect to partnership property located in or transactions that occur in this State.

(b) A certified copy of a statement that has been filed in the office of the [Secretary of State] and recorded in the office for recording transfers of real property has the effect provided for recorded statements in this [Act]. A recorded statement that is not a certified copy of a statement filed in the office of the [Secretary of State] does not have the effect provided for recorded statements in this [Act].

(c) A statement filed by a partnership must be executed by at least two partners. Other statements must be executed by a partner or other person authorized by this [Act]. An individual who executes a statement as, or on behalf of, a partner or other person named as a partner in a statement shall personally declare under penalty of perjury that the contents of the statement are accurate.

(d) A person authorized by this [Act] to file a statement may amend or cancel the statement by filing an amendment or cancellation that names the partnership, identifies the statement, and states the substance of the amendment or cancellation.

(e) A person who files a statement pursuant to this section shall promptly send a copy of the statement to every nonfiling partner and to any other person named as a partner in the statement. Failure to send a copy of a statement to a partner or other person does not limit the effectiveness of the statement as to a person not a partner.

(f) The [Secretary of State] may collect a fee for filing or providing a certified copy of a statement. The [officer responsible for] recording transfers of real property may collect a fee for recording a statement.

Comment:

1.   Section 105 is new.   It mandates the procedural rules for the execution, filing, and recording of the various "statements" (see Section 101(11)) authorized by RUPA. . . .

No filings are mandatory under RUPA.   In all cases, the filing of a statement is optional and voluntary.   A system of mandatory filing and disclosure for partnerships, similar to that required for corporations and limited partnerships, was rejected for several reasons.   First, RUPA is designed to accommodate the needs of small partnerships, which often have unwritten or sketchy agreements and limited resources.   Furthermore, inadvertent partnerships are also governed by the Act, as the default form of business organization, in which case filing would be unlikely.

The RUPA filing provisions are, however, likely to encourage the voluntary use of partnership statements.   There are a number of strong incentives for the partnership or the partners to file statements or for third parties, such as lenders or transferees of partnership property, to compel them to do so.

Only statements that are executed, filed, and, if appropriate (such as the authority to transfer real property), recorded in conformity with Section 105 have the legal consequences accorded statements by RUPA.   The requirements of Section 105 cannot be varied in the partnership agreement, except the duty to provide copies of statements to all the partners.   See Section 103(b)(1). . . .

SECTION 106.   GOVERNING LAW.

(a) Except as otherwise provided in subsection (b), the law of the jurisdiction in which a partnership has its chief executive office governs relations among the partners and between the partners and the partnership.

(b) The law of this State governs relations among the partners and between the partners and the partnership and the liability of partners for an obligation of a limited liability partnership.

Comment:

The subsection (a) internal relations rule is new. . . .

RUPA looks to the jurisdiction in which a partnership's chief executive office is located to provide the law governing the internal relations among the partners and between the partners and the partnership.   The concept of the partnership's "chief executive office" is drawn from UCC Section 9–103(3)(d).   It was chosen in lieu of the State of organization because no filing is necessary to form a general partnership, and thus the situs of its organization is not always clear, unlike a limited partnership, which is organized in the State where its certificate is filed.

The term "chief executive office" is not defined in the Act, nor is it defined in the UCC. Paragraph 5 of the Official Comment to UCC Section 9–103(3)(d) explains:

"Chief executive office" ... means the place from which in fact the debtor manages the main part of his business operations.... Doubt may arise as to which is the "chief executive office" of a multi-state enterprise, but it would be rare that there could be more than two possibilities.... [The rule] will be simple to apply in most cases....

In the absence of any other clear rule for determining a partnership's legal situs, it seems convenient to use that rule for choice of law purposes as well.

The choice-of-law rule provided by Section 106 is only a default rule, and the partners may by agreement select the law of another State to govern their internal affairs, subject to generally applicable conflict of laws requirements. For example, where the partners may not resolve a particular issue by an explicit provision of the partnership agreement, such as the rights and duties set forth in Section 103(b), the law chosen will not be applied if the partners or the partnership have no substantial relationship to the chosen State or other reasonable basis for their choice or if application of the law of the chosen State would be contrary to a fundamental policy of a State that has a materially greater interest than the chosen State. See Restatement (Second) of Conflict of Laws § 187(2) (1971). The partners must ... select only one State to govern their internal relations. They cannot select one State for some aspects of their internal relations and another State for others.

Contrasted with the variable choice-of-law rule provided by subsection (a), the law of the State where a limited liability partnership files its statement of qualification applies to such a partnership and may not be varied by the agreement of the partners. See Section 103(b)(9). Also, a partnership that files a statement of qualification in another state is not defined as a limited liability partnership in this state. See Section 101(5). Unlike a general partnership which may be formed without any filing, a partnership may only become a limited liability partnership by filing a statement of qualification. Therefore, the situs of its organization is clear. Because it is often unclear where a general partnership is actually formed, the decision to file a statement of qualification in a particular state constitutes a choice-of-law for the partnership which cannot be altered by the partnership agreement. See Comments to Section 103(b)(9). If the partnership agreement of an existing partnership specifies the law of a particular state as its governing law, and the partnership thereafter files a statement of qualification in another state, the partnership agreement choice is no longer controlling. In such cases, the filing of a statement of qualification "amends" the partnership agreement on this limited matter. Accordingly, if a statement of qualification is revoked or canceled for a limited liability partnership, the law of the state of filing would continue to apply unless the partnership agreement thereafter altered the applicable law rule.

SECTION 107. PARTNERSHIP SUBJECT TO AMENDMENT OR REPEAL OF [ACT].

A partnership governed by this [Act] is subject to any amendment to or repeal of this [Act].

Comment:

The reservation of power provision is new. It is adapted from Section 1.02 of the Revised Model Business Corporation Act (RMBCA) and Section 1106 of RULPA.

As explained in the Official Comment to the RMBCA, the genesis of those provisions is Trustees of Dartmouth College v. Woodward, 17 U.S. (4 Wheat) 518 (1819), which held that the United States Constitution prohibits the application of newly enacted statutes to existing corporations, while suggesting the efficacy of a reservation of power provision. Its purpose is to avoid any possible argument that a legal entity created pursuant to statute or its members have a contractual or vested right in any specific statutory provision and to ensure that the State may in the future modify its enabling statute as it deems appropriate and require existing entities to comply with the statutes as modified.

ARTICLE 2

NATURE OF PARTNERSHIP

Section 201. Partnership As Entity.
Section 202. Formation of Partnership.
Section 203. Partnership Property.
Section 204. When Property Is Partnership Property.

SECTION 201. PARTNERSHIP AS ENTITY.

(a) A partnership is an entity distinct from its partners.

(b) A limited liability partnership continues to be the same entity that existed before the filing of a statement of qualification under Section 1001.

Comment:

RUPA embraces the entity theory of the partnership. In light of the UPA's ambivalence on the nature of partnerships, the explicit statement provided by subsection (a) is deemed appropriate as an expression of the increased emphasis on the entity theory as the dominant model. *But see* Section 306 (partners' liability joint and several unless the partnership has filed a statement of qualification to become a limited liability partnership).

Giving clear expression to the entity nature of a partnership is intended to allay previous concerns stemming from the aggregate theory, such as the necessity of a deed to convey title from the "old" partnership to the "new" partnership every time there is a change of cast among the partners. Under RUPA, there is no "new" partnership just because of membership changes. That will avoid the result in cases such as Fairway Development Co. v. Title Insurance Co., 621 F.Supp. 120 (N.D.Ohio 1985), which held that the "new" partnership resulting from a partner's death did not have standing to enforce a title insurance policy issued to the "old" partnership.

Subsection (b) makes clear that the explicit entity theory provided by subsection (a) applies to a partnership both before and after it files a statement of qualification to become a limited liability partnership. Thus, just as there is no "new" partnership resulting from membership changes, the filing of a statement of qualification does not create a "new" partnership. The filing partnership continues to be the same partnership entity that existed before the filing. Similarly, the amendment or cancellation of a statement of qualification under Section 105(d) or the revocation of a statement of qualification under Section 1003(c) does not terminate the partnership and create a "new" partnership. See Section 1003(d). Accordingly, a partnership remains the same entity regardless of a filing, cancellation, or revocation of a statement of qualification.

SECTION 202. FORMATION OF PARTNERSHIP.

(a) Except as otherwise provided in subsection (b), the association of two or more persons to carry on as co-owners a business for profit forms a partnership, whether or not the persons intend to form a partnership.

(b) An association formed under a statute other than this [Act], a predecessor statute, or a comparable statute of another jurisdiction is not a partnership under this [Act].

(c) In determining whether a partnership is formed, the following rules apply:

(1) Joint tenancy, tenancy in common, tenancy by the entireties, joint property, common property, or part ownership does not by

itself establish a partnership, even if the co-owners share profits made by the use of the property.

(2) The sharing of gross returns does not by itself establish a partnership, even if the persons sharing them have a joint or common right or interest in property from which the returns are derived.

(3) A person who receives a share of the profits of a business is presumed to be a partner in the business, unless the profits were received in payment:

(i) of a debt by installments or otherwise;

(ii) for services as an independent contractor or of wages or other compensation to an employee;

(iii) of rent;

(iv) of an annuity or other retirement or health benefit to a beneficiary, representative, or designee of a deceased or retired partner;

(v) of interest or other charge on a loan, even if the amount of payment varies with the profits of the business, including a direct or indirect present or future ownership of the collateral, or rights to income, proceeds, or increase in value derived from the collateral; or

(vi) for the sale of the goodwill of a business or other property by installments or otherwise.

Comment:

1. Section 202 combines UPA Sections 6 and 7. The traditional UPA Section 6(1) "definition" of a partnership is recast as an operative rule of law. No substantive change in the law is intended. The UPA "definition" has always been understood as an operative rule, as well as a definition. The addition of the phrase, "whether or not the persons intend to form a partnership," merely codifies the universal judicial construction of UPA Section 6(1) that a partnership is created by the association of persons whose intent is to carry on as co-owners a business for profit, regardless of their subjective intention to be "partners." Indeed, they may inadvertently create a partnership despite their expressed subjective intention not to do so. The new language alerts readers to this possibility.

As under the UPA, the attribute of co-ownership distinguishes a partnership from a mere agency relationship. A business is a series of acts directed toward an end. Ownership involves the power of ultimate control. To state that partners are co-owners of a business is to state that they each have the power of ultimate control. See Official Comment to UPA § 6(1). On the other hand, as subsection (c)(1) makes clear, passive co-ownership of property by itself, as distinguished from the carrying on of a business, does not establish a partnership.

2.   Subsection (b) provides that business associations organized under other statutes are not partnerships. Those statutory associations include corporations, limited partnerships, and limited liability companies. That continues the UPA concept that general partnership is the residual form of for profit business association, existing only if another form does not.

A limited partnership is not a partnership under this definition. Nevertheless, certain provisions of RUPA will continue to govern limited partnerships because RULPA itself, in Section 1105, so requires "in any case not provided for" in RULPA. For example, the rules applicable to a limited liability partnership will generally apply to limited partnerships. See Comment to Section 101(5) (definition of a limited liability partnership). In light of ... RULPA Section 1105, UPA Section 6(2), which provides that limited partnerships are governed by the UPA, is redundant and has not been carried over to RUPA. It is also more appropriate that the applicability of RUPA to limited partnerships be governed exclusively by RULPA. For example, a RULPA amendment may clarify certain linkage questions regarding the application of the limited liability partnership rules to limited partnerships. See Comment to Section 101(5) for a suggested form of such an amendment....

Relationships that are called "joint ventures" are partnerships if they otherwise fit the definition of a partnership. An association is not classified as a partnership, however, simply because it is called a "joint venture."

An unincorporated nonprofit organization is not a partnership under RUPA, even if it qualifies as a business, because it is not a "for profit" organization.

3.   Subsection (c) provides three rules of construction that apply in determining whether a partnership has been formed under subsection (a). They are largely derived from UPA Section 7, and to that extent no substantive change is intended. The sharing of profits is recast as a rebuttable presumption of a partnership, a more contemporary construction, rather than as prima facie evidence thereof. The protected categories, in which receipt of a share of the profits is not presumed to create a partnership, apply whether the profit share is a single flat percentage or a ratio which varies, for example, after reaching a dollar floor or different levels of profits.

Like its predecessor, RUPA makes no attempt to answer in every case whether a partnership is formed. Whether a relationship is more properly characterized as that of borrower and lender, employer and employee, or landlord and tenant is left to the trier of fact. As under the UPA, a person may function in both partner and nonpartner capacities....

SECTION 203. PARTNERSHIP PROPERTY.

Property acquired by a partnership is property of the partnership and not of the partners individually.

Comment:

All property acquired by a partnership, by transfer or otherwise, becomes partnership property and belongs to the partnership as an entity, rather than to the individual partners. This expresses the substantive result of UPA Sections 8(1) and 25.

Neither UPA Section 8(1) nor RUPA Section 203 provides any guidance concerning when property is "acquired by" the partnership. That problem is dealt with in Section 204....

SECTION 204. WHEN PROPERTY IS PARTNERSHIP PROPERTY.

(a) Property is partnership property if acquired in the name of:

(1) the partnership; or

(2) one or more partners with an indication in the instrument transferring title to the property of the person's capacity as a partner or of the existence of a partnership but without an indication of the name of the partnership.

(b) Property is acquired in the name of the partnership by a transfer to:

(1) the partnership in its name; or

(2) one or more partners in their capacity as partners in the partnership, if the name of the partnership is indicated in the instrument transferring title to the property.

(c) Property is presumed to be partnership property if purchased with partnership assets, even if not acquired in the name of the partnership or of one or more partners with an indication in the instrument transferring title to the property of the person's capacity as a partner or of the existence of a partnership.

(d) Property acquired in the name of one or more of the partners, without an indication in the instrument transferring title to the property of the person's capacity as a partner or of the existence of a partnership and without use of partnership assets, is presumed to be separate property, even if used for partnership purposes.

Comment: ...

3. Ultimately, it is the intention of the partners that controls whether property belongs to the partnership or to one or more of the partners in their individual capacities, at least as among the partners themselves. RUPA sets forth two rebuttable presumptions that apply when the partners have failed to express their intent.

First, under subsection (c), property purchased with partnership funds is presumed to be partnership property, notwithstanding the name in which title is held. The presumption is intended to apply if partnership credit is used to obtain financing, as well as the use of partnership cash or property for payment. Unlike the rule in subsection (b), under which property is *deemed* to be partnership property if the partnership's name or the partner's capacity as a partner is disclosed in the instrument of conveyance, subsection (c) raises only a *presumption* that the property is partnership property if it is purchased with partnership assets.

That presumption is also subject to an important caveat. Under Section 302(b), partnership property held in the name of individual partners, without an indication of their capacity as partners or of the existence of a partnership, that is transferred by the partners in whose name title is held to a purchaser without knowledge that it is partnership property is free of any claims of the partnership.

Second, under subsection (d), property acquired in the name of one or more of the partners, without an indication of their capacity as partners and without use of partnership funds or credit, is presumed to be the partners' separate property, even if used for partnership purposes. In effect, it is presumed in that case that only the use of the property is contributed to the partnership....

ARTICLE 3

RELATIONS OF PARTNERS TO PERSONS DEALING WITH PARTNERSHIP

SECTION 301. PARTNER AGENT OF PARTNERSHIP.

Subject to the effect of a statement of partnership authority under Section 303:

(1) Each partner is an agent of the partnership for the purpose of its business. An act of a partner, including the execution of an instrument in the partnership name, for apparently carrying on in the ordinary course the partnership business or business of the kind carried on by the partnership binds the partnership, unless the partner had no authority to act for the partnership in the particular matter and the person with whom the partner was dealing knew or had received a notification that the partner lacked authority.

(2) An act of a partner which is not apparently for carrying on in the ordinary course the partnership business or business of the kind carried on by the partnership binds the partnership only if the act was authorized by the other partners.

Comment: ...

2. Section 301(1) retains the basic principles reflected in UPA Section 9(1). It declares that each partner is an agent of the partnership and that, by virtue of partnership status, each partner has apparent authority to bind the partnership in ordinary course transactions. The effect of Section 301(1) is to characterize a partner as a general managerial agent having both actual and apparent authority co-extensive in scope with the firm's ordinary business, at least in the absence of a contrary partnership agreement.

Section 301(1) effects two changes from UPA Section 9(1). First, it clarifies that a partner's apparent authority includes acts for carrying on in the ordinary course "business of the kind carried on by the partnership," not just the business of the particular partnership in question. The UPA is ambiguous on this point, but there is some authority for an expanded construction in accordance with the so-called English rule. See, e.g., Burns v. Gonzalez, 439 S.W.2d 128, 131 (Tex.Civ.App.1969) (dictum); Commercial Hotel Co. v. Weeks, 254 S.W. 521 (Tex.Civ.App.1923). No substantive change is intended by use of the more customary phrase "carrying on in the ordinary course" in lieu of the UPA phrase "in the usual way." The UPA and the case law use both terms without apparent distinction.

The other change from the UPA concerns the allocation of risk of a partner's lack of authority. RUPA draws the line somewhat differently from the UPA.

Under UPA Section 9(1) and (4), only a person with knowledge of a restriction on a partner's authority is bound by it. Section 301(1) provides that a person who has received a notification of a partner's lack of authority is also bound. The meaning of "receives a notification" is explained in Section 102(d). Thus, the partnership may protect itself from unauthorized acts by giving a notification of a restriction on a partner's authority to a person dealing with that partner. A notification may be effective upon delivery, whether or not it actually comes to the other person's attention. To that extent, the risk of lack of authority is shifted to those dealing with partners.

On the other hand, as used in the UPA, the term "knowledge" embodies the concept of "bad faith" knowledge arising from other known facts. As used in RUPA, however, "knowledge" is limited to actual knowledge. See Section 102(a). Thus, RUPA does not expose persons dealing with a partner to the greater risk of being bound by a restriction based on their purported reason to know of the partner's lack of authority from all the facts they did know. Compare Section 102(b)(3) (notice).

With one exception, this result is not affected even if the partnership files a statement of partnership authority containing a limitation on a partner's authority. Section 303(f) makes clear that a person dealing with a partner is not deemed to know of such a limitation merely because it is contained in a filed statement of authority. Under Section 303(e), however, all persons are deemed to know of a limitation on the authority of a partner to transfer real property contained in a recorded statement. Thus, a recorded limitation on authority concerning real property constitutes constructive knowledge of the limitation to the whole world.

3. Section 301(2) is drawn directly from UPA Section 9(2), with conforming changes to mirror the new language of subsection (1). Subsection (2) makes it clear that the partnership is bound by a partner's actual authority, even if the partner has no apparent authority. Section 401(j) requires the unanimous consent of the partners for a grant of authority outside the ordinary course of business, unless the partnership agreement provides otherwise. Under general agency principles, the partners can subsequently ratify a partner's unauthorized act. See Section 104(a).

4. UPA Section 9(3) contains a list of five extraordinary acts that require unanimous consent of the partners before the partnership is bound. RUPA omits that section. That leaves it to the courts to decide the outer limits of the agency power of a partner. Most of the acts listed in UPA Section 9(3) probably remain outside the apparent authority of a partner under RUPA, such as disposing of the goodwill of the business, but elimination of a statutory rule will afford more flexibility in some situations specified in UPA Section 9(3). In particular, it seems archaic that the submission of a partnership claim to arbitration always requires unanimous consent. See UPA § 9(3)(e).....

SECTION 302. TRANSFER OF PARTNERSHIP PROPERTY.

(a) Partnership property may be transferred as follows:

(1) Subject to the effect of a statement of partnership authority under Section 303, partnership property held in the name of the partnership may be transferred by an instrument of transfer executed by a partner in the partnership name.

(2) Partnership property held in the name of one or more partners with an indication in the instrument transferring the property to them of their capacity as partners or of the existence of a partnership, but without an indication of the name of the partnership, may be transferred by an instrument of transfer executed by the persons in whose name the property is held.

(3) Partnership property held in the name of one or more persons other than the partnership, without an indication in the instrument transferring the property to them of their capacity as partners or of the existence of a partnership, may be transferred by an instrument of transfer executed by the persons in whose name the property is held.

(b) A partnership may recover partnership property from a transferee only if it proves that execution of the instrument of initial transfer did not bind the partnership under Section 301 and:

(1) as to a subsequent transferee who gave value for property transferred under subsection (a)(1) and (2), proves that the subsequent transferee knew or had received a notification that the person who executed the instrument of initial transfer lacked authority to bind the partnership; or

(2) as to a transferee who gave value for property transferred under subsection (a)(3), proves that the transferee knew or had received a notification that the property was partnership property and that the person who executed the instrument of initial transfer lacked authority to bind the partnership.

(c) A partnership may not recover partnership property from a subsequent transferee if the partnership would not have been entitled to recover the property, under subsection (b), from any earlier transferee of the property.

(d) If a person holds all of the partners' interests in the partnership, all of the partnership property vests in that person. The person may execute a document in the name of the partnership to evidence vesting of the property in that person and may file or record the document.

SECTION 303. STATEMENT OF PARTNERSHIP AUTHORITY.

(a) A partnership may file a statement of partnership authority, which:

(1) must include:

(i) the name of the partnership;

(ii) the street address of its chief executive office and of one office in this State, if there is one;

(iii) the names and mailing addresses of all of the partners or of an agent appointed and maintained by the partnership for the purpose of subsection (b); and

(iv) the names of the partners authorized to execute an instrument transferring real property held in the name of the partnership; and

(2) may state the authority, or limitations on the authority, of some or all of the partners to enter into other transactions on behalf of the partnership and any other matter.

(b) If a statement of partnership authority names an agent, the agent shall maintain a list of the names and mailing addresses of all of the partners and make it available to any person on request for good cause shown.

(c) If a filed statement of partnership authority is executed pursuant to Section 105(c) and states the name of the partnership but does not contain all of the other information required by subsection (a), the statement nevertheless operates with respect to a person not a partner as provided in subsections (d) and (e).

(d) Except as otherwise provided in subsection (g), a filed statement of partnership authority supplements the authority of a partner to enter into transactions on behalf of the partnership as follows:

(1) Except for transfers of real property, a grant of authority contained in a filed statement of partnership authority is conclusive in favor of a person who gives value without knowledge to the contrary, so long as and to the extent that a limitation on that authority is not then contained in another filed statement. A filed cancellation of a limitation on authority revives the previous grant of authority.

(2) A grant of authority to transfer real property held in the name of the partnership contained in a certified copy of a filed statement of partnership authority recorded in the office for recording transfers of that real property is conclusive in favor of a person who gives value without knowledge to the contrary, so long as and to the extent that a certified copy of a filed statement containing a limitation on that authority is not then of record in the office for recording transfers of that real property. The recording in the office for recording transfers of that real property of a certified copy of a filed cancellation of a limitation on authority revives the previous grant of authority.

(e) A person not a partner is deemed to know of a limitation on the authority of a partner to transfer real property held in the name of the partnership if a certified copy of the filed statement containing the limitation on authority is of record in the office for recording transfers of that real property.

(f) Except as otherwise provided in subsections (d) and (e) and Sections 704 and 805, a person not a partner is not deemed to know of a limitation on the authority of a partner merely because the limitation is contained in a filed statement.

(g) Unless earlier canceled, a filed statement of partnership authority is canceled by operation of law five years after the date on which the statement, or the most recent amendment, was filed with the [Secretary of State].

Comment:

1.   Section 303 is new.   It provides for an optional statement of partnership authority specifying the names of the partners authorized to execute instruments transferring real property held in the name of the partnership.   It may also grant supplementary authority to partners, or limit their authority, to enter into other transactions on behalf of the partnership.   The execution, filing, and recording of statements is governed by Section 105....

2.   The most important goal of the statement of authority is to facilitate the transfer of real property held in the name of the partnership.   A statement must specify the names of the partners authorized to execute an instrument transferring that property.

Under subsection (d)(2), a recorded grant of authority to transfer real property held in the name of the partnership is conclusive in favor of a transferee for value without actual knowledge to the contrary....

Under subsection (e), third parties are deemed to know of a recorded limitation on the authority of a partner to transfer real property held in the partnership name.   Since transferees are bound under Section 301 by knowledge of a limitation on a partner's authority, they are bound by such a recorded limitation.   Of course, a transferee with actual knowledge of a limitation on a partner's authority is bound under Section 301, whether or not there is a recorded statement of limitation.

3.   A statement of partnership authority may have effect beyond the transfer of real property held in the name of the partnership.   Under subsection (a)(2), a statement of authority may contain any other matter the partnership chooses, including a grant of authority, or a limitation on the authority, of some or all of the partners to enter into other transactions on behalf of the partnership.   Since Section 301 confers authority on all partners to act for

the partnership in ordinary matters, the real import of such a provision is to grant extraordinary authority, or to limit the ordinary authority, of some or all of the partners.

The effect given to such a provision is different from that accorded a provision regarding the transfer of real property. Under subsection (d)(1), a filed grant of authority is binding on the partnership, in favor of a person who gives value without actual knowledge to the contrary, unless limited by another filed statement. That is the same rule as for statements involving real property under subsection 301(d)(2). There is, however, no counterpart to subsection (e) regarding a filed limitation of authority. To the contrary, subsection (f) makes clear that filing a limitation of authority does not operate as constructive knowledge of a partner's lack of authority with respect to non-real property transactions.

Under Section 301, only a third party who knows or has received a notification of a partner's lack of authority in an ordinary course transaction is bound. Thus, a limitation on a partner's authority to transfer personal property or to enter into other non-real property transactions on behalf of the partnership, contained in a filed statement of partnership authority, is effective only against a third party who knows or has received a notification of it. The fact of the statement being filed has no legal significance in those transactions, although the filed statement is a potential source of actual knowledge to third parties.

4. It should be emphasized that Section 303 concerns the authority of partners to bind the partnership to third persons. As among the partners, the authority of a partner to take any action is governed by the partnership agreement, or by the provisions of RUPA governing the relations among partners, and is not affected by the filing or recording of a statement of partnership authority. . . .

SECTION 304. STATEMENT OF DENIAL.

A partner or other person named as a partner in a filed statement of partnership authority or in a list maintained by an agent pursuant to Section 303(b) may file a statement of denial stating the name of the partnership and the fact that it is being denied, which may include denial of a person's authority or status as a partner. A statement of denial is a limitation on authority as provided in Section 303(d) and (e).

SECTION 305. PARTNERSHIP LIABLE FOR PARTNER'S AC-TIONABLE CONDUCT.

(a) A partnership is liable for loss or injury caused to a person, or for a penalty incurred, as a result of a wrongful act or omission, or other actionable conduct, of a partner acting in the ordinary course of business of the partnership or with authority of the partnership.

(b) If, in the course of the partnership's business or while acting with authority of the partnership, a partner receives or causes the partnership to receive money or property of a person not a partner, and the money or property is misapplied by a partner, the partnership is liable for the loss.

Comment:

Section 305(a), which is derived from UPA Section 13, imposes liability on the partnership for the wrongful acts of a partner acting in the ordinary course of the partnership's business or otherwise within the partner's authority. The scope of the section has been expanded by deleting from UPA Section 13, "not being a partner in the partnership." This is intended to permit a partner to sue the partnership on a tort or other theory during the term of the partnership, rather than being limited to the remedies of dissolution and an accounting. See also Comment 2 to Section 405.

The section has also been broadened to cover no-fault torts by the addition of the phrase, "or other actionable conduct."

The partnership is liable for the actionable conduct or omission of a partner acting in the ordinary course of its business or "with the authority of the partnership." This is intended to include a partner's apparent, as well as actual, authority....

Section 305(b).... imposes strict liability on the partnership for the misapplication of money or property received by a partner in the course of the partnership's business or otherwise within the scope of the partner's actual authority.

SECTION 306. PARTNER'S LIABILITY.

(a) Except as otherwise provided in subsection (b), all partners are liable jointly and severally for all obligations of the partnership unless otherwise agreed by the claimant or provided by law.

(b) A person admitted as a partner into an existing partnership is not personally liable for any partnership obligation incurred before the person's admission as a partner.

(c) An obligation of a partnership incurred while the partnership is a limited liability partnership, whether arising in contract, tort, or otherwise, is solely the obligation of the partnership. A partner is not personally liable, directly or indirectly, by way of contribution or other-wise, for such a partnership obligation solely by reason of being or so acting as a partner. This subsection applies notwithstanding anything inconsistent in the partnership agreement that existed immediately before the vote required to become a limited liability partnership under Section 1001(b).

Comment:

1. Section 306(a) changes the UPA rule by imposing joint and several liability on the partners for all partnership obligations where the partnership is not a limited liability partnership. Under UPA Section 15, partners' liability for torts is joint and several, while their liability for contracts is joint but not several. About ten States that have adopted the UPA already provide for joint and several liability. The UPA reference to "debts and obligations" is redundant, and no change is intended by RUPA's reference solely to "obligations."

Joint and several liability under RUPA differs, however, from the classic model, which permits a judgment creditor to proceed immediately against any of the joint and several judgment debtors. Generally, Section 307(d) requires the judgment creditor to exhaust the partnership's assets before enforcing a judgment against the separate assets of a partner. . . .

3. Subsection (c) alters classic joint and several liability of general partners for obligations of a partnership that is a limited liability partnership. Like shareholders of a corporation and members of a limited liability company, partners of a limited liability partnership are not personally liable for partnership obligations incurred while the partnership liability shield is in place solely because they are partners. As with shareholders of a corporation and members of a limited liability company, partners remain personally liable for their personal misconduct.

In cases of partner misconduct, Section 401(c) sets forth a partnership's obligation to indemnify the culpable partner where the partner's liability was incurred in the ordinary course of the partnership's business. When indemnification occurs, the assets of both the partnership and the culpable partner are available to a creditor. However, Sections 306(c), 401(b), and 807(b) make clear that a partner who is not otherwise liable under Section 306(c) is not obligated to contribute assets to the partnership in excess of agreed contributions to share the loss with the culpable partner. (See Comments to Sections 401(b) and 807(b) regarding a slight variation in the context of priority of payment of partnership obligations.) Accordingly, Section 306(c) makes clear that an innocent partner is not personally liable for specified partnership obligations, directly or indirectly, by way of contribution or otherwise.

Although the liability shield protections of Section 306(c) may be modified in part or in full in a partnership agreement (and by way of private contractual guarantees), the modifications must constitute an intentional waiver of the liability protections. See Sections 103(b), 104(a), and 902(b). Since the mere act of filing a statement of qualification reflects the assumption that the partners intend to modify the otherwise applicable partner liability rules, the final sentence of subsection (c) makes clear that the filing negates inconsistent aspects of the partnership agreement that existed immediately before the vote to approve becoming a limited liability partnership. The negation only applies to a partner's personal liability for future partnership obligations. The filing however has no effect as to previously created partner obligations to the partnership in the form of specific capital contribution requirements.

Inter se contribution agreements may erode part or all of the effects of the liability shield. For example, Section 807(f) provides that an assignee for the benefit of creditors of a partnership or a partner may enforce a partner's obligation to contribute to the partnership. The ultimate effect of such contribution obligations may make each partner jointly and severally liable for all partnership obligations—even those incurred while the partnership is a limited liability partnership. Although the final sentence of subsection (c) negates such provisions existing before a statement of qualification is filed, it will have no effect on any amendments to the partnership agreement after the statement is filed....

SECTION 307. ACTIONS BY AND AGAINST PARTNERSHIP AND PARTNERS.

(a) A partnership may sue and be sued in the name of the partnership.

(b) An action may be brought against the partnership and, to the extent not inconsistent with section 306, any or all of the partners in the same action or in separate actions.

(c) A judgment against a partnership is not by itself a judgment against a partner. A judgment against a partnership may not be satisfied from a partner's assets unless there is also a judgment against the partner.

(d) A judgment creditor of a partner may not levy execution against the assets of the partner to satisfy a judgment based on a claim against the partnership unless the partner is personally liable for the claim under Section 306 and:

(1) a judgment based on the same claim has been obtained against the partnership and a writ of execution on the judgment has been returned unsatisfied in whole or in part;

(2) the partnership is a debtor in bankruptcy;

(3) the partner has agreed that the creditor need not exhaust partnership assets;

(4) a court grants permission to the judgment creditor to levy execution against the assets of a partner based on a finding that partnership assets subject to execution are clearly insufficient to satisfy the judgment, that exhaustion of partnership assets is excessively burdensome, or that the grant of permission is an appropriate exercise of the court's equitable powers; or

(5) liability is imposed on the partner by law or contract independent of the existence of the partnership.

(e) This section applies to any partnership liability or obligation resulting from a representation by a partner or purported partner under Section 308.

Comment:

1. Section 307 is new. Subsection (a) provides that a partnership may sue and be sued in the partnership name. That entity approach is designed to simplify suits by and against a partnership.

At common law, a partnership, not being a legal entity, could not sue or be sued in the firm name. The UPA itself is silent on this point, so in the absence of another enabling statute, it is generally necessary to join all the partners in an action against the partnership.

Most States have statutes or rules authorizing partnerships to sue or be sued in the partnership name. Many of those statutes, however, are found in the state provisions dealing with civil procedure rather than in the partnership act. . . .

3. Subsection (c) provides that a judgment against the partnership is not, standing alone, a judgment against the partners, and it cannot be satisfied from a partner's personal assets unless there is a judgment against the partner. Thus, a partner must be individually named and served, either in the action against the partnership or in a later suit, before his personal assets may be subject to levy for a claim against the partnership.

RUPA leaves it to the law of judgments, as did the UPA, to determine the collateral effects to be accorded a prior judgment for or against the partnership in a subsequent action against a partner individually. . . .

SECTION 308. LIABILITY OF PURPORTED PARTNER.

(a) If a person, by words or conduct, purports to be a partner, or consents to being represented by another as a partner, in a partnership or with one or more persons not partners, the purported partner is liable to a person to whom the representation is made, if that person, relying on the representation, enters into a transaction with the actual or purported partnership. If the representation, either by the purported partner or by a person with the purported partner's consent, is made in a public manner, the purported partner is liable to a person who relies upon the purported partnership even if the purported partner is not aware of being held out as a partner to the claimant. If partnership liability results, the purported partner is liable with respect to that liability as if the purported partner were a partner. If no partnership liability results, the purported partner is liable with respect to that liability jointly and severally with any other person consenting to the representation.

(b) If a person is thus represented to be a partner in an existing partnership, or with one or more persons not partners, the purported partner is an agent of persons consenting to the representation to bind them to the same extent and in the same manner as if the purported partner were a partner, with respect to persons who enter into transactions in reliance upon the representation. If all of the partners of the existing partnership consent to the representation, a partnership act or obligation results. If fewer than all of the partners of the existing partnership consent to the representation, the person acting and the partners consenting to the representation are jointly and severally liable.

(c) A person is not liable as a partner merely because the person is named by another in a statement of partnership authority.

(d) A person does not continue to be liable as a partner merely because of a failure to file a statement of dissociation or to amend a statement of partnership authority to indicate the partner's dissociation from the partnership.

(e) Except as otherwise provided in subsections (a) and (b), persons who are not partners as to each other are not liable as partners to other persons.

ARTICLE 4

RELATIONS OF PARTNERS TO EACH OTHER AND TO PARTNERSHIP

Section 401. Partner's Rights and Duties.
Section 402. Distributions in Kind.
Section 403. Partner's Rights and Duties With Respect to Information.
Section 404. General Standards of Partner's Conduct.
Section 405. Actions by Partnership and Partners.
Section 406. Continuation of Partnership Beyond Definite Term or Particular Undertaking.

SECTION 401. PARTNER'S RIGHTS AND DUTIES.

(a) Each partner is deemed to have an account that is:

(1) credited with an amount equal to the money plus the value of any other property, net of the amount of any liabilities, the

partner contributes to the partnership and the partner's share of the partnership profits; and

(2) charged with an amount equal to the money plus the value of any other property, net of the amount of any liabilities, distributed by the partnership to the partner and the partner's share of the partnership losses.

(b) Each partner is entitled to an equal share of the partnership profits and is chargeable with a share of the partnership losses in proportion to the partner's share of the profits.

(c) A partnership shall reimburse a partner for payments made and indemnify a partner for liabilities incurred by the partner in the ordinary course of the business of the partnership or for the preservation of its business or property.

(d) A partnership shall reimburse a partner for an advance to the partnership beyond the amount of capital the partner agreed to contribute.

(e) A payment or advance made by a partner which gives rise to a partnership obligation under subsection (c) or (d) constitutes a loan to the partnership which accrues interest from the date of the payment or advance.

(f) Each partner has equal rights in the management and conduct of the partnership business.

(g) A partner may use or possess partnership property only on behalf of the partnership.

(h) A partner is not entitled to remuneration for services performed for the partnership, except for reasonable compensation for services rendered in winding up the business of the partnership.

(i) A person may become a partner only with the consent of all of the partners.

(j) A difference arising as to a matter in the ordinary course of business of a partnership may be decided by a majority of the partners. An act outside the ordinary course of business of a partnership and an amendment to the partnership agreement may be undertaken only with the consent of all of the partners.

(k) This section does not affect the obligations of a partnership to other persons under Section 301.

Comment: ...

3. Subsection (b) establishes the default rules for the sharing of partnership profits and losses. The UPA Section 18(a) rules that profits are shared equally and that losses, whether capital or operating, are shared in proportion to each partner's share of the profits are continued. Thus, under the default rule, partners share profits

per capita and not in proportion to capital contribution as do corporate shareholders or partners in limited partnerships. Compare RULPA Section 504. With respect to losses, the qualifying phrase, "whether capital or operating," has been deleted as inconsistent with contemporary partnership accounting practice and terminology; no substantive change is intended.

If partners agree to share profits other than equally, losses will be shared similarly to profits, absent agreement to do otherwise. That rule, carried over from the UPA, is predicated on the assumption that partners would likely agree to share losses on the same basis as profits, but may fail to say so. Of course, by agreement, they may share losses on a different basis from profits.

The default rules apply, as does UPA Section 18(a), where one or more of the partners contribute no capital, although there is case law to the contrary. See, e.g., Kovacik v. Reed, 49 Cal.2d 166, 315 P.2d 314 (1957); Becker v. Killarney, 177 Ill.App.3d 793, 523 N.E.2d 467 (1988). It may seem unfair that the contributor of services, who contributes little or no capital, should be obligated to contribute toward the capital loss of the large contributor who contributed no services. In entering a partnership with such a capital structure, the partners should foresee that application of the default rule may bring about unusual results and take advantage of their power to vary by agreement the allocation of capital losses.

Subsection (b) provides that each partner "is chargeable" with a share of the losses, rather than the UPA formulation that each partner shall "contribute" to losses. Losses are charged to each partner's account as provided in subsection (a)(2). It is intended to make clear that a partner is not obligated to contribute to partnership losses before his withdrawal or the liquidation of the partnership, unless the partners agree otherwise. In effect, unless related to an obligation for which the partner is not personally liable under Section 306(c), a partner's negative account represents a debt to the partnership unless the partners agree to the contrary. Similarly, each partner's share of the profits is credited to his account under subsection (a)(1). Absent an agreement to the contrary, however, a partner does not have a right to receive a current distribution of the profits credited to his account, the interim distribution of profits being a matter arising in the ordinary course of business to be decided by majority vote of the partners.

However, where a liability to contribute at dissolution and winding up relates to a partnership obligation governed by the limited liability rule of Section 306(c), a partner is not obligated to contribute additional assets even at dissolution and winding up. See Section 807(b). In such a case, although a partner is not personally liable for the partnership obligation, that partner's interest in the partnership remains at risk.   See also Comment to Section 401(c) relating to indemnification.

In the case of an operating limited liability partnership, the Section 306 liability shield may be partially eroded where the limited liability partnership incurs both shielded and unshielded liabilities. Where the limited liability partnership uses its assets to pay shielded liabilities before paying unshielded liabilities, each partner's obligation to contribute to the limited liability partnership for that partner's share of the unpaid and unshielded obligations at dissolution and winding up remains intact.   The same issue is less likely to occur in the context of the termination of a limited liability partnership since a partner's contribution obligation is based only on that partner's share of unshielded obligations and the partnership will ordinarily use the contributed assets to pay unshielded claims first as they were the basis of the contribution obligations.   See Comments to Section 807(b).

4.   Subsection (c) is derived from UPA Section 18(b) and provides that the partnership shall reimburse partners for payments made and indemnify them for liabilities incurred in the ordinary course of the partnership's business or for the preservation of its business or property.   Reimbursement and indemnification is an obligation of the partnership.   Indemnification may create a loss toward which the partners must contribute.   Although the right to indemnification is usually enforced in the settlement of accounts among partners upon dissolution and winding up of the partnership business, the right accrues when the liability is incurred and thus may be enforced during the term of the partnership in an appropriate case.   See Section 405 and Comment.   A partner's right to indemnification under this Act is not affected by the partnership becoming a limited liability partnership.   Accordingly, partners continue to share partnership losses to the extent of partnership assets....

7.   Under subsection (f), each partner has equal rights in the management and conduct of the business.   It is based on UPA Section 18(e), which has been interpreted broadly to mean that, absent contrary agreement, each partner has a continuing right to participate in the management of the partnership and to be informed about the partnership business even if his assent to partnership business decisions is not required.   There are special rules regarding the partner vote necessary to approve a partnership becoming (or canceling its status as) a limited liability partnership. See Section 1001(b)....

11.   Subsection (j) continues with one important clarification the UPA Section 18(h) scheme of allocating management authority among the partners.   In the absence of an agreement to the con-

trary, matters arising in the ordinary course of the business may be decided by a majority of the partners. Amendments to the partnership agreement and matters outside the ordinary course of the partnership business require unanimous consent of the partners. Although the text of the UPA is silent regarding extraordinary matters, courts have generally required the consent of all partners for those matters. See, e.g., Paciaroni v. Crane, 408 A.2d 946 (Del.Ch.1989); Thomas v. Marvin E. Jewell & Co., 232 Neb. 261, 440 N.W.2d 437 (1989); Duell v. Hancock, 83 A.D.2d 762, 443 N.Y.S.2d 490 (1981)....

SECTION 402. DISTRIBUTIONS IN KIND.

A partner has no right to receive, and may not be required to accept, a distribution in kind.

Comment: ...

This section is complemented by Section 807(a) which provides that, in winding up the partnership business on dissolution, any surplus after the payment of partnership obligations must be applied to pay in cash the net amount distributable to each partner.

SECTION 403. PARTNER'S RIGHTS AND DUTIES WITH RESPECT TO INFORMATION.

(a) A partnership shall keep its books and records, if any, at its chief executive office.

(b) A partnership shall provide partners and their agents and attorneys access to its books and records. It shall provide former partners and their agents and attorneys access to books and records pertaining to the period during which they were partners. The right of access provides the opportunity to inspect and copy books and records during ordinary business hours. A partnership may impose a reasonable charge, covering the costs of labor and material, for copies of documents furnished.

(c) Each partner and the partnership shall furnish to a partner, and to the legal representative of a deceased partner or partner under legal disability:

(1) without demand, any information concerning the partnership's business and affairs reasonably required for the proper exercise of the partner's rights and duties under the partnership agreement or this [Act]; and

(2) on demand, any other information concerning the partnership's business and affairs, except to the extent the demand or the information demanded is unreasonable or otherwise improper under the circumstances.

Comment: ...

2.   ... A partner's right to inspect and copy the partnership's books and records is not conditioned on the partner's purpose or motive.   Compare RMBCA Section 16.02(c)(1) (shareholder must have proper purpose to inspect certain corporate records).   A partner's unlimited personal liability justifies an unqualified right of access to the partnership books and records.   An abuse of the right to inspect and copy might constitute a violation of the obligation of good faith and fair dealing for which the other partners would have a remedy.   See Sections 404(d) and 405.

Under Section 103(b)(2), a partner's right of access to partnership books and records may not be unreasonably restricted by the partnership agreement.   Thus, to preserve a partner's core information rights despite unequal bargaining power, an agreement limiting a partner's right to inspect and copy partnership books and records is subject to judicial review.   Nevertheless, reasonable restrictions on access to partnership books and records by agreement are authorized.   For example, a provision in a partnership agreement denying partners access to the compensation of other partners should be upheld, absent any abuse such as fraud or duress....

3.   ... Paragraph (2) continues the UPA rule that partners are entitled, on demand, to any other information concerning the partnership's business and affairs.   The demand may be refused if either the demand or the information demanded is unreasonable or otherwise improper.   That qualification is new to the statutory formulation.   The burden is on the partnership or partner from whom the information is requested to show that the demand is unreasonable or improper....

The Section 403(c) information rights can be waived or varied by agreement of the partners, since there is no Section 103(b) limitation on the variation of those rights as there is with respect to the Section 403(b) access rights to books and records.   See Section 103(b)(2).

SECTION 404.   GENERAL STANDARDS OF PARTNER'S CONDUCT.

(a) The only fiduciary duties a partner owes to the partnership and the other partners are the duty of loyalty and the duty of care set forth in subsections (b) and (c).

(b) A partner's duty of loyalty to the partnership and the other partners is limited to the following:

(1) to account to the partnership and hold as trustee for it any property, profit, or benefit derived by the partner in the conduct and winding up of the partnership business or derived from a use by the

partner of partnership property, including the appropriation of a partnership opportunity;

(2) to refrain from dealing with the partnership in the conduct or winding up of the partnership business as or on behalf of a party having an interest adverse to the partnership; and

(3) to refrain from competing with the partnership in the conduct of the partnership business before the dissolution of the partnership.

(c) A partner's duty of care to the partnership and the other partners in the conduct and winding up of the partnership business is limited to refraining from engaging in grossly negligent or reckless conduct, intentional misconduct, or a knowing violation of law.

(d) A partner shall discharge the duties to the partnership and the other partners under this [Act] or under the partnership agreement and exercise any rights consistently with the obligation of good faith and fair dealing.

(e) A partner does not violate a duty or obligation under this [Act] or under the partnership agreement merely because the partner's conduct furthers the partner's own interest.

(f) A partner may lend money to and transact other business with the partnership, and as to each loan or transaction the rights and obligations of the partner are the same as those of a person who is not a partner, subject to other applicable law.

(g) This section applies to a person winding up the partnership business as the personal or legal representative of the last surviving partner as if the person were a partner.

Comment:

1. Section 404 is new. The title, "General Standards of Partner's Conduct," is drawn from RMBCA Section 8.30. Section 404 is both comprehensive and exclusive. In that regard, it is structurally different from the UPA which touches only sparingly on a partner's duty of loyalty and leaves any further development of the fiduciary duties of partners to the common law of agency. Compare UPA Sections 4(3) and 21.

Section 404 begins by stating that the **only** fiduciary duties a partner owes to the partnership and the other partners are the duties of loyalty and care set forth in subsections (b) and (c) of the Act. Those duties may not be waived or eliminated in the partnership agreement, but the agreement may identify activities and determine standards for measuring performance of the duties, if not manifestly unreasonable. See Sections 103(b)(3)–(5). . . .

[2.] Under Section 103(b)(3), the partnership agreement may not "eliminate" the duty of loyalty. Section 103(b)(3)(i) expressly empowers the partners, however, to identify specific types or categories of activities that do not violate the duty of loyalty, if not manifestly unreasonable. As under UPA Section 21, the other partners may also consent to a specific act or transaction that otherwise violates one of the rules. For the consent to be effective under Section 103(b)(3)(ii), there must be full disclosure of all material facts regarding the act or transaction and the partner's conflict of interest. See Comment 5 to Section 103.

3. Subsection (c) is new and establishes the duty of care that partners owe to the partnership and to the other partners. There is no statutory duty of care under the UPA, although a common law duty of care is recognized by some courts. See, e.g., Rosenthal v. Rosenthal, 543 A.2d 348, 352 (Me.1988) (duty of care limited to acting in a manner that does not constitute gross negligence or wilful misconduct).

The standard of care imposed by RUPA is that of gross negligence, which is the standard generally recognized by the courts. See, e.g., Rosenthal v. Rosenthal, supra. Section 103(b)(4) provides that the duty of care may not be eliminated entirely by agreement, but the standard may be reasonably reduced. See Comment 6 to Section 103.

4. Subsection (d) is also new. It provides that partners have an obligation of good faith and fair dealing in the discharge of all their duties, including those arising under the Act, such as their fiduciary duties of loyalty and care, and those arising under the partnership agreement. The exercise of any rights by a partner is also subject to the obligation of good faith and fair dealing. The obligation runs to the partnership and to the other partners in all matters related to the conduct and winding up of the partnership business.

The obligation of good faith and fair dealing is a contract concept, imposed on the partners because of the consensual nature of a partnership. See Restatement (Second) of Contracts § 205 (1981). It is not characterized, in RUPA, as a fiduciary duty arising out of the partners' special relationship. Nor is it a separate and independent obligation. It is an ancillary obligation that applies whenever a partner discharges a duty or exercises a right under the partnership agreement or the Act.

The meaning of "good faith and fair dealing" is not firmly fixed under present law. "Good faith" clearly suggests a subjective element, while "fair dealing" implies an objective component. It was decided to leave the terms undefined in the Act and allow the courts to develop their meaning based on the experience of real cases. . . .

In some situations the obligation of good faith includes a disclosure component. Depending on the circumstances, a partner may have an affirmative disclosure obligation that supplements the Section 403 duty to render information.

Under Section 103(b)(5), the obligation of good faith and fair dealing may not be eliminated by agreement, but the partners by agreement may determine the standards by which the performance of the obligation is to be measured, if the standards are not manifestly unreasonable. See Comment 7 to Section 103.

5. Subsection (e) is new and deals expressly with a very basic issue on which the UPA is silent. A partner as such is not a trustee and is not held to the same standards as a trustee. Subsection (e) makes clear that a partner's conduct is not deemed to be improper merely because it serves the partner's own individual interest.

That admonition has particular application to the duty of loyalty and the obligation of good faith and fair dealing. It underscores the partner's rights as an owner and principal in the enterprise, which must always be balanced against his duties and obligations as an agent and fiduciary. For example, a partner who, with consent, owns a shopping center may, under subsection (e), legitimately vote against a proposal by the partnership to open a competing shopping center.

6. Subsection (f) authorizes partners to lend money to and transact other business with the partnership and, in so doing, to enjoy the same rights and obligations as a nonpartner. That language is drawn from RULPA Section 107. The rights and obligations of a partner doing business with the partnership as an outsider are expressly made subject to the usual laws governing those transactions. They include, for example, rules limiting or qualifying the rights and remedies of inside creditors, such as fraudulent transfer law, equitable subordination, and the law of avoidable preferences, as well as general debtor-creditor law. The reference to "other applicable law" makes clear that subsection (f) is not intended to displace those laws, and thus they are preserved under Section 104(a).

It is unclear under the UPA whether a partner may, for the partner's own account, purchase the assets of the partnership at a foreclosure sale or upon the liquidation of the partnership. Those purchases are clearly within subsection (f)'s broad approval. It is also clear under that subsection that a partner may purchase partnership assets at a foreclosure sale, whether the partner is the mortgagee or the mortgagee is an unrelated third party. Similarly, a partner may purchase partnership property at a tax sale. The obligation of good faith requires disclosure of the partner's interest in the transaction, however. . . .

SECTION 405. ACTIONS BY PARTNERSHIP AND PARTNERS.

(a) A partnership may maintain an action against a partner for a breach of the partnership agreement, or for the violation of a duty to the partnership, causing harm to the partnership.

(b) A partner may maintain an action against the partnership or another partner for legal or equitable relief, with or without an accounting as to partnership business, to:

(1) enforce the partner's rights under the partnership agreement;

(2) enforce the partner's rights under this [Act], including:

(i) the partner's rights under Sections 401, 403, or 404;

(ii) the partner's right on dissociation to have the partner's interest in the partnership purchased pursuant to Section 701 or enforce any other right under [Article] 6 or 7; or

(iii) the partner's right to compel a dissolution and winding up of the partnership business under Section 801 or enforce any other right under [Article] 8; or

(3) enforce the rights and otherwise protect the interests of the partner, including rights and interests arising independently of the partnership relationship.

(c) The accrual of, and any time limitation on, a right of action for a remedy under this section is governed by other law. A right to an accounting upon a dissolution and winding up does not revive a claim barred by law.

Comment:

1. Section 405(a) is new and reflects the entity theory of partnership. It provides that the partnership itself may maintain an action against a partner for any breach of the partnership agreement or for the violation of any duty owed to the partnership, such as a breach of fiduciary duty.

2. Section 405(b) is the successor to UPA Section 22, but with significant changes. At common law, an accounting was generally not available before dissolution. That was modified by UPA Section 22 which specifies certain circumstances in which an accounting action is available without requiring a partner to dissolve the partnership. Section 405(b) goes far beyond the UPA rule. It provides that, during the term of the partnership, partners may maintain a variety of legal or equitable actions, including an action for an accounting, as well as a final action for an accounting upon dissolution and winding up. It reflects a new policy choice that partners should have access to the courts during the term of the partnership to resolve claims against the partnership and the other

partners, leaving broad judicial discretion to fashion appropriate remedies. . . .

Under subsection (b), a partner may bring a direct suit against the partnership or another partner for almost any cause of action arising out of the conduct of the partnership business. That eliminates the present procedural barriers to suits between partners filed independently of an accounting action. In addition to a formal account, the court may grant any other appropriate legal or equitable remedy. Since general partners are not passive investors like limited partners, RUPA does not authorize derivative actions, as does RULPA Section 1001. . . .

3. Generally, partners may limit or contract away their Section 405 remedies. They may not, however, eliminate entirely the remedies for breach of those duties that are mandatory under Section 103(b). See Comment 1 to Section 103. . . .

SECTION 406. CONTINUATION OF PARTNERSHIP BEYOND DEFINITE TERM OR PARTICULAR UNDERTAKING.

(a) If a partnership for a definite term or particular undertaking is continued, without an express agreement, after the expiration of the term or completion of the undertaking, the rights and duties of the partners remain the same as they were at the expiration or completion, so far as is consistent with a partnership at will.

(b) If the partners, or those of them who habitually acted in the business during the term or undertaking, continue the business without any settlement or liquidation of the partnership, they are presumed to have agreed that the partnership will continue.

ARTICLE 5

TRANSFEREES AND CREDITORS OF PARTNER

SECTION 501. PARTNER NOT CO–OWNER OF PARTNERSHIP PROPERTY.

A partner is not a co-owner of partnership property and has no interest in partnership property which can be transferred, either voluntarily or involuntarily.

Comment:

Section 501 provides that a partner is not a co-owner of partnership property and has no interest in partnership property that can be transferred, either voluntarily or involuntarily. Thus, the section abolishes the UPA Section 25(1) concept of tenants in partnership and reflects the adoption of the entity theory. Partnership property is owned by the entity and not by the individual partners. See also Section 203, which provides that property transferred to or otherwise acquired by the partnership is property of the partnership and not of the partners individually....

Adoption of the entity theory also has the effect of protecting partnership property from execution or other process by a partner's personal creditors. That continues the result under UPA Section 25(2)(c). Those creditors may seek a charging order under Section 504 to reach the partner's transferable interest in the partnership....

SECTION 502. PARTNER'S TRANSFERABLE INTEREST IN PARTNERSHIP.

The only transferable interest of a partner in the partnership is the partner's share of the profits and losses of the partnership and the partner's right to receive distributions. The interest is personal property.

Comment:

Section 502 continues the UPA Section 26 concept that a partner's only transferable interest in the partnership is the partner's share of profits and losses and right to receive distributions, that is, the partner's financial rights. The term "distribution" is defined in Section 101(3)....

Under Section 503(b)(3), a transferee of a partner's transferable interest has standing to seek judicial dissolution of the partnership business.

A partner has other interests in the partnership that may not be transferred, such as the right to participate in the management of the business. Those rights are included in the broader concept of a "partner's interest in the partnership." See Section 101(7).

SECTION 503. TRANSFER OF PARTNER'S TRANSFERABLE INTEREST.

(a) A transfer, in whole or in part, of a partner's transferable interest in the partnership:

(1) is permissible;

(2) does not by itself cause the partner's dissociation or a dissolution and winding up of the partnership business; and

(3) does not, as against the other partners or the partnership, entitle the transferee, during the continuance of the partnership, to participate in the management or conduct of the partnership business, to require access to information concerning partnership transactions, or to inspect or copy the partnership books or records.

(b) A transferee of a partner's transferable interest in the partnership has a right:

(1) to receive, in accordance with the transfer, distributions to which the transferor would otherwise be entitled;

(2) to receive upon the dissolution and winding up of the partnership business, in accordance with the transfer, the net amount otherwise distributable to the transferor; and

(3) to seek under Section 801(6) a judicial determination that it is equitable to wind up the partnership business.

(c) In a dissolution and winding up, a transferee is entitled to an account of partnership transactions only from the date of the latest account agreed to by all of the partners.

(d) Upon transfer, the transferor retains the rights and duties of a partner other than the interest in distributions transferred.

(e) A partnership need not give effect to a transferee's rights under this section until it has notice of the transfer.

(f) A transfer of a partner's transferable interest in the partnership in violation of a restriction on transfer contained in the partnership agreement is ineffective as to a person having notice of the restriction at the time of transfer.

Comment:

1. ... Subsection (a)(1) states explicitly that a partner has the right to transfer his transferable interest in the partnership. The term "transfer" is used throughout RUPA in lieu of the term "assignment." See Section 101(10).

Subsection (a)(2) continues the UPA Section 27(1) rule that an assignment of a partner's interest in the partnership does not of itself cause a winding up of the partnership business. Under Section 601(4)(ii), however, a partner who has transferred substantially all of his partnership interest may be expelled by the other partners....

4. Subsection (d) is new. It makes clear that unless otherwise agreed the partner whose interest is transferred retains all of the rights and duties of a partner, other than the right to receive distributions. That means the transferor is entitled to participate

in the management of the partnership and remains personally liable for all partnership obligations, unless and until he withdraws as a partner, is expelled under Section 601(4)(ii), or is otherwise dissociated under Section 601....

6. Subsection (f) is new and provides that a transfer of a partner's transferable interest in the partnership in violation of a restriction on transfer contained in a partnership agreement is ineffective as to a person with timely notice of the restriction. Under Section 103(a), the partners may agree among themselves to restrict the right to transfer their partnership interests. Subsection (f) makes explicit that a transfer in violation of such a restriction is ineffective as to a transferee with notice of the restriction. See Section 102(b) for the meaning of "notice." RUPA leaves to general law and the UCC the issue of whether a transfer in violation of a valid restriction is effective as to a transferee without notice of the restriction.

Whether a particular restriction will be enforceable, however, must be considered in light of other law. See 11 U.S.C. § 541(c)(1) (property owned by bankrupt passes to trustee regardless of restrictions on transfer); UCC § 9–318(4) (agreement between account debtor and assignor prohibiting creation of security interest in a general intangible or requiring account debtor's consent is ineffective); Battista v. Carlo, 57 Misc.2d 495, 293 N.Y.S.2d 227 (1968) (restriction on transfer of partnership interest subject to rules against unreasonable restraints on alienation of property) (dictum); Tupper v. Kroc, 88 Nev. 146, 494 P.2d 1275 (1972) (partnership interest subject to charging order even if partnership agreement prohibits assignments). Cf. Tu–Vu Drive–In Corp. v. Ashkins, 61 Cal.2d 283, 38 Cal.Rptr. 348, 391 P.2d 828 (1964) (restraints on transfer of corporate stock must be reasonable). Even if a restriction on the transfer of a partner's transferable interest in a partnership were held to be unenforceable, the transfer might be grounds for expelling the partner-transferor from the partnership under Section 601(5)(ii).

7. Other rules that apply in the case of transfers include Section 601(4)(ii) (expulsion of partner who transfers substantially all of partnership interest); Section 601(6) (dissociation of partner who makes an assignment for benefit of creditors); and Section 801(6) (transferee has standing to seek judicial winding up).

SECTION 504. PARTNER'S TRANSFERABLE INTEREST SUBJECT TO CHARGING ORDER.

(a) On application by a judgment creditor of a partner or of a partner's transferee, a court having jurisdiction may charge the transferable interest of the judgment debtor to satisfy the judgment. The court may appoint a receiver of the share of the distributions due or to become due to the judgment debtor in respect of the partnership and make all other orders, directions, accounts, and inquiries the judgment debtor might have made or which the circumstances of the case may require.

(b) A charging order constitutes a lien on the judgment debtor's transferable interest in the partnership. The court may order a foreclosure of the interest subject to the charging order at any time. The purchaser at the foreclosure sale has the rights of a transferee.

(c) At any time before foreclosure, an interest charged may be redeemed:

(1) by the judgment debtor;

(2) with property other than partnership property, by one or more of the other partners; or

(3) with partnership property, by one or more of the other partners with the consent of all of the partners whose interests are not so charged.

(d) This [Act] does not deprive a partner of a right under exemption laws with respect to the partner's interest in the partnership.

(e) This section provides the exclusive remedy by which a judgment creditor of a partner or partner's transferee may satisfy a judgment out of the judgment debtor's transferable interest in the partnership.

ARTICLE 6

PARTNER'S DISSOCIATION

SECTION 601. EVENTS CAUSING PARTNER'S DISSOCIATION.

A partner is dissociated from a partnership upon the occurrence of any of the following events:

(1) the partnership's having notice of the partner's express will to withdraw as a partner [upon the date of notice] or on a later date specified by the partner;

(2) an event agreed to in the partnership agreement as causing the partner's dissociation;

(3) the partner's expulsion pursuant to the partnership agreement;

(4) the partner's expulsion by the unanimous vote of the other partners if:

(i) it is unlawful to carry on the partnership business with that partner;

(ii) there has been a transfer of all or substantially all of that partner's transferable interest in the partnership, other than a transfer for security purposes, or a court order charging the partner's interest, which has not been foreclosed;

(iii) within 90 days after the partnership notifies a corporate partner that it will be expelled because it has filed a certificate of dissolution or the equivalent, its charter has been revoked, or its right to conduct business has been suspended by the jurisdiction of its incorporation, [and] there is no revocation of the certificate of dissolution or no reinstatement of its charter or its right to conduct business; or

(iv) a partnership that is a partner has been dissolved and its business is being wound up;

(5) on application by the partnership or another partner, the partner's expulsion by judicial determination because:

(i) the partner engaged in wrongful conduct that adversely and materially affected the partnership business;

(ii) the partner willfully or persistently committed a material breach of the partnership agreement or of a duty owed to the partnership or the other partners under Section 404; or

(iii) the partner engaged in conduct relating to the partnership business which makes it not reasonably practicable to carry on the business in partnership with the partner;

(6) the partner's:

(i) becoming a debtor in bankruptcy;

(ii) executing an assignment for the benefit of creditors;

(iii) seeking, consenting to, or acquiescing in the appointment of a trustee, receiver, or liquidator of that partner or of all or substantially all of that partner's property; or

(iv) failing, within 90 days after the appointment, to have vacated or stayed the appointment of a trustee, receiver, or liquidator of the partner or of all or substantially all of the partner's property obtained without the partner's consent or acquiescence, or failing within 90 days after the expiration of a stay to have the appointment vacated;

(7) in the case of a partner who is an individual:

(i) the partner's death;

(ii) the appointment of a guardian or general conservator for the partner; or

(iii) a judicial determination that the partner has otherwise become incapable of performing the partner's duties under the partnership agreement;

(8) in the case of a partner that is a trust or is acting as a partner by virtue of being a trustee of a trust, distribution of the trust's entire transferable interest in the partnership, but not merely by reason of the substitution of a successor trustee;

(9) in the case of a partner that is an estate or is acting as a partner by virtue of being a personal representative of an estate, distribution of the estate's entire transferable interest in the partnership, but not merely by reason of the substitution of a successor personal representative; or

(10) termination of a partner who is not an individual, partnership, corporation, trust, or estate.

Comment:

1. RUPA dramatically changes the law governing partnership breakups and dissolution. An entirely new concept, "dissociation," is used in lieu of the UPA term "dissolution" to denote the change in the relationship caused by a partner's ceasing to be associated in the carrying on of the business. "Dissolution" is retained but with a different meaning. See Section 802. The entity theory of partnership provides a conceptual basis for continuing the firm itself despite a partner's withdrawal from the firm.

Under RUPA, unlike the UPA, the dissociation of a partner does not necessarily cause a dissolution and winding up of the business of the partnership. Section 801 identifies the situations in which the dissociation of a partner causes a winding up of the business. Section 701 provides that in all other situations there is a buyout of the partner's interest in the partnership, rather than a windup of the partnership business. In those other situations, the partnership entity continues, unaffected by the partner's dissociation.

A dissociated partner remains a partner for some purposes and still has some residual rights, duties, powers, and liabilities. Although Section 601 determines when a partner is dissociated from the partnership, the consequences of the partner's dissociation do not all occur at the same time. Thus, it is more useful to think of a dissociated partner as a partner for some purposes, but as a former partner for others. For example, see Section 403(b) (former partner's access to partnership books and records). The consequences of a partner's dissociation depend on whether the partnership continues or is wound up, as provided in Articles 6, 7 and 8.

Section 601 enumerates all of the events that cause a partner's dissociation....

2. Section 601(1) provides that a partner is dissociated when the partnership has notice of the partner's express will to withdraw as a partner, unless a later date is specified by the partner. If a future date is specified by the partner, other partners may dissociate

before that date; specifying a future date does not bind the others to remain as partners until that date. See also Section 801(2)(i).

Section 602(a) provides that a partner has the power to withdraw at any time. The power to withdraw is immutable under Section 103(b)(6), with the exception that the partners may agree the notice must be in writing. This continues the present rule that a partner has the power to withdraw at will, even if not the right. See UPA Section 31(2). Since no writing is required to create a partner relationship, it was felt unnecessarily formalistic, and a trap for the unwary, to require a writing to end one. If a written notification is given, Section 102(d) clarifies when it is deemed received.

RUPA continues the UPA "express will" concept, thus preserving existing case law. Section 601(1) clarifies existing law by providing that the partnership must have notice of the partner's expression of will before the dissociation is effective. See Section 102(b) for the meaning of "notice." ...

4. Section 601(3) provides that a partner may be expelled by the other partners pursuant to a power of expulsion contained in the partnership agreement. That continues the basic rule of UPA Section 31(1)(d). The expulsion can be with or without cause. As under existing law, the obligation of good faith under Section 404(d) does not require prior notice, specification of cause, or an opportunity to be heard. See Holman v. Coie, 11 Wash.App. 195, 522 P.2d 515, cert. denied, 420 U.S. 984 (1974).

5. Section 601(4) empowers the partners, by unanimous vote, to expel a partner for specified causes, even if not authorized in the partnership agreement. This changes the UPA Section 31(1)(d) rule that authorizes expulsion only if provided in the partnership agreement. A partner may be expelled from a term partnership, as well as from a partnership at will. Under Section 103(a), the partnership agreement may change or abolish the partners' power of expulsion....

Subsection (4)(ii) provides that a partner may be expelled for transferring substantially all of his transferable interest in the partnership, other than as security for a loan. (He may, however, be expelled upon foreclosure.) This rule is derived from UPA Section 31(1)(c). To avoid the presence of an unwelcome transferee, the remaining partners may dissolve the partnership under Section 801(2)(ii), after first expelling the transferor partner....

6. ... Subsection (5)(iii) provides for judicial expulsion of a partner who engaged in conduct relating to the partnership business that makes it not reasonably practicable to carry on the business in partnership with that partner. Expulsion for such misconduct makes the partner's dissociation wrongful under Section 602(a)(ii)

and may also support a judicial decree of dissolution under Section 801(5)(ii).

7. Section 601(6) provides that a partner is dissociated upon becoming a debtor in bankruptcy or upon taking or suffering other action evidencing the partner's insolvency or lack of financial responsibility. . . .

Initially, upon the filing of the bankruptcy petition, the debtor partner's transferable interest in the partnership will pass to the bankruptcy trustee as property of the estate under Section 541(a)(1) of the Bankruptcy Code, notwithstanding any restrictions on transfer provided in the partnership agreement. In most Chapter 7 cases, that will result in the eventual buyout of the partner's interest.

The application of various provisions of the federal Bankruptcy Code to Section 601(6)(i) is unclear. In particular, there is uncertainty as to the validity of UPA Section 31(5), and thus its RUPA counterpart, under Sections 365(e) and 541(c)(1) of the Bankruptcy Code. Those sections generally invalidate so-called *ipso facto* laws that cause a termination or modification of the debtor's contract or property rights because of the bankruptcy filing. As a consequence, RUPA Section 601(6)(i), which provides for a partner's dissociation by operation of law upon becoming a debtor in bankruptcy, may be invalid under the Supremacy Clause. . . .

8. UPA Section 31(4) provides for the dissolution of a partnership upon the death of any partner, although by agreement the remaining partners may continue the partnership business. RUPA Section 601(7)(i), on the other hand, provides for dissociation upon the death of a partner who is an individual, rather than dissolution of the partnership. . . . Normally, under RUPA, the deceased partner's transferable interest in the partnership will pass to his estate and be bought out under Article 7. . . .

SECTION 602. PARTNER'S POWER TO DISSOCIATE; WRONGFUL DISSOCIATION.

(a) A partner has the power to dissociate at any time, rightfully or wrongfully, by express will pursuant to Section 601(1).

(b) A partner's dissociation is wrongful only if:

(1) it is in breach of an express provision of the partnership agreement; or

(2) in the case of a partnership for a definite term or particular undertaking, before the expiration of the term or the completion of the undertaking;

(i) the partner withdraws by express will, unless the withdrawal follows within 90 days after another partner's dissociation by death or otherwise under Section 601(6) through (10) or wrongful dissociation under this subsection;

(ii) the partner is expelled by judicial determination under Section 601(5);

(iii) the partner is dissociated by becoming a debtor in bankruptcy; or

(iv) in the case of a partner who is not an individual, trust other than a business trust, or estate, the partner is expelled or otherwise dissociated because it willfully dissolved or terminated.

(c) A partner who wrongfully dissociates is liable to the partnership and to the other partners for damages caused by the dissociation. The liability is in addition to any other obligation of the partner to the partnership or to the other partners.

Comment:

1. Subsection (a) states explicitly what is implicit in UPA Section 31(2) and RUPA Section 601(1)—that a partner has the power to dissociate at any time by expressing a will to withdraw, even in contravention of the partnership agreement. The phrase "rightfully or wrongfully" reflects the distinction between a partner's *power* to withdraw in contravention of the partnership agreement and a partner's *right* to do so. In this context, although a partner can not be enjoined from exercising the power to dissociate, the dissociation may be wrongful under subsection (b).

2. Subsection (b) provides that a partner's dissociation is wrongful only if it results from one of the enumerated events. The significance of a wrongful dissociation is that it may give rise to damages under subsection (c) and, if it results in the dissolution of the partnership, the wrongfully dissociating partner is not entitled to participate in winding up the business under Section 804.

Under subsection (b), a partner's dissociation is wrongful if (1) it breaches an express provision of the partnership agreement or (2), in a term partnership, before the expiration of the term or the completion of the undertaking (i) the partner voluntarily withdraws by express will, except a withdrawal following *another* partner's wrongful dissociation or dissociation by death or otherwise under Section 601(6) through (10); (ii) the partner is expelled for misconduct under Section 601(5); (iii) the partner becomes a debtor in bankruptcy (see Section 101(2)); or (iv) a partner that is an entity (other than a trust or estate) is expelled or otherwise dissociated because its dissolution or termination was willful. Since subsection (b) is merely a default rule, the partnership agreement may eliminate or expand the dissociations that are wrongful or modify the effects of wrongful dissociation.

The exception in subsection (b)(2)(i) is intended to protect a partner's reactive withdrawal from a term partnership after the premature departure of another partner, such as the partnership's rainmaker or main supplier of capital, under the same circumstances that may result in the dissolution of the partnership under Section 801(2)(i). Under that section, a term partnership is dissolved 90 days after the bankruptcy, incapacity, death (or similar dissociation of a partner that is an entity), or wrongful dissociation of any partner, unless a majority in interest (see Comment 5(i) to Section 801 for a discussion of the term "majority in interest") of the remaining partners agree to continue the partnership. Under Section 602(b)(2)(i), a partner's exercise of the right of withdrawal by express will under those circumstances is rendered "rightful," even if the partnership is continued by others, and does not expose the withdrawing partner to damages for wrongful dissociation under Section 602(c).

A partner wishing to withdraw prematurely from a term partnership for any other reason, such as another partner's misconduct, can avoid being treated as a wrongfully dissociating partner by applying to a court under Section 601(5)(iii) to have the offending partner expelled. Then, the partnership could be dissolved under Section 801(2)(i) or the remaining partners could, by unanimous vote, dissolve the partnership under Section 801(2)(ii).

3. Subsection (c) provides that a wrongfully dissociating partner is liable to the partnership and to the other partners for any damages caused by the wrongful nature of the dissociation. That liability is in addition to any other obligation of the partner to the partnership or to the other partners. For example, the partner would be liable for any damage caused by breach of the partnership agreement or other misconduct. The partnership might also incur substantial expenses resulting from a partner's premature withdrawal from a term partnership, such as replacing the partner's expertise or obtaining new financing. The wrongfully dissociating partner would be liable to the partnership for those and all other expenses and damages that are causally related to the wrongful dissociation.

Section 701(c) provides that any damages for wrongful dissociation may be offset against the amount of the buyout price due to the partner under Section 701(a), and Section 701(h) provides that a partner who wrongfully dissociates from a term partnership is not entitled to payment of the buyout price until the term expires.

Under UPA Section 38(2)(c)(II), in addition to an offset for damages, the goodwill value of the partnership is excluded in determining the value of a wrongfully dissociating partner's partnership interest. Under RUPA, however, unless the partnership's goodwill is damaged by the wrongful dissociation, the value of the wrongfully dissociating partner's interest will include any goodwill value of the partnership. If the firm's goodwill is damaged, the amount of the damages suffered by the partnership and the remaining partners will be offset against the buyout price. See Section 701 and Comments.

SECTION 603. EFFECT OF PARTNER'S DISSOCIATION.

(a) If a partner's dissociation results in a dissolution and winding up of the partnership business, [Article] 8 applies; otherwise, [Article] 7 applies.

(b) Upon a partner's dissociation:

(1) the partner's right to participate in the management and conduct of the partnership business terminates, except as otherwise provided in Section 803;

(2) the partner's duty of loyalty under Section 404(b)(3) terminates; and

(3) the partner's duty of loyalty under Section 404(b)(1) and (2) and duty of care under Section 404(c) continue only with regard to matters arising and events occurring before the partner's dissociation, unless the partner participates in winding up the partnership's business pursuant to Section 803.

Comment:

1. Section 603(a) is a "switching" provision. It provides that, after a partner's dissociation, the partner's interest in the partnership must be purchased pursuant to the buyout rules in Article 7 *unless* there is a dissolution and winding up of the partnership business under Article 8. Thus, a partner's dissociation will always result in either a buyout of the dissociated partner's interest or a dissolution and winding up of the business.

By contrast, under the UPA, every partner dissociation results in the dissolution of the partnership, most of which trigger a right to have the business wound up unless the partnership agreement provides otherwise. See UPA § 38. The only exception in which the remaining partners have a statutory right to continue the business is when a partner wrongfully dissolves the partnership in breach of the partnership agreement. See UPA § 38(2)(b).

2. Section 603(b) is new and deals with some of the internal effects of a partner's dissociation. Subsection (b)(1) makes it clear that one of the consequences of a partner's dissociation is the immediate loss of the right to participate in the management of the business, unless it results in a dissolution and winding up of the business. In that case, Section 804(a) provides that all of the

partners who have not wrongfully dissociated may participate in winding up the business.

Subsection[s] (b)(2) and (3) clarify a partner's fiduciary duties upon dissociation. No change from current law is intended. With respect to the duty of loyalty, the Section 404(b)(3) duty not to compete terminates upon dissociation, and the dissociated partner is free immediately to engage in a competitive business, without any further consent. With respect to the partner's remaining loyalty duties under Section 404(b) and duty of care under Section 404(c), a withdrawing partner has a continuing duty after dissociation, but it is limited to matters that arose or events that occurred before the partner dissociated. For example, a partner who leaves a brokerage firm may immediately compete with the firm for new clients, but must exercise care in completing on-going client transactions and must account to the firm for any fees received from the old clients on account of those transactions. As the last clause makes clear, there is no contraction of a dissociated partner's duties under subsection (b)(3) if the partner thereafter participates in the dissolution and winding up the partnership's business.

ARTICLE 7

PARTNER'S DISSOCIATION WHEN BUSINESS NOT WOUND UP

SECTION 701. PURCHASE OF DISSOCIATED PARTNER'S INTEREST.

(a) If a partner is dissociated from a partnership without resulting in a dissolution and winding up of the partnership business under Section 801, the partnership shall cause the dissociated partner's interest in the partnership to be purchased for a buyout price determined pursuant to subsection (b).

(b) The buyout price of a dissociated partner's interest is the amount that would have been distributable to the dissociating partner under Section 807(b) if, on the date of dissociation, the assets of the partnership were sold at a price equal to the greater of the liquidation value or the value based on a sale of the entire business as a going concern without the dissociated partner and the partnership were wound up as of that date. Interest must be paid from the date of dissociation to the date of payment.

(c) Damages for wrongful dissociation under Section 602(b), and all other amounts owing, whether or not presently due, from the dissociated partner to the partnership, must be offset against the buyout price. Interest must be paid from the date the amount owed becomes due to the date of payment.

(d) A partnership shall indemnify a dissociated partner whose interest is being purchased against all partnership liabilities, whether incurred before or after the dissociation, except liabilities incurred by an act of the dissociated partner under Section 702.

(e) If no agreement for the purchase of a dissociated partner's interest is reached within 120 days after a written demand for payment, the partnership shall pay, or cause to be paid, in cash to the dissociated partner the amount the partnership estimates to be the buyout price and accrued interest, reduced by any offsets and accrued interest under subsection (c).

(f) If a deferred payment is authorized under subsection (h), the partnership may tender a written offer to pay the amount it estimates to be the buyout price and accrued interest, reduced by any offsets under subsection (c), stating the time of payment, the amount and type of security for payment, and the other terms and conditions of the obligation.

(g) The payment or tender required by subsection (e) or (f) must be accompanied by the following:

    (1) a statement of partnership assets and liabilities as of the date of dissociation;

    (2) the latest available partnership balance sheet and income statement, if any;

    (3) an explanation of how the estimated amount of the payment was calculated; and

    (4) written notice that the payment is in full satisfaction of the obligation to purchase unless, within 120 days after the written notice, the dissociated partner commences an action to determine the buyout price, any offsets under subsection (c), or other terms of the obligation to purchase.

(h) A partner who wrongfully dissociates before the expiration of a definite term or the completion of a particular undertaking is not entitled to payment of any portion of the buyout price until the expiration of the term or completion of the undertaking, unless the partner establishes to the satisfaction of the court that earlier payment will not cause undue hardship to the business of the partnership. A deferred payment must be adequately secured and bear interest.

(i) A dissociated partner may maintain an action against the partnership, pursuant to Section 405(b)(2)(ii), to determine the buyout price of that partner's interest, any offsets under subsection (c), or other terms of the obligation to purchase. The action must be commenced within 120 days after the partnership has tendered payment or an offer to pay or within one year after written demand for payment if no payment or offer to pay is tendered. The court shall determine the buyout price of the dissociated partner's interest, any offset due under subsection (c), and accrued interest, and enter judgment for any additional payment or refund. If deferred payment is authorized under subsection (h), the court shall also determine the security for payment and other terms of the obligation to purchase. The court may assess reasonable attorney's fees and the fees and expenses of appraisers or other experts for a party to the action, in amounts the court finds equitable, against a party that the court finds acted arbitrarily, vexatiously, or not in good faith. The finding may be based on the partnership's failure to tender payment or an offer to pay or to comply with subsection (g).

Comment:

1. Article 7 is new and provides for the buyout of a dissociated partner's interest in the partnership when the partner's dissociation does not result in a dissolution and winding up of its business under Article 8. See Section 603(a). If there is no dissolution, the remaining partners have a right to continue the business and the dissociated partner has a right to be paid the value of his partnership interest. These rights can, of course, be varied in the partnership agreement. See Section 103. A dissociated partner has a continuing relationship with the partnership and third parties as provided in Sections 603(b), 702, and 703. See also Section 403(b) (former partner's access to partnership books and records).

2. Subsection (a) provides that, if a partner's dissociation does not result in a windup of the business, the partnership shall cause the interest of the dissociating partner to be purchased for a buyout price determined pursuant to subsection (b). The buyout is mandatory. The "cause to be purchased" language is intended to accommodate a purchase by the partnership, one or more of the remaining partners, or a third party. . . .

3. Subsection (b) provides how the "buyout price" is to be determined. The terms "fair market value" or "fair value" were not used because they are often considered terms of art having a special meaning depending on the context, such as in tax or corporate law. "Buyout price" is a new term. It is intended that the term be developed as an independent concept appropriate to the partnership buyout situation, while drawing on valuation principles developed elsewhere.

115

Under subsection (b), the buyout price is the amount that would have been distributable to the dissociating partner under Section 807(b) if, on the date of dissociation, the assets of the partnership were sold at a price equal to the greater of liquidation value or going concern value without the departing partner. Liquidation value is not intended to mean distress sale value. Under general principles of valuation, the hypothetical selling price in either case should be the price that a willing and informed buyer would pay a willing and informed seller, with neither being under any compulsion to deal. The notion of a minority discount in determining the buyout price is negated by valuing the business as a going concern. Other discounts, such as for a lack of marketability or the loss of a key partner, may be appropriate, however.

Since the buyout price is based on the value of the business at the time of dissociation, the partnership must pay interest on the amount due from the date of dissociation until payment to compensate the dissociating partner for the use of his interest in the firm. Section 104(b) provides that interest shall be at the legal rate unless otherwise provided in the partnership agreement. . . .

UPA Section 38(2)(c)(II) provides that the good will of the business not be considered in valuing a wrongfully dissociating partner's interest. The forfeiture of good will rule is implicitly rejected by RUPA. See Section 602(c) and Comment 3.

The Section 701 rules are merely default rules. The partners may, in the partnership agreement, fix the method or formula for determining the buyout price and all of the other terms and conditions of the buyout right. Indeed, the very right to a buyout itself may be modified, although a provision providing for a complete forfeiture would probably not be enforceable. See Section 104(a).

4. Subsection (c) provides that the partnership may offset against the buyout price all amounts owing by the dissociated partner to the partnership, whether or not presently due, including any damages for wrongful dissociation under Section 602(c). This has the effect of accelerating payment of amounts not yet due from the departing partner to the partnership, including a long-term loan by the partnership to the dissociated partner. Where appropriate, the amounts not yet due should be discounted to present value. A dissociating partner, on the other hand, is not entitled to an add-on for amounts owing to him by the partnership. Thus, a departing partner who has made a long-term loan to the partnership must wait for repayment, unless the terms of the loan agreement provide for acceleration upon dissociation.

It is not intended that the partnership's right of setoff be construed to limit the amount of the damages for the partner's wrongful dissociation and any other amounts owing to the partnership to the value of the dissociated partner's interest. Those amounts may result in a net sum due to the partnership from the dissociated partner.

5. Subsection (d) follows the UPA Section 38 rule and provides that the partnership must indemnify a dissociated partner against all partnership liabilities, whether incurred before or after the dissociation, except those incurred by the dissociated partner under Section 702.

6. Subsection (e) provides that, if no agreement for the purchase of the dissociated partner's interest is reached within 120 days after the dissociated partner's written demand for payment, the partnership must pay, or cause to be paid, in cash the amount it estimates to be the buyout price, adjusted for any offsets allowed and accrued interest. Thus, the dissociating partner will receive in cash within 120 days of dissociation the undisputed minimum value of the partner's partnership interest. If the dissociated partner claims that the buyout price should be higher, suit may thereafter be brought as provided in subsection (i) to have the amount of the buyout price determined by the court. This is similar to the procedure for determining the value of dissenting shareholders' shares under RMBCA Sections 13.20–13.28.

The "cause to be paid" language of subsection (a) is repeated here to permit either the partnership, one or more of the continuing partners, or a third-party purchaser to tender payment of the estimated amount due.

7. Subsection (f) provides that, when deferred payment is authorized in the case of a wrongfully dissociating partner, a written offer stating the amount the partnership estimates to be the purchase price should be tendered within the 120–day period, even though actual payment of the amount may be deferred, possibly for many years.... The dissociated partner is entitled to know at the time of dissociation what amount the remaining partners think is due, including the estimated amount of any damages allegedly caused by the partner's wrongful dissociation that may be offset against the buyout price....

9. Subsection (h) replaces UPA Section 38(2)(c) and provides a somewhat different rule for payment to a partner whose dissociation before the expiration of a definite term or the completion of a particular undertaking is wrongful under Section 602(b). Under subsection (h), a wrongfully dissociating partner is not entitled to receive any portion of the buyout price before the expiration of the term or completion of the undertaking, unless the dissociated partner establishes to the satisfaction of the court that earlier payment will not cause undue hardship to the business of the partnership. In all other cases, there must be an immediate payment in cash.

10. Subsection (i) provides that a dissociated partner may maintain an action against the partnership to determine the buyout price, any offsets, or other terms of the purchase obligation. The action must be commenced within 120 days after the partnership tenders payment of the amount it estimates to be due or, if deferred payment is authorized, its written offer. This provision creates a 120–day "cooling off" period. It also allows the parties an opportunity to negotiate their differences after disclosure by the partnership of its financial statements and other required information.

If the partnership fails to tender payment of the estimated amount due (or a written offer, if deferred payment is authorized), the dissociated partner has one year after written demand for payment in which to commence suit.

If the parties fail to reach agreement, the court must determine the buyout price of the partner's interest, any offsets, including damages for wrongful dissociation, and the amount of interest accrued. If payment to a wrongfully dissociated partner is deferred, the court may also require security for payment and determine the other terms of the obligation....

SECTION 702.   DISSOCIATED PARTNER'S POWER TO BIND AND LIABILITY TO PARTNERSHIP.

(a) For two years after a partner dissociates without resulting in a dissolution and winding up of the partnership business, the partnership, including a surviving partnership under [Article] 9, is bound by an act of the dissociated partner which would have bound the partnership under Section 301 before dissociation only if at the time of entering into the transaction the other party:

(1) reasonably believed that the dissociated partner was then a partner;

(2) did not have notice of the partner's dissociation; and

(3) is not deemed to have had knowledge under Section 303(e) or notice under Section 704(c).

(b) A dissociated partner is liable to the partnership for any damage caused to the partnership arising from an obligation incurred by the dissociated partner after dissociation for which the partnership is liable under subsection (a).

Comment:

1. Section 702 deals with a dissociated partner's lingering apparent authority to bind the partnership in ordinary course partnership transactions and the partner's liability to the partnership for any loss caused thereby. It also applies to partners who withdraw incident to a merger under Article 9. See Section 906(e).

A dissociated partner has no *actual* authority to act for the partnership. See Section 603(b)(1). Nevertheless, in order to protect innocent third parties, Section 702(a) provides that the partnership remains bound, for two years after a partner's dissociation, by that partner's acts that would, before his dissociation, have bound the partnership under Section 301 if, and only if, the other party to the transaction reasonably believed that he was still a partner, did not have notice of the partner's dissociation, and is not deemed to have had knowledge of the dissociation under Section 303(e) or notice thereof under Section 704(c).

Under Section 301, every partner has *apparent* authority to bind the partnership by any act for carrying on the partnership business in the ordinary course, unless the other party knows that the partner has no actual authority to act for the partnership or has received a notification of the partner's lack of authority. Section 702(a) continues that general rule for two years after a partner's dissociation, subject to three modifications.

After a partner's dissociation, the general rule is modified, first, by requiring the other party to show reasonable reliance on the partner's status as a partner. Section 301 has no explicit reliance requirement, although the partnership is bound only if the partner purports to act on its behalf. Thus, the other party will normally be aware of the partnership and presumably the partner's status as such.

The second modification is that, under Section 702(a), the partnership is not bound if the third party has *notice* of the partner's dissociation, while under the general rule of Section 301 the partnership is bound unless the third party *knows* of the partner's lack of authority. Under Section 102(b), a person has "notice" of a fact if he knows or has reason to know it exists from all the facts that are known to him or he has received a notification of it. Thus, the partnership may protect itself by sending a notification of the dissociation to a third party, and a third party may, in any event, have a duty to inquire further based on what is known. That provides the partnership with greater protection from the unauthorized acts of a dissociated partner than from those of partners generally.

The third modification of the general apparent authority rule under Section 702(a) involves the effect of a statement of dissociation. Section 704(c) provides that, for the purposes of Sections 702(a)(3) and 703(b)(3), third parties are deemed to have notice of a partner's dissociation 90 days after the filing of a statement of dissociation. Thus, the filing of a statement operates as constructive notice of the dissociated partner's lack of authority after 90 days, conclusively terminating the dissociated partner's Section 702 apparent authority. . . .

Under RUPA, therefore, a partnership should notify all known creditors of a partner's dissociation and may, by filing a statement of dissociation, conclusively limit to 90 days a dissociated partner's lingering agency power. Moreover, under Section 703(b), a dissociated partner's lingering liability for post-dissociation partnership liabilities may be limited to 90 days by filing a statement of dissociation. These incentives should encourage both partnerships and dissociating partners to file statements routinely. Those transacting substantial business with partnerships can protect themselves from the risk of dealing with dissociated partners, or relying on their credit, by checking the partnership records at least every 90 days.

2. Section 702(b) is a corollary to subsection (a) and provides that a dissociated partner is liable to the partnership for any loss resulting from an obligation improperly incurred by the partner under subsection (a). In effect, the dissociated partner must indemnify the partnership for any loss, meaning a loss net of any gain from the transaction. The dissociated partner is also personally liable to the third party for the unauthorized obligation.

SECTION 703. DISSOCIATED PARTNER'S LIABILITY TO OTHER PERSONS.

(a) A partner's dissociation does not of itself discharge the partner's liability for a partnership obligation incurred before dissociation. A dissociated partner is not liable for a partnership obligation incurred after dissociation, except as otherwise provided in subsection (b).

(b) A partner who dissociates without resulting in a dissolution and winding up of the partnership business is liable as a partner to the other party in a transaction entered into by the partnership, or a surviving partnership under [Article] 9, within two years after the partner's dissociation, only if at the time of entering into the transaction the other party:

(1) reasonably believed that the dissociated partner was then a partner;

(2) did not have notice of the partner's dissociation; and

(3) is not deemed to have had knowledge under Section 303(e) or notice under Section 704(c).

(c) By agreement with the partnership creditor and the partners continuing the business, a dissociated partner may be released from liability for a partnership obligation.

(d) A dissociated partner is released from liability for a partnership obligation if a partnership creditor, with notice of the partner's dissociation but without the partner's consent, agrees to a material alteration in the nature or time of payment of a partnership obligation.

SECTION 704. STATEMENT OF DISSOCIATION.

(a) A dissociated partner or the partnership may file a statement of dissociation stating the name of the partnership and that the partner is dissociated from the partnership.

(b) A statement of dissociation is a limitation on the authority of a dissociated partner for the purposes of Section 303(d) and (e).

(c) For the purposes of Sections 702(a)(3) and 703(b)(3), a person not a partner is deemed to have notice of the dissociation 90 days after the statement of dissociation is filed.

SECTION 705. CONTINUED USE OF PARTNERSHIP NAME.

Continued use of a partnership name, or a dissociated partner's name as part thereof, by partners continuing the business does not of itself make the dissociated partner liable for an obligation of the partners or the partnership continuing the business.

ARTICLE 8

WINDING UP PARTNERSHIP BUSINESS

SECTION 801. EVENTS CAUSING DISSOLUTION AND WINDING UP OF PARTNERSHIP BUSINESS.

A partnership is dissolved, and its business must be wound up, only upon the occurrence of any of the following events:

(1) in a partnership at will, the partnership's having notice from a partner, other than a partner who is dissociated under Section 601(2) through (10), of that partner's express will to withdraw as a partner [as of the time of the notice], or on a later date specified by the partner;

(2) in a partnership for a definite term or particular undertaking:

(i) the expiration of 90 days after a partner's dissociation by death or otherwise under Section 601(6) through (10) or wrongful dissociation under Section 602(b), unless before that time a majority in interest of the remaining partners, including partners who have rightfully dissociated pursuant to Section 602(b)(2)(i), agree to continue the partnership;

(ii) the express will of all of the partners to wind up the partnership business; or

(iii) the expiration of the term or the completion of the undertaking;

(3) an event agreed to in the partnership agreement resulting in the winding up of the partnership business;

(4) an event that makes it unlawful for all or substantially all of the business of the partnership to be continued, but a cure of illegality within 90 days after notice to the partnership of the event is effective retroactively to the date of the event for purposes of this section;

(5) on application by a partner, a judicial determination that:

(i) the economic purpose of the partnership is likely to be unreasonably frustrated;

(ii) another partner has engaged in conduct relating to the partnership business which makes it not reasonably practicable to carry on the business in partnership with that partner; or

(iii) it is not otherwise reasonably practicable to carry on the partnership business in conformity with the partnership agreement; or

(6) on application by a transferee of a partner's transferable interest, a judicial determination that it is equitable to wind up the partnership business:

(i) after the expiration of the term or completion of the undertaking, if the partnership was for a definite term or particular undertaking at the time of the transfer or entry of the charging order that gave rise to the transfer; or

(ii) at any time, if the partnership was a partnership at will at the time of the transfer or entry of the charging order that gave rise to the transfer.

Comment:

1. Under UPA Section 29, a partnership is dissolved every time a partner leaves. That reflects the aggregate nature of the partnership under the UPA. Even if the business of the partnership is continued by some of the partners, it is technically a new partnership. The dissolution of the old partnership and creation of a new partnership causes many unnecessary problems. . . .

RUPA's move to the entity theory is driven in part by the need to prevent a technical dissolution or its consequences. Under RUPA, not every partner dissociation causes a dissolution of the partnership.   Only certain departures trigger a dissolution.   The basic rule is that a partnership is dissolved, and its business must be wound up, only upon the occurrence of one of the events listed in Section 801.   All other dissociations result in a buyout of the partner's interest under Article 7 and a continuation of the partnership entity and business by the remaining partners.   See Section 603(a).

With only three exceptions, the provisions of Section 801 are merely default rules and may by agreement be varied or eliminated as grounds for dissolution.   The first exception is dissolution under Section 801(4) resulting from carrying on an illegal business.   The other two exceptions cover the power of a court to dissolve a partnership under Section 801(5) on application of a partner and under Section 801(6) on application of a transferee....

2.   Under RUPA, "dissolution" is merely the commencement of the winding up process.   The partnership continues for the limited purpose of winding up the business.   In effect, that means the scope of the partnership business contracts to completing work in process and taking such other actions as may be necessary to wind up the business.   Winding up the partnership business entails selling its assets, paying its debts, and distributing the net balance, if any, to the partners in cash according to their interests.   The partnership entity continues, and the partners are associated in the winding up of the business until winding up is completed.   When the winding up is completed, the partnership entity terminates.

3.   Section 801 continues two basic rules from the UPA.   First, it continues the rule that any member of an *at-will* partnership has the right to force a liquidation.   Second, by negative implication, it continues the rule that the partners who wish to continue the business of a *term* partnership can not be forced to liquidate the business by a partner who withdraws prematurely in violation of the partnership agreement....

4.   Section 801(1) provides that a partnership at will is dissolved and its business must be wound up upon the partnership's having notice of a partner's express will to withdraw as a partner, unless a later effective date is specified by the partner....

If, after dissolution, none of the partners wants the partnership wound up, Section 802(b) provides that, with the consent of all the partners, including the withdrawing partner, the remaining partners may continue the business.   In that event, although there is a technical dissolution of the partnership and, at least in theory, a temporary contraction of the scope of the business, the partnership entity continues and the scope of its business is restored.   See Section 802(b) and Comment 2.

5. Section 801(2) provides three ways in which a term partnership may be dissolved before the expiration of the term:

(i) Subsection (2)(i) provides for dissolution upon the expiration of 90 days after any partner's dissociation by death or otherwise under Section 601(6) to (10) or wrongful dissociation under Section 602(b), unless within that 90–day period a majority in interest of the remaining partners agree to continue the partnership. This reactive dissolution of a term partnership protects the remaining partners where the dissociating partner is crucial to the successful continuation of the business. The corresponding UPA Section 38(2)(b) rule requires unanimous consent of the remaining partners to continue the business, thus giving each partner an absolute right to a reactive liquidation. Under RUPA, if the partnership is continued by the majority, any dissenting partner who wants to withdraw may do so rightfully under the exception to Section 602(b)(2)(i), in which case his interest in the partnership will be bought out under Article 7. By itself, however, a partner's vote not to continue the business is not necessarily an expression of the partner's will to withdraw, and a dissenting partner may still elect to remain a partner and continue in the business.

The Section 601 dissociations giving rise to a reactive dissolution are: (6) a partner's bankruptcy or similar financial impairment; (7) a partner's death or incapacity; (8) the distribution by a trust-partner of its entire partnership interest; (9) the distribution by an estate-partner of its entire partnership interest; and (10) the termination of an entity-partner. Any dissociation during the term of the partnership that is wrongful under Section 602(b), including a partner's voluntary withdrawal, expulsion or bankruptcy, also gives rise to a reactive dissolution. Those statutory grounds may be varied by agreement or the reactive dissolution may be abolished entirely.

Under subsection (2)(i), a term partnership is dissolved 90 days after the first partner's dissociation unless within that time a majority in interest of the remaining partners have agreed to continue the partnership. Continuation under subsection (2)(i) requires the agreement of at least a majority in interest of the remaining partners. The interest and vote of a partner who dissociates rightfully under Section 602(b)(2)(i) is counted in determining whether a majority in interest agrees to continue.

Decision-making by a majority in interest is not the normal RUPA default rule. Section 401(j) requires a majority in number, rather than a majority in interest, for ordinary business decisions and unanimity for extraordinary matters and amendments to the partnership agreement. Requiring only majority approval to continue the partnership, rather than unanimity, in effect treats the decision as an ordinary business matter, thereby enhancing firm stability. At the same time, requiring a majority in interest, rather than a majority in number, satisfies Internal Revenue Service concerns regarding a partnership's continuity of life. See Treas.Reg. § 301.7701–2(b)(1).

"Majority in interest" is not defined in the Act, but is intended to satisfy Internal Revenue Service regulations regarding continuity of life. Under Rev.Proc. 94–46 (June 29, 1994), the "in-interest" concept refers to the partners' economic interests in both the profits and capital of the partnership.

Under Section 601(6)(i), a partner is dissociated upon becoming a debtor in bankruptcy. The bankruptcy of a partner or of the partnership is not, however, an event of dissolution under Section 801. That is a change from UPA Section 31(5). A partner's bankruptcy does, however, cause dissolution of a term partnership under Section 801(2)(i), unless a majority in interest of the remaining partners thereafter agree to continue the partnership. Affording the other partners the option of buying out the bankrupt partner's interest avoids the necessity of winding up a term partnership every time a partner becomes a debtor in bankruptcy.

Similarly, under Section 801(2)(i), the death of any partner will result in the dissolution of a term partnership, unless a majority in interest of the remaining partners agree to continue the business. In that case, the deceased partner's transferable interest in the partnership passes to his estate and must be bought out under Article 7. See Comment 8 to Section 601.

(ii) Section 801(2)(ii) provides that a term partnership may be dissolved and wound up at any time by the express will of all the partners. That is merely an expression of the general rule that the partnership agreement may override the statutory default rules and that the partnership agreement, like any contract, can be amended at any time by unanimous consent.

UPA Section 31(1)(c) provides that a term partnership may be wound up by the express will of all the partners whose transferable interests have not been assigned or charged for a partner's separate debts. That rule reflects the belief that the remaining partners may find transferees very intrusive. This provision has been deleted, however, because the liquidation is easily accomplished under Section 801(2)(ii) by first expelling the transferor partner under Section 601(4)(ii).

(iii) Section 801(2)(iii) ... provides for winding up a term partnership upon the expiration of the term or the completion of the undertaking. ...

8. Section 801(5) provides for judicial dissolution on application by a partner.... A court may order a partnership dissolved upon a judicial determination that: (i) the economic purpose of the partnership is likely to be unreasonably frustrated; (ii) another partner has engaged in conduct relating to the partnership business which makes it not reasonably practicable to carry on the business in partnership with that partner; or (iii) it is not otherwise reasonably practicable to carry on the partnership business in conformity with the partnership agreement. The court's power to wind up the partnership under Section 801(5) cannot be varied in the partnership agreement. See Section 103(b)(8)....

SECTION 802. PARTNERSHIP CONTINUES AFTER DISSOLUTION.

(a) Subject to subsection (b), a partnership continues after dissolution only for the purpose of winding up its business. The partnership is terminated when the winding up of its business is completed.

(b) At any time after the dissolution of a partnership and before the winding up of its business is completed, all of the partners, including any dissociating partner other than a wrongfully dissociating partner, may waive the right to have the partnership's business wound up and the partnership terminated. In that event:

(1) the partnership resumes carrying on its business as if dissolution had never occurred, and any liability incurred by the partnership or a partner after the dissolution and before the waiver is determined as if dissolution had never occurred; and

(2) the rights of a third party accruing under Section 804(1) or arising out of conduct in reliance on the dissolution before the third party knew or received a notification of the waiver may not be adversely affected.

Comment:

1. Section 802(a) is derived from UPA Section 30 and provides that a partnership continues after dissolution only for the purpose of winding up its business, after which it is terminated. RUPA continues the concept of "termination" to mark the completion of the winding up process. Since no filing or other formality is required, the date will often be determined only by hindsight. No legal rights turn on the partnership's termination or the date thereof. Even after termination, if a previously unknown liability is asserted, all of the partners are still liable.

2. Section 802(b) makes explicit the right of the remaining partners to continue the business after an event of dissolution if all of the partners, including the dissociating partner or partners, waive the right to have the business wound up and the partnership

terminated. Only those "dissociating" partners whose dissociation was the immediate cause of the dissolution must waive the right to have the business wound up. The consent of wrongfully dissociating partners is not required.

3. Upon waiver of the right to have the business wound up, paragraph (1) of the subsection provides that the partnership entity may resume carrying on its business as if dissolution had never occurred, thereby restoring the scope of its business to normal. "Resumes" is intended to mean that acts appropriate to winding up, authorized when taken, are in effect ratified, and the partnership remains liable for those acts, as provided explicitly in paragraph (2). . . .

SECTION 803. RIGHT TO WIND UP PARTNERSHIP BUSINESS.

(a) After dissolution, a partner who has not wrongfully dissociated may participate in winding up the partnership's business, but on application of any partner, partner's legal representative, or transferee, the [designate the appropriate court], for good cause shown, may order judicial supervision of the winding up.

(b) The legal representative of the last surviving partner may wind up a partnership's business.

(c) A person winding up a partnership's business may preserve the partnership business or property as a going concern for a reasonable time, prosecute and defend actions and proceedings, whether civil, criminal, or administrative, settle and close the partnership's business, dispose of and transfer the partnership's property, discharge the partnership's liabilities, distribute the assets of the partnership pursuant to Section 807, settle disputes by mediation or arbitration, and perform other necessary acts.

SECTION 804. PARTNER'S POWER TO BIND PARTNERSHIP AFTER DISSOLUTION.

Subject to Section 805, a partnership is bound by a partner's act after dissolution that:

(1) is appropriate for winding up the partnership business; or

(2) would have bound the partnership under Section 301 before dissolution, if the other party to the transaction did not have notice of the dissolution.

SECTION 805. STATEMENT OF DISSOLUTION.

(a) After dissolution, a partner who has not wrongfully dissociated may file a statement of dissolution stating the name of the partnership and that the partnership has dissolved and is winding up its business.

(b) A statement of dissolution cancels a filed statement of partnership authority for the purposes of Section 303(d) and is a limitation on authority for the purposes of Section 303(e).

(c) For the purposes of Sections 301 and 804, a person not a partner is deemed to have notice of the dissolution and the limitation on the partners' authority as a result of the statement of dissolution 90 days after it is filed.

(d) After filing and, if appropriate, recording a statement of dissolution, a dissolved partnership may file and, if appropriate, record a statement of partnership authority which will operate with respect to a person not a partner as provided in Section 303(d) and (e) in any transaction, whether or not the transaction is appropriate for winding up the partnership business.

Comment:

1. Section 805 is new. Subsection (a) provides that, after an event of dissolution, any partner who has not wrongfully dissociated may file a statement of dissolution on behalf of the partnership. The filing and recording of a statement of dissolution is optional. The execution, filing, and recording of the statement is governed by Section 105. The legal consequences of filing a statement of dissolution are similar to those of a statement of dissociation under Section 704. . . .

SECTION 806. PARTNER'S LIABILITY TO OTHER PARTNERS AFTER DISSOLUTION.

(a) Except as otherwise provided in subsection (b) and Section 306, after dissolution a partner is liable to the other partners for the partner's share of any partnership liability incurred under Section 804.

(b) A partner who, with knowledge of the dissolution, incurs a partnership liability under Section 804(2) by an act that is not appropriate for winding up the partnership business is liable to the partnership for any damage caused to the partnership arising from the liability.

Comment: . . .

Subsection (a) provides that, except as provided in Section 306(a) and subsection (b), after dissolution each partner is liable to the other partners by way of contribution for his share of any partnership liability incurred under Section 804. That includes not only obligations that are appropriate for winding up the business, but also obligations that are inappropriate if within the partner's apparent authority. Consistent with other provisions of this Act, Section 806(a) makes clear that a partner does not have a contribution obligation with regard to limited liability partnership obligations for which the partner is not liable under Section 306. See Comments to Section 401(b) . . . .

Section 806 is merely a default rule and may be varied in the partnership agreement. See Section 103(a).

SECTION 807. SETTLEMENT OF ACCOUNTS AND CONTRIBUTIONS AMONG PARTNERS.

(a) In winding up a partnership's business, the assets of the partnership, including the contributions of the partners required by this section, must be applied to discharge its obligations to creditors, including, to the extent permitted by law, partners who are creditors. Any surplus must be applied to pay in cash the net amount distributable to partners in accordance with their right to distributions under subsection (b).

(b) Each partner is entitled to a settlement of all partnership accounts upon winding up the partnership business. In settling accounts among the partners, the profits and losses that result from the liquidation of the partnership assets must be credited and charged to the partners' accounts. The partnership shall make a distribution to a partner in an amount equal to any excess of the credits over the charges in the partner's account. A partner shall contribute to the partnership an amount equal to any excess of the charges over the credits in the partner's account but excluding from the calculation charges attributable to an obligation for which the partner is not personally liable under Section 306.

(c) If a partner fails to contribute the full amount required under subsection (b), all of the other partners shall contribute, in the proportions in which those partners share partnership losses, the additional amount necessary to satisfy the partnership obligations for which they are personally liable under Section 306. A partner or partner's legal representative may recover from the other partners any contributions the partner makes to the extent the amount contributed exceeds that partner's share of the partnership obligations for which the partner is personally liable under Section 306.

(d) After the settlement of accounts, each partner shall contribute, in the proportion in which the partner shares partnership losses, the amount necessary to satisfy partnership obligations that were not known at the time of the settlement and for which the partner is personally liable under Section 306.

(e) The estate of a deceased partner is liable for the partner's obligation to contribute to the partnership.

(f) An assignee for the benefit of creditors of a partnership or a partner, or a person appointed by a court to represent creditors of a partnership or a partner, may enforce a partner's obligation to contribute to the partnership.

Comment:

1. Section 807 provides the default rules for the settlement of accounts and contributions among the partners in winding up the business. It is derived in part from UPA Sections 38(1) and 40.

2. Subsection (a) continues the rule in UPA Section 38(1) that, in winding up the business, the partnership assets must first be applied to discharge partnership liabilities to creditors. For this purpose, any required contribution by the partners is treated as an asset of the partnership. After the payment of all partnership liabilities, any surplus must be applied to pay in cash the net amount due the partners under subsection (b) by way of a liquidating distribution.

RUPA continues the "in-cash" rule of UPA Section 38(1) and is consistent with Section 402, which provides that a partner has no right to receive, and may not be required to accept, a distribution in kind, unless otherwise agreed. The in-cash rule avoids the valuation problems that afflict unwanted in-kind distributions.

The partnership must apply its assets to discharge the obligations of partners who are creditors on a parity with other creditors. See Section 404(f). . . . In effect, that abolishes the priority rules in UPA Section 40(b) and (c) which subordinate the payment of inside debt to outside debt. Both RULPA and the RMBCA do likewise. See RULPA § 804; RMBCA §§ 6.40(f), 14.05(a). Ultimately, however, a partner whose "debt" has been repaid by the partnership is personally liable, as a partner, for any outside debt remaining unsatisfied, unlike a limited partner or corporate shareholder. Accordingly, the obligation to contribute sufficient funds to satisfy the claims of outside creditors may result in the equitable subordination of inside debt when partnership assets are insufficient to satisfy all obligations to non-partners.

RUPA in effect abolishes the "dual priority" or "jingle" rule of UPA Section 40(h) and (i). Those sections gave partnership creditors priority as to partnership property and separate creditors priority as to separate property. The jingle rule has already been preempted by the Bankruptcy Code, at least as to Chapter 7 partnership liquidation proceedings. Under Section 723(c) of the Bankruptcy Code, and under RUPA, partnership creditors share pro rata with the partners' individual creditors in the assets of the partners' estates.

3. Subsection (b) provides that each partner is entitled to a settlement of all partnership accounts upon winding up. It also establishes the default rules for closing out the partners' accounts. First, the profits and losses resulting from the liquidation of the partnership assets must be credited or charged to the partners' accounts, according to their respective shares of profits and losses.

Then, the partnership must make a final liquidating distribution to those partners with a positive account balance. That distribution should be in the amount of the excess of credits over the charges in the account. Any partner with a negative account balance must contribute to the partnership an amount equal to the excess of charges over the credits in the account provided the excess relates to an obligation for which the partner is personally liable under Section 306. The partners may, however, agree that a negative account does not reflect a debt to the partnership and need not be repaid in settling the partners' accounts.

Section 807(b) makes clear that a partner's contribution obligation to a partnership in dissolution only considers the partner's share of obligations for which the partner was personally liable under Section 306 ("unshielded obligations"). See Comments to Section 401(b) (partner contribution obligation to an operating partnership). Properly determined under this Section, the total required partner contributions will be sufficient to satisfy the partnership's total unshielded obligations. In special circumstances where a partnership has both shielded and unshielded obligations and the [partners] required contributions are used to first pay shielded partnership obligations, the partners may be required to make further contributions to satisfy the partnership unpaid unshielded obligations. The proper resolution of this matter is left to debtor-creditor law as well as the law governing the fiduciary obligations of the partners. See Section 104(a).

RUPA eliminates the distinction in UPA Section 40(b) between the liability owing to a partner in respect of capital and the liability owing in respect of profits. Section 807(b) speaks simply of the right of a partner to a liquidating distribution. That implements the logic of RUPA Sections 401(a) and 502 under which contributions to capital and shares in profits and losses combine to determine the right to distributions. The partners may, however, agree to share "operating" losses differently from "capital" losses, thereby continuing the UPA distinction.

4. Subsection (c) continues the UPA Section 40(d) rule that solvent partners share proportionately in the shortfall caused by insolvent partners who fail to contribute their proportionate share. The partnership may enforce a partner's obligation to contribute. See Section 405(a). A partner is entitled to recover from the other partners any contributions in excess of that partner's share of the partnership's liabilities. See Section 405(b)(iii).

5. Subsection (d) provides that, after settling the partners' accounts, each partner must contribute, in the proportion in which he shares losses, the amount necessary to satisfy partnership obligations that were not known at the time of the settlement. That

continues the basic rule of UPA Section 40(d) and underscores that the obligation to contribute exists independently of the partnership's books of account. It specifically covers the situation of a partnership liability that was unknown when the partnership books were closed....

ARTICLE 9

CONVERSIONS AND MERGERS

SECTION 901. DEFINITIONS.

In this [article]:

(1) "General partner" means a partner in a partnership and a general partner in a limited partnership.

(2) "Limited partner" means a limited partner in a limited partnership.

(3) "Limited partnership" means a limited partnership created under the [State Limited Partnership Act], predecessor law, or comparable law of another jurisdiction.

(4) "Partner" includes both a general partner and a limited partner.

Comment: ...

2. As Section 908 makes clear, the requirements of Article 9 are not mandatory, and a partnership may convert or merge in any other manner provided by law. Article 9 is merely a "safe harbor." If the requirements of the article are followed, the conversion or merger is legally valid. Since most States have no other established procedure for the conversion or merger of partnerships, it is likely that the Article 9 procedures will be used in virtually all cases....

SECTION 902. CONVERSION OF PARTNERSHIP TO LIMITED PARTNERSHIP.

(a) A partnership may be converted to a limited partnership pursuant to this section.

(b) The terms and conditions of a conversion of a partnership to a limited partnership must be approved by all of the partners or by a number or percentage specified for conversion in the partnership agreement.

(c) After the conversion is approved by the partners, the partnership shall file a certificate of limited partnership in the jurisdiction in which the limited partnership is to be formed. The certificate must include:

(1) a statement that the partnership was converted to a limited partnership from a partnership;

(2) its former name; and

(3) a statement of the number of votes cast by the partners for and against the conversion and, if the vote is less than unanimous, the number or percentage required to approve the conversion under the partnership agreement.

(d) The conversion takes effect when the certificate of limited partnership is filed or at any later date specified in the certificate.

(e) A general partner who becomes a limited partner as a result of the conversion remains liable as a general partner for an obligation incurred by the partnership before the conversion takes effect. If the other party to a transaction with the limited partnership reasonably believes when entering the transaction that the limited partner is a general partner, the limited partner is liable for an obligation incurred by the limited partnership within 90 days after the conversion takes effect. The limited partner's liability for all other obligations of the limited partnership incurred after the conversion takes effect is that of a limited partner as provided in the [State Limited Partnership Act].

SECTION 903. CONVERSION OF LIMITED PARTNERSHIP TO PARTNERSHIP.

(a) A limited partnership may be converted to a partnership pursuant to this section.

(b) Notwithstanding a provision to the contrary in a limited partnership agreement, the terms and conditions of a conversion of a limited partnership to a partnership must be approved by all of the partners.

(c) After the conversion is approved by the partners, the limited partnership shall cancel its certificate of limited partnership.

(d) The conversion takes effect when the certificate of limited partnership is canceled.

(e) A limited partner who becomes a general partner as a result of the conversion remains liable only as a limited partner for an obligation incurred by the limited partnership before the conversion takes effect. Except as otherwise provided in Section 306, the partner is liable as a general partner for an obligation of the partnership incurred after the conversion takes effect.

SECTION 904. EFFECT OF CONVERSION; ENTITY UNCHANGED.

(a) A partnership or limited partnership that has been converted pursuant to this [article] is for all purposes the same entity that existed before the conversion.

(b) When a conversion takes effect:

(1) all property owned by the converting partnership or limited partnership remains vested in the converted entity;

(2) all obligations of the converting partnership or limited partnership continue as obligations of the converted entity; and

(3) an action or proceeding pending against the converting partnership or limited partnership may be continued as if the conversion had not occurred.

SECTION 905. MERGER OF PARTNERSHIPS.

(a) Pursuant to a plan of merger approved as provided in subsection (c), a partnership may be merged with one or more partnerships or limited partnerships.

(b) The plan of merger must set forth:

(1) the name of each partnership or limited partnership that is a party to the merger;

(2) the name of the surviving entity into which the other partnerships or limited partnerships will merge;

(3) whether the surviving entity is a partnership or a limited partnership and the status of each partner;

(4) the terms and conditions of the merger;

(5) the manner and basis of converting the interests of each party to the merger into interests or obligations of the surviving entity, or into money or other property in whole or part; and

(6) the street address of the surviving entity's chief executive office.

(c) The plan of merger must be approved:

(1) in the case of a partnership that is a party to the merger, by all of the partners, or a number or percentage specified for merger in the partnership agreement; and

(2) in the case of a limited partnership that is a party to the merger, by the vote required for approval of a merger by the law of the State or foreign jurisdiction in which the limited partnership is organized and, in the absence of such a specifically applicable law, by all of the partners, notwithstanding a provision to the contrary in the partnership agreement.

(d) After a plan of merger is approved and before the merger takes effect, the plan may be amended or abandoned as provided in the plan.

(e) The merger takes effect on the later of:

(1) the approval of the plan of merger by all parties to the merger, as provided in subsection (c);

(2) the filing of all documents required by law to be filed as a condition to the effectiveness of the merger; or

(3) any effective date specified in the plan of merger.

Comment:

Section 905 provides a "safe harbor" for the merger of a general partnership and one or more general or limited partnerships. The surviving entity may be either a general or a limited partnership. . . .

SECTION 906. EFFECT OF MERGER.

(a) When a merger takes effect:

(1) the separate existence of every partnership or limited partnership that is a party to the merger, other than the surviving entity, ceases;

(2) all property owned by each of the merged partnerships or limited partnerships vests in the surviving entity;

(3) all obligations of every partnership or limited partnership that is a party to the merger become the obligations of the surviving entity; and

(4) an action or proceeding pending against a partnership or limited partnership that is a party to the merger may be continued as if the merger had not occurred, or the surviving entity may be substituted as a party to the action or proceeding.

(b) The [Secretary of State] of this State is the agent for service of process in an action or proceeding against a surviving foreign partnership or limited partnership to enforce an obligation of a domestic partnership or limited partnership that is a party to a merger. The surviving entity shall promptly notify the [Secretary of State] of the mailing address of its chief executive office and of any change of address. Upon receipt of process, the [Secretary of State] shall mail a copy of the process to the surviving foreign partnership or limited partnership.

(c) A partner of the surviving partnership or limited partnership is liable for:

(1) all obligations of a party to the merger for which the partner was personally liable before the merger;

(2) all other obligations of the surviving entity incurred before the merger by a party to the merger, but those obligations may be satisfied only out of property of the entity; and

(3) except as otherwise provided in Section 306, all obligations of the surviving entity incurred after the merger takes effect, but those obligations may be satisfied only out of property of the entity if the partner is a limited partner.

(d) If the obligations incurred before the merger by a party to the merger are not satisfied out of the property of the surviving partnership or limited partnership, the general partners of that party immediately before the effective date of the merger shall contribute the amount necessary to satisfy that party's obligations to the surviving entity, in the manner provided in Section 807 or in the [Limited Partnership Act] of the jurisdiction in which the party was formed, as the case may be, as if the merged party were dissolved.

(e) A partner of a party to a merger who does not become a partner of the surviving partnership or limited partnership is dissociated from the entity, of which that partner was a partner, as of the date the merger takes effect. The surviving entity shall cause the partner's interest in the entity to be purchased under Section 701 or another statute specifically applicable to that partner's interest with respect to a merger. The surviving entity is bound under Section 702 by an act of a general partner dissociated under this subsection, and the partner is liable under Section 703 for transactions entered into by the surviving entity after the merger takes effect.

SECTION 907.   STATEMENT OF MERGER.

(a) After a merger, the surviving partnership or limited partnership may file a statement that one or more partnerships or limited partnerships have merged into the surviving entity.

(b) A statement of merger must contain:

(1) the name of each partnership or limited partnership that is a party to the merger;

(2) the name of the surviving entity into which the other partnerships or limited partnership were merged;

(3) the street address of the surviving entity's chief executive office and of an office in this State, if any; and

(4) whether the surviving entity is a partnership or a limited partnership.

(c) Except as otherwise provided in subsection (d), for the purposes of Section 302, property of the surviving partnership or limited partnership which before the merger was held in the name of another party to the merger is property held in the name of the surviving entity upon filing a statement of merger.

(d) For the purposes of Section 302, real property of the surviving partnership or limited partnership which before the merger was held in the name of another party to the merger is property held in the name of the surviving entity upon recording a certified copy of the statement of merger in the office for recording transfers of that real property.

(e) A filed and, if appropriate, recorded statement of merger, executed and declared to be accurate pursuant to Section 105(c), stating the name of a partnership or limited partnership that is a party to the merger in whose name property was held before the merger and the name of the surviving entity, but not containing all of the other information required by subsection (b), operates with respect to the partnerships or limited partnerships named to the extent provided in subsections (c) and (d).

SECTION 908. NONEXCLUSIVE.

This [article] is not exclusive. Partnerships or limited partnerships may be converted or merged in any other manner provided by law.

[ARTICLE] 10

LIMITED LIABILITY PARTNERSHIP

Section 1001. Statement of Qualification.
Section 1002. Name.
Section 1003. Annual Report.

SECTION 1001. STATEMENT OF QUALIFICATION.

(a) A partnership may become a limited liability partnership pursuant to this section.

(b) The terms and conditions on which a partnership becomes a limited liability partnership must be approved by the vote necessary to amend the partnership agreement except, in the case of a partnership agreement that expressly considers contribution obligations, the vote necessary to amend those provisions.

(c) After the approval required by subsection (b), a partnership may become a limited liability partnership by filing a statement of qualification. The statement must contain:

(1) the name of the partnership;

(2) the street address of the partnership's chief executive office and, if different, the street address of an office in this State, if any;

(3) if there is no office in this State, the name and street address of the partnership's agent for service of process who must be an individual resident of this State or any other person authorized to do business in this State;

(4) a statement that the partnership elects to be a limited liability partnership; and

(5) a deferred effective date, if any.

(d) The status of a partnership as a limited liability partnership is effective on the later of the filing of the statement or a date specified in the statement. The status remains effective, regardless of changes in the partnership, until it is canceled pursuant to Section 105(d) or revoked pursuant to Section 1003.

(e) The status of a partnership as a limited liability partnership and the liability of its partners is not affected by errors or later changes in the information required to be contained in the statement of qualification under subsection (c).

(f) The filing of a statement of qualification establishes that a partnership has satisfied all conditions precedent to the qualification of the partnership as a limited liability partnership.

(g) An amendment or cancellation of a statement of qualification is effective when it is filed or on a deferred effective date specified in the amendment or cancellation.

Comment:

Any partnership may become a limited liability partnership by filing a statement of qualification. See Comments to Sections 101(6) and 202(b) regarding a limited partnership filing a statement of qualification to become a limited liability limited partnership. Section 1001 sets forth the required contents of a statement of qualification. The section also sets forth requirements for the approval of a statement of qualification, establishes the effective date of the filing (and any amendments) which remains effective until canceled or revoked, and provides that the liability of the partners of a limited liability partnership is not affected by errors or later changes in the statement information.

Subsection (b) provides that the terms and conditions on which a partnership becomes a limited liability partnership must . . . generally be approved by the vote necessary to amend the partnership agreement. This means that the act of becoming a limited liability partnership is equivalent to an amendment of the partnership agreement. Where the partnership agreement is silent as to how it may be amended, the subsection (b) vote requires the approval of every partner. Since the limited liability partnership rules are not intended to increase the vote necessary to amend the partnership agreement, where the partnership agreement specifically sets forth an amendment process, that process may be used. Where a partnership agreement sets forth several amendment procedures depending upon the nature of the amendment, the required vote will be that necessary to amend the contribution obligations of the partners. The specific "contribution" vote is preferred because the filing of the statement directly affects partner contribution obligations. Therefore, the language "considers contribution" should be broadly interpreted to include any amendment vote that indirectly affects any partner's contribution obligation such as a partner's obligation to "indemnify" other partners.

The unanimous vote default rule reflects the significance of a partnership becoming a limited liability partnership. In general, upon such a filing each partner is released from the personal contribution obligation imposed under this Act in exchange for relinquishing the right to enforce the contribution obligations of other partners under this Act. See Comments to Sections 306(c) and 401(b). The wisdom of this bargain will depend on many factors including the relative risks of the partners' duties and the assets of the partnership.

Subsection (c) sets forth the information required in a statement of qualification. The [information] must include the name of the partnership which must comply with Section 1002 to identify the partnership as a limited liability partnership. The statement must also include the address of the partnership's chief executive office and, if different, the street address of any other office in this State. A statement must include the name and street address of an agent for service of process only if it does not have any office in this State.

As with other statements, a statement of qualification must be filed in the office of the Secretary of State. See Sections 101(13) and 105(a). Accordingly, a statement of qualification is executed, filed, and otherwise regarded as a statement under this Act. For example, a copy of a filed statement must be sent to every nonfiling partner unless otherwise provided in the partnership agreement. See Sections 105(e) and 103(b)(1). A statement of qualification must be executed by at least two partners under penalties of perjury that the contents of the statement are accurate. See Section 105(c). A person who files the statement must promptly send a copy of the statement to every nonfiling partner but failure to send the copy does not limit the effectiveness of the filed statement to a nonpartner. Section 105(e). The filing must be accompanied by the fee required by the Secretary of State. Section 105(f).

Subsection (d) makes clear that once a statement is filed and effective, the status of the partnership as a limited liability partnership remains effective until the partnership status is either canceled or revoked "regardless of changes in the partnership." Accordingly, a partnership that dissolves but whose business is continued under a business continuation agreement retains its status as a limited liability partnership without the need to refile a new statement. Also, limited liability partnership status remains even though a partnership may be dissolved, wound up, and terminated. Even after the termination of the partnership, the former partners of a terminated partnership would not be personally liable for partnership obligations incurred while the partnership was a limited liability partnership.

Subsection (d) also makes clear that limited liability partnership status remains effective until actual cancellation under Section 1003 or revocation under Section 105(d). Ordinarily the terms and conditions of becoming a limited liability partnership must be approved by the vote necessary to amend the partnership agreement. See Sections 1001(b), 306(c), and 401(j). Since the statement of cancellation may be filed by a person authorized to file the original statement of qualification, the same vote necessary to approve the filing of the statement of qualification must be obtained to file the statement of cancellation. See Section 105(d).

Subsection (f) provides that once a statement of qualification is executed and filed under subsection (c) and Section 105, the partnership assumes the status of a limited liability partnership. This status is intended to be conclusive with regard to third parties dealing with the partnership. It is not intended to affect the rights of partners. For example, a properly executed and filed statement of qualification conclusively establishes the limited liability shield described in Section 306(c). If the partners executing and filing the statement exceed their authority, the internal abuse of authority has no effect on the liability shield with regard to third parties. Partners may challenge the abuse of authority for purposes of establishing the liability of the culpable partners but may not effect the liability shield as to third parties. Likewise, third parties may not challenge the existence of the liability shield because the decision to file the statement lacked the proper vote. As a result, the filing of the statement creates the liability shield even when the required subsection (b) vote is not obtained.

SECTION 1002. NAME.

The name of a limited liability partnership must end with "Registered Limited Liability Partnership", "Limited Liability Partnership", "R.L.L.P.", "L.L.P.", "RLLP," or "LLP".

Comment:

The name provisions are intended to alert persons dealing with a limited liability partnership of the presence of the liability shield. Because many jurisdictions have adopted the naming concept of a "registered" limited liability partnership, this aspect has been retained. These name requirements also distinguish limited partnerships and general partnerships that become limited liability partnerships because the new name must be at the end of and in addition to the general or limited partnership's regular name. See Comments to Section 101(6). Since the name identification rules of this section do not alter the regular name of the partnership, they do not disturb historic notions of apparent authority of partners in both general and limited partnerships.

SECTION 1003. ANNUAL REPORT.

(a) A limited liability partnership, and a foreign limited liability partnership authorized to transact business in this State, shall file an annual report in the office of the [Secretary of State] which contains:

(1) the name of the limited liability partnership and the State or other jurisdiction under whose laws the foreign limited liability partnership is formed;

(2) the current street address of the partnership's chief executive office and, if different, the current street address of an office in this State, if any; and

(3) if there is no current office in this State, the name and street address of the partnership's current agent for service of process who must be an individual resident of this State or any other person authorized to do business in this State.

(b) An annual report must be filed between [January 1 and April 1] of each year following the calendar year in which a partnership files a statement of qualification or a foreign partnership becomes authorized to transact business in this State.

(c) The [Secretary of State] may administratively revoke the statement of qualification of a partnership that fails to file an annual report when due or to pay the required filing fee. The [Secretary of State] shall provide the partnership at least 60 days' written notice of intent to revoke the statement. The notice must be mailed to the partnership at its chief executive office set forth in the last filed statement of qualification or annual report. The notice must specify the annual report that has not been filed, the fee that has not been paid, and the effective date of the revocation. The revocation is not effective if the annual report is filed and the fee is paid before the effective date of the revocation.

(d) A revocation under subsection (c) only affects a partnership's status as a limited liability partnership and is not an event of dissolution of the partnership.

(e) A partnership whose statement of qualification has been administratively revoked may apply to the [Secretary of State] for reinstatement within two years after the effective date of the revocation. The application must state:

(1) the name of the partnership and the effective date of the revocation; and

(2) that the ground for revocation either did not exist or has been corrected.

(f) A reinstatement under subsection (e) relates back to and takes effect as of the effective date of the revocation, and the partnership's status as a limited liability partnership continues as if the revocation had never occurred.

Comment:

Section 1003 sets forth the requirements of an annual report that must be filed by all limited liability partnerships and any foreign limited liability partnership authorized to transact business in this State. See Sections 101(5) (definition of a limited liability partnership) and 101(4) (definition of a foreign limited liability partnership). The failure of a limited liability partnership to file an annual report is a basis for the Secretary of State to administratively revoke its statement of qualification. See Section 1003(c). A foreign limited liability partnership that fails to file an annual report may not maintain an action or proceeding in this State. See Section 1103(a).

Subsection (a) generally requires that an annual report contain the same information required in a statement of qualification. Compare Sections 1001(a) and 1003(a). The differences are that the annual report requires disclosure of the state of formation of a foreign limited liability partnership but deletes the delayed effective date and limited liability partnership election statement provisions of a statement of qualification. As such, the annual report serves to update the information required in a statement of qualification. Under subsection (b), the annual report must be filed between January 1 and April 1 of each calendar year following the year in which a statement of qualification was filed or a foreign limited liability partnership becomes authorized to transact business. This timing requirement means that a limited liability partnership must make an annual filing and may not prefile multiple annual reports in a single year.

Subsection (c) sets forth the procedure for the Secretary of State to administratively revoke a partnership's statement of qualification for the failure to file an annual report when due or pay the required filing fee. The Secretary of State must provide a partnership at least 60 days' written notice of the intent to revoke the statement. The notice must be mailed to the partnership at the address of its chief executive office set forth in the last filed statement or annual report and must state the grounds for revocation as well as the effective date of revocation. The revocation is not effective if the stated problem is cured before the stated effective date.

Under subsection (d), a revocation only terminates the partnership's status as a limited liability partnership but is not an event of dissolution of the partnership itself. Where revocation occurs, a partnership may apply for reinstatement under subsection (e) within two years after the effective date of the revocation. The application must state that the grounds for revocation either did not exist or have been corrected. The Secretary of State may grant the application on the basis of the statements alone or require proof of correction. Under subsection (f), when the application is granted, the reinstatement relates back to and takes effect as of the effective date of the revocation. The relation back doctrine prevents gaps in a reinstated partnership's liability shield. See Comments to Section 306(c).

[ARTICLE] 11

FOREIGN LIMITED LIABILITY PARTNERSHIP

Section 1101. Law Governing Foreign Limited Liability Partnership.
Section 1102. Statement of Foreign Qualification.
Section 1103. Effect of Failure to Qualify.
Section 1104. Activities Not Constituting Transacting Business.
Section 1105. Action By [Attorney General].

SECTION 1101. LAW GOVERNING FOREIGN LIMITED LIABILITY PARTNERSHIP.

(a) The laws under which a foreign limited liability partnership is formed govern relations among the partners and between the partners and the partnership and the liability of partners for obligations of the partnership.

(b) A foreign limited liability partnership may not be denied a statement of foreign qualification by reason of any difference between the laws under which the partnership was formed and the laws of this State.

(c) A statement of foreign qualification does not authorize a foreign limited liability partnership to engage in any business or exercise any power that a partnership may not engage in or exercise in this State as a limited liability partnership.

Comment:

Section 1101 provides that the laws where a foreign limited liability partnership is formed rather than the laws of this State govern both the internal relations of the partnership and liability of its partners for the obligations of the partnership. See Section 101(4) (definition of a foreign limited liability partnership). Section 106(b) provides that the laws of this State govern the internal relations of a domestic limited liability and the liability of its partners for the obligations of the partnership. See Sections 101(5) (definition of a domestic limited liability partnership). A partnership may therefore choose the laws of a particular jurisdiction by filing a statement of qualification in that jurisdiction. But there are limitations on this choice.

Subsections (b) and (c) together make clear that although a foreign limited liability partnership may not be denied a statement of foreign qualification simply because of a difference between the laws of its foreign jurisdiction and the laws of this State, it may not engage in any business or exercise any power in this State that a domestic limited liability partnership may not engage in or exercise. Under subsection (c), a foreign limited liability partnership that engages in a business or exercises a power in this State that a domestic may not engage in or exercise, does so only as an ordinary partnership without the benefit of the limited liability partnership liability shield set forth in Section 306(c). In this sense, a foreign limited liability partnership is treated the same as a domestic limited liability partnership. Also, the Attorney General may maintain an action to restrain a foreign limited liability partnership from transacting an unauthorized business in this State. See Section 1105.

SECTION 1102. STATEMENT OF FOREIGN QUALIFICATION.

(a) Before transacting business in this State, a foreign limited liability partnership must file a statement of foreign qualification. The statement must contain:

(1) the name of the foreign limited liability partnership which satisfies the requirements of the State or other jurisdiction under whose laws it is formed and ends with "Registered Limited Liability Partnership", "Limited Liability Partnership", "R.L.L.P.", "L.L.P.", "RLLP," or "LLP";

(2) the street address of the partnership's chief executive office and, if different, the street address of an office in this State, if any;

(3) if there is no office in this State, the name and street address of the partnership's agent for service of process who must be an individual resident of this State or any other person authorized to do business in this State; and

(4) a deferred effective date, if any.

(b) The status of a partnership as a foreign limited liability partnership is effective on the later of the filing of the statement of foreign qualification or a date specified in the statement. The status remains effective, regardless of changes in the partnership, until it is canceled pursuant to Section 105(d) or revoked pursuant to Section 1003.

(c) An amendment or cancellation of a statement of foreign qualification is effective when it is filed or on a deferred effective date specified in the amendment or cancellation.

Comment:

Section 1102 provides that a foreign limited liability partnership must file a statement of foreign qualification before transacting business in this State. The section also sets forth the information required in the statement. As with other statements, a statement of foreign qualification must be filed in the office of the Secretary of State. See Sections 101(13), 105(a), and 1001(c). Accordingly, a statement of foreign qualification is executed, filed, and otherwise regarded as a statement under this Act. See Section 101(13) (definition of a statement includes a statement of foreign qualification).

Subsection (a) generally requires the same information in a statement of foreign qualification as is required in a statement of qualification. Compare Sections 1001(c). The statement of foreign qualification must include a name that complies with the requirements for domestic limited liability partnership under Section 1002 and must include the address of the partnership's chief executive office and, if different, the street address of any other office in this State. If a foreign limited liability partnership does not have any office in this State, the statement of foreign qualification must include the name and street address of an agent for service of process.

As with a statement of qualification, a statement of foreign qualification (and amendments) is effective when filed or at a later specified filing date. Compare Sections 1102(b) and (c) with Sections 1001(e) and (h). Likewise, a statement of foreign qualification remains effective until canceled by the partnership or revoked by the Secretary of State, regardless of changes in the partnership. See Sections 105(d) (statement cancellation) and Section 1003 (revocation for failure to file annual report or pay annual filing fee) and compare Sections 1102(b) and 1001(e). Statement of qualification provisions regarding the relationship of the status of a foreign partnership relative to its initial filing of a statement are governed by foreign law and are therefore omitted from this section. See Sections 1001(f) (effect of errors and omissions) and (g) (filing establishes all conditions precedent to qualification).

SECTION 1103. EFFECT OF FAILURE TO QUALIFY.

(a) A foreign limited liability partnership transacting business in this State may not maintain an action or proceeding in this State unless it has in effect a statement of foreign qualification.

(b) The failure of a foreign limited liability partnership to have in effect a statement of foreign qualification does not impair the validity of a contract or act of the foreign limited liability partnership or preclude it from defending an action or proceeding in this State.

(c) Limitations on personal liability of partners are not waived solely by transacting business in this State without a statement of foreign qualification.

(d) If a foreign limited liability partnership transacts business in this State without a statement of foreign qualification, the [Secretary of State] is its agent for service of process with respect to [claims for relief] arising out of the transaction of business in this State.

Comment:

Section 1103 makes clear that the only consequence of a failure to file a statement of foreign qualification is that the foreign limited liability partnership will not be able to maintain an action or proceeding in this State. The partnership's contracts remain valid, it may defend an action or proceeding, personal liability of the partners is not waived, and the Secretary of State is the agent for service of process with respect to claims arising out of transacting business in this State. Sections 1103(b)–(d). Once a statement of foreign qualification is filed, the Secretary of State may revoke the statement for failure to file an annual report but the partnership has the right to cure the failure for two years. See Section 1003(c) and (e). Since the failure to file a statement of foreign qualification has no impact on the liability shield of the partners, a revocation of a statement of foreign qualification also has no impact on the liability shield created under foreign laws. Compare Sections 1103(c) and 1003(f) (revocation of the statement of qualification of a domestic limited liability partnership removes partner liability shield unless filing problems cured within two years).

SECTION 1104. ACTIVITIES NOT CONSTITUTING TRANSACTING BUSINESS.

(a) Activities of a foreign limited liability partnership which do not constitute transacting business within the meaning of this [article] include:

(1) maintaining, defending, or settling an action or proceeding;

(2) holding meetings of its partners or carrying on any other activity concerning its internal affairs;

(3) maintaining bank accounts;

(4) maintaining offices or agencies for the transfer, exchange, and registration of the partnership's own securities or maintaining trustees or depositories with respect to those securities;

(5) selling through independent contractors;

(6) soliciting or obtaining orders, whether by mail or through employees or agents or otherwise, if the orders require acceptance outside this State before they become contracts;

(7) creating or acquiring indebtedness, mortgages, or security interests in real or personal property;

(8) securing or collecting debts or foreclosing mortgages or other security interests in property securing the debts, and holding, protecting, and maintaining property so acquired;

(9) conducting an isolated transaction that is completed within 30 days and is not one in the course of similar transactions of like nature; and

(10) transacting business in interstate commerce.

(b) For purposes of this [article], the ownership in this State of income-producing real property or tangible personal property, other than property excluded under subsection (a), constitutes transacting business in this State.

(c) This section does not apply in determining the contacts or activities that may subject a foreign limited liability partnership to service of process, taxation, or regulation under any other law of this State.

Comment:

Because the Attorney General may restrain a foreign limited liability partnership from transacting an unauthorized business in this State and a foreign partnership may not maintain an action or proceeding in this State, the concept of "transacting business" in this State is important. To provide more certainty, subsection (a) sets forth ten separate categories of activities that do not constitute transacting business. Subsection (c) makes clear that the section only considers the definition of "transacting business" and as no impact on whether a foreign limited liability partnership's activities in this State subject it to service of process, taxation, or regulation under any other law of this State.

SECTION 1105. ACTION BY [ATTORNEY GENERAL].

The [Attorney General] may maintain an action to restrain a foreign limited liability partnership from transacting business in this State in violation of this [article].

Comment:

Section 1105 makes clear that the Attorney General may restrain a foreign limited liability from transacting an unauthorized business in this State. As a threshold matter, a foreign limited liability partnership must be "transacting business" in this State within the meaning of Section 1104. Secondly, the business transacted in this State must be that which could not be engaged in by a domestic limited liability partnership. See Section 1101(c). The fact that a foreign limited liability partnership has a statement of foreign qualification does not permit it to engage in any unauthorized business in this State or impair the power of the Attorney General to restrain the foreign partnership from engaging in the unauthorized business. See Section 1101(c).

ARTICLE 12

MISCELLANEOUS PROVISIONS

SECTION 1201. UNIFORMITY OF APPLICATION AND CONSTRUCTION.

This [Act] shall be applied and construed to effectuate its general purpose to make uniform the law with respect to the subject of this [Act] among States enacting it.

SECTION 1202. SHORT TITLE.

This [Act] may be cited as the Uniform Partnership Act (1994).

SECTION 1203. SEVERABILITY CLAUSE.

If any provision of this [Act] or its application to any person or circumstance is held invalid, the invalidity does not affect other provisions or applications of this [Act] which can be given effect without the invalid provision or application, and to this end the provisions of this [Act] are severable.

SECTION 1204. EFFECTIVE DATE.

This [Act] takes effect _____.

SECTION 1205. REPEALS.

Effective January 1, 199__, the following acts and parts of acts are repealed: [the State Partnership Act as amended and in effect immediately before the effective date of this Act].

SECTION 1206. APPLICABILITY.

(a) Before January 1, 199__, this [Act] governs only a partnership formed:

(1) after the effective date of this [Act], unless that partnership is continuing the business of a dissolved partnership under [Section 41 of the prior Uniform Partnership Act]; and

(2) before the effective date of this [Act], that elects, as provided by subsection (c), to be governed by this [Act].

(b) After January 1, 199__, this [Act] governs all partnerships.

(c) Before January 1, 199__, a partnership voluntarily may elect, in the manner provided in its partnership agreement or by law for amending the partnership agreement, to be governed by this [Act]. The provisions of this [Act] relating to the liability of the partnership's partners to third parties apply to limit those partners' liability to a third party who had done business with the partnership within one year preceding the partnership's election to be governed by this [Act], only if the third party knows or has received a notification of the partnership's election to be governed by this [Act].

SECTION 1207. SAVINGS CLAUSE.

This [Act] does not affect an action or proceeding commenced or right accrued before this [Act] takes effect.

FORM OF PARTNERSHIP AGREEMENT

[From M. Volz, C. Trower & D. Reiss, The Drafting of Partnership Agreements 65–85 (7th ed. 1986).]

General Partnership Agreement of

[Insert Name]

This is a general Partnership Agreement, made and entered into by and between [list partners' full names], (collectively, the "Partners").

SECTION 1

FORMATION OF PARTNERSHIP

The Partners hereby form a partnership (the "Partnership") pursuant to the [name of state] Uniform Partnership Act. The rights and duties of the Partners shall be as provided in that Act except as modified by this Agreement.

SECTION 2

NAME

The business of the Partnership shall be conducted under the name "[insert name]" or such other name as the Managing Partner shall hereafter designate in writing to the Partners.

SECTION 3

DEFINITIONS

"Act" means the [insert jurisdiction of formation] Uniform Partnership Act, [insert citation to official state statute].

"Agreement" means this Partnership Agreement, as amended, modified, or supplemented from time to time.

"Bankruptcy" shall be deemed to have occurred with respect to any Partner 60 days after the happening of any of the following: (1) the filing of an application by a Partner for, or a consent to, the appointment of a trustee of the Partner's assets; (2) the filing by a Partner of a voluntary petition in bankruptcy or the filing of a pleading in any court of record admitting in writing the Partner's inability to pay the Partner's debts as they become due; (3) the making by a Partner of a general assignment for the benefit of creditors; (4) the filing by a Partner of an answer admitting the material allegations of, or consenting to, or defaulting in answering a bankruptcy petition filed against the Partner in any bankruptcy proceeding; or (5) the entry of an order, judgment, or decree by any court of competent jurisdiction adjudicating a Partner a bankrupt or appointing a trustee of the Partner's assets, and that order, judgment, or decree continuing unstayed and in effect for a period of 60 days.

"Capital Account" means with respect to each Partner, the account established on the books and records of the Partnership for each Partner under Section 11.01. Each Partner's Capital Account shall initially equal the cash and the agreed value of property (net of liabilities assumed or to which the property is subject) contributed by the Partner to the Partnership, and during the term of the Partnership shall be (1) *increased* by the amount of (a) Taxable Income allocated to the Partner, other than Taxable Income attributable to the difference between the agreed value and adjusted basis of the property at contribution, and (b) any money and the agreed value of property (net of any liabilities assumed or to which the property is subject) subsequently contributed to the Partnership, and (2) *decreased* by the amount of (a) Tax Losses allocated to the Partner, *except* (i) Tax Losses attributable to depreciation of contributed property, which shall decrease Capital Accounts only to the extent of depreciation computed as if the property were purchased by the Partnership at its agreed value, and (ii) Tax Losses attributable to the difference between the agreed value and adjusted basis of property at contribution (which shall not decrease the contributing Partner's Capital Account), and (b) all cash and the agreed value of property (net of liabilities assumed or to which the property is subject) distributed to such Partner, and shall otherwise be kept in accordance with applicable Treasury Regulations.

"Capital Contribution" means the amount of money or the agreed value of other property contributed to the Partnership by a Partner.

"Code" means the Internal Revenue Code . . . as amended, modified, or rescinded from time to time, or any similar provision of succeeding law.

"Incapacity" or "Incapacitated" means the incompetence, insanity, interdiction, death, disability, or incapacity, as the case may be, of any Partner.

"Interest" means the entire ownership interest of a Partner in the Partnership.

"Managing Partner" means [insert name] but in the event that he is at any time no longer a Partner, or is replaced by vote of the Partners, the term shall mean the party or parties then acting in that capacity.

"Net Cash Flow" with respect to any fiscal period means all cash revenues of the Partnership during that period (including interest or other earnings on the funds of the Partnership), *less* the sum of the following to the extent made from those cash revenues:

(1) All principal and interest payments on any indebtedness of the Partnership.

(2) All cash expenses incurred incident to the operations of the Partnership's business.

(3) Funds set aside as reserves for contingencies, working capital, debt service, taxes, insurance, or other costs or expenses incident to the conduct of the Partnership's business, which the Managing Partner deems reasonably necessary or appropriate.

"Partners" means [insert names]; any person admitted as a substituted Partner pursuant to Section 16; and, with respect to those provisions of this Agreement concerning a Partner's right to receive a share of profits or other compensation by way of income or the return of a Partner's contribution, any assignee of a Partner's Interest (except that an assignee who does not become a substituted Partner shall have only those rights specified in Section 27 of the Act).

"Partnership Percentage" means the following percentages:

Name	*Percentage*
[insert]	[insert]

Distributions or allocations made in proportion to or in accordance with the Partnership Percentages of the Partners shall be based upon relative Partnership Percentages as of the record date for distributions and in accordance with Section 706(c) and (d) of the Code for allocations.

"Taxable Income" and "Tax Losses," respectively, shall mean the net income or net losses of the Partnership as determined for federal income tax purposes, and all items required to be separately stated by Section 702 of the Code and the Regulations thereunder.

SECTION 4

BUSINESS OF THE PARTNERSHIP

The business of the Partnership is to [insert specific purposes] and to engage in any and all activities related or incidental thereto.

SECTION 5

NAMES AND ADDRESSES OF PARTNERS

The names and addresses of the Partners are:

[Insert name and addresses where partners wish to be contacted about partnership-related business.]

SECTION 6

TERM

The term of the Partnership shall begin [*or*: began] on [insert] and shall continue until the earlier of [date] or until dissolved by an act or event specified in this Agreement or by the law as one effecting dissolution.

SECTION 7

BUSINESS OFFICES

The principal place of business of the Partnership shall be [insert]. The Managing Partner may, from time to time, change the principal place of business of the Partnership, and in such event the Managing Partner shall notify the other Partners in writing within 30 days of the effective date of such change. The Managing Partner may in his discretion establish additional places of business of the Partnership.

SECTION 8

CAPITAL AND CONTRIBUTIONS

8.01. *Initial Capital Contributions.* The Partners shall initially make Capital Contributions totaling $_____ and among them in accordance with their Partnership Percentages. The Partners' initial Capital Contributions shall be made as soon as practicable after execution of this Agreement.

8.02. *Partners' Assessments.* In addition to the Capital Contributions required by Section 8.01, each Partner shall be obligated to make additional Capital Contributions, as called for by the Managing Partner. All additional Capital Contributions shall be made in accordance with the Partnership Percentages and within 30 days after the Partners have received notice thereof from the Managing Partner. The Managing Partner shall call these assessments based upon his estimate of all costs, expenses, or charges with respect to operation of the Partnership, *less* the expected revenues from such operations. Any increases in the Capital Contributions of the Partners pursuant to this

154

Section 8.02 shall be noted on Annex A attached hereto and incorporated by reference.

8.03. *Default in Payment of Capital Contributions.* If any Partner fails to pay all or any portion of an additional assessment called pursuant to Section 8.02 (an "Assessment Payment") within 60 days after notification of the assessment, the remaining Partners shall advance an additional amount to the Partnership equal to the unpaid Assessment Payment (and as between them in accordance with their respective Partnership Percentages), which amount shall be deemed a loan to the defaulting Partner and a subsequent Capital Contribution to the Partnership. Thereafter, the Managing Partner shall withhold any distributions to which the defaulting Partner would otherwise be entitled and pay that amount to the other Partners in accordance with their respective Partnership Percentages, until the entire Assessment Payment, plus interest computed at _____ per cent shall have been repaid in full.

8.04. *Interest on Capital Contributions.* No Partner shall be paid interest on any Capital Contribution.

8.05. *Withdrawal and Return of Capital Contributions.* No Partner shall be entitled to withdraw any part of his Capital Contribution, or to receive any distributions from the Partnership except as provided by this Agreement.

8.06. *Loans by Partner.* The Partners may (but shall not be obligated to) [*or:* the Partners shall, in accordance with their Partnership Percentages,] loan or advance to the Partnership such funds as they deem advisable [*or:* as are necessary for the Partnership's operations]; provided, however, that interest on those loans or advances shall not be in excess of _____ per cent.

SECTION 9

DISTRIBUTIONS

9.01. *Distributions as Between Partners.* Net Cash Flow shall be distributed among the Partners in accordance with their respective Partnership Percentages.

9.02. *Timing of Distributions and Discretion of Partners as to Reinvestment.* Partnership distributions, if any, will be made to those persons recognized on the books of the Partnership as Partners or as assignees of Interests on the day of the distribution. To the extent permitted by law and as permitted by any loan agreements entered into by the Partnership, the Partnership's Net Cash Flow may in whole or in part be reinvested in the Partnership's business or distributed to the Partners, as the Managing Partner determines.

SECTION 10

ALLOCATION OF PROFITS AND LOSSES FOR TAX PURPOSES

The Taxable Income and Tax Losses to be allocated among the Partners shall be allocated among them in accordance with their respective Partnership Percentages.

SECTION 11

BOOKS OF ACCOUNT, RECORDS, AND REPORTS

11.01. ***Responsibility for Books and Records.*** Proper and complete records and books of account shall be kept by the Managing Partner in which shall be entered fully and accurately all transactions and other matters relative to the Partnership's business as are usually entered into records and books of account maintained by persons engaged in businesses of a like character, including a Capital Account for each Partner. The Partnership books and records shall be prepared in accordance with generally accepted accounting practices, consistently applied, and shall be kept on the cash [*or*: accrual] basis except in circumstances in which the Managing Partner determines that another basis of accounting will be in the best interests of the Partnership [*or*: on the basis determined in the best interests of the Partnership by the Managing Partner]. The books and records shall at all times be maintained at the principal place of business of the Partnership and shall be open to the inspection and examination of the Partners or their duly authorized representatives during reasonable business hours.

11.02. ***Reports to Partners.*** As soon as practicable in the particular case, the Managing Partner shall deliver to every other Partner

(1) Such information concerning the Partnership after the end of each fiscal year as shall be necessary for the preparation by such a Partner of his income or other tax returns.

(2) An unaudited statement prepared by the Managing Partner setting forth, as of the end of and for each fiscal year, a profit and loss statement and a balance sheet of the Partnership and a statement showing the amounts allocated to or against each Interest during that year.

(3) If feasible, on or before October 15 of each year, a statement setting forth projected Taxable Income or Tax Losses to be generated by the Partnership for the fiscal year.

(4) Other information as in the judgment of the Managing Partner shall be reasonably necessary for the other Partners to be advised of the results of operations of the Partnership.

11.03. Additional Reports. The Managing Partner may prepare and deliver to the Partners from time to time during each fiscal year, in connection with distributions or otherwise, unaudited statements showing the results of operations of the Partnership to the date of that statement.

SECTION 12

FISCAL YEAR

The fiscal year of the Partnership shall end on the thirty-first day of December in each year.

SECTION 13

PARTNERSHIP FUNDS

The funds of the Partnership shall be deposited in such bank account or accounts, or invested in such interest-bearing or noninterest-bearing investments, as shall be designated by the Managing Partner. All withdrawals from any such bank accounts shall be made by the duly authorized agent or agents of the Managing Partner. Partnership funds shall be held in the name of the Partnership and shall not be commingled with those of any other person.

SECTION 14

RIGHTS OF PARTNERS

14.01. Incapacity. Within 90 days after a Partner becomes Incapacitated, his executor, administrator, committee, or analogous fiduciary (the "Representative") shall elect whether to retain the Incapacitated Partner's Interest in the Partnership or whether to sell that Interest to the remaining Partners. If the Representative elects to retain that Interest, the Interest shall remain bound by all the provisions of this Agreement, and the Partnership shall continue. If the Representative elects to sell the Incapacitated Partner's Interest to the other Partners, he shall so notify the other Partners in writing within the 90 day period and the other Partners must purchase the Incapacitated Partner's Interest. Any Interest shall be purchased by the remaining Partners in proportion to their respective Partnership Percentages at that time, or in such other proportion as they may mutually agree. The purchase price of an Interest sold pursuant to this Section 14.01 shall be the Contract Price as defined by Section 14.06, and payment for the Interest shall be made in the manner set forth in Section 14.07.

14.02. Bankruptcy. At the Bankruptcy of any Partner, that Partner (an "Inactive Partner") or his representative shall cease to have any voice in the conduct of the affairs of the Partnership and all acts, consents, and decisions with respect to the Partnership shall thereafter be made by the other Partners. The Inactive Partner shall, nonetheless, remain liable for his share of any losses of the Partnership or contributions to the Partnership as provided herein, and shall be entitled to receive his share of Taxable Income, Tax Losses, and Net Cash Flow. For six months from and after the date of the Bankruptcy of any Partner, the other Partners shall have the irrevocable option to purchase the Inactive Partner's Interest in the Partnership. That purchase shall be made in proportion to the respective Partnership Percentages of the other Partners at the time or in such other proportion as they may mutually agree. Should the other Partners exercise their option to purchase the Inactive Partner's Interest, they shall notify the Inactive Partner or his representative of their intention to do so within this six-month period. The purchase price of any Interest purchased pursuant to this Section 14.02 shall be the Contract Price as defined by Section 14.06 and shall be payable at the time and in the manner specified in Section 14.07. Should the other Partners not exercise the option to purchase the Inactive Partner's Interest, the Inactive Partner shall remain such in accordance with the provisions set forth above.

14.03. *Limitation on Sale of Interests.* If a Partner desires to offer for sale his Interest in the Partnership, such Partner (the "Selling Partner") shall give written notice of all material terms and conditions of the offer to the other Partners (the "Buying Partners"). Within 30 days after receipt of the notice, the Buying Partners shall notify the Selling Partner of their intent to purchase the Interest of the Selling Partner upon the terms and conditions contained in the offer. The Buying Partners shall purchase the Interest of the Selling Partner in proportion to their respective Partnership Percentages, or in such other proportion as the Buying Partners may mutually agree. If the Buying Partners fail to notify the Selling Partner that they elect to purchase his Interest within the 30–day period, the Selling Partner shall have the right (1) to sell his Interest within 90 days to a third party on the same terms offered to the Buying Partners, *if* all Partners consent to the specific sale pursuant to Section 14.04, or (2) failing this consent, to withdraw from the Partnership.

If a Partner withdraws pursuant to the immediately preceding sentence, the Partner shall be entitled to a payment from the Partnership equal to the Contract Price and payable at the time and in the manner set forth in Section 14.07. Any amounts received pursuant to this Section 14.03 shall constitute complete and full discharge of all amounts owing to the withdrawing Partner on account of his Interest as a Partner in the Partnership.

14.04. *Assignment.* Subject to the right of first refusal in Section 14.03, a Partner may assign all or a portion of his Interest *provided that* the other Partners unanimously consent, in writing, to the assignment (which consent may be withheld in their absolute discretion). The assignment shall confer upon the assignee the right to become a substituted Partner, in the following manner and subject to the following conditions:

(1) Each assignment shall be effective as of the day on which all Partners accept the transfer.

(2) No assignment shall be effective if the assignment would, in the opinion of counsel to the Partnership, result in the termination of the Partnership for purposes of the then applicable provisions of the Code.

(3) No assignment to a minor or incompetent shall be effective in any respect except that this limitation shall not apply to a transfer in trust for the benefit of a minor or in custodianship under the Uniform Gifts to Minors Act or similar legislation.

Unless an assignee becomes a substituted Partner, the assignee shall have no right to interfere in the management or administration of the Partnership's business or affairs, or to require any information or account of Partnership transactions, or to inspect the Partnership's books. The assignment merely entitles the assignee to receive the share of distributions, income, and losses to which the assigning Partner would otherwise be entitled.

14.05. *Transferees Bound by Agreement.* Any assignee and any person admitted to the Partnership as a substituted Partner shall be subject to and bound by all the provisions of this Agreement as if originally a party to this Agreement.

14.06. *Contract Price.* The Contract Price shall be equal to the fair market value of the selling Partner's Interest as of the date of the event triggering the sale. The fair market value shall be determined within 60 days by (1) an appraisal (to be performed by [insert name]) of the fair market value of the Partnership's assets, less its liabilities, and (2) a valuation of the selling Partner's Interest as if the net assets of the Partnership were sold for cash and the cash distributed in accordance with Section 17.02 (dissolution).

14.07. *Payment—Time and Manner.*

(a) Any Interest transferred to other Partners or the Partnership pursuant to Sections 14.01, 14.02, or 14.03 of this Agreement shall be paid for, at the purchaser's option, either (1) all in cash at the time of transfer of the Interest, or (2) by a downpayment computed in accordance with Section 14.07(b) and delivery of a promissory note signed by the purchaser(s).

(b) If the purchaser(s) elects the second option in Section 14.07(a) above, he shall pay as a downpayment 33 per cent of the Contract Price. The remaining unpaid portion of the Contract Price shall be represented by a promissory note of the purchasers, in such form as shall be acceptable to the purchasers, and providing for four equal annual installments of the remaining unpaid portion of the Contract Price, each installment due on the anniversary of the transfer of the interest. The promissory note shall provide that interest at an annual rate of 9 per cent (compounded semi-annually) shall be paid with each payment of principal (or such higher interest rate as shall be necessary to avoid the imputation of interest pursuant to Section 483 of the Code), from the date of acquisition of the Interest on the portion of the note remaining unpaid from time to time.

14.08. *Adjustment of Partnership Percentages.* If a Partner withdraws pursuant to Section 14.03, the Partnership Percentages of the remaining Partners shall immediately be recalculated so that each Partner's Partnership Percentage is equal to (1) his Capital Contribution as stated on Annex A, *divided by* (2) the aggregate Capital Contributions of all remaining Partners. If the Partners or a third party purchases an Interest pursuant to Sections 14.01, 14.02, or 14.03, the Partnership Percentage of the selling Partner shall be added to that of the purchasing Partners, pro rata, or shall become the Partnership Percentage of the third-party purchaser, as the case may be.

14.09. *Voting.* All decisions required to be made or actions required to be taken by the Partners pursuant to this Agreement (including amendment hereof) shall be made or taken by the affirmative vote (at a meeting or, in lieu thereof, by written consent of the required percentage in Interest) of Partners having _____ per cent of the aggregate Partnership Percentages.

SECTION 15

MANAGEMENT AND ADMINISTRATION OF BUSINESS

15.01. *Authority of Managing Partner.* The Managing Partner shall have the authority to manage the day-to-day operations and affairs of the Partnership and to make decisions regarding the business of the Partnership. Any action taken by the Managing Partner shall constitute the act of and serve to bind the Partnership. In dealing with the Managing Partner acting on behalf of the Partnership, no person shall be required to inquire into the authority of the Managing Partner to bind the Partnership. Persons dealing with the Partnership are entitled to rely conclusively on the power and authority of the Managing Partner as set forth in this Agreement.

15.02. *Power of Managing Partner.* The powers of the Managing Partner shall include, but shall not be limited to, the power to

(1) Create, by grant or otherwise, easements and servitudes relating to the Partnership's property.

(2) Employ and dismiss from employment any and all employees, agents, independent contractors, real estate managers, brokers, attorneys, and accountants.

(3) To let or lease all or any portion of any Partnership property for any purpose and without limit as to the term thereof, whether or not that term (including renewal terms) shall extend beyond the date of termination of the Partnership and whether or not the portion so leased is to be occupied by the lessee or, in turn, subleased in whole or in part to others.

(4) Construct, alter, improve, repair, raze, replace, or rebuild any property.

(5) Obtain replacements of any mortgage or mortgages related in any way to the property owned by the Partnership, and to repay in whole or in part, refinance, recast, modify, consolidate, or extend any mortgages affecting any such property.

(6) Take such action on behalf of the Partnership as may be necessary to acquire real or personal property for the Partnership as the Partners deem advisable or beneficial to the purposes and goals of the Partnership.

(7) Sell or exchange Partnership property.

(8) Be reimbursed for all expenses incurred in conducting the Partnership business, all taxes paid by the Managing Partner in connection with the Partnership business, and all costs associated with the development, organization, and initial operation of the Partnership.

(9) Do any and all of the foregoing at such a price, rental or amount, for cash, securities, or other property and upon those terms as the Partners deem proper.

(10) Deposit Partnership funds in an account or accounts to be established at that time or times in such financial institutions (including any state or federally chartered bank or savings and loan association), and authorize withdrawals of those funds by such persons, at such times, and in those amounts, as the Managing Partner may designate.

(11) Place record title to any property in its name or in the name of a nominee or a trustee for the purpose of mortgage financing or any other convenience or benefit of the Partnership.

(12) Cause the Partnership to carry such indemnification insurance as the Managing Partner deems necessary to protect himself and any other persons entitled to indemnification by the Partnership under Section 15.06.

(13) Keep, or cause to be kept, full and accurate records of all transactions of the Partnership.

(14) Prepare, or cause to be prepared, all tax returns and reports for the Partnership and, in connection therewith, make any elections that the Partners deem advisable, including but not limited to the election referred to in Section 754 of the Code, and act as "tax matters partner"

for the Partnership, within the meaning of Sections 6221 through 6232 of the Code.

(15) Prepare, or cause to be prepared, and deliver to each Partner (A) the reports and other information described by Section 11, and (B) such other information as in the Managing Partner's judgment shall be reasonably necessary for the Partners to be advised of the results of operations of the Partnership.

(16) Execute, acknowledge, and deliver any and all instruments to effectuate any and all of the foregoing.

15.03. *Time to Be Devoted to Business.* The Managing Partner shall devote such time to the Partnership's business as the Managing Partner, in his sole discretion, shall deem necessary [*or:* such time as is necessary] [*or:* all of his time and attention] to manage and supervise the Partnership business and affairs in an efficient manner. Nothing in this Agreement shall preclude the employment, at the expense of the Partnership, of any agent or third party to manage or provide other services with respect to the Partnership's property or administrative business, subject to the control of the Managing Partner.

15.04. *Other Activities and Competition.* The Partners shall not be required to manage the Partnership as their sole and exclusive functions. The Partners may have other business interests and may engage in other activities in addition to and in competition with those relating to the Partnership. Neither the Partnership nor any Partner shall have any right by virtue of this Agreement, or the partnership relationship created hereby, in or to such other ventures or activities of any Partner or to the income or proceeds derived therefrom.

15.05. *Liability.* No Partner shall be liable, responsible, or accountable in damages or otherwise to the Partnership or any Partner for any action taken or failure to act on behalf of the Partnership within the scope of the authority conferred on any Partner by this Agreement or by law unless the act or omission was performed or omitted fraudulently or in bad faith or constituted negligence.

15.06. *Indemnification.* The Partnership shall indemnify and hold harmless the Partners from and against any loss, expense, damage, or injury suffered or sustained by them by reason of any acts, omissions, or alleged acts or omissions arising out of their activities on behalf of the Partnership or in furtherance of the interests of the Partnership, including but not limited to any judgment, award, settlement, reasonable attorneys' fees, and other costs or expenses incurred in connection with the defense of any actual or threatened action, proceeding, or claim, if the acts, omissions, or alleged acts or omissions upon which the actual or threatened action, proceeding, or claims are based were for a purpose reasonably believed to be in the best interests of the Partnership and were not performed or omitted fraudulently or in bad faith or as a result of negligence by a Partner and were not in violation of the Partner's fiduciary obligation to the Partnership. Any such indemnification shall be first from the assets of the Partnership, and then from all Partners and borne among them in accordance with their Partnership Percentages.

15.07. ***Termination of Management Powers.*** The other Partners may terminate all management powers, duties, and responsibilities of the Managing Partner by a vote of Partners having _____ per cent or more of the aggregate Partnership Percentages.

15.08. ***Limits on Managing Partner's Powers.*** Anything in this Agreement to the contrary notwithstanding, the Managing Partner shall not cause or permit the Partnership to

(1) Commingle the Partnership's funds with those of any other person, or employ or permit another to employ those funds or assets in any manner except for the exclusive benefit of the Partnership (except to the extent that funds are temporarily retained by agents of the Partnership).

(2) Reimburse the Managing Partner for expenses incurred by the Managing Partner except for the actual cost to the Managing Partner of goods, materials, or services (including reasonable travel and entertainment expenses) used for or by the Partnership.

15.09. ***Employment and Compensation of Managing Partner.*** The Managing Partner shall receive $_____ per annum, payable in advance on January 1 of each year, for services performed in his capacity as a Managing Partner, which amount shall be deemed a payment to the Managing Partner for services not in his capacity as a Partner with the meaning of Section 707(c) of the Code.

SECTION 16

DISSOLUTION OF THE PARTNERSHIP

The happening of any one of the following events shall work an immediate dissolution of the Partnership:

(1) The sale or other disposition of all or substantially all of the assets of the Partnership.

(2) The affirmative vote for dissolution of the Partnership by Partners having at least _____ per cent of the aggregate Partnership Percentages.

(3) The Bankruptcy or Incapacity of any Partner; *provided that* the remaining Partners shall continue the business of the Partnership within the meaning of Section 38 of the Act unless the Partnership is dissolved under subparagraph (2) above.

(4) The expiration of the term of the Partnership.

SECTION 17

WINDING UP, TERMINATION, AND
LIQUIDATING DISTRIBUTIONS

17.01. *Winding Up.* If the Partnership is dissolved and its business is not continued under Section 16(3), the Managing Partner or his successor shall commence to wind up the affairs of the Partnership and to liquidate the Partnership's assets. The Partners shall continue to share profits and losses during the period of liquidation in accordance with Section 10. Following the occurrence of any of the events set forth in Section 16, the Partners shall determine whether the assets of the Partnership are to be sold or whether the assets are to be distributed to the Partners. If assets are distributed to the Partners, all such assets shall be valued at their then fair market value as determined by the Partners and the difference, if any, of the fair market value over (or under) the adjusted basis of such property to the Partnership shall be credited (or charged) to the Capital Accounts of the Partners in accordance with the provisions of Section 10. Such fair market value shall be used for purposes of determining the amount of any distribution to a Partner pursuant to Section 17.02. If the Partners are unable to agree on the fair market value of any asset of the Partnership, the fair market value shall be the average of two appraisals, one prepared by a qualified appraiser selected by Partners having 50 per cent or more of the aggregate Partnership Percentages, and the other selected by the remaining Partners.

17.02. *Distributions.* Subject to the right of the Partners to set up such cash reserves as may be deemed reasonably necessary for any contingent or unforeseen liabilities or obligations of the Partnership, the proceeds of the liquidation and any other funds of the Partnership shall be distributed.

(1) To creditors, in the order of priority as provided by law except those liabilities to Partners in their capacities as Partners.

(2) To the Partners for loans, if any, made by them to the Partnership, or reimbursement for Partnership expenses paid by them.

(3) To the Partners in proportion to their respective Capital Accounts until they have received an amount equal to their Capital Accounts immediately prior to such distribution, but *after* adjustment for gain or loss with respect to the disposition of the Partnership's assets incident to the dissolution of the Partnership and the winding up of its affairs, whether or not the disposition occurs prior to the dissolution of the Partnership.

(4) To the Partners in accordance with their Partnership Percentages.

17.03. ***Deficit Capital Account Restoration.*** If, upon the dissolution and liquidation of the Partnership, after crediting all income upon sale of the Partnership's assets that have been sold and after making the allocations provided for in Section 17.01, any Partner has a negative Capital Account, then the Partner shall be obligated to contribute to the Partnership an amount equal to the negative Capital Account for distribution to creditors, or to Partners with positive Capital Account balances, in accordance with this Section.

17.04. ***Final Reports.*** Within a reasonable time following the completion of the liquidation of the Partnership's properties, the Managing Partner shall supply to each of the other Partners a statement that shall set forth the assets and liabilities of the Partnership as of the date of complete liquidation, each Partner's portion of distributions pursuant to Section 17.02, and the amounts paid to the Managing Partner pursuant to Section 17.02.

17.05. ***Rights of Partners.*** Each Partner shall look solely to the assets of the Partnership for all distributions with respect to the Partnership and his Capital Contribution (including the return thereof), and share of profits, and shall have no recourse therefor (upon dissolution [or] otherwise) against any other Partner except as provided in Section 17.03.

17.06. ***Termination.*** Upon the completion of the liquidation of the Partnership and the distribution of all Partnership funds, the Partnership shall terminate.

SECTION 18

NOTICES

All notices and demands required or permitted under this Agreement shall be in writing and may be sent by certified or registered mail or similar delivery service, postage prepaid, to the Partners at their addresses as shown from time to time on the records of the Partnership, and shall be deemed given when mailed or delivered to the service. Any Partner may specify a different address by notifying the Managing Partner in writing of the different address.

.   .   .

IN WITNESS WHEREOF, the undersigned have executed this Agreement as of this _____ day of _____, 19__.

[Partner's signature]	[Partner's signature]
[Partner's signature]	[Partner's signature]

UNIFORM LIMITED PARTNERSHIP ACT (1976) WITH 1985 AMENDMENTS

ARTICLE 1. GENERAL PROVISIONS

ARTICLE 2. FORMATION; CERTIFICATE OF LIMITED PARTNERSHIP

ARTICLE 3. LIMITED PARTNERS

ARTICLE 4. GENERAL PARTNERS

ARTICLE 5. FINANCE

* Omitted.

Sec.   Page

ARTICLE 6. DISTRIBUTIONS AND WITHDRAWAL

ARTICLE 7. ASSIGNMENT OF PARTNERSHIP INTERESTS

ARTICLE 8. DISSOLUTION

ARTICLE 9. FOREIGN LIMITED PARTNERSHIPS*

ARTICLE 10. DERIVATIVE ACTIONS

ARTICLE 11. MISCELLANEOUS

* Omitted.

ARTICLE 1

GENERAL PROVISIONS

§ 101. Definitions

As used in this [Act], unless the context otherwise requires:

(1) "Certificate of limited partnership" means the certificate referred to in Section 201, and the certificate as amended or restated.

(2) "Contribution" means any cash, property, services rendered, or a promissory note or other binding obligation to contribute cash or property or to perform services, which a partner contributes to a limited partnership in his capacity as a partner.

(3) "Event of withdrawal of a general partner" means an event that causes a person to cease to be a general partner as provided in Section 402.

(4) "Foreign limited partnership" means a partnership formed under the laws of any state other than this State and having as partners one or more general partners and one or more limited partners.

(5) "General partner" means a person who has been admitted to a limited partnership as a general partner in accordance with the partnership agreement and named in the certificate of limited partnership as a general partner.

(6) "Limited partner" means a person who has been admitted to a limited partnership as a limited partner in accordance with the partnership agreement.

(7) "Limited partnership" and "domestic limited partnership" mean a partnership formed by two or more persons under the laws of this State and having one or more general partners and one or more limited partners.

(8) "Partner" means a limited or general partner.

(9) "Partnership agreement" means any valid agreement, written or oral, of the partners as to the affairs of a limited partnership and the conduct of its business.

(10) "Partnership interest" means a partner's share of the profits and losses of a limited partnership and the right to receive distributions of partnership assets.

(11) "Person" means a natural person, partnership, limited partnership (domestic or foreign), trust, estate, association, or corporation.

(12) "State" means a state, territory, or possession of the United States, the District of Columbia, or the Commonwealth of Puerto Rico.

§ 102. Name

The name of each limited partnership as set forth in its certificate of limited partnership:

(1) shall contain without abbreviation the words "limited partnership";

(2) may not contain the name of a limited partner unless (i) it is also the name of a general partner or the corporate name of a corporate general partner, or (ii) the business of the limited partnership had been carried on under that name before the admission of that limited partner;

(3) may not be the same as, or deceptively similar to, the name of any corporation or limited partnership organized under the laws of this State or licensed or registered as a foreign corporation or limited partnership in this State; and

(4) may not contain the following words [here insert prohibited words]. . . .

§ 105. Records to Be Kept

(a) Each limited partnership shall keep at the office referred to in Section 104(1) the following:

(1) a current list of the full name and last known business address of each partner, separately identifying the general partners (in alphabetical order) and the limited partners (in alphabetical order);

(2) a copy of the certificate of limited partnership and all certificates of amendment thereto, together with executed copies of any powers of attorney pursuant to which any certificate has been executed;

(3) copies of the limited partnership's federal, state and local income tax returns and reports, if any, for the three most recent years;

(4) copies of any then effective written partnership agreements and of any financial statements of the limited partnership for the three most recent years; and

(5) unless contained in a written partnership agreement, a writing setting out:

(i) the amount of cash and a description and statement of the agreed value of the other property or services contributed by each partner and which each partner has agreed to contribute;

(ii) the times at which or events on the happening of which any additional contributions agreed to be made by each partner are to be made;

169

(iii) any right of a partner to receive, or of a general partner to make, distributions to a partner which include a return of all or any part of the partner's contribution; and

(iv) any events upon the happening of which the limited partnership is to be dissolved and its affairs wound up.

(b) Records kept under this section are subject to inspection and copying at the reasonable request and at the expense of any partner during ordinary business hours.

§ 106. Nature of Business

A limited partnership may carry on any business that a partnership without limited partners may carry on except [here designate prohibited activities].

§ 107. Business Transactions of Partner With Partnership

Except as provided in the partnership agreement, a partner may lend money to and transact other business with the limited partnership and, subject to other applicable law, has the same rights and obligations with respect thereto as a person who is not a partner.

ARTICLE 2

FORMATION; CERTIFICATE OF LIMITED PARTNERSHIP

§ 201. Certificate of Limited Partnership

(a) In order to form a limited partnership, a certificate of limited partnership must be executed and filed in the office of the Secretary of State. The certificate shall set forth:

(1) the name of the limited partnership;

(2) the address of the office and the name and address of the agent for service of process required to be maintained by Section 104;

(3) the name and the business address of each general partner;

(4) the latest date upon which the limited partnership is to dissolve; and

(5) any other matters the general partners determine to include therein.

(b) A limited partnership is formed at the time of the filing of the certificate of limited partnership in the office of the Secretary of State or at any later time specified in the certificate of limited partnership if, in either case, there has been substantial compliance with the requirements of this section.

Comment

The 1985 Act requires far fewer matters to be set forth in the certificate of limited partnership than did Section 2 of the 1916 Act and Section 201 of the 1976 Act. This is in recognition of the fact that the partnership agreement, not the certificate of limited partnership, has become the authoritative and comprehensive document for most limited partnerships, and that creditors and potential creditors of the partnership do and should refer to the partnership agreement and to other information furnished to them directly by the partnership and by others, not to the certificate of limited partnership, to obtain facts concerning the capital and finances of the partnership and other matters of concern. Subparagraph (b), which is based upon the 1916 Act, has been retained to make it clear that existence of the limited partnership depends only upon compliance with this section. Its continued existence is not dependent upon compliance with other provisions of this Act.

§ 202. Amendment to Certificate

(a) A certificate of limited partnership is amended by filing a certificate of amendment thereto in the office of the Secretary of State. The certificate shall set forth:

(1) the name of the limited partnership;

(2) the date of filing the certificate; and

(3) the amendment to the certificate.

(b) Within 30 days after the happening of any of the following events, an amendment to a certificate of limited partnership reflecting the occurrence of the event or events shall be filed:

(1) the admission of a new general partner;

(2) the withdrawal of a general partner; or

(3) the continuation of the business under Section 801 after an event of withdrawal of a general partner.

(c) A general partner who becomes aware that any statement in a certificate of limited partnership was false when made or that any arrangements or other facts described have changed, making the certificate inaccurate in any respect, shall promptly amend the certificate.

(d) A certificate of limited partnership may be amended at any time for any other proper purpose the general partners determine.

(e) No person has any liability because an amendment to a certificate of limited partnership has not been filed to reflect the occurrence of any event referred to in subsection (b) of this section if the amendment is filed within the 30–day period specified in subsection (b).

(f) A restated certificate of limited partnership may be executed and filed in the same manner as a certificate of amendment. . . .

§ 204. Execution of Certificates

(a) Each certificate required by this Article to be filed in the office of the Secretary of State shall be executed in the following manner:

(1) an original certificate of limited partnership must be signed by all general partners;

(2) a certificate of amendment must be signed by at least one general partner and by each other general partner designated in the certificate as a new general partner; and

(3) a certificate of cancellation must be signed by all general partners.

(b) Any person may sign a certificate by an attorney-in-fact, but a power of attorney to sign a certificate relating to the admission of a general partner must specifically describe the admission.

(c) The execution of a certificate by a general partner constitutes an affirmation under the penalties of perjury that the facts stated therein are true.

§ 206. Filing in Office of Secretary of State

(a) Two signed copies of the certificate of limited partnership and of any certificates of amendment or cancellation (or of any judicial decree of amendment or cancellation) shall be delivered to the Secretary of State. A person who executes a certificate as an agent or fiduciary need not exhibit evidence of his [or her] authority as a prerequisite to filing. Unless the Secretary of State finds that any certificate does not conform to law, upon receipt of all filing fees required by law he [or she] shall:

(1) endorse on each duplicate original the word "Filed" and the day, month, and year of the filing thereof;

(2) file one duplicate original in his [or her] office; and

(3) return the other duplicate original to the person who filed it or his [or her] representative.

(b) Upon the filing of a certificate of amendment (or judicial decree of amendment) in the office of the Secretary of State, the certificate of limited partnership shall be amended as set forth therein, and upon the effective date of a certificate of cancellation (or a judicial decree thereof), the certificate of limited partnership is cancelled.

§ 207. Liability for False Statement in Certificate

If any certificate of limited partnership or certificate of amendment or cancellation contains a false statement, one who suffers loss by reliance on the statement may recover damages for the loss from:

(1) any person who executes the certificate, or causes another to execute it on his behalf, and knew, and any general partner who knew or

should have known, the statement to be false at the time the certificate was executed; and

(2) any general partner who thereafter knows or should have known that any arrangement or other fact described in the certificate has changed, making the statement inaccurate in any respect within a sufficient time before the statement was relied upon reasonably to have enabled that general partner to cancel or amend the certificate, or to file a petition for its [judicial] cancellation or amendment ....

§ 208. Scope of Notice

The fact that a certificate of limited partnership is on file in the office of the Secretary of State is notice that the partnership is a limited partnership and the persons designated therein as general partners are general partners, but it is not notice of any other fact.

Comment

... By stating that the filing of a certificate of limited partnership only results in notice of the general liability of the general partners, Section 208 obviates the concern that third parties may be held to have notice of special provisions set forth in the certificate. While this section is designed to preserve by implication the limited liability of limited partners, the implicit protection provided is not intended to change any liability of a limited partner which may be created by his action or inaction under the law of estoppel, agency, fraud or the like.

§ 209. Delivery of Certificates to Limited Partners

Upon the return by the Secretary of State pursuant to Section 206 of a certificate marked "Filed," the general partners shall promptly deliver or mail a copy of the certificate of limited partnership and each certificate of amendment or cancellation to each limited partner unless the partnership agreement provides otherwise.

ARTICLE 3

LIMITED PARTNERS

§ 301. Admission of Limited Partners

(a) A person becomes a limited partner:

(1) at the time the limited partnership is formed; or

(2) at any later time specified in the records of the limited partnership for becoming a limited partner.

(b) After the filing of a limited partnership's original certificate of limited partnership, a person may be admitted as an additional limited partner:

(1) in the case of a person acquiring a partnership interest directly from the limited partnership, upon compliance with the partnership agreement or, if the partnership agreement does not so provide, upon the written consent of all partners; and

(2) in the case of an assignee of a partnership interest of a partner who has the power, as provided in Section 704, to grant the assignee the right to become a limited partner, upon the exercise of that power and compliance with any conditions limiting the grant or exercise of the power.

§ 302. Voting

Subject to Section 303, the partnership agreement may grant to all or a specified group of the limited partners the right to vote (on a per capita or other basis) upon any matter.

Comment

Section 302 first appeared in the 1976 Act, and must be read together with subdivision (b)(6) of Section 303. Although the 1916 Act did not speak specifically of the voting powers of limited partners, it was not uncommon for partnership agreements to grant such powers to limited partners. Section 302 is designed only to make it clear that the partnership agreement may grant such power to limited partners. If such powers are granted to limited partners beyond the "safe harbor" of subdivision (6) or (8) of Section 303(b), a court may (but of course need not) hold that, under the circumstances, the limited partners have participated in "control of the business" within the meaning of Section 303(a). Section 303(c) makes clear that the exercise of powers beyond the ambit of Section 303(b) is not ipso facto to be taken as taking part in the control of the business.

§ 303. Liability to Third Parties

(a) Except as provided in subsection (d), a limited partner is not liable for the obligations of a limited partnership unless he [or she] is also a general partner or, in addition to the exercise of his [or her] rights and powers as a limited partner, he [or she] participates in the control of the business. However, if the limited partner participates in the control of the business, he [or she] is liable only to persons who transact business with the limited partnership reasonably believing, based upon the limited partner's conduct, that the limited partner is a general partner.

(b) A limited partner does not participate in the control of the business within the meaning of subsection (a) solely by doing one or more of the following:

(1) being a contractor for or an agent or employee of the limited partnership or of a general partner or being an officer, director, or shareholder of a general partner that is a corporation;

(2) consulting with and advising a general partner with respect to the business of the limited partnership;

(3) acting as surety for the limited partnership or guaranteeing or assuming one or more specific obligations of the limited partnership;

(4) taking any action required or permitted by law to bring or pursue a derivative action in the right of the limited partnership;

(5) requesting or attending a meeting of partners;

(6) proposing, approving, or disapproving, by voting or otherwise, one or more of the following matters:

(i) the dissolution and winding up of the limited partnership;

(ii) the sale, exchange, lease, mortgage, pledge, or other transfer of all or substantially all of the assets of the limited partnership;

(iii) the incurrence of indebtedness by the limited partnership other than in the ordinary course of its business;

(iv) a change in the nature of the business;

(v) the admission or removal of a general partner;

(vi) the admission or removal of a limited partner;

(vii) a transaction involving an actual or potential conflict of interest between a general partner and the limited partnership or the limited partners;

(viii) an amendment to the partnership agreement or certificate of limited partnership; or

(ix) matters related to the business of the limited partnership not otherwise enumerated in this subsection (b), which the partnership agreement states in writing may be subject to the approval or disapproval of limited partners;

(7) winding up the limited partnership pursuant to Section 803; or

(8) exercising any right or power permitted to limited partners under this [Act] and not specifically enumerated in this subsection (b).

(c) The enumeration in subsection (b) does not mean that the possession or exercise of any other powers by a limited partner constitutes participation by him [or her] in the business of the limited partnership.

(d) A limited partner who knowingly permits his [or her] name to be used in the name of the limited partnership, except under circumstances permitted by Section 102(2), is liable to creditors who extend credit to the limited partnership without actual knowledge that the limited partner is not a general partner.

Comment

... The second sentence of Section 303(a) .... was adopted partly because of the difficulty of determining when the "control" line has been overstepped, but also (and more importantly) because of a determination that it is not sound public policy to hold a limited partner who is not also a general partner liable for the obligations of the partnership except to persons who have done business with the limited partnership reasonably believing, based on the limited partner's conduct, that he is a general partner. Paragraph (b) is intended to provide a "safe harbor" by enumerating certain activities which a limited partner may carry on for the partnership without being deemed to have taken part in control of the business. This "safe harbor" list has been expanded beyond that set out in the 1976 Act to reflect case law and statutory developments and more clearly to assure that limited partners are not subjected to general liability where such liability is inappropriate. Paragraph (d) is derived from Section 5 of the 1916 Act, but adds as a condition to the limited partner's liability the requirement that a limited partner must have knowingly permitted his name to be used in the name of the limited partnership.

§ 304. Person Erroneously Believing Himself [or Herself] Limited Partner

(a) Except as provided in subsection (b), a person who makes a contribution to a business enterprise and erroneously but in good faith believes that he [or she] has become a limited partner in the enterprise is not a general partner in the enterprise and is not bound by its obligations by reason of making the contribution, receiving distributions from the enterprise, or exercising any rights of a limited partner, if, on ascertaining the mistake, he [or she]:

(1) causes an appropriate certificate of limited partnership or a certificate of amendment to be executed and filed; or

(2) withdraws from future equity participation in the enterprise by executing and filing in the office of the Secretary of State a certificate declaring withdrawal under this section.

(b) A person who makes a contribution of the kind described in subsection (a) is liable as a general partner to any third party who transacts business with the enterprise (i) before the person withdraws and an appropriate certificate is filed to show withdrawal, or (ii) before an appropriate certificate is filed to show that he [or she] is not a general partner, but in either case only if the third party actually believed in good faith that the person was a general partner at the time of the transaction.

§ 305. Information

Each limited partner has the right to:

(1) inspect and copy any of the partnership records required to be maintained by Section 105; and

(2) obtain from the general partners from time to time upon reasonable demand (i) true and full information regarding the state of the business and financial condition of the limited partnership, (ii) promptly after becoming available, a copy of the limited partnership's federal, state, and local income tax returns for each year, and (iii) other information regarding the affairs of the limited partnership as is just and reasonable.

ARTICLE 4

GENERAL PARTNERS

§ 401. Admission of Additional General Partners

After the filing of a limited partnership's original certificate of limited partnership, additional general partners may be admitted as provided in writing in the partnership agreement or, if the partnership agreement does not provide in writing for the admission of additional general partners, with the written consent of all partners.

§ 402. Events of Withdrawal

Except as approved by the specific written consent of all partners at the time, a person ceases to be a general partner of a limited partnership upon the happening of any of the following events:

(1) the general partner withdraws from the limited partnership as provided in Section 602;

(2) the general partner ceases to be a member of the limited partnership as provided in Section 702;

(3) the general partner is removed as a general partner in accordance with the partnership agreement;

(4) unless otherwise provided in writing in the partnership agreement, the general partner: (i) makes an assignment for the benefit of creditors; (ii) files a voluntary petition in bankruptcy; (iii) is adjudicated a bankrupt or insolvent; (iv) files a petition or answer seeking for himself [or herself] any reorganization, arrangement, composition, readjustment, liquidation, dissolution, or similar relief under any statute, law, or regulation; (v) files an answer or other pleading admitting or

failing to contest the material allegations of a petition filed against him [or her] in any proceeding of this nature; or (vi) seeks, consents to, or acquiesces in the appointment of a trustee, receiver, or liquidator of the general partner or of all or any substantial part of his [or her] properties;

(5) unless otherwise provided in writing in the partnership agreement, [120] days after the commencement of any proceeding against the general partner seeking reorganization, arrangement, composition, readjustment, liquidation, dissolution, or similar relief under any statute, law, or regulation, the proceeding has not been dismissed, or if within [90] days after the appointment without his [or her] consent or acquiescence of a trustee, receiver, or liquidator of the general partner or of all or any substantial part of his [or her] properties, the appointment is not vacated or stayed or within [90] days after the expiration of any such stay, the appointment is not vacated;

(6) in the case of a general partner who is a natural person,

(i) his [or her] death; or

(ii) the entry of an order by a court of competent jurisdiction adjudicating him [or her] incompetent to manage his [or her] person or his [or her] estate;

(7) in the case of a general partner who is acting as a general partner by virtue of being a trustee of a trust, the termination of the trust (but not merely the substitution of a new trustee);

(8) in the case of a general partner that is a separate partnership, the dissolution and commencement of winding up of the separate partnership;

(9) in the case of a general partner that is a corporation, the filing of a certificate of dissolution, or its equivalent, for the corporation or the revocation of its charter; or

(10) in the case of an estate, the distribution by the fiduciary of the estate's entire interest in the partnership.

Comment

Section 402 expands considerably the provisions of Section 20 of the 1916 Act, which provided for dissolution in the event of the retirement, death or insanity of a general partner. Subdivisions (1), (2) and (3) recognize that the general partner's agency relationship is terminable at will, although it may result in a breach of the partnership agreement giving rise to an action for damages. Subdivisions (4) and (5) reflect a judgment that, unless the limited partners agree otherwise, they ought to have the power to rid themselves of a general partner who is in such dire financial straits that he is the subject of proceedings under the National Bankruptcy Code or a similar provision of law. Subdivisions

(6) through (10) simply elaborate on the notion of death in the case of a general partner who is not a natural person. ...

§ 403. General Powers and Liabilities

(a) Except as provided in this [Act] or in the partnership agreement, a general partner of a limited partnership has the rights and powers and is subject to the restrictions of a partner in a partnership without limited partners.

(b) Except as provided in this [Act], a general partner of a limited partnership has the liabilities of a partner in a partnership without limited partners to persons other than the partnership and the other partners. Except as provided in this [Act] or in the partnership agreement, a general partner of a limited partnership has the liabilities of a partner in a partnership without limited partners to the partnership and to the other partners.

§ 404. Contributions by General Partner

A general partner of a limited partnership may make contributions to the partnership and share in the profits and losses of, and in distributions from, the limited partnership as a general partner. A general partner also may make contributions to and share in profits, losses, and distributions as a limited partner. A person who is both a general partner and a limited partner has the rights and powers, and is subject to the restrictions and liabilities, of a general partner and, except as provided in the partnership agreement, also has the powers, and is subject to the restrictions, of a limited partner to the extent of his [or her] participation in the partnership as a limited partner.

§ 405. Voting

The partnership agreement may grant to all or certain identified general partners the right to vote (on a per capita or any other basis), separately or with all or any class of the limited partners, on any matter.

ARTICLE 5

FINANCE

§ 501. Form of Contribution

The contribution of a partner may be in cash, property, or services rendered, or a promissory note or other obligation to contribute cash or property or to perform services.

§ 502. Liability for Contribution

(a) A promise by a limited partner to contribute to the limited partnership is not enforceable unless set out in a writing signed by the limited partner.

(b) Except as provided in the partnership agreement, a partner is obligated to the limited partnership to perform any enforceable promise to contribute cash or property or to perform services, even if he [or she] is unable to perform because of death, disability, or any other reason. If a partner does not make the required contribution of property or services, he [or she] is obligated at the option of the limited partnership to contribute cash equal to that portion of the value, as stated in the partnership records required to be kept pursuant to Section 105, of the stated contribution which has not been made.

(c) Unless otherwise provided in the partnership agreement, the obligation of a partner to make a contribution or return money or other property paid or distributed in violation of this [Act] may be compromised only by consent of all partners. Notwithstanding the compromise, a creditor of a limited partnership who extends credit or otherwise acts in reliance on that obligation after the partner signs a writing which reflects the obligation, and before the amendment or cancellation thereof to reflect the compromise, may enforce the original obligation.

§ 503. Sharing of Profits and Losses

The profits and losses of a limited partnership shall be allocated among the partners, and among classes of partners, in the manner provided in writing in the partnership agreement. If the partnership agreement does not so provide in writing, profits and losses shall be allocated on the basis of the value, as stated in the partnership records required to be kept pursuant to Section 105, of the contributions made by each partner to the extent they have been received by the partnership and have not been returned.

§ 504. Sharing of Distributions

Distributions of cash or other assets of a limited partnership shall be allocated among the partners and among classes of partners in the manner provided in writing in the partnership agreement. If the partnership agreement does not so provide in writing, distributions shall be made on the basis of the value, as stated in the partnership records required to be kept pursuant to Section 105, of the contributions made by each partner to the extent they have been received by the partnership and have not been returned.

ARTICLE 6

DISTRIBUTIONS AND WITHDRAWAL

§ 601. Interim Distributions

Except as provided in this Article, a partner is entitled to receive distributions from a limited partnership before his [or her] withdrawal from the limited partnership and before the dissolution and winding up thereof to the extent and at the times or upon the happening of the events specified in the partnership agreement.

§ 602. Withdrawal of General Partner

A general partner may withdraw from a limited partnership at any time by giving written notice to the other partners, but if the withdrawal violates the partnership agreement, the limited partnership may recover from the withdrawing general partner damages for breach of the partnership agreement and offset the damages against the amount otherwise distributable to him [or her].

§ 603. Withdrawal of Limited Partner

A limited partner may withdraw from a limited partnership at the time or upon the happening of events specified in writing in the partnership agreement. If the agreement does not specify in writing the time or the events upon the happening of which a limited partner may withdraw or a definite time for the dissolution and winding up of the limited partnership, a limited partner may withdraw upon not less than six months' prior written notice to each general partner at his [other] address on the books of the limited partnership at its office in this State.

§ 604. Distribution Upon Withdrawal

Except as provided in this Article, upon withdrawal any withdrawing partner is entitled to receive any distribution to which he [or she] is entitled under the partnership agreement and, if not otherwise provided in the agreement, he [or she] is entitled to receive, within a reasonable time after withdrawal, the fair value of his [or her] interest in the limited partnership as of the date of withdrawal based upon his [or her] right to share in distributions from the limited partnership.

§ 605. Distribution in Kind

Except as provided in writing in the partnership agreement, a partner, regardless of the nature of his [or her] contribution, has no right to demand and receive any distribution from a limited partnership in any form other than cash. Except as provided in writing in the partnership agreement, a partner may not be compelled to accept a distribution of any asset in kind from a limited partnership to the extent that the percentage of the asset distributed to him [or her] exceeds a percentage of that asset which is equal to the percentage in which he [or she] shares in distributions from the limited partnership.

§ 606. Right to Distribution

At the time a partner becomes entitled to receive a distribution, he [or she] has the status of, and is entitled to all remedies available to, a creditor of the limited partnership with respect to the distribution.

§ 607. Limitations on Distribution

A partner may not receive a distribution from a limited partnership to the extent that, after giving effect to the distribution, all liabilities of the limited partnership, other than liabilities to partners on account of their partnership interests, exceed the fair value of the partnership assets.

§ 608. Liability Upon Return of Contribution

(a) If a partner has received the return of any part of his [or her] contribution without violation of the partnership agreement or this [Act], he [or she] is liable to the limited partnership for a period of one year thereafter for the amount of the returned contribution, but only to the extent necessary to discharge the limited partnership's liabilities to creditors who extended credit to the limited partnership during the period the contribution was held by the partnership.

(b) If a partner has received the return of any part of his [or her] contribution in violation of the partnership agreement or this [Act], he [or she] is liable to the limited partnership for a period of six years thereafter for the amount of the contribution wrongfully returned.

(c) A partner receives a return of his [or her] contribution to the extent that a distribution to him [or her] reduces his [or her] share of the fair value of the net assets of the limited partnership below the value, as set forth in the partnership records required to be kept pursuant to Section 105, of his contribution which has not been distributed to him [or her].

ARTICLE 7

ASSIGNMENT OF PARTNERSHIP INTERESTS

§ 701. Nature of Partnership Interest

A partnership interest is personal property.

§ 702. Assignment of Partnership Interest

Except as provided in the partnership agreement, a partnership interest is assignable in whole or in part. An assignment of a partnership interest does not dissolve a limited partnership or entitle the assignee to become or to exercise any rights of a partner. An assignment entitles the assignee to receive, to the extent assigned, only the distribution to which the assignor would be entitled. Except as provided in the partnership agreement, a partner ceases to be a partner upon assignment of all his [or her] partnership interest.

§ 703. Rights of Creditor

On application to a court of competent jurisdiction by any judgment creditor of a partner, the court may charge the partnership interest of the partner with payment of the unsatisfied amount of the judgment with interest. To the extent so charged, the judgment creditor has only the rights of an assignee of the partnership interest. This [Act] does not deprive any partner of the benefit of any exemption laws applicable to his [or her] partnership interest.

§ 704. Right of Assignee to Become Limited Partner

(a) An assignee of a partnership interest, including an assignee of a general partner, may become a limited partner if and to the extent that (i) the assignor gives the assignee that right in accordance with authority described in the partnership agreement, or (ii) all other partners consent.

(b) An assignee who has become a limited partner has, to the extent assigned, the rights and powers, and is subject to the restrictions and liabilities, of a limited partner under the partnership agreement and this [Act]. An assignee who becomes a limited partner also is liable for the obligations of his [or her] assignor to make and return contributions as provided in Articles 5 and 6. However, the assignee is not obligated for liabilities unknown to the assignee at the time he [or she] became a limited partner.

(c) If an assignee of a partnership interest becomes a limited partner, the assignor is not released from his [or her] liability to the limited partnership under Sections 207 and 502.

§ 705. Power of Estate of Deceased or Incompetent Partner

If a partner who is an individual dies or a court of competent jurisdiction adjudges him [or her] to be incompetent to manage his [or her] person or his [or her] property, the partner's executor, administrator, guardian, conservator, or other legal representative may exercise all of the partner's rights for the purpose of settling his [or her] estate or administering his [or her] property, including any power the partner had to give an assignee the right to become a limited partner. If a partner is a corporation, trust, or other entity and is dissolved or terminated, the powers of that partner may be exercised by its legal representative or successor.

ARTICLE 8

DISSOLUTION

§ 801. Nonjudicial Dissolution

A limited partnership is dissolved and its affairs shall be wound up upon the happening of the first to occur of the following:

(1) at the time specified in the certificate of limited partnership;

(2) upon the happening of events specified in writing in the partnership agreement;

(3) written consent of all partners;

(4) an event of withdrawal of a general partner unless at the time there is at least one other general partner and the written provisions of the partnership agreement permit the business of the limited partnership to be carried on by the remaining general partner and that partner does so, but the limited partnership is not dissolved and is not required to be wound up by reason of any event of withdrawal, if, within 90 days after the withdrawal, all partners agree in writing to continue the business of the limited partnership and to the appointment of one or more additional general partners if necessary or desired; or

(5) entry of a decree of judicial dissolution under Section 802.

§ 802. Judicial Dissolution

On application by or for a partner the [designate the appropriate court] court may decree dissolution of a limited partnership whenever it is not reasonably practicable to carry on the business in conformity with the partnership agreement.

§ 803. Winding Up

Except as provided in the partnership agreement, the general partners who have not wrongfully dissolved a limited partnership or, if none, the limited partners, may wind up the limited partnership's affairs; but the [designate the appropriate court] court may wind up the limited partnership's affairs upon application of any partner, his [or her] legal representative, or assignee.

§ 804. Distribution of Assets

Upon the winding up of a limited partnership, the assets shall be distributed as follows:

(1) to creditors, including partners who are creditors, to the extent permitted by law, in satisfaction of liabilities of the limited partnership other than liabilities for distributions to partners under Section 601 or 604;

(2) except as provided in the partnership agreement, to partners and former partners in satisfaction of liabilities for distributions under Section 601 or 604; and

(3) except as provided in the partnership agreement, to partners first for the return of their contributions and secondly respecting their partnership interests, in the proportions in which the partners share in distributions. . . .

ARTICLE 10

DERIVATIVE ACTIONS

§ 1001. Right of Action

A limited partner may bring an action in the right of a limited partnership to recover a judgment in its favor if general partners with authority to do so have refused to bring the action or if an effort to cause those general partners to bring the action is not likely to succeed.

§ 1002. Proper Plaintiff

In a derivative action, the plaintiff must be a partner at the time of bringing the action and (i) must have been a partner at the time of the transaction of which he [or she] complains or (ii) his [or her] status as a partner must have devolved upon him [or her] by operation of law or pursuant to the terms of the partnership agreement from a person who was a partner at the time of the transaction.

§ 1003. Pleading

In a derivative action, the complaint shall set forth with particularity the effort of the plaintiff to secure initiation of the action by a general partner or the reasons for not making the effort.

§ 1004. Expenses

If a derivative action is successful, in whole or in part, or if anything is received by the plaintiff as a result of a judgment, compromise, or settlement of an action or claim, the court may award the plaintiff reasonable expenses, including reasonable attorney's fees, and shall direct him [or her] to remit to the limited partnership the remainder of those proceeds received by him [or her].

ARTICLE 11

MISCELLANEOUS

§ 1105. Rules for Cases Not Provided for in This [Act]

In any case not provided for in this [Act] the provisions of the Uniform Partnership Act govern.

DELAWARE LIMITED LIABILITY PARTNERSHIP ACT

(Excerpts)

[Delaware Code Annotated, Title 6, Chapter 15]

§ 1502. Definitions ...

(4) "Foreign registered limited liability partnership" means a registered limited liability partnership or a limited liability partnership formed pursuant to an agreement governed by the laws of a jurisdiction other than this state and registered as such under the laws of such other jurisdiction....

(7) "Registered limited liability partnership" means a partnership formed pursuant to an agreement governed by the laws of this State, registered under § 1544 of this title and complying with §§ 1545, 1546 and 1549 of this title.

§ 1515. Nature of Partner's Liability

(a) Except as provided in Subsection (b) of this Section, all partners are liable:

(1) Jointly and severally for everything chargeable to the partnership under §§ 1513 and 1514 of this title [UPA §§ 13, 14]; and

(2) Jointly for all other debts and obligations of the partnership; but any partner may enter into a separate obligation to perform a partnership contract.

* Omitted.

(b) Subject to Subsection (c) of this Section, a partner in a registered limited liability partnership is not liable either directly or indirectly, by way of indemnification, contribution, assessment or otherwise, for debts, obligations and liabilities of or chargeable to the partnership, arising from negligence, wrongful acts or misconduct whether characterized as tort, contract or otherwise, committed while the partnership is a registered limited liability partnership and in the course of the partnership business by another partner or an employee, agent or representative of the partnership.

(c) Subsection (b) of this Section shall not affect the liability of a partner in a registered limited liability partnership for his own negligence, wrongful acts or misconduct or that of any person under his direct supervision and control. . . .

§ 1544. Registered Limited Liability Partnerships

(a) To become and to continue as a registered limited liability partnership, a partnership shall file with the Secretary of State an application or a renewal application, as the case may be, stating the name of the partnership; the address of its principal office; the address of a registered office and the name and address of a registered agent for service of process required to be maintained by Section 1549 of this title; the number of partners; a brief statement of the business in which the partnership engages; that the partnership thereby applies for status or renewal of this status, as the case may be, as a registered limited liability partnership and any other matters the partnership determines to include therein. A partnership becomes a registered limited liability partnership at the time of the filing of the initial application in the Office of the Secretary of State or at any later date or time specified in the application if, in either case, there has been substantial compliance with the requirements of this chapter. A partnership continues as a registered limited liability partnership if there has been substantial compliance with the requirements of this chapter.

(b) The application or renewal application shall be executed by a majority in interest of the partners or by one or more partners authorized to execute an application or renewal application. . . .

(e) Registration is effective for one year after the date an application is filed. . . . Registration, whether pursuant to an original application or a renewal application, as a registered limited liability partnership is renewed if, during the sixty-day period preceding the date the application or renewal application otherwise would have expired, the partnership files with the Secretary of State a renewal application. . . . .

§ 1545. Name of Registered Limited Liability Partnerships

The name of a registered limited liability partnership shall contain the words "Registered Limited Liability Partnership" or the abbreviation "L.L.P." or the designation "LLP" as the last words or letters of its name. . . .

§ 1546. Insurance or Financial Responsibility of Registered Limited Liability Partnerships

(a) A registered limited liability partnership shall carry at least $1,000,000 of liability insurance of a kind that is designed to cover the kinds of negligence, wrongful acts, and misconduct for which liability is limited by § 1515(b) of this title and which insures the partnership and its partners.

(b) If, in any proceeding, compliance by a partnership with the requirements of subsection (a) of this section is disputed, (1) that issue shall be determined by the court, and (2) the burden of proof of compliance shall be on the person who claims the limitation of liability in § 1515(b) of this title.

(c) If a registered limited liability partnership is in compliance with the requirements of subsection (a) of this section, the requirements of this section shall not be admissible or in any way be made known to a jury in determining an issue of liability for or extent of the debt or obligation or damages in question.

(d) A registered limited liability partnership is considered to be in compliance with subsection (a) of this section if the partnership provides $1,000,000 of funds specifically designated and segregated for the satisfaction of judgments against the partnership or its partners based on the kinds of negligence, wrongful acts, and misconduct for which liability is limited by § 1515(b) of this title by:

    (1) deposit in trust or in bank escrow of cash, bank certificates of deposit, or United States Treasury obligations; or

    (2) a bank letter of credit or insurance company bond.

(e) Notwithstanding the pendency of other claims against the partnership, a registered limited liability partnership is in compliance with this section if:

    (1) at the time a claim arising out of the kinds of negligence, wrongful acts or misconduct for which liability is limited by section 1515(b) of this title is asserted through service of a complaint or comparable pleading in a judicial or administrative proceeding, the partnership has in effect insurance, in the amount set forth in subsection (a) of this section, that is applicable to (A) claims made as of the date such claim is asserted or (B) events occurring on the date of the conduct giving rise to such claim; or

    (2) within 30 days after the day such a claim is asserted as described in (1) above, the partnership has designated and segregated funds in the amount set forth in subsection (d) of this section.

(f) Notwithstanding any other provision of this section, if a registered limited liability partnership is otherwise in compliance with the terms of this section 1546 at the time that a bankruptcy or other insolvency proceeding is commenced with respect to the registered limited liability partnership, it shall be deemed to be in compliance with section 1546 during the pendency of the proceeding. A registered limited liability partnership which has been the subject of such a proceeding and which conducts business after the proceeding has ended must thereafter comply with section 1546(a) or (d) in order to thereafter obtain the limitations on liability afforded by section 1515(b) hereof.

§ 1547. Applicability of Chapter to Foreign and Interstate Commerce

(a) A partnership, including a registered limited liability partnership, formed and existing under this chapter, may conduct its business, carry on its operations, and have and exercise the powers granted by this chapter in any state, territory, district, or possession of the United States or in any foreign country.

(b) It is the policy of this state that the internal affairs of partnerships, including registered limited liability partnerships, formed and existing under this chapter, including the liability of partners for debts and obligations of partnerships, shall be subject to and governed by the laws of this state.

§ 1553. Limited Partnerships as Registered Limited Liability Limited Partnerships

A domestic limited partnership may become a registered limited liability limited partnership by complying with the applicable provisions of the Delaware Revised Uniform Limited Partnership Act....

TEXAS LIMITED LIABILITY PARTNERSHIP ACT

[TEXAS REVISED PARTNERSHIP ACT]

Section 1.01. General Definitions

In this Act: ...

(10) "Partnership" means an entity created as described by Section 2.02(a). The term includes a registered limited liability partnership formed under Section 3.08 or under the Texas Uniform Partnership Act and its subsequent amendments....

Section 3.08. Liability in and Registration of Registered Limited Liability Partnership

(a) LIABILITY OF PARTNER. (1) A partner in a registered limited liability partnership is not individually liable for debts and obligations of the partnership arising from errors, omissions, negligence, incompetence, or malfeasance committed while the partnership is a registered limited liability partnership and in the course of the partnership business by another partner or a representative of the partnership not working under the supervision or direction of the first partner unless the first partner:

(A) was directly involved in the specific activity in which the errors, omissions, negligence, incompetence, or malfeasance were committed by the other partner or representative; or

(B) had notice or knowledge of the errors, omissions, negligence, incompetence, or malfeasance by the other partner or representative at the time of occurrence and then failed to take reasonable steps to prevent or cure the errors, omissions, negligence, incompetence, or malfeasance.

(2) Subsection (a)(1) does not affect:

(A) the joint and several liability of a partner for debts and obligations of the partnership arising from a cause other than the causes specified by Subsection (a)(1);

(B) the liability of a partnership to pay its debts and obligations out of partnership property; or

(C) the manner in which service of citation or other civil process may be served in an action against a partnership.

(3) In this subsection, "representative" includes an agent, servant, or employee of a registered limited liability partnership.

(b) REGISTRATION. (1) In addition to complying with Subsections (c) and (d)(1), to become a registered limited liability partnership, a partnership must file with the secretary of state an application stating:

(A) the name of the partnership;

(B) the federal tax identification number of the partnership;

(C) the street address of the partnership's principal office in this state and outside this state, as applicable;

(D) the number of partners at the date of application; and

(E) in brief, the partnership's business.

(2) The application must be executed by a majority-in-interest of the partners or by one or more partners authorized by a majority-in-interest of the partners.

(3) Two copies of the application must be filed, accompanied by a fee of $100 for each partner.

(4) A partnership is registered as a registered limited liability partnership on filing a completed initial or renewal application, in duplicate with the required fee, or on a later date specified in the application. A registration is not affected by later changes in the partners of the partnership.

(5) An initial application filed under this subsection and registered by the secretary of state expires one year after the date of registration or later effective date unless earlier withdrawn or revoked or unless renewed in accordance with Subdivision (7).

(6) A registration may be withdrawn by filing in duplicate with the secretary of state a written withdrawal notice executed by a majority-in-interest of the partners or by one or more partners authorized by a majority-in-interest of the partners. A withdrawal notice must include the name of the partnership, the federal tax identification number of the partnership, the date of registration of the partnership's last application under this section, and a current street address of the partnership's principal office in this state and outside this state, if applicable. A withdrawal notice terminates the status of the partnership as a registered limited liability partnership as of the date of filing the notice or a later date specified in the notice, but not later than the expiration date under Subdivision (5).

(7) An effective registration may be renewed before its expiration by filing in duplicate with the secretary of state an application containing current information of the kind required in an initial application and the most recent date of registration of the partnership. The renewal application must be accompanied by a fee of $200 for each partner on the date of renewal. A renewal application filed under this section continues an effective registration for one year after the date the effective registration would otherwise expire....

(c) NAME. A registered limited liability partnership's name must contain the words "registered limited liability partnership" or the abbreviation "L.L.P." as the last words or letters of its name.

(d) INSURANCE OR FINANCIAL RESPONSIBILITY. (1) A registered limited liability partnership must:

　　(A) carry at least $100,000 of liability insurance of a kind that is designed to cover the kinds of errors, omissions, negligence, incompetence, or malfeasance for which liability is limited by Subsection (a)(1); or

　　(B) provide $100,000 of funds specifically designated and segregated for the satisfaction of judgments against the partnership based on the kinds of errors, omissions, negligence, incompetence, or malfeasance for which liability is limited by Subsection (a)(1) by:

　　　　(i) deposit in trust or in bank escrow of cash, bank certificates of deposit, or United States Treasury obligations; or

　　　　(ii) a bank letter of credit or insurance company bond.

(2) If the registered limited liability partnership is in compliance with Subdivision (1), the requirements of this subsection shall not be admissible or in any way be made known to the jury in determining an issue of liability for or extent of the debt or obligation or damages in question.

(3) If compliance with Subdivision (1) is disputed:

　　(A) compliance must be determined separately from the trial or proceeding to determine the partnership debt or obligation in question, its amount, or partner liability for the debt or obligation; and

　　(B) the burden of proof of compliance is on the person claiming limitation of liability under Subsection (a)(1).

(e) LIMITED PARTNERSHIP. A limited partnership may become a registered limited liability partnership by complying with applicable provisions of the Texas Revised Limited Partnership Act and its subsequent amendments.

[TEXAS REVISED LIMITED PARTNERSHIP ACT]

Section 2.14. Limited Partnership as Registered Limited Liability Partnership

(a) A limited partnership is a registered limited liability partnership as well as a limited partnership if it:

　　(1) registers as a registered limited liability partnership as provided by Section 3.08(b), Texas Revised Partnership Act, as permitted by its partnership agreement or, if its partnership agreement does not include provisions for becoming a registered limited

liability partnership, with the consent of partners required to amend its partnership agreement;

(2) complies with Section 3.08(d), Texas Revised Partnership Act; and

(3) has as the last words or letters of its name the words "Limited Partnership" or the abbreviation "Ltd." followed by the words "registered limited liability partnership" or the abbreviation "L.L.P."

(b) In applying Section 3.08(b), Texas Revised Partnership Act, to a limited partnership:

(1) an application to become a registered limited liability partnership or to withdraw a registration must be executed by at least one general partner; and

(2) all other references to partners mean general partners only.

(c) If a limited partnership is a registered limited liability partnership, Section 3.08(a), Texas Revised Partnership Act, applies to its general partners and to any of its limited partners who, under other provisions of this Act, are liable for the debts or obligations of the limited partnership.

DELAWARE LIMITED LIABILITY COMPANY ACT
DEL.CODE ANN. TITLE 6, CHAPTER 18

SUBCHAPTER I. GENERAL PROVISIONS

SUBCHAPTER II. FORMATION; CERTIFICATE OF FORMATION

* Omitted.

SUBCHAPTER I. GENERAL PROVISIONS

§ 18–101. Definitions.

As used in this chapter unless the context otherwise requires:

(1) "Bankruptcy" means an event that causes a person to cease to be a member as provided in § 18–304 of this title.

(2) "Certificate of formation" means the certificate referred to in § 18–201 of this title, and the certificate as amended.

* Omitted.

(3) "Contribution" means any cash, property, services rendered or a promissory note or other obligation to contribute cash or property or to perform services, which a person contributes to a limited liability company in his capacity as a member.

(4) "Foreign limited liability company" means a limited liability company formed under the laws of any state or under the laws of any foreign country or other foreign jurisdiction and denominated as such under the laws of such state or foreign country or other foreign jurisdiction.

(5) "Knowledge" means a person's actual knowledge of a fact, rather than the person's constructive knowledge of the fact.

(6) "Limited liability company" and "domestic limited liability company" means a limited liability company formed under the laws of the State of Delaware and having 1 or more members.

(7) "Limited liability company agreement" means any agreement, written or oral, of the members as to the affairs of a limited liability company and the conduct of its business. A written limited liability company agreement or another written agreement or writing:

    a. May provide that a person shall be admitted as a member of a limited liability company, or shall become an assignee of a limited liability company interest or other rights or powers of a member to the extent assigned, and shall become bound by the limited liability company agreement:

        1. If such person (or a representative authorized by such person orally, in writing or by other action such as payment for a limited liability company interest) executes the limited liability company agreement or any other writing evidencing the intent of such person to become a member or assignee; or

        2. Without such execution, if such person (or a representative authorized by such person orally, in writing or by other action such as payment for a limited liability company interest) complies with the conditions for becoming a member or assignee as set forth in the limited liability company agreement or any other writing and requests (orally, in writing or by other action such as payment for a limited liability company interest) that the records of the limited liability company reflect such admission or assignment; and

    b. Shall not be unenforceable by reason of its not having been signed by a person being admitted as a member or becoming an assignee as provided in subparagraph a. of this paragraph, or by reason of its having been signed by a representative as provided in this chapter.

(8) "Limited liability company interest" means a member's share of the profits and losses of a limited liability company and a member's right to receive distributions of the limited liability company's assets.

(9) "Liquidating trustee" means a person carrying out the winding up of a limited liability company.

(10) "Manager" means a person who is named as a manager of a limited liability company in, or designated as a manager of a limited liability company pursuant to, a limited liability company agreement or similar instrument under which the limited liability company is formed.

(11) "Member" means a person who has been admitted to a limited liability company as a member as provided in § 18–301 of this title or, in the case of a foreign limited liability company, in accordance with the laws of the state or foreign country or other foreign jurisdiction under which the foreign limited liability company is organized.

(12) "Person" means a natural person, partnership (whether general or limited and whether domestic or foreign), limited liability company, foreign limited liability company, trust, estate, association, corporation, custodian, nominee or any other individual or entity in its own or any representative capacity.

(13) "State" means the District of Columbia or the Commonwealth of Puerto Rico or any state, territory, possession or other jurisdiction of the United States other than the State of Delaware.

§ 18–102. Name Set Forth in Certificate

The name of each limited liability company as set forth in its certificate of formation:

(1) Shall contain the words "Limited Liability Company" or the abbreviation "L.L.C." or the designation LLC;

(2) May contain the name of a member or manager;

(3) Must be such as to distinguish it upon the records in the office of the Secretary of State from the name of any corporation, limited partnership, business trust, registered limited liability partnership or limited liability company reserved, registered, formed or organized under the laws of the State of Delaware or qualified to do business or registered as a foreign corporation, foreign limited partnership or foreign limited liability company in the State of Delaware; provided however, that a limited liability company may register under any name which is not such as to distinguish it upon

the records in the office of the Secretary of State from the name of any domestic or foreign corporation, limited partnership, business trust, registered limited liability partnership or limited liability company reserved, registered, formed or organized under the laws of the State of Delaware with the written consent of the other corporation, limited partnership, business trust, registered limited liability partnership or limited liability company, which written consent shall be filed with the Secretary of State; and

(4) May contain the following words: "Company," "Association," "Club," "Foundation," "Fund," "Institute," "Society," "Union," "Syndicate," "Limited" or "Trust" (or abbreviations of like import).

§ 18–104. Registered Office; Registered Agent

(a) Each limited liability company shall have and maintain in the State of Delaware:

(1) A registered office, which may but need not be a place of its business in the State of Delaware; and

(2) A registered agent for service of process on the limited liability company, which agent may be either an individual resident of the State of Delaware whose business office is identical with the limited liability company's registered office, or a domestic corporation, or a foreign corporation authorized to do business in the State of Delaware having a business office identical with such registered office, or the limited liability company itself. . . .

§ 18–105. Service of Process on Domestic Limited Liability Companies

(a) Service of legal process upon any domestic limited liability company shall be made by delivering a copy personally to any manager of the limited liability company in the State of Delaware or the registered agent of the limited liability company in the State of Delaware, or by leaving it at the dwelling house or usual place of abode in the State of Delaware of any such manager or registered agent (if the registered agent be an individual), or at the registered office or other place of business of the limited liability company in the State of Delaware. If the registered agent be a corporation, service of process upon it as such may be made by serving, in the State of Delaware, a copy thereof on the president, vice-president, secretary, assistant secretary or any director of the corporate registered agent. Service by copy left at the dwelling house or usual place of abode of a manager or registered agent, or at the registered office or other place of business of the limited liability company in the State of Delaware, to be effective, must be delivered thereat at least 6 days before the return date of the process, and in the presence of an adult person, and the officer serving the process shall distinctly state the manner of service in his return thereto. Process returnable forthwith must be delivered personally to the manager or registered agent.

(b) In case the officer whose duty it is to serve legal process cannot by due diligence serve the process in any manner provided for by subsection (a) of this section, it shall be lawful to serve the process against the limited liability company upon the Secretary of State, and such service shall be as effectual for all intents and purposes as if made in any of the ways provided for in subsection (a) of this section. In the event that service is effected through the Secretary of State in accordance with this subsection, the Secretary of State shall forthwith notify the limited liability company by letter, certified mail, return receipt requested, directed to the limited liability company at its address as it appears on the records relating to such limited liability company on file with the Secretary of State or, if no such address appears, at its last registered office. Such letter shall enclose a copy of the process and any other papers served on the Secretary of State pursuant to this subsection. It shall be the duty of the plaintiff in the event of such service to serve process and any other papers in duplicate, to notify the Secretary of State that service is being effected pursuant to this subsection, and to pay the Secretary of State the sum of $50 for the use of the State of Delaware, which sum shall be taxed as part of the costs in the proceeding if the plaintiff shall prevail therein. The Secretary of State shall maintain an alphabetical record of any such service setting forth the name of the plaintiff and defendant, the title, docket number and nature of the proceeding in which process has been served upon him, the fact that service has been effected pursuant to this subsection, the return date thereof, and the day and hour when the service was made. The Secretary of State shall not be required to retain such information for a period longer than 5 years from his receipt of the service of process.

§ 18–106. Nature of Business Permitted; Powers

(a) A limited liability company may carry on any lawful business, purpose or activity with the exception of the business of granting policies of insurance, or assuming insurance risks or banking as defined in § 126 of Title 8.

(b) A limited liability company shall possess and may exercise all the powers and privileges granted by this chapter or by any other law or by its limited liability company agreement, together with any powers incidental thereto, so far as such powers and privileges are necessary or convenient to the conduct, promotion or attainment of the business, purposes or activities of the limited liability company.

§ 18–107. Business Transactions of Member or Manager With the Limited Liability Company

Except as provided in a limited liability company agreement, a member or manager may lend money to, borrow money from, act as a surety, guarantor or endorser for, guarantee or assume 1 or more obligations of, provide collateral for, and transact other business with, a limited liability company and, subject to other applicable law, has the same rights and obligations with respect to any such matter as a person who is not a member or manager.

§ 18–108. Indemnification

Subject to such standards and restrictions, if any, as are set forth in its limited liability company agreement, a limited liability company may, and shall have the power to, indemnify and hold harmless any member or manager or other person from and against any and all claims and demands whatsoever.

§ 18–109. Service of Process on Managers and Liquidating Trustees

(a) A manager or a liquidating trustee of a limited liability company may be served with process in the manner prescribed in this section in all civil actions or proceedings brought in the State of Delaware involving or relating to the business of the limited liability company or a violation by the manager or the liquidating trustee of a duty to the limited liability company, or any member of the limited liability company, whether or not the manager or the liquidating trustee is a manager or a liquidating trustee at the time suit is commenced. A manager's or a liquidating trustee's serving as such constitutes such person's consent to the appointment of the registered agent of the limited liability company (or, if there is none, the Secretary of State) as such person's agent upon whom service of process may be made as provided in this section. Such service as a manager or a liquidating trustee shall signify the consent of such manager or liquidating trustee that any process when so served shall be of the same legal force and validity as if served upon such manager or liquidating trustee within the State of Delaware and such appointment of the registered agent (or, if there is none, the Secretary of State) shall be irrevocable.

(b) Service of process shall be effected by serving the registered agent (or, if there is none, the Secretary of State) with 1 copy of such process in the manner provided by law for service of writs of summons. In the event service is made under this subsection upon the Secretary of State, the plaintiff shall pay to the Secretary of State the sum of $50 for the use of the State of Delaware, which sum shall be taxed as part of the costs of the proceeding if the plaintiff shall prevail therein. In addition, the Prothonotary or the Register in Chancery of the court in which the civil action or proceeding is pending shall, within 7 days of such service, deposit in the United States mails, by registered mail, postage prepaid, true and attested copies of the process, together with a statement that service is being made pursuant to this section, addressed to such manager or liquidating trustee at the registered office of the limited liability company and at his address last known to the party desiring to make such service.

(c) In any action in which any such manager or liquidating trustee has been served with process as hereinabove provided, the time in which a defendant shall be required to appear and file a responsive pleading shall be computed from the date of mailing by the Prothonotary or the Register in Chancery as provided in subsection (b) of this section; however, the court in which such action has been commenced may order such continuance or continuances as may be necessary to afford such manager or liquidating trustee reasonable opportunity to defend the action.

(d) In a written limited liability company agreement or other writing, a manager or member may consent to be subject to the nonexclusive jurisdiction of the courts of, or arbitration in, a specified jurisdiction, or the exclusive jurisdiction of the courts of, or the exclusivity of arbitration in, the State of Delaware, and to be served with legal process in the manner prescribed in such limited liability company agreement or other writing.

(e) Nothing herein contained limits or affects the right to serve process in any other manner now or hereafter provided by law. This section is an extension of and not a limitation upon the right otherwise existing of service of legal process upon nonresidents.

(f) The Court of Chancery and the Superior Court may make all necessary rules respecting the form of process, the manner of issuance and return thereof and such other rules which may be necessary to implement this section and are not inconsistent with this section.

§ 18–110. Contested Matters Relating to Managers; Contested Votes

(a) Upon application of any member or manager, the Court of Chancery may hear and determine the validity of any admission, election, appointment or withdrawal of a manager of a limited liability company, and the right of any person to be a manager of a limited liability company, and, in case the right to serve as a manager is claimed by more than 1 person, may determine the person or persons entitled to serve as managers; and to that end make such order or decree in any such case as may be just and proper, with power to enforce the production of any books, papers and records of the limited liability company relating to the issue. In any such application, service of copies of the application upon the registered agent of the limited liability company shall be deemed to be service upon the limited liability company and upon the person or persons whose right to serve as a manager is contested and upon the person or persons, if any, claiming to be a manager or claiming the right to be a manager; and the registered agent shall forward immediately a copy of the application to the limited liability company and to the person or persons whose right to serve as a manager is contested and to the person or persons, if any, claiming to be a manager or the right to be a manager, in a postpaid, sealed, registered letter addressed to such limited liability company and such person or persons at their post-office addresses last known to the registered agent or furnished to the registered agent by the applicant member or manager. The Court may make such order respecting further or other notice of such application as it deems proper under [the] circumstances.

(b) Upon application of any member or manager, the Court of Chancery may hear and determine the result of any vote of members or managers upon matters as to which the members or managers of the limited liability company, or any class or group of members or managers, have the right to vote pursuant to the limited liability company agreement or other agreement or this chapter (other than the admission, election, appointment or withdrawal of managers). Service of the application upon the registered agent of the limited liability company shall be deemed to be service upon the limited liability company, and no other party need be joined in order for the Court to adjudicate the result of the vote. The Court may make such order respecting further or other notice of such application as it deems proper under [the] circumstances.

(c) Nothing herein contained limits or affects the right to serve process in any other manner now or hereafter provided by law. This section is an extension of and not a limitation upon the right otherwise existing of service of legal process upon nonresidents.

§ 18–111. Interpretation and Enforcement of Limited Liability Company Agreement

Any action to interpret, apply or enforce the provisions of a limited liability company agreement, or the duties, obligations or liabilities of a limited liability company to the members or managers of the limited liability company, or the duties, obligations or liabilities among members or managers and of members or managers to the limited liability company, or the rights or powers of, or restrictions on, the limited liability company, members or managers, may be brought in the Court of Chancery.

SUBCHAPTER II. FORMATION; CERTIFICATE OF FORMATION

§ 18–201. Certificate of Formation

(a) In order to form a limited liability company, 1 or more authorized persons must execute a certificate of formation. The certificate of formation shall be filed in the office of the Secretary of State and set forth:

(1) The name of the limited liability company;

(2) The address of the registered office and the name and address of the registered agent for service of process required to be maintained by § 18–104 of this title; and

(3) Any other matters the members determine to include therein.

(b) A limited liability company is formed at the time of the filing of the initial certificate of formation in the office of the Secretary of State or at any later date or time specified in the certificate of formation if, in either case, there has been substantial compliance with the requirements of this section. A limited liability company formed under this chapter shall be a separate legal entity, the existence of which as a separate legal entity shall continue until cancellation of the limited liability company's certificate of formation.

(c) The filing of the certificate of formation in the office of the Secretary of State shall make it unnecessary to file any other documents under Chapter 31 of this title.

(d) A limited liability company agreement may be entered into either before, after or at the time of the filing of a certificate of formation and, whether entered into before, after or at the time of such filing, may be made effective as of the formation of the limited liability company or at such other time or date as provided in the limited liability company agreement.

§ 18–202. Amendment to Certificate of Formation

(a) A certificate of formation is amended by filing a certificate of amendment thereto in the office of the Secretary of State. The certificate of amendment shall set forth:

(1) The name of the limited liability company; and

(2) The amendment to the certificate of formation.

(b) A manager or, if there is no manager, then any member who becomes aware that any statement in a certificate of formation was false when made, or that any matter described has changed making the certificate of formation false in any material respect, shall promptly amend the certificate of formation.

(c) A certificate of formation may be amended at any time for any other proper purpose.

(d) Unless otherwise provided in this chapter or unless a later effective date or time (which shall be a date or time certain) is provided for in the certificate of amendment, a certificate of amendment shall be effective at the time of its filing with the Secretary of State.

§ 18–203. Cancellation of Certificate

A certificate of formation shall be cancelled upon the dissolution and the completion of winding up of a limited liability company, or at any other time there are no members, or as provided in § 18–104(d) or § 18–1108 [cancellation of certificate of formation for failure to pay taxes] of this chapter, or upon the filing of a certificate of merger or consolidation if the limited liability company is not the surviving or resulting entity in a merger or consolidation. A certificate of cancellation shall be filed in the office of the Secretary of State to accomplish the cancellation of a certificate of formation upon the dissolution and the completion of winding up of a limited liability company or at any other time there are no members and shall set forth:

(1) The name of the limited liability company;

(2) The date of filing of its certificate of formation;

(3) The reason for filing the certificate of cancellation;

(4) The future effective date or time (which shall be a date or time certain) of cancellation if it is not to be effective upon the filing of the certificate; and

(5) Any other information the person filing the certificate of cancellation determines.

§ 18–204. Execution

(a) Each certificate required by this subchapter to be filed in the office of the Secretary of State shall be executed by 1 or more authorized persons.

(b) Unless otherwise provided in a limited liability company agreement, any person may sign any certificate or amendment thereof or enter into a limited liability company agreement or amendment thereof by an agent, including an attorney-in-fact. An authorization, including a power of attorney, to sign any certificate or amendment thereof or to enter into a limited liability company agreement or amendment thereof need not be in writing, need not be sworn to, verified or acknowledged, and need not be filed in the office of the Secretary of State, but if in writing, must be retained by the limited liability company.

(c) The execution of a certificate by an authorized person constitutes an oath or affirmation, under the penalties of perjury in the third degree, that, to the best of the authorized person's knowledge and belief, the facts stated therein are true.

§ 18–205. Execution, Amendment or Cancellation by Judicial Order

(a) If a person required to execute a certificate required by this subchapter fails or refuses to do so, any other person who is adversely affected by the failure or refusal may petition the Court of Chancery to direct the execution of the certificate. If the Court finds that the execution of the certificate is proper and that any person so designated has failed or refused to execute the certificate, it shall order the Secretary of State to record an appropriate certificate.

(b) If a person required to execute a limited liability company agreement or amendment thereof fails or refuses to do so, any other person who is adversely affected by the failure or refusal may petition the Court of Chancery to direct the execution of the limited liability company agreement or amendment thereof. If the Court finds that the limited liability company agreement or amendment thereof should be executed and that any person required to execute the limited liability company agreement or amendment thereof has failed or refused to do so, it shall enter an order granting appropriate relief.

§ 18-206. Filing

(a) The original signed copy of the certificate of formation and of any certificates of amendment, correction, amendment of a certificate of merger or consolidation, termination of a merger or consolidation or cancellation (or of any judicial decree of amendment or cancellation), and of any certificate of merger or consolidation, any restated certificate, certificate of conversion to limited liability company, any certificate of transfer, any certificate of limited liability company domestication, and of any certificate of revival shall be delivered to the Secretary of State. A person who executes a certificate as an agent or fiduciary need not exhibit evidence of his authority as a prerequisite to filing. Any signature on any certificate authorized to be filed with the Secretary of State under any provision of this chapter may be a facsimile, a conformed signature or an electronically transmitted signature. Unless the Secretary of State finds that any certificate does not conform to law, upon receipt of all filing fees required by law he shall:

(1) Certify that the certificate of formation, the certificate of amendment, the certificate of correction, the certificate of amendment or a certificate of merger or consolidation, the certificate of termination of a merger or consolidation, the certificate of cancellation (or of any judicial decree of amendment or cancellation), the certificate of merger or consolidation, the restated certificate, the certificate of conversion to limited liability company, the certificate of transfer, the certificate of limited liability company domestication or the certificate of revival has been filed in his office by endorsing upon the original certificate the word "Filed", and the date and hour of the filing. This endorsement is conclusive of the date and time of its filing in the absence of actual fraud;

(2) File and index the endorsed certificate; and

(3) Prepare and return to the person who filed it or his representative a copy of the original signed instrument, similarly endorsed, and shall certify such copy as a true copy of the original signed instrument.

(b) Upon the filing of a certificate of amendment (or judicial decree of amendment) or restated certificate in the office of the Secretary of State, or upon the future effective date or time of a certificate of amendment (or judicial decree thereof) or restated certificate, as provided for therein, the certificate of formation shall be amended or restated as set forth therein. Upon the filing of a certificate of cancellation (or a judicial decree thereof), or a certificate of merger or consolidation which acts as a certificate of cancellation, or a certificate of transfer, or upon the future effective date or time of a certificate of cancellation (or a judicial decree thereof) or of a certificate of merger or consolidation which acts as a certificate of cancellation, or a certificate of transfer, as provided for therein, or as specified in § 18–104(d) of this title, the certificate of formation is cancelled. Upon the filing of a certificate of limited liability company domestication, or upon the future effective date or time of a certificate of limited liability company domestication, the entity filing the certificate of limited liability company domestication is domesticated as a limited liability company with the effect provided in § 18–212 of this title. Upon the filing of a certificate of conversion to limited liability company, or upon the future effective date or time of a certificate of conversion to limited liability company, the entity filing the certificate of conversion to limited liability company is converted to a limited liability company with the effect provided in § 18–214 of this chapter. Upon the filing of a certificate of amendment of a certificate of merger or consolidation, the certificate of merger or consolidation identified in the certificate of amendment of a certificate of merger or consolidation is amended. Upon the filing of a certificate of termination of a merger or consolidation, the certificate of merger or consolidation identified in the certificate of termination of a merger or consolidation is terminated. . . .

§ 18–207. Notice

The fact that a certificate of formation is on file in the office of the Secretary of State is notice that the entity formed in connection with the filing of the certificate of formation is a limited liability company formed under the laws of the State of Delaware and is notice of all other facts set forth therein which are required to be set forth in a certificate of formation by § 18–201(a)(1) and (2) of this title and which are permitted to be set forth in a certificate of formation by § 18–215(b) of this chapter.

§ 18–209. Merger and Consolidation

(a) As used in this section, "other business entity" means a corporation, or a business trust or association, a real estate investment trust, a common-law trust, or any other unincorporated business, including a partnership (whether general (including a registered limited liability partnership) or limited (including a registered limited liability partnership)), and a foreign limited liability company, but excluding a domestic limited liability company.

(b) Pursuant to an agreement of merger or consolidation, a domestic limited liability company may merge or consolidate with or into 1 or more domestic limited liability companies or other business entities formed or organized under the laws of the State of Delaware or any other state or the United States or any foreign country or other foreign jurisdiction, with such domestic limited liability company or other business entity as the agreement shall provide being the surviving or resulting domestic limited liability company or other business entity. Unless otherwise provided in the limited liability company agreement, a merger or consolidation shall be approved by each domestic limited liability company which is to merge or consolidate by the members or, if there is more than one class or group of members, then by each class or group of members, in either case, by members who own more than 50 percent of the then current percentage or other interest in the profits of the domestic limited liability company owned by all of the members or by the members in each class or group, as appropriate. In connection with a merger or consolidation hereunder, rights or securities of, or interests in, a domestic limited liability company or other business entity which is a constituent party to the merger or consolidation may be exchanged for or converted into cash, property, rights or securities of, or interests in, the surviving or resulting domestic limited liability company or other business entity or, in addition to or in lieu thereof, may be exchanged for or converted into cash, property, rights or securities of, or interests in, a domestic limited liability company or other business entity which is not the surviving or resulting limited liability company or other business entity in the merger or consolidation. Notwithstanding prior approval, an agreement of merger or consolidation may be terminated or amended pursuant to a provision for such termination or amendment contained in the agreement of merger or consolidation.

(c) If a domestic limited liability company is merging or consolidating under this section, the domestic limited liability company or other business entity surviving or resulting in or from the merger or consolidation shall file a certificate of merger or consolidation in the office of the Secretary of State. The certificate of merger or consolidation shall state:

(1) The name and jurisdiction of formation or organization of each of the domestic limited liability companies or other business entities which is to merge or consolidate;

(2) That an agreement of merger or consolidation has been approved and executed by each of the domestic limited liability

208

companies or other business entities which is to merge or consolidate;

(3) The name of the surviving or resulting domestic limited liability company or other business entity;

(4) The future effective date or time (which shall be a date or time certain) of the merger or consolidation if it is not to be effective upon the filing of the certificate of merger or consolidation;

(5) That the agreement of merger or consolidation is on file at a place of business of the surviving or resulting domestic limited liability company or other business entity, and shall state the address thereof;

(6) That a copy of the agreement of merger or consolidation will be furnished by the surviving or resulting domestic limited liability company or other business entity, on request and without cost, to any member of any domestic limited liability company or any person holding an interest in any other business entity which is to merge or consolidate; and

(7) If the surviving or resulting entity is not a domestic limited liability company, or a corporation or limited partnership organized under the laws of the State of Delaware, or a business trust organized under Chapter 38 of Title 12, a statement that such surviving or resulting other business entity agrees that it may be served with process in the State of Delaware in any action, suit or proceeding for the enforcement of any obligation of any domestic limited liability company which is to merge or consolidate, irrevocably appointing the Secretary of State as its agent to accept service of process in any such action, suit or proceeding and specifying the address to which a copy of such process shall be mailed to it by the Secretary of State. In the event of service hereunder upon the Secretary of State, the procedures set forth in § 18–911(c) of this title shall be applicable, except that the plaintiff in any such action, suit or proceeding shall furnish the Secretary of State with the address specified in the certificate of merger or consolidation provided for in this section and any other address which the plaintiff may elect to furnish, together with copies of such process as required by the Secretary of State, and the Secretary of State shall notify such surviving or resulting other business entity at all such addresses furnished by the plaintiff in accordance with the procedures set forth in § 18–911(c) of this title.

(d) Unless a future effective date or time is provided in a certificate of merger or consolidation, in which event a merger or consolidation shall be effective at any such future effective date or time, a merger or consolidation shall be effective upon the filing in the office of the Secretary of State of a certificate of merger or consolidation. . . .

(e) A certificate of merger or consolidation shall act as a certificate of cancellation for a domestic limited liability company which is not the surviving or resulting entity in the merger or consolidation.

(f) An agreement of merger or consolidation approved in accordance with subsection (b) of this section may:

(1) Effect any amendment to the limited liability company agreement; or

(2) Effect the adoption of a new limited liability company agreement ... for a limited liability company if it is the surviving or resulting limited liability company in the merger or consolidation.

Any amendment to a limited liability company agreement or adoption of a new limited liability company agreement made pursuant to the foregoing sentence shall be effective at the effective time or date of the merger or consolidation. The provisions of this subsection shall not be construed to limit the accomplishment of a merger or of any of the matters referred to herein by any other means provided for in a limited liability company agreement or other agreement or as otherwise permitted by law, including that the limited liability company agreement of any constituent limited liability company to the merger or consolidation (including a limited liability company formed for the purpose of consummating a merger or consolidation) shall be the limited liability company agreement of the surviving or resulting limited liability company.

(g) When any merger or consolidation shall have become effective under this section, for all purposes of the laws of the State of Delaware, all of the rights, privileges and powers of each of the domestic limited liability companies and other business entities that have merged or consolidated, and all property, real, personal and mixed, and all debts due to any of said domestic limited liability companies and other business entities, as well as all other things and causes of action belonging to each of such domestic limited liability companies and other business entities, shall be vested in the surviving or resulting domestic limited liability company or other business entity, and shall thereafter be the property of the surviving or resulting domestic limited liability company or other business entity as they were of each of the domestic limited liability companies and other business entities that have merged or consolidated, and the title to any real property vested by deed or otherwise, under the laws of the State of Delaware, in any of such domestic limited liability companies and other business entities, shall not revert or be in any way impaired by reason of this chapter; but all rights of creditors and all liens upon any property of any of said domestic limited liability companies and other business entities shall be preserved unimpaired, and all debts, liabilities and duties of each of the said domestic limited liability companies and other business entities that have merged or consolidated shall thenceforth attach to the surviving or resulting domestic limited liability company or other business entity, and may be enforced against it to the same extent as if said debts, liabilities and duties had been incurred or contracted by it. Unless otherwise agreed, a merger or consolidation of a domestic limited liability company, including a domestic limited liability company which is not the surviving or resulting entity in the merger or consolidation, shall not require such domestic limited liability company to wind up its affairs under § 18–803 of this title or pay its liabilities and distribute its assets under § 18–804 of this title.

§ 18–210. Contractual Appraisal Rights

A limited liability company agreement or an agreement of merger or consolidation may provide that contractual appraisal rights with respect to a limited liability company shall be available for any class or group of members or limited liability company interests in connection with any amendment of a limited liability company agreement, any merger or consolidation in which the limited liability company is a constituent party to the merger or consolidation, or the sale of all or substantially all of the limited liability company's assets. The Court of Chancery shall have jurisdiction to hear and determine any matter relating to any such appraisal rights.

§ 18–211. Certificate of Correction

Whenever any certificate authorized to be filed with the office of the Secretary of State under any provision of this chapter has been so filed and is an inaccurate record of the action therein referred to, or was defectively or erroneously executed, such certificate may be corrected by filing with the office of the Secretary of State a certificate of correction of such certificate. The certificate of correction shall specify the inaccuracy or defect to be corrected, shall set forth the portion of the certificate in corrected form and shall be executed and filed as required by this chapter. The corrected certificate shall be effective as of the date the original certificate was filed, except as to those persons who are substantially and adversely affected by the correction, and as to those persons the corrected certificate shall be effective from the filing date.

§ 18–212. Domestication of Non–United States Entities

(a) As used in this section, "non-United States entity" means a foreign limited liability company (other than one formed under the laws of a state) or a corporation, a business trust or association, a real estate investment trust, a common-law trust or any other unincorporated business, including a partnership (whether general (including a registered limited liability partnership) or limited (including a registered limited liability limited partnership)) formed, incorporated, created or that otherwise came into being under the laws of any foreign country or other foreign jurisdiction (other than any state).

(b) Any non-United States entity may become domesticated as a limited liability company in the State of Delaware by complying with subsection (g) of this section and filing in the office of the Secretary of State in accordance with § 18–206 of this title:

(1) A certificate of limited liability company domestication that has been executed by 1 or more authorized persons in accordance with § 18–204 of this title; and

(2) A certificate of formation that complies with § 18–201 of this title and has been executed by 1 or more authorized persons in accordance with § 18–204 of this title.

(c) The certificate of limited liability company domestication shall state:

(1) The date on which and jurisdiction where the non-United States entity was first formed, incorporated, created or otherwise came into being;

(2) The name of the non-United States entity immediately prior to the filing of the certificate of limited liability company domestication;

(3) The name of the limited liability company as set forth in the certificate of formation filed in accordance with subsection (b) of this section;

(4) The future effective date or time (which shall be a date or time certain) of the domestication as a limited liability company if it is not to be effective upon the filing of the certificate of limited liability company domestication and the certificate of formation; and

(5) The jurisdiction that constituted the seat, siege social, or principal place of business or central administration of the non-United States entity, or any other equivalent thereto under applicable law, immediately prior to the filing of the certificate of limited liability company domestication.

(d) Upon the filing in the office of the Secretary of State of the certificate of limited liability company domestication and the certificate of formation or upon the future effective date or time of the certificate of limited liability company domestication and the certificate of formation, the non-United States entity shall be domesticated as a limited liability company in the State of Delaware and the limited liability company shall thereafter be subject to all of the provisions of this chapter, except that notwithstanding § 18–201 of this title, the existence of the limited liability company shall be deemed to have commenced on the date the non-United States entity commenced its existence in the jurisdiction in which the non-United States entity was first formed, incorporated, created or otherwise came into being.

(e) The domestication of any non-United States entity as a limited liability company in the State of Delaware shall not be deemed to affect any obligations or liabilities of the non-United States entity incurred prior to its domestication as a limited liability company in the State of Delaware, or the personal liability of any person therefor.

(f) The filing of a certificate of limited liability company domestication shall not affect the choice of law applicable to the non-United States entity, except that from the effective date or time of the domestication, the law of the State of Delaware, including the provisions of this chapter, shall apply to the non-United States entity to the same extent as if the non-United States entity had been formed as a limited liability company on that date.

(g) Prior to filing a certificate of limited liability company domestication with the Office of the Secretary of State, a limited liability company agreement shall be approved in the manner provided for by the document, instrument, agreement or other writing, as the case may be, governing the internal affairs of the non-United States entity and the conduct of its business or by applicable non-Delaware law, as appropriate.

(h) When any domestication shall have become effective under this section, for all purposes of the laws of the State of Delaware, all of the rights, privileges and powers of the non-United States entity that has been domesticated, and all property, real, personal and mixed, and all debts due to such non-United States entity, as well as all other things and causes of action belonging to such non-United States entity, shall be vested in the domestic limited liability company and shall thereafter be the property of the domestic limited liability company as they were of the non-United States entity immediately prior to its domestication, and the title to any real property vested by deed or otherwise in such non-United States entity shall not revert or be in any way impaired by reason of this chapter, but all rights of creditors and all liens upon any property of such non-United States entity shall be preserved unimpaired, and all debts, liabilities and duties of the non-United States entity that has been domesticated shall thenceforth attach to the domestic limited liability company and may be enforced against it to the same extent as if said debts, liabilities and duties had been incurred or contracted by the domestic limited liability company.

§ 18–213. Transfer and Continuance of Domestic Limited Liability Companies

(a) Upon compliance with the provisions of this section, any limited liability company may transfer to any jurisdiction, other than any state, that permits the transfer to or domestication or continuance in such jurisdiction of a limited liability company.

(b) Notwithstanding anything to the contrary in this chapter or a limited liability company agreement, a transfer described in subsection (a) of this section shall be approved in writing by all of the managers and all of the members. If all of the managers and all of the members of the limited liability company shall approve the transfer described in subsection (a) of this section, a certificate of transfer, executed in accordance with § 18–204 of this title, shall be filed in the office of the Secretary of State in accordance with § 18–206 of this title. The certificate of transfer shall state:

(1) The name of the limited liability company and, if it has been changed, the name under which it was originally filed;

(2) The date of the filing of its original certificate of formation with the Secretary of State;

(3) The jurisdiction to which the limited liability company will transfer;

(4) The future effective date or time (which shall be a date or time certain) of the transfer to the jurisdiction specified in subsection (b)(3) of this section if it is not to be effective upon the filing of the certificate of transfer;

(5) That the transfer of the limited liability company has been approved in accordance with the provisions of this section;

(6) The agreement of the limited liability company that it may be served with process in the State of Delaware in any action, suit or proceeding for enforcement of any obligation of the limited liability company arising while it was a limited liability company of the State of Delaware, and that it irrevocably appoints the Secretary of State as its agent to accept service of process in any such action, suit or proceeding; and

(7) The address to which a copy of the process referred to in subsection (b)(6) of this section shall be mailed to it by the Secretary of State. In the event of service hereunder upon the Secretary of State, the procedures set forth in § 18–911(c) of this title [Service of Process on Unregistered Foreign Limited Liability Companies] shall be applicable, except that the plaintiff in any such action, suit or proceeding shall furnish the Secretary of State with the address specified in this subsection and any other address that the plaintiff may elect to furnish, together with copies of such process as required by the Secretary of State, and the Secretary of State shall notify the limited liability company that has transferred out of the State of Delaware at all such addresses furnished by the plaintiff in accordance with the procedures set forth in § 18–911(c) of this title.

(c) Upon the filing in the office of the Secretary of State of the certificate of transfer or upon the future effective date or time of the certificate of transfer and payment to the Secretary of State of all fees prescribed in this chapter, the Secretary of State shall certify that the limited liability company has filed all documents and paid all fees required by this chapter, and thereupon the limited liability company shall cease to exist as a limited liability company of the State of Delaware. Such certificate of the Secretary of State shall be prima facie evidence of the transfer by such limited liability company out of the State of Delaware.

(d) The transfer of a limited liability company out of the State of Delaware in accordance with this section shall not be deemed to affect any obligations or liabilities of the limited liability company incurred prior to such transfer or the personal liability of any person incurred prior to such transfer, nor shall it be deemed to affect the choice of law applicable to the limited liability company with respect to matters arising prior to such transfer.

§ 18–214. Conversion of Certain Entities to a Limited Liability Company

(a) As used in this section, the term "other entity" means a business trust or association, a real estate investment trust, a common-law trust or any other unincorporated business, including a partnership (whether general (including a registered limited liability partnership) or limited (including a registered limited liability limited partnership)) or a foreign limited liability company.

(b) Any other entity may convert to a domestic limited liability company by complying with subsection (h) of this section and filing in the office of the Secretary of State in accordance with § 18–206 of this title:

(1) A certificate of conversion to limited liability company that has been executed by 1 or more authorized persons in accordance with § 18–204 of this title; and

(2) A certificate of formation that complies with § 18–201 of this title and has been executed by 1 or more authorized persons in accordance with § 18–204 of this title.

(c) The certificate of conversion to limited liability company shall state:

(1) The date on which and jurisdiction where the other entity was first created, formed, incorporated or otherwise came into being and, if it has changed, its jurisdiction immediately prior to its conversion to a domestic limited liability company;

(2) The name of the other entity immediately prior to the filing of the certificate of conversion to limited liability company;

(3) The name of the limited liability company as set forth in its certificate of formation filed in accordance with subsection (b) of this section; and

215

(4) The future effective date or time (which shall be a date or time certain) of the conversion to a limited liability company if it is not to be effective upon the filing of the certificate of conversion to limited liability company and the certificate of formation.

(d) Upon the filing in the office of the Secretary of State of the certificate of conversion to limited liability company and the certificate of formation or upon the future effective date or time of the certificate of conversion to limited liability company and the certificate of formation, the other entity shall be converted into a domestic limited liability company and the limited liability company shall thereafter be subject to all of the provisions of this chapter, except that notwithstanding § 18–201 of this title, the existence of the limited liability company shall be deemed to have commenced on the date the other entity commenced its existence in the jurisdiction in which the other entity was first created, formed, incorporated or otherwise came into being.

(e) The conversion of any other entity into a domestic limited liability company shall not be deemed to affect any obligations or liabilities of the other entity incurred prior to its conversion to a domestic limited liability company or the personal liability of any person incurred prior to such conversion.

(f) When any conversion shall have become effective under this section, for all purposes of the laws of the State of Delaware, all of the rights, privileges and powers of the other entity that has converted, and all property, real, personal and mixed, and all debts due to such other entity, as well as all other things and causes of action belonging to such other entity, shall be vested in the domestic limited liability company and shall thereafter be the property of the domestic limited liability company as they were of the other entity that has converted, and the title to any real property vested by deed or otherwise in such other entity shall not revert or be in any way impaired by reason of this chapter, but all rights of creditors and all liens upon any property of such other entity shall be preserved unimpaired, and all debts, liabilities and duties of the other entity that has converted shall thenceforth attach to the domestic limited liability company and may be enforced against it to the same extent as if said debts, liabilities and duties had been incurred or contracted by it.

(g) Unless otherwise agreed, or as required under applicable non-Delaware law, the converting other entity shall not be required to wind up its affairs or pay its liabilities and distribute its assets, and the conversion shall not be deemed to constitute a dissolution of such other entity.

(h) Prior to filing a certificate of conversion to limited liability company with the office of the Secretary of State, a limited liability company agreement shall be approved in the manner provided for by the document, instrument, agreement or other writing, as the case may be, governing the internal affairs of the other entity and the conduct of its business or by applicable law, as appropriate.

(i) The provisions of this section shall not be construed to limit the accomplishment of a change in the law governing, or the domicile of, an other entity to the State of Delaware by any other means provided for in a limited liability company agreement or other agreement or as otherwise permitted by law, including by the amendment of a limited liability company agreement or other agreement.

§ 18–215. Series of Members, Managers or Limited Liability Company Interests

(a) A limited liability company agreement may establish or provide for the establishment of designated series of members, managers or limited liability company interests having separate rights, powers or duties with respect to specified property or obligations of the limited liability company or profits and losses associated with specified property or obligations, and, to the extent provided in the limited liability company agreement, any such series may have a separate business purpose or investment objective.

(b) Notwithstanding anything to the contrary set forth in this chapter or under other applicable law, in the event that a limited liability company agreement creates 1 or more series, and if separate and distinct records are maintained for any such series and the assets associated with any such series are held and accounted for separately from the other assets of the limited liability company, or any other series thereof, and if the limited liability company agreement so provides, and notice of the limitation on liabilities of a series as referenced in this subsection is set forth in the certificate of formation of the limited liability company, then the debts, liabilities and obligations incurred, contracted for or otherwise existing with respect to a particular series shall be enforceable against the assets of such series only, and not against the assets of the limited liability company generally. The fact that a certificate of formation that contains the foregoing notice of the limitation on liabilities of a series is on file in the office of the Secretary of State shall constitute notice of the limitation on liabilities of such series.

(c) Notwithstanding § 18–303(a) of this title, under a limited liability company agreement or under another agreement, a member or manager may agree to be obligated personally for any or all of the debts, obligations and liabilities of one or more series.

(d) A limited liability company agreement may provide for classes or groups of members or managers associated with a series having such relative rights, powers and duties as the limited liability company agreement may provide, and may make provision for the future creation in the manner provided in the limited liability company agreement of additional classes or groups of members or managers associated with the series having such relative rights, powers and duties as may from time to time be established, including rights, powers and duties senior to existing classes and groups of members or managers associated with the series. A limited liability company agreement may provide for the taking of an action, including the amendment of the limited liability company agreement, without the vote or approval of any member or manager or class or group of members or managers, including an action to create under the provisions of the limited liability company agreement a class or group of [a] series of limited liability company interests that was not previously outstanding. A limited liability company agreement may provide that any member or class or group of members associated with a series shall have no voting rights.

(e) A limited liability company agreement may grant to all or certain identified members or managers or a specified class or group of the members or managers associated with a series the right to vote separately or with all or any class or group of the members or managers associated with the series, on any matter. Voting by members or managers associated with a series may be on a per capita, number, financial interest, class, group or any other basis.

(f) Unless otherwise provided in a limited liability company agreement, the management of a series shall be vested in the members associated with such series in proportion to the then current percentage or other interest of members in the profits of the series owned by all of the members associated with such series, the decision of members owning more than 50 percent of the said percentage or other interest in the profits controlling; provided, however, that if a limited liability company agreement provides for the management of the series, in whole or in part, by a manager, the management of the series, to the extent so provided, shall be vested in the manager who shall be chosen in the manner provided in the limited liability company agreement. The manager of the series shall also hold the offices and have the responsibilities accorded to the manager as set forth in a limited liability company agreement. A series may have more than 1 manager. Subject to § 18–602 of this title, a manager shall cease to be a manager with respect to a series as provided in a limited liability company agreement. Except as otherwise provided in a limited liability company agreement, any event under this chapter or in a limited liability company agreement that causes a manager to cease to be a manager with respect to a series shall not, in itself, cause such manager to cease to be a manager of the limited liability company or with respect to any other series thereof.

(g) Notwithstanding § 18–606 of this title, but subject to subsections (h) and (k) of this section, and unless otherwise provided in a limited liability company agreement, at the time a member associated with a series that has been established in accordance with subsection (b) of this section becomes entitled to receive a distribution with respect to such series, the member has the status of, and is entitled to all remedies available to, a creditor of the series, with respect to the distribution. A limited liability company agreement may provide for the establishment of a record date with respect to allocations and distributions with respect to a series.

(h) Notwithstanding § 18–607(a) of this title, a limited liability company may make a distribution with respect to a series that has been established in accordance with subsection (b) of this section; provided, that a limited liability company shall not make a distribution with respect to a series that has been established in accordance with subsection (b) of this section to a member to the extent that at the time of the distribution, after giving effect to the distribution, all liabilities of such series, other than liabilities to members on account of their limited liability company interests with respect to such series and liabilities for which the recourse of creditors is limited to specified property of such series, exceed the fair value of the assets associated with such series, except that the fair value of property of the series that is subject to a liability for which the recourse of creditors is limited shall be included in the assets associated with such series only to the extent that the fair value of that property exceeds that liability. A member who receives a distribution in violation of this subsection, and who knew at the time of the distribution that the distribution violated this subsection, shall be liable to a series for the amount of the distribution. A member who receives a distribution in violation of this subsection, and who did not know at the time of the distribution that the distribution violated this subsection, shall not be liable for the amount of the distribution. Subject to § 18–607(c) of this title, which shall apply to any distribution made with respect to a series under this subsection, this subsection shall not affect any obligation or liability of a member under an agreement or other applicable law for the amount of a distribution.

(i) Unless otherwise provided in the limited liability company agreement, a member shall cease to be associated with a series and to have the power to exercise any rights or powers of a member with respect to such series upon the assignment of all of the member's limited liability company interest with respect to such series. Except as otherwise provided in a limited liability company agreement, any event under this chapter or a limited liability company agreement that causes a member to cease to be associated with a series shall not, in itself, cause such member to cease to be associated with any other series or terminate the continued membership of a member in the limited liability company.

(j) Subject to § 18–801 of this title, except to the extent otherwise provided in the limited liability company agreement, a series may be terminated and its affairs wound up without causing the dissolution of the limited liability company. The termination of a series established in accordance with subsection (b) of this section shall not affect the limitation on liabilities of such series provided by subsection (b) of this section. A series is terminated and its affairs shall be wound up upon the dissolution of the limited liability company under § 18–801 of this title or otherwise upon the first to occur of the following:

(1) At the time specified in the limited liability company agreement;

(2) Upon the happening of events specified in the limited liability company agreement;

(3) Unless otherwise provided in the limited liability company agreement, upon the written consent of all members associated with such series; or

(4) The termination of such series under subsection (*l*) of this section.

(k) Notwithstanding § 18–803(a) of this title, unless otherwise provided in the limited liability company agreement, a manager associated with a series who has not wrongfully terminated the series or, if none, the members associated with the series or a person approved by the members associated with the series or, if there is more than 1 class or group of members associated with the series, then by each class or group of members associated with the series, in either case, by members who own more than 50 percent of the then current percentage or other interest in the profits of the series owned by all of the members associated with the series or by the members in each class or group associated with the series, as appropriate, may wind up the affairs of the series; but, if the series has been established in accordance with subsection (b) of this section, the Court of Chancery, upon cause shown, may wind up the affairs of the series upon application of any member associated with the series, the member's legal representative or assignee, and in connection therewith, may appoint a liquidating trustee. The persons winding up the affairs of a series may, in the name of the limited liability company and for and on behalf of the limited liability company and such series, take all actions with respect to the series as are permitted under § 18–803(b) of this title. The persons winding up the affairs of a series shall provide for the claims and obligations of the series as provided in § 18–804(b) of this title and distribute the assets of the series as provided in § 18–804(a) of this title. Actions taken in accordance with this subsection shall not affect the liability of members and shall not impose liability on a liquidating trustee.

(*l*) On application by or for a member or manager associated with a series established in accordance with subsection (b) of this section, the Court of Chancery may decree dissolution of such series whenever it is not reasonably practicable to carry on the business of the series in conformity with a limited liability company agreement.

(m) If a foreign limited liability company that is registering to do business in the State of Delaware in accordance with § 18–902 of this title is governed by a limited liability company agreement that establishes or provides for the establishment of designated series of members, managers or limited liability company interests having separate rights, powers or duties with respect to specified property or obligations of the foreign limited liability company or profits and losses associated with specified property or obligations, that fact shall be so stated on the application for registration as a foreign limited liability company. In addition, the foreign limited liability company shall state on such application whether the debts, liabilities and obligations incurred, contracted for or otherwise existing with respect to a particular series, if any, shall be enforceable against the assets of such series only, and not against the assets of the foreign limited liability company generally.

§ 18–216. Approval of Conversion of a Limited Liability Company

A domestic limited liability company may convert to a business trust or association, a real estate investment trust, a common-law trust, a general partnership (including a registered limited liability partnership) or a limited partnership (including a registered limited liability limited partnership), organized, formed or created under the laws of the State of Delaware, upon the authorization of such conversion in accordance with this section. If the limited liability company agreement specifies the manner of authorizing a conversion of the limited liability company, the conversion shall be authorized as specified in the limited liability company agreement. If the limited liability company agreement does not specify the manner of authorizing a conversion of the limited liability company and does not prohibit a conversion of the limited liability company, the conversion shall be authorized in the same manner as is specified in the limited liability company agreement for authorizing a merger or consolidation that involves the limited liability company as a constituent party to the merger or consolidation. If the limited liability company agreement does not specify the manner of authorizing a conversion of the limited liability company or a merger or consolidation that involves the limited liability company as a constituent party and does not prohibit a conversion of the limited liability company, the conversion shall be authorized by the approval by the members or, if there is more than 1 class or group of members, then by each class or group of members, in either case, by members who own more than 50 percent of the then current percentage or other interest in the profits of the domestic limited liability company owned by all of the members or by the members in each class or group, as appropriate.

SUBCHAPTER III. MEMBERS

§ 18–301. Admission of Members

(a) In connection with the formation of a limited liability company, a person is admitted as a member of the limited liability company upon the later to occur of:

(1) The formation of the limited liability company; or

(2) The time provided in and upon compliance with the limited liability company agreement or, if the limited liability company agreement does not so provide, when the person's admission is reflected in the records of the limited liability company.

(b) After the formation of a limited liability company, a person is admitted as a member of the limited liability company:

(1) In the case of a person who is not an assignee of a limited liability company interest, including a person acquiring a limited liability company interest directly from the limited liability company and a person to be admitted as a member of the limited liability company without acquiring a limited liability company interest in the limited liability company, at the time provided in and upon compliance with the limited liability company agreement or, if the limited liability company agreement does not so provide, upon the consent of all members and when the person's admission is reflected in the records of the limited liability company;

(2) In the case of an assignee of a limited liability company interest, as provided in § 18–704(a) of this title and at the time provided in and upon compliance with the limited liability company agreement or, if the limited liability company agreement does not so provide, when any such person's permitted admission is reflected in the records of the limited liability company; or

(3) Unless otherwise provided in an agreement of merger or consolidation, in the case of a person acquiring a limited liability company interest in a surviving or resulting limited liability company pursuant to a merger or consolidation approved in accordance with Section 18–209(b) of this chapter, at the time provided in and upon compliance with the limited liability company agreement of the surviving or resulting limited liability company.

(c) A person may be admitted to a limited liability company as a member of the limited liability company and may receive a limited liability company interest in the limited liability company without making a contribution or being obligated to make a contribution to the limited liability company. Unless otherwise provided in a limited liability company agreement, a person may be admitted to a limited liability company as a member of the limited liability company without acquiring a limited liability company interest in the limited liability company.

§ 18–302. Classes and Voting

(a) A limited liability company agreement may provide for classes or groups of members having such relative rights, powers and duties as the limited liability company agreement may provide, and may make provision for the future creation in the manner provided in the limited liability company agreement of additional classes or groups of members having such relative rights, powers and duties as may from time to time be established, including rights, powers and duties senior to existing classes and groups of members. A limited liability company agreement may provide for the taking of an action, including the amendment of the limited liability company agreement, without the vote or approval of any member or class or group of members, including an action to create under the provisions of the limited liability company agreement a class or group of limited liability company interests that was not previously outstanding. A limited liability company agreement may provide that any member or class or group of members shall have no voting rights.

(b) A limited liability company agreement may grant to all or certain identified members or a specified class or group of the members the right to vote separately or with all or any class or group of the members or managers, on any matter. Voting by members may be on a per capita, number, financial interest, class, group or any other basis.

(c) A limited liability company agreement which grants a right to vote may set forth provisions relating to notice of the time, place or purpose of any meeting at which any matter is to be voted on by any members, waiver of any such notice, action by consent without a meeting, the establishment of a record date, quorum requirements, voting in person or by proxy, or any other matter with respect to the exercise of any such right to vote.

§ 18–303. Liability to 3rd Parties

(a) Except as otherwise provided by this chapter, the debts, obligations and liabilities of a limited liability company, whether arising in contract, tort or otherwise, shall be solely the debts, obligations and liabilities of the limited liability company, and no member or manager of a limited liability company shall be obligated personally for any such debt, obligation or liability of the limited liability company solely by reason of being a member or acting as a manager of the limited liability company.

(b) Notwithstanding the provisions of Section 18–303(a) of this chapter, under a limited liability company agreement or under another agreement, a member or manager may agree to be obligated personally for any or all of the debts, obligations and liabilities of the limited liability company.

§ 18–304. Events of Bankruptcy

A person ceases to be a member of a limited liability company upon the happening of any of the following events:

(1) Unless otherwise provided in a limited liability company agreement, or with the written consent of all members, a member:

    a. Makes an assignment for the benefit of creditors;

    b. Files a voluntary petition in bankruptcy;

    c. Is adjudged a bankrupt or insolvent, or has entered against him an order for relief, in any bankruptcy or insolvency proceeding;

    d. Files a petition or answer seeking for himself any reorganization, arrangement, composition, readjustment, liquidation, dissolution or similar relief under any statute, law or regulation;

    e. Files an answer or other pleading admitting or failing to contest the material allegations of a petition filed against him in any proceeding of this nature;

    f. Seeks, consents to or acquiesces in the appointment of a trustee, receiver or liquidator of the member or of all or any substantial part of his properties; or

(2) Unless otherwise provided in a limited liability company agreement, or with the written consent of all members, 120 days after the commencement of any proceeding against the member seeking reorganization, arrangement, composition, readjustment, liquidation, dissolution or similar relief under any statute, law or regulation, if the proceeding has not been dismissed, or if within 90 days after the appointment without his consent or acquiescence of a trustee, receiver or liquidator of the member or of all or any substantial part of his properties, the appointment is not vacated or stayed, or within 90 days after the expiration of any such stay, the appointment is not vacated.

§ 18–305. Access to and Confidentiality of Information; Records

(a) Each member of a limited liability company has the right, subject to such reasonable standards (including standards governing what information and documents are to be furnished at what time and location and at whose expense) as may be set forth in a limited liability company agreement or otherwise established by the manager or, if there is no manager, then by the members, to obtain from the limited liability company from time to time upon reasonable demand for any purpose reasonably related to the member's interest as a member of the limited liability company:

(1) True and full information regarding the status of the business and financial condition of the limited liability company;

(2) Promptly after becoming available, a copy of the limited liability company's federal, state and local income tax returns for each year;

(3) A current list of the name and last known business, residence or mailing address of each member and manager;

(4) A copy of any written limited liability company agreement and certificate of formation and all amendments thereto, together with executed copies of any written powers of attorney pursuant to which the limited liability company agreement and any certificate and all amendments thereto have been executed;

(5) True and full information regarding the amount of cash and a description and statement of the agreed value of any other property or services contributed by each member and which each member has agreed to contribute in the future, and the date on which each became a member; and

(6) Other information regarding the affairs of the limited liability company as is just and reasonable.

(b) Each manager shall have the right to examine all of the information described in subsection (a) of this section for a purpose reasonably related to his position as a manager.

(c) The manager of a limited liability company shall have the right to keep confidential from the members, for such period of time as the manager deems reasonable, any information which the manager reasonably believes to be in the nature of trade secrets or other information the disclosure of which the manager in good faith believes is not in the best interest of the limited liability company or could damage the limited liability company or its business or which the limited liability company is required by law or by agreement with a 3rd party to keep confidential.

(d) A limited liability company may maintain its records in other than a written form if such form is capable of conversion into written form within a reasonable time.

(e) Any demand by a member under this section shall be in writing and shall state the purpose of such demand.

(f) Any action to enforce any right arising under this section shall be brought in the Court of Chancery. If the limited liability company refuses to permit a member to obtain or a manager to examine the information described in subsection (a)(3) of this section or does not reply to the demand that has been made within 5 business days after the demand has been made, the demanding member or manager may apply to the Court of Chancery for an order to compel such disclosure. The Court of Chancery is hereby vested with exclusive jurisdiction to determine whether or not the person seeking such information is entitled to the information sought. The Court of Chancery may summarily order the limited liability company to permit the demanding member to obtain or manager to examine the information described in subsection (a)(3) of this section and to make copies or abstracts therefrom; or the Court of Chancery may summarily order the limited liability company to furnish to the demanding member or manager the information described in subsection (a)(3) of this section on the condition that the demanding member or manager first pay to the limited liability company the reasonable cost of obtaining and furnishing such information and on such other conditions as the Court of Chancery deems appropriate. When a demanding member seeks to obtain or a manager seeks to examine the information described in subsection (a)(3) of this section, the demanding member or manager shall first establish (1) that the demanding member or manager has complied with the provisions of this section respecting the form and manner of making demand for obtaining or examining of such information, and (2) that the information the demanding member or manager seeks is reasonably related to the member's interest as a member or the manager's position as a manager, as the case may be. The Court of Chancery may, in its discretion, prescribe any limitations or conditions with reference to the obtaining or examining of information, or award such other or further relief as the Court of Chancery may deem just and proper. The Court of Chancery may order books, documents and records, pertinent extracts therefrom, or duly authenticated copies thereof, to be brought within the State of Delaware and kept in the State of Delaware upon such terms and conditions as the order may prescribe.

§ 18–306. Remedies for Breach of Limited Liability Company Agreement by Member

A limited liability company agreement may provide that:

(1) A member who fails to perform in accordance with, or to comply with the terms and conditions of, the limited liability company agreement shall be subject to specified penalties or specified consequences; and

(2) At the time or upon the happening of events specified in the limited liability company agreement, a member shall be subject to specified penalties or specified consequences.

SUBCHAPTER IV. MANAGERS

§ 18–401. Admission of Managers

A person may be named or designated as a manager of the limited liability company as provided in § 18–101(10) of this title.

§ 18–402. Management of Limited Liability Company

Unless otherwise provided in a limited liability company agreement, the management of a limited liability company shall be vested in its members in proportion to the then current percentage or other interest of members in the profits of the limited liability company owned by all of the members, the decision of members owning more than 50 percent of the said percentage or other interest in the profits controlling; provided however, that if a limited liability company agreement provides for the management, in whole or in part, of a limited liability company by a manager, the management of the limited liability company, to the extent so provided, shall be vested in the manager who shall be chosen by the members in the manner provided in the limited liability company agreement. The manager shall also hold the offices and have the responsibilities accorded to him by the members and set forth in a limited liability company agreement. Subject to § 18–602 of this title, a manager shall cease to be a manager as provided in a limited liability company agreement. A limited liability company may have more than 1 manager. Unless otherwise provided in a limited liability company agreement, each member and manager has the authority to bind the limited liability company.

§ 18–403. Contributions by a Manager

A manager of a limited liability company may make contributions to the limited liability company and share in the profits and losses of, and in distributions from, the limited liability company as a member. A person who is both a manager and a member has the rights and powers, and is subject to the restrictions and liabilities, of a manager and, except as provided in a limited liability company agreement, also has the rights and powers, and is subject to the restrictions and liabilities, of a member to the extent of his participation in the limited liability company as a member.

§ 18–404. Classes and Voting

(a) A limited liability company agreement may provide for classes or groups of managers having such relative rights, powers and duties as the limited liability company agreement may provide, and may make provision for the future creation in the manner provided in the limited liability company agreement of additional classes or groups of managers having such relative rights, powers and duties as may from time to time be established, including rights, powers and duties senior to existing classes and groups of managers. A limited liability company agreement may provide for the taking of an action, including the amendment of the limited liability company agreement, without the vote or approval of any manager or class or group of managers, including an action to create under the provisions of the limited liability company agreement a class or group of limited liability company interests that was not previously outstanding.

(b) A limited liability company agreement may grant to all or certain identified managers or a specified class or group of the managers the right to vote, separately or with all or any class or group of managers or members, on any matter. Voting by managers may be on a per capita, number, financial interest, class, group or any other basis.

(c) A limited liability company agreement which grants a right to vote may set forth provisions relating to notice of the time, place or purpose of any meeting at which any matter is to be voted on by any manager or class or group of managers, waiver of any such notice, action by consent without a meeting, the establishment of a record date, quorum requirements, voting in person or by proxy, or any other matter with respect to the exercise of any such right to vote.

§ 18–405. Remedies for Breach of Limited Liability Company Agreement by Manager

A limited liability company agreement may provide that:

(1) A manager who fails to perform in accordance with, or to comply with the terms and conditions of, the limited liability company agreement shall be subject to specified penalties or specified consequences; and

(2) At the time or upon the happening of events specified in the limited liability company agreement, a manager shall be subject to specified penalties or specified consequences.

§ 18–406. Reliance on Reports and Information by Member or Manager

A member or manager of a limited liability company shall be fully protected in relying in good faith upon the records of the limited liability company and upon such information, opinions, reports or statements presented to the limited liability company by any of its other managers, members, officers, employees or committees of the limited liability company, or by any other person, as to matters the member or manager reasonably believes are within such other person's professional or expert competence and who has been selected with reasonable care by or on behalf of the limited liability company, including information, opinions, reports or statements as to the value and amount of the assets, liabilities, profits or losses of the limited liability company or any other facts pertinent to the existence and amount of assets from which distributions to members might properly be paid.

§ 18–407. Delegation of Rights and Powers to Manage

Unless otherwise provided in the limited liability company agreement, a member or manager of limited liability company has the power and authority to delegate to one or more other persons the member's or manager's, as the case may be, rights and powers to manage and control the business and affairs of the limited liability company, including to delegate to agents and employees of a member or manager [of] the limited liability company, and to delegate by a management agreement or another agreement with, or otherwise to, other persons. Unless otherwise provided in the limited liability company agreement, such delegation by a member or manager of a limited liability company shall not cause the member or manager to cease to be a member or manager, as the case may be, of the limited liability company.

SUBCHAPTER V.   FINANCE

§ 18–501.   Form of Contribution

The contribution of a member to a limited liability company may be in cash, property or services rendered, or a promissory note or other obligation to contribute cash or property or to perform services.

§ 18–502.   Liability for Contribution

(a) Except as provided in a limited liability company agreement, a member is obligated to a limited liability company to perform any promise to contribute cash or property or to perform services, even if he is unable to perform because of death, disability or any other reason. If a member does not make the required contribution of property or services, he is obligated at the option of the limited liability company to contribute cash equal to that portion of the agreed value (as stated in the records of the limited liability company) of the contribution that has not been made. The foregoing option shall be in addition to, and not in lieu of, any other rights, including the right to specific performance, that the limited liability company may have against such member under the limited liability company agreement or applicable law.

(b) Unless otherwise provided in a limited liability company agreement, the obligation of a member to make a contribution or return money or other property paid or distributed in violation of this chapter may be compromised only by consent of all the members. Notwithstanding the compromise, a creditor of a limited liability company who extends credit, after the entering into of a limited liability company agreement or an amendment thereto which, in either case, reflects the obligation, and before the amendment thereof to reflect the compromise, may enforce the original obligation to the extent that, in extending credit, the creditor reasonably relied on the obligation of a member to make a contribution or return. A conditional obligation of a member to make a contribution or return money or other property to a limited liability company may not be enforced unless the conditions of the obligation have been satisfied or waived as to or by such member.

Conditional obligations include contributions payable upon a discretionary call of a limited liability company prior to the time the call occurs.

(c) A limited liability company agreement may provide that the interest of any member who fails to make any contribution that he is obligated to make shall be subject to specified penalties for, or specified consequences of, such failure. Such penalty or consequence may take the form of reducing or eliminating the defaulting member's proportionate interest in a limited liability company, subordinating his limited liability company interest to that of nondefaulting members, a forced sale of his limited liability company interest, forfeiture of his limited liability company interest, the lending by other members of the amount necessary to meet his commitment, a fixing of the value of his limited liability company interest by appraisal or by formula and redemption or sale of his limited liability company interest at such value, or other penalty or consequence.

§ 18–503. Allocation of Profits and Losses

The profits and losses of a limited liability company shall be allocated among the members, and among classes or groups of members, in the manner provided in a limited liability company agreement. If the limited liability company agreement does not so provide, profits and losses shall be allocated on the basis of the agreed value (as stated in the records of the limited liability company) of the contributions made by each member to the extent they have been received by the limited liability company and have not been returned.

§ 18–504. Allocation of Distributions

Distributions of cash or other assets of a limited liability company shall be allocated among the members, and among classes or groups of members, in the manner provided in a limited liability company agreement. If the limited liability company agreement does not so provide, distributions shall be made on the basis of the agreed value (as stated in the records of the limited liability company) of the contributions made by each member to the extent they have been received by the limited liability company and have not been returned.

SUBCHAPTER VI. DISTRIBUTIONS AND RESIGNATION

§ 18–601. Interim Distributions

Except as provided in this subchapter, to the extent and at the times or upon the happening of the events specified in a limited liability company agreement, a member is entitled to receive from a limited liability company distributions before his resignation from the limited liability company and before the dissolution and winding up thereof.

§ 18–602. Resignation of Manager

A manager may resign as a manager of a limited liability company at the time or upon the happening of events specified in a limited liability company agreement and in accordance with the limited liability company agreement. A limited liability company agreement may provide that a manager shall not have the right to resign as a manager of a limited liability company. Notwithstanding that a limited liability company agreement provides that a manager does not have the right to resign as a manager of a limited liability company, a manager may resign as a manager of a limited liability company at any time by giving written notice to the members and other managers. If the resignation of a manager violates a limited liability company agreement, in addition to any remedies otherwise available under applicable law, a limited liability company may recover from the resigning manager damages for breach of the limited liability company agreement and offset the damages against the amount otherwise distributable to the resigning manager.

§ 18–603. Resignation of Member

A member may resign from a limited liability company only at the time or upon the happening of events specified in a limited liability company agreement and in accordance with the limited liability company agreement. Notwithstanding anything to the contrary under applicable law, unless a limited liability company agreement provides otherwise, a member may not resign from a limited liability company prior to the dissolution and winding up of the limited liability company. Notwithstanding anything to the contrary under applicable law, a limited liability company agreement may provide that a limited liability company interest may not be assigned prior to the dissolution and winding up of the limited liability company. . . .

§ 18–604. Distribution Upon Resignation

Except as provided in this subchapter, upon resignation any resigning member is entitled to receive any distribution to which he is entitled under a limited liability company agreement and, if not otherwise provided in a limited liability company agreement, he is entitled to receive, within a reasonable time after resignation, the fair value of his limited liability company interest as of the date of resignation based upon his right to share in distributions from the limited liability company.

§ 18–605. Distribution in Kind

Except as provided in a limited liability company agreement, a member, regardless of the nature of his contribution, has no right to demand and receive any distribution from a limited liability company in any form other than cash. Except as provided in a limited liability company agreement, a member may not be compelled to accept a distribution of any asset in kind from a limited liability company to the extent that the percentage of the asset distributed to him exceeds a percentage of that asset which is equal to the percentage in which he shares in distributions from the limited liability company. Except as provided in the limited liability company agreement, a member may be compelled to accept a distribution of any asset in kind from a limited liability company to the extent that the percentage of the asset distributed to him is equal to a percentage of that asset which is equal to the percentage in which he shares in distributions from the limited liability company.

§ 18–606. Right to Distribution

Subject to §§ 18–607 and 18–804 of this title, and unless otherwise provided in a limited liability company agreement, at the time a member becomes entitled to receive a distribution, he has the status of, and is entitled to all remedies available to, a creditor of a limited liability company with respect to the distribution. A limited liability company agreement may provide for the establishment of a record date with respect to allocations and distributions by a limited liability company.

§ 18–607. Limitations on Distribution

(a) A limited liability company shall not make a distribution to a member to the extent that at the time of the distribution, after giving effect to the distribution, all liabilities of the limited liability company, other than liabilities to members on account of their limited liability company interests and liabilities for which the recourse of creditors is limited to specified property of the limited liability company, exceed the fair value of the assets of the limited liability company, except that the fair value of property that is subject to a liability for which the recourse of creditors is limited shall be included in the assets of the limited liability company only to the extent that the fair value of that property exceeds that liability.

(b) A member who receives a distribution in violation of subsection (a) of this section, and who knew at the time of the distribution that the distribution violated subsection (a) of this section, shall be liable to a limited liability company for the amount of the distribution. A member who receives a distribution in violation of subsection (a) of this section, and who did not know at the time of the distribution that the distribution violated subsection (a) of this section, shall not be liable for the amount of the distribution. Subject to subsection (c) of this section, this subsection shall not affect any obligation or liability of a member under agreement or other applicable law for the amount of a distribution.

(c) Unless otherwise agreed, a member who receives a distribution from a limited liability company shall have no liability under this chapter or other applicable law for the amount of the distribution after the expiration of 3 years from the date of the distribution unless an action to recover the distribution from such member is commenced prior to the expiration of the said 3–year period and an adjudication of liability against such member is made in the said action.

SUBCHAPTER VII.   ASSIGNMENT OF LIMITED LIABILITY COMPANY INTERESTS

§ 18–701.   Nature of Limited Liability Company Interest

A limited liability company interest is personal property.   A member has no interest in specific limited liability company property.

§ 18–702.   Assignment of Limited Liability Company Interest

(a) A limited liability company interest is assignable in whole or in part except as provided in a limited liability company agreement.   The assignee of a member's limited liability company interest shall have no right to participate in the management of the business and affairs of a limited liability company except as provided in a limited liability company agreement and upon:

(1) The approval of all of the members of the limited liability company other than the member assigning his limited liability company interest; or

(2) Compliance with any procedure provided for in the limited liability company agreement.

(b) Unless otherwise provided in a limited liability company agreement:

(1) An assignment of a limited liability company interest does not entitle the assignee to become or to exercise any rights or powers of a member;

(2) An assignment of a limited liability company interest entitles the assignee to share in such profits and losses, to receive such distribution or distributions, and to receive such allocation of income, gain, loss, deduction, or credit or similar item to which the assignor was entitled, to the extent assigned; and

(3) A member ceases to be a member and to have the power to exercise any rights or powers of a member upon assignment of all of his limited liability company interest.   Unless otherwise provided in a limited liability company agreement, the pledge of, or granting of a security interest, lien or other encumbrance in or against, any or all of the limited liability company interest of a member shall not cause the member to cease to be a member or to have the power to exercise any rights or powers of a member.

(c) A limited liability company agreement may provide that a member's interest in a limited liability company may be evidenced by a certificate of limited liability company interest issued by the limited liability company.

(d) Unless otherwise provided in a limited liability company agreement and except to the extent assumed by agreement, until an assignee of a limited liability company interest becomes a member, the assignee shall have no liability as a member solely as a result of the assignment.

(e) Unless otherwise provided in the limited liability company agreement, a limited liability company may acquire, by purchase, redemption or otherwise, any limited liability company interest or other interest of a member or manager in the limited liability company. Unless otherwise provided in the limited liability company agreement, any such interest so acquired by the limited liability company shall be deemed canceled.

§ 18–703. Rights of Judgment Creditor

On application to a court of competent jurisdiction by any judgment creditor of a member, the court may charge the limited liability company interest of the member with payment of the unsatisfied amount of the judgment with interest. To the extent so charged, the judgment creditor has only the rights of an assignee of the limited liability company interest. This chapter does not deprive any member of the benefit of any exemption laws applicable to his limited liability company interest.

§ 18–704. Right of Assignee to Become Member

(a) An assignee of a limited liability company interest may become a member as provided in a limited liability company agreement and upon:

(1) The approval of all of the members of the limited liability company other than the member assigning his limited liability company interest; or

(2) Compliance with any procedure provided for in the limited liability company agreement.

(b) An assignee who has become a member has, to the extent assigned, the rights and powers, and is subject to the restrictions and liabilities, of a member under a limited liability company agreement and this chapter. Notwithstanding the foregoing, unless otherwise provided in a limited liability company agreement, an assignee who becomes a member is liable for the obligations of his assignor to make contributions as provided in § 18–502 of this title, but shall not be liable for the obligations of his assignor under subchapter VI of this chapter. However, the assignee is not obligated for liabilities, including the obligations of his assignor to make contributions as provided in § 18–502 of this title, unknown to the assignee at the time he became a member and which could not be ascertained from a limited liability company agreement.

(c) Whether or not an assignee of a limited liability company interest becomes a member, the assignor is not released from his liability to a limited liability company under subchapters V and VI of this chapter.

§ 18–705. Powers of Estate of Deceased or Incompetent Member

If a member who is an individual dies or a court of competent jurisdiction adjudges him to be incompetent to manage his person or his property, the member's executor, administrator, guardian, conservator or other legal representative may exercise all of the member's rights for the purpose of settling his estate or administering his property, including any power under a limited liability company agreement of an assignee to become a member. If a member is a corporation, trust or other entity and is dissolved or terminated, the powers of that member may be exercised by its legal representative or successor.

SUBCHAPTER VIII. DISSOLUTION

§ 18–801. Dissolution

A limited liability company is dissolved and its affairs shall be wound up upon the first to occur of the following:

(1) At the time specified in a limited liability company agreement, which limited liability company agreement may include a provision providing for the perpetual existence of the limited liability company, or thirty (30) years from the date of the formation of the limited liability company if no such time is set forth in the limited liability company agreement or the limited liability company agreement does not provide for the perpetual existence of the limited liability company;

(2) Upon the happening of events specified in a limited liability company agreement;

(3) Unless otherwise provided in the limited liability company agreement, upon the written consent of all members;

(4) The death, retirement, resignation, expulsion, bankruptcy or dissolution of any member or only the member, members or class or classes or group or groups of members specified in the limited liability company agreement, or the occurrence of any other event that terminates the continued membership of any member, or only such member, members or class or classes or group or groups of members specified in the limited liability company agreement, unless the business of the limited liability company is continued (i) within 90 days following the occurrence of any such event either (A) by the vote or written consent of the percentage in interest of the members or class or classes or group or groups of members stated in the limited liability company agreement, or (B) if no such percentage

is specified in the limited liability company agreement, by the vote or written consent of not less than a majority in interest of the remaining members, or (ii) pursuant to a right to continue stated in the limited liability company agreement; or

(5) The entry of a decree of judicial dissolution under § 18–802 of this title.

§ 18–802. Judicial Dissolution

On application by or for a member or manager the Court of Chancery may decree dissolution of a limited liability company whenever it is not reasonably practicable to carry on the business in conformity with a limited liability company agreement.

§ 18–803. Winding Up

(a) Unless otherwise provided in a limited liability company agreement, a manager who has not wrongfully dissolved a limited liability company or, if none, the members or a person approved by the members or, if there is more than 1 class or group of members, then by each class or group of members, in either case, by members who own more than 50 percent of the then current percentage or other interest in the profits of the limited liability company owned by all of the members or by the members in each class or group, as appropriate, may wind up the limited liability company's affairs; but the Court of Chancery, upon cause shown, may wind up the limited liability company's affairs upon applica- tion of any member or manager, his legal representative or assignee, and in connection therewith, may appoint a liquidating trustee.

(b) Upon dissolution of a limited liability company and until the filing of a certificate of cancellation as provided in § 18–203 of this title, the persons winding up the limited liability company's affairs may, in the name of, and for and on behalf of, the limited liability company, prosecute and defend suits, whether civil, criminal or administrative, gradually settle and close the limited liability company's business, dispose of and convey the limited liability company's property, discharge or make reasonable provision for the limited liability company's liabilities, and distribute to the members any remaining assets of the limited liability company, all without affecting the liability of members and managers and without imposing liability on a liquidating trustee.

§ 18–804. Distribution of Assets

(a) Upon the winding up of a limited liability company, the assets shall be distributed as follows:

(1) To creditors, including members and managers who are creditors, to the extent otherwise permitted by law, in satisfaction of liabilities of the limited liability company (whether by payment or the making of reasonable provision for payment thereof) other than

liabilities for which reasonable provision for payment has been made and liabilities for distributions to members and former members under § 18–601 or § 18–604 of this title;

(2) Unless otherwise provided in a limited liability company agreement, to members and former members in satisfaction of liabilities for distributions under § 18–601 or § 18–604 of this title; and

(3) Unless otherwise provided in a limited liability company agreement, to members first for the return of their contributions and second respecting their limited liability company interests, in the proportions in which the members share in distributions.

(b) A limited liability company which has dissolved shall pay or make reasonable provision to pay all claims and obligations, including all contingent, conditional or unmatured claims and obligations, known to the limited liability company and all claims and obligations which are known to the limited liability company but for which the identity of the claimant is unknown. If there are sufficient assets, such claims and obligations shall be paid in full and any such provision for payment made shall be made in full. If there are insufficient assets, such claims and obligations shall be paid or provided for according to their priority and, among claims and obligations of equal priority, ratably to the extent of assets available therefor. Unless otherwise provided in a limited liability company agreement, any remaining assets shall be distributed as provided in this chapter. Any liquidating trustee winding up a limited liability company's affairs who has complied with this section shall not be personally liable to the claimants of the dissolved limited liability company by reason of such person's actions in winding up the limited liability company.

SUBCHAPTER IX. FOREIGN LIMITED LIABILITY COMPANIES

§ 18–901. Law Governing

(a) Subject to the Constitution of the State of Delaware:

(1) The laws of the state, territory, possession, or other jurisdiction or country under which a foreign limited liability company is organized govern its organization and internal affairs and the liability of its members and managers; and

(2) A foreign limited liability company may not be denied registration by reason of any difference between those laws and the laws of the State of Delaware.

(b) A foreign limited liability company shall be subject to § 18–106 of this title.

§ 18–902. Registration Required; Application

(a) Before doing business in the State of Delaware, a foreign limited liability company shall register with the Secretary of State. . . .

SUBCHAPTER X.   DERIVATIVE ACTIONS

§ 18–1001.   Right to Bring Action

A member may bring an action in the Court of Chancery in the right of a limited liability company to recover a judgment in its favor if managers or members with authority to do so have refused to bring the action or if an effort to cause those managers or members to bring the action is not likely to succeed.

§ 18–1002.   Proper Plaintiff

In a derivative action, the plaintiff must be a member at the time of bringing the action and:

(1) At the time of the transaction of which he complains; or

(2) His status as a member had devolved upon him by operation of law or pursuant to the terms of a limited liability company agreement from a person who was a member at the time of the transaction.

§ 18–1003.   Complaint

In a derivative action, the complaint shall set forth with particularity the effort, if any, of the plaintiff to secure initiation of the action by a manager or member or the reasons for not making the effort.

§ 18–1004.   Expenses

If a derivative action is successful, in whole or in part, as a result of a judgment, compromise or settlement of any such action, the court may award the plaintiff reasonable expenses, including reasonable attorney's fees, from any recovery in any such action or from a limited liability company.

SUBCHAPTER XI.   MISCELLANEOUS

§ 18–1101.   Construction and Application of Chapter and Limited Liability Company Agreement

(a) The rule that statutes in derogation of the common law are to be strictly construed shall have no application to this chapter.

(b) It is the policy of this chapter to give the maximum effect to the principle of freedom of contract and to the enforceability of limited liability company agreements.

(c) To the extent that, at law or in equity, a member or manager or other person has duties (including fiduciary duties) and liabilities relating thereto to a limited liability company or to another member or manager:

(1) Any such member or manager or other person acting under a limited liability company agreement shall not be liable to the limited liability company or to any such other member or manager for the member's or manager's or other person's good faith reliance on the provisions of the limited liability company agreement; and

(2) The member's or manager's or other person's duties and liabilities may be expanded or restricted by provisions in a limited liability company agreement.

(d) Unless the context otherwise requires, as used herein, the singular shall include the plural and the plural may refer to only the singular. The use of any gender shall be applicable to all genders. The captions contained herein are for purposes of convenience only and shall not control or affect the construction of this chapter.

§ 18–1102. Short Title

This chapter may be cited as the "Delaware Limited Liability Company Act."

§ 18–1104. Cases Not Provided for in This Chapter

In any case not provided for in this chapter, the rules of law and equity, including the law merchant, shall govern.

§ 18–1106. Reserved Power of State of Delaware to Alter or Repeal Chapter

All provisions of this chapter may be altered from time to time or repealed and all rights of members and managers are subject to this reservation.

§ 18–1107. Taxation of Limited Liability Companies

(a) For purposes of any tax imposed by the State of Delaware or any instrumentality, agency or political subdivision of the State of Delaware, a limited liability company formed under this chapter or qualified to do business in the State of Delaware as a foreign limited liability company shall be classified as a partnership unless classified otherwise for federal income tax purposes, in which case the limited liability company shall be classified in the same manner as it is classified for federal income tax purposes. . . .

UNIFORM LIMITED LIABILITY COMPANY ACT (1995) †

TABLE OF CONTENTS

Prefatory Note*

Sec.

† As amended July 1996.

* Omitted.

* Omitted.

[ARTICLE] 1

GENERAL PROVISIONS

Section 101. Definitions.

In this [Act]:

(1) "Articles of organization" means initial, amended, and restated articles of organization and articles of merger. In the case of a foreign limited liability company, the term includes all records serving a similar function required to be filed in the office of the [Secretary of State] or other official having custody of company records in the State or country under whose law it is organized.

(2) "At-will company" means a limited liability company other than a term company.

(3) "Business" includes every trade, occupation, profession, and other lawful purpose, whether or not carried on for profit.

(4) "Debtor in bankruptcy" means a person who is the subject of an order for relief under Title 11 of the United States Code or a comparable order under a successor statute of general application or a comparable order under federal, state, or foreign law governing insolvency.

(5) "Distribution" means a transfer of money, property, or other benefit from a limited liability company to a member in the member's capacity as a member or to a transferee of the member's distributional interest.

(6) "Distributional interest" means all of a member's interest in distributions by the limited liability company.

(7) "Entity" means a person other than an individual.

(8) "Foreign limited liability company" means an unincorporated entity organized under laws other than the laws of this State which afford limited liability to its owners comparable to the liability under Section 303 and is not required to obtain a certificate of authority to transact business under any law of this State other than this [Act].

(9) "Limited liability company" means a limited liability company organized under this [Act].

(10) "Manager" means a person, whether or not a member of a manager-managed company, who is vested with authority under Section 301.

(11) "Manager-managed company" means a limited liability company which is so designated in its articles of organization.

(12) "Member-managed company" means a limited liability company other than a manager-managed company.

(13) "Operating agreement" means the agreement under Section 103 concerning the relations among the members, managers, and limited liability company. The term includes amendments to the agreement.

(14) "Person" means an individual, corporation, business trust, estate, trust, partnership, limited liability company, association, joint venture, government, governmental subdivision, agency, or instrumentality, or any other legal or commercial entity.

(15) "Principal office" means the office, whether or not in this State, where the principal executive office of a domestic or foreign limited liability company is located.

(16) "Record" means information that is inscribed on a tangible medium or that is stored in an electronic or other medium and is retrievable in perceivable form.

(17) "Sign" means to identify a record by means of a signature, mark, or other symbol, with intent to authenticate it.

(18) "State" means a State of the United States, the District of Columbia, the Commonwealth of Puerto Rico, or any territory or insular possession subject to the jurisdiction of the United States.

(19) "Term company" means a limited liability company in which its members have agreed to remain members until the expiration of a term specified in the articles of organization.

(20) "Transfer" includes an assignment, conveyance, deed, bill of sale, lease, mortgage, security interest, encumbrance, and gift.

Comment:

Uniform Limited Liability Company Act ("ULLCA") definitions, like the rest of the Act, are a blend of terms and concepts derived from the Uniform Partnership Act ("UPA"), the Uniform Partnership Act (1994) ("UPA 1994", also previously known as the Revised Uniform Partnership Act or "RUPA"), the Revised Uniform Limited Partnership Act ("RULPA"), the Uniform Commercial Code ("UCC"), and the Model Business Corporation Act ("MBCA"), or their revisions from time to time; some are tailored specially for this Act.

"Business." A limited liability company may be organized to engage in an activity either for or not for profit. The extent to which contributions to a nonprofit company may be deductible for Federal income tax purposes is determined by federal law. Other state law determines the extent of exemptions from state and local income and property taxes.

"Debtor in bankruptcy." The filing of a voluntary petition operates immediately as an "order for relief." See Sections 601(7)(i) and 602(b)(2)(iii).

"Distribution." This term includes all sources of a member's distributions including the member's capital contributions, undistributed profits, and residual interest in the assets of the company after all claims, including those of third parties and debts to members, have been paid.

"Distributional interest." The term does not include a member's broader rights to participate in the management of the company. See Comments to Article 5.

"Foreign limited liability company." The term is not restricted to companies formed in the United States.

"Manager." The rules of agency apply to limited liability companies. Therefore, managers may designate agents with whatever titles, qualifications, and responsibilities they desire. For example, managers may designate an agent as "President."

"Manager-managed company." The term includes only a company designated as such in the articles of organization. In a manager-managed company agency authority is vested exclusively in one or more managers and not in the members. See Sections 101(10) (manager), 203(a)(6) (articles designation), and 301(b) (agency authority of members and managers).

"Member-managed limited liability company." The term includes every company not designated as "manager-managed" under Section 203(a)(6) in its articles of organization.

"Operating agreement." This agreement may be oral. Members may agree upon the extent to which their relationships are to be governed by writings.

"Principal office." The address of the principal office must be set forth in the annual report required under Section 211(a)(3).

"Record." This Act is the first Uniform Act promulgated with a definition of this term. The definition brings this Act in conformity with the present state of technology and accommodates prospective future technology in the communication and storage of information other than by human memory. Modern methods of communicating and storing information employed in commercial practices are no longer confined to physical documents.

The term includes any writing. A record need not be permanent or indestructible, but an oral or other unwritten communication must be stored or preserved on some medium to qualify as a record. Information that has not been retained other than through human memory does not qualify as a record. A record may be signed or may be created without the knowledge or intent of a particular person. Other law must be consulted to determine admissibility in evidence, the applicability of statute of frauds, and other questions regarding the use of records. Under Section 206(a), electronic filings may be permitted and even encouraged.

Section 102. Knowledge and Notice.

(a) A person knows a fact if the person has actual knowledge of it.

(b) A person has notice of a fact if the person:

(1) knows the fact;

(2) has received a notification of the fact; or

(3) has reason to know the fact exists from all of the facts known to the person at the time in question.

(c) A person notifies or gives a notification of a fact to another by taking steps reasonably required to inform the other person in ordinary course, whether or not the other person knows the fact.

(d) A person receives a notification when the notification:

(1) comes to the person's attention; or

(2) is duly delivered at the person's place of business or at any other place held out by the person as a place for receiving communications.

(e) An entity knows, has notice, or receives a notification of a fact for purposes of a particular transaction when the individual conducting the transaction for the entity knows, has notice, or receives a notification of the fact, or in any event when the fact would have been brought to the individual's attention had the entity exercised reasonable diligence. An entity exercises reasonable diligence if it maintains reasonable routines for communicating significant information to the individual conducting the transaction for the entity and there is reasonable compliance with

246

the routines. Reasonable diligence does not require an individual acting for the entity to communicate information unless the communication is part of the individual's regular duties or the individual has reason to know of the transaction and that the transaction would be materially affected by the information.

Comment:

Knowledge requires cognitive awareness of a fact, whereas notice is based on a lesser degree of awareness. The Act imposes constructive knowledge under limited circumstances. See Comments to Sections 301(c), 703, and 704.

Section 103. Effect of Operating Agreement; Nonwaivable Provisions.

(a) Except as otherwise provided in subsection (b), all members of a limited liability company may enter into an operating agreement, which need not be in writing, to regulate the affairs of the company and the conduct of its business, and to govern relations among the members, managers, and company. To the extent the operating agreement does not otherwise provide, this [Act] governs relations among the members, managers, and company.

(b) The operating agreement may not:

(1) unreasonably restrict a right to information or access to records under Section 408;

(2) eliminate the duty of loyalty under Section 409(b) or 603(b)(3), but the agreement may:

(i) identify specific types or categories of activities that do not violate the duty of loyalty, if not manifestly unreasonable; and

(ii) specify the number or percentage of members or disinterested managers that may authorize or ratify, after full disclosure of all material facts, a specific act or transaction that otherwise would violate the duty of loyalty;

(3) unreasonably reduce the duty of care under Section 409(c) or 603(b)(3);

(4) eliminate the obligation of good faith and fair dealing under Section 409(d), but the operating agreement may determine the standards by which the performance of the obligation is to be measured, if the standards are not manifestly unreasonable;

(5) vary the right to expel a member in an event specified in Section 601(6);

(6) vary the requirement to wind up the limited liability company's business in a case specified in Section 801(3); or

(7) restrict rights of a person, other than a manager, member, and transferee of a member's distributional interest, under this [Act].

Comment:

The operating agreement is the essential contract that governs the affairs of a limited liability company. Since it is binding on all members, amendments must be approved by all members unless otherwise provided in the agreement. Although many agreements will be in writing, the agreement and any amendments may be oral or may be in the form of a record. Course of dealing, course of performance and usage of trade are relevant to determine the meaning of the agreement unless the agreement provides that all amendments must be in writing.

This section makes clear that the only matters an operating agreement may not control are specified in subsection (b). Accordingly, an operating agreement may modify or eliminate any rule specified in any section of this Act except matters specified in subsection (b). To the extent not otherwise mentioned in subsection (b), every section of this Act is simply a default rule, regardless of whether the language of the section appears to be otherwise mandatory. This approach eliminates the necessity of repeating the phrase "unless otherwise agreed" in each section and its commentary.

Under subsection (b)(1), an operating agreement may not unreasonably restrict the right to information or access to any records under Section 408. This does not create an independent obligation beyond Section 408 to maintain any specific records. Under subsections (b)(2) to (4), an irreducible core of fiduciary responsibilities survive any contrary provision in the operating agreement. Subsection (b)(2)(i) authorizes an operating agreement to modify, but not eliminate, the three specific duties of loyalty set forth in Section 409(b)(1) to (3) provided the modification itself is not manifestly unreasonable, a question of fact. Subsection (b)(2)(ii) preserves the common law right of the members to authorize future or ratify past violations of the duty of loyalty provided there has been a full disclosure of all material facts. The authorization or ratification must be unanimous unless otherwise provided in an operating agreement, because the authorization or ratification itself constitutes an amendment to the agreement. The authorization or ratification of specific past or future conduct may sanction conduct that would have been manifestly unreasonable under subsection (b)(2)(i).

Section 104.   Supplemental Principles of Law.

(a) Unless displaced by particular provisions of this [Act], the principles of law and equity supplement this [Act].

(b) If an obligation to pay interest arises under this [Act] and the rate is not specified, the rate is that specified in [applicable statute].

Comment:

Supplementary principles include, but are not limited to, the law of agency, estoppel, law merchant, and all other principles listed in UCC Section 1–103, including the law relative to the capacity to contract, fraud, misrepresentation, duress, coercion, mistake, bankruptcy, and other validating and invalidating clauses. Other principles such as those mentioned in UCC Section 1–205 (Course of Dealing and Usage of Trade) apply as well as course of performance. As with UPA 1994 Section 104, upon which this provision is based, no substantive change from either the UPA or the UCC is intended. Section 104(b) establishes the applicable rate of interest in the absence of an agreement among the members.

Section 105. Name.

(a) The name of a limited liability company must contain "limited liability company" or "limited company" or the abbreviation "L.L.C.", "LLC", "L.C.", or "LC". "Limited" may be abbreviated as "Ltd.", and "company" may be abbreviated as "Co.".

(b) Except as authorized by subsections (c) and (d), the name of a limited liability company must be distinguishable upon the records of the [Secretary of State] from:

(1) the name of any corporation, limited partnership, or company incorporated, organized or authorized to transact business, in this State;

(2) a name reserved or registered under Section 106 or 107;

(3) a fictitious name approved under Section 1005 for a foreign company authorized to transact business in this State because its real name is unavailable.

(c) A limited liability company may apply to the [Secretary of State] for authorization to use a name that is not distinguishable upon the records of the [Secretary of State] from one or more of the names described in subsection (b). The [Secretary of State] shall authorize use of the name applied for if:

(1) the present user, registrant, or owner of a reserved name consents to the use in a record and submits an undertaking in form satisfactory to the [Secretary of State] to change the name to a name that is distinguishable upon the records of the [Secretary of State] from the name applied for; or

(2) the applicant delivers to the [Secretary of State] a certified copy of the final judgment of a court of competent jurisdiction

establishing the applicant's right to use the name applied for in this State.

(d) A limited liability company may use the name, including a fictitious name, of another domestic or foreign company which is used in this State if the other company is organized or authorized to transact business in this State and the company proposing to use the name has:

(1) merged with the other company;

(2) been formed by reorganization with the other company; or

(3) acquired substantially all of the assets, including the name, of the other company.

Section 106. Reserved Name.

(a) A person may reserve the exclusive use of the name of a limited liability company, including a fictitious name for a foreign company whose name is not available, by delivering an application to the [Secretary of State] for filing. The application must set forth the name and address of the applicant and the name proposed to be reserved. If the [Secretary of State] finds that the name applied for is available, it must be reserved for the applicant's exclusive use for a nonrenewable 120–day period.

(b) The owner of a name reserved for a limited liability company may transfer the reservation to another person by delivering to the [Secretary of State] a signed notice of the transfer which states the name and address of the transferee.

Comment:

A foreign limited liability company that is not presently authorized to transact business in the State may reserve a fictitious name for a nonrenewable 120–day period. When its actual name is available, a company will generally register that name under Section 107 because the registration is valid for a year and may be extended indefinitely.

Section 107. Registered Name.

(a) A foreign limited liability company may register its name subject to the requirements of Section 1005, if the name is distinguishable upon the records of the [Secretary of State] from names that are not available under Section 105(b).

(b) A foreign limited liability company registers its name, or its name with any addition required by Section 1005, by delivering to the [Secretary of State] for filing an application:

(1) setting forth its name, or its name with any addition required by Section 1005, the State or country and date of its organi-

zation, and a brief description of the nature of the business in which it is engaged; and

(2) accompanied by a certificate of existence, or a record of similar import, from the State or country of organization.

(c) A foreign limited liability company whose registration is effective may renew it for successive years by delivering for filing in the office of the [Secretary of State] a renewal application complying with subsection (b) between October 1 and December 31 of the preceding year. The renewal application renews the registration for the following calendar year.

(d) A foreign limited liability company whose registration is effective may qualify as a foreign company under its name or consent in writing to the use of its name by a limited liability company later organized under this [Act] or by another foreign company later authorized to transact business in this State. The registered name terminates when the limited liability company is organized or the foreign company qualifies or consents to the qualification of another foreign company under the registered name.

Section 108. Designated Office and Agent for Service of Process.

(a) A limited liability company and a foreign limited liability company authorized to do business in this State shall designate and continuously maintain in this State:

(1) an office, which need not be a place of its business in this State; and

(2) an agent and street address of the agent for service of process on the company.

(b) An agent must be an individual resident of this State, a domestic corporation, another limited liability company, or a foreign corporation or foreign company authorized to do business in this State.

Comment:

Limited liability companies organized under Section 202 or authorized to transact business under Section 1004 are required to designate and continuously maintain an office in the State. Although the designated office need not be a place of business, it most often will be the only place of business of the company. The company must also designate an agent for service of process within the State and the agent's street address. The agent's address need not be the same as the company's designated office address. The initial office and agent designations must be set forth in the articles of organization, including the address of the designated office. See Section 203(a)(2) to (3). The current office and agent designations

251

must be set forth in the company's annual report. See Section 211(a)(2). See also Section 109 (procedure for changing the office or agent designations), Section 110 (procedure for an agent to resign), and Section 111(b) (the filing officer is the service agent for the company if it fails to maintain its own service agent).

Section 109. Change of Designated Office or Agent for Service of Process.

A limited liability company may change its designated office or agent for service of process by delivering to the [Secretary of State] for filing a statement of change which sets forth:

(1) the name of the company;

(2) the street address of its current designated office;

(3) if the current designated office is to be changed, the street address of the new designated office;

(4) the name and address of its current agent for service of process; and

(5) if the current agent for service of process or street address of that agent is to be changed, the new address or the name and street address of the new agent for service of process.

Section 110. Resignation of Agent for Service of Process.

(a) An agent for service of process of a limited liability company may resign by delivering to the [Secretary of State] for filing a record of the statement of resignation.

(b) After filing a statement of resignation, the [Secretary of State] shall mail a copy to the designated office and another copy to the limited liability company at its principal office.

(c) An agency is terminated on the 31st day after the statement is filed in the office of the [Secretary of State].

Section 111. Service of Process.

(a) An agent for service of process appointed by a limited liability company or a foreign limited liability company is an agent of the company for service of any process, notice, or demand required or permitted by law to be served upon the company.

(b) If a limited liability company or foreign limited liability company fails to appoint or maintain an agent for service of process in this State or the agent for service of process cannot with reasonable diligence be found at the agent's address, the [Secretary of State] is an agent of the company upon whom process, notice, or demand may be served.

(c) Service of any process, notice, or demand on the [Secretary of State] may be made by delivering to and leaving with the [Secretary of

State], the [Assistant Secretary of State], or clerk having charge of the limited liability company department of the [Secretary of State's] office duplicate copies of the process, notice, or demand. If the process, notice, or demand is served on the [Secretary of State], the [Secretary of State] shall forward one of the copies by registered or certified mail, return receipt requested, to the company at its designated office. Service is effected under this subsection at the earliest of:

(1) the date the company receives the process, notice, or demand;

(2) the date shown on the return receipt, if signed on behalf of the company; or

(3) five days after its deposit in the mail, if mailed postpaid and correctly addressed.

(d) The [Secretary of State] shall keep a record of all processes, notices, and demands served pursuant to this section and record the time of and the action taken regarding the service.

(e) This section does not affect the right to serve process, notice, or demand in any manner otherwise provided by law.

Comment:

Service of process on a limited liability company and a foreign company authorized to transact business in the State must be made on the company's agent for service of process whose name and address should be on file with the filing office. If for any reason a company fails to appoint or maintain an agent for service of process or the agent cannot be found with reasonable diligence at the agent's address, the filing officer will be deemed the proper agent.

Section 112.   Nature of Business and Powers.

(a) A limited liability company may be organized under this [Act] for any lawful purpose, subject to any law of this State governing or regulating business.

(b) Unless its articles of organization provide otherwise, a limited liability company has the same powers as an individual to do all things necessary or convenient to carry on its business or affairs, including power to:

(1) sue and be sued, and defend in its name;

(2) purchase, receive, lease, or otherwise acquire, and own, hold, improve, use, and otherwise deal with real or personal property, or any legal or equitable interest in property, wherever located;

(3) sell, convey, mortgage, grant a security interest in, lease, exchange, and otherwise encumber or dispose of all or any part of its property;

(4) purchase, receive, subscribe for, or otherwise acquire, own, hold, vote, use, sell, mortgage, lend, grant a security interest in, or otherwise dispose of and deal in and with, shares or other interests in or obligations of any other entity;

(5) make contracts and guarantees, incur liabilities, borrow money, issue its notes, bonds, and other obligations, which may be convertible into or include the option to purchase other securities of the limited liability company, and secure any of its obligations by a mortgage on or a security interest in any of its property, franchises, or income;

(6) lend money, invest and reinvest its funds, and receive and hold real and personal property as security for repayment;

(7) be a promoter, partner, member, associate, or manager of any partnership, joint venture, trust, or other entity;

(8) conduct its business, locate offices, and exercise the powers granted by this [Act] within or without this State;

(9) elect managers and appoint officers, employees, and agents of the limited liability company, define their duties, fix their compensation, and lend them money and credit;

(10) pay pensions and establish pension plans, pension trusts, profit sharing plans, bonus plans, option plans, and benefit or incentive plans for any or all of its current or former members, managers, officers, employees, and agents;

(11) make donations for the public welfare or for charitable, scientific, or educational purposes; and

(12) make payments or donations, or do any other act, not inconsistent with law, that furthers the business of the limited liability company.

Comment:

A limited liability company may be organized for any lawful purpose unless the State has specifically prohibited a company from engaging in a specific activity. For example, many States require that certain regulated industries, such as banking and insurance, be conducted only by organizations that meet the special requirements. Also, many States impose restrictions on activities in which a limited liability company may engage. For example, the practice of certain professionals is often subject to special conditions.

A limited liability company has the power to engage in and perform important and necessary acts related to its operation and function. A company's power to enter into a transaction is distinguishable from the authority of an agent to enter into the transaction. See Section 301 (agency rules).

[ARTICLE] 2

ORGANIZATION

Section 201.   Limited Liability Company as Legal Entity.

A limited liability company is a legal entity distinct from its members.

Comment:

A limited liability company is legally distinct from its members who are not normally liable for the debts, obligations, and liabilities of the company. See Section 303. Accordingly, members are not proper parties to suits against the company unless an object of the proceeding is to enforce members' rights against the company or to enforce their liability to the company.

Section 202.   Organization.

(a) One or more persons may organize a limited liability company, consisting of one or more members, by delivering articles of organization to the office of the [Secretary of State] for filing.

(b) Unless a delayed effective date is specified, the existence of a limited liability company begins when the articles of organization are filed.

(c) The filing of the articles of organization by the [Secretary of State] is conclusive proof that the organizers satisfied all conditions precedent to the creation of a limited liability company.

Comment:

Any person may organize a limited liability company by performing the ministerial act of signing and filing the articles of organization. The person need not be a member. As a matter of flexibility, a company may be organized and operated with only one member to enable sole proprietors to obtain the benefit of a liability shield. The effect of organizing or operating a company with one member on the Federal tax classification of the company is determined by federal law.

The existence of a company begins when the articles are filed. Therefore, the filing of the articles of organization is conclusive as to the existence of the limited liability shield for persons who enter into transactions on behalf of the company. Until the articles are filed, a firm is not organized under this Act and is not a "limited liability company" as defined in Section 101(9). In that case, the parties' relationships are not governed by this Act unless they have expressed a contractual intent to be bound by the provisions of the Act. Third parties would also not be governed by the provisions of this Act unless they have expressed a contractual intent to extend a limited liability shield to the members of the would-be limited liability company.

Section 203. Articles of Organization.

(a) Articles of organization of a limited liability company must set forth:

(1) the name of the company;

(2) the address of the initial designated office;

(3) the name and street address of the initial agent for service of process;

(4) the name and address of each organizer;

(5) whether the company is to be a term company and, if so, the term specified;

(6) whether the company is to be manager-managed, and, if so, the name and address of each initial manager; and

(7) whether one or more of the members of the company are to be liable for its debts and obligations under Section 303(c).

(b) Articles of organization of a limited liability company may set forth:

(1) provisions permitted to be set forth in an operating agreement; or

(2) other matters not inconsistent with law.

(c) Articles of organization of a limited liability company may not vary the nonwaivable provisions of Section 103(b). As to all other matters, if any provision of an operating agreement is inconsistent with the articles of organization:

(1) the operating agreement controls as to managers, members, and members' transferees; and

(2) the articles of organization control as to persons, other than managers, members and their transferees, who reasonably rely on the articles to their detriment.

Comment:

The articles serve primarily a notice function and generally do not reflect the substantive agreement of the members regarding the business affairs of the company. Those matters are generally reserved for an operating agreement which may be unwritten. Under Section 203(b), the articles may contain provisions permitted to be set forth in an operating agreement. Where the articles and operating agreement conflict, the operating agreement controls as to members but the articles control as to third parties. The articles may also contain any other matter not inconsistent with law. The most important is a Section 301(c) limitation on the authority of a member or manager to transfer interests in the company's real property.

A company will be at-will unless it is designated as a term company and the duration of its term is specified in its articles under Section 203(a)(5). The duration of a term company may be specified in any manner which sets forth a specific and final date for the dissolution of the company. For example, the period specified may be in the form of "50 years from the date of filing of the articles" or "the period ending on January 1, 2020." Mere specification of a particular undertaking of an uncertain business duration is not sufficient unless the particular undertaking is within a longer fixed period. An example of this type of designation would include "2020 or until the building is completed, whichever occurs first." When the specified period is incorrectly specified, the company will be an at-will company. Notwithstanding the correct specification of a term in the articles, a company will be an at-will company among the members under Section 203(c)(1) if an operating agreement so provides. A term company that continues after the expiration of its term specified in its articles will also be an at-will company.

A term company possesses several important default rule characteristics that differentiate it dramatically from an at-will company. An operating agreement may alter any of these rules. Any dissociation of an at-will member dissolves a member-managed company unless a specified percentage of the remaining members agree to continue the business of the company. Before the expiration of its term, only specified dissociation events (excluding voluntary withdrawal) of a term member will dissolve a member-managed company unless a specified percentage of the remaining members agree to continue the business of the company. See Comments to Sections

601 and 801(b)(3). Also, even if the dissociation of an at-will member does not result in a dissolution of a member-managed company, the dissociated member is entitled to have the company purchase that member's interest for its fair value. Unless the company earlier dissolves, a term member must generally await the expiration of the agreed term to withdraw the fair value of the interest. See Comments to Section 701(a).

A company will be member-managed unless it is designated as manager-managed under Section 203(a)(6). Absent further designation in the articles, a company will be a member-managed at-will company. The designation of a limited liability company as either member- or manager-managed is important because it defines who are agents and have the apparent authority to bind the company under Section 301 and determines whether the dissociation of members who are not managers will threaten dissolution of the company. In a member-managed company, the members have the agency authority to bind the company. In a manager-managed company only the managers have that authority. The effect of the agency structure of a company on the Federal tax classification of the company is determined by federal law. The agency designation relates only to agency and does not preclude members of a manager-managed company from participating in the actual management of company business. See Comments to Section 404(b).

In a member-managed company, the dissociation of any member will cause the company to dissolve unless a specified percentage of the remaining members agree to continue the business of the company. In a manager-managed company, only the dissociation of any member who is also a manager threatens dissolution of the company. Only where there are no members who are also managers will the dissociation of members who are not managers threaten dissolution of a manager-managed company. See Comments to Section 801.

Section 204. Amendment or Restatement of Articles of Organization.

(a) Articles of organization of a limited liability company may be amended at any time by delivering articles of amendment to the [Secretary of State] for filing. The articles of amendment must set forth the:

    (1) name of the limited liability company;

    (2) date of filing of the articles of organization; and

    (3) amendment to the articles.

(b) A limited liability company may restate its articles of organization at any time. Restated articles of organization must be signed and filed in the same manner as articles of amendment. Restated articles of organization must be designated as such in the heading and state in the heading or in an introductory paragraph the limited liability company's present name and, if it has been changed, all of its former names and the date of the filing of its initial articles of organization.

Comment:

An amendment to the articles requires the consent of all the members unless an operating agreement provides for a lesser number. See Section 404(c)(3).

Section 205. Signing of Records.

(a) Except as otherwise provided in this [Act], a record to be filed by or on behalf of a limited liability company in the office of the [Secretary of State] must be signed in the name of the company by a:

(1) manager of a manager-managed company;

(2) member of a member-managed company;

(3) person organizing the company, if the company has not been formed; or

(4) fiduciary, if the company is in the hands of a receiver, trustee, or other court-appointed fiduciary.

(b) A record signed under subsection (a) must state adjacent to the signature the name and capacity of the signer.

(c) Any person may sign a record to be filed under subsection (a) by an attorney-in-fact. Powers of attorney relating to the signing of records to be filed under subsection (a) by an attorney-in-fact need not be filed in the office of the [Secretary of State] as evidence of authority by the person filing but must be retained by the company.

Comment:

Both a writing and a record may be signed. An electronic record is signed when a person adds a name to the record with the intention to authenticate the record. See Sections 101(16) ("record" definition) and 101(17) ("signed" definition).

Other provisions of this Act also provide for the filing of records with the filing office but do not require signing by the persons specified in clauses (1) to (3). Those specific sections prevail.

Section 206. Filing in Office of [Secretary of State].

(a) Articles of organization or any other record authorized to be filed under this [Act] must be in a medium permitted by the [Secretary of State] and must be delivered to the office of the [Secretary of State]. Unless the [Secretary of State] determines that a record fails to comply as to form with the filing requirements of this [Act], and if all filing fees have been paid, the [Secretary of State] shall file the record and send a receipt for the record and the fees to the limited liability company or its representative.

(b) Upon request and payment of a fee, the [Secretary of State] shall send to the requester a certified copy of the requested record.

(c) Except as otherwise provided in subsection (d) and Section 207(c), a record accepted for filing by the [Secretary of State] is effective:

(1) at the time of filing on the date it is filed, as evidenced by the [Secretary of State's] date and time endorsement on the original record; or

(2) at the time specified in the record as its effective time on the date it is filed.

(d) A record may specify a delayed effective time and date, and if it does so the record becomes effective at the time and date specified. If a delayed effective date but no time is specified, the record is effective at the close of business on that date. If a delayed effective date is later than the 90th day after the record is filed, the record is effective on the 90th day.

Comment:

The definition and use of the term "record" permits filings with the filing office under this Act to conform to technological advances that have been adopted by the filing office. However, since Section 206(a) provides that the filing "must be in a medium permitted by the [Secretary of State]", the Act simply conforms to filing changes as they are adopted.

Section 207.   Correcting Filed Record.

(a) A limited liability company or foreign limited liability company may correct a record filed by the [Secretary of State] if the record contains a false or erroneous statement or was defectively signed.

(b) A record is corrected:

(1) by preparing articles of correction that:

(i) describe the record, including its filing date, or attach a copy of it to the articles of correction;

(ii) specify the incorrect statement and the reason it is incorrect or the manner in which the signing was defective; and

(iii) correct the incorrect statement or defective signing; and

(2) by delivering the corrected record to the [Secretary of State] for filing.

(c) Articles of correction are effective retroactively on the effective date of the record they correct except as to persons relying on the uncorrected record and adversely affected by the correction. As to those persons, articles of correction are effective when filed.

Section 208. Certificate of Existence or Authorization.

(a) A person may request the [Secretary of State] to furnish a certificate of existence for a limited liability company or a certificate of authorization for a foreign limited liability company.

(b) A certificate of existence for a limited liability company must set forth:

(1) the company's name;

(2) that it is duly organized under the laws of this State, the date of organization, whether its duration is at-will or for a specified term, and, if the latter, the period specified;

(3) if payment is reflected in the records of the [Secretary of State] and if nonpayment affects the existence of the company, that all fees, taxes, and penalties owed to this State have been paid;

(4) whether its most recent annual report required by Section 211 has been filed with the [Secretary of State];

(5) that articles of termination have not been filed; and

(6) other facts of record in the office of the [Secretary of State] which may be requested by the applicant.

(c) A certificate of authorization for a foreign limited liability company must set forth:

(1) the company's name used in this State;

(2) that it is authorized to transact business in this State;

(3) if payment is reflected in the records of the [Secretary of State] and if nonpayment affects the authorization of the company, that all fees, taxes, and penalties owed to this State have been paid;

(4) whether its most recent annual report required by Section 211 has been filed with the [Secretary of State];

(5) that a certificate of cancellation has not been filed; and

(6) other facts of record in the office of the [Secretary of State] which may be requested by the applicant.

(d) Subject to any qualification stated in the certificate, a certificate of existence or authorization issued by the [Secretary of State] may be relied upon as conclusive evidence that the domestic or foreign limited liability company is in existence or is authorized to transact business in this State.

Section 209.   Liability for False Statement in Filed Record.

If a record authorized or required to be filed under this [Act] contains a false statement, one who suffers loss by reliance on the statement may recover damages for the loss from a person who signed the record or caused another to sign it on the person's behalf and knew the statement to be false at the time the record was signed.

Section 210.   Filing by Judicial Act.

If a person required by Section 205 to sign any record fails or refuses to do so, any other person who is adversely affected by the failure or refusal may petition the [designate the appropriate court] to direct the signing of the record.   If the court finds that it is proper for the record to be signed and that a person so designated has failed or refused to sign the record, it shall order the [Secretary of State] to sign and file an appropriate record.

Section 211.   Annual Report for [Secretary of State].

(a) A limited liability company, and a foreign limited liability company authorized to transact business in this State, shall deliver to the [Secretary of State] for filing an annual report that sets forth:

    (1) the name of the company and the State or country under whose law it is organized;

    (2) the address of its designated office and the name and address of its agent for service of process in this State;

    (3) the address of its principal office; and

    (4) the names and business addresses of any managers.

(b) Information in an annual report must be current as of the date the annual report is signed on behalf of the limited liability company.

(c) The first annual report must be delivered to the [Secretary of State] between [January 1 and April 1] of the year following the calendar year in which a limited liability company was organized or a foreign company was authorized to transact business.   Subsequent annual reports must be delivered to the [Secretary of State] between [January 1 and April 1] of the ensuing calendar years.

(d) If an annual report does not contain the information required in subsection (a), the [Secretary of State] shall promptly notify the reporting limited liability company or foreign limited liability company and return the report to it for correction.   If the report is corrected to contain the information required in subsection (a) and delivered to the [Secretary of State] within 30 days after the effective date of the notice, it is timely filed.

Comment:

Failure to deliver the annual report within 60 days after its due date is a primary ground for administrative dissolution of the company under Section 809. See Comments to Sections 809 to 812.

[ARTICLE] 3

RELATIONS OF MEMBERS AND MANAGERS TO PERSONS DEALING WITH LIMITED LIABILITY COMPANY

Sec.

301. Agency of Members and Managers.
302. Limited Liability Company Liable for Member's or Manager's Actionable Conduct.
303. Liability of Members and Managers.

Section 301. Agency of Members and Managers.

(a) Subject to subsections (b) and (c):

(1) Each member is an agent of the limited liability company for the purpose of its business, and an act of a member, including the signing of an instrument in the company's name, for apparently carrying on in the ordinary course the company's business or business of the kind carried on by the company binds the company, unless the member had no authority to act for the company in the particular matter and the person with whom the member was dealing knew or had notice that the member lacked authority.

(2) An act of a member which is not apparently for carrying on in the ordinary course the company's business or business of the kind carried on by the company binds the company only if the act was authorized by the other members.

(b) Subject to subsection (c), in a manager-managed company:

(1) A member is not an agent of the company for the purpose of its business solely by reason of being a member. Each manager is an agent of the company for the purpose of its business, and an act of a manager, including the signing of an instrument in the company's name, for apparently carrying on in the ordinary course the company's business or business of the kind carried on by the company binds the company, unless the manager had no authority to act for the company in the particular matter and the person with whom the manager was dealing knew or had notice that the manager lacked authority.

(2) An act of a manager which is not apparently for carrying on in the ordinary course the company's business or business of the

263

kind carried on by the company binds the company only if the act was authorized under Section 404.

(c) Unless the articles of organization limit their authority, any member of a member-managed company or manager of a manager-managed company may sign and deliver any instrument transferring or affecting the company's interest in real property. The instrument is conclusive in favor of a person who gives value without knowledge of the lack of the authority of the person signing and delivering the instrument.

Comment:

Members of a member-managed and managers of manager-managed company, as agents of the firm, have the apparent authority to bind a company to third parties. Members of a manager-managed company are not as such agents of the firm and do not have the apparent authority, as members, to bind a company. Members and managers with apparent authority possess actual authority by implication unless the actual authority is restricted in an operating agreement. Apparent authority extends to acts for carrying on in the ordinary course the company's business and business of the kind carried on by the company. Acts beyond this scope bind the company only where supported by actual authority created before the act or ratified after the act.

Ordinarily, restrictions on authority in an operating agreement do not affect the apparent authority of members and managers to bind the company to third parties without notice of the restriction. However, the restriction may make a member or manager's conduct wrongful and create liability to the company for the breach. This rule is subject to three important exceptions. First, under Section 301(c), a limitation reflected in the articles of organization on the authority of any member or manager to sign and deliver an instrument affecting an interest in company real property is effective when filed, even to persons without knowledge of the agent's lack of authority. The effect of such a limitation on authority on the Federal tax classification of the company is determined by federal law. Secondly, under Section 703, a dissociated member's apparent authority terminates two years after dissociation, even to persons without knowledge of the dissociation. Thirdly, under Section 704, a dissociated member's apparent authority may be terminated earlier than the two years by filing a statement of dissociation. The statement is effective 90 days after filing, even to persons without knowledge of the filing. Together, these three provisions provide constructive knowledge to the world of the lack of apparent authority of an agent to bind the company.

Section 302. Limited Liability Company Liable for Member's or Manager's Actionable Conduct.

A limited liability company is liable for loss or injury caused to a person, or for a penalty incurred, as a result of a wrongful act or omission, or other actionable conduct, of a member or manager acting in the ordinary course of business of the company or with authority of the company.

Comment:

Since a member of a manager-managed company is not as such an agent, the acts of the member are not imputed to the company unless the member is acting under actual or apparent authority created by circumstances other than membership status.

Section 303. Liability of Members and Managers.

(a) Except as otherwise provided in subsection (c), the debts, obligations, and liabilities of a limited liability company, whether arising in contract, tort, or otherwise, are solely the debts, obligations, and liabilities of the company. A member or manager is not personally liable for a debt, obligation, or liability of the company solely by reason of being or acting as a member or manager.

(b) The failure of a limited liability company to observe the usual company formalities or requirements relating to the exercise of its company powers or management of its business is not a ground for imposing personal liability on the members or managers for liabilities of the company.

(c) All or specified members of a limited liability company are liable in their capacity as members for all or specified debts, obligations, or liabilities of the company if:

(1) a provision to that effect is contained in the articles of organization; and

(2) a member so liable has consented in writing to the adoption of the provision or to be bound by the provision.

Comment:

A member or manager, as an agent of the company, is not liable for the debts, obligations, and liabilities of the company simply because of the agency. A member or manager is responsible for acts or omissions to the extent those acts or omissions would be actionable in contract or tort against the member or manager if that person were acting in an individual capacity. Where a member or manager delegates or assigns the authority or duty to exercise appropriate company functions, the member or manager is ordinarily not personally liable for the acts or omissions of the officer,

265

employee, or agent if the member or manager has complied with the duty of care set forth in Section 409(c).

Under Section 303(c), the usual liability shield may be waived, in whole or in part, provided the waiver is reflected in the articles of organization and the member has consented in writing to be bound by the waiver. The importance and unusual nature of the waiver consent requires that the consent be evidenced by a writing and not merely an unwritten record. See Comments to Section 205. The effect of a waiver on the Federal tax classification of the company is determined by federal law.

[ARTICLE] 4

RELATIONS OF MEMBERS TO EACH OTHER AND TO LIMITED LIABILITY COMPANY

Sec.

Section 401.   Form of Contribution.

A contribution of a member of a limited liability company may consist of tangible or intangible property or other benefit to the company, including money, promissory notes, services performed, or other agreements to contribute cash or property, or contracts for services to be performed.

Comment:

Unless otherwise provided in an operating agreement, admission of a member and the nature and valuation of a would-be member's contribution are matters requiring the consent of all of the other members. See Section 404(c)(7). An agreement to contribute to a company is controlled by the operating agreement and therefore may not be created or modified without amending that agreement through the unanimous consent of all the members, including the member to be bound by the new contribution terms. See 404(c)(1).

Section 402. Member's Liability for Contributions.

(a) A member's obligation to contribute money, property, or other benefit to, or to perform services for, a limited liability company is not excused by the member's death, disability, or other inability to perform personally. If a member does not make the required contribution of property or services, the member is obligated at the option of the company to contribute money equal to the value of that portion of the stated contribution which has not been made.

(b) A creditor of a limited liability company who extends credit or otherwise acts in reliance on an obligation described in subsection (a), and without notice of any compromise under Section 404(c)(5), may enforce the original obligation.

Comment:

An obligation need not be in writing to be enforceable. Given the informality of some companies, a writing requirement may frustrate reasonable expectations of members based on a clear oral agreement. Obligations may be compromised with the consent of all of the members under Section 404(c)(5), but the compromise is generally effective only among the consenting members. Company creditors are bound by the compromise only as provided in Section 402(b).

Section 403. Member's and Manager's Rights to Payments and Reimbursement.

(a) A limited liability company shall reimburse a member or manager for payments made and indemnify a member or manager for liabilities incurred by the member or manager in the ordinary course of the business of the company or for the preservation of its business or property.

(b) A limited liability company shall reimburse a member for an advance to the company beyond the amount of contribution the member agreed to make.

(c) A payment or advance made by a member which gives rise to an obligation of a limited liability company under subsection (a) or (b) constitutes a loan to the company upon which interest accrues from the date of the payment or advance.

(d) A member is not entitled to remuneration for services performed for a limited liability company, except for reasonable compensation for services rendered in winding up the business of the company.

Comment:

The presence of a liability shield will ordinarily prevent a member or manager from incurring personal liability on behalf of the company in the ordinary course of the company's business. Where a member of a member-managed or a manager of a manager-managed company incurs such liabilities, Section 403(a) provides that the company must indemnify the member or manager where that person acted in the ordinary course of the company's business or the preservation of its property. A member or manager is therefore entitled to indemnification only if the act was within the member or manager's actual authority. A member or manager is therefore not entitled to indemnification for conduct that violates the duty of care set forth in Section 409(c) or for tortious conduct against a third party. Since members of a manager-managed company do not possess the apparent authority to bind the company, it would be more unusual for such a member to incur a liability for indemnification in the ordinary course of the company's business.

Section 404.   Management of Limited Liability Company.

(a) In a member-managed company:

(1) each member has equal rights in the management and conduct of the company's business; and

(2) except as otherwise provided in subsection (c), any matter relating to the business of the company may be decided by a majority of the members.

(b) In a manager-managed company:

(1) each manager has equal rights in the management and conduct of the company's business;

(2) except as otherwise provided in subsection (c), any matter relating to the business of the company may be exclusively decided by the manager or, if there is more than one manager, by a majority of the managers; and

(3) a manager:

(i) must be designated, appointed, elected, removed, or replaced by a vote, approval, or consent of a majority of the members; and

(ii) holds office until a successor has been elected and qualified, unless the manager sooner resigns or is removed.

(c) The only matters of a member or manager-managed company's business requiring the consent of all of the members are:

(1) the amendment of the operating agreement under Section 103;

(2) the authorization or ratification of acts or transactions under Section 103(b)(2)(ii) which would otherwise violate the duty of loyalty;

(3) an amendment to the articles of organization under Section 204;

(4) the compromise of an obligation to make a contribution under Section 402(b);

(5) the compromise, as among members, of an obligation of a member to make a contribution or return money or other property paid or distributed in violation of this [Act];

(6) the making of interim distributions under Section 405(a), including the redemption of an interest;

(7) the admission of a new member;

(8) the use of the company's property to redeem an interest subject to a charging order;

(9) the consent to dissolve the company under Section 801(b)(2);

(10) a waiver of the right to have the company's business wound up and the company terminated under Section 802(b);

(11) the consent of members to merge with another entity under Section 904(c)(1); and

(12) the sale, lease, exchange, or other disposal of all, or substantially all, of the company's property with or without goodwill.

(d) Action requiring the consent of members or managers under this [Act] may be taken without a meeting.

(e) A member or manager may appoint a proxy to vote or otherwise act for the member or manager by signing an appointment instrument, either personally or by the member's or manager's attorney-in-fact.

Comment:

In a member-managed company, each member has equal rights in the management and conduct of the company's business unless otherwise provided in an operating agreement. For example, an operating agreement may allocate voting rights based upon capital contributions rather than the subsection (a) per capita rule. Also, member disputes as to any matter relating to the company's business may be resolved by a majority of the members unless the matter relates to a matter specified either in subsection (c) (unanimous consent required) or in Section 801(b)(3)(i) (special consent required). Regardless of how the members allocate management rights, each member is an agent of the company with the apparent authority to bind the company in the ordinary course of its business.

See Comments to Section 301(a). A member's right to participate in management terminates upon dissociation. See Section 603(b)(1).

In a manager-managed company, the members, unless also managers, have no rights in the management and conduct of the company's business unless otherwise provided in an operating agreement. If there is more than one manager, manager disputes as to any matter relating to the company's business may be resolved by a majority of the managers unless the matter relates to a matter specified either in subsection (c) (unanimous member consent required) or Section 801(b)(3)(i) (special consent required). Managers must be designated, appointed, or elected by a majority of the members. A manager need not be a member and is an agent of the company with the apparent authority to bind the company in the ordinary course of its business. See Sections 101(10) and 301(b).

To promote clarity and certainty, subsection (c) specifies those exclusive matters requiring the unanimous consent of the members, whether the company is member- or manager-managed. For example, interim distributions, including redemptions, may not be made without the unanimous consent of all the members. Unless otherwise agreed, all other company matters are to be determined under the majority of members or managers rules of subsections (a) and (b).

Section 405.   Sharing of and Right to Distributions.

(a) Any distributions made by a limited liability company before its dissolution and winding up must be in equal shares.

(b) A member has no right to receive, and may not be required to accept, a distribution in kind.

(c) If a member becomes entitled to receive a distribution, the member has the status of, and is entitled to all remedies available to, a creditor of the limited liability company with respect to the distribution.

Comment:

Recognizing the informality of many limited liability companies, this section creates a simple default rule regarding interim distributions. Any interim distributions made must be in equal shares and approved by all members. See Section 404(c)(6). The rule assumes that: profits will be shared equally; some distributions will constitute a return of contributions that should be shared equally rather than a distribution of profits; and property contributors should have the right to veto any distribution that threatens their return of contributions on liquidation. In the simple case where the members make equal contributions of property or equal contributions of services, those assumptions avoid the necessity of maintaining a complex capital account or determining profits. Where some members contribute services and others property, the unanimous vote necessary to approve interim distributions protects against unwanted distributions of contributions to service contributors. Consistently, Section 408(a) does not require the company to maintain a separate account for each member, the Act does not contain a default rule for allocating profits and losses, and Section 806(b) requires that liquidating distributions to members be made in equal shares after the return of contributions not previously returned. See Comments to Section 806(b).

Section 405(c) governs distributions declared or made when the company was solvent. Section 406 governs distributions declared or made when the company is insolvent.

Section 406. Limitations on Distributions.

(a) A distribution may not be made if:

(1) the limited liability company would not be able to pay its debts as they become due in the ordinary course of business; or

(2) the company's total assets would be less than the sum of its total liabilities plus the amount that would be needed, if the company were to be dissolved, wound up, and terminated at the time of the distribution, to satisfy the preferential rights upon dissolution, winding up, and termination of members whose preferential rights are superior to those receiving the distribution.

(b) A limited liability company may base a determination that a distribution is not prohibited under subsection (a) on financial statements prepared on the basis of accounting practices and principles that are reasonable in the circumstances or on a fair valuation or other method that is reasonable in the circumstances.

(c) Except as otherwise provided in subsection (e), the effect of a distribution under subsection (a) is measured:

(1) in the case of distribution by purchase, redemption, or other acquisition of a distributional interest in a limited liability company, as of the date money or other property is transferred or debt incurred by the company; and

(2) in all other cases, as of the date the:

(i) distribution is authorized if the payment occurs within 120 days after the date of authorization; or

(ii) payment is made if it occurs more than 120 days after the date of authorization.

(d) A limited liability company's indebtedness to a member incurred by reason of a distribution made in accordance with this section is at parity with the company's indebtedness to its general, unsecured creditors.

(e) Indebtedness of a limited liability company, including indebtedness issued in connection with or as part of a distribution, is not considered a liability for purposes of determinations under subsection (a) if its terms provide that payment of principal and interest are made only if and to the extent that payment of a distribution to members could then be made under this section. If the indebtedness is issued as a distribution, each payment of principal or interest on the indebtedness is treated as a distribution, the effect of which is measured on the date the payment is made.

Comment:

This section establishes the validity of company distributions, which in turn determines the potential liability of members and managers for improper distributions under Section 407. Distributions are improper if the company is insolvent under subsection (a) at the time the distribution is measured under subsection (c). In recognition of the informality of many limited liability companies, the solvency determination under subsection (b) may be made on the basis of a fair valuation or other method reasonable under the circumstances.

The application of the equity insolvency and balance sheet tests present special problems in the context of the purchase, redemption, or other acquisition of a company's distributional interests. Special rules establish the time of measurement of such transfers. Under Section 406(c)(1), the time for measuring the effect of a distribution to purchase a distributional interest is the date of payment. The company may make payment either by transferring property or incurring a debt to transfer property in the future. In the latter case, subsection (c)(1) establishes a clear rule that the legality of the distribution is tested when the debt is actually incurred, not later when the debt is actually paid. Under Section 406(e), indebtedness is not considered a liability for purposes of subsection (a) if the terms of the indebtedness itself provide that payments can be made only if and to the extent that a payment of a distribution could then be made under this section. The effect makes the holder of the indebtedness junior to all other creditors but senior to members in their capacity as members.

Section 407. Liability for Unlawful Distributions.

(a) A member of a member-managed company or a member or manager of a manager-managed company who votes for or assents to a distribution made in violation of Section 406, the articles of organization, or the operating agreement is personally liable to the company for the amount of the distribution which exceeds the amount that could have been distributed without violating Section 406, the articles of organization, or the operating agreement if it is established that the member or manager did not perform the member's or manager's duties in compliance with Section 409.

(b) A member of a manager-managed company who knew a distribution was made in violation of Section 406, the articles of organization, or the operating agreement is personally liable to the company, but only to the extent that the distribution received by the member exceeded the amount that could have been properly paid under Section 406.

(c) A member or manager against whom an action is brought under this section may implead in the action all:

(1) other members or managers who voted for or assented to the distribution in violation of subsection (a) and may compel contribution from them; and

(2) members who received a distribution in violation of subsection (b) and may compel contribution from the member in the amount received in violation of subsection (b).

(d) A proceeding under this section is barred unless it is commenced within two years after the distribution.

Comment:

Whenever members or managers fail to meet the standards of conduct of Section 409 and vote for or assent to an unlawful distribution, they are personally liable to the company for the portion of the distribution that exceeds the maximum amount that could have been lawfully distributed. The recovery remedy under this section extends only to the company, not the company's creditors. Under subsection (a), members and managers are not liable for an unlawful distribution provided their vote in favor of the distribution satisfies the duty of care of Section 409(c).

Subsection (a) creates personal liability in favor of the company against members or managers who approve an unlawful distribution for the entire amount of a distribution that could not be lawfully distributed. Subsection (b) creates personal liability against only members who knowingly received the unlawful distribution, but only in the amount measured by the portion of the actual distribution received that was not lawfully made. Members who both vote for or assent to an unlawful distribution and receive a portion or all of the distribution will be liable, at the election of the company, under either but not both subsections.

A member or manager who is liable under subsection (a) may seek contribution under subsection (c)(1) from other members and managers who also voted for or assented to the same distribution and may also seek recoupment under subsection (c)(2) from members who received the distribution, but only if they accepted the payments knowing they were unlawful.

The two-year statute of limitations of subsection (d) is measured from the date of the distribution. The date of the distribution is determined under Section 406(c).

Section 408. Member's Right to Information.

(a) A limited liability company shall provide members and their agents and attorneys access to its records, if any, at the company's principal office or other reasonable locations specified in the operating agreement. The company shall provide former members and their agents and attorneys access for proper purposes to records pertaining to the period during which they were members. The right of access provides the opportunity to inspect and copy records during ordinary business hours. The company may impose a reasonable charge, limited to the costs of labor and material, for copies of records furnished.

(b) A limited liability company shall furnish to a member, and to the legal representative of a deceased member or member under legal disability:

(1) without demand, information concerning the company's business or affairs reasonably required for the proper exercise of the member's rights and performance of the member's duties under the operating agreement or this [Act]; and

(2) on demand, other information concerning the company's business or affairs, except to the extent the demand or the information demanded is unreasonable or otherwise improper under the circumstances.

(c) A member has the right upon written demand given to the limited liability company to obtain at the company's expense a copy of any written operating agreement.

Comment:

Recognizing the informality of many limited liability companies, subsection (a) does not require a company to maintain any records. In general, a company should maintain records necessary to enable members to determine their share of profits and losses and their rights on dissociation. If inadequate records are maintained to determine those and other critical rights, a member may maintain an action for an accounting under Section 410(a). Normally, a company will maintain at least records required by state or federal authorities regarding tax and other filings.

The obligation to furnish access includes the obligation to insure that all records, if any, are accessible in intelligible form. For example, a company that switches computer systems has an obligation either to convert the records from the old system or retain at least one computer capable of accessing the records from the old system.

The right to inspect and copy records maintained is not conditioned on a member or former member's purpose or motive. However, an abuse of the access and copy right may create a remedy in favor of the other members as a violation of the requesting member or former member's obligation of good faith and fair dealing. See Section 409(d).

Although a company is not required to maintain any records under subsection (a), it is nevertheless subject to a disclosure duty to furnish specified information under subsection (b)(1). A company must therefore furnish to members, without demand, information reasonably needed for members to exercise their rights and duties as members. A member's exercise of these duties justifies an unqualified right of access to the company's records. The member's right to company records may not be unreasonably restricted by the operating agreement. See Section 103(b)(1).

Section 409. General Standards of Member's and Manager's Conduct.

(a) The only fiduciary duties a member owes to a member-managed company and its other members are the duty of loyalty and the duty of care imposed by subsections (b) and (c).

(b) A member's duty of loyalty to a member-managed company and its other members is limited to the following:

(1) to account to the company and to hold as trustee for it any property, profit, or benefit derived by the member in the conduct or winding up of the company's business or derived from a use by the member of the company's property, including the appropriation of a company's opportunity;

(2) to refrain from dealing with the company in the conduct or winding up of the company's business as or on behalf of a party having an interest adverse to the company; and

(3) to refrain from competing with the company in the conduct of the company's business before the dissolution of the company.

(c) A member's duty of care to a member-managed company and its other members in the conduct of and winding up of the company's business is limited to refraining from engaging in grossly negligent or reckless conduct, intentional misconduct, or a knowing violation of law.

(d) A member shall discharge the duties to a member-managed company and its other members under this [Act] or under the operating agreement and exercise any rights consistently with the obligation of good faith and fair dealing.

(e) A member of a member-managed company does not violate a duty or obligation under this [Act] or under the operating agreement merely because the member's conduct furthers the member's own interest.

(f) A member of a member-managed company may lend money to and transact other business with the company. As to each loan or transaction, the rights and obligations of the member are the same as those of a person who is not a member, subject to other applicable law.

(g) This section applies to a person winding up the limited liability company's business as the personal or legal representative of the last surviving member as if the person were a member.

(h) In a manager-managed company:

(1) a member who is not also a manager owes no duties to the company or to the other members solely by reason of being a member;

(2) a manager is held to the same standards of conduct prescribed for members in subsections (b) through (f);

(3) a member who pursuant to the operating agreement exercises some or all of the rights of a manager in the management and conduct of the company's business is held to the standards of conduct in subsections (b) through (f) to the extent that the member exercises the managerial authority vested in a manager by this [Act]; and

(4) a manager is relieved of liability imposed by law for violation of the standards prescribed by subsections (b) through (f) to the extent of the managerial authority delegated to the members by the operating agreement.

Comment:

Under subsections (a), (c), and (h), members and managers, and their delegatees, owe to the company and to the other members and managers only the fiduciary duties of loyalty and care set forth in subsections (b) and (c) and the obligation of good faith and fair dealing set forth in subsection (d). An operating agreement may not waive or eliminate the duties or obligation, but may, if not manifestly unreasonable, identify activities and determine standards for measuring the performance of them. See Section 103(b)(2) to (4).

Upon a member's dissociation, the duty to account for personal profits under subsection (b)(1), the duty to refrain from acting as or representing adverse interests under subsection (b)(2), and the duty of care under subsection (c) are limited to those derived from matters arising or events occurring before the dissociation unless the member participates in winding up the company's business. Also, the duty not to compete terminates upon dissociation. See Section 603(b)(3) and (b)(2). However, a dissociated member is not free to use confidential company information after dissociation. For example, a dissociated member of a company may immediately compete with the company for new clients but must exercise care in completing on-going client transactions and must account to the company for any fees from the old clients on account of those transactions. Subsection (c) adopts a gross negligence standard for the duty of care, the standard actually used in most partnerships and corporations.

Subsection (b)(2) prohibits a member from acting adversely or representing an adverse party to the company. The rule is based on agency principles and seeks to avoid the conflict of opposing interests in the mind of the member agent whose duty is to act for the benefit of the principal company. As reflected in subsection (f), the rule does not prohibit the member from dealing with the company other than as an adversary. A member may generally deal with the company under subsection (f) when the transaction is approved by the company.

Subsection (e) makes clear that a member does not violate the obligation of good faith under subsection (d) merely because the member's conduct furthers that member's own interest. For example, a member's refusal to vote for an interim distribution because of negative tax implications to that member does not violate that member's obligation of good faith to the other members. Likewise, a member may vote against a proposal by the company to open a shopping center that would directly compete with another shopping center in which the member owns an interest.

Section 410. Actions by Members.

(a) A member may maintain an action against a limited liability company or another member for legal or equitable relief, with or without an accounting as to the company's business, to enforce:

    (1) the member's rights under the operating agreement;

    (2) the member's rights under this [Act]; and

    (3) the rights and otherwise protect the interests of the member, including rights and interests arising independently of the member's relationship to the company.

(b) The accrual, and any time limited for the assertion, of a right of action for a remedy under this section is governed by other law. A right to an accounting upon a dissolution and winding up does not revive a claim barred by law.

Comment:

During the existence of the company, members have under this section access to the courts to resolve claims against the company and other members, leaving broad judicial discretion to fashion appropriate legal remedies. A member pursues only that member's claim against the company or another member under this section. Article 11 governs a member's derivative pursuit of a claim on behalf of the company.

A member may recover against the company and the other members under subsection (a)(3) for personal injuries or damage to the member's property caused by another member. One member's negligence is therefore not imputed to bar another member's action.

Section 411.   Continuation of Term Company After Expiration of Specified Term.

(a) If a term company is continued after the expiration of the specified term, the rights and duties of the members and managers remain the same as they were at the expiration of the term except to the extent inconsistent with rights and duties of members and managers of an at-will company.

(b) If the members in a member-managed company or the managers in a manager-managed company continue the business without any winding up of the business of the company, it continues as an at-will company.

Comment:

A term company will generally dissolve upon the expiration of its term unless either its articles are amended before the expiration of the original specified term to provide for an additional specified term or the members or managers simply continue the company as an at-will company under this section. Amendment of the articles specifying an additional term requires the unanimous consent of the members. See Section 404(c)(3). Therefore, any member has the right to block the amendment. Absent an amendment to the articles, a company may only be continued under subsection (b) as an at-will company. The decision to continue a term company as an at-will company does not require the unanimous consent of the members and is treated as an ordinary business matter with disputes resolved by a simple majority vote of either the members or managers. See Section 404. In that case, subsection (b) provides that the members' conduct amends or becomes part of an operating agreement to "continue" the company as an at-will company. The amendment to the operating agreement does not alter the rights of creditors who suffer detrimental reliance because the company does not liquidate after the expiration of its specified term. See Section 203(c)(2).

Preexisting operating-agreement provisions continue to control the relationship of the members under subsection (a) except to the extent inconsistent with the rights and duties of members of an at-will company with an operating agreement containing the same provisions. However, the members could agree in advance that, if the company's business continues after the expiration of its specified term, the company continues as a company with a new specified term or that the provisions of its operating agreement survive the expiration of the specified term.

[ARTICLE] 5

TRANSFEREES AND CREDITORS OF MEMBER

Sec.
501. Member's Distributional Interest.
502. Transfer of Distributional Interest.
503. Rights of Transferee.
504. Rights of Creditor.

Section 501.   Member's Distributional Interest.

(a) A member is not a co-owner of, and has no transferable interest in, property of a limited liability company.

(b) A distributional interest in a limited liability company is personal property and, subject to Sections 502 and 503, may be transferred in whole or in part.

(c) An operating agreement may provide that a distributional interest may be evidenced by a certificate of the interest issued by the limited liability company and, subject to Section 503, may also provide for the transfer of any interest represented by the certificate.

Comment:

Members have no property interest in property owned by a limited liability company. A distributional interest is personal property and is defined under Section 101(6) as a member's interest in distributions only and does not include the member's broader rights to participate in management under Section 404 and to inspect company records under Section 408.

Under Section 405(a), distributions are allocated in equal shares unless otherwise provided in an operating agreement. Whenever it is desirable to allocate distributions in proportion to contributions rather than per capita, certification may be useful to reduce valuation issues. The effect of certification on the Federal tax classification of the company is determined by federal law.

Section 502.   Transfer of Distributional Interest.

A transfer of a distributional interest does not entitle the transferee to become or to exercise any rights of a member. A transfer entitles the transferee to receive, to the extent transferred, only the distributions to which the transferor would be entitled.

Comment:

Under Sections 501(b) and 502, the only interest a member may freely transfer is that member's distributional interest. A member's transfer of part, all, or substantially all of a distributional interest will threaten the dissolution of the company under Section 801(b)(3)(i) only if the transfer constitutes an event of dissociation. See Section 601(3). Member dissociation has defined dissolution consequences under Section 801(b)(3)(i) depending upon whether the company is an at-will or term company and whether it is member- or manager-managed. Only the transfer of all or substantially all of a member's distributional interest constitutes or may constitute a member dissociation. A transfer of less than substantially all of a member's distributional interest is not an event of dissociation. A member ceases to be a member upon the transfer of all that member's distributional interest and that transfer is also an event of dissociation under Section 601(3). Relating the event of dissociation to the member's transfer of all of the member's distributional interest avoids the need for the company to track potential future dissociation events associated with a member no longer financially interested in the company. Also, all the remaining members may expel a member upon the transfer of "substantially all" the member's distributional interest. The expulsion is an event of dissociation under Section 601(5)(ii).

Section 503.   Rights of Transferee.

(a) A transferee of a distributional interest may become a member of a limited liability company if and to the extent that the transferor gives the transferee the right in accordance with authority described in the operating agreement or all other members consent.

(b) A transferee who has become a member, to the extent transferred, has the rights and powers, and is subject to the restrictions and liabilities, of a member under the operating agreement of a limited liability company and this [Act]. A transferee who becomes a member also is liable for the transferor member's obligations to make contributions under Section 402 and for obligations under Section 407 to return unlawful distributions, but the transferee is not obligated for the transferor member's liabilities unknown to the transferee at the time the transferee becomes a member.

(c) Whether or not a transferee of a distributional interest becomes a member under subsection (a), the transferor is not released from liability to the limited liability company under the operating agreement or this [Act].

(d) A transferee who does not become a member is not entitled to participate in the management or conduct of the limited liability company's business, require access to information concerning the company's transactions, or inspect or copy any of the company's records.

(e) A transferee who does not become a member is entitled to:

(1) receive, in accordance with the transfer, distributions to which the transferor would otherwise be entitled;

(2) receive, upon dissolution and winding up of the limited liability company's business:

(i) in accordance with the transfer, the net amount otherwise distributable to the transferor;

(ii) a statement of account only from the date of the latest statement of account agreed to by all the members;

(3) seek under Section 801(5) a judicial determination that it is equitable to dissolve and wind up the company's business.

(f) A limited liability company need not give effect to a transfer until it has notice of the transfer.

Comment:

The only interest a member may freely transfer is the member's distributional interest. A transferee may acquire the remaining rights of a member only by being admitted as a member of the company by all of the remaining members. The effect of these default rules and any modifications on the Federal tax classification of the company is determined by federal law.

A transferee not admitted as a member is not entitled to participate in management, require access to information, or inspect or copy company records. The only rights of a transferee are to receive the distributions the transferor would otherwise be entitled, receive a limited statement of account, and seek a judicial dissolution under Section 801(b)(6).

Subsection (e) sets forth the rights of a transferee of an existing member. Although the rights of a dissociated member to participate in the future management of the company parallel the rights of a transferee, a dissociated member retains additional rights that accrued from that person's membership such as the right to enforce Article 7 purchase rights. See and compare Sections 603(b)(1) and 801(b)(5) and Comments.

Section 504. Rights of Creditor.

(a) On application by a judgment creditor of a member of a limited liability company or of a member's transferee, a court having jurisdiction may charge the distributional interest of the judgment debtor to satisfy the judgment. The court may appoint a receiver of the share of the distributions due or to become due to the judgment debtor and make all other orders, directions, accounts, and inquiries the judgment debtor might have made or which the circumstances may require to give effect to the charging order.

(b) A charging order constitutes a lien on the judgment debtor's distributional interest. The court may order a foreclosure of a lien on a distributional interest subject to the charging order at any time. A purchaser at the foreclosure sale has the rights of a transferee.

(c) At any time before foreclosure, a distributional interest in a limited liability company which is charged may be redeemed:

(1) by the judgment debtor;

(2) with property other than the company's property, by one or more of the other members; or

(3) with the company's property, but only if permitted by the operating agreement.

(d) This [Act] does not affect a member's right under exemption laws with respect to the member's distributional interest in a limited liability company.

(e) This section provides the exclusive remedy by which a judgment creditor of a member or a transferee may satisfy a judgment out of the judgment debtor's distributional interest in a limited liability company.

Comment:

A charging order is the only remedy by which a judgment creditor of a member or a member's transferee may reach the distributional interest of a member or member's transferee. Under Section 503(e), the distributional interest of a member or transferee is limited to the member's right to receive distributions from the company and to seek judicial liquidation of the company.

[ARTICLE] 6

MEMBER'S DISSOCIATION

Sec.
601. Events Causing Member's Dissociation.
602. Member's Power to Dissociate; Wrongful Dissociation.
603. Effect of Member's Dissociation.

Section 601. Events Causing Member's Dissociation.

A member is dissociated from a limited liability company upon the occurrence of any of the following events:

(1) the company's having notice of the member's express will to withdraw upon the date of notice or on a later date specified by the member;

(2) an event agreed to in the operating agreement as causing the member's dissociation;

(3) upon transfer of all of a member's distributional interest, other than a transfer for security purposes or a court order charging the member's distributional interest which has not been foreclosed;

(4) the member's expulsion pursuant to the operating agreement;

(5) the member's expulsion by unanimous vote of the other members if:

(i) it is unlawful to carry on the company's business with the member;

(ii) there has been a transfer of substantially all of the member's distributional interest, other than a transfer for security purposes or a court order charging the member's distributional interest which has not been foreclosed;

(iii) within 90 days after the company notifies a corporate member that it will be expelled because it has filed a certificate of dissolution or the equivalent, its charter has been revoked, or its right to conduct business has been suspended by the jurisdiction of its incorporation, the member fails to obtain a revocation of the certificate of dissolution or a reinstatement of its charter or its right to conduct business; or

(iv) a partnership or a limited liability company that is a member has been dissolved and its business is being wound up;

(6) on application by the company or another member, the member's expulsion by judicial determination because the member:

(i) engaged in wrongful conduct that adversely and materially affected the company's business;

(ii) willfully or persistently committed a material breach of the operating agreement or of a duty owed to the company or the other members under Section 409; or

(iii) engaged in conduct relating to the company's business which makes it not reasonably practicable to carry on the business with the member;

(7) the member's:

(i) becoming a debtor in bankruptcy;

(ii) executing an assignment for the benefit of creditors;

(iii) seeking, consenting to, or acquiescing in the appointment of a trustee, receiver, or liquidator of the member or of all or substantially all of the member's property; or

(iv) failing, within 90 days after the appointment, to have vacated or stayed the appointment of a trustee, receiver, or liquidator of the member or of all or substantially all of the member's property obtained without the member's consent or acquiescence, or failing within 90 days after the expiration of a stay to have the appointment vacated;

(8) in the case of a member who is an individual:

(i) the member's death;

(ii) the appointment of a guardian or general conservator for the member; or

(iii) a judicial determination that the member has otherwise become incapable of performing the member's duties under the operating agreement;

(9) in the case of a member that is a trust or is acting as a member by virtue of being a trustee of a trust, distribution of the trust's entire rights to receive distributions from the company, but not merely by reason of the substitution of a successor trustee;

(10) in the case of a member that is an estate or is acting as a member by virtue of being a personal representative of an estate, distribution of the estate's entire rights to receive distributions from the company, but not merely the substitution of a successor personal representative; or

(11) termination of the existence of a member if the member is not an individual, estate, or trust other than a business trust.

Comment:

The term "dissociation" refers to the change in the relationships among the dissociated member, the company and the other members caused by a member's ceasing to be associated in the carrying on of the company's business. Member dissociation for any reason from a member-managed at-will company will cause a dissolution of the company under Section 801(b)(3) unless a specified percentage of the remaining members agree to continue the business of the company. If the dissociation does not dissolve the company, the dissociated member's distributional interest must be immediately purchased by the company under Article 7. Member dissociation from a member-managed term company, but only for the reasons specified in paragraphs (7) to (11), will cause a dissolution of the company under Section 801(b)(3) unless a specified percentage of the remaining members agree to continue the business of the company. Member dissociations specified in paragraphs (1) to (6) do not threaten dissolution under Section 801(b)(3) of a member-managed term company. If the dissociation does not dissolve the company, it is not required to purchase the dissociated member's distributional interest until the expiration of the specified term that existed on the date of the member's dissociation. If an at-will company or a term company is manager-managed, only the dissociation of a member who is also a manager or, if there is none, any member specified above threatens dissolution. The effect on the Federal tax classification of the company creating a member-manager with a minimal interest in the company is determined by federal law.

A member may be expelled from the company under paragraph (5)(ii) by the unanimous vote of the other members upon a transfer of "substantially all" of the member's distributional interest other than for a transfer as security for a loan. A transfer of "all" of the member's distributional interest is an event of dissociation under paragraph (3).

Although a member is dissociated upon death, the effect of the dissociation where the company does not dissolve depends upon whether the company is at-will or term and whether manager-managed. Only the decedent's distributional interest transfers to the decedent's estate which does not acquire the decedent member's management rights. See Section 603(b)(1). Unless otherwise agreed, if the company was at-will, the estate's distributional interest must be purchased by the company at fair value determined at the date of death. However, if a term company, the estate and its transferees continue only as the owner of the distributional interest with no management rights until the expiration of the specified term that existed on the date of death. At the expiration of that term, the company must purchase the interest of a dissociated member if the company continues for an additional term by amending its articles or simply continues as an at-will company. See Sections 411 and 701(a)(2) and Comments. Before that time, the estate and its transferees have the right to make application for a judicial dissolution of the company under Section 801(b)(5) as successors in interest to a dissociated member. See Comments to Sections 801, 411, and 701. Where the members have allocated management rights on the basis of contributions rather than simply the number of members, a member's death will result in a transfer of management rights to the remaining members on a proportionate basis. This transfer of rights may be avoided by a provision in an operating agreement extending the Section 701(a)(1) at-will purchase right to a decedent member of a term company.

Section 602. Member's Power to Dissociate; Wrongful Dissociation.

(a) Unless otherwise provided in the operating agreement, a member has the power to dissociate from a limited liability company at any time, rightfully or wrongfully, by express will pursuant to Section 601(1).

(b) If the operating agreement has not eliminated a member's power to dissociate, the member's dissociation from a limited liability company is wrongful only if:

    (1) it is in breach of an express provision of the agreement; or

    (2) before the expiration of the specified term of a term company:

        (i) the member withdraws by express will;

        (ii) the member is expelled by judicial determination under Section 601(6);

        (iii) the member is dissociated by becoming a debtor in bankruptcy; or

        (iv) in the case of a member who is not an individual, trust other than a business trust, or estate, the member is expelled or otherwise dissociated because it willfully dissolved or terminated its existence.

(c) A member who wrongfully dissociates from a limited liability company is liable to the company and to the other members for damages caused by the dissociation. The liability is in addition to any other obligation of the member to the company or to the other members.

(d) If a limited liability company does not dissolve and wind up its business as a result of a member's wrongful dissociation under subsection (b), damages sustained by the company for the wrongful dissociation must be offset against distributions otherwise due the member after the dissociation.

Comment:

A member has the power to withdraw from both an at-will company and a term company although the effects of the withdrawal are remarkably different. See Comments to Section 601. At a minimum, the exercise of a power to withdraw enables members to terminate their continuing duties of loyalty and care. See Section 603(b)(2) to (3).

A member's power to withdraw by express will may be eliminated by an operating agreement. The effect of such a provision on the Federal tax classification of the company is determined by federal law. An operating agreement may eliminate a member's power to withdraw by express will to promote the business continuity of an at-will company by removing the threat of dissolution and to eliminate the member's right to force the company to purchase the member's distributional interest. See Sections 801(b)(3) and 701(a)(1). However, such a member retains the ability to seek a judicial dissolution of the company. See Section 801(b)(5).

If a member's power to withdraw by express will is not eliminated in an operating agreement, the withdrawal may nevertheless be made wrongful under subsection (b). All dissociations, including withdrawal by express will, may be made wrongful under subsection (b)(1) in both an at-will and term company by the inclusion of a provision in an operating agreement. Even where an operating agreement does not eliminate the power to withdraw by express will or make any dissociation wrongful, the dissociation of a member of a term company for the reasons specified under subsection (b)(2) is wrongful. The member is liable to the company and other members for damages caused by a wrongful dissociation under subsection (c) and, under subsection (d), the damages may be offset against all distributions otherwise due the member after the dissociation. Section 701(f) provides a similar rule permitting damages for wrongful dissociation to be offset against any company purchase of the member's distributional interest.

Section 603. Effect of Member's Dissociation.

(a) Upon a member's dissociation;

(1) in an at-will company, the company must cause the dissociated member's distributional interest to be purchased under [Article] 7; and

(2) in a term company:

(i) if the company dissolves and winds up its business on or before the expiration of its specified term, [Article] 8 applies to determine the dissociated member's rights to distributions; and

(ii) if the company does not dissolve and wind up its business on or before the expiration of its specified term, the company must cause the dissociated member's distributional interest to be purchased under [Article] 7 on the date of the expiration of the term specified at the time of the member's dissociation.

(b) Upon a member's dissociation from a limited liability company:

(1) the member's right to participate in the management and conduct of the company's business terminates, except as otherwise provided in Section 803, and the member ceases to be a member and is treated the same as a transferee of a member;

(2) the member's duty of loyalty under Section 409(b)(3) terminates; and

(3) the member's duty of loyalty under Section 409(b)(1) and (2) and duty of care under Section 409(c) continue only with regard to matters arising and events occurring before the member's dissociation, unless the member participates in winding up the company's business pursuant to Section 803.

Comment:

Dissociation from an at-will company that does not dissolve the company causes the dissociated member's distributional interest to be immediately purchased under Article 7. See Comments to Sections 602 and 603. Dissociation from a term company that does not dissolve the company does not cause the dissociated member's distributional interest to be purchased under Article 7 until the expiration of the specified term that existed on the date of dissociation.

Subsection (b)(1) provides that a dissociated member forfeits the right to participate in the future conduct of the company's business. Dissociation does not however forfeit that member's right to enforce the Article 7 rights that accrue by reason of the dissociation. Similarly, where dissociation occurs by death, the decedent member's successors in interest may enforce that member's Article 7 rights. See and compare Comments to Section 503(e).

Dissociation terminates the member's right to participate in management, including the member's actual authority to act for the company under Section 301, and begins the two-year period after which a member's apparent authority conclusively ends. See Comments to Section 703. Dissociation also terminates a member's continuing duties of loyalty and care, except with regard to continuing transactions, to the company and other members unless the member participates in winding up the company's business. See Comments to Section 409.

[ARTICLE] 7

MEMBER'S DISSOCIATION WHEN BUSINESS NOT WOUND UP

Section 701. Company Purchase of Distributional Interest.

(a) A limited liability company shall purchase a distributional interest of a:

(1) member of an at-will company for its fair value determined as of the date of the member's dissociation if the member's dissociation does not result in a dissolution and winding up of the company's business under Section 801; or

(2) member of a term company for its fair value determined as of the date of the expiration of the specified term that existed on the

date of the member's dissociation if the expiration of the specified term does not result in a dissolution and winding up of the company's business under Section 801.

(b) A limited liability company must deliver a purchase offer to the dissociated member whose distributional interest is entitled to be purchased not later than 30 days after the date determined under subsection (a). The purchase offer must be accompanied by:

(1) a statement of the company's assets and liabilities as of the date determined under subsection (a);

(2) the latest available balance sheet and income statement, if any; and

(3) an explanation of how the estimated amount of the payment was calculated.

(c) If the price and other terms of a purchase of a distributional interest are fixed or are to be determined by the operating agreement, the price and terms so fixed or determined govern the purchase unless the purchaser defaults. If a default occurs, the dissociated member is entitled to commence a proceeding to have the company dissolved under Section 801(4)(iv).

(d) If an agreement to purchase the distributional interest is not made within 120 days after the date determined under subsection (a), the dissociated member, within another 120 days, may commence a proceeding against the limited liability company to enforce the purchase. The company at its expense shall notify in writing all of the remaining members, and any other person the court directs, of the commencement of the proceeding. The jurisdiction of the court in which the proceeding is commenced under this subsection is plenary and exclusive.

(e) The court shall determine the fair value of the distributional interest in accordance with the standards set forth in Section 702 together with the terms for the purchase. Upon making these determinations, the court shall order the limited liability company to purchase or cause the purchase of the interest.

(f) Damages for wrongful dissociation under Section 602(b), and all other amounts owing, whether or not currently due, from the dissociated member to a limited liability company, must be offset against the purchase price.

Comment:

This section sets forth default rules regarding an otherwise mandatory company purchase of a distributional interest. Even though a dissociated member's rights to participate in the future management of the company are equivalent to those of a transferee of a member, the dissociation does not forfeit that member's right to enforce the Article 7 purchase right. Similarly, if the dissociation occurs by reason of death, the decedent member's successors in interest may enforce the Article 7 rights. See Comments to Sections 503(e) and 603(b)(1).

An at-will company must purchase a dissociated member's distributional interest under subsection (a)(1) when that member's dissociation does not result in a dissolution of the company. The purchase price is equal to the fair value of the interest determined as of the date of dissociation. Any damages for wrongful dissociation must be offset against the purchase price.

Dissociation from a term company does not require an immediate purchase of the member's interest but certain types of dissociation may cause the dissolution of the company. See Section 801(b)(3). A term company must only purchase the dissociated member's distributional interest under subsection (a)(2) on the expiration of the specified term that existed on the date of the member's dissociation. The purchase price is equal to the fair value of the interest determined as of the date of the expiration of that specified term. Any damages for wrongful dissociation must be offset against the purchase price.

The valuation dates differ between subsections (a)(1) and (a)(2) purchases. The former is valued on the date of member dissociation whereas the latter is valued on the date of the expiration of the specified term that existed on the date of dissociation. A subsection (a)(2) dissociated member therefore assumes the risk of loss between the date of dissociation and the expiration of the then stated specified term. See Comments to Section 801 (dissociated member may file application to dissolve company under Section 801(b)(6)).

The default valuation standard is fair value. See Comments to Section 702. An operating agreement may fix a method or formula for determining the purchase price and the terms of payment. The purchase right may be modified. For example, an operating agreement may eliminate a member's power to withdraw from an at-will company which narrows the dissociation events contemplated under subsection (a)(1). See Comments to Section 602(a). However, a provision in an operating agreement providing for complete forfeiture of the purchase right may be unenforceable where the power to dissociate has not also been eliminated. See Section 104(a).

The company must deliver a purchase offer to the dissociated member within 30 days after the date determined under subsection (a). The offer must be accompanied by information designed to enable the dissociated member to evaluate the fairness of the offer. The subsection (b)(3) explanation of how the offer price was calculated need not be elaborate. For example, a mere statement of the basis of the calculation, such as "book value," may be sufficient.

The company and the dissociated member must reach an agreement on the purchase price and terms within 120 days after the date determined under subsection (a). Otherwise, the dissociated member may file suit within another 120 days to enforce the purchase under subsection (d). The court will then determine the fair value and terms of purchase under subsection (e). See Section 702. The member's lawsuit is not available under subsection (c) if the parties have previously agreed to price and terms in an operating agreement.

Section 702. Court Action to Determine Fair Value of Distributional Interest.

(a) In an action brought to determine the fair value of a distributional interest in a limited liability company, the court shall:

(1) determine the fair value of the interest, considering among other relevant evidence the going concern value of the company, any agreement among some or all of the members fixing the price or specifying a formula for determining value of distributional interests for any other purpose, the recommendations of any appraiser appointed by the court, and any legal constraints on the company's ability to purchase the interest;

(2) specify the terms of the purchase, including, if appropriate, terms for installment payments, subordination of the purchase obligation to the rights of the company's other creditors, security for a deferred purchase price, and a covenant not to compete or other restriction on a dissociated member; and

(3) require the dissociated member to deliver an assignment of the interest to the purchaser upon receipt of the purchase price or the first installment of the purchase price.

(b) After the dissociated member delivers the assignment, the dissociated member has no further claim against the company, its members, officers, or managers, if any, other than a claim to any unpaid balance of the purchase price and a claim under any agreement with the company or the remaining members that is not terminated by the court.

(c) If the purchase is not completed in accordance with the specified terms, the company is to be dissolved upon application under Section 801(b)(5)(iv). If a limited liability company is so dissolved, the dissociated member has the same rights and priorities in the company's assets as if the sale had not been ordered.

(d) If the court finds that a party to the proceeding acted arbitrarily, vexatiously, or not in good faith, it may award one or more other parties their reasonable expenses, including attorney's fees and the expenses of appraisers or other experts, incurred in the proceeding. The finding may be based on the company's failure to make an offer to pay or to comply with Section 701(b).

(e) Interest must be paid on the amount awarded from the date determined under Section 701(a) to the date of payment.

Comment:

The default valuation standard is fair value. Under this broad standard, a court is free to determine the fair value of a distributional interest on a fair market, liquidation, or any other method deemed appropriate under the circumstances. A fair market value standard is not used because it is too narrow, often inappropriate, and assumes a fact not contemplated by this section—a willing buyer and a willing seller.

The court has discretion under subsection (a)(2) to include in its order any conditions the court deems necessary to safeguard the interests of the company and the dissociated member or transferee. The discretion may be based on the financial and other needs of the parties.

If the purchase is not consummated or the purchaser defaults, the dissociated member or transferee may make application for dissolution of the company under subsection (c). The court may deny the petition for good cause but the proceeding affords the company an opportunity to be heard on the matter and avoid dissolution. See Comments to Section 801(b)(5).

The power of the court to award all costs and attorney's fees incurred in the suit under subsection (d) is an incentive for both parties to act in good faith. See Section 701(c).

Section 703. Dissociated Member's Power to Bind Limited Liability Company.

For two years after a member dissociates without the dissociation resulting in a dissolution and winding up of a limited liability company's business, the company, including a surviving company under [Article] 9, is bound by an act of the dissociated member which would have bound the company under Section 301 before dissociation only if at the time of entering into the transaction the other party:

(1) reasonably believed that the dissociated member was then a member;

(2) did not have notice of the member's dissociation; and

(3) is not deemed to have had notice under Section 704.

Comment:

A dissociated member of a member-managed company does not have actual authority to act for the company. See Section 603(b)(1). Under Section 301(a), a dissociated member of a member-managed company has apparent authority to bind the company in ordinary course transactions except as to persons who knew or had notice of the dissociation. This section modifies that rule by requiring the person to show reasonable reliance on the member's status as a member provided a Section 704 statement has not been filed within the previous 90 days. See also Section 804 (power to bind after dissolution).

Section 704. Statement of Dissociation.

(a) A dissociated member or a limited liability company may file in the office of the [Secretary of State] a statement of dissociation stating the name of the company and that the member is dissociated from the company.

(b) For the purposes of Sections 301 and 703, a person not a member is deemed to have notice of the dissociation 90 days after the statement of dissociation is filed.

[ARTICLE] 8

WINDING UP COMPANY'S BUSINESS

Section 801. Events Causing Dissolution and Winding Up of Company's Business.

A limited liability company is dissolved, and its business must be wound up, upon the occurrence of any of the following events:

(1) an event specified in the operating agreement;

(2) consent of the number or percentage of members specified in the operating agreement;

(3) an event that makes it unlawful for all or substantially all of the business of the company to be continued, but any cure of

illegality within 90 days after notice to the company of the event is effective retroactively to the date of the event for purposes of this section;

(4) on application by a member or a dissociated member, upon entry of a judicial decree that:

(i) the economic purpose of the company is likely to be unreasonably frustrated;

(ii) another member has engaged in conduct relating to the company's business that makes it not reasonably practicable to carry on the company's business with that member;

(iii) it is not otherwise reasonably practicable to carry on the company's business in conformity with the articles of organization and the operating agreement;

(iv) the company failed to purchase the petitioner's distributional interest as required by Section 701; or

(v) the managers or members in control of the company have acted, are acting, or will act in a manner that is illegal, oppressive, fraudulent, or unfairly prejudicial to the petitioner; or

(5) on application by a transferee of a member's interest, a judicial determination that it is equitable to wind up the company's business:

(i) after the expiration of the specified term, if the company was for a specified term at the time the applicant became a transferee by member dissociation, transfer, or entry of a charging order that gave rise to the transfer; or

(ii) at any time, if the company was at will at the time the applicant became a transferee by member dissociation, transfer, or entry of a charging order that gave rise to the transfer.

Section 802. Limited Liability Company Continues After Dissolution.

(a) Subject to subsection (b), a limited liability company continues after dissolution only for the purpose of winding up its business.

(b) At any time after the dissolution of a limited liability company and before the winding up of its business is completed, the members, including a dissociated member whose dissociation caused the dissolution, may unanimously waive the right to have the company's business wound up and the company terminated. In that case:

(1) the limited liability company resumes carrying on its business as if dissolution had never occurred and any liability incurred by the company or a member after the dissolution and before the waiver is determined as if the dissolution had never occurred; and

(2) the rights of a third party accruing under Section 804(a) or arising out of conduct in reliance on the dissolution before the third party knew or received a notification of the waiver are not adversely affected.

Comment:

The liability shield continues in effect for the winding up period because the legal existence of the company continues under subsection (a). The company is terminated on the filing of articles of termination. See Section 805.

Section 803. Right to Wind Up Limited Liability Company's Business.

(a) After dissolution, a member who has not wrongfully dissociated may participate in winding up a limited liability company's business, but on application of any member, member's legal representative, or transferee, the [designate the appropriate court], for good cause shown, may order judicial supervision of the winding up.

(b) A legal representative of the last surviving member may wind up a limited liability company's business.

(c) A person winding up a limited liability company's business may preserve the company's business or property as a going concern for a reasonable time, prosecute and defend actions and proceedings, whether civil, criminal, or administrative, settle and close the company's business, dispose of and transfer the company's property, discharge the company's liabilities, distribute the assets of the company pursuant to Section 806, settle disputes by mediation or arbitration, and perform other necessary acts.

Section 804. Member's or Manager's Power and Liability as Agent After Dissolution.

(a) A limited liability company is bound by a member's or manager's act after dissolution that:

(1) is appropriate for winding up the company's business; or

(2) would have bound the company under Section 301 before dissolution, if the other party to the transaction did not have notice of the dissolution.

(b) A member or manager who, with knowledge of the dissolution, subjects a limited liability company to liability by an act that is not appropriate for winding up the company's business is liable to the company for any damage caused to the company arising from the liability.

Comment:

After dissolution, members and managers continue to have the authority to bind the company that they had prior to dissolution provided that the third party did not have notice of the dissolution. See Section 102(b) (notice defined). Otherwise, they have only the authority appropriate for winding up the company's business. See Section 703 (agency power of member after dissociation).

Section 805.   Articles of Termination.

(a) At any time after dissolution and winding up, a limited liability company may terminate its existence by filing with the [Secretary of State] articles of termination stating:

(1) the name of the company;

(2) the date of the dissolution; and

(3) that the company's business has been wound up and the legal existence of the company has been terminated.

(b) The existence of a limited liability company is terminated upon the filing of the articles of termination, or upon a later effective date, if specified in the articles of termination.

Comment:

The termination of legal existence also terminates the company's liability shield. See Comments to Section 802 (liability shield continues in effect during winding up). It also ends the company's responsibility to file an annual report. See Section 211.

Section 806.   Distribution of Assets in Winding Up Limited Liability Company's Business.

(a) In winding up a limited liability company's business, the assets of the company must be applied to discharge its obligations to creditors, including members who are creditors. Any surplus must be applied to pay in money the net amount distributable to members in accordance with their right to distributions under subsection (b).

(b) Each member is entitled to a distribution upon the winding up of the limited liability company's business consisting of a return of all contributions which have not previously been returned and a distribution of any remainder in equal shares.

Section 807.   Known Claims Against Dissolved Limited Liability Company.

(a) A dissolved limited liability company may dispose of the known claims against it by following the procedure described in this section.

(b) A dissolved limited liability company shall notify its known claimants in writing of the dissolution. The notice must:

(1) specify the information required to be included in a claim;

(2) provide a mailing address where the claim is to be sent;

(3) state the deadline for receipt of the claim, which may not be less than 120 days after the date the written notice is received by the claimant; and

(4) state that the claim will be barred if not received by the deadline.

(c) A claim against a dissolved limited liability company is barred if the requirements of subsection (b) are met, and:

(1) the claim is not received by the specified deadline; or

(2) in the case of a claim that is timely received but rejected by the dissolved company, the claimant does not commence a proceeding to enforce the claim within 90 days after the receipt of the notice of the rejection.

(d) For purposes of this section, "claim" does not include a contingent liability or a claim based on an event occurring after the effective date of dissolution.

Comment:

A known claim will be barred when the company provides written notice to a claimant that a claim must be filed with the company no later than at least 120 days after receipt of the written notice and the claimant fails to file the claim. If the claim is timely received but is rejected by the company, the claim is nevertheless barred unless the claimant files suit to enforce the claim within 90 days after the receipt of the notice of rejection. A claim described in subsection (d) is not a "known" claim and is governed by Section 808. This section does not extend any other applicable statutes of limitation. See Section 104. Depending on the management of the company, members or managers must discharge or make provision for discharging all of the company's known liabilities before distributing the remaining assets to the members. See Sections 806(a), 406, and 407.

Section 808. Other Claims Against Dissolved Limited Liability Company.

(a) A dissolved limited liability company may publish notice of its dissolution and request persons having claims against the company to present them in accordance with the notice.

(b) The notice must:

(1) be published at least once in a newspaper of general circulation in the [county] in which the dissolved limited liability compa-

ny's principal office is located or, if none in this State, in which its designated office is or was last located;

(2) describe the information required to be contained in a claim and provide a mailing address where the claim is to be sent; and

(3) state that a claim against the limited liability company is barred unless a proceeding to enforce the claim is commenced within five years after publication of the notice.

(c) If a dissolved limited liability company publishes a notice in accordance with subsection (b), the claim of each of the following claimants is barred unless the claimant commences a proceeding to enforce the claim against the dissolved company within five years after the publication date of the notice:

(1) a claimant who did not receive written notice under Section 807;

(2) a claimant whose claim was timely sent to the dissolved company but not acted on; and

(3) a claimant whose claim is contingent or based on an event occurring after the effective date of dissolution.

(d) A claim not barred under this section may be enforced:

(1) against the dissolved limited liability company, to the extent of its undistributed assets; or

(2) if the assets have been distributed in liquidation, against a member of the dissolved company to the extent of the member's proportionate share of the claim or the company's assets distributed to the member in liquidation, whichever is less, but a member's total liability for all claims under this section may not exceed the total amount of assets distributed to the member.

Comment:

An unknown claim will be barred when the company publishes notice requesting claimants to file claims with the company and stating that claims will be barred unless the claimant files suit to enforce the claim within five years after the date of publication. The procedure also bars known claims where the claimant either did not receive written notice described in Section 807 or received notice [and] mailed a claim, but the company did not act on the claim.

Depending on the management of the company, members or managers must discharge or make provision for discharging all of the company's known liabilities before distributing the remaining assets to the members. See Comment to Section 807. This section does not contemplate that a company will postpone member distributions until all unknown claims are barred under this section. In appropriate cases, the company may purchase insurance or set aside funds permitting a distribution of the remaining assets. Where winding up distributions have been made to members, subsection (d)(2) authorizes recovery against those members. However, a claimant's recovery against a member is limited to the lesser of the member's proportionate share of the claim or the amount received in the distribution. This section does not extend any other applicable statutes of limitation. See Section 104.

Section 809. Grounds for Administrative Dissolution.

The [Secretary of State] may commence a proceeding to dissolve a limited liability company administratively if the company does not:

> (1) pay any fees, taxes, or penalties imposed by this [Act] or other law within 60 days after they are due; or

> (2) deliver its annual report to the [Secretary of State] within 60 days after it is due.

Comment:

Administrative dissolution is an effective enforcement mechanism for a variety of statutory obligations under this Act and it avoids the more expensive judicial dissolution process. When applicable, administrative dissolution avoids wasteful attempts to compel compliance by a company abandoned by its members.

Section 810. Procedure for and Effect of Administrative Dissolution.

(a) If the [Secretary of State] determines that a ground exists for administratively dissolving a limited liability company, the [Secretary of State] shall enter a record of the determination and serve the company with a copy of the record.

(b) If the company does not correct each ground for dissolution or demonstrate to the reasonable satisfaction of the [Secretary of State] that each ground determined by the [Secretary of State] does not exist within 60 days after service of the notice, the [Secretary of State] shall administratively dissolve the company by signing a certification of the dissolution that recites the ground for dissolution and its effective date. The [Secretary of State] shall file the original of the certificate and serve the company with a copy of the certificate.

(c) A company administratively dissolved continues its existence but may carry on only business necessary to wind up and liquidate its business and affairs under Section 802 and to notify claimants under Sections 807 and 808.

(d) The administrative dissolution of a company does not terminate the authority of its agent for service of process.

Comment:

A company's failure to comply with a ground for administrative dissolution may simply occur because of oversight. Therefore, subsections (a) and (b) set forth a mandatory notice by the filing officer to the company of the ground for dissolution and a 60 day grace period for correcting the ground.

Section 811. Reinstatement Following Administrative Dissolution.

(a) A limited liability company administratively dissolved may apply to the [Secretary of State] for reinstatement within two years after the effective date of dissolution. The application must:

(1) recite the name of the company and the effective date of its administrative dissolution;

(2) state that the ground for dissolution either did not exist or have been eliminated;

(3) state that the company's name satisfies the requirements of Section 105; and

(4) contain a certificate from the [taxing authority] reciting that all taxes owed by the company have been paid.

(b) If the [Secretary of State] determines that the application contains the information required by subsection (a) and that the information is correct, the [Secretary of State] shall cancel the certificate of dissolution and prepare a certificate of reinstatement that recites this determination and the effective date of reinstatement, file the original of the certificate, and serve the company with a copy of the certificate.

(c) When reinstatement is effective, it relates back to and takes effect as of the effective date of the administrative dissolution and the company may resume its business as if the administrative dissolution had never occurred.

Section 812. Appeal From Denial of Reinstatement.

(a) If the [Secretary of State] denies a limited liability company's application for reinstatement following administrative dissolution, the [Secretary of State] shall serve the company with a record that explains the reason or reasons for denial.

(b) The company may appeal the denial of reinstatement to the [name appropriate] court within 30 days after service of the notice of denial is perfected. The company appeals by petitioning the court to set aside the dissolution and attaching to the petition copies of the [Secretary of State's] certificate of dissolution, the company's application for reinstatement, and the [Secretary of State's] notice of denial.

(c) The court may summarily order the [Secretary of State] to reinstate the dissolved company or may take other action the court considers appropriate.

(d) The court's final decision may be appealed as in other civil proceedings.

[ARTICLE] 9

CONVERSIONS AND MERGERS

Section 901. Definitions.

In this [article]:

(1) "Corporation" means a corporation under [the State Corporation Act], a predecessor law, or comparable law of another jurisdiction.

(2) "General partner" means a partner in a partnership and a general partner in a limited partnership.

(3) "Limited partner" means a limited partner in a limited partnership.

(4) "Limited partnership" means a limited partnership created under [the State Limited Partnership Act], a predecessor law, or comparable law of another jurisdiction.

(5) "Partner" includes a general partner and a limited partner.

(6) "Partnership" means a general partnership under [the State Partnership Act], a predecessor law, or comparable law of another jurisdiction.

(7) "Partnership agreement" means an agreement among the partners concerning the partnership or limited partnership.

(8) "Shareholder" means a shareholder in a corporation.

Comment:

Section 907 makes clear that the provisions of Article 9 are not mandatory. Therefore, a partnership or a limited liability company

301

may convert or merge in any other manner provided by law. However, if the requirements of Article 9 are followed, the conversion or merger is legally valid. Article 9 is not restricted to domestic business entities.

Section 902. Conversion of Partnership or Limited Partnership to Limited Liability Company.

(a) A partnership or limited partnership may be converted to a limited liability company pursuant to this section.

(b) The terms and conditions of a conversion of a partnership or limited partnership to a limited liability company must be approved by all of the partners or by a number or percentage of the partners required for conversion in the partnership agreement.

(c) An agreement of conversion must set forth the terms and conditions of the conversion of the interests of partners of a partnership or of a limited partnership, as the case may be, into interests in the converted limited liability company or the cash or other consideration to be paid or delivered as a result of the conversion of the interests of the partners, or a combination thereof.

(d) After a conversion is approved under subsection (b), the partnership or limited partnership shall file articles of organization in the office of the [Secretary of State] which satisfy the requirements of Section 203 and contain:

    (1) a statement that the partnership or limited partnership was converted to a limited liability company from a partnership or limited partnership, as the case may be;

    (2) its former name;

    (3) a statement of the number of votes cast by the partners entitled to vote for and against the conversion and, if the vote is less than unanimous, the number or percentage required to approve the conversion under subsection (b); and

    (4) in the case of a limited partnership, a statement that the certificate of limited partnership is to be canceled as of the date the conversion took effect.

(e) In the case of a limited partnership, the filing of articles of organization under subsection (d) cancels its certificate of limited partnership as of the date the conversion took effect.

(f) A conversion takes effect when the articles of organization are filed in the office of the [Secretary of State] or at any later date specified in the articles of organization.

(g) A general partner who becomes a member of a limited liability company as a result of a conversion remains liable as a partner for an obligation incurred by the partnership or limited partnership before the conversion takes effect.

(h) A general partner's liability for all obligations of the limited liability company incurred after the conversion takes effect is that of a member of the company. A limited partner who becomes a member as a result of a conversion remains liable only to the extent the limited partner was liable for an obligation incurred by the limited partnership before the conversion takes effect.

Comment:

Subsection (b) makes clear that the terms and conditions of the conversion of a general or limited partnership to a limited liability company must be approved by all of the partners unless the partnership agreement specifies otherwise.

Section 903. Effect of Conversion; Entity Unchanged.

(a) A partnership or limited partnership that has been converted pursuant to this [article] is for all purposes the same entity that existed before the conversion.

(b) When a conversion takes effect:

(1) all property owned by the converting partnership or limited partnership vests in the limited liability company;

(2) all debts, liabilities, and other obligations of the converting partnership or limited partnership continue as obligations of the limited liability company;

(3) an action or proceeding pending by or against the converting partnership or limited partnership may be continued as if the conversion had not occurred;

(4) except as prohibited by other law, all of the rights, privileges, immunities, powers, and purposes of the converting partnership or limited partnership vest in the limited liability company; and

(5) except as otherwise provided in the agreement of conversion under Section 902(c), all of the partners of the converting partnership continue as members of the limited liability company.

Comment:

A conversion is not a conveyance or transfer and does not give rise to claims of reverter or impairment of title based on a prohibited conveyance or transfer. Under subsection (b)(1), title to all partnership property, including real estate, vests in the limited liability company as a matter of law without reversion or impairment.

Section 904. Merger of Entities.

(a) Pursuant to a plan of merger approved under subsection (c), a limited liability company may be merged with or into one or more limited liability companies, foreign limited liability companies, corporations, foreign corporations, partnerships, foreign partnerships, limited partnerships, foreign limited partnerships, or other domestic or foreign entities.

(b) A plan of merger must set forth:

(1) the name of each entity that is a party to the merger;

(2) the name of the surviving entity into which the other entities will merge;

(3) the type of organization of the surviving entity;

(4) the terms and conditions of the merger;

(5) the manner and basis for converting the interests of each party to the merger into interests or obligations of the surviving entity, or into money or other property in whole or in part; and

(6) the street address of the surviving entity's principal place of business.

(c) A plan of merger must be approved:

(1) in the case of a limited liability company that is a party to the merger, by all of the members or by a number or percentage of members specified in the operating agreement;

(2) in the case of a foreign limited liability company that is a party to the merger, by the vote required for approval of a merger by the law of the State or foreign jurisdiction in which the foreign limited liability company is organized;

(3) in the case of a partnership or domestic limited partnership that is a party to the merger, by the vote required for approval of a conversion under Section 902(b); and

(4) in the case of any other entities that are parties to the merger, by the vote required for approval of a merger by the law of this State or of the State or foreign jurisdiction in which the entity is organized and, in the absence of such a requirement, by all the owners of interests in the entity.

(d) After a plan of merger is approved and before the merger takes effect, the plan may be amended or abandoned as provided in the plan.

(e) The merger is effective upon the filing of the articles of merger with the [Secretary of State], or at such later date as the articles may provide.

Comment:

This section sets forth a "safe harbor" for cross-entity mergers of limited liability companies with both domestic and foreign: corporations, general and limited partnerships, and other limited liability companies. Subsection (c) makes clear that the terms and conditions of the plan of merger must be approved by all of the partners unless applicable state law specifies otherwise for the merger.

Section 905. Articles of Merger.

(a) After approval of the plan of merger under Section 904(c), unless the merger is abandoned under Section 904(d), articles of merger must be signed on behalf of each limited liability company and other entity that is a party to the merger and delivered to the [Secretary of State] for filing. The articles must set forth:

(1) the name and jurisdiction of formation or organization of each of the limited liability companies and other entities that are parties to the merger;

(2) for each limited liability company that is to merge, the date its articles of organization were filed with the [Secretary of State];

(3) that a plan of merger has been approved and signed by each limited liability company and other entity that is to merge;

(4) the name and address of the surviving limited liability company or other surviving entity;

(5) the effective date of the merger;

(6) if a limited liability company is the surviving entity, such changes in its articles of organization as are necessary by reason of the merger;

(7) if a party to a merger is a foreign limited liability company, the jurisdiction and date of filing of its initial articles of organization and the date when its application for authority was filed by the [Secretary of State] or, if an application has not been filed, a statement to that effect; and

(8) if the surviving entity is not a limited liability company, an agreement that the surviving entity may be served with process in this State and is subject to liability in any action or proceeding for the enforcement of any liability or obligation of any limited liability company previously subject to suit in this State which is to merge, and for the enforcement, as provided in this [Act], of the right of members of any limited liability company to receive payment for their interest against the surviving entity.

(b) If a foreign limited liability company is the surviving entity of a merger, it may not do business in this State until an application for that authority is filed with the [Secretary of State].

(c) The surviving limited liability company or other entity shall furnish a copy of the plan of merger, on request and without cost, to any member of any limited liability company or any person holding an interest in any other entity that is to merge.

(d) Articles of merger operate as an amendment to the limited liability company's articles of organization.

Section 906.   Effect of Merger.

(a) When a merger takes effect:

(1) the separate existence of each limited liability company and other entity that is a party to the merger, other than the surviving entity, terminates;

(2) all property owned by each of the limited liability companies and other entities that are party to the merger vests in the surviving entity;

(3) all debts, liabilities, and other obligations of each limited liability company and other entity that is party to the merger become the obligations of the surviving entity;

(4) an action or proceeding pending by or against a limited liability company or other party to a merger may be continued as if the merger had not occurred or the surviving entity may be substituted as a party to the action or proceeding; and

(5) except as prohibited by other law, all the rights, privileges, immunities, powers, and purposes of every limited liability company and other entity that is a party to a merger vest in the surviving entity.

(b) The [Secretary of State] is an agent for service of process in an action or proceeding against the surviving foreign entity to enforce an obligation of any party to a merger if the surviving foreign entity fails to appoint or maintain an agent designated for service of process in this State or the agent for service of process cannot with reasonable diligence be found at the designated office.   Upon receipt of process, the [Secretary of State] shall send a copy of the process by registered or certified mail, return receipt requested, to the surviving entity at the address set forth in the articles of merger.   Service is effected under this subsection at the earliest of:

(1) the date the company receives the process, notice, or demand;

(2) the date shown on the return receipt, if signed on behalf of the company; or

(3) five days after its deposit in the mail, if mailed postpaid and correctly addressed.

(c) A member of the surviving limited liability company is liable for all obligations of a party to the merger for which the member was personally liable before the merger.

(d) Unless otherwise agreed, a merger of a limited liability company that is not the surviving entity in the merger does not require the limited liability company to wind up its business under this [Act] or pay its liabilities and distribute its assets pursuant to this [Act].

(e) Articles of merger serve as articles of dissolution for a limited liability company that is not the surviving entity in the merger.

Section 907.   [Article] Not Exclusive.

This [article] does not preclude an entity from being converted or merged under other law.

[ARTICLE] 10

FOREIGN LIMITED LIABILITY COMPANIES

Section 1001.   Law Governing Foreign Limited Liability Companies.

(a) The laws of the State or other jurisdiction under which a foreign limited liability company is organized govern its organization and internal affairs and the liability of its managers, members, and their transferees.

(b) A foreign limited liability company may not be denied a certificate of authority by reason of any difference between the laws of another jurisdiction under which the foreign company is organized and the laws of this State.

(c) A certificate of authority does not authorize a foreign limited liability company to engage in any business or exercise any power that a limited liability company may not engage in or exercise in this State.

Comment:

The law where a foreign limited liability company is organized, rather than this Act, governs that company's internal affairs and the liability of its owners. Accordingly, any difference between the laws of the foreign jurisdiction and this Act will not constitute grounds for denial of a certificate of authority to transact business in this State. However, a foreign limited liability company transacting business in this State by virtue of a certificate of authority is limited to the business and powers that a limited liability company may lawfully pursue and exercise under Section 112.

Section 1002.   Application for Certificate of Authority.

(a) A foreign limited liability company may apply for a certificate of authority to transact business in this State by delivering an application to the [Secretary of State] for filing. The application must set forth:

(1) the name of the foreign company or, if its name is unavailable for use in this State, a name that satisfies the requirements of Section 1005;

(2) the name of the State or country under whose law it is organized;

(3) the street address of its principal office;

(4) the address of its initial designated office in this State;

(5) the name and street address of its initial agent for service of process in this State;

(6) whether the duration of the company is for a specified term and, if so, the period specified;

(7) whether the company is manager-managed, and, if so, the name and address of each initial manager; and

(8) whether the members of the company are to be liable for its debts and obligations under a provision similar to Section 303(c).

(b) A foreign limited liability company shall deliver with the completed application a certificate of existence or a record of similar import authenticated by the secretary of state or other official having custody of company records in the State or country under whose law it is organized.

Comment:

As with articles of organization, the application must be signed and filed with the filing office. See Sections 105, 107 (name registration), 205, 206, 209 (liability for false statements), and 1005.

Section 1003.   Activities Not Constituting Transacting Business.

(a) Activities of a foreign limited liability company that do not constitute transacting business in this State within the meaning of this [article] include:

(1) maintaining, defending, or settling an action or proceeding;

(2) holding meetings of its members or managers or carrying on any other activity concerning its internal affairs;

(3) maintaining bank accounts;

(4) maintaining offices or agencies for the transfer, exchange, and registration of the foreign company's own securities or maintaining trustees or depositories with respect to those securities;

(5) selling through independent contractors;

(6) soliciting or obtaining orders, whether by mail or through employees or agents or otherwise, if the orders require acceptance outside this State before they become contracts;

(7) creating or acquiring indebtedness, mortgages, or security interests in real or personal property;

(8) securing or collecting debts or enforcing mortgages or other security interests in property securing the debts, and holding, protecting, and maintaining property so acquired;

(9) conducting an isolated transaction that is completed within 30 days and is not one in the course of similar transactions of a like manner; and

(10) transacting business in interstate commerce.

(b) For purposes of this [article], the ownership in this State of income-producing real property or tangible personal property, other than property excluded under subsection (a), constitutes transacting business in this State.

(c) This section does not apply in determining the contacts or activities that may subject a foreign limited liability company to service of process, taxation, or regulation under any other law of this State.

Section 1004. Issuance of Certificate of Authority.

Unless the [Secretary of State] determines that an application for a certificate of authority fails to comply as to form with the filing requirements of this [Act], the [Secretary of State], upon payment of all filing fees, shall file the application and send a receipt for it and the fees to the limited liability company or its representative.

Section 1005. Name of Foreign Limited Liability Company.

(a) If the name of a foreign limited liability company does not satisfy the requirements of Section 105, the company, to obtain or maintain a certificate of authority to transact business in this State, must use a fictitious name to transact business in this State if its real name is unavailable and it delivers to the [Secretary of State] for filing a copy of the resolution of its managers, in the case of a manager-managed company, or of its members, in the case of a member-managed company, adopting the fictitious name.

(b) Except as authorized by subsections (c) and (d), the name, including a fictitious name to be used to transact business in this State, of a foreign limited liability company must be distinguishable upon the records of the [Secretary of State] from:

(1) the name of any corporation, limited partnership, or company incorporated, organized, or authorized to transact business in this State;

(2) a name reserved or registered under Section 106 or 107; and

(3) the fictitious name of another foreign limited liability company authorized to transact business in this State.

(c) A foreign limited liability company may apply to the [Secretary of State] for authority to use in this State a name that is not distinguishable upon the records of the [Secretary of State] from a name described in subsection (b). The [Secretary of State] shall authorize use of the name applied for if:

(1) the present user, registrant, or owner of a reserved name consents to the use in a record and submits an undertaking in form satisfactory to the [Secretary of State] to change its name to a name that is distinguishable upon the records of the [Secretary of State] from the name of the foreign applying limited liability company; or

(2) the applicant delivers to the [Secretary of State] a certified copy of a final judgment of a court establishing the applicant's right to use the name applied for in this State.

(d) A foreign limited liability company may use in this State the name, including the fictitious name, of another domestic or foreign entity that is used in this State if the other entity is incorporated, organized, or authorized to transact business in this State and the foreign limited liability company:

(1) has merged with the other entity;

(2) has been formed by reorganization of the other entity; or

(3) has acquired all or substantially all of the assets, including the name, of the other entity.

(e) If a foreign limited liability company authorized to transact business in this State changes its name to one that does not satisfy the requirements of Section 105, it may not transact business in this State under the name as changed until it adopts a name satisfying the requirements of Section 105 and obtains an amended certificate of authority.

Section 1006.   Revocation of Certificate of Authority.

(a) A certificate of authority of a foreign limited liability company to transact business in this State may be revoked by the [Secretary of State] in the manner provided in subsection (b) if:

(1) the company fails to:

(i) pay any fees, taxes, and penalties owed to this State;

(ii) deliver its annual report required under Section 211 to the [Secretary of State] within 60 days after it is due;

(iii) appoint and maintain an agent for service of process as required by this [article]; or

(iv) file a statement of a change in the name or business address of the agent as required by this [article]; or

(2) a misrepresentation has been made of any material matter in any application, report, affidavit, or other record submitted by the company pursuant to this [article].

(b) The [Secretary of State] may not revoke a certificate of authority of a foreign limited liability company unless the [Secretary of State] sends the company notice of the revocation, at least 60 days before its effective date, by a record addressed to its agent for service of process in this State, or if the company fails to appoint and maintain a proper agent in this State, addressed to the office required to be maintained by Section 108. The notice must specify the cause for the revocation of the certificate of authority. The authority of the company to transact business in this State ceases on the effective date of the revocation unless the foreign limited liability company cures the failure before that date.

Section 1007. Cancellation of Authority.

A foreign limited liability company may cancel its authority to transact business in this State by filing in the office of the [Secretary of State] a certificate of cancellation. Cancellation does not terminate the authority of the [Secretary of State] to accept service of process on the company for [claims for relief] arising out of the transactions of business in this State.

Section 1008. Effect of Failure to Obtain Certificate of Authority.

(a) A foreign limited liability company transacting business in this State may not maintain an action or proceeding in this State unless it has a certificate of authority to transact business in this State.

(b) The failure of a foreign limited liability company to have a certificate of authority to transact business in this State does not impair the validity of a contract or act of the company or prevent the foreign limited liability company from defending an action or proceeding in this State.

(c) Limitations on personal liability of managers, members, and their transferees are not waived solely by transacting business in this State without a certificate of authority.

311

(d) If a foreign limited liability company transacts business in this State without a certificate of authority, it appoints the [Secretary of State] as its agent for service of process for [claims for relief] arising out of the transaction of business in this State.

Section 1009.   Action by [Attorney General].

The [Attorney General] may maintain an action to restrain a foreign limited liability company from transacting business in this State in violation of this [article].

[ARTICLE] 11

DERIVATIVE ACTIONS

Sec.
1101.   Right of Action.
1102.   Proper Plaintiff.
1103.   Pleading.
1104.   Expenses.

Section 1101.   Right of Action.

A member of a limited liability company may maintain an action in the right of the company if the members or managers having authority to do so have refused to commence the action or an effort to cause those members or managers to commence the action is not likely to succeed.

Comment:

A member may bring an action on behalf of the company when the members or managers having the authority to pursue the company recovery refuse to do so or an effort to cause them to pursue the recovery is not likely to succeed. See Comments to Section 411(a) (personal action of member against company or another member).

Section 1102.   Proper Plaintiff.

In a derivative action for a limited liability company, the plaintiff must be a member of the company when the action is commenced; and:

(1) must have been a member at the time of the transaction of which the plaintiff complains; or

(2) the plaintiff's status as a member must have devolved upon the plaintiff by operation of law or pursuant to the terms of the operating agreement from a person who was a member at the time of the transaction.

Section 1103. Pleading.

In a derivative action for a limited liability company, the complaint must set forth with particularity the effort of the plaintiff to secure initiation of the action by a member or manager or the reasons for not making the effort.

Comment:

There is no obligation of the company or its members or managers to respond to a member demand to bring an action to pursue a company recovery. However, if a company later decides to commence the demanded action or assume control of the derivative litigation, the member's right to commence or control the proceeding ordinarily ends.

Section 1104. Expenses.

If a derivative action for a limited liability company is successful, in whole or in part, or if anything is received by the plaintiff as a result of a judgment, compromise, or settlement of an action or claim, the court may award the plaintiff reasonable expenses, including reasonable attorney's fees, and shall direct the plaintiff to remit to the limited liability company the remainder of the proceeds received.

[ARTICLE] 12

MISCELLANEOUS PROVISIONS

Sec.

Section 1201.   Uniformity of Application and Construction.

This [Act] shall be applied and construed to effectuate its general purpose to make uniform the law with respect to the subject of this [Act] among States enacting it.

Section 1202.   Short Title.

This [Act] may be cited as the Uniform Limited Liability Company Act (1995).

Section 1203.   Severability Clause.

If any provision of this [Act] or its application to any person or circumstance is held invalid, the invalidity does not affect other provisions or applications of this [Act] which can be given effect without the invalid provision or application, and to this end the provisions of this [Act] are severable ...

Section 1204.　Effective Date.

This [Act] takes effect [_____].

FORM OF LIMITED LIABILITY COMPANY OPERATING AGREEMENT

BY

ROBERT R. KEATINGE

Operating Agreement † of _____ Limited Liability Company [1]

(Member–Manager Managed) [2]

ARTICLE I. FORMATION

ARTICLE II. DEFINITIONS

† © Copyright 1995, Robert R. Keatinge, all rights reserved. This Operating Agreement is for discussion only and is not intended for use without thorough review by a competent professional.

1. The name must include the words required by the appropriate statute such as "limited liability company," "limited company," "L.L.C.," or "L.C.," See § **4.11** (all references are to the **Ribstein and Keat-** **inge on Limited Liability Companies** (Shepard's/McGraw–Hill, Inc. 1992)).

2. This operating agreement is designed for a limited liability company that has elected to be managed by managers (a "manager-managed LLC"). Note that the decision of whether to be member-managed or manager-managed will have several tax consequences, both in classification and operation....

ARTICLE III.   NATURE OF BUSINESS

ARTICLE IV.   ACCOUNTING AND RECORDS

ARTICLE V.   NAMES AND ADDRESSES OF MEMBERS AND MEMBER–MANAGERS

ARTICLE VI.   RIGHTS AND DUTIES OF MEMBERS

ARTICLE VII.   MANAGERS

ARTICLE VIII.   CONTRIBUTIONS AND CAPITAL ACCOUNTS

ARTICLE IX.   ALLOCATIONS AND DISTRIBUTIONS

ARTICLE X.   TAXES

This Operating Agreement of _____ Limited Liability Company, a limited liability company organized pursuant to the Act, is entered into and shall be effective as of the Effective Date, by and among the Company and the persons executing this Agreement as Members.

ARTICLE I.

FORMATION

1. **Organization**—The Members hereby organize the Company as a State limited liability company pursuant to the provisions of the Act.

2. **Agreement, Effect of Inconsistencies With Act**—For and in consideration of the mutual covenants herein contained and for other good and valuable consideration, the receipt and sufficiency of which is

hereby acknowledged, the Members executing this Company Agreement hereby agree to the terms and conditions of this Company Agreement, as it may from time to time be amended according to its terms. It is the express intention of the Members that this Company Agreement shall be the sole source of agreement of the parties, and, except to the extent a provision of this Company Agreement expressly incorporates federal income tax rules by reference to sections of the Code or Regulations or is expressly prohibited or ineffective under the Act, this Company Agreement shall govern, even when inconsistent with, or different than, the provisions of the Act or any other law or rule.[5] To the extent any provision of this Company Agreement is prohibited or ineffective under the Act, this Company Agreement shall be considered amended to the smallest degree possible in order to make the agreement effective under the Act. In the event the Act is subsequently amended or interpreted in such a way to make any provision of this Company Agreement that was formerly invalid valid, such provision shall be considered to be valid from the effective date of such interpretation or amendment. The Members hereby agree that each Member shall be entitled to rely on the provisions of this Company Agreement, and no Member shall be liable to the Company or to any Member for any action or refusal to act taken in good faith reliance on the terms of this Company Agreement. The Members and the Company hereby agree that the duties and obligations imposed on the Members of the Company as such shall be those set forth in this Company Agreement, which is intended to govern the relationship among the Company, the Members, notwithstanding any provision of the Act or common law to the contrary.

3. **Name**—The name of the Company is _____ Limited Liability Company, and all business of the Company shall be conducted under that name or under any other name, but in any case, only to the extent permitted by applicable law.

4. **Effective Date**—This Company Agreement shall become effective upon the filing of the Articles with the Secretary of State of the State.[9]

5. **Term**—The Company shall be dissolved and its affairs wound up in accordance with the Act and this Company Agreement on _____,

5. Several statutes make clear that the statute merely provides default provisions that may be modified by the agreement....

9. Because filing may [be] necessary for recognition of the limited liability aspects of the entity ..., it is prudent to delay the Effective Date until the effective date of filing or a later date if specified in the articles of organization. Under the statutes that require at least two members, it is essential that there be at least two members at the time of filing .... By analogy to the limited partnership, if the agreement is effective prior to, or in the absence of filing, a general partnership may result. Security Equities v. Giamba, 210 Conn. 71, 553 A.2d 1135 (1989). Under some statutes, the articles are not effectively "filed" until they are accepted by the secretary of state. If this is the case, the term "acceptance of the Articles by" should be substituted for "filing of the Articles with."

20__,[10] unless the term shall be extended by amendment to this Company Agreement and the Articles, or unless the Company shall be sooner dissolved and its affairs wound up in accordance with the Act or this Company Agreement.

6. **Registered Agent and Office**—The registered agent for the service of process and the registered office shall be that Person and location reflected in the Articles as filed in the office of the Secretary of State. The Member–Managers, may, from time to time, change the registered agent or office through appropriate filings with the Secretary of State. In the event the registered agent ceases to act as such for any reason or the registered office shall change, the Member–Managers shall promptly designate a replacement registered agent or file a notice of change of address as the case may be. If the Member–Managers shall fail to designate a replacement registered agent or change of address of the registered office, any Member may designate a replacement registered agent or file a notice of change of address.[12]

7. **Principal Office**—The Principal Office of the Company shall be located at _____

_____.

ARTICLE II.

DEFINITIONS

For purposes of this operating agreement, unless the context clearly indicates otherwise, the following terms shall have the following meanings:

1. **Act**—The State Limited Liability Company Act and all amendments to the Act.

2. **Additional Member**—A Member other than an Initial Member or a Substitute Member who has acquired a Membership Interest from the Company.

3. **Admission Agreement**—The Agreement between an Additional Member and the Company described in Article XIII.

10. Some statutes provide that an LLC may be perpetual; others require that some term be set forth, but allow the members to select any term they desire; while still others provide for a thirty year maximum term. ... In an LLC organized under a statute that limits the term to thirty years, it is questionable whether an extension of the term beyond thirty years by amendment to the articles of organization would be effective. As the articles of organization are evolving into a disclosure document rather than a substantive agreement, it may be appropriate to set forth the term in the operating agreement, which is the actual agreement of the members, even though the term will also have to be reflected in the articles of organization....

12. The failure to maintain a registered agent at a designated registered office may not only cause delay in the receipt of notice, but may even rise to the level of failure to observe "corporate" formalities, thereby supporting a piercing the "corporate" veil argument, cause an administrative dissolution. Therefore, it should be as easy as possible for any member-manager or other member to file a designation or change....

4. **Articles**—The Articles of Organization of the Company as properly adopted and amended from time to time by the Members and filed with the Secretary of State.[13]

5. **Assignee**—A Person to whom a Membership Interest has been transferred who has not been admitted as a Substituted Member.

6. **Bankrupt Member**—A Member who: (1) has become the subject of an Order for Relief under the United States Bankruptcy Code, (2) has initiated, either in an original Proceeding or by way of answer in any state insolvency or receivership proceeding, an action for liquidation arrangement, composition, readjustment, dissolution, or similar relief.

7. **Book Adjustments**—Adjustments with respect to the Book Value of Partnership Property for depreciation, depletion, amortization, and gain or loss, as computed in accordance with section 1.704–1(b)(2)(iv)(g) of the Regulations.

8. **Book Value**—With respect to Property Contributed to the Company, the fair market value of the Property at the time of Contribution as adjusted by Book Adjustments.

9. **Business Day**—Any day other than Saturday, Sunday or any legal holiday observed in the State.

10. **Capital Account**—The account maintained for a Member or Assignee determined in accordance with Article VIII.

11. **Code**—The Internal Revenue Code of 1986 as amended from time to time.

12. **Commitment**—The obligation of a Member or Assignee to make a Capital Contribution in the future.

13. **Company**—The _____ Limited Liability Company, a limited liability company formed under the laws of the State, and any successor limited liability company.

14. **Company Agreement**—This operating agreement including all amendments adopted in accordance with this Company Agreement and the Act.[15]

15. **Company Liability**—Any enforceable debt or obligation for which the Company is liable or which is secured by any Company Property.

16. **Company Minimum Gain**—An amount determined by first computing for each Company Nonrecourse Liability any gain the Company would realize if it disposed of the Company Property subject to that liability for no consideration other than full satisfac-

---

13. In some states this document will be known as certificate of formation.

15. ... The term *Company Agreement* (which is similar to *limited liability compa-* *ny agreement,* the term used in the Delaware statute) is used to distinguish it from other types of agreements.

tion of the liability, and then aggregating the separately computed gains. The amount of Company Minimum Gain includes such minimum gain arising from a conversion, refinancing, or other change to a debt instrument, only to the extent a Member is allocated a share of that minimum gain. For any Taxable Year, the net increase or decrease in Company Minimum Gain is determined by comparing the Company Minimum Gain on the last day of the immediately preceding Taxable Year with the Minimum Gain on the last day of the current Taxable Year. Notwithstanding any provision to the contrary contained herein, Company Minimum Gain and increases and decreases in Company Minimum Gain are intended to be computed in accordance with section 704 of the Code [and] the Regulations issued thereunder, as the same may be issued and interpreted from time to time. **A Member's share of Company Minimum Gain** at the end of any Taxable Year equals: the sum of Nonrecourse Deductions allocated to that Member (and to that Member's predecessors in interest) up to that time and the distributions made to that Member (and to that Member's predecessors in interest) up to that time of proceeds of a nonrecourse liability allocable to an increase in Company Minimum Gain minus the sum of that Member's (and of that Member's predecessors in interest) aggregate share of the net decreases in Company Minimum Gain plus their aggregate share of decreases resulting from Revaluations of Company Property subject to one or more Company Nonrecourse Liabilities.

17. **Company Nonrecourse Liability**—A Company Liability to the extent that no Member or Related Person bears the economic risk of loss (as defined in section 1.752–2 of the Regulations) with respect to the liability.

18. **Company Property**—Any Property owned by the Company.

19. **Contributing Members**—Members making Capital Contributions as a result of the failure of a Delinquent Member to perform a Commitment as described in Article VIII.

20. **Contribution**—Any contribution of Property made by or on behalf of a new or existing Member or Assignee as consideration for a Membership Interest.

21. **Default Interest Rate**—The higher of the legal rate or the then-current prime rate quoted by the largest commercial bank in the jurisdiction of the Principal Office plus three percent.

22. **Delinquent Member**—A Member or Assignee who has failed to meet the Commitment of that Member or Assignee.

23. **Distribution**—A transfer of Property to a member on account of a Membership Interest as described in Article IX.

24. **Disposition (Dispose)**—Any sale, assignment, transfer, exchange, mortgage, pledge, grant, hypothecation, or other transfer, absolute or as security or encumbrance (including dispositions by operation of law).

25. **Dissociation**—Any action which causes a Person to cease to be Member as described in Article XII hereof.

26. **Dissociated Member**—A Person who has ceased to be Member as a result of Dissociation in Article XII hereof.

27. **Immediate Family**—A Member's Immediate Family includes the Member's spouse, children (including natural, adopted and stepchildren), grandchildren, and parents.

28. **Initial Contribution**—The Contribution agreed to be made by the Initial Members as described in Article VIII.

29. **Initial Members**—Those persons identified on Exhibit A attached hereto and made a part hereof by this reference who have executed this Company Agreement.

30. **Liquidating Distribution**—A Distribution made as consideration for a Membership Interest.

31. **Majority of the Member–Managers**—A majority by number of all of the Member–Managers.

32. **Majority of the Members**—Members having Sharing Ratios in excess of one-half of the Sharing Ratios of all the Members entitled to vote on, consent to, or approve a particular matter. Assignees shall not be considered Members entitled to vote for the purpose of determining a Majority. In the case of a Member–Manager who has Disposed of that Member's entire Membership Interest to an Assignee, but has not ceased to be a Member as provided below, the Sharing Ratio of such Assignee shall be considered in determining a Majority of the Members and such Member's vote or consent shall be determined by such Sharing Ratio.[19]

33. **Majority of the Remaining Member–Managers**—A majority by number of all the Remaining Member–Managers.

34. **Majority of the Remaining Members**—Remaining Members having Sharing Ratios equal to more than one-half of the Sharing Ratios of all the Remaining Members entitled to vote on, consent to,

---

19. Many of the statutes include a provision that requires a dissolution upon any event that terminates the continued membership of a member in a limited liability company. See § 11.03. As a result, the agreement gives the remaining members the right to remove a member who has assigned all of that member's capital interest in the firm. In order to lack continuity of life, the Remaining Members should be required to vote to continue the LLC after the dissociation of a member (or in this case, a member-manager). Thus, rather than having a dissociation on a member's assignment of that member's entire membership interest, the operating agreement provides that the member will remain as such until removed by an affirmative act (at which time the continuing members will vote to continue the Company).

or approve a particular matter. Assignees shall not be considered Members entitled to vote for the purpose of determining a Majority of Remaining Members. A Member who has Disposed of that Member's entire Membership Interest to an Assignee, but has not been ceased to be a Member as provided below, shall be considered a Member for the purpose of determining a Majority of Remaining Members.

35. **Management Right**—The right of a Member to participate in the management of the Company, including the rights to information and to consent or approve actions of the Company. The rights and authority of a Member–Manager that exceed those of a Member who is not a Member–Manager are not considered Management Rights for purposes of this Company Agreement.[21]

36. **Member–Manager**—A Member selected to manage the affairs of the Company under Article VII hereof. Notwithstanding the foregoing, at any time the Member–Managers do not own at least 21 percent of the total Membership Interests of the Company and 21 percent of the total positive Capital Accounts (taking into account the Membership Interests and Capital Accounts of all Members and Assignees), all Members shall be Member–Managers.[22]

37. **Member**—An Initial Member, Substituted Member or Additional Member, including, unless the context expressly indicates to the contrary, a Member–Manager or Assignee.[23]

38. **Member Minimum Gain**—An amount determined by first computing for each Member Nonrecourse Liability any gain the Company would realize if it disposed of the Company Property subject to that liability for no consideration other than full satisfaction of the liability, and then aggregating the separately computed gains. The amount of Member Minimum Gain includes such minimum gain arising from a conversion, refinancing, or other change to a debt instrument, only to the extent a Member is allocated a share of that minimum gain. For any Taxable Year, the net increase or decrease in Member Minimum Gain is determined by comparing the Member Minimum Gain on the last day of the immediately preceding Taxable Year with the Minimum Gain on the last day of the current Taxable Year. Notwithstanding any provision to the contrary contained herein, Member Minimum Gain and increases and decreases in Member Minimum Gain are intended to be computed in accordance with section 704 of the Code [and] the Regulations

---

21. A Member owns a Membership Interest (economic rights) and a Management Right (rights of a member other than economic rights). A Member–Manager has Management Rights in excess of those of a Member.

22. For the implications of this definition see Section VII.1 below.

23. Because Assignees are entitled to participate in distributions and will be treated as partners....

issued thereunder, as the same may be issued and interpreted from time to time.

39. **Member Nonrecourse Liability**—Any Company Liability to the extent the liability is nonrecourse under state law, and on which a Member or Related Person bears the economic risk of loss under section 1.752–2 of the Regulations because, for example, the Member or Related Person is the creditor or a guarantor.

40. **Membership Interest**—The rights of a Member or, in the case of an Assignee, the rights of the assigning Member in Distributions (liquidating or otherwise) and allocations of the profits, losses, gains, deductions, and credits of the Company.[25]

41. **Money**—Cash or other legal tender of the United States, or any obligation that is immediately reducible to legal tender without delay or discount. Money shall be considered to have a fair market value equal to its face amount.

42. **Net Losses**—The losses and deductions of the Company determined in accordance with accounting principles consistently applied from year to year employed under the method of accounting adopted by the Company and as reported separately or in the aggregate, as appropriate, on the tax return of the Company filed for federal income tax purposes.

43. **Net Profits**—The income and gains of the Company determined in accordance with accounting principles consistently applied from year to year employed under the method of accounting adopted by the Company and as reported separately or in the aggregate, as appropriate, on the tax return of the Company filed for federal income tax purposes. Net Profits includes taxable income, capital gain, and income exempt from taxation.

44. **Nonrecourse Liabilities**—Nonrecourse liabilities include Company Nonrecourse Liabilities and Member Nonrecourse Liabilities.

45. **Notice**—Notice shall be in writing. Notice to the Company shall be considered given when mailed by first class mail postage prepaid addressed to any Member–Manager in care of the Company at the address of Principal Office. Notice . . . to a Member shall be considered given when mailed by first class mail postage prepaid addressed to the Member at the address reflected in this Company

---

25. This definition is intended to encompass the *assignable* portion of a member's interest, that portion of the Member's rights that may be assigned without the consent of the other members under the act. This definition is in contradistinction to the Management Rights which may not be assigned without the consent of the other members. Under this agreement, the membership interest may not be disposed of without the consent of managing members or the other members as a control device. . . .

Agreement unless the Member has given the Company a Notice of a different address.

46. **Organization**—A Person other than a natural person. Organization includes, without limitation, corporations (both non-profit and other corporations), partnerships (both limited and general), joint ventures, limited liability companies, and unincorporated associations, but the term does not include joint tenancies and tenancies by the entirety.

47. **Organization Expenses**—Those expenses incurred in the organization of the Company including the costs of preparation of this Company Agreement and Articles.

48. **Property**—Any property real or personal, tangible or intangible (including goodwill), including Money and any legal or equitable interest in such property, but excluding services and promises to perform services in the future.

49. **Permitted Transferee**—Any member of the Member's Immediate Family, or an Organization controlled by such Member or by members of the Member's Immediate Family.

50. **Person**—An individual, trust, estate, or any incorporated or unincorporated organization permitted to be a member of a limited liability company under the laws of the State.

51. **Proceeding**—Any judicial or administrative trial, hearing or other activity, civil[,] criminal or investigative, the result of which may be that a court, arbitrator, or governmental agency may enter a judgment, order, decree, or other determination which, if not appealed and reversed, would be binding upon the Company, a Member or other Person subject to the jurisdiction of such court, arbitrator, or governmental agency.

52. **Regulations**—Except where the context indicates otherwise, the permanent, temporary, proposed, or proposed and temporary regulations of Department of the Treasury under the Code as such regulations may be lawfully changed from time to time.

53. **Related Person**—A person having a relationship to a Member that is described in section 1.752–4(b) of the Regulations. . . .

54. **Remaining Member–Managers**—In the event of a Member–Manager who has any potential conflict of interest or transaction between a Member–Manager and the Company, the Member–Managers not having the potential conflict of interest [or] participating in the transaction. In the event of the transfer of a Restricted Membership Interest, all of the Member–Managers other than the Member who has transferred the Membership Interest. If the Restricted Membership Interest is not held by a Member–Manager, Remaining Member–Managers means all the Member–Managers.

55. **Remaining Members**—In the event of the Dissociation of a Member–Manager, all of the Members at the time of such Dissociation other than the Member who has dissociated. In the event of a Member–Manager who has any potential conflict of interest or transaction between a Member–Manager and the Company, the Members not having the potential conflict of interest or participating in the transaction.

56. **Removal**—The act of the Remaining Members by which a Member–Manager is Removed as a Member–Manager but continues to be a Member.

57. **Resignation**—The act of a Member–Manager by which such Member ceases to be a Member–Manager but continues to be a Member.

58. **Restricted Membership Interest**—The Membership Interests so designated on Exhibit A. [If at] any time less than 21% of all of the Membership Interests would be Restricted Membership Interests as defined in the previous sentence, then, notwithstanding such previous sentence, all Membership Interests shall be Restricted Membership Interests.[29]

59. **Revaluation**—The adjustment to the Book Value of Partnership Property as provided in section VIII.7 of this Company Agreement.

60. **Revaluation Date**—The date on which a Revaluation Event occurs.

61. **Revaluation Event**—(1) a Contribution (other than a *de minimis* amount), (2) a Liquidating Distribution (other than a *de minimis* amount), or (3) a Liquidation of the Company.

62. **Sharing Ratio**—With respect to any Member, a fraction (expressed as a percentage), the numerator of which is the total of the Member's Capital Account and the denominator is the total of all Capital Accounts of all Members and Assignees.

63. **Substitute Member**—An Assignee who has been admitted to all of the rights of membership pursuant to this Company Agreement.

64. **Taxable Year**—The taxable year of the Company as determined pursuant to section 706 of the Code.

---

29. This provision should be approached carefully, Rev.Proc. 95–10 provides that an LLC will lack free transferability of interests if more than twenty percent of the interests are restricted. While more than twenty percent may be restricted at the outset, that percentage will be reduced by (1) Restricted Interests that are transferred to unadmitted Assignees and (2) Increases in unrestricted Membership Interests through the admission of new Members, additional contributions or allocations of income to holders of unrestricted interests, or distributions or allocations of loss to holders of Restricted Interests.

65. **Taxing Jurisdiction**—Any state, local, or foreign government that collects tax, interest or penalties, however designated, on any Member's share of the income or gain attributable to the Company.

ARTICLE III.

NATURE OF BUSINESS

The Company may engage in any lawful business permitted by the Act or the laws of any jurisdiction in which the Company may do business. The Company shall have the authority to do all things necessary or convenient to the accomplish its purpose and operate its business as described in this Article III. The Company exists only for the purpose specified in this Article III, and may not conduct any other business without the unanimous consent of the Members. The authority granted to the Members hereunder to bind the Company shall be limited to actions necessary or convenient to this business.[31]

ARTICLE IV.

ACCOUNTING AND RECORDS

1. **Records to Be Maintained**—The Member–Managers shall maintain the following records at the Principal Office.

    1.1. A current list of the full name and last known business address of each Member, former Member and other holder of a Membership Interest;

    1.2. A copy of the Articles and all amendments thereto, together with executed copies of any powers of attorney pursuant to which Articles has been executed;

    1.3. Copies of the Company's federal, foreign, state and local income tax returns and reports, if any, for the three most recent years;

    1.4. Copies of this Company Agreement including all amendments thereto;

    1.5. Any financial statements of the Company for the three most recent years;

---

31. Some statutes do not impose the "for profit" requirement applicable to general and limited partnerships. If the members desire to have the flexibility to enter into an activity not for profit, it may be advisable to include this provision. On the other hand, if the limited liability company is to be engaged in a narrower purpose, as for example, the practice of a profession, that limitation should be identified here. Finally, if the Nature of Business or Purpose is required to be included in the articles of organization, this section should merely refer to the articles so that the inadvertent failure to change the operating agreement when the articles of organization are changed will not lead to a conflict....

1.6. If not set forth in this Company Agreement, a writing or other data compilation from which information can be obtained through retrieval devices into reasonably usable form setting forth the following:

   a. The amount of cash and a description and statement of the agreed value of the other property or services contributed by each Member and which each Member has agreed to contribute;

   b. The times at which or events on the happening of which any additional Commitments agreed to be made by each Member are to be made;

   c. Any right of a Member to receive, or of the Company to make, distributions to a Member which include a return of all or any part of the Member's Capital Contribution; and

   d. Any events upon the happening of which the Company is to be dissolved and its affairs wound up.

2. **Reports to Members:**

2.1. The Member–Managers shall provide reports at least annually to the Members at such time and in such manner as the Member–Managers may determine reasonable.

2.2. The Member–Managers shall provide all Members and Assignees with those information returns required by the Code and the laws of any state.

ARTICLE V.

NAMES AND ADDRESSES OF MEMBERS AND MEMBER–MANAGERS

The names and addresses of the Initial Members and the designation of Member–Managers are as reflected on Exhibit A attached hereto and by this reference made a part hereof as if set forth fully herein.

ARTICLE VI.

RIGHTS AND DUTIES OF MEMBERS

1. **Management Rights**—All Members who are not Dissociated Members shall be entitled to vote on any matter submitted to a vote of the Members. Except as otherwise provided in this Company Agreement, in the case of any difference with respect to the ordinary course of the business action may be taken on the approval or consent, either in writing or at a meeting of the Member–Managers, of a Majority of the Member–Managers and any other action may be taken on the consent or affirmative vote on the approval or consent, either in writing or at a

meeting of the Members, of a Majority of Members.[35]

2. **Liability of Members**—No Member shall be liable as either Member or as Manager for the liabilities of the Company. The failure of the Company to observe any formalities or requirements relating to the exercise of its powers or management of its business or affairs under this Company Agreement or the Act shall not be grounds for imposing personal liability on the Members for liabilities of the Company.[37]

3. **Indemnification**—The Company shall indemnify the Members, and agents for all costs, losses, liabilities, and damages paid or accrued by such Member (either as Member or as Manager) or agent in connection with the business of the Company, to the fullest extent provided or allowed by the laws of the State.[38]

4. **Representations and Warranties**—Each Member, and in the case of an organization, the person(s) executing this Company Agreement on behalf of the organization, hereby represents and warrants to the Company and each other Member that: (a) if that Member is a organization, that it is duly organized, validly existing, and in good standing under the law of its state of organization and that it has full organizational power to execute and agree to this Company Agreement to perform its obligations hereunder; (b) that the Member is acquiring its interest in the Company for the Member's own account as an investment and without an intent to distribute the interest; (c) the Member acknowledges that the interests have not been registered under the Securities Act of 1933 or any state securities laws, and may not be resold or transferred by the Member without appropriate registration or the availability of an exemption from such requirements.[39]

5. **Conflicts of Interest**

5.1. A Member (regardless of whether such Member is a Member–Manager) shall be entitled to enter into transactions that may be considered to be competitive with, or a business opportunity that

---

35. Certain items, such as admission of an assignee and consent to continue the LLC may require specific consent, which differs from simple majority. In a large LLC, it may be appropriate to set forth rules for meetings and voting. Note that this provision requires that the consent be in writing if not taken at a meeting.

37. The efficacy of this language, based on Section 25 of the Statutory Close Corporation Supplement to the MBCA is open to question, however it is prudent to attempt to avoid veil piercing arguments if possible.

38. Like corporations and partnerships, many limited liability company statutes set limits and conditions on indemnification, these indemnification statutes are going to apply regardless of the language of the agreement. By adding the concept of a

liability accrued, it may be possible to have indemnification for an expense prior to the time it is paid by the indemnitee. In this circumstance, the Company would probably pay the expense directly to the claimant. Note that this provision makes indemnification mandatory if permitted by the statute. To the extent the Members agree that they wish to evaluate the right to indemnification in close cases, and the statute does not otherwise require such evaluation, this language may preclude a post hoc evaluation.

39. This language is included to provide some compliance with the rules under Regulation D (particularly Rule 502(d)) promulgated pursuant to the Securities Act of 1933.

may be beneficial to, the Company, it being expressly understood that some of the Members may enter into transactions that are similar to the transactions into which the Company may enter. Notwithstanding the foregoing, Members shall account to the Company and hold as trustee for it any property, profit, or benefit derived by the Member, without the consent of a Majority of the Remaining Member–Managers, or, if none, a Majority of the Remaining Members, in the conduct and winding up of the Company business or from a use or appropriation by the Member of Company property including information developed exclusively for the Company and opportunities expressly offered to the Company.

5.2.   A Member (regardless of whether such Member is a Member–Manager) does not violate a duty or obligation to the Company merely because the Member's conduct furthers the Member's own interest.   A Member may lend money to and transact other business with the Company.   The rights and obligations of a Member who lends money to or transacts business with the Company are the same as those of a person who is not a Member, subject to other applicable law.   No transaction with the Company shall be voidable solely because a Member has a direct or indirect interest in the transaction if either the transaction is fair to the Company or a Majority of the Remaining Member–Managers or, if none, a Majority of the Remaining Members, in either case knowing the material facts of the transaction and the Member's interest, authorize, approve, or ratify the transaction.

ARTICLE VII.

MANAGERS

1.   **Managers**—The ordinary and usual decisions concerning the business affairs of the Company shall be made by the Managers, each of whom shall be a Member–Manager.   There shall be three Member–Managers who must be Members of the Company.[40]   The initial Member–Managers are identified on Exhibit A.   Notwithstanding the foregoing, at any time the Member–Managers do not own at least 21 percent of the total Membership Interests of the Company and 21 percent of the total positive Capital Accounts (taking into account the Membership Interests and Capital Accounts of all Members and Assignees), all Members shall be Member–Managers.[41]

---

40.   While neither Rev.Proc. 95–10 nor Prop.Reg. § 1.1402(a)–18 define "member-managers" it appears that they must be both members and managers.

41.   This provision is added to ensure that the LLC lacks the corporate characteristic of centralized management.   Section

5.03 of Rev.Proc. 95–10 requires that the Member–Managers own at least 20 percent "of the total interests in the LLC."   This provision is similar to section 4.06 of Rev. Proc. 89–12.   This provision will be burdensome and should only be included if the Company is relying on lacking centralized

331

2. **Term of Member–Manager**—No Member–Manager shall have any contractual right to such position.[42] Each Member–Manager shall serve until the earliest of:

    2.1.   The Dissociation of such Member–Manager;

    2.2.   The Resignation of such Member–Manager; or

    2.3.   Removal of the Member–Manager for gross negligence, self-dealing, or embezzlement by a Majority of the Remaining Members.[43]

3. **Authority of Members to Bind the Company**—Only the Member–Managers and agents of the Company authorized by the Member–Managers shall have the authority to bind the Company. No Member who is not either a Member–Manager or otherwise authorized as an agent shall take any action to bind the Company, and each Member shall indemnify the Company for any costs or damages incurred by the Company as a result of the unauthorized action of such Member.[44] Subject to section VI.1 of this Company Agreement, each Member–Manager has the power, on behalf of the Company, to do all things necessary or convenient to carry out the business and affairs of the Company, including, without limitation:

    3.1.   The institution, prosecution and defense of any Proceeding in the Company's name;

    3.2.   The purchase, receipt, lease or other acquisition, ownership, holding, improvement, use and other dealing with, Property, wherever located;

    3.3.   The sale, conveyance, mortgage, pledge, lease, exchange, and other disposition of Property;

management. Note that when this default rule is triggered, all of the Members will probably be subject to self-employment tax. See Treas.Reg. § 1.1402(a)–18. If this provision is included, the fallback provisions of sections XIII.2 (dealing with admission of an assignee) or XIV.1.3 (relating to the persons the dissociation of whom will trigger dissolution) will probably not be necessary.

42. It is important to make clear the difference between the management right that is an inherent portion of any Member's status as such, and the rights that a Member may have when acting as a Member–Manager.

43. Rev.Proc. 95–10, section 5.03(2) provides that "[t]he Service will not rule that the LLC lacks centralized management if the member-managers are subject to periodic elections by the members, or, alternatively, the non-managing members have a sub-stantially non-restricted power to remove the member-managers." Treas.Reg. § 301.7701–2(c)(4) provides that a "substantially restricted right of the limited partners to remove the general partner (e.g., in the event of the general partner's gross negligence, self-dealing or negligence) will not itself cause the partnership to possess centralized management." This consideration will be of less significance ... if the LLC does not need to lack centralized management. If the LLC needs to lack centralized management, the Member–Managers should own at least 20% of the interests in the LLC.

44. This phrase is intended to at least provide an internal check on the activities of members who are not Member–Managers. This should not be an issue, as members or a manager-managed LLC do not have apparent authority as do members of a member-managed LLC (See § 8.06).

3.4.   The entering into contracts and guaranties; incurring of liabilities; borrowing [of] money, issuance of notes, bonds, and other obligations; and the securing of any of its obligations by mortgage or pledge of any of its Property or income;

3.5.   The lending of money, investment and reinvestment of the Company's funds, and receipt and holding of Property as security for repayment, including, without limitation, . . . loaning money to, and otherwise helping Members, officers, employees, and agents;

3.6.   The conduct of the Company's business, the establishment of Company offices, and the exercise of the powers of the Company within or without the State;

3.7.   The appointment of employees and agents of the Company, the defining of their duties, the establishment of their compensation;

3.8.   The payment of pensions and establishment of pension plans, pension trusts, profit sharing plans, and benefit and incentive plans for all or any of the current or former Members, employees, and agents of the Company;

3.9.   The making of donations to the public welfare or for religious, charitable, scientific, literary or educational purposes;

3.10.   The payment or donation, or any other act that furthers the business and affairs of the Company;

3.11.   The payment of compensation, or additional compensation to any or all Members, and employees on account of services previously rendered to the limited liability company, whether or not an agreement to pay such compensation was made before such services were rendered;

3.12.   The purchase of insurance [on] the life of any of its Members, or employees for the benefit of the Company;

3.14.   The indemnification of Members or any other Person.

4.   **Actions of the Member–Managers**—Each Member–Manager has the power to bind the Company as provided in this Article VII. Any difference arising as to any matter within the Authority of the Member–Managers shall be decided by a Majority of the Member–Managers. No act of a Member–Manager in contravention of such determination shall bind the Company to Persons having knowledge of such determination. Notwithstanding such determination, the act of Member–Manager for the purpose of apparently carrying on the usual way the business or affairs of the Company, including the exercise of the authority indicated in this Article VII shall bind the Company, and no person dealing with the Company shall have any obligation to inquire into the power or authority of the Member–Manager acting on behalf of the Company.[45]

45. In seeking to avoid the corporate characteristic of centralization of manage-   ment, drafters may want to go further and state that the action of all *members* will

5. **Compensation of Member–Manager**—Each Member–Manager shall be reimbursed all reasonable expenses incurred in managing the Company and shall be entitled to compensation, in an amount to be determined from time to time by the affirmative vote of a Majority of the Members.

6. **Member–Managers' Standard of Care**—A Member–Manager's duty of care in the discharge of the Member–Manager's duties to the Company and the other Members is limited to refraining from engaging in grossly negligent or reckless conduct, intentional misconduct, or a knowing violation of law.[46] In discharging its duties, a Member–Manager shall be fully protected in relying in good faith upon the records required to be maintained under Article IV and upon such information, opinions, reports or statements by any of its other Members, or agents, or by any other person, as to matters the Member–Manager reasonably believes are within such other person's professional or expert competence and who has been selected with reasonable care by or on behalf of the Company, including information, opinions, reports or statements as to the value and amount of the assets, liabilities, profits or losses of the Company or any other facts pertinent to the existence and amount of assets from which distributions to members might properly be paid.

7. **Removal of Member–Manager**—Any Member–Manager may be Removed by the affirmative vote of a Majority of the Members for gross negligence, self-dealing, or embezzlement by a Majority of the Remaining Members.

ARTICLE VIII.

CONTRIBUTIONS AND CAPITAL ACCOUNTS

1. **Initial Contributions**—Each Initial Member shall make the Contribution described for that Member on Exhibit A at the time and on the terms specified on Exhibit A and shall perform that Member's Commitment. If no time for the Contribution is specified, the Contributions shall be made upon the filing of the Articles with the Secretary of State. The value of the Contributions shall be as set forth on Exhibit A. No interest shall accrue on any Contribution and no Member shall have the right to withdraw or be repaid any Contribution except as provided in this Company Agreement. Each Additional Member shall make the Contribution and shall perform the Commitment described in the Admission Agreement. The value of the Additional Member's Contribution

---

bind the LLC to persons without knowledge of the limitations of authority to managing members. See Treas.Reg. § 301.7701–2(c).

46. This standard is taken from the RUPA § 404, and differs significantly from the standards set forth in MBCA § 8.30, which calls for the care an ordinary prudent person in a like position would exercise under similar circumstances.

and the time for making such contribution shall be set forth in the Admission Agreement.

2. **Additional Contributions**—In addition to the Initial Contributions and Commitments, the Member–Managers may determine from time to time that additional contributions are needed to enable the Company to conduct its business. Upon making such a determination, the Member–Managers shall give Notice to all Members in writing at least ten Business Days prior to the date on which such contribution is due. Such Notice shall set forth the amount of additional contribution needed, the purpose for which the contribution is needed, and the date by which the Members should contribute. Each Member shall be entitled to contribute a proportionate share of such additional contribution. Except to the extent of a Member's unpaid Commitment, no Member shall be obligated to make any such additional contributions. In the event any one or more Members do not make their additional contribution, the other members shall be given the opportunity to make the contributions. Each Additional Member shall make the Capital Contribution to which such Member has agreed, at the time or times and upon the terms to which the Member–Managers and the Additional Member agree.

3. **Enforcement of Commitments**—In the event any Member (a Delinquent Member) fails to perform the Delinquent Member's Commitment, the Member–Managers shall give the Delinquent Member a Notice of the failure to meet the Commitment. If the Delinquent Member fails to perform the Commitment (including any costs associated with the [need] to demand compliance with the Commitment and interest on such obligation at the Default Interest Rate) within ten Business days of the giving of Notice, the Member–Managers may take such action, including but not limited to enforcing the Commitment in the court of appropriate jurisdiction in the state in which the Principal Office is located or the state of the Delinquent Member's address as reflected in this Company Agreement. Each Member expressly agrees to the jurisdiction of such courts but only for the enforcement of Commitments.[48] The Member–Managers may elect to allow the other Members to contribute the amount of the Commitment in proportion to such Members' sharing ratios, with those Members who contribute (Contributing Members) to contribute additional amounts equal to any amount of the Commitment not contributed. The Contributing Members shall be entitled to treat the amounts contributed pursuant to this section as a loan from the Contributing Members bearing interest at the Default Interest Rate secured by the Delinquent Member's interest in the Company. Until they are fully repaid the Contributing Members shall be entitled to all

48. Whether a partner (or in this case a member) subjects himself or herself to personal jurisdiction in any jurisdiction in which the partner does business is an open question. While the Company will want to sue a Member in its home jurisdiction, the Members will probably be reluctant to grant general jurisdiction to such courts.

Distributions to which the Delinquent Member would have been entitled. Notwithstanding the foregoing, no Commitment or other obligation to make an additional contribution may be enforced by a creditor of the Company or other Person other than the Company unless the Member expressly consents to such enforcement or to the assignment of the obligation to such creditor.

4. **Maintenance of Capital Accounts**—The Company shall establish and maintain a Capital Account for each Member and Assignee.[51] Each Member's Capital Account shall be increased by (1) the amount of any Money actually contributed by the Member to the capital of the Company, (2) the fair market value of any Property (other than Money) contributed, as determined by the Company and the Contributing Member at arm's length at the time of contribution (net of liabilities assumed by the Company or subject to which the company takes such Property, within the meaning of Section 752 of the Code), and (3) the Member's share of Net Profits and of any separately allocated items of income or gain except adjustments of the Code (including income and gain exempt from tax and adjustments to income and gain as a result of a Revaluation or in connection with Property Contributed in the manner described in section 1.704–1(b)(2)(iv)(g) to reflect the difference between the Book Value and the adjusted basis of Company Property, but excluding allocations of income and gain described in section 1.704–1(b)(4)(i) of the Regulations under which such difference is reflected for tax purposes). Each Member's Capital Account shall be decreased by (1) the amount of any Money distributed to the Member by the Company, (2) the fair market value of any Property distributed to the Member, as determined by the Company and the Member receiving the Distribution at arm's length at the time of Distribution (net of liabilities of the Company assumed by the Member or subject to which the Member takes such Property within the meaning of Section 752 of the Code), and (3) the Member's share of Net Losses and of any separately allocated items of Net Loss (including adjustments for depreciation, depletion, amortization, and loss as a result of a Revaluation or in connection with Property Contributed in the manner described in section 1.704–1(b)(2)(iv)(g) [of the Regulations] to reflect the difference between the difference between the Book Value and the adjusted basis of Company Property, but excluding allocations of depreciation, depletion, amortization, and loss described in section 1.704–1(b)(4)(i) of the Regulations under which such difference is reflected for tax purposes).

5. **Distribution of Assets**—If the Company at any time Distributes any of the Company Property (other than Money) in-kind to any Member, the Capital Account of each Member shall be adjusted to

---

51. Although Assignees are not Members, they are treated as partners for tax purposes, so that allocations should take into account their economic interests. See Rev.Rul. 77–137, 1977–1 C.B. 178. See, 1 Arthur B. Willis, John S. Pennell, Philip F. Postlewaite, Partnership Taxation, 5/e § 307 (1994 and Supp.).

account for the that Member's allocable share (as determined under Article IX below) of the Net Profits or Net Losses that would have been realized by the Company had it sold the assets that were distributed at their respective fair market values immediately prior to their distribution.

6. **Sale or Exchange of Interest**—In the event of a sale or exchange of some or all of a Membership Interest, the Capital Account of the Transferring Member shall become the Capital Account of the Assignee, to the extent it relates to the portion of the Interest Transferred.

7. **Revaluation of Partnership Property**—The Capital Accounts of the Members shall be increased or decreased to reflect a revaluation of Company Property (including intangible assets such as goodwill) on the Company's books in connection with a Revaluation Event. Upon such Revaluation: (1) the Book Value of Company Property shall be adjusted based on the fair market value of Company Property (taking section 7701(g) of the Code into account) on the Revaluation Date; (2) the unrealized income, gain, loss, or deduction inherent in such Company Property (that has not been reflected in the Capital Accounts previously) [shall] be allocated among the Members as if there were a taxable disposition of such Company property for such fair market value on the Revaluation Date.

8. **Compliance With Section 704(b) of the Code**—The provisions of this Article VIII as they relate to the maintenance of Capital Accounts are intended, and shall be construed, and, if necessary, modified to cause the allocations of profits, losses, income, gain and credit pursuant to Article IX to have substantial economic effect under the Regulations promulgated under Section 704(b) of the Code, in light of the Distributions made pursuant to Articles IX and XIV and the Contributions made pursuant to this Article VIII. Notwithstanding anything herein to the contrary, this Company Agreement shall not be construed as creating a deficit restoration obligation or otherwise personally [obligating] any Member or Assignee to make a Contribution in excess of the Initial Contribution, Additional Contribution, and Commitment of the Member or Assignee.

ARTICLE IX.

ALLOCATIONS AND DISTRIBUTIONS

1. **Allocations of Net Profits and Net Losses From Operations**—Except as may be required by section 704(c) of the Code, and sections 2, 3, and 4 of this Article IX, net profits, net losses, and other items of income, gain, loss, deduction and credit shall be apportioned among the Members in proportion to their Sharing Ratios.

2. **Company Minimum Gain Chargeback**—If there is a net decrease in Company Minimum Gain for a Taxable Year, each Member

must be allocated items of income and gain for that Taxable year equal to that Member's share of the net decrease in Company Minimum Gain. A Member's share of the net decrease in Company Minimum Gain is the amount of the total net decrease multiplied by the Member's percentage share of the Company Minimum Gain at the end of the immediately preceding Taxable Year. A Member's share of any decrease in Company Minimum Gain resulting from a Revaluation of Company Property equals the increase in the Member's Capital Account attributable to the Revaluation to the extent the reduction in minimum gain is caused by the Revaluation. A Member is not subject to the Company Minimum Gain Chargeback Requirement to the extent the Member's share of the net decrease in Company Minimum Gain is caused by a guarantee, refinancing, or other change in the debt instrument causing it to become partially or wholly a Recourse Liability or a Member Nonrecourse Liability, and the Member bears the economic risk of loss (within the meaning of section 1.752–2 of the Regulations) for the newly guaranteed, refinanced, or otherwise changed liability.

3. **Member Minimum Gain Chargeback**—If during a Taxable Year there is a net decrease in Member Minimum Gain, any Member with a share of that Member Minimum Gain ("partner minimum gain" as determined under section 1.704–2(i)(5) of the Regulations) as of the beginning of that Taxable Year must be allocated items of income and gain for that Taxable Year (and, if necessary, for succeeding Taxable Years) equal to that Member's share of the net decrease in the Company Minimum Gain. A Member's share of the net decrease in Member Minimum Gain is determined in a manner consistent with the provisions of section 1.704–2(g)(2) of the Regulations. A Member is not subject to this Member Minimum Gain Chargeback, however, to the extent the net decrease in Member Minimum Gain arises because the liability ceases to be Member Nonrecourse Liability due to a conversion, refinancing, or other change in the debt instrument that causes it to become partially or wholly a Company Nonrecourse Liability. The amount that would otherwise be subject to the Member Minimum Gain Chargeback is added to the Member's share of Company Minimum Gain. In addition, rules consistent with those applicable to Company Minimum Gain shall be applied to determine the shares of Member Minimum Gain and Member Minimum Gain Chargeback to the extent provided under the Regulations issued pursuant to section 704(b) of the Code.

4. **Qualified Income Offset**—Notwithstanding any provision of this Company Agreement to the contrary (other than sections IX.2 and IX.3 above), in the event that a deficit in a Member's Capital Account is created or increased (taking into account any allocations, adjustments, or distributions described in section 1.704–1(b)(2)(ii)(d)(4), (5), or (6)) in excess of such Member's share of Company Minimum Gain and Member Minimum Gain, plus any amount that the Member is obligated to restore to the Company, such Member will be allocated items of income and gain

338

(consisting of a pro rata portion of each item of partnership income and gain for such year) in an amount and manner sufficient to offset such Offsettable Decrease as quickly as possible. . . .

5. **Interim Distributions**—From time to time, the Member–Managers shall determine in their reasonable judgment to what extent, if any, the Company's cash on hand exceeds the current and anticipated needs, including, without limitation, needs for operating expenses, debt service, acquisitions, reserves, and mandatory distributions, if any. To the extent such excess exists, the Member–Managers may make distributions to the Members in accordance with their Sharing Ratios. Such distributions shall be in cash or Property (which need not be distributed proportionately) or partly in both, as determined by the Member–Managers.[52] All interim distributions which, when made, exceed the recipient Member's basis in that Member's Membership interest shall be considered advances or drawings against the Member's distributive share of net income. To the extent it is determined at the end of the Taxable Year of the Company that the recipient Member has not been allocated net income that equals or exceeds the total of such advances or drawings for such year, the recipient Member shall be obligated to restore any such advances or drawings to the Company. Notwithstanding the foregoing sentence, the Member will not be required to restore such advances or drawings to the extent that, on the last day of the Taxable Year, the recipient Member's basis in the Member's interest in the Company has increased from the time of such advance or drawing.[53]

6. **Limitations on Distributions**—No distribution shall be declared and paid unless, after the distribution is made, the assets of the Company are in excess of all liabilities of the Company, except liabilities to Members on account of their Capital Accounts.[54]

ARTICLE X.

TAXES

1. **Elections**—The Member–Managers may make any tax elections for the Company allowed under the Code or the tax laws of any state or other jurisdiction having taxing jurisdiction over the Company.

52. Most statutes provide that members are not required to accept disproportionate distributions in kind unless the operating agreement or articles of organization provide otherwise. See § 6.04. This provision allowing in kind distributions is intended to afford the Managing Members the flexibility to distribute property in kind to avoid the application of the disguised sale rules. See § 17.05.

53. This provision is intended to avoid the recognition of gain at a time when a member does not have sufficient basis to cover the distribution, but will have such basis at the end of the year when income is credited to the member's basis. See section 1.731–1(a)(ii) of the Regulations.

54. This provision is added as a point of reference. Many statutes provide that distributions rendering the LLC insolvent are invalid. See § 6.05. This provision may give rise to additional liability, when such liability is best left to the statute and fraudulent conveyance law.

2. **Taxes of Taxing Jurisdictions**—To the extent that the laws of any Taxing Jurisdiction [require], each Member and Economic Interest Holder (or such Members as may be required by the Taxing Jurisdiction) will submit an agreement indicating that the Member will make timely income tax payments to the Taxing Jurisdiction and that the Member accepts personal jurisdiction of the Taxing Jurisdiction with regard to the collection of income taxes attributable to the Member's income, and interest, and penalties assessed on such income. If the Member fails to provide such agreement, the Company may withhold and pay over to such Taxing Jurisdiction the amount of tax, penalty and interest determined under the laws of the Taxing Jurisdiction with respect to such income. Any such payments with respect to the income of a Member shall be treated as a distribution for purposes of Article IX.

The Member–Managers may, where permitted by the rules of any Taxing Jurisdiction, file a composite, combined or aggregate tax return reflecting the income of the Company and pay the tax, interest and penalties of some or all of the Members on such income to the Taxing Jurisdiction, in which case the Company shall inform the Members of the amount of such tax interest and penalties so paid.

3. **Tax Matters Partner**—The Member–Managers shall designate one of their number or, if there are no Member–Managers eligible to act as tax matters partner any other Member, as the *tax matters partner* of the Company pursuant to Section 6231(a)(7) of the Code. Any Member designated as tax matters partner shall take such action as many be necessary to cause each other Member to become a *notice partner* within the meaning of Section 6223 of the Code. Any Member who is designated tax matter partner may not take any action contemplated by sections 6222 through 6232 of the Code without the consent of the Member–Managers.

4. **Cash Method of Accounting**—The records of the Company shall be maintained on a cash receipts and disbursements method of accounting.[55]

ARTICLE XI.

DISPOSITION OF MEMBERSHIP INTERESTS

1. **Disposition**—Any Member or Assignee may dispose of all or a portion of the Member's or Assignee's Membership Interest upon compliance with this Section 1. No Membership Interest shall be Disposed of:

   1.1. if such disposition, alone or when combined with other transactions, would result in a termination of the Company within the meaning of Section 708 of the Code;

---

55. Not all LLCs will be entitled to use the cash method of accounting. See § 17.11.

1.2.   without an opinion of counsel satisfactory to the Member–Managers that such assignment is subject to an effective registration under, or exempt from the registration requirements of, the applicable state and federal securities laws;

1.3.   unless and until the Company receives from the Assignee the information and agreements that the Member–Managers may reasonably require, including but not limited to any taxpayer identification number and any agreement that may be required by any Taxing Jurisdiction.

2.   **Dispositions Not in Compliance With This Article Void**— Any attempted Disposition of a Membership Interest, or any part thereof, not in compliance with ... Section 1 ... shall be, and is declared to be, null and void *ab initio*.

ARTICLE XII.

DISSOCIATION OF A MEMBER

1.   **Dissociation**—A Person shall cease to be a Member upon the happening of any of the following events: [56]

1.1.   the Member's becoming a Bankrupt Member,[57]

1.2.   in the case of a Member who is a natural person, the death of the Member or the entry of an order by a court of competent jurisdiction adjudicating the Member incompetent to manage the Member's [personal] estate;[58]

1.3.   in the case of a Member who is acting as a Member by virtue of being a trustee of a trust, the termination of the trust (but not merely the substitution of a new trustee);

1.4.   in the case of a Member that is a separate Organization other than a corporation, the dissolution and commencement of winding up of the separate Organization; [59]

1.5.   in the case of a Member that is a corporation, the filing of a certificate of dissolution, or its equivalent, for the corporation or the revocation of its charter; or

---

56. Under Rev.Proc. 95–10, section 5.01(4) the events of Dissociation may be limited without causing the LLC to possess continuity of life so long as the event provides a "meaningful possibility of dissolution."

57. See §§ 7.06 and 11.14 as well as section XIV.1.3 of this agreement. Note that the voluntary dissociation of a member is not included. Members do not have the right to voluntarily resign. Member-Managers who desire to reduce their fiduciary duties may resign (i.e., cease to be Member-Managers, but continue to be Members).

58. There is a question of whether the insanity or incompetence of a Member should be sufficient to cause the dissolution of the limited liability company. In a member managed limited liability company, each member is an agent, which would suggest that it should still constitute an event of dissociation. See §§ 11.06 and 11.14.

59. This provision is intended to be sufficiently broad to deal with new and different forms of organization, as there should be no limit on the nature of the owners.

1.6.   in the case of an estate, the distribution by the fiduciary of the estate's entire interest in the limited liability company.

2.   **Purchase of Dissociated Member's Membership Interest**—Upon the Dissociation of a Member, when the Remaining Members elect to continue the business of the Company, a Majority of the Remaining Members, shall, subject to the provisions of the Act, elect one of the two following provisions:

2.1.   The Disassociated Member's Membership Interest shall be purchased by the Company for a purchase price equal to the aggregate fair market value of the Member's Interest determined according to the provisions of [sections] XII.3, XII.4.   The purchase price of such interest shall be paid by the Company to the Member in cash within 60 days of determination of the aggregate fair market value or, at the Company's option, said debt may be evidenced by a promissory note bearing interest at the Prime Rate, which shall be due and payable upon the earlier of (i) expiration of five years or (ii) the sale or other disposition of all of the Property; or

2.2.   The Dissociated Member, or assignee of Dissociated Member's Interest, shall hold the Dissociated Member's Membership Interest as an Assignee.

3.   **Purchase Price of Dissociated Member's Membership Interest**—The fair market value of a Member's Interest to be purchased by the Company pursuant to section XII.2.1 shall be determined by agreement between the Dissociated Member (or the Assignee of the Dissociated Member's Membership Interest, as the case may be) and the Company, which agreement is subject to approval by a Majority of the Remaining Members.   For this purpose, the fair market value [60] of the Dissociated Member's Membership Interest shall be computed as the amount which could reasonably be expected to be realized by such Member upon the sale of the Company Property in the ordinary course of business at the time of Dissociation.   If the Dissociated Member (or the Assignee of the Dissociated Member's Membership Interest, as the case may be) and the Company cannot agree upon the fair market value of such Membership Interest within 30 days, the fair market value thereof shall be determined by appraisal, the Company and the terminated Member each to choose one appraiser and the two appraisers so chosen to choose a third appraiser.   The decision of a majority of the appraisers as to the fair market value of such Membership Interest shall be final and binding and may be enforced by legal proceedings.   The Dissociated Member and the Company shall each compensate the appraiser appointed by it and the compensation of the third appraiser shall be borne equally by such parties.

---

60. The default rule, under Colo.Rev. Stat. § 7–80–603 (1990) is "fair value," based on the Member's right to share in distributions. The provision allows the operating agreement to provide otherwise as this does.

4. **Damages**—The provision set forth herein shall not effect any claim for damages the Company may have against the Dissociated Member if such Dissociation is in violation of this Company Agreement. The Company shall have the right to offset any payments due under this Article XII by any damages that the Company may incur as a result of a Dissociation of a Member in contravention of this Company Agreement.

ARTICLE XIII.

ADMISSION OF ASSIGNEES AND ADDITIONAL MEMBERS

1. **Rights of Assignees**—The Assignee of a Membership Interest has no right to participate in the management of the business and affairs of the Company or to become a Member. The Assignee is only entitled to receive the Distributions and return of capital, and to be allocated the Net Profits and Net Losses attributable [to] the Membership Interest.

2. **Admission of Substitute Members**—An Assignee of a Membership Interest shall be admitted as a Substitute Member and admitted to all the rights of the Member who initially assigned the Membership Interest, but an Assignee of a Restricted Membership Interest shall be so admitted only with the approval, which may be withheld in their sole and absolute discretion, of a Majority of the Remaining Member–Managers (or of a Majority of the Remaining Members at any time Member–Managers own in the aggregate: (1) an interest in each material item of the income, gain, loss, deduction, or credit of the LLC equal to at least the lesser of one percent or $500,000 divided by total contributions to the LLC, and (2) maintain a Capital Account balance equal to at least the lesser of one percent of total positive capital account balances or $500,000). The Remaining Member–Managers may grant or withhold the approval of such admission ... in their sole and absolute discretion.[62] If so admitted, the Substitute Member has all the rights and powers and is subject to all the restrictions and liabilities of the Member originally assigning the Membership Interest. The admission of a Substitute Member, without more, shall not release the Member originally assigning the Membership Interest from any liability to Company that may [have] existed prior to the approval.

---

62. See Priv.Ltr.Rul. 9219022 (February 6, 1992) (the LLC lacked free transferability of interests where the operating agreement further provided that no transferee, designee or legal representative of a member shall become a substitute member without the consent of a majority, by sharing ratios, of the non-transferring members). See also, Rev.Proc. 92–33, (a partnership lacks free transferability of interests if, through- out the life of the partnership, the partnership agreement expressly restricts the transferability of partnership interests representing more than 20 percent of all interests in partnership capital, income, gain, loss, deduction, and credit.) This may provide an opportunity to apply the restrictions in this section to less than all of the membership interests.

3. **Admission of Permitted Transferees**—Notwithstanding Section 2. hereof, the Membership Interest of any Member shall be transferable without the consent of the Member–Managers if (i) the transfer occurs by reason of or incident to the death, dissolution, divorce, liquidation, merger or termination of the transferor Member, and (ii) the Transferee is a Permitted Transferee.[63]

4. **Admission of Additional Members**—The Managing–Members may admit Additional Members and determine the Capital Contributions of such Members.

ARTICLE XIV.

DISSOLUTION AND WINDING UP

1. **Dissolution**—The Company shall be dissolved and its affairs wound up, upon the first to occur of the following events:

1.1. the expiration of the Term;

1.2. the unanimous written consent of all of the Members;

1.3. the Dissociation of any Member–Manager (or of any Member at any time Member–Managers do not in the aggregate both: (1) own an interest in each material item of the income, gain, loss, deduction, or credit of the LLC equal to at least the lesser of one percent or $500,000 divided by total contributions to the LLC, and (2) maintain a Capital Account balance equal to at least the lesser of one percent of total positive capital account balances or $500,000), unless the business of the Company is continued with the consent of:

(1) Remaining Members holding a majority of the Sharing Ratios of all the Remaining Members based on any reasonable estimate of profits from the date of the dissociation to the projected termination of the Company, taking into account present and future allocations of profits under the . . . agreement that is in effect as of the date of the dissolution event; and

(2) Remaining Members holding a majority of the Capital Accounts of all of the Remaining Members determined as of the

---

63. See Priv.Ltr.Rul. 9210019 (December 6, 1991). **NOTE: THIS CLAUSE SHOULD BE USED WITH CARE, WHILE THE PRIVATE LETTER RULING SANCTIONS SOME EXCLUSIONS FROM THE DEFINITION OF TRANSFER, THE EFFECT OF THIS SECTION ON THE CORPORATE CHARACTERISTIC OF FREE TRANSFERABILITY IS STILL OPEN TO QUESTION.** There is no authority for this sort of exception in Rev.Proc. 95–10. As an alternative, the operating agreement could provide only for date of the dissociation.[64]

2. **Effect of Dissolution**—Upon dissolution, the Company shall cease carrying on as distinguished from the winding up of the Company business, but the Company is not terminated, but continues until the winding up of the affairs of the Company is completed and the Certificate of Dissolution has [been] issued by the Secretary of State.[65]

3. **Distribution of Assets on Dissolution**—Upon the winding up of the Company, the Company Property shall be distributed:

3.1. to creditors, including Members who are creditors, to the extent permitted by law, in satisfaction of Company Liabilities;

3.2. to Members in accordance with positive Capital Account balances taking into account all Capital Account adjustments for the Company's taxable year in which the liquidation occurs. Liquidation proceeds shall be paid within 60 days of the end of the Company's taxable year or, if later, within 90 days after the date of liquidation. Such distributions shall be in cash or Property (which need not be distributed proportionately) or partly in both, as determined by the Member–Managers.

4. **Winding Up and Certificate of Dissolution**—The winding up of a limited liability company shall be completed when all debts, liabilities, and obligations of the limited liability company have been paid and discharged or reasonably adequate provision therefor has been made, and all of the remaining property and assets of the limited liability company have been distributed to the members. Upon the completion of winding up of the Company, a certificate of dissolution shall be delivered to the Secretary of State for filing. The certificate of dissolution shall set forth the information required by the Act.

ARTICLE XV.

AMENDMENT

1. **Company Agreement May Be Modified**—This Company Agreement may be modified as provided in this Article XV (as the same may, from time to time be amended). No Member or Member–Manager

---

transfer of membership interests other than Restricted Interests.

64. See § 16.14, Rev.Procs. 94–46, 95–10.

65. Most statutes do not define *dissolution,* as does UPA § 29 (1914) (the change in the relation of the partners caused by any partner ceasing to be associated in the carrying on as distinguished from the winding up of the business.). UPA § 30 (1914) makes clear that the dissolution does not terminate the partnership. Because the concept of dissolution is important to the regulations, it may be appropriate to include some reference to what dissolution is. Treas.Reg. § 301.7701–2(b)(2) ("an alteration of the identity of an organization by reason of a change in the relationship between its members as determined under local law"). Dissolution is not normally defined except by reference to the consequences of dissolution under most of the statutes.

shall have any vested rights in this Company Agreement which may not be modified through an amendment to this Company Agreement.

2. **Amendment or Modification of Company Agreement**— This Company Agreement may be amended or modified from time to time only by a written instrument adopted by the Member–Managers and executed by a Majority of the Members, but, without the written consent of each Member adversely affected thereby (the Affected Member), no amendment of the Company Agreement shall be made that (i) increases the obligations of the Affected Member to make contributions, (ii) alters the allocation to the Affected Member for tax purposes of any items of income, gain, loss, deduction or credit, or (iii) alters the manner of computing the distributions of the Affected Member.[66]

ARTICLE XVI.

MISCELLANEOUS PROVISIONS

1. **Entire Agreement**—This Company Agreement represents the entire agreement among all the Members and between the Members and the Company.

2. **No Partnership Intended for Nontax Purposes**—The Members have formed the Company under the Act, and expressly do not intend hereby to form a partnership under either the State Uniform Partnership Act nor the State Uniform Limited Partnership Act. The Members do not intend to be partners one to another, or partners as to any third party. To the extent any Member, by word or action, represents to another person that any other Member is a partner or that the Company is a partnership, the Member making such wrongful representation shall be liable to any other Member who incurs personal liability by reason of such wrongful representation.

3. **Rights of Creditors and Third Parties Under Company Agreement**—This Company Agreement is entered into among the Company and the Members for the exclusive benefit of the Company, its Members, and their successors and assignees. This Company Agreement is expressly not intended for the benefit of any creditor of the Company or any other Person. Except and only to the extent provided by applicable statute, no such creditor or third party shall have any rights under this Company Agreement, Admission Agreement or any agreement between the Company and any Member with respect to any Capital Contribution or otherwise.[68]

---

66. This provision is based on N.Y. Partnership Law Chapter 34 § 417(b) (1994). It will make the readjustment of the financial arrangement difficult, and should not be used if such adjustments are anticipated.

68. This provision is intended to reduce the ability of third parties to enforce capital contribution obligations. This provides the Company with the flexibility to adjust contribution obligations without the possibility that some creditors of the Company could

IN WITNESS WHEREOF, we have hereunto set out hand and seals on the date set forth beside out names.

_____ Limited Liability Company

_____
Member

_____   _____
                                     Date

_____   _____
                                     Date

_____   _____
                                     Date

_____   _____
                                     Date

_____   _____
                                     Date

_____   _____
                                     Date

_____   _____
                                     Date

EXHIBIT A

Member   Initial Contribution   Interests
                           and Value

Member–Managers

Members

... enforce the unadjusted capital contribution obligations.

INTERNAL REVENUE CODE § 7701 AND REGULATIONS THEREUNDER

IRC § 7701

Sec. 7701. (a) When used in this title, where not otherwise distinctly expressed or manifestly incompatible with the intent thereof—

(1) PERSON.—The term "person" shall be construed to mean and include an individual, a trust, estate, partnership, association, company or corporation.

(2) PARTNERSHIP AND PARTNER.—The term "partnership" includes a syndicate, group, pool, joint venture, or other unincorporated organization, through or by means of which any business, financial operation, or venture is carried on, and which is not, within the meaning of this title, a trust or estate or a corporation; and the term "partner" includes a member in such a syndicate, group, pool, joint venture, or organization.

(3) CORPORATION.—The term "corporation" includes associations, joint-stock companies, and insurance companies. . . .

————

REGULATIONS UNDER IRC § 7701

Regulation 7701–1. **Classification of organizations for federal tax purposes.**—(a) *Organizations for federal tax purposes*—

(1) *In general.* The Internal Revenue Code prescribes the classification of various organizations for federal tax purposes. Whether an organization is an entity separate from its owners for federal tax purposes is a matter of federal tax law and does not depend on whether the organization is recognized as an entity under local law.

(2) *Certain joint undertakings give rise to entities for federal tax purposes.* A joint venture or other contractual arrangement may create a separate entity for federal tax purposes if the participants carry on a trade, business, financial operation, or venture and divide the profits therefrom. For example, a separate entity exists for federal tax purposes if co-owners of an apartment building lease space and in addition provide services to the occupants either directly or through an agent. Nevertheless, a joint undertaking merely to share expenses does not create a separate entity for federal tax purposes. For example, if two or more persons jointly construct a ditch merely to drain surface water from their properties, they have not created a separate entity for federal tax purposes. Similarly, mere co-ownership of property that is maintained, kept in

repair, and rented or leased does not constitute a separate entity for federal tax purposes. For example, if an individual owner, or tenants in common, of farm property lease it to a farmer for a cash rental or a share of the crops, they do not necessarily create a separate entity for federal tax purposes. . . .

(4) *Single owner organizations.* Under Regulations 7701–2 and 7701–3, certain organizations that have a single owner can choose to be recognized or disregarded as entities separate from their owners.

(b) *Classification of organizations.* The classification of organizations that are recognized as separate entities is determined under Regulations 7701–2, 7701–3, and 7701–4. . . .

Regulation 7701–2. **Business entities; definitions.**—(a) *Business entities.* For purposes of this section and Regulation 7701–3, a *business entity* is any entity recognized for federal tax purposes (including an entity with a single owner that may be disregarded as an entity separate from its owner under Regulation 7701–3) that is not properly classified as a trust under Regulation 7701–4 or otherwise subject to special treatment under the Internal Revenue Code. A business entity with two or more members is classified for federal tax purposes as either a corporation or a partnership. A business entity with only one owner is classified as a corporation or is disregarded; if the entity is disregarded, its activities are treated in the same manner as a sole proprietorship, branch, or division of the owner.

(b) *Corporations.* For federal tax purposes, the term *corporation* means—

(1) A business entity organized under a Federal or State statute, or under a statute of a federally recognized Indian tribe, if the statute describes or refers to the entity as incorporated or as a corporation, body corporate, or body politic;

(2) An association (as determined under Regulation 7701–3);

(3) A business entity organized under a State statute, if the statute describes or refers to the entity as a joint-stock company or joint-stock association;

(4) An insurance company;

(5) A State-chartered business entity conducting banking activities, if any of its deposits are insured under the Federal Deposit Insurance Act, as amended, 12 U.S.C. 1811 et seq., or a similar federal statute;

(6) A business entity wholly owned by a State or any political subdivision thereof;

(7) A business entity that is taxable as a corporation under a provision of the Internal Revenue Code other than section 7701(a)(3); and

(8) *Certain foreign entities*—...

Regulation 7701–3. **Classification of certain business entities.**—(a) *In general.* A business entity that is not classified as a corporation under Regulations 7701–2(b)(1), (3), (4), (5), (6), (7), or (8) (an *eligible entity*) can elect its classification for federal tax purposes as provided in this section. An eligible entity with at least two members can elect to be classified as either an association (and thus a corporation under Regulation 7701–2(b)(2)) or a partnership, and an eligible entity with a single owner can elect to be classified as an association or to be disregarded as an entity separate from its owner. Paragraph (b) of this section provides a default classification for an eligible entity that does not make an election. Thus, elections are necessary only when an eligible entity chooses to be classified initially as other than the default classification or when an eligible entity chooses to change its classification. An entity whose classification is determined under the default classification retains that classification (regardless of any changes in the members' liability that occurs at any time during the time that the entity's classification is relevant as defined in paragraph (d) of this section) until the entity makes an election to change that classification under paragraph (c)(1) of this section. Paragraph (c) of this section provides rules for making express elections....

(b) *Classification of eligible entities that do not file an election*—(1) *Domestic eligible entities.* Except as provided in paragraph (b)(3) of this section, unless the entity elects otherwise, a domestic eligible entity is—

(i) A partnership if it has two or more members; or

(ii) Disregarded as an entity separate from its owner if it has a single owner....

(3) *Existing eligible entities*—(i) *In general.* Unless the entity elects otherwise, an eligible entity in existence prior to the effective date of this section will have the same classification that the entity claimed under Regulations 7701–1 through 7701–3 as in effect on the date prior to the effective date of this section; except that if an eligible entity with a single owner claimed to be a partnership under those regulations, the entity will be disregarded as an entity separate from its owner under this paragraph (b)(3)(i)....

(c) *Elections*—(1) *Time and place for filing*—

(i) *In general.* Except as provided in paragraphs (c)(1)(iv) and (v) of this section, an eligible entity may elect to be classified other than as provided under paragraph (b) of this section, or to change its classification, by filing Form 8832, Entity Classification Election, with the service center designated on Form 8832....

(iv) *Limitation.* If an eligible entity makes an election under paragraph (c)(1)(i) of this section to change its classification (other than an election made by an existing entity to change its classification as of the effective date of this section), the entity cannot change its classification by election again during the sixty months succeeding the effective date of the election. However, the Commissioner may permit the entity to change its classification by election within the sixty months if more than fifty percent of the ownership interests in the entity as of the effective date of the subsequent election are owned by persons that did not own any interests in the entity on the filing date or on the effective date of the entity's prior election....

DELAWARE GENERAL
CORPORATION LAW

SUBCHAPTER I. FORMATION

SUBCHAPTER II. POWERS

SUBCHAPTER III. REGISTERED OFFICE
AND REGISTERED AGENT

SUBCHAPTER IV. DIRECTORS AND OFFICERS

* Omitted.

* Omitted.

353

* Omitted.

SUBCHAPTER X. SALE OF ASSETS, DISSOLUTION AND WINDING UP

* Omitted.

* Omitted.

SUBCHAPTER XIV. CLOSE CORPORATIONS; SPECIAL PROVISIONS

SUBCHAPTER XV. FOREIGN CORPORATIONS

* Omitted.

SUBCHAPTER I. FORMATION

§ 101. Incorporators; How Corporation Formed; Purposes

(a) Any person, partnership, association or corporation, singly or jointly with others, and without regard to his or their residence, domicile or state of incorporation, may incorporate or organize a corporation under this chapter by filing with the Secretary of State a certificate of incorporation which shall be executed, acknowledged and filed in accordance with section 103 of this title.

(b) A corporation may be incorporated or organized under this chapter to conduct or promote any lawful business or purposes, except as may otherwise be provided by the constitution or other law of this State.

(c) Corporations for constructing, maintaining and operating public utilities, whether in or outside of this State, may be organized under this chapter, but corporations for constructing, maintaining and operating public utilities within this State shall be subject to, in addition to the provisions of this chapter, the special provisions and requirements of Title 26 applicable to such corporations.

§ 102. Certificate of Incorporation; Contents

(a) The certificate of incorporation shall set forth—

* Omitted.

(1) The name of the corporation which (i) shall contain one of the words "association", "company", "corporation", "club", "foundation", "fund", "incorporated", "institute", "society", "union", "syndicate", or "limited", or one of the abbreviations "co.", "corp.", "inc.", "ltd.", or words or abbreviations of like import in other languages (provided they are written in Roman characters or letters); provided, however, that the Division of Corporations in the Department of State may waive such requirement (unless it determines that such name is, or might otherwise appear to be, that of a natural person) if such corporation executes, acknowledges and files with the Secretary of State in accordance with § 103 of this title a certificate stating that its total assets, as defined in subsection (ii) of § 503 of this title, are not less than 10 million dollars, and (2) shall be such as to distinguish it upon the records in the office of the Secretary of State from the names of other corporations or limited partnerships organized, reserved or registered as a foreign corporation or foreign limited partnership under the laws of this State except with the written consent of such other foreign corporation or domestic or foreign limited partnership, executed, acknowledged, and filed with the Secretary of State in accordance with section 103 of this title;

(2) The address (which shall include the street, number, city and county) of the corporation's registered office in this State, and the name of its registered agent at such address;

(3) The nature of the business or purposes to be conducted or promoted. It shall be sufficient to state, either alone or with other businesses or purposes, that the purpose of the corporation is to engage in any lawful act or activity for which corporations may be organized under the General Corporation Law of Delaware, and by such statement all lawful acts and activities shall be within the purposes of the corporation, except for express limitations, if any;

(4) If the corporation is to be authorized to issue only one class of stock, the total number of shares of stock which the corporation shall have authority to issue and the par value of each of such shares, or a statement that all such shares are to be without par value. If the corporation is to be authorized to issue more than one class of stock, the certificate of incorporation shall set forth the total number of shares of all classes of stock which the corporation shall have authority to issue and the number of shares of each class, and shall specify each class the shares of which are to be without par value and each class the shares of which are to have par value and the par value of the shares of each such class. The certificate of incorporation shall also set forth a statement of the designations and the powers, preferences and rights, and the qualifications, limitations or restrictions thereof, which are permitted by § 151 of this Title in respect of any class or classes of stock or any series of any class of stock of the corporation and the fixing of which by the certificate of incorporation is desired, and an express grant of such authority as it may then be desired to grant to the board of directors to fix by resolution

or resolutions any thereof that may be desired but which shall not be fixed by the certificate of incorporation.   . . .;

(5) The name and mailing address of the incorporator or incorporators;

(6) If the powers of the incorporator or incorporators are to terminate upon the filing of the certificate of incorporation, the names and mailing addresses of the persons who are to serve as directors until the first annual meeting of stockholders or until their successors are elected and qualify.

(b) In addition to the matters required to be set forth in the certificate of incorporation by subsection (a) of this section the certificate of incorporation may also contain any or all of the following matters—

(1) Any provision for the management of the business and for the conduct of the affairs of the corporation, and any provision creating, defining, limiting and regulating the powers of the corporation, the directors, and the stockholders, or any class of the stockholders, or the members of a non-stock corporation; if such provisions are not contrary to the laws of this State. Any provision which is required or permitted by any section of this chapter to be stated in the by-laws may instead be stated in the certificate of incorporation;

(2) The following provisions, in haec verba, viz.—

"Whenever a compromise or arrangement is proposed between this corporation and its creditors or any class of them and/or between this corporation and its stockholders or any class of them, any court of equitable jurisdiction within the State of Delaware may, on the application in a summary way of this corporation or of any creditor or stockholder thereof or on the application of any receiver or receivers appointed for this corporation under the provisions of section 291 of Title 8 of the Delaware Code or on the application of trustees in dissolution or of any receiver or receivers appointed for this corporation under the provisions of section 279 of Title 8 of the Delaware Code order a meeting of the creditors or class of creditors, and/or of the stockholders or class of stockholders of this corporation, as the case may be, to be summoned in such manner as the said court directs. If a majority in number representing three-fourths in value of the creditors or class of creditors, and/or of the stockholders or class of stockholders of this corporation, as the case may be, agree to any compromise or arrangement and to any reorganization of this corporation as consequence of such compromise or arrangement, the said compromise or arrangement and the said reorganization shall, if sanctioned by the court to which the said application has been made, be binding on all the creditors or class of creditors, and/or on all the stockholders or class of stockholders, of this corporation, as the case may be, and also on this corporation";

(3) Such provisions as may be desired granting to the holders of the stock of the corporation, or the holders of any class or series of a class thereof, the preemptive right to subscribe to any or all additional issues of stock of the corporation of any or all classes or series thereof, or to any securities of the corporation convertible into such stock. No stockholder shall have any preemptive right to subscribe to an additional issue of stock or to any security convertible into such stock unless, and except to the extent that, such right is expressly granted to him in the certificate of incorporation. All such rights in existence on July 3, 1967, shall remain in existence unaffected by this paragraph (3) unless and until changed or terminated by appropriate action which expressly provides for such change or termination;

(4) Provisions requiring for any corporate action, the vote of a larger portion of the stock or of any class or series thereof, or of any other securities having voting power, or a larger number of the directors, that is required by this chapter;

(5) A provision limiting the duration of the corporation's existence to a specified date; otherwise, the corporation shall have perpetual existence;

(6) A provision imposing personal liability for the debts of the corporation on its stockholders or members to a specified extent and upon specified conditions; otherwise, the stockholders or members of a corporation shall not be personally liable for the payment of the corporation's debts except as they may be liable by reason of their own conduct or acts;

(7) A provision eliminating or limiting the personal liability of a director to the corporation or its stockholders for monetary damages for breach of fiduciary duty as a director, provided that such provision shall not eliminate or limit the liability of a director (i) for any breach of the director's duty of loyalty to the corporation or its stockholders, (ii) for acts or omissions not in good faith or which involve intentional misconduct or a knowing violation of law, (iii) under section 174 of this Title, or (iv) for any transaction from which the director derived an improper personal benefit. No such provision shall eliminate or limit the liability of a director for any act or omission occurring prior to the date when such provision becomes effective. All references in this paragraph to a director shall also be deemed to refer (x) to a member of the governing body of a corporation which is not authorized to issue capital stock, and (y) to such other person or persons, if any, who, pursuant to a provision of the certificate of incorporation in accordance with § 141(a) of this title, exercise or perform any of the powers or duties otherwise conferred or imposed upon the board of directors by this title.

(c) It shall not be necessary to set forth in the certificate of incorporation any of the powers conferred on corporations by this chapter.

§ 103. Execution, Acknowledgment, Filing, Recording and Effective Date of Original Certificate of Incorporation and Other Instruments; Exceptions

(a) Whenever any provision of this chapter requires any instrument to be filed with the Secretary of State or in accordance with this section or chapter, such instrument shall be executed as follows:

(1) The certificate of incorporation, and any other instrument to be filed before the election of the initial board of directors if the initial directors were not named in the certificate of incorporation, shall be signed by the incorporator or incorporators.

(2) All other instruments shall be signed:

a. By any authorized officer of the corporation; or

b. If it shall appear from the instrument that there are no such officers, then by a majority of the directors or by such directors as may be designated by the board; or

c. If it shall appear from the instrument that there are no such officers or directors, then by the holders of record, or such of them as may be designated by the holders of record, of a majority of all outstanding shares of stock; or

d. By the holders of record of all outstanding shares of stock.

(b) Whenever any provision of this chapter requires any instrument to be acknowledged, such requirement is satisfied by either:

(1) The formal acknowledgment by the person or one of the persons signing the instrument that it is his act and deed or the act and deed of the corporation, as the case may be, and that the facts stated therein are true. Such acknowledgment shall be made before a person who is authorized by the law of the place of execution to take acknowledgments of deeds and who, if he has a seal of office, shall affix it to the instrument.

(2) The signature, without more, of the person or persons signing the instrument, in which case such signature or signatures shall constitute the affirmation or acknowledgment of the signatory, under penalties of perjury, that the instrument is his act and deed or the act and deed of the corporation, as the case may be, and that the facts stated therein are true.

(c) Whenever any provision of this chapter requires any instrument to be filed with the Secretary of State or in accordance with this section or chapter, such requirement means that:

(1) The original signed instrument shall be delivered to the office of the Secretary of State.

(2) All taxes and fees authorized by law to be collected by the Secretary of State in connection with the filing of the instrument shall be tendered to the Secretary of State.

(3) Upon delivery of the instrument, and upon tender of the required taxes and fees, the Secretary of State shall certify that the instrument has been filed in his office by endorsing upon the original signed instrument the word "Filed", and the date and hour of its filing. This endorsement is the "filing date" of the instrument, and is conclusive of the date and time of its filing in the absence of actual fraud. The Secretary of State shall thereupon file and index the endorsed instrument.

(4) The Secretary of State, acting as agent for the recorders of each of the counties, shall collect and deposit in a separate account established exclusively for that purpose a county assessment fee with respect to each filed instrument, and shall thereafter weekly remit from such account to the recorder of each of the said counties the amount or amounts of such fees as provided for in paragraph (c)(5) of this section or as elsewhere provided by law. Said fees shall be for the purposes of defraying certain costs incurred by the counties in merging the information and images of such filed documents with the document information systems of each of the recorder's offices in the counties, and in retrieving, maintaining and displaying such information and images in the offices of the recorders and at remote locations in each of such counties. In consideration for its acting as the agent for the recorders with respect to the collection and payment of the county assessment fees, the Secretary of State shall retain and pay over to the general fund of the State an administrative charge of one percent of the total fees collected.

(5) The assessment fee to the counties shall be $24 for each one-page instrument filed with the Secretary of State in accordance with this section and $9 for each additional page for instruments with more than one page. The recorder's office to receive the assessment fee shall be the recorder's office in the county in which the corporation's registered office in this State is, or is to be, located, except that an assessment fee shall not be charged for either a certificate of dissolution qualifying for treatment under § 391(a)(5)(b) ... [short-form dissolution], or a document filed in accordance with subchapter XV of this title.

(6) The Secretary of State shall enter such information from each instrument as he deems appropriate into the Delaware Corporation Information System or any system which is a successor thereto in the office of the Secretary of State, and such information shall be permanently maintained. A copy of each instrument shall be permanently maintained on optical disk or by other suitable medium.

(d) Any instrument filed in accordance with subsection (c) of this section shall be effective upon its filing date. Any instrument may provide that it is not to become effective until a specified time subsequent to the time it is filed, but such time shall not be later than a time on the 90th day after the date of its filing. ...

(f) Whenever any instrument authorized to be filed with the Secretary of State under any provision of this title has been so filed and is an inaccurate record of the corporate action therein referred to, or was defectively or erroneously executed, sealed or acknowledged, such instrument may be corrected by filing with the Secretary of State a certificate of correction of such instrument which shall be executed, acknowledged and filed in accordance with this section. The certificate of correction shall specify the inaccuracy or defect to be corrected and shall set forth the portion of the instrument in corrected form. In lieu of filing a certificate of correction the instrument may be corrected by filing with the Secretary of State a corrected instrument which shall be executed, acknowledged and filed in accordance with this section. The corrected instrument shall be specifically designated as such in its heading, shall specify the inaccuracy or defect to be corrected, and shall set forth the entire instrument in corrected form. An instrument corrected in accordance with this section shall be effective as of the date the original instrument was filed, except as to those persons who are substantially and adversely affected by the correction and as to those persons the instrument as corrected shall be effective from the filing date.

(g) Notwithstanding that any instrument authorized to be filed with the Secretary of State under any provision of this title is when filed inaccurately, defectively or erroneously executed, sealed or acknowledged, or otherwise defective in any respect, the Secretary of State shall have no liability to any person for the preclearance for filing, the acceptance for filing, or the filing and indexing of such instrument by the Secretary of State.

(h) Any signature or any instrument authorized to be filed with the Secretary of State under any provision of this title may be a facsimile, a conformed signature or an electronically transmitted signature.

§ 105. Certificate of Incorporation and Other Certificates; Evidence

A copy of a certificate of incorporation, or a restated certificate of incorporation, or of any other certificate which has been filed in the office of the Secretary of State as required by any provision of this title shall, when duly certified by the Secretary of State, be received in all courts, public offices, and official bodies as prima facie evidence of:

(1) Due execution, acknowledgment and filing of the instrument;

(2) Observance and performance of all acts and conditions necessary to have been observed and performed precedent to the instrument becoming effective; and of

(3) Any other facts required or permitted by law to be stated in the instrument.

§ 106. Commencement of Corporate Existence

Upon the filing with the Secretary of State of the certificate of incorporation, executed and acknowledged in accordance with section 103, the incorporator or incorporators who signed the certificate, and his or their successors and assigns, shall, from the date of such filing, be and constitute a body corporate, by the name set forth in the certificate, subject to the provisions of section 103(d) of this title and subject to dissolution or other termination of its existence as provided in this chapter.

§ 107. Powers of Incorporators

If the persons who are to serve as directors until the first annual meeting of stockholders have not been named in the certificate of incorporation, the incorporator or incorporators, until the directors are elected, shall manage the affairs of the corporation and may do whatever is necessary and proper to perfect the organization of the corporation, including the adoption of the original by-laws of the corporation and the election of directors.

§ 108. Organization Meeting of Incorporators or Directors Named in Certificate of Incorporation

(a) After the filing of the certificate of incorporation an organization meeting of the incorporator or incorporators, or of the board of directors if the initial directors were named in the certificate of incorporation, shall be held, either within or without this State, at the call of a majority of the incorporators or directors, as the case may be, for the purposes of adopting by-laws, electing directors (if the meeting is of the incorporators) to serve or hold office until the first annual meeting of stockholders or until their successors are elected and qualify, electing officers if the meeting is of the directors, doing any other or further acts to perfect the organization of the corporation, and transacting such other business as may come before the meeting.

(b) The persons calling the meeting shall give to each other incorporator or director, as the case may be, at least 2 days written notice thereof by any usual means of communication, which notice shall state the time, place and purposes of the meeting as fixed by the persons calling it. Notice of the meeting need not be given to anyone who attends the meeting or who signs a waiver of notice either before or after the meeting.

(c) Any action permitted to be taken at the organization meeting of the incorporators or directors, as the case may be, may be taken without a meeting if each incorporator or director, where there is more than one, or the sole incorporator or director where there is only one, signs an instrument which states the action so taken.

§ 109. By–Laws

(a) The original or other by-laws of a corporation may be adopted, amended, or repealed by the incorporators, by the initial directors if they were named in the certificate of incorporation, or, before a corporation has received any payment for any of its stock, by its board of directors. After a corporation has received any payment for any of its stock, the power to adopt, amend or repeal by-laws shall be in the stockholders entitled to vote, or, in the case of a non-stock corporation, in its members entitled to vote; provided, however, any corporation may, in its certificate of incorporation, confer the power to adopt, amend, or repeal by-laws upon the directors or, in the case of a non-stock corporation, upon its governing body by whatever name designated. The fact that such power has been so conferred upon the directors or governing body, as the case may be, shall not divest the stockholders or members of the power, nor limit their power to adopt, amend or repeal by-laws.

(b) The by-laws may contain any provision, not inconsistent with law or with the certificate of incorporation, relating to the business of the corporation, the conduct of its affairs, and its rights or powers or the rights or powers of its stockholders, directors, officers or employees.

§ 110. Emergency By–Laws and Other Powers in Emergency

The board of directors of any corporation may adopt emergency by-laws, subject to repeal or change by action of the stockholders, which shall notwithstanding any different provision elsewhere in this chapter or in Chapters 3 and 5 of Title 26, or in Chapter 7 of Title 5, or in the certificate of incorporation or by-laws, be operative during any emergency resulting from an attack on the United States or on a locality in which the corporation conducts its business or customarily holds meetings of its board of directors or its stockholders, or during any nuclear or atomic disaster, or during the existence of any catastrophe, or other similar emergency condition, as a result of which a quorum of the board of directors or a standing committee thereof cannot readily be convened for action. The emergency by-laws may make any provision that may be practical and necessary for the circumstances of the emergency.

SUBCHAPTER II. POWERS

§ 121. General Powers

(a) In addition to the powers enumerated in Section 122 of this title, every corporation, its officers, directors, and stockholders shall possess and may exercise all the powers and privileges granted by this chapter or by any other law or by its certificate of incorporation, together with any powers incidental thereto, so far as such powers and privileges are necessary or convenient to the conduct, promotion or attainment of the business or purposes set forth in its certificate of incorporation.

(b) Every corporation shall be governed by the provisions and be subject to the restrictions and liabilities contained in this chapter.

§ 122. Specific Powers

Every corporation created under this chapter shall have power to—

(1) Have perpetual succession by its corporate name, unless a limited period of duration is stated in its certificate of incorporation;

(2) Sue and be sued in all courts and participate, as a party or otherwise, in any judicial, administrative, arbitrative or other proceeding, in its corporate name;

(3) Have a corporate seal, which may be altered at pleasure, and use the same by causing it or a facsimile thereof, to be impressed or affixed or in any other manner reproduced;

(4) Purchase, receive, take by grant, gift, devise, bequest or otherwise, lease, or otherwise acquire, own, hold, improve, employ, use and otherwise deal in and with real or personal property, or any interest therein, wherever situated, and to sell, convey, lease, exchange, transfer or otherwise dispose of, or mortgage or pledge, all or any of its property and assets, or any interest therein, wherever situated;

(5) Appoint such officers and agents as the business of the corporation requires and to pay or otherwise provide for them suitable compensation;

(6) Adopt, amend and repeal by-laws;

(7) Wind up and dissolve itself in the manner provided in this chapter;

(8) Conduct its business, carry on its operations, and have offices and exercise its powers within or without this State;

(9) Make donations for the public welfare or for charitable, scientific or educational purposes, and in time of war or other national emergency in aid thereof;

(10) Be an incorporator, promoter, or manager of other corporations of any type or kind;

(11) Participate with others in any corporation, partnership, limited partnership, joint venture, or other association of any kind, or in any transaction, undertaking or arrangement which the participating corporation would have power to conduct by itself, whether or not such participation involves sharing or delegation of control with or to others;

(12) Transact any lawful business which the corporation's board of directors shall find to be in aid of governmental authority;

(13) Make contracts, including contracts of guaranty and suretyship, incur liabilities, borrow money at such rates of interest as the corporation may determine, issue its notes, bonds and other obligations, and secure any of its obligations by mortgage, pledge or other encumbrance of all or any of its property, franchises and income, and make contracts of guaranty and suretyship which are necessary or convenient to the conduct, promotion or attainment of the business of (a) a corporation all of the outstanding stock of which is owned, directly or indirectly, by the contracting corporation, or (b) a corporation which owns, directly or indirectly, all of the outstanding stock of the contracting corporation, or (c) a corporation all of the outstanding stock of which is owned, directly or indirectly, by a corporation which owns, directly or indirectly, all of the outstanding stock of the contracting corporation, which contracts of guaranty and suretyship shall be deemed to be necessary or convenient to the conduct, promotion or attainment of the business of the contracting corporation, and make other contracts of guaranty and suretyship which are necessary or convenient to the conduct, promotion or attainment of the business of the contracting corporation;

(14) Lend money for its corporate purposes, invest and reinvest its funds, and take, hold and deal with real and personal property as security for the payment of funds so loaned or invested;

(15) Pay pensions and establish and carry out pension, profit sharing, stock option, stock purchase, stock bonus, retirement, benefit, incentive and compensation plans, trusts and provisions for any or all of its directors, officers, and employees, and for any or all of the directors, officers, and employees of its subsidiaries;

(16) Provide insurance for its benefit on the life of any of its directors, officers, or employees, or on the life of any stockholder for the purpose of acquiring at his death shares of its stock owned by such stockholder.

§ 123. Powers Respecting Securities of Other Corporations or Entities

Any corporation organized under the laws of this State may guarantee, purchase, take, receive, subscribe for or otherwise acquire; own, hold, use or otherwise employ; sell, lease, exchange, transfer, or otherwise dispose of; mortgage, lend, pledge or otherwise deal in and with, bonds and other obligations of, or shares or other securities or interests in, or issued by, any other domestic or foreign corporation, partnership, association, or individual, or by any government or agency or instrumentality thereof. A corporation while owner of any such securities may exercise all the rights, powers and privileges of ownership, including the right to vote.

§ 124. Lack of Corporate Capacity or Power; Effect; Ultra Vires

No act of a corporation and no conveyance or transfer of real or personal property to or by a corporation shall be invalid by reason of the fact that the corporation was without capacity or power to do such act or to make or receive such conveyance or transfer, but such lack of capacity or power may be asserted:

(1) In a proceeding by a stockholder against the corporation to enjoin the doing of any act or acts or the transfer of real or personal property by or to the corporation. If the unauthorized acts or transfer sought to be enjoined are being, or are to be, performed or made pursuant to any contract to which the corporation is a party, the court may, if all of the parties to the contract are parties to the proceeding and if it deems the same to be equitable, set aside and enjoin the performance of such contract, and in so doing may allow to the corporation or to the other parties to the contract, as the case may be, such compensation as may be equitable for the loss or damage sustained by any of them which may result from the action of the court in setting aside and enjoining the performance of such contract, but anticipated profits to be derived from the performance of the contract shall not be awarded by the court as a loss or damage sustained.

(2) In a proceeding by the corporation, whether acting directly or through a receiver, trustee, or other legal representative, or through stockholders in a representative suit, against an incumbent or former officer or director of the corporation, for loss or damage due to his unauthorized act.

(3) In a proceeding by the Attorney General to dissolve the corporation, or to enjoin the corporation from the transaction of unauthorized business.

SUBCHAPTER III. REGISTERED OFFICE AND REGISTERED AGENT

§ 131. Registered Office in State; Principal Office or Place of Business in State

(a) Every corporation shall have and maintain in this State a registered office which may, but need not be, the same as its place of business.

(b) Whenever the term "corporation's principal office or place of business in this State" or "principal office or place of business of the corporation in this State", or other term of like import, is or has been used in a corporation's certificate of incorporation, or in any other document, or in any statute, it shall be deemed to mean and refer to, unless the context indicates otherwise, the corporation's registered office required by this section; and it shall not be necessary for any corporation to amend its certificate of incorporation or any other document to comply with this section.

§ 132.   Registered Agent in State; Resident Agent

(a) Every corporation shall have and maintain in this State a registered agent, which agent may be either an individual resident in this State whose business office is identical with the corporation's registered office, or a domestic corporation (which may be itself), or a foreign corporation authorized to transact business in this State, having a business office identical with such registered office.

(b) Whenever the term "resident agent" or "resident agent in charge of a corporation's principal office or place of business in this State", or other term of like import which refers to a corporation's agent required by statute to be located in this State, is or has been used in a corporation's certificate of incorporation, or in any other document, or in any statute, it shall be deemed to mean and refer to, unless the context indicates otherwise, the corporation's registered agent required by this section; and it shall not be necessary for any corporation to amend its certificate of incorporation or any other document to comply with this section.

SUBCHAPTER IV.   DIRECTORS AND OFFICERS

§ 141.   Board of Directors; Powers; Number, Qualifications, Terms and Quorum; Committees; Classes of Directors; ... Reliance Upon Books; Action Without Meeting, etc.

(a) The business and affairs of every corporation organized under this chapter shall be managed by or under the direction of a board of directors, except as may be otherwise provided in this chapter or in its certificate of incorporation. If any such provision is made in the certificate of incorporation, the powers and duties conferred or imposed upon the board of directors by this chapter shall be exercised or performed to such extent and by such person or persons as shall be provided in the certificate of incorporation.

(b) The board of directors of a corporation shall consist of one or more members. The number of directors shall be fixed by, or in the manner provided in, the by-laws, unless the certificate of incorporation fixes the number of directors, in which case a change in the number of directors shall be made only by amendment of the certificate. Directors need not be stockholders unless so required by the certificate of incorporation or the by-laws. The certificate of incorporation or by-laws may prescribe other qualifications for directors. Each director shall hold office until his successor is elected and qualified or until his earlier resignation or removal. Any director may resign at any time upon written notice to the corporation. A majority of the total number of directors shall constitute a quorum for the transaction of business unless the certificate of incorporation or the by-laws require a greater number. Unless the certificate of incorporation provides otherwise, the by-laws may provide that a number less than a majority shall constitute a quorum which in no case shall be less than one-third of the total number of directors except that when a board of one director is authorized under the provisions of this section, then one director shall constitute a quorum. The vote of the majority of the directors present at a meeting at which a quorum is present shall be the act of the board of directors unless the certificate of incorporation or the by-laws shall require a vote of a greater number.

(c)(1) All corporations incorporated prior to July 1, 1996, shall be governed by subsection (1) of this section, provided that any such corporation may by a resolution adopted by a majority of the whole board elect to be governed by subsection (2) of this section, in which case subsection (1) of this section shall not apply to such corporation. All corporations incorporated on or after July 1, 1996, shall be governed by subsection (2) of this section. The board of directors may, by resolution passed by a majority of the whole board, designate one or more committees, each committee to consist of one or more of the directors of the corporation. The board may designate one or more directors as alternate members of any committee, who may replace any absent or disqualified member at any meeting of the committee. The by-laws may provide that in the absence or disqualification of a member of a committee, the member or members thereof present at any meeting and not disqualified from voting, whether or not he or they constitute a quorum, may unanimously appoint another member of the board of directors to act at the meeting in the place of any such absent or disqualified member. Any such committee, to the extent provided in the resolution of the board of directors, or in the by-laws of the corporation, shall have and may exercise all the powers and authority of the board of directors in the management of the business and affairs of the corporation, and may authorize the seal of the corporation to be affixed to all papers which may require it; but no such committee shall have the power or authority in reference to amending the certificate of incorporation (except that a committee may, to the extent authorized in the resolution or resolutions providing for the issuance of shares of stock adopted by the board of directors as provided in Section 151(a) of this title, fix the designations and any of the preferences or rights of such shares relating to dividends, redemption, dissolution, any distribution of assets of the corporation or the conversion into, or the exchange of such shares for, shares of any other class or classes or any other series of the same or any other class or classes of stock of the corporation or fix the number of shares of any series of stock or authorize the increase or decrease of the shares of any series), adopting an agreement of merger or consolidation under Sections 251, 252, 254, 255, 256, 257, 258, 263 or 264 of this title, recommending to the stockholders the sale, lease or exchange of all or substantially all of the corporation's property and assets, recommending to the stockholders a dissolution of the corporation or a revocation of a dissolution, or amending the by-laws of the corporation; and, unless the resolution, by-laws, or certificate of incorporation expressly so provide, no such committee shall have the power or authority to declare a dividend, to authorize the issuance of stock, or to adopt a certificate of ownership and merger pursuant to Section 253 of this title.

(2) The board of directors may designate 1 or more committees, each committee to consist of 1 or more of the directors of the corporation. The board may designate one or more directors as alternate members of any committee, who may replace any absent or disqualified member at any meeting of the committee. The bylaws may provide that in the absence or disqualification of a member of a committee, the member or members present at any meeting and not disqualified from voting, whether or not such member or members constitute a quorum, may unanimously appoint another member of the board of directors to act at the meeting in the place of any such absent or disqualified member. Any such committee, to the extent provided in the resolution of the board of directors, or in the bylaws of the corporation, shall have and may exercise all the powers and authority of the board of directors in the management of the business and affairs of the corporation, and may authorize the seal of the corporation to be affixed to all papers which may require it; but no such committee shall have the power or authority in reference to the following matters: (i) approving or adopting, or recommending to the stockholders, any action or matter expressly required by this chapter to be submitted to stockholders for approval or (ii) adopting, amending or repealing any bylaw of the corporation.

(d) The directors of any corporation organized under this chapter may, by the certificate of incorporation or by an initial by-law, or by a by-law adopted by a vote of the stockholders, be divided into one, two or three classes; the term of office of those of the first class to expire at the annual meeting next ensuing; of the second class one year thereafter; of the third class two years thereafter; and at each annual election held after such classification and election, directors shall be chosen for a full term, as the case may be, to succeed those whose terms expire. The certificate of incorporation may confer upon holders of any class or series of stock the right to elect one or more directors who shall serve for such term, and have such voting powers as shall be stated in the certificate of incorporation. The terms of office and voting powers of the directors elected in the manner so provided in the certificate of incorporation may be greater than or less than those of any other director or class of directors. If the certificate of incorporation provides that directors elected by the holders of a class or series of stock shall have more or less than 1 vote per director on any matter, every reference in this chapter to a majority or other proportion of directors shall refer to a majority or other proportion of the votes of such directors.

(e) A member of the board of directors, or a member of any committee designated by the board of directors, shall, in the performance of his duties, be fully protected in relying in good faith upon the records of the corporation and upon such information, opinions, reports or statements presented to the corporation by any of the corporation's officers or employees, or committees of the board of directors, or by any other person as to matters the member reasonably believes are within such other person's professional or expert competence and who has been selected with reasonable care by or on behalf of the corporation.

(f) Unless otherwise restricted by the certificate of incorporation or by-laws, any action required or permitted to be taken at any meeting of the board of directors, or of any committee thereof may be taken without a meeting if all members of the board or committee, as the case may be, consent thereto in writing, and the writing or writings are filed with the minutes of proceedings of the board or committee.

(g) Unless otherwise restricted by the certificate of incorporation or by-laws, the board of directors of any corporation organized under this chapter may hold its meetings, and have an office or offices, outside of this State.

(h) Unless otherwise restricted by the certificate of incorporation or by-laws, the board of directors shall have the authority to fix the compensation of directors.

(i) Unless otherwise restricted by the certificate of incorporation or by-laws, members of the board of directors of any corporation, or any committee designated by such board, may participate in a meeting of such board or committee by means of conference telephone or similar communications equipment by means of which all persons participating in the meeting can hear each other, and participation in a meeting pursuant to this subsection shall constitute presence in person at such meeting. ...

(k) Any director or the entire board of directors may be removed, with or without cause, by the holders of a majority of the shares then entitled to vote at an election of directors, except as follows:

(i) Unless the certificate of incorporation otherwise provides, in the case of a corporation whose board is classified as provided in subsection (d) of this section, shareholders may effect such removal only for cause; or

(ii) In the case of a corporation having cumulative voting, if less than the entire board is to be removed, no director may be removed without cause if the votes cast against his removal would be sufficient to elect him if then cumulatively voted at an election of the entire board of directors, or, if there be classes of directors, at an election of the class of directors of which he is a part.

Whenever the holders of any class or series are entitled to elect one or more directors by the provisions of the certificate of incorporation, the provisions of this subsection shall apply, in respect to the removal without cause of a director or directors so elected, to the vote of the holders of the outstanding shares of that class or series and not to the vote of the outstanding shares as a whole.

§ 142. Officers; Titles, Duties, Selection, Term; Failure to Elect; Vacancies

(a) Every corporation organized under this chapter shall have such officers with such titles and duties as shall be stated in the by-laws or in a resolution of the board of directors which is not inconsistent with the by-laws and as may be necessary to enable it to sign instruments and stock certificates which comply with sections 103(a)(2) and 158 of this chapter. One of the officers shall have the duty to record the proceedings of the meetings of the stockholders and directors in a book to be kept for that purpose. Any number of offices may be held by the same person unless the certificate of incorporation or bylaws otherwise provide.

(b) Officers shall be chosen in such manner and shall hold their offices for such terms as are prescribed by the by-laws or determined by the board of directors or other governing body. Each officer shall hold his office until his successor is elected and qualified or until his earlier resignation or removal. Any officer may resign at any time upon written notice to the corporation.

(c) The corporation may secure the fidelity of any or all of its officers or agents by bond or otherwise.

(d) A failure to elect officers shall not dissolve or otherwise affect the corporation.

(e) Any vacancy occurring in any office of the corporation by death, resignation, removal or otherwise, shall be filled as the by-laws provide. In the absence of such provision, the vacancy shall be filled by the board of directors or other governing body.

§ 143. Loans to Employees and Officers; Guaranty of Obligations of Employees and Officers

Any corporation may lend money to, or guarantee any obligation of, or otherwise assist any officer or other employee of the corporation or of its subsidiary, including any officer or employee who is a director of the corporation or its subsidiary, whenever, in the judgment of the directors, such loan, guaranty or assistance may reasonably be expected to benefit the corporation. The loan, guaranty or other assistance may be with or without interest, and may be unsecured, or secured in such manner as the board of directors shall approve, including, without limitation, a pledge of shares of stock of the corporation. Nothing in this section contained shall be deemed to deny, limit or restrict the powers of guaranty or warranty of any corporation at common law or under any statute.

§ 144. Interested Directors; Quorum

(a) No contract or transaction between a corporation and one or more of its directors or officers, or between a corporation and any other corporation, partnership, association, or other organization in which one or more of its directors or officers are directors or officers, or have a financial interest, shall be void or voidable solely for this reason, or solely because the director or officer is present at or participates in the meeting of the board or committee thereof which authorizes the contract or transaction, or solely because his or their votes are counted for such purpose, if:

(1) The material facts as to his relationship or interest and as to the contract or transaction are disclosed or are known to the board of directors or the committee, and the board or committee in good faith authorizes the contract or transaction by the affirmative votes of a majority of the disinterested directors, even though the disinterested directors be less than a quorum; or

(2) The material facts as to his relationship or interest and as to the contract or transaction are disclosed or are known to the shareholders entitled to vote thereon, and the contract or transaction is specifically approved in good faith by vote of the shareholders; or

(3) The contract or transaction is fair as to the corporation as of the time it is authorized, approved or ratified, by the board of directors, a committee thereof, or the shareholders.

(b) Common or interested directors may be counted in determining the presence of a quorum at a meeting of the board of directors or of a committee which authorizes the contract or transaction.

§ 145. Indemnification of Officers, Directors, Employees and Agents; Insurance

(a) A corporation shall have power to indemnify any person who was or is a party or is threatened to be made a party to any threatened, pending or completed action, suit or proceeding, whether civil, criminal, administrative or investigative (other than an action by or in the right of the corporation) by reason of the fact that he is or was a director, officer, employee or agent of the corporation, or is or was serving at the request of the corporation as a director, officer, employee or agent of another corporation, partnership, joint venture, trust or other enterprise, against expenses (including attorneys' fees), judgments, fines and amounts paid in settlement actually and reasonably incurred by him in connection with such action, suit or proceeding if he acted in good faith and in a manner he reasonably believed to be in or not opposed to the best interests of the corporation, and, with respect to any criminal action or proceeding, had no reasonable cause to believe his conduct was unlawful. The termination of any action, suit or proceeding by judgment, order, settlement, conviction, or upon a plea of *nolo contendere* or its equivalent, shall not, of itself, create a presumption that the person did not act in good faith and in a manner which he reasonably believed to be in or not opposed to the best interests of the corporation, and, with respect to any criminal action or proceeding, had reasonable cause to believe that his conduct was unlawful.

(b) A corporation shall have power to indemnify any person who was or is a party or is threatened to be made a party to any threatened, pending or completed action or suit by or in the right of the corporation to procure a judgment in its favor by reason of the fact that he is or was a director, officer, employee or agent of the corporation, or is or was serving at the request of the corporation as a director, officer, employee or agent of another corporation, partnership, joint venture, trust or other enterprise against expenses (including attorneys' fees) actually and reasonably incurred by him in connection with the defense or settlement of such action or suit if he acted in good faith and in a manner he reasonably believed to be in or not opposed to the best interests of the corporation and except that no indemnification shall be made in respect of any claim, issue or matter as to which such person shall have been adjudged to be liable to the corporation unless and only to the extent that the Court of Chancery or the court in which such action or suit was brought shall determine upon application that, despite the adjudication of liability but in view of all the circumstances of the case, such person is fairly and reasonably entitled to indemnity for such expenses which the Court of Chancery or such other court shall deem proper.

(c) To the extent that a director, officer, employee or agent of a corporation has been successful on the merits or otherwise in defense of any action, suit or proceeding referred to in subsections (a) and (b), or in defense of any claim, issue or matter therein, he shall be indemnified against expenses (including attorneys' fees) actually and reasonably incurred by him in connection therewith.

(d) Any indemnification under subsections (a) and (b) of this section (unless ordered by a court) shall be made by the corporation only as authorized in the specific case upon a determination that indemnification of the director, officer, employee or agent is proper in the circumstances because he has met the applicable standard of conduct set forth in subsections (a) and (b) of this section. Such determination shall be made (1) by a majority vote of the directors who are not parties to such action, suit or proceeding, even though less than a quorum, or (2) if there are no such directors, or if such directors so direct, by independent legal counsel in a written opinion, or (3) by the stockholders.

(e) Expenses (including attorneys' fees) incurred by an officer or director in defending any civil, criminal, administrative, or investigative action, suit or proceeding may be paid by the corporation in advance of the final disposition of such action, suit or proceeding upon receipt of an undertaking by or on behalf of such director or officer to repay such amount if it shall ultimately be determined that he is not entitled to be indemnified by the corporation as authorized in this Section. Such expenses (including attorneys' fees) incurred by other employees and agents may be so paid upon such terms and conditions, if any, as the board of directors deems appropriate.

(f) The indemnification and advancement of expenses provided by, or granted pursuant to, the other subsections of this section shall not be deemed exclusive of any other rights to which those seeking indemnification or advancement of expenses may be entitled under any by-law, agreement, vote of stockholders or disinterested directors or otherwise, both as to action in his official capacity and as to action in another capacity while holding such office.

(g) A corporation shall have power to purchase and maintain insurance on behalf of any person who is or was a director, officer, employee or agent of the corporation, or is or was serving at the request of the corporation as a director, officer, employee or agent of another corporation, partnership, joint venture, trust or other enterprise against any liability asserted against him and incurred by him in any such capacity, or arising out of his status as such, whether or not the corporation would have the power to indemnify him against such liability under the provisions of this section.

(h) For purposes of this Section, references to "the corporation" shall include, in addition to the resulting corporation, any constituent corporation (including any constituent of a constituent) absorbed in a consolidation or merger which, if its separate existence had continued, would have had power and authority to indemnify its directors, officers, and employees or agents, so that any person who is or was a director, officer, employee or agent of such constituent corporation, or is or was serving at the request of such constituent corporation as a director, officer, employee or agent of another corporation, partnership, joint venture, trust or other enterprise, shall stand in the same position under the provisions of this Section with respect to the resulting or surviving corporation as he would have with respect to such constituent corporation if its separate existence had continued.

(i) For purposes of this Section, references to "other enterprises" shall include employee benefit plans; references to "fines" shall include any excise taxes assessed on a person with respect to an employee benefit plan; and references to "serving at the request of the corporation" shall include any service as a director, officer, employee or agent of the corporation which imposes duties on, or involves services by, such director, officer, employee, or agent with respect to an employee benefit plan, its participants, or beneficiaries; and a person who acted in good faith and in a manner he reasonably believed to be in the interest of the participants and beneficiaries of an employee benefit plan shall be deemed to have acted in a manner "not opposed to the best interests of the corporation" as referred to in this Section.

(j) The indemnification and advancement of expenses provided by, or granted pursuant to, this section shall, unless otherwise provided when authorized or ratified, continue as to a person who has ceased to be a director, officer, employee or agent and shall inure to the benefit of the heirs, executors and administrators of such a person.

(k) The Court of Chancery is hereby vested with exclusive jurisdiction to hear and determine all actions for advancement of expenses or indemnification brought under this section or under any bylaw, agreement, vote of stockholders or disinterested directors, or otherwise. The Court of Chancery may summarily determine a corporation's obligation to advance expenses (including attorneys' fees).

SUBCHAPTER V.   STOCK AND DIVIDENDS

§ 151.   Classes and Series of Stock; Rights, etc.

(a) Every corporation may issue one or more classes of stock or one or more series of stock within any class thereof, any or all of which classes may be of stock with par value or stock without par value and which classes or series may have such voting powers, full or limited, or no voting powers, and such designations, preferences and relative, participating, optional or other special rights, and qualifications, limitations or restrictions thereof, as shall be stated and expressed in the certificate of incorporation or of any amendment thereto, or in the resolution or resolutions providing for the issue of such stock adopted by the board of directors pursuant to authority expressly vested in it by the provisions of its certificate of incorporation. Any of the voting powers, designations, preferences, rights and qualifications, limitations or restrictions of any such class or series of stock may be made dependent upon facts ascertainable outside the certificate of incorporation or of any amendment thereto, or outside the resolution or resolutions providing for the issue of such stock adopted by the board of directors pursuant to authority expressly vested in it by the provisions of its certificate of incorporation, provided that the manner in which such facts shall operate upon the voting powers, designations, preferences, rights and qualifications, limitations or restrictions of such class or series of stock is clearly and expressly set forth in the certificate of incorporation or in the resolution or resolutions providing for the issue of such stock adopted by the board of directors. The term "facts," as used in this subsection, includes, but is not limited to, the occurrence of any event, including a determination or action by any person or body, including the corporation. The power to increase or decrease or otherwise adjust the capital stock as provided in this chapter shall apply to all or any such classes of stock.

(b) The stock of any class or series may be made subject to redemption by the corporation at its option or at the option of the holders of such stock or upon the happening of a specified event; provided however, that at the time of such redemption the corporation shall have outstanding shares of at least 1 class or series of stock with full voting powers which shall not be subject to redemption. Notwithstanding the limitation stated in the foregoing proviso:

(1) Any stock of a regulated investment company registered under the Investment Company Act of 1940, as heretofore or hereafter amended, may be made subject to redemption by the corporation at its option or at the option of the holders of such stock.

(2) Any stock of a corporation which holds (directly or indirectly) a license or franchise from a governmental agency to conduct its business or is a member of a national securities exchange, which license, franchise or membership is conditioned upon some or all of the holders of its stock possessing prescribed qualifications, may be made subject to redemption by the corporation to the extent necessary to prevent the loss of such license, franchise or membership or to reinstate it.

Any stock which may be made redeemable under this section may be redeemed for cash, property or rights, including securities of the same or another corporation, at such time or times, price or prices, or rate or rates, and with such adjustments, as shall be stated in the certificate of incorporation or in the resolution or resolutions providing for the issue of such stock adopted by the board of directors pursuant to subsection (a) of this section.

(c) The holders of preferred or special stock of any class or of any series thereof shall be entitled to receive dividends at such rates, on such conditions and at such times as shall be stated in the certificate of incorporation or in the resolution or resolutions providing for the issue of such stock adopted by the board of directors as hereinabove provided, payable in preference to, or in such relation to, the dividends payable on any other class or classes or of any other series of stock, and cumulative or non-cumulative as shall be so stated and expressed. When dividends upon the preferred and special stocks, if any, to the extent of the preference to which such stocks are entitled, shall have been paid or declared and set apart for payment, a dividend on the remaining class or classes or series of stock may then be paid out of the remaining assets of the corporation available for dividends as elsewhere in this chapter provided.

(d) The holders of the preferred or special stock of any class or of any series thereof shall be entitled to such rights upon the dissolution of, or upon any distribution of the assets of, the corporation as shall be stated in the certificate of incorporation or in the resolution or resolutions providing for the issue of such stock adopted by the board of directors as hereinabove provided.

(e) Any stock of any class or of any series thereof may be made convertible into, or exchangeable for, at the option of either the holder or the corporation or upon the happening of a specified event, shares of any other class or classes or any other series of the same or any other class or classes of stock of the corporation, at such price or prices or at such rate or rates of exchange and with such adjustments as shall be stated in the certificate of incorporation or in the resolution or resolutions providing for the issue of such stock adopted by the board of directors as hereinabove provided.

(f) If any corporation shall be authorized to issue more than one class of stock or more than one series of any class, the powers, designations, preferences and relative, participating, optional or other special rights of each class of stock or series thereof and the qualifications, limitations or restrictions of such preferences and/or rights shall be set forth in full or summarized on the face or back of the certificate which the corporation shall issue to represent such class or series of stock, provided that, except as otherwise provided in section 202 of this title, in lieu of the foregoing requirements, there may be set forth on the face or back of the certificate which the corporation shall issue to represent such class or series of stock, a statement that the corporation will furnish without charge to each stockholder who so requests the powers, designations, preferences and relative, participating, optional or other special rights of each class of stock or series thereof and the qualifications, limitations or restrictions of such preferences and/or rights. Within a reasonable time after the issuance or transfer of uncertificated stock, the corporation shall send to the registered owner thereof a written notice containing the information required to be set forth or stated on certificates pursuant to this Section or Sections 156, 202(a) or 218(a) or with respect to this Section a statement that the corporation will furnish without charge to each stockholder who so requests the powers, designations, preferences and relative participating, optional or other special rights of each class of stock or series thereof and the qualifications, limitations or restrictions of such preferences and/or rights. Except as otherwise expressly provided by law, the rights and obligations of the holders of uncertificated stock and the rights and obligations of the holders of certificates representing stock of the same class and series shall be identical.

(g) When any corporation desires to issue any shares of stock of any class or of any series of any class of which the powers, designations, preferences and relative, participating, optional or other rights, if any, or the qualifications, limitations or restrictions thereof, if any, shall not have been set forth in the certificate of incorporation or in any amendment thereto but shall be provided for in a resolution or resolutions adopted by the board of directors pursuant to authority expressly vested in it by the provisions of the certificate of incorporation or any amendment thereto, a certificate of designations setting forth a copy of such resolution or resolutions and the number of shares of stock of such class or series as to which the resolution or resolutions apply shall be executed, acknowledged, filed, and shall become effective, in accordance with § 103 of this Title. Unless otherwise provided in any such resolution or resolutions, the number of shares of stock of any such series to which such resolution or resolutions apply may be increased (but not above the total number of authorized shares of the class) or decreased (but not below the number of shares thereof then outstanding) by a certificate likewise executed, acknowledged and filed setting forth a statement that a specified increase or decrease therein had been authorized and directed by a resolution or resolutions likewise adopted by the board of directors. In case the number of such shares shall be decreased the number of shares so specified in the certificate shall resume the status which they had prior to the adoption of the first resolution or resolutions. When no shares of any such class or series are outstanding, either because none were issued or because no issued shares of any such class or series remain outstanding, a certificate setting forth a resolution or resolutions adopted by the board of directors that none of the authorized shares of such class or series are outstanding, and that none will be issued subject to the certificate of designations previously filed with respect to such class or series, may be executed, acknowledged and filed in accordance with § 103 of this Title and, when such certificate becomes effective, it shall have the effect of eliminating from the certificate of incorporation all matters set forth in the certificate of designations with respect to such class or series of stock. Unless otherwise provided in the certificate of incorporation, if no shares of stock have been issued of a class or series of stock established by a resolution of the board of directors, the voting powers, designations, preferences and relative, participating, optional or other rights, if any, or the qualifications, limitations or restrictions thereof, may be amended by a resolution or resolutions adopted by the board of directors. A certificate which (1) states that no shares of the class or series have been issued, (2) sets forth a copy of the resolution or resolutions and (3) if the designation of the class or series is being changed, indicates the original designation and the new designation, shall be executed, acknowledged and filed, and shall become effective, in accordance with § 103 of this title. When any certificate filed under this subsection becomes effective, it shall have the effect of amending the certificate of incorporation; except that neither the filing of such certificate nor the filing of a restated certificate of incorporation pursuant to § 245 of this title shall prohibit the board of directors from subsequently adopting such resolutions as authorized by this subsection.

§ 152. Issuance of Stock, Lawful Consideration; Fully Paid Stock

The consideration, as determined pursuant to subsections (a) and (b) of section 153 of this title, for subscriptions to, or the purchase of, the capital stock to be issued by a corporation shall be paid in such form and in such manner as the board of directors shall determine. In the absence of actual fraud in the transaction, the judgment of the directors as to the value of such consideration shall be conclusive. The capital stock so issued shall be deemed to be fully paid and nonassessable stock, if: (1) the entire amount of such consideration has been received by the corporation in the form of cash, services rendered, personal property, real property, leases of real property, or a combination thereof; or (2) not less than the amount of the consideration determined to be capital pursuant to section 154 of this title has been received by the corporation in such form and the corporation has received a binding obligation of the subscriber or purchaser to pay the balance of the subscription or purchase price; provided, however, nothing contained herein shall prevent the board of directors from issuing partly paid shares under section 156 of this title.

§ 153. Consideration for Stock

(a) Shares of stock with par value may be issued for such consideration, having a value not less than the par value thereof, as is determined from time to time by the board of directors, or by the stockholders if the certificate of incorporation so provides.

(b) Shares of stock without par value may be issued for such consideration as is determined from time to time by the board of directors, or by the stockholders if the certificate of incorporation so provides.

(c) Treasury shares may be disposed of by the corporation for such consideration as may be determined from time to time by the board of directors, or by the stockholders if the certificate of incorporation so provides.

(d) If the certificate of incorporation reserves to the stockholders the right to determine the consideration for the issue of any shares, the stockholders shall, unless the certificate requires a greater vote, do so by a vote of a majority of the outstanding stock entitled to vote thereon.

§ 154. Determination of Amount of Capital; Capital, Surplus and Net Assets Defined

Any corporation may, by resolution of its board of directors, determine that only a part of the consideration which shall be received by the corporation for any of the shares of its capital stock which it shall issue from time to time shall be capital; but, in case any of the shares issued shall be shares having a par value, the amount of the part of such consideration so determined to be capital shall be in excess of the aggregate par value of the shares issued for such consideration having a par value, unless all the shares issued shall be shares having a par value, in which case the amount of the part of such consideration so determined to be capital need be only equal to the aggregate par value of such shares. In each such case the board of directors shall specify in dollars the part of such consideration which shall be capital. If the board of directors shall not have determined (1) at the time of issue of any shares of the capital stock of the corporation issued for cash or (2) within 60 days after the issue of any shares of the capital stock of the corporation issued for property other than cash what part of the consideration for such shares shall be capital, the capital of the corporation in respect of such shares shall be an amount equal to the aggregate par value of such shares having a par value, plus the amount of the consideration for such shares without par value. The amount of the consideration so determined to be capital in respect of any shares without par value shall be the stated capital of such shares. The capital of the corporation may be increased from time to time by resolution of the board of directors directing that a portion of the net assets of the corporation in excess of the amount so determined to be capital be transferred to the capital account. The board of directors may direct that the portion of such net assets so transferred shall be treated as capital in respect of any shares of the corporation of any designated class or classes. The excess, if any, at any given time, of the net assets of the corporation over the amount so determined to be capital shall be surplus. Net assets means the amount by which total assets exceed total liabilities. Capital and surplus are not liabilities for this purpose.

§ 155. Fractions of Shares

A corporation may, but shall not be required to, issue fractions of a share. If it does not issue fractions of a share, it shall (1) arrange for the disposition of fractional interests by those entitled thereto, (2) pay in cash the fair value of fractions of a share as of the time when those entitled to receive such fractions are determined or (3) issue scrip or warrants in registered form (either represented by a certificate or uncertificated) or in bearer form (represented by a certificate) which shall entitle the holder to receive a full share upon the surrender of such scrip or warrants aggregating a full share. A certificate for a fractional share or an uncertificated fractional share shall, but scrip or warrants shall not unless otherwise provided therein, entitle the holder to exercise voting rights, to receive dividends thereon, and to participate in any of the assets of the corporation in the event of liquidation. The board of directors may cause scrip or warrants to be issued subject to the conditions that they shall become void if not exchanged for certificates representing the full shares or uncertificated full shares before a specified date, or subject to the conditions that the shares for which scrip or warrants are exchangeable may be sold by the corporation and the proceeds thereof distributed to the holders of scrip or warrants, or subject to any other conditions which the board of directors may impose.

§ 156. Partly Paid Shares

Any corporation may issue the whole or any part of its shares as partly paid and subject to call for the remainder of the consideration to be paid therefor. Upon the face or back of each stock certificate issued to represent any such partly paid shares, or upon the books and records of the corporation in the case of uncertificated partly paid shares, the total amount of the consideration to be paid therefor and the amount paid thereon shall be stated. Upon the declaration of any dividend on fully paid shares, the corporation shall declare a dividend upon partly paid shares of the same class, but only upon the basis of the percentage of the consideration actually paid thereon.

§ 157. Rights and Options Respecting Stock

Subject to any provisions in the certificate of incorporation, every corporation may create and issue, whether or not in connection with the issue and sale of any shares of stock or other securities of the corporation, rights or options entitling the holders thereof to purchase from the corporation any shares of its capital stock of any class or classes, such rights or options to be evidenced by or in such instrument or instruments as shall be approved by the board of directors. The terms upon which, including the time or times, which may be limited or unlimited in duration, at or within which, and the price or prices at which any such shares may be purchased from the corporation upon the exercise of any such right or option, shall be such as shall be stated in the certificate of incorporation, or in a resolution adopted by the board of directors providing for the creation and issue of such rights or options, and, in every case, shall be set forth or incorporated by reference in the instrument or instruments evidencing such rights or options. In the absence of actual fraud in the transaction, the judgment of the directors as to the consideration for the issuance of such rights or options and the sufficiency thereof shall be conclusive. In case the shares of stock of the corporation to be issued upon the exercise of such rights or options shall be shares having a par value, the price or prices so to be received therefor shall not be less than the par value thereof. In case the shares of stock so to be issued shall be shares of stock without par value, the consideration therefor shall be determined in the manner provided in section 153 of this title.

§ 158. Stock Certificates; Uncertificated Shares

The shares of a corporation shall be represented by certificates, provided that the board of directors of the corporation may provide by resolution or resolutions that some or all of any or all classes or series of its stock shall be uncertificated shares. Any such resolution shall not apply to shares represented by a certificate until such certificate is surrendered to the corporation. Notwithstanding the adoption of such a resolution by the board of directors, every holder of stock represented by certificates and upon request every holder of uncertificated shares shall be entitled to have a certificate signed by, or in the name of the corporation by the chairman or vice-chairman of the board of directors, or the president or vice-president, and by the treasurer or an assistant treasurer, or the secretary or an assistant secretary of such corporation representing the number of shares registered in certificate form. Any or all the signatures on the certificate may be a facsimile. In case any officer, transfer agent, or registrar who has signed or whose facsimile signature has been placed upon a certificate shall have ceased to be such officer, transfer agent or registrar before such certificate is issued, it may be issued by the corporation with the same effect as if he were such officer, transfer agent or registrar at the date of issue.

§ 160. Corporation's Powers Respecting Ownership, Voting, etc. of Its Own Stock; Rights of Stock Called for Redemption

(a) Every corporation may purchase, redeem, receive, take or otherwise acquire, own and hold, sell, lend, exchange, transfer or otherwise dispose of, pledge, use and otherwise deal in and with its own shares; provided, however, that no corporation shall—

1. Purchase or redeem its own shares of capital stock for cash or other property when the capital of the corporation is impaired or when such purchase or redemption would cause any impairment of the capital of the corporation, except that a corporation may purchase or redeem out of capital any of its own shares which are entitled upon any distribution of its assets, whether by dividend or in liquidation, to a preference over another class or series of its stock or, if no shares entitled to such a preference are outstanding, any of its own shares, if such shares will be retired upon their acquisition and the capital of the corporation reduced in accordance with Sections 243 and 244 of this title. Nothing in this subsection shall invalidate or otherwise affect a note, debenture or other obligation of a corporation given by it as consideration for its acquisition by purchase, redemption or exchange of its shares of stock if at the time such note, debenture or obligation was delivered by the corporation its capital was not then impaired or did not thereby become impaired;

2. Purchase, for more than the price at which they may then be redeemed, any of its shares which are redeemable at the option of the corporation; or,

3. Redeem any of its shares unless their redemption is authorized by Section 151(b) of this title and then only in accordance with such Section and the certificate of incorporation.

(b) Nothing in this section limits or affects a corporation's right to resell any of its shares theretofore purchased or redeemed out of surplus and which have not been retired, for such consideration as shall be fixed by the board of directors.

(c) Shares of its own capital stock belonging to the corporation or to another corporation, if a majority of the shares entitled to vote in the election of directors of such other corporation is held, directly or indirectly, by the corporation, shall neither be entitled to vote nor be counted for quorum purposes. Nothing in this section shall be construed as limiting the right of any corporation to vote stock, including but not limited to its own stock, held by it in a fiduciary capacity.

(d) Shares which have been called for redemption shall not be deemed to be outstanding shares for the purpose of voting or determining the total number of shares entitled to vote on any matter on and after the date on which written notice of redemption has been sent to holders thereof and a sum sufficient to redeem such shares has been irrevocably deposited or set aside to pay the redemption price to the holders of the shares upon surrender of certificates therefor.

§ 161. Issuance of Additional Stock; When and by Whom

The directors may, at any time and from time to time, if all of the shares of capital stock which the corporation is authorized by its certificate of incorporation to issue have not been issued, subscribed for, or otherwise committed to be issued, issue or take subscriptions for additional shares of its capital stock up to the amount authorized in its certificate of incorporation.

§ 162. Liability of Stockholder or Subscriber for Stock Not Paid in Full

(a) When the whole of the consideration payable for shares of a corporation has not been paid in, and the assets shall be insufficient to satisfy the claims of its creditors, each holder of or subscriber for such shares shall be bound to pay on each share held or subscribed for by him the sum necessary to complete the amount of the unpaid balance of the consideration for which such shares were issued or to be issued by the corporation.

(b) The amounts which shall be payable as provided in subsection (a) of this section may be recovered as provided in section 325 of this title, after a writ of execution against the corporation has been returned unsatisfied as provided in that section.

(c) Any person becoming an assignee or transferee of shares or of a subscription for shares in good faith and without knowledge or notice that the full consideration therefor has not been paid shall not be personally liable for any unpaid portion of such consideration, but the transferor shall remain liable therefor.

(d) No person holding shares in any corporation as collateral security shall be personally liable as a stockholder but the person pledging such shares shall be considered the holder thereof and shall be so liable. No executor, administrator, guardian, trustee or other fiduciary shall be personally liable as a stockholder, but the estate or funds held by such executor, administrator, guardian, trustee or other fiduciary in such fiduciary capacity shall be liable.

(e) No liability under this section or under section 325 of this title shall be asserted more than six years after the issuance of the stock or the date of the subscription upon which the assessment is sought.

(f) In any action by a receiver or trustee of an insolvent corporation or by a judgment creditor to obtain an assessment under this section, any stockholder or subscriber for stock of the insolvent corporation may appear and contest the claim or claims of such receiver or trustee.

§ 163. Payment for Stock Not Paid in Full

The capital stock of a corporation shall be paid for in such amounts and at such times as the directors may require. The directors may, from time to time, demand payment, in respect of each share of stock not fully paid, of such sum of money as the necessities of the business may, in the judgment of the board of directors, require, not exceeding in the whole the balance remaining unpaid on said stock, and such sum so demanded shall be paid to the corporation at such times and by such installments as the directors shall direct. The directors shall give written notice of the time and place of such payments, which notice shall be mailed at least 30 days before the time for such payment, to each holder of or subscriber for stock which is not fully paid at his last known post-office address.

§ 164. Failure to Pay for Stock; Remedies

When any stockholder fails to pay any installment or call upon his stock which may have been properly demanded by the directors, at the time when such payment is due, the directors may collect the amount of any such installment or call or any balance thereof remaining unpaid, from the said stockholder by an action at law, or they shall sell at public sale such part of the shares of such delinquent stockholder as will pay all demands then due from him with interest and all incidental expenses, and shall transfer the shares so sold to the purchaser, who shall be entitled to a certificate therefor. Notice of the time and place of such sale and of the sum due on each share shall be given by advertisement at least one week before the sale, in a newspaper of the county in this State where such corporation's registered office is located, and such notice shall be mailed by the corporation to such delinquent stockholder at his last known postoffice address, at least 20 days before such sale. If no bidder can be had to pay the amount due on the stock, and if the amount is not collected by an action at law, which may be brought within the county where the corporation has its registered office, within one year from the date of the bringing of such action at law, the said stock and the amount previously paid in by the delinquent stockholder on the stock shall be forfeited to the corporation.

§ 165. Revocability of Pre-incorporation Subscriptions

Unless otherwise provided by the terms of the subscription, a subscription for stock of a corporation to be formed shall be irrevocable, except with the consent of all other subscribers or the corporation, for a period of six months from its date.

§ 166. Formalities Required of Stock Subscriptions

A subscription for stock of a corporation, whether made before or after the formation of a corporation, shall not be enforceable against a subscriber, unless in writing and signed by the subscriber or by his agent.

§ 169. Situs of Ownership of Stock

For all purposes of title, action, attachment, garnishment and jurisdiction of all courts held in this State, but not for the purpose of taxation, the situs of the ownership of the capital stock of all corporations existing under the laws of this State, whether organized under this chapter or otherwise, shall be regarded as in this State.

§ 170. Dividends; Payment; Wasting Asset Corporations

(a) The directors of every corporation, subject to any restrictions contained in its certificate of incorporation, may declare and pay dividends upon the shares of its capital stock ... either (1) out of its surplus, as defined in and computed in accordance with sections 154 and 244 of this title, or (2) in case there shall be no such surplus, out of its net profits for the fiscal year in which the dividend is declared and/or the preceding fiscal year. If the capital of the corporation, computed in accordance with sections 154 and 244 of this title, shall have been diminished by depreciation in the value of its property, or by losses, or otherwise, to an amount less than the aggregate amount of the capital represented by the issued and outstanding stock of all classes having a preference upon the distribution of assets, the directors of such corporation shall not declare and pay out of such net profits any dividends upon any shares of any classes of its capital stock until the deficiency in the amount of capital represented by the issued and outstanding stock of all classes having a preference upon the distribution of assets shall have been repaired. Nothing in this subsection shall invalidate or otherwise affect a note, debenture or other obligation of the corporation paid by it as a dividend on shares of its stock, or any payment made thereon, if at the time such note, debenture or obligation was delivered by the corporation, the corporation had either surplus or net profits as provided in clause (1) or (2) of this subsection from which the dividend could lawfully have been paid.

(b) Subject to any restrictions contained in its certificate of incorporation, the directors of any corporation engaged in the exploitation of wasting assets (including but not limited to a corporation engaged in the exploitation of natural resources or other wasting assets, including patents, or engaged primarily in the liquidation of specific assets) may determine the net profits derived from the exploitation of such wasting assets or the net proceeds derived from such liquidation without taking into consideration the depletion of such assets resulting from lapse of time, consumption, liquidation or exploitation of such assets.

§ 171. Special Purpose Reserves

The directors of a corporation may set apart out of any of the funds of the corporation available for dividends a reserve or reserves for any proper purpose and may abolish any such reserve.

§ 172. Liability of Directors as to Dividends or Stock Redemption

A member of the board of directors, or a member of any committee designated by the board of directors, shall be fully protected in relying in good faith upon the records of the corporation and upon such information, opinions, reports or statements presented to the corporation by any of its officers or employees, or committees of the board of directors, or by any other person as to matters the director reasonably believes are within such other person's professional or expert competence and who has been selected with reasonable care by or on behalf of the corporation, as to the value and amount of the assets, liabilities and/or net profits of the corporation, or any other facts pertinent to the existence and amount of surplus or other funds from which dividends might properly be declared and paid, or with which the corporation's stock might properly be purchased or redeemed.

§ 173. Declaration and Payment of Dividends

No corporation shall pay dividends except in accordance with the provisions of this chapter. Dividends may be paid in cash, in property, or in shares of the corporation's capital stock. If the dividend is to be paid in shares of the corporation's theretofore unissued capital stock the board of directors shall, by resolution, direct that there be designated as capital in respect of such shares an amount which is not less than the aggregate par value of par value shares being declared as a dividend and, in the case of shares without par value being declared as a dividend, such amount as shall be determined by the board of directors. No such designation as capital shall be necessary if shares are being distributed by a corporation pursuant to a split-up or division of its stock rather than as payment of a dividend declared payable in stock of the corporation.

§ 174. Liability of Directors for Unlawful Payment of Dividend or Unlawful Stock Purchase or Redemption; Exoneration From Liability; Contribution Among Directors; Subrogation

(a) In case of any willful or negligent violation of the provisions of sections 160 or 173 of this title, the directors under whose administration the same may happen shall be jointly and severally liable, at any time within six years after paying such unlawful dividend or after such unlawful stock purchase or redemption, to the corporation, and to its creditors in the event of its dissolution or insolvency, to the full amount of the dividend unlawfully paid, or to the full amount unlawfully paid for the purchase or redemption of the corporation's stock, with interest from the time such liability accrued. Any director who may have been absent when the same was done, or who may have dissented from the act or resolution by which the same was done, may exonerate himself from such liability by causing his dissent to be entered on the books containing the minutes of the proceedings of the directors at the time the same was done, or immediately after he has notice of the same.

(b) Any director against whom a claim is successfully asserted under this section shall be entitled to contribution from the other directors who voted for or concurred in the unlawful dividend, stock purchase or stock redemption.

(c) Any director against whom a claim is successfully asserted under this section shall be entitled, to the extent of the amount paid by him as a result of such claim, to be subrogated to the rights of the corporation against stockholders who received the dividend on, or assets for the sale or redemption of, their stock with knowledge of facts indicating that such dividend, stock purchase or redemption was unlawful under this chapter, in proportion to the amounts received by such stockholders respectively.

SUBCHAPTER VI. STOCK TRANSFERS

§ 201. Transfer of Stock, Stock Certificates and Uncertificated Stock

Except as otherwise provided in this Chapter, the transfer of stock and the certificates of stock which represent the stock or uncertificated stock shall be governed by Article 8 of Subtitle I of Title 6.* To the extent that any provision of this Chapter is inconsistent with any provision of Subtitle I of Title 6, the provisions of this Chapter shall be controlling.

§ 202. Restriction on Transfer of Securities

(a) A written restriction on the transfer or registration of transfer of a security of a corporation, if permitted by this Section and noted conspicuously on the certificate representing the security or, in the case of uncertificated shares, contained in the notice sent pursuant to Section 151(f) of this Title, may be enforced against the holder of the restricted security or any successor or transferee of the holder including an executor, administrator, trustee, guardian or other fiduciary entrusted with like responsibility for the person or estate of the holder. Unless noted conspicuously on the certificate representing the security or, in the case of uncertificated shares, contained in the notice sent pursuant to Section 151(f) of this Title, a restriction, even though permitted by this Section, is ineffective except against a person with actual knowledge of the restriction.

(b) A restriction on the transfer or registration of transfer of securities of a corporation may be imposed either by the certificate of incorporation or by the by-laws or by an agreement among any number of security holders or among such holders and the corporation. No restriction so imposed shall be binding with respect to securities issued prior to the adoption of the restriction unless the holders of the securities are parties to an agreement or voted in favor of the restriction.

(c) A restriction on the transfer of securities of a corporation is permitted by this section if it:

(1) Obligates the holder of the restricted securities to offer to the corporation or to any other holders of securities of the corporation or to any other person or to any combination of the foregoing, a prior opportunity, to be exercised within a reasonable time, to acquire the restricted securities; or

(2) Obligates the corporation or any holder of securities of the corporation or any other person or any combination of the foregoing, to

---

* The Article referred to is UCC Article 8.
[Footnote by ed.]

purchase the securities which are the subject of an agreement respecting the purchase and sale of the restricted securities; or

(3) Requires the corporation or the holders of any class of securities of the corporation to consent to any proposed transfer of the restricted securities or to approve the proposed transferee of the restricted securities; or

(4) Prohibits the transfer of the restricted securities to designated persons or classes of persons, and such designation is not manifestly unreasonable.

(d) Any restriction on the transfer of the shares of a corporation for the purpose of maintaining its status as an electing small business corporation under subchapter S of the United States Internal Revenue Code or of maintaining any other tax advantage to the corporation is conclusively presumed to be for a reasonable purpose.

(e) Any other lawful restriction on transfer or registration of transfer of securities is permitted by this section.

§ 203. Business Combinations With Interested Stockholders

(a) Notwithstanding any other provisions of this chapter, a corporation shall not engage in any business combination with any interested stockholder for a period of 3 years following the time that such stockholder became an interested stockholder, unless (1) prior to such time the board of directors of the corporation approved either the business combination or the transaction which resulted in the stockholder becoming an interested stockholder, or (2) upon consummation of the transaction which resulted in the stockholder becoming an interested stockholder, the interested stockholder owned at least 85% of the voting stock of the corporation outstanding at the time the transaction commenced, excluding for purposes of determining the number of shares outstanding those shares owned (i) by persons who are directors and also officers and (ii) employee stock plans in which employee participants do not have the right to determine confidentially whether shares held subject to the plan will be tendered in a tender or exchange offer, or (3) at or subsequent to such time the business combination is approved by the board of directors and authorized at an annual or special meeting of stockholders, and not by written consent, by the affirmative vote of at least 66⅔% of the outstanding voting stock which is not owned by the interested stockholder.

(b) The restrictions contained in this section shall not apply if:

(1) the corporation's original certificate of incorporation contains a provision expressly electing not to be governed by this section;

(2) the corporation, by action of its board of directors, adopts an amendment to its bylaws within 90 days of the effective date of this

section, expressly electing not to be governed by this section, which amendment shall not be further amended by the board of directors;

(3) the corporation, by action of its stockholders, adopts an amendment to its certificate of incorporation or bylaws expressly electing not to be governed by this section, provided that, in addition to any other vote required by law, such amendment to the certificate of incorporation or bylaws must be approved by the affirmative vote of a majority of the shares entitled to vote. An amendment adopted pursuant to this paragraph shall be effective immediately in the case of a corporation that both (i) has never had a class of voting stock that falls within any of the three categories set out in subsection (b)(4) hereof, and (ii) has not elected by a provision in its original certificate of incorporation or any amendment thereto to be governed by this section. In all other cases, an amendment adopted pursuant to this paragraph shall not be effective until 12 months after the adoption of such amendment and shall not apply to any business combination between such corporation and any person who became an interested stockholder of such corporation on or prior to such adoption. A bylaw amendment adopted pursuant to this paragraph shall not be further amended by the board of directors;

(4) the corporation does not have a class of voting stock that is (i) listed on a national securities exchange, (ii) authorized for quotation on The NASDAQ Stock Market or (iii) held of record by more than 2,000 stockholders, unless any of the foregoing results from action taken, directly or indirectly, by an interested stockholder or from a transaction in which a person becomes an interested stockholder;

(5) a stockholder becomes an interested stockholder inadvertently and (i) as soon as practicable divests itself of ownership of sufficient shares so that the stockholder ceases to be an interested stockholder and (ii) would not, at any time within the 3 year period immediately prior to a business combination between the corporation and such stockholder, have been an interested stockholder but for the inadvertent acquisition of ownership;

(6) the business combination is proposed prior to the consummation or abandonment of and subsequent to the earlier of the public announcement or the notice required hereunder of a proposed transaction which (i) constitutes one of the transactions described in the second sentence of this paragraph; (ii) is with or by a person who either was not an interested stockholder during the previous 3 years or who became an interested stockholder with the approval of the corporation's board of directors or during the period described in paragraph (7) of this subsection (b); and (iii) is approved or not opposed by a majority of the members of the board of directors then in office (but not less than 1) who were directors prior to any person becoming an interested stockholder during the previous 3 years or were recommended for election or elected to succeed such directors by a majority of such directors. The

proposed transactions referred to in the preceding sentence are limited to (x) a merger or consolidation of the corporation (except for a merger in respect of which, pursuant to section 251(f) of the chapter, no vote of the stockholders of the corporation is required); (y) a sale, lease, exchange, mortgage, pledge, transfer or other disposition (in one transaction or a series of transactions), whether as part of a dissolution or otherwise, of assets of the corporation or of any direct or indirect majority-owned subsidiary of the corporation (other than to any direct or indirect wholly-owned subsidiary or to the corporation) having an aggregate market value equal to 50% or more of either [the] aggregate market value of all of the assets of the corporation determined on a consolidated basis or the aggregate market value of all the outstanding stock of the corporation; or (z) a proposed tender or exchange offer for 50% or more of the outstanding voting stock of the corporation. The corporation shall give not less then 20 days notice to all interested stockholders prior to the consummation of any of the transactions described in clauses (x) or (y) of the second sentence of this paragraph; or

(7) The business combination is with an interested stockholder who became an interested stockholder at a time when the restrictions contained in this section did not apply by reason of any of paragraphs (1) through (4) of this subsection (b), provided, however, that this paragraph (7) shall not apply if, at the time such interested stockholder became an interested stockholder, the corporation's certificate of incorporation contained a provision authorized by the last sentence of this subsection (b).

Notwithstanding paragraphs (1), (2), (3) and (4) of this subsection, a corporation may elect by a provision of its original certificate of incorporation or any amendment thereto to be governed by this section; provided that any such amendment to the certificate of incorporation shall not apply to restrict a business combination between the corporation and an interested stockholder of the corporation if the interested stockholder became such prior to the effective date of the amendment.

(c) As used in this section only, the term:

(1) "affiliate" means a person that directly, or indirectly through one or more intermediaries, controls, or is controlled by, or is under common control with, another person.

(2) "associate," when used to indicate a relationship with any person, means (i) any corporation, partnership, unincorporated association or other entity of which such person is a director, officer or partner or is, directly or indirectly, the owner of 20% or more of any class of voting stock, (ii) any trust or other estate in which such person has at least a 20% beneficial interest or as to which such person serves as trustee or in a similar fiduciary capacity, and (iii) any relative or spouse of such person, or any relative of such spouse, who has the same residence as such person.

(3) "business combination," when used in reference to any corporation and any interested stockholder of such corporation, means:

(i) any merger or consolidation of the corporation or any direct or indirect majority-owned subsidiary of the corporation with (A) the interested stockholder, or (B) with any other corporation, partnership, unincorporated association or other entity if the merger or consolidation is caused by the interested stockholder and as a result of such merger or consolidation subsection (a) of this section is not applicable to the surviving entity;

(ii) any sale, lease, exchange, mortgage, pledge, transfer or other disposition (in one transaction or a series of transactions), except proportionately as a stockholder of such corporation, to or with the interested stockholder, whether as part of a dissolution or otherwise, of assets of the corporation or of any direct or indirect majority-owned subsidiary of the corporation which assets have an aggregate market value equal to 10% or more of either the aggregate market value of all the assets of the corporation determined on a consolidated basis or the aggregate market value of all the outstanding stock of the corporation;

(iii) any transaction which results in the issuance or transfer by the corporation or by any direct or indirect majority-owned subsidiary of the corporation of any stock of the corporation or of such subsidiary to the interested stockholder, except (A) pursuant to the exercise, exchange or conversion of securities exercisable for, exchangeable for or convertible into stock of such corporation or any such subsidiary which securities were outstanding prior to the time that the interested stockholder became such, (B) pursuant to a merger under Section 251(g) of this title, (C) pursuant to a dividend or distribution paid or made, or the exercise, exchange or conversion of securities exercisable for, exchangeable for or convertible into stock of such corporation or any such subsidiary which security is distributed, pro rata to all holders of a class or series of stock of such corporation subsequent to the time the interested stockholder became such, (D) pursuant to an exchange offer by the corporation to purchase stock made on the same terms to all holders of said stock, or (E) any issuance or transfer of stock by the corporation, provided however, that in no case under (C)–(E) above shall there be an increase in the interested stockholder's proportionate share of the stock of any class or series of the corporation or of the voting stock of the corporation;

(iv) any transaction involving the corporation or any direct or indirect majority-owned subsidiary of the corporation which has the effect, directly or indirectly, of increasing the proportionate share of the stock of any class or series, or securities convertible into the stock of any class or series, of the corporation or of any such subsidiary which is owned by the interested stockholder, except as a result of immaterial changes due to fractional share adjustments or as a result of any purchase or redemption of any shares of stock not caused, directly or indirectly, by the interested stockholder; or

(v) any receipt by the interested stockholder of the benefit, directly or indirectly (except proportionately as a stockholder of such corporation) of any loans, advances, guarantees, pledges or other financial benefits (other than those expressly permitted in subparagraphs (i)–(iv) above) provided by or through the corporation or any direct or indirect majority-owned subsidiary.

(4) "control," including the term "controlling," "controlled by" and "under common control with," means the possession, directly or indirectly, of the power to direct or cause the direction of the management and policies of a person, whether through the ownership of voting stock, by contract, or otherwise. A person who is the owner of 20% or more of the outstanding voting stock of any corporation, partnership, unincorporated association or other entity shall be presumed to have control of such entity, in the absence of proof by a preponderance of the evidence to the contrary. Notwithstanding the foregoing, a presumption of control shall not apply where such person holds voting stock, in good faith and not for the purpose of circumventing this section, as an agent, bank, broker, nominee, custodian or trustee for one or more owners who do not individually or as a group have control of such entity.

(5) "interested stockholder" means any person (other than the corporation and any direct or indirect majority-owned subsidiary of the corporation) that (i) is the owner of 15% or more of the outstanding voting stock of the corporation, or (ii) is an affiliate or associate of the corporation and was the owner of 15% or more of the outstanding voting stock of the corporation at any time within the 3-year period immediately prior to the date on which it is sought to be determined whether such person is an interested stockholder; and the affiliates and associates of such person; provided, however, that the term "interested stockholder" shall not include (x) any person who (A) owned shares in excess of the 15% limitation set forth herein as of, or acquired such shares pursuant to a tender offer commenced prior to, December 23, 1987 or pursuant to an exchange offer announced prior to the aforesaid date and commenced within 90 days thereafter and either (I) continued to own shares in excess of such 15% limitation or would have but for action by the corporation or (II) is an affiliate or associate of the corporation and so continued (or so would have continued but for action by the corporation) to be the owner of 15% or more of the outstanding voting stock of the corporation at any time within the 3–year period immediately prior to the date on which it is sought to be determined whether such a person is an interested stockholder or (B) acquired said shares from a person described in (A) above by gift, inheritance or in a transaction in which no consideration was exchanged; or (y) any person whose ownership of

shares in excess of the 15% limitation set forth herein [is] the result of action taken solely by the corporation provided that such person shall be an interested stockholder if thereafter such person acquires additional shares of voting stock of the corporation, except as a result of further corporate action not caused, directly or indirectly, by such person. For the purpose of determining whether a person is an interested stockholder, the voting stock of the corporation deemed to be outstanding shall include stock deemed to be owned by the person through application of paragraph (8) of this subsection but shall not include any other unissued stock of such corporation which may be issuable pursuant to any agreement, arrangement or understanding, or upon exercise of conversion rights, warrants or options, or otherwise.

(6) "person" means any individual, corporation, partnership, unincorporated association or other entity.

(7) "stock" means, with respect to any corporation, capital stock and, with respect to any other entity, any equity interest.

(8) "voting stock" means, with respect to any corporation, stock of any class or series entitled to vote generally in the election of directors and, with respect to any entity that is not a corporation, any equity interest entitled to vote generally in the election of the governing body of such entity.

(9) "owner" including the terms "own" and "owned" when used with respect to any stock means a person that individually or with or through any of its affiliates or associates:

(i) beneficially owns such stock, directly or indirectly; or

(ii) has (A) the right to acquire such stock (whether such right is exercisable immediately or only after the passage of time) pursuant to any agreement, arrangement or understanding, or upon the exercise of conversion rights, exchange rights, warrants or options, or otherwise; provided, however, that a person shall not be deemed the owner of stock tendered pursuant to a tender or exchange offer made by such person or any of such person's affiliates or associates until such tendered stock is accepted for purchase or exchange; or (B) the right to vote such stock pursuant to any agreement, arrangement or understanding; provided, however, that a person shall not be deemed the owner of any stock because of such person's right to vote such stock if the agreement, arrangement or understanding to vote such stock arises solely from a revocable proxy or consent given in response to a proxy or consent solicitation made to 10 or more persons; or

(iii) has any agreement, arrangement or understanding for the purpose of acquiring, holding, voting (except voting pursuant to a revocable proxy or consent as described in item (B) of clause (ii) of this paragraph), or disposing of such stock with any other person that beneficially owns, or whose affiliates or associates beneficially own, directly or indirectly, such stock.

(d) No provision of a certificate of incorporation or bylaw shall require, for any vote of stockholders required by this section a greater vote of stockholders than that specified in this section.

(e) The Court of Chancery is hereby vested with exclusive jurisdiction to hear and determine all matters with respect to this section.

SUBCHAPTER VII. MEETINGS, ELECTIONS, VOTING AND NOTICE

§ 211. Meetings of Stockholders

(a) Meetings of stockholders may be held at such place, either within or without this State, as may be designated by or in the manner provided in the by-laws or, if not so designated, at the registered office of the corporation in this State.

(b) An annual meeting of stockholders shall be held for the election of directors on a date and at a time designated by or in the manner provided in the by-laws. Any other proper business may be transacted at the annual meeting.

(c) A failure to hold the annual meeting at the designated time or to elect a sufficient number of directors to conduct the business of the corporation shall not affect otherwise valid corporate acts or work a forfeiture or dissolution of the corporation except as may be otherwise specifically provided in this chapter. If the annual meeting for election of directors is not held on the date designated therefor, the directors shall cause the meeting to be held as soon thereafter as convenient. If there be a failure to hold the annual meeting for a period of thirty days after the date designated therefor, or if no date has been designated, for a period of thirteen months after the organization of the corporation or after its last annual meeting, the Court of Chancery may summarily order a meeting to be held upon the application of any stockholder or director. The shares of stock represented at such meeting, either in person or by proxy, and entitled to vote thereat, shall constitute a quorum for the purpose of such meeting, notwithstanding any provision of the certificate of incorporation or by-laws to the contrary. The Court of Chancery may issue such orders as may be appropriate, including, without limitation, orders designating the time and place of such meeting, the record date for determination of stockholders entitled to vote, and the form of notice of such meeting.

(d) Special meetings of the stockholders may be called by the board of directors or by such person or persons as may be authorized by the certificate of incorporation or by the by-laws.

(e) All elections of directors shall be by written ballot, unless otherwise provided in the certificate of incorporation.

§ 212. Voting Rights of Stockholders; Proxies; Limitations

(a) Unless otherwise provided in the certificate of incorporation and subject to the provisions of section 213 of this title, each stockholder shall be entitled to one vote for each share of capital stock held by such stockholder. If the certificate of incorporation provides for more or less than one vote for any share on any matter, every reference in this chapter to a majority or other proportion of stock shall refer to such majority or other proportion of the votes of such stock.

(b) Each stockholder entitled to vote at a meeting of stockholders or to express consent or dissent to corporate action in writing without a meeting may authorize another person or persons to act for him by proxy, but no such proxy shall be voted or acted upon after three years from its date, unless the proxy provides for a longer period.

(c) Without limiting the manner in which a stockholder may authorize another person or persons to act for him as proxy pursuant to subsection (b) of this section, the following shall constitute a valid means by which a stockholder may grant such authority:

(1) A stockholder may execute a writing authorizing another person or persons to act for him as proxy. Execution may be accomplished by the stockholder or his authorized officer, director, employee or agent signing such writing or causing his or her signature to be affixed to such writing by any reasonable means including, but not limited to, by facsimile signature.

(2) A stockholder may authorize another person or persons to act for him as proxy by transmitting or authorizing the transmission of a telegram, cablegram, or other means of electronic transmission to the person who will be the holder of the proxy or to a proxy solicitation firm, proxy support service organization or like agent duly authorized by the person who will be the holder of the proxy to receive such transmission, provided that any such telegram, cablegram or other means of electronic transmission must either set forth or be submitted with information from which it can be determined that the telegram, cablegram or other electronic transmission was authorized by the stockholder. If it is determined that such telegrams, cablegrams or other electronic transmissions are valid, the inspectors or, if there are no inspectors, such other persons making that determination shall specify the information upon which they relied.

(d) Any copy, facsimile telecommunication or other reliable reproduction of the writing or transmission created pursuant to subsection (c) of this section may be substituted or used in lieu of the original writing or transmission for any and all purposes for which the original writing or transmission could be used, provided that such copy, facsimile telecommunication or other reproduction shall be a complete reproduction of the entire original writing or transmission.

(e) A duly executed proxy shall be irrevocable if it states that it is irrevocable and if, and only as long as, it is coupled with an interest sufficient in law to support an irrevocable power. A proxy may be made irrevocable regardless of whether the interest with which it is coupled is an interest in the stock itself or an interest in the corporation generally.

§ 213. Fixing Date for Determination of Stockholders of Record

(a) In order that the corporation may determine the stockholders entitled to notice of or to vote at any meeting of stockholders or any adjournment thereof, the board of directors may fix a record date, which record date shall not precede the date upon which the resolution fixing the record date is adopted by the board of directors, and which record date shall not be more than sixty nor less than ten days before the date of such meeting. If no record date is fixed by the board of directors, the record date for determining stockholders entitled to notice of or to vote at a meeting of stockholders shall be at the close of business on the day next preceding the day on which notice is given, or, if notice is waived, at the close of business on the day next preceding the day on which the meeting is held. A determination of stockholders of record entitled to notice of or to vote at a meeting of stockholders shall apply to any adjournment of the meeting; provided, however, that the board of directors may fix a new record date for the adjourned meeting.

(b) In order that the corporation may determine the stockholders entitled to consent to corporate action in writing without a meeting, the board of directors may fix a record date, which record date shall not precede the date upon which the resolution fixing the record date is adopted by the board of directors, and which date shall not be more than ten days after the date upon which the resolution fixing the record date is adopted by the board of directors. If no record date has been fixed by the board of directors, the record date for determining stockholders entitled to consent to corporate action in writing without a meeting, when no prior action by the board of directors is required by this chapter, shall be the first date on which a signed written consent setting forth the action taken or proposed to be taken is delivered to the corporation by delivery to its registered office in this State, its principal place of business, or an officer or agent of the corporation having custody of the book in which proceedings of meetings of stockholders are recorded. Delivery made to a corporation's registered office shall be by hand or by certified or registered mail, return receipt requested. If no record date has been fixed by the board of directors and prior action by the board of directors is required by this chapter, the record date for determining stockholders entitled to consent to corporate action in writing without a meeting shall be at the close of business on the day on which the board of directors adopts the resolution taking such prior action.

(c) In order that the corporation may determine the stockholders entitled to receive payment of any dividend or other distribution or allotment of any rights or the stockholders entitled to exercise any rights in respect of any change, conversion or exchange of stock, or for the purpose of any other lawful action, the board of directors may fix a record date, which record date shall not precede the date upon which the resolution fixing the record date is adopted, and which record date shall be not more than sixty days prior to such action. If no record date is fixed, the record date for determining stockholders for any such purpose shall be at the close of business on the day on which the board of directors adopts the resolution relating thereto.

§ 214. Cumulative Voting

The certificate of incorporation of any corporation may provide that at all elections of directors of the corporation, or at elections held under specified circumstances, each holder of stock or of any class or classes or of a series or series thereof shall be entitled to as many votes as shall equal the number of votes which (except for such provision as to cumulative voting) he would be entitled to cast for the election of directors with respect to his shares of stock multiplied by the number of directors to be elected by him, and that he may cast all of such votes for a single director or may distribute them among the number to be voted for, or for any two or more of them as he may see fit.

§ 216. Quorum and Required Vote for Stock Corporations

Subject to this chapter in respect of the vote that shall be required for a specified action, the certificate of incorporation or by-laws of any corporation authorized to issue stock may specify the number of shares and/or the amount of other securities having voting power the holders of which shall be present or represented by proxy at any meeting in order to constitute a quorum for, and the votes that shall be necessary for, the transaction of any business, but in no event shall a quorum consist of less than one-third of the shares entitled to vote at the meeting. In the absence of such specification in the certificate of incorporation or by-laws of the corporation, (i) a majority of the shares entitled to vote, present in person or represented by proxy, shall constitute a quorum at a meeting of stockholders; (ii) In all matters other than the election of directors, the affirmative vote of the majority of shares present in person or represented by proxy at the meeting and entitled to vote on the subject matter shall be the act of the stockholders; [iii] Directors shall be elected by a plurality of the votes of the shares present in person or represented by proxy at the meeting and entitled to vote on the election of directors; and [iv] Where a separate vote by a class or classes is required, a majority of the outstanding shares of such class or classes, present in person or represented by proxy, shall constitute a quorum entitled to take action with respect to that vote on that matter and the affirmative vote of the majority of shares of such class or classes present in person or represented by proxy at the meeting shall be the act of such class.

§ 217. Voting Rights of Fiduciaries, Pledgors and Joint Owners of Stock

(a) Persons holding stock in a fiduciary capacity shall be entitled to vote the shares so held. Persons whose stock is pledged shall be entitled to vote, unless in the transfer by the pledgor on the books of the corporation he has expressly empowered the pledgee to vote thereon, in which case only the pledgee, or his proxy, may represent such stock and vote thereon.

(b) If shares or other securities having voting power stand of record in the names of two or more persons, whether fiduciaries, members of a partnership, joint tenants, tenants in common, tenants by the entirety or otherwise, or if two or more persons have the same fiduciary relationship respecting the same shares, unless the secretary of the corporation is given written notice to the contrary and is furnished with a copy of the instrument or order appointing them or creating the relationship wherein it is so provided, their acts with respect to voting shall have the following effect:

(1) If only one votes, his act binds all;

(2) If more than one vote, the act of the majority so voting binds all;

(3) If more than one vote, but the vote is evenly split on any particular matter, each faction may vote the securities in question proportionally, or any person voting the shares, or a beneficiary, if any, may apply to the Court of Chancery or such other court as may have jurisdiction to appoint an additional person to act with the persons so voting the shares, which shall then be voted as determined by a majority of such persons and the person appointed by the Court. If the instrument so filed shows that any such tenancy is held in unequal interests, a majority or even-split for the purpose of this subsection shall be a majority or even-split in interest.

§ 218. Voting Trusts and Other Voting Agreements

(a) One stockholder or 2 or more stockholders may by agreement in writing deposit capital stock of an original issue with or transfer capital stock to any person or persons, or corporation or corporations authorized to act as trustee, for the purpose of vesting in such person or persons, corporation or corporations, who may be designated voting trustee, or voting trustees, the right to vote thereon for any period of time determined by such agreement, upon the terms and conditions stated in such agreement. The agreement may contain any other lawful provisions not inconsistent with such purpose. After the filing of a copy of the agreement in the registered office of the corporation in this State, which copy shall be open to the inspection of any stockholder of the corporation or any beneficiary of the trust under the agreement daily during business hours, certificates of stock or uncertificated stock shall be issued to the voting trustee or trustees to represent any stock of an original issue so deposited with him or them, and any certificates of stock or uncertificated stock so transferred to the voting trustee or trustees shall be surrendered and cancelled and new certificates or uncertificated stock shall be issued therefore to the voting trustee or trustees. In the certificate so issued, if any, it shall be stated that it is issued pursuant to such agreement, and that fact shall also be stated in the stock ledger of the corporation. The voting trustee or trustees may vote the stock so issued or transferred during the period specified in the agreement. Stock standing in the name of the voting trustee or trustees may be voted either in person or by proxy, and in voting the stock, the voting trustee or trustees shall incur no responsibility as stockholder, trustee or otherwise, except for his or their own individual malfeasance. In any case where two or more persons are designated as voting trustees, and the right and method of voting any stock standing in their names at any meeting of the corporation are not fixed by the agreement appointing the trustees, the right to vote the stock and the manner of voting it at the meeting shall be determined by a majority of the trustees, or if they be equally divided as to the right and manner of voting the stock in any particular case, the vote of the stock in such case shall be divided equally among the trustees.

(b) Any amendment to a voting trust agreement shall be made by a written agreement, a copy of which shall be filed in the registered office of the corporation in this State.

(c) An agreement between two or more stockholders, if in writing and signed by the parties thereto, may provide that in exercising any voting rights, the shares held by them shall be voted as provided by the agreement, or as the parties may agree, or as determined in accordance with a procedure agreed upon by them.

(d) This section shall not be deemed to invalidate any voting or other agreement among stockholders or any irrevocable proxy which is not otherwise illegal.

§ 219. List of Stockholders Entitled to Vote; Penalty for Refusal to Produce; Stock Ledger

(a) The officer who has charge of the stock ledger of a corporation shall prepare and make, at least ten days before every meeting of stockholders, a complete list of the stockholders entitled to vote at the meeting, arranged in alphabetical order, and showing the address of each stockholder and the number of shares registered in the name of each stockholder. Such list shall be open to the examination of any stockholder, for any purpose germane to the meeting, during ordinary business hours, for a period of at least ten days prior to the meeting, either at a place within the city where the meeting is to be held, which place shall be specified in the notice of the meeting, or, if not so specified, at the place where the meeting is to be held. The list shall also be produced and kept at the time and place of the meeting during the whole time thereof, and may be inspected by any stockholder who is present.

(b) Upon the willful neglect or refusal of the directors to produce such a list at any meeting for the election of directors, they shall be ineligible for election to any office at such meeting.

(c) The stock ledger shall be the only evidence as to who are the stockholders entitled to examine the stock ledger, the list required by this section or the books of the corporation, or to vote in person or by proxy at any meeting of stockholders.

§ 220. Inspection of Books and Records

(a) As used in this section, "stockholder" means a stockholder of record of stock in a stock corporation . . . .

(b) Any stockholder, in person or by attorney or other agent, shall, upon written demand under oath stating the purpose thereof, have the right during the usual hours for business to inspect for any proper purpose the corporation's stock ledger, a list of its stockholders, and its other books and records, and to make copies or extracts therefrom. A proper purpose shall mean a purpose reasonably related to such person's interest as a stockholder. In every instance where an attorney or other agent shall be the person who seeks the right to inspection, the demand under oath shall be accompanied by a power of attorney or such other writing which authorizes the attorney or other agent to so act on behalf of the stockholder. The demand under oath shall be directed to the corporation at its registered office in this State or at its principal place of business.

(c) If the corporation, or an officer or agent thereof, refuses to permit an inspection sought by a stockholder or attorney or other agent acting for the stockholder pursuant to sub-section (b) or does not reply to the demand within five business days after the demand has been made, the stockholder may apply to the Court of Chancery for an order to compel such inspection. The Court of Chancery is hereby vested with exclusive jurisdiction to determine whether or not the person seeking inspection is entitled to the inspection sought. The court may summarily order the corporation to permit the stockholder to inspect the corporation's stock ledger, an existing list of stockholders, and its other books and records, and to make copies or extracts therefrom; or the Court may order the corporation to furnish to the stockholder a list of its stockholders as of a specific date on condition that the stockholder first pay to the corporation the reasonable cost of obtaining and furnishing such list and on such other conditions as the Court deems appropriate. Where the stockholder seeks to inspect the corporation's books and records, other than its stock ledger or list of stockholders, he shall first establish (1) that he has complied with the provisions of this section respecting the form and manner of making demand for inspection of such documents; and (2) that the inspection he seeks is for a proper purpose. Where the stockholder seeks to inspect the corporation's stock ledger or list of stockholders and he has complied with the provisions of this section respecting the form and manner of making demand for inspection of such documents, the burden of proof shall be upon the corporation to establish that the inspection he seeks is for an improper purpose. The court may, in its discretion, prescribe any limitations or conditions with reference to the inspection, or award such other or further relief as the court may deem just and proper. The court may order books, documents and records, pertinent extracts therefrom, or duly authenticated copies thereof, to be brought within this State and kept in this State upon such terms and conditions as the order may prescribe.

(d) Any director ... shall have the right to examine the corporation's stock ledger, a list of its stockholders and its other books and records for a purpose reasonably related to his position as a director. The Court of Chancery is hereby vested with the exclusive jurisdiction to determine whether a director is entitled to the inspection sought. The court may summarily order the corporation to permit the director to inspect any and all books and records, the stock ledger and the list of stockholders and to make copies or extracts therefrom. The court may, in its discretion, prescribe any limitations or conditions with reference to the inspection, or award such other and further relief as the court may deem just and proper.

§ 221. Voting, Inspection and Other Rights of Bondholders and Debenture Holders

Every corporation may in its certificate of incorporation confer upon the holders of any bonds, debentures, or other obligations issued or to be issued by the corporation the power to vote in respect to the corporate affairs and management of the corporation to the extent and in the manner provided in the certificate of incorporation, and may confer upon such holders of bonds, debentures or other obligations the same right of inspection of its books, accounts and other records, and also any other rights, which the stockholders of the corporation have or may have by reason of the provisions of this chapter or of its certificate of incorporation. If the certificate of incorporation so provides, such holders of bonds, debentures or other obligations shall be deemed to be stockholders, and their bonds, debentures or other obligations shall be deemed to be shares of stock, for the purpose of any provision of this chapter which requires the vote of stockholders as a prerequisite to any corporate action and the certificate of incorporation may divest the holders of capital stock, in whole or in part, of their right to vote on any corporate matter whatsoever, except as set forth in § 242(b)(2) of this chapter.

§ 222. Notice of Meetings and Adjourned Meetings

(a) Whenever stockholders are required or permitted to take any action at a meeting, a written notice of the meeting shall be given which shall state the place, date and hour of the meeting, and, in the case of a special meeting, the purpose or purposes for which the meeting is called.

(b) Unless otherwise provided in this chapter, the written notice of any meeting shall be given not less than ten nor more than sixty days before the date of the meeting to each stockholder entitled to vote at such meeting. If mailed, notice is given when deposited in the United States mail, postage prepaid, directed to the stockholder at his address as it appears on the records of the corporation. An affidavit of the secretary or an assistant secretary or of the transfer agent of the corporation that the notice has been given shall, in the absence of fraud, be prima facie evidence of the facts stated therein.

(c) When a meeting is adjourned to another time or place, unless the by-laws otherwise require, notice need not be given of the adjourned meeting if the time and place thereof are announced at the meeting at which the adjournment is taken. At the adjourned meeting the corporation may transact any business which might have been transacted at the original meeting. If the adjournment is for more than thirty days, or if after the adjournment a new record date is fixed for the adjourned meeting, a notice of the adjourned meeting shall be given to each stockholder of record entitled to vote at the meeting.

§ 223. Vacancies and Newly Created Directorships

(a) Unless otherwise provided in the certificate of incorporation or by-laws:

(1) vacancies and newly created directorships resulting from any increase in the authorized number of directors elected by all of the stockholders having the right to vote as a single class may be filled by a majority of the directors then in office, although less than a quorum, or by a sole remaining director;

(2) whenever the holders of any class or classes of stock or series thereof are entitled to elect one or more directors by the provisions of the certificate of incorporation, vacancies and newly created directorships of such class or classes or series may be filled by a majority of the directors elected by such class or classes or series thereof then in office, or by a sole remaining director so elected.

If at any time, by reason of death or resignation or other cause, a corporation should have no directors in office, then any officer or any stockholder or an executor, administrator, trustee or guardian of a stockholder, or other fiduciary entrusted with like responsibility for the person or estate of a stockholder, may call a special meeting of stockholders in accordance with the provisions of the certificate of incorporation or the by-laws, or may apply to the Court of Chancery for a decree summarily ordering an election as provided in section 211 of this title.

(b) In the case of a corporation the directors of which are divided into classes, any directors chosen under subsection (a) of this section shall hold office until the next election of the class for which such directors shall have been chosen, and until their successors shall be elected and qualified.

(c) If, at the time of filling any vacancy or any newly created directorship, the directors then in office shall constitute less than a majority of the whole board (as constituted immediately prior to any such increase), the Court of Chancery may, upon application of any stockholder or stockholders holding at least ten percent of the total number of the shares at the time outstanding having the right to vote for such directors, summarily order an election to be held to fill any such vacancies or newly created directorships, or to replace the directors chosen by the directors then in office as aforesaid, which election shall be governed by the provisions of section 211 of this title as far as applicable.

(d) Unless otherwise provided in the certificate of incorporation or by-laws, when one or more directors shall resign from the board, effective at a future date, a majority of the directors then in office, including those who have so resigned, shall have power to fill such vacancy or vacancies, the vote thereon to take effect when such resignation or resignations shall become effective, and each director so chosen shall hold office as provided in this section in the filling of other vacancies.

§ 225. Contested Election of Directors; Proceedings to Determine Validity

(a) Upon application of any stockholder or director, or any officer whose title to office is contested, or any member of a corporation without capital stock, the Court of Chancery may hear and determine the validity of any election of any director, member of the governing body, or officer of any corporation, and the right of any person to hold such office, and, in case any such office is claimed by more than one person, may determine the person entitled thereto; and to that end make such order or decree in any such case as may be just and proper, with power to enforce the production of any books, papers and records of the corporation relating to the issue. In case it should be determined that no valid election has been held, the Court of Chancery may order an election to be held in accordance with sections 211 or 215 of this title. In any such application, service of copies of the application upon the registered agent of the corporation shall be deemed to be service upon the corporation and upon the person whose title to office is contested and upon the person, if any, claiming such office; and the registered agent shall forward immediately a copy of the application to the corporation and to the person whose title to office is contested and to the person, if any, claiming such office, in a postpaid, sealed, registered letter addressed to such corporation and such person at their post-office addresses last known to the registered agent or furnished to the registered agent by the applicant stockholder. The Court may make such order respecting further or other notice of such application as it deems proper under the circumstances.

(b) Upon application of any stockholder or any member of a corporation without capital stock, the Court of Chancery may hear and determine the result of any vote of stockholders or members, as the case may be, upon matters other than the election of directors, officers or members of the governing body. Service of the application upon the registered agent of the corporation shall be deemed to be service upon the corporation, and no other party need be joined in order for the Court to adjudicate the result of the vote. The Court may make such order respecting notice of the application as it deems proper under the circumstances.

§ 226. Appointment of Custodian or Receiver of Corporation on Deadlock or for Other Cause

(a) The Court of Chancery, upon application of any stockholder, may appoint one or more persons to be custodians, and, if the corporation is insolvent, to be receivers, of and for any corporation when:

(1) At any meeting held for the election of directors the stockholders are so divided that they have failed to elect successors to directors whose terms have expired or would have expired upon qualification of their successors; or

(2) The business of the corporation is suffering or is threatened with irreparable injury because the directors are so divided respecting the management of the affairs of the corporation that the required vote for action by the board of directors cannot be obtained and the stockholders are unable to terminate this division; or

(3) The corporation has abandoned its business and has failed within a reasonable time to take steps to dissolve, liquidate or distribute its assets.

(b) A custodian appointed under this section shall have all the powers and title of a receiver appointed under section 291 of this title, but the authority of the custodian is to continue the business of the corporation and not to liquidate its affairs and distribute its assets, except when the Court shall otherwise order and except in cases arising under subparagraph (a)(3) of this section or section 352(a)(2) of this title.

§ 227. Powers of Court in Elections of Directors

(a) The Court of Chancery, in any proceeding instituted under sections 211, 215 or 225 of this title may determine the right and power of persons claiming to own stock, or in the case of a corporation without capital stock, of the persons claiming to be members, to vote at any meeting of the stockholders or members.

(b) The Court of Chancery may appoint a master to hold any election provided for in sections 211, 215 or 225 of this title under such orders and powers as it deems proper; and it may punish any officer or director for contempt in case of disobedience of any order made by the Court; and, in case of disobedience by a corporation of any order made by the Court, may enter a decree against such corporation for a penalty of not more than $5,000.

§ 228. Consent of Stockholders in Lieu of Meeting

(a) Unless otherwise provided in the certificate of incorporation, any action required by this chapter to be taken at any annual or special meeting of stockholders of a corporation, or any action which may be taken at any annual or special meeting of such stockholders, may be taken without a meeting, without prior notice and without a vote, if a consent or consents in writing, setting forth the action so taken, shall be signed by the holders of outstanding stock having not less than the minimum number of votes that would be necessary to authorize or take such action at a meeting at which all shares entitled to vote thereon were present and voted and shall be delivered to the corporation by delivery to its registered office in this State, its principal place of business, or an officer or agent of the corporation having custody of the book in which proceedings of meetings of stockholders are recorded. Delivery made to a corporation's registered office shall be by hand or by certified or registered mail, return receipt requested. . . .

(c) Every written consent shall bear the date of signature of each stockholder . . . who signs the consent and no written consent shall be effective to take the corporate action referred to therein unless, within sixty days of the earliest dated consent delivered in the manner required by this Section to the corporation, written consents signed by a sufficient number of holders . . . to take action are delivered to the corporation by delivery to its registered office in this State, its principal place of business, or an officer or agent of the corporation having custody of the book in which proceedings of meetings of stockholders . . . are recorded. Delivery made to a corporation's registered office shall be by hand or by certified or registered mail, return receipt requested.

(d) Prompt notice of the taking of the corporate action without a meeting by less than unanimous written consent shall be given to those stockholders ... who have not consented in writing and who, if the action had been taken at a meeting, would have been entitled to notice of the meeting if the record date for such meeting had been the date that written consents signed by a sufficient number of holders or members to take the action were delivered to the corporation as provided in subsection (c) of this section. In the event that the action which is consented to is such as would have required the filing of a certificate under any other section of this title, if such action had been voted on by stockholders ... at a meeting thereof, the certificate filed under such other section shall state, in lieu of any statement required by such section concerning any vote of stockholders ..., that written consent has been given in accordance with the provisions of this section.

§ 229. Waiver of Notice

Whenever notice is required to be given under any provision of this chapter or of the certificate of incorporation or by-laws, a written waiver thereof, signed by the person entitled to notice, whether before or after the time stated therein, shall be deemed equivalent to notice. Attendance of a person at a meeting shall constitute a waiver of notice of such meeting, except when the person attends a meeting for the express purpose of objecting, at the beginning of the meeting, to the transaction of any business because the meeting is not lawfully called or convened. Neither the business to be transacted at, nor the purpose of, any regular or special meeting of the stockholders, directors, or members of a committee of directors need be specified in any written waiver of notice unless so required by the certificate of incorporation or the by-laws.

§ 231. Voting Procedures and Inspectors of Elections

(a) The corporation shall, in advance of any meeting of stockholders, appoint 1 or more inspectors to act at the meeting and make a written report thereof. The corporation may designate 1 or more persons as alternate inspectors to replace any inspector who fails to act. If no inspector or alternate is able to act at a meeting of stockholders, the person presiding at the meeting shall appoint 1 or more inspectors to act at the meeting. Each inspector, before entering upon the discharge of his duties, shall take and sign an oath faithfully to execute the duties of inspector with strict impartiality and according to the best of his ability.

(b) The inspectors shall:

(1) Ascertain the number of shares outstanding and the voting power of each;

(2) Determine the shares represented at a meeting and the validity of proxies and ballots;

(3) Count all votes and ballots;

(4) Determine and retain for a reasonable period a record of the disposition of any challenges made to any determination by the inspectors; and

(5) Certify their determination of the number of shares represented at the meeting, and their count of all votes and ballots.

The inspectors may appoint or retain other persons or entities to assist the inspectors in the performance of the duties of the inspectors.

(c) The date and time of the opening and the closing of the polls for each matter upon which the stockholders will vote at a meeting shall be announced at the meeting. No ballot, proxies or votes, nor any revocations thereof or changes thereto, shall be accepted by the inspectors after the closing of the polls unless the Court of Chancery upon application by a stockholder shall determine otherwise.

(d) In determining the validity and counting of proxies and ballots, the inspectors shall be limited to an examination of the proxies, any envelopes submitted with those proxies, any information provided in accordance with § 212(c)(2) of this title, ballots and the regular books and records of the corporation, except that the inspectors may consider other reliable information for the limited purpose of reconciling proxies and ballots submitted by or on behalf of banks, brokers, their nominees or similar persons which represent more votes than the holder of a proxy is authorized by the record owner to cast or more votes than the stockholder holds of record. If the inspectors consider other reliable information for the limited purpose permitted herein, the inspectors at the time they make their certification pursuant to subsection (b)(5) of this section shall specify the precise information considered by them including the person or persons from whom they obtained the information, when the information was obtained, the means by which the information was obtained and the basis for the inspectors' belief that such information is accurate and reliable.

(e) Unless otherwise provided in the certificate of incorporation or bylaws, this section shall not apply to a corporation that does not have a class of voting stock that is:

(1) Listed on a national securities exchange;

(2) Authorized for quotation on an interdealer quotation system of a registered national securities association; or

(3) Held of record by more than 2,000 stockholders.

SUBCHAPTER VIII. AMENDMENT OF CERTIFICATE OF INCORPORATION; CHANGES IN CAPITAL AND CAPITAL STOCK

§ 241. Amendment of Certificate of Incorporation Before Receipt of Payment for Stock

(a) Before a corporation has received any payment for any of its stock, it may amend its certificate of incorporation at any time or times, in any and as many respects as may be desired, so long as its certificate of incorporation as amended would contain only such provisions as it would be lawful and proper to insert in an original certificate of incorporation filed at the time of filing the amendment.

(b) The amendment of a certificate of incorporation authorized by this section shall be adopted by a majority of the incorporators, if directors were not named in the original certificate of incorporation or have not yet been elected, or, if directors were named in the original certificate of incorporation or have been elected and have qualified, by a majority of the directors. A certificate setting forth the amendment and certifying that the corporation has not received any payment for any of its stock and that the amendment has been duly adopted in accordance with the provisions of this section shall be executed, acknowledged and filed in accordance with section 103 of this title. Upon such filing, the corporation's certificate of incorporation shall be deemed to be amended accordingly as of the date on which the original certificate of incorporation became effective, except as to those persons who are substantially and adversely affected by the amendment and as to those persons the amendment shall be effective from the filing date.

§ 242. Amendment of Certificate of Incorporation After Receipt of Payment for Stock ...

(a) After a corporation has received payment for any of its capital stock, it may amend its certificate of incorporation, from time to time, in any and as many respects as may be desired, so long as its certificate of incorporation as amended would contain only such provisions as it would be lawful and proper to insert in an original certificate of incorporation filed at the time of the filing of the amendment; and, if a change in stock or the rights of stockholders, or an exchange, reclassification, subdivision, combination or cancellation of stock or rights of stockholders is to be made, such provisions as may be necessary to effect such change, exchange, reclassification, subdivision, combination or cancellation. In particular, and without limitation upon such general power of amendment, a corporation may amend its certificate of incorporation, from time to time, so as:

(1) To change its corporate name; or

(2) To change, substitute, enlarge or diminish the nature of its business or its corporate powers and purposes; or

(3) To increase or decrease its authorized capital stock or to reclassify the same, by changing the number, par value, designations, preferences, or relative, participating, optional, or other special rights of the shares, or the qualifications, limitations or restrictions of such rights, or by changing shares with par value into shares without par value, or shares without par value into shares with par value either with or without increasing or decreasing the number of shares, or by subdividing or combining the outstanding shares of any class or series of a class of shares into a greater or lesser number of outstanding shares; or

(4) To cancel or otherwise affect the right of the holders of the shares of any class to receive dividends which have accrued but have not been declared; or

(5) To create new classes of stock having rights and preferences either prior and superior or subordinate and inferior to the stock of any class then authorized, whether issued or unissued; or

(6) To change the period of its duration.

Any or all such changes or alterations may be effected by one certificate of amendment.

(b) Every amendment authorized by subsection (a) of this section shall be made and effected in the following manner—

(1) If the corporation has capital stock, its board of directors shall adopt a resolution setting forth the amendment proposed, declaring its advisability, and either calling a special meeting of the stockholders entitled to vote in respect thereof for the consideration of such amendment or directing that the amendment proposed be considered at the next annual meeting of the stockholders. Such special or annual meeting shall be called and held upon notice in accordance with section 222 of this title. The notice shall set forth such amendment in full or a brief summary of the changes to be effected thereby, as the directors shall deem advisable. At the meeting a vote of the stockholders entitled to vote thereon shall be taken for and against the proposed amendment. If a majority of the outstanding stock entitled to vote thereon, and a majority of the outstanding stock of each class entitled to vote thereon as a class has been voted in favor of the amendment, a certificate setting forth the amendment and certifying that such amendment has been duly adopted in accordance with the provisions of this section shall be executed, acknowledged and filed, and shall become effective in accordance with section 103 of this title.

(2) The holders of the outstanding shares of a class shall be entitled to vote as a class upon a proposed amendment, whether or not entitled to vote thereon by the provisions of the certificate of incorporation, if the

amendment would increase or decrease the aggregate number of authorized shares of such class, increase or decrease the par value of the shares of such class, or alter or change the powers, preferences or special rights of the shares of such class so as to affect them adversely. If any proposed amendment would alter or change the powers, preferences, or special rights of one or more series of any class so as to affect them adversely, but shall not so affect the entire class, then only the shares of the series so affected by the amendment shall be considered a separate class for the purposes of this paragraph. The number of authorized shares of any such class or classes of stock may be increased or decreased (but not below the number of shares thereof then outstanding) by the affirmative vote of the holders of a majority of the stock of the corporation entitled to vote irrespective of the provisions of this paragraph (b)(2), if so provided in the original certificate of incorporation, in any amendment thereto which created such class or classes of stock or which was adopted prior to the issuance of any shares of such class or classes of stock, or in any amendment thereto which was authorized by a resolution or resolutions adopted by the affirmative vote of the holders of a majority of such class or classes of stock....

(4) Whenever the certificate of incorporation shall require for action by the board of directors, by the holders of any class or series of shares or by the holders of any other securities having voting power the vote of a greater number or proportion than is required by any section of this title, the provision of the certificate of incorporation requiring such greater vote shall not be altered, amended or repealed except by such greater vote.

(c) The resolution authorizing a proposed amendment to the certificate of incorporation may provide that at any time prior to the effectiveness of the filing of the amendment with the Secretary of State, notwithstanding authorization of the proposed amendment by the stockholders of the corporation ..., the board of directors ... may abandon such proposed amendment without further action by the stockholders ....

§ 243. Retirement of Stock

(a) A corporation, by resolution of its board of directors, may retire any shares of its capital stock that are issued but are not outstanding.

(b) Whenever any shares of the capital stock of a corporation are retired, they shall resume the status of authorized and unissued shares of the class or series to which they belong unless the certificate of incorporation otherwise provides. If the certificate of incorporation prohibits the reissuance of such shares, or prohibits the reissuance of such shares as a part of a specific series only, a certificate stating that reissuance of the shares (as part of the class or series) is prohibited[,] identifying the shares and reciting their retirement shall be executed, acknowledged and filed and shall become effective in accordance with

§ 103 of this Title. When such certificate becomes effective, it shall have the effect of amending the certificate of incorporation so as to reduce accordingly the number of authorized shares of the class or series to which such shares belong or, if such retired shares constitute all of the authorized shares of the class or series to which they belong, of eliminating from the certificate of incorporation all reference to such class or series of stock.

(c) If the capital of the corporation will be reduced by or in connection with the retirement of shares, the reduction of capital shall be effected pursuant to Section 244 of this title.

§ 244. Reduction of Capital

(a) A corporation, by resolution of its board of directors, may reduce its capital in any of the following ways:

1. By reducing or eliminating the capital represented by shares of capital stock which have been retired;

2. By applying to an otherwise authorized purchase or redemption of outstanding shares of its capital stock some or all of the capital represented by the shares being purchased or redeemed, or any capital that has not been allocated to any particular class of its capital stock;

3. By applying to an otherwise authorized conversion or exchange of outstanding shares of its capital stock some or all of the capital represented by the shares being converted or exchanged, or some or all of any capital that has not been allocated to any particular class of its capital stock, or both, to the extent that such capital in the aggregate exceeds the total aggregate par value or the stated capital of any previously unissued shares issuable upon such conversion or exchange; or,

4. By transferring to surplus (i) some or all of the capital not represented by any particular class of its capital stock; (ii) some or all of the capital represented by issued shares of its par value capital stock, which capital is in excess of the aggregate par value of such shares; or (iii) some of the capital represented by issued shares of its capital stock without par value.

(b) Notwithstanding the other provisions of this section, no reduction of capital shall be made or effected unless the assets of the corporation remaining after such reduction shall be sufficient to pay any debts of the corporation for which payment has not been otherwise provided. No reduction of capital shall release any liability of any stockholder whose shares have not been fully paid.

SUBCHAPTER IX.   MERGER OR CONSOLIDATION

§ 251.   Merger or Consolidation of Domestic Corporations

(a) Any two or more corporations existing under the laws of this State may merge into a single corporation, which may be any one of the constituent corporations or may consolidate into a new corporation formed by the consolidation, pursuant to an agreement of merger or consolidation, as the case may be, complying and approved in accordance with this section.

(b) The board of directors of each corporation which desires to merge or consolidate shall adopt a resolution approving an agreement of merger or consolidation. The agreement shall state: (1) the terms and conditions of the merger or consolidation; (2) the mode of carrying the same into effect; (3) in the case of a merger, such amendments or changes in the certificate of incorporation of the surviving corporation as are desired to be effected by the merger, or, if no such amendments or changes are desired, a statement that the certificate of incorporation of the surviving corporation shall be its certificate of incorporation; (4) in the case of a consolidation, that the certificate of incorporation of the resulting corporation shall be as is set forth in an attachment to the agreement; (5) the manner of converting the shares of each of the constituent corporations into shares or other securities of the corporation surviving or resulting from the merger or consolidation, and, if any shares of any of the constituent corporations are not to be converted solely into shares or other securities of the surviving or resulting corporation, the cash, property, rights or securities of any other corporation or entity which the holders of such shares are to receive in exchange for, or upon conversion of such shares and the surrender of any certificates evidencing them, which cash, property, rights or securities of any other corporation or entity may be in addition to or in lieu of shares or other securities of the surviving or resulting corporation; and (6) such other details or provisions as are deemed desirable, including, without limiting the generality of the foregoing, a provision for the payment of cash in lieu of the issuance or recognition of fractional shares, interests or rights, or for any other arrangement with respect thereto, consistent with the provisions of section 155 of this title. The agreement so adopted shall be executed and acknowledged in accordance with section 103 of this title. Any of the terms of the agreement of merger or consolidation may be made dependent upon facts ascertainable outside of such agreement, provided that the manner in which such facts shall operate upon the terms of the agreement is clearly and expressly set forth in the agreement of merger or consolidation. The term "facts," as used in the preceding sentence, includes, but is not limited to, the occurrence of any event, including a determination or action by any person or body, including the corporation.

(c) The agreement required by subsection (b) shall be submitted to the stockholders of each constituent corporation at an annual or special meeting thereof for the purpose of acting on the agreement. Due notice of the time, place and purpose of the meeting shall be mailed to each holder of stock, whether voting or non-voting, of the corporation at his address as it appears on the records of the corporation, at least 20 days prior to the date of the meeting. The notice shall contain a copy of the agreement or a brief summary thereof, as the directors shall deem advisable. At the meeting the agreement shall be considered and a vote taken for its adoption or rejection. If a majority of the outstanding stock of the corporation entitled to vote thereon shall be voted for the adoption of the agreement, that fact shall be certified on the agreement by the secretary or assistant secretary of the corporation. If the agreement shall be so adopted and certified by each constituent corporation, it shall then be filed, and shall become effective, in accordance with section 103 of this title. In lieu of filing the agreement of merger or consolidation required by this Section, the surviving or resulting corporation may file a certificate of merger or consolidation, executed in accordance with section 103 of this title, which states:

(1) The name and state of incorporation of each of the constituent corporations;

(2) That an agreement of merger or consolidation has been approved, adopted, certified, executed and acknowledged by each of the constituent corporations in accordance with this section;

(3) The name of the surviving or resulting corporation;

(4) In the case of a merger, such amendments or changes in the certificate of incorporation of the surviving corporation as are desired to be effected by the merger, or, if no such amendments or changes are desired, a statement that the certificate of incorporation of the surviving corporation shall be its certificate of incorporation;

(5) In the case of a consolidation, that the certificate of incorporation of the resulting corporation shall be as set forth in an attachment to the certificate;

(6) That the executed agreement of consolidation or merger is on file at an office of the surviving corporation, stating the address thereof; and

(7) That a copy of the agreement of consolidation or merger will be furnished by the surviving corporation, on request and without cost, to any stockholder of any constituent corporation.

(d) Any agreement of merger or consolidation may contain a provision that at any time prior to the time that the agreement (or a certificate in lieu thereof) filed with the Secretary of State becomes effective in accordance with § 103 of this title, the agreement may be terminated by the board of directors of any constituent corporation notwithstanding approval of the agreement by the stockholders of all or any of the constituent corporations; in the event the agreement of merger or consolidation is terminated after the filing of the agreement (or a certificate in lieu thereof) with the Secretary of State but before the agreement (or a certificate in lieu thereof) has become effective, a certificate of termination or merger or consolidation shall be filed in accordance with § 103 of this title. Any agreement of merger or consolidation may contain a provision that the boards of directors of the constituent corporations may amend the agreement at any time prior to the time that the agreement (or a certificate in lieu thereof) filed with the Secretary of State becomes effective in accordance with § 103 of this title, provided that an amendment made subsequent to the adoption of the agreement by the stockholders of any constituent corporation shall not (1) alter or change the amount or kind of shares, securities, cash, property and/or rights to be received in exchange for or on conversion of all or any of the shares of any class or or series thereof of such constituent corporation, (2) alter or change any term of the certificate of incorporation of the surviving corporation to be effected by the merger or consolidation, or (3) alter or change any of the terms and conditions of the agreement if such alteration or change would adversely affect the holder of any class or series thereof of such constituent corporation; in the event the agreement of merger or consolidation is amended after the filing thereof with the Secretary of State but before the agreement has become effective, a certificate of amendment of merger or consolidation shall be filed in accordance with § 103 of this title.

(e) In the case of a merger, the certificate of incorporation of the surviving corporation shall automatically be amended to the extent, if any, that changes in the certificate of incorporation are set forth in the agreement of merger.

(f) Notwithstanding the requirements of subsection (c), unless required by its certificate of incorporation, no vote of stockholders of a constituent corporation surviving a merger shall be necessary to authorize a merger if (1) the agreement of merger does not amend in any respect the certificate of incorporation of such constituent corporation, (2) each share of stock of such constituent corporation outstanding immediately prior to the effective date of the merger is to be an identical outstanding or treasury share of the surviving corporation after the effective date of the merger, and (3) either no shares of common stock of the surviving corporation and no shares, securities or obligations convertible into such stock are to be issued or delivered under the plan of merger, or the authorized unissued shares or the treasury shares of common stock of the surviving corporation to be issued or delivered under the plan of merger plus those initially issuable upon conversion of any other shares, securities or obligations to be issued or delivered under such plan do not exceed 20 percent of the shares of common stock of such constituent corporation outstanding immediately prior to the effective date of the merger. No vote of stockholders of a constituent corporation shall be necessary to authorize a merger or consolidation if no shares of the stock of such corporation shall have been issued prior to the adoption by the board of directors of the resolution approving the agreement of merger or consolidation. If an agreement of merger is adopted by the constituent corporation surviving the merger, by action of its board of directors and without any vote of its stockholders pursuant to this subsection, the secretary or assistant secretary of that corporation shall certify on the agreement that the agreement has been adopted pursuant to this subsection and, (1) if it has been adopted pursuant to the first sentence of this subsection, that the conditions specified in that sentence have been satisfied, or (2) if it has been adopted pursuant to the second sentence of this subsection, that no shares of stock of such corporation were issued prior to the adoption by the board of directors of the resolution approving the agreement of merger or consolidation. The agreement so adopted and certified shall then be filed and shall become effective, in accordance with section 103 of this title. Such filing shall constitute a representation by the person who executes the agreement that the facts stated in the certificate remain true immediately prior to such filing.

(g) Notwithstanding the requirements of subsection (c) of this section, unless expressly required by its certificate of incorporation, no vote of stockholders of a constituent corporation shall be necessary to authorize a merger with or into a single direct or indirect wholly-owned subsidiary of such constituent corporation if: (1) such constituent corporation and the direct or indirect wholly-owned subsidiary of such constituent corporation are the only constituent corporations to the merger; (2) each share or fraction of a share of the capital stock of the constituent corporation outstanding immediately prior to the effective time of the merger is converted in the merger into a share or equal fraction of [a] share of capital stock of a holding company having the same designations, rights, powers and preferences, and the qualifications, limitations and restrictions thereof, as the share of stock of the constituent corporation being converted in the merger; (3) the holding company and each of the constituent corporations to the merger are corporations of this State; (4) the certificate of incorporation and by-laws of the holding company immediately following the effective time of the merger contain provisions identical to the certificate of incorporation and by-laws of the constituent corporation immediately prior to the effective time of the merger (other than provisions, if any, regarding the incorporator or incorporators, the corporate name, the registered office and agent, the initial board of directors and the initial subscribers for shares and such provisions contained in any amendment to the certificate of incorporation as were necessary to effect a change, exchange, reclassification or cancellation of stock, if such change, exchange, reclassification or cancellation has become effective); (5) as a result of the merger the constituent corporation or its successor corporation becomes or remains a direct or indirect wholly-owned subsidiary of the holding company; (6) the directors of the constituent corporation become or remain the directors of the holding company upon the effective time of the merger; (7) the certificate of incorporation of the surviving corporation immediately following the effective time of the merger is identical to the certificate of incorporation of the constituent corporation immediately prior to the effective time of the merger (other than provisions, if any, regarding the incorporator or incorporators, the corporate name, the registered office and agent, the initial board of directors and the initial subscribers for shares and such provisions contained in any amendment to the certificate of incorporation as were necessary to effect a change, exchange, reclassification or cancellation of stock, if such change, exchange, reclassification or cancellation has become effective); provided, however, that (i) the certificate of incorporation of the surviving corporation shall be amended in the merger to contain a provision requiring that any act or transaction by or involving the surviving corporation that requires for its adoption under this Chapter or its certificate of incorporation the approval of the stockholders of the surviving corporation shall, by specific reference to this subsection, require, in addition, the approval of the stockholders of the holding company (or any successor by merger), by the same vote as is required by this Chapter and/or by the certificate of incorporation of the surviving corporation, and (ii) the certificate of incorporation of the surviving corporation may be amended in the merger to reduce the number of classes and shares of capital stock that the surviving corporation is authorized to issue; and (8) the stockholders of the constituent corporation do not recognize gain or loss for United States federal income tax purposes as determined by the board of directors of the constituent corporation. As used in this subsection only, the term "holding company" means a corporation which, from its incorporation until consummation of a merger governed by this subsection, was at all times a direct or indirect wholly-owned subsidiary of the constituent corporation and whose capital stock is issued in such merger. From and after the effective time of a merger adopted by a constituent corporation by action of its board of directors and without any vote of stockholders pursuant to this subsection: (i) to the extent the restrictions of § 203 of this Chapter applied to the constituent corporation and its stockholders at the effective time of the merger, such restrictions shall apply to the holding company and its stockholders immediately after the effective time of the merger as though it were the constituent corporation, and all shares of stock of the holding company acquired in the merger shall for purposes of § 203 be deemed to have been acquired at the time that the shares of stock of the constituent corporation converted in the merger were acquired, and provided further that any stockholder who immediately prior to the effective time of the merger was not an interested stockholder within the meaning of § 203 shall not solely by reason of the merger become an interested stockholder of the holding company, and

(ii) if the corporate name of the holding company immediately following the effective time of the merger is the same as the corporate name of the constituent corporation immediately prior to the effective time of the merger, the shares of capital stock of the holding company into which the shares of capital stock of the constituent corporation are converted in the merger shall be represented by the stock certificates that previously represented shares of capital stock of the constituent corporation. If an agreement of merger is adopted by a constituent corporation by action of its board of directors and without any vote of stockholders pursuant to this subsection, the secretary or assistant secretary of the constituent corporation shall certify on the agreement that the agreement has been adopted pursuant to this subsection and that the conditions specified in the first sentence of this subsection have been satisfied. The agreement so adopted and certified shall then be filed and become effective, in accordance with § 103 of this title. Such filing shall constitute a representation by the person who executes the agreement that the facts stated in the certificate remain true immediately prior to such filing.

§ 253. Merger of Parent Corporation and Subsidiary or Subsidiaries

(a) In any case in which at least 90 percent of the outstanding shares of each class of the stock of a corporation or corporations (other than a corporation which has in its certificate of incorporation the provision required by subsection (g)(7)(i) of Section 251 of this title) is owned by another corporation and one of such corporations is a corporation of this State and the other or others are corporations of this State or of any other state or states or of the District of Columbia and the laws of such other state or states or of the District permit a corporation of such jurisdiction to merge with a corporation of another jurisdiction, the corporation having such stock ownership may either merge such other corporation or corporations into itself and assume all of its or their obligations, or merge itself, or itself and one or more of such other corporations, into one of such other corporations by executing, acknowledging and filing, in accordance with section 103 of this title, a certificate of such ownership and merger setting forth a copy of the resolution of its board of directors to so merge and the date of the adoption thereof; provided, however, that in case the parent corporation shall not own all the outstanding stock of all the subsidiary corporations, parties to a merger as aforesaid, the resolution of the board of directors of the parent corporation shall state the terms and conditions of the merger, including the securities, cash, property, or rights to be issued, paid, delivered or granted by the surviving corporation upon surrender of each share of the subsidiary corporation or corporations not owned by the parent corporation. Any of the terms of the resolution of the board of directors to so merge may be made dependent upon facts ascertainable outside of such resolution, provided that the manner in which such facts shall operate upon the terms of the resolution is clearly and expressly set forth in the resolution. The term "facts", as used in the preceding sentence, includes, but is not limited to, the occurrence of any event, including a determination or action by any person or body, including the corporation. If the parent corporation be not the surviving corporation, the resolution shall include provision for the pro rata issuance of stock of the surviving corporation to the holders of the stock of the parent corporation on surrender of any certificates therefor, and the certificate of ownership and merger shall state that the proposed merger has been approved by a majority of the outstanding stock of the parent corporation entitled to vote thereon at a meeting thereof duly called and held after 20 days' notice of the purpose of the meeting mailed to each such stockholder at his address as it appears on the records of the corporation if the parent corporation is a corporation of this State or state that the proposed merger has been adopted, approved, certified, executed and acknowledged by the parent corporation in accordance with the laws under which it is organized if the parent corporation is not a corporation of this State. If the surviving corporation exists under the laws of the District of Columbia or any state or jurisdiction other than this State, the provisions of section 252(d) of this title shall also apply to a merger under this section.

(b) If the surviving corporation is a Delaware corporation, it may change its corporate name by the inclusion of a provision to that effect in the resolution of merger adopted by the directors of the parent corporation and set forth in the certificate of ownership and merger, and upon the effective date of the merger, the name of the corporation shall be so changed.

(c) The provisions of Section 251(d) of this title shall apply to a merger under this section, and the provisions of Section 251(e) shall apply to a merger under this section in which the surviving corporation is the subsidiary corporation and is a corporation of this State. References to "agreement of merger" in Sections 251(d) and 251(e) of this title shall mean for purposes of this Section 253(c) the resolution of merger adopted by the board of directors of the parent corporation. Any merger which effects any changes other than those authorized by this section or made applicable by this subsection shall be accomplished under the provisions of Section 251 or Section 252 of this title. The provisions of Section 262 of this title shall not apply to any merger effected under this section, except as provided in subsection (d) of this section.

(d) In the event all of the stock of a subsidiary Delaware corporation party to a merger effected under this Section is not owned by the parent corporation immediately prior to the merger, the stockholders of the subsidiary Delaware corporation party to the merger shall have appraisal rights as set forth in Section 262 of this Title.

(e) A merger may be effected under this section although one or more of the corporations parties to the merger is a corporation organized under the laws of a jurisdiction other than one of the United States; provided that the laws of such jurisdiction permit a corporation of such jurisdiction to merge with a corporation of another jurisdiction.

§ 259. Status, Rights, Liabilities, etc. of Constituent and Surviving or Resulting Corporations Following Merger or Consolidation

(a) When any merger or consolidation shall have become effective under this chapter, for all purposes of the laws of this State the separate existence of all the constituent corporations, or of all such constituent corporations except the one into which the other or others of such constituent corporations have been merged, as the case may be, shall cease and the constituent corporations shall become a new corporation, or be merged into one of such corporations, as the case may be, possessing all the rights, privileges, powers and franchises as well of a public as of a private nature, and being subject to all the restrictions, disabilities and duties of each of such corporations so merged or consolidated; and all and singular, the rights, privileges, powers and franchises of each of said corporations, and all property, real, personal and mixed, and all debts due to any of said constituent corporations on whatever account, as well for stock subscriptions as all other things in action or belonging to each of such corporations shall be vested in the corporation surviving or resulting from such merger or consolidation; and all property, rights, privileges, powers and franchises, and all and every other interest shall be thereafter as effectually the property of the surviving or resulting corporation as they were of the several and respective constituent corporations, and the title to any real estate vested by deed or otherwise, under the laws of this State, in any of such constituent corporations, shall not revert or be in any way impaired by reason of this chapter; but all rights of creditors and all liens upon any property of any of said constituent corporations shall be preserved unimpaired, and all debts, liabilities and duties of the respective constituent corporations shall thenceforth attach to said surviving or resulting corporation, and may be enforced against it to the same extent as if said debts, liabilities and duties had been incurred or contracted by it. . . .

§ 260. Powers of Corporation Surviving or Resulting From Merger or Consolidation; Issuance of Stock, Bonds or Other Indebtedness

When two or more corporations are merged or consolidated, the corporation surviving or resulting from the merger may issue bonds or other obligations, negotiable or otherwise, and with or without coupons or interest certificates thereto attached, to an amount sufficient with its capital stock to provide for all the payments it will be required to make, or obligations it will be required to assume, in order to effect the merger or consolidation. For the purpose of securing the payment of any such bonds and obligations, it shall be lawful for the surviving or resulting corporation to mortgage its corporate franchise, rights, privileges and property, real, personal or mixed. The surviving or resulting corporation may issue certificates of its capital stock or uncertificated stock if authorized to do so and other securities to the stockholders of the constituent corporations in exchange or payment for the original shares, in such amount as shall be necessary in accordance with the terms of the agreement of merger or consolidation in order to effect such merger or consolidation in the manner and on the terms specified in the agreement.

§ 261. Effect of Merger Upon Pending Actions

Any action or proceeding, whether civil, criminal or administrative, pending by or against any corporation which is a party to a merger or consolidation shall be prosecuted as if such merger or consolidation had not taken place, or the corporation surviving or resulting from such merger or consolidation may be substituted in such action or proceeding.

§ 262. Appraisal Rights

(a) Any stockholder of a corporation of this State who holds shares of stock on the date of the making of a demand pursuant to subsection (d) of this section with respect to such shares, who continuously holds such shares through the effective date of the merger or consolidation, who has otherwise complied with subsection (d) of this section and who has neither voted in favor of the merger or consolidation nor consented thereto in writing pursuant to § 228 of this title shall be entitled to an appraisal by the Court of Chancery of the fair value of his shares of stock under the circumstances described in subsections (b) and (c) of this section. As used in this section, the word "stockholder" means a holder of record of stock in a stock corporation and also a member of record of a nonstock corporation; the words "stock" and "share" mean and include what is ordinarily meant by those words and also membership or membership interest of a member of a nonstock corporation; and the words "depository receipt" mean a receipt or other instrument issued by a depository representing an interest in one or more shares, or fractions thereof, solely of stock of a corporation, which stock is deposited with the depository.

(b) Appraisal rights shall be available for the shares of any class or series of stock of a constituent corporation in a merger or consolidation to be effected pursuant to § 251 (other than a merger effected pursuant to subsection (g) of § 251), § 252, § 254, § 257, § 258, § 263 or § 264 of this title:

(1) Provided, however, that no appraisal rights under this section shall be available for the shares of any class or series of stock, which stock, or depository receipts in respect thereof, at the record date fixed to determine the stockholders entitled to receive notice of and to vote at the meeting of stockholders to act upon the agreement of merger or consolidation, were either (i) listed on a national securities exchange or designated as a national market system security on an interdealer quotation system by the National Association of Securities Dealers, Inc. or (ii) held of record by more than 2,000 holders; and further provided that no appraisal rights shall be available for any shares of stock of the constituent corporation surviving a merger if the merger did not require for its approval the vote of the stockholders of the surviving corporation as provided in subsection (f) of § 251 of this title.

(2) Notwithstanding paragraph (1) of this subsection, appraisal rights under this section shall be available for the shares of any class or series of stock of a constituent corporation if the holders thereof are required by the terms of an agreement of merger or consolidation pursuant to §§ 251, 252, 254, 257, 258, 263 and 264 of this title to accept for such stock anything except:

    a. Shares of stock of the corporation surviving or resulting from such merger or consolidation, or depository receipts in respect thereof;

    b. Shares of stock of any other corporation, or depository receipts in respect thereof, which shares of stock or depository receipts at the effective date of the merger or consolidation will be either listed on a national securities exchange or designated as a national market system security on an interdealer quotation system by the National Association of Securities Dealers, Inc. or held of record by more than 2,000 holders;

    c. Cash in lieu of fractional shares or fractional depository receipts described in the foregoing subparagraphs a. and b. of this paragraph; or

    d. Any combination of the shares of stock, depository receipts and cash in lieu of fractional shares or fractional depository receipts described in the foregoing subparagraphs a., b. and c. of this paragraph.

(3) In the event all of the stock of a subsidiary Delaware corporation party to a merger effected under Section 253 of this chapter is not owned by the parent corporation immediately prior to the merger, appraisal rights shall be available for the shares of the subsidiary Delaware corporation.

(c) Any corporation may provide in its certificate of incorporation that appraisal rights under this Section shall be available for the shares of any class or series of its stock as a result of an amendment to its certificate of incorporation, any merger or consolidation in which the corporation is a constituent corporation or the sale of all or substantially all of the assets of the corporation. If the certificate of incorporation contains such a provision, the procedures of this Section, including those set forth in subsections (d) and (e), shall apply as nearly as is practicable.

(d) Appraisal rights shall be perfected as follows:

(1) If a proposed merger or consolidation for which appraisal rights are provided under this Section is to be submitted for approval at a meeting of stockholders, the corporation, not less than 20 days prior to the meeting, shall notify each of its stockholders who was such on the record date for such meeting with respect to shares for which appraisal rights are available pursuant to subsections (b) or (c) hereof that appraisal rights are available for any or all of the shares of the constituent corporations, and shall include in such notice a copy of this Section. Each stockholder electing to demand the appraisal of his shares shall deliver to the corporation, before the taking of the vote on the merger or consolidation, a written demand for appraisal of his shares. Such demand will be sufficient if it reasonably informs the corporation of the identify of the stockholder and that the stockholder intends thereby to demand the appraisal of his shares. A proxy or vote against the merger or consolidation shall not constitute such a demand. A stockholder electing to take such action must do so by a separate written demand as herein provided. Within 10 days after the effective date of such merger or consolidation, the surviving or resulting corporation shall notify each stockholder of each constituent corporation who has complied with the provisions of this subsection and has not voted in favor of or consented to the merger or consolidation of the date that the merger or consolidation has become effective; or

(2) If the merger or consolidation was approved pursuant to § 228 or § 253 of this title, each constituent corporation, either before the effective date of the merger or consolidation or within ten days thereafter, shall notify each of the holders of any class or series of stock of such constituent corporation who are entitled to appraisal rights of the approval of the merger or consolidation and that appraisal rights are available for any or all shares of such class or series of stock of such constituent corporation, and shall include in such notice a copy of this section; provided that, if the notice is given on or after the effective date of the merger or consolidation, such notice shall be given by the surviving or resulting corporation to all such holders of any class or series of stock of a constituent corporation that are entitled to appraisal rights. Such notice may, and, if given on or after the effective date of the merger or consolidation, shall, also notify such stockholders of the effective date of the merger or consolidation. Any stockholder entitled to appraisal rights may, within twenty days after the date of mailing of such notice, demand in writing from the surviving or resulting corporation the appraisal of such holder's shares. Such demand will be suffi-

cient if it reasonably informs the corporation of the identity of the stockholder and that the stockholder intends thereby to demand the appraisal of such holder's shares. If such notice did not notify stockholders of the effective date of the merger or consolidation, either (i) each such constituent corporation shall send a second notice before the effective date of the merger or consolidation notifying each of the holders of any class or series of stock of such constituent corporation that are entitled to appraisal rights of the effective date of the merger or consolidation or (ii) the surviving or resulting corporation shall send such a second notice to all such holders on or within 10 days after such effective date; provided, however, that if such second notice is sent more than 20 days following the sending of the first notice, such second notice need only be sent to each stockholder who is entitled to appraisal rights and who has demanded appraisal of such holder's shares in accordance with this subsection. An affidavit of the secretary or assistant secretary or of the transfer agent of the corporation that is required to give either notice that such notice has been given shall, in the absence of fraud, be prima facie evidence of the facts stated therein. For purposes of determining the stockholders entitled to receive either notice, each constituent corporation may fix, in advance, a record date that shall be not more than 10 days prior to the date the notice is given; provided that, if the notice is given on or after the effective date of the merger or consolidation, the record date shall be such effective date. If no record date is fixed and the notice is given prior to the effective date, the record date shall be the close of business on the day next preceding the day on which the notice is given.

(e) Within 120 days after the effective date of the merger or consolidation, the surviving or resulting corporation or any stockholder who has complied with the provisions of subsections (a) and (d) hereof and who is otherwise entitled to appraisal rights, may file a petition in the Court of Chancery demanding a determination of the value of the stock of all such stockholders. Notwithstanding the foregoing, at any time within 60 days after the effective date of the merger or consolidation, any stockholder shall have the right to withdraw his demand for appraisal and to accept the terms offered upon the merger or consolidation. Within 120 days after the effective date of the merger or consolidation, any stockholder who has complied with the requirements of subsections (a) and (d) hereof, upon written request, shall be entitled to receive from the corporation surviving the merger or resulting from the consolidation a statement setting forth the aggregate number of shares not voted in favor of the merger or consolidation and with respect to which demands for appraisal have been received and the aggregate number of holders of such shares. Such written statement shall be mailed to the stockholder within 10 days after his written request for such a statement is received by the surviving or resulting corporation or within 10 days after expiration of the period for delivery of demands for appraisal under subsection (d) hereof, whichever is later.

(f) Upon the filing of any such petition by a stockholder, service of a copy thereof shall be made upon the surviving or resulting corporation, which shall within 20 days after such service file in the office of the Register in Chancery in which the petition was filed a duly verified list containing the names and addresses of all stockholders who have demanded payment for their shares and with whom agreements as to the value of their shares have not been reached by the surviving or resulting corporation. If the petition shall be filed by the surviving or resulting corporation, the petition shall be accompanied by such a duly verified list. The Register in Chancery, if so ordered by the Court, shall give notice of the time and place fixed for the hearing of such petition by registered or certified mail to the surviving or resulting corporation and to the stockholders shown on the list at the addresses therein stated. Such notice shall also be given by one or more publications at least one week before the day of the hearing, in a newspaper of general circulation published in the City of Wilmington, Delaware or such publication as the Court deems advisable. The forms of the notices by mail and by publication shall be approved by the Court, and the costs thereof shall be borne by the surviving or resulting corporation.

(g) At the hearing on such petition, the Court shall determine the stockholders who have complied with the provisions of this Section and who have become entitled to appraisal rights. The Court may require the stockholders who have demanded an appraisal for their shares and who hold stock represented by certificates to submit their certificates of stock to the Register in Chancery for notation thereon of the pendency of the appraisal proceedings; and if any stockholder fails to comply with such direction, the Court may dismiss the proceedings as to such stockholder.

(h) After determining the stockholders entitled to an appraisal, the Court shall appraise the shares, determining their fair value exclusive of any element of value arising from the accomplishment or expectation of the merger or consolidation, together with a fair rate of interest, if any, to be paid upon the amount determined to be the fair value. In determining such fair value, the Court shall take into account all relevant factors. In determining the fair rate of interest, the Court may consider all relevant factors, including the rate of interest which the surviving or resulting corporation would have had to pay to borrow money during the pendency of the proceeding. Upon application by the surviving or resulting corporation or by any stockholder entitled to participate in the appraisal proceeding, the Court may, in its discretion, permit discovery or other pretrial proceedings and may proceed to trial upon the appraisal prior to the final determination of the stockholder entitled to an appraisal. Any stockholder whose name appears on the list filed by the surviving or resulting corporation pursuant to subsection

(f) of this Section and who has submitted his certificates of stock to the Register in Chancery, if such is required, may participate fully in all proceedings until it is finally determined that he is not entitled to appraisal rights under this Section.

(i) The Court shall direct the payment of the fair value of the shares, together with interest, if any, by the surviving or resulting corporation to the stockholders entitled thereto. Interest may be simple or compound, as the Court may direct. Payment shall be so made to each such stockholder, in the case of holders of uncertificated stock forthwith, and in the case of holders of shares represented by certificates upon the surrender to the corporation of the certificates representing such stock. The Court's decree may be enforced as other decrees in the Court of Chancery may be enforced, whether such surviving or resulting corporation be a corporation of this State or of any other state.

(j) The costs of the proceeding may be determined by the Court and taxed upon the parties as the Court deems equitable in the circumstances. Upon application of a stockholder, the Court may order all or a portion of the expenses incurred by any stockholder in connection with the appraisal proceeding, including, without limitation, reasonable attorney's fees and the fees and expenses of experts, to be charged pro rata against the value of all of the shares entitled to an appraisal.

(k) From and after the effective date of the merger or consolidation, no stockholder who has demanded his appraisal rights as provided in subsection (d) of this Section shall be entitled to vote such stock for any purpose or to receive payment of dividends or other distributions on the stock (except dividends or other distributions payable to stockholders of record at a date which is prior to the effective date of the merger or consolidation); provided, however, that if no petition for an appraisal shall be filed within the time provided in subsection (e) of this Section, or if such stockholder shall deliver to the surviving or resulting corporation a written withdrawal of his demand for an appraisal and an acceptance of the merger or consolidation, either within 60 days after the effective date of the merger or consolidation as provided in subsection (e) of this Section or thereafter with the written approval of the corporation, then the right of such stockholder to an appraisal shall cease. Notwithstanding the foregoing, no appraisal proceeding in the Court of Chancery shall be dismissed as to any stockholder without the approval of the Court, and such approval may be conditioned upon such terms as the Court deems just.

(*l*) The shares of the surviving or resulting corporation into which the shares of such objecting stockholders would have been converted had they assented to the merger or consolidation shall have the status of authorized and unissued shares of the surviving or resulting corporation.

§ 263. Merger or Consolidation of Domestic Corporation and Limited Partnership

(a) Any 1 or more corporations of this State may merge or consolidate with 1 or more limited partnerships, of this State or of any other state or states of the United States, or of the District of Columbia, unless the laws of such other state or states or the District of Columbia forbid such merger or consolidation. Such corporation or corporations and such 1 or more limited partnerships may merge with or into a corporation, which may be any 1 of such corporations, or they may merge with or into a limited partnership, which may be any 1 of such limited partnerships, or they may consolidate into a new corporation or limited partnership formed by the consolidation, which shall be a corporation or limited partnership of this State or any other state of the United States, or the District of Columbia, which permits such merger or consolidation, pursuant to an agreement of merger or consolidation, as the case may be, complying and approved in accordance with this section.

(b) Each such corporation and limited partnership shall enter into a written agreement of merger or consolidation. The agreement shall state: (1) The terms and conditions of the merger or consolidation; (2) the mode of carrying the same into effect; (3) the manner of converting the shares of stock of each such corporation and the partnership interests of each such limited partnership into shares, partnership interests or other securities of the entity surviving or resulting from such merger or consolidation, and if any shares of any such corporation or any partnership interests of any such limited partnership are not to be converted solely into shares, partnership interests or other securities of the entity surviving or resulting from such merger or consolidation, the cash, property, rights or securities of any other corporation or entity which the holders of such shares or partnership interests are to receive in exchange for, or upon conversion of such shares or partnership interests and the surrender of any certificates evidencing them, which cash, property, rights or securities of any other corporation or entity may be in addition to or in lieu of shares, partnership interests or other securities of the entity surviving or resulting from such merger or consolidation; and (4) such other details or provisions as are deemed desirable, including, without limiting the generality of the foregoing, a provision for the payment of cash in lieu of the issuance of fractional shares or interests of the surviving or resulting corporation or limited partnership. Any of the terms of the agreement of merger or consolidation may be made dependent upon facts ascertainable outside of such agreement, provided that the manner in which such facts shall operate upon the terms of the agreement is clearly and expressly set forth in the agreement of merger or consolidation. The term "facts," as used in the preceding sentence, includes, but is not limited to, the occurrence of any event, including a determination or action by any person or body, including the corporation.

(c) The agreement required by subsection (b) of this section shall be adopted, approved, certified, executed and acknowledged by each of the corporations in the same manner as is provided in § 251 of this title and, in the case of the limited partnerships, in accordance with their limited partnership agreements and in accordance with the laws of the state under which they are formed, as the case may be. The agreement shall be filed and shall become effective for all purposes of the laws of this State when and as provided in § 251 of this title with respect to the merger or consolidation of corporations of this State. In lieu of filing the agreement of merger or consolidation, the surviving or resulting corporation or limited partnership may file a certificate of merger or consolidation, executed in accordance with § 103 of this title, if the surviving or resulting entity is a corporation, or by a general partner, if the surviving or resulting entity is a limited partnership, which states: (1) The name and state of domicile of each of the constituent entities; (2) that an agreement of merger or consolidation has been approved, adopted, certified, executed and acknowledged by each of the constituent entities in accordance with this subsection; (3) the name of the surviving or resulting corporation or limited partnership; (4) in the case of a merger in which a corporation is the surviving entity, such amendments or changes in the certificate of incorporation of the surviving corporation as are desired to be effected by the merger, or, if no such amendments or changes are desired, a statement that the certificate of incorporation of the surviving corporation shall be its certificate of incorporation; (5) in the case of a consolidation in which a corporation is the resulting entity, that the certificate of incorporation of the resulting corporation shall be as is set forth in an attachment to the certificate; (6) that the executed agreement of consolidation or merger is on file at an office of the surviving corporation or limited partnership and the address thereof; (7) that a copy of the agreement of consolidation or merger will be furnished by the surviving or resulting entity, on request and without cost, to any stockholder of any constituent corporation or any partner of any constituent limited partnership; and (8) the agreement, if any, required by subsection (d) of this section.

(d) If the entity surviving or resulting from the merger or consolidation is to be governed by the laws of the District of Columbia or any state other than this State, it shall agree that it may be served with process in this State in any proceeding for enforcement of any obligation of any constituent corporation or limited partnership of this State, as well as for enforcement of any obligation of the surviving or resulting corporation or limited partnership arising from the merger or consolidation, including any suit or other proceeding to enforce the right of any stockholders as determined in appraisal proceedings pursuant to § 262 of this title, and shall irrevocably appoint the Secretary of State as its agent to accept service of process in any such suit or other proceedings and shall specify the address to which a copy of such process shall be mailed by the Secretary of State. In the event of such service upon the Secretary of State in accordance with this subsection, the Secretary of State shall forthwith notify such surviving or resulting corporation or limited partnership thereof by letter, certified mail, return receipt requested, directed to such surviving or resulting corporation or limited partnership at its address so specified, unless such surviving or resulting corporation or limited partnership shall have designated in writing to the Secretary of State a different address for such purpose, in which case it shall be mailed to the last address so designated. Such letter shall enclose a copy of the process and any other papers served on the Secretary of State pursuant to this subsection. It shall be the duty of the plaintiff in the event of such service to serve process and any other papers in duplicate, to notify the Secretary of State that service is being effected pursuant to this subsection and to pay the Secretary of State the sum of $50 for the use of the State, which sum shall be taxed as part of the costs in the proceeding, if the plaintiff shall prevail therein. The Secretary of State shall maintain an alphabetical record of any such service setting forth the name of the plaintiff and the defendant, the title, docket number and nature of the proceeding in which process has been served upon him, the fact that service has been effected pursuant to this subsection, the return date thereof, and the day and hour service was made. The Secretary of State shall not be required to retain such information longer than 5 years from his receipt of the service of process.

(e) Sections 251(d)–(f), 259–261 and 328 of this title shall, insofar as they are applicable, apply to mergers or consolidations between corporations and limited partnerships.

§ 264. Merger or Consolidation of Domestic Corporation and Limited Liability Company

(a) Any one or more corporations of this State may merge or consolidate with one or more limited liability companies, of this State or of any other state or states of the United States, or of the District of Columbia, unless the laws of such other state or states or the District of Columbia forbid such merger or consolidation. Such corporation or corporations and such one or more limited liability companies may merge with or into a corporation, which may be any one of such corporations, or they may merge with or into a limited liability company, which may be any one of such limited liability companies, or they may consolidate into a new corporation or limited liability company formed by the consolidation, which shall be a corporation or limited liability company of this State or any other state of the United States, or the District of Columbia, which permits such merger or consolidation, pursuant to an agreement of merger or consolidation, as the case may be, complying and approved in accordance with this section.

(b) Each such corporation and limited liability company shall enter into a written agreement of merger or consolidation. The agreement shall state:

(1) The terms and conditions of the merger or consolidation;

(2) The mode of carrying the same into effect;

(3) The manner of converting the shares of stock of each such corporation and the limited liability company interests of each such limited liability company into shares, limited liability company interests or other securities of the entity surviving or resulting from such merger or consolidation, and if any shares of any such corporation or any limited liability company interests of any such limited liability company are not to be converted solely into shares, limited liability company interests or other securities of the entity surviving or resulting from such merger or consolidation, the cash, property, rights or securities of any other corporation or entity which the holders of such shares or limited liability company interests are to receive in exchange for, or upon conversion of such shares or limited liability company interests and the surrender of any certificates evidencing them, which cash, property, rights or securities of any other corporation or entity may be in addition to or in lieu of shares, limited liability company interests or other securities of the entity surviving or resulting from such merger or consolidation; and

(4) Such other details or provisions as are deemed desirable, including, without limiting the generality of the foregoing, a provision for the payment of cash in lieu of the issuance of fractional shares or interests of the surviving or resulting corporation or limited liability company. Any of the terms of the agreement of merger or consolidation may be made dependent upon facts ascertainable outside of such agreement, provided that the manner in which such facts shall operate upon the terms of the agreement is clearly and expressly set forth in the agreement of merger or consolidation. The term "facts," as used in the preceding sentence, includes, but is not limited to, the occurrence of any event, including a determination or action by any person or body, including the corporation.

(c) The agreement required by subsection (b) shall be adopted, approved, certified, executed and acknowledged by each of the corporations in the same manner as is provided in § 251 of this title and, in the case of the limited liability companies, in accordance with their limited liability company agreements and in accordance with the laws of the state under which they are formed, as the case may be. The agreement shall be filed and shall become effective for all purposes of the laws of this State when and as provided in § 251 of this title with respect to the merger or consolidation of corporations of this State. In lieu of filing the agreement of merger or consolidation, the surviving or resulting corporation or limited liability company may file a certificate of merger or consolidation, executed in accordance with § 103 of this title, if the surviving or resulting entity is a corporation, or by an authorized person, if the surviving or resulting entity is a limited liability company, which states:

> (1) The name and state of domicile of each of the constituent entities;

> (2) That an agreement of merger or consolidation has been approved, adopted, certified, executed and acknowledged by each of the constituent entities in accordance with this subsection;

> (3) The name of the surviving or resulting corporation or limited liability company;

> (4) In the case of a merger in which a corporation is the surviving entity, such amendments or changes in the certificate of incorporation of the surviving corporation as are desired to be effected by the merger, or, if no such amendments or changes are desired, a statement that the certificate of incorporation of the surviving corporation shall be its certificate of incorporation;

> (5) In the case of a consolidation in which a corporation is the resulting entity, that the certificate of incorporation of the resulting corporation shall be as is set forth in an attachment to the certificate;

> (6) That the executed agreement of consolidation or merger is on file at an office of the surviving corporation or limited liability company and the address thereof;

> (7) That a copy of the agreement of consolidation or merger will be furnished by the surviving or resulting entity, on request and without cost, to any stockholder of any constituent corporation or any member of any constituent limited liability company; and

> (8) The agreement, if any, required by subsection (d) of this section.

(d) If the entity surviving or resulting from the merger or consolidation is to be governed by the laws of the District of Columbia or any state other than this State, it shall agree that it may be served with process in this State in any proceeding for enforcement of any obligation of any constituent corporation or limited liability company of this State, as well as for enforcement of any obligation of the surviving or resulting corporation or limited liability company arising from the merger or consolidation, including any suit or other proceeding to enforce the right of any stockholders as determined in appraisal proceedings pursuant to the provisions of § 262 of this title, and shall irrevocably appoint the Secretary of State as its agent to accept service of process in any such suit or other proceedings and shall specify the address to which a copy of such process shall be mailed by the Secretary of State. In the event of such service upon the Secretary of State in accordance with this subsection, the Secretary of State shall forthwith notify such surviving or resulting corporation or limited liability company thereof by letter, certified mail, return receipt requested, directed to such surviving or resulting corporation or limited liability company at its address so specified, unless such surviving or resulting corporation or limited liability company shall have designated in writing to the Secretary of State a different address for such purpose, in which case it shall be mailed to the last address so designated.   Such letter shall enclose a copy of the process and any other papers served on the Secretary of State pursuant to this subsection.   It shall be the duty of the plaintiff in the event of such service to serve process and any other papers in duplicate, to notify the Secretary of State that service is being effected pursuant to this subsection and to pay the Secretary of State the sum of $50 for the use of the State, which sum shall be taxed as part of the costs in the proceeding, if the plaintiff shall prevail therein.   The Secretary of State shall maintain an alphabetical record of any such service setting forth the name of the plaintiff and the defendant, the title, docket number and nature of the proceeding in which process has been served upon him, the fact that service has been effected pursuant to this subsection, the return date thereof, and the day and hour service was made.   The Secretary of State shall not be required to retain such information longer than 5 years from his receipt of the service of process.

(e) Sections 251(d)–(f), 259–261 and 328 of this title shall, insofar as they are applicable, apply to mergers or consolidations between corporations and limited liability companies.

SUBCHAPTER X.   SALE OF ASSETS, DISSOLUTION AND WINDING UP

§ 271.   Sale, Lease or Exchange of Assets;   Consideration;   Procedure

(a) Every corporation may at any meeting of its board of directors or governing body sell, lease, or exchange all or substantially all of its property and assets, including its goodwill and its corporate franchises, upon such terms and conditions and for such consideration, which may consist in whole or in part of money or other property, including shares of stock in, and/or other securities of, any other corporation or corporations, as its board of directors or governing body deems expedient and for the best interests of the corporation, when and as authorized by a resolution adopted by the holders of a majority of the outstanding stock of the corporation entitled to vote thereon or, if the corporation is a nonstock corporation, by a majority of the members having the right to vote for the election of the members of the governing body, at a meeting duly called upon at least 20 days notice. The notice of the meeting shall state that such a resolution will be considered.

(b) Notwithstanding authorization or consent to a proposed sale, lease or exchange of a corporation's property and assets by the stockholders or members, the board of directors or governing body may abandon such proposed sale, lease or exchange without further action by the stockholders or members, subject to the rights, if any, of third parties under any contract relating thereto.

§ 272.　Mortgage or Pledge of Assets

The authorization or consent of stockholders to the mortgage or pledge of a corporation's property and assets shall not be necessary, except to the extent that the certificate of incorporation otherwise provides.

§ 273.　Dissolution of Joint Venture Corporation Having Two Stockholders

(a) If the stockholders of a corporation of this State, having only two stockholders each of which owns 50% of the stock therein, shall be engaged in the prosecution of a joint venture and if such stockholders shall be unable to agree upon the desirability of discontinuing such joint venture and disposing of the assets used in such venture, either stockholder may unless otherwise provided in the certificate of incorporation of the corporation or in a written agreement between the stockholders, file with the Court of Chancery a petition stating that it desires to discontinue such joint venture and to dispose of the assets used in such venture in accordance with a plan to be agreed upon by both stockholders or that, if no such plan shall be agreed upon by both stockholders, the corporation be dissolved. Such petition shall have attached thereto a copy of the proposed plan of discontinuance and distribution and a certificate stating that copies of such petition and plan have been transmitted in writing to the other stockholder and to the directors and officers of such corporation. The petition and certificate shall be executed and acknowledged in accordance with section 103 of this title.

(b) Unless both stockholders file with the Court of Chancery (i) within three months of the date of the filing of such petition, a certificate similarly executed and acknowledged stating that they have agreed on such plan, or a modification thereof, and (ii) within one year from the date of the filing of such petition, a certificate similarly executed and acknowledged stating that the distribution provided by such plan has been completed, the Court of Chancery may dissolve such corporation and may by appointment of one or more trustees or receivers with all the powers and title of a trustee or receiver appointed under section 279 of this title, administer and wind up its affairs. Either or both of the above periods may be extended by agreement of the stockholders, evidenced by a certificate similarly executed, acknowledged and filed with the Court of Chancery prior to the expiration of such period.

§ 275. Dissolution; Procedure

(a) If it should be deemed advisable in the judgment of the board of directors of any corporation that it should be dissolved, the board, after the adoption of a resolution to that effect by a majority of the whole board at any meeting called for that purpose, shall cause notice to be mailed to each stockholder entitled to vote thereon of the adoption of the resolution and of a meeting of stockholders to take action upon the resolution.

(b) At the meeting a vote shall be taken upon the proposed dissolution. If a majority of the outstanding stock of the corporation entitled to vote thereon shall vote for the proposed dissolution, a certification of dissolution shall be filed with the Secretary of State pursuant to subsection (d) of this Section.

(c) Dissolution of a corporation may also be authorized without action of the directors if all the stockholders entitled to vote thereon shall consent in writing and a certificate of dissolution shall be filed with the Secretary of State pursuant to subsection (d) of this Section.

(d) If dissolution is authorized in accordance with this Section, a certificate of dissolution shall be executed, acknowledged and filed, and shall become effective, in accordance with § 103 of this Title. Such certificate of dissolution shall set forth:

(i) the name of the corporation;

(ii) the date dissolution was authorized;

(iii) that the dissolution has been authorized by the board of directors and stockholders of the corporation, in accordance with subsections (a) and (b) of this Section, or that the dissolution has been authorized by all of the stockholders of the corporation entitled to vote on a dissolution, in accordance with subsection (c) of this section; and

(iv) the names and addresses of the directors and officers of the corporation.

(e) The resolution authorizing a proposed dissolution may provide that notwithstanding authorization or consent to the proposed dissolution by the stockholders ... the board of directors or governing body may abandon such proposed dissolution without further action by the stockholders or members.

(f) Upon a certificate of dissolution becoming effective in accordance with § 103 of this title, the corporation shall be dissolved.

§ 278. Continuation of Corporation After Dissolution for Purposes of Suit and Winding Up Affairs

All corporations, whether they expire by their own limitation or are otherwise dissolved, shall nevertheless be continued, for the term of three years from such expiration or dissolution or for such longer period as the Court of Chancery shall in its discretion direct, bodies corporate for the purpose of prosecuting and defending suits, whether civil, criminal or administrative, by or against them, and of enabling them gradually to settle and close their business, to dispose of and convey their property, to discharge their liabilities, and to distribute to their stockholders any remaining assets, but not for the purpose of continuing the business for which the corporation was organized. With respect to any action, suit or proceeding begun by or against the corporation either prior to or within 3 years after the date of its expiration or dissolution the action shall not abate by reason of the dissolution of the corporation; the corporation shall, solely for the purpose of such action, suit or proceeding, be continued as a body corporate beyond the 3–year period and until any judgments, orders or decrees therein shall be fully executed, without the necessity for any special direction to that effect by the Court of Chancery.

§ 279. Trustees or Receivers for Dissolved Corporations; Appointment; Powers; Duties

When any corporation organized under this chapter shall be dissolved in any manner whatever, the Court of Chancery, on application of any creditor, stockholder or director of the corporation, or any other person who shows good cause therefor, at any time, may either appoint one or more of the directors of the corporation to be trustees, or appoint one or more persons to be receivers, of and for the corporation, to take charge of the corporation's property, and to collect the debts and property due and belonging to the corporation, with power to prosecute and defend, in the name of the corporation, or otherwise, all such suits as may be necessary or proper for the purposes aforesaid, and to appoint an agent or agents under them, and to do all other acts which might be done by the corporation, if in being, that may be necessary for the final settlement of the unfinished business of the corporation. The powers of the trustees or receivers may be continued as long as the Court of Chancery shall think necessary for the purposes aforesaid.

§ 280. Notice of Claimants; Filing of Claims

(a)(1) After a corporation has been dissolved in accordance with the procedures set forth in this chapter, the corporation or any successor entity may give notice of the dissolution, requiring all persons having a claim against the corporation other than a claim against the corporation in a pending action, suit or proceeding to which the corporation is a party to present their claims against the corporation in accordance with such notice. Such notice shall state:

a. That all such claims must be presented in writing and must contain sufficient information reasonably to inform the corporation or successor entity of the identity of the claimant and the substance of the claim;

b. The mailing address to which such a claim must be sent;

c. The date by which such a claim must be received by the corporation or successor entity, which date shall be no earlier than 60 days from the date thereof; and

d. That such claim will be barred if not received by the date referred to in subparagraph c. of this subsection; and

e. That the corporation or a successor entity may make distributions to other claimants and the corporation's stockholders or persons interested as having been such without further notice to the claimant; and

f. The aggregate amount, on an annual basis, of all distributions made by the corporation to its stockholders for each of the 3 years prior to the date the corporation dissolved.

Such notice shall also be published at least once a week for 2 consecutive weeks in a newspaper of general circulation in the county in which the office of the corporation's last registered agent in this State is located and in the corporation's principal place of business and, in the case of a corporation having $10,000,000 or more in total assets at the time of its dissolution, at least once in all editions of a daily newspaper with a national circulation. On or before the date of the first publication of such notice, the corporation or successor entity shall mail a copy of such notice by certified or registered mail, return receipt requested, to each known claimant of the corporation including persons with claims asserted against the corporation in a pending action, suit or proceeding to which the corporation is a party.

(2) Any claim against the corporation required to be presented pursuant to this subsection is barred if a claimant who was given actual notice under this subsection does not present the claim to the dissolved corporation or successor entity by the date referred to in subparagraph (1)c. of this subsection.

(3) A corporation or successor entity may reject, in whole or in part, any claim made by a claimant pursuant to this subsection by mailing notice of such rejection by certified or registered mail, return receipt requested, to the claimant within 90 days after receipt of such claim and, in all events, at least 150 days before the expiration of the period described in § 278 of this title; provided however, that in the case of a claim filed pursuant to § 295 of this title against a corporation or successor entity for which a receiver or trustee has been appointed by

the Court of Chancery the time period shall be as provided in § 296 of this title, and the 30–day appeal period provided for in § 296 of this title shall be applicable. A notice sent by a corporation or successor entity pursuant to this subsection shall state that any claim rejected therein will be barred if an action, suit or proceeding with respect to the claim is not commenced within 120 days of the date thereof, and shall be accompanied by a copy of §§ 278–283 of this title and, in the case of a notice sent by a court-appointed receiver or trustee and as to which a claim has been filed pursuant to § 295 of this title, copies of §§ 295 and 296 of this title.

(4) A claim against a corporation is barred if a claimant whose claim is rejected pursuant to paragraph (3) of this subsection does not commence an action, suit or proceeding with respect to the claim no later than 120 days after the mailing of the rejection notice.

(b)(1) A corporation or successor entity electing to follow the procedures described in subsection (a) of this section shall also give notice of the dissolution of the corporation to persons with contractual claims contingent upon the occurrence or nonoccurrence of future events or otherwise conditional or unmatured, and request that such persons present such claims in accordance with the terms of such notice. Provided however, that as used in this section and in § 281 of this title, the term "contractual claims" shall not include any implied warranty as to any product manufactured, sold, distributed or handled by the dissolved corporation. Such notice shall be in substantially the form, and sent and published in the same manner, as described in subsection (a)(1) of this section.

(2) The corporation or successor entity shall offer any claimant on a contract whose claim is contingent, conditional or unmatured such security as the corporation or successor entity determines is sufficient to provide compensation to the claimant if the claim matures. The corporation or successor entity shall mail such offer to the claimant by certified or registered mail, return receipt requested, within 90 days of receipt of such claim and, in all events, at least 150 days before the expiration of the period described in § 278 of this title. If the claimant offered such security does not deliver in writing to the corporation or successor entity a notice rejecting the offer within 120 days after receipt of such offer for security, the claimant shall be deemed to have accepted such security as the sole source from which to satisfy his claim against the corporation.

(c)(1) A corporation or successor entity which has given notice in accordance with subsection (a) of this section shall petition the Court of Chancery to determine the amount and form of security that will be reasonably likely to be sufficient to provide compensation for any claim against the corporation which is the subject of a pending action, suit or proceeding to which the corporation is a party other than a claim barred pursuant to subsection (a) of this section.

(2) A corporation or successor entity which has given notice in accordance with subsections (a) and (b) of this section shall petition the Court of Chancery to determine the amount and form of security that will be sufficient to provide compensation to any claimant who has rejected the offer for security made pursuant to subsection (b)(2) of this section.

(3) A corporation or successor entity which has given notice in accordance with subsection (a) of this section shall petition the Court of Chancery to determine the amount and form of security which will be reasonably likely to be sufficient to provide compensation for claims that have not been made known to the corporation or that have not arisen but that, based on facts known to the corporation or successor entity, are likely to arise or to become known to the corporation or successor entity within 5 years after the date of dissolution or such longer period of time as the Court of Chancery may determine not to exceed 10 years after the date of dissolution. The Court of Chancery may appoint a guardian ad litem in respect of any such proceeding brought under this subsection. The reasonable fees and expenses of such guardian, including all reasonable expert witness fees, shall be paid by the petitioner in such proceeding.

(d) The giving of any notice or making of any offer pursuant to the provisions of this section shall not revive any claim then barred or constitute acknowledgment by the corporation or successor entity that any person to whom such notice is sent is a proper claimant and shall not operate as a waiver of any defense or counterclaim in respect of any claim asserted by any person to whom such notice is sent.

(e) As used in this section, the term "successor entity" shall include any trust, receivership or other legal entity governed by the laws of this State to which the remaining assets and liabilities of a dissolved corporation are transferred and which exists solely for the purposes of prosecuting and defending suits, by or against the dissolved corporation, enabling the dissolved corporation to settle and close the business of the dissolved corporation, to dispose of and convey the property of the dissolved corporation, to discharge the liabilities of the dissolved corporation, and to distribute to the dissolved corporation's stockholders any remaining assets, but not for the purpose of continuing the business for which the dissolved corporation was organized.

(f) The time periods and notice requirements of this section shall, in the case of a corporation or successor entity for which a receiver or trustee has been appointed by the Court of Chancery, be subject to variation by, or in the manner provided in, the Rules of the Court of Chancery.

§ 281. Payment and Distribution to Claimants and Stockholders

(a) A dissolved corporation or successor entity which has followed the procedures described in § 280 of this title (i) shall pay the claims made and not rejected in accordance with § 280(a) of this title, (ii) shall post the security offered and not rejected pursuant to § 280(b)(2) of this title, (iii) shall post any security ordered by the Court of Chancery in any proceeding under § 280(c) of this title and (iv) shall pay or make provision for all other claims that are mature, known and uncontested or that have been finally determined to be owing by the corporation or such successor entity. Such claims or obligations shall be paid in full and any such provision for payment shall be made in full if there are sufficient funds. If there are insufficient funds, such claims and obligations shall be paid or provided for according to their priority, and, among claims of equal priority, ratably to the extent of funds legally available therefor. Any remaining funds shall be distributed to the stockholders of the dissolved corporation; provided, however, that such distribution shall not be made before the expiration of 150 days from the date of the last notice of rejections given pursuant to § 280(a)(3) of this title. In the absence of actual fraud, the judgment of the directors of the dissolved corporation or the governing persons of such successor entity as to the provision made for the payment of all obligations under (iv) above shall be conclusive.

(b) A dissolved corporation or successor entity which has not followed the procedures described in § 280 of this title shall, prior to the expiration of the period described in § 278 of this title, adopt a plan of distribution pursuant to which the dissolved corporation or successor entity (i) shall pay or make reasonable provision to pay all claims and obligations, including all contingent, conditional or unmatured contractual claims known to the corporation or such successor entity, (ii) shall make such provision as will be reasonably likely to be sufficient to provide compensation for any claim against the corporation which is the subject of a pending action, suit or proceeding to which the corporation is a party and (iii) shall make such provision as will be reasonably likely to be sufficient to provide compensation for claims that have not been made known to the corporation or that have not arisen but that, based on facts known to the corporation or successor entity, are likely to arise or to become known to the corporation or successor entity within 10 years after the date of dissolution. The plan of distribution shall provide that such claims shall be paid in full and any such provision for payment made shall be made in full if there are sufficient funds. If there are insufficient funds, such plan shall provide that such claims and obligations shall be paid or provided for according to their priority and, among claims of equal priority, ratably to the extent of funds legally available therefor. Any remaining funds shall be distributed to the stockholders of the dissolved corporation.

(c) Directors of a dissolved corporation or governing persons of a successor entity which has complied with subsections (a) or (b) of this section shall not be personally liable to the claimants of the dissolved corporation.

(d) As used in this section, the term "successor entity" has the meaning set forth in § 280(e) of this title.

(e) The term "priority", as used in this section, does not refer either to the order of payments set forth in subsection (a)(1)–(4) of this section or to the relative times at which any claims mature or are reduced to judgment.

§ 282. Liability of Stockholders of Dissolved Corporations

(a) A stockholder of a dissolved corporation the assets of which were distributed pursuant to § 281(a) or (b) of this title shall not be liable for any claim against the corporation in an amount in excess of such stockholder's pro rata share of the claim or the amount so distributed to him, whichever is less.

(b) A stockholder of a dissolved corporation the assets of which were distributed pursuant to § 281(a) of this title shall not be liable for any claim against the corporation on which an action, suit or proceeding is not begun prior to the expiration of the period described in § 278 of this title.

(c) The aggregate liability of any stockholder of a dissolved corporation for claims against the dissolved corporation shall not exceed the amount distributed to him in dissolution.

§ 283. Jurisdiction of the Court

The Court of the Chancery shall have jurisdiction of any application prescribed in this subchapter and of all questions arising in the proceedings thereon, and may make such orders and decrees and issue injunctions therein as justice and equity shall require.

§ 284. Revocation or Forfeiture of Charter; Proceedings

(a) The Court of Chancery shall have jurisdiction to revoke or forfeit the charter of any corporation for abuse, misuse or nonuse of its corporate powers, privileges or franchises. The Attorney General shall, upon his own motion or upon the relation of a proper party, proceed for this purpose by complaint in the County in which the registered office of the corporation is located.

(b) The Court of Chancery shall have power, by appointment of receivers or otherwise, to administer and wind up the affairs of any corporation whose charter shall be revoked or forfeited by any court under any section of this title or otherwise, and to make such orders and decrees with respect thereto as shall be just and equitable respecting its affairs and assets and the rights of its stockholders and creditors.

(c) No proceeding shall be instituted under this section for non-use of any corporation's powers, privileges or franchises during the first two years after its incorporation.

SUBCHAPTER XIII. SUITS AGAINST COR-PORATIONS, DIRECTORS, OFFICERS OR STOCKHOLDERS

§ 325. Actions Against Officers, Directors or Stockholders to Enforce Liability of Corporation; Unsatisfied Judgment Against Corporation

(a) When the officers, directors or stockholders of any corporation shall be liable by the provisions of this chapter to pay the debts of the corporation, or any part thereof, any person to whom they are liable may have an action, at law or in equity, against any one or more of them, and the complaint shall state the claim against the corporation, and the ground on which the plaintiff expects to charge the defendants personally.

(b) No suit shall be brought against any officer, director, or stockholder for any debt of a corporation of which he is an officer, director or stockholder, until judgment be obtained therefor against the corporation and execution thereon returned unsatisfied.

§ 327. Stockholder's Derivative Action; Allegation of Stock Ownership

In any derivative suit instituted by a stockholder of a corporation, it shall be averred in the complaint that the plaintiff was a stockholder of the corporation at the time of the transaction of which he complains or that his stock thereafter devolved upon him by operation of law.

§ 328. Liability of Corporation, etc., Impairment by Certain Transactions

The liability of a corporation of this State, or the stockholders, directors or officers thereof, or the rights or remedies of the creditors thereof, or of persons doing or transacting business with the corporation, shall not in any way be lessened or impaired by the sale of its assets, or by the increase or decrease in the capital stock of the corporation, or by its merger or consolidation with one or more corporations or by any change or amendment in its certificate of incorporation.

§ 329. Defective Organization of Corporation as Defense

(a) No corporation of this State and no person sued by any such corporation shall be permitted to assert the want of legal organization as a defense to any claim.

(b) This section shall not be construed to prevent judicial inquiry into the regularity or validity of the organization of a corporation, or its lawful possession of any corporate power it may assert in any other suit or proceeding where its corporate existence or the power to exercise the corporate rights it asserts is challenged, and evidence tending to sustain the challenge shall be admissible in any such suit or proceeding....

SUBCHAPTER XIV. CLOSE CORPORATIONS; SPECIAL PROVISIONS

§ 341. Law Applicable to Close Corporation

(a) This subchapter applies to all close corporations, as defined in section 342 of this title. Unless a corporation elects to become a close corporation under this subchapter in the manner prescribed in this subchapter, it shall be subject in all respects to the provisions of this chapter, except the provisions of this subchapter.

(b) All provisions of this chapter shall be applicable to all close corporations, as defined in section 342 of this title, except insofar as this subchapter otherwise provides.

§ 342. Close Corporation Defined; Contents of Certificate of Incorporation

(a) A close corporation is a corporation organized under this chapter whose certificate of incorporation contains the provisions required by section 102 of this title and, in addition, provides that:

(1) All of the corporation's issued stock of all classes, exclusive of treasury shares, shall be represented by certificates and shall be held of record by not more than a specified number of persons, not exceeding thirty; and

(2) All of the issued stock of all classes shall be subject to one or more of the restrictions on transfer permitted by section 202 of this title; and

(3) The corporation shall make no offering of any of its stock of any class which would constitute a "public offering" within the meaning of the United States Securities Act of 1933, as it may be amended from time to time.

(b) The certificate of incorporation of a close corporation may set forth the qualifications of stockholders, either by specifying classes of persons who shall be entitled to be holders of record of stock of any class, or by specifying classes of persons who shall not be entitled to be holders of stock of any class or both.

(c) For purposes of determining the number of holders of record of the stock of a close corporation, stock which is held in joint or common tenancy or by the entireties shall be treated as held by one stockholder.

§ 343.   Formation of a Close Corporation

A close corporation shall be formed in accordance with sections 101, 102 and 103 of this title, except that:

(a) Its certificate of incorporation shall contain a heading stating the name of the corporation and that it is a close corporation, and

(b) Its certificate of incorporation shall contain the provisions required by section 342 of this title.

§ 344.   Election of Existing Corporation to Become a Close Corporation

Any corporation organized under this chapter may become a close corporation under this subchapter by executing, acknowledging and filing in accordance with section 103 of this title, a certificate of amendment of its certificate of incorporation which shall contain a statement that it elects to become a close corporation, the provisions required by section 342 of this title to appear in the certificate of incorporation of a close corporation, and a heading stating the name of the corporation and that it is a close corporation. Such amendment shall be adopted in accordance with the requirements of section 241 or 242 of this title, except that it must be approved by a vote of the holders of record of at least two-thirds of the shares of each class of stock of the corporation which are outstanding.

§ 345.   Limitations on Continuation of Close Corporation Status

A close corporation continues to be such and to be subject to this subchapter until:

(a) It files with the Secretary of State a certificate of amendment deleting from its certificate of incorporation the provisions required or permitted by section 342 of this title to be stated in the certificate of incorporation to qualify it as a close corporation, or

(b) Any one of the provisions or conditions required or permitted by section 342 of this title to be stated in a certificate of incorporation to qualify a corporation as a close corporation has in fact been breached and neither the corporation nor any of its stockholders takes the steps required by section 348 of this title to prevent such loss of status or to remedy such breach.

§ 346.   Voluntary Termination of Close Corporation Status by Amendment of Certificate of Incorporation; Vote Required

(a) A corporation may voluntarily terminate its status as a close corporation and cease to be subject to this subchapter by amending its certificate of incorporation to delete therefrom the additional provisions required or permitted by section 342 of this title to be stated in the certificate of incorporation of a close corporation. Any such amendment shall be adopted and shall become effective in accordance with section 242 of this title, except that it must be approved by a vote of the holders of record of at least two-thirds of the shares of each class of stock of the corporation which are outstanding.

(b) The certificate of incorporation of a close corporation may provide that on any amendment to terminate its status as a close corporation, a vote greater than two-thirds or a vote of all shares of any class shall be required; and if the certificate of incorporation contains such a provision, that provision shall not be amended, repealed or modified by any vote less than that required to terminate the corporation's status as a close corporation.

§ 347. Issuance or Transfer of Stock of a Close Corporation in Breach of Qualifying Conditions

(a) If stock of a close corporation is issued or transferred to any person who is not entitled under any provision of the certificate of incorporation permitted by section 342(b) of this title to be a holder of record of stock of such corporation, and if the certificate for such stock conspicuously notes the qualifications of the persons entitled to be holders of record thereof, such person is conclusively presumed to have notice of the fact of his ineligibility to be a stockholder.

(b) If the certificate of incorporation of a close corporation states the number of persons, not in excess of thirty, who are entitled to be holders of record of its stock, and if the certificate for such stock conspicuously states such number, and if the issuance or transfer of stock to any person would cause the stock to be held by more than such number of persons, the person to whom such stock is issued or transferred is conclusively presumed to have notice of this fact.

(c) If a stock certificate of any close corporation conspicuously notes the fact of a restriction on transfer of stock of the corporation, and the restriction is one which is permitted by section 202 of this title, the transferee of the stock is conclusively presumed to have notice of the fact that he has acquired stock in violation of the restriction, if such acquisition violates the restriction.

(d) Whenever any person to whom stock of a close corporation has been issued or transferred has, or is conclusively presumed under this section to have, notice either (i) that he is a person not eligible to be a holder of stock of the corporation, or (ii) that transfer of stock to him would cause the stock of the corporation to be held by more than the number of persons permitted by its certificate of incorporation to hold stock of the corporation, or (iii) that the transfer of stock is in violation of a restriction on transfer of stock, the corporation may, at its option, refuse to register transfer of the stock into the name of the transferee.

(e) The provisions of subsection (d) shall not be applicable if the transfer of stock, even though otherwise contrary to subsections (a), (b) or (c), has been consented to by all the stockholders of the close corporation, or if the close corporation has amended its certificate of incorporation in accordance with section 346 of this title.

(f) The term "transfer", as used in this section, is not limited to a transfer for value.

(g) The provisions of this section do not in any way impair any rights of a transferee regarding any right to rescind the transaction or to recover under any applicable warranty express or implied.

§ 348. Involuntary Termination of Close Corporation Status; Proceeding to Prevent Loss of Status

(a) If any event occurs as a result of which one or more of the provisions or conditions included in a close corporation's certificate of incorporation pursuant to section 342 of this title to qualify it as a close corporation has been breached, the corporation's status as a close corporation under this subchapter shall terminate unless

(1) within thirty days after the occurrence of the event, or within thirty days after the event has been discovered, whichever is later, the corporation files with the Secretary of State a certificate, executed and acknowledged in accordance with section 103 of this title, stating that a specified provision or condition included in its certificate of incorporation pursuant to section 342 of this title to qualify it as a close corporation has ceased to be applicable, and furnishes a copy of such certificate to each stockholder, and

(2) the corporation concurrently with the filing of such certificate takes such steps as are necessary to correct the situation which threatens its status as a close corporation, including, without limitation, the refusal to register the transfer of stock which has been wrongfully transferred as provided by section 347 of this title, or a proceeding under subsection (b) of this section.

(b) The Court of Chancery, upon the suit of the corporation or any stockholder, shall have jurisdiction to issue all orders necessary to prevent the corporation from losing its status as a close corporation, or to restore its status as a close corporation by enjoining or setting aside any act or threatened act on the part of the corporation or a stockholder which would be inconsistent with any of the provisions or conditions required or permitted by section 342 of this title to be stated in the certificate of incorporation of a close corporation, unless it is an act approved in accordance with section 346 of this title. The Court of Chancery may enjoin or set aside any transfer or threatened transfer of stock of a close corporation which is contrary to the terms of its certificate of incorporation or of any transfer restriction permitted by section 202 of this title, and may enjoin any public offering, as defined in section 342 of this title, or threatened public offering of stock of the close corporation.

§ 349. Corporate Option Where a Restriction on Transfer of a Security Is Held Invalid

If a restriction on transfer of a security of a close corporation is held not to be authorized by section 202 of this title, the corporation shall nevertheless have an option, for a period of thirty days after the judgment setting aside the restriction becomes final, to acquire the restricted security at a price which is agreed upon by the parties, or if no agreement is reached as to price, then at the fair value as determined by the Court of Chancery. In order to determine fair value, the Court may appoint an appraiser to receive evidence and report to the Court his findings and recommendation as to fair value.

§ 350. Agreements Restricting Discretion of Directors

A written agreement among the stockholders of a close corporation holding a majority of the outstanding stock entitled to vote, whether solely among themselves or with a party not a stockholder, is not invalid, as between the parties to the agreement, on the ground that it so relates to the conduct of the business and affairs of the corporation as to restrict or interfere with the discretion or powers of the board of directors. The effect of any such agreement shall be to relieve the directors and impose upon the stockholders who are parties to the agreement the liability for managerial acts or omissions which is imposed on directors to the extent and so long as the discretion or powers of the board in its management of corporate affairs is controlled by such agreement.

§ 351. Management by Stockholders

The certificate of incorporation of a close corporation may provide that the business of the corporation shall be managed by the stockholders of the corporation rather than by a board of directors. So long as this provision continues in effect,

(1) No meeting of stockholders need be called to elect directors;

(2) Unless the context clearly requires otherwise, the stockholders of the corporation shall be deemed to be directors for purposes of applying provisions of this chapter; and

(3) The stockholders of the corporation shall be subject to all liabilities of directors.

Such a provision may be inserted in the certificate of incorporation by amendment if all incorporators and subscribers or all holders of record of all of the outstanding stock, whether or not having voting power, authorize such a provision. An amendment to the certificate of incorporation to delete such a provision shall be adopted by a vote of the holders of a majority of all outstanding stock of the corporation, whether or not otherwise entitled to vote. If the certificate of incorporation contains a provision authorized by this section, the existence of such provision shall be noted conspicuously on the face or back of every stock certificate issued by such corporation.

§ 352. Appointment of Custodian for Close Corporation

(a) In addition to the provisions of section 226 of this title respecting the appointment of a custodian for any corporation, the Court of Chancery, upon application of any stockholder, may appoint one or more persons to be custodians, and, if the corporation is insolvent, to be receivers, of any close corporation when:

(1) Pursuant to section 351 of this title the business and affairs of the corporation are managed by the stockholders and they are so divided that the business of the corporation is suffering or is threatened with irreparable injury and any remedy with respect to such deadlock provided in the certificate of incorporation or by-laws or in any written agreement of the stockholders has failed; or

(2) The petitioning stockholder has the right to the dissolution of the corporation under a provision of the certificate of incorporation permitted by section 355 of this title.

(b) In lieu of appointing a custodian for a close corporation under this section or section 226 of this title the Court of Chancery may appoint a provisional director, whose powers and status shall be as provided in section 353 of this title if the Court determines that it would be in the best interest of the corporation. Such appointment shall not preclude any subsequent order of the Court appointing a custodian for such corporation.

§ 353. Appointment of a Provisional Director in Certain Cases

(a) Notwithstanding any contrary provision of the certificate of incorporation or the by-laws or agreement of the stockholders, the Court of Chancery may appoint a provisional director for a close corporation if the directors are so divided respecting the management of the corporation's business and affairs that the votes required for action by the board of directors cannot be obtained with the consequence that the business and affairs of the corporation can no longer be conducted to the advantage of the stockholders generally.

(b) An application for relief under this section must be filed (1) by at least one-half of the number of directors then in office, (2) by the holders of at least one-third of all stock then entitled to elect directors, or, (3) if there be more than one class of stock then entitled to elect one or more directors, by the holders of two-thirds of the stock of any such class; but the certificate of incorporation of a close corporation may provide that a lesser proportion of the directors or of the stockholders or of a class of stockholders may apply for relief under this section.

(c) A provisional director shall be an impartial person who is neither a stockholder nor a creditor of the corporation or of any subsidiary or affiliate of the corporation, and whose further qualifications, if any, may be determined by the Court of Chancery. A provisional director is not a receiver of the corporation and does not have the title and powers of a custodian or receiver appointed under sections 226 and 291 of this title. A provisional director shall have all the rights and powers of a duly elected director of the corporation, including the right to notice of and to vote at meetings of directors, until such time as he shall be removed by order of the Court of Chancery or by the holders of a majority of all shares then entitled to vote to elect directors or by the holders of two-thirds of the shares of that class of voting shares which filed the application for appointment of a provisional director. His compensation shall be determined by agreement between him and the corporation subject to approval of the Court of Chancery, which may fix his compensation in the absence of agreement or in the event of disagreement between the provisional director and the corporation.

(d) Even though the requirements of subsection (b) of this section relating to the number of directors or stockholders who may petition for appointment of a provisional director are not satisfied, the Court of Chancery may nevertheless appoint a provisional director if permitted by subsection (b) of section 352 of this title.

§ 354. Operating Corporation as Partnership

No written agreement among stockholders of a close corporation, nor any provision of the certificate of incorporation or of the by-laws of the corporation, which agreement or provision relates to any phase of the affairs of such corporation, including but not limited to the management of its business or declaration and payment of dividends or other division of profits or the election of directors or officers or the employment of stockholders by the corporation or the arbitration of disputes, shall be invalid on the ground that it is an attempt by the parties to the agreement or by the stockholders of the corporation to treat the corporation as if it were a partnership or to arrange relations among the stockholders or between the stockholders and the corporation in a manner that would be appropriate only among partners.

§ 355. Stockholders' Option to Dissolve Corporation

(a) The certificate of incorporation of any close corporation may include a provision granting to any stockholder, or to the holders of any specified number or percentage of shares of any class of stock, an option to have the corporation dissolved at will or upon the occurrence of any specified event or contingency. Whenever any such option to dissolve is exercised, the stockholders exercising such option shall give written notice thereof to all other stockholders. After the expiration of 30 days following the sending of such notice, the dissolution of the corporation shall proceed as if the required number of stockholders having voting power had consented in writing to dissolution of the corporation as provided by section 228 of this title.

(b) If the certificate of incorporation as originally filed does not contain a provision authorized by subsection (a), the certificate may be amended to include such provision if adopted by the affirmative vote of the holders of all the outstanding stock, whether or not entitled to vote, unless the certificate of incorporation specifically authorizes such an amendment by a vote which shall be not less than two-thirds of all the outstanding stock whether or not entitled to vote.

(c) Each stock certificate in any corporation whose certificate of incorporation authorizes dissolution as permitted by this section shall conspicuously note on the face thereof the existence of the provision. Unless noted conspicuously on the face of the stock certificate, the provision is ineffective.

§ 356. Effect of This Subchapter on Other Laws

The provisions of this subchapter shall not be deemed to repeal any statute or rule of law which is or would be applicable to any corporation which is organized under the provisions of this chapter but is not a close corporation.

SUBCHAPTER XV. FOREIGN CORPORATIONS

§ 371. Definition; Qualification to Do Business in State; Procedure

(a) As used in this chapter, the words "foreign corporation" mean a corporation organized under the laws of any jurisdiction other than this State.

(b) No foreign corporation shall do any business in this State, through or by branch offices, agents or representatives located in this State, until it shall have paid to the Secretary of State of this State for the use of the State, $80, and shall have filed in the Office of the Secretary of State:

(1) A certificate issued by an authorized officer of the jurisdiction of its incorporation evidencing its corporate existence. If such certificate is in a foreign language, a translation thereof, under oath of the translator, shall be attached thereto.

(2) A statement executed by an authorized officer of each corporation setting forth (i) the name and address of its registered agent in this State, which agent shall be either an individual resident in this State

when appointed or another corporation authorized to transact business in this State, (ii) a statement, as of a date not earlier than six months prior to the filing date, of the assets and liabilities of the corporation, and (iii) the business it proposes to do in this State and a statement that it is authorized to do that business in the jurisdiction of its incorporation. The statement shall be acknowledged in accordance with § 103 of this Title.

(c) The certificate of the Secretary of State, under his seal of office, of the filing of the certificates required by subsection (b) of this section, shall be delivered to the registered agent upon the payment to the Secretary of State of the fee prescribed for his certificates and the certificate shall be prima facie evidence of the right of the corporation to do business in this State; provided that the Secretary of State shall not issue such certificate unless the name of the corporation is such as to distinguish it upon the records of the office of the Secretary of State from the names of other corporations or limited partnerships organized under the laws of this State or reserved or registered as a foreign corporation or foreign limited partnership under the laws of this State except with the written consent of such other corporation or limited partnership, executed, acknowledged, and filed with the Secretary of State in accordance with section 103 of this title. If the name of the foreign corporation conflicts with the name of a corporation, limited partnership, limited liability company, registered limited liability partnership or business trust organized under the laws of this State, or a name reserved for a corporation, limited partnership, limited liability company, registered limited liability partnership or business trust to be organized under the laws of this State, or a name reserved or registered as that of a foreign corporation, foreign limited partnership or foreign limited liability company under the laws of this State, the foreign corporation may qualify to do business if it adopts an assumed name which shall be used when doing business in this State as long as the assumed name is authorized for use by this section.

§ 383. Actions by and Against Unqualified Foreign Corporations

(a) A foreign corporation which is required to comply with the provisions of sections 371 and 372 of this title and which has done business in this State without authority shall not maintain any action or special proceeding in this State unless and until such corporation has been authorized to do business in this State and has paid to the State all fees, penalties and franchise taxes for the years or parts thereof during which it did business in this State without authority. This prohibition shall not apply to any successor in interest of such foreign corporation.

(b) The failure of a foreign corporation to obtain authority to do business in this State shall not impair the validity of any contract or act of the foreign corporation or the right of any other party to the contract to maintain any action or special proceeding thereon, and shall not prevent the foreign corporation from defending any action or special proceeding in this State.

SUBCHAPTER XVI. TRANSFER AND CONTINUANCE OF CORPORATIONS

§ 390. Transfer and Continuance of Domestic Corporations

(a) Upon compliance with the provisions of this section any corporation existing under the laws of this State may transfer to any jurisdiction other than the United States, any State, the District of Columbia, Puerto Rico, Guam or any possession or territory of the United States, which permits the transfer to or domestication or continuance in such jurisdiction of a corporation existing under the laws of this State.

(b) The board of directors of the corporation which desires to transfer to another jurisdiction shall adopt a resolution approving such transfer specifying the jurisdiction in which the corporation shall be domesticated or continued and recommending the approval of such transfer by the stockholders of the corporation. Such resolution shall be submitted to the stockholders of the corporation at an annual or special meeting. Due notice of the time, place and purpose of the meeting shall be mailed to each holder of stock, whether voting or nonvoting, of the corporation at the address of the stockholder as it appears on the records of the corporation, at least 20 days prior to the date of the meeting. At the meeting, the resolution shall be considered and a vote taken for its adoption or rejection. If all outstanding shares of stock of the corporation, whether voting or nonvoting, shall be voted for the adoption of the resolution, the corporation shall file with the Secretary of State a certificate of transfer, executed in accordance with § 103 of this title, which certifies:

(1) The name of the corporation, and if it has been changed, the name under which it was originally incorporated.

(2) The date of filing of its original certificate of incorporation with the Secretary of State.

(3) The jurisdiction to which the corporation will transfer or in which it will be domesticated or continued.

(4) That the transfer of the corporation has been approved in accordance with the provisions of this section.

(5) The agreement of the corporation that it may be served with process in this State in any proceeding for enforcement of any obligation of the corporation arising while it was a corporation of this State which shall also appoint the Secretary of State as its agent to accept service of process in any such proceeding and specify the

address to which a copy of such process shall be mailed by the Secretary of State.

(c) Upon compliance by the corporation with subsection (b) of this section and payment to the Secretary of State of all fees prescribed under this title, the Secretary of State shall certify that the corporation has filed all documents and paid all fees required by this title, and thereupon the corporation shall cease to exist as a corporation of this State. Such certificate of the Secretary of State shall be *prima facie* evidence of the transfer by such corporation out of this State.

(d) The transfer of a corporation out of this State shall not be deemed to affect any obligations or liabilities of the corporation incurred prior to such transfer, nor shall it be deemed to affect the choice of law applicable to the corporation with respect to matters arising prior to such transfer.

SUBCHAPTER XVII. MISCELLANEOUS PROVISIONS

§ 394. Reserved Power of State to Amend or Repeal Chapter; Chapter Part of Corporation's Charter or Certificate of Incorporation

This chapter may be amended or repealed, at the pleasure of the Legislature, but any amendment or repeal shall not take away or impair any remedy under this chapter against any corporation or its officers for any liability which shall have been previously incurred. This chapter and all amendments thereof shall be a part of the charter or certificate of incorporation of every corporation except so far as the same are inapplicable and inappropriate to the objects of the corporation.

REVISED MODEL BUSINESS CORPORATION ACT

CHAPTER 1. GENERAL PROVISIONS

Subchapter A. Short Title and Reservation of Power

Subchapter B. Filing Documents

Subchapter C. Secretary of State*

Subchapter D. Definitions

CHAPTER 2. INCORPORATION

CHAPTER 3. PURPOSES AND POWERS

* Omitted.

* Omitted.

CHAPTER 10.   AMENDMENT OF ARTICLES OF INCORPORATION AND BYLAW

Subchapter A.   Amendment of Articles of Incorporation

** Sections 8.31 and 8.32 have been superseded, in the Revised Model Business Corporation Act, by Subchapter F, sections 8.60–8.63, infra. Sections 8.31 and 8.32 are nevertheless included in this Supplement because many states that had adopted sections 8.31 and 8.32 as part of their corporation statutes did not decide to adopt Subchapter F.

* Omitted.

Chapter 1

GENERAL PROVISIONS

Subchapter A

Short Title and Reservation of Power

§ 1.01   Short Title

This Act shall be known and may be cited as the "[name of state] Business Corporation Act."

§ 1.02   Reservation of Power to Amend or Repeal

The [name of state legislature] has power to amend or repeal all or part of this Act at any time and all domestic and foreign corporations subject to this Act are governed by the amendment or repeal.

* Omitted.

Subchapter B

Filing Documents

§ 1.20   Filing Requirements

(a) A document must satisfy the requirements of this section, and of any other section that adds to or varies these requirements, to be entitled to filing by the secretary of state.

(b) This Act must require or permit filing the document in the office of the secretary of state.

(c) The document must contain the information required by this Act.   It may contain other information as well.

(d) The document must be typewritten or printed.

(e) The document must be in the English language.   A corporate name need not be in English if written in English letters or Arabic or Roman numerals, and the certificate of existence required of foreign corporations need not be in English if accompanied by a reasonably authenticated English translation.

(f) The document must be executed:

    (1) by the chairman of the board of directors of a domestic or foreign corporation, by its president, or by another of its officers;

    (2) if directors have not been selected or the corporation has not been formed, by an incorporator;   or

    (3) if the corporation is in the hands of a receiver, trustee, or other court-appointed fiduciary, by that fiduciary.

(g) The person executing the document shall sign it and state beneath or opposite his signature his name and the capacity in which he signs. The document may but need not contain: (1) the corporate seal, (2) an attestation by the secretary or an assistant secretary, (3) an acknowledgement, verification, or proof.

(h) If the secretary of state has prescribed a mandatory form for the document under section 1.21, the document must be in or on the prescribed form.

(i) The document must be delivered to the office of the secretary of state for filing and must be accompanied by one exact or conformed copy (except as provided in sections 5.03 and 15.09), the correct filing fee, and any franchise tax, license fee, or penalty required by this Act or other law.

§ 1.21   Forms

(a) The secretary of state may prescribe and furnish on request forms for: (1) an application for a certificate of existence, (2) a foreign corporation's application for a certificate of authority to transact business in this state, (3) a foreign corporation's application for a certificate of withdrawal, and (4) the annual report. If the secretary of state so requires, use of these forms is mandatory.

(b) The secretary of state may prescribe and furnish on request forms for other documents required or permitted to be filed by this Act but their use is not mandatory.

§ 1.23   Effective Time and Date of Document

(a) Except as provided in subsection (b) and section 1.24(c), a document accepted for filing is effective:

   (1) at the time of filing on the date it is filed, as evidenced by the secretary of state's date and time endorsement on the original document; or

   (2) at the time specified in the document as its effective time on the date it is filed.

(b) A document may specify a delayed effective time and date, and if it does so the document becomes effective at the time and date specified. If a delayed effective date but no time is specified, the document is effective at the close of business on that date. A delayed effective date for a document may not be later than the 90th day after the date it is filed.

§ 1.24   Correcting Filed Document

(a) A domestic or foreign corporation may correct a document filed by the secretary of state if the document (1) contains an incorrect statement or (2) was defectively executed, attested, sealed, verified, or acknowledged.

(b) A document is corrected:

   (1) by preparing articles of correction that (i) describe the document (including its filing date) or attach a copy of it to the articles, (ii) specify the incorrect statement and the reason it is incorrect or the manner in which the execution was defective, and (iii) correct the incorrect statement or defective execution; and

   (2) by delivering the articles to the secretary of state for filing.

(c) Articles of correction are effective on the effective date of the document they correct except as to persons relying on the uncorrected document and adversely affected by the correction. As to those persons, articles of correction are effective when filed.

§ 1.25   Filing Duty of Secretary of State

(a) If a document delivered to the office of the secretary of state for filing satisfies the requirements of section 1.20, the secretary of state shall file it.

(b) The secretary of state files a document by stamping or otherwise endorsing "Filed," together with his name and official title and the date and time of receipt, on both the original and the document copy and on the receipt for the filing fee. After filing a document, except as provided in sections 5.03 and 15.10, the secretary of state shall deliver the document copy, with the filing fee receipt (or acknowledgement of receipt if no fee is required) attached, to the domestic or foreign corporation or its representative.

(c) If the secretary of state refuses to file a document, he shall return it to the domestic or foreign corporation or its representative within five days after the document was delivered, together with a brief, written explanation of the reason for his refusal.

(d) The secretary of state's duty to file documents under this section is ministerial. His filing or refusing to file a document does not:

(1) affect the validity or invalidity of the document in whole or part;

(2) relate to the correctness or incorrectness of information contained in the document;

(3) create a presumption that the document is valid or invalid or that information contained in the document is correct or incorrect.

§ 1.27 Evidentiary Effect of Copy of Filed Document

A certificate attached to a copy of a document filed by the secretary of state, bearing his signature (which may be in facsimile) and the seal of this state, is conclusive evidence that the original document is on file with the secretary of state.

Subchapter D

Definitions

§ 1.40 Act Definitions

In this Act:

(1) "Articles of incorporation" include amended and restated articles of incorporation and articles of merger.

(2) "Authorized shares" means the shares of all classes a domestic or foreign corporation is authorized to issue.

(3) "Conspicuous" means so written that a reasonable person against whom the writing is to operate should have noticed it. For example, printing in italics or boldface or contrasting color, or typing in capitals or underlined, is conspicuous.

(4) "Corporation" or "domestic corporation" means a corporation for profit, which is not a foreign corporation, incorporated under or subject to the provisions of this Act.

(5) "Deliver" includes mail.

(6) "Distribution" means a direct or indirect transfer of money or other property (except its own shares) or incurrence of indebtedness by a corporation to or for the benefit of its shareholders in respect of any of its shares. A distribution may be in the form of a declaration or payment of a dividend; a purchase, redemption, or other acquisition of shares; a distribution of indebtedness; or otherwise.

(7) "Effective date of notice" is defined in section 1.41.

(7A) "Electronic transmission" or "transmitted electronically" means any process of communication not directly involving the physical transfer of paper that is suitable for the retention, retrieval, and reproduction of information by the recipient.

(8) "Employee" includes an officer but not a director. A director may accept duties that make him also an employee.

(9) "Entity" includes corporation and foreign corporation; not-for-profit corporation; profit and not-for-profit unincorporated association; business trust, estate, partnership, trust, and two or more persons having a joint or common economic interest; and state, United States, and foreign government.

(10) "Foreign corporation" means a corporation for profit incorporated under a law other than the law of this state.

(11) "Governmental subdivision" includes authority, county, district, and municipality.

(12) "Includes" denotes a partial definition.

(13) "Individual" includes the estate of an incompetent or deceased individual.

(14) "Means" denotes an exhaustive definition.

(15) "Notice" is defined in section 1.41.

(16) "Person" includes individual and entity.

(17) "Principal office" means the office (in or out of this state) so designated in the annual report where the principal executive offices of a domestic or foreign corporation are located.

(18) "Proceeding" includes civil suit and criminal, administrative, and investigatory action.

(19) "Record date" means the date established under chapter 6 or 7 on which a corporation determines the identity of its shareholders and their shareholdings for purposes of this Act. The determinations shall be made as of the close of business on the record date unless another time for doing so is specified when the record date is fixed.

(20) "Secretary" means the corporate officer to whom the board of directors has delegated responsibility under section 8.40(c) for cus-

tody of the minutes of the meetings of the board of directors and of the shareholders and for authenticating records of the corporation.

(21) "Shares" means the units into which the proprietary interests in a corporation are divided.

(22) "Shareholder" means the person in whose name shares are registered in the records of a corporation or the beneficial owner of shares to the extent of the rights granted by a nominee certificate on file with a corporation.

(23) "State," when referring to a part of the United States, includes a state and commonwealth (and their agencies and governmental subdivisions) and a territory and insular possession (and their agencies and governmental subdivisions) of the United States.

(24) "Subscriber" means a person who subscribes for shares in a corporation, whether before or after incorporation.

(25) "United States" includes district, authority, bureau, commission, department, and any other agency of the United States.

(26) "Voting group" means all shares of one or more classes or series that under the articles of incorporation or this Act are entitled to vote and be counted together collectively on a matter at a meeting of shareholders. All shares entitled by the articles of incorporation or this Act to vote generally on the matter are for that purpose a single voting group.

Official Comment

3. Distribution

The term "distribution" defined in section 1.40(6) is a fundamental element of the financial provisions of the Model Act as amended in 1980. Section 6.40 sets forth a single, unitary test for the validity of any "distribution." Section 1.40(6) in turn defines "distribution" to include all transfers of money or other property made by a corporation to any shareholder in respect of the corporation's shares, except mere changes in the unit of interest such as share dividends and share splits. Thus, a "distribution" includes the declaration or payment of a dividend, a purchase by a corporation of its own shares, a distribution of evidences of indebtedness or promissory notes of the corporation, and a distribution in voluntary or involuntary liquidation. If a corporation incurs indebtedness in connection with a distribution (as in the case of a distribution of a debt instrument or an installment purchase of shares), the creation, incurrence, or distribution of the indebtedness is the event which constitutes the distribution rather than the subsequent payment of the debt by the corporation.

The term "indirect" in the definition of "distribution" is intended to include transactions like the repurchase of parent company shares by a subsidiary whose actions are controlled by the parent. It also is intended to include any other transaction in which the substance is clearly the same as a typical dividend or share repurchase, no matter how structured or labeled. . . .

9. Voting Group

Section 1.40(26) defines "voting group" for purposes of the Act as a matter of convenient reference. A "voting group" consists of all shares of one or more classes or series that under the articles of incorporation or the revised Model Act are entitled to vote and be counted together collectively on a matter. Shares entitled to vote "generally" on a matter under the articles of incorporation or this Act are for that purpose a single voting group. The word "generally" signifies all shares entitled to vote on the matter by the articles of incorporation or this Act that do not expressly have the right to be counted or tabulated separately. "Voting groups" are thus the basic units of collective voting at a shareholders' meeting, and voting by voting groups may provide essential protection to one or more classes or series of shares against actions that are detrimental to the rights or interests of that class or series.

The determination of which shares form part of a single voting group must be made from the provisions of the articles of incorporation and of this Act. In a few instances under the Model Act, the board of directors may establish the right to vote by voting groups. On most matters coming before shareholders' meetings, only a single voting group, consisting of a class of voting or common shares, will be involved, and action on such a matter is effective when approved by that voting group pursuant to section 7.25. See section 7.26(a). If a second class of shares is also entitled to vote on the matter, then a further determination must be made as to whether that class is to vote as a separate voting group or whether it is to vote along with the other voting shares as part of a single voting group.

Members of the board of directors are usually elected by the single voting group of shares entitled to vote generally; in some circumstances, however, some members of the board may be selected by one voting group and other members by one or more different voting groups. See section 8.03.

The definition of a voting group permits the establishment by statute of quorum and voting requirements for a variety of matters considered at shareholders' meetings in corporations with multiple classes of shares. See sections 7.25 and 7.26. Depending on the circumstances, two classes or series of shares may vote together collectively on a matter as a single voting group, they may be entitled to vote on the matter separately as two voting groups, or one or both of them may not be entitled to vote on the matter at all.

468

§ 1.41 Notice

(a) Notice under this Act must be in writing unless oral notice is reasonable under the circumstances.

(b) Notice may be communicated in person; by telephone, telegraph, teletype, or other form of wire or wireless communication; or by mail or private carrier. If these forms of personal notice are impracticable, notice may be communicated by a newspaper of general circulation in the area where published; or by radio, television, or other form of public broadcast communication.

(c) Written notice by a domestic or foreign corporation to its shareholder, if in a comprehensible form, is effective when mailed, if mailed postpaid and correctly addressed to the shareholder's address shown in the corporation's current record of shareholders.

(d) Written notice to a domestic or foreign corporation (authorized to transact business in this state) may be addressed to its registered agent at its registered office or to the corporation or its secretary at its principal office shown in its most recent annual report or, in the case of a foreign corporation that has not yet delivered an annual report, in its application for a certificate of authority.

(e) Except as provided in subsection (c), written notice, if in a comprehensible form, is effective at the earliest of the following:

    (1) when received;

    (2) five days after its deposit in the United States Mail, as evidenced by the postmark, if mailed postpaid and correctly addressed;

    (3) On the date shown on the return receipt, if sent by registered or certified mail, return receipt requested, and the receipt is signed by or on behalf of the addressee.

(f) Oral notice is effective when communicated if communicated in a comprehensible manner.

(g) If this Act prescribes notice requirements for particular circumstances, those requirements govern. If articles of incorporation or bylaws prescribe notice requirements, not inconsistent with this section or other provisions of this Act, those requirements govern.

§ 1.42 Number of Shareholders

(a) For purposes of this Act, the following identified as a shareholder in a corporation's current record of shareholders constitutes one shareholder:

    (1) three or fewer coowners;

    (2) a corporation, partnership, trust, estate, or other entity;

    (3) the trustees, guardians, custodians, or other fiduciaries of a single trust, estate, or account.

(b) For purposes of this Act, shareholdings registered in substantially similar names constitute one shareholder if it is reasonable to believe that the names represent the same person.

Chapter 2

INCORPORATION

§ 2.01 Incorporators

One or more persons may act as the incorporator or incorporators of a corporation by delivering articles of incorporation to the secretary of state for filing.

§ 2.02 Articles of Incorporation

(a) The articles of incorporation must set forth:

    (1) a corporate name for the corporation that satisfies the requirements of section 4.01;

    (2) the number of shares the corporation is authorized to issue;

    (3) the street address of the corporation's initial registered office and the name of its initial registered agent at that office; and

    (4) the name and address of each incorporator.

(b) The articles of incorporation may set forth:

    (1) the names and addresses of the individuals who are to serve as the initial directors;

    (2) provisions not inconsistent with law regarding:

        (i) the purpose or purposes for which the corporation is organized;

        (ii) managing the business and regulating the affairs of the corporation;

        (iii) defining, limiting, and regulating the powers of the corporation, its board of directors, and shareholders;

        (iv) a par value for authorized shares or classes of shares;

        (v) the imposition of personal liability on shareholders for the debts of the corporation to a specified extent and upon specified conditions;

    (3) any provision that under this Act is required or permitted to be set forth in the bylaws;

    (4) a provision eliminating or limiting the liability of a director to the corporation or its shareholders for money damages for any action taken, or any failure to take any action, as a director, except liability for (A) the amount of a financial benefit received by a director to which he is not entitled; (B) an intentional infliction

of harm on the corporation or the shareholders; (C) a violation of section 8.33; or (D) an intentional violation of criminal law; and

(5) a provision permitting or making obligatory indemnification of a director for liability (as defined in section 8.50(5)) to any person for any action taken, or any failure to take any action, as a director, except liability for (A) receipt of a financial benefit to which he is not entitled, (B) an intentional infliction of harm on the corporation or its shareholders, (C) a violation of section 8.33, or (D) an intentional violation of criminal law.

(c) The articles of incorporation need not set forth any of the corporate powers enumerated in this Act.

Official Comment

1. Introduction

Section 2.02(a) sets forth the minimum mandatory requirements for all articles of incorporation while section 2.02(b) describes optional provisions that may be included. A corporation that is formed solely pursuant to the mandatory requirements will generally have the broadest powers and least restrictions on activities permitted by the Model Act. The Model Act thus permits the creation of a "standard" corporation by a simple and easily prepared one-page document.

No reference is made in section 2.02(a) either to the period of duration of the corporation or to its purposes. A corporation formed under these provisions will automatically have perpetual duration under section 3.02(1) unless a special provision is included providing a shorter period. Similarly, a corporation formed without reference to a purpose clause will automatically have the purpose of engaging in any lawful business under section 3.01(a). The option of providing a narrower purpose clause is also preserved in sections 2.02(b)(2) and 3.01, with the effect described in the Official Comment to section 3.01....

2. Optional Provisions ...

e. *Shareholder liability*

The basic tenet of modern corporation law is that shareholders are not liable for the corporation's debts by reason of their status as shareholders. Section 2.02(b)(2)(v) nevertheless permits a corporation to impose that liability under specified circumstances if that is desirable. If no provision of this type is included shareholders have no liability for corporate debts except to the extent they become liable by reason of their own conduct or acts. See section 6.22(b). ...

i. *Director liability*

Section 2.02(b)(4) authorizes the inclusion of a provision in the articles of incorporation eliminating or limiting, with certain exceptions, the liability of the directors to the corporation or its shareholders for money damages. This grant of authority to the shareholders is consistent with the more general authorization of section 2.02(b)(2) for the articles to include a wide range of provisions regulating various matters affecting the corporation, including allocating power between the directors and the shareholders. Developments in the mid- and late 1980s highlighted the need to permit reasonable protection of directors from exposure to personal liability, in addition to indemnification, so that directors would not be discouraged from fully and freely carrying out their duties, including responsible entrepreneurial risk-taking. These developments included increased costs and reduced availability of director and officer liability insurance, the decision of the Delaware Supreme Court in Smith v. Van Gorkom, 488 A.2d 858 (1985), and the resulting reluctance of qualified individuals to serve as directors.

. . . [S]ection 2.02(b)(4) is optional rather than self-executing. In addition, it follows the path of virtually all the states that have adopted charter option statutes and is applicable only to money damages and not to equitable relief. Likewise, nothing in section 2.02(b)(4) in any way affects the right of the shareholders to remove directors, under section 8.08(a), with or without cause.

The language "any action taken, or any failure to take any action, as a director" parallels section 8.30(d). It is recognized that in the case of individuals who are both directors and officers it will often not be clear in which capacity the individual is acting. The phrase "as a director" emphasizes that section 2.02(b)(4) applies to a director's actions or failures to take action in his capacity as a director and not in any other capacity, such as officer, employee, or controlling shareholder. However, it is not intended to exclude coverage of conduct by individuals, even though they are officers, when they are acting in their capacity as directors.

§ 2.03   Incorporation

(a) Unless a delayed effective date is specified, the corporate existence begins when the articles of incorporation are filed.

(b) The secretary of state's filing of the articles of incorporation is conclusive proof that the incorporators satisfied all conditions precedent to incorporation except in a proceeding by the state to cancel or revoke the incorporation or involuntarily dissolve the corporation.

Official Comment

5. Conclusiveness of Secretary of State's Action on Question of Individual Liability for Corporate Actions

Under section 2.03(b) the filing of the articles of incorporation as evidenced by return of the stamped copy of the articles with the fee receipt is conclusive proof that all conditions precedent to incorporation have been met, except in proceedings brought by the state. Thus the filing of the articles of incorporation is conclusive as to the existence of limited liability for persons who enter into transactions on behalf of the corporation. If articles of incorporation have not been filed, section 2.04 generally imposes personal liability on all persons who prematurely act as or on behalf of a "corporation" knowing that articles have not been filed. Section 2.04 may protect some of these persons to a limited extent, however; see the Official Comment to that section.

§ 2.04 Liability for Preincorporation Transactions

All persons purporting to act as or on behalf of a corporation, knowing there was no incorporation under this Act, are jointly and severally liable for all liabilities created while so acting.

Official Comment

Earlier versions of the Model Act, and the statutes of many states, have long provided that corporate existence begins only with the acceptance of articles of incorporation by the secretary of state. Many states also have statutes that provide expressly that those who prematurely act as or on behalf of a corporation are personally liable on all transactions entered into or liabilities incurred before incorporation. A review of recent case law indicates, however, that even in states with such statutes courts have continued to rely on common law concepts of de facto corporations, de jure corporations, and corporations by estoppel that provide uncertain protection against liability for preincorporation transactions. These cases caused a review of the underlying policies represented in earlier versions of the Model Act and the adoption of a slightly more flexible or relaxed standard.

Incorporation under modern statutes is so simple and inexpensive that a strong argument may be made that nothing short of filing articles of incorporation should create the privilege of limited liability. A number of situations have arisen, however, in which the protection of limited liability arguably should be recognized even though the simple incorporation process established by modern statutes has not been completed.

(1) The strongest factual pattern for immunizing participants from personal liability occurs in cases in which the participant honestly and reasonably but erroneously believed the articles had been filed. In Cranson v. International Business Machines Corp., 234 Md. 477, 200 A.2d 33 (1964), for example, the defendant had been shown executed articles of incorporation some months earlier before he invested in the corporation and became an officer and director. He was also told by the corporation's attorney that the articles had been filed, but in fact they had not been filed because of a mix-up in the

attorney's office.   The defendant was held not liable on the "corporate" obligation.

(2) Another class of cases, which is less compelling but in which the participants sometimes have escaped personal liability, involves the defendant who mails in articles of incorporation and then enters into a transaction in the corporate name; the letter is either delayed or the secretary of state's office refuses to file the articles after receiving them or returns them for correction.   E.g., Cantor v. Sunshine Greenery, Inc., 165 N.J.Super. 411, 398 A.2d 571 (1979).   Many state filing agencies adopt the practice of treating the date of receipt as the date of issuance of the certificate even though delays and the review process may result in the certificate being backdated.   The finding of nonliability in cases of this second type can be considered an extension of this principle by treating the date of original mailing or original filing as the date of incorporation.

(3) A third class of cases in which the participants sometimes have escaped personal liability involves situations where the third person has urged immediate execution of the contract in the corporate name even though he knows that the other party has not taken any steps toward incorporating.   E.g., Quaker Hill v. Parr, 148 Colo. 45, 364 P.2d 1056 (1961).

(4) In another class of cases the defendant has represented that a corporation exists and entered into a contract in the corporate name when he knows that no corporation has been formed, either because no attempt has been made to file articles of incorporation or because he has already received rejected articles of incorporation from the filing agency.   In these cases, the third person has dealt solely with the "corporation" and has not relied on the personal assets of the defendant.   The imposition of personal liability in this class of case, it has sometimes been argued, gives the plaintiff more than he originally bargained for.   On the other hand, to recognize limited liability in this situation threatens to undermine the incorporation process, since one then may obtain limited liability by consistently conducting business in the corporate name.   Most courts have imposed personal liability in this situation.   E.g., Robertson v. Levy, 197 A.2d 443 (D.C.App.1964).

(5) A final class of cases involves inactive investors who provide funds to a promoter with the instruction, "Don't start doing business until you incorporate."   After the promoter does start business without incorporating, attempts have been made, sometimes unsuccessfully, to hold the investors liable as partners.   E.g., Frontier Refining Co. v. Kunkels, Inc., 407 P.2d 880 (Wyo.1965).   One case held that the language of section 146 of the 1969 Model Act ["*persons who assume to act* as a corporation are liable for preincorporation transactions"] creates a distinction between active and inactive participants, makes

only the former liable as partners, and therefore relieves the latter of personal liability. Nevertheless, "active" participation was defined to include all investors who actively participate in the policy and operational decisions of the organization and is, therefore, a larger group than merely the persons who incurred the obligation in question on behalf of the "corporation." Timberline Equipment Co. v. Davenport, 267 Or. 64, 72–76, 514 P.2d 1109, 1113–14 (1973).

After a review of these situations, it seemed appropriate to impose liability only on persons who act as or on behalf of corporations "knowing" that no corporation exists. Analogous protection has long been accorded under the uniform limited partnership acts to limited partners who contribute capital to a partnership in the erroneous belief that a limited partnership certificate has been filed. Uniform Limited Partnership Act § 12 (1916); Revised Uniform Limited Partnership Act § 3.04 (1976). Persons protected under § 3.04 of the latter are persons who "erroneously but in good faith" believe that a limited partnership certificate has been filed. The language of section 2.04 has essentially the same meaning.

While no special provision is made in section 2.04, the section does not foreclose the possibility that persons who urge defendants to execute contracts in the corporate name knowing that no steps to incorporate have been taken may be estopped to impose personal liability on individual defendants. This estoppel may be based on the inequity perceived when persons, unwilling or reluctant to enter into a commitment under their own name, are persuaded to use the name of a nonexistent corporation, and then are sought to be held personally liable under section 2.04 by the party advocating that form of execution. By contrast, persons who knowingly participate in a business under a corporate name are jointly and severally liable on "corporate" obligations under section 2.04 and may not argue that plaintiffs are "estopped" from holding them personally liable because all transactions were conducted on a corporate basis.

§ 2.05 Organization of Corporation

(a) After incorporation:

   (1) if initial directors are named in the articles of incorporation, the initial directors shall hold an organizational meeting, at the call of a majority of the directors, to complete the organization of the corporation by appointing officers, adopting bylaws, and carrying on any other business brought before the meeting;

   (2) if initial directors are not named in the articles, the incorporator or incorporators shall hold an organizational meeting at the call of a majority of the incorporators:

      (i) to elect directors and complete the organization of the corporation; or

(ii) to elect a board of directors who shall complete the organization of the corporation.

(b) Action required or permitted by this Act to be taken by incorporators at an organizational meeting may be taken without a meeting if the action taken is evidenced by one or more written consents describing the action taken and signed by each incorporator.

(c) An organizational meeting may be held in or out of this state.

§ 2.06 Bylaws

(a) The incorporators or board of directors of a corporation shall adopt initial bylaws for the corporation.

(b) The bylaws of a corporation may contain any provision for managing the business and regulating the affairs of the corporation that is not inconsistent with law or the articles of incorporation.

Chapter 3

PURPOSES AND POWERS

§ 3.01 Purposes

(a) Every corporation incorporated under this Act has the purpose of engaging in any lawful business unless a more limited purpose is set forth in the articles of incorporation.

(b) A corporation engaging in a business that is subject to regulation under another statute of this state may incorporate under this Act only if permitted by, and subject to all limitations of, the other statute.

§ 3.02 General Powers

Unless its articles of incorporation provide otherwise, every corporation has perpetual duration and succession in its corporate name and has the same powers as an individual to do all things necessary or convenient to carry out its business and affairs, including without limitation power:

(1) to sue and be sued, complain and defend in its corporate name;

(2) to have a corporate seal, which may be altered at will, and to use it, or a facsimile of it, by impressing or affixing it or in any other manner reproducing it;

(3) to make and amend bylaws, not inconsistent with its articles of incorporation or with the laws of this state, for managing the business and regulating the affairs of the corporation;

(4) to purchase, receive, lease, or otherwise acquire, and own, hold, improve, use, and otherwise deal with, real or personal property, or any legal or equitable interest in property, wherever located;

(5) to sell, convey, mortgage, pledge, lease, exchange, and otherwise dispose of all or any part of its property;

(6) to purchase, receive, subscribe for, or otherwise acquire; own, hold, vote, use, sell, mortgage, lend, pledge, or otherwise dispose of; and deal in and with shares or other interests in, or obligations of, any other entity;

(7) to make contracts and guarantees, incur liabilities, borrow money, issue its notes, bonds, and other obligations (which may be convertible into or include the option to purchase other securities of the corporation), and secure any of its obligations by mortgage or pledge of any of its property, franchises, or income;

(8) to lend money, invest and reinvest its funds, and receive and hold real and personal property as security for repayment;

(9) to be a promoter, partner, member, associate, or manager of any partnership, joint venture, trust, or other entity;

(10) to conduct its business, locate offices, and exercise the powers granted by this Act within or without this state;

(11) to elect directors and appoint officers, employees, and agents of the corporation, define their duties, fix their compensation, and lend them money and credit;

(12) to pay pensions and establish pension plans, pension trusts, profit sharing plans, share bonus plans, share option plans, and benefit or incentive plans for any or all of its current or former directors, officers, employees, and agents;

(13) to make donations for the public welfare or for charitable, scientific, or educational purposes;

(14) to transact any lawful business that will aid governmental policy;

(15) to make payments or donations, or do any other act, not inconsistent with law, that furthers the business and affairs of the corporation.

Official Comment

Section 3.02(15) permits payments or donations or other acts "that further the business and affairs of the corporation." This clause, which is in addition to and independent of the power to make charitable and similar donations under section 3.02(13), permits contributions for purposes that may not be charitable, such as for political purposes or to influence elections. This power exists only to the extent consistent with law other than the Model Act. It is the purpose of this section to authorize all corporate actions that are lawful or not against public policy....

§ 3.04 Ultra Vires

(a) Except as provided in subsection (b), the validity of corporate action may not be challenged on the ground that the corporation lacks or lacked power to act.

(b) A corporation's power to act may be challenged:

    (1) in a proceeding by a shareholder against the corporation to enjoin the act;

    (2) in a proceeding by the corporation, directly, derivatively, or through a receiver, trustee, or other legal representative, against an incumbent or former director, officer, employee, or agent of the corporation; or

    (3) in a proceeding by the Attorney General under section 14.30.

(c) In a shareholder's proceeding under subsection (b)(1) to enjoin an unauthorized corporate act, the court may enjoin or set aside the act, if equitable and if all affected persons are parties to the proceeding, and may award damages for loss (other than anticipated profits) suffered by the corporation or another party because of enjoining the unauthorized act.

Official Comment

The basic purpose of section 3.04—as has been the purpose of all similar statutes during the 20th century—is to eliminate all vestiges of the doctrine of inherent incapacity of corporations. ... Under this section it is unnecessary for persons dealing with a corporation to inquire into limitations on its purposes or powers that may appear in its articles of incorporation. A person who is unaware of these limitations when dealing with the corporation is not bound by them. The phrase in section 3.04(a) that the "validity of corporate action may not be challenged on the ground that the corporation lacks or lacked power to act" applies equally to the use of the doctrine as a sword or as a shield: a third person may no more avoid an undesired contract with a corporation on the ground the corporation was without authority to make the contract than a corporation may defend a suit on a contract on the ground that the contract is ultra vires.

The language of section 3.04 extends beyond contracts and conveyances of property; "corporate action" of any kind cannot be challenged on the ground of ultra vires. For this reason it makes no difference whether a limitation in articles of incorporation is considered to be a limitation on a purpose or a limitation on a power; both are equally subject to section 3.04. Corporate action also includes inaction or refusal to act. The common law of ultra vires distinguished between executory contracts, partially executed contracts, and fully executed ones; section 3.04 treats all corporate action the same—except to the extent described in section 3.04(b)—and the same rules apply to all contracts no matter at what stage of performance.

Section 3.04, however, does not validate corporate conduct that is made illegal or unlawful by statute or common law decision. This conduct is subject to whatever sanction, criminal or civil, that is provided by the statute or decision. Whether or not illegal corporate conduct is voidable or rescindable depends on the applicable statute or substantive law and is not affected by section 3.04....

... [Under subsection (c)] an ultra vires act may be enjoined only if all "affected parties" are parties to the suit. The requirement that the action be "equitable" generally means that only third persons dealing with a corporation while specifically aware that the corporation's action was ultra vires will be enjoined. The general phrase "if equitable" was retained because of the possibility that other circumstances may exist in which it may be equitable to refuse to enforce an ultra vires contract....

Chapter 4

NAME

§ 4.01 Corporate Name

(a) A corporate name:

   (1) must contain the word "corporation," "incorporated," "company," or "limited," or the abbreviation "corp.," "inc.," "co.," or "ltd.," or words or abbreviations of like import in another language; and

   (2) may not contain language stating or implying that the corporation is organized for a purpose other than that permitted by section 3.01 and its articles of incorporation....

Chapter 5

OFFICE AND AGENT

§ 5.01 Registered Office and Registered Agent

Each corporation must continuously maintain in this state:

(1) a registered office that may be the same as any of its places of business; and

(2) a registered agent, who may be:

   (i) an individual who resides in this state and whose business office is identical with the registered office;

   (ii) a domestic corporation or not-for-profit domestic corporation whose business office is identical with the registered office; or

(iii) a foreign corporation or not-for-profit foreign corporation authorized to transact business in this state whose business office is identical with the registered office.

Chapter 6

SHARES AND DISTRIBUTIONS

Subchapter A

Shares

§ 6.01 Authorized Shares

(a) The articles of incorporation must prescribe the classes of shares and the number of shares of each class that the corporation is authorized to issue. If more than one class of shares is authorized, the articles of incorporation must prescribe a distinguishing designation for each class, and, prior to the issuance of shares of a class, the preferences, limitations, and relative rights of that class must be described in the articles of incorporation. All shares of a class must have preferences, limitations, and relative rights identical with those of other shares of the same class except to the extent otherwise permitted by section 6.02.

(b) The articles of incorporation must authorize (1) one or more classes of shares that together have unlimited voting rights, and (2) one or more classes of shares (which may be the same class or classes as those with voting rights) that together are entitled to receive the net assets of the corporation upon dissolution.

(c) The articles of incorporation may authorize one or more classes of shares that:

(1) have special, conditional, or limited voting rights, or no right to vote, except to the extent prohibited by this Act;

(2) are redeemable or convertible as specified in the articles of incorporation (i) at the option of the corporation, the shareholder, or another person or upon the occurrence of a designated event; (ii) for cash, indebtedness, securities, or other property; (iii) in a designated amount or in an amount determined in accordance with a designated formula or by reference to extrinsic data or events;

(3) entitle the holders to distributions calculated in any manner, including dividends that may be cumulative, noncumulative, or partially cumulative;

(4) have preference over any other class of shares with respect to distributions, including dividends and distributions upon the dissolution of the corporation.

(d) The description of the designations, preferences, limitations, and relative rights of share classes in subsection (c) is not exhaustive.

Official Comment

Section 6.01 adopts a new terminology from that traditionally used in corporation statutes to describe classes of shares that may be created, but makes only limited substantive changes from earlier versions of the Model Act. Traditional corporation statutes work from a perceived inheritance of concepts of "common shares" and "preferred shares" that at one time may have had considerable meaning but that today often do not involve significant distinctions. It is possible under modern corporation statutes to create classes of "common" shares that have important preferential rights and classes of "preferred" shares that are subordinate in all important economic aspects or that are indistinguishable from common shares in either voting rights or entitlement to participate in the assets of the corporation upon dissolution. The revised Model Act breaks away from the inherited concepts of "common" and "preferred" shares and develops more general language to reflect the actual flexibility in the creation of classes of shares that exists in modern corporate practice. The words "common shares" or "preferred shares" are no longer used in the revised Model Act, though the words appear in a few instances in examples appearing in the Official Comment. . . .

Section 6.01(a) requires that the articles of incorporation prescribe the classes of shares and the number of shares of each class that the corporation is authorized to issue. If the articles authorize the issue of only one class of shares, no designation or description of the shares is required, it being understood that these shares have both the power to vote and the power to receive the net assets of the corporation upon dissolution. See section 6.01(b). Shares with both of these characteristics are usually referred to as "common shares" or "common stock," but no specific designation is required by the Model Act.

If more than one class of shares is authorized, the preferences, limitations, and relative rights of each class of shares must be described in the articles of incorporation before any shares of that class are issued, or the board of directors may be given authority to establish them under section 6.02. These descriptions constitute the "contract" of the holders of those classes of shares with respect to their interest in the corporation and must be set forth in sufficient detail reasonably to define their interest. The designations, preferences, limitations, and relative rights of shares with one or more special or preferential rights which may be authorized are further described in section 6.01(c).

§ 6.02 Terms of Class or Series Determined by Board of Directors

(a) If the articles of incorporation so provide, the board of directors may determine, in whole or part, the preferences, limitations, and relative rights (within the limits set forth in section 6.01) of (1) any class of shares before the issuance of any shares of that class or (2) one or more series within a class before the issuance of any shares of that series.

(b) Each series of a class must be given a distinguishing designation.

(c) All shares of a series must have preferences, limitations, and relative rights identical with those of other shares of the same series and, except to the extent otherwise provided in the description of the series, with those of other series of the same class.

(d) Before issuing any shares of a class or series created under this section, the corporation must deliver to the secretary of state for filing articles of amendment, which are effective without shareholder action, that set forth:

    (1) the name of the corporation;

    (2) the text of the amendment determining the terms of the class or series of shares;

    (3) the date it was adopted; and

    (4) a statement that the amendment was duly adopted by the board of directors.

§ 6.03 Issued and Outstanding Shares

(a) A corporation may issue the number of shares of each class or series authorized by the articles of incorporation. Shares that are issued are outstanding shares until they are reacquired, redeemed, converted, or cancelled.

(b) The reacquisition, redemption, or conversion of outstanding shares is subject to the limitations of subsection (c) of this section and to section 6.40.

(c) At all times that shares of the corporation are outstanding, one or more shares that together have unlimited voting rights and one or more shares that together are entitled to receive the net assets of the corporation upon dissolution must be outstanding.

§ 6.04 Fractional Shares

(a) A corporation may:

    (1) issue fractions of a share or pay in money the value of fractions of a share;

    (2) arrange for disposition of fractional shares by the shareholders;

(3) issue scrip in registered or bearer form entitling the holder to receive a full share upon surrendering enough scrip to equal a full share.

(b) Each certificate representing scrip must be conspicuously labeled "scrip" and must contain the information required by section 6.25(b).

(c) The holder of a fractional share is entitled to exercise the rights of a shareholder, including the right to vote, to receive dividends, and to participate in the assets of the corporation upon liquidation. The holder of scrip is not entitled to any of these rights unless the scrip provides for them.

(d) The board of directors may authorize the issuance of scrip subject to any condition considered desirable, including:

(1) that the scrip will become void if not exchanged for full shares before a specified date; and

(2) that the shares for which the scrip is exchangeable may be sold and the proceeds paid to the scripholders.

Subchapter B

Issuance of Shares

§ 6.20 Subscription for Shares Before Incorporation

(a) A subscription for shares entered into before incorporation is irrevocable for six months unless the subscription agreement provides a longer or shorter period or all the subscribers agree to revocation.

(b) The board of directors may determine the payment terms of subscriptions for shares that were entered into before incorporation, unless the subscription agreement specifies them. A call for payment by the board of directors must be uniform so far as practicable as to all shares of the same class or series, unless the subscription agreement specifies otherwise.

(c) Shares issued pursuant to subscriptions entered into before incorporation are fully paid and nonassessable when the corporation receives the consideration specified in the subscription agreement.

(d) If a subscriber defaults in payment of money or property under a subscription agreement entered into before incorporation, the corporation may collect the amount owed as any other debt. Alternatively, unless the subscription agreement provides otherwise, the corporation may rescind the agreement and may sell the shares if the debt remains unpaid more than 20 days after the corporation sends written demand for payment to the subscriber.

(e) A subscription agreement entered into after incorporation is a contract between the subscriber and the corporation subject to section 6.21.

Official Comment

Agreements for the purchase of shares to be issued by a corporation are typically referred to as "subscriptions" or "subscription agreements." Section 6.20 deals exclusively with preincorporation subscriptions, that is, subscriptions entered into before the corporation was formed. Preincorporation subscriptions have often been considered to be revocable offers rather than binding contracts. Since the corporation is not in existence, it cannot be a party to the agreement and the consideration established for the shares is not determined by the board of directors. While preincorporation subscriptions entered into simultaneously by several subscribers may be considered a binding contract between or among the subscribers, not all factual situations lend themselves to contractual analysis. Because of the uncertainty of the legal enforceability of these transactions, section 6.20 provides a simple set of legal rules applicable to the enforcement of preincorporation subscriptions by the corporation after its formation. It does not address the extent to which preincorporation subscriptions may constitute a contract between or among subscribers, and other subscribers may enforce whatever contract rights they have without regard to section 6.20.

Section 6.20(a) provides that preincorporation subscriptions are irrevocable for six months unless the subscription agreement provides that they are revocable or that they are irrevocable for some other period. Nevertheless, all the subscribers to shares may agree at any time that a subscriber may withdraw in part from his commitment to subscribe for shares, that a subscriber may revoke his subscription entirely, or that the period of irrevocability may continue for an additional stated period. If the corporation accepts the subscription during the period of irrevocability, the subscription becomes a contract binding on both the subscribers and the corporation. The terms of this contract are set forth in sections 6.20(b) and (d). . . .

Postincorporation subscriptions are contracts between the corporation and the investor by which the corporation agrees to issue shares for a stated consideration and the investor agrees to purchase the shares for that consideration. Postincorporation subscriptions are simple contracts subject to the power of the board of directors and they may contain any mutually acceptable provisions subject to section 6.21. Section 6.20(e) states, for completeness, that postincorporation subscriptions are contracts between the corporation and the subscriber subject to section 6.21.

§ 6.21 Issuance of Shares

(a) The powers granted in this section to the board of directors may be reserved to the shareholders by the articles of incorporation.

(b) The board of directors may authorize shares to be issued for consideration consisting of any tangible or intangible property or benefit to the corporation, including cash, promissory notes, services performed, contracts for services to be performed, or other securities of the corporation.

(c) Before the corporation issues shares, the board of directors must determine that the consideration received or to be received for shares to be issued is adequate. That determination by the board of directors is conclusive insofar as the adequacy of consideration for the issuance of shares relates to whether the shares are validly issued, fully paid, and nonassessable.

(d) When the corporation receives the consideration for which the board of directors authorized the issuance of shares, the shares issued therefor are fully paid and nonassessable.

(e) The corporation may place in escrow shares issued for a contract for future services or benefits or a promissory note, or make other arrangements to restrict the transfer of the shares, and may credit distributions in respect of the shares against their purchase price, until the services are performed, the note is paid, or the benefits received. If the services are not performed, the note is not paid, or the benefits are not received, the shares escrowed or restricted and the distributions credited may be cancelled in whole or part.

Official Comment

The financial provisions of the Model Act reflect a modernization of the concepts underlying the capital structure and limitations on distributions of corporations. This process of modernization began with amendments in 1980 to the 1969 Model Act that eliminated the concepts of "par value" and "stated capital," and further modernization occurred in connection with the development of the revised Act in 1984. Practitioners and legal scholars have long recognized that the statutory structure embodying "par value" and "legal capital" concepts is not only complex and confusing but also fails to serve the original purpose of protecting creditors and senior security holders from payments to junior security holders. Indeed, to the extent security holders are led to believe that it provides this protection, these provisions may be affirmatively misleading. The Model Act has therefore eliminated these concepts entirely and substituted a simpler and more flexible structure that provides more realistic protection to these interests. Major aspects of this new structure are:

(1) the provisions relating to the issuance of shares set forth in this and the following sections;

(2) the provisions limiting distributions by corporations set forth in section 6.40 and discussed in the Official Comment to that section; and

(3) the elimination of the concept of treasury shares described in the Official Comment to section 6.31.

Section 6.21 incorporates not only the elimination of the concepts of par value and stated capital from the Model Act in 1980 but also eliminates the earlier rule declaring certain kinds of property ineligible as consideration for shares. . . .

Since shares need not have a par value, under section 6.21 there is no minimum price at which specific shares must be issued and therefore there can be no "watered stock" liability for issuing shares below an arbitrarily fixed price. The price at which shares are issued is primarily a matter of concern to other shareholders whose interests may be diluted if shares are issued at unreasonably low prices or for overvalued property. This problem of equality of treatment essentially involves honest and fair judgments by directors and cannot be effectively addressed by an arbitrary doctrine establishing a minimum price for shares such as "par value" provided under older statutes.

Section 6.21(b) specifically validates contracts for future services (including promoters' services), promissory notes, or "any tangible or intangible property or benefit to the corporation," as consideration for the present issue of shares. The term "benefit" should be broadly construed to include, for example, a reduction of a liability, a release of a claim, or benefits obtained by a corporation by contribution of its shares to a charitable organization or as a prize in a promotion. In the realities of commercial life, there is sometimes a need for the issuance of shares for contract rights or such intangible property or benefits. And, as a matter of business economics, contracts for future services, promissory notes, and intangible property or benefits often have value that is as real as the value of tangible property or past services, the only types of property that many older statutes permit as consideration for shares. Thus, only business judgment should determine what kind of property should be obtained for shares, and a determination by the directors meeting the requirements of section 8.30 to accept a specific kind of valuable property for shares should be accepted and not circumscribed by artificial or arbitrary rules.

The issuance of some shares for cash and other shares for promissory notes, contracts for past or future services, or for tangible or intangible property or benefits, like the issuance of shares for an inadequate consideration, opens the possibility of dilution of the interests of other shareholders. For example, persons acquiring shares for cash may be unfairly treated if optimistic values are placed on past or future services or intangible benefits being provided by other persons. The problem is particularly acute if the persons providing services, promissory notes, or property or benefits of debatable value are themselves connected with the promoters of the corporation or with its directors. Protection of shareholders against abuse of the power granted to the board of directors to determine that shares should be issued for intangible property or benefits is provided in part by the requirement that the board must act in accordance with the requirements of section 8.30, and, if applicable, section 8.31, in determining that the consideration received for shares is adequate, and in part by the requirement of section 16.21 that the corporation must inform all shareholders annually of all shares issued during the previous year for promissory notes or promises of future services.

Accounting principles are not specified in the Model Act, and the board of directors is not required by the statute to determine the "value" of noncash consideration received by the corporation (as was the case in earlier versions of the Model Act). In many instances, property or benefit received by the corporation will be of uncertain value; if the board of directors determines that the issuance of shares for the property or benefit is an appropriate transaction that protects the shareholders from dilution, that is sufficient under section 6.21. The board of directors does not have to make an explicit "adequacy" determination by formal resolution; that determination may be inferred from a determination to authorize the issuance of shares for a specified consideration.

Section 6.21 also does not require that the board of directors determine the value of the consideration to be entered on the books of the corporation, though the board of directors may do so if it wishes. Of course, a specific value must be placed on the consideration received for the shares for bookkeeping purposes, but bookkeeping details are not the statutory responsibility of the board of directors. The statute also does not require the board of directors to determine the corresponding entry on the right-hand side of the balance sheet under owner's equity to be designated as "stated capital" or be allocated among "stated capital" and other surplus accounts. The corporation, however, may determine that the shareholders' equity accounts should be divided into these traditional categories if it wishes.

The second sentence of section 6.21(c) describes the effect of the determination by the board of directors that consideration is adequate for the issuance of shares. That determination, without more, is conclusive to the extent that adequacy is relevant to the question whether the shares are validly issued, fully paid, and nonassessable. Section 6.21(c) provides that shares are fully paid and nonassessable when the corporation receives the consideration for which the board of directors authorized their issuance. Whether shares are validly issued may depend on compliance with corporate procedural requirements, such as issuance within the amount authorized in the articles of incorporation or holding a directors' meeting upon proper notice and with a quorum present. The Model Act does not address the remedies that may be available for issuances that are subject to challenge. . . .

The revised Model Act does not address the question whether validly issued shares may thereafter be cancelled on the grounds of fraud or bad faith if the shares are in the hands of the original shareholder or other persons who were aware of the circumstances under which they were issued when they acquired the shares. It also leaves to the Uniform Commercial Code other questions relating to the rights of persons other than the person acquiring the shares from the corporation....

§ 6.22   Liability of Shareholders

(a) A purchaser from a corporation of its own shares is not liable to the corporation or its creditors with respect to the shares except to pay the consideration for which the shares were authorized to be issued (section 6.21) or specified in the subscription agreement (section 6.20).

(b) Unless otherwise provided in the articles of incorporation, a shareholder of a corporation is not personally liable for the acts or debts of the corporation except that he may become personally liable by reason of his own acts or conduct.

§ 6.23   Share Dividends

(a) Unless the articles of incorporation provide otherwise, shares may be issued pro rata and without consideration to the corporation's shareholders or to the shareholders of one or more classes or series. An issuance of shares under this subsection is a share dividend.

(b) Shares of one class or series may not be issued as a share dividend in respect of shares of another class or series unless (1) the articles of incorporation so authorize, (2) a majority of the votes entitled to be cast by the class or series to be issued approve the issue, or (3) there are no outstanding shares of the class or series to be issued.

(c) If the board of directors does not fix the record date for determining shareholders entitled to a share dividend, it is the date the board of directors authorizes the share dividend.

Official Comment

A share dividend is solely a paper transaction: No assets are received by the corporation for the shares and any "dividend" paid in shares does not involve the distribution of property by the corporation to its shareholders. Section 6.23 therefore recognizes that such a transaction involves the issuance of shares "without consideration," and section 1.40(6) excludes it from the definition of a "distribution." Such transactions were treated in a fictional way under the old "par value" and "stated capital" statutes, which treated a share dividend as involving transfers from a surplus account to stated capital and assumed that par value shares could be issued without receiving any consideration by reason of that transfer of surplus.

The par value statutory treatment of share dividend transactions distinguished a share "split" from a dividend. In a share "split" the par value of the former shares was divided among the new shares and there was no transfer of surplus into the stated capital account as in the case of a share "dividend." Since the Model Act has eliminated the concept of par value, the distinction between a "split" and a "dividend" has not been retained and both types of transactions are referred to simply as "share dividends." A distinction between "share dividends" and "share splits," however, continues to exist in other contexts—for example, in connection with transactions by publicly held corporations, see N.Y.S.E. Listed Company Manual § 703.02(a), or corporations that have optionally retained par value for their shares. The change made in the Model Act is not intended to affect the manner in which transactions by these corporations are handled or described but simply reflects the elimination of artificial legal distinctions based on the par value statutes. . . .

§ 6.24 Share Options

A corporation may issue rights, options, or warrants for the purchase of shares of the corporation. The board of directors shall determine the terms upon which the rights, options, or warrants are issued, their form and content, and the consideration for which the shares are to be issued.

§ 6.25 Form and Content of Certificates

(a) Shares may but need not be represented by certificates. Unless this Act or another statute expressly provides otherwise, the rights and obligations of shareholders are identical whether or not their shares are represented by certificates.

(b) At a minimum each share certificate must state on its face:

    (1) the name of the issuing corporation and that it is organized under the law of this state;

    (2) the name of the person to whom issued; and

    (3) the number and class of shares and the designation of the series, if any, the certificate represents.

(c) If the issuing corporation is authorized to issue different classes of shares or different series within a class, the designations, relative rights, preferences, and limitations applicable to each class and the variations in rights, preferences, and limitations determined for each series (and the authority of the board of directors to determine variations for future series) must be summarized on the front or back of each certificate. Alternatively, each certificate may state conspicuously on its front or back that the corporation will furnish the shareholder this information on request in writing and without charge.

(d) Each share certificate (1) must be signed (either manually or in facsimile) by two officers designated in the bylaws or by the board of directors and (2) may bear the corporate seal or its facsimile.

(e) If the person who signed (either manually or in facsimile) a share certificate no longer holds office when the certificate is issued, the certificate is nevertheless valid.

§ 6.26   Shares Without Certificates

(a) Unless the articles of incorporation or bylaws provide otherwise, the board of directors of a corporation may authorize the issue of some or all of the shares of any or all of its classes or series without certificates. The authorization does not affect shares already represented by certificates until they are surrendered to the corporation.

(b) Within a reasonable time after the issue or transfer of shares without certificates, the corporation shall send the shareholder a written statement of the information required on certificates by section 6.25(b) and (c), and, if applicable, section 6.27.

§ 6.27   Restriction on Transfer of Shares and Other Securities

(a) The articles of incorporation, bylaws, an agreement among shareholders, or an agreement between shareholders and the corporation may impose restrictions on the transfer or registration of transfer of shares of the corporation. A restriction does not affect shares issued before the restriction was adopted unless the holders of the shares are parties to the restriction agreement or voted in favor of the restriction.

(b) A restriction on the transfer or registration of transfer of shares is valid and enforceable against the holder or a transferee of the holder if the restriction is authorized by this section and its existence is noted conspicuously on the front or back of the certificate or is contained in the information statement required by section 6.26(b). Unless so noted, a restriction is not enforceable against a person without knowledge of the restriction.

(c) A restriction on the transfer or registration of transfer of shares is authorized:

   (1) to maintain the corporation's status when it is dependent on the number or identity of its shareholders;

   (2) to preserve exemptions under federal or state securities law;

   (3) for any other reasonable purpose.

(d) A restriction on the transfer or registration of transfer of shares may:

   (1) obligate the shareholder first to offer the corporation or other persons (separately, consecutively, or simultaneously) an opportunity to acquire the restricted shares;

   (2) obligate the corporation or other persons (separately, consecutively, or simultaneously) to acquire the restricted shares;

(3) require the corporation, the holders of any class of its shares, or another person to approve the transfer of the restricted shares, if the requirement is not manifestly unreasonable;

(4) prohibit the transfer of the restricted shares to designated persons or classes of persons, if the prohibition is not manifestly unreasonable.

(e) For purposes of this section, "shares" includes a security convertible into or carrying a right to subscribe for or acquire shares.

§ 6.28   Expense of Issue

A corporation may pay the expenses of selling or underwriting its shares, and of organizing or reorganizing the corporation, from the consideration received for shares.

Subchapter C

Subsequent Acquisition of Shares by Shareholders and Corporation

§ 6.30   Shareholders' Preemptive Rights

(a) The shareholders of a corporation do not have a preemptive right to acquire the corporation's unissued shares except to the extent the articles of incorporation so provide.

(b) A statement included in the articles of incorporation that "the corporation elects to have preemptive rights" (or words of similar import) means that the following principles apply except to the extent the articles of incorporation expressly provide otherwise:

(1) The shareholders of the corporation have a preemptive right, granted on uniform terms and conditions prescribed by the board of directors to provide a fair and reasonable opportunity to exercise the right, to acquire proportional amounts of the corporation's unissued shares upon the decision of the board of directors to issue them.

(2) A shareholder may waive his preemptive right. A waiver evidenced by a writing is irrevocable even though it is not supported by consideration.

(3) There is no preemptive right with respect to:

(i)   shares issued as compensation to directors, officers, agents, or employees of the corporation, its subsidiaries or affiliates;

(ii) shares issued to satisfy conversion or option rights created to provide compensation to directors, officers, agents, or employees of the corporation, its subsidiaries or affiliates;

(iii) shares authorized in articles of incorporation that are issued within six months from the effective date of incorporation;

(iv) shares sold otherwise than for money.

(4) Holders of shares of any class without general voting rights but with preferential rights to distributions or assets have no preemptive rights with respect to shares of any class.

(5) Holders of shares of any class with general voting rights but without preferential rights to distributions or assets have no preemptive rights with respect to shares of any class with preferential rights to distributions or assets unless the shares with preferential rights are convertible into or carry a right to subscribe for or acquire shares without preferential rights.

(6) Shares subject to preemptive rights that are not acquired by shareholders may be issued to any person for a period of one year after being offered to shareholders at a consideration set by the board of directors that is not lower than the consideration set for the exercise of preemptive rights. An offer at a lower consideration or after the expiration of one year is subject to the shareholders' preemptive rights.

(c) For purposes of this section, "shares" includes a security convertible into or carrying a right to subscribe for or acquire shares.

Official Comment

Section 6.30(a) adopts an "opt in" provision for preemptive rights: Unless an affirmative reference to these rights appears in the articles of incorporation, no preemptive rights exist. Whether or not preemptive rights are elected, however, the directors' fiduciary duties extend to the issuance of shares. Issuance of shares at favorable prices to directors (but excluding other shareholders) or the issuance of shares on a nonproportional basis for the purpose of affecting control rather than raising capital may violate that duty. These duties, it is believed, form a more rational structure of regulation than the technical principles of traditional preemptive rights.

Section 6.30(b) provides a standard model for preemptive rights if the corporation desires to exercise the "opt in" alternative of section 6.30(a). The simple phrase, "the corporation elects to have preemptive rights," or words of similar import, results in the rest of subsection (b) becoming applicable to the corporation. But a corporation may qualify or limit any of the rules set forth in subsection (b) by express provisions in the articles of incorporation if the rules are felt to be undesirable or inappropriate for the specific corporation. The purposes of this standard model for preemptive rights are (1) to simplify drafting articles of incorporation and (2) to provide a simple checklist of business considerations for the benefit of attorneys who are considering the inclusion of preemptive rights in articles of incorporation....

§ 6.31 Corporation's Acquisition of Its Own Shares

(a) A corporation may acquire its own shares and shares so acquired constitute authorized but unissued shares.

(b) If the articles of incorporation prohibit the reissue of acquired shares, the number of authorized shares is reduced by the number of shares acquired, effective upon amendment of the articles of incorporation.

(c) The board of directors may adopt articles of amendment under this section without shareholder action and deliver them to the secretary of state for filing. The articles must set forth:

(1) the name of the corporation;

(2) the reduction in the number of authorized shares, itemized by class and series; and

(3) the total number of authorized shares, itemized by class and series, remaining after reduction of the shares.

Official Comment

The elimination of the concepts of "par value" and "stated capital" in the 1980 amendments to the Model Act (see the Official Comment to section 6.21) permitted the simplification of a number of other sections of the Act and the elimination of several historical concepts that primarily served the purpose of ameliorating problems created by retention of the concepts of "par value" and "stated capital."

One concept eliminated by the 1980 amendments was that of treasury shares. The status of once-issued but reacquired shares was an uneasy one under the traditional statutes. It was universally recognized that a corporation's shares in its own hands are not an asset any more than authorized but unissued shares. As an economic matter payments made by a corporation to repurchase its own shares must be viewed as a distribution of corporate assets by the corporation rather than as an acquisition of an asset. Further, conventional statutes gave treasury shares an intermediate status between issued and unissued: they were treated as outstanding shares for some purposes, and they could be resold or disposed of by the corporation (presumably) without regard to restrictions that might be imposed on the original issuance of shares by the corporation. Finally, the accounting treatment for treasury shares was complex, confusing, and to some extent unrealistic since the capital accounts often did not reflect transactions in treasury shares.

Under the 1980 revisions of the financial provisions in the Model Act the concept of treasury shares is unnecessary. . . .

Section 6.31(a) restates the fundamental power of a corporation to reacquire its own shares. Such a transaction constitutes a "distribution" by the corporation (see the definition of that term in section 1.40) and is subject to the limitations of section 6.40.

Shares that are reacquired by the corporation become authorized but unissued shares under section 6.31(b) unless the articles prohibit reissue, in which event they are cancelled. Section 6.31(c) requires a simplified official filing to reflect the reduction of authorized shares. This provision is included in order that there be a public record of the number of authorized shares that a corporation may issue. The amendment may be made without shareholder action. See section 10.02....

Subchapter D

Distributions

§ 6.40   Distributions to Shareholders

(a) A board of directors may authorize and the corporation may make distributions to its shareholders subject to restriction by the articles of incorporation and the limitation in subsection (c).

(b) If the board of directors does not fix the record date for determining shareholders entitled to a distribution (other than one involving a purchase, redemption, or other acquisition of the corporation's shares), it is the date the board of directors authorizes the distribution.

(c) No distribution may be made if, after giving it effect:

(1) the corporation would not be able to pay its debts as they become due in the usual course of business; or

(2) the corporation's total assets would be less than the sum of its total liabilities plus (unless the articles of incorporation permit otherwise) the amount that would be needed, if the corporation were to be dissolved at the time of the distribution, to satisfy the preferential rights upon dissolution of shareholders whose preferential rights are superior to those receiving the distribution.

(d) The board of directors may base a determination that a distribution is not prohibited under subsection (c) either on financial statements prepared on the basis of accounting practices and principles that are reasonable in the circumstances or on a fair valuation or other method that is reasonable in the circumstances.

(e) Except as provided in subsection (g), the effect of a distribution under subsection (c) is measured:

(1) in the case of distribution by purchase, redemption, or other acquisition of the corporation's shares, as of the earlier of (i) the date money or other property is transferred or debt incurred by the corporation or (ii) the date the shareholder ceases to be a shareholder with respect to the acquired shares;

(2) in the case of any other distribution of indebtedness, as of the date the indebtedness is distributed; and

(3) in all other cases, as of (i) the date the distribution is authorized if the payment occurs within 120 days after the date of authorization or (ii) the date the payment is made if it occurs more than 120 days after the date of authorization.

(f) A corporation's indebtedness to a shareholder incurred by reason of a distribution made in accordance with this section is at parity with the corporation's indebtedness to its general, unsecured creditors except to the extent subordinated by agreement.

(g) Indebtedness of a corporation, including indebtedness issued as a distribution, is not considered a liability for purposes of determinations under subsection (c) if its terms provide that payment of principal and interest are made only if and to the extent that payment of a distribution to shareholders could then be made under this section. If the indebtedness is issued as a distribution, each payment of principal or interest is treated as a distribution, the effect of which is measured on the date the payment is actually made.

Official Comment

The reformulation of the statutory standards governing distributions is another important change made by the 1980 revisions to the financial provisions of the Model Act. It has long been recognized that the traditional "par value" and "stated capital" statutes do not provide significant protection against distributions of capital to shareholders. While most of these statutes contained elaborate provisions establishing "stated capital," "capital surplus," and "earned surplus" (and often other types of surplus as well), the net effect of most statutes was to permit the distribution to shareholders of most or all of the corporation's net assets—its capital along with its earnings—if the shareholders wished this to be done. However, statutes also generally imposed an equity insolvency test on distributions that prohibited distributions of assets if the corporation was insolvent or if the distribution had the effect of making the corporation insolvent or unable to meet its obligations as they were projected to arise.

The financial provisions of the revised Model Act, which are based on the 1980 amendments, sweep away all the distinctions among the various types of surplus but retain restrictions on distributions built around both the traditional equity insolvency and balance sheet tests of earlier statutes.

1. The Scope of Section 6.40

Section 1.40 defines "distribution" to include virtually all transfers of money, indebtedness of the corporation or other property to a shareholder in respect of the corporation's shares. It thus includes cash or property dividends, payments by a corporation to purchase its own shares, distributions of promissory notes or indebtedness, and distributions in partial or complete liquidation or voluntary or involuntary dissolution. Section 1.40 excludes from the definition of "distribution" transactions by the corporation in which only its own shares are distributed to its shareholders. These transactions are called "share dividends" in the revised Model Business Corporation Act. See section 6.23.

Section 6.40 imposes a single, uniform test on all distributions. Many of the old "par value" and "stated capital" statutes provided tests that varied with the type of distribution under consideration or did not cover certain types of distributions at all.

2. Equity Insolvency Test

As noted above, older statutes prohibited payments of dividends if the corporation was, or as a result of the payment would be, insolvent in the equity sense. This test is retained, appearing in section 6.40(c)(1).

In most cases involving a corporation operating as a going concern in the normal course, information generally available will make it quite apparent that no particular inquiry concerning the equity insolvency test is needed. While neither a balance sheet nor an income statement can be conclusive as to this test, the existence of significant shareholders' equity and normal operating conditions are of themselves a strong indication that no issue should arise under that test. Indeed, in the case of a corporation having regularly audited financial statements, the absence of any qualification in the most recent auditor's opinion as to the corporation's status as a "going concern," coupled with a lack of subsequent adverse events, would normally be decisive.

It is only when circumstances indicate that the corporation is encountering difficulties or is in an uncertain position concerning its liquidity and operations that the board of directors or, more commonly, the officers or others upon whom they may place reliance under section 8.30(b), may need to address the issue. Because of the overall judgment required in evaluating the equity insolvency test, no one or more "bright line" tests can be employed. However, in determining whether the equity insolvency test has been met, certain judgments or assumptions as to the future course of the corporation's business are customarily justified, absent clear evidence to the contrary. These include the likelihood that (a) based on existing and contemplated demand for the corporation's products or services, it will be able to generate funds over a period of time sufficient to satisfy its existing and reasonably anticipated obligations as they mature, and (b) indebtedness which matures in the near-term will be refinanced where, on the basis of the corporation's financial condition and future prospects and the general availability of credit to businesses similarly situated, it is reasonable to assume that such refinancing may be accomplished. To the extent that the corporation may be subject to asserted or unasserted contingent liabilities, reasonable judgments as to the likelihood, amount, and time of any recovery against the corporation, after giving consideration to the extent to which the corporation is insured or otherwise protected against loss, may be utilized. There may be occasions when it would be useful to consider a cash flow analysis, based on a business forecast and budget, covering a sufficient period of time to permit a conclusion that known obligations of the corporation can reasonably be expected to be satisfied over the period of time that they will mature.

In exercising their judgment, the directors are entitled to rely, under section 8.30(b) as noted above, on information, opinions, reports, and statements prepared by others. Ordinarily, they should not be expected to become involved in the details of the various analyses or market or economic projections that may be relevant. Judgments must of necessity be made on the basis of information in the hands of the directors when a distribution is authorized. They should not, of course, be held responsible as a matter of hindsight for unforeseen developments. This is particularly true with respect to assumptions as to the ability of the corporation's business to repay long-term obligations which do not mature for several years, since the primary focus of the directors' decision to make a distribution should normally be on the corporation's prospects and obligations in the shorter term, unless special factors concerning the corporation's prospects require the taking of a longer term perspective.

3. Relationship to the Federal Bankruptcy Act and Other Fraudulent Conveyance Statutes

The revised Model Business Corporation Act establishes the validity of distributions from the corporate law standpoint under section 6.40 and determines the potential liability of directors for improper distributions under sections 8.30 and 8.33. The federal Bankruptcy Act and state fraudulent conveyance statutes, on the other hand, are designed to enable the trustee or other representative to recapture for the benefit of creditors funds distributed to others in some circumstances. In light of these diverse purposes, it was not thought necessary to make the tests of section 6.40 identical to the tests for insolvency under these various statutes.

4. Balance Sheet Test

Section 6.40(c)(2) requires that, after giving effect to any distribution, the corporation's assets equal or exceed its liabilities plus (with some exceptions) the dissolution preferences of senior equity securities. Section 6.40(d) authorizes asset and liability determinations to be made for this purpose on the basis of either (1) financial statements prepared on the basis of accounting practices and principles that are reasonable in the circumstances or (2) a fair valuation or other method that is reasonable in the circumstances. The determination of a corporation's assets and liabilities and the choice of the permissible basis on which to do so are left to the judgment of its board of directors. In making a judgment under section 6.40(d), the board may rely under section 8.30 upon opinions, reports, or statements, including financial statements and other financial data prepared or presented by public accountants or others.

Section 6.40 does not utilize particular accounting terminology of a technical nature or specify accounting concepts. In making determinations under this section, the board of directors may make judgments about accounting matters, giving full effect to its right to rely upon professional or expert opinion.

In a corporation with subsidiaries, the board of directors may rely on unconsolidated statements prepared on the basis of the equity method of accounting (see American Institute of Certified Public Accountants, APB Opinion No. 18 (1971)) as to the corporation's investee corporations, including corporate joint ventures and subsidiaries, although other evidence would be relevant in the total determination.

a. *Generally Accepted Accounting Principles*

The board of directors should in all circumstances be entitled to rely upon reasonably current financial statements prepared on the basis of generally accepted accounting principles in determining whether or not the balance sheet test of section 6.40(c)(2) has been met, unless the board is then aware that it would be unreasonable to rely on the financial statements because of newly-discovered or subsequently arising facts or circumstances. But section 6.40 does not mandate the use of generally accepted accounting principles; it only requires the use of accounting practices and principles that are reasonable in the circumstances. While publicly-owned corporations subject to registration under the Securities Exchange Act of 1934 must, and many other corporations in fact do, utilize financial statements prepared on the basis of generally accepted accounting principles, a great number of smaller or closely-held corporations do not. Some of these corporations maintain records solely on a tax accounting basis and their financial statements are of necessity prepared on that basis. Others prepare financial statements that substantially reflect generally accepted accounting principles but may depart from them in some respects (e.g., footnote disclosure). These facts of corporate life indicate that a statutory standard of reasonableness, rather than stipulating generally accepted accounting principles as the normative standard, is appropriate in order to achieve a reasonable degree of flexibility and to accommodate the needs of the many different types of business corporations which might be subject to these provisions, including in particular closely-held corporations. Accordingly, the revised Model Business Corporation Act contemplates that generally acceptable accounting principles are always "reasonable in the circumstances" and that other accounting principles may be perfectly acceptable, under a general standard of reasonableness, even if they do not involve the "fair value" or "current value" concepts that are also contemplated by section 6.40(d).

b. Other Principles

Section 6.40(d) specifically permits determinations to be made under section 6.40(c)(2) on the basis of a fair valuation or other method that is reasonable in the circumstances. Thus the statute authorizes departures from historical cost accounting and sanctions the use of appraisal and current value methods to determine the amount available for distribution. No particular method of valuation is prescribed in the statute, since different methods may have validity depending upon the circumstances, including the type of enterprise and the purpose for which the determination is made. For example, it is inappropriate in most cases to apply a "quick-sale liquidation" method to value an enterprise, particularly with respect to the payment of normal dividends. On the other hand, a "quick-sale liquidation" valuation method might be appropriate in certain circumstances for an enterprise in the course of reducing its asset or business base by a material degree. In most cases, a fair valuation method or a going-concern basis would be appropriate if it is believed that the enterprise will continue as a going concern.

Ordinarily a corporation should not selectively revalue assets. It should consider the value of all its material assets, whether or not reflected in the financial statements (e.g., a valuable executory contract). Likewise, all of a corporation's material obligations should be considered and revalued to the extent appropriate and possible. In any event, section 6.40(d) calls for the application under section 6.40(c)(2) of a method of determining the aggregate amount of assets and liabilities that is reasonable in the circumstances.

Section 6.40(d) also refers to some "other method that is reasonable in the circumstances." This phrase is intended to comprehend within section 6.40(c)(2) the wide variety of possibilities that might not be considered to fall under a "fair valuation" or "current value" but might be reasonable in the circumstances of a particular case.

5. Preferential Dissolution Rights and the Balance Sheet Test

Section 6.40(c)(2) provides that a distribution may not be made unless the total assets of the corporation exceed its liabilities plus the amount that would be needed to satisfy any shareholders' superior preferential rights upon dissolution if the corporation were to be dissolved at the time of the distribution. This requirement in effect treats preferential dissolution rights of shares for distribution purposes as if they were liabilities for the sole purpose of determining the amount available for distributions, and carries forward analogous treatment of shares having preferential dissolution rights from earlier versions of the Model Act. In making the calculation of the amount that must be added to the liabilities of the corporation to reflect the preferential dissolution rights, the assumption should be made that the preferential dissolution rights are to be established pursuant to the articles of incorporation, as of the date of the distribution or proposed distribution. The amount so determined must include arrearages in preferential dividends if the articles of incorporation or resolution require that they be paid upon the dissolution of the corporation. In the case of shares having both a preferential right upon dissolution and other nonpreferential rights, only the preferential right should be taken into account. The treatment of preferential dissolution rights of classes of shares set forth in section 6.40(c)(2) is applicable only to the balance sheet test and is not applicable to the equity insolvency test of section 6.40(c)(1). The treatment of preferential rights mandated by this section may always be eliminated by an appropriate provision in the articles of incorporation.

6.   Time of Measurement

Section 6.40(e)(3) provides that the time for measuring the effect of a distribution for compliance with the equity insolvency and balance sheet tests for all distributions not involving the reacquisition of shares or the distribution of indebtedness is the date of authorization, if the payment occurs within 120 days following the authorization; if the payment occurs more than 120 days after the authorization, however, the date of payment must be used. If the corporation elects to make a distribution in the form of its own indebtedness under section 6.40(e)(2) the validity of that distribution must be measured as of the time of distribution, unless the indebtedness qualifies under section 6.40(g).

Section 6.40(e)(1) provides a different rule for the time of measurement when the distribution involves a reacquisition of shares. See below, Application to Reacquisition of Shares—Time of Measurement.

7.   Record Date

Section 6.40(b) fixes the record date (if the board of directors does not otherwise fix it) for distributions other than those involving a reacquisition of shares as the date the board of directors authorizes the distribution. No record date is necessary for a reacquisition of shares from one or more specific shareholders. The board of directors has discretion to set a record date for a reacquisition if it is to be pro rata and to be offered to all shareholders as of a specified date.

8.   Application to Reacquisition of Shares

The application of the equity insolvency and balance sheet tests to distributions that involve the purchase, redemption, or other acquisition of the corporation's shares creates unique problems; section 6.40 provides a specific rule for the resolution of these problems as described below.

a. Time of Measurement

Section 6.40(e)(1) provides that the time for measuring the effect of a distribution under section 6.40(c), if shares of the corporation are reacquired, is the earlier of (i) the payment date, or (ii) the date the shareholder ceased to be a shareholder with respect to the shares, except as provided in section 6.40(g).

b. When Tests Are Applied to Redemption–Related Debt

In an acquisition of its shares, a corporation may transfer property or incur debt to the former holder of the shares. The case law on the status of this debt is conflicting. However, share repurchase agreements involving payment for shares over a period of time are of special importance in closely-held corporate enterprises. Section 6.40(e) provides a clear rule for this situation: the legality of the distribution must be measured at the time of the issuance [or] incurrence of the debt, not at a later date when the debt is actually paid, except as provided in section 6.40(g). Of course, this does not preclude a later challenge of a payment on account of redemption-related debt by a bankruptcy trustee on the ground that it constitutes a preferential payment to a creditor.

c. Priority of Debt Distributed Directly or Incurred in Connection With a Reacquisition of Shares

Section 6.40(f) provides that indebtedness created to acquire the corporation's shares or issued as a distribution is on a parity with the indebtedness of the corporation to its general, unsecured creditors, except to the extent subordinated by agreement. General creditors are better off in these situations than they would have been if cash or other property had been paid out for the shares or distributed (which is proper under the statute), and no worse off than if cash had been paid or distributed and then lent back to the corporation, making the shareholders (or former shareholders) creditors. The parity created by section 6.40(f) therefore is logically consistent with the rule established by section 6.40(e) that these transactions should be judged at the time of the issuance of the debt.

Chapter 7

SHAREHOLDERS

Subchapter A

Meetings

§ 7.01 Annual Meeting

(a) A corporation shall hold a meeting of shareholders annually at a time stated in or fixed in accordance with the bylaws.

(b) Annual shareholders' meetings may be held in or out of this state at the place stated in or fixed in accordance with the bylaws. If no place is stated in or fixed in accordance with the bylaws, annual meetings shall be held at the corporation's principal office.

(c) The failure to hold an annual meeting at the time stated in or fixed in accordance with a corporation's bylaws does not affect the validity of any corporate action.

§ 7.02   Special Meeting

(a) A corporation shall hold a special meeting of shareholders:

    (1) on call of its board of directors or the person or persons authorized to do so by the articles of incorporation or bylaws; or

    (2) if the holders of at least 10 percent of all the votes entitled to be cast on any issue proposed to be considered at the proposed special meeting sign, date, and deliver to the corporation's secretary one or more written demands for the meeting describing the purpose or purposes for which it is to be held, provided that the articles of incorporation may fix a lower percentage or a higher percentage not exceeding 25 percent of all the votes entitled to be cast on any issue proposed to be considered. Unless otherwise provided in the articles of incorporation, a written demand for a special meeting may be revoked by a writing to that effect received by the corporation prior to the receipt by the corporation of demands sufficient in number to require the holding of a special meeting.

(b) If not otherwise fixed under section 7.03 or 7.07, the record date for determining shareholders entitled to demand a special meeting is the date the first shareholder signs the demand.

(c) Special shareholders' meetings may be held in or out of this state at the place stated in or fixed in accordance with the bylaws. If no place is stated or fixed in accordance with the bylaws, special meetings shall be held at the corporation's principal office.

(d) Only business within the purpose or purposes described in the meeting notice required by section 7.05(c) may be conducted at a special shareholders' meeting.

§ 7.03   Court–Ordered Meeting

(a) The [name or describe] court of the county where a corporation's principal office (or, if none in this state, its registered office) is located may summarily order a meeting to be held:

    (1) on application of any shareholder of the corporation entitled to participate in an annual meeting if an annual meeting was not held within the earlier of 6 months after the end of the corporation's fiscal year or 15 months after its last annual meeting; or

(2) on application of a shareholder who signed a demand for a special meeting valid under section 7.02, if:

    (i) notice of the special meeting was not given within 30 days after the date the demand was delivered to the corporation's secretary; or

    (ii) the special meeting was not held in accordance with the notice.

(b) The court may fix the time and place of the meeting, determine the shares entitled to participate in the meeting, specify a record date for determining shareholders entitled to notice of and to vote at the meeting, prescribe the form and content of the meeting notice, fix the quorum required for specific matters to be considered at the meeting (or direct that the votes represented at the meeting constitute a quorum for action on those matters), and enter other orders necessary to accomplish the purpose or purposes of the meeting.

§ 7.04 Action Without Meeting

(a) Action required or permitted by this Act to be taken at a shareholders' meeting may be taken without a meeting if the action is taken by all the shareholders entitled to vote on the action. The action must be evidenced by one or more written consents bearing the date of signature and describing the action taken, signed by all the shareholders entitled to vote on the action, and delivered to the corporation for inclusion in the minutes or filing with the corporate records.

(b) If not otherwise fixed under section 7.03 or 7.07, the record date for determining shareholders entitled to take action without a meeting is the date the first shareholder signs the consent under subsection (a). No written consent shall be effective to take the corporate action referred to therein unless, within 60 days of the earliest date appearing on a consent delivered to the corporation in the manner required by this section, written consents signed by all shareholders entitled to vote on the action are received by the corporation. A written consent may be revoked by a writing to that effect received by the corporation prior to the receipt by the corporation of unrevoked written consents sufficient in number to take corporate action.

(c) A consent signed under this section has the effect of a meeting vote and may be described as such in any document.

(d) If this Act requires that notice of proposed action be given to nonvoting shareholders and the action is to be taken by unanimous consent of the voting shareholders, the corporation must give its nonvoting shareholders written notice of the proposed action at least 10 days before the action is taken. The notice must contain or be accompanied by the same material that, under this Act, would have been required to be sent to nonvoting shareholders in a notice of meeting at which the proposed action would have been submitted to the shareholders for action.

Official Comment ...

2. Revocation of Consent

Action by unanimous written consent is effective only when the last shareholder has signed the appropriate written consent and all consents have been delivered to the corporation in the manner contemplated by section 1.41(d). Before that time, any shareholder may withdraw his consent simply by advising the corporation in writing of that fact. Cf. Calumet Industries, Inc. v. MacClure, 464 F.Supp. 19 (N.D.Ill.1978). The withdrawal of a single consent, of course, destroys the unanimous written consent required by this section. If a shareholder seeks to withdraw his consent after all shareholders have signed written consents and filed them with the corporation, such withdrawal will be a nullity and shall be given no effect.

§ 7.05   Notice of Meeting

(a) A corporation shall notify shareholders of the date, time, and place of each annual and special shareholders' meeting no fewer than 10 nor more than 60 days before the meeting date. Unless this Act or the articles of incorporation require otherwise, the corporation is required to give notice only to shareholders entitled to vote at the meeting.

(b) Unless this Act or the articles of incorporation require otherwise, notice of an annual meeting need not include a description of the purpose or purposes for which the meeting is called.

(c) Notice of a special meeting must include a description of the purpose or purposes for which the meeting is called.

(d) If not otherwise fixed under section 7.03 or 7.07, the record date for determining shareholders entitled to notice of and to vote at an annual or special shareholders' meeting is the day before the first notice is delivered to shareholders.

(e) Unless the bylaws require otherwise, if an annual or special shareholders' meeting is adjourned to a different date, time, or place, notice need not be given of the new date, time, or place if the new date, time, or place is announced at the meeting before adjournment. If a new record date for the adjourned meeting is or must be fixed under section 7.07, however, notice of the adjourned meeting must be given under this section to persons who are shareholders as of the new record date.

Official Comment ...

2. Statement of Matters to Be Considered at an Annual Meeting

Notice of all special meetings must include a description of the purpose or purposes for which the meeting is called and the matters acted upon at the meeting are limited to those within the notice of meeting. By contrast, the Model Act does not require that the notice of an annual meeting refer to any specific purpose or purposes, and any matter appropriate for shareholder action may be considered. As recognized in subsection (b), however, other provisions of the Model Act provide that certain types of fundamental corporate changes may be considered at an annual meeting only if specific reference to the proposed action appears in the notice of meeting. See sections 10.03, 11.03, 12.02, and 14.02. In addition, as a condition to relying upon shareholder action to establish the safe harbor protection of section 8.61(b), section 8.63 requires notice to shareholders providing information regarding any director's conflicting interest in a transaction. If the board of directors chooses, a notice of an annual meeting may also contain references to purposes or proposals not required by statute. In the event that management intends to present non-routine proposals for a shareholder vote and shareholders have not otherwise been informed of such proposals, good corporate practice suggests that references to such proposals be made in the notice. In any event, if a notice of an annual meeting refers specifically to one or more purposes, the meeting is not limited to those purposes. . . .

§ 7.06 Waiver of Notice

(a) A shareholder may waive any notice required by this Act, the articles of incorporation, or bylaws before or after the date and time stated in the notice. The waiver must be in writing, be signed by the shareholder entitled to the notice, and be delivered to the corporation for inclusion in the minutes or filing with the corporate records.

(b) A shareholder's attendance at a meeting:

(1) waives objection to lack of notice or defective notice of the meeting, unless the shareholder at the beginning of the meeting objects to holding the meeting or transacting business at the meeting;

(2) waives objection to consideration of a particular matter at the meeting that is not within the purpose or purposes described in the meeting notice, unless the shareholder objects to considering the matter when it is presented.

§ 7.07 Record Date

(a) The bylaws may fix or provide the manner of fixing the record date for one or more voting groups in order to determine the shareholders entitled to notice of a shareholders' meeting, to demand a special meeting, to vote, or to take any other action. If the bylaws do not fix or provide for fixing a record date, the board of directors of the corporation may fix a future date as the record date.

(b) A record date fixed under this section may not be more than 70 days before the meeting or action requiring a determination of shareholders.

(c) A determination of shareholders entitled to notice of or to vote at a shareholders' meeting is effective for any adjournment of the meeting unless the board of directors fixes a new record date, which it must do if the meeting is adjourned to a date more than 120 days after the date fixed for the original meeting.

(d) If a court orders a meeting adjourned to a date more than 120 days after the date fixed for the original meeting, it may provide that the original record date continues in effect or it may fix a new record date.

§ 7.08   Conduct of the Meeting

(a) At each meeting of shareholders, a chair shall preside. The chair shall be appointed as provided in the bylaws or, in the absence of such provision, by the board.

(b) The chair, unless the articles of incorporation or bylaws provide otherwise, shall determine the order of business and shall establish rules for the conduct of the meeting.

(c) Any rules adopted for, and the conduct of, the meeting shall be fair to shareholders.

(d) The chair of the meeting shall announce at the meeting when the polls close for each matter voted upon. If no announcement is made, the polls shall be deemed to have closed upon the final adjournment of the meeting. After the polls close, no ballots, proxies or votes nor any revocations or changes thereto may be accepted.

Official Comment ...

The Act provides that only business within the purpose or purposes described in the meeting notice may be conducted at a special shareholders' meeting. See sections 7.02(d) and 7.05(c). In addition, a corporation's articles of incorporation or, more typically, its bylaws, may contain advance notice provisions requiring that shareholder nominations for election to the board of directors or resolutions intended to be voted on at the annual meeting must be made in writing and received by the corporation a prescribed number of days in advance of the meeting. Such advance notice bylaws are permitted provided (1) there is reasonable opportunity for shareholders to comply with them in a timely fashion, and (2) the requirements of the bylaws are reasonable in relationship to corporate needs. . . .

Among the considerations to be taken into account in determining reasonableness are (a) how and with what frequency shareholders are advised of the specific bylaw provisions, and (b) whether the time frame within which director nominations or shareholder resolutions must be submitted is consistent with the corporation's need, if any, (i) to prepare and publish a proxy statement, (ii) to verify that the director nominee meets any established qualifications for director and is willing to serve, (iii) to determine that a proposed resolution is a proper subject for shareholder action under the Act or other state law, or (iv) to give interested parties adequate opportunity to communicate a recommendation or response with respect to such matters, or to solicit proxies. Whether or not an advance notice provision has been adopted, if a public company receives advance notice of a matter to be raised for a vote at an annual meeting, management may exercise its discretionary proxy authority only in compliance with SEC Rule 14a–4(c)(1) adopted under the Securities Exchange Act of 1934. . . .

Subchapter B

Voting

§ 7.20 Shareholders' List for Meeting

(a) After fixing a record date for a meeting, a corporation shall prepare an alphabetical list of the names of all its shareholders who are entitled to notice of a shareholders' meeting. The list must be arranged by voting group (and within each voting group by class or series of shares) and show the address of and number of shares held by each shareholder.

(b) The shareholders' list must be available for inspection by any shareholder, beginning two business days after notice of the meeting is given for which the list was prepared and continuing through the meeting, at the corporation's principal office or at a place identified in the meeting notice in the city where the meeting will be held. A shareholder, his agent, or attorney is entitled on written demand to inspect and, subject to the requirements of section 16.02(c), to copy the list, during regular business hours and at his expense, during the period it is available for inspection.

(c) The corporation shall make the shareholders' list available at the meeting, and any shareholder, his agent, or attorney is entitled to inspect the list at any time during the meeting or any adjournment.

(d) If the corporation refuses to allow a shareholder, his agent, or attorney to inspect the shareholders' list before or at the meeting (or copy the list as permitted by subsection (b)), the [name or describe] court of the county where a corporation's principal office (or, if none in this state, its registered office) is located, on application of the shareholder, may summarily order the inspection or copying at the corporation's expense and may postpone the meeting for which the list was prepared until the inspection or copying is complete.

(e) Refusal or failure to prepare or make available the shareholders' list does not affect the validity of action taken at the meeting.

Official Comment ...

5. The Right to Obtain a Copy of the List

Section 7.20(b) permits shareholders to "inspect" the list without limitation, but permits the shareholder to "copy" the list only if the shareholder complies with the requirement of section 16.02(c), that the demand be "made in good faith and for a proper purpose." The right to copy the list includes, if reasonable, the right to receive a copy of the list upon payment of a reasonable charge. See sections 16.03(b) and (c). The distinction between "inspection" and "copying" set forth in section 7.20(b) reflects an accommodation between competing considerations of permitting shareholders access to the list before a meeting and possible misuse of the list.

6. Relationship to Right to Inspect Corporate Records Generally

Section 7.20 creates a right of shareholders to inspect a list of shareholders in advance of and at a meeting that is independent of the rights of shareholders to inspect corporate records under chapter 16A. A shareholder may obtain the right to inspect the list of shareholders as provided in chapter 16A without regard to the provisions relating to the pendency of a meeting in section 7.20, and similarly the limitations of chapter 16A are not applicable to the right of inspection created by section 7.20 except to the extent the shareholder seeks to copy the list in advance of the meeting.

The right to inspect under chapter 16A is also broader in the sense that in some circumstances the shareholder may be entitled to receive copies of the documents he may inspect. See section 16.03.

§ 7.21   Voting Entitlement of Shares

(a) Except as provided in subsections (b) and (c) or unless the articles of incorporation provide otherwise, each outstanding share, regardless of class, is entitled to one vote on each matter voted on at a shareholders' meeting. Only shares are entitled to vote.

(b) Absent special circumstances, the shares of a corporation are not entitled to vote if they are owned, directly or indirectly, by a second corporation, domestic or foreign, and the first corporation owns, directly or indirectly, a majority of the shares entitled to vote for directors of the second corporation.

(c) Subsection (b) does not limit the power of a corporation to vote any shares, including its own shares, held by it in a fiduciary capacity.

(d) Redeemable shares are not entitled to vote after notice of redemption is mailed to the holders and a sum sufficient to redeem the shares has been deposited with a bank, trust company, or other financial institution under an irrevocable obligation to pay the holders the redemption price on surrender of the shares.

Official Comment

Section 7.21 deals with the entitlement of shareholders to vote, while section 7.22 deals with voting by proxy and section 7.24 establishes rules for the corporation's acceptance or rejection of proxy votes.

1. Voting Power of Shares

Section 7.21(a) provides that each outstanding share, regardless of class, is entitled to one vote per share unless otherwise provided in the articles of incorporation. See section 6.01 and its Official Comment. The articles of incorporation may provide for multiple or fractional votes per share, and may provide that some classes of shares are nonvoting on some or all matters, or that some classes have multiple or fractional votes per share while other classes have a single vote per share or different multiple or fractional votes per share, or that some classes constitute one or more separate voting groups and are entitled to vote separately on the matter.

The articles of incorporation may also authorize the board of directors to create classes or series of shares with preferential rights, which may be voting or nonvoting in whole or in part. See section 6.02 and its Official Comment.

Fractional or multiple votes per share, or nonvoting shares, are often used in the planning of business ventures, particularly closely held ventures, when the contributions of participants vary in kind or quality. It is possible through these devices, for example, to give persons with relatively small financial contributions a relatively large voting power within the corporation.

The power to vary or condition voting power is also often used to give increased protection to financial interests in the corporation. It is customary, for example, to make classes of shares with preferential rights nonvoting, but the power to vote may be granted to those classes if distributions are omitted for a specified period. This conditional right to vote may permit the class of shares with preferential rights to vote separately as a voting group to elect one or more directors or to vote with the shares having general voting rights in the election of the directors.

In order to reflect the possibility that shares may have multiple or fractional votes per share, all provisions relating to quorums, voting, and similar matters in the Model Act are phrased in terms of "votes" rather than "shares."

2.   Voting Power of Nonshareholders

Under the last sentence of section 7.21(a), the power to vote cannot be granted generally to nonshareholders. The statutes of some states permit bondholders to be given the power to vote under certain specified circumstances; this option is not available under the Model Act. But creditors may in effect be given the power to vote, e.g., by creating a special class of redeemable voting shares for them, by creating a voting trust at the time the credit is extended with power in the creditors to name the voting trustees, by registering the shares in the name of the creditors as pledgees with power to vote, or by granting the creditors a revocable or irrevocable proxy to vote some or all of the outstanding shares. See the Official Comment to section 7.22.

3.   Circular Holdings

Section 7.21(b) prohibits the voting of shares held by a domestic or foreign corporation that is itself a majority-owned subsidiary of the corporation issuing the shares. The purpose of this prohibition is to prevent management from using a corporate investment to perpetuate itself in power. Similar public policy considerations may be present in situations where the issuing corporation owns a large but not a majority interest in the corporation voting the shares. The inclusion of section 7.21(b) is not intended to affect the possible application of common law principles that may invalidate circular holding situations not within its literal prohibition. As to the possible existence of these common law principles, see, e.g., Cleveland Trust Co. v. Eaton, 11 Ohio Misc. 151, 229 N.E.2d 850 (1967), rev'd on the basis of statutory amendment, 21 Ohio St.2d 129, 256 N.E.2d 198 (1970). The phrase "absent special circumstances" is included to enable a court to permit the voting of shares where it deems that the purpose of the section is not violated.

4.   Shares Held in a Fiduciary Capacity

Section 7.21(c) makes the prohibition against voting of circularly-owned shares of section 7.21(b) inapplicable to shares held in a fiduciary capacity. Compare Del.Gen.Corp.Law § 160(c). The Ohio statute involved in the Eaton case authorized a bank to vote its own shares that were held by it in a fiduciary capacity. A state may grant or prohibit such voting by another statute; section 7.21(c) provides only that such voting is not prohibited by the Model Act....

§ 7.22   Proxies

(a) A shareholder may vote his shares in person or by proxy.

(b) A shareholder or his agent or attorney-in-fact may appoint a proxy to vote or otherwise act for the shareholder by signing an appointment form, or by an electronic transmission. An electronic transmission must contain or be accompanied by information from which one can determine that the shareholder, the shareholder's agent, or the shareholder's attorney-in-fact authorized the electronic transmission.

(c) An appointment of a proxy is effective when a signed appointment form or an electronic transmission of the appointment is received by the inspector of election or the officer or agent of the corporation authorized to tabulate votes. An appointment is valid for 11 months unless a longer period is expressly provided in the appointment.

(d) An appointment of a proxy is revocable unless the appointment form or electronic transmission conspicuously states that it is irrevocable and the appointment is coupled with an interest. Appointments coupled with an interest include the appointment of:

(1) a pledgee;

(2) a person who purchased or agreed to purchase the shares;

(3) a creditor of the corporation who extended it credit under terms requiring the appointment;

(4) an employee of the corporation whose employment contract requires the appointment; or

(5) a party to a voting agreement created under section 7.31.

(e) The death or incapacity of the shareholder appointing a proxy does not affect the right of the corporation to accept the proxy's authority unless notice of the death or incapacity is received by the secretary or other officer or agent authorized to tabulate votes before the proxy exercises his authority under the appointment.

(f) An appointment made irrevocable under subsection (d) is revoked when the interest with which it is coupled is extinguished.

(g) A transferee for value of shares subject to an irrevocable appointment may revoke the appointment if he did not know of its existence when he acquired the shares and the existence of the irrevocable appointment was not noted conspicuously on the certificate representing the shares or on the information statement for shares without certificates.

(h) Subject to section 7.24 and to any express limitation on the proxy's authority stated in the appointment form or electronic transmission, a corporation is entitled to accept the proxy's vote or other action as that of the shareholder making the appointment.

Official Comment ...

1. Nomenclature

The word "proxy" is often used ambiguously, sometimes referring to the grant of authority to vote, sometimes to the document granting the authority, and sometimes to the person to whom the authority is granted. In the Model Act the word "proxy" is used only in the last sense; the terms "appointment form" and "electronic transmission" are used to describe the document or communication appointing the proxy; and the word "appointment" is used to describe the grant of authority to vote. . . .

§ 7.23   Shares Held by Nominees

(a) A corporation may establish a procedure by which the beneficial owner of shares that are registered in the name of a nominee is recognized by the corporation as the shareholder. The extent of this recognition may be determined in the procedure.

(b) The procedure may set forth:

   (1) the types of nominees to which it applies;

   (2) the rights or privileges that the corporation recognizes in a beneficial owner;

   (3) the manner in which the procedure is selected by the nominee;

   (4) the information that must be provided when the procedure is selected;

   (5) the period for which selection of the procedure is effective; and

   (6) other aspects of the rights and duties created.

§ 7.24   Corporation's Acceptance of Votes

(a) If the name signed on a vote, consent, waiver, or proxy appointment corresponds to the name of a shareholder, the corporation if acting in good faith is entitled to accept the vote, consent, waiver, or proxy appointment and give it effect as the act of the shareholder.

(b) If the name signed on a vote, consent, waiver, or proxy appointment does not correspond to the name of its shareholder, the corporation if acting in good faith is nevertheless entitled to accept the vote, consent, waiver, or proxy appointment and give it effect as the act of the shareholder if:

   (1) the shareholder is an entity and the name signed purports to be that of an officer or agent of the entity;

   (2) the name signed purports to be that of an administrator, executor, guardian, or conservator representing the shareholder and, if the corporation requests, evidence of fiduciary status acceptable to the corporation has been presented with respect to the vote, consent, waiver, or proxy appointment;

   (3) the name signed purports to be that of a receiver or trustee in bankruptcy of the shareholder and, if the corporation requests, evidence of this status acceptable to the corporation has been

presented with respect to the vote, consent, waiver, or proxy appointment;

(4) the name signed purports to be that of a pledgee, beneficial owner, or attorney-in-fact of the shareholder and, if the corporation requests, evidence acceptable to the corporation of the signatory's authority to sign for the shareholder has been presented with respect to the vote, consent, waiver, or proxy appointment;

(5) two or more persons are the shareholder as cotenants or fiduciaries and the name signed purports to be the name of at least one of the coowners and the person signing appears to be acting on behalf of all the coowners.

(c) The corporation is entitled to reject a vote, consent, waiver, or proxy appointment if the secretary or other officer or agent authorized to tabulate votes, acting in good faith, has reasonable basis for doubt about the validity of the signature on it or about the signatory's authority to sign for the shareholder.

(d) The corporation and its officer or agent who accepts or rejects a vote, consent, waiver, or proxy appointment in good faith and in accordance with the standards of this section or section 7.22(b) are not liable in damages to the shareholder for the consequences of the acceptance or rejection.

(e) Corporate action based on the acceptance or rejection of a vote, consent, waiver, or proxy appointment under this section or section 7.22(b) is valid unless a court of competent jurisdiction determines otherwise.

§ 7.25 Quorum and Voting Requirements for Voting Groups

(a) Shares entitled to vote as a separate voting group may take action on a matter at a meeting only if a quorum of those shares exists with respect to that matter. Unless the articles of incorporation or this Act provide otherwise, a majority of the votes entitled to be cast on the matter by the voting group constitutes a quorum of that voting group for action on that matter.

(b) Once a share is represented for any purpose at a meeting, it is deemed present for quorum purposes for the remainder of the meeting and for any adjournment of that meeting unless a new record date is or must be set for that adjourned meeting.

(c) If a quorum exists, action on a matter (other than the election of directors) by a voting group is approved if the votes cast within the voting group favoring the action exceed the votes cast opposing the action, unless the articles of incorporation or this Act require a greater number of affirmative votes.

(d) An amendment of articles of incorporation adding, changing, or deleting a quorum or voting requirement for a voting group greater than specified in subsection (a) or (c) is governed by section 7.27.

(e) The election of directors is governed by section 7.28.

Official Comment ....

3.   Quorum Requirements for Action by Voting Group ....

Section 7.25(b) retains the common law view that once a share is present at a meeting, it is deemed present for quorum purposes throughout the meeting. Thus, a voting group may continue to act despite the withdrawal of persons having the power to vote one or more shares in an effort "to break the quorum." In this respect, a meeting of shareholders is governed by a different rule than a meeting of directors, where a sufficient number of directors must be present to constitute a quorum at the time action is taken. See section 8.24 and its Official Comment.

Once a share is present at a meeting it is also deemed to be present at any adjourned meeting unless a new record date is or must be set for that adjourned meeting. See section 7.07. If a new record date is set, new notice must be given to holders of shares of a voting group and a quorum must be established from within the holders of shares of that voting group on the new record date.

The shares owned by a shareholder who comes to the meeting to object on grounds of lack of notice may be counted toward the presence of a quorum. Similarly, the holdings of a shareholder who attends a meeting solely for purposes of raising the objection that a quorum is not present is counted toward the presence of a quorum. Attendance at a meeting, however, does not constitute a waiver of other objections to the meeting such as the lack of notice. Such waivers are governed by section 7.06(b).

As used in sections 7.25 and 7.26, "represented at the meeting" means the physical presence of the shareholder (whether in person or by his written authorization) in the meeting room after the meeting has been called to order or the presiding officer has commenced consideration of the business of the meeting, and before the final adjournment of the meeting....

4.   Voting Requirements for Approval by Voting Group

Section 7.25(c) provides that an action (other than the election of directors, which is governed by section 7.28) is approved by a voting group at a meeting at which a quorum is present if the votes cast in favor of the action exceed the votes cast opposing the action. This section changes the traditional rule appearing in earlier versions of the Model Act and many state statutes that an action is approved at a meeting at which a quorum is present if it receives the affirmative vote "of a majority of the shares represented at that meeting." The traditional rule in effect treated abstentions as negative votes; the Revised Model Act treats them truly as abstentions....

5. Modification of Standard Requirements

... The articles of incorporation may increase the quorum and voting requirements to any extent desired up to and including unanimity upon compliance with section 7.27 .... The articles may also decrease the quorum requirement as desired. Earlier versions of the Model Act limited the power to reduce the quorum to a minimum of one-third; this restriction, was eliminated from the Revised Model Act because it was thought to be unreasonably confining in certain situations, such as where a class of shares with preferential rights is given a limited right to vote that may be exercisable only rarely....

§ 7.26 Action by Single and Multiple Voting Groups

(a) If the articles of incorporation or this Act provide for voting by a single voting group on a matter, action on that matter is taken when voted upon by that voting group as provided in section 7.25.

(b) If the articles of incorporation or this Act provide for voting by two or more voting groups on a matter, action on that matter is taken only when voted upon by each of those voting groups counted separately as provided in section 7.25. Action may be taken by one voting group on a matter even though no action is taken by another voting group entitled to vote on the matter.

Official Comment

Section 7.26(a) provides that when a matter is to be voted upon by a single voting group, action is taken when the voting group votes upon the action as provided in section 7.25. In most instances the single voting group will consist of all the shares of the class or classes entitled to vote by the articles of incorporation; voting by two or more voting groups as contemplated by section 7.26(b) is the exceptional case.

Section 7.26(b) basically requires that if more than one voting group is entitled to vote on a matter, favorable action on a matter is taken only when it is voted upon favorably by each voting group, counted separately. Implicit in this section are the concepts that (1) different quorum and voting requirements may be applicable to different matters considered at a single meeting and (2) different quorum and voting requirements may be applicable to different voting groups voting on the same matter. See the Official Comment to section 7.25. Thus, each group entitled to vote must independently meet the quorum and voting requirements established by section 7.25....

2. Participation of Shares in Multiple Voting Groups

As described in section 7.26(b), if voting by multiple voting groups is required, the votes of members of each voting group must be separately tabulated. Normally, each class or series of shares will participate in only a single voting group. But since holders of shares entitled by the articles of incorporation to vote generally on a matter are always entitled to vote in the voting group consisting of the general voting shares, in some instances classes or series of shares may be entitled to be counted simultaneously in two voting groups. This will occur whenever a class or series of shares entitled to vote generally on a matter under the articles of incorporation is affected by the matter in a way that gives rise to the right to have its vote counted separately as an independent voting group under the Act. For example, assume that corporation Y has outstanding one class of general voting shares without preferential rights ("common shares"), 500 shares issued, and one class of shares with preferential rights ("preferred shares"), 100 shares issued, that also have full voting rights under the articles of incorporation, i.e., the preferred may vote for election of directors and on all other matters on which common may vote. The preferred and the common therefore are part of the general voting group. The directors propose to amend the articles of incorporation to change the preferential dividend rights of the preferred from cumulative to noncumulative. All shares are present at the meeting and they divide as follows on the proposal to adopt the amendment:

Yes — Common   230
    — Preferred   80
No — Common   270
    — Preferred   20.

Both the preferred and the common are entitled to vote on the amendment to the articles of incorporation since they are part of a general voting group pursuant to the articles. But the vote of the preferred is also entitled to be counted separately on the proposal by section 10.04(a)(4) of the Model Act. The result is that the proposal passes by a vote of 310 to 290 in the voting group consisting of the shares entitled to vote generally and 80 to 20 in the voting group consisting solely of the preferred shares:

(a) First voting group

Yes: Common   230
      Preferred   80
                  310
No: Common   270
      Preferred   20
                  290

(b) Second voting group (preferred)

Yes: Preferred   80
No: Preferred   20

In this situation, in the absence of a special quorum requirement, a meeting could approve the proposal to amend the articles of incorporation if—and only if—a quorum of each voting group is present, i.e., at least 51 shares of preferred and 301 shares of common and preferred were represented at the meeting. . . .

§ 7.27 Greater Quorum or Voting Requirements

(a) The articles of incorporation may provide for a greater quorum or voting requirement for shareholders (or voting groups of shareholders) than is provided for by this Act.

(b) An amendment to the articles of incorporation that adds, changes, or deletes a greater quorum or voting requirement must meet the same quorum requirement and be adopted by the same vote and voting groups required to take action under the quorum and voting requirements then in effect or proposed to be adopted, whichever is greater.

Official Comment

Section 7.27(a) permits the articles of incorporation to increase the quorum or voting requirements for approval of an action by shareholders up to any desired amount including unanimity. These provisions may relate to ordinary or routine actions by the general voting group . . . or to one or more other voting groups or to actions for which the Model Act provides a greater voting requirement—for example, changes of a fundamental nature in the corporation like certain amendments to articles of incorporation (section 10.03) . . . .

A provision that increases the requirement for approval of an ordinary matter or a fundamental change is usually referred to as a "supermajority" provision.

Section 7.27(b) requires any amendment of the articles of incorporation that adds, modifies, or repeals any supermajority provision to be approved by the greater of the proposed quorum and vote requirement or by the quorum and vote required by the articles before their amendment. Thus, a supermajority provision that requires an 80 percent affirmative vote of all eligible votes of a voting group present at the meeting may not be removed from the articles of incorporation or reduced in any way except by an 80 percent affirmative vote. If the 80 percent requirement is coupled with a quorum requirement for a voting group that shares representing two-thirds of the total votes must be present in person or by proxy, both the 80 percent voting requirement and the two-thirds quorum requirement are immune from reduction except at a meeting of the voting group at which the two-thirds quorum requirement is met and the reduction is approved by an 80 percent affirmative vote. If the proposal is to increase the 80 percent voting requirement to 90 percent, that proposal must be approved by a 90 percent affirmative vote at a meeting of the voting group at which the two-thirds quorum requirement is met; if the proposal is to increase the two-thirds quorum requirement to three-fourths without changing the

80 percent voting requirement, that proposal must be approved by an 80 percent affirmative vote at a meeting of the voting group at which a three-fourths quorum requirement is met.

§ 7.28   Voting for Directors; Cumulative Voting

(a) Unless otherwise provided in the articles of incorporation, directors are elected by a plurality of the votes cast by the shares entitled to vote in the election at a meeting at which a quorum is present.

(b) Shareholders do not have a right to cumulate their votes for directors unless the articles of incorporation so provide.

(c) A statement included in the articles of incorporation that "[all] [a designated voting group of] shareholders are entitled to cumulate their votes for directors" (or words of similar import) means that the shareholders designated are entitled to multiply the number of votes they are entitled to cast by the number of directors for whom they are entitled to vote and cast the product for a single candidate or distribute the product among two or more candidates.

(d) Shares otherwise entitled to vote cumulatively may not be voted cumulatively at a particular meeting unless:

   (1) the meeting notice or proxy statement accompanying the notice states conspicuously that cumulative voting is authorized; or

   (2) a shareholder who has the right to cumulate his votes gives notice to the corporation not less than 48 hours before the time set for the meeting of his intent to cumulate his votes during the meeting, and if one shareholder gives this notice all other shareholders in the same voting group participating in the election are entitled to cumulate their votes without giving further notice.

§ 7.29   Inspectors of Election

(a) A corporation having any shares listed on a national securities exchange or regularly traded in a market maintained by one or more members of a national or affiliated securities association shall, and any other corporation may, appoint one or more inspectors to act at a meeting of shareholders and make a written report of the inspectors' determinations. Each inspector shall take and sign an oath faithfully to execute the duties of inspector with strict impartiality and according to the best of the inspector's ability.

(b) The inspectors shall
   (1) ascertain the number of shares outstanding and the voting power of each;
   (2) determine the shares represented at a meeting;
   (3) determine the validity of proxies and ballots;
   (4) count all votes; and
   (5) determine the result.

(c) An inspector may be an officer or employee of the corporation.

Official Comment

Section 7.29(a) requires that, if a corporation has shares which are listed on a national securities exchange or regularly traded in a market maintained by one or more members of a national or affiliated securities association, one or more inspectors of election must be appointed to act at each meeting of shareholders and make a written report of the determinations made pursuant to section 7.29(b). It is contemplated that the selection of inspectors would be made by responsible officers or by the directors, as authorized either generally or specifically in the corporation's bylaws. Alternate inspectors could also be designated to replace any inspector who fails to act. The requirement of a written report is to facilitate judicial review of determinations made by inspectors.

Section 7.29(b) specifies the duties of inspectors of election. If no challenge of a determination by the inspectors within the authority given them under this section is timely made, such determination shall be conclusive. In the event of a challenge of any determination by the inspectors in a court of competent jurisdiction, the court should give such weight to determinations of fact by the inspectors as it shall deem appropriate, taking into account the relationship of the inspectors, if any, to the management of the company and other persons interested in the outcome of the vote, the evidence available to the inspectors, whether their determinations appear to be reasonable, and such other circumstances as the court shall regard as relevant. The court should review de novo all determinations of law made implicitly or explicitly by the inspectors....

Section 7.29(c) provides that an inspector may be an officer or employee of the corporation. However, in the case of publicly-held corporations, good corporate practice suggests that such inspectors should be independent persons who are neither employees nor officers if there is a contested matter or a shareholder proposal to be considered. Not only will the issue of independent inspectors enhance investor perception as to the fairness of the voting process, but also the report of independent inspectors can be expected to be given greater evidentiary weight by any court reviewing a contested vote.

Subchapter C

Voting Trusts and Agreements

§ 7.30 Voting Trusts

(a) One or more shareholders may create a voting trust, conferring on a trustee the right to vote or otherwise act for them, by signing an agreement setting out the provisions of the trust (which may include anything consistent with its purpose) and transferring their shares to the trustee. When a voting trust agreement is signed, the trustee shall prepare a list of the names and addresses of all owners of beneficial interests in the trust, together with the number and class of shares each transferred to the trust, and deliver copies of the list and agreement to the corporation's principal office.

(b) A voting trust becomes effective on the date the first shares subject to the trust are registered in the trustee's name. A voting trust is valid for not more than 10 years after its effective date unless extended under subsection (c).

(c) All or some of the parties to a voting trust may extend it for additional terms of not more than 10 years each by signing an extension agreement and obtaining the voting trustee's written consent to the extension. An extension is valid for 10 years from the date the first shareholder signs the extension agreement. The voting trustee must deliver copies of the extension agreement and list of beneficial owners to the corporation's principal office. An extension agreement binds only those parties signing it.

§ 7.31   Voting Agreements

(a) Two or more shareholders may provide for the manner in which they will vote their shares by signing an agreement for that purpose. A voting agreement created under this section is not subject to the provisions of section 7.30.

(b) A voting agreement created under this section is specifically enforceable.

Official Comment

Section 7.31(a) explicitly recognizes agreements among two or more shareholders as to the voting of shares and makes clear that these agreements are not subject to the rules relating to a voting trust. These agreements are often referred to as "pooling agreements." The only formal requirements are that they be in writing and signed by all the participating shareholders; in other respects their validity is to be judged as any other contract. They are not subject to the 10–year limitation applicable to voting trusts.

Section 7.31(b) provides that voting agreements may be specifically enforceable. A voting agreement may provide its own enforcement mechanism, as by the appointment of a proxy to vote all shares subject to the agreement; the appointment may be made irrevocable under section 7.22. If no enforcement mechanism is provided, a court may order specific enforcement of the agreement and order the votes cast as the agreement contemplates. This section recognizes that damages are not likely to be an appropriate remedy for breach of a voting agreement, and also avoids the result reached in Ringling Bros. Barnum & Bailey Combined Shows v. Ringling, 53 A.2d 441 (Del.1947), where the court held that the appropriate remedy to enforce a pooling agreement was to refuse to permit any voting of the breaching party's shares.

§ 7.32 Shareholder Agreements

(a) An agreement among the shareholders of a corporation that complies with this section is effective among the shareholders and the corporation even though it is inconsistent with one or more other provisions of this Act in that it:

(1) eliminates the board of directors or restricts the discretion or powers of the board of directors;

(2) governs the authorization or making of distributions whether or not in proportion to ownership of shares, subject to the limitations in section 6.40;

(3) establishes who shall be directors or officers of the corporation, or their terms of office or manner of selection or removal;

(4) governs, in general or in regard to specific matters, the exercise or division of voting power by or between the shareholders and directors or by or among any of them, including use of weighted voting rights or director proxies;

(5) establishes the terms and conditions of any agreement for the transfer or use of property or the provision of services between the corporation and any shareholder, director, officer or employee of the corporation or among any of them;

(6) transfers to one or more shareholders or other persons all or part of the authority to exercise the corporate powers or to manage the business and affairs of the corporation, including the resolution of any issue about which there exists a deadlock among directors or shareholders;

(7) requires dissolution of the corporation at the request of one or more of the shareholders or upon the occurrence of a specified event or contingency; or

(8) otherwise governs the exercise of the corporate powers or the management of the business and affairs of the corporation or the relationship among the shareholders, the directors and the corporation, or among any of them, and is not contrary to public policy.

(b) An agreement authorized by this section shall be:

(1) set forth (A) in the articles of incorporation or bylaws and approved by all persons who are shareholders at the time of the agreement or (B) in a written agreement that is signed by all persons who are shareholders at the time of the agreement and is made known to the corporation;

    (2) subject to amendment only by all persons who are shareholders at the time of the amendment, unless the agreement provides otherwise; and

    (3) valid for 10 years, unless the agreement provides otherwise.

(c) The existence of an agreement authorized by this section shall be noted conspicuously on the front or back of each certificate for outstanding shares or on the information statement required by section 6.26(b). If at the time of the agreement the corporation has shares outstanding represented by certificates, the corporation shall recall the outstanding certificates and issue substitute certificates that comply with this subsection. The failure to note the existence of the agreement on the certificate or information statement shall not affect the validity of the agreement or any action taken pursuant to it. Any purchaser of shares who, at the time of purchase, did not have knowledge of the existence of the agreement shall be entitled to rescission of the purchase. A purchaser shall be deemed to have knowledge of the existence of the agreement if its existence is noted on the certificate or information statement for the shares in compliance with this subsection and, if the shares are not represented by a certificate, the information statement is delivered to the purchaser at or prior to the time of purchase of the shares. An action to enforce the right of rescission authorized by this subsection must be commenced within the earlier of 90 days after discovery of the existence of the agreement or two years after the time of purchase of the shares.

(d) An agreement authorized by this section shall cease to be effective when shares of the corporation are listed on a national securities exchange or regularly traded in a market maintained by one or more members of a national or affiliated securities association. If the agreement ceases to be effective for any reason, the board of directors may, if the agreement is contained or referred to in the corporation's articles of incorporation or bylaws, adopt an amendment to the articles of incorporation or bylaws, without shareholder action, to delete the agreement and any references to it.

(e) An agreement authorized by this section that limits the discretion or powers of the board of directors shall relieve the directors of, and impose upon the person or persons in whom such discretion or powers are vested, liability for acts or omissions imposed by law on directors to the extent that the discretion or powers of the directors are limited by the agreement.

(f) The existence or performance of an agreement authorized by this section shall not be a ground for imposing personal liability on any shareholder for the acts or debts of the corporation even if the agreement or its performance treats the corporation as if it were a partnership or results in failure to observe the corporate formalities otherwise applicable to the matters governed by the agreement.

(g) Incorporators or subscribers for shares may act as shareholders with respect to an agreement authorized by this section if no shares have been issued when the agreement is made.

Official Comment

Shareholders of closely-held corporations, ranging from family businesses to joint ventures owned by large public corporations, frequently enter into agreements that govern the operation of the enterprise. In the past, various types of shareholder agreements were invalidated by courts for a variety of reasons, including so-called "sterilization" of the board of directors and failure to follow the statutory norms of the applicable corporation act. See, e.g., Long Park, Inc. v. Trenton–New Brunswick Theatres Co., 297 N.Y. 174, 77 N.E.2d 633 (1948). The more modern decisions reflect a greater willingness to uphold shareholder agreements. See, e.g., Galler v. Galler, 32 Ill.2d 16, 203 N.E.2d 577 (1964)....

Rather than relying on further uncertain and sporadic development of the law in the courts, section 7.32 rejects the older line of cases. It adds an important element of predictability currently absent from the Model Act and affords participants in closely-held corporations greater contractual freedom to tailor the rules of their enterprise.

Section 7.32 is not intended to establish or legitimize an alternative form of corporation. Instead, it is intended to add, within the context of the traditional corporate structure, legal certainty to shareholder agreements that embody various aspects of the business arrangement established by the shareholders to meet their business and personal needs. The subject matter of these arrangements includes governance of the entity, allocation of the economic return from the business, and other aspects of the relationships among shareholders, directors, and the corporation which are part of the business arrangement. Section 7.32 also recognizes that many of the corporate norms contained in the Model Act, as well as the corporation statutes of most states, were designed with an eye towards public companies, where management and share ownership are quite distinct. *Cf.* 1 O'Neal & Thompson, O'Neal's Close Corporations, section 5.06 (3d ed.). These functions are often conjoined in the close corporation. Thus, section 7.32 validates for nonpublic corporations various types of agreements among shareholders even when the agreements are inconsistent with the statutory norms contained in the Act.

Importantly, section 7.32 only addresses the parties to the shareholder agreement, their transferees, and the corporation, and does not have any binding legal effect on the state, creditors, or other third persons. ...

The types of provisions validated by section 7.32 are many and varied. Section 7.32(a) defines the range of permissible subject matter for shareholder agreements largely by illustration, enumerating seven types of agreements that are expressly validated to the extent they would not be valid absent section 7.32. The enumeration of these types of agreements is not exclusive; nor should it give rise to a negative inference that an agreement of a type that is or might be embraced by one of the categories of section 7.32(a) is, ipso facto, a type of agreement that is not valid unless it complies with section 7.32. Section 7.32(a) also contains a "catch all" which adds a measure of flexibility to the seven enumerated categories. . . .

1. Section 7.32(a)

Subsection (a) is the heart of section 7.32. It states that certain types of agreements are effective among the shareholders and the corporation even if inconsistent with another provision of the Model Act. Thus, an agreement authorized by section 7.32 is, by virtue of that section, "not inconsistent with law" within the meaning of sections 2.02(b)(2) and 2.06(b) of the Act. In contrast, a shareholder agreement that is not inconsistent with any provisions of the Model Act is not subject to the requirements of section 7.32.

The range of agreements validated by section 7.32(a) is expansive though not unlimited. The most difficult problem encountered in crafting a shareholder agreement validation provision is to determine the reach of the provision. Some states have tried to articulate the limits of a shareholder agreement validation provision in terms of negative grounds, stating that no shareholder agreement shall be invalid on certain specified grounds. See, e.g., Del.Code Ann. tit. 8, sections 350, 354 (1983); N.C.Gen.Stat. section 55–73(b) (1982). The deficiency in this type of statute is the uncertainty introduced by the ever present possibility of articulating another ground on which to challenge the validity of the agreement. Other states have provided that shareholder agreements may waive or alter all provisions in the corporation act except certain enumerated provisions that cannot be varied. See, e.g., Cal.Corp.Code section 300(b)–(c) (West 1989 and Supp.1990). The difficulty with this approach is that any enumeration of the provisions that can never be varied will almost inevitably be subjective, arbitrary, and incomplete.

The approach chosen in section 7.32 is more pragmatic. It defines the types of agreements that can be validated largely by illustration. The seven specific categories that are listed are designed to cover the most frequently used arrangements. The outer boundary is provided by section 7.32(a)(8), which provides an additional "catch all" for any provisions that, in a manner inconsistent with any other provision of the Model Act, otherwise govern the exercise of the corporate powers, the management of the business and affairs of the corporation, or the relationship between and among the shareholders, the directors, and the corporation or any of them. Section 7.32(a) validates virtually all types of shareholder agreements that, in practice, normally concern shareholders and their advisors.

Given the breadth of section 7.32(a), any provision that may be contained in the articles of incorporation with a majority vote under sections 2.02(b)(2)(ii) and (iii), as well as under section 2.02(b)(4), may also be effective if contained in a shareholder agreement that complies with section 7.32.

The provisions of a shareholder agreement authorized by section 7.32(a) will often, in operation, conflict with the literal language of more than one section of the Act, and courts should in such cases construe all related sections of the Act flexibly and in a manner consistent with the underlying intent of the shareholder agreement. Thus, for example, in the case of an agreement that provides for weighted voting by directors, every reference in the Act to a majority or other proportion of directors should be construed to refer to a majority or other proportion of the votes of the directors.

While the outer limits of the catch-all provision of subsection 7.32(a)(8) are left uncertain, there are provisions of the Model Act that cannot be overridden by resort to the catch-all. Subsection (a)(8), introduced by the term "otherwise," is intended to be read in context with the preceding seven subsections and to be subject to a *ejusdem generis* rule of construction. Thus, in defining the outer limits, courts should consider whether the variation from the Model Act under consideration is similar to the variations permitted by the first seven subsections. Subsection (a)(8) is also subject to a public policy limitation, intended to give courts express authority to restrict the scope of the catch-all where there are substantial issues of public policy at stake. For example, a shareholder agreement that provides that the directors of the corporation have no duties of care or loyalty to the corporation or the shareholders would not be within the purview of section 7.32(a)(8), because it is not sufficiently similar to the types of arrangements suggested by the first seven subsections of section 7.32(a) and because such a provision could be viewed as contrary to a public policy of substantial importance. Similarly, a provision that exculpates directors from liability more broadly than permitted by section 2.02(b)(4) likely would not be validated under section 7.32, because, as the Official Comment to section 2.02(b)(4) states, there are serious public policy reasons which support the few limitations that remain on the right to exculpate directors from liability. Further development of the outer limits is left, however, for the courts.

As noted above, shareholder agreements otherwise validated by section 7.32 are not legally binding on the state, on creditors, or on other third parties. For example, an agreement that dispenses with the need to make corporate filings required by the Act would be ineffective. Similarly, an agreement among shareholders that provides that only the president has authority to enter into contracts for the corporation would not, without more, be binding against third parties, and ordinary principles of agency, including the concept of apparent authority, would continue to apply.

2. Section 7.32(b) ...

Section 7.32(b) requires unanimous shareholder approval regardless of entitlement to vote. Unanimity is required because an agreement authorized by section 7.32 can effect material organic changes in the corporation's operation and structure, and in the rights and obligations of shareholders....

3. Section 7.32(c)

Section 7.32(c) addresses the effect of a shareholder agreement on subsequent purchasers or transferees of shares. Typically, corporations with shareholder agreements also have restrictions on the transferability of the shares as authorized by section 6.27 of the Model Act, thus lessening the practical effects of the problem in the context of voluntary transferees. Transferees of shares without knowledge of the agreement or those acquiring shares upon the death of an original participant in a close corporation may, however, be heavily impacted. Weighing the burdens on transferees against the burdens on the remaining shareholders in the enterprise, section 7.32(c) affirms the continued validity of the shareholder agreement on all transferees, whether by purchase, gift, operation of law, or otherwise. Unlike restrictions on transfer, it may be impossible to enforce a shareholder agreement against less than all of the shareholders. Thus, under section 7.32, one who inherits shares subject to a shareholder agreement must continue to abide by the agreement. If that is not the desired result, care must be exercised at the initiation of the shareholder agreement to ensure a different outcome, such as providing for a buy-back upon death.

Where shares are transferred to a purchaser without knowledge of a shareholder agreement, the validity of the agreement is similarly unaffected, but the purchaser is afforded a rescission remedy against the seller....

Section 7.32(c) contains an affirmative requirement that the share certificate or information statement for the shares be legended to note the existence of a shareholder agreement. No specified form of legend is required, and a simple statement that "[t]he shares represented by this certificate are subject to a shareholder agreement" is sufficient. At that point a purchaser must obtain a copy of the shareholder agreement from his transferor or proceed at his peril. In the event a corporation fails to legend share certificates or information statements, a court may, in an appropriate case, imply a cause of action against the corporation in favor of an injured purchaser without knowledge of a shareholder agreement. The circumstances under which such a remedy would be implied, the proper measure of damages, and other attributes of and limitations on such an implied remedy are left to development in the courts.

If the purchaser has no actual knowledge of a shareholder agreement, and is not charged with knowledge by virtue of a legend on the certificate or information statement, he has a rescission remedy against his transferor (which would be the corporation in the case of a new issue of shares). While the statutory rescission remedy provided in subsection (c) is nonexclusive, it is intended to be a purchaser's primary remedy. . . .

4. Section 7.32(d)

Section 7.32(d) contains a self-executing termination provision for a shareholder agreement when the shares of the corporation become publicly held. The statutory norms in the Model Act become more necessary and appropriate as the number of shareholders increases, as there is greater opportunity to acquire or dispose of an investment in the corporation, and as there is less opportunity for negotiation over the terms under which the enterprise will be conducted. Given that section 7.32 requires unanimity, however, in most cases a practical limit on the availability of a shareholder agreement will be reached before a public market develops. Subsection (d), coupled with a parallel change in section 8.01, rejects the use of an absolute number of shareholders in determining when the shelter of section 7.32 is lost. . . .

Subchapter D

Derivative Proceedings . . .

§ 7.40 Subchapter Definitions

In this subchapter:

(1) "Derivative proceeding" means a civil suit in the right of a domestic corporation or, to the extent provided in section 7.47, in the right of a foreign corporation.

(2) "Shareholder" includes a beneficial owner whose shares are held in a voting trust or held by a nominee on the beneficial owner's behalf.

Official Comment

The definition of "derivative proceeding" makes it clear that the subchapter applies to foreign corporations only to the extent provided in section 7.47. Section 7.47 provides that the law of the jurisdiction of incorporation governs except for sections 7.43 (stay of proceedings), 7.45 (discontinuance or settlement) and 7.46 (payment of expenses). See the Official Comment to section 7.47.

The definition of "shareholder", which applies only to subchapter D, includes all beneficial owners and therefore goes beyond the definition in section 1.40(22) which includes only record holders and beneficial owners who are certified by a nominee pursuant to the procedure specified in section 7.23. Similar definitions are found in section 13.01 (dissenters' rights) and section 16.02(f) (inspection of records by a shareholder). In the context of subchapter D, beneficial owner means a person having a direct economic interest in the shares. The definition is not intended to adopt the broad definition of beneficial ownership in SEC rule 13d–2 under the Securities Exchange Act of 1934 which includes persons with the right to vote or dispose of the shares even though they have no economic interest in them.

§ 7.41   Standing

A shareholder may not commence or maintain a derivative proceeding unless the shareholder:

(1) was a shareholder of the corporation at the time of the act or omission complained of or became a shareholder through transfer by operation of law from one who was a shareholder at that time; and

(2) fairly and adequately represents the interests of the corporation in enforcing the right of the corporation.

Official Comment...

Section 7.41 requires the plaintiff to be a shareholder and therefore does not permit creditors or holders of options, warrants, or conversion rights to commence a derivative proceeding.

Section 7.41(2) follows the requirement of Federal Rule of Civil Procedure 23.1 with the exception that the plaintiff must fairly and adequately represent the interests of *the corporation* rather than *shareholders similarly situated* as provided in the rule. The clarity of the rule's language in this regard has been questioned by the courts. See Nolen v. Shaw-Walker Company, 449 F.2d 506, 508 n. 4 (6th Cir.1971). Furthermore, it is believed that the reference to the corporation in section 7.41(2) more properly reflects the nature of the derivative suit.

The introductory language of section 7.41 refers both to the commencement and maintenance of the proceeding to make it clear that the proceeding should be dismissed if, after commencement, the plaintiff ceases to be a shareholder or a fair and adequate representative. The latter would occur, for example, if the plaintiff were using the proceeding for personal advantage. If a plaintiff no longer has standing, courts have in a number of instances provided an opportunity for one or more other shareholders to intervene.

§ 7.42   Demand

No shareholder may commence a derivative proceeding until:

(1) a written demand has been made upon the corporation to take suitable action; and

(2) 90 days have expired from the date the demand was made unless the shareholder has earlier been notified that the demand has been rejected by the corporation or unless irreparable injury to the corporation would result by waiting for the expiration of the 90 day period.

Official Comment

Section 7.42 requires a written demand on the corporation in all cases. The demand must be made at least 90 days before commencement of suit unless irreparable injury to the corporation would result. This approach has been adopted for two reasons. First, even though no director may be independent, the demand will give the board of directors the opportunity to reexamine the act complained of in the light of a potential lawsuit and take corrective action. Secondly, the provision eliminates the time and expense of the litigants and the court involved in litigating the question whether demand is required. It is believed that requiring a demand in all cases does not impose an onerous burden since a relatively short waiting period of 90 days is provided and this period may be shortened if irreparable injury to the corporation would result by waiting for the expiration of the 90 day period. Moreover, the cases in which demand is excused are relatively rare. Many plaintiffs' counsel as a matter of practice make a demand in all cases rather than litigate the issue whether demand is excused.

1. Form of Demand

Section 7.42 specifies only that the demand shall be in writing. The demand should, however, set forth the facts concerning share ownership and be sufficiently specific to apprise the corporation of the action sought to be taken and the grounds for that action so that the demand can be evaluated. See Allison v. General Motors Corp., 604 F.Supp. 1106, 1117 (D. Del.1985). Detailed pleading is not required since the corporation can contact the shareholder for clarification if there are any questions. In keeping with the spirit of this section, the specificity of the demand should not become a new source of dilatory motions.

2. Upon Whom Demand Should Be Made

Section 7.42 states that demand shall be made upon the corporation. Reference is not made specifically to the board of directors as in previous section 7.40(b) since there may be instances, such as a decision to sue a third party for an injury to the corporation, in which the taking of, or refusal to take, action would fall within the authority of an officer of the corporation. Nevertheless, it is expected that in most cases the board of directors will be the appropriate body to review the demand.

To ensure that the demand reaches the appropriate person for review, it should be addressed to the board of directors, chief executive officer or corporate secretary of the corporation at its principal office.

3.   The 90 Day Period...

Two exceptions are provided to the 90 day waiting period. The first exception is the situation where the shareholder has been notified of the rejection of the demand prior to the end of the 90 days. The second exception is where irreparable injury to the corporation would otherwise result if the commencement of the proceeding is delayed for the 90 day period. The standard to be applied is intended to be the same as that governing the entry of a preliminary injunction. Compare Gimbel v. Signal Cos., 316 A.2d 599 (Del. Ch.1974) with Gelco Corp. v. Coniston Partners, 811 F.2d 414 (8th Cir.1987). Other factors may also be considered such as the possible expiration of the statute of limitations although this would depend on the period of time during which the shareholder was aware of the grounds for the proceeding.

It should be noted that the shareholder bringing suit does not necessarily have to be the person making the demand. Only one demand need be made in order for the corporation to consider whether to take corrective action.

4.   Response by the Corporation

There is no obligation on the part of the corporation to respond to the demand. However, if the corporation, after receiving the demand, decides to institute litigation or, after a derivative proceeding has commenced, decides to assume control of the litigation, the shareholder's right to commence or control the proceeding ends unless it can be shown that the corporation will not adequately pursue the matter....

§ 7.43   Stay of Proceedings

If the corporation commences an inquiry into the allegations made in the demand or complaint, the court may stay any derivative proceeding for such period as the court deems appropriate.

Official Comment

Section 7.43 provides that if the corporation undertakes an inquiry, the court may in its discretion stay the proceeding for such period as the court deems appropriate. This might occur where the complaint is filed 90 days after demand but the inquiry into the matters raised by the demand has not been completed or where a demand has not been investigated but the corporation commences the inquiry after the complaint has been filed. In either case, it is expected that the court will monitor the course of the inquiry to ensure that it is proceeding expeditiously and in good faith.

§ 7.44 Dismissal

(a) A derivative proceeding shall be dismissed by the court on motion by the corporation if one of the groups specified in subsections (b) or (f) has determined in good faith after conducting a reasonable inquiry upon which its conclusions are based that the maintenance of the derivative proceeding is not in the best interests of the corporation.

(b) Unless a panel is appointed pursuant to subsection (f), the determination in subsection (a) shall be made by:

    (1) a majority vote of independent directors present at a meeting of the board of directors if the independent directors constitute a quorum; or

    (2) a majority vote of a committee consisting of two or more independent directors appointed by majority vote of independent directors present at a meeting of the board of directors, whether or not such independent directors constituted a quorum.

(c) None of the following shall by itself cause a director to be considered not independent for purposes of this section:

    (1) the nomination or election of the director by persons who are defendants in the derivative proceeding or against whom action is demanded;

    (2) the naming of the director as a defendant in the derivative proceeding or as a person against whom action is demanded; or

    (3) the approval by the director of the act being challenged in the derivative proceeding or demand if the act resulted in no personal benefit to the director.

(d) If a derivative proceeding is commenced after a determination has been made rejecting a demand by a shareholder, the complaint shall allege with particularity facts establishing either (1) that a majority of the board of directors did not consist of independent directors at the time the determination was made or (2) that the requirements of subsection (a) have not been met.

(e) If a majority of the board of directors does not consist of independent directors at the time the determination is made, the corporation shall have the burden of proving that the requirements of subsection (a) have been met. If a majority of the board of directors consists of independent directors at the time the determination is made, the plaintiff shall have the burden of proving that the requirements of subsection (a) have not been met.

(f) The court may appoint a panel of one or more independent persons upon motion by the corporation to make a determination whether the maintenance of the derivative proceeding is in the best interests of the corporation. In such case, the plaintiff shall have the burden of proving that the requirements of subsection (a) have not been met.

Official Comment . . .

1. The Persons Making the Determination

Section 7.44(b) prescribes the persons by whom the determination in subsection (a) may be made. The subsection provides that the determination may be made by a majority vote of independent directors if there is a quorum of independent directors, or by a committee of independent directors. These provisions parallel the mechanics for determining entitlement to indemnification in section 8.55 of the Model Act except that clause (2) provides that the committee of independent directors shall be appointed by a vote of the independent directors only, rather than the entire board. In this respect this clause is an exception to section 8.25 of the Model Act which requires the approval of at least a majority of all the directors in office to create a committee and appoint members. This approach has been taken to respond to the criticism expressed in a few cases that special litigation committees suffer from a structural bias because of their appointment by vote of non-independent directors. See Hasan v. CleveTrust Realty Investors, 729 F.2d 372, 376–77 (6th Cir.1984).

The decisions which have examined the qualifications of directors making the determination have required that they be both "disinterested" in the sense of not having a personal interest in the transaction being challenged as opposed to a benefit which devolves upon the corporation or all shareholders generally, and "independent" in the sense of not being influenced in favor of the defendants by reason of personal or other relationships. See, e.g., Aronson v. Lewis, 473 A.2d 805, 812–16 (Del.1984). Only the word "independent" has been used in section 7.44(b) because it is believed that this word necessarily also includes the requirement that a person have no interest in the transaction. The concept of an independent director is not intended to be limited to non-officer or "outside" directors but may in appropriate circumstances include directors who are also officers.

Many of the special litigation committees involved in the reported cases consisted of directors who were elected after the alleged wrongful acts by the directors who were named as defendants in the action. Subsection (c)(1) makes it clear that the participation of non-independent directors or shareholders in the nomination or election of a new director shall not prevent the new director from being considered independent. This sentence therefore rejects the concept that the mere appointment of new directors by the non-independent directors makes the new directors not independent in making the necessary determination because of an inherent structural bias. Clauses (2) and (3) also confirm the decisions by a number of courts that the mere fact that a director has been named as a defendant or approved the action being challenged does not cause the director to be considered not independent.

See Aronson v. Lewis, 473 A.2d 805, 816 (Del.1984); Lewis v. Graves, 701 F.2d 245 (2d Cir.1983). It is believed that a court will be able to assess any actual bias in deciding whether the director is independent without any presumption arising out of the method of the director's appointment, the mere naming of the director as a defendant or the director's approval of the act where the director received no personal benefit from the transaction. . . .

2. Standard to Be Applied

Section 7.44(a) requires that the determination be made by the appropriate persons in good faith after conducting a reasonable inquiry upon which their conclusions are based. The word "inquiry" rather than "investigation" has been used to make it clear that the scope of the inquiry will depend upon the issues raised and the knowledge of the group making the determination with respect to the issues. In some cases, the issues may be so simple or the knowledge of the group so extensive that little additional inquiry is required. In other cases, the group may need to engage counsel and other professionals to make an investigation and assist the group in its evaluation of the issues.

The phrase "in good faith" modifies both the determination and the inquiry. The test, which is also included in sections 8.30 (general standards of conduct for directors) and 8.51 (authority to indemnify), is a subjective one, meaning "honestly or in an honest manner." The Corporate Director's Guidebook, 33 Bus.Law. 1595, 1601 (1978). As stated in Abella v. Universal Leaf Tobacco Co., 546 F.Supp. 795, 800 (E.D.Va.1982), "the inquiry intended by this phrase goes to the spirit and sincerity with which the investigation was conducted, rather than the reasonableness of its procedures or basis for conclusions."

The phrase "upon which its conclusions are based" requires that the inquiry and the conclusions follow logically. This provision authorizes the court to examine the determination to ensure that it has some support in the findings of the inquiry. The burden of convincing the court about this issue lies with whichever party has the burden under section 7.44(e). This phrase does not require the persons making the determination to prepare a written report that sets forth their determination and the bases therefor, since circumstances will vary as to the need for such a report. There may, however, be many instances where good corporate practice will commend such a procedure.

Section 7.44 is not intended to modify the general standards of conduct for directors set forth in section 8.30 of the Model Act, but rather to make those standards somewhat more explicit in the derivative proceeding context. In this regard, the independent directors making the determination would be entitled to rely on information and reports from other persons in accordance with section 8.30(b).

Section 7.44 is similar in several respects and differs in certain other respects from the law as it has developed in Delaware and been followed in a number of other states. Under the Delaware cases, the role of the court in reviewing the board's determination varies depending upon whether the plaintiff is in a demand required or demand excused situation. Demand is excused only if the plaintiff pleads particularized facts that create a reasonable doubt that a majority of directors at the time demand would be made are independent or disinterested, or alternatively, that the challenged transaction was the product of a valid exercise of business judgment by the approving board. Aronson v. Lewis, 473 A.2d 805, 814 (Del.1984); Pogostin v. Rice, 480 A.2d 619, 624 (Del.1984). If the plaintiff fails to make either of these two showings, demand is required. Since the *Aronson* requirements are difficult to satisfy, the plaintiff normally must make demand on the board.

In the unusual case where the plaintiff's demand is excused under either of the *Aronson* tests, the plaintiff has standing to bring the derivative suit. If the corporation seeks to reassert its right to control the litigation, the corporation will form a special litigation committee to determine if the litigation is in the best interests of the corporation. If the corporation files a motion to dismiss the litigation based upon the recommendation of the special committee, Delaware law requires the corporation to bear the burden of proving the independence of the committee, the reasonableness of its investigation, and the reasonableness of the bases of its decision reflected in the motion. Zapata Corp. v. Maldonado, 430 A.2d 779 (Del.1981). *Zapata* also permits the court a discretionary second step to review the special committee's decision by invoking the court's "independent business judgment." Id. at 789.

In the usual scenario where demand is not excused, the shareholder must demand that the board take action and the *Zapata* principles do not apply. The board or special committee of independent directors decides whether the corporation should take the action the shareholder requests or respond in some other way. As in the case of all board decisions, the board's response to the shareholder's demand is presumptively protected by the traditional business judgment rule. Allison v. General Motors Corp., 604 F.Supp. 1106, 1122 (D.Del.1985). As a result, the shareholder in filing suit bears the normal burden of creating by particularized pleadings a reasonable doubt that the board's response to the demand was wrongful. Levine v. Smith, C.A. No. 8833, n. 5 (Del.Ch. Nov. 27, 1989) (available on LEXIS). The plaintiff must allege with particularity a lack of good faith, care, independence or disinterestedness by the directors in responding to the demand.

In contrast to Delaware's approach, some jurisdictions have adopted uniform tests to judge both demand required and demand excused situations. For example, in New York judicial review is always limited to an analysis of the independence and good faith of the board or committee and the reasonableness of its investigation; the court does not examine the reasonableness of the bases for the board's decision, nor does the court have the discretionary authority to use its independent business judgment. Auerbach v. Bennett, 47 N.Y.2d 619, 633–34, 419 N.Y.S.2d 920, 928–29, 393 N.E.2d 994, 1002–03 (1979). In contrast, the North Carolina Supreme Court has interpreted that state's statutory provisions on derivative actions as requiring the application of the *Zapata* criteria in both demand required and demand excused cases. Alford v. Shaw, [320 N.C. 465], 358 S.E.2d 323, 327 (1987).

Since section 7.42 requires demand in all cases, the distinction between demand excused and demand required cases does not apply. Subsections (d) and (e) of section 7.44 carry forward the distinction, however, by establishing pleading rules and allocating the burden of proof depending on whether there is a majority of independent directors. Subsection (d), like Delaware law, assigns the plaintiff the threshold burden of alleging facts establishing that a majority of the board is not independent. If there is an independent majority, the burden remains with the plaintiff to plead and establish that the requirements of section 7.44(a) have not been met. If there is no independent majority, the burden is on the corporation on the issues delineated in section 7.44(a). In this case, the corporation must prove both the independence of the decisionmakers and the propriety of the inquiry and determination.

Subsections (d) and (e) of section 7.44 thus follow the first *Aronson* standard in allocating the burden of proof depending on whether the majority of the board is independent. The Committee decided, however, not to adopt the second *Aronson* standard for excusing demand (and thus shifting the burden to the corporation) based on whether the decision of the board that decided the challenged transaction is protected by the business judgment rule. The Committee believes that the only appropriate concern in the context of derivative litigation is whether the board considering the demand has a disabling conflict. See Starrels v. First Nat'l Bank, 870 F.2d 1168, 1172–76 (7th Cir.1989) (Easterbrook, J., concurring).

Thus, the burden of proving that the requirements of 7.44(a) have not been met will remain with the plaintiff in several situations. First, in subsection (b)(1), the burden of proof will generally remain with the plaintiff since the subsection requires a quorum of independent directors and a quorum is normally a majority. See § 8.24. The burden will also remain with the plaintiff if there is a majority of independent directors which appoints the committee under subsection (b)(2). Under section 7.44(f), the burden of proof also remains with the plaintiff in the case of a determination by a panel appointed by the court.

The burden of proof will shift to the corporation, however, where a majority of directors is not independent, and the determination is made by the group specified in subsection (b)(2). It can be argued that, if the directors making the determination under subsection (b)(2) are independent and have been delegated full responsibility for making the decision, the composition of the entire board is irrelevant. This argument is buttressed by the section's method of appointing the group specified in subsection (b)(2) since subsection (b)(2) departs from the general method of appointing committees and allows only independent directors, rather than a majority of the entire board, to appoint the committee which will make the determination. Nevertheless, despite the argument that the composition of the board is irrelevant in these circumstances, the Committee adopted the provisions of subsections (b)(2) and (e) of section 7.44 to respond to concerns of structural bias.

Finally, section 7.44 does not authorize the court to review the reasonableness of the determination. As discussed above, the phrase in section 7.44(a) "upon which its conclusions are based" limits judicial review to whether the determination has some support in the findings of the inquiry.

3. Pleading

Former section 7.40(b) provided that the complaint in a derivative proceeding must allege with particularity whether demand has been made on the board of directors and the board's response or why demand was excused. This requirement is similar to rule 23.1 of the Federal Rules of Civil Procedure. Since demand is now required in all cases, this provision is no longer necessary.

Subsection (d) sets forth a modified pleading rule to cover the typical situation where plaintiff makes demand on the board, the board rejects that demand, and the plaintiff commences an action. In that scenario, in order to state a cause of action, subsection (d) requires the complaint to allege facts with particularity demonstrating either (1) that no majority of independent directors exists or (2) why the determination does not meet the standards in subsection (a). Discovery is available to the plaintiff only after the plaintiff has successfully stated a cause of action by making either of these two showings.

§ 7.45 Discontinuance or Settlement

A derivative proceeding may not be discontinued or settled without the court's approval. If the court determines that a proposed discontinuance or settlement will substantially affect the interests of the corporation's shareholders or a class of shareholders, the court shall direct that notice be given to the shareholders affected.

Official Comment

Unlike the statutes of some states, section 7.45 does not address the issue of which party should bear the cost of giving this notice. That is a matter left to the discretion of the court reviewing the proposed settlement.

§ 7.46 Payment of Expenses

On termination of the derivative proceeding the court may:

(1) order the corporation to pay the plaintiff's reasonable expenses (including counsel fees) incurred in the proceeding if it finds that the proceeding has resulted in a substantial benefit to the corporation;

(2) order the plaintiff to pay any defendant's reasonable expenses (including counsel fees) incurred in defending the proceeding if it finds that the proceeding was commenced or maintained without reasonable cause or for an improper purpose; or

(3) order a party to pay an opposing party's reasonable expenses (including counsel fees) incurred because of the filing of a pleading, motion or other paper, if it finds that the pleading, motion or other paper was not well grounded in fact, after reasonable inquiry, or warranted by existing law or a good faith argument for the extension, modification or reversal of existing law and was interposed for an improper purpose, such as to harass or to cause unnecessary delay or needless increase in the cost of litigation.

§ 7.47 Applicability to Foreign Corporations

In any derivative proceeding in the right of a foreign corporation, the matters covered by this subchapter shall be governed by the laws of the jurisdiction of incorporation of the foreign corporation except for sections 7.43, 7.45, and 7.46.

Chapter 8

DIRECTORS AND OFFICERS

Subchapter A

Board of Directors

§ 8.01 Requirement for and Duties of Board of Directors

(a) Except as provided in section 7.32, each corporation must have a board of directors.

(b) All corporate powers shall be exercised by or under the authority of, and the business and affairs of the corporation managed under the direction of, its board of directors, subject to any limitation set forth in the articles of incorporation or in an agreement authorized under section 7.32.

Official Comment

Section 8.01 requires that every corporation have a board of directors except that a corporation with a shareholder agreement authorized by section 7.32 may dispense with or limit the authority of the board of directors.

Obviously, some form of governance is necessary for every corporation. The board of directors is the traditional form of corporate governance but it need not be the exclusive form. Patterns of management may also be tailored to specific needs in connection with family controlled enterprises, wholly or partially owned subsidiaries, or corporate joint ventures through a shareholder agreement under section 7.32.

Under section 7.32, an agreement among all shareholders can provide for a nontraditional form of corporate governance until there is a regular market for the corporation's shares .... As the number of shareholders increases and a market for the shares develops, there is (i) an opportunity for unhappy shareholders to dispose of shares—a "market out," (ii) a correlative opportunity for others to acquire shares with related expectations regarding the applicability of the statutory norms of governance, and (iii) no real opportunity to negotiate over the terms upon which the enterprise will be conducted.... If a corporation does not have a shareholders agreement that satisfies the requirements of section 7.32 or a market exists for its shares as specified in section 7.32, it must adopt the traditional board of directors as its sole form of governance....

§ 8.02   Qualifications of Directors

The articles of incorporation or bylaws may prescribe qualifications for directors. A director need not be a resident of this state or a shareholder of the corporation unless the articles of incorporation or bylaws so prescribe.

§ 8.03   Number and Election of Directors

(a) A board of directors must consist of one or more individuals, with the number specified in or fixed in accordance with the articles of incorporation or bylaws.

(b) If a board of directors has power to fix or change the number of directors, the board may increase or decrease by 30 percent or less the number of directors last approved by the shareholders, but only the shareholders may increase or decrease by more than 30 percent the number of directors last approved by the shareholders.

(c) The articles of incorporation or bylaws may establish a variable range for the size of the board of directors by fixing a minimum and maximum number of directors. If a variable range is established, the number of directors may be fixed or changed from time to time, within the minimum and maximum, by the shareholders or the board of directors. After shares are issued, only the shareholders may change the range for the size of the board or change from a fixed to a variable-range size board or vice versa.

(d) Directors are elected at the first annual shareholders' meeting and at each annual meeting thereafter unless their terms are staggered under section 8.06.

§ 8.04 Election of Directors by Certain Classes of Shareholders

If the articles of incorporation authorize dividing the shares into classes, the articles may also authorize the election of all or a specified number of directors by the holders of one or more authorized classes of shares. A class (or classes) of shares entitled to elect one or more directors is a separate voting group for purposes of the election of directors.

Official Comment

Section 8.04 makes explicit that the articles of incorporation may provide that a specified number (or all) of the directors may be elected by the holders of one or more classes of shares. This approach is widely used in closely held corporations to effect an agreed upon allocation of control, for example, to ensure minority representation on the board of directors by issuing to that minority a class of shares entitled to elect one or more directors. A class (or classes) of shares entitled to elect separately one or more directors constitutes a separate voting group for purposes of the election of directors; within each voting group directors are elected by a plurality of votes and quorum and voting requirements must be separately met by each voting group. See sections 7.25, 7.26, and 7.28.

§ 8.05 Terms of Directors Generally

(a) The terms of the initial directors of a corporation expire at the first shareholders' meeting at which directors are elected.

(b) The terms of all other directors expire at the next annual shareholders' meeting following their election unless their terms are staggered under section 8.06.

(c) A decrease in the number of directors does not shorten an incumbent director's term.

(d) The term of a director elected to fill a vacancy expires at the next shareholders' meeting at which directors are elected.

(e) Despite the expiration of a director's term, he continues to serve until his successor is elected and qualifies or until there is a decrease in the number of directors.

§ 8.06 Staggered Terms for Directors

If there are nine or more directors, the articles of incorporation may provide for staggering their terms by dividing the total number of directors into two or three groups, with each group containing one half or one-third of the total, as near as may be. In that event, the terms of directors in the first group expire at the first annual shareholders' meeting after their election, the terms of the second group expire at the second annual shareholders' meeting after their election, and the terms of the third group, if any, expire at the third annual shareholders' meeting after their election. At each annual shareholders' meeting held thereafter, directors shall be chosen for a term of two years or three years, as the case may be, to succeed those whose terms expire.

§ 8.07   Resignation of Directors

(a) A director may resign at any time by delivering written notice to the board of directors, its chairman, or to the corporation.

(b) A resignation is effective when the notice is delivered unless the notice specifies a later effective date.

§ 8.08   Removal of Directors by Shareholders

(a) The shareholders may remove one or more directors with or without cause unless the articles of incorporation provide that directors may be removed only for cause.

(b) If a director is elected by a voting group of shareholders, only the shareholders of that voting group may participate in the vote to remove him.

(c) If cumulative voting is authorized, a director may not be removed if the number of votes sufficient to elect him under cumulative voting is voted against his removal. If cumulative voting is not authorized, a director may be removed only if the number of votes cast to remove him exceeds the number of votes cast not to remove him.

(d) A director may be removed by the shareholders only at a meeting called for the purpose of removing him and the meeting notice must state that the purpose, or one of the purposes, of the meeting is removal of the director.

§ 8.09   Removal of Directors by Judicial Proceeding

(a) The [name or describe] court of the county where a corporation's principal office (or, if none in this state, its registered office) is located may remove a director of the corporation from office in a proceeding commenced either by the corporation or by its shareholders holding at least 10 percent of the outstanding shares of any class if the court finds that (1) the director engaged in fraudulent or dishonest conduct, or gross abuse of authority or discretion, with respect to the corporation and (2) removal is in the best interest of the corporation.

(b) The court that removes a director may bar the director from reelection for a period prescribed by the court.

(c) If shareholders commence a proceeding under subsection (a), they shall make the corporation a party defendant.

Official Comment

Section 8.09 authorizes the removal of a director who is found in a judicial proceeding to have engaged in fraudulent or dishonest conduct or gross abuse of office. For example, a judicial proceeding (as contrasted with removal under section 8.08) may be necessary or appropriate in the following situations:

(1) In a closely held corporation, the director charged with misconduct is elected by voting group or cumulative voting, and the shareholders with power to prevent his removal exercise that power despite the existence of fraudulent or dishonest conduct. The classic example is where the director charged with misconduct himself possesses sufficient votes to prevent his own removal and exercises his voting power to that end.

(2) In a publicly held corporation, the director charged with misconduct declines to resign, though urged to do so, and because of the large number of widely scattered shareholders, a special shareholders' meeting can be held only after a period of delay and at considerable expense.

A shareholder who owns less than 10 percent of the outstanding shares of the corporation may bring suit derivatively in the name of the corporation under this section upon compliance with the requirements of section 7.40. A shareholder who owns at least 10 percent of the outstanding shares of the corporation may maintain suit in his own name and in his own right without compliance with section 7.40. The corporation, however, must be made a party to the proceeding. See section 8.09(c).

The purpose of section 8.09 is to permit the prompt and efficient elimination of dishonest directors. It is not intended to permit judicial resolution of internal corporate struggles for control except in those cases in which a court finds that the director has been guilty of wrongful conduct of the type described.

§ 8.10 Vacancy on Board

(a) Unless the articles of incorporation provide otherwise, if a vacancy occurs on a board of directors, including a vacancy resulting from an increase in the number of directors:

(1) the shareholders may fill the vacancy;

(2) the board of directors may fill the vacancy; or

(3) if the directors remaining in office constitute fewer than a quorum of the board, they may fill the vacancy by the affirmative vote of a majority of all the directors remaining in office.

(b) If the vacant office was held by a director elected by a voting group of shareholders, only the holders of shares of that voting group are entitled to vote to fill the vacancy if it is filled by the shareholders.

(c) A vacancy that will occur at a specific later date (by reason of a resignation effective at a later date under section 8.07(b) or otherwise) may be filled before the vacancy occurs but the new director may not take office until the vacancy occurs.

Official Comment

Section 8.10(a)(3) allows the directors remaining in office to fill vacancies even though they are fewer than a quorum. The test for the exercise of this power is whether the directors remaining in office are fewer than a quorum, not whether the directors seeking to act are fewer than a quorum. For example, on a board of six directors where a quorum is four, if there are two vacancies, they may not be filled under section 8.10(a)(3) at a "meeting" attended by only three directors. Even though the three directors are fewer than a quorum, section 8.10(a)(3) is not applicable because the number of directors remaining in office—four—is not fewer than a quorum. . . .

§ 8.11   Compensation of Directors

Unless the articles of incorporation or bylaws provide otherwise, the board of directors may fix the compensation of directors.

Subchapter B

Meetings and Action of the Board

§ 8.20   Meetings

(a) The board of directors may hold regular or special meetings in or out of this state.

(b) Unless the articles of incorporation or bylaws provide otherwise, the board of directors may permit any or all directors to participate in a regular or special meeting by, or conduct the meeting through the use of, any means of communication by which all directors participating may simultaneously hear each other during the meeting. A director participating in a meeting by this means is deemed to be present in person at the meeting.

§ 8.21   Action Without Meeting

(a) Unless the articles of incorporation or bylaws provide otherwise, action required or permitted by this Act to be taken at a board of directors' meeting may be taken without a meeting if the action is taken by all members of the board. The action must be evidenced by one or more written consents describing the action taken, signed by each director, and included in the minutes or filed with the corporate records reflecting the action taken.

(b) Action taken under this section is effective when the last director signs the consent, unless the consent specifies a different effective date.

(c) A consent signed under this section has the effect of a meeting vote and may be described as such in any document.

Official Comment

The power of the board of directors to act unanimously without a meeting is based on the pragmatic consideration that in many situations a formal meeting is a waste of time. For example, in a closely held corporation there will often be informal discussion by the manager-owners of the venture before a decision is made. And, of course, if there is only a single director (as is permitted by section 8.03), a written consent is the natural method of signifying director action. Consent may be signified on one or more documents if desirable.

In publicly held corporations, formal meetings of the board of directors may be appropriate for many actions. But there will always be situations where prompt action is necessary and the decision noncontroversial, so that approval without a formal meeting may be appropriate.

Under section 8.21 the requirement of unanimous consent precludes the possibility of stifling or ignoring opposing argument. A director opposed to an action that is proposed to be taken by unanimous consent, or uncertain about the desirability of that action, may compel the holding of a directors' meeting to discuss the matter simply by withholding his consent.

§ 8.22 Notice of Meeting

(a) Unless the articles of incorporation or bylaws provide otherwise, regular meetings of the board of directors may be held without notice of the date, time, place, or purpose of the meeting.

(b) Unless the articles of incorporation or bylaws provide for a longer or shorter period, special meetings of the board of directors must be preceded by at least two days' notice of the date, time, and place of the meeting. The notice need not describe the purpose of the special meeting unless required by the articles of incorporation or bylaws.

§ 8.23 Waiver of Notice

(a) A director may waive any notice required by this Act, the articles of incorporation, or bylaws before or after the date and time stated in the notice. Except as provided by subsection (b), the waiver must be in writing, signed by the director entitled to the notice, and filed with the minutes or corporate records.

(b) A director's attendance at or participation in a meeting waives any required notice to him of the meeting unless the director at the beginning of the meeting (or promptly upon his arrival) objects to holding the meeting or transacting business at the meeting and does not thereafter vote for or assent to action taken at the meeting.

§ 8.24   Quorum and Voting

(a) Unless the articles of incorporation or bylaws require a greater number or unless otherwise specifically provided in this Act, a quorum of a board of directors consists of:

    (1) a majority of the fixed number of directors if the corporation has a fixed board size; or

    (2) a majority of the number of directors prescribed, or if no number is prescribed the number in office immediately before the meeting begins, if the corporation has a variable-range size board.

(b) The articles of incorporation or bylaws may authorize a quorum of a board of directors to consist of no fewer than one-third of the fixed or prescribed number of directors determined under subsection (a).

(c) If a quorum is present when a vote is taken, the affirmative vote of a majority of directors present is the act of the board of directors unless the articles of incorporation or bylaws require the vote of a greater number of directors.

(d) A director who is present at a meeting of the board of directors or a committee of the board of directors when corporate action is taken is deemed to have assented to the action taken unless: (1) he objects at the beginning of the meeting (or promptly upon his arrival) to holding it or transacting business at the meeting; (2) his dissent or abstention from the action taken is entered in the minutes of the meeting; or (3) he delivers written notice of his dissent or abstention to the presiding officer of the meeting before its adjournment or to the corporation immediately after adjournment of the meeting. The right of dissent or abstention is not available to a director who votes in favor of the action taken.

§ 8.25   Committees

(a) Unless the articles of incorporation or bylaws provide otherwise, a board of directors may create one or more committees and appoint members of the board of directors to serve on them. Each committee must have two or more members, who serve at the pleasure of the board of directors.

(b) The creation of a committee and appointment of members to it must be approved by the greater of (1) a majority of all the directors in office when the action is taken or (2) the number of directors required by the articles of incorporation or bylaws to take action under section 8.24.

(c) Sections 8.20 through 8.24, which govern meetings, action without meetings, notice and waiver of notice, and quorum and voting requirements of the board of directors, apply to committees and their members as well.

(d) To the extent specified by the board of directors or in the articles of incorporation or bylaws, each committee may exercise the authority of the board of directors under section 8.01.

(e) A committee may not, however:

(1) authorize distributions;

(2) approve or propose to shareholders action that this Act requires be approved by shareholders;

(3) fill vacancies on the board of directors or on any of its committees;

(4) amend articles of incorporation pursuant to section 10.02;

(5) adopt, amend, or repeal bylaws;

(6) approve a plan of merger not requiring shareholder approval;

(7) authorize or approve reacquisition of shares, except according to a formula or method prescribed by the board of directors; or

(8) authorize or approve the issuance or sale or contract for sale of shares, or determine the designation and relative rights, preferences, and limitations of a class or series of shares, except that the board of directors may authorize a committee (or a senior executive officer of the corporation) to do so within limits specifically prescribed by the board of directors.

(f) The creation of, delegation of authority to, or action by a committee does not alone constitute compliance by a director with the standards of conduct described in section 8.30.

Official Comment

Section 8.25 makes explicit the common law power of a board of directors to act through committees of directors and specifies the powers of the board of directors that are nondelegable, that is, powers that only the full board of directors may exercise. Section 8.25 deals only with committees of the board of directors exercising the functions of the board of directors; the board of directors or management, independently of section 8.25, may establish nonboard committees composed of directors, employees, or others to deal with corporate powers not required to be exercised by the board of directors.

Section 8.25(b) provides that a committee of the board of directors may be created only by the affirmative vote of a majority of the board of directors then in office, or, if greater, by the number of directors required to take action by the articles of incorporation or the bylaws. This supermajority requirement reflects the importance of the decision to invest board committees with power to act under section 8.25.

Committees of the board of directors are assuming increasingly important roles in the governance of publicly held corporations. See "The Corporate Director's Guidebook," 33 Bus.Law. 1591 (1978); "The Overview Committees of the Board of Directors," 35 Bus.Law. 1335 (1980). Executive committees have long provided guidance to management between meetings of the full board of directors. Audit committees also have a long history of performing essential review and control functions on behalf of the board of directors. In recent years nominating and compensation committees, composed primarily or entirely of nonmanagement directors, have also become more widely used by publicly held corporations.

Section 8.25 establishes the desirable and appropriate role of director committees in light of competing considerations: on the one hand, it seems clear that appropriate board committee action is not only desirable but also is likely to improve the functioning of larger and more diffuse boards of directors; on the other hand, wholesale delegation of authority to a board committee, to the point of abdication of director responsibility as a board of directors, is manifestly inappropriate and undesirable. Overbroad delegation also increases the potential, where the board of directors is divided, for usurpation of basic board functions by means of delegation to a committee dominated by one faction....

Section 8.25(e) prohibits delegation of authority with respect to most mergers, sales of substantially all the assets, amendments to articles of incorporation and voluntary dissolution under section 8.25(e)(2) since these require shareholder action.... On the other hand, under section 8.25(e) many actions of a material nature, such as the authorization of long-term debt and capital investment or the pricing of shares, may properly be made the subject of committee delegation.

The statutes of several states make nondelegable certain powers not listed in section 8.25(e)—for example, the power to change the principal corporate office, to appoint or remove officers, to fix director compensation, or to remove agents. These are not prohibited by section 8.25(e) since the whole board of directors may reverse or rescind the committee action taken, if it should wish to do so, without undue risk that implementation of the committee action might be irrevocable or irreversible.

Section 8.25(f) makes clear that although the board of directors may delegate to a committee the authority to take action, the designation of the committee, the delegation of authority to it, and action by the committee will not alone constitute compliance by a noncommittee board member with his responsibility under section 8.30. On the other hand, a noncommittee director also will not automatically incur liability should the action of the particular committee fail to meet the standard of care set out in section 8.30. The noncommittee member's liability in these cases will depend upon whether he failed to comply with section

8.30(b)(3). Factors to be considered in this regard will include the care used in the delegation to and supervision over the committee, and the amount of knowledge regarding the particular matter which the noncommittee director has available to him. Care in delegation and supervision include appraisal of the capabilities and diligence of the committee directors in light of the subject and its relative importance and may be facilitated, in the usual case, by review of minutes and receipt of other reports concerning committee activities. The enumeration of these factors is intended to emphasize that directors may not abdicate their responsibilities and secure exoneration from liability simply by delegating authority to board committees. Rather, a director against whom liability is asserted based upon acts of a committee of which he is not a member avoids liability if the standards contained in section 8.30 are met.

Section 8.25(f) has no application to a member of the committee itself. The standard applicable to a committee member is set forth in section 8.30(a).

Subchapter C

Standards of Conduct

§ 8.30   General Standards for Directors

(a) A director shall discharge his duties as a director, including his duties as a member of a committee:

(1) in good faith;

(2) with the care an ordinarily prudent person in a like position would exercise under similar circumstances; and

(3) in a manner he reasonably believes to be in the best interests of the corporation.

(b) In discharging his duties a director is entitled to rely on information, opinions, reports, or statements, including financial statements and other financial data, if prepared or presented by:

(1) one or more officers or employees of the corporation whom the director reasonably believes to be reliable and competent in the matters presented;

(2) legal counsel, public accountants, or other persons as to matters the director reasonably believes are within the person's professional or expert competence; or

(3) a committee of the board of directors of which he is not a member if the director reasonably believes the committee merits confidence.

(c) A director is not acting in good faith if he has knowledge concerning the matter in question that makes reliance otherwise permitted by subsection (b) unwarranted.

(d) A director is not liable for any action taken as a director, or any failure to take any action, if he performed the duties of his office in compliance with this section.

Official Comment

Section 8.30 defines the general standard of conduct for directors. It sets forth the standard by focusing on the manner in which the director performs his duties, not the correctness of his decisions. Section 8.30(a) thus requires a director to perform his duties in good faith, with the care of an ordinarily prudent person in a like position and in a manner he believes to be in the best interests of the corporation....

Even before statutory formulations of directors' duty of care, courts sometimes invoked the business judgment rule in determining whether to impose liability in a particular case. In doing so, courts have sometimes used language similar to the standards set forth in section 8.30(a). The elements of the business judgment rule and the circumstances for its application are continuing to be developed by the courts. In view of that continuing judicial development, section 8.30 does not try to codify the business judgment rule or to delineate the differences, if any, between that rule and the standards of director conduct set forth in this section. That is a task left to the courts and possibly to later revisions of this Model Act....

1. Section 8.30(a)

Section 8.30(a) establishes a general standard of care for all directors. It requires a director to exercise "the care an ordinarily prudent person in a like position would exercise." Some state statutes use the words "diligence," "care," and "skill" to define this duty. E.g., N.C.Gen.Stat.Ann. § 55–35 (1975). There is very little authority as to what "skill" and "diligence," as distinguished from "care," can be required or properly expected of corporate directors in the performance of their duties. "Skill," in the sense of technical competence in a particular field, should not be a qualification for the office of director. The concept of "diligence" is sufficiently subsumed within the concept of "care." Accordingly, the words "diligence" and "skill" were omitted from the standard adopted.

Likewise, section 8.30 does not use the term "fiduciary" in the standard for directors' conduct, because that term could be confused with the unique attributes and obligations of a fiduciary imposed by the law of trusts, some of which are not appropriate for directors of a corporation.

Several of the phrases chosen to define the general standard of care in section 8.30(a) deserve specific mention.

(1) The reference to "ordinarily prudent person" embodies long traditions of the common law, in contrast to suggested standards that

might call for some undefined degree of expertise, like "ordinarily prudent businessman." The phrase recognizes the need for innovation, essential to profit orientation, and focuses on the basic director attributes of common sense, practical wisdom, and informed judgment.

(2) The phrase "in a like position" recognizes that the "care" under consideration is that which would be used by the "ordinarily prudent person" if he were a director of the particular corporation.

(3) The combined phrase "in a like position ... under similar circumstances" is intended to recognize that (a) the nature and extent of responsibilities will vary, depending upon such factors as the size, complexity, urgency, and location of activities carried on by the particular corporation, (b) decisions must be made on the basis of the information known to the directors without the benefit of hindsight, and (c) the special background, qualifications, and management responsibilities of a particular director may be relevant in evaluating his compliance with the standard of care. Even though the quoted phrase takes into account the special background, qualifications and management responsibilities of a particular director, it does not excuse a director lacking business experience or particular expertise from exercising the common sense, practical wisdom, and informed judgment of an "ordinarily prudent person."

The process by which a director informs himself will vary but the duty of care requires every director to take steps to become informed about the background facts and circumstances before taking action on the matter at hand. In relying upon the performance by management of delegated or assigned duties pursuant to section 8.01 (including, for example, matters of law and legal compliance), the director may depend upon the presumption of regularity, absent knowledge or notice to the contrary. A director may also rely on information, opinions, reports, and statements prepared or presented by others as set forth in section 8.30(b). Furthermore, a director should not be expected to anticipate the problems which the corporation may face except in those circumstances where something has occurred to make it obvious to the director that the corporation should be addressing a particular problem.

2. Section 8.30(b)

A director complying with the standards expressed in section 8.30(a) is entitled to rely upon information, opinions, reports or statements, including financial statements and other financial data, prepared or presented by the persons or committees described in section 8.30(b). The right to rely under this section applies to the entire range of matters for which the board of directors is responsible. Under section 8.30(c), however, a director so relying must be without knowledge concerning the matter in question that would cause his reliance to be unwarranted. Also inherent in the concept of good faith is the requirement that, in order to be entitled to rely on a report, statement, opinion, or other matter, the director must have read the report or statement in question, or have been present at a meeting at which it was orally presented, or have taken other steps to become generally familiar with its contents. In short, the director must comply with the general standard of care of section 8.30(a) in making a judgment as to the reliability and competence of the source of information upon which he proposes to rely.

Section 8.30(b) permits reliance upon outside advisers, including not only those in the professional disciplines customarily supervised by state authorities, such as lawyers, accountants, and engineers, but also those in other fields involving special experience and skills, such as investment bankers, geologists, management consultants, actuaries, and real estate appraisers. The concept of "expert competence" in section 8.30(b)(2) embraces a wide variety of qualifications and is not limited to the more precise and narrower recognition of experts under the Securities Act of 1933. In this respect section 8.30(b) goes beyond any existing state business corporation act, although several state statutes permit reliance on reports of appraisers selected with reasonable care by the board of directors and deal with the scope and nature of corporate reports and records generally.

Section 8.30(b) permits reliance upon a committee of the board of directors when performing a supervisory or other functions in instances where neither the full board of directors nor the committee takes dispositive action. For example, there may be reliance upon an investigation undertaken by a board committee and reported to the full board of directors, which forms the basis for action by the board of directors itself. Another example is reliance upon a committee of the board of directors, such as a corporate audit committee, with respect to the ongoing role of oversight of the accounting and auditing functions of the corporation. . . .

In conditioning reliance upon reasonable belief that the board committee merits the director's "confidence," section 8.30(b)(3) recognizes a difference between a board committee and an expert. In sections 8.30(b)(1) and (2) the reference is to "competence of an expert," which recognizes the expectation of experience and in most instances technical skills on the part of those upon whom the director may rely. In section 8.30(b)(3), the concept of "confidence" is substituted for "competence" in order to avoid any inference that technical skills are a prerequisite. . . .

3.   Section 8.30(c)

Section 8.30(c) expressly prevents a director from "hiding his head in the sand" and relying on information, opinions, reports, or statements when he has actual knowledge which makes reliance unwarranted.

4. Section 8.30(d) ....

Section 8.30(d) makes clear that the section will apply whether or not affirmative action was in fact taken. If the board of directors or a committee considers an issue (such as a recommendation of independent auditors concerning the corporation's internal accounting controls) and determines not to take action, the determination not to act is protected by section 8.30. Similarly, if the board of directors or committee delegates responsibility for handling a matter to subordinates, the delegation constitutes "action" under section 8.30. Section 8.30(d) applies (assuming its requirements are satisfied) to any conscious consideration of matters involving the affairs of the corporation. It also applies to the determination by the board of directors of which matters to address and which not to address. Section 8.30(d) does not apply only when the director has failed to consider taking action which under the circumstances he is obliged to consider taking.

5. Application to Officers

Section 8.30 generally deals only with directors. Section 8.42 and its Official Comment explain the extent to which the provisions of section 8.30 apply to officers.

§ 8.31 Director Conflict of Interest *

(a) A conflict of interest transaction is a transaction with the corporation in which a director of the corporation has a direct or indirect interest. A conflict of interest transaction is not voidable by the corporation solely because of the director's interest in the transaction if any one of the following is true:

   (1) the material facts of the transaction and the director's interest were disclosed or known to the board of directors or a committee of the board of directors and the board of directors or committee authorized, approved, or ratified the transaction;

   (2) the material facts of the transaction and the director's interest were disclosed or known to the shareholders entitled to vote and they authorized, approved, or ratified the transaction; or

   (3) the transaction was fair to the corporation.

(b) For purposes of this section, a director of the corporation has an indirect interest in a transaction if (1) another entity in which he has a material financial interest or in which he is a general partner is a party to the transaction or (2) another entity of which he is a director, officer, or trustee is a party to the transaction and the

---

* Sections 8.31 and 8.32 have been superseded, in the Revised Model Business Corporation Act, by Subchapter F, sections 8.60–8.63, infra. Sections 8.31 and 8.32 are nevertheless included in this Supplement because many states that had adopted sections 8.31 and 8.32 as part of their corporation statutes did not decide to adopt Subchapter F.

transaction is or should be considered by the board of directors of the corporation.

(c) For purposes of subsection (a)(1), a conflict of interest transaction is authorized, approved, or ratified if it receives the affirmative vote of a majority of the directors on the board of directors (or on the committee) who have no direct or indirect interest in the transaction, but a transaction may not be authorized, approved, or ratified under this section by a single director. If a majority of the directors who have no direct or indirect interest in the transaction vote to authorize, approve, or ratify the transaction, a quorum is present for the purpose of taking action under this section. The presence of, or a vote cast by, a director with a direct or indirect interest in the transaction does not affect the validity of any action taken under subsection (a)(1) if the transaction is otherwise authorized, approved, or ratified as provided in that subsection.

(d) For purposes of subsection (a)(2), a conflict of interest transaction is authorized, approved, or ratified if it receives the vote of a majority of the shares entitled to be counted under this subsection. Shares owned by or voted under the control of a director who has a direct or indirect interest in the transaction, and shares owned by or voted under the control of an entity described in subsection (b)(1), may not be counted in a vote of shareholders to determine whether to authorize, approve, or ratify a conflict of interest transaction under subsection (a)(2). The vote of those shares, however, is counted in determining whether the transaction is approved under other sections of this Act. A majority of the shares, whether or not present, that are entitled to be counted in a vote on the transaction under this subsection constitutes a quorum for the purpose of taking action under this section.

Official Comment

1. Conflict of Interest Transactions in General

Section 8.31 deals only with "conflict of interest" transactions by a director with the corporation, that is, transactions in which the director has an interest either (1) directly or (2) indirectly through an entity in which the director has a financial or managerial interest covered by section 8.31(b). A conflict of interest transaction does not include transactions in which the director participates in the transaction only as a shareholder and receives only a proportionate share of the advantage or benefit of the transaction. Section 8.31 deals only with conflict of interest transactions involving directors; it does not address analogous transactions entered into by officers, employees, or substantial or dominating shareholders unless they are also directors.

Section 8.31 rejects the common law view that all conflict of interest transactions entered into by directors are automatically voidable at the option of the corporation without regard to the fairness of the transaction or the manner in which the transaction was approved by the corporation. Section 8.31(a) makes any automatic rule of voidability inapplicable to transactions that are fair or that have been approved by directors or shareholders in the manner provided by the balance of section 8.31. The approval mechanisms set forth in section 8.31(c) and (d) relate only to the elimination of this automatic rule of voidability and do not address the manner in which the transactions must be approved under other sections of this Act. This is made clear by the express limitations in sections 8.31(c) and (d) that they are applicable only "for the purposes of this section" as well as the language of the second and third sentences of section 8.31(d).

The elimination of the automatic rule of voidability does not mean that all transactions that meet one or more of the tests set forth in section 8.31(a) are automatically valid. These transactions may be subject to attack on a variety of grounds independent of section 8.31—for example, that the transaction constituted waste, that it was not authorized by the appropriate corporate body, that it violated other sections of the Model Business Corporation Act, or that it was unenforceable under other common law principles. The sole purpose of section 8.31 is to sharply limit the common law principle of automatic voidability and in this respect section 8.31 follows earlier versions of the Model Act and the statutes of many states dealing with conflict of interest transactions.

2. Requirements for Approval of Conflict of Interest Transactions

Sections 8.31(c) and (d) provide special rules for determining whether the board of directors (or a committee thereof) or the shareholders have authorized, approved, or ratified a conflict of interest transaction so as to bring subsections (a)(1) or (a)(2) into play. Basically, these subsections require the transaction in question to be approved by an absolute majority of the directors (on the board of directors, or on the committee, as the case may be) or shares whose votes may be counted in determining whether the transaction should be authorized, approved, or ratified. If these votes are not obtained the transaction is tested under the fairness test of subsection (a)(3). The vote required for authorization, approval, or ratification of a conflict of interest transaction is more onerous than the standard applicable to normal voting requirements for approval of corporate actions—i.e., that a quorum be present and only the votes of directors or shares present or represented at that meeting be considered—because of the importance of assuring that conflict of interest transactions receive as broad consideration within the corporation as possible if independent review on the basis of fairness is to be avoided. . . .

    b. Consideration by the shareholders. . . .

In some situations, the prohibition of section 8.31(d) will result in the conflict of interest issue being resolved by a majority of a minority of the shares. This will occur, for example, whenever a director who is the majority shareholder of the corporation is interested in a transaction. The vote on the conflict of interest issue under section 8.31, however, must be distinguished from the vote on the approval of the transaction itself under other sections of the Model Act, in which there is no prohibition against the voting of shares owned or controlled by an interested director. For example, if a parent corporation wishes to merge its 60–percent–owned subsidiary into itself, and the majority shareholder of the parent is a director of the subsidiary, the votes of the shares owned by the parent corporation may not be counted under section 8.31(d) (since the shares are owned by an entity which is a party to the transaction and which the director controls). The shares nevertheless may be voted on the merger proposal itself under chapter 11 of the Model Act, and the merger will, of course, normally be approved solely by the vote of the shares owned by the parent corporation. On the other hand, the test of section 8.31(a)(2) is not met unless the transaction is approved by at least a majority of the votes cast by the holders of the 40 percent of the shares not owned by the parent corporation. If this requirement is not met, the transaction may be evaluated under the fairness test of section 8.31(a)(3).

3. Indirect Conflicts of Interest

Section 8.31 is applicable to "indirect" as well as direct conflicts; "indirect" is defined in section 8.31(b) to cover transactions between the corporation and an entity in which the director has a material financial interest or is a general partner. Further, section 8.31(b) covers indirect conflicts where the director is an officer or director of another entity (but does not have a material financial interest in the transaction) if the transaction is of sufficient importance that it is or should be considered by the board of directors of the corporation. The purpose of this last clause is to permit normal business transactions between large business entities that may have a common director to go forward without concern about the technical rules relating to conflict of interest unless the transaction is of such importance that it is or should be considered by the board of directors or the director may be deemed to have a material financial interest in the transaction. Thus, section 8.31 covers transactions between corporations with interlocking or common directors as well as the direct "interested director" transaction.

4. "Fairness" of a Transaction

The fairness of a transaction for purposes of section 8.31 should be evaluated on the basis of the facts and circumstances as they were known or should have been known at the time the transaction was entered into. For example, the terms of a transaction subject to section

8.31 should normally be deemed "fair" if they are within the range that might have been entered into at arm's-length by disinterested persons.

5. An "Interested" Director

The Model Act does not attempt to define precisely when a director should be viewed as "interested" for purposes of participating in the decision to adopt, approve, or ratify a conflict of interest transaction. Section 8.31(b) does, however, define one aspect of this concept—the "indirect" interest. For purposes of section 8.31 a director should normally be viewed as interested in a transaction if he or the immediate members of his family have a financial interest in the transaction or a relationship with the other parties to the transaction such that the relationship might reasonably be expected to affect his judgment in the particular matter in a manner adverse to the corporation.

§ 8.32 Loans to Directors *

(a) Except as provided by subsection (c), a corporation may not lend money to or guarantee the obligation of a director of the corporation unless:

 (1) the particular loan or guarantee is approved by a majority of the votes represented by the outstanding voting shares of all classes, voting as a single voting group, except the votes of shares owned by or voted under the control of the benefited director; or

 (2) the corporation's board of directors determines that the loan or guarantee benefits the corporation and either approves the specific loan or guarantee or a general plan authorizing loans and guarantees.

(b) The fact that a loan or guarantee is made in violation of this section does not affect the borrower's liability on the loan.

(c) This section does not apply to loans and guarantees authorized by statute regulating any special class of corporations.

§ 8.33 Liability for Unlawful Distributions

(a) A director who votes for or assents to a distribution made in violation of section 6.40 or the articles of incorporation is personally liable to the corporation for the amount of the distribution that exceeds what could have been distributed without violating section 6.40 or the articles of incorporation if it is established that he did not perform his duties in compliance with section 8.30. In any proceed-

---

* Sections 8.31 and 8.32 have been superseded, in the Revised Model Business Corporation Act, by Subchapter F, sections 8.60–8.63, infra. Sections 8.31 and 8.32 are nevertheless included in this Supplement because many states that had adopted sections 8.31 and 8.32 as part of their corporation statutes did not decide to adopt Subchapter F.

ing commenced under this section, a director has all of the defenses ordinarily available to a director.

(b) A director held liable under subsection (a) for an unlawful distribution is entitled to contribution:

   (1) from every other director who could be held liable under subsection (a) for the unlawful distribution; and

   (2) from each shareholder for the amount the shareholder accepted knowing the distribution was made in violation of section 6.40 or the articles of incorporation.

(c) A proceeding under this section is barred unless it is commenced within two years after the date on which the effect of the distribution was measured under section 6.40(e) or (g).

Subchapter D

Officers

§ 8.40   Required Officers

(a) A corporation has the officers described in its bylaws or appointed by the board of directors in accordance with the bylaws.

(b) A duly appointed officer may appoint one or more officers or assistant officers if authorized by the bylaws or the board of directors.

(c) The bylaws or the board of directors shall delegate to one of the officers responsibility for preparing minutes of the directors' and shareholders' meetings and for authenticating records of the corporation.

(d) The same individual may simultaneously hold more than one office in a corporation.

§ 8.41   Duties of Officers

Each officer has the authority and shall perform the duties set forth in the bylaws or, to the extent consistent with the bylaws, the duties prescribed by the board of directors or by direction of an officer authorized by the board of directors to prescribe the duties of other officers.

§ 8.42   Standards of Conduct for Officers

(a) An officer with discretionary authority shall discharge his duties under that authority:

   (1) in good faith;

   (2) with the care an ordinarily prudent person in a like position would exercise under similar circumstances; and

   (3) in a manner he reasonably believes to be in the best interests of the corporation.

(b) In discharging his duties an officer is entitled to rely on information, opinions, reports, or statements, including financial statements and other financial data, if prepared or presented by:

(1) one or more officers or employees of the corporation whom the officer reasonably believes to be reliable and competent in the matters presented; or

(2) legal counsel, public accountants, or other persons as to matters the officer reasonably believes are within the person's professional or expert competence.

(c) An officer is not acting in good faith if he has knowledge concerning the matter in question that makes reliance otherwise permitted by subsection (b) unwarranted.

(d) An officer is not liable for any action taken as an officer, or any failure to take any action, if he performed the duties of his office in compliance with this section.

§ 8.43 Resignation and Removal of Officers

(a) An officer may resign at any time by delivering notice to the corporation. A resignation is effective when the notice is delivered unless the notice specifies a later effective date. If a resignation is made effective at a later date and the corporation accepts the future effective date, its board of directors may fill the pending vacancy before the effective date if the board of directors provides that the successor does not take office until the effective date.

(b) A board of directors may remove any officer at any time with or without cause.

§ 8.44 Contract Rights of Officers

(a) The appointment of an officer does not itself create contract rights.

(b) An officer's removal does not affect the officer's contract rights, if any, with the corporation. An officer's resignation does not affect the corporation's contract rights, if any, with the officer.

Subchapter E

Indemnification

Introductory Comment

The provisions for indemnification and advance for expenses of the Model Act are among the most complex and important in the entire Act. Subchapter E of chapter 8 is an integrated treatment of this subject and strikes a balance among important social policies. Its substance is based almost entirely on an amendment to the 1969 Model Act adopted in 1980 and substantially revised in 1994.

1. Policy Issues Raised by Indemnification and Advance for Expenses

Indemnification (including advance for expenses) provides financial protection by the corporation for its directors against exposure to expenses and liabilities that may be incurred by them in connection with legal proceedings based on an alleged breach of duty in their service to or on behalf of the corporation. Today, when both the volume and the cost of litigation have increased dramatically, it would be difficult to persuade responsible persons to serve as directors if they were compelled to bear personally the cost of vindicating the propriety of their conduct in every instance in which it might be challenged. While reasonable people may differ as to what constitutes a meritorious case, almost all would agree that corporate directors should have appropriate protection against personal risk and that the rule of New York Dock Co. v. McCollom, 173 Misc. 106, 16 N.Y.S.2d 844 (Sup.Ct.1939), which denied reimbursement to directors who successfully defended their case on the merits, should as a matter of policy be overruled by statute.

The concept of indemnification recognizes that there will be situations in which the director does not satisfy all of the elements of the standard of conduct set forth in section 8.30(a) or the requirements of some other applicable law but where the corporation should nevertheless be permitted (or required) to absorb the economic costs of any ensuing litigation. A carefully constructed indemnification statute should identify these situations.

If permitted too broadly, however, indemnification may violate equally basic tenets of public policy. It is inappropriate to permit management to use corporate funds to avoid the consequences of certain conduct. For example, a director who intentionally inflicts harm on the corporation should not expect to receive assistance from the corporation for legal or other expenses and should be required to satisfy from his personal assets not only any adverse judgment but also expenses incurred in connection with the proceeding. Any other rule would tend to encourage socially undesirable conduct.

A further policy issue is raised in connection with indemnification against liabilities or sanctions imposed under state or federal civil or criminal statutes. A shift of the economic cost of these liabilities from the individual director to the corporation by way of indemnification may in some instances frustrate the public policy of those statutes.

The fundamental issue that must be addressed by an indemnification statute is the establishment of policies consistent with these broad principles: to ensure that indemnification is permitted only where it will further sound corporate policies and to prohibit indemnification where it might protect or encourage wrongful or improper conduct. As phrased by one commentator, the goal of indemnification is to "seek the middle ground between encouraging fiduciaries to violate their trust, and discouraging them from serving at all." Johnston, "Corporate Indemnification and Liability Insurance for Directors and Officers," 33 BUS.LAW. 1993, 1994 (1978). The increasing number of suits against directors, the increasing cost of defense, and the increasing emphasis on diversifying the membership of boards of directors all militate in favor of workable arrangements to protect directors against liability to the extent consistent with established principles.

Some of the same policy considerations apply to the indemnification of officers and, in many cases, employees and agents. The indemnification of officers, whose duties are specified in section 8.42, is dealt with separately in section 8.56. However, other considerations apply to employees and agents, who have significantly different roles and responsibilities and as to whom the spectre of structural bias (sympathetic directors approving indemnification for themselves or for colleagues on the board or for officers, who may work closely with board members) is not present. The indemnification of employees and agents, whose duties are prescribed by sources of law other than corporation law (e.g., contract and agency law), is beyond the scope of this subchapter. Section 8.58(d), however, makes clear that the absence in subchapter E of provisions concerning employees and agents is not intended to limit a corporation's power to indemnify or advance expenses to them in accordance with applicable law.

2. Relationship of Indemnification to Other Policies Established in the Model Act

Indemnification is closely related to the standards of conduct for directors and officers established elsewhere in chapter 8. The structure of the Model Act is based on the assumption that if a director acts consistently with the standards of conduct described in section 8.30 or with the standards of a liability-limitation provision in the articles of incorporation (as authorized by section 2.02(b)(4)), he will not have exposure to liability to the corporation or to shareholders and any expenses necessary to establish his defense will be borne by the corporation (under section 8.52). But the converse is not necessarily true. The basic standards for indemnification set forth in this subchapter for a civil action, in the absence of an indemnification provision in the corporation's articles (as authorized by section 2.02(b)(5)), are good faith and reasonable belief that the conduct was in or not opposed to the best interests of the corporation. See section 8.51. In some circumstances, a director or officer may be found to have violated a statutory or common law duty and yet be able to establish eligibility for indemnification under these standards of conduct. In addition, this subchapter permits a director or officer who is held liable for violating a statutory or common law duty, but who does not meet the relevant standard of conduct, to petition a court to order indemnification under section 8.54(a)(3) on the ground that it would be fair and reasonable to do so. . . .

§ 8.50 Subchapter Definitions

In this subchapter:

(1) "Corporation" includes any domestic or foreign predecessor entity of a corporation in a merger.

(2) "Director" or "officer" means an individual who is or was a director or officer, respectively, of a corporation or who, while a director or officer of the corporation, is or was serving at the corporation's request as a director, officer, partner, trustee, employee, or agent of another domestic or foreign corporation, partnership, joint venture, trust, employee benefit plan, or other entity. A director or officer is considered to be serving an employee benefit plan at the corporation's request if his duties to the corporation also impose duties on, or otherwise involve services by, him to the plan or to participants in or beneficiaries of the plan. "Director" or "officer" includes, unless the context requires otherwise, the estate or personal representative of a director or officer.

(3) "Disinterested director" means a director who, at the time of a vote referred to in section 8.53(c) or a vote or selection referred to in section 8.55(b) or (c), is not (i) a party to the proceeding, or (ii) an individual having a familial, financial, professional or employment relationship with the director whose indemnification or advance for expenses is the subject of the decision being made, which relationship would, in the circumstances, reasonably be expected to exert an influence on the director's judgment when voting on the decision being made.

(4) "Expenses" includes counsel fees.

(5) "Liability" means the obligation to pay a judgment, settlement, penalty, fine (including an excise tax assessed with respect to an employee benefit plan), or reasonable expenses incurred with respect to a proceeding.

(6) "Official capacity" means: (i) when used with respect to a director, the office of director in a corporation; and (ii) when used with respect to an officer, as contemplated in section 8.56, the office in a corporation held by the officer. "Official capacity" does not include service for any other domestic or foreign corporation or any partnership, joint venture, trust, employee benefit plan, or other entity.

(7) "Party" means an individual who was, is, or is threatened to be made, a defendant or respondent in a proceeding.

(8) "Proceeding" means any threatened, pending, or completed action, suit, or proceeding, whether civil, criminal, administrative, arbitrative, or investigative and whether formal or informal.

Official Comment

The definitions set forth in section 8.50 apply only to subchapter E and have no application elsewhere in the Model Act (except as set forth in section 2.02(b)(5))....

2. Director and Officer

A special definition of "director" and "officer" is included in subchapter E to cover individuals who are made parties to proceedings because they are or were directors or officers or, while serving as directors or officers, also serve or served at the corporation's request in another capacity for another entity. The purpose of the latter part of this definition is to give directors and officers the benefits of the protection of this subchapter while serving at the corporation's request in a responsible position for employee benefit plans, trade associations, nonprofit or charitable entities, domestic or foreign entities, or other kinds of profit or nonprofit ventures.... The definition covers an individual who is or was either a director or officer so that further references in the remainder of subchapter E to an individual who is a director or officer necessarily include former directors or officers.

3. Disinterested Director

This term identifies, for subchapter E purposes, those members of the board who are eligible to make, in the first instance, the authorizations and determinations required in connection with decisions on advance for expenses and indemnification. It is used only in sections 8.53(c) and 8.55(b) and (c) and is not applicable to any other sections of the Act. (See section 8.62 where the term "qualified director" is used in connection with conflicting interest transactions.)

To be a "disinterested director," a member of the board must not be a party to the proceeding at the time the board makes the determination or authorization and he must not be the subject of the request for advance or indemnification with respect to which action is being taken. He must also not have a familial, financial, professional or employment relationship that could reasonably be expected to influence his decision. The fact that a director was nominated for the board by directors who are parties to the proceeding or are interested in the request or is a director of another corporation of which the director who is a party to the proceeding or is interested in the request is also a director should not, absent unusual circumstances, constitute a disqualifying relationship.

4. Expenses

"Expenses" is defined to include counsel fees in order to avoid repeated references to such fees every time "expenses" appears throughout the subchapter. "Expenses" does not include the other items listed in the definition of "liability," such as judgments or amounts paid in settlement.

5.   Liability

"Liability" is defined for convenience in order to avoid repeated references to recoverable items throughout the subchapter.   Even though the definition of "liability" includes amounts paid in settlement or to satisfy a judgment, indemnification against certain types of settlements and judgments is not allowed under several provisions of subchapter E.   For example, indemnification in suits brought by or in the right of the corporation is limited to expenses (see section 8.51(d)(1)), unless indemnification for a settlement is ordered by a court under section 8.54(a)(3).

The definition of "liability" permits the indemnification only of "reasonable expenses incurred."   The intention is that any portion of expenses falling outside the perimeter of reasonableness should not be advanced or indemnified.   In contrast, unlike earlier versions of the Model Act and statutes of many states, section 8.50(5) provides that amounts paid to settle or satisfy substantive claims are not subject to a reasonableness test.   Since payment of these amounts is permissive— mandatory indemnification is available under section 8.52 only where the defendant is "wholly successful"—a special limitation of "reasonableness" for settlements is inappropriate.

"Penalties" and "fines" are expressly included within the definition of "liability" so that, in appropriate cases, these items may also be indemnified.   The purpose of this definition is to cover every type of monetary obligation that may be imposed upon a director, including civil penalties, restitution, and obligations to give notice.   This definition also expressly includes as a "fine" the levy of excise taxes under the Internal Revenue Code pursuant to ERISA.

6.   Official Capacity

The definition of "official capacity" is necessary because the term determines which of the two alternative standards of conduct set forth in section 8.51(a)(1)(ii) applies: If action is taken in an "official capacity," the person to be indemnified must have reasonably believed he was acting in the best interests of the corporation, while if the action in question was not taken in his "official capacity," he need only have reasonably believed that the conduct was not opposed to the best interests of the corporation.   See also the Official Comment to section 8.51(a).

7.   Party

The definition of "party" includes every "individual who was, is, or is threatened to be made, a defendant or respondent in a proceeding." Thus, the definition includes present and former parties in addition to individuals currently or formerly threatened with being made a party. An individual who is only called as a witness is not a "party" within this definition and, as specifically provided in section 8.58(d), payment or reimbursement of his expenses is not limited by this subchapter.

8. Proceeding

The broad definition of "proceeding" ensures that the benefits of this subchapter will be available to directors in new and unexpected, as well as traditional, types of litigation or other adversarial matters, whether civil, criminal, administrative, or investigative. It also includes arbitration and other dispute resolution proceedings, lawsuit appeals and petitions to review administrative actions.

§ 8.51 Permissible Indemnification

(a) Except as otherwise provided in this section, a corporation may indemnify an individual who is a party to a proceeding because he is a director against liability incurred in the proceeding if:

  (1) (i) he conducted himself in good faith; and

   (ii) he reasonably believed:

     (A) in the case of conduct in his official capacity, that his conduct was in the best interests of the corporation; and

     (B) in all other cases, that his conduct was at least not opposed to the best interests of the corporation; and

   (iii) in the case of any criminal proceeding, he had no reasonable cause to believe his conduct was unlawful; or

  (2) he engaged in conduct for which broader indemnification has been made permissible or obligatory under a provision of the articles of incorporation (as authorized by section 2.02(b)(5)).

(b) A director's conduct with respect to an employee benefit plan for a purpose he reasonably believed to be in the interests of the participants in, and the beneficiaries of, the plan is conduct that satisfies the requirement of subsection (a)(1)(ii)(B).

(c) The termination of a proceeding by judgment, order, settlement, or conviction, or upon a plea of nolo contendere or its equivalent, is not, of itself, determinative that the director did not meet the relevant standard of conduct described in this section.

(d) Unless ordered by a court under section 8.54(a)(3), a corporation may not indemnify a director:

  (1) in connection with a proceeding by or in the right of the corporation, except for reasonable expenses incurred in connection with the proceeding if it is determined that the director has met the relevant standard of conduct under subsection (a); or

(2) in connection with any proceeding with respect to conduct for which he was adjudged liable on the basis that he received a financial benefit to which he was not entitled, whether or not involving action in his official capacity.

Official Comment

1. Section 8.51(a)

Subsection 8.51(a) permits, but does not require, a corporation to indemnify directors if the standards of subsection (a)(1) or of a provision of the articles referred to in subsection (a)(2) are met. This authorization is subject to any limitations set forth in the articles of incorporation pursuant to section 8.58(c). Absent any such limitation, the standards for indemnification of directors contained in this subsection define the outer limits for which discretionary indemnification is permitted under the Model Act. Conduct which does not meet one of these standards is not eligible for permissible indemnification under the Model Act, although court-ordered indemnification may be available under section 8.54(a)(3). Conduct that falls within these outer limits does not automatically entitle directors to indemnification, although a corporation may obligate itself to indemnify directors to the maximum extent permitted by applicable law. See section 8.58(a). No such obligation, however, may exceed these outer limits. Absent such an obligatory provision, section 8.52 defines much narrower circumstances in which directors are entitled as a matter of right to indemnification.

Some state statutes provide separate, but usually similarly worded, standards for indemnification in third-party suits and indemnification in suits brought by or in the right of the corporation. Section 8.51 makes clear that the outer limits of conduct for which indemnification is permitted should not be dependent on the type of proceeding in which the claim arises. To prevent circularity in recovery, however, section 8.51(d)(1) limits indemnification in connection with suits brought by or in the right of the corporation to expenses incurred and excludes amounts paid to settle such suits or to satisfy judgments. In addition, to discourage wrongdoing, section 8.51(d)(2) bars indemnification where the director has been adjudged to have received a financial benefit to which he is not entitled. Nevertheless, a court may order certain relief from these limitations under section 8.54(a)(3).

The standards of conduct described in subsections (a)(1)(i) and (a)(1)(ii)(A) that must be met in order to permit the corporation to indemnify a director are closely related, but not identical, to the standards of conduct imposed on directors by section 8.30. Section 8.30(a) requires a director acting in his official capacity to discharge his duties in good faith, with due care (i.e., that which an ordinarily prudent person in a like position would exercise under similar circumstances) and in a manner he reasonably believes to be in the corporation's best interests.

Unless authorized by a charter provision adopted pursuant to subsection (a)(2), it would be difficult to justify indemnifying a director who has not met any of these standards. It would not, however, make sense to require a director to meet all these standards in order to be indemnified because a director who meets all three of these standards would have no liability, at least to the corporation, under the terms of section 8.30(d).

Section 8.51(a) adopts a middle ground by authorizing discretionary indemnification in the case of a failure to meet the due care standard of section 8.30(a) because public policy would not be well served by an absolute bar. A director's potential liability for conduct which does not on each and every occasion satisfy the due care requirement of section 8.30(a), or which with the benefit of hindsight could be so viewed, would in all likelihood deter qualified individuals from serving as directors and inhibit some who serve from taking risks. Permitting indemnification against such liability tends to counter these undesirable consequences. Accordingly, section 8.51(a) authorizes indemnification at the corporation's option even though section 8.30's due care requirement is not met, but only if the director satisfies the "good faith" and "corporation's best interests" standards. This reflects a judgment that, balancing public policy considerations, the corporation may indemnify a director who does not satisfy the due care test but not one who fails either of the other two standards.

As in the case of section 8.30, where the concept of good faith is also used, no attempt is made in section 8.51 to provide a definition. The concept involves a subjective test, which would permit indemnification for "a mistake of judgment," in the words of the Official Comment to section 8.30, even though made unwisely or negligently by objective standards. Section 8.51 also requires, as does section 8.30, a "reasonable" belief by a director acting in his official capacity that his conduct was in the corporation's best interests. It then adds a provision, not found in section 8.30, relating to criminal proceedings that requires the director to have had no "reasonable cause" to believe that his conduct was unlawful. These both involve objective standards applicable to the director's belief concerning the effect of his conduct. Conduct includes both acts and omissions.

Section 8.51(a)(1)(ii)(B) requires, if a director is not acting in his official capacity, that his action be "at least not opposed to" the corporation's best interests. This standard is applicable to the director when serving another entity at the request of the corporation or when sued simply because of his status as a director. The words "at least" qualify "not opposed to" in order to make it clear that this standard is an outer limit for conduct other than in an official capacity. While this subsection is directed at the interests of the indemnifying (i.e., requesting) corporation, a director serving another entity by request remains subject to the provisions of the law governing his service to that entity, including provisions dealing with conflicts of interest. Compare sections

8.60–8.63. Should indemnification from the requesting corporation be sought by a director for acts done while serving another entity, which acts involved breach of the duty of loyalty owed to that entity, nothing in section 8.51(a)(1)(ii)(B) would preclude the requesting corporation from considering, in assessing its own best interests, whether the fact that its director had engaged in a violation of the duty owed to the other entity was in fact "opposed to" the interests of the indemnifying corporation. Receipt of an improper financial benefit from a subsidiary would normally be opposed to the best interests of the parent.

Section 8.51 also permits indemnification in connection with a proceeding involving an alleged failure to satisfy legal standards other than the standards of conduct in section 8.30, e.g., violations of federal securities laws and environmental laws. It should be noted, however, that the Securities and Exchange Commission takes the position that indemnification against liabilities under the Securities Act of 1933 is against public policy and requires that, as a condition for accelerating the effectiveness of a registration statement under the Act, the issuer must undertake that, unless in the opinion of its counsel the matter has been settled by controlling precedent, it will submit to a court the question whether such indemnification is against public policy as expressed in the Act. 17 C.F.R. § 229.512(h) (1993).

In addition to indemnification under section 8.51(a)(1), section 8.51(a)(2) permits indemnification under the standard of conduct set forth in a charter provision adopted pursuant to section 2.02(b)(5). Based on such a charter provision, section 8.51(a)(2) permits indemnification in connection with claims by third parties and, through section 8.56, applies to officers as well as directors. (This goes beyond the scope of a charter provision adopted pursuant to section 2.02(b)(4), which can only limit liability of directors against claims by the corporation or its shareholders.) Section 8.51(a)(2) is subject to the prohibition of subsection (d)(1) against indemnification of settlements and judgments in derivative suits. It is also subject to the prohibition of subsection (d)(2) against indemnification for receipt of an improper financial benefit; however, this prohibition is already subsumed in the exception contained in section 2.02(b)(5)(A).

Notice of any indemnification under this section (or sections 8.52, 8.53 or 8.54) in a derivative proceeding must be given to the shareholders pursuant to section 16.21(a).

2. Section 8.51(b)

As discussed in the Official Comment to Section 8.50(2), ERISA requires that a "fiduciary" (as defined in ERISA) discharge his duties "solely in the interest" of the participants in and beneficiaries of an employee benefit plan. Section 8.51(b) makes clear that a director who is serving as a trustee or fiduciary for an employee benefit plan under ERISA meets the standard for indemnification under section 8.51(a) if he reasonably believes his conduct was in the best interests of the participants in and beneficiaries of the plan.

This standard is arguably an exception to the more general standard that conduct not in an official corporate capacity is indemnifiable if it is "at least not opposed to" the best interests of the corporation. However, a corporation that causes a director to undertake fiduciary duties in connection with an employee benefit plan should expect the director to act in the best interests of the plan's beneficiaries or participants. Thus, subsection (b) establishes and provides a standard for indemnification that is consistent with the statutory policies embodied in ERISA. See Official Comment to section 8.50(2).

3. Section 8.51(c)

The purpose of section 8.51(c) is to reject the argument that indemnification is automatically improper whenever a proceeding has been concluded on a basis that does not exonerate the director claiming indemnification. Even though a final judgment or conviction is not automatically determinative of the issue of whether the minimum standard of conduct was met, any judicial determination of substantive liability would in most instances be entitled to considerable weight. By the same token, it is clear that the termination of a proceeding by settlement or plea of nolo contendere should not of itself create a presumption either that conduct met or did not meet the relevant standard of subsection (a) since a settlement or nolo plea may be agreed to for many reasons unrelated to the merits of the claim. On the other hand, a final determination of non-liability (including one based on a liability-limitation provision adopted under section 2.02(b)(4)) or an acquittal in a criminal case automatically entitles the director to indemnification of expenses under section 8.52.

Section 8.51(c) applies to the indemnification of expenses in derivative proceedings (as well as to indemnification in third party suits). The most likely application of this subsection in connection with a derivative proceeding will be to a settlement since a judgment or order would normally result in liability to the corporation and thereby preclude indemnification for expenses under section 8.51(d)(1), unless ordered by a court under section 8.54(a)(3). In the rare event that a judgment or order entered against the director did not include a determination of liability to the corporation, the entry of the judgment or order would not be determinative that the director failed to meet the relevant standard of conduct.

4. Section 8.51(d)

This subsection makes clear that indemnification is not permissible under section 8.51 in two situations: (i) a proceeding brought by or in the right of a corporation that results in a settlement or a judgment against the director and (ii) a proceeding that results in a judgment that the director received an improper financial benefit as a result of his conduct.

Permitting indemnification of settlements and judgments in derivative proceedings would give rise to a circularity in which the corporation receiving payment of damages by the director in the settlement or judgment (less attorneys' fees) would then immediately return the same amount to the director (including attorneys' fees) as indemnification. Thus, the corporation would be in a poorer economic position than if there had been no proceeding. This situation is most egregious in the case of a judgment against the director. Even in the case of a settlement, however, prohibiting indemnification is not unfair. Under the revised procedures of section 7.44, upon motion by the corporation, the court must dismiss any derivative proceeding which independent directors (or a court-appointed panel) determine in good faith, after a reasonable inquiry, is not in the best interests of the corporation. Furthermore, under section 2.02(b)(4), the directors have the opportunity to propose to shareholders adoption of a provision limiting the liability of directors in derivative proceedings. In view of these considerations, it is unlikely that directors will be unnecessarily exposed to meritless actions. In addition, if directors were to be indemnified for amounts paid in settlement, the dismissal procedures in section 7.44 might not be fully employed since it could be less expensive for the corporation to indemnify the directors immediately for the amount of the claimed damages rather than bear the expense of the inquiry required by section 7.44. The result could increase the filing of meritless derivative proceedings in order to generate small but immediately paid attorneys' fees. Despite the prohibition on indemnification of a settlement or a judgment in a derivative proceeding, subsection (d)(1) permits indemnification of the related reasonable expenses incurred in the proceeding so long as the director meets the relevant standard of conduct set forth in section 8.51(a). In addition, indemnification of derivative proceeding expenses and amounts paid in settlement where the relevant standard was not met may be ordered by a court under section 8.54(a)(3).

If a corporation indemnifies a director in connection with a derivative proceeding, the corporation must report that fact to the shareholders prior to their next meeting. See section 16.21(a).

Indemnification under section 8.51 is also prohibited if there has been an adjudication that a director received an improper financial benefit (i.e., a benefit to which he is not entitled), even if, for example, he acted in a manner not opposed to the best interests of the corporation. For example, improper use of inside information for financial benefit should not be an action for which the corporation may elect to provide indemnification, even if the corporation was not thereby harmed. Given the express language of section 2.02(b)(5) establishing the outer limit of an indemnification provision contained in the articles of incorporation, a director found to have received an improper financial benefit would not be permitted indemnification under subsection (a)(2). Although it is unlikely that a director found to have received an improper financial benefit could meet the standard in subsection (a)(1)(ii)(B), this limitation is made explicit in section 8.51(d)(2). Section 8.54(a)(3) permits a director found liable in a proceeding referred to in subsection (d)(2) to petition a court for a judicial determination of entitlement to indemnification for reasonable expenses. The language of section 8.51(d)(2) is based on section 2.02(b)(4)(A) and, thus, the same standards should be used in interpreting the application of both provisions. Although a settlement may create an obligation to pay money, it should not be construed for purposes of this subchapter as an adjudication of liability.

§ 8.52 Mandatory Indemnification

A corporation shall indemnify a director who was wholly successful, on the merits or otherwise, in the defense of any proceeding to which he was a party because he was a director of the corporation against reasonable expenses incurred by him in connection with the proceeding.

Official Comment

Section 8.51 determines whether indemnification may be made voluntarily by a corporation if it elects to do so. Section 8.52 determines whether a corporation must indemnify a director for his expenses; in other words, section 8.52 creates a statutory right of indemnification in favor of the director who meets the requirements of that section. Enforcement of this right by judicial proceeding is specifically contemplated by section 8.54(a)(1). Section 8.54(b) gives the director a statutory right to recover expenses incurred by him in enforcing his statutory right to indemnification under section 8.52.

The basic standard for mandatory indemnification is that the director has been "wholly successful, on the merits or otherwise," in the defense of the proceeding. The word "wholly" is added to avoid the argument accepted in Merritt–Chapman & Scott Corp. v. Wolfson, 321 A.2d 138 (Del.1974), that a defendant may be entitled to partial mandatory indemnification if, by plea bargaining or otherwise, he was able to obtain the dismissal of some but not all counts of an indictment. A defendant is "wholly successful" only if the entire proceeding is disposed of on a basis which does not involve a finding of liability. A director who is precluded from mandatory indemnification by this requirement may still be entitled to permissible indemnification under section 8.51(a) or court-ordered indemnification under section 8.54(a)(3).

The language in earlier versions of the Model Act and in many other state statutes that the basis of success may be "on the merits or otherwise" is retained. While this standard may result in an occasional defendant becoming entitled to indemnification because of procedural defenses not related to the merits, e.g., the statute of limitations or disqualification of the plaintiff, it is unreasonable to require a defendant with a valid procedural defense to undergo a possibly prolonged and expensive trial on the merits in order to establish eligibility for mandatory indemnification.

If the corporation indemnifies or advances expenses to a director in connection with a derivative proceeding, the corporation must report that fact to the shareholders prior to their next meeting. See section 16.21(a).

§ 8.53 Advance for Expenses

(a) A corporation may, before final disposition of a proceeding, advance funds to pay for or reimburse the reasonable expenses incurred by a director who is a party to a proceeding because he is a director if he delivers to the corporation:

   (1) a written affirmation of his good faith belief that he has met the relevant standard of conduct described in section 8.51 or that the proceeding involves conduct for which liability has been eliminated under a provision of the articles of incorporation as authorized by section 2.02(b)(4); and

   (2) his written undertaking to repay any funds advanced if he is not entitled to mandatory indemnification under section 8.52 and it is ultimately determined under section 8.54 or section 8.55 that he has not met the relevant standard of conduct described in section 8.51.

(b) The undertaking required by subsection (a)(2) must be an unlimited general obligation of the director but need not be secured and may be accepted without reference to the financial ability of the director to make repayment.

(c) Authorizations under this section shall be made:

   (1) by the board of directors:

      (i) if there are two or more disinterested directors, by a majority vote of all the disinterested directors (a majority of whom shall for such purpose constitute a quorum) or by a majority of the members of a committee of two or more disinterested directors appointed by such a vote; or

      (ii) if there are fewer than two disinterested directors, by the vote necessary for action by the board in accordance with section 8.24(c), in which authorization directors who do not qualify as disinterested directors may participate; or

   (2) by the shareholders, but shares owned by or voted under the control of a director who at the time does not qualify as a disinterested director may not be voted on the authorization.

Official Comment

Section 8.53 authorizes, but does not require, a corporation to pay for or reimburse, in advance, a director's reasonable expenses if two conditions are met. This authorization is subject to any limitations set forth in the articles of incorporation pursuant to section 8.58(c).

Section 8.53 recognizes an important difference between indemnification and an advance for expenses: Indemnification is retrospective and, therefore, enables the persons determining whether to indemnify to do so on the basis of known facts, including the outcome of the proceeding. Advance for expenses is necessarily prospective and the individuals making the decision whether to advance expenses generally have fewer known facts on which to base their decision. Indemnification may include reimbursement for non-advanced expenses.

Section 8.53 reflects a determination that it is sound public policy to permit the corporation to advance (by direct payment or by reimbursement) the defense expenses of a director so long as the director believes in good faith that he was acting in accordance with the relevant standard for indemnification set forth in section 8.51 or that the proceeding involves conduct for which liability has been eliminated pursuant to section 2.02(b)(4) and agrees to repay any amounts advanced if it is ultimately determined that he is not entitled to indemnification. This policy is based upon the view that a person who serves an entity in a representative capacity should not be required to finance his own defense. Moreover, adequate legal representation often requires substantial expenses during the proceeding and many individuals are willing to serve as directors only if they have the assurance that the corporation has the power to advance these expenses. In fact, many corporations contractually obligate themselves (by a provision in the articles or bylaws or otherwise) to advance expenses for directors. See section 8.58(a).

Section 8.53(a) requires a written affirmation by the director of his good faith belief that he has met the relevant standard of conduct necessary for indemnification by the corporation and a written undertaking by the director to repay any funds advanced if it is ultimately determined that he has not met the standard of conduct. A single undertaking may cover all funds advanced in connection with the proceeding. Under section 8.53(b), the undertaking need not be secured and financial ability to repay is not a prerequisite. The theory underlying this subsection is that wealthy directors should not be favored over directors whose financial resources are modest. The undertaking must be made by the director and not by a third party. If the director or the corporation wishes some third party to be responsible for the director's obligation in this regard, either of them is free to make those arrangements separately with the third party.

In the absence of an obligatory provision established pursuant to section 8.58(a), the decision to advance expenses must be made in accordance with section 8.53(c). Section 8.53 does not address the question of the standard by which the decision to advance expenses is to be made. Accordingly, the standards of section 8.30 should, in general, govern. The conditions for advance for expenses are different from the conditions for indemnification. Directors normally meet the standards of section 8.30 in approving an advance for expenses if they limit their consideration to the financial ability of the corporation to pay the amounts in question and do not have actual knowledge of facts sufficient to cause them to believe that the subsection (a)(1) affirmation was not made in good faith. The directors are not required by section 8.30 to make any inquiry into the merits of the proceeding or the good faith of the belief stated in that affirmation. Thus, in the great majority of cases, no special inquiry will be required. The directors acting on a decision to advance expenses may, but are not required to, consider any additional matters they deem appropriate and may condition the advance of expenses upon compliance with any additional requirements they desire to impose.

Advance for expenses under section 8.53 may be made obligatory upon a corporation pursuant to section 8.58(a) by a provision set forth in its articles of incorporation or bylaws, in a resolution of its shareholders or board of directors, in a contract or otherwise. However, any such provision must comply with the requirements of subsection (a) of section 8.53 regarding furnishing of an affirmation and undertaking. No other procedures are contemplated, although obligatory provisions may include notice and other procedures in connection with advancement of expenses and indemnification requests.

At least one court has held that a general obligatory provision requiring indemnification to the extent permitted by law does not include advance for expenses if not specifically mentioned. E.g., Advanced Mining Systems, Inc. v. Fricke, 623 A.2d 82 (Del.1992). Section 8.58(a) requires the opposite result, unless provided otherwise.

The decision to advance expenses is required to be made only one time with respect to each proceeding rather than each time a request for payment of expenses is received by the corporation. The directors are, however, free to reconsider the decision at any time, e.g., upon a change in the financial ability of the corporation to pay the amounts in question. The decision as to the reasonableness of any expenses may be made by any officer or agent of the corporation duly authorized to do so.

The procedures set forth in subsection (c) for authorizing an advance for expenses parallel the procedures set forth in section 8.55(b) for selecting the person or persons to make the determination that indemnification is permissible. Unless the authorization is made by the shareholders under subsection (c)(2), first resort must be made to subsection (c)(1)(i). If it is unavailable, then resort may be made to subsection (c)(1)(ii).

Under subsection (c)(1)(i), the vote required when the disinterested directors act as a group is an absolute majority of their number. A majority of the disinterested directors constitutes a quorum for board action for this purpose.

The committee of two or more disinterested directors referred to in subsection (c)(1)(i) may include a standing committee of the board of directors to which the power to authorize advances for expenses has been delegated, so long as (1) the committee was appointed by a majority vote of directors who were, at the time of appointment of the committee, not parties to the proceeding in connection with which the advance is being sought and (2) the advance is authorized by a majority vote of members of the committee who, at the time of the vote, are disinterested directors.

Under subsection (c)(1)(ii), which is available only if subsection (c)(1)(i) is not available, the board's action must be taken in accordance with sections 8.20 or 8.21, as the case may be, and directors who are not disinterested directors may participate in the vote. Allowing non-disinterested directors to participate in the authorization decision, if there is no or only one disinterested director, is a principle of prudence that is based on the concept that if there are not at least two disinterested directors, then it is preferable to return the power to make the decision to the full board (even though it includes non-disinterested directors) rather than to leave it with one disinterested director. An interested director should absent himself from any meeting considering a request for advance for expenses by him or the appointment of a committee to consider such a request.

Illustration 1: The board consists of 15 directors, four of whom are interested. Of the eleven disinterested directors, nine are present at the meeting at which the authorization is made or the committee is appointed.

Under subsection (c)(1)(i), a quorum is present and at least six of the nine disinterested directors present at the board meeting must authorize any advance for expenses because six is an absolute majority of the eleven disinterested directors. Alternatively, six of the nine disinterested directors present at the board meeting may appoint a committee of two to all (eleven) of the disinterested directors to decide whether to authorize the advance. Action by the committee requires an absolute majority of the members appointed.

Illustration 2: The board consists of 15 directors, 14 of whom are interested.

Subsection (c)(1)(i) is not available because the number of disinterested directors, one, is less than two. Accordingly, the decision must be made by the board under subsection (c)(1)(ii) (or, as is always permitted, by the shareholders under subsection (c)(2)).

Authorizations by shareholders rather than by directors are permitted by section 8.53(c)(2), but shares owned by or voted under the control of directors who at the time do not qualify as disinterested directors may not be voted on the authorizations of eligibility for indemnification. This does not affect rules governing the authorization as to the presence of a quorum at the meeting.

The fact that there has been an advance for expenses does not determine whether a director is entitled to indemnification. Repayment of any advance is required only if it is ultimately determined that the director did not meet the relevant standard of conduct in section 8.51. A proceeding will often terminate without a judicial or other determination of whether the director's conduct met that standard. Nevertheless, the board of directors should make, or cause to be made, an affirmative determination of entitlement to indemnification at the conclusion of the proceeding. This decision should be made in accordance with the procedures set forth in section 8.55.

If the corporation advances expenses to a director in connection with a derivative proceeding, the corporation must report that fact to the shareholders prior to their next meeting. See section 16.21(a).

Judicial enforcement of rights granted by or pursuant to section 8.53 is specifically contemplated by section 8.54.

§ 8.54 Court–Ordered Indemnification and Advance for Expenses

(a) A director who is a party to a proceeding because he is a director may apply for indemnification or an advance for expenses to the court conducting the proceeding or to another court of competent jurisdiction. After receipt of an application and after giving any notice it considers necessary, the court shall:

(1) order indemnification if the court determines that the director is entitled to mandatory indemnification under section 8.52;

(2) order indemnification or advance for expenses if the court determines that the director is entitled to indemnification or advance for expenses pursuant to a provision authorized by section 8.58(a); or

(3) order indemnification or advance for expenses if the court determines, in view of all the relevant circumstances, that it is fair and reasonable

(i) to indemnify the director, or

(ii) to advance expenses to the director,

even if he has not met the relevant standard of conduct set forth in section 8.51(a), failed to comply with section 8.53 or was adjudged liable in a proceeding referred to in subsection 8.51(d)(1) or (d)(2), but if he was adjudged so liable his indemnification shall be limited to reasonable expenses incurred in connection with the proceeding.

(b) If the court determines that the director is entitled to indemnification under subsection (a)(1) or to indemnification or advance for expenses under subsection (a)(2), it shall also order the corporation to pay the director's reasonable expenses incurred in connection with obtaining court-ordered indemnification or advance for expenses. If the court determines that the director is entitled to indemnification or advance for expenses under subsection (a)(3), it may also order the corporation to pay the director's reasonable expenses to obtain court-ordered indemnification or advance for expenses.

Official Comment

Section 8.54(a) provides for court-ordered indemnification in three situations:

(1) A director is entitled to mandatory indemnification under section 8.52. If so, the director may enforce that right by judicial proceeding.

(2) A director is entitled to indemnification or advance for expenses pursuant to a provision in the articles or bylaws, board or shareholder resolution or contract. If so, the director may enforce that right by judicial proceeding. To the extent that these rights are contractual, the corporation may have contractual defenses. If the corporation has contracted to indemnify a director to the fullest extent permitted by law, a court may, nevertheless, deny an advance for expenses if it determines that the director did not have, at the time he delivered the affirmation required by section 8.53(a)(1), a good faith belief that he met the relevant standard of conduct.

(3) A court in its discretion determines that it is fair and reasonable under all the relevant circumstances to order an advance for expenses or indemnification for the amount of a settlement or judgment (in addition to expenses), whether or not the director met the relevant standard of conduct in section 8.51 or is otherwise ineligible for indemnification. However, there are two exceptions: an adverse judgment in a derivative proceeding (section 8.51(d)(1)) and an adverse judgment in a proceeding charging receipt of an improper financial benefit (section 8.51(d)(2)), although in either case the court may order payment of expenses. Thus, with these exceptions, section 8.54(a)(3) permits a court to order indemnification for amounts paid in settlement of and expenses incurred in connection with a derivative proceeding or a proceeding charging receipt of an improper financial benefit. Section 8.54(a)(3) applies to (a) a situation in which a provision in the articles of incorporation, bylaws, resolution or contract obligates the corporation to indemnify or to

advance expenses but the relevant standard of conduct has not been met and (b) a situation involving a permissive provision pursuant to which the board declines to exercise its authority to indemnify or to advance expenses. However, in determining whether indemnification or expense advance would be "fair and reasonable," a court should give appropriate deference to an informed decision of a board or committee made in good faith and based upon full information. Ordinarily, a court should not determine that it is "fair and reasonable" to order indemnification or expense advance where the director has not met conditions and procedures to which he agreed.

The discretionary authority of the court to order indemnification of a derivative proceeding settlement under section 8.54(a)(3) contrasts with the denial of similar authority under section 145(b) of the Delaware General Corporation Law. A director seeking court-ordered indemnification or expense advance under section 8.54(a)(3) must show that there are facts peculiar to his situation that make it fair and reasonable to both the corporation and to the director to override an intra-corporate declination or any otherwise applicable statutory prohibition against indemnification, e.g., sections 8.51(a) or (d).

Aside from the two exceptions noted above and other than the fairness and reasonableness requirement, there are no statutory outer limits on the court's power to order indemnification under section 8.54(a)(3). In an appropriate case, a court may wish to refer to the provisions of section 2.02(b)(4) establishing the outer limits of a liability-limiting charter provision. It would be an extraordinary situation in which a court would want to provide indemnification going beyond the limits of section 2.02(b)(4), but if the court, as the independent decision-maker, finds that it is "fair and reasonable," then the court is permitted to do so. It should be emphasized again, however, that the director seeking indemnification must make a showing of fairness and reasonableness and that exercise of the power granted by section 8.54(a)(3) is committed to the court's discretion.

Among the factors a court may want to consider are the gravity of the offense, the financial impact upon the corporation, the occurrence of a change in control or, in the case of an advance for expenses, the inability of the director to finance his defense. A court may want to give special attention to certain other issues. First, has the corporation joined in the application to the court for indemnification or an advance for expenses? This factor may be particularly important where under section 8.51(d) indemnification is not permitted for an amount paid in settlement of a proceeding brought by or in the right of the corporation. Second, in a case where indemnification would have been available under section 8.51(a)(2) if the corporation had adopted a provision authorized by section 2.02(b)(5), was the decision to adopt such a provision presented to and rejected by the shareholders and, if not, would exculpation of the director's conduct have resulted under a section 2.02(b)(4) provision?

Third, in connection with considering indemnification for expenses under section 8.51(d)(2) in a proceeding in which a director was adjudged liable for receiving a financial benefit to which he was not entitled, was such financial benefit insubstantial—particularly in relation to the other aspects of the transaction involved—and what was the degree of the director's involvement in the transaction and the decision to participate?

Under section 8.54(b), if a director successfully sues to enforce his right to indemnification of expenses under subsection (a)(1) or to indemnification or advance for expenses under subsection (a)(2), then the court must order the corporation to pay the director's expenses in the enforcement proceeding. However, if a director successfully sues for indemnification or advance for expenses under subsection (a)(3), then the court may (but is not required to) order the corporation to pay the director's expenses in the proceeding under subsection (a)(3). The basis for the distinction is that the corporation breached its obligation in the first two cases but not in the third.

Application for indemnification under section 8.54 may be made either to the court in which the proceeding was heard or to another court of appropriate jurisdiction. For example, a defendant in a criminal proceeding who has been convicted but believes that indemnification would be proper could apply either to the court which heard the criminal proceeding or bring an action against the corporation in another forum.

A decision by the board of directors not to oppose the request for indemnification is governed by the general standards of conduct of section 8.30. Even if the corporation decided not to oppose the request, the court must satisfy itself that the person seeking indemnification is deserving of receiving it under section 8.54.

As provided in section 8.58(c), a corporation may limit the rights of a director under section 8.54 by a provision in its articles of incorporation. In the absence of such a provision, the court has general power to exercise the authority granted under this section.

If the corporation provides indemnification or advances expenses to a director in connection with a derivative proceeding, the corporation must report that fact to the shareholders prior to their next meeting. See section 16.21(a).

§ 8.55 Determination and Authorization of Indemnification

(a) A corporation may not indemnify a director under section 8.51 unless authorized for a specific proceeding after a determination has been made that indemnification of the director is permissible because he has met the relevant standard of conduct set forth in section 8.51.

(b) The determination shall be made:

    (1) if there are two or more disinterested directors, by the board of directors by a majority vote of all the disinterested directors (a

majority of whom shall for such purpose constitute a quorum), or by a majority of the members of a committee of two or more disinterested directors appointed by such a vote;

(2) by special legal counsel:

(i) selected in the manner prescribed in subdivision (1); or

(ii) if there are fewer than two disinterested directors, selected by the board of directors (in which selection directors who do not qualify as disinterested directors may participate); or

(3) by the shareholders, but shares owned by or voted under the control of a director who at the time does not qualify as a disinterested director may not be voted on the determination.

(c) Authorization of indemnification shall be made in the same manner as the determination that indemnification is permissible, except that if there are fewer than two disinterested directors or if the determination is made by special legal counsel, authorization of indemnification shall be made by those entitled under subsection (b)(2)(ii) to select special legal counsel.

Official Comment

Section 8.55 provides the method for determining whether a corporation should indemnify a director under section 8.51. In this section a distinction is made between a "determination" and an "authorization." A "determination" involves a decision whether under the circumstances the person seeking indemnification has met the relevant standard of conduct under section 8.51 and is therefore eligible for indemnification. This decision may be made by the individuals or groups described in section 8.55(b). In addition, after a favorable "determination" has been made, the corporation must decide whether to "authorize" indemnification except to the extent that an obligatory provision under section 8.58(a) is applicable. This decision includes a review of the reasonableness of the expenses, the financial ability of the corporation to make the payment, and the judgment whether limited financial resources should be devoted to this or some other use by the corporation. While special legal counsel may make the "determination" of eligibility for indemnification, counsel may not "authorize" the indemnification. The existence of an obligation to "authorize" indemnification is subject to the existence of an obligatory provision under section 8.58(a).

Section 8.55(b) establishes procedures for selecting the person or persons who will make the determination of permissibility of indemnification. As indicated in the Official Comment to section 8.53(c), the committee referred to in subsection (b)(1) may include a standing committee of the board to which the power to determine whether to indemnify a director has been delegated so long as the appointment and composition of the committee members comply with subsection (b)(1).

In selecting special legal counsel under subsection (b)(2), directors who are parties to the proceeding may participate in the decision if there are insufficient disinterested directors to satisfy subsection (b)(1). Directors who do not qualify as disinterested directors may also participate in the decision to "authorize" indemnification on the basis of a favorable "determination" if necessary to permit action by the board of directors. The authorization of indemnification is the decision that results in payment of any amounts to be indemnified. This limited participation of interested directors in the authorization decision is justified by the principle of necessity.

Under subsection (b)(1), the vote required when the disinterested directors act as a group is an absolute majority of their number. A majority of the disinterested directors constitutes a quorum for board action for this purpose.

If there are not at least two disinterested directors, then the determination of entitlement to indemnification must be made by special legal counsel or by the shareholders.

Legal counsel authorized to make the required determination is referred to as "special legal counsel." In earlier versions of the Model Act, and in the statutes of many states, reference is made to "independent" legal counsel. The word "special" is felt to be more descriptive of the role to be performed; it is intended that the counsel selected should be independent in accordance with governing legal precepts. "Special legal counsel" normally should be counsel having no prior professional relationship with those seeking indemnification, should be retained for the specific occasion, and should not be or have been either inside counsel or regular outside counsel to the corporation. Special legal counsel should also not have any familial, financial or other relationship with any of those seeking indemnification that would, in the circumstances, reasonably be expected to exert an influence on counsel in making the determination. It is important that the process be sufficiently flexible to permit selection of counsel in light of the particular circumstances and so that unnecessary expense may be avoided. Hence the phrase "special legal counsel" is not defined in the statute.

Determinations by shareholders rather than by directors or special legal counsel are permitted by section 8.55(b)(3), but shares owned by or voted under the control of directors who at the time do not qualify as disinterested directors may not be voted on the determination of eligibility for indemnification. This does not affect rules governing the determination as to the presence of a quorum at the meeting.

Section 8.55 is subject to section 8.58(a), which permits the corporation to obligate itself in advance to provide indemnification or to advance expenses.

§ 8.56 Officers

(a) A corporation may indemnify and advance expenses under this subchapter to an officer of the corporation who is a party to a proceeding because he is an officer of the corporation.

  (1) to the same extent as a director; and

  (2) if he is an officer but not a director, to such further extent as may be provided by the articles of incorporation, the bylaws, a resolution of the board of directors, or contract except for (A) liability in connection with a proceeding by or in the right of the corporation other than for reasonable expenses incurred in connection with the proceeding or (B) liability arising out of conduct that constitutes (i) receipt by him of a financial benefit to which he is not entitled, (ii) an intentional infliction of harm on the corporation or the shareholders, or (iii) an intentional violation of criminal law.

(b) The provisions of subsection (a)(2) shall apply to an officer who is also a director if the basis on which he is made a party to the proceeding is an act or omission solely as an officer.

(c) An officer of a corporation who is not a director is entitled to mandatory indemnification under section 8.52, and may apply to a court under section 8.54 for indemnification or an advance for expenses, in each case to the same extent to which a director may be entitled to indemnification or advance for expenses under those provisions.

Official Comment

Section 8.56 correlates the general legal principles relating to the indemnification of officers of the corporation with the limitations on indemnification in subchapter E. This correlation may be summarized in general terms as follows:

  (1) An officer of a corporation who is *not* a director may be indemnified by the corporation on a discretionary basis to the same extent as though he were a director, and, in addition, may have additional indemnification rights apart from subchapter E, but the outer limits of such rights are specified. (See section 8.56(a)(2) and (c).)

  (2) An officer who is *also* a director of the corporation is entitled to the indemnification rights of a director and of an officer who is not a director (see preceding paragraph) if his conduct that is the subject of the proceeding was solely in his capacity as an officer. (See section 8.56(b).)

  (3) An *officer* of a corporation who is not a director has the right of mandatory indemnification granted to directors under section

8.52 and the right to apply for court-ordered indemnification under section 8.54. (See section 8.56(c).)

Section 8.56 does not deal with indemnification of employees and agents because the concerns of self-dealing that arise when directors provide for their own indemnification and expense advance (and sometimes for senior executive officers) are not present when directors (or officers) provide for indemnification and expense advance for employees and agents who are not directors or officers. Moreover, the rights of employees and agents to indemnification and advance for expenses derive from principles of agency, the doctrine of respondeat superior, collective bargaining or other contractual arrangements rather than from a corporation statute. It would be presumptuous for a corporation statute to seek to limit the indemnification bargain that a corporation may wish to make with those it hires or retains. The same standard applicable to directors and officers may not be appropriate for office workers and hazardous waste workers, brokers and custodians, engineers and farm workers. None of their roles or responsibilities are prescribed by the Model Act.

Section 3.02 grants broad powers to corporations, including powers to make contracts, appoint and fix the compensation of employees and agents and to make payments furthering the business and affairs of the corporation. Many corporations provide for the exercise of these powers in the same provisions in the articles, bylaws or otherwise in which they provide for expense advance and indemnification for directors and officers.

Indemnification may also be provided to protect employees or agents from liabilities incurred while serving at a corporation's request as a director, officer, partner, trustee, or agent of another commercial, charitable, or nonprofit venture.

Although employees and agents are not covered by subchapter E, the principles and procedures set forth in the subchapter for indemnification and advance for expenses for directors and officers may be helpful to counsel and courts in dealing with indemnification and expense advance for employees and agents.

Careful consideration should be given to extending mandatory maximum indemnification and expense advance to employees and agents. The same considerations that may favor mandatory maximum indemnification for directors and officers—e.g., encouraging qualified individuals to serve—may not be present in the cases of employees and agents. Many corporations may prefer to retain the discretion to decide, on a case-by-case basis, whether to indemnify and advance expenses to employees and agents (and perhaps even officers, especially non-executive officers) rather than binding themselves in advance to do so.

1. Officers Who Are Not Directors

While Section 8.56 does not prescribe the standards governing the rights of officers to indemnification, subsection (a) does set outer limits beyond which the corporation may not indemnify. These outer limits for officers (see subsection (a)(2)) are substantially the same as the outer limits on the corporation's power to indemnify directors: (i) in a proceeding by or in the right of the corporation, indemnification is not allowed other than for reasonable expenses incurred in connection therewith and (ii) in any proceeding, indemnification is not allowed in those situations in which directors' liability to the corporation or its shareholders could not be eliminated by a provision included in the articles pursuant to section 2.02(b)(4), i.e., where there has been receipt of a financial benefit to which he is not entitled, intentional infliction of harm on the corporation or shareholders or intentional violation of criminal law. Since officers are held to substantially the same standards of conduct as directors (see section 8.42), there does not appear to be any reasoned basis for granting officers greater indemnification rights as a substantive matter. Procedurally, however, there is an important difference. To permit greater flexibility, officers may be indemnified (within the above-mentioned outer limits) with respect to conduct that does not meet the standards set by section 8.51(a)(1) simply by authorization of the board of directors, whereas directors' indemnification can reach beyond those standards, as contemplated by section 8.51(a)(2), only with a shareholder-approved provision included in the articles pursuant to section 2.02(b)(5). This procedural difference reflects the reduced risk of self-dealing as to officers.

Section 8.56(c) grants non-director officers the same rights to mandatory indemnification under section 8.52 and to apply to a court for indemnification under section 8.54 as are granted to directors. Since their substantive rights to indemnification are essentially the same as those of directors, it is appropriate to grant officers the same affirmative procedural rights to judicial relief as are provided to directors.

The broad authority in section 8.56(a)(2) to grant indemnification may be limited by appropriate provisions in the articles of incorporation. See section 8.58(c).

2. Officers Who Are Also Directors

Subsection (b) provides, in effect, that an officer of the corporation who is also a director is subject to the same standards of indemnification as other directors and cannot avail himself of the provisions of subsection (a) unless he can establish that the act or omission that is the subject of the proceeding was committed solely in his capacity as officer. Thus, a vice president for sales who is also a director and whose actions failed to meet section 8.51(a) standards could be indemnified provided that his conduct was within the outer limits of subsection (a)(2) and involved only his officer capacity.

This more flexible approach for situations where the individual is not acting as a director seems appropriate as a matter of fairness. There are many instances where officers who also serve as directors assume responsibilities and take actions in their non-director capacities. It is hard to justify a denial of indemnification to an officer who failed to meet a standard applicable only to directors when the officer can establish that he did not act as a director. Nor are there likely to be complications or difficulties because some directors are treated differently than others where the high burden of proof—solely as officer—is met. Obviously, the burden will be especially difficult to meet where the roles of officer and director are closely intertwined, as is often the case with a chief executive officer.

For a director-officer to be indemnified under section 8.51 for conduct in his capacity as a director when he has not satisfied the standards of section 8.51(a), a provision in the articles under section 2.02(b)(5) is required. If such a provision is included in the articles, the standards for indemnification are those specified in section 2.02(b)(5). For a director-officer to be indemnified for conduct solely in his capacity as an officer, even though the director-officer has not satisfied the standards of section 8.56(a), only a resolution of the board authorizing such indemnification is required, rather than a provision in the articles. If such a resolution is adopted, the standards for indemnification are those specified in subsection (a)(2). However, when a director-officer seeks indemnification or expense advance under subsections (b) and (a)(2) on the basis of having acted solely in his capacity as an officer, indemnification or expense advance must be approved through the same procedures as set forth in sections 8.55 or 8.53(c), as the case may be, for approval of indemnification or expense advance for a director when acting in his capacity as a director.

§ 8.57 Insurance

A corporation may purchase and maintain insurance on behalf of an individual who is a director or officer of the corporation, or who, while a director or officer of the corporation, serves at the corporation's request as a director, officer, partner, trustee, employee, or agent of another domestic or foreign corporation, partnership, joint venture, trust, employee benefit plan, or other entity, against liability asserted against or incurred by him in that capacity or arising from his status as a director or officer, whether or not the corporation would have power to indemnify or advance expenses to him against the same liability under this subchapter.

Official Comment

Section 8.57 authorizes a corporation to purchase and maintain insurance on behalf of directors and officers against liabilities imposed on them by reason of actions in their official capacity, or their status as such, or arising from their service to the corporation or another entity at the corporation's request. Insurance is not limited to claims against which a corporation is entitled to indemnify under this subchapter. This insurance, usually referred to as "D & O Liability Insurance," provides protection to directors and officers in addition to the rights of indemnification created by or pursuant to this subchapter (as well as typically protecting the individual insureds against the corporation's failure to pay indemnification required or permitted by this subchapter) and provides a source of reimbursement for corporations which indemnify directors and others for conduct covered by the insurance. On the other hand, policies typically do not cover uninsurable matters, such as actions involving dishonesty, self-dealing, bad faith, knowing violations of the securities acts, or other willful misconduct. Johnston, "Corporate Indemnification and Liability Insurance for Directors and Officers," 33 Bus.Law. 1993, 2024–29 (1978). See also Knepper & Bailey, Liability of Corporate Officers and Directors § 21.07 (4th ed. 1988).

Although this section does not include employees and agents for the reasons stated in the Official Comment to section 8.56, the corporation has the power under section 3.02 to purchase and maintain insurance on their behalf. This power is confirmed in section 8.58(d).

This section is not intended to set the outer limits on the type of insurance which a corporation may maintain or the persons to be covered. Rather, it is included to remove "any doubt as to the power to carry insurance and to maintain it on behalf of directors, officers, employees and agents." Sebring, "Recent Legislative Changes in the Law of Indemnification of Directors, Officers and Others," 23 Bus.Law. 95, 106 (1967).

§ 8.58 Variation by Corporate Action; Application of Subchapter

(a) A corporation may, by a provision in its articles of incorporation or bylaws or in a resolution adopted or a contract approved by its board of directors or shareholders, obligate itself in advance of the act or omission giving rise to a proceeding to provide indemnification in accordance with section 8.51 or advance funds to pay for or reimburse expenses in accordance with section 8.53. Any such obligatory provision shall be deemed to satisfy the requirements for authorization referred to in section 8.53(c) and in section 8.55(c). Any such provision that obligates the corporation to provide indemnification to the fullest extent permitted by law shall be deemed to obligate the corporation to advance funds to pay for or reimburse expenses in accordance with section 8.53 to the fullest extent permitted by law, unless the provision specifically provides otherwise.

(b) Any provision pursuant to subsection (a) shall not obligate the corporation to indemnify or advance expenses to a director of a predecessor of the corporation, pertaining to conduct with respect to the predecessor, unless otherwise specifically provided. Any provision for indemnification or advance for expenses in the articles of incorporation, bylaws, or a resolution of the board of directors or shareholders of a predecessor of the corporation in a merger or in a contract to which the predecessor is a party, existing at the time the merger takes effect, shall be governed by section 11.06(a)(3).

(c) A corporation may, by a provision in its articles of incorporation, limit any of the rights to indemnification or advance for expenses created by or pursuant to this subchapter.

(d) This subchapter does not limit a corporation's power to pay or reimburse expenses incurred by a director or an officer in connection with his appearance as a witness in a proceeding at a time when he is not a party.

(e) This subchapter does not limit a corporation's power to indemnify, advance expenses to or provide or maintain insurance on behalf of an employee or agent.

Official Comment

Section 8.58(a) authorizes a corporation to make obligatory the permissive provisions of subchapter E in advance of the conduct giving rise to the request for assistance. Many corporations have adopted such provisions, often with shareholder approval. An obligatory provision satisfies the requirements for authorization in subsection (c) of sections 8.53 and 8.55, but compliance would still be required with subsections (a) and (b) of these sections.

Section 8.58(a) further provides that a provision requiring indemnification to the fullest extent permitted by law shall be deemed, absent an express statement to the contrary, to include an obligation to advance expenses under section 8.53. This provision of the statute is intended to avoid a decision such as that of the Delaware Supreme Court in Advanced Mining Systems, Inc. v. Fricke, 623 A.2d 82 (Del.1992). If a corporation provides for obligatory indemnification and not for obligatory advance for expenses, the provision should be reviewed to ensure that it properly reflects the intent in light of the second sentence of section 8.58(a). Also, a corporation should consider whether obligatory expense advance is intended for direct suits by the corporation as well as for derivative suits by shareholders in the right of the corporation. In the former case, assuming compliance with subsections (a) and (b) of section 8.53, the corporation could be required to fund the defense of a defendant director even where the board of directors has already concluded that he has engaged in significant wrongdoing. See Official Comment to section 8.53.

Section 8.58(b) provides that an obligatory indemnification provision as authorized by subsection (a) does not, unless specific provision is made to the contrary, bind the corporation with respect to a predecessor. An obligatory indemnification provision of a predecessor is treated as a liability (to the extent it is one) under section 11.06(a)(3), which governs the effect of a merger.

Section 8.58(c) permits a corporation to limit the right of the corporation to indemnify or advance expenses by a provision in its articles of incorporation. As provided in section 10.09, no such limitation will affect rights in existence when the provision becomes effective pursuant to section 1.23.

Section 8.58(d) makes clear that subchapter E deals only with actual or threatened defendants or respondents in a proceeding, and that expenses incurred by a director in connection with appearance as a witness may be indemnified without regard to the limitations of subchapter E. Indeed, most of the standards described in sections 8.51 and 8.54(a) by their own terms can have no meaningful application to a director whose only connection with a proceeding is that he has been called as a witness.

Subchapter E does not regulate the power of the corporation to indemnify or advance expenses to employees and agents. That subject is governed by the law of agency and related principles and frequently by contractual arrangements between the corporation and the employee or agent. Section 8.58(e) makes clear that, while indemnification, advance for expenses and insurance for employees and agents are beyond the scope of this subchapter, the elaboration in subchapter E of standards and procedures for indemnification, expense advance and insurance for directors and officers is not in any way intended to cast doubt on the power of the corporation to indemnify or advance expenses to or purchase and maintain insurance for employees and agents under section 3.02 or otherwise.

§ 8.59 Exclusivity of Subchapter

A corporation may provide indemnification or advance expenses to a director or an officer only as permitted by this subchapter.

Official Comment

This subchapter is the exclusive source for the power of a corporation to indemnify or advance expenses to a director or an officer.

Section 8.59 does not preclude provisions in articles of incorporation, bylaws, resolutions, or contracts designed to provide procedural machinery in addition to (but not inconsistent with) that provided by this subchapter. For example, a corporation may properly obligate the board of directors to consider and act expeditiously on an application for indemnification or advance for expenses or to cooperate in the procedural steps required to obtain a judicial determination under section 8.54.

Subchapter F *

Directors' Conflicting Interest Transactions

Introductory Comment ...

2. Scope of Subchapter F

The focus of subchapter F is sharply defined and limited.

First, the subchapter is targeted on legal challenges based on interest conflicts only. Subchapter F does not undertake to define, regulate, or provide any form of procedure regarding other possible claims. For example, subchapter F does not address a claim that a controlling shareholder has violated a duty owed to the corporation or minority shareholders.

Second, the subchapter is applicable only when there is a "transaction" by or with the corporation. For purposes of subchapter F, "transaction" generally connotes negotiations or a consensual bilateral arrangement between the corporation and another party or parties that concern their respective and differing economic rights or interests—not simply a unilateral action by the corporation but rather a "deal." See the discussion regarding "transaction" under clause (2) of Section 8.60(2)....

Third, subchapter F deals with directors only. ...

Subchapter F contemplates deletion of former Model Act section 8.32 dealing specially with loans to directors; a loan to a director is simply a subspecies of directors' conflicting interest transactions and is procedurally governed by subchapter F. See the Note on Fair Transactions in the Official Comment to section 8.61(b).

3. Structure of Subchapter F

The skeleton of subchapter F has only four parts. Definitions are in section 8.60. Section 8.61 prescribes what a court may or may not do in various situations. Section 8.62 prescribes procedures for action by boards of directors regarding a director's conflicting interest transaction. Section 8.63 prescribes corresponding procedures for shareholders. Thus, the most important operative section of the subchapter is section 8.61. ...

Note ...

In the Official Comments to subchapter F, the director who has a conflicting interest is for convenience referred to as "the director" or

---

* Subchapter F, sections 8.60–8.63, replaces former sections 8.31 and 8.32 in the Revised Model Business Corporation Act. Sections 8.31 and 8.32 are nevertheless included in this Supplement, supra, because many states that had adopted sections 8.31 and 8.32 as part of their corporation statutes did not decide to adopt Subchapter F.

"D", the corporation of which he is a director is referred to as "the corporation" or "X Co.," and another corporation dealing with X Co. is referred to as "Y Co."

§ 8.60   Subchapter Definitions

In this subchapter:

(1) "Conflicting interest" with respect to a corporation means the interest a director of the corporation has respecting a transaction effected or proposed to be effected by the corporation (or by a subsidiary of the corporation or any other entity in which the corporation has a controlling interest) if

> (i) whether or not the transaction is brought before the board of directors of the corporation for action, the director knows at the time of commitment that he or a related person is a party to the transaction or has a beneficial financial interest in or so closely linked to the transaction and of such financial significance to the director or a related person that the interest would reasonably be expected to exert an influence on the director's judgment if he were called upon to vote on the transaction; or

> (ii) the transaction is brought (or is of such character and significance to the corporation that it would in the normal course be brought) before the board of directors of the corporation for action, and the director knows at the time of commitment that any of the following persons is either a party to the transaction or has a beneficial financial interest in or so closely linked to the transaction and of such financial significance to the person that the interest would reasonably be expected to exert an influence on the director's judgment if he were called upon to vote on the transaction: (A) an entity (other than the corporation) of which the director is a director, general partner, agent, or employee; (B) a person that controls one or more of the entities specified in subclause (A) or an entity that is controlled by, or is under common control with, one or more of the entities specified in subclause (A); or (C) an individual who is a general partner, principal, or employer of the director.

(2) "Director's conflicting interest transaction" with respect to a corporation means a transaction effected or proposed to be effected by the corporation (or by a subsidiary of the corporation or any other entity in which the corporation has a controlling interest) respecting which a director of the corporation has a conflicting interest.

(3) "Related person" of a director means (i) the spouse (or a parent or sibling thereof) of the director, or a child, grandchild, sibling, parent (or spouse of any thereof) of the director, or an individual having the same home as the director, or a trust or estate of which an individual specified in this clause (i) is a substantial beneficiary; or (ii) a trust,

estate, incompetent, conservatee, or minor of which the director is a fiduciary.

(4) "Required disclosure" means disclosure by the director who has a conflicting interest of (i) the existence and nature of his conflicting interest, and (ii) all facts known to him respecting the subject matter of the transaction that an ordinarily prudent person would reasonably believe to be material to a judgment about whether or not to proceed with the transaction.

(5) "Time of commitment" respecting a transaction means the time when the transaction is consummated or, if made pursuant to contract, the time when the corporation (or its subsidiary or the entity in which it has a controlling interest) becomes contractually obligated so that its unilateral withdrawal from the transaction would entail significant loss, liability, or other damage.

Official Comment ...

The definitions set forth in section 8.60 apply to subchapter F only and have no application elsewhere in the Model Act.

1. Conflicting Interest

The definition of conflicting interest requires that the director know of the transaction. More than that, it requires that he know of his interest conflict at the time of the corporation's commitment to the transaction. Absent that knowledge by the director, the risk to the corporation addressed by subchapter F is not present. In a corporation of significant size, routine transactions in the ordinary course of business, involving decisionmaking at lower management levels, will usually not be known to the director and will thus be excluded by the "knowledge" criterion in the definition.

The term "conflicting interest" as defined in subchapter F is never abstract or freestanding; its use must always be linked to a particular director, to a particular transaction and to a particular corporation.

The definition of "conflicting interest" is exclusive. An interest of a director is a conflicting interest *if and only if* it meets the requirements of subdivision (1).

D can have a conflicting interest in only three ways.

First a conflicting interest of D will obviously arise if the transaction is between D and X Co.

A conflicting interest will also arise under subdivision (1)(i) if D is not a party but has a beneficial financial interest in the transaction that is separate from his interest as a director or shareholder and is of such significance to the director that it would reasonably be expected to exert an influence on his judgment if he were called upon to vote on the matter. The personal economic stake of the director must be in or closely linked to the transaction—that is, his gain must hinge directly on the transaction itself. A contingent or remote gain (such as a future reduction in tax rates in the local community) is not enough to give rise to a conflicting interest under subdivision (1)(i). See the discussion of "transaction" under the Official Comment to subdivision (2).

If Y Co. is a party to or interested in the transaction with X Co. and Y Co. is somehow linked to D, the matter is in general governed by subdivision (1)(ii). But D's economic interest in Y Co. could be so substantial and the impact of the transaction so important to Y Co. that D could also have a conflicting interest under subdivision (1)(i).

Note that basic standard set by subdivision (1)(i) and throughout subchapter F—"would reasonably be expected to exert an influence"—is an objective, not a subjective, criterion.

Second, a conflicting interest of D can arise under subdivision (1)(i) from the involvement in the transaction of a "related person" of D. "Related person" is defined in subdivision (3).

Third, in limited circumstances, subsequently discussed, a conflicting interest of D can arise through the economic involvement of certain other persons specified in subdivision (1)(ii). These are any entity (other than X Co.) of which the director is a director, general partner, agent, or employee; a person that controls, or an entity that is controlled by, or is under common control with one or more of the entities specified in the preceding clause; and any individual who is a general partner, principal, or employer of D.

The terms "principal" and "employer" as used in subdivision (1)(ii) are not separately defined but should be interpreted sensibly in the context of the purpose of the subdivision. The key question is whether D is, by force of an overt or covert tie to an employer or a principal who has a significant stake in the outcome of the transaction, beholden to act in the interest of that outside employer or principal rather than in the interest of X Co.

The "would reasonably be expected" criterion of subdivision (1)(i) applies also to subdivision (1)(ii).

Any director will, of course, have countless relationships and linkages to persons and institutions other than those specified in subdivision (1)(ii) and those defined in subdivision (3) to be related persons. But ... the subcategories of persons encompassed by subdivision (1)(ii) are expressly intended to be exclusive and to cover the field for purposes of subchapter F and particularly section 8.61(a). Thus, if, in a case involving a transaction between X Co. and Y Co., a court is presented with the argument that D, a director of X Co., is also a major creditor of Y Co. and that that stake in Y Co. gives D a conflicting interest, the court should reply that D's creditor interest in Y Co. does not fit any subcategory of subdivision (1)(ii) or subdivision (3) and therefore the conflict of interest claim must be rejected by force of section 8.61(a). The result would be otherwise if Y Co.'s debt to D is of such economic significance to D that it would fall under subdivision (1)(i) or put him in control of Y Co. and thus come within subdivision (1)(ii).

Subdivision (1)(ii) has a differentiated threshold keyed to the significance of the transaction. See the Official Comment to subdivision (2).

It is to be noted that under subdivision (1) of Section 8.60, any interest that the director has that meets the criteria set forth is considered a "conflicting interest". If a director has an interest that meets those criteria, subchapter F draws no further distinction between a director's interest that clashes with the interests of the corporation and a director's interest that coincides with or is parallel to the interests of the corporation. If the director's "interest" is present, "conflict" is assumed.

2. Director's Conflicting Interest Transaction

The definition of "director's conflicting interest transaction" in subdivision (2) is the key concept of subchapter F, establishing the area that lies within—and without—the scope of the subchapter's provisions. The definition operates preclusively; it not only designates the area within which the rules of subchapter F are to be applied but also denies the power of the court to act with respect to conflict of interest claims against directors in circumstances that lie outside the statutory definition of "director's conflicting interest transaction." See section 8.61(a).

(1) Transaction

To constitute a director's conflicting interest transaction, there must first be a transaction by the corporation, its subsidiary, or controlled entity in which the director has a financial interest. As discussed earlier, the safe harbor provisions provided by subchapter F have no application to circumstances in which there is no "transaction" by the corporation, however apparent the director's conflicting interest. Other strictures of the law prohibit a director from seizing corporate opportunities for himself and from competing against the corporation of which he is a director; subchapter F has no application to such situations. Moreover, a director might personally benefit if the corporation takes no action, as where the corporation decides not to make a bid. Subchapter F has no application to such instances. The limited thrust of the subchapter is to establish procedures which, if followed, immunize a corporate transaction and the interested director against the common law doctrine of voidability grounded on the director's conflicting interest.

. . .

However, a policy decision and a transactional decision can blur and overlap. Assume X Co. operates a steel mini-mill that is running at a loss. A real estate developer offers to buy the land on which the mill is located and the X Co. board, having no other use for the land, accepts the offer. This corporate action can readily be characterized either as a transaction—the sale of the land—or as a business policy decision—to go out of an unprofitable business. If D is a partner of the real estate developer, D has a stake in the sale transaction and subdivisions (1)(i) and (1)(ii) and all of subchapter F apply. But what if D, having no such interest, is in the local trucking business and a predictable consequence of closing the local mini-mill is that D will benefit from a future increase in demand for hauling services to bring in steel from more distant supply sources. An intent of the words "in or so closely linked to the transaction" in subdivisions (1)(i) and (1)(ii) is to focus subchapter F on the transaction itself. D's financial stake as a trucker in this situation lies not in the transaction, which is governed by subchapter F, but in the corporate business decision, which is not; accordingly, section 8.61(a) is inapplicable and imposes no bar to the court's discretion. Board action, though in compliance with section 8.62, will not, ipso facto, yield safe harbor protection for D or the transaction under section 8.61(b). ...

As another feature of the key term "transaction", the text of subdivision (1) emphasizes that the term implies and is limited to action by the corporation itself. The language of subchapter F has no application one way or the other to economic actions by the director in which the corporation is not a party or in which the corporation takes no action. Thus, a purchase by the director of the corporation's shares on the open market or from a third party is not a "transaction" within the scope of subchapter F and the subchapter does not govern an attack made on the propriety of such a share purchase.

If the board of directors of X Co. decides to distribute "poison pill" rights in order to fend off a possible takeover, that occurrence does not constitute a "transaction" as contemplated by subchapter F. ... If, on the other hand, a board of directors commits the corporation to a "crown jewel" option granted to a third party, there would be a "transaction".

But as noted earlier, for the transaction to be covered by subchapter F, the director (or other person designated by Section 8.60(i)) must have a beneficial interest respecting the transaction. Subchapter F would obviously govern such a crown jewel contract if a director was himself (or had a defined relationship to) the third party. But the fact that the crown jewel contract was in part motivated by the directors' desire to keep themselves on the board would not, taken alone, constitute a sufficiently direct interest in the transaction to bring it with subchapter F.

(2) Party to the Transaction—The Corporation

Transaction by what entity? In the usual case, the transaction in question would be by X Co. But assume that X Co. is the controlling corporation of S Co. (i.e., it controls the vote for directors of S Co.). D wishes to sell a building he owns to X Co. and X Co. is willing to buy it.

As a business matter, it will often make no difference to X Co. whether it takes the title itself or places it with its subsidiary S Co. or another entity that X Co. controls. The applicability of subchapter F cannot be allowed to depend upon that formal distinction. The subchapter therefore includes within its operative framework transactions by a subsidiary or controlled entity of X Co. See the Note on Parent Companies and Subsidiaries below.

(3) *Party to the Transaction—The Director*

Subdivision (1)(i) and subdivision (1)(ii) differ as to the persons covered and as to the threshold of transactional significance. Subdivision (1)(i), addressed to D and related persons of D, includes as directors' conflicting interest transactions *all* transactions that meet the substantive criteria prescribed. By contrast, subdivision (1)(ii), addressed to transactions involving other designated persons, excludes from its coverage transactions that are not sufficiently significant to the corporation to warrant decision at the boardroom level.

As a generalization, the linkage between a director and a "related person" is closer than that between the director and those persons and entities specified in subdivision (1)(ii). Correspondingly, the threshold of conflicting interest under subdivision (1)(i) is lower than that set for subdivision (1)(ii). Thus, all routine transactions of X Co. are excluded from the definition of director's conflicting interest transaction unless they fall within subdivision (1)(i). If Y Co., a computer company of which D is also an outside director, sells office machinery to X Co., the transaction will not normally give rise to a conflicting interest for D from the perspective of either company since the transaction is a routine matter that would not come before either board. If, however, the transaction is of such significance to one of the two companies that it would come before the board of that company, then D has a conflicting interest in the transaction with respect to that company.

Implicit in subdivision (1)(ii) is a recognition that X Co. and Y Co., particularly if large enterprises, are likely to have routine, perhaps frequent, business dealings with each other as they buy and sell goods and services in the marketplace. The terms of these dealings are dictated by competitive market forces and the transactions are conducted at personnel levels far below the boardroom. The fact that D has some relationship with Y Co. is not in itself sufficient reason to open these smaller scale impersonal business transactions to challenge if not passed through the board in accordance with section 8.62 procedures. It would be doubly impractical to do so twice where X Co. and Y Co. have a common director.

Subchapter F takes the practical position. The definition in subdivision (1)(ii) excludes most such transactions both by its "knowledge" requirement and by its higher threshold of economic significance. In almost all cases, any such transaction, if challenged, would be easily defensible as being "fair." In respect of day-to-day business dealings, the main practical risk of impropriety would be that a director having a conflicting interest might seek to exert inappropriate influence upon the interior operations of the enterprise, might try to use his status as a director to pressure lower level employees to divert their business out of ordinary channels to his advantage. But a director's affirmative misconduct goes well beyond a claim that he has a conflicting interest, and judicial action against such improper behavior remains available. See also the Official Comment to section 8.62(b) regarding common directors.

The absence of the significance threshold in subdivision (1)(i) does not impose an inappropriate burden on directors and related persons. The commonplace and oftentimes recurring transaction will involve purchase of the corporation's product line; it will usually not be difficult for D to show that the transaction was on commercial terms and was fair, or indeed, that he had no knowledge of the transaction. As a result, these transactions do not invite harassing lawsuits against the director. A purchase by D of a product of X Co. at a usual "employee's discount," while technically assailable as a conflicting interest transaction, would customarily be viewed as "fair" to the corporation as a routine incident of the office of director. For other transactions between the corporation and the director or those close to him, D can, and should, have the burden of establishing the fairness of the transaction if it is not passed upon by the arm's length review of qualified directors or the holders of qualified shares. If there are any reasons to believe that the terms of the transaction might be questioned as unfair to X Co., D is well advised to pass the transaction through the safe harbor procedures for subchapter F.

Note on Parent Companies and Subsidiaries

If a subsidiary is wholly owned, there is no outside holder of shares of the subsidiary to be injured with respect to transactions between the two corporations.

Transactions between a parent corporation and a partially-owned subsidiary may raise the possibility of abuse of power by a majority shareholder to the disadvantage of a minority shareholder. Subchapter F has no relevance as to how a court should deal with that claim.

If there are not at least two outside directors of the subsidiary, the subsidiary and the board of directors must operate on the basis that any transaction between the subsidiary and the parent that reaches the significance threshold in subdivision (1)(ii) may, as a technical matter, be challengeable by a minority shareholder of the subsidiary on grounds that it is a director's conflicting interest transaction. In that case, the directors of the subsidiary will have to establish the fairness of the transaction to the subsidiary. In practice, however, the case law has dealt with such claims under the rubric of the duties of a majority shareholder and that is, in reality, the better approach. See the Official Comment to section 8.61(b).

3. Related Person

Two subcategories of "related person" of the director are set out in subdivision (3). These subcategories are specified, exclusive, and preemptive.

The first subcategory is made up of closely related family, or near-family, individuals, trusts, and estates as specified in clause (i). The clause is exclusive insofar as family relationships are concerned. The references to a "spouse" are intended to include a common law spouse or unrelated cohabitant.

The second subcategory is made up of persons specified in clause (ii) to whom or which the director is linked in a fiduciary capacity as, for example, in his status as a trustee or administrator. (Note that the definition of "person" in the Model Act includes both individuals and entities. See section 1.40(16).) From the perspective of X Co., D's fiduciary relationships are always a sensitive concern. A conscientious director may be able to control his own greed arising from a conflicting personal interest. And he may resist the temptation to assist his wife or child. But he can never escape his legal obligation to act in the best interests of another person for whom he is a trustee or other fiduciary.

4. Required Disclosure

Two separate elements make up the defined term "required disclosure." They are disclosure of the existence of the conflicting interest and then disclosure of the material facts known to D about the subject of the transaction.

Subdivision (4) calls for disclosure of all facts known to D about the subject of the transaction that an ordinarily prudent person would reasonably believe to be material to a judgment by the person acting for the corporation as to whether to proceed or not to proceed with the transaction. If a director knows that the land the corporation is buying from him is sinking into an abandoned coal mine, he must disclose not only that he is the owner and that he has an interest in the transaction but also that the land is subsiding; as a director of X Co. he may not invoke caveat emptor. But in the same circumstances the director is *not* under an obligation to reveal the price he paid for the property ten years ago, or that he inherited it, since that information is not material to the corporation's business judgment as to whether or not to proceed with the transaction. Further, while material facts that pertain to the *subject* of the transaction must be disclosed, a director is not required to reveal personal or subjective information that bears upon his negotiating position (such as, for example, his urgent need for cash, or the lowest price he would be willing to accept). This is true despite the fact that such information would obviously be relevant to the corporation's decision-making in the sense that, if known to the corporation, it could equip the corporation to hold out for terms more favorable to it.

Underlying the definition of the twin components of "required disclosure" is the critically important provision contained in subdivision (1) that a basic precondition for the existence of a "conflicting interest" is that the director *know* of the transaction and also that he *know* of the existence of his conflicting interest.

5.   Time of Commitment

The time of the commitment by the corporation (or its subsidiary or other controlled entity) to the transaction is defined in operational terms geared to change of economic position.

§ 8.61   Judicial Action

(a) A transaction effected or proposed to be effected by a corporation (or by a subsidiary of the corporation or any other entity in which the corporation has a controlling interest) that is not a director's conflicting interest transaction may not be enjoined, set aside, or give rise to an award of damages or other sanctions, in a proceeding by a shareholder or by or in the right of the corporation, because a director of the corporation, or any person with whom or which he has a personal, economic, or other association, has an interest in the transaction.

(b) A director's conflicting interest transaction may not be enjoined, set aside, or give rise to an award of damages or other sanctions, in a proceeding by a shareholder or by or in the right of the corporation, because the director, or any person with whom or which he has a personal, economic, or other association, has an interest in the transaction, if:

(1) directors' action respecting the transaction was at any time taken in compliance with section 8.62;

(2) shareholders' action respecting the transaction was at any time taken in compliance with section 8.63;

(3) the transaction, judged according to the circumstances at the time of commitment, is established to have been fair to the corporation.

Official Comment ...

Section 8.61 is the operational section of subchapter F as it prescribes the judicial consequences of the other sections.

Speaking generally:

(i) If the procedure set forth in section 8.62 or in section 8.63 is complied with, or if the transaction is fair to the corporation, then a director's conflicting interest transaction is immune from attack on any ground of a personal interest or conflict of interest of the director. However, the narrow scope of subchapter F must again be strongly emphasized; if the transaction is vulnerable to attack on some other ground, subchapter F does not make it less so for having been passed through the procedures of subchapter F. . . .

(ii) If a transaction is *not* a director's conflicting interest transaction as defined in section 8.60, then the transaction may *not* be enjoined, rescinded, or made the basis of other sanction *on the ground of a conflict of interest of a director, whether or not it went through the procedures of subchapter F*. In that sense, subchapter F is specifically intended to be both comprehensive and exclusive.

(iii) If a transaction that is a director's conflicting interest transaction was not at any time the subject of action taken in compliance with section 8.62 or section 8.63, and it is attacked on grounds of a director's conflicting interest and is not shown to be fair to the corporation, then the court may grant such remedial action as it considers appropriate under the applicable law of the jurisdiction. If the attack is on other grounds, subchapter F has no relevance to the issue(s) before the court.

1. Section 8.61(a)

Section 8.61(a) is a key component in the design of subchapter F. It draws a bright-line circle, declaring that the definitions of section 8.60 wholly occupy and preempt the field of directors' conflicting interest transactions. Of course, outside this circle there is a penumbra of director interests, desires, goals, loyalties, and prejudices that may, in a particular context, run at odds with the best interests of the corporation, but section 8.61(a) forbids a court to ground remedial action on any of them. If a plaintiff charges that a director had a conflict of interest with respect to a transaction of the corporation because the other party was his cousin, the answer of the court should be: "No. A cousin, as such and without more, is not included in section 8.60(3) as a related person— and under section 8.61(a), I have no authority to reach out farther." If a plaintiff contends that the director had a conflict of interest in a corporate transaction because the other party is president of the golf club the director wants desperately to join, the court should respond: "No. The only director's conflicting interest on the basis of which I can set aside a corporate transaction or impose other sanctions is a financial interest as defined in section 8.60." . . .

2. Section 8.61(b)

Section 8.61(b) is the heart of subchapter F—the fundamental section that provides for the safe harbor.

Clause (1) of subsection (b) provides that if a director has a conflicting interest respecting a transaction, neither the transaction nor the director is legally vulnerable if the procedures of section 8.62 have been properly followed. Subsection (b)(1) is, however, subject to a critically important predicate condition.

The condition—an obvious one—is that the board's action must comply with the care, best interests and good faith criteria prescribed in section 8.30(a) for all directors' actions. If the directors who voted for the conflicting interest transaction were qualified directors under subchapter F, but approved the transaction merely as an accommodation to the director with the conflicting interest, going through the motions of board action without complying with the requirements of section 8.30(a), the action of the board would not be given effect for purposes of section 8.61(b)(1).

Board action on a director's conflicting interest transaction provides a context in which the function of the "best interests of the corporation" language in section 8.30(a) is brought into clear focus. Consider, for example, a situation in which it is established that the board of a manufacturing corporation approved a cash loan to a director where the duration, security and interest terms of the loan were at prevailing commercial rates, but (i) the loan was not made in the course of the corporation's ordinary business and (ii) the loan required a commitment of limited working capital that would otherwise have been used in furtherance of the corporation's business activities. Such a loan transaction would not be afforded safe-harbor protection by section 8.62(b)(1) since the board did not comply with the requirement in section 8.30(a) that the board's action be, in its reasonable judgment, in the best interests of the corporation—that is, that the action will, as the board judges the circumstances at hand, yield favorable results (or reduce detrimental results) as judged from the perspective of furthering the corporation's business activities.

If a determination is made that the terms of a director's conflicting interest transaction, judged according to the circumstances at the time of commitment, were manifestly unfavorable to the corporation, that determination would be relevant to an allegation that the directors' action was not taken in good faith and therefore did not comply with section 8.30(a). . . .

Note on Fair Transactions

(1) *Terms of the Transaction.* If the issue in a transaction is the "fairness" of a price, "fair" is not to be taken to imply that there is a single "fair" price, all others being "unfair." It has long been settled that a "fair" price is any price in that broad range which an unrelated party might have been willing to pay or willing to accept, as the case may be, for the property, following a normal arm's-length business negotiation, in the light of the knowledge that would have been reasonably acquired in the course of such negotiations, any result within that range being "fair." The same statement applies not only to price but to any other key term of the deal.

Although the "fair" criterion applied by the court is a range rather than a point, the width of that range is only a segment of the full spectrum of the directors' discretion associated with the exercise of business judgment under section 8.30(a). That is to say, the scope of decisional discretion that a court would have allowed to the directors if they had acted and had complied with section 8.30(a) is wider than the range of "fairness" contemplated for judicial determination where section 8.61(b)(3) is the governing provision.

(2) *Benefit to the Corporation.* In considering the "fairness" of the transaction, the court will in addition be required to consider not only the market fairness of the terms of the deal, but also, as the board would have been required to do, whether the transaction was one that was reasonably likely to yield favorable results (or reduce detrimental results) from the perspective of furthering the corporation's business activities. Thus, if a manufacturing company that is short of working capital allocates some of its scarce funds to purchase a sailing yacht owned by one of its directors, it will not be easy to persuade the court that the transaction is "fair" in the sense that it was reasonably made to further the business interests of the corporation; the fact that the price paid for the yacht was stipulated to be a "fair" market price will not be enough alone to uphold the transaction. See also the discussion above regarding section 8.30(a).

(3) *Process of Decision.* In some circumstances, the behavior of the director having the conflicting interest can itself affect the finding and content of "fairness." The most obvious illustration of unfair dealing arises out of the director's failure to disclose fully his interest or hidden defects known to him regarding the transaction. Another illustration could be the exertion of improper pressure by the director upon the other directors. When the facts of such unfair dealing become known, the court should offer the corporation its option as to whether to rescind the transaction on grounds of "unfairness" even if it appears that the terms were "fair" by market standards and the corporation profited from it. If the corporation decides not to rescind the transaction because of business advantages accruing to the corporation from it, the court may still find in the director's misconduct a basis for judicially imposed sanction against the director personally. Thus, the course of dealing—or process—is a key component to a "fairness" determination under subsection (b)(3). . . .

§ 8.62 Directors' Action

(a) Directors' action respecting a transaction is effective for purposes of section 8.61(b)(1) if the transaction received the affirmative vote of a majority (but no fewer than two) of those qualified directors on the board of directors or on a duly empowered committee of the board who voted on the transaction after either required disclosure to them (to the extent the information was not known by them) or compliance with subsection (b); provided that action by a committee is so effective only if (1) all its members are qualified directors, and (2) its members are either all the qualified directors on the board or are appointed by the affirmative vote of a majority of the qualified directors on the board.

(b) If a director has a conflicting interest respecting a transaction, but neither he nor a related person of the director specified in section 8.60(3)(i) is a party to the transaction, and if the director has a duty under law or professional canon, or a duty of confidentiality to another person, respecting information relating to the transaction such that the director may not make the disclosure described in section 8.60(4)(ii), then disclosure is sufficient for purposes of subsection (a) if the director (1) discloses to the directors voting on the transaction the existence and nature of his conflicting interest and informs them of the character and limitations imposed by that duty before their vote on the transaction, and (2) plays no part, directly or indirectly, in their deliberations or vote.

(c) A majority (but no fewer than two) of all the qualified directors on the board of directors, or on the committee, constitutes a quorum for purposes of action that complies with this section. Directors' action that otherwise complies with this section is not affected by the presence or vote of a director who is not a qualified director.

(d) For purposes of this section, "qualified director" means, with respect to a director's conflicting interest transaction, any director who does not have either (1) a conflicting interest respecting the transaction, or (2) a familial, financial, professional, or employment relationship with a second director who does have a conflicting interest respecting the transaction, which relationship would, in the circumstances, reasonably be expected to exert an influence on the first director's judgment when voting on the transaction.

Official Comment ...

Section 8.62 provides the procedure for action of the board of directors under subchapter F. In the normal course, this section, taken together with section 8.61(b), will be the key provision for dealing with directors' conflicting interest transactions.

All discussion of section 8.62 must be conducted in light of the overarching provisions of section 8.30(a) prescribing the criteria for decisions by directors. Board action that does not comply with the requirements of section 8.30(a) will not, of course, be given effect under section 8.62. See the Official Comment to section 8.61(b).

1. Section 8.62(a)

A transaction in which a director has a conflicting interest is approved under section 8.62 if and only if it is approved by qualified directors, as defined in subsection 8.62(d). Action by the board of directors as a whole is effective if approved by the affirmative vote of a majority (but not less than two) of the qualified directors on the board. Action may also be taken by a duly authorized committee of the board but, to be effective, all members of the committee must be qualified directors and the committee must either contain all of the qualified directors on the board or must have been appointed by the affirmative vote of a majority of the qualified directors on the board. The effect of the limitation on committee action is to make it impossible to handpick as committee members a favorably inclined minority from among the qualified directors.

Except to the limited extent provided in subsection (b), approval by the board or committee must be preceded by required disclosure.

Action complying with subsection 8.62(a) may be taken by the board of directors at any time, before or after the transaction, and may deal with a single transaction or a specified category of similar transactions.

2. Section 8.62(b)

Subsection (b) is a new provision designed to deal, in a practical way, with situations in which a director who has a conflicting interest is not able to comply fully with the disclosure requirement of subsection (a) because of an extrinsic duty of confidentiality. The director may, for example, be prohibited from making full disclosure because of restrictions of law that happen to apply to the transaction (e.g., grand jury seal or national security statute) or professional canon (e.g., lawyers' or doctors' client privilege). The most frequent use of subsection (b), however, will undoubtedly be in connection with common directors who find themselves in a position of dual fiduciary obligations that clash. If D is also a director of Y Co., D may have acquired privileged confidential information from one or both sources relevant to a transaction between X Co. and Y Co. that he cannot reveal to one without violating his fiduciary duty to the other. In such circumstance, subsection (b) makes it possible for such a matter to be brought to the board for consideration under subsection (a) and thus enable X Co. to secure the protection afforded by subchapter F for the transaction despite the fact that D cannot make the full disclosure usually required.

To comply with subsection (b), D must disclose that he has a conflicting interest, inform the directors who vote on the transaction of the nature of his duty of confidentiality (e.g., inform them that it arises out of an attorney-client privilege or his duty as a director of Y Co. that prevents him from making the disclosure called for by clause (ii) of section 8.60(4)), and then play no personal part in the board's deliberations. The point of subsection (b) is simply to make clear that the provisions of subchapter F may be employed with regard to a transaction in circumstances where an interested director cannot, because of enforced fiduciary silence, make disclosure of the facts known to him. Of course, if D invokes subsection (b) and then remains silent before leaving the boardroom, the remaining directors may decline to act on the transaction if troubled by a concern that D knows (or may know) something they do not. On the other hand, if D is subject to an extrinsic duty of confidentiality but has no knowledge of facts that should be disclosed, he would normally so state and disregard subsection (b), and (having disclosed the existence and nature of his conflicting interest) thereby comply with section 8.60(4). . . .

Subsection (b) is not available to D if the transaction is directly between the corporation and D or his related person—if, that is, the director or a related person is a party to the transaction. If D or a related person is a party to the transaction, D's only options are required disclosure on an unqualified basis, abandonment of the transaction, or acceptance of the risk of establishing fairness in a court proceeding if the transaction is challenged.

Whenever D proceeds as provided in subsection 8.62(b), the board should recognize that he may well have information that in usual circumstances he would be required to reveal to the board—information that may well indicate that the transaction is a favorable or unfavorable one for X Co. . . .

4.   Section 8.62(d)

Obviously, a director's conflicting interest transaction and D cannot be provided safe harbor protection by fellow directors who themselves have conflicting interests; only "qualified directors" can provide such safe harbor protection pursuant to subsection (a). "Qualified director" is defined in subsection (d). The definition is broad. It excludes not only any director who has a conflicting interest respecting the matter, but also—going significantly beyond the persons specified in the subcategories of section 8.60(1)(ii) for purposes of the "conflicting interest" definition—any director whose familial or financial relationship with D or whose employment or professional relationship with D would be likely to influence the director's vote on the transaction.

The determination of whether there is a financial, employment or professional relationship should be based on the practicalities of the situation rather than formalistic circumstances. For example, a director employed by a corporation controlled by D should be regarded as having an employment relationship with D.

§ 8.63   Shareholders' Action

(a) Shareholders' action respecting a transaction is effective for purposes of section 8.61(b)(2) if a majority of the votes entitled to be cast by the holders of all qualified shares were cast in favor of the transaction after (1) notice to shareholders describing the director's conflicting interest transaction, (2) provision of the information referred to in subsection (d), and (3) required disclosure to the shareholders who voted on the transaction (to the extent the information was not known by them).

(b) For purposes of this section, "qualified shares" means any shares entitled to vote with respect to the director's conflicting interest transaction except shares that, to the knowledge, before the vote, of the secretary (or other officer or agent of the corporation authorized to tabulate votes), are beneficially owned (or the voting of which is controlled) by a director who has a conflicting interest respecting the transaction or by a related person of the director, or both.

(c) A majority of the votes entitled to be cast by the holders of all qualified shares constitutes a quorum for purposes of action that complies with this section. Subject to the provisions of subsections (d) and (e), shareholders' action that otherwise complies with this section is not affected by the presence of holders, or the voting, of shares that are not qualified shares.

(d) For purposes of compliance with subsection (a), a director who has a conflicting interest respecting the transaction shall, before the shareholders' vote, inform the secretary (or other office or agent of the corporation authorized to tabulate votes) of the number, and the identity of persons holding or controlling the vote, of all shares that the director knows are beneficially owned (or the voting of which is controlled) by the director or by a related person of the director, or both.

(e) If a shareholders' vote does not comply with subsection (a) solely because of a failure of a director to comply with subsection (d), and if the director establishes that his failure did not determine and was not intended by him to influence the outcome of the vote, the court may, with or without further proceedings respecting section 8.61(b)(3), take such action respecting the transaction and the director, and give such effect, if any, to the shareholders' vote, as it considers appropriate in the circumstances.

Official Comment ...

1. Section 8.63(a) ....

Note that section 8.63 does not contain a provision comparable to section 8.62(b). Thus, the safe harbor protection of subchapter F cannot be made available through shareholder action under section 8.63 in a case where D remains silent because of an extrinsic duty of confidentiality. This is advertent. While it is believed that the section 8.62(b) procedure is workable in the collegial setting of the boardroom, one must have reservations whether the same is true vis-a-vis the shareholder body, especially in larger corporations where there is heavy reliance upon the proxy mechanic. In most situations no opportunity exists for shareholders to quiz D about his duty and to discuss the implications of acting without the benefit of D's knowledge concerning the transaction.

In a case involving a closely-held corporation where section 8.63 procedures are followed, but with D acting as provided in section 8.62(b), a court could, of course, attach significance to a favorable shareholder vote in evaluating the fairness of the transaction to the corporation....

2. Section 8.63(b) ....

The category of persons whose shares are excluded from the vote count under subsection (b) is not the same as the category of persons specified in section 8.60(1)(ii) for purposes of defining D's "conflicting interest" and—*importantly*—is not the same as the category of persons excluded for purposes of the definition of non-qualified directors under section 8.62(d). The distinctions among these three categories are deliberate and carefully drawn.

The definition of "qualified shares" excludes shares owned by D or a related person as defined in section 8.60(3). If D is an employee or director of Y Co., Y Co. is *not* prevented by that fact from exercising its usual voting rights as to any shares it may hold in X Co. D's linkage to a related person is close. But the net of section 8.60(1)(ii) specifying other persons and entities for purposes of the "conflicting interest" definition is cast so wide that D will never be able to know whether, nor have a reason to try to monitor whether, some person within those subcategories holds X Co. shares. Typically, moreover, D will have no control over those persons and how they vote their X Co. shares. There is, in reality, no reason to strip those persons of their voting rights as shareholders, for in the usual commercial situation they will vote in accordance with their own interests, which may well not coincide with the personal interest of D.

To illustrate the operation of subsection (b), consider a case in which D is also a director of Y Co., and to his knowledge: thirty percent of Y Co.'s stock is owned by X Co.; D, his wife, a trust of which D is the trustee, and a corporation he controls, together own ten percent of X Co.'s stock but not stock of Y Co.; and X Co. and Y Co. wish to enter into a transaction that is of major significance to both.

From the perspective of X Co., D has a conflicting interest since he is a director of Y Co. If X Co. submits the transaction to a vote of its shareholders under section 8.63, the shares held by D, his wife, the trust of which he is the trustee, and the corporation he controls are not qualified shares and may not be counted in the vote.

From the perspective of Y Co., D has a conflicting interest since he is a director of X Co. If Y Co. submits the transaction to a vote of its shareholders under section 8.63, the thirty percent of Y Co. shares held by X Co. *are* qualified shares and may be counted for purposes of section 8.63. The same would be equally true if X Co. were the majority shareholder of Y Co., but as emphasized elsewhere, the vote under section 8.63 has no effect whatever of exonerating or protecting X Co. if

X Co. fails to meet any legal obligation that, as the majority shareholder of Y Co., it may owe to the minority shareholders of Y Co.

3. Section 8.63(c) . . . .

The fact that certain shares are not qualified and are not countable for purposes of subsection (a) says nothing as to whether they are properly countable for other purposes such as, for example, a statutory requirement that a certain fraction of the total vote or a special majority vote be obtained.

4. Section 8.63(d)

In most circumstances, the secretary of X Co. will have no way to know whether certain of X Co.'s outstanding shares should be excluded from the teller's count because of the identity of the owners or of those persons who control the voting of the shares. Subsection (a) together with subsection (d) therefore impose on a director who has a conflicting interest respecting the transaction, as a prerequisite to safe harbor protection by shareholder vote, the obligation to inform the secretary, or other officer or agent authorized to tabulate votes, of the number and holders of shares known by him to be owned by him or by a related person of his. Thus, a director who has a conflicting interest respecting the transaction, because he stands to make a commission from it, is obligated to report shares owned or the vote of which is controlled by him and by all related persons of his; a director who has a conflicting interest respecting the transaction because his brother stands to make a commission from it has the same reporting obligation. The tabulator may also, of course, have other independent knowledge of shares that are owned or controlled by a related person of the director.

If the tabulator of votes knows that particular shares should be excluded but fails to exclude them from the count and their inclusion in the vote does not affect its outcome, subsection (c) governs and the shareholders' vote stands. If the improper inclusion determines the outcome, the shareholders' vote fails to comply with subsection (a). If the tabulator *does not know* that certain shares are owned or controlled by the director who has the conflicting interest or a related person of his, the shares are "qualified" pursuant to the definition in subsection (b), and the vote cannot be attacked on that ground for failure to comply with subsection (a); but see subsection (e).

5. Section 8.63(e)

If D did not provide the information required under subsection (d), on the face of it shareholders' action is not in compliance with subsection (a) and D has no safe harbor under subsection (a). In the absence of such safe harbor D can be put to the challenge of establishing the fairness of the transaction under section 8.61(b)(3).

That result is the proper one where D's failure to inform was determinative of the vote or, worse, was part of a deliberate effort on D's part to influence the outcome of the vote. But if D's omission was essentially an act of negligence, if the number of unreported shares was not determinative of the outcome of the vote, and if the omission was not motivated by D's effort to influence the integrity of the voting process, the court should be free to fashion an appropriate response to the situation in the light of all the considerations at the time of trial. The court should not be automatically forced by the mechanics of the subchapter to a lengthy and retrospective trial on "fairness." Subsection (e) grants the court that discretion in those circumstances and permits it to accord such effect, if any, to the shareholders' vote, or grant such relief respecting the transaction or D, as the court may find appropriate. . . .

Chapter 10

AMENDMENT OF ARTICLES OF INCORPORATION AND BYLAW

Subchapter A

Amendment of Articles of Incorporation

§ 10.01   Authority to Amend

(a) A corporation may amend its articles of incorporation at any time to add or change a provision that is required or permitted in the articles of incorporation or to delete a provision not required in the articles of incorporation. Whether a provision is required or permitted in the articles of incorporation is determined as of the effective date of the amendment.

(b) A shareholder of the corporation does not have a vested property right resulting from any provision in the articles of incorporation, including provisions relating to management, control, capital structure, dividend entitlement, or purpose or duration of the corporation.

§ 10.02   Amendment by Board of Directors

Unless the articles of incorporation provide otherwise, a corporation's board of directors may adopt one or more amendments to the corporation's articles of incorporation without shareholder action:

(1) to extend the duration of the corporation if it was incorporated at a time when limited duration was required by law;

(2) to delete the names and addresses of the initial directors;

(3) to delete the name and address of the initial registered agent or registered office, if a statement of change is on file with the secretary of state;

(4) to change each issued and unissued authorized share of an outstanding class into a greater number of whole shares if the corporation has only shares of that class outstanding;

(5) to change the corporate name by substituting the word "corporation," "incorporated," "company," "limited," or the abbreviation "corp.," "inc.," "co.," or "ltd.," for a similar word or abbreviation in the name, or by adding, deleting, or changing a geographical attribution for the name; or

(6) to make any other change expressly permitted by this Act to be made without shareholder action.

§ 10.03   Amendment by Board of Directors and Shareholders

(a) A corporation's board of directors may propose one or more amendments to the articles of incorporation for submission to the shareholders.

(b) For the amendment to be adopted:

(1) the board of directors must recommend the amendment to the shareholders unless the board of directors determines that because of conflict of interest or other special circumstances it should make no recommendation and communicates the basis for its determination to the shareholders with the amendment; and

(2) the shareholders entitled to vote on the amendment must approve the amendment as provided in subsection (e).

(c) The board of directors may condition its submission of the proposed amendment on any basis.

(d) The corporation shall notify each shareholder, whether or not entitled to vote, of the proposed shareholders' meeting in accordance with section 7.05. The notice of meeting must also state that the purpose, or one of the purposes, of the meeting is to consider the proposed amendment and contain or be accompanied by a copy or summary of the amendment.

(e) Unless this Act, the articles of incorporation, or the board of directors (acting pursuant to subsection (c)) require a greater vote or a vote by voting groups, the amendment to be adopted must be approved by:

(1) a majority of the votes entitled to be cast on the amendment by any voting group with respect to which the amendment would create dissenters' rights; and

(2) the votes required by sections 7.25 and 7.26 by every other voting group entitled to vote on the amendment.

§ 10.04   Voting on Amendments by Voting Groups

(a) The holders of the outstanding shares of a class are entitled to vote as a separate voting group (if shareholder voting is otherwise required by this Act) on a proposed amendment if the amendment would:

(1) increase or decrease the aggregate number of authorized shares of the class;

(2) effect an exchange or reclassification of all or part of the shares of the class into shares of another class;

(3) effect an exchange or reclassification, or create the right of exchange, of all or part of the shares of another class into shares of the class;

(4) change the designation, rights, preferences, or limitations of all or part of the shares of the class;

(5) change the shares of all or part of the class into a different number of shares of the same class;

(6) create a new class of shares having rights or preferences with respect to distributions or to dissolution that are prior, superior, or substantially equal to the shares of the class;

(7) increase the rights, preferences, or number of authorized shares of any class that, after giving effect to the amendment, have rights or preferences with respect to distributions or to dissolution that are prior, superior, or substantially equal to the shares of the class;

(8) limit or deny an existing preemptive right of all or part of the shares of the class; or

(9) cancel or otherwise affect rights to distributions or dividends that have accumulated but not yet been declared on all or part of the shares of the class.

(b) If a proposed amendment would affect a series of a class of shares in one or more of the ways described in subsection (a), the shares of that series are entitled to vote as a separate voting group on the proposed amendment.

(c) If a proposed amendment that entitles two or more series of shares to vote as separate voting groups under this section would affect those two or more series in the same or a substantially similar way, the shares of all the series so affected must vote together as a single voting group on the proposed amendment.

(d) A class or series of shares is entitled to the voting rights granted by this section although the articles of incorporation provide that the shares are nonvoting shares.

§ 10.05 Amendment Before Issuance of Shares

If a corporation has not yet issued shares, its incorporators or board of directors may adopt one or more amendments to the corporation's articles of incorporation.

§ 10.06 Articles of Amendment

A corporation amending its articles of incorporation shall deliver to the secretary of state for filing articles of amendment setting forth:

(1) the name of the corporation;

(2) the text of each amendment adopted;

(3) if an amendment provides for an exchange, reclassification, or cancellation of issued shares, provisions for implementing the amendment if not contained in the amendment itself;

(4) the date of each amendment's adoption;

(5) if an amendment was adopted by the incorporators or board of directors without shareholder action, a statement to that effect and that shareholder action was not required;

(6) if an amendment was approved by the shareholders:

    (i) the designation, number of outstanding shares, number of votes entitled to be cast by each voting group entitled to vote separately on the amendment, and number of votes of each voting group indisputably represented at the meeting;

    (ii) either the total number of votes cast for and against the amendment by each voting group entitled to vote separately on the amendment or the total number of undisputed votes cast for the amendment by each voting group and a statement that the number cast for the amendment by each voting group was sufficient for approval by that voting group.

§ 10.09 Effect of Amendment

An amendment to articles of incorporation does not affect a cause of action existing against or in favor of the corporation, a proceeding to which the corporation is a party, or the existing rights of persons other than shareholders of the corporation. An amendment changing a corporation's name does not abate a proceeding brought by or against the corporation in its former name.

Subchapter B

Amendment of Bylaws

§ 10.20   Amendment by Board of Directors or Shareholders

(a) A corporation's board of directors may amend or repeal the corporation's bylaws unless:

    (1) the articles of incorporation or this Act reserve this power exclusively to the shareholders in whole or part; or

    (2) the shareholders in amending or repealing a particular bylaw provide expressly that the board of directors may not amend or repeal that bylaw.

(b) A corporation's shareholders may amend or repeal the corporation's bylaws even though the bylaws may also be amended or repealed by its board of directors.

§ 10.21   Bylaw Increasing Quorum or Voting Requirement for Shareholders

(a) If authorized by the articles of incorporation, the shareholders may adopt or amend a bylaw that fixes a greater quorum or voting requirement for shareholders (or voting groups of shareholders) than is required by this Act.   The adoption or amendment of a bylaw that adds, changes, or deletes a greater quorum or voting requirement for shareholders must meet the same quorum requirement and be adopted by the same vote and voting groups required to take action under the quorum and voting requirement then in effect or proposed to be adopted, whichever is greater.

(b) A bylaw that fixes a greater quorum or voting requirement for shareholders under subsection (a) may not be adopted, amended, or repealed by the board of directors.

§ 10.22   Bylaw Increasing Quorum or Voting Requirement for Directors

(a) A bylaw that fixes a greater quorum or voting requirement for the board of directors may be amended or repealed:

    (1) if originally adopted by the shareholders, only by the shareholders;

    (2) if originally adopted by the board of directors, either by the shareholders or by the board of directors.

(b) A bylaw adopted or amended by the shareholders that fixes a greater quorum or voting requirement for the board of directors may provide that it may be amended or repealed only by a specified vote of either the shareholders or the board of directors.

(c) Action by the board of directors under subsection (a)(2) to adopt or amend a bylaw that changes the quorum or voting requirement for the board of directors must meet the same quorum requirement and be adopted by the same vote required to take action under the quorum and voting requirement then in effect or proposed to be adopted, whichever is greater.

Chapter 11

MERGER AND SHARE EXCHANGE

§ 11.01 Merger

(a) One or more corporations may merge into another corporation if the board of directors of each corporation adopts and its shareholders (if required by section 11.03) approve a plan of merger.

(b) The plan of merger must set forth:

    (1) the name of each corporation planning to merge and the name of the surviving corporation into which each other corporation plans to merge;

    (2) the terms and conditions of the merger; and

    (3) the manner and basis of converting the shares of each corporation into shares, obligations, or other securities of the surviving or any other corporation or into cash or other property in whole or part.

(c) The plan of merger may set forth:

    (1) amendments to the articles of incorporation of the surviving corporation; and

    (2) other provisions relating to the merger.

Official Comment . . .

2. Equivalent Nonstatutory Transactions

A transaction may have the same economic effect as a statutory merger even though it is cast in the form of a nonstatutory transaction. For example, assets of the disappearing corporations may be sold for consideration in the form of shares of the surviving corporation, followed by the distribution of those shares by the disappearing corporations to their shareholders and their subsequent dissolution. Transactions have sometimes been structured in nonstatutory form for tax reasons or in an effort to avoid some of the consequences of a statutory merger, particularly appraisal rights to dissenting shareholders. Faced with these transactions, a few courts have developed or accepted the "de facto merger" concept which, to some uncertain extent, grants to dissenting shareholders the rights they would have had if the transaction had been structured as a statutory merger. See Folk, "De Facto Mergers in Delaware: Hariton v. Arco Electronics, Inc.," 49 Va.L.Rev. 1261 (1963). These problems should not occur under the Model Act since the procedural requirements for authorization and consequences of various types of transactions are largely standardized. For example, dissenters' rights are granted not only in mergers but also in share exchanges, in sales of all or substantially all the corporate assets, and in amendments to articles of incorporation that significantly affect rights of shareholders.

§ 11.02 Share Exchange

(a) A corporation may acquire all of the outstanding shares of one or more classes or series of another corporation if the board of directors of each corporation adopts and its shareholders (if required by section 11.03) approve the exchange.

(b) The plan of exchange must set forth:

(1) the name of the corporation whose shares will be acquired and the name of the acquiring corporation;

(2) the terms and conditions of the exchange;

(3) the manner and basis of exchanging the shares to be acquired for shares, obligations, or other securities of the acquiring or any other corporation or for cash or other property in whole or part.

(c) The plan of exchange may set forth other provisions relating to the exchange.

(d) This section does not limit the power of a corporation to acquire all or part of the shares of one or more classes or series of another corporation through a voluntary exchange or otherwise.

§ 11.03 Action on Plan

(a) After adopting a plan of merger or share exchange, the board of directors of each corporation party to the merger, and the board of directors of the corporation whose shares will be acquired in the share exchange, shall submit the plan of merger (except as provided in subsection (g)) or share exchange for approval by its shareholders.

(b) For a plan of merger or share exchange to be approved:

(1) the board of directors must recommend the plan of merger or share exchange to the shareholders, unless the board of directors determines that because of conflict of interest or other special circumstances it should make no recommendation and communicates the basis for its determination to the shareholders with the plan; and

(2) the shareholders entitled to vote must approve the plan.

(c) The board of directors may condition its submission of the proposed merger or share exchange on any basis.

(d) The corporation shall notify each shareholder, whether or not entitled to vote, of the proposed shareholders' meeting in accordance with section 7.05. The notice must also state that the purpose, or one of the purposes, of the meeting is to consider the plan of merger or share exchange and contain or be accompanied by a copy or summary of the plan.

(e) Unless this Act, the articles of incorporation, or the board of directors (acting pursuant to subsection (c)) require a greater vote or a vote by voting groups, the plan of merger or share exchange to be authorized must be approved by each voting group entitled to vote separately on the plan by a majority of all the votes entitled to be cast on the plan by that voting group.

(f) Separate voting by voting groups is required:

    (1) on a plan of merger if the plan contains a provision that, if contained in a proposed amendment to articles of incorporation, would require action by one or more separate voting groups on the proposed amendment under section 10.04;

    (2) on a plan of share exchange by each class or series of shares included in the exchange, with each class or series constituting a separate voting group.

(g) Action by the shareholders of the surviving corporation on a plan of merger is not required if:

    (1) the articles of incorporation of the surviving corporation will not differ (except for amendments enumerated in section 10.02) from its articles before the merger;

    (2) each shareholder of the surviving corporation whose shares were outstanding immediately before the effective date of the merger will hold the same number of shares, with identical designations, preferences, limitations, and relative rights, immediately after;

    (3) the number of voting shares outstanding immediately after the merger, plus the number of voting shares issuable as a result of the merger (either by the conversion of securities issued pursuant to the merger or the exercise of rights and warrants issued pursuant to the merger), will not exceed by more than 20 percent the total number of voting shares of the surviving corporation outstanding immediately before the merger; and

    (4) the number of participating shares outstanding immediately after the merger, plus the number of participating shares issuable as a result of the merger (either by the conversion of securities issued pursuant to the merger or the exercise of rights and warrants issued pursuant to the merger), will not exceed by more than 20 percent the total number of participating shares outstanding immediately before the merger.

(h) As used in subsection (g):
  (1) "Participating shares" means shares that entitle their holders to participate without limitation in distributions.
  (2) "Voting shares" means shares that entitle their holders to vote unconditionally in elections of directors.

(i) After a merger or share exchange is authorized, and at any time before articles of merger or share exchange are filed, the planned merger or share exchange may be abandoned (subject to any contractual rights), without further shareholder action, in accordance with the procedure set forth in the plan of merger or share exchange or, if none is set forth, in the manner determined by the board of directors.

Official Comment ....

2. When Surviving Corporation Shareholder Approval is Not Required

Section 11.03(g) describes when approval by the shareholders of the surviving corporation is not required. The theory behind this subsection is that shareholders' votes should be required only if the transaction fundamentally alters the character of the enterprise or substantially reduces the shareholders' participation in voting or profit distribution. It is believed that the transactions for which shareholder approval is not required by subsection (g) do not alter the investors' prospects any more than many other management decisions, and thus should not require a shareholder vote. In particular, the 20 percent requirement of subsections (g)(3) and (4) is broadly consistent with the statutes of several states, including Delaware (20 percent), Michigan (20 percent), and Pennsylvania (15 percent), and also with the New York Stock Exchange requirement that shareholders must be consulted if the number of outstanding shares is to be increased by more than 18.5 percent.

The requirement that shareholders of the surviving corporation in a statutory merger have a right to vote if the increase in the number of shares exceeds 20 percent may be avoided by arranging the transaction in the form of a merger involving a subsidiary of the acquiring corporation or as a share exchange under section 11.02. This anomaly reflects a compromise among basically conflicting points of view.

The 20 percent requirement is applicable only if the corporation has available enough authorized shares to permit it to issue the shares without amending its articles of incorporation to increase authorized capital. If it must amend its articles of incorporation to authorize the shares necessary to complete the transaction, a shareholder vote on the amendment will be necessary in all cases. See section 10.03....

§ 11.04 Merger of Subsidiary

(a) A parent corporation owning at least 90 percent of the outstanding shares of each class of a subsidiary corporation may merge the subsidiary into itself without approval of the shareholders of the parent or subsidiary.

(b) The board of directors of the parent shall adopt a plan of merger that sets forth:

    (1) the names of the parent and subsidiary; and

    (2) the manner and basis of converting the shares of the subsidiary into shares, obligations, or other securities of the parent or any other corporation or into cash or other property in whole or part.

(c) The parent shall mail a copy or summary of the plan of merger to each shareholder of the subsidiary who does not waive the mailing requirement in writing.

(d) The parent may not deliver articles of merger to the secretary of state for filing until at least 30 days after the date it mailed a copy of the plan of merger to each shareholder of the subsidiary who did not waive the mailing requirement.

(e) Articles of merger under this section may not contain amendments to the articles of incorporation of the parent corporation (except for amendments enumerated in section 10.02).

Official Comment

Section 11.04(a) defines a "parent" corporation as one that owns at least 90 percent of the outstanding shares of each class of another corporation, and a "subsidiary" corporation as one whose shares are so owned. Section 11.04 permits merger of a subsidiary into its parent corporation upon adoption of a plan of merger by the board of directors of the parent alone. Separate action by the board of directors of the subsidiary is unnecessary because the share ownership of the parent corporation is normally sufficient to permit it to elect or remove the subsidiary's board of directors.

Further, the merger transaction need not be approved by the shareholders of either corporation. Approval by the shareholders of the subsidiary is meaningless because the parent's share ownership is sufficient to ensure the plan will be approved. Approval by the parent's shareholders is also unnecessary because the transaction does not materially change their rights: the ownership of the parent corporation is being changed only from 90 percent indirect ownership to 100 percent direct ownership of the same assets, and no significant amendment of the parent's articles of incorporation is being made. For the same reason, shareholders of the parent corporation do not have the right to dissent from the transaction under chapter 13.

Minority shareholders of the subsidiary corporation may receive shares, obligations, or other securities of the parent or any other corporation, or cash or other property in whole or in part in exchange for their shares. These shareholders are entitled to 30 days' notice of the plan of merger before it is effectuated.

Shareholders of the subsidiary corporation have a right to dissent from the merger transaction under chapter 13....

§ 11.05 Articles of Merger or Share Exchange

(a) After a plan of merger or share exchange is approved by the shareholders, or adopted by the board of directors if shareholder approval is not required, the surviving or acquiring corporation shall deliver to the secretary of state for filing articles of merger or share exchange setting forth:

   (1) the plan of merger or share exchange;

   (2) if shareholder approval was not required, a statement to that effect;

   (3) if approval of the shareholders of one or more corporations party to the merger or share exchange was required:

      (i) the designation, number of outstanding shares, and number of votes entitled to be cast by each voting group entitled to vote separately on the plan as to each corporation; and

      (ii) either the total number of votes cast for and against the plan by each voting group entitled to vote separately on the plan or the total number of undisputed votes cast for the plan separately by each voting group and a statement that the number cast for the plan by each voting group was sufficient for approval by that voting group.

(b) A merger or share exchange takes effect upon the effective date of the articles of merger or share exchange.

§ 11.06 Effect of Merger or Share Exchange

(a) When a merger takes effect:

   (1) every other corporation party to the merger merges into the surviving corporation and the separate existence of every corporation except the surviving corporation ceases;

   (2) the title to all real estate and other property owned by each corporation party to the merger is vested in the surviving corporation without reversion or impairment;

   (3) the surviving corporation has all liabilities of each corporation party to the merger;

   (4) a proceeding pending against any corporation party to the merger may be continued as if the merger did not occur or the surviving corporation may be substituted in the proceeding for the corporation whose existence ceased;

(5) the articles of incorporation of the surviving corporation are amended to the extent provided in the plan of merger; and

(6) the shares of each corporation party to the merger that are to be converted into shares, obligations, or other securities of the surviving or any other corporation or into cash or other property are converted, and the former holders of the shares are entitled only to the rights provided in the articles of merger or to their rights under chapter 13.

(b) When a share exchange takes effect, the shares of each acquired corporation are exchanged as provided in the plan, and the former holders of the shares are entitled only to the exchange rights provided in the articles of share exchange or to their rights under chapter 13.

Chapter 12

SALE OF ASSETS

§ 12.01   Sale of Assets in Regular Course of Business and Mortgage of Assets

(a) A corporation may, on the terms and conditions and for the consideration determined by the board of directors:

(1) sell, lease, exchange, or otherwise dispose of all, or substantially all, of its property in the usual and regular course of business;

(2) mortgage, pledge, dedicate to the repayment of indebtedness (whether with or without recourse), or otherwise encumber any or all of its property whether or not in the usual and regular course of business; or

(3) transfer any or all of its property to a corporation all the shares of which are owned by the corporation.

(b) Unless the articles of incorporation require it, approval by the shareholders of a transaction described in subsection (a) is not required.

Official Comment

A sale of "all or substantially all" the corporate assets in the regular course of business is governed by section 12.01. Mortgages of all of the corporation's assets or redeployment of those assets through a wholly owned subsidiary are also covered by section 12.01. All other sales of "all or substantially all" the corporate assets are governed by section 12.02. Dispositions or transfers of property that do not involve "all or substantially all" the property of the corporation are not controlled by statute and may be approved by the board of directors (or authorized corporate officer) in the same manner as any other corporate transaction.

1. The Meaning of "All or Substantially All"

The phrase "all or substantially all," chosen by the draftsmen of the Model Act, is intended to mean what it literally says, "all or substantially all." The phrase "substantially all" is synonymous with "nearly all" and was added merely to make it clear that the statutory requirements could not be avoided by retention of some minimal or nominal residue of the original assets. A sale of all the corporate assets other than cash or cash equivalents is normally the sale of "all or substantially all" of the corporation's property. A sale of several distinct manufacturing lines while retaining one or more lines is normally not a sale of "all or substantially all" even though the lines being sold are substantial and include a significant fraction of the corporation's former business. If the lines retained are viewed only as a temporary operation or as a pretext to avoid the "all or substantially all" requirements, however, the statutory requirements of chapter 12 must be complied with. Similarly, a sale of a plant but retention of operating assets (e.g., machinery and equipment), accounts receivable, good will, and the like with a view toward continuing the operation at another location is not a sale of "all or substantially all" the corporation's property.

Some court decisions have adopted a narrower construction of somewhat similar statutory language. These decisions should be viewed as resting on the diverse statutory language involved in those cases and should not be viewed as illustrating the meaning of "all or substantially all" intended by the draftsmen of the Model Act.

2. Transfers of "All or Substantially All" of a Corporation's Assets That Do Not Require Shareholder Approval ....

b.   Sales in the Usual and Regular Course of Business

Most transfers of "all or substantially all" the corporate property (as defined above) are, almost by definition, not in the usual and regular course of business; sales by real estate corporations and by corporations organized to liquidate a business are examples of sales that may be included in this part of section 12.01(a). Typically, sales falling within the usual and regular course of business do not involve the sale of the corporate name or good will....

§ 12.02   Sale of Assets Other Than in Regular Course of Business

(a) A corporation may sell, lease, exchange, or otherwise dispose of all, or substantially all, of its property (with or without the good will), otherwise than in the usual and regular course of business, on the terms and conditions and for the consideration determined by the corporation's board of directors, if the board of directors proposes and its shareholders approve the proposed transaction.

(b) For a transaction to be authorized:

(1) the board of directors must recommend the proposed transaction to the shareholders unless the board of directors determines that because of conflict of interest or other special circumstances it should make no recommendation and communicates the basis for its determination to the shareholders with the submission of the proposed transaction; and

(2) the shareholders entitled to vote must approve the transaction.

(c) The board of directors may condition its submission of the proposed transaction on any basis.

(d) The corporation shall notify each shareholder, whether or not entitled to vote, of the proposed shareholders' meeting in accordance with section 7.05. The notice must also state that the purpose, or one of the purposes, of the meeting is to consider the sale, lease, exchange, or other disposition of all, or substantially all, the property of the corporation and contain or be accompanied by a description of the transaction.

(e) Unless the articles of incorporation or the board of directors (acting pursuant to subsection (c)) require a greater vote or a vote by voting groups, the transaction to be authorized must be approved by a majority of all the votes entitled to be cast on the transaction.

(f) After a sale, lease, exchange, or other disposition of property is authorized, the transaction may be abandoned (subject to any contractual rights) without further shareholder action.

(g) A transaction that constitutes a distribution is governed by section 6.40 and not by this section.

Official Comment

Certain corporate divisions, often called "spin offs," "split offs," or "split ups," sometimes involve transactions that may be formally characterized as sales of "all or substantially all" the corporate assets when in fact they are only a step in a corporate division that does not give rise to the problem of a major change in corporate direction and therefore does not need shareholder approval. Section 12.02(g) is designed to make clear that transactions like this, which actually constitute a distribution, are not subject to section 12.02. See Siegal, "When Corporations Divide: A Statutory and Financial Analysis," 79 Harv.L.Rev. 534 (1966).

Chapter 13

DISSENTERS' RIGHTS

Subchapter A

Right to Dissent and Obtain Payment for Shares

§ 13.01   Definitions

In this chapter:

(1) "Corporation" means the issuer of the shares held by a dissenter before the corporate action, or the surviving or acquiring corporation by merger or share exchange of that issuer.

(2) "Dissenter" means a shareholder who is entitled to dissent from corporate action under section 13.02 and who exercises that right when and in the manner required by sections 13.20 through 13.28.

(3) "Fair value," with respect to a dissenter's shares, means the value of the shares immediately before the effectuation of the corporate action to which the dissenter objects, excluding any appreciation or depreciation in anticipation of the corporate action unless exclusion would be inequitable.

(4) "Interest" means interest from the effective date of the corporate action until the date of payment, at the average rate currently paid by the corporation on its principal bank loans or, if none, at a rate that is fair and equitable under all the circumstances.

(5) "Record shareholder" means the person in whose name shares are registered in the records of a corporation or the beneficial owner of shares to the extent of the rights granted by a nominee certificate on file with a corporation.

(6) "Beneficial shareholder" means the person who is a beneficial owner of shares held in a voting trust or by a nominee as the record shareholder.

(7) "Shareholder" means the record shareholder or the beneficial shareholder.

Official Comment

Section 13.01 contains specialized definitions applicable only to chapter 13....

(2) The definition of "dissenter" in section 13.01(2) is phrased in terms of a "shareholder," a term that is itself specially defined in section 13.01(7)....

... Under this definition, a shareholder who initially objects but fails to perform any of these conditions within the times specified by this chapter loses his status as "dissenter" under this section.

(3) The definition of "fair value" in section 13.01(3) leaves to the parties (and ultimately to the courts) the details by which "fair value" is to be determined within the broad outlines of the definition. This definition thus leaves untouched the accumulated case law about market value, value based on prior sales, capitalized earnings value, and asset value. It specifically preserves the former language excluding appreciation and depreciation in anticipation of the proposed corporate action, but permits an exception for equitable considerations. The purpose of this exception ("unless exclusion would be inequitable") is to permit consideration of factors similar to those approved by the Supreme Court of Delaware in Weinberger v. UOP, Inc., 457 A.2d 701 (Del.1983), a case in which the court found that the transaction did not involve fair dealing or fair price: "In our view this includes the elements of [rescissory] damages if the Chancellor considers them susceptible of proof and a remedy appropriate to all the issues of fairness before him." Consideration of appreciation or depreciation which might result from other corporate actions is permitted; these effects in the past have often been reflected either in market value or capitalized earnings value.

"Fair value" is to be determined immediately before the effectuation of the corporate action, instead of the date of the shareholder's vote, as is the case under most state statutes that address the issue. This comports with the plan of this chapter to preserve the dissenter's prior rights as a shareholder until the effective date of the corporate action, rather than leaving him in a twilight zone where he has lost his former rights, but has not yet gained his new ones.

(4) The definition of "interest" in section 13.01(4) is included to make interest computations under this chapter more realistic. The right to receive interest is based on the elementary consideration that the corporation has the use of the dissenter's money, and the dissenter has no use of it, from the effective date of the corporate action until the date of payment....

§ 13.02 Right to Dissent

(a) A shareholder is entitled to dissent from, and obtain payment of the fair value of his shares in the event of, any of the following corporate actions:

    (1) consummation of a plan of merger to which the corporation is a party (i) if shareholder approval is required for the merger by section 11.03 or the articles of incorporation and the shareholder is entitled to vote on the merger or (ii) if the corporation is a subsidiary that is merged with its parent under section 11.04;

(2) consummation of a plan of share exchange to which the corporation is a party as the corporation whose shares will be acquired, if the shareholder is entitled to vote on the plan;

(3) consummation of a sale or exchange of all, or substantially all, of the property of the corporation other than in the usual and regular course of business, if the shareholder is entitled to vote on the sale or exchange, including a sale in dissolution, but not including a sale pursuant to court order or a sale for cash pursuant to a plan by which all or substantially all of the net proceeds of the sale will be distributed to the shareholders within one year after the date of sale;

(4) an amendment of the articles of incorporation that materially and adversely affects rights in respect of a dissenter's shares because it:

(i)   alters or abolishes a preferential right of the shares;

(ii) creates, alters, or abolishes a right in respect of redemption, including a provision respecting a sinking fund for the redemption or repurchase, of the shares;

(iii) alters or abolishes a preemptive right of the holder of the shares to acquire shares or other securities;

(iv) excludes or limits the right of the shares to vote on any matter, or to cumulate votes, other than a limitation by dilution through issuance of shares or other securities with similar voting rights; or

(v)   reduces the number of shares owned by the shareholder to a fraction of a share if the fractional share so created is to be acquired for cash under section 6.04; or

(5) any corporate action taken pursuant to a shareholder vote to the extent the articles of incorporation, bylaws, or a resolution of the board of directors provides that voting or nonvoting shareholders are entitled to dissent and obtain payment for their shares.

(b) A shareholder entitled to dissent and obtain payment for his shares under this chapter may not challenge the corporate action creating his entitlement unless the action is unlawful or fraudulent with respect to the shareholder or the corporation.

Official Comment

1. Transactions Giving Rise to Dissenters' Rights

Section 13.02(a) establishes the scope of a shareholder's right to dissent (and his resulting right to obtain payment for his shares) by defining the transactions with respect to which a right to dissent exists. These transactions are:

(1) A plan of merger if the shareholder (i) is entitled to vote on the merger under section 11.03 or pursuant to provisions in the articles of incorporation, or (ii) is a shareholder of a subsidiary that is merged with a parent under section 11.04. The right to vote on a merger under section 11.03 extends to corporations whose separate existence disappears in the merger and to the surviving corporations if the number of its outstanding shares is increased by more than 20 percent as a result of the merger.

(2) A share exchange under section 11.02 if the corporation is a party whose shares are being acquired by the plan and the shareholder is entitled to vote on the exchange.

(3) A sale or exchange of all or substantially all of the property of the corporation not in the usual course of business under section 12.02 if the shareholder is entitled to vote on the sale or exchange. Section 13.02(a)(3) generally grants dissenters' rights in connection with sales in the process of dissolution but excludes them in connection with sales by court order and sales for cash that require substantially all the proceeds to be distributed to the shareholders within one year. The inclusion of sales in dissolution is designed to ensure that the right to dissent cannot be avoided by characterizing sales as made in the process of dissolution long before distribution is made. An exception is provided for sales for cash pursuant to a plan that provides for distribution within one year. These transactions are unlikely to be unfair to minority shareholders since majority and minority are being treated in precisely the same way and all shareholders will ultimately receive cash for their shares. A sale other than for cash gives rise to a right of dissent since property sometimes cannot be converted into cash until long after receipt and a minority shareholder should not be compelled to assume the risk of delays or market declines. Similarly, a plan that provides for a prompt distribution of the property received gives rise to the right of dissent since the minority shareholder should not be compelled to accept for his shares different securities or other property that may not be readily marketable.

The exclusion of court-ordered sales from the dissenter's right is based on the view that court review and approval ensures that an independent appraisal of the fairness of the transaction has been made.

(4) Amendments to articles of incorporation that impair the shareholders' rights as shareholders in any of the enumerated ways. The reasons for granting a right of dissent in these situations are similar to those granting such rights in cases of merger and transfer of assets. The grant of these rights increases the security of investors by allowing them to escape when the nature of their investment rights is fundamentally altered or they are compelled to accept cash

for their investment in an amount established by the corporation. The grant also enhances the freedom of the majority to make changes, because the existence of an escape hatch makes fair and reasonable a change that might be unfair if it forced a fundamental change of rights upon unwilling investors without giving them a reasonable alternative. . . .

Generally, only shareholders who are entitled to vote on the transaction are entitled to assert dissenters' rights with respect to the transaction. The right to vote may be based on the articles of incorporation or other provisions of the Model Act. For example, a class of nonvoting shares may nevertheless be entitled to vote (either as a separate voting group or as part of the general voting group) on an amendment to the articles of incorporation that affects them as provided in one of the ways set forth in section 10.04; such a class is entitled to assert dissenters' rights if the transaction also falls within section 13.02. On the other hand, such a class does not have the right to vote on a sale of substantially all the corporation's assets not in the ordinary course of business, and therefore that class is not entitled to assert dissenters' rights with respect to that sale. One exception to this principle is the merger of a subsidiary into its parent under section 11.04 in which minority shareholders of the subsidiary have the right to assert dissenters' rights even though they have no right to vote.

2. Exclusivity of Dissenters' Rights

Section 13.02(b) basically adopts the New York formula as to exclusivity of the dissenters' remedy of this chapter. The remedy is the exclusive remedy unless the transaction is "unlawful" or "fraudulent." The theory underlying this section is as follows: when a majority of shareholders has approved a corporate change, the corporation should be permitted to proceed even if a minority considers the change unwise or disadvantageous, and persuades a court that this is correct. Since dissenting shareholders can obtain the fair value of their shares, they are protected from pecuniary loss. Thus in general terms an exclusivity principle is justified. But the prospect that shareholders may be "paid off" does not justify the corporation in proceeding unlawfully or fraudulently. If the corporation attempts an action in violation of the corporation law on voting, in violation of clauses in articles of incorporation prohibiting it, by deception of shareholders, or in violation of a fiduciary duty—to take some examples—the court's freedom to intervene should be unaffected by the presence or absence of dissenters' rights under this chapter. Because of the variety of situations in which unlawfulness and fraud may appear, this section makes no attempt to specify particular illustrations. Rather, it is designed to recognize and preserve the principles that have developed in the case law of Delaware, New York and other states with regard to the effect of dissenters' rights on other remedies of dissident shareholders. See Weinberger v. UOP, Inc., 457

A.2d 701 (Del.1983) (appraisal remedy may not be adequate "where fraud, misrepresentation, self-dealing, deliberate waste of corporate assets, or gross or palpable overreaching are involved"). See also Vorenberg, "Exclusiveness of the Dissenting Stockholders' Appraisal Right," 77 Harv.L.Rev. 1189 (1964).

§ 13.03 Dissent by Nominees and Beneficial Owners

(a) A record shareholder may assert dissenters' rights as to fewer than all the shares registered in his name only if he dissents with respect to all shares beneficially owned by any one person and notifies the corporation in writing of the name and address of each person on whose behalf he asserts dissenters' rights. The rights of a partial dissenter under this subsection are determined as if the shares as to which he dissents and his other shares were registered in the names of different shareholders.

(b) A beneficial shareholder may assert dissenters' rights as to shares held on his behalf only if:

   (1) he submits to the corporation the record shareholder's written consent to the dissent not later than the time the beneficial shareholder asserts dissenters' rights; and

   (2) he does so with respect to all shares of which he is the beneficial shareholder or over which he has power to direct the vote.

Subchapter B

Procedure for Exercise of Dissenters' Rights

§ 13.20 Notice of Dissenters' Rights

(a) If proposed corporate action creating dissenters' rights under section 13.02 is submitted to a vote at a shareholders' meeting, the meeting notice must state that shareholders are or may be entitled to assert dissenters' rights under this chapter and be accompanied by a copy of this chapter.

(b) If corporate action creating dissenters' rights under section 13.02 is taken without a vote of shareholders, the corporation shall notify in writing all shareholders entitled to assert dissenters' rights that the action was taken and send them the dissenters' notice described in section 13.22.

§ 13.21 Notice of Intent to Demand Payment

(a) If proposed corporate action creating dissenters' rights under section 13.02 is submitted to a vote at a shareholders' meeting, a shareholder who wishes to assert dissenters' rights (1) must deliver to the corporation before the vote is taken written notice of his intent to demand payment for his shares if the proposed action is effectuated and (2) must not vote his shares in favor of the proposed action.

(b) A shareholder who does not satisfy the requirements of subsection (a) is not entitled to payment for his shares under this chapter.

§ 13.22   Dissenters' Notice

(a) If proposed corporate action creating dissenters' rights under section 13.02 is authorized at a shareholders' meeting, the corporation shall deliver a written dissenters' notice to all shareholders who satisfied the requirements of section 13.21.

(b) The dissenters' notice must be sent no later than 10 days after the corporate action was taken, and must:

    (1) state where the payment demand must be sent and where and when certificates for certificated shares must be deposited;

    (2) inform holders of uncertificated shares to what extent transfer of the shares will be restricted after the payment demand is received;

    (3) supply a form for demanding payment that includes the date of the first announcement to news media or to shareholders of the terms of the proposed corporate action and requires that the person asserting dissenters' rights certify whether or not he acquired beneficial ownership of the shares before that date;

    (4) set a date by which the corporation must receive the payment demand, which date may not be fewer than 30 nor more than 60 days after the date the subsection (a) notice is delivered; and

    (5) be accompanied by a copy of this chapter.

§ 13.23   Duty to Demand Payment

(a) A shareholder sent a dissenters' notice described in section 13.22 must demand payment, certify whether he acquired beneficial ownership of the shares before the date required to be set forth in the dissenters' notice pursuant to section 13.22(b)(3), and deposit his certificates in accordance with the terms of the notice.

(b) The shareholder who demands payment and deposits his share certificates under section (a) retains all other rights of a shareholder until these rights are cancelled or modified by the taking of the proposed corporate action.

(c) A shareholder who does not demand payment or deposit his share certificates where required, each by the date set in the dissenters' notice, is not entitled to payment for his shares under this chapter.

§ 13.24   Share Restrictions

(a) The corporation may restrict the transfer of uncertificated shares from the date the demand for their payment is received until the proposed corporate action is taken or the restrictions released under section 13.26.

(b) The person for whom dissenters' rights are asserted as to uncertificated shares retains all other rights of a shareholder until these rights are cancelled or modified by the taking of the proposed corporate action.

§ 13.25 Payment

(a) Except as provided in section 13.27, as soon as the proposed corporate action is taken, or upon receipt of a payment demand, the corporation shall pay each dissenter who complied with section 13.23 the amount the corporation estimates to be the fair value of his shares, plus accrued interest.

(b) The payment must be accompanied by:

(1) the corporation's balance sheet as of the end of a fiscal year ending not more than 16 months before the date of payment, an income statement for that year, a statement of changes in shareholders' equity for that year, and the latest available interim financial statements, if any;

(2) a statement of the corporation's estimate of the fair value of the shares;

(3) an explanation of how the interest was calculated;

(4) a statement of the dissenter's right to demand payment under section 13.28; and

(5) a copy of this chapter.

Official Comment

Section 13.25 changes the relative balance between corporation and dissenting shareholders by requiring immediate payment by the corporation upon the completion of the transaction or (if the transaction did not need shareholder approval and has been completed) upon receipt of the demand for payment. The corporation may not wait for a final agreement on value before making payment, and the shareholder has the immediate use of the amount determined by the corporation to represent fair value without waiting for the conclusion of appraisal proceedings.

This obligation to make immediate payment is based on the view that since the person's rights as a shareholder are terminated with the completion of the transaction, he should have immediate use of the money to which the corporation agrees it has no further claim. A difference of opinion over the total amount to be paid should not delay payment of the amount that is undisputed. . . .

§ 13.26 Failure to Take Action

(a) If the corporation does not take the proposed action within 60 days after the date set for demanding payment and depositing share certificates, the corporation shall return the deposited certificates and release the transfer restrictions imposed on uncertificated shares.

(b) If after returning deposited certificates and releasing transfer restrictions, the corporation takes the proposed action, it must send a new dissenters' notice under section 13.22 and repeat the payment demand procedure.

§ 13.27   After–Acquired Shares

(a) A corporation may elect to withhold payment required by section 13.25 from a dissenter unless he was the beneficial owner of the shares before the date set forth in the dissenters' notice as the date of the first announcement to news media or to shareholders of the terms of the proposed corporate action.

(b) To the extent the corporation elects to withhold payment under subsection (a), after taking the proposed corporate action, it shall estimate the fair value of the shares, plus accrued interest, and shall pay this amount to each dissenter who agrees to accept it in full satisfaction of his demand. The corporation shall send with its offer a statement of its estimate of the fair value of the shares, an explanation of how the interest was calculated, and a statement of the dissenter's right to demand payment under section 13.28.

§ 13.28   Procedure if Shareholder Dissatisfied With Payment or Offer

(a) A dissenter may notify the corporation in writing of his own estimate of the fair value of his shares and amount of interest due, and demand payment of his estimate (less any payment under section 13.25), or reject the corporation's offer under section 13.27 and demand payment of the fair value of his shares and interest due, if:

   (1) the dissenter believes that the amount paid under section 13.25 or offered under section 13.27 is less than the fair value of his shares or that the interest due is incorrectly calculated;

   (2) the corporation fails to make payment under section 13.25 within 60 days after the date set for demanding payment; or

   (3) the corporation, having failed to take the proposed action, does not return the deposited certificates or release the transfer restrictions imposed on uncertificated shares within 60 days after the date set for demanding payment.

(b) A dissenter waives his right to demand payment under this section unless he notifies the corporation of his demand in writing under subsection (a) within 30 days after the corporation made or offered payment for his shares.

Subchapter C

Judicial Appraisal of Shares

§ 13.30 Court Action

(a) If a demand for payment under section 13.28 remains unsettled, the corporation shall commence a proceeding within 60 days after receiving the payment demand and petition the court to determine the fair value of the shares and accrued interest. If the corporation does not commence the proceeding within the 60–day period, it shall pay each dissenter whose demand remains unsettled the amount demanded.

(b) The corporation shall commence the proceeding in the [name or describe] court of the county where a corporation's principal office (or, if none in this state, its registered office) is located. If the corporation is a foreign corporation without a registered office in this state, it shall commence the proceeding in the county in this state where the registered office of the domestic corporation merged with or whose shares were acquired by the foreign corporation was located.

(c) The corporation shall make all dissenters (whether or not residents of this state) whose demands remain unsettled parties to the proceeding as in an action against their shares and all parties must be served with a copy of the petition. Nonresidents may be served by registered or certified mail or by publication as provided by law.

(d) The jurisdiction of the court in which the proceeding is commenced under subsection (b) is plenary and exclusive. The court may appoint one or more persons as appraisers to receive evidence and recommend decision on the question of fair value. The appraisers have the powers described in the order appointing them, or in any amendment to it. The dissenters are entitled to the same discovery rights as parties in other civil proceedings.

(e) Each dissenter made a party to the proceeding is entitled to judgment (1) for the amount, if any, by which the court finds the fair value of his shares, plus interest, exceeds the amount paid by the corporation or (2) for the fair value, plus accrued interest, of his after-acquired shares for which the corporation elected to withhold payment under section 13.27.

Official Comment

All demands for payment made under section 13.28 are to be resolved in a single proceeding brought in the county where the corporation's principal office is located or, if none, in other specified counties. All shareholders making section 13.28 demands must be made parties, with service by publication authorized if necessary. . . .

§ 13.31   Court Costs and Counsel Fees

(a) The court in an appraisal proceeding commenced under section 13.30 shall determine all costs of the proceeding, including the reasonable compensation and expenses of appraisers appointed by the court. The court shall assess the costs against the corporation, except that the court may assess costs against all or some of the dissenters, in amounts the court finds equitable, to the extent the court finds the dissenters acted arbitrarily, vexatiously, or not in good faith in demanding payment under section 13.28.

(b) The court may also assess the fees and expenses of counsel and experts for the respective parties, in amounts the court finds equitable:

   (1) against the corporation and in favor of any or all dissenters if the court finds the corporation did not substantially comply with the requirements of sections 13.20 through 13.28; or

   (2) against either the corporation or a dissenter, in favor of any other party, if the court finds that the party against whom the fees and expenses are assessed acted arbitrarily, vexatiously, or not in good faith with respect to the rights provided by this chapter.

(c) If the court finds that the services of counsel for any dissenter were of substantial benefit to other dissenters similarly situated, and that the fees for those services should not be assessed against the corporation, the court may award to these counsel reasonable fees to be paid out of the amounts awarded the dissenters who were benefited.

Chapter 14

DISSOLUTION

Subchapter A

Voluntary Dissolution

§ 14.01   Dissolution by Incorporators or Initial Directors

A majority of the incorporators or initial directors of a corporation that has not issued shares or has not commenced business may dissolve the corporation by delivering to the secretary of state for filing articles of dissolution that set forth:

(1) the name of the corporation;

(2) the date of its incorporation;

(3) either (i) that none of the corporation's shares has been issued or (ii) that the corporation has not commenced business;

(4) that no debt of the corporation remains unpaid;

(5) that the net assets of the corporation remaining after winding up have been distributed to the shareholders, if shares were issued; and

(6) that a majority of the incorporators or initial directors authorized the dissolution.

§ 14.02 Dissolution by Board of Directors and Shareholders

(a) A corporation's board of directors may propose dissolution for submission to the shareholders.

(b) For a proposal to dissolve to be adopted:

(1) the board of directors must recommend dissolution to the shareholders unless the board of directors determines that because of conflict of interest or other special circumstances it should make no recommendation and communicates the basis for its determination to the shareholders; and

(2) the shareholders entitled to vote must approve the proposal to dissolve as provided in subsection (e).

(c) The board of directors may condition its submission of the proposal for dissolution on any basis.

(d) The corporation shall notify each shareholder, whether or not entitled to vote, of the proposed shareholders' meeting in accordance with section 7.05. The notice must also state that the purpose, or one of the purposes, of the meeting is to consider dissolving the corporation.

(e) Unless the articles of incorporation or the board of directors (acting pursuant to subsection (c)) require a greater vote or a vote by voting groups, the proposal to dissolve to be adopted must be approved by a majority of all the votes entitled to be cast on that proposal.

§ 14.03 Articles of Dissolution

(a) At any time after dissolution is authorized, the corporation may dissolve by delivering to the secretary of state for filing articles of dissolution setting forth:

(1) the name of the corporation;

(2) the date dissolution was authorized;

(3) if dissolution was approved by the shareholders:

(i) the number of votes entitled to be cast on the proposal to dissolve; and

(ii) either the total number of votes cast for and against dissolution or the total number of undisputed votes cast for dissolution and a statement that the number cast for dissolution was sufficient for approval.

(4) If voting by voting groups was required, the information required by subparagraph (3) must be separately provided for each voting group entitled to vote separately on the plan to dissolve.

(b) A corporation is dissolved upon the effective date of its articles of dissolution.

§ 14.04   Revocation of Dissolution

(a) A corporation may revoke its dissolution within 120 days of its effective date.

(b) Revocation of dissolution must be authorized in the same manner as the dissolution was authorized unless that authorization permitted revocation by action of the board of directors alone, in which event the board of directors may revoke the dissolution without shareholder action.

(c) After the revocation of dissolution is authorized, the corporation may revoke the dissolution by delivering to the secretary of state for filing articles of revocation of dissolution, together with a copy of its articles of dissolution, that set forth:

(1) the name of the corporation;

(2) the effective date of the dissolution that was revoked;

(3) the date that the revocation of dissolution was authorized;

(4) if the corporation's board of directors (or incorporators) revoked the dissolution, a statement to that effect;

(5) if the corporation's board of directors revoked a dissolution authorized by the shareholders, a statement that revocation was permitted by action by the board of directors alone pursuant to that authorization; and

(6) if shareholder action was required to revoke the dissolution, the information required by section 14.03(a)(3) or (4).

(d) Revocation of dissolution is effective upon the effective date of the articles of revocation of dissolution.

(e) When the revocation of dissolution is effective, it relates back to and takes effect as of the effective date of the dissolution and the corporation resumes carrying on its business as if dissolution had never occurred.

§ 14.05   Effect of Dissolution

(a) A dissolved corporation continues its corporate existence but may not carry on any business except that appropriate to wind up and liquidate its business and affairs, including:

(1) collecting its assets;

(2) disposing of its properties that will not be distributed in kind to its shareholders;

(3) discharging or making provision for discharging its liabilities;

(4) distributing its remaining property among its shareholders according to their interests; and

(5) doing every other act necessary to wind up and liquidate its business and affairs.

(b) Dissolution of a corporation does not:

(1) transfer title to the corporation's property;

(2) prevent transfer of its shares or securities, although the authorization to dissolve may provide for closing the corporation's share transfer records;

(3) subject its directors or officers to standards of conduct different from those prescribed in chapter 8;

(4) change quorum or voting requirements for its board of directors or shareholders; change provisions for selection, resignation, or removal of its directors or officers or both; or change provisions for amending its bylaws;

(5) prevent commencement of a proceeding by or against the corporation in its corporate name;

(6) abate or suspend a proceeding pending by or against the corporation on the effective date of dissolution; or

(7) terminate the authority of the registered agent of the corporation.

Official Comment

Section 14.05(a) provides that dissolution does not terminate the corporate existence but simply requires the corporation thereafter to devote itself to winding up its affairs and liquidating its assets; after dissolution, the corporation may not carry on its business except as may be appropriate for winding-up.

The Model Act uses the term "dissolution" in the specialized sense described above and not to describe the final step in the liquidation of the corporate business. This is made clear by section 14.05(b), which provides that chapter 14 dissolution does not have any of the characteristics of common law dissolution, which treated corporate dissolution as analogous to the death of a natural person and abated lawsuits, vested equitable title to corporate property in the shareholders, imposed the fiduciary duty of trustees on directors who had custody of corporate assets, and revoked the authority of the registered agent. Section 14.05(b) expressly reverses all of these common law attributes of dissolution and makes clear that the rights, powers, and duties of shareholders, the directors, and the registered agent are not affected by dissolution and that suits by or against the corporation are not affected in any way.

§ 14.06 Known Claims Against Dissolved Corporation

(a) A dissolved corporation may dispose of the known claims against it by following the procedure described in this section.

(b) The dissolved corporation shall notify its known claimants in writing of the dissolution at any time after its effective date. The written notice must:

    (1) describe information that must be included in a claim;

    (2) provide a mailing address where a claim may be sent;

    (3) state the deadline, which may not be fewer than 120 days from the effective date of the written notice, by which the dissolved corporation must receive the claim; and

    (4) state that the claim will be barred if not received by the deadline.

(c) A claim against the dissolved corporation is barred:

    (1) if a claimant who was given written notice under subsection (b) does not deliver the claim to the dissolved corporation by the deadline;

    (2) if a claimant whose claim was rejected by the dissolved corporation does not commence a proceeding to enforce the claim within 90 days from the effective date of the rejection notice.

(d) For purposes of this section, "claim" does not include a contingent liability or a claim based on an event occurring after the effective date of dissolution.

Official Comment

Sections 14.06 and 14.07 provide a new and simplified system for handling known and unknown claims against a dissolved corporation, including claims based on events that occur after the dissolution of the corporation. Section 14.06 deals solely with known claims while section 14.07 deals with unknown or subsequently arising claims. A claim is a "known" claim even if it is unliquidated (see section 14.06(d)); a claim that is contingent or has not matured so that there is no immediate right to bring suit is not a "known" claim.

Known claims are handled in section 14.06 through a process of written notice to claimants; the written notice must contain the information described in section 14.06(b). Section 14.06(c) then provides fixed deadlines by which claims are barred under various circumstances, as follows:

    (1) If a claimant receives written notice satisfying section 14.06(b) but fails to file the claim by the deadline specified by the corporation, the claim is barred by section 14.06(c)(1).

    (2) If a claimant receives written notice satisfying section 14.06(b) and files the claim as required:

        (i) but the corporation rejects the claim, the claimant must commence a proceeding to enforce the claim within 90 days of the rejection or the claim is barred by section 14.06(c)(2); or

(ii) if the corporation does not act on the claim or fails to notify the claimant of the rejection, the claimant is not barred by section 14.06(c) until the corporation notifies the claimant.

(3) If the corporation publishes notice under section 14.07, a claimant who was not notified in writing is barred unless he commences a proceeding within five years after publication of the notice.

(4) If the corporation does not publish notice, a claimant who was not notified in writing is not barred by section 14.06(c) from pursuing his claim. . . .

Even though the directors are not trustees of the assets of a dissolved corporation (see section 14.05(b)(3)), they must discharge or make provision for discharging all of the corporation's known liabilities before distributing the remaining assets to the shareholders. See sections 14.05(a)(3) and (4). See also sections 6.40 and 8.33.

§ 14.07 Unknown Claims Against Dissolved Corporation

(a) A dissolved corporation may also publish notice of its dissolution and request that persons with claims against the corporation present them in accordance with the notice.

(b) The notice must:

(1) be published one time in a newspaper of general circulation in the county where the dissolved corporation's principal office (or, if none in this state, its registered office) is or was last located;

(2) describe the information that must be included in a claim and provide a mailing address where the claim may be sent; and

(3) state that a claim against the corporation will be barred unless a proceeding to enforce the claim is commenced within five years after the publication of the notice.

(c) If the dissolved corporation publishes a newspaper notice in accordance with subsection (b), the claim of each of the following claimants is barred unless the claimant commences a proceeding to enforce the claim against the dissolved corporation within five years after the publication date of the newspaper notice:

(1) a claimant who did not receive written notice under section 14.06;

(2) a claimant whose claim was timely sent to the dissolved corporation but not acted on;

(3) a claimant whose claim is contingent or based on an event occurring after the effective date of dissolution.

635

(d) A claim may be enforced under this section:

    (1) against the dissolved corporation, to the extent of its undistributed assets; or

    (2) if the assets have been distributed in liquidation, against a shareholder of the dissolved corporation to the extent of his pro rata share of the claim or the corporate assets distributed to him in liquidation, whichever is less, but a shareholder's total liability for all claims under this section may not exceed the total amount of assets distributed to him.

Subchapter B

Administrative Dissolution

§ 14.20 Grounds for Administrative Dissolution

The secretary of state may commence a proceeding under section 14.21 to administratively dissolve a corporation if:

(1) the corporation does not pay within 60 days after they are due any franchise taxes or penalties imposed by this Act or other law;

(2) the corporation does not deliver its annual report to the secretary of state within 60 days after it is due;

(3) the corporation is without a registered agent or registered office in this state for 60 days or more;

(4) the corporation does not notify the secretary of state within 60 days that its registered agent or registered office has been changed, that its registered agent has resigned, or that its registered office has been discontinued; or

(5) the corporation's period of duration stated in its articles of incorporation expires.

Subchapter C

Judicial Dissolution

§ 14.30 Grounds for Judicial Dissolution

The [name or describe court or courts] may dissolve a corporation:

(1) in a proceeding by the attorney general if it is established that:

    (i) the corporation obtained its articles of incorporation through fraud; or

    (ii) the corporation has continued to exceed or abuse the authority conferred upon it by law;

(2) in a proceeding by a shareholder if it is established that:

    (i) the directors are deadlocked in the management of the corporate affairs, the shareholders are unable to break the deadlock, and irreparable injury to the corporation is threatened or being suffered, or the business and affairs of the corporation can no longer be conducted to the advantage of the shareholders generally, because of the deadlock;

(ii) the directors or those in control of the corporation have acted, are acting, or will act in a manner that is illegal, oppressive, or fraudulent;

(iii) the shareholders are deadlocked in voting power and have failed, for a period that includes at least two consecutive annual meeting dates, to elect successors to directors whose terms have expired; or

(iv) the corporate assets are being misapplied or wasted;

(3) in a proceeding by a creditor if it is established that:

(i) the creditor's claim has been reduced to judgment, the execution on the judgment returned unsatisfied, and the corporation is insolvent; or

(ii) the corporation has admitted in writing that the creditor's claim is due and owing and the corporation is insolvent; or

(4) in a proceeding by the corporation to have its voluntary dissolution continued under court supervision.

§ 14.31   Procedure for Judicial Dissolution

(a) Venue for a proceeding by the attorney general to dissolve a corporation lies in [name the county or counties]. Venue for a proceeding brought by any other party named in section 14.30 lies in the county where a corporation's principal office (or, if none in this state, its registered office) is or was last located.

(b) It is not necessary to make shareholders parties to a proceeding to dissolve a corporation unless relief is sought against them individually.

(c) A court in a proceeding brought to dissolve a corporation may issue injunctions, appoint a receiver or custodian pendente lite with all powers and duties the court directs, take other action required to preserve the corporate assets wherever located, and carry on the business of the corporation until a full hearing can be held.

(d) Within 10 days of the commencement of a proceeding under section 14.30(2) to dissolve a corporation that has no shares listed on a national securities exchange or regularly traded in a market maintained by one or more members of a national securities exchange, the corporation must send to all shareholders, other than the petitioner, a notice stating that the shareholders are entitled to avoid the dissolution of the corporation by electing to purchase the petitioner's shares under section 14.34 and accompanied by a copy of section 14.34.

§ 14.32   Receivership or Custodianship

(a) A court in a judicial proceeding brought to dissolve a corporation may appoint one or more receivers to wind up and liquidate, or one or more custodians to manage, the business and affairs of the corporation. The court shall hold a hearing, after notifying all parties to the proceeding and any interested persons designated by the court, before appointing a receiver or custodian. The court appointing a receiver or custodian has exclusive jurisdiction over the corporation and all of its property wherever located.

(b) The court may appoint an individual or a domestic or foreign corporation (authorized to transact business in this state) as a receiver or custodian. The court may require the receiver or custodian to post bond, with or without sureties, in an amount the court directs.

(c) The court shall describe the powers and duties of the receiver or custodian in its appointing order, which may be amended from time to time. Among other powers:

(1) the receiver (i) may dispose of all or any part of the assets of the corporation wherever located, at a public or private sale, if authorized by the court; and (ii) may sue and defend in his own name as receiver of the corporation in all courts of this state;

(2) the custodian may exercise all of the powers of the corporation, through or in place of its board of directors or officers, to the extent necessary to manage the affairs of the corporation in the best interests of its shareholders and creditors.

(d) The court during a receivership may redesignate the receiver a custodian, and during a custodianship may redesignate the custodian a receiver, if doing so is in the best interests of the corporation, its shareholders, and creditors.

(e) The court from time to time during the receivership or custodianship may order compensation paid and expense disbursements or reimbursements made to the receiver or custodian and his counsel from the assets of the corporation or proceeds from the sale of the assets.

§ 14.33   Decree of Dissolution

(a) If after a hearing the court determines that one or more grounds for judicial dissolution described in section 14.30 exist, it may enter a decree dissolving the corporation and specifying the effective date of the dissolution, and the clerk of the court shall deliver a certified copy of the decree to the secretary of state, who shall file it.

(b) After entering the decree of dissolution, the court shall direct the winding up and liquidation of the corporation's business and affairs in accordance with section 14.05 and the notification of claimants in accordance with sections 14.06 and 14.07.

§ 14.34 Election to Purchase in Lieu of Dissolution

(a) In a proceeding under section 14.30(2) to dissolve a corporation that has no shares listed on a national securities exchange or regularly traded in a market maintained by one or more members of a national or affiliated securities association, the corporation may elect or, if it fails to elect, one or more shareholders may elect to purchase all shares owned by the petitioning shareholder at the fair value of the shares. An election pursuant to this section shall be irrevocable unless the court determines that it is equitable to set aside or modify the election.

(b) An election to purchase pursuant to this section may be filed with the court at any time within 90 days after the filing of the petition under section 14.30(2) or at such later time as the court in its discretion may allow. If the election to purchase is filed by one or more shareholders, the corporation shall, within 10 days thereafter, give written notice to all shareholders, other than the petitioner. The notice must state the name and number of shares owned by the petitioner and the name and number of shares owned by each electing shareholder and must advise the recipients of their right to join in the election to purchase shares in accordance with this section. Shareholders who wish to participate must file notice of their intention to join in the purchase no later than 30 days after the effective date of the notice to them. All shareholders who have filed an election or notice of their intention to participate in the election to purchase thereby become parties to the proceeding and shall participate in the purchase in proportion to their ownership of shares as of the date the first election was filed, unless they otherwise agree or the court otherwise directs. After an election has been filed by the corporation or one or more shareholders, the proceeding under section 14.30(2) may not be discontinued or settled, nor may the petitioning shareholder sell or otherwise dispose of his shares, unless the court determines that it would be equitable to the corporation and the shareholders, other than the petitioner, to permit such discontinuance, settlement, sale, or other disposition.

(c) If, within 60 days of the filing of the first election, the parties reach agreement as to the fair value and terms of purchase of the petitioner's shares, the court shall enter an order directing the purchase of petitioner's shares upon the terms and conditions agreed to by the parties.

(d) If the parties are unable to reach an agreement as provided for in subsection (c), the court, upon application of any party, shall stay the section 14.30(2) proceedings and determine the fair value of the petitioner's shares as of the day before the date on which the petition under section 14.30(2) was filed or as of such other date as the court deems appropriate under the circumstances.

(e) Upon determining the fair value of the shares, the court shall enter an order directing the purchase upon such terms and conditions as the court deems appropriate, which may include payment of the purchase price in installments, where necessary in the interests of equity, provision for security to assure payment of the purchase price and any additional costs, fees, and expenses as may have been awarded, and, if the shares are to be purchased by shareholders, the allocation of shares among them. In allocating petitioner's shares among holders of different classes of shares, the court should attempt to preserve the existing distribution of voting rights among holders of different classes insofar as practicable and may direct that holders of a specific class or classes shall not participate in the purchase. Interest may be allowed at the rate and from the date determined by the court to be equitable, but if the court finds that the refusal of the petitioning shareholder to accept an offer of payment was arbitrary or otherwise not in good faith, no interest shall be allowed. If the court finds that the petitioning shareholder had probable grounds for relief under paragraphs (ii) or (iv) of section 14.30(2), it may award to the petitioning shareholder reasonable fees and expenses of counsel and of any experts employed by him.

(f) Upon entry of an order under subsections (c) or (e), the court shall dismiss the petition to dissolve the corporation under section 14.30, and the petitioning shareholder shall no longer have any rights or status as a shareholder of the corporation, except the right to receive the amounts awarded to him by the order of the court which shall be enforceable in the same manner as any other judgment.

(g) The purchase ordered pursuant to subsection (e), shall be made within 10 days after the date the order becomes final unless before that time the corporation files with the court a notice of its intention to adopt articles of dissolution pursuant to sections 14.02 and 14.03, which articles must then be adopted and filed within 50 days thereafter. Upon filing of such articles of dissolution, the corporation shall be dissolved in accordance with the provisions of sections 14.05 through 07, and the order entered pursuant to subsection (e) shall no longer be of any force or effect, except that the court may award the petitioning shareholder reasonable fees and expenses in accordance with the provisions of the last sentence of subsection (e) and the petitioner may continue to pursue any claims previously asserted on behalf of the corporation.

(h) Any payment by the corporation pursuant to an order under subsections (c) or (e), other than an award of fees and expenses pursuant to subsection (e), is subject to the provisions of section 6.40.

Official Comment

The proceeding for judicial dissolution has become an increasingly important remedy for minority shareholders of closely-held corporations who believe that the value of their investment is threatened by reason of circumstances or conduct described in section 14.30(2). If the petitioning shareholder proves one or more grounds under section 14.30(2), he is entitled to some form of relief but many courts have hesitated to award dissolution, the only form of relief explicitly provided, because of its adverse effects on shareholders, employees, and others who may have an interest in the continuation of the business.

Commentators have observed that it is rarely necessary to dissolve the corporation and liquidate its assets in order to provide relief: the rights of the petitioning shareholder are fully protected by liquidating only his interest and paying the fair value of his shares while permitting the remaining shareholders to continue the business. In fact, it appears that most dissolution proceedings result in a buyout of one or another of the disputants' shares either pursuant to a statutory buyout provision or a negotiated settlement. See generally Hetherington & Dooley, Illiquidity and Exploitation: A Proposed Statutory Solution to the Remaining Close Corporation Problem, 63 Va.L.Rev. 1 (1977); Haynsworth, The Effectiveness of Involuntary Dissolution Suits As a Remedy for Close Corporation Dissension, 35 Clev.St.L.Rev. 25 (1987). Accordingly, section 14.34 affords an orderly procedure by which a dissolution proceeding under section 14.30(2) can be terminated upon payment of the fair value of the petitioner's shares.

1. Availability

There are three prerequisites to filing an election to purchase under section 14.34. First, a proceeding to dissolve the corporation under section 14.30(2) must have been commenced. Second, the corporation must have no shares of any class listed on a national securities exchange or regularly traded over the counter. Finally, the election may be made only by the corporation or by shareholders other than the shareholder who is seeking to dissolve the corporation under section 14.30(2).

As a practical matter, the remedy of judicial dissolution under section 14.30(2) is appropriate only for shareholders of closely-held firms who have no ready market for their shares. Shareholders of publicly-traded firms are protected by their right to sell out if they are dissatisfied with current management or they may seek traditional remedies for breach of fiduciary duty. In contrast, a resort to litigation may result in an irreparable breach of personal relationships among the shareholders of a closely-held firm, making it impossible for them to continue in business to their mutual advantage.

2. Effect of Filing

The election to purchase is wholly voluntary, but it can be made as a matter of right within 90 days after the filing of the petition under section 14.30(2). After 90 days, leave of court is required. Once an election is filed:

(i) The election is irrevocable and may not be set aside or modified (as to one or more parties) unless the court determines it is equitable to do so; and

(ii) The dissolution proceeding under section 14.30(2) may not be discontinued or settled and the petitioning shareholder may not dispose of his shares without court approval.

These provisions are intended to reduce the risk that either the dissolution proceeding or the buyout election will be used for strategic purposes. For example, the Official Comment to section 14.30 cautions courts to distinguish between dissolution petitions predicated on "genuine abuse" and those brought for other reasons. Section 14.34 makes strategic use of section 14.30(2) a high-risk proposition for the petitioning shareholder because his shares are, in effect, subject to a "call" for 90 days after commencement of the section 14.30(2) proceeding. The petitioner becomes irrevocably committed to sell his shares pursuant to section 14.34 once an election is filed and may not thereafter discontinue the dissolution proceeding or dispose of his shares outside of section 14.34 without permission of the court, which is specifically directed to consider whether such action would be equitable from the standpoint of the corporation and the other shareholders.

By the same token, if the corporation or the other shareholders fail to elect to purchase the petitioner's shares within the first 90 days, they run the risk that the court will decline to accept a subsequent election and will, instead, allow the dissolution proceeding to go forward. Note also that the dissolution proceeding is not affected by the mere filing of an election; it will be stayed only upon application to the court to determine the fair value of the petitioner's shares after the expiration of the 60 day negotiating period provided for in section 14.34(c).

Once an election is filed, it may be set aside or modified only for reasons that the court finds equitable. If the court sets aside the election, the corporation or the electing shareholders are released from their obligation to purchase the petitioner's shares. Under section 14.34(a), the court also has discretion to "modify" the election by releasing one or more electing shareholders without releasing the others.

3.   Election by Corporation or Shareholders

Any change in the allocation of shareholdings in a closely-held corporation may upset control or other arrangements that have been previously negotiated by the parties. It is therefore desirable that the purchase of petitioner's shares under section 14.34 be made in ways that are least disruptive of existing arrangements. Accordingly, an election by the corporation is given preference during the 90 day period provided for in section 14.34(b). This preference does not affect the order of filing, and any shareholder may file an election (thus triggering the provisions of subsection (b)) as soon as the dissolution proceeding is commenced. If the corporation thereafter files an election within the 90 day period, its election takes precedence over any previously filed election by shareholders. An election by the corporation after 90 days may be filed only with the court's approval and would not be entitled to the same preemptive weight. Section 14.34 does not affect an agreement between the corporation and the other shareholders to participate jointly in the purchase of the petitioner's shares.

Concern over preserving existing control arrangements makes it inadvisable to extend purchase rights to holders of shares that have only preferential rights to distributions or assets but do not have any right to vote (other than as provided by law). On the other hand, control arrangements are not disturbed if shareholders having voting rights elect to purchase nonvoting shares of a petitioning shareholder, and such elections are permitted. If the election to purchase is made by one or more shareholders, section 14.34(b) requires the corporation to notify all other shareholders of their right to join in the purchase "in proportion to their ownership of shares as of the date the first election was filed." This raises the question of whether shareholders of a class different from the class of shares owned by the petitioner may participate in the purchase. Given the wide variety of capital structures adopted by closely-held corporations, it is not possible to state a general rule that would be appropriate in all cases. Any allocation that is agreed to by the electing shareholders controls regardless of whether the other terms and conditions of the purchase are set by the parties' agreement pursuant to subsection (c) or are determined by the court pursuant to subsection (e). If electing shareholders cannot agree, the court, under subsection (e), must determine an allocation.

In making this determination, the court should be guided by the desirability of preserving existing arrangements, so far as that is practicable....

4. Court Order

If the parties are unable to reach agreement, any or all terms of the purchase may be set by the court under subsection (d). Section 14.34 does not specify the components of "fair value," and the court may find it useful to consider valuation methods that would be relevant to a judicial appraisal of shares under section 13.30. The two proceedings are not wholly analogous, however, and the court should consider all relevant facts and circumstances of the particular case in determining fair value. For example, liquidating value may be relevant in cases of deadlock but an inappropriate measure in other cases. If the court finds that the value of the corporation has been diminished by the wrongful conduct of controlling shareholders, it would be appropriate to include as an element of fair value the petitioner's proportional claim for any compensable corporate injury. In cases where there is dissension but no evidence of wrongful conduct, "fair value" should be determined with reference to what the petitioner would likely receive in a voluntary sale of shares to a third party, taking into account his minority status. If the parties have previously entered into a shareholders' agreement that defines or provides a method for determining the fair value of shares to be sold, the court should look to such definition or method unless the court decides it would be unjust or inequitable to do so in light of the facts and circumstances of the particular case. The valuation date is set as the day before the filing of the petition under section 14.30, although the court may choose an earlier or later date if appropriate under the circumstances of the particular case. . . .

Chapter 15

FOREIGN CORPORATIONS

Subchapter A

Certificate of Authority

§ 15.01   Authority to Transact Business Required

(a) A foreign corporation may not transact business in this state until it obtains a certificate of authority from the secretary of state. . . .

§ 15.02   Consequences of Transacting Business Without Authority

(a) A foreign corporation transacting business in this state without a certificate of authority may not maintain a proceeding in any court in this state until it obtains a certificate of authority.

(b) The successor to a foreign corporation that transacted business in this state without a certificate of authority and the assignee of a cause of action arising out of that business may not maintain a proceeding based on that cause of action in any court in this state until the foreign corporation or its successor obtains a certificate of authority.

(c) A court may stay a proceeding commenced by a foreign corporation, its successor, or assignee until it determines whether the foreign corporation or its successor requires a certificate of authority. If it so determines, the court may further stay the proceeding until the foreign corporation or its successor obtains the certificate.

(d) A foreign corporation is liable for a civil penalty of $_____ for each day, but not to exceed a total of $_____ for each year, it transacts business in this state without a certificate of authority. The attorney general may collect all penalties due under this subsection.

(e) Notwithstanding subsections (a) and (b), the failure of a foreign corporation to obtain a certificate of authority does not impair the validity of its corporate acts or prevent it from defending any proceeding in this state.

Chapter 16

RECORDS AND REPORTS

Subchapter A

Records

§ 16.01 Corporate Records

(a) A corporation shall keep as permanent records minutes of all meetings of its shareholders and board of directors, a record of all actions taken by the shareholders or board of directors without a meeting, and a record of all actions taken by a committee of the board of directors in place of the board of directors on behalf of the corporation.

(b) A corporation shall maintain appropriate accounting records.

(c) A corporation or its agent shall maintain a record of its shareholders, in a form that permits preparation of a list of the names and addresses of all shareholders, in alphabetical order by class of shares showing the number and class of shares held by each.

(d) A corporation shall maintain its records in written form or in another form capable of conversion into written form within a reasonable time.

(e) A corporation shall keep a copy of the following records at its principal office:

(1) its articles or restated articles of incorporation and all amendments to them currently in effect;

(2) its bylaws or restated bylaws and all amendments to them currently in effect;

(3) resolutions adopted by its board of directors creating one or more classes or series of shares, and fixing their relative rights, preferences, and limitations, if shares issued pursuant to those resolutions are outstanding;

(4) the minutes of all shareholders' meetings, and records of all action taken by shareholders without a meeting, for the past three years;

(5) all written communications to shareholders generally within the past three years, including the financial statements furnished for the past three years under section 16.20;

(6) a list of the names and business addresses of its current directors and officers; and

(7) its most recent annual report delivered to the secretary of state under section 16.22.

§ 16.02 Inspection of Records by Shareholders

(a) A shareholder of a corporation is entitled to inspect and copy, during regular business hours at the corporation's principal office, any of the records of the corporation described in section 16.01(e) if he gives the corporation written notice of his demand at least five business days before the date on which he wishes to inspect and copy.

(b) A shareholder of a corporation is entitled to inspect and copy, during regular business hours at a reasonable location specified by the corporation, any of the following records of the corporation if the shareholder meets the requirements of subsection (c) and gives the corporation written notice of his demand at least five business days before the date on which he wishes to inspect and copy:

(1) excerpts from minutes of any meeting of the board of directors, records of any action of a committee of the board of directors while acting in place of the board of directors on behalf of the corporation, minutes of any meeting of the shareholders, and records of action taken by the shareholders or board of directors without a meeting, to the extent not subject to inspection under section 16.02(a);

(2) accounting records of the corporation; and

(3) the record of shareholders.

(c) A shareholder may inspect and copy the records described in subsection (b) only if:

(1) his demand is made in good faith and for a proper purpose;

(2) he describes with reasonable particularity his purpose and the records he desires to inspect; and

(3) the records are directly connected with his purpose.

(d) The right of inspection granted by this section may not be abolished or limited by a corporation's articles of incorporation or bylaws.

(e) This section does not affect:

(1) the right of a shareholder to inspect records under section 7.20 or, if the shareholder is in litigation with the corporation, to the same extent as any other litigant;

(2) the power of a court, independently of this Act, to compel the production of corporate records for examination.

(f) For purposes of this section, "shareholder" includes a beneficial owner whose shares are held in a voting trust or by a nominee on his behalf.

§ 16.03 Scope of Inspection Right

(a) A shareholder's agent or attorney has the same inspection and copying rights as the shareholder he represents.

(b) The right to copy records under section 16.02 includes, if reasonable, the right to receive copies made by photographic, xerographic, or other means.

(c) The corporation may impose a reasonable charge, covering the costs of labor and material, for copies of any documents provided to the shareholder. The charge may not exceed the estimated cost of production or reproduction of the records.

(d) The corporation may comply with a shareholder's demand to inspect the record of shareholders under section 16.02(b)(3) by providing him with a list of its shareholders that was compiled no earlier than the date of the shareholder's demand.

§ 16.04 Court–Ordered Inspection

(a) If a corporation does not allow a shareholder who complies with section 16.02(a) to inspect and copy any records required by that subsection to be available for inspection, the [name or describe court] of the county where the corporation's principal office (or, if none in this state, its registered office) is located may summarily order inspection and copying of the records demanded at the corporation's expense upon application of the shareholder.

(b) If a corporation does not within a reasonable time allow a shareholder to inspect and copy any other record, the shareholder who complies with sections 16.02(b) and (c) may apply to the [name or describe court] in the county where the corporation's principal office (or, if none in this state, its registered office) is located for an order to permit inspection and copying of the records demanded. The court shall dispose of an application under this subsection on an expedited basis.

(c) If the court orders inspection and copying of the records demanded, it shall also order the corporation to pay the shareholder's costs (including reasonable counsel fees) incurred to obtain the order unless the corporation proves that it refused inspection in good faith because it had a reasonable basis for doubt about the right of the shareholder to inspect the records demanded.

(d) If the court orders inspection and copying of the records demanded, it may impose reasonable restrictions on the use or distribution of the records by the demanding shareholder.

Official Comment ....

Earlier versions of the Model Act and the statutes of many states imposed a penalty upon the corporation or its officers for refusal to permit inspection of books and records by shareholders who (1) had been shareholders for at least six months or (2) owned five percent or more of the outstanding shares. This provision has been omitted. A penalty unrelated to the costs of securing inspection was arbitrary and, as a result, was seldom actually enforced; further, a qualification based on the size or duration of the shareholder's holding unrelated to his actual purpose was subject to the criticism that it constituted unreasonable discrimination against small shareholders.

Subchapter B

Reports

§ 16.20   Financial Statements for Shareholders

(a) A corporation shall furnish its shareholders annual financial statements, which may be consolidated or combined statements of the corporation and one or more of its subsidiaries, as appropriate, that include a balance sheet as of the end of the fiscal year, an income statement for that year, and a statement of changes in shareholders' equity for the year unless that information appears elsewhere in the financial statements. If financial statements are prepared for the corporation on the basis of generally accepted accounting principles, the annual financial statements must also be prepared on that basis.

(b) If the annual financial statements are reported upon by a public accountant, his report must accompany them. If not, the statements must be accompanied by a statement of the president or the person responsible for the corporation's accounting records:

    (1) stating his reasonable belief whether the statements were prepared on the basis of generally accepted accounting principles and, if not, describing the basis of preparation; and

    (2) describing any respects in which the statements were not prepared on a basis of accounting consistent with the statements prepared for the preceding year.

(c) A corporation shall mail the annual financial statements to each shareholder within 120 days after the close of each fiscal year. Thereafter, on written request from a shareholder who was not mailed the statements, the corporation shall mail him the latest financial statements.

§ 16.21   Other Reports to Shareholders

(a) If a corporation indemnifies or advances expenses to a director under section 8.51, 8.52, 8.53, or 8.54 in connection with a proceeding by or in the right of the corporation, the corporation shall report the indemnification or advance in writing to the shareholders with or before the notice of the next shareholders' meeting.

(b) If a corporation issues or authorizes the issuance of shares for promissory notes or for promises to render services in the future, the corporation shall report in writing to the shareholders the number of shares authorized or issued, and the consideration received by the corporation, with or before the notice of the next shareholders' meeting.

§ 16.22 Annual Report for Secretary of State

(a) Each domestic corporation, and each foreign corporation authorized to transact business in this state, shall deliver to the secretary of state for filing an annual report that sets forth:

(1) the name of the corporation and the state or country under whose law it is incorporated;

(2) the address of its registered office and the name of its registered agent at that office in this state;

(3) the address of its principal office;

(4) the names and business addresses of its directors and principal officers;

(5) a brief description of the nature of its business;

(6) the total number of authorized shares, itemized by class and series, if any, within each class; and

(7) the total number of issued and outstanding shares, itemized by class and series, if any, within each class.

(b) Information in the annual report must be current as of the date the annual report is executed on behalf of the corporation.

(c) The first annual report must be delivered to the secretary of state between January 1 and April 1 of the year following the calendar year in which a domestic corporation was incorporated or a foreign corporation was authorized to transact business. Subsequent annual reports must be delivered to the secretary of state between January 1 and April 1 of the following calendar years.

(d) If an annual report does not contain the information required by this section, the secretary of state shall promptly notify the reporting domestic or foreign corporation in writing and return the report to it for correction. If the report is corrected to contain the information required by this section and delivered to the secretary of state within 30 days after the effective date of notice, it is deemed to be timely filed.

MODEL STATUTORY CLOSE CORPORATION SUPPLEMENT

Subchapter A. Creation

Subchapter B. Shares

Subchapter C. Governance

Subchapter D. Reorganization and Termination

Subchapter E. Judicial Supervision

Subchapter F. Transition Provisions *

* Omitted.

Subchapter A

Creation

§ 1. Short Title

This Supplement shall be known and may be cited as the "[name of state] Statutory Close Corporation Supplement."

§ 2. Application of [Model] Business Corporation Act ...

(a) The [Model] Business Corporation Act applies to statutory close corporations to the extent not inconsistent with the provisions of this Supplement. . . .

§ 3. Definition and Election of Statutory Close Corporation Status

(a) A statutory close corporation is a corporation whose articles of incorporation contain a statement that the corporation is a statutory close corporation.

(b) A corporation having 50 or fewer shareholders may become a statutory close corporation by amending its articles of incorporation to include the statement required by subsection (a). The amendment must be approved by the holders of at least two-thirds of the votes of each class or series of shares of the corporation, voting as separate voting groups, whether or not otherwise entitled to vote on amendments. If the amendment is adopted, a shareholder who voted against the amendment is entitled to assert dissenters' rights under [MBCA ch. 13].

Official Comment

1. 50–Shareholder Limit

The danger that a large corporation with numerous shareholders might attempt to elect close corporation status in order to operate without a board of directors, although highly unlikely as a practical matter, is the reason for the 50 shareholder limit in section 3(b). A new corporation that wishes to elect statutory close corporation status at the time of its initial incorporation is eligible, however, regardless of the number of subscribers. Likewise, a new or existing corporation that becomes a statutory close corporation at a time when it has fewer than 50 shareholders may continue to operate as a statutory close corporation even though it subsequently has more than 50 shareholders. The

* Omitted.

651

potential for abuse by evasion of the normal rules governing corporations is not considered to be sufficiently great to justify an absolute numerical limitation, which inevitably creates the possibility of an unknowing change in status, and complexity of statutory provisions designed to deal with those changes of status. . . .

Subchapter B

Shares

§ 10. Notice of Statutory Close Corporation Status on Issued Shares

(a) The following statement must appear conspicuously on each share certificate issued by a statutory close corporation:

> The rights of shareholders in a statutory close corporation may differ materially from the rights of shareholders in other corporations. Copies of the articles of incorporation and bylaws, shareholders' agreements, and other documents, any of which may restrict transfers and affect voting and other rights, may be obtained by a shareholder on written request to the corporation.

(b) Within a reasonable time after the issuance or transfer of uncertificated shares, the corporation shall send to the shareholders a written notice containing the information required by subsection (a).

(c) The notice required by this section satisfies all requirements of this Act and of [MBCA § 6.27] that notice of share transfer restrictions be given.

(d) A person claiming an interest in shares of a statutory close corporation which has complied with the notice requirement of this section is bound by the documents referred to in the notice. A person claiming an interest in shares of a statutory close corporation which has not complied with the notice requirement of this section is bound by any documents of which he, or a person through whom he claims, has knowledge or notice.

(e) A corporation shall provide to any shareholder upon his written request and without charge copies of provisions that restrict transfer or affect voting or other rights of shareholders appearing in articles of incorporation, bylaws, or shareholders' or voting trust agreements filed with the corporation.

§ 11. Share Transfer Prohibition

(a) An interest in shares of a statutory close corporation may not be voluntarily or involuntarily transferred, by operation of law or otherwise, except to the extent permitted by the articles of incorporation or under section 12.

(b) Except to the extent the articles of incorporation provide otherwise, this section does not apply to a transfer:

(1) to the corporation or to any other holder of the same class or series of shares;

(2) to members of the shareholder's immediate family (or to a trust, all of whose beneficiaries are members of the shareholder's immediate family), which immediate family consists of his spouse, parents, lineal descendants (including adopted children and stepchildren) and the spouse of any lineal descendant, and brothers and sisters;

(3) that has been approved in writing by all of the holders of the corporation's shares having general voting rights;

(4) to an executor or administrator upon the death of a shareholder or to a trustee or receiver as the result of a bankruptcy, insolvency, dissolution, or similar proceeding brought by or against a shareholder;

(5) by merger or share exchange [under MBCA ch. 11] or an exchange of existing shares for other shares of a different class or series in the corporation;

(6) by a pledge as collateral for a loan that does not grant the pledgee any voting rights possessed by the pledgor;

(7) made after termination of the corporation's status as a statutory close corporation.

Official Comment ...

2. Exempt Transfers

Subsection (b) describes a number of exemptions to the prohibition of subsection (a). Intrashareholder and intrafamily transfers are exempt on the assumption that most "typical" close corporation shareholders would want these transfers to be exempt. Transfers to executors, administrators, trustees, or receivers that result from death, bankruptcy, liquidation, or dissolution of a shareholder are also exempt. In addition, transfers that are in effect merely internal recapitalizations and transfers having the approval of all the shareholders are exempt. Transactions in which the stock is pledged or hypothecated are also exempt when no voting rights are given to the pledgee. In all these situations, however, further attempted transfers by the transferees are subject to the prohibitions unless the subsequent transfer qualifies under one of the exemptions. For example, although a pledge of shares as collateral for a loan is an exempt transaction (unless the pledgee is given the power to vote the shares), a subsequent sale of the pledged stock by the pledgee in a foreclosure proceeding can only be made in accordance with section 12 unless the transfer is exempt under subsection (b)....

§ 12. **Share Transfer After First Refusal by Corporation**

(a) A person desiring to transfer shares of a statutory close corporation subject to the transfer prohibition of section 11 must first offer them to the corporation by obtaining an offer to purchase the shares for cash from a third person who is eligible to purchase the shares under subsection (b). The offer by the third person must be in writing and state the offeror's name and address, the number and class (or series) of shares offered, the offering price per share, and the other terms of the offer.

(b) A third person is eligible to purchase the shares if:

   (1) he is eligible to become a qualified shareholder under any federal or state tax statute the corporation has adopted and he agrees in writing not to terminate his qualification without the approval of the remaining shareholders; and

   (2) his purchase of the shares will not impose a personal holding company tax or similar federal or state penalty tax on the corporation.

(c) The person desiring to transfer shares shall deliver the offer to the corporation, and by doing so offers to sell the shares to the corporation on the terms of the offer. Within 20 days after the corporation receives the offer, the corporation shall call a special shareholders' meeting, to be held not more than 40 days after the call, to decide whether the corporation should purchase all (but not less than all) of the offered shares. The offer must be approved by the affirmative vote of the holders of a majority of votes entitled to be cast at the meeting, excluding votes in respect of the shares covered by the offer.

(d) The corporation must deliver to the offering shareholder written notice of acceptance within 75 days after receiving the offer or the offer is rejected. If the corporation makes a counteroffer, the shareholder must deliver to the corporation written notice of acceptance within 15 days after receiving the counteroffer or the counteroffer is rejected. If the corporation accepts the original offer or the shareholder accepts the corporation's counteroffer, the shareholder shall deliver to the corporation duly endorsed certificates for the shares, or instruct the corporation in writing to transfer the shares if uncertificated, within 20 days after the effective date of the notice of acceptance. The corporation may specifically enforce the shareholder's delivery or instruction obligation under this subsection.

(e) A corporation accepting an offer to purchase shares under this section may allocate some or all of the shares to one or more of its shareholders or to other persons if all the shareholders voting in favor of the purchase approve the allocation. If the corporation has more than one class (or series) of shares, however, the remaining holders of the class (or series) of shares being purchased are entitled to a first option to purchase the shares not purchased by the corporation in proportion to their shareholdings or in some other proportion agreed to by all the shareholders participating in the purchase.

(f) If an offer to purchase shares under this section is rejected, the offering shareholder, for a period of 120 days after the corporation received his offer, is entitled to transfer to the third person offeror all (but not less than all) of the offered shares in accordance with the terms of his offer to the corporation.

§ 13. Attempted Share Transfer in Breach of Prohibition

(a) An attempt to transfer shares in a statutory close corporation in violation of a prohibition against transfer binding on the transferee is ineffective.

(b) An attempt to transfer shares in a statutory close corporation in violation of a prohibition against transfer that is not binding on the transferee, either because the notice required by section 10 was not given or because the prohibition is held unenforceable by a court, gives the corporation an option to purchase the shares from the transferee for the same price and on the same terms that he purchased them. To exercise its option, the corporation must give the transferee written notice within 30 days after they are presented for registration in the transferee's name. The corporation may specifically enforce the transferee's sale obligation upon exercise of its purchase option.

Official Comment

This section provides additional protection for the effectiveness of the transfer restrictions applicable to the shares of a statutory close corporation. If the required notice of the restrictions has not been given (see section 10) and the transferee does not have actual notice of the restrictions, the corporation is given a 30–day option to purchase the shares. If the corporation exercises its option, the proposed transferee may pursue a breach of warranty claim or any other appropriate remedy against the proposed transferor. Section 13 is derived from the Delaware law.

This section also gives the corporation an option to purchase shares attempted to be transferred in violation of a transfer restriction that has been held unenforceable by a court.

§ 14. Compulsory Purchase of Shares After Death of Shareholder

(a) This section, and sections 15 through 17, apply to a statutory close corporation only if so provided in its articles of incorporation. If these sections apply, the executor or administrator of the estate of a deceased shareholder may require the corporation to purchase or cause to be purchased all (but not less than all) of the decedent's shares or to be dissolved.

(b) The provisions of sections 15 through 17 may be modified only if the modification is set forth or referred to in the articles of incorporation.

(c) An amendment to the articles of incorporation to provide for application of sections 15 through 17, or to modify or delete the provisions of these sections, must be approved by the holders of at least two-thirds of the votes of each class or series of shares of the statutory close corporation, voting as separate voting groups, whether or not otherwise entitled to vote on amendments. If the corporation has no shareholders when the amendment is proposed, it must be approved by at least two-thirds of the subscribers for shares, if any, or, if none, by all of the incorporators.

(d) A shareholder who votes against an amendment to modify or delete the provisions of sections 15 through 17 is entitled to dissenters' rights under [MBCA chapter 13] if the amendment upon adoption terminates or substantially alters his existing rights under these sections to have his shares purchased.

(e) A shareholder may waive his and his estate's rights under sections 15 through 17 by a signed writing.

(f) Sections 15 through 17 do not prohibit any other agreement providing for the purchase of shares upon a shareholder's death, nor do they prevent a shareholder from enforcing any remedy he has independently of these sections.

Official Comment

1. Introduction

Sections 14 through 17, which are operative only if the articles of incorporation specifically so provide, guarantee a buy-out at the death of a shareholder. ... The optional sell-mandatory purchase option was chosen on the ground that it was the one most likely to be chosen by a shareholder in a closely held corporation, all other factors being equal. . . .

These sections are intended to work in tandem with the share transfer prohibition of section 11. Under the share transfer prohibition there is no obligation to purchase, while under sections 14 through 17 there is an obligation to purchase by the corporation or the other shareholders if the estate wants to sell; if this obligation is not met, the corporation will be dissolved.

The statute grants the estate of a deceased shareholder the right to compel a purchase of the decedent's shares since this is the situation most often covered in privately drafted contractual buy-outs. The problem of illiquidity of close corporation shares is most acute in this situation because the estate frequently needs cash for estate taxes and other purposes. At the same time the remaining shareholders are often concerned about having the decedent's spouse and children involved in the management of the corporation. ... Life insurance may be used to fund part or all of the purchase obligation. In the absence of available cash, an installment arrangement may help to alleviate any financial strain on the corporation. ... Furthermore, if the parties do not have an existing agreement containing a binding price formula or other terms often contained in buy-out agreements and are unable to agree voluntarily on the price or other terms, a court action may be brought in which a judge in his discretion may resolve the differences and structure a buy-out plan that is realistic in light of the corporation's finances.

In summary, assuming some sort of mandatory buy-out in a particular situation is desirable, the major advantage of electing sections 14 through 17 is that they provide basic protection in the event the shareholders have failed to enter into an appropriate private agreement, or have entered into a buy-out agreement but have failed to agree upon a buy-out price formula, or have agreed upon a formula but have neglected to provide other necessary terms such as interest rates or number of installments in the event deferred purchases are authorized or necessary. . . .

2. Redemption Problems

The ability of a corporation to redeem its shares is subject to legal limitations. Section 6.40 of the revised Model Business Corporation Act sets forth a clear set of principles dealing with permissible redemptions of shares. . . .

§ 15. Exercise of Compulsory Purchase Right

(a) A person entitled and desiring to exercise the compulsory purchase right described in section 14 must deliver a written notice to the corporation, within 120 days after the death of the shareholder, describing the number and class or series of shares beneficially owned by the decedent and requesting that the corporation offer to purchase the shares.

(b) Within 20 days after the effective date of the notice, the corporation shall call a special shareholders' meeting, to be held not more than 40 days after the call, to decide whether the corporation should offer to purchase the shares. A purchase offer must be approved by the affirmative vote of the holders of a majority of votes entitled to be cast at the meeting, excluding votes in respect of the shares covered by the notice.

(c) The corporation must deliver a purchase offer to the person requesting it within 75 days after the effective date of the request notice. A purchase offer must be accompanied by the corporation's balance sheet as of the end of a fiscal year ending not more than 16 months before the effective date of the request notice, an income statement for that year, a statement of changes in shareholders' equity for that year, and the latest available interim financial statements, if any. The person must accept the purchase offer in writing within 15 days after receiving it or the offer is rejected.

(d) A corporation agreeing to purchase shares under this section may allocate some or all of the shares to one or more of its shareholders or to other persons if all the shareholders voting in favor of the purchase offer approve the allocation. If the corporation has more than one class or series of shares, however, the remaining holders of the class or series of shares being purchased are entitled to a first option to purchase the shares not purchased by the corporation in proportion to their shareholdings or in some other proportion agreed to by all the shareholders participating in the purchase.

(e) If price and other terms of a compulsory purchase of shares are fixed or are to be determined by the articles of incorporation, bylaws, or a written agreement, the price and terms so fixed or determined govern the compulsory purchase unless the purchaser defaults, in which event the buyer is entitled to commence a proceeding for dissolution under section 16.

§ 16. Court Action to Compel Purchase

(a) If an offer to purchase shares made under section 15 is rejected, or if no offer is made, the person exercising the compulsory purchase right may commence a proceeding against the corporation to compel the purchase in the [name or describe] court of the county where the corporation's principal office (or, if none in this state, its registered office) is located. The corporation at its expense shall notify in writing all of its shareholders, and any other person the court directs, of the commencement of the proceeding. The jurisdiction of the court in which the proceeding is commenced under this subsection is plenary and exclusive.

(b) The court shall determine the fair value of the shares subject to compulsory purchase in accordance with the standards set forth in section 42 together with terms for the purchase. Upon making these determinations the court shall order the corporation to purchase or cause the purchase of the shares or empower the person exercising the compulsory purchase right to have the corporation dissolved.

(c) After the purchase order is entered, the corporation may petition the court to modify the terms of purchase and the court may do so if it finds that changes in the financial or legal ability of the corporation or other purchaser to complete the purchase justify a modification.

(d) If the corporation or other purchaser does not make a payment required by the court's order within 30 days of its due date, the seller may petition the court to dissolve the corporation and, absent a showing of good cause for not making the payment, the court shall do so.

(e) A person making a payment to prevent or cure a default by the corporation or other purchaser is entitled to recover the payment from the defaulter.

§ 17. Court Costs and Other Expenses

(a) The court in a proceeding commenced under section 16 shall determine the total costs of the proceeding, including the reasonable compensation and expenses of appraisers appointed by the court and of counsel and experts employed by the parties. Except as provided in subsection (b), the court shall assess these costs equally against the corporation and the party exercising the compulsory purchase right.

(b) The court may assess all or a portion of the total costs of the proceeding:

(1) against the person exercising the compulsory purchase right if the court finds that the fair value of the shares does not substantially exceed the corporation's last purchase offer made before commencement of the proceeding and that the person's failure to accept the offer was arbitrary, vexatious, or otherwise not in good faith; or

(2) against the corporation if the court finds that the fair value of the shares substantially exceeds the corporation's last sale offer made before commencement of the proceeding and that the offer was arbitrary, vexatious, or otherwise not made in good faith.

Subchapter C

Governance

§ 20. Shareholder Agreements

(a) All the shareholders of a statutory close corporation may agree in writing to regulate the exercise of the corporate powers and the management of the business and affairs of the corporation or the relationship among the shareholders of the corporation.

(b) An agreement authorized by this section is effective although:

(1) it eliminates a board of directors;

(2) it restricts the discretion or powers of the board or authorizes director proxies or weighted voting rights;

(3) its effect is to treat the corporation as a partnership; or

(4) it creates a relationship among the shareholders or between the shareholders and the corporation that would otherwise be appropriate only among partners.

(c) If the corporation has a board of directors, an agreement authorized by this section restricting the discretion or powers of the board relieves directors of liability imposed by law, and imposes that liability on each person in whom the board's discretion or power is vested, to the extent that the discretion or powers of the board of directors are governed by the agreement.

(d) A provision eliminating a board of directors in an agreement authorized by this section is not effective unless the articles of incorporation contain a statement to that effect as required by section 21.

(e) A provision entitling one or more shareholders to dissolve the corporation under section 33 is effective only if a statement of this right is contained in the articles of incorporation.

(f) To amend an agreement authorized by this section, all the shareholders must approve the amendment in writing unless the agreement provides otherwise.

(g) Subscribers for shares may act as shareholders with respect to an agreement authorized by this section if shares are not issued when the agreement was made.

(h) This section does not prohibit any other agreement between or among shareholders in a statutory close corporation.

§ 21. Elimination of Board of Directors

(a) A statutory close corporation may operate without a board of directors if its articles of incorporation contain a statement to that effect.

(b) An amendment to articles of incorporation eliminating a board of directors must be approved by all the shareholders of the corporation, whether or not otherwise entitled to vote on amendments, or if no shares have been issued, by all the subscribers for shares, if any, or if none, by all the incorporators.

(c) While a corporation is operating without a board of directors as authorized by subsection (a):

(1) all corporate powers shall be exercised by or under the authority of, and the business and affairs of the corporation managed under the direction of, the shareholders;

(2) unless the articles of incorporation provide otherwise, (i) action requiring director approval or both director and shareholder approval is authorized if approved by the shareholders and (ii) action requiring a majority or greater percentage vote of the board of directors is authorized if approved by the majority or

greater percentage of the votes of shareholders entitled to vote on the action;

(3) a shareholder is not liable for his act or omission, although a director would be, unless the shareholder was entitled to vote on the action;

(4) a requirement by a state or the United States that a document delivered for filing contain a statement that specified action has been taken by the board of directors is satisfied by a statement that the corporation is a statutory close corporation without a board of directors and that the action was approved by the shareholders;

(5) the shareholders by resolution may appoint one or more shareholders to sign documents as "designated directors."

(d) An amendment to articles of incorporation deleting the statement eliminating a board of directors must be approved by the holders of at least two-thirds of the votes of each class or series of shares of the corporation, voting as separate voting groups, whether or not otherwise entitled to vote on amendments. The amendment must also specify the number, names, and addresses of the corporation's directors or describe who will perform the duties of a board under [MBCA § 8.01].

§ 22. Bylaws

(a) A statutory close corporation need not adopt bylaws if provisions required by law to be contained in bylaws are contained in either the articles of incorporation or a shareholder agreement authorized by section 20.

(b) If a corporation does not have bylaws when its statutory close corporation status terminates under section 31, the corporation shall immediately adopt bylaws under [MBCA § 2.06].

§ 23. Annual Meeting

(a) The annual meeting date for a statutory close corporation is the first business day after May 31st unless its articles of incorporation, bylaws, or a shareholder agreement authorized by section 20 fixes a different date.

(b) A statutory close corporation need not hold an annual meeting unless one or more shareholders deliver written notice to the corporation requesting a meeting at least 30 days before the meeting date determined under subsection (a).

§ 24. Execution of Documents in More Than One Capacity

Notwithstanding any law to the contrary, an individual who holds more than one office in a statutory close corporation may execute, acknowledge, or verify in more than one capacity any document required to be executed, acknowledged, or verified by the holders of two or more offices.

§ 25. Limited Liability

The failure of a statutory close corporation to observe the usual corporate formalities or requirements relating to the exercise of its corporate powers or management of its business and affairs is not a ground for imposing personal liability on the shareholders for liabilities of the corporation.

Official Comment

The purpose of this section is to eliminate the possible argument that the shareholders in a statutory close corporation are individually liable for the debts and torts of the business because the corporation did not follow the classical model of a corporation. Pursuant to sections 20, 21, and 33, a statutory close corporation may in effect function like a partnership, although legally the business is still a corporation. This section does not prevent a court from "piercing the corporate veil" of a statutory close corporation if the circumstances should justify imposing personal liability on the shareholders were the corporation not a statutory close corporation. It merely prevents a court from "piercing the corporate veil" because it is a statutory close corporation....

Subchapter D

Reorganization and Termination

§ 30. Merger, Share Exchange, and Sale of Assets

(a) A plan of merger or share exchange:

    (1) that if effected would terminate statutory close corporation status must be approved by the holders of at least two-thirds of the votes of each class or series of shares of the statutory close corporation, voting as separate voting groups, whether or not the holders are otherwise entitled to vote on the plan;

    (2) that if effected would create the surviving corporation as a statutory close corporation must be approved by the holders of at least two-thirds of the votes of each class or series of shares of the surviving corporation, voting as separate voting groups, whether or not the holders are otherwise entitled to vote on the plan.

(b) A sale, lease, exchange, or other disposition of all or substantially all of the property (with or without the good will) of a statutory close corporation, if not made in the usual and regular course of business, must be approved by the holders of at least two-thirds of the votes of each class or series of shares of the corporation, voting as separate voting groups, whether or not the holders are otherwise entitled to vote on the transaction.

Official Comment ...

The exceptions to shareholder approval of mergers or share exchanges for subsidiary mergers and some other types of transactions (in MBCA chapter 11) do not apply to statutory close corporations since a shareholder vote is required in all circumstances where statutory close corporation status is elected or terminated.

Shareholders of a statutory close corporation who vote against the merger, share exchange, or sale not in the regular course of business of all or substantially all the assets have dissenters' rights under MBCA chapter 13. . . .

§ 31. Termination of Statutory Close Corporation Status

(a) A statutory close corporation may terminate its statutory close corporation status by amending its articles of incorporation to delete the statement that it is a statutory close corporation. If the statutory close corporation has elected to operate without a board of directors under section 21, the amendment must either comply with [MBCA § 8.01] or delete the statement dispensing with the board of directors from its articles of incorporation.

(b) An amendment terminating statutory close corporation status must be approved by the holders of at least two-thirds of the votes of each class or series of shares of the corporation, voting as separate voting groups, whether or not the holders are otherwise entitled to vote on amendments.

(c) If an amendment to terminate statutory close corporation status is adopted, each shareholder who voted against the amendment is entitled to assert dissenters' rights under [MBCA ch. 13].

Official Comment

Sections 31 and 32 deal with issues that arise when it is decided to terminate a corporation's status as a statutory close corporation. . . .

In the absence of agreement upon rights and duties of the shareholders, the corporation upon termination automatically becomes subject to the state's general business corporation statute, or professional corporation act if the corporation was organized as a professional corporation. Further, except for transfer restrictions under section 11 and authority to operate without a board of directors under MBCA section 8.01(c), any existing rights of the shareholders established by agreement ... between the shareholders or with the corporation and any rights granted to the shareholders in the articles of incorporation that are valid under the general business or professional corporation acts remain in effect.

If the shareholders desire to have transfer restrictions applicable under section 11 to continue after termination of statutory close corporation status, the restrictions must meet all requirements specified in MBCA section 6.27, or analogous section of the state's general corporation statute. . . .

If the Revised Model Business Corporation Act . . . [has] been enacted, most of the special control and distribution arrangements among the shareholders and the optional provisions that may be included in the articles of incorporation are not affected by the termination. For example, if sections 14 through 17 have been elected, the buy-out purchase option at the death of a shareholder continues to apply, unless the articles of incorporation are amended to terminate the option. . . . Some provisions, however, may be of doubtful validity after termination. One that may be in this category is a provision in the articles of incorporation giving one or more minority shareholders the right to dissolve the corporation as authorized by section 33. . . .

§ 32. Effect of Termination of Statutory Close Corporation Status

(a) A corporation that terminates its status as a statutory close corporation is thereafter subject to all provisions of the [Model] Business Corporation Act or, if incorporated under the [Model] Professional Corporation Supplement, to all provisions of that Supplement.

(b) Termination of statutory close corporation status does not affect any right of a shareholder or of the corporation under an agreement or the articles of incorporation unless this Act, the [Model] Business Corporation Act, or another law of this state invalidates the right.

§ 33. Shareholder Option to Dissolve Corporation

(a) The articles of incorporation of a statutory close corporation may authorize one or more shareholders, or the holders of a specified number or percentage of shares of any class or series, to dissolve the corporation at will or upon the occurrence of a specified event or contingency. The shareholder or shareholders exercising this authority must give written notice of the intent to dissolve to all the other shareholders. Thirty-one days after the effective date of the notice, the corporation shall begin to wind up and liquidate its business and affairs and file articles of dissolution under [MBCA sections 14.03 through 14.07].

(b) Unless the articles of incorporation provide otherwise, an amendment to the articles of incorporation to add, change, or delete the authority to dissolve described in subsection (a) must be approved by the holders of all the outstanding shares, whether or not otherwise entitled to vote on amendments, or if no shares have been issued, by all the subscribers for shares, if any, or if none, by all the incorporators.

Official Comment

The purpose of this section is to give shareholders in a statutory close corporation, if they so elect, basically the same power to dissolve the business as general partners have under the Uniform Partnership Act. The section applies only if it is elected in the corporation's original or amended articles of incorporation. The right may be given to a single shareholder or to any group of shareholders and may be exercisable at will or restricted to certain designated circumstances. Rights under this section are in addition to other rights a shareholder may have under the state's general business corporation or professional corporation acts or this Supplement to dissolve the corporation. . . .

Subchapter E

Judicial Supervision

§ 40. Court Action to Protect Shareholders

(a) Subject to satisfying the conditions of subsections (c) and (d), a shareholder of a statutory close corporation may petition the [name or describe] court for any of the relief described in section 41, 42, or 43 if:

   (1) the directors or those in control of the corporation have acted, are acting, or will act in a manner that is illegal, oppressive, fraudulent, or unfairly prejudicial to the petitioner, whether in his capacity as shareholder, director, or officer, of the corporation;

   (2) the directors or those in control of the corporation are deadlocked in the management of the corporation's affairs, the shareholders are unable to break the deadlock, and the corporation is suffering or will suffer irreparable injury or the business and affairs of the corporation can no longer be conducted to the advantage of the shareholders generally because of the deadlock; or

   (3) there exists one or more grounds for judicial dissolution of the corporation under [MBCA § 14.30].

(b) A shareholder must commence a proceeding under subsection (a) in the [name or describe] court of the county where the corporation's principal office (or, if none in this state, its registered office) is located. The jurisdiction of the court in which the proceeding is commenced is plenary and exclusive.

(c) If a shareholder has agreed in writing to pursue a nonjudicial remedy to resolve disputed matters, he may not commence a proceeding under this section with respect to the matters until he has exhausted the nonjudicial remedy.

(d) If a shareholder has dissenters' rights under this Act or [MBCA ch. 13] with respect to proposed corporate action, he must commence a proceeding under this section before he is required to give notice of his intent to demand payment under [MBCA § 13.21] or to demand payment under [MBCA § 13.23] or the proceeding is barred.

(e) Except as provided in subsections (c) and (d), a shareholder's right to commence a proceeding under this section and the remedies available under sections 41 through 43 are in addition to any other right or remedy he may have.

Official Comment

1. Introduction

Sections 40 through 43 are derived from similar provisions in the California, Michigan, Minnesota, New Jersey, and South Carolina statutes, which in turn are derived from former section 210 of the 1948 English Companies Act (reenacted as section 75 of the 1980 English Companies Act). There are two major differences between these statutes and sections 40 through 43: (1) the statutes, either specifically or by implication, provide that a shareholder may obtain relief only if he has statutory grounds therefor, whereas section 43 does not tie relief either to a suit to compel dissolution or to the establishment of grounds for dissolution; and (2) the range of relief available to the court is spelled out in greater detail.

The primary danger in granting relief for oppression and related conduct by dissolution is that the remedy is drastic and courts have usually refused to order dissolution of a solvent corporation, except in extreme cases of fraudulent conduct. Moreover, even though authority may exist to grant relief other than dissolution, courts have often been reluctant to grant any relief unless the fact situation itself justifies dissolution. This approach makes the grounds for relief too narrow to protect in an adequate fashion the rights of minority shareholders. At the same time the threat of dissolution gives minority shareholders a powerful weapon to hold over the head of the majority. Under this Supplement, dissolution is one form of relief that may be ordered by the court, but it is appropriate only as a last resort after other possibilities of resolving the dispute have failed. If a shareholder is actually seeking liquidation of the corporation, he may bring an action for dissolution under the state's general business corporation act (assuming he qualifies to bring the proceeding) or under the option-to-dissolve provisions of section 33.

Although sections 40 through 43 probably will be invoked most frequently by minority shareholders, the ground for relief described in section 40(a)(2) may be used by the holders of the majority of shares to seek relief from deadlocks created by veto rights given minority shareholders which threaten the corporation's continued existence. Moreover, even in suits brought by minority shareholders, the court has power under section 42 to order the petitioning shareholders to sell their shares to the corporation or to the remaining shareholders, even if this is not the relief requested.

Relief available under sections 40 through 43 is circumscribed to minimize the danger of abuse by shareholders. No relief of any kind may be ordered unless the court affirmatively finds that one or more of the specific conditions listed in section 40(a)—fraud, oppression, unfairly prejudicial conduct, deadlock, or grounds for involuntary dissolution— exist. The petitioner has the burden of proof on this issue. The court may award expenses and counsel fees to either side under section 41(b) in order to discourage or punish the bringing of harassment suits. Finally, if the complaining shareholder has agreed to arbitrate the dispute in question or to resolve it in some other nonjudicial manner, these remedies must be exhausted under section 40(c) before a suit under this section may be filed.

2. Grounds for Relief

Section 40(a)(1) provides relief from oppression and related conduct that adversely affects a minority shareholder in any relationship with the corporation. Attempted squeeze-outs in close corporations often involve removing a shareholder from his various offices or diminishing his compensation. The subsection makes clear that relief is not limited to those situations in which the value of the shareholder's share interest has been adversely affected.

No attempt has been made to define oppression, fraud, or unfairly prejudicial conduct. These are elastic terms whose meaning varies with the circumstances presented in a particular case, and it is felt that existing case law provides sufficient guidelines for courts and litigants. . . .

Section 40(a)(2) allows relief when the corporation is deadlocked. Whether a deadlock is created by majority or minority shareholders is immaterial and either majority or minority shareholders may claim relief under this subsection. Relief may be granted even though the corporation's financial condition is not threatened with irreparable injury if the court finds that the interest of all the shareholders is being damaged by the deadlock.

Section 40(a)(3) permits a shareholder to claim relief under this section if grounds for involuntary dissolution exist (see MBCA section 14.30). By filing an action under this section, a greater range of relief is made available to the shareholder. For example, the petitioning shareholder may not wish the corporation dissolved, even though grounds for dissolution exist....

§ 41. Ordinary Relief

(a) If the court finds that one or more of the grounds for relief described in section 40(a) exist, it may order one or more of the following types of relief:

    (1) the performance, prohibition, alteration, or setting aside of any action of the corporation or of its shareholders, directors, or officers of or any other party to the proceeding;

    (2) the cancellation or alteration of any provision in the corporation's articles of incorporation or bylaws;

    (3) the removal from office of any director or officer;

    (4) the appointment of any individual as a director or officer;

    (5) an accounting with respect to any matter in dispute;

    (6) the appointment of a custodian to manage the business and affairs of the corporation;

    (7) the appointment of a provisional director (who has all the rights, powers, and duties of a duly elected director) to serve for the term and under the conditions prescribed by the court;

    (8) the payment of dividends;

    (9) the award of damages to any aggrieved party.

(b) If the court finds that a party to the proceeding acted arbitrarily, vexatiously, or otherwise not in good faith, it may award one or more other parties their reasonable expenses, including counsel fees and the expenses of appraisers or other experts, incurred in the proceeding.

Official Comment

The purpose of listing the types of relief available, in this section and in sections 42 and 43, is to overcome the reluctance some courts have shown in the past to ordering anything other than dissolution, or possibly a buy-out. See, e.g., Gruenberg v. Goldmine Plantation, Inc., 360 So.2d 884 (La.Ct.App.1978); Harkey v. Mobley, 552 S.W.2d 79 (Mo.Ct.App.1977); White v. Perkins, 213 Va. 129, 189 S.E.2d 315 (1972). A court should have broad discretion to fashion the most appropriate remedy to resolve the dispute. What works in one case may not work in another. Detailed standards are not provided since they might encourage litigation and also unduly restrict the court's discretion. The dangers of including detailed standards, however, outweigh the advantages. Existing cases applying principles of equity, are, of course, precedents for the exercise of a judge's discretion under this section....

§ 42. Extraordinary Relief: Share Purchase

(a) If the court finds that the ordinary relief described in section 41(a) is or would be inadequate or inappropriate, it may order the corporation dissolved under section 43 unless the corporation or one or more of its shareholders purchases all the shares of the shareholder for their fair value and on terms determined under subsection (b).

(b) If the court orders a share purchase, it shall:

    (1) determine the fair value of the shares, considering among other relevant evidence the going concern value of the corporation, any agreement among some or all of the shareholders fixing the price or specifying a formula for determining share value for any purpose, the recommendations of appraisers (if any) appointed by the court, and any legal constraints on the corporation's ability to purchase the shares;

    (2) specify the terms of the purchase, including if appropriate terms for installment payments, subordination of the purchase obligation to the rights of the corporation's other creditors, security for a deferred purchase price, and a covenant not to compete or other restriction on the seller;

    (3) require the seller to deliver all his shares to the purchaser upon receipt of the purchase price or the first installment of the purchase price;

    (4) provide that after the seller delivers his shares he has no further claim against the corporation, its directors, officers, or shareholders, other than a claim to any unpaid balance of the purchase price and a claim under any agreement with the corporation or the remaining shareholders that is not terminated by the court; and

    (5) provide that if the purchase is not completed in accordance with the specified terms, the corporation is to be dissolved under section 43.

(c) After the purchase order is entered, any party may petition the court to modify the terms of the purchase and the court may do so if it finds that changes in the financial or legal ability of the corporation or other purchaser to complete the purchase justify a modification.

(d) If the corporation is dissolved because the share purchase was not completed in accordance with the court's order, the selling shareholder has the same rights and priorities in the corporation's assets as if the sale had not been ordered.

Official Comment

... [T]he buy-out and dissolution remedies provided by this section and section 43 are cumulative of ordinary remedies available under section 41; for example, a court may award damages in addition to compelling a buy-out. See the Official Comment to section 40.

§ 43. Extraordinary Relief: Dissolution

(a) The court may dissolve the corporation if it finds:

   (1) there are one or more grounds for judicial dissolution under [MBCA § 14.30]; or

   (2) all other relief ordered by the court under section 41 or 42 has failed to resolve the matters in dispute.

(b) In determining whether to dissolve the corporation, the court shall consider among other relevant evidence the financial condition of the corporation but may not refuse to dissolve solely because the corporation has accumulated earnings or current operating profits.

CALIFORNIA CORPORATIONS CODE
(SELECTED PROVISIONS)

TITLE 1

CORPORATIONS

Chapter 1

GENERAL PROVISIONS AND DEFINITIONS

Chapter 2

ORGANIZATION AND BYLAWS

Chapter 6

SHAREHOLDERS' MEETINGS AND CONSENTS

Chapter 7

VOTING OF SHARES

Chapter 8

SHAREHOLDER DERIVATIVE ACTIONS

Chapter 9

AMENDMENT OF ARTICLES

Chapter 10

SALES OF ASSETS

TITLE 1

CORPORATIONS

Chapter 1

GENERAL PROVISIONS AND DEFINITIONS

§ 114. Financial Statements and Accounting Items

All references in this division to financial statements, balance sheets, income statements and statements of changes in financial position of a corporation and all references to assets, liabilities, earnings, retained earnings and similar accounting items of a corporation mean such financial statements or such items prepared or determined in conformity with generally accepted accounting principles then applicable, fairly presenting in conformity with generally accepted accounting principles the matters which they purport to present, subject to any specific accounting treatment required by a particular section of this division. Unless otherwise expressly stated, all references in this division to such financial statements mean, in the case of a corporation which has subsidiaries, consolidated statements of the corporation and such of its subsidiaries as are required ... to be included in such consolidated statements under generally accepted accounting principles then applicable and all references to such accounting items mean such items determined on a consolidated basis in accordance with such consolidated financial statements. Financial statements other than annual statements may be condensed or otherwise presented as permitted by authoritative accounting pronouncements.

§ 150. Affiliate; Affiliated

A corporation is an "affiliate" of, or a corporation is "affiliated" with, another specified corporation if it directly, or indirectly through one or more intermediaries, controls, is controlled by or is under common control with the other specified corporation.

§ 151. Approved by (or Approval of) the Board

"Approved by (or approval of) the board" means approved or ratified by the vote of the board or by the vote of a committee authorized to exercise the powers of the board ....

§ 152. Approved by (or Approval of) the Outstanding Shares

"Approved by (or approval of) the outstanding shares" means approved by the affirmative vote of a majority of the outstanding shares entitled to vote. Such approval shall include the affirmative vote of a majority of the outstanding shares of each class or series entitled, by any provision of the articles or of this division, to vote as a class or series on the subject matter being voted upon and shall also include the affirmative vote of such greater proportion (including all) of the outstanding shares of any class or series if such greater proportion is required by the articles or this division.

§ 153. Approved by (or Approval of) the Shareholders

"Approved by (or approval of) the shareholders" means approved or ratified by the affirmative vote of a majority of the shares . . . represented and voting at a duly held meeting at which a quorum is present (which shares voting affirmatively also constitute at least a majority of the required quorum) or by the written consent of shareholders . . . or by the affirmative vote or written consent of such greater proportion (including all) of the shares of any class or series as may be provided in the articles or in this division for all or any specified shareholder action.

§ 158. Close Corporation

(a) "Close corporation" means a corporation whose articles contain, in addition to the provisions required by Section 202 [Articles of Incorporation; Required Provisions], a provision that all of the corporation's issued shares of all classes shall be held of record by not more than a specified number of persons, not exceeding 35, and a statement "This corporation is a close corporation."

(b) The special provisions referred to in subdivision (a) may be included in the articles by amendment, but if such amendment is adopted after the issuance of shares only by the affirmative vote of all of the issued and outstanding shares of all classes.

(c) The special provisions referred to in subdivision (a) may be deleted from the articles by amendment, or the number of shareholders specified may be changed by amendment, but if such amendment is adopted after the issuance of shares only by the affirmative vote of at least two-thirds of each class of the outstanding shares; provided, however, that the articles may provide for a lesser vote, but not less than a majority of the outstanding shares, or may deny a vote to any class, or both.

(d) In determining the number of shareholders for the purposes of the provision in the articles authorized by this section, a husband and wife and the personal representative of either shall be counted as one regardless of how shares may be held by either or both of them, a trust or personal representative of a decedent holding shares shall be counted as one regardless of the number of trustees or beneficiaries and a partnership or corporation or business association holding shares shall be counted as one (except that any such trust or entity the primary purpose of which was the acquisition or voting of the shares shall be counted according to the number of beneficial interests therein).

(e) A corporation shall cease to be a close corporation upon the filing of an amendment to its articles pursuant to subdivision (c) or if it shall have more than the maximum number of holders of record of its shares specified in its articles as a result of an inter vivos transfer of shares which is not void under subdivision (d) of Section 418, the transfer of shares on distribution by will or pursuant to the laws of descent and distribution, the dissolution of a partnership or corporation or business association or the termination of a trust which holds shares, by court decree upon dissolution of a marriage or otherwise by operation of law. Promptly upon acquiring more than the specified number of holders of record of its shares, a close corporation shall execute and file an amendment to its articles deleting the special provisions referred to in subdivision (a) and deleting any other provisions not permissible for a corporation which is not a close corporation, which amendment shall be promptly approved and filed by the board and need not be approved by the outstanding shares.

(f) Nothing contained in this section shall invalidate any agreement among the shareholders to vote for the deletion from the articles of the special provisions referred to in subdivision (a) upon the lapse of a specified period of time or upon the occurrence of a certain event or condition or otherwise. . . .

§ 160. Control

(a) Except as provided in subdivision (b), "control" means the possession, direct or indirect, of the power to direct or cause the direction of the management and policies of a corporation.

(b) "Control" in Sections 181, 1001 and 1200 means the ownership directly or indirectly of shares possessing more than 50 percent of the voting power.

§ 161. Constituent Corporation

"Constituent corporation" means a corporation which is merged with or into one or more other corporations or one or more other business entities and includes a surviving corporation.

§ 161.7 Constituent Other Business Entity

"Constituent other business entity" means an other business entity that is merged with or into one or more corporations and includes the surviving other business entity.

§ 165. Disappearing Corporation

"Disappearing corporation" means a constituent corporation which is not the surviving corporation.

§ 166. Distribution to Its Shareholders

"Distribution to its shareholders" means the transfer of cash or property by a corporation to its shareholders without consideration, whether by way of dividend or otherwise, except a dividend in shares of the corporation, or the purchase or redemption of its shares for cash or property, including the transfer, purchase, or redemption by a subsidiary of the corporation. The time of any distribution by way of dividend shall be the date of declaration thereof and the time of any distribution by purchase or redemption of shares shall be the date cash or property is transferred by the corporation, whether or not pursuant to a contract of an earlier date; provided, that where a debt obligation that is a security (as defined in Section 8102 of the Commercial Code) is issued in exchange for shares the time of the distribution is the date when the corporation acquires the shares in the exchange. In the case of a sinking fund payment, cash or property is transferred within the meaning of this section at the time that it is delivered to a trustee for the holders of preferred shares to be used for the redemption of the shares or physically segregated by the corporation in trust for that purpose. "Distribution to its shareholders" shall not include (a) satisfaction of a final judgment of a court or tribunal of appropriate jurisdiction ordering the rescission of the issuance of shares, (b) the rescission by a corporation of the issuance of its shares, if the board determines (with any director who is, or would be, a party to the transaction not being entitled to vote) that (1) it is reasonably likely that the holder or holders of the shares in question could legally enforce a claim for the rescission, (2) that the rescission is in the best interests of the corporation, and (3) the corporation is likely to be able to meet its liabilities (except those for which payment is otherwise adequately provided) as they mature, or (c) the repurchase by a corporation of its shares issued by it pursuant to Section 408 [Employee Stock Purchase or Stock Option Plans], if the board determines (with any director who is, or would be, a party to the transaction not being entitled to vote) that (1) the repurchase is in the best interests of the corporation and that (2) the corporation is likely to be able to meet its liabilities (except those for which payment is otherwise adequately provided) as they mature.

§ 167.8 Disappearing Other Business Entity

"Disappearing other business entity" means a constituent other business entity that is not the surviving other business entity.

§ 168. Equity Security

"Equity security" in Sections 181, 1200 and 1201 means any share, any security convertible, with or without consideration, into shares or any warrant or right to subscribe to or purchase any of the foregoing.

§ 171.1 Initial Transaction Statement

"Initial transaction statement" means a statement signed by or on behalf of the issuer sent to the new registered owner or registered pledgee, and "written statements," when used in connection with uncertificated securities, means the written statements that are periodically, or at the request of the registered owner or registered pledgee, sent by the issuer to the registered owner or registered pledgee describing the issue of which the uncertificated security is a part.

§ 172. Liquidation Price; Liquidation Preference

"Liquidation price" or "liquidation preference" means amounts payable on shares of any class upon voluntary or involuntary dissolution, winding up or distribution of the entire assets of the corporation, including any cumulative dividends accrued and unpaid, in priority to shares of another class or classes.

§ 174.5 Other Business Entity

"Other business entity" means a limited liability company [or] a limited partnership . . . .

§ 175. Parent

Except as used in Sections 1001, 1101 and 1200, a "parent" of a specified corporation is an affiliate controlling such corporation directly or indirectly through one or more intermediaries. In Sections 1001 and 1101, "parent" means a person in control of a corporation as defined in subdivision (b) of Section 160.

§ 180. Redemption Price

"Redemption price" means the amount or amounts (in cash, property or securities, or any combination thereof) payable on shares of any class or series upon the redemption of the shares. Unless otherwise expressly provided, the redemption price is payable in cash.

§ 181. Reorganization

"Reorganization" means either:

(a) A merger pursuant to Chapter 11 (commencing with Section 1100) other than a short-form merger (a "merger reorganization").

(b) The acquisition by one corporation in exchange in whole or in part for its equity securities (or the equity securities of a corporation which is in control of the acquiring corporation) of shares of another corporation if, immediately after the acquisition, the acquiring corporation has control of the other corporation (an "exchange reorganization").

(c) The acquisition by one corporation in exchange in whole or in part for its equity securities (or the equity securities of a corporation which is in control of the acquiring corporation) or for its debt securities (or debt securities of a corporation which is in control of the acquiring corporation) which are not adequately secured and which have a maturity date in excess of five years after the consummation of the reorganization, or both, of all or substantially all of the assets of another corporation (a "sale-of-assets reorganization").

§ 183.5   Share Exchange Tender Offer

"Share exchange tender offer" means any acquisition by one corporation in exchange in whole or in part for its equity securities (or the equity securities of a corporation which is in control of the acquiring corporation) of shares of another corporation, other than an exchange reorganization (subdivision (b) of Section 181).

§ 186.   Shareholders' Agreement

"Shareholders' agreement" means a written agreement among all of the shareholders of a close corporation, or if a close corporation has only one shareholder between such shareholder and the corporation, as authorized by subdivision (b) of Section 300.

§ 187.   Short Form Merger

"Short-form merger" means a merger pursuant to Section 1110.

§ 189.   Subsidiary

(a) Except as provided in subdivision (b), "subsidiary" of a specified corporation means a corporation shares of which possessing more than 50 percent of the voting power are owned directly or indirectly through one or more subsidiaries by the specified corporation.

(b) For the purpose of Section 703, "subsidiary" of a specified corporation means a corporation shares of which possessing more than 25 percent of the voting power are owned directly or indirectly through one or more subsidiaries as defined in subdivision (a) by the specified corporation.

§ 190.   Surviving Corporation

"Surviving corporation" means a corporation into which one or more other corporations or one or more other business entities are merged.

§ 190.5   Surviving Limited Partnership

"Surviving limited partnership" means a limited partnership into which one or more other limited partnerships or one or more corporations are merged.

§ 190.7   Surviving Other Business Entity

"Surviving other business entity" means an other business entity into which one or more other business entities or one or more corporations are merged.

§ 194.   Vote

"Vote" includes authorization by written consent, subject to the provisions of subdivision (b) of Section 307 and subdivision (d) of Section 603.*

§ 194.5   Voting Power

"Voting power" means the power to vote for the election of directors at the time any determination of voting power is made and does not include the right to vote upon the happening of some condition or event which has not yet occurred. In any case where different classes of shares are entitled to vote as separate classes for different members of the board, the determination of percentage of voting power shall be made on the basis of the percentage of the total number of authorized directors which the shares in question (whether of one or more classes) have the power to elect in an election at which all shares then entitled to vote for the election of any directors are voted.

§ 194.7   Voting Shift

"Voting shift" means a change, pursuant to or by operation of a provision of the articles, in the relative rights of the holders of one or more classes or series of shares, voting as one or more separate classes or series, to elect one or more directors.

Chapter 2

ORGANIZATION AND BYLAWS

§ 204.   Articles of Incorporation; Optional Provisions

The articles of incorporation may set forth:

(a) Any or all of the following provisions, which shall not be effective unless expressly provided in the articles:

(1) Granting, with or without limitations, the power to levy assessments upon the shares or any class of shares.

(2) Granting to shareholders preemptive rights to subscribe to any or all issues of shares or securities.

(3) Special qualifications of persons who may be shareholders.

---

*Section 603(d) provides that directors may not be elected by written consent except by unanimous written consent. (Footnote by ed.)

(4) A provision limiting the duration of the corporation's existence to a specified date.

(5) A provision requiring, for any or all corporate actions (except as provided in Section 303, subdivision (b) of Section 402.5, subdivision (c) of Section 708 and Section 1900) the vote of a larger proportion or of all of the shares of any class or series, or the vote or quorum for taking action of a larger proportion or of all of the directors, than is otherwise required by this division.

(6) A provision limiting or restricting the business in which the corporation may engage or the powers which the corporation may exercise or both.

(7) A provision conferring upon the holders of any evidences of indebtedness, issued or to be issued by the corporation, the right to vote in the election of directors and on any other matters on which shareholders may vote.

(8) A provision conferring upon shareholders the right to determine the consideration for which shares shall be issued.

(9) A provision requiring the approval of the shareholders (Section 153) or the approval of the outstanding shares (Section 152) for any corporate action, even though not otherwise required by this division.

(10) Provisions eliminating or limiting the personal liability of a director for monetary damages in an action brought by or in the right of the corporation for breach of a director's duties to the corporation and its shareholders, as set forth in Section 309, provided, however, that (A) such a provision may not eliminate or limit the liability of directors (i) for acts or omissions that involve intentional misconduct or a knowing and culpable violation of law, (ii) for acts or omissions that a director believes to be contrary to the best interests of the corporation or its shareholders or that involve the absence of good faith on the part of the director, (iii) for any transaction from which a director derived an improper personal benefit, (iv) for acts or omissions that show a reckless disregard for the director's duty to the corporation or its shareholders in circumstances in which the director was aware, or should have been aware, in the ordinary course of performing a director's duties, of a risk of serious injury to the corporation or its shareholders, (v) for acts or omissions that constitute an unexcused pattern of inattention that amounts to an abdication of the director's duty to the corporation or its shareholders, (vi) under Section 310, or (vii) under Section 316, (B) no such provision shall eliminate or limit the liability of a director for any act or omission occurring prior to the date when the provision becomes effective, and (C) no such provision shall eliminate or limit the liability of an officer for any act or omission as an officer, notwithstanding that the officer is also a director or that his or her actions, if negligent or improper, have been ratified by the directors.

(11) A provision authorizing, whether by bylaw, agreement, or otherwise, the indemnification of agents (as defined in Section 317) in excess of that expressly permitted by Section 317 for those agents of the corporation for breach of duty to the corporation and its stockholders, provided, however, that the provision may not provide for indemnification of any agent for any acts or omissions or transactions from which a director may not be relieved of liability as set forth in the exception to paragraph (10) or as to circumstances in which indemnity is expressly prohibited by Section 317.

Notwithstanding this subdivision, in the case of a close corporation any of the provisions referred to above may be validly included in a shareholders' agreement. Notwithstanding this subdivision, bylaws may require for all or any actions by the board the affirmative vote of a majority of the authorized number of directors. Nothing contained in this subdivision shall affect the enforceability, as between the parties thereto, of any lawful agreement not otherwise contrary to public policy.

(b) Reasonable restrictions upon the right to transfer or hypothecate shares of any class or classes or series, but no restriction shall be binding with respect to shares issued prior to the adoption of the restriction unless the holders of such shares voted in favor of the restriction.

(c) The names and addresses of the persons appointed to act as initial directors.

(d) Any other provision, not in conflict with law, for the management of the business and for the conduct of the affairs of the corporation, including any provision which is required or permitted by this division to be stated in the bylaws.

§ 212. Bylaws; Contents

(a) The bylaws shall set forth (unless such provision is contained in the articles, in which case it may only be changed by an amendment of the articles) the number of directors of the corporation; or that the number of directors shall be not less than a stated minimum nor more than a stated maximum (which in no case shall be greater than two times the stated minimum minus one), with the exact number of directors to be fixed, within the limits specified, by approval of the board or the shareholders (Section 153) in the manner provided in the bylaws, subject to paragraph (5) of subdivision (a) of Section 204. The number or minimum number of directors shall not be less than three; provided, however, that (1) before shares are issued, the number may be one, (2) before shares are issued, the number may be two, (3) so long as the corporation has only one shareholder, the number may be one, (4) so long as the corporation has only one shareholder, the number may be two, and (5) so long as the corporation has only two shareholders, the number may be two. After the issuance of shares, a bylaw specifying or changing a fixed number of directors or the maximum or minimum number or changing from a fixed to a variable board or vice versa may only be adopted by approval of the outstanding shares (Section 152); provided, however that a bylaw or amendment of the articles reducing the fixed number or the minimum number of directors to a number less than five cannot be adopted if the votes cast against its adoption at a meeting or the shares not consenting in the case of action by written consent are equal to more than 16⅔ percent of the outstanding shares entitled to vote.

(b) The bylaws may contain any provision, not in conflict with law or the articles for the management of the business and for the conduct of the affairs of the corporation, including but not limited to:

(1) Any provision referred to in subdivision (b), (c) or (d) of Section 204.

(2) The time, place and manner of calling, conducting and giving notice of shareholders', directors' and committee meetings.

(3) The manner of execution, revocation and use of proxies.

(4) The qualifications, duties and compensation of directors; the time of their annual election; and the requirements of a quorum for directors' and committee meetings.

(5) The appointment and authority of committees of the board.

(6) The appointment, duties, compensation and tenure of officers.

(7) The mode of determination of holders of record of its shares.

(8) The making of annual reports and financial statements to the shareholders.

Chapter 3

DIRECTORS AND MANAGEMENT

§ 300. Powers of Board; Delegation; Close Corporations; Shareholders' Agreements; Validity; Liability; Failure to Observe Formalities

(a) Subject to the provisions of this division and any limitations in the articles relating to action required to be approved by the shareholders (Section 153) or by the outstanding shares (Section 152), or by a less than majority vote of a class or series of preferred shares (Section 402.5), the business and affairs of the corporation shall be managed and all corporate powers shall be exercised by or under the direction of the board. The board may delegate the management of the day-to-day operation of the business of the corporation to a management company or other person provided that the business and affairs of the corporation shall be managed and all corporate powers shall be exercised under the ultimate direction of the board.

(b) Notwithstanding subdivision (a) or any other provision of this division, but subject to subdivision (c), no shareholders' agreement, which relates to any phase of the affairs of a close corporation, including but not limited to management of its business, division of its profits or distribution of its assets on liquidation, shall be invalid as between the parties thereto on the ground that it so relates to the conduct of the affairs of the corporation as to interfere with the discretion of the board or that it is an attempt to treat the corporation as if it were a partnership or to arrange their relationships in a manner that would be appropriate only between partners. A transferee of shares covered by such an agreement which is filed with the secretary of the corporation for inspection by any prospective purchaser of shares, who has actual knowledge thereof or notice thereof by a notation on the certificate pursuant to Section 418, is bound by its provisions and is a party thereto for the purposes of subdivision (d). Original issuance of shares by the corporation to a new shareholder who does not become a party to the agreement terminates the agreement, except that if the agreement so provides it shall continue to the extent it is enforceable apart from this subdivision. The agreement may not be modified, extended or revoked without the consent of such a transferee, subject to any provision of the agreement permitting modification, extension or revocation by less than unanimous agreement of the parties. A transferor of shares covered by such an agreement ceases to be a party thereto upon ceasing to be a shareholder of the corporation unless the transferor is a party thereto other than as a shareholder. An agreement made pursuant to this subdivision shall terminate when the corporation ceases to be a close corporation, except that if the agreement so provides it shall continue to the extent it is enforceable apart from this subdivision. This subdivision does not apply to an agreement authorized by subdivision (a) of Section 706.

(c) No agreement entered into pursuant to subdivision (b) may alter or waive any of the provisions of Sections 158, 417, 418, 500, 501, and 1111, subdivision (e) of Section 1201, Sections 2009, 2010, and 2011, or of Chapters 15 (commencing with Section 1500), 16 (commencing with Section 1600), 18 (commencing with Section 1800), and 22 (commencing with Section 2200). All other provisions of this division may be altered or waived as between the parties thereto in a shareholders' agreement, except the required filing of any document with the Secretary of State.

(d) An agreement of the type referred to in subdivision (b) shall, to the extent and so long as the discretion or powers of the board in its management of corporate affairs is controlled by such agreement, impose upon each shareholder who is a party thereto liability for managerial acts performed or omitted by such person pursuant thereto that is otherwise imposed by this division upon directors, and the directors shall be relieved to that extent from such liability.

(e) The failure of a close corporation to observe corporate formalities relating to meetings of directors or shareholders in connection with the management of its affairs, pursuant to an agreement authorized by subdivision (b), shall not be considered a factor tending to establish that the shareholders have personal liability for corporate obligations.

§ 301. Directors; Election; Term

(a) Except as provided in Section 301.5, at each annual meeting of shareholders, directors shall be elected to hold office until the next annual meeting. However, to effectuate a voting shift (Section 194.7) the articles may provide that directors hold office for a shorter term. The articles may provide for the election of one or more directors by the holders of the shares of any class or series voting as a class or series.

(b) Each director, including a director elected to fill a vacancy, shall hold office until the expiration of the term for which elected and until a successor has been elected and qualified.

§ 301.5 Listed Corporations; Classes of Directors; Cumulative Voting; Election of Directors; Amendment of Articles and Bylaws

(a) A listed corporation may, by amendment of its articles or bylaws, adopt provisions to divide the board of directors into two or three classes to serve for terms of two or three years respectively, or to eliminate cumulative voting, or both. After the issuance of shares, a corporation which is not a listed corporation may, by amendment of its articles or bylaws, adopt provisions to be effective when the corporation becomes a listed corporation to divide the board of directors into two or three classes to serve for terms of two or three years respectively, or to eliminate cumulative voting, or both. An article or bylaw amendment providing for division of the board of directors into classes, or any change in the number of classes, or the elimination of cumulative voting may only be adopted by the approval of the board and the outstanding shares (Section 152) voting as a single class ....

(b) If the board of directors is divided into two classes pursuant to subdivision (a), the authorized number of directors shall be no less than six and one-half of the directors or as close an approximation as possible shall be elected at each annual meeting of shareholders. If the board of directors is divided into three classes, the authorized number of directors shall be no less than nine and one-third of the directors or as close an approximation as possible shall be elected at each annual meeting of shareholders. Directors of a listed corporation may be elected by classes at a meeting of shareholders at which an amendment to the articles or bylaws described in subdivision (a) is approved, but the extended terms for directors are contingent on that approval, and in the case of an amendment to the articles, the filing of any necessary amendment to the articles . . . .

(c) If directors for more than one class are to be elected by the shareholders at any one meeting of shareholders and the election is by cumulative voting pursuant to Section 708, votes may be cumulated only for directors to be elected within each class.

(d) For purposes of this section, a "listed corporation" means any of the following:

(1) A corporation with outstanding shares listed on the New York Stock Exchange or the American Stock Exchange.

(2) A corporation with outstanding securities designated as qualified for trading as a national market system security on the National Association of Securities Dealers Automatic Quotation System (or any successor national market system) if the corporation has at least 800 holders of its equity securities as of the record date of the corporation's most recent annual meeting of shareholders. . . .

(e) If an article amendment referred to in subdivision (a) is adopted by a listed corporation, the certificate of amendment shall include a statement of the facts showing that the corporation is a listed corporation within the meaning of subdivision (d). If an article or bylaw amendment referred to in subdivision (a) is adopted by a corporation which is not a listed corporation, the provision as adopted, shall include the following statement or the substantial equivalent: "This provision shall become effective only when the corporation becomes a listed corporation within the meaning of Section 301.5 of the Corporations Code."

§ 302. Directors; Vacancy; Grounds for Declaration

The board may declare vacant the office of a director who has been declared of unsound mind by an order of court or convicted of a felony.

§ 303. Directors; Removal Without Cause

(a) Any or all of the directors may be removed without cause if such removal is approved by the outstanding shares (Section 152), subject to the following:

(1) Except for a corporation to which paragraph (3) is applicable, no director may be removed (unless the entire board is removed) when the votes cast against removal, or not consenting in writing to the removal, would be sufficient to elect the director if voted cumulatively at an election at which the same total number of votes were cast (or, if the action is taken by written consent, all shares entitled to vote were voted) and the entire number of directors authorized at the time of the director's most recent election were then being elected.

(2) When by the provisions of the articles the holders of the shares of any class or series, voting as a class or series, are entitled to elect one or more directors, any director so elected may be removed only by the applicable vote of the holders of the shares of that class or series.

(3) A director of a corporation whose board of directors is classified pursuant to Section 301.5 may not be removed if the votes cast against removal of the director, or not consenting in writing to the removal, would be sufficient to elect the director if voted cumulatively (without regard to whether shares may otherwise be voted cumulatively) at an election at which the same total number of votes were cast (or, if the action is taken by written consent, all shares entitled to vote were voted) and either the number of directors elected at the most recent annual meeting of shareholders, or if greater, the number of directors for whom removal is being sought, were then being elected.

(b) Any reduction of the authorized number of directors or amendment reducing the number of classes of directors does not remove any director prior to the expiration of such director's term of office.

(c) Except as provided in this section and Sections 302 and 304, a director may not be removed prior to the expiration of the director's term of office.

§ 304. Removal for Cause; Shareholders Suit

The superior court of the proper county may, at the suit of shareholders holding at least 10 percent of the number of outstanding shares of any class, remove from office any director in case of fraudulent or dishonest acts or gross abuse of authority or discretion with reference to the corporation and may bar from reelection any director so removed for a period prescribed by the court. The corporation shall be made a party to such action.

§ 307. Meetings

(a) Unless otherwise provided in the articles or (subject to paragraph (5) of subdivision (a) of Section 204) in the bylaws . . . .

(7) A majority of the authorized number of directors constitutes a quorum of the board for the transaction of business. The articles or bylaws may not provide that a quorum shall be less than one-third the authorized number of directors or less than two, whichever is larger, unless the authorized number of directors is one, in which case one director constitutes a quorum.

(8) [An] act or decision done or made by a majority of the directors present at a meeting duly held at which a quorum is present is the act of the board, subject to the provisions of Section 310 and subdivision (e) of Section 317 [authorization of indemnification]. The articles or bylaws may not provide that a lesser vote than a majority of the directors

present at a meeting is the act of the board. A meeting at which a quorum is initially present may continue to transact business notwithstanding the withdrawal of directors, if any action taken is approved by at least a majority of the required quorum for [that] meeting....

§ 308. Deadlock on Board With Even Number of Directors; Provisional Director; Appointment; Powers

(a) If a corporation has an even number of directors who are equally divided and cannot agree as to the management of its affairs, so that its business can no longer be conducted to advantage or so that there is danger that its property and business will be impaired or lost, the superior court of the proper county may, notwithstanding any provisions of the articles or bylaws and whether or not an action is pending for an involuntary winding up or dissolution of the corporation, appoint a provisional director pursuant to this section. Action for such appointment may be brought by any director or by the holders of not less than 33⅓ percent of the voting power.

(b) If the shareholders of a corporation are deadlocked so that they cannot elect the directors to be elected at an annual meeting of shareholders, the superior court of the proper county may, notwithstanding any provisions of the articles or bylaws, upon petition of a shareholder or shareholders holding 50 percent of the voting power, appoint a provisional director or directors pursuant to this section or order such other equitable relief as the court deems appropriate.

(c) A provisional director shall be an impartial person, who is neither a shareholder nor a creditor of the corporation, nor related by consanguinity or affinity within the third degree according to the common law to any of the other directors of the corporation or to any judge of the court by which such provisional director is appointed. A provisional director shall have all the rights and powers of a director until the deadlock in the board or among shareholders is broken or until such provisional director is removed by order of the court or by approval of the outstanding shares (Section 152). Such person shall be entitled to such compensation as shall be fixed by the court unless otherwise agreed with the corporation....

§ 309. Performance of Duties by Director; Liability

(a) A director shall perform the duties of a director, including duties as a member of any committee of the board upon which the director may serve, in good faith, in a manner such director believes to be in the best interests of the corporation and its shareholders and with such care, including reasonable inquiry, as an ordinarily prudent person in a like position would use under similar circumstances.

(b) In performing the duties of a director, a director shall be entitled to rely on information, opinions, reports or statements, including financial statements and other financial data, in each case prepared or presented by any of the following:

(1) One or more officers or employees of the corporation whom the director believes to be reliable and competent in the matters presented.

(2) Counsel, independent accountants or other persons as to matters which the director believes to be within such person's professional or expert competence.

(3) A committee of the board upon which the director does not serve, as to matters within its designated authority, which committee the director believes to merit confidence, so long as, in any such case, the director acts in good faith, after reasonable inquiry when the need therefor is indicated by the circumstances and without knowledge that would cause such reliance to be unwarranted.

(c) A person who performs the duties of a director in accordance with subdivisions (a) and (b) shall have no liability based upon any alleged failure to discharge the person's obligations as a director. In addition, the liability of a director for monetary damages may be eliminated or limited in a corporation's articles to the extent provided in paragraph (10) of subdivision (a) of Section 204.

§ 310. Contracts in Which Director Has Material Financial Interest; Validity

(a) No contract or other transaction between a corporation and one or more of its directors, or between a corporation and any corporation, firm or association in which one or more of its directors has a material financial interest, is either void or voidable because such director or directors or such other corporation, firm or association are parties or because such director or directors are present at the meeting of the board or a committee thereof which authorizes, approves or ratifies the contract or transaction, if

(1) The material facts as to the transaction and as to such director's interest are fully disclosed or known to the shareholders and such contract or transaction is approved by the shareholders (Section 153) in good faith, with the shares owned by the interested director or directors not being entitled to vote thereon, or

(2) The material facts as to the transaction and as to such director's interest are fully disclosed or known to the board or committee, and the board or committee authorizes, approves or ratifies the contract or transaction in good faith by a vote sufficient without counting the vote of the interested director or directors and the contract or transaction is just and reasonable as to the corporation at the time it is authorized, approved or ratified, or

(3) As to contracts or transactions not approved as provided in paragraph (1) or (2) of this subdivision, the person asserting the validity

of the contract or transaction sustains the burden of proving that the contract or transaction was just and reasonable as to the corporation at the time it was authorized, approved or ratified.

A mere common directorship does not constitute a material financial interest within the meaning of this subdivision. A director is not interested within the meaning of this subdivision in a resolution fixing the compensation of another director as a director, officer or employee of the corporation, notwithstanding the fact that the first director is also receiving compensation from the corporation.

(b) No contract or other transaction between a corporation and any corporation or association of which one or more of its directors are directors is either void or voidable because such director or directors are present at the meeting of the board or a committee thereof which authorizes, approves or ratifies the contract or transaction, if

(1) The material facts as to the transaction and as to such director's other directorship are fully disclosed or known to the board or committee, and the board or committee authorizes, approves or ratifies the contract or transaction in good faith by a vote sufficient without counting the vote of the common director or directors or the contract or transaction is approved by the shareholders (Section 153) in good faith, or

(2) As to contracts or transactions not approved as provided in paragraph (1) of this subdivision, the contract or transaction is just and reasonable as to the corporation at the time it is authorized, approved or ratified.

This subdivision does not apply to contracts or transactions covered by subdivision (a).

(c) Interested or common directors may be counted in determining the presence of a quorum at a meeting of the board or a committee thereof which authorizes, approves or ratifies a contract or transaction.

§ 312. Officers; Election; Term; Resignation

(a) A corporation shall have a chairman of the board or a president or both, a secretary, a chief financial officer and such other officers with such titles and duties as shall be stated in the bylaws or determined by the board and as may be necessary to enable it to sign instruments and share certificates. The president, or if there is no president the chairman of the board, is the general manager and chief executive officer of the corporation, unless otherwise provided in the articles or bylaws. Any number of offices may be held by the same person unless the articles or bylaws provide otherwise.

(b) Except as otherwise provided by the articles or bylaws, officers shall be chosen by the board and serve at the pleasure of the board, subject to the rights, if any, of an officer under any contract of employment. Any officer may resign at any time upon written notice to the corporation without prejudice to the rights, if any, of the corporation under any contract to which the officer is a party.

§ 313. Instrument in Writing and Assignment or Endorsement Thereof; Signatures; Validity

Subject to the provisions of subdivision (a) of Section 208, any note, mortgage, evidence of indebtedness, contract, share certificate, initial transaction statement or written statement, conveyance, or other instrument in writing, and any assignment or endorsement thereof, executed or entered into between any corporation and any other person, when signed by the chairman of the board, the president or any vice president and the secretary, any assistant secretary, the chief financial officer or any assistant treasurer of such corporation, is not invalidated as to the corporation by any lack of authority of the signing officers in the absence of actual knowledge on the part of the other person that the signing officers had no authority to execute the same.

§ 316. Corporate Actions Subjecting Directors to Joint and Several Liability; Actions; Damages

(a) Subject to the provisions of Section 309, directors of a corporation who approve any of the following corporate actions shall be jointly and severally liable to the corporation for the benefit of all of the creditors or shareholders entitled to institute an action under subdivision (c):

(1) The making of any distribution to its shareholders to the extent that it is contrary to the provisions of Sections 500 to 503, inclusive.

(2) The distribution of assets to shareholders after institution of dissolution proceedings of the corporation, without paying or adequately providing for all known liabilities of the corporation, excluding any claims not filed by creditors within the time limit set by the court in a notice given to creditors under Chapters 18 (commencing with Section 1800), 19 (commencing with Section 1900) and 20 (commencing with Section 2000).

(3) The making of any loan or guaranty contrary to Section 315 [Loans or guarantees of obligations of directors, officers, or other persons].

(b) A director who is present at a meeting of the board, or any committee thereof, at which action specified in subdivision (a) is taken and who abstains from voting shall be considered to have approved the action.

(c) Suit may be brought in the name of the corporation to enforce the liability (1) under paragraph (1) of subdivision (a) against any or all directors liable by the persons entitled to sue under subdivision (b) of

Section 506, (2) under paragraph (2) or (3) of subdivision (a) against any or all directors liable by any one or more creditors of the corporation whose debts or claims arose prior to the time of any of the corporate actions specified in paragraph (2) or (3) of subdivision (a) and who have not consented to the corporate action, whether or not they have reduced their claims to judgment, or (3) under paragraph (3) of subdivision (a) against any or all directors liable by any one or more holders of shares outstanding at the time of any corporate action specified in paragraph (3) of subdivision (a) who have not consented to the corporate action, without regard to the provisions of Section 800.

(d) The damages recoverable from a director under this section shall be the amount of the illegal distribution (or if the illegal distribution consists of property, the fair market value of that property at the time of the illegal distribution) plus interest thereon from the date of the distribution at the legal rate on judgments until paid, together with all reasonably incurred costs of appraisal or other valuation, if any, of that property or loss suffered by the corporation as a result of the illegal loan or guaranty, as the case may be, but not exceeding the liabilities of the corporation owed to nonconsenting creditors at the time of the violation and the injury suffered by nonconsenting shareholders, as the case may be.

(e) Any director sued under this section may implead all other directors liable and may compel contribution, either in that action or in an independent action against directors not joined in that action.

(f) Directors liable under this section shall also be entitled to be subrogated to the rights of the corporation:

(1) With respect to paragraph (1) of subdivision (a), against shareholders who received the distribution.

(2) With respect to paragraph (2) of subdivision (a), against shareholders who received the distribution of assets.

(3) With respect to paragraph (3) of subdivision (a), against the person who received the loan or guaranty. Any director sued under this section may file a cross-complaint against the person or persons who are liable to the director as a result of the subrogation provided for in this subdivision or may proceed against them in an independent action.

§ 317. Indemnification of Agent of Corporation in Proceedings or Actions

(a) For the purposes of this section, "agent" means any person who is or was a director, officer, employee or other agent of the corporation, or is or was serving at the request of the corporation as a director, officer, employee or agent of another foreign or domestic corporation, partnership, joint venture, trust or other enterprise, or was a director, officer, employee or agent of a foreign or domestic corporation which was a predecessor corporation of the corporation or of another enterprise at the request of the predecessor corporation; "proceeding" means any threatened, pending or completed action or proceeding, whether civil, criminal, administrative or investigative; and "expenses" includes without limitation attorneys' fees and any expenses of establishing a right to indemnification under subdivision (d) or paragraph (4) of subdivision (e).

(b) A corporation shall have power to indemnify any person who was or is a party or is threatened to be made a party to any proceeding (other than an action by or in the right of the corporation to procure a judgment in its favor) by reason of the fact that the person is or was an agent of the corporation, against expenses, judgments, fines, settlements, and other amounts actually and reasonably incurred in connection with the proceeding if that person acted in good faith and in a manner the person reasonably believed to be in the best interests of the corporation and, in the case of a criminal proceeding, had no reasonable cause to believe the conduct of the person was unlawful. The termination of any proceeding by judgment, order, settlement, conviction, or upon a plea of nolo contendere or its equivalent shall not, of itself, create a presumption that the person did not act in good faith and in a manner which the person reasonably believed to be in the best interests of the corporation or that the person had reasonable cause to believe that the person's conduct was unlawful.

(c) A corporation shall have power to indemnify any person who was or is a party or is threatened to be made a party to any threatened, pending, or completed action by or in the right of the corporation to procure a judgment in its favor by reason of the fact that the person is or was an agent of the corporation, against expenses actually and reasonably incurred by that person in connection with the defense or settlement of the action if the person acted in good faith, in a manner the person believed to be in the best interests of the corporation and its shareholders.

No indemnification shall be made under this subdivision for any of the following:

(1) In respect of any claim, issue or matter as to which the person shall have been adjudged to be liable to the corporation in the performance of that person's duty to the corporation and its shareholders, unless and only to the extent that the court in which the proceeding is or was pending shall determine upon application that, in view of all the circumstances of the case, the person is fairly and reasonably entitled to indemnity for expenses and then only to the extent that the court shall determine.

(2) Of amounts paid in settling or otherwise disposing of a pending action without court approval.

(3) Of expenses incurred in defending a pending action which is settled or otherwise disposed of without court approval.

(d) To the extent that an agent of a corporation has been successful on the merits in defense of any proceeding referred to in subdivision (b) or (c) or in defense of any claim, issue, or matter therein, the agent shall be indemnified against expenses actually and reasonably incurred by the agent in connection therewith.

(e) Except as provided in subdivision (d), any indemnification under this section shall be made by the corporation only if authorized in the specific case, upon a determination that indemnification of the agent is proper in the circumstances because the agent has met the applicable standard of conduct set forth in subdivision (b) or (c), by any of the following:

(1) A majority vote of a quorum consisting of directors who are not parties to such proceeding.

(2) If such a quorum of directors is not obtainable, by independent legal counsel in a written opinion.

(3) Approval of the shareholders (Section 153), with the shares owned by the person to be indemnified not being entitled to vote thereon.

(4) The court in which the proceeding is or was pending upon application made by the corporation or the agent or the attorney or other person rendering services in connection with the defense, whether or not the application by the agent, attorney or other person is opposed by the corporation.

(f) Expenses incurred in defending any proceeding may be advanced by the corporation prior to the final disposition of the proceeding upon receipt of an undertaking by or on behalf of the agent to repay that amount if it shall be determined ultimately that the agent is not entitled to be indemnified as authorized in this section. The provisions of subdivision (a) of Section 315 do not apply to advances made pursuant to this subdivision.

(g) The indemnification authorized by this section shall not be deemed exclusive of any additional rights to indemnification for breach of duty to the corporation and its shareholders while acting in the capacity of a director or officer of the corporation to the extent the additional rights to indemnification are authorized in an article provision adopted pursuant to paragraph (11) of subdivision (a) of Section 204. The indemnification provided by this section for acts, omissions, or transactions while acting in the capacity of, or while serving as, a director or officer of the corporation but not involving breach of duty to the corporation and its shareholders shall not be deemed exclusive of any other rights to which those seeking indemnification may be entitled under any bylaw, agreement, vote of shareholders or disinterested directors, or otherwise, to the extent the additional rights to indemnification are authorized in the articles of the corporation. An article provision authorizing indemnification "in excess of that otherwise permitted by Section 317" or "to the fullest extent permissible under California law" or the substantial equivalent thereof shall be construed to be both a provision for additional indemnification for breach of duty to the corporation and its shareholders as referred to in, and with the limitations required by, paragraph (11) of subdivision (a) of Section 204 and a provision for additional indemnification as referred to in the second sentence of this subdivision. The rights to indemnity hereunder shall continue as to a person who has ceased to be a director, officer, employee, or agent and shall inure to the benefit of the heirs, executors, and administrators of the person. Nothing contained in this section shall affect any right to indemnification to which persons other than the directors and officers may be entitled by contract or otherwise.

(h) No indemnification or advance shall be made under this section, except as provided in subdivision (d) or paragraph (4) of subdivision (e), in any circumstance where it appears:

(1) That it would be inconsistent with a provision of the articles, bylaws, a resolution of the shareholders, or an agreement in effect at the time of the accrual of the alleged cause of action asserted in the proceeding in which the expenses were incurred or other amounts were paid, which prohibits or otherwise limits indemnification.

(2) That it would be inconsistent with any condition expressly imposed by a court in approving a settlement.

(i) A corporation shall have power to purchase and maintain insurance on behalf of any agent of the corporation against any liability asserted against or incurred by the agent in that capacity or arising out of the agent's status as such whether or not the corporation would have the power to indemnify the agent against that liability under this section. The fact that a corporation owns all or a portion of the shares of the company issuing a policy of insurance shall not render this subdivision inapplicable if either of the following conditions are satisfied: (1) if the articles authorize indemnification in excess of that authorized in this section and the insurance provided by this subdivision is limited as indemnification is required to be limited by paragraph (11) of subdivision (a) of Section 204; or (2)(A) the company issuing the insurance policy is organized, licensed, and operated in a manner that complies with the insurance laws and regulations applicable to its jurisdiction of organization, (B) the company issuing the policy provides procedures for processing claims that do not permit that company to be subject to the direct control of the corporation that purchased that policy, and (C) the policy issued provides for some manner of risk sharing between the issuer and purchaser of the policy, on one hand, and some unaffiliated person or persons, on the other, such as by providing for more than one unaffiliated owner of the company issuing the policy or by providing that a portion of the coverage furnished will be obtained from some unaffiliated insurer or reinsurer.

(j) This section does not apply to any proceeding against any trustee, investment manager, or other fiduciary of an employee benefit plan in that person's capacity as such, even though the person may also be an agent as defined in subdivision (a) of the employer corporation. A corporation shall have power to indemnify such a trustee, investment manager or other fiduciary to the extent permitted by subdivision (f) of Section 207 [corporate powers].

Chapter 4

SHARES AND SHARE CERTIFICATES

§ 407. Fractional Shares

A corporation may, but is not required to, issue fractions of a share originally or upon transfer. If it does not issue fractions of a share, it shall in connection with any original issuance of shares (a) arrange for the disposition of fractional interests by those entitled thereto, (b) pay in cash the fair value of fractions of a share as of the time when those entitled to receive such fractions are determined or (c) issue scrip or warrants in registered form, as certificated securities or uncertificated securities, or [in] bearer form as certificated securities, which shall entitle the holder to receive a certificate for a full share upon the surrender of such script or warrants aggregating a full share; provided, however, that, if the fraction of a share which any person would otherwise be entitled to receive in a merger or reorganization is less than one-half of 1 percent of the total shares such person is entitled to receive, a merger or reorganization agreement may provide that fractions of a share will be disregarded or that shares issuable in the merger will be rounded off to the nearest whole share; and provided, further, that a corporation may not pay cash for fractional shares if such action would result in the cancellation of more than 10 percent of the outstanding shares of any class. A determination by the board of the fair value of fractions of a share shall be conclusive in the absence of fraud. A certificate for a fractional share shall, but scrip or warrants shall not unless otherwise provided therein, entitle the holder to exercise voting rights, to receive dividends thereon and to participate in any of the assets of the corporation in the event of liquidation. The board may cause scrip or warrants to be issued subject to the condition that they shall become void if not exchanged for full shares before a specified date or that the shares for which scrip or warrants are exchangeable may be sold by the corporation and the proceeds thereof distributed to the holder of the scrip or warrants or any other condition which the board may impose.

§ 418. Certificates or Initial Transaction Statements; Required Contents of Statements on Face of Documents; Failure to State; Enforceability; Close Corporations; Validity of Transfers

(a) There shall also appear on the certificate, the initial transaction statement, and written statements (unless stated or summarized under subdivision (a) or (b) of Section 417) the statements required by all of the following clauses to the extent applicable:

(1) The fact that the shares are subject to restrictions upon transfer.

(2) If the shares are assessable or are not fully paid, a statement that they are assessable or the statements required by subdivision (d) of Section 409 if they are not fully paid.

(3) The fact that the shares are subject to a voting agreement under subdivision (a) of Section 706 or an irrevocable proxy under subdivision (e) of Section 705 or restrictions upon voting rights contractually imposed by the corporation.

(4) The fact that the shares are redeemable.

(5) The fact that the shares are convertible and the period for conversion.

Any such statement or reference thereto (Section 174) on the face of the certificate, the initial transaction statement, and written statements required by paragraph (1) or (2) shall be conspicuous.

(b) Unless stated on the certificate, the initial transaction statement, and written statements as required by subdivision (a), no restriction upon transfer, no right of redemption and no voting agreement under subdivision (a) of Section 706, no irrevocable proxy under subdivision (e) of Section 705, and no voting restriction imposed by the corporation shall be enforceable against a transferee of the shares without actual knowledge of such restriction, right, agreement of proxy. With regard only to liability to assessment or for the unpaid portion of the subscription price, unless stated on the certificate as required by subdivision (a), that liability shall not be enforceable against a transferee of the shares. For the purpose of this subdivision, "transferee" includes a purchaser from the corporation.

(c) All certificates representing shares of a close corporation shall contain in addition to any other statements required by this section, the following conspicuous legend on the face thereof: "This corporation is a close corporation. The number of holders of record of its shares of all classes cannot exceed _____ [a number not in excess of 35]. Any attempted voluntary inter vivos transfer which would violate this requirement is void. Refer to the articles, bylaws and any agreements on file with the secretary of the corporation for further restrictions."

(d) Any attempted voluntary inter vivos transfer of the shares of a close corporation which would result in the number of holders of record of its shares exceeding the maximum number specified in its articles is void if the certificate contains the legend required by subdivision (c).

Chapter 5

DIVIDENDS AND REACQUISITIONS OF SHARES

§ 500. Distributions; Retained Earnings or Assets Remaining After Completion

Neither a corporation nor any of its subsidiaries shall make any distribution to the corporation's shareholders (Section 166) except as follows:

(a) The distribution may be made if the amount of the retained earnings of the corporation immediately prior thereto equals or exceeds the amount of the proposed distribution; or

(b) The distribution may be made if immediately after giving effect thereto:

(1) The sum of the assets of the corporation (exclusive of goodwill, capitalized research and development expenses and deferred charges) would be at least equal to $1\frac{1}{4}$ times its liabilities (not including deferred taxes, deferred income and other deferred credits); and

(2) The current assets of the corporation would be at least equal to its current liabilities or, if the average of the earnings of the corporation before taxes on income and before interest expense for the two preceding fiscal years was less than the average of the interest expense of the corporation for those fiscal years, at least equal to $1\frac{1}{4}$ times its current liabilities; provided, however, that in determining the amount of the assets of the corporation profits derived from an exchange of assets shall not be included unless the assets received are currently realizable in cash; and provided, further, that for the purpose of this subdivision "current assets" may include net amounts which the board has determined in good faith may reasonably be expected to be received from customers during the 12–month period used in calculating current liabilities pursuant to existing contractual relationships obligating those customers to make fixed or periodic payments during the term of the contract or, in the case of public utilities, pursuant to service connections with customers, after in each case giving effect to future costs not then included in current liabilities but reasonably expected to be incurred by the corporation in performing those contracts or providing service to utility customers. Paragraph (2) of subdivision (b) is not applicable to a corporation which does not classify its assets into current and fixed under generally accepted accounting principles.

(c) The amount of any distribution payable in property shall, for the purposes of this chapter, be determined on the basis of the value at which such property is carried on the corporation's financial statements in accordance with generally accepted accounting principles.

(d) For the purpose of applying this section to a distribution by a corporation of cash or property in payment by the corporation in connection with the purchase of its shares, there shall be added to retained earnings all amounts that had been previously deducted therefrom with respect to obligations incurred in connection with the corporation's repurchase of its shares and reflected on the corporation's balance sheet, but not in excess of the principal of the obligations that remain unpaid immediately prior to the distribution. In addition, there shall be deducted from liabilities all amounts that had been previously added thereto with respect to the obligations incurred in connection with the corporation's repurchase of its shares and reflected on the corporation's balance sheet, but not in excess of the principal of the obligations that will remain unpaid after the distribution, provided that no addition to retained earnings or deduction from liabilities under this subdivision shall occur on account of any obligation that is a distribution to the corporation's shareholders (Section 166) at the time the obligation is incurred. . . .

Legislative Committee Comment . . .

. . . Under prior law dividends may generally be declared only out of earned surplus . . . . There are several exceptions to this general rule. Dividends may be paid in some circumstances out of net profits for a six to twelve month period ("nimble" dividends), paid-in surplus or surplus resulting from the reduction of stated capital . . . . However, a dividend may not be declared in any event where the corporation would thereby be rendered insolvent . . . .

As a practical matter, these general restrictions do not provide adequate protection to creditors, particularly trade creditors. This results from the fact that all but an insignificant amount of the money originally received from the shareholders can be designated as paid-in surplus rather than stated capital.

Similarly, the general rule under prior law is that a corporation may acquire shares issued by it only from earned surplus . . . . Exceptions to this rule permit purchases of such shares from reduction surplus, and redemption of shares subject to redemption from any surplus . . . .

This distinction between the sources from which shares may be purchased and those from which dividends may be paid is anomalous, as a purchase of shares on a pro rata basis has exactly the same effect as a dividend with regard to the protection of creditors and senior shareholders.

For the purpose of establishing meaningful protection for creditors and shareholders and to rationalize restrictions upon the payment of dividends and repurchase of shares, this section provides restrictions upon a corporation in the making of any "distribution to its shareholders" based upon the current financial condition of the corporation ["Distribution to its shareholder" is a defined term. See § 166]. This approach eliminates the concepts of "stated capital" and "surplus" in favor of balance sheet tests.

The corporation may make a distribution to its shareholders if either of two tests is met. First, a corporation may make a distribution out of its retained earnings.

Second, if there are not retained earnings, a corporation may make a distribution provided that after giving effect to the distribution the assets of the corporation (exclusive of certain intangibles) are at least equal to one and a quarter times its liabilities (excluding certain deferred items) and its current assets are at least equal to its current liabilities.

With regard to the liquidity portion of this test, if the average of the earnings of the corporation before taxes on income and before interest expense for the two proceeding fiscal years is not at least equal to the average of the interest expense of the corporation for such years, the current assets must be at least one and a quarter times the current liabilities. However, this liquidity test is inapplicable to any corporation not classifying its assets into current and fixed under generally accepted accounting principles.

This section prohibits, in determining the amount of the assets of a corporation, the inclusion of any appreciation in value not yet realized (except with respect to readily marketable securities) and profits derived from exchange of assets unless the assets received are currently realizable in cash. ... The amount of any distribution payable in property is the value at which such property is carried on the corporation's financial statements [All references to financial statements, as well as other specified terms, mean consolidated financial statements or other items prepared or determined in accordance with generally accepted accounting principles then applicable. See § 114.].

In appropriate cases where income within a "current" period is definitely assured and determinable, such income although not yet received may be included in the calculation of current assets subject to certain adjustments.

Any distribution to the corporation's shareholders permitted by this section is subject to the solvency limitation of § 501.

§ 501. Inability to Meet Liabilities as They Mature; Prohibition of Distribution

Neither a corporation nor any of its subsidiaries shall make any distribution to the corporation's shareholders (Section 166) if the corporation or the subsidiary making the distribution is, or as a result thereof would be, likely to be unable to meet its liabilities (except those whose payment is otherwise adequately provided for) as they mature.

§ 502. Distribution to Junior Shares if Excess of Assets Over Liabilities Less Than Liquidation Preference of Senior Shares; Prohibition

Neither a corporation nor any of its subsidiaries shall make any distribution to the corporation's shareholders (Section 166) on any shares of its stock of any class or series that are junior to outstanding shares of any class or series with respect to distribution of assets on liquidation if, after giving effect thereto, the excess of its assets (exclusive of goodwill, capitalized research and development expenses and deferred charges) over its liabilities (not including deferred taxes, deferred income and other deferred credits) would be less than the liquidation preference of all shares having a preference on liquidation over the class or series to which the distribution is made; provided, however, that for the purpose of applying this section to a distribution by a corporation of cash or property in payment by the corporation in connection with the purchase of its shares, there shall be deducted from liabilities all amounts that had been previously added thereto with respect to obligations incurred in connection with the corporation's repurchase of its shares and reflected on the corporation's balance sheet, but not in excess of the principal of the obligations that will remain unpaid after the distribution; provided, further, that no deduction from liabilities shall occur on account of any obligation that is a distribution to the corporation's shareholders (Section 166) at the time the obligation is incurred.

§ 503. Retained Earnings Necessary to Allow Distribution to Junior Shares

Neither a corporation nor any of its subsidiaries shall make any distribution to the corporation's shareholders (Section 166) on any shares of its stock of any class or series that are junior to outstanding shares of any other class or series with respect to payment of dividends unless the amount of the retained earnings of the corporation immediately prior thereto equals or exceeds the amount of the proposed distribution plus the aggregate amount of the cumulative dividends in arrears on all shares having a preference with respect to payment of dividends over the class or series to which the distribution is made; provided, however, that for the purpose of applying this section to a distribution by a corporation of cash or property in payment by the corporation in connection with the purchase of its shares, there shall be added to retained earnings all amounts that had been previously deducted therefrom with respect to obligations incurred in connection with the corporation's repurchase of its shares and reflected on the corporation's balance sheet, but not in excess of the principal of the obligations that remain unpaid immediately prior to the distribution; provided, further, that no addition to retained earnings shall occur on account of any obligation that is a distribution to the corporation's shareholders (Section 166) at the time the obligation is incurred.

§ 506.　Receipt of Prohibited Dividend;　Liability of Shareholder;　Suit by Creditors or Other Shareholders;　Fraudulent Transfers

(a) Any shareholder who receives any distribution prohibited by this chapter with knowledge of facts indicating the impropriety thereof is liable to the corporation for the benefit of all of the creditors or shareholders entitled to institute an action under subdivision (b) for the amount so received by such shareholder with interest thereon at the legal rate on judgments until paid, but not exceeding the liabilities of the corporation owed to nonconsenting creditors at the time of the violation and the injury suffered by nonconsenting shareholders, as the case may be. For purposes of this chapter, in the event that any shareholder receives any distribution of the corporation's property that is prohibited by this chapter, the shareholder receiving that illegal distribution shall be liable to the corporation for an amount equal to the fair market value of the property at the time of the illegal distribution plus interest thereon from the date of the distribution at the legal rate on judgments until paid, together with all reasonably incurred costs of appraisal or other valuation, if any, of that property, but not exceeding the liabilities of the corporation owed to nonconsenting creditors at the time of the violation and the injury suffered by nonconsenting shareholders, as the case may be.

(b) Suit may be brought in the name of the corporation to enforce the liability (1) to creditors arising under subdivision (a) for a violation of Section 500 or 501 against any or all shareholders liable by any one or more creditors of the corporation whose debts or claims arose prior to the time of the distribution to shareholders and who have not consented thereto, whether or not they have reduced their claims to judgment, or (2) to shareholders arising under subdivision (a) for a violation of Section 502 or 503 against any or all shareholders liable by any one or more holders of preferred shares outstanding at the time of the distribution who have not consented thereto, without regard to the provisions of Section 800.

(c) Any shareholder sued under this section may implead all other shareholders liable under this section and may compel contribution, either in that action or in an independent action against shareholders not joined in that action.

(d) Nothing contained in this section affects any liability which any shareholder may have under Chapter 1 (commencing with Section 3439) of Title 2 of Part 2 of Division 4 of the Civil Code [Uniform Fraudulent Transfer Act].

§ 507. Dividend Not Chargeable to Retained Earnings; Notice to Shareholders

Each dividend other than one chargeable to retained earnings shall be identified in a notice to shareholders as being made from a source other than retained earnings, stating the accounting treatment thereof. The notice shall accompany the dividend or shall be given within three months after the end of the fiscal year in which the dividend is paid.

§ 510. Acquisition of Own Shares; Status; Prohibition of Reissue by Articles; Reduction in Authorized Shares; Amendment of Articles; Filing

(a) When a corporation reacquires its own shares, those shares are restored to the status of authorized but unissued shares, unless the articles prohibit the reissuance thereof.

(b) When a corporation reacquires authorized shares of a class or series and the articles prohibit the reissuance of those shares:

(1) If all of the authorized shares of that class or series, as the case may be, are reacquired, then (A) that class or series is automatically eliminated, (B) in the case of reacquisition of all of the authorized shares of a series, the authorized number of shares of the class to which the shares belonged is reduced by the number of shares so reacquired, and (C) the articles shall be amended to eliminate any statement of rights, preferences, privileges, and restrictions relating solely to that class or series.

(2) If less than all of the authorized shares but all of the issued and outstanding shares of that class or series, as the case may be, are reacquired, the authorized number of shares of the class or series is automatically reduced by the number of shares so reacquired, and the board shall determine either (A) to eliminate that class or series, whereupon the articles shall be amended to eliminate any statement of rights, preferences, privileges, and restrictions relating solely to that class or series, or (B) not to eliminate that class or series, whereupon the articles shall be amended to reflect that reduction of the number of authorized shares of that class or series by the shares so reacquired.

(3) If less than all of the authorized shares and less than all of the issued and outstanding shares of a class or series, as the case may be, are reacquired, the authorized number of shares of that class or series shall be automatically reduced by the number of shares reacquired, and the articles shall be amended to reflect that reduction.

(c) When a corporation reacquires authorized shares of a series of shares and the articles only prohibit the reissuance of those shares as shares of the same series:

(1) If all of the authorized shares of that series are reacquired, then that series is automatically eliminated, the articles shall be amended to eliminate any statement of rights, preferences, privileges, and restrictions relating solely to that series, and the board shall determine either (A) to return those shares to the status of authorized but undesignated shares of the class to which they belong or (B) to eliminate those shares entirely, whereupon the articles in either case shall be amended to reflect the reduction in the authorized shares of that series and the effect, if any, on the class to which that series belongs.

(2) If all of the issued and outstanding shares of that series (but less than all of the authorized shares of that series) are reacquired, the board shall determine either (A) to eliminate that series, whereupon the articles shall be amended to eliminate any statement of rights, preferences, privileges, and restrictions relating solely to that series, or (B) not to eliminate that series, whereupon the articles shall be amended to reflect the return of the reacquired shares to the status of authorized but undesignated shares of the class to which they belong.

(3) If less than all of the issued and outstanding shares of that series are reacquired, the authorized number of shares of that series shall be automatically reduced by the number of shares reacquired, and the board shall determine either (A) to return those shares to the status of authorized but undesignated shares of the class to which they belong, or (B) to eliminate those shares entirely, whereupon the articles in either case shall be amended to reflect the reduction in the authorized shares of that series and the effect, if any, on the class to which that series belongs.

(d) "Reacquires" as used in this section means that a corporation purchases, redeems, acquires by way of conversion to another class or series, or otherwise acquires its own shares or that issued and outstanding shares cease to be outstanding.

(e) The provisions of this section are subject to any contrary or inconsistent provision in the articles.

(f) A certificate of amendment shall be filed in accordance with the requirements of Chapter 9 (commencing with Section 900) reflecting any elimination or reduction of authorized shares set forth in subdivisions (b) and (c), and any related elimination from the articles of the designation and the rights, preferences, privileges, and restrictions of any series or class of stock that is eliminated, except that approval by the outstanding shares (Section 152) shall not be required to adopt any such amendment. . . .

Chapter 6

SHAREHOLDERS' MEETINGS AND CONSENTS

§ 602. Quorum; Votes; Withdrawal During Meeting Leaving Less Than Quorum

(a) Unless otherwise provided in the articles, a majority of the shares entitled to vote, represented in person or by proxy, shall constitute a quorum at a meeting of the shareholders, but in no event shall a quorum consist of less than one-third ... of the shares entitled to vote at the meeting or, except in the case of a close corporation, of more than a majority of the shares entitled to vote at the meeting. Except as provided in subdivision (b), the affirmative vote of a majority of the shares represented and voting at a duly held meeting at which a quorum is present (which shares voting affirmatively also constitute at least a majority of the required quorum) shall be the act of the shareholders, unless the vote of a greater number or voting by classes is required by this division or the articles.

(b) The shareholders present at a duly called or held meeting at which a quorum is present may continue to transact business until adjournment notwithstanding the withdrawal of enough shareholders to leave less than a quorum, if any action taken (other than adjournment) is approved by at least a majority of the shares required to constitute a quorum.

(c) In the absence of a quorum, any meeting of shareholders may be adjourned from time to time by the vote of a majority of the shares represented either in person or by proxy, but no other business may be transacted, except as provided in subdivision (b).

§ 604. Proxies or Written Consents; Contents; Form

(a) Any form of proxy or written consent distributed to 10 or more shareholders of a corporation with outstanding shares held of record by 100 or more persons shall afford an opportunity on the proxy or form of written consent to specify a choice between approval and disapproval of each matter or group of related matters intended to be acted upon at the meeting for which the proxy is solicited or by such written consent, other than elections to office, and shall provide, subject to reasonable specified conditions, that where the person solicited specifies a choice with respect to any such matter the shares will be voted in accordance therewith.

(b) In any election of directors, any form of proxy in which the directors to be voted upon are named therein as candidates and which is marked by a shareholder "withhold" or otherwise marked in a manner indicating that the authority to vote for the election of directors is withheld shall not be voted for the election of a director.

(c) Failure to comply with this section shall not invalidate any corporate action taken, but may be the basis for challenging any proxy at a meeting and the superior court may compel compliance therewith at the suit of any shareholder.

(d) This section does not apply to any corporation with an outstanding class of securities registered under Section 12 of the Securities Exchange Act of 1934 or whose securities are exempted from such registration by Section 12(g)(2) of that act.

Chapter 7

VOTING OF SHARES

§ 703. Shares in Name of Other Corporations, [Shares Owned by] Subsidiary or Held in Fiduciary Capacity by Issuing Corporation

(a) Shares standing in the name of another corporation, domestic or foreign, may be voted by an officer, agent, or proxyholder as the bylaws of the other corporation may prescribe or, in the absence of such provision, as the board of the other corporation may determine or, in the absence of that determination, by the chairman of the board, president or any vice president of the other corporation, or by any other person authorized to do so by the chairman of the board, president, or any vice president of the other corporation. Shares which are purported to be voted or any proxy purported to be executed in the name of a corporation (whether or not any title of the person signing is indicated) shall be presumed to be voted or the proxy executed in accordance with the provisions of this subdivision, unless the contrary is shown.

(b) Shares of a corporation owned by its subsidiary shall not be entitled to vote on any matter.

(c) Shares held by the issuing corporation in a fiduciary capacity, and shares of an issuing corporation held in a fiduciary capacity by its subsidiary, shall not be entitled to vote on any matter, except as follows:

(1) To the extent that the settlor or beneficial owner possesses and exercises a right to vote or to give the corporation binding instructions as to how to vote such shares.

(2) Where there are one or more cotrustees who are not affected by the prohibition of this subdivision, in which case the shares may be voted by the cotrustees as if it or they are the sole trustee.

§ 705. Proxies; Validity; Expiration; Revocation; Irrevocable Proxies

(a) Every person entitled to vote shares may authorize another person or persons to act by proxy with respect to such shares. Any proxy purporting to be executed in accordance with the provisions of this division shall be presumptively valid.

(b) No proxy shall be valid after the expiration of 11 months from the date thereof unless otherwise provided in the proxy. Every proxy continues in full force and effect until revoked by the person executing it prior to the vote pursuant thereto, except as otherwise provided in this section. Such revocation may be effected by a writing delivered to the corporation stating that the proxy is revoked or by a subsequent proxy executed by the person executing the prior proxy and presented to the meeting, or as to any meeting by attendance at such meeting and voting in person by the person executing the proxy. The dates contained on the forms of proxy presumptively determine the order of execution, regardless of the postmark dates on the envelopes in which they are mailed.

(c) A proxy is not revoked by the death or incapacity of the maker unless, before the vote is counted, written notice of such death or incapacity is received by the corporation.

(d) Except when other provision shall have been made by written agreement between the parties, the recordholder of shares which such person holds as pledgee or otherwise as security or which belong to another shall issue to the pledgor or to the owner of such shares, upon demand therefor and payment of necessary expenses thereof, a proxy to vote or take other action thereon.

(e) A proxy which states that it is irrevocable is irrevocable for the period specified therein (notwithstanding subdivision (c)) when it is held by any of the following or a nominee of any of the following:

(1) A pledgee.

(2) A person who has purchased or agreed to purchase or holds an option to purchase the shares or a person who has sold a portion of such person's shares in the corporation to the maker of the proxy.

(3) A creditor or creditors of the corporation or the shareholder who extended or continued credit to the corporation or the shareholder in consideration of the proxy if the proxy states that it was given in consideration of such extension or continuation of credit and the name of the person extending or continuing credit.

(4) A person who has contracted to perform services as an employee of the corporation, if a proxy is required by the contract of employment and if the proxy states that it was given in consideration of such contract of employment, the name of the employee and the period of employment contracted for.

(5) A person designated by or under an agreement under Section 706.

(6) A beneficiary of a trust with respect to shares held by the trust.

Notwithstanding the period of irrevocability specified, the proxy becomes revocable when the pledge is redeemed, the option or agreement to purchase is terminated or the seller no longer owns any shares of the corporation or dies, the debt of the corporation or the shareholder is paid, the period of employment provided for in the contract of employment has terminated, the agreement under Section 706 has terminated, or the person ceases to be a beneficiary of the trust. In addition to the foregoing clauses (1) through (5), a proxy may be made irrevocable (notwithstanding subdivision (c)) if it is given to secure the performance of a duty or to protect a title, either legal or equitable, until the happening of events which, by its terms, discharge the obligations secured by it.

(f) A proxy may be revoked, notwithstanding a provision making it irrevocable, by a transferee of shares without knowledge of the existence of the provision unless the existence of the proxy and its irrevocability appears, in the case of certificated securities, on the certificate representing such shares, or in the case of uncertificated securities, on the initial transaction statement and written statements.

§ 706. Agreement Between Two or More Shareholders of Close Corporation; Voting Trust Agreements

(a) Notwithstanding any other provision of this division, an agreement between two or more shareholders of a close corporation, if in writing and signed by the parties thereto, may provide that in exercising any voting rights the shares held by them shall be voted as provided by the agreement, or as the parties may agree or as determined in accordance with a procedure agreed upon by them, and the parties may transfer the shares covered by such an agreement to a third party or parties with authority to vote them in accordance with the terms of the agreement. Such an agreement shall not be denied specific performance by a court on the ground that the remedy at law is adequate or on other grounds relating to the jurisdiction of a court of equity. An agreement made pursuant to this subdivision between shareholders of a close corporation shall terminate when the corporation ceases to be a close corporation, except that if the agreement so provides it shall continue to the extent it is enforceable apart from this subdivision.

(b) Shares in any corporation may be transferred by written agreement to trustees in order to confer upon them the right to vote and otherwise represent the shares for such period of time, not exceeding 10 years, as may be specified in the agreement. The validity of a voting trust agreement, otherwise lawful, shall not be affected during a period of 10 years from the date when it was created or last extended as hereinafter provided by the fact that under its terms it will or may last beyond such 10–year period. At any time within two years prior to the time of expiration of any voting trust agreement as originally fixed or as last extended as provided in this subdivision, one or more beneficiaries under the voting trust agreement may, by written agreement and with the written consent of the voting trustee or trustees, extend the duration of the voting trust agreement with respect to their shares for an additional period not exceeding 10 years from the expiration date of the trust as originally fixed or as last extended as provided in this subdivision. A duplicate of the voting trust agreement and any extension thereof shall be filed with the secretary of the corporation and shall be open to inspection by a shareholder, a holder of a voting trust certificate or the agent of either, upon the same terms as the record of shareholders of the corporation is open to inspection.

(c) No agreement made pursuant to subdivision (a) shall be held to be invalid or unenforceable on the ground that it is a voting trust which does not comply with subdivision (b).

(d) This section shall not invalidate any voting or other agreement among shareholders or any irrevocable proxy complying with subdivision (e) of Section 705, which agreement or proxy is not otherwise illegal.

§ 708. Directors; Cumulative Voting; Election by Ballot

(a) Except as provided in Section 301.5, every shareholder complying with subdivision (b) and entitled to vote at any election of directors may cumulate such shareholder's votes and give one candidate a number of votes equal to the number of directors to be elected multiplied by the number of votes to which the shareholder's shares are normally entitled, or distribute the shareholder's votes on the same principle among as many candidates as the shareholder thinks fit.

(b) No shareholder shall be entitled to cumulate votes (i.e., cast for any candidate a number of votes greater than the number of votes which such shareholder normally is entitled to cast) unless such candidate or candidates' names have been placed in nomination prior to the voting and the shareholder has given notice at the meeting prior to the voting of the shareholder's intention to cumulate the shareholder's votes. If any one shareholder has given such notice, all shareholders may cumulate their votes for candidates in nomination.

(c) In any election of directors, the candidates receiving the highest number of affirmative votes of the shares entitled to be voted for them up to the number of directors to be elected by such shares are elected; votes against the director and votes withheld shall have no legal effect. . . .

(e) Elections for directors need not be by ballot unless a shareholder demands election by ballot at the meeting and before the voting begins or unless the bylaws so require.

§ 710. Supermajority Vote Requirement; Approval; Duration; Readoption

(a) This section applies to a corporation with outstanding shares held of record by 100 or more persons (determined as provided in Section

605) [shares deemed "held of record"] which files an amendment of articles or certificate of determination containing a "supermajority vote" provision on or after January 1, 1989; provided that this section shall not apply to a corporation which files an amendment of articles or certificate of determination on or after January 1, 1994, if, at the time of filing, the corporation has (1) outstanding shares of more than one class or series of stock; (2) no class of equity securities registered under Section 12(b) or 12(g) of the Securities Exchange Act of 1934; (3) outstanding securities held of record by fewer than 300 persons determined as provided by Section 605; and (4) no supermajority vote provision, and has never had a supermajority vote provision, subject to the requirement of readoption under subdivision (c).

(b) A "supermajority vote" is a requirement set forth in the articles or in a certificate of determination authorized under any provision of this division that specified corporate action or actions be approved by a larger proportion of the outstanding shares than a majority, or by a larger proportion of the outstanding shares of a class or series than a majority, but no supermajority vote which is subject to this section shall require a vote in excess of 66⅔ percent of the outstanding shares or 66⅔ percent of the outstanding shares of any class or series of such shares.

(c) An amendment of the articles or a certificate of determination that includes a supermajority vote requirement shall be approved by at least as large a proportion of the outstanding shares (Section 152) as is required pursuant to that amendment or certificate of determination for the approval of the specified corporate action or actions. The supermajority vote requirement shall cease to be effective two years after the filing of the most recent filing of the amendment or certificate of determination to adopt or readopt the supermajority vote requirement. At any time within one year before the applicable expiration date, a supermajority vote requirement may be renewed, and at any time after the expiration date, a supermajority vote requirement may again be made effective for another two-year period, by readopting the provision and filing a certificate of amendment pursuant to, and subject to the limitations of, this subdivision. If the provision is not readopted in this manner, then the particular corporate action or actions previously subject to the supermajority vote shall thereafter require a vote of only a majority of either the outstanding shares or the shares of the specified class or series which had previously been subject to the supermajority vote provision, whichever the case may be.

§ 711. Maintenance by Holding Legal Owners and Disclosure to Persons on Whose Behalf Shares Are Voted; Charges; Actions to Enforce Section; Payment of Costs and Attorney's Fees ...

(a) The Legislature finds and declares that:

Many of the residents of this state are the legal and beneficial owners or otherwise the ultimate beneficiaries of shares of stock of domestic and foreign corporations, title to which may be held by a variety of intermediate owners as defined in subdivision (b). The informed and active involvement of such beneficial owners and beneficiaries in holding legal owners and, through them, management, accountable in their exercise of corporate power is essential to the interest of those beneficiaries and beneficial owners and to the economy and well-being of this state.

The purpose of this section is to serve the public interest by ensuring that voting records are maintained and disclosed as provided in this section. In the event that by statute or regulation pursuant to the federal Employee Retirement Income Security Act of 1974 (29 U.S.C. Sec. 1001 et seq.), there are imposed upon investment managers as defined in Sec. 2(38) thereof, duties substantially the same as those set forth in this section, compliance with those statutory or regulatory requirements by persons subject to this section shall be deemed to fulfill the obligations contained in this section.

This section shall be construed liberally to achieve that purpose.

(b) For purposes of this section, a person on whose behalf shares are voted includes, but is not limited to:

(1) A participant or beneficiary of an employee benefit plan with regard to shares held for the benefit of the participant or beneficiary.

(2) A shareholder, beneficiary, or contract owner of any entity (or of any portfolio of any entity) as defined in Section 3(a) of the federal Investment Company Act of 1940 (15 U.S.C. Sec. 80a–1 et seq.), as amended, to the extent the entity (or portfolio) holds the shares for which the record is requested.

(c) For the purposes of this section, a person on whose behalf shares are voted does not include:

(1) A person who possesses the right to terminate or withdraw from the shareholder, contract owner, participant, or beneficiary relationship with any entity (or any portfolio of any entity) defined in subdivision (b). This exclusion does not apply in the event the right of termination or withdrawal cannot be exercised without automatic imposition of a tax penalty. The right to substitute a relationship with an entity or portfolio, the shares of which are voted by or subject to the direction of the investment adviser (as defined in Section 2 of the federal Investment Company Act of 1940 (15 U.S.C. Sec. 80a–1 et seq.), as amended), of the prior entity or portfolio, or an affiliate of the investment adviser, shall not be deemed to be a right of termination or withdrawal within the meaning of this subdivision.

(2) A person entitled to receive information about a trust pursuant to Section 16061 of the Probate Code.

(3) A beneficiary, participant, contract owner, or shareholder whose interest is funded through the general assets of a life insurance company authorized to conduct business in this state.

(d) Every person possessing the power to vote shares of stock on behalf of another shall maintain a record of the manner in which the shares were voted. The record shall be maintained for a period of 12 consecutive months from the effective date of the vote.

(e) Upon a reasonable written request, the person possessing the power to vote shares of stock on behalf of another, or a designated agent, shall disclose the voting record with respect to any matter involving a specific security or securities in accordance with the following procedures:

(1) Except as set forth in paragraph (2), disclosure shall be made to the person making the request. The person making the disclosure may require identification sufficient to identify the person making the request as a person on whose behalf the shares were voted. A request for identification, if made, shall be reasonable, shall be made promptly, and may include a request for the person's social security number.

(2) If the person possessing the power to vote shares on behalf of another holds that power pursuant to an agreement entered into with a party other than the person making the request for disclosure, the person maintaining and disclosing the record pursuant to this section may, instead, make the requested disclosure to that party. Disclosure to that party shall be deemed compliance with the disclosure requirement of this section. If disclosure is made to that party and not to the person making the request, subdivision (i) shall not apply. However, nothing herein shall prohibit that party and the person possessing the power to vote on shares from entering into an agreement between themselves for the payment or assessment of a reasonable charge to defray expenses of disclosing the record.

(f) Where the entity subject to the requirements of this section is organized as a unit investment trust as defined in Section 4(2) of the federal Investment Company Act of 1940 (15 U.S.C. Sec. 80a–1 et seq.), the open-ended investment companies underlying the unit investment trust shall promptly make available their proxy voting records to the unit investment trust upon evidence of a bona fide request for voting record information pursuant to subdivision (e).

(g) Signing a proxy on another's behalf and forwarding it for disposition or receiving voting instructions does not constitute the power to vote. A person forwarding proxies or receiving voting instructions shall disclose the identity of the person having the power to vote shares upon reasonable written request by a person entitled to request a voting record under subdivision (c).

(h) For purposes of this section, if one or more persons has the power to vote shares on behalf of another, unless a governing instrument provides otherwise, the person or persons may designate an agent who shall maintain and disclose the record in accordance with subdivisions (b) and (c).

(i) Except as provided in paragraph (2) of subdivision (e), or as otherwise provided by law or a governing instrument, a person maintaining and disclosing a record pursuant to this section may assess a reasonable charge to the requesting person in order to defray expenses of disclosing the record in accordance with subdivision (e). Disclosure shall be made within a reasonable period after payment is received.

(j) Upon the petition of any person who successfully brings an action pursuant to or to enforce this section, the court may award costs and reasonable attorney's fees if the court finds that the defendant willfully violated this section. . . .

Chapter 8

SHAREHOLDER DERIVATIVE ACTIONS

§ 800. Conditions; Security; Motion for Order; Determination

. . . .

(b) No action may be instituted or maintained in right of any domestic or foreign corporation by any holder of shares or of voting trust certificates of . . . the corporation unless both of the following conditions exist:

(1) The plaintiff alleges in the complaint that plaintiff was a shareholder, of record or beneficially, or the holder of voting trust certificates at the time of the transaction or any part thereof of which plaintiff complains or that plaintiff's shares or voting trust certificates thereafter devolved upon plaintiff by operation of law from a holder who was a holder at the time of the transaction or any part thereof complained of; provided, that any shareholder who does not meet . . . these requirements may nevertheless be allowed in the discretion of the court to maintain . . . the action on a preliminary showing to and determination by the court, by motion and after a hearing, at which the court shall consider such evidence, by affidavit or testimony, as it deems material, that (i) there is a strong prima facie case in favor of the claim asserted on behalf of the corporation, (ii) no other similar action has been or is likely to be instituted, (iii) the plaintiff acquired the shares before there was disclosure to the public or to the plaintiff of the wrongdoing of which plaintiff complains, (iv) unless the action can be maintained the defendant may retain a gain derived from defendant's willful breach of a fiduciary duty, and (v) the requested relief will not result in unjust

enrichment of the corporation or any shareholder of the corporation; and

(2) The plaintiff alleges in the complaint with particularity plaintiff's efforts to secure from the board such action as plaintiff desires, or the reasons for not making such effort, and alleges further that plaintiff has either informed the corporation or the board in writing of the ultimate facts of each cause of action against each defendant or delivered to the corporation or the board a true copy of the complaint which plaintiff proposes to file.

(c) In any action referred to in subdivision (b), at any time within 30 days after service of summons upon the corporation or upon any defendant who is an officer or director of the corporation, or held such office at the time of the acts complained of, the corporation or ... the defendant may move the court for an order, upon notice and hearing, requiring the plaintiff to furnish ... a bond as hereinafter provided. The motion shall be based upon one or both of the following grounds:

(1) That there is no reasonable possibility that the prosecution of the cause of action alleged in the complaint against the moving party will benefit the corporation or its shareholders.

(2) That the moving party, if other than the corporation, did not participate in the transaction complained of in any capacity.

The court on application of the corporation or any defendant may, for good cause shown, extend the 30–day period for an additional period or periods not exceeding 60 days.

(d) At the hearing upon any motion pursuant to subdivision (c), the court shall consider such evidence, written or oral, by witnesses or affidavit, as may be material (1) to the ground or grounds upon which the motion is based, or (2) to a determination of the probable reasonable expenses, including attorneys' fees, of the corporation and the moving party which will be incurred in the defense of the action. If the court determines, after hearing the evidence adduced by the parties, that the moving party has established a probability in support of any of the grounds upon which the motion is based, the court shall fix the ... amount of the bond, not to exceed fifty thousand dollars ($50,000), to be furnished by the plaintiff for reasonable expenses, including attorneys' fees, which may be incurred by the moving party and the corporation in connection with the action, including expenses for which the corporation may become liable pursuant to Section 317 [Indemnification]. A ruling by the court on the motion shall not be a determination of any issue in the action or of the merits thereof. ... If the court, upon the motion, makes a determination that ... a bond shall be furnished by the plaintiff as to any one or more defendants, the action shall be dismissed as to ... the defendant or defendants, unless the bond required by the court ... has been furnished within such reasonable time as may be fixed by the court. ...

(e) If the plaintiff shall, either before or after a motion is made pursuant to subdivision (c), or any order or determination pursuant to ... the motion, ... furnish a bond in the aggregate amount of fifty thousand dollars ($50,000) to secure the reasonable expenses of the parties entitled to make the motion, the plaintiff has complied with the requirements of this section and with any order for ... a bond theretofore made ..., and any such motion then pending shall be dismissed and no further or additional bond ... shall be required.

(f) If a motion is filed pursuant to subdivision (c), no pleadings need be filed by the corporation or any other defendant and the prosecution of the action shall be stayed until 10 days after the motion has been disposed of.

Chapter 9

AMENDMENT OF ARTICLES

§ 900. Authorization; Prohibited Amendments

(a) By complying with the provisions of this chapter, a corporation may amend its articles from time to time, in any and as many respects as may be desired, so long as its articles as amended contain only such provisions as it would be lawful to insert in original articles filed at the time of the filing of the amendment and, if a change in shares or the rights of shareholders or an exchange, reclassification or cancellation of shares or rights of shareholders is to be made, such provisions as may be necessary to effect such change, exchange, reclassification or cancellation. It is the intent of the Legislature in adopting this section to exercise to the fullest extent the reserve power of the state over corporations and to authorize any amendment of the articles covered by the preceding sentence regardless of whether any provision contained in the amendment was permissible at the time of the original incorporation of the corporation.

(b) A corporation shall not amend its articles to alter any statement which may appear in the original articles of the names and addresses of the first directors, nor the name and address of the initial agent, except to correct an error in the statement or to delete either after the corporation has filed a statement under Section 1502 [Annual statement of general information and agents for service of process].

Chapter 10

SALES OF ASSETS

§ 1001. Sale, Lease, Exchange, etc. . . . .; of Property or Assets; Approval; Abandonment; Terms, Conditions and Consideration

(a) A corporation may sell, lease, convey, exchange, transfer or otherwise dispose of all or substantially all of its assets when the principal terms are

(1) Approved by the board, and

(2) Unless the transaction is in the usual and regular course of its business, approved by the outstanding shares (Section 152), either before or after approval by the board and before or after the transaction.

A transaction constituting a reorganization (Section 181) is subject to the provisions of Chapter 12 (commencing with Section 1200) and not this section (other than subdivision (d) hereof).

(b) Notwithstanding approval of the outstanding shares (Section 152), the board may abandon the proposed transaction without further action by the shareholders, subject to the contractual rights, if any, of third parties.

(c) Such sale, lease, conveyance, exchange, transfer or other disposition may be made upon such terms and conditions and for such consideration as the board may deem in the best interests of the corporation. The consideration may be money, property or securities of any other corporation, domestic or foreign, or any of them.

(d) If the buyer in a sale of assets pursuant to subdivision (a) of this section or subdivision (g) of Section 2001 [sale of assets in dissolution] is in control of or under common control with the seller, the principal terms of the sale must be approved by at least 90 percent of the voting power unless the sale is to a domestic or foreign corporation in consideration of the nonredeemable common shares of the purchasing corporation or its parent.

(e) Subdivision (d) does not apply to any transaction if the Commissioner of Corporations, the Commissioner of Financial Institutions, the Insurance Commissioner or the Public Utilities Commission has approved the terms and conditions . . . .

Chapter 11

MERGER

§ 1101. Agreement of Merger; Approval of Boards; Contents

The board of each corporation which desires to merge shall approve an agreement of merger. The constituent corporations shall be parties to the agreement of merger and other persons, including a parent party corporation (Section 1200), may be parties to the agreement of merger. The agreement shall state all of the following:

(a) The terms and conditions of the merger.

(b) The amendments ... to the articles of the surviving corporation to be effected by the merger, if any; if any amendment changes the name of the surviving corporation the new name may be the same as or similar to the name of a disappearing domestic or foreign corporation ....

(c) The name and place of incorporation of each constituent corporation and which of the constituent corporations is the surviving corporation.

(d) The manner of converting the shares of each of the constituent corporations into shares or other securities of the surviving corporation and, if any shares of any of the constituent corporations are not to be converted solely into shares or other securities of the surviving corporation, the cash, property, rights or securities of any corporation which the holders of those shares are to receive in exchange for the shares, which cash, property, rights or securities of any corporation may be in addition to or in lieu of shares or other securities of the surviving corporation, or that the shares are cancelled without consideration.

(e) Such other details or provisions as are desired, if any, including, without limitation, a provision for the payment of cash in lieu of fractional shares or for any other arrangement with respect thereto consistent with the provisions of Section 407.

Each share of the same class or series of any constituent corporation (other than the cancellation of shares held by a constituent corporation or its parent or a wholly owned subsidiary of either in another constituent corporation) shall, unless all shareholders of the class or series consent and except as provided in Section 407, be treated equally with respect to any distribution of cash, property, rights or securities. Notwithstanding subdivision (d), except in a short-form merger, and in the merger of a corporation into its subsidiary in which it owns at least 90 percent of the outstanding shares of each class, the nonredeemable common shares of a constituent corporation may be converted only into nonredeemable common shares of the surviving corporation or a parent

719

party if a constituent corporation or its parent owns, directly or indirectly, shares of another constituent corporation representing more than 50 percent of the voting power of the other constituent corporation prior to the merger, unless all of the shareholders of the class consent and except as provided in Section 407.

§ 1101.1   Agreement of Merger; Approval by Governmental Officer or Commission

. . . [T]he last two sentences of Section 1101 do not apply to any transaction if the Commissioner of Corporations, the Commissioner of Financial Institutions, the Insurance Commissioner . . . or the Public Utilities Commission has approved the terms and conditions of the transaction and the fairness of such terms and conditions . . . .

Chapter 12

REORGANIZATIONS

§ 1200.   Approval by Board

A reorganization (Section 181) or a share exchange tender offer (Section 183.5) shall be approved by the board of:

(a) Each constituent corporation in a merger reorganization;

(b) The acquiring corporation in an exchange reorganization;

(c) The acquiring corporation and the corporation whose property and assets are acquired in a sale-of-assets reorganization;

(d) The acquiring corporation in a share exchange tender offer (Section 183.5); and

(e) The corporation in control of any constituent or acquiring corporation under subdivision (a), (b) or (c) and whose equity securities are issued or transferred in the reorganization (a "parent party").

Legislative Committee Comment . . .

Under the new law, various methods of corporate fusion are treated as different means to the same end for the purpose of codifying the "de facto merger" doctrine.

As a basis for this approach, "reorganization" is defined to encompass the three basic methods of combination . . . . This section generally requires a reorganization to be approved by the board of each party, as well as the board of any "parent party" to the transaction.   Taken together, these provisions specify the transactions (including the so-called "upside-down" and "triangular" transactions) in which § 1201 may require shareholder approval and, in turn, § 1300 may require dissenters' rights.

§ 1201. Approval of Shareholders; Abandonment by Board; Actions to Attack Validity if Party Directly or Indirectly Controlled by Other Party

(a) The principal terms of a reorganization shall be approved by the outstanding shares (Section 152) of each class of each corporation the approval of whose board is required under Section 1200, except as provided in subdivision (b) and except that (unless otherwise provided in the articles) no approval of any class of outstanding preferred shares of the surviving or acquiring corporation or parent party shall be required if the rights, preferences, privileges and restrictions granted to or imposed upon such class of shares remain unchanged (subject to the provisions of subdivision (c)). For the purpose of this subdivision, two classes of common shares differing only as to voting rights shall be considered as a single class of shares.

(b) No approval of the outstanding shares (Section 152) is required by subdivision (a) in the case of any corporation if such corporation, or its shareholders immediately before the reorganization, or both, shall own (immediately after the reorganization) equity securities, other than any warrant or right to subscribe to or purchase such equity securities, of the surviving or acquiring corporation or a parent party (subdivision (d) of Section 1200) possessing more than five-sixths of the voting power of the surviving or acquiring corporation or parent party. In making the determination of ownership by the shareholders of a corporation, immediately after the reorganization, of equity securities pursuant to the preceding sentence, equity securities which they owned immediately before the reorganization as shareholders of another party to the transaction shall be disregarded. For the purpose of this section only, the voting power of a corporation shall be calculated by assuming the conversion of all equity securities convertible (immediately or at some future time) into shares entitled to vote but not assuming the exercise of any warrant or right to subscribe to or purchase such shares.

(c) Notwithstanding the provisions of subdivision (b), the principal terms of a reorganization shall be approved by the outstanding shares (Section 152) of the surviving corporation in a merger reorganization if any amendment is made to its articles which would otherwise require such approval.

(d) Notwithstanding the provisions of subdivision (b), the principal terms of a reorganization shall be approved by the outstanding shares (Section 152) of any class of a corporation which is a party to a merger or sale-of-assets reorganization if holders of shares of that class receive shares of the surviving or acquiring corporation or parent party having different rights, preferences, privileges or restrictions than those surrendered. Shares in a foreign corporation received in exchange for shares in a domestic corporation have different rights, preferences, privileges and restrictions within the meaning of the preceding sentence.

(e) Notwithstanding the provisions of subdivisions (a) and (b), the principal terms of a reorganization shall be approved by the affirmative vote of at least two-thirds of each class of the outstanding shares of any close corporation if the reorganization would result in their receiving shares of a corporation which is not a close corporation; provided, however, that the articles may provide for a lesser vote, but not less than a majority of the outstanding shares of each class.

(f) Notwithstanding the provisions of subdivisions (a) and (b), the principal terms of a reorganization shall be approved by the outstanding shares (Section 152) of any class of a corporation which is a party to a merger reorganization if holders or shares of that class receive interests of a surviving other business entity [§ 174.5] in the merger.

(g) Any approval required by this section may be given before or after the approval by the board. Notwithstanding approval required by this section, the board may abandon the proposed reorganization without further action by the shareholders, subject to the contractual rights, if any, of third parties.

§ 1201.5　Share Exchange Tender Offer; Approval of Principal Terms

(a) The principal terms of a share exchange tender offer (Section 183.5) shall be approved by the outstanding shares (Section 152) of each class of the corporation making the tender offer or whose shares are to be used in the tender offer, except as provided in subdivision (b) and except that (unless otherwise provided in the articles) no approval of any class of outstanding preferred shares of either corporation shall be required, if the rights, preferences, privileges, and restrictions granted to or imposed upon that class of shares remain unchanged. For the purpose of this subdivision, two classes of common shares differing only as to voting rights shall be considered as a single class of shares.

(b) No approval of the outstanding shares (Section 152) is required by subdivision (a) in the case of any corporation if the corporation, or its shareholders immediately before the tender offer, or both, shall own (immediately after the completion of the share exchange proposed in the tender offer) equity securities, (other than any warrant or right to subscribe to or purchase the equity securities), of the corporation making the tender offer or of the corporation whose shares were used in the tender offer, possessing more than five-sixths of the voting power of either corporation. In making the determination of ownership by the shareholders of a corporation, immediately after the tender offer, of equity securities pursuant to the preceding sentence, equity securities which they owned immediately before the tender offer as shareholders of another party to the transaction shall be disregarded. For the purpose of this section only, the voting power of a corporation shall be calculated by assuming the conversion of all equity securities convertible (immediately or at some future time) into shares entitled to vote but not assuming the exercise of any warrant or right to subscribe to, or purchase, shares.

§ 1202. Terms of Merger Reorganization or Sale-of-Assets Reorganization; Approval by Shareholders; Foreign Corporations

(a) In addition to the requirements of Section 1201, the principal terms of a merger reorganization shall be approved by all the outstanding shares of a corporation if the agreement of merger provides that all the outstanding shares of that corporation are canceled without consideration in the merger.

(b) In addition to the requirements of Section 1201, if the terms of a merger reorganization or sale-of-assets reorganization provide that a class or series of preferred shares is to have distributed to it a lesser amount than would be required by applicable article provisions, the principal terms of the reorganization shall be approved by the same percentage of outstanding shares of that class or series which would be required to approve an amendment of the article provisions to provide for the distribution of that lesser amount.

(c) If a parent party within the meaning of Section 1200 is a foreign corporation (other than a foreign corporation to which subdivision (a) of Section 2115 is applicable), any requirement or lack of a requirement for approval by the outstanding shares of the foreign corporation shall be based, not on the application of Sections 1200 and 1201, but on the application of the laws of the state or place of incorporation of the foreign corporation.

§ 1203. Interested Party Proposal or Tender Offer to Shareholders; Affirmative Opinion; Delivery; Approval; Later Proposal or Tender Offer; Withdrawal of Vote, Consent, or Proxy; Procedures

(a) If a tender offer, including a share exchange tender offer (Section 183.5), or a written proposal for approval of a reorganization subject to Section 1200 or for a sale of assets subject to subdivision (a) of Section 1001 is made to some or all of a corporation's shareholders by an interested party (herein referred to as an "Interested Party Proposal"), an affirmative opinion in writing as to the fairness of the consideration to the shareholders of that corporation shall be delivered as follows:

(1) If no shareholder approval or acceptance is required for the consummation of the transaction, the opinion shall be delivered to the corporation's board of directors not later than the time that consummation of the transaction is authorized and approved by the board of directors.

(2) If a tender offer is made to the corporation's shareholders, the opinion shall be delivered to the shareholders at the time that the tender offer is first made in writing to the shareholders. However, if the tender offer is commenced by publication and tender offer materials are subsequently mailed or otherwise distributed to the shareholders, the opinion may be omitted in that publication if the opinion is included in the materials distributed to the shareholders.

(3) If a shareholders' meeting is to be held to vote on approval of the transaction, the opinion shall be delivered to the shareholders with the notice of the meeting (Section 601).

(4) If consents of all shareholders entitled to vote are solicited in writing (Section 603), the opinion shall be delivered at the same time as that solicitation.

(5) If the consents of all shareholders are not solicited in writing, the opinion shall be delivered to each shareholder whose consent is solicited prior to that shareholder's consent being given, and to all other shareholders at the time they are given the notice required by subdivision (b) of Section 603.

For purposes of this section, the term "interested party" means a person who is a party to the transaction and (A) directly or indirectly controls the corporation that is the subject of the tender offer or proposal, (B) is, or is directly or indirectly controlled by, an officer or director of the subject corporation, or (C) is an entity in which a material financial interest (subdivision (a) of Section 310) is held by any director or executive officer of the subject corporation. For purposes of the preceding sentence, "any executive officer" means the president, any vice president in charge of a principal business unit, division, or function such as sales, administration, research or development, or finance, and any other officer or other person who performs a policymaking function or has the same duties as those of a president or vice president. The opinion required by this subdivision shall be provided by a person who is not affiliated with the offeror and who, for compensation, engages in the business of advising others as to the value of properties, businesses, or securities. The fact that the opining person previously has provided services to the offeror or a related entity or is simultaneously engaged in providing advice or assistance with respect to the proposed transaction in a manner which makes its compensation contingent on the success of the proposed transaction shall not, for those reasons, be deemed to affiliate the opining person with the offeror. Nothing in this subdivision shall limit the applicability of the standards of review of the transaction in the event of a challenge thereto under Section 310 or subdivision (c) of Section 1312.

This subdivision shall not apply to an Interested Party Proposal if the corporation that is the subject thereof does not have shares held of record by 100 or more persons ... , or if the transaction has been qualified under Section 25113 [Qualification by permit; application; contents; effective date] or 25120 [Necessity of qualification of security or exemption of security or transaction] and no order under Section 25140 [Issuance of stop orders affecting qualification of securities; refusal to issue or suspension or revocation of permits; grounds] or subdivision (a) of Section 25143 [Postponement or suspension of effectiveness of qualification; notice; hearing] is in effect with respect to that qualification.

(b) If a tender of shares or a vote or written consent is being sought pursuant to an Interested Party Proposal and a later tender offer or written proposal for a reorganization subject to Section 1200 or sale of assets subject to subdivision (a) of Section 1001 that would require a vote or written consent of shareholders is made to the corporation or its shareholders (herein referred to as a "Later Proposal") by any other person at least 10 days prior to the date for acceptance of the tendered shares or the vote or notice of shareholder approval on the Interested Party Proposal, then each of the following shall apply:

(1) The shareholders shall be informed of the Later Proposal and any written material provided for this purpose by the later offeror shall be forwarded to the shareholders at that offeror's expense.

(2) The shareholders shall be afforded a reasonable opportunity to withdraw any vote, consent, or proxy previously given before the vote or written consent on the Interested Party Proposal becomes effective, or a reasonable time to withdraw any tendered shares before the purchase of the shares pursuant to the Interested Party Proposal. For purposes of this subdivision, a delay of 10 days from the notice or publication of the Later Proposal shall be deemed to provide a reasonable opportunity or time to effect that withdrawal.

Chapter 13

DISSENTERS' RIGHTS

§ 1300. Reorganization or Short–Form Merger; Dissenting Shares; Corporate Purchase at Fair Market Value; Definitions

(a) If the approval of the outstanding shares (Section 152) of a corporation is required for a reorganization under subdivisions (a) and (b) or subdivision (e) or (f) of Section 1201, each shareholder of the corporation entitled to vote on the transaction and each shareholder of a subsidiary corporation in a short-form merger may, by complying with this chapter, require the corporation in which the shareholder holds shares to purchase for cash at their fair market value the shares owned by the shareholder which are dissenting shares as defined in subdivision (b). The fair market value shall be determined as of the day before the

725

first announcement of the terms of the proposed reorganization or short-form merger, excluding any appreciation or depreciation in consequence of the proposed action, but adjusted for any stock split, reverse stock split or share dividend which becomes effective thereafter.

(b) As used in this chapter, "dissenting shares" means shares which come within all of the following descriptions:

(1) Which were not immediately prior to the reorganization or short-form merger either (A) listed on any national securities exchange certified by the Commissioner of Corporations under subdivision (*o*) of Section 25100 or (B) listed on the list of OTC margin stocks issued by the Board of Governors of the Federal Reserve System, and the notice of meeting of shareholders to act upon the reorganization summarizes this section and Sections 1301, 1302, 1303 and 1304; provided, however, that this provision does not apply to any shares with respect to which there exists any restriction on transfer imposed by the corporation or by any law or regulation; and provided, further, that this provision does not apply to any class of shares described in subparagraph (A) or (B) if demands for payment are filed with respect to 5 percent or more of the outstanding shares of that class.

(2) Which were outstanding on the date for the determination of shareholders entitled to vote on the reorganization and (A) were not voted in favor of the reorganization or, (B) if described in subparagraph (A) or (B) of paragraph (1) (without regard to the provisos in that paragraph), were voted against the reorganization, or which were held of record on the effective date of a short-form merger; provided, however, that subparagraph (A) rather than subparagraph (B) of this paragraph applies in any case where the approval required by Section 1201 is sought by written consent rather than at a meeting.

(3) Which the dissenting shareholder has demanded that the corporation purchase at their fair market value, in accordance with Section 1301.

(4) Which the dissenting shareholder has submitted for endorsement, in accordance with Section 1302.

(c) As used in this chapter, "dissenting shareholder" means the recordholder of dissenting shares and includes a transferee of record.

§ 1311. Exempt Shares

This chapter, except Section 1312, does not apply to classes of shares whose terms and provisions specifically set forth the amount to be paid in respect to such shares in the event of a reorganization or merger.

§ 1312. Right of Dissenting Shareholder to Attack, Set Aside or Rescind Merger or Reorganization; Restraining Order or Injunction; Conditions

(a) No shareholder of a corporation who has a right under this chapter to demand payment of cash for the shares held by the shareholder shall have any right at law or in equity to attack the validity of the reorganization or short-form merger, or to have the reorganization or short-form merger set aside or rescinded, except in an action to test whether the number of shares required to authorize or approve the reorganization have been legally voted in favor thereof; but any holder of shares of a class whose terms and provisions specifically set forth the amount to be paid in respect to them in the event of a reorganization or short-form merger is entitled to payment in accordance with those terms and provisions, or, if the principal terms of the reorganization are approved pursuant to subdivision (b) or Section 1202, is entitled to payment in accordance with the terms and provisions of the approved reorganization.

(b) If one of the parties to a reorganization or short-form merger is directly or indirectly controlled by, or under common control with, another party to the reorganization or short-form merger, subdivision (a) shall not apply to any shareholder of such party who has not demanded payment of cash for such shareholder's shares pursuant to this chapter; but if the shareholder institutes any action to attack the validity of the reorganization or short-form merger or to have the reorganization or short-form merger set aside or rescinded, the shareholder shall not thereafter have any right to demand payment of cash for the shareholder's shares pursuant to this chapter. The court in any action attacking the validity of the reorganization or short-form merger or to have the reorganization or short-form merger set aside or rescinded shall not restrain or enjoin the consummation of the transaction except upon 10 days' prior notice to the corporation and upon a determination by the court that clearly no other remedy will adequately protect the complaining shareholder or the class of shareholders of which such shareholder is a member.

(c) If one of the parties to a reorganization or short-form merger is directly or indirectly controlled by, or under common control with, another party to the reorganization or short-form merger, in any action to attack the validity of the reorganization or short-form merger or to have the reorganization or short-form merger set aside or rescinded, (1) a party to a reorganization or short-form merger which controls another party to the reorganization or short-form merger shall have the burden of proving that the transaction is just and reasonable as to the shareholders of the controlled party, and (2) a person who controls two or more parties to a reorganization shall have the burden of proving that the transaction is just and reasonable as to the shareholders of any party so controlled.

Chapter 15

RECORDS AND REPORTS

§ 1501. Annual Report; Time of Sending to Shareholders; Contents; Quarterly Financial Statements; Written Request; Inspection; Expenses in Actions

(a) The board shall cause an annual report to be sent to the shareholders not later than 120 days after the close of the fiscal year, unless in the case of a corporation with less than 100 holders of record of its shares ... this requirement is expressly waived in the bylaws. This report shall contain a balance sheet as of the end of that fiscal year and an income statement and statement of changes in financial position for that fiscal year, accompanied by any report thereon of independent accountants or, if there is no such report, the certificate of an authorized officer of the corporation that the statements were prepared without audit from the books and records of the corporation.

Unless so waived, the report shall be sent to the shareholders at least 15 (or, if sent by third-class mail, 35) days prior to the annual meeting of shareholders to be held during the next fiscal year, but this requirement shall not limit the requirement for holding an annual meeting as required by Section 600.

Notwithstanding Section 114, the financial statements of any corporation with fewer than 100 holders of record of its shares ... required to be furnished by this subdivision and subdivision (c) ... are not required to be prepared in conformity with generally accepted accounting principles if they reasonably set forth the assets and liabilities and the income and expense of the corporation and disclose the accounting basis used in their preparation.

(b) In addition to the financial statements required by subdivision (a), the annual report of any corporation having 100 or more holders of record of its shares ... either not subject to the reporting requirements of Section 13 of the Securities Exchange Act of 1934, or exempted from those reporting requirements by Section 12(g)(2) of that act, shall also describe briefly both of the following:

(1) Any transaction (excluding compensation of officers and directors) during the previous fiscal year involving an amount in excess of forty thousand dollars ($40,000) (other than contracts let at competitive bid or services rendered at prices regulated by law) to which the corporation or its parent or subsidiary was a party and in which any director or officer of the corporation or of a subsidiary or (if known to the corporation or its parent or subsidiary) any holder of more than 10 percent of the outstanding voting shares of the corporation had a direct or indirect material interest, naming the person and stating the person's

relationship to the corporation, the nature of the person's interest in the transaction and, where practicable, the amount of the interest; provided . . . that in the case of a transaction with a partnership of which the person is a partner, only the interest of the partnership need be stated; and provided . . . further that no such report need be made in the case of any transaction approved by the shareholders (Section 153).

(2) The amount and circumstances of any indemnification or advances aggregating more than ten thousand dollars ($10,000) paid during the fiscal year to any officer or director of the corporation . . . ; provided . . . that no such report need be made in the case of indemnification approved by the shareholders . . . .

(c) If no annual report for the last fiscal year has been sent to shareholders, the corporation shall, upon the written request of any shareholder made more than 120 days after the close of that fiscal year, deliver or mail to the person making the request within 30 days thereafter the financial statements required by subdivision (a) for that year. A shareholder or shareholders holding at least 5 percent of the outstanding shares of any class of a corporation may make a written request to the corporation for an income statement of the corporation for the three-month, six-month or nine-month period of the current fiscal year ended more than 30 days prior to the date of the request and a balance sheet of the corporation as of the end of the period and, in addition, if no annual report for the last fiscal year has been sent to shareholders, the statements referred to in subdivision (a) for the last fiscal year. The statements shall be delivered or mailed to the person making the request within 30 days thereafter. A copy of the statements shall be kept on file in the principal office of the corporation for 12 months and it shall be exhibited at all reasonable times to any shareholder demanding an examination of the statements or a copy shall be mailed to the shareholder.

(d) The quarterly income statements and balance sheets referred to in this section shall be accompanied by the report thereon, if any, of any independent accountants engaged by the corporation or the certificate of an authorized officer of the corporation that the financial statements were prepared without audit from the books and records of the corporation.

(e) In addition to the [financial] penalties provided for in Section 2200, the superior court of the proper county shall enforce the duty of making and mailing or delivering the information and financial statements required by this section and, for good cause shown, may extend the time therefor.

(f) In any action or proceeding under this section, if the court finds the failure of the corporation to comply with the requirements of this section to have been without justification, the court may award an amount sufficient to reimburse the shareholder for the reasonable expenses incurred by the shareholder, including attorneys' fees, in connection with the action or proceeding.

(g) This section applies to any domestic corporation and also to a foreign corporation having its principal executive office in this state or customarily holding meetings of its board in this state.

Chapter 16

RIGHTS OF INSPECTION

§ 1600. List of Shareholders' Names, Addresses and Shareholdings; Time for Compliance After Demand; Delay; Postponement of Shareholders' Meeting; Inspection and Copying

(a) A shareholder or shareholders holding at least 5 percent in the aggregate of the outstanding voting shares of a corporation or who hold at least 1 percent of those voting shares and have filed a Schedule 14A with the United States Securities and Exchange Commission ... shall have an absolute right to do either or both of the following: (1) inspect and copy the record of shareholders' names and addresses and shareholdings during usual business hours upon five business days' prior written demand upon the corporation, or (2) obtain from the transfer agent for the corporation, upon written demand and upon the tender of its usual charges for such a list (the amount of which charges shall be stated to the shareholder by the transfer agent upon request), a list of the shareholders' names and addresses, who are entitled to vote for the election of directors, and their shareholdings, as of the most recent record date for which it has been compiled or as of a date specified by the shareholder subsequent to the date of demand. The list shall be made available on or before the later of five business days after the demand is received or the date specified therein as the date as of which the list is to be compiled. A corporation shall have the responsibility to cause its transfer agent to comply with this subdivision.

(b) Any delay by the corporation or the transfer agent in complying with a demand under subdivision (a) beyond the time limits specified therein shall give the shareholder or shareholders properly making the demand a right to obtain from the superior court, upon the filing of a verified complaint in the proper county and after a hearing, notice of which shall be given to such persons and in such manner as the court may direct, an order postponing any shareholders' meeting previously noticed for a period equal to the period of such delay. Such right shall be in addition to any other legal or equitable remedies to which the shareholder may be entitled.

(c) The record of shareholders shall also be open to inspection and copying by any shareholder or holder of a voting trust certificate at any time during usual business hours upon written demand on the corporation, for a purpose reasonably related to such holder's interests as a shareholder or holder of a voting trust certificate.

(d) Any inspection and copying under this section may be made in person or by agent or attorney. The rights provided in this section may not be limited by the articles or bylaws. This section applies to any domestic corporation and to any foreign corporation having its principal executive office in this state or customarily holding meetings of its board in this state.

§ 1601. Accounting Books and Records and Minutes of Meetings; Inspection Upon Demand by Shareholder or Holder of Voting Trust Certificate; Nature of Right

(a) The accounting books and records and minutes of proceedings of the shareholders and the board and committees of the board of any domestic corporation, and of any foreign corporation keeping any such records in this state or having its principal executive office in this state, shall be open to inspection upon the written demand on the corporation of any shareholder or holder of a voting trust certificate at any reasonable time during usual business hours, for a purpose reasonably related to such holder's interests as a shareholder or as the holder of such voting trust certificate. The right of inspection created by this subdivision shall extend to the records of each subsidiary of a corporation subject to this subdivision.

(b) Such inspection by a shareholder or holder of a voting trust certificate may be made in person or by agent or attorney, and the right of inspection includes the right to copy and make extracts. The right of the shareholders to inspect the corporate records may not be limited by the articles or bylaws.

§ 1602. Directors

Every director shall have the absolute right at any reasonable time to inspect and copy all books, records and documents of every kind and to inspect the physical properties of the corporation of which such person is a director and also of its subsidiary corporations, domestic or foreign. Such inspection by a director may be made in person or by agent or attorney and the right of inspection includes the right to copy and make extracts. This section applies to a director of any foreign corporation having its principal executive office in this state or customarily holding meetings of its board in this state.

§ 1603. Action to Enforce Right; Appointment of Inspector or Accountant; Report; Penalty for Failure to Produce Records; Expenses of Suit

(a) Upon refusal of a lawful demand for inspection, the superior court of the proper county, may enforce the right of inspection with just and proper conditions or may, for good cause shown, appoint one or more competent inspectors or accountants to audit the books and records kept in this state and investigate the property, funds and affairs of any domestic corporation or any foreign corporation keeping records in this state and of any subsidiary corporation thereof, domestic or foreign, keeping records in this state and to report thereon in such manner as the court may direct.

(b) All officers and agents of the corporation shall produce to the inspectors or accountants so appointed all books and documents in their custody or power, under penalty of punishment for contempt of court.

(c) All expenses of the investigation or audit shall be defrayed by the applicant unless the court orders them to be paid or shared by the corporation.

Chapter 18

INVOLUNTARY DISSOLUTION

§ 1800. Verified Complaint; Plaintiffs; Grounds; Intervention by Shareholder or Creditor; Exempt Corporations

(a) A verified complaint for involuntary dissolution of a corporation on any one or more of the grounds specified in subdivision (b) may be filed in the superior court of the proper county by any of the following persons:

(1) One-half or more of the directors in office.

(2) A shareholder or shareholders who hold shares representing not less than 33⅓ percent of (i) the total number of outstanding shares (assuming conversion of any preferred shares convertible into common shares) or (ii) the outstanding common shares or (iii) the equity of the corporation, exclusive in each case of shares owned by persons who have personally participated in any of the transactions enumerated in paragraph (4) of subdivision (b), or any shareholder or shareholders of a close corporation.

(3) Any shareholder if the ground for dissolution is that the period for which the corporation was formed has terminated without extension thereof.

(4) Any other person expressly authorized to do so in the articles.

(b) The grounds for involuntary dissolution are that:

(1) The corporation has abandoned its business for more than one year.

(2) The corporation has an even number of directors who are equally divided and cannot agree as to the management of its affairs, so that its business can no longer be conducted to advantage or so that

there is danger that its property and business will be impaired or lost, and the holders of the voting shares of the corporation are so divided into factions that they cannot elect a board consisting of an uneven number.

(3) There is internal dissension and two or more factions of shareholders in the corporation are so deadlocked that its business can no longer be conducted with advantage to its shareholders or the shareholders have failed at two consecutive annual meetings at which all voting power was exercised, to elect successors to directors whose terms have expired or would have expired upon election of their successors.

(4) Those in control of the corporation have been guilty of or have knowingly countenanced persistent and pervasive fraud, mismanagement or abuse of authority or persistent unfairness toward any shareholders or its property is being misapplied or wasted by its directors or officers.

(5) In the case of any corporation with 35 or fewer shareholders (determined as provided in Section 605), liquidation is reasonably necessary for the protection of the rights or interests of the complaining shareholder or shareholders.

(6) The period for which the corporation was formed has terminated without extension of such period.

(c) At any time prior to the trial of the action any shareholder or creditor may intervene therein.

(d) This section does not apply to any corporation subject to the Banking Law ... , the Public Utilities Act ... , [or] the Savings and Loan Association Law ....

(e) For the purposes of this section, "shareholder" includes a beneficial owner of shares who has entered into an agreement under Section 300 or 706.

§ 1802. Provisional Director; Appointment; Deadlocked Board

If the ground for the complaint for involuntary dissolution of the corporation is a deadlock in the board as set forth in subdivision (b)(2) of Section 1800, the court may appoint a provisional director. The provisions of subdivision (c) of Section 308 apply to any such provisional director so appointed.

§ 1804. Decree for Winding Up and Dissolution; Other Judicial Relief

After hearing the court may decree a winding up and dissolution of the corporation if cause therefor is shown or, with or without winding up and dissolution, may make such orders and decrees and issue such injunctions in the case as justice and equity require.

Chapter 19

VOLUNTARY DISSOLUTION

§ 1900. Election by Shareholders; Required Vote; Election by Board; Grounds

(a) Any corporation may elect voluntarily to wind up and dissolve by the vote of shareholders holding shares representing 50 percent or more of the voting power.

(b) Any corporation which comes within one of the following descriptions may elect by approval by the board to wind up and dissolve:

(1) A corporation ... as to which an order for relief has been entered under Chapter 7 of the federal bankruptcy law.

(2) A corporation which has disposed of all its assets and has not conducted any business for a period of five years immediately preceding the adoption of the resolution electing to dissolve the corporation.

(3) A corporation which has issued no shares.

Chapter 20

GENERAL PROVISIONS RELATING TO DISSOLUTION

§ 2000. Avoidance of Dissolution by Purchase of Plaintiffs' Shares; Valuation; Vote Required; Stay of Dissolution Proceedings; Appraisal Under Court Order; Confirmation by Court; Appeal

(a) Subject to any contrary provision in the articles, in any suit for involuntary dissolution, or in any proceeding for voluntary dissolution initiated by the vote of shareholders representing only 50 percent of the voting power, the corporation or, if it does not elect to purchase, the holders of 50 percent or more of the voting power of the corporation (the "purchasing parties") may avoid the dissolution of the corporation and the appointment of any receiver by purchasing for cash the shares owned by the plaintiffs or by the shareholders so initiating the proceeding (the "moving parties") at their fair value. The fair value shall be determined on the basis of the liquidation value as of the valuation date but taking into account the possibility, if any, of sale of the entire business as a going concern in a liquidation. In fixing the value, the amount of any damages resulting if the initiation of the dissolution is a breach by any moving party or parties of an agreement with the purchasing party or parties may be deducted from the amount payable to such moving party or parties, unless the ground for dissolution is that specified in paragraph (4) of subdivision (b) of Section 1800. The election of the corporation to purchase may be made by the approval of the outstanding shares (Section 152) excluding shares held by the moving parties.

(b) If the purchasing parties (1) elect to purchase the shares owned by the moving parties, and (2) are unable to agree with the moving parties upon the fair value of such shares, and (3) give bond with sufficient security to pay the estimated reasonable expenses (including attorneys' fees) of the moving parties if such expenses are recoverable under subdivision (c), the court upon application of the purchasing parties, either in the pending action or in a proceeding initiated in the superior court of the proper county by the purchasing parties in the case of a voluntary election to wind up and dissolve, shall stay the winding up and dissolution proceeding and shall proceed to ascertain and fix the fair value of the shares owned by the moving parties.

(c) The court shall appoint three disinterested appraisers to appraise the fair value of the shares owned by the moving parties, and shall make an order referring the matter to the appraisers so appointed for the purpose of ascertaining such value. The order shall prescribe the time and manner of producing evidence, if evidence is required. The award of the appraisers or of a majority of them, when confirmed by the court, shall be final and conclusive upon all parties. The court shall enter a decree which shall provide in the alternative for winding up and dissolution of the corporation unless payment is made for the shares within the time specified by the decree. If the purchasing parties do not make payment for the shares within the time specified, judgment shall be entered against them and the surety or sureties on the bond for the amount of the expenses (including attorneys' fees) of the moving parties. Any shareholder aggrieved by the action of the court may appeal therefrom.

(d) If the purchasing parties desire to prevent the winding up and dissolution, they shall pay to the moving parties the value of their shares ascertained and decreed within the time specified pursuant to this section, or, in case of an appeal, as fixed on appeal. On receiving such payment or the tender thereof, the moving parties shall transfer their shares to the purchasing parties.

(e) For the purposes of this section, "shareholder" includes a beneficial owner of shares who has entered into an agreement under Section 300 or 706.

(f) For the purposes of this section, the valuation date shall be (1) in the case of a suit for involuntary dissolution under Section 1800, the date upon which that action was commenced, or (2) in the case of a proceeding for voluntary dissolution initiated by the vote of shareholders representing only 50 percent of the voting power, the date upon which that proceeding was initiated. However, in either case the court may, upon the hearing of a motion by any party, and for good cause shown, designate some other date as the valuation date.

Chapter 21

FOREIGN CORPORATIONS

§ 2115. Foreign Corporations Subject to Corporate Laws of State; Tests to Determine Subject Corporations; Laws Applicable; Time of Application

(a) A foreign corporation (other than a foreign association or foreign nonprofit corporation but including a foreign parent corporation even though it does not itself transact intrastate business) is subject to this section if the average of the property factor, the payroll factor and the sales factor (as defined in Sections 25129, 25132 and 25134 of the Revenue and Taxation Code) with respect to it is more than 50 percent during its latest full income year and if more than one-half of its outstanding voting securities are held of record by persons having addresses in this state. The property factor, payroll factor and sales factor shall be those used in computing the portion of its income allocable to this state in its franchise tax return or, with respect to corporations the allocation of whose income is governed by special formulas or which are not required to file separate or any tax returns, which would have been so used if they were governed by such three-factor formula. The determination of these factors with respect to any parent corporation shall be made on a consolidated basis, including in a unitary computation (after elimination of intercompany transactions) the property, payroll and sales of the parent and all of its subsidiaries in which it owns directly or indirectly more than 50 percent of the outstanding shares entitled to vote for the election of directors, but deducting a percentage of the property, payroll and sales of any subsidiary equal to the percentage minority ownership, if any, in the subsidiary. For the purpose of this subdivision, any securities held to the knowledge of the issuer in the names of broker-dealers or nominees for broker-dealers (including clearing corporations) or banks, associations, or other entities holding securities in a nominee name or otherwise on behalf of a beneficial owner (collectively "Nominee Holders"), shall not be considered outstanding. However, if the foreign corporation requests all Nominee Holders to certify, with respect to all beneficial owners for whom securities are held, the number of shares held for those beneficial owners having addresses (as shown on the records of the Nominee Holder) in this state and outside of this state, then all shares so certified shall be considered outstanding and held of record by persons having addresses either in this state or outside of this state as so certified, provided that the certification so provided shall be retained with the record of shareholders and made available for inspection and copying in the same manner as provided in Section 1600 with respect to that record. A current list of beneficial owners of a foreign corporation's securities provided to the corporation by one or more Nominee Holders or their agent pursuant to the requirements of Rule 14b–1(b)(3) or 14b–2(b)(3) as adopted on January 6, 1992, promulgated under the Securities Exchange Act of 1934 shall constitute an acceptable certification with respect to beneficial owners for the purposes of this subdivision.

(b) The following chapters and sections of this division shall apply to a foreign corporation subject to this section (to the exclusion of the law of the jurisdiction in which it is incorporated):

Chapter 1 (general provisions and definitions), to the extent applicable to the following provisions;

Section 301 (annual election of directors);

Section 303 (removal of directors without cause);

Section 304 (removal of directors by court proceedings);

Section 305, subdivision (c) (filing of director vacancies where less than a majority in office elected by shareholders);

Section 309 (directors' standard of care);

Section 310 (super-majority requirement);

Section 316 (excluding paragraph (3) of subdivision (a) and paragraph (3) of subdivision (f)) (liability of directors for unlawful distributions);

Section 317 (indemnification of directors, officers and others);

Sections 500 to 505, inclusive (limitations on corporate distributions in cash or property);

Section 506 (liability of shareholder who receives unlawful distribution);

Section 600, subdivisions (b) and (c) (requirement for annual shareholders' meeting and remedy if same not timely held);

Section 708, subdivisions (a), (b) and (c) (shareholder's right to cumulate votes at any election of directors);

Section 710 (supermajority vote requirement);

Section 1001, subdivision (d) (limitations on sale of assets);

Section 1101 (provisions following subdivision (e)) (limitations on mergers);

Chapter 12 (commencing with Section 1200) (reorganizations);

Chapter 13 (commencing with Section 1300) (dissenters' rights);

Sections 1500 and 1501 (records and reports);

Section 1508 (action by Attorney General);

Chapter 16 (commencing with Section 1600) (rights of inspection).

(c) Subdivision (a) shall become applicable to any foreign corporation only upon the first day of the first income year of the corporation commencing on or after the 30th day after the filing by it of the report pursuant to Section 2108 [certificate of state connections] showing that the tests referred to in subdivision (a) have been met or on or after the entry of a final order by a court of competent jurisdiction declaring that such tests have been met.

(d) Subdivision (a) shall cease to be applicable at the end of any income year during which a report pursuant to Section 2108 shall have been filed showing that at least one of the tests referred to in subdivision (a) is not met or a final order shall have been entered by a court of competent jurisdiction declaring that one of such tests is not met, provided that such filing or order shall be ineffective if a contrary report or order shall be made or entered before the end of such income year.

(e) This section does not apply to any corporation (1) with outstanding securities listed on the New York Stock Exchange or the American Stock Exchange, or (2) with outstanding securities designated as qualified for trading as a national market security on the National Association of Securities Dealers Automatic Quotation System (or any successor national market system) if such corporation has at least 800 holders of its equity securities as of the record date of its most recent annual meeting of shareholders, or (3) if all of its voting shares (other than directors' qualifying shares) are owned directly or indirectly by a corporation or corporations not subject to this section. For purposes of determining the number of holders of a corporation's equity securities under clause (2) of this subdivision, there shall be included, in addition to the number of recordholders reflected on the corporation's stock records, the number of holders of the equity securities held in the name of any Nominee Holder which furnishes the corporation with a certification pursuant to subdivision (a), provided that the corporation retains the certification with the record of shareholders and makes it available for inspection and copying in the same manner as is provided in Section 1600 with respect to that record.

TITLE 4

SECURITIES

§ 25402. Purchase or Sale of Securities by Person Having Access to Material Information Not Available to Public Through Special Relationship With Issuer

It is unlawful for an issuer or any person who is an officer, director or controlling person of an issuer or any other person whose relationship to the issuer gives him access, directly or indirectly, to material information about the issuer not generally available to the public, to purchase or sell any security of the issuer in this state at a time when he knows material information about the issuer gained from such relationship which would significantly affect the market price of that security and which is not generally available to the public, and which he knows is not intended to be so available, unless he has reason to believe that the person selling to or buying from him is also in possession of the information.

§ 25502. Violation of Section 25402; Damages

Any person who violates Section 25402 shall be liable to the person who purchases a security from him or sells a security to him, for damages equal to the difference between the price at which such security was purchased or sold and the market value which such security would have had at the time of the purchase or sale if the information known to the defendant had been publicly disseminated prior to that time and a reasonable time had elapsed for the market to absorb the information, plus interest at the legal rate, unless the defendant proves that the plaintiff knew the information or that the plaintiff would have purchased or sold at the same price even if the information had been revealed to him.

§ 25502.5 Liability to Issuer of Violator of Insider Trading Prohibitions; Allegation by Shareholder; Consideration by Board

(a) Any person other than the issuer who violates Section 25402 shall be liable to the issuer of the security purchased or sold in violation of Section 25402 for damages in an amount up to three times the difference between the price at which the security was purchased or sold and the market value which the security would have had at the time of the purchase or sale if the information known to the defendant had been publicly disseminated prior to that time and a reasonable time had elapsed for the market to absorb the information and shall be liable to the issuer of the security or to a person who institutes an action under this section in the right of the issuer of the security for reasonable costs and attorney's fees.

(b) The amounts recoverable under this section by the issuer shall be reduced by any amount paid by the defendant in a proceeding brought by the Securities and Exchange Commission with respect to the same transaction or transactions under the federal Insider Trading Sanctions Act of 1984 (15 U.S.C. Secs. 78a, 78c, 78o, 78t, 78u, and 78ff) or any other act regardless of whether the amount was paid pursuant to a judgment or settlement or paid before or after the filing of an action by the plaintiff against the defendant. If a proceeding has been commenced by the Securities and Exchange Commission but has not been finally resolved, the court shall delay entering a judgment for the plaintiff under this section until that proceeding is resolved.

(c) If any shareholder of an issuer alleges to the board that there has been a violation of this section, the board shall be required to consider the allegation in good faith, and if the allegation involves misconduct by any director, that director shall not be entitled to vote on any matter involving the allegation. However, that director may be counted in determining the presence of a quorum at a meeting of the board or a committee of the board.

(d) This section shall only apply to issuers who have total assets in excess of one million dollars ($1,000,000) and have a class of equity security held of record by 500 or more persons.

CONNECTICUT GENERAL STATUTES ANN. § 33–756

§ 33–756. General standards for directors

(a) A director shall discharge his duties as a director, including his duties as a member of a committee: (1) In good faith; (2) with the care an ordinarily prudent person in a like position would exercise under similar circumstances; and (3) in a manner he reasonably believes to be in the best interests of the corporation.

(b) In discharging his duties a director is entitled to rely on information, opinions, reports or statements, including financial statements and other financial data, if prepared or presented by: (1) One or more officers or employees of the corporation whom the director reasonably believes to be reliable and competent in the matters presented; (2) legal counsel, public accountants or other persons as to matters the director reasonably believes are within the person's professional or expert competence; or (3) a committee of the board of directors of which he is not a member if the director reasonably believes the committee merits confidence.

(c) A director is not acting in good faith if he has knowledge concerning the matter in question that makes reliance otherwise permitted by subsection (b) of this section unwarranted.

(d) For purposes of sections 134 [merger], 139 [sale of substantially all assets in the usual course of business], 140 [sale of substantially all assets otherwise than in the regular course of business], 142 [certain business combinations] and 145 [certain business combinations] of this act, a director of a corporation which has a class of voting stock registered pursuant to Section 12 of the Securities Exchange Act of 1934, as the same has been or hereafter may be amended from time to time, in addition to complying with the provisions of subsections (a) to (c), inclusive, of this section, shall consider, in determining what he reasonably believes to be in the best interests of the corporation, (1) the long-term as well as the short-term interests of the corporation, (2) the interests of the shareholders, long-term as well as short-term, including the possibility that those interests may be best served by the continued independence of the corporation, (3) the interests of the corporation's employees, customers, creditors and suppliers, and (4) community and societal considerations including those of any community in which any office or other facility of the corporation is located. A director may also in his discretion consider any other factors he reasonably considers appropriate in determining what he reasonably believes to be in the best interests of the corporation.

(e) A director is not liable for any action taken as a director, or any failure to take any action, if he performed the duties of his office in compliance with this section.

IND. CODE ANN.

[Standards of Conduct for Directors;
Control Share Acquisitions]

Chapter 35

STANDARDS OF CONDUCT FOR DIRECTORS

§ 23-1-35-1 Standards of conduct; liability; reaffirmation of corporate governance rules; presumption

(a) A director shall, based on facts then known to the director, discharge the duties as a director, including the director's duties as a member of a committee:

(1) in good faith;

(2) with the care an ordinarily prudent person in a like position would exercise under similar circumstances; and

(3) in a manner the director reasonably believes to be in the best interests of the corporation.

(b) In discharging the director's duties a director is entitled to rely on information, opinions, reports, or statements, including financial statements and other financial data, if prepared or presented by:

(1) one (1) or more officers or employees of the corporation whom the director reasonably believes to be reliable and competent in the matters presented;

(2) legal counsel, public accountants, or other persons as to matters the director reasonably believes are within the person's professional or expert competence; or

(3) a committee of the board of directors of which the director is not a member if the director reasonably believes the committee merits confidence.

(c) A director is not acting in good faith if the director has knowledge concerning the matter in question that makes reliance otherwise permitted by subsection (b) unwarranted.

(d) A director may, in considering the best interests of a corporation, consider the effects of any action on shareholders, employees, suppliers, and customers of the corporation, and communities in which offices or other facilities of the corporation are located, and any other factors the director considers pertinent.

(e) A director is not liable for any action taken as a director, or any failure to take any action, unless:

(1) the director has breached or failed to perform the duties of the director's office in compliance with this section; and

(2) the breach or failure to perform constitutes willful misconduct or recklessness.

(f) In enacting this article, the general assembly established corporate governance rules for Indiana corporations, including in this chapter, the standards of conduct applicable to directors of Indiana corporations, and the corporate constituent groups and interests that a director may take into account in exercising the director's business judgment. The general assembly intends to reaffirm certain of these corporate governance rules to ensure that the directors of Indiana corporations, in exercising their business judgment, are not required to approve a proposed corporate action if the directors in good faith determine, after considering and weighing as they deem appropriate the effects of such action on the corporation's constituents, that such action is not in the best interests of the corporation. In making such determination, directors are not required to consider the effects of a proposed corporate action on any particular corporate constituent group or interest as a dominant or controlling factor. Without limiting the generality of the foregoing, directors are not required to render inapplicable any of the provisions of [§] 23–1–43 [business combinations], to redeem any rights under or to render inapplicable a shareholder rights plan adopted pursuant to [§] 23–1–26–5 [rights, options or warrants], or to take or decline to take any other action under this article, solely because of the effect such action might have on a proposed acquisition of control of the corporation or the amounts that might be paid to shareholders under such an acquisition. Certain judicial decisions in Delaware and other jurisdictions, which might otherwise be looked to for guidance in interpreting Indiana corporate law, including decisions relating to potential change of control transactions that impose a different or higher degree of scrutiny on actions taken by directors in response to a proposed acquisition of control of the corporation, are inconsistent with the proper application of the business judgment rule under this article. Therefore, the general assembly intends:

(1) to reaffirm that this section allows directors the full discretion to weigh the factors enumerated in subsection (d) as they deem appropriate; and

(2) to protect both directors and the validity of corporate action taken by them in the good faith exercise of their business judgment after reasonable investigation.

(g) In taking or declining to take any action, or in making or declining to make any recommendation to the shareholders of the corporation with respect to any matter, a board of directors may, in its discretion, consider both the short term and long term best interests of the corporation, taking into account, and weighing as the directors deem appropriate, the effects thereof on the corporation's shareholders and the other corporate constituent groups and interests listed or described in subsection (d), as well as any other factors deemed pertinent by the directors under subsection (d). If a determination is made with respect to the foregoing with the approval of a majority of the disinterested directors of the board of directors, that determination shall conclusively be presumed to be valid unless it can be demonstrated that the determination was not made in good faith after reasonable investigation.

(h) For the purposes of subsection (g), a director is disinterested if:

(1) the director does not have a conflict of interest, within the meaning of section 2 of this chapter [conflict-of-interest transactions], in connection with the action or recommendation in question;

(2) in connection with matters described in [§] 23–1–32 [derivative actions] the director is disinterested (as defined in [§] 23–1–32–4(d);

(3) in connection with any matter involving or otherwise affecting:

(A) a control share acquisition (as defined in [§] 23–1–42–2) or any matter related to a control share acquisition ...;

(B) a business combination (as defined in [§] 23–1–43–5) or any matter related to a business combination ...;

(C) any transaction that may result in a change of control (as defined in [§] 23–1–22–4) of the corporation;

the director is not an employee of the corporation; and

(4) in connection with any matter involving or otherwise affecting:

(A) a control share acquisition (as defined in [§] 23–1–42–2) or any matter related to a control share acquisition ...;

(B) a business combination (as defined in [§] 23–1–43–5) or any matter related to a business combination ...;

(C) any transaction that may result in a change of control (as defined in [§] 23–1–22–4) of the corporation;

the director is not an affiliate or associate of, or was not nominated or designated as a director by, a person proposing any of the transactions described in clause (A), (B), or (C).

(i) A person may be disinterested under this section even though the person is a director or shareholder of the corporation....

Chapter 42

CONTROL SHARE ACQUISITIONS

§ 23–1–42–1 "Control shares" defined

As used in this chapter, "control shares" means shares that, except for this chapter, would have voting power with respect to shares of an issuing public corporation that, when added to all other shares of the issuing public corporation owned by a person or in respect to which that person may exercise or direct the exercise of voting power, would entitle that person, immediately after acquisition of the shares (directly or indirectly, alone or as a part of a group), to exercise or direct the exercise of the voting power of the issuing public corporation in the election of directors within any of the following ranges of voting power:

(1) One-fifth (⅕) or more but less than one-third (⅓) of all voting power.

(2) One-third (⅓) or more but less than a majority of all voting power.

(3) A majority or more of all voting power.

§ 23–1–42–2 "Control share acquisition" defined

(a) As used in this chapter, "control share acquisition" means the acquisition (directly or indirectly) by any person of ownership of, or the power to direct the exercise of voting power with respect to, issued and outstanding control shares.

(b) For purposes of this section, shares acquired within ninety (90) days or shares acquired pursuant to a plan to make a control share acquisition are considered to have been acquired in the same acquisition.

(c) For purposes of this section, a person who acquires shares in the ordinary course of business for the benefit of others in good faith and not for the purpose of circumventing this chapter has voting power only of

746

shares in respect of which that person would be able to exercise or direct the exercise of votes without further instruction from others.

(d) The acquisition of any shares of an issuing public corporation does not constitute a control share acquisition if the acquisition is consummated in any of the following circumstances: . . .

(3) Pursuant to the laws of descent and distribution.

(4) Pursuant to the satisfaction of a pledge or other security interest created in good faith and not for the purpose of circumventing this chapter.

(5) Pursuant to a merger or plan of share exchange effected in compliance with [Indiana Code] 23–1–40 [merger and share exchange] if the issuing public corporation is a party to the agreement of merger or plan of share exchange.

(e) The acquisition of shares of an issuing public corporation in good faith and not for the purpose of circumventing this chapter by or from:

(1) any person whose voting rights had previously been authorized by shareholders in compliance with this chapter; or

(2) any person whose previous acquisition of shares of an issuing public corporation would have constituted a control share acquisition but for subsection (d);

does not constitute a control share acquisition, unless the acquisition entitles any person (directly or indirectly, alone or as a part of a group) to exercise or direct the exercise of voting power of the corporation in the election of directors in excess of the range of the voting power otherwise authorized.

§ 23–1–42–3 "Interested shares" defined

As used in this chapter, "interested shares" means the shares of an issuing public corporation in respect of which any of the following persons may exercise or direct the exercise of the voting power of the corporation in the election of directors:

(1) An acquiring person or member of a group with respect to a control share acquisition.

(2) Any officer of the issuing public corporation.

(3) Any employee of the issuing public corporation who is also a director of the corporation.

§ 23–1–42–4 "Issuing public corporation" defined

(a) As used in this chapter, "issuing public corporation" means a corporation that has:

(1) one hundred (100) or more shareholders;

(2) its principal place of business, its principal office, or substantial assets within Indiana; and

(3) either:

(A) more than ten percent (10%) of its shareholders resident in Indiana;

(B) more than ten percent (10%) of its shares owned by Indiana residents; or

(C) ten thousand (10,000) shareholders resident in Indiana.

(b) The residence of a shareholder is presumed to be the address appearing in the records of the corporation.

(c) Shares held by banks (except as trustee or guardian), brokers or nominees shall be disregarded for purposes of calculating the percentages or numbers described in this section.*

§ 23–1–42–5 Voting rights under [§] 23–1–42–9

Unless the corporation's articles of incorporation or bylaws provide that this chapter does not apply to control share acquisitions of shares of the corporation before the control share acquisition, control shares of an issuing public corporation acquired in a control share acquisition have only such voting rights as are conferred by section 9 of this chapter.

§ 23–1–42–6 Acquiring person statement

Any person who proposes to make or has made a control share acquisition may at the person's election deliver an acquiring person statement to the issuing public corporation at the issuing public corporation's principal office. The acquiring person statement must set forth all of the following:

(1) The identity of the acquiring person and each other member of any group of which the person is a part for purposes of determining control shares.

(2) A statement that the acquiring person statement is given pursuant to this chapter.

(3) The number of shares of the issuing public corporation owned (directly or indirectly) by the acquiring person and each other member of the group.

(4) The range of voting power under which the control share acquisition falls or would, if consummated, fall.

(5) If the control share acquisition has not taken place:

(A) a description in reasonable detail of the terms of the proposed control share acquisition; and

* Under   § 23–1–20–5,   "corporation"   Indiana. [Footnote by ed.]
means   a   corporation   incorporated   in

(B) representations of the acquiring person, together with a statement in reasonable detail of the facts upon which they are based, that the proposed control share acquisition, if consummated, will not be contrary to law, and that the acquiring person has the financial capacity to make the proposed control share acquisition.

§ 23–1–42–7 Special meeting of shareholders

(a) If the acquiring person so requests at the time of delivery of an acquiring person statement and gives an undertaking to pay the corporation's expenses of a special meeting, within ten (10) days thereafter, the directors of the issuing public corporation shall call a special meeting of shareholders of the issuing public corporation for the purpose of considering the voting rights to be accorded the shares acquired or to be acquired in the control share acquisition.

(b) Unless the acquiring person agrees in writing to another date, the special meeting of shareholders shall be held within fifty (50) days after receipt by the issuing public corporation of the request.

(c) If no request is made, the voting rights to be accorded the shares acquired in the control share acquisition shall be presented to the next special or annual meeting of shareholders.

(d) If the acquiring person so requests in writing at the time of delivery of the acquiring person statement, the special meeting must not be held sooner than thirty (30) days after receipt by the issuing public corporation of the acquiring person statement.

§ 23–1–42–8 Notice

(a) If a special meeting is requested, notice of the special meeting of shareholders shall be given as promptly as reasonably practicable by the issuing public corporation to all shareholders of record as of the record date set for the meeting, whether or not entitled to vote at the meeting.

(b) Notice of the special or annual shareholder meeting at which the voting rights are to be considered must include or be accompanied by both of the following:

(1) A copy of the acquiring person statement delivered to the issuing public corporation pursuant to this chapter.

(2) A statement by the board of directors of the corporation, authorized by its directors, of its position or recommendation, or that it is taking no position or making no recommendation, with respect to the proposed control share acquisition.

§ 23–1–42–9 Voting rights of acquired control shares; resolution

(a) Control shares acquired in a control share acquisition have the same voting rights as were accorded the shares before the control share acquisition only to the extent granted by resolution approved by the shareholders of the issuing public corporation.

(b) To be approved under this section, the resolution must be approved by:

(1) each voting group entitled to vote separately on the proposal by a majority of all the votes entitled to be cast by that voting group, with the holders of the outstanding shares of a class being entitled to vote as a separate voting group if the proposed control share acquisition would, if fully carried out, result in any of the changes described in [Indiana Code] 23–1–38–4(a) [class voting on amendments]; and

(2) each voting group entitled to vote separately on the proposal by a majority of all the votes entitled to be cast by that group, excluding all interested shares.

§ 23–1–42–10   Redemption of acquired control shares

(a) If authorized in a corporation's articles of incorporation or bylaws before a control share acquisition has occurred, control shares acquired in a control share acquisition with respect to which no acquiring person statement has been filed with the issuing public corporation may, at any time during the period ending sixty (60) days after the last acquisition of control shares by the acquiring person, be subject to redemption by the corporation at the fair value thereof pursuant to the procedures adopted by the corporation.

(b) Control shares acquired in a control share acquisition are not subject to redemption after an acquiring person statement has been filed unless the shares are not accorded full voting rights by the shareholders as provided in section 9 of this chapter.

§ 23–1–42–11   Dissenters' rights; "fair value" defined

(a) Unless otherwise provided in a corporation's articles of incorporation or bylaws before a control share acquisition has occurred, in the event control shares acquired in a control share acquisition are accorded full voting rights and the acquiring person has acquired control shares with a majority or more of all voting power, all shareholders of the issuing public corporation have dissenters' rights as provided in this chapter.

(b) As soon as practicable after such events have occurred, the board of directors shall cause a notice to be sent to all shareholders of the corporation advising them of the facts and that they have dissenters' rights to receive the fair value of their shares pursuant to [Indiana Code] 23–1–44 [dissenters' rights].

(c) As used in this section, "fair value" means a value not less than the highest price paid per share by the acquiring person in the control share acquisition.

MARYLAND ANN. CODE CORPORATIONS AND ASSOCIATIONS, TITLE 4

[Close Corporations]

TITLE 4.

CLOSE CORPORATIONS.

751

Subtitle 1.   Definitions; General Provisions.

§ 4–101. Definitions

(a) *In general.*—In this title the following words have the meanings indicated.

(b) *Close corporation.*—"Close corporation" means a corporation which elects to be a close corporation in accordance with § 4–201 of this title.

(c) *Unanimous stockholders' agreement.*—"Unanimous stockholders' agreement" means an agreement to which every stockholder of a close corporation actually has assented and which is contained in its charter or bylaws or in a written instrument signed by all the stockholders.

§ 4–102. Execution of documents

Notwithstanding any contrary provision of law, an individual who holds more than one office in a close corporation may act in more than one capacity to execute, acknowledge, or verify any instrument required to be executed, acknowledged, or verified by more than one officer.

Subtitle 2.   Election to Be a Close Corporation.

§ 4–201. Statement of election

(a) *Statement to be contained in charter.*—A corporation may elect to be a close corporation under this title by including in its charter a statement that it is a close corporation.

(b) *Procedure.*—The statement that a corporation is a close corporation shall be:

(1) Contained in the articles of incorporation originally filed with the Department; or

(2) Added to the charter by an amendment which is approved:

(i) Under the provisions of § 2–603 [Charter amendment— No stock outstanding or subscribed for] of this article, if at the time of the adoption of the amendment no stock of the corporation is either outstanding or subscribed for; or

(ii) By the affirmative vote of every stockholder and every subscriber for stock of the corporation.

§ 4–202. Required references to close corporation status

(a) *Clear reference required.*—Clear reference to the fact that the corporation is a close corporation shall appear prominently:

(1) At the head of the charter document in which the election to be a close corporation is made;

(2) In each subsequent charter document of the corporation; and

(3) On each certificate representing outstanding stock of the corporation.

(b) *Absence of reference.*—The status of a corporation as a close corporation is not affected by the failure of any charter document or stock certificate to contain the reference required by this section.

§ 4–203. Removal of statement from charter

The charter of a close corporation may be amended to remove the statement of election to be a close corporation, but only by the affirmative vote of every stockholder and every subscriber for stock of the corporation.

Subtitle 3. Board of Directors.

§ 4–301. At least one director required initially

A close corporation shall have at least one director until an election by the corporation in its charter to have no board of directors becomes effective.

§ 4–302. Election to have no board of directors

(a) *Effective time of election.*—An election to have no board of directors becomes effective at the later of:

(1) The time that the organization meeting of directors and the issuance of at least one share of stock of the corporation are completed;

(2) The time the charter document in which the election is made becomes effective; or

(3) The time specified in the charter document in which the election is made.

(b) *Cessation of director's status.*—A director automatically ceases to be a director when an election to have no board of directors becomes effective.

§ 4–303. Effect of election to have no board of directors

If there is an election to have no board of directors:

(1) The stockholders may exercise all powers of directors, and the business and affairs of the corporation shall be managed under their direction;

(2) The stockholders of the corporation are responsible for taking any action required by law to be taken by the board of directors;

(3) Action by stockholders shall be taken by the voting of shares of stock as provided in this article;

(4) The stockholders may take any action for which this article otherwise would require both a resolution of directors and a vote of stockholders;

(5) By the affirmative vote of a majority of all the votes entitled to be cast, the stockholders may take any action for which this article otherwise would require a vote of a majority of the entire board of directors;

(6) A statement that the corporation is a close corporation which has no board of directors satisfies any requirement that an instrument filed with the Department contain a statement that a specified action was taken by the board of directors;

(7) The special liabilities imposed on directors by § 2–312(a) of this article and the provisions of §§ 2–312(b) and 2–410 of this article apply to the stockholders of the corporation and, for this purpose, "present" in § 2–410 of this article means present in person or by proxy *; and

(8) A stockholder is not liable for any action taken as a result of a vote of the stockholders, unless he was entitled to vote on the action.

Subtitle 4.　Stockholders.

§ 4–401.　Unanimous stockholders' agreement

(a) *Governing the corporation.*—Under a unanimous stockholders' agreement, the stockholders of a close corporation may regulate any aspect of the affairs of the corporation or the relations of the stockholders, including:

(1) The management of the business and affairs of the corporation;

(2) Restrictions on the transfer of stock;

(3) The right of one or more stockholders to dissolve the corporation at will or on the occurrence of a specified event or contingency;

* Section 2–312 concerns the liability of directors.　Section 2–410 concerns the dissent of a director to an action of the board. (Footnote by ed.)

(4) The exercise or division of voting power;

(5) The terms and conditions of employment of an officer or employee of the corporation, without regard to the period of his employment;

(6) The individuals who are to be directors and officers of the corporation; and

(7) The payment of dividends or the division of profits.

(b) *Amending unanimous stockholders' agreement.*—A unanimous stockholders' agreement may be amended, but only by the unanimous written consent of the stockholders then parties to the agreement.

(c) *Acquisition of stock subject to unanimous stockholders' agreement.*—A stockholder who acquires his stock after a unanimous stockholders' agreement becomes effective is considered to have actually assented to the agreement and is a party to it:

(1) Whether or not he has actual knowledge of the existence of the agreement at the time he acquires the stock, if acquired by gift or bequest from a person who was a party to the agreement; and

(2) If he has actual knowledge of the existence of the agreement at the time he acquires the stock, if acquired in any other manner.

(d) *Enforcement of unanimous stockholders' agreement.*—(1) A court of equity may enforce a unanimous stockholders' agreement by injunction or by any other relief which the court in its discretion determines to be fair and appropriate in the circumstances.

(2) As an alternative to the granting of an injunction or other equitable relief, on motion of a party to the proceeding, the court may order dissolution of the corporation under the provisions of Subtitle 6 of this title.

(e) *Inapplicability of section to other agreements.*—This section does not affect any otherwise valid agreement among stockholders of a close corporation or of any other corporation.

§ 4–402. Stockholders' annual meeting

(a) *General rule.*—The bylaws of a close corporation shall provide for an annual meeting of stockholders in accordance with Title 2 of this article, but the meeting need not be held unless requested by a stockholder.

(b) *Written request for annual meeting.*—A request for an annual meeting shall be in writing and delivered to the president or secretary of the corporation:

(1) At least 30 days before the date specified in the bylaws for the meeting; or

(2) If the bylaws specify a period during which the date for the meeting may be set, at least 30 days before the beginning of that period.

§ 4–403. Stockholders' right of inspection

A stockholder of a close corporation or his agent may inspect and copy during usual business hours any records or documents of the corporation relevant to its business and affairs, including any:

(1) Bylaws;

(2) Minutes of the proceedings of the stockholders and directors;

(3) Annual statement of affairs;

(4) Stock ledger; and

(5) Books of account.

§ 4–404. Statement of affairs

(a) *Stockholders' right to request.*—Once during each calendar year, each stockholder of a close corporation may present to any officer of the corporation a written request for a statement of its affairs.

(b) *Duty to prepare and file; verification.*—Within 20 days after a request is made for a statement of a close corporation's affairs, the corporation shall prepare and have available on file at its principal office a statement verified under oath by its president or treasurer or one of its vice-presidents or assistant treasurers which sets forth in reasonable detail the corporation's assets and liabilities as of a reasonably current date.

Subtitle 5.   Stock Restrictions.

§ 4–501. Restriction on issuance or sale of stock

If there is any stock of a close corporation outstanding, the corporation may not issue or sell any of its stock, including treasury stock, unless the issuance or sale is:

(1) Approved by the affirmative vote of the holders of all outstanding stock; or

(2) Permitted by a unanimous stockholders' agreement.

§ 4–502. Certain securities and stock options prohibited

A close corporation may not have outstanding any:

(1) Securities which are convertible into its stock;

(2) Voting securities other than stock; or

(3) Options, warrants, or other rights to subscribe for or purchase any of its stock, unless they are nontransferable.

§ 4–503. Restrictions on transfer of stock

(a) *"Transfer" defined.*—(1) In this section, "transfer" means the transfer of any interest in the stock of a close corporation, except:

(i) A transfer by operation of law to a personal representative, trustee in bankruptcy, receiver, guardian, or similar legal representative;

(ii) The acquisition of a lien or power of sale by an attachment, levy, or similar procedure; or

(iii) The creation or assignment of a security interest.

(2) A foreclosure sale or other transfer by a person who acquired his interest or power in a transaction described in paragraph (1) of this subsection is a transfer subject to all the provisions of this section. For purposes of the transfer, the person effecting the foreclosure sale or other transfer shall be treated as and have the rights of a holder of the stock under this section and § 4–602(b) of this title.

(b) *Enumeration of restrictions.*—A transfer of the stock of a close corporation is invalid unless:

(1) Every stockholder of the corporation consents to the transfer in writing within the 90 days before the date of the transfer; or

(2) The transfer is made under a provision of a unanimous stockholders' agreement permitting the transfer to the corporation or to or in trust for the principal benefit of:

(i) One or more of the stockholders or security holders of the corporation or their wives, children, or grandchildren; or

(ii) One or more persons named in the agreement.

§ 4–504. Denial or restriction of voting rights; unanimous stockholder vote

(a) *Denial or restriction of voting rights.*—A close corporation may deny or restrict the voting rights of any of its stock as provided in this article. Notwithstanding any denial or restriction, all stock has voting rights on any matter required by this title to be authorized by the affirmative vote of every stockholder or every subscriber for stock of a close corporation.

(b) *Unanimous stockholder vote.*—Notwithstanding the provisions of § 2–104(b)(5) * of this article, the charter of a close corporation may not lower the proportion of votes required to approve any action for which this title requires the affirmative vote or assent of every stockholder or every subscriber for stock of the corporation.

* Section 2–104(b)(5) provides that the articles of incorporation may include certain provisions that reduce the shareholder note that would otherwise be required. (Footnote by ed.)

Subtitle 6.　Termination of Existence.

§ 4–601. Consolidation, merger, share exchange, or transfer of assets

A consolidation, merger, share exchange, or transfer of assets of a close corporation shall be made in accordance with the provisions of Title 3 of this article [Extraordinary Actions]. However, approval of a proposed consolidation or merger, a transfer of its assets, or an acquisition of its stock in a share exchange requires the affirmative vote of every stockholder of the corporation.

§ 4–602. Involuntary dissolution

(a) *Dissolution by stockholder generally.*—Any stockholder of a close corporation may petition a court of equity for dissolution of the corporation on the grounds set forth in § 3–413 of this article [Grounds for petition for involuntary dissolution] or on the ground that there is such internal dissension among the stockholders of the corporation that the business and affairs of the corporation can no longer be conducted to the advantage of the stockholders generally.

(b) *Dissolution by stockholder desiring to transfer stock.*—(1) Unless a unanimous stockholders' agreement provides otherwise, a stockholder of a close corporation has the right to require dissolution of the corporation if:

(i) The stockholder made a written request for consent to a proposed bona fide transfer of his stock in accordance with the provisions of § 4–503(b)(1) of this title, specifying the proposed transferee and consideration, and the consent was not received by him within 30 days after the date of the request; or

(ii) Another party to a unanimous stockholders' agreement defaulted in an obligation, set forth in or arising under the agreement, to purchase or cause to be purchased stock of the stockholder, and the default was not remedied within 30 days after the date for performance of the obligation.

(2) A petition for dissolution under this subsection shall be filed within 60 days after the date of the request or the default, as the case may be.

(c) *Proceeding to be in accordance with § 3–414.*—A proceeding for dissolution authorized by this section shall be in accordance with the provisions of § 3–414 of this article [Appointment of receiver in involuntary dissolution].

§ 4–603. Avoidance of dissolution by purchase of petitioner's stock

(a) *Stockholder's right to avoid dissolution.*—Any one or more stockholders who desire to continue the business of a close corporation may avoid the dissolution of the corporation or the appointment of a receiver by electing to purchase the stock owned by the petitioner at a price equal to its fair value.

(b) *Court to determine fair value of stock.*—

(1) If a stockholder who makes the election is unable to reach an agreement with the petitioner as to the fair value of the stock, then, if the electing stockholder gives bond or other security sufficient to assure payment to the petitioner of the fair value of the stock, the court shall stay the proceeding and determine the fair value of the stock.

(2) Fair value shall be determined in accordance with the procedure set forth in Title 3, Subtitle 2 of this article [Rights of Objecting Shareholders], as of the close of business on the day on which the petition for dissolution was filed.

(c) *Court order.*—After the fair value of the stock is determined, the order of the court directing the purchase shall set the purchase price and the time within which payment shall be made. The court may order other appropriate terms and conditions of sale, including:

(1) Payment of the purchase price in installments; and

(2) The allocation of shares of stock among electing stockholders.

(d) *Interest on purchase price; cessation of other rights.*—The petitioner:

(1) Is entitled to interest on the purchase price of his stock from the date the petition is filed; and

(2) Ceases to have any other rights with respect to the stock, except the right to receive payment of its fair value.

(e) *Costs of proceeding.*—The costs of the proceeding, as determined by the court, shall be divided between the petitioner and the purchasing stockholder. The costs shall include the reasonable compensation and expenses of appraisers, but may not include fees and expenses of counsel or of other experts retained by a party.

(f) *Transfer of stock.*—The petitioner shall transfer his shares of stock to the purchasing stockholder:

(1) At a time set by the court; or

(2) If the court sets no time, at the time the purchase price is paid in full.

MICH. COMP. LAWS § 450.1489

450.1489. Shareholders' actions; relief; exclusions

Sec. 489. (1) A shareholder may bring an action in the circuit court of the county in which the principal place of business or registered office of the corporation is located, to establish that the acts of the directors or those in control of the corporation are illegal, fraudulent, or willfully unfair and oppressive to the corporation, or to the shareholder. If the shareholder establishes grounds for relief, the circuit court may make an order or grant relief as it considers appropriate, including, without limitation, an order providing for any of the following:

(a) The dissolution and liquidation of the assets and business of the corporation.

(b) The cancellation or alteration of a provision contained in the articles of incorporation, or an amendment of the articles, or in the bylaws of the corporation.

(c) The cancellation, alteration, or injunction against a resolution or other act of the corporation.

(d) The direction or prohibition of an act of the corporation or of shareholders, directors, officers, or other persons party to the action.

(e) The purchase at fair value of the shares of a shareholder, either by the corporation or by the officers, directors, or other shareholders responsible for the wrongful acts.

(f) Award of damages to the corporation or a shareholder.

(2) No action under this section shall be brought by a shareholder whose shares are listed on a national securities exchange or regularly quoted in an over-the-counter market by 1 or more members of a national or affiliated securities association.

MINNESOTA STATS. ANN. § 302A.751

302A.751. Judicial intervention; equitable remedies or dissolution

Subdivision 1. When permitted. A court may grant any equitable relief it deems just and reasonable in the circumstances or may dissolve a corporation and liquidate its assets and business:

(a) In a supervised voluntary dissolution pursuant to section 302A.741;

(b) In an action by a shareholder when it is established that:

(1) the directors or the persons having the authority otherwise vested in the board are deadlocked in the management of the corporate affairs and the shareholders are unable to break the deadlock;

(2) the directors or those in control of the corporation have acted fraudulently or illegally toward one or more shareholders in their capacities as shareholders or directors, or as officers or employees of a closely held corporation;

(3) the directors or those in control of the corporation have acted in a manner unfairly prejudicial toward one or more shareholders in their capacities as shareholders or directors of a corporation that is not a publicly held corporation, or as officers or employees of a closely held corporation;

(4) the shareholders of the corporation are so divided in voting power that, for a period the includes the time when two consecutive regular meetings were held, they have failed to elect successors to directors whose terms have expired or would have expired upon the election and qualification of their successors;

(5) the corporate assets are being misapplied or wasted; or

(6) the period of duration as provided in the articles has expired and has not been extended as provided in section 302A.801;

(c) In an action by a creditor when:

(1) the claim of the creditor has been reduced to judgment and an execution thereon has been returned unsatisfied; or

(2) the corporation has admitted in writing that the claim of the creditor is due and owing and it is established that the corporation is unable to pay its debts in the ordinary course of business; or

(d) In an action by the attorney general to dissolve the corporation in accordance with section 302A.757 when it is established that a decree of dissolution is appropriate.

Subd. 2. Buy-out on motion. In an action under subdivision 1, clause (b), involving a corporation that is not a publicly held corporation at the time the action is commenced and in which one or more of the circumstances described in that clause is established, the court may, upon motion of a corporation or a shareholder or beneficial owner of shares of the corporation, order the sale by plaintiff or a defendant of all shares of the corporation held by the plaintiff or defendant to either the corporation or the moving shareholders, whichever is specified in the motion, if the court determines in its discretion that an order would be fair and equitable to all parties under all of the circumstances of the case.

The purchase price of any shares so sold shall be the fair value of the shares as of the date of the commencement of the action or as of another date found equitable by the court, provided that, if the shares in question are then subject to sale and purchase pursuant to the bylaws of the corporation, a shareholder control agreement, the terms of the shares, or otherwise, the court shall order the sale for the price and on the terms set forth in them, unless the court determines that the price or terms are unreasonable under all the circumstances of the case.

Within five days after the entry of the order, the corporation shall provide each selling shareholder or beneficial owner with the information it is required to provide under section 302A.473, subdivision 5, paragraph (a).

If the parties are unable to agree on fair value within 40 days of entry of the order, the court shall determine the fair value of the shares under the provisions of section 302A.473, subdivision 7, and may allow interest or costs as provided in section 302A.473, subdivisions 1 and 8.

The purchase price shall be paid in one or more installments as agreed on by the parties, or, if no agreement can be reached within 40 days of entry of the order, as ordered by the court. Upon entry of an order for the sale of shares under this subdivision and provided that the corporation or the moving shareholders post a bond in adequate amount with sufficient sureties or otherwise satisfy the court that the full purchase price of the shares, plus such additional costs, expenses, and fees as may be awarded, will be paid when due and payable, the selling shareholders shall no longer have any rights or status as shareholders, officers, or directors, except the right to receive the fair value of their shares plus such other amounts as might be awarded.

Subd. 3. Condition of corporation. In determining whether to order equitable relief, dissolution, or a buy-out, the court shall take into consideration the financial condition of the corporation but shall not refuse to order equitable relief, dissolution, or a buy-out solely on the ground that the corporation has accumulated or current operating profits.

Subd. 3a. Considerations in granting relief involving closely held corporations. In determining whether to order equitable relief, dissolution, or a buy-out, the court shall take into consideration the duty which all shareholders in a closely held corporation owe one another to act in an honest, fair, and reasonable manner in the operation of the corporation and the reasonable expectations of all shareholders as they exist at the inception and develop during the course of the shareholders' relationship with the corporation and with each other. For purposes of this section, any written agreements, including employment agreements and buy-sell agreements, between or among shareholders or between or among one or more shareholders and the corporation are presumed to reflect the parties' reasonable expectations concerning matters dealt with in the agreements.

Subd. 3b. Dissolution as remedy. In deciding whether to order dissolution, the court shall consider whether lesser relief suggested by one or more parties, such as any form of equitable relief, a buy-out, or a partial liquidation, would be adequate to permanently relieve the circumstances established under subdivision 1, clause (b) or (c). Lesser relief may be ordered in any case where it would be appropriate under all the facts and circumstances of the case.

Subd. 4. Expenses. If the court finds that a party to a proceeding brought under this section has acted arbitrarily, vexatiously, or otherwise not in good faith, it may in its discretion award reasonable expenses, including attorneys' fees and disbursements, to any of the other parties.

Subd. 5. Venue; parties. Proceedings under this section shall be brought in a court within the county in which the registered office of the corporation is located. It is not necessary to make shareholders parties to the action or proceeding unless relief is sought against them personally.

NEW YORK BUSINESS CORPORATION LAW (SELECTED PROVISIONS)

ARTICLE 1. SHORT TITLE; DEFINITIONS; APPLICATION; CERTIFICATES; MISCELLANEOUS

ARTICLE 4. FORMATION OF CORPORATIONS

ARTICLE 5. CORPORATE FINANCE

ARTICLE 6. SHAREHOLDERS

ARTICLE 1

SHORT TITLE; DEFINITIONS; APPLICATION; CERTIFICATES; MISCELLANEOUS

§ 102. Definitions

(a) As used in this chapter, unless the context otherwise requires, the term....

(2) "Capital surplus" means the surplus other than earned surplus....

(6) "Earned surplus" means the portion of the surplus that represents the net earnings, gains or profits, after deduction of all losses, that have not been distributed to the shareholders as dividends, or transferred to stated capital or capital surplus, or applied to other purposes permitted by law. Unrealized appreciation of assets is not included in earned surplus....

(8) "Insolvent" means being unable to pay debts as they become due in the usual course of the debtor's business.

(9) "Net assets" means the amount by which the total assets exceed the total liabilities. Stated capital and surplus are not liabilities....

(12) "Stated capital" means the sum of (A) the par value of all shares with par value that have been issued, (B) the amount of the consideration received for all shares without par value that have been issued, except such part of the consideration therefor as may have been allocated to surplus in a manner permitted by law, and (C) such amounts not included in clauses (A) and (B) as have been transferred to stated capital, whether upon the distribution of shares or otherwise, minus all reductions from such sums as have been effected in a manner permitted by law.

(13) "Surplus" means the excess of net assets over stated capital.

(14) "Treasury shares" means shares which have been issued, have been subsequently acquired, and are retained uncancelled by the corporation. Treasury shares are issued shares, but not outstanding shares, and are not assets....

ARTICLE 4

FORMATION OF CORPORATIONS

§ 402. Certificate of Incorporation; Contents

(a) A certificate, entitled "Certificate of incorporation of _____ (name of corporation) under section 402 of the Business Corporation Law", shall be signed by each incorporator, with his name and address stated beneath or opposite his signature, acknowledged and delivered to the department of state. It shall set forth:

(1) The name of the corporation.

(2) The purpose or purposes for which it is formed, it being sufficient to state, either alone or with other purposes, that the purpose of the corporation is to engage in any lawful act or activity for which corporations may be organized under this chapter, provided that it also state that it is not formed to engage in any act or activity requiring the consent or approval of any state official, department, board, agency or other body without such consent or approval first being obtained. By such statement all lawful acts and activities shall be within the purposes of the corporation, except for express limitations therein or in this chapter, if any.

(3) The county within this state in which the office of the corporation is to be located.

(4) The aggregate number of shares which the corporation shall have the authority to issue; if such shares are to consist of one class only, the par value of the shares or a statement that the shares are without par value; or, if the shares are to be divided into classes, the number of shares of each class and the par value of the shares having par value and a statement as to which shares, if any, are without par value.

(5) If the shares are to be divided into classes, the designation of each class and a statement of the relative rights, preferences and limitations of the shares of each class.

(6) If the shares of any preferred class are to be issued in series, the designation of each series and a statement of the variations in the relative rights, preferences and limitations as between series insofar as the same are to be fixed in the certificate of incorporation, and a statement of any authority to be vested in the board to establish and designate series and to fix the variations in the relative rights, preferences and limitations as between series.

(7) A designation of the secretary of state as agent of the corporation upon whom process against it may be served and the post office address within or without this state to which the secretary of state shall mail a copy of any process against it served upon him.

(8) If the corporation is to have a registered agent, his name and address within this state and a statement that the registered agent is to be the agent of the corporation upon whom process against it may be served.

(9) The duration of the corporation if other than perpetual.

(b) The certificate of incorporation may set forth a provision eliminating or limiting the personal liability of directors to the corporation or its shareholders for damages for any breach of duty in such capacity, provided that no such provision shall eliminate or limit:

(1) the liability of any director if a judgment or other final adjudication adverse to him establishes that his acts or omissions were in bad faith or involved intentional misconduct or a knowing violation of law or that he personally gained in fact a financial profit or other advantage to which he was not legally entitled or that his acts violated section 719, or

(2) the liability of any director for any act or omission prior to the adoption of a provision authorized by this paragraph.

(c) The certificate of incorporation may set forth any provision, not inconsistent with this chapter or any other statute of this state, relating to the business of the corporation, its affairs, its rights or powers, or the rights or powers of its shareholders, directors or officers including any provision relating to matters which under this chapter are required or permitted to be set forth in the by-laws. It is not necessary to set forth in the certificate of incorporation any of the powers enumerated in this chapter.

ARTICLE 5

CORPORATE FINANCE

§ 501. Authorized Shares

(a) Every corporation shall have power to create and issue the number of shares stated in its certificate of incorporation. Such shares may be all of one class or may be divided into two or more classes. Each class shall consist of either shares with par value or shares without par value, having such designation and such relative voting, dividend, liquidation and other rights, preferences and limitations, consistent with this chapter, as shall be stated in the certificate of incorporation. The certificate of incorporation may deny, limit or otherwise define the voting rights and may limit or otherwise define the dividend or liquidation rights of shares of any class, but no such denial, limitation or definition of voting rights shall be effective unless at the time one or more classes of outstanding shares or bonds, singly or in the aggregate, are entitled to full voting rights, and no such limitation or definition of dividend or liquidation rights shall be effective unless at the time one or more classes of outstanding shares, singly or in the aggregate, are entitled to unlimited dividend and liquidation rights.

(b) If the shares are divided into two or more classes, the shares of each class shall be designated to distinguish them from the shares of all other classes. Shares which are entitled to preference in the distribution of dividends or assets shall not be designated as common shares. Shares which are not entitled to preference in the distribution of dividends or assets shall be common shares, even if identified by a class or other designation, and shall not be designated as preferred shares.

(c) Subject to the designations, relative rights, preferences and limitations applicable to separate series and except as otherwise permitted by subparagraph two of paragraph (a) of section five hundred five of this article, each share shall be equal to every other share of the same class....

§ 504. Consideration and Payment for Shares

(a) Consideration for the issue of shares shall consist of money or other property, tangible or intangible, or labor or services actually received by or performed for the corporation or for its benefit or in its formation or reorganization, or a combination thereof. In the absence of fraud in the transaction, the judgment of the board or shareholders, as the case may be, as to the value of the consideration received for shares shall be conclusive.

(b) Neither obligations of the subscriber for future payments nor future services shall constitute payment or part payment for shares of a corporation.

(c) Shares with par value may be issued for such consideration, not less than the par value thereof, as is fixed from time to time by the board.

(d) Shares without par value may be issued for such consideration as is fixed from time to time by the board unless the certificate of incorporation reserves to the shareholders the right to fix the consideration. If such right is reserved as to any shares, a vote of the shareholders shall either fix the consideration to be received for the shares or authorize the board to fix such consideration.

(e) Treasury shares may be disposed of by a corporation on such terms and conditions as are fixed from time to time by the board.

(f) Upon distribution of authorized but unissued shares to shareholders, that part of the surplus of a corporation which is concurrently transferred to stated capital shall be the consideration for the issue of such shares.

(g) In the event of a conversion of bonds or shares into shares, or in the event of an exchange of bonds or shares for shares, with or without par value, the consideration for the shares so issued in exchange or conversion shall be the sum of (1) either the principal sum of, and accrued interest on, the bonds so exchanged or converted, or the stated capital then represented by the shares so exchanged or converted, plus (2) any additional consideration paid to the corporation for the new shares, plus (3) any stated capital not theretofore allocated to any designated class or series which is thereupon allocated to the new shares, plus (4) any surplus thereupon transferred to stated capital and allocated to the new shares.

(h) Certificates for shares may not be issued until the full amount of the consideration therefor has been paid, except as provided in paragraphs (e) and (f) of section 505 (Rights and options to purchase shares; issue of rights and options to directors, officers and employees).

(i) When the consideration for shares has been paid in full, the subscriber shall be entitled to all the rights and privileges of a holder of such shares and to a certificate representing his shares, and such shares shall be fully paid and nonassessable.

§ 505. Rights and Options to Purchase Shares; Issue of Rights and Options to Directors, Officers and Employees

(a)(1) Except as otherwise provided in this section or in the certificate of incorporation, a corporation may create and issue, whether or not in connection with the issue and sale of any of its shares or bonds, rights or options entitling the holders thereof to purchase from the corporation, upon such consideration, terms and conditions as may be fixed by the board, shares of any class or series, whether authorized but unissued shares, treasury shares or shares to be purchased or acquired or assets of the corporation.

(2)(i) In the case of a domestic corporation that has a class of voting stock registered with the Securities and Exchange Commission pursuant to section twelve of the Exchange Act, the terms and conditions of such rights or options may include, without limitation, restrictions or conditions that preclude or limit the exercise, transfer or receipt of such rights or options by an interested shareholder or any transferee of any such interested shareholder or that invalidate or void such rights or options held by any such interested shareholder or any such transferee. For the purposes of this subparagraph, the terms "voting stock", "Exchange Act" and "interested shareholder" shall have the same meanings as set forth in section nine hundred twelve of this chapter.

(ii) Determinations of the board of directors whether to impose, enforce or waive or otherwise render ineffective such limitations or conditions as are permitted by clause (i) of this subparagraph shall be subject to judicial review in an appropriate proceeding in which the courts formulate or apply appropriate standards in order to insure that such limitations or conditions are imposed, enforced or waived in the best long-term interests and short-term interests of the corporation and its shareholders considering, without limitation, the prospects for potential growth, development, productivity and profitability of the corporation.

(b) The consideration for shares to be purchased under any such right or option shall comply with the requirements of section 504 (Consideration and payment for shares).

(c) The terms and conditions of such rights or options, including the time or times at or within which and the price or prices at which they may be exercised and any limitations upon transferability, shall be set forth or incorporated by reference in the instrument or instruments evidencing such rights or options.

(d) The issue of such rights or options to one or more directors, officers or employees of the corporation or a subsidiary or affiliate thereof, as an incentive to service or continued service with the corporation, a subsidiary or affiliate thereof, or to a trustee on behalf of such directors, officers or employees, shall be authorized at a meeting of shareholders by the vote of the holders of a majority of all outstanding shares entitled to vote thereon, or authorized by and consistent with a plan adopted by such vote of shareholders. If, under the certificate of incorporation, there are preemptive rights to any of the shares to be thus subject to rights or options to purchase, either such issue or such plan, if any shall also be approved by the vote or written consent of the holders of a majority of the shares entitled to exercise preemptive rights with respect to such shares and such vote or written consent shall operate to release the preemptive rights with respect thereto of the holders of all the shares that were entitled to exercise such preemptive rights.

In the absence of preemptive rights, nothing in this paragraph shall require shareholder approval for the issuance of rights or options to purchase shares of the corporation in substitution for, or upon the assumption of, rights or options issued by another corporation, if such substitution or assumption is in connection with such other corporation's merger or consolidation with, or the acquisition of its shares or all or part of its assets by, the corporation or its subsidiary.

(e) A plan adopted by the shareholders for the issue of rights or options to directors, officers or employees shall include the material terms and conditions upon which such rights or options are to be issued, such as, but without limitation thereof, any restrictions on the number of shares that eligible individuals may have the right or option to purchase, the method of administering the plan, the terms and conditions of payment for shares in full or in installments, the issue of certificates for shares to be paid for in installments, any limitations upon the transferability of such shares and the voting and dividend rights to which the holders of such shares may be entitled, though the full amount of the consideration therefor has not been paid; provided that under this section no certificate for shares shall be delivered to a shareholder, prior to full payment therefor, unless the fact that the shares are partly paid is noted conspicuously on the face or back of such certificate.

(f) If there is shareholder approval for the issue of rights or options to individual directors, officers or employees, but not under an approved plan under paragraph (e), the terms and conditions of issue set forth in paragraph (e) shall be permissible except that the grantees of such rights or options shall not be granted voting or dividend rights until the consideration for the shares to which they are entitled under such rights or options has been fully paid.

(g) If there is shareholder approval for the issue of rights and options, such approval may provide that the board is authorized by certificate of amendment under section 805 (Certificate of amendment; contents) to increase the authorized shares of any class or series to such number as will be sufficient, when added to the previously authorized but unissued shares of such class or series, to satisfy any such rights or options entitling the holders thereof to purchase from the corporation authorized but unissued shares of such class or series.

(h) In the absence of fraud in the transaction, the judgment of the board shall be conclusive as to the adequacy of the consideration, tangible or intangible, received or to be received by the corporation for the issue of rights or options for the purchase from the corporation of its shares.

(i) The provisions of this section are inapplicable to the rights of the holders of convertible shares or bonds to acquire shares upon the exercise of conversion privileges under section 519 (Convertible shares and bonds).

§ 506. Determination of Stated Capital

(a) Upon issue by a corporation of shares with a par value, the consideration received therefor shall constitute stated capital to the extent of the par value of such shares.

(b) Upon issue by a corporation of shares without par value, the entire consideration received therefor shall constitute stated capital unless the board within a period of sixty days after issue allocates to surplus a portion, but not all, of the consideration received for such shares. No such allocation shall be made of any portion of the consideration received for shares without par value having a preference in the assets of the corporation upon involuntary liquidation except all or part of the amount, if any, of such consideration in excess of such preference, nor shall such allocation be made of any portion of the consideration for the issue of shares without par value which is fixed by the shareholders pursuant to a right reserved in the certificate of incorporation, unless such allocation is authorized by vote of the shareholders.

(c) The stated capital of a corporation may be increased from time to time by resolution of the board transferring all or part of the surplus of the corporation to stated capital. The board may direct that the amount so transferred shall be stated capital in respect of any designated class or series of shares.

§ 510. Dividends or Other Distributions in Cash or Property

(a) A corporation may declare and pay dividends or make other distributions in cash or its bonds or its property, including the shares or bonds of other corporations, on its outstanding shares, except when currently the corporation is insolvent or would thereby be made insolvent, or when the declaration, payment or distribution would be contrary to any restrictions contained in the certificate of incorporation.

(b) Dividends may be declared or paid and other distributions may be made out of surplus only, so that the net assets of the corporation remaining after such declaration, payment or distribution shall at least equal the amount of its stated capital; except that a corporation engaged in the exploitation of natural resources or other wasting assets, including patents, or formed primarily for the liquidation of specific assets, may declare and pay dividends or make other distributions in excess of its surplus, computed after taking due account of depletion and amortization, to the extent that the cost of the wasting or specific assets has been recovered by depletion reserves, amortization or sale, if the net assets remaining after such dividends or distributions are sufficient to cover the liquidation preferences of shares having such preferences in involuntary liquidation.

(c) When any dividend is paid or any other distribution is made, in whole or in part, from sources other than earned surplus, it shall be accompanied by a written notice (1) disclosing the amounts by which such dividend or distribution affects stated capital, capital surplus and earned surplus, or (2) if such amounts are not determinable at the time of such notice, disclosing the approximate effect of such dividend or distribution upon stated capital, capital surplus and earned surplus and stating that such amounts are not yet determinable.

§ 511. Share Distributions and Changes

(a) A corporation may make pro rata distributions of its authorized but unissued shares to holders of any class or series of its outstanding shares, subject to the following conditions:

(1) If a distribution of shares having a par value is made, such shares shall be issued at not less than the par value thereof and there shall be transferred to stated capital at the time of such distribution an amount of surplus equal to the aggregate par value of such shares.

(2) If a distribution of shares without par value is made, the amount of stated capital to be represented by each such share shall be fixed by the board, unless the certificate of incorporation reserves to the shareholders the right to fix the consideration for the issue of such shares, and there shall be transferred to stated capital at the time of such distribution an amount of surplus equal to the aggregate stated capital represented by such shares.

(3) A distribution of shares of any class or series may be made only to holders of the same class or series of shares unless the certificate of incorporation permits distribution, subject to the preemptive rights of holders of any outstanding shares, to holders of another class or series,

or unless such distribution is approved, when there are no outstanding preemptive rights, by the affirmative vote or the written consent of the holders of a majority of the outstanding shares of the class or series to be distributed.

(b) A corporation making a pro rata distribution of authorized but unissued shares to the holders of any class or series of outstanding shares may at its option make an equivalent distribution upon treasury shares of the same class or series, and any shares so distributed shall be treasury shares.

(c) A change of issued shares of any class which increases the stated capital represented by those shares may be made if the surplus of the corporation is sufficient to permit the transfer, and a transfer is concurrently made, from surplus to stated capital, of an amount equal to such increase.

(d) No transfer from surplus to stated capital need be made by a corporation making a distribution of its treasury shares to holders of any class of outstanding shares; nor upon a split up or division of issued shares of any class into a greater number of shares of the same class, or a combination of issued shares of any class into a lesser number of shares of the same class, if there is no increase in the aggregate stated capital represented by them.

(e) Nothing in this section shall prevent a corporation from making other transfers from earned surplus to stated capital or capital surplus in connection with share distributions or otherwise.

(f) Every distribution to shareholders of certificates representing a share distribution or a change of shares which affects stated capital, capital surplus or earned surplus shall be accompanied by a written notice (1) disclosing the amounts by which such distribution or change affects stated capital, capital surplus and earned surplus, or (2) if such amounts are not determinable at the time of such notice, disclosing the approximate effect of such distribution or change upon stated capital, capital surplus and earned surplus and stating that such amounts are not yet determinable.

(g) When issued shares are changed in any manner which affects stated capital, capital surplus or earned surplus, and no distribution to shareholders of certificates representing any shares resulting from such change is made, disclosure of the effect of such change upon the stated capital, capital surplus and earned surplus shall be made in the next financial statement covering the period in which such change is made that is furnished by the corporation to holders of shares of the class or series so changed or, if practicable, in the first notice of dividend or share distribution or change that is furnished to such shareholders between the date of the change of shares and the next such financial statement, and in any event within six months of the date of such change.

§ 513. Purchase or Redemption by a Corporation of Its Own Shares

(a) A corporation, subject to any restrictions contained in its certificate of incorporation, may purchase its own shares, or redeem its redeemable shares, out of surplus except when currently the corporation is insolvent or would thereby be made insolvent.

(b) A corporation may purchase its own shares out of stated capital except when currently the corporation is insolvent or would thereby be made insolvent, if the purchase is made for the purpose of:

(1) Eliminating fractions of shares;

(2) Collecting or compromising indebtedness to the corporation; or

(3) Paying shareholders entitled to receive payment for their shares under section 623 (Procedure to enforce shareholder's right to receive payment for shares).

(c) A corporation, subject to any restrictions contained in its certificate of incorporation, may redeem or purchase its redeemable shares out of stated capital except when currently the corporation is insolvent or would thereby be made insolvent and except when such redemption or purchase would reduce net assets below the stated capital remaining after giving effect to the cancellation of such redeemable shares.

(d) When its redeemable shares are purchased by a corporation within the period of redeemability, the purchase price thereof shall not exceed the applicable redemption price stated in the certificate of incorporation. Upon a call for redemption, the amount payable by the corporation for shares having a cumulative preference on dividends may include the stated redemption price plus accrued dividends to the next dividend date following the date of redemption of such shares.

(e) No domestic corporation which is subject to the provisions of section nine hundred twelve of this chapter shall purchase or agree to purchase more than ten percent of the stock of the corporation from a shareholder for more than the market value thereof unless such purchase or agreement to purchase is approved by the affirmative vote of the board of directors followed by the affirmative vote of the holders of a majority of all outstanding shares entitled to vote thereon at a meeting of shareholders unless the certificate of incorporation requires a greater percentage of the outstanding shares to approve.

The provisions of this paragraph shall not apply when the corporation offers to purchase shares from all holders of stock or for stock which the holder has been the beneficial owner of for more than two years.

The terms "stock", "beneficial owner", and "market value" shall be as defined in section nine hundred twelve of this chapter.

§ 514. Agreements for Purchase by a Corporation of Its Own Shares

(a) An agreement for the purchase by a corporation of its own shares shall be enforceable by the shareholder and the corporation to the extent such purchase is permitted at the time of purchase by section 513 (Purchase or redemption by a corporation of its own shares).

(b) The possibility that a corporation may not be able to purchase its shares under section 513 shall not be a ground for denying to either party specific performance of an agreement for the purchase by a corporation of its own shares, if at the time for performance the corporation can purchase all or part of such shares under section 513.

§ 515. Reacquired Shares

(a) Shares that have been issued and have been purchased, redeemed or otherwise reacquired by a corporation shall be cancelled if they are reacquired out of stated capital, or if they are converted shares, or if the certificate of incorporation requires that such shares be cancelled upon reacquisition.

(b) Any shares reacquired by the corporation and not required to be cancelled may be either retained as treasury shares or cancelled by the board at the time of reacquisition or at any time thereafter.

(c) Neither the retention of reacquired shares as treasury shares, nor their subsequent distribution to shareholders or disposition for a consideration shall change the stated capital. When treasury shares are disposed of for a consideration, the capital surplus shall be increased by the full amount of the consideration received unless the corporation exercises the option granted in subparagraph (a)(5) of section 517 (Special provisions relative to surplus and reserves).

(d) When reacquired shares other than converted shares are cancelled, the stated capital of the corporation is thereby reduced by the amount of stated capital then represented by such shares plus any stated capital not theretofore allocated to any designated class or series which is thereupon allocated to the shares cancelled. The amount by which stated capital has been reduced by cancellation of reacquired shares during a stated period of time shall be disclosed in the next financial statement covering such period that is furnished by the corporation to all its shareholders or, if practicable, in the first notice of dividend or share distribution that is furnished to the holders of each class or series of its shares between the end of the period and the next such financial statement, and in any event to all its shareholders within six months of the date of the reduction of capital.

(e) Shares cancelled under this section are restored to the status of authorized but unissued shares. However, if the certificate of incorporation prohibits the reissue of any shares required or permitted to be cancelled under this section, the board by certificate of amendment under section 805 (Certificate of amendment; contents) shall reduce the number of authorized shares accordingly.

§ 516. Reduction of Stated Capital in Certain Cases

(a) Except as otherwise provided in the certificate of incorporation, the board may at any time reduce the stated capital of a corporation by eliminating from stated capital amounts previously transferred by the board from surplus to stated capital and not allocated to any designated class or series of shares, or by eliminating any amount of stated capital represented by issued shares having a par value which exceeds the aggregate par value of such shares, or by reducing the amount of stated capital represented by issued shares without par value. However, if the consideration for the issue of shares without par value was fixed by the shareholders under section 504 (Consideration and payment for shares), the board shall not reduce the stated capital represented by such shares except to the extent, if any, that the board was authorized by the shareholders to allocate any portion of such consideration to surplus.

(b) No reduction of stated capital shall be made under this section unless after such reduction the stated capital exceeds the aggregate preferential amounts payable upon involuntary liquidation upon all issued shares having preferential rights in the assets plus the par value of all other issued shares with par value.

(c) When a reduction of stated capital has been effected under this section, the amount of such reduction shall be disclosed in the next financial statement covering the period in which such reduction is made that is furnished by the corporation to all its shareholders or, if practicable, in the first notice of dividend or share distribution that is furnished to the holders of each class or series of its shares between the date of such reduction and the next such financial statement, and in any event to all its shareholders within six months of the date of such reduction.

§ 517. Special Provisions Relative to Surplus and Reserves

(a) Whenever under this chapter it is necessary for a corporation to determine the amount or availability of its earned surplus, the following rules shall apply:

(1) The amount of the earned surplus of a corporation may be computed either from the date of formation or from the latest date when a deficit was eliminated as permitted in this section by an application of the corporation's capital surplus provided that:

(A) The board of any corporation formed before the effective date of this chapter may determine the amount of the corporation's earned surplus before the declaration of the first dividend after the effective date of this chapter, and such determination if made in good faith shall be conclusive; and

(B) After merger, consolidation or combination of two or more corporations by purchase or otherwise, the amount of the earned surplus of the surviving, consolidated or purchasing corporation shall not exceed the aggregate net earned surplus of the component corporations as it existed immediately prior to such merger, consolidation or combination, reduced by such distributions to shareholders and transfers of earned surplus to stated capital or capital surplus as were made in connection with the issue of shares or otherwise at the time of merger, consolidation or combination.

(2) All or part of the earned surplus of a corporation may be transferred by the board at any time to capital surplus or to stated capital.

(3) Any surplus resulting from reduction of stated capital shall be capital surplus.

(4) A corporation may apply any part or all of its capital surplus to the elimination of any deficit in the earned surplus account, upon approval by vote of the shareholders. The application of capital surplus to the elimination of a deficit in the earned surplus account shall be disclosed in the next financial statement covering the period in which such elimination is made that is furnished by the corporation to all its shareholders or, if practicable, in the first notice of dividend or share distribution that is furnished to holders of each class or series of its shares between the date of such elimination and the next such financial statement, and in any event to all its shareholders within six months of the date of such action.

(5) When a corporation has applied its earned surplus to the acquisition of treasury shares and such shares are subsequently disposed of for a consideration, the corporation may, at its option, restore to earned surplus, out of the consideration received and on an appropriate basis per share, all or part of the amount by which earned surplus was reduced at the time of acquisition of such shares. If the consideration received exceeds the amount by which earned surplus was reduced with respect to such shares, the excess shall be capital surplus.

(b) Nothing in this section shall prevent a corporation from creating reserves from its earned surplus or capital surplus for any proper purpose or purposes, or from increasing, decreasing or abolishing any such reserve.

§ 518. Corporate Bonds

(a) No corporation shall issue bonds except for money or other property, tangible or intangible, or labor or services actually received by or performed for the corporation or for its benefit or in its formation or reorganization, or a combination thereof. In the absence of fraud in the transaction, the judgment of the board as to the value of the consideration received shall be conclusive.

(b) If a distribution of its own bonds is made by a corporation to holders of any class or series of its outstanding shares, there shall be concurrently transferred to the liabilities of the corporation in respect of such bonds an amount of surplus equal to the principal amount of, and any accrued interest on, such bonds. The amount of the surplus so transferred shall be the consideration for the issue of such bonds.

(c) A corporation may, in its certificate of incorporation, confer upon the holders of any bonds issued or to be issued by the corporation, rights to inspect the corporate books and records and to vote in the election of directors and on any other matters on which shareholders of the corporation may vote.

§ 520. Liability for Failure to Disclose Required Information

Failure of the corporation to comply in good faith with the notice or disclosure provisions of paragraph (c) of section 510 (Dividends or other distributions in cash or property), ... or paragraph (d) of section 515 (Reacquired shares), or paragraph (c) of section 516 (Reduction of stated capital in certain cases), or subparagraph (a)(4) of section 517 (Special provisions relative to surplus and reserves), ... shall make the corporation liable for any damage sustained by any shareholder in consequence thereof.

ARTICLE 6

SHAREHOLDERS

§ 601. By–Laws

(a) The initial by-laws of a corporation shall be adopted by its incorporator or incorporators at the organization meeting. Thereafter, subject to section 613 (Limitations on right to vote), by-laws may be adopted, amended or repealed by vote of the holders of the shares at the time entitled to vote in the election of any directors. When so provided in the certificate of incorporation or a by-law adopted by the shareholders, by-laws may also be adopted, amended or repealed by the board by such vote as may be therein specified, which may be greater than the vote otherwise prescribed by this chapter, but any by-law adopted by the board may be amended or repealed by the shareholders entitled to vote thereon as herein provided. Any reference in this chapter to a "by-law adopted by the shareholders" shall include a by-law adopted by the incorporator or incorporators.

(b) If any by-law regulating an impending election of directors is adopted, amended or repealed by the board, there shall be set forth in the notice of the next meeting of shareholders for the election of directors the by-law so adopted, amended or repealed, together with a concise statement of the changes made.

(c) The by-laws may contain any provision relating to the business of the corporation, the conduct of its affairs, its rights or powers or the rights or powers of its shareholders, directors or officers, not inconsistent with this chapter or any other statute of this state or the certificate of incorporation.

§ 609. Proxies

(a) Every shareholder entitled to vote at a meeting of shareholders or to express consent or dissent without a meeting may authorize another person or persons to act for him by proxy.

(b) Every proxy must be signed by the shareholder or his attorney-in-fact. No proxy shall be valid after the expiration of eleven months from the date thereof unless otherwise provided in the proxy. Every proxy shall be revocable at the pleasure of the shareholder executing it, except as otherwise provided in this section.

(c) The authority of the holder of a proxy to act shall not be revoked by the incompetence or death of the shareholder who executed the proxy unless, before the authority is exercised, written notice of an adjudication of such incompetence or of such death is received by the corporate officer responsible for maintaining the list of shareholders.

(d) Except when other provision shall have been made by written agreement between the parties, the record holder of shares which he holds as pledgee or otherwise as security or which belong to another, shall issue to the pledgor or to such owner of such shares, upon demand therefor and payment of necessary expenses thereof, a proxy to vote or take other action thereon.

(e) A shareholder shall not sell his vote or issue a proxy to vote to any person for any sum of money or anything of value, except as authorized in this section and section 620 (Agreements as to voting; provision in certificate of incorporation as to control of directors).

(f) A proxy which is entitled "irrevocable proxy" and which states that it is irrevocable, is irrevocable when it is held by any of the following or a nominee of any of the following:

(1) A pledgee;

(2) A person who has purchased or agreed to purchase the shares;

(3) A creditor or creditors of the corporation who extend or continue credit to the corporation in consideration of the proxy if the proxy states that it was given in consideration of such extension or continuation of credit, the amount thereof, and the name of the person extending or continuing credit;

(4) A person who has contracted to perform services as an officer of the corporation, if a proxy is required by the contract of employment, if the proxy states that it was given in consideration of such contract of

employment, the name of the employee and the period of employment contracted for;

(5) A person designated by or under an agreement under paragraph (a) of section 620.

(g) Notwithstanding a provision in a proxy, stating that it is irrevocable, the proxy becomes revocable after the pledge is redeemed, or the debt of the corporation is paid, or the period of employment provided for in the contract of employment has terminated, or the agreement under paragraph (a) of section 620 has terminated; and, in a case provided for in subparagraphs (f)(3) or (4), becomes revocable three years after the date of the proxy or at the end of the period, if any, specified therein, whichever period is less, unless the period of irrevocability is renewed from time to time by the execution of a new irrevocable proxy as provided in this section. This paragraph does not affect the duration of a proxy under paragraph (b).

(h) A proxy may be revoked, notwithstanding a provision making it irrevocable, by a purchaser of shares without knowledge of the existence of the provision unless the existence of the proxy and its irrevocability is noted conspicuously on the face or back of the certificate representing such shares.

§ 614. Vote of Shareholders

(a) Directors shall, except as otherwise required by this chapter or by the certificate of incorporation as permitted by this chapter, be elected by a plurality of the votes cast at a meeting of shareholders by the holders of shares entitled to vote in the election.

(b) Whenever any corporate action, other than the election of directors, is to be taken under this chapter by vote of the shareholders, it shall, except as otherwise required by this chapter or by the certificate of incorporation as permitted by this chapter, be authorized by a majority of the votes cast at a meeting of shareholders by the holders of shares entitled to vote thereon.

§ 616. Greater Requirement as to Quorum and Vote of Shareholders

(a) The certificate of incorporation may contain provisions specifying either or both of the following:

(1) That the proportion of shares, or the proportion of shares of any class or series thereof, the holders of which shall be present in person or by proxy at any meeting of shareholders ... in order to constitute a quorum for the transaction of any business or of any specified item of business, including amendments to the certificate of incorporation, shall be greater than the proportion prescribed by this chapter in the absence of such provision.

(2) That the proportion of votes of the holders of shares, or of the holders of shares of any class or series thereof, that shall be necessary at any meeting of shareholders for the transaction of any business or of any specified item of business, including amendments to the certificate of incorporation, shall be greater than the proportion prescribed by this chapter in the absence of such provision.

(b) An amendment of the certificate of incorporation which changes or strikes out a provision permitted by this section, shall be authorized at a meeting of shareholders by vote of the holders of two-thirds of all outstanding shares entitled to vote thereon, or of such greater proportion of shares, or class or series of shares, as may be provided specifically in the certificate of incorporation for changing or striking out a provision permitted by this section.

(c) If the certificate of incorporation of any corporation contains a provision authorized by this section, the existence of such provision shall be noted conspicuously on the face or back of every certificate for shares issued by such corporation, except that this requirement shall not apply to any corporation having any class of any equity security registered pursuant to Section twelve of the Securities Exchange Act of 1934, as amended.

§ 620. Agreements as to Voting; Provision in Certificate of Incorporation as to Control of Directors

(a) An agreement between two or more shareholders, if in writing and signed by the parties thereto, may provide that in exercising any voting rights, the shares held by them shall be voted as therein provided, or as they may agree, or as determined in accordance with a procedure agreed upon by them.

(b) A provision in the certificate of incorporation otherwise prohibited by law because it improperly restricts the board in its management of the business of the corporation, or improperly transfers to one or more shareholders or to one or more persons or corporations to be selected by him or them, all or any part of such management otherwise within the authority of the board under this chapter, shall nevertheless be valid:

(1) If all the incorporators or holders of record of all outstanding shares, whether or not having voting power, have authorized such provision in the certificate of incorporation or an amendment thereof; and

(2) If, subsequent to the adoption of such provision, shares are transferred or issued only to persons who had knowledge or notice thereof or consented in writing to such provision.

(c) A provision authorized by paragraph (b) shall be valid only so long as no shares of the corporation are listed on a national securities exchange or regularly quoted in an over-the-counter market by one or more members of a national or affiliated securities association.

(d) Except as provided in paragraph (e), an amendment to strike out a provision authorized by paragraph (b) shall be authorized at a meeting of shareholders by vote of the holders of two-thirds of all outstanding shares entitled to vote thereon or by the holders of such greater proportion of shares as may be required by the certificate of incorporation for that purpose.

(e) Alternatively, if a provision authorized by paragraph (b) shall have ceased to be valid under this section, the board may authorize a certificate of amendment under section 805 (Certificate of amendment; contents) striking out such provision. Such certificate shall set forth the event by reason of which the provision ceased to be valid.

(f) The effect of any such provision authorized by paragraph (b) shall be to relieve the directors and impose upon the shareholders authorizing the same or consenting thereto the liability for managerial acts or omissions that is imposed on directors by this chapter to the extent that and so long as the discretion or powers of the board in its management of corporate affairs is controlled by any such provision.

(g) If the certificate of incorporation of any corporation contains a provision authorized by paragraph (b), the existence of such provision shall be noted conspicuously on the face or back of every certificate for shares issued by such corporation.

§ 622. Preemptive Rights

(a) As used in this section, the term:

(1) "Unlimited dividend rights" means the right without limitation as to amount either to all or to a share of the balance of current or liquidating dividends after the payment of dividends on any shares entitled to a preference.

(2) "Equity shares" means shares of any class, whether or not preferred as to dividends or assets, which have unlimited dividend rights.

(3) "Voting rights" means the right to vote for the election of one or more directors, excluding a right so to vote which is dependent on the happening of an event specified in the certificate of incorporation which would change the voting rights of any class of shares.

(4) "Voting shares" means shares of any class which have voting rights, but does not include bonds on which voting rights are conferred under section 518 (Corporate bonds).

(5) "Preemptive right" means the right to purchase shares or other securities to be issued or subject to rights or options to purchase, as such right is defined in this section.

(b) Except as otherwise provided in the certificate of incorporation, and except as provided in this section, the holders of equity shares of any class, in case of the proposed issuance by the corporation of, or the proposed granting by the corporation of rights or options to purchase, its equity shares of any class or any shares or other securities convertible into or carrying rights or options to purchase its equity shares of any class, shall, if the issuance of the equity shares proposed to be issued or issuable upon exercise of such rights or options or upon conversion of such other securities would adversely affect the unlimited dividend rights of such holders, have the right during a reasonable time and on reasonable conditions, both to be fixed by the board, to purchase such shares or other securities in such proportions as shall be determined as provided in this section.

(c) Except as otherwise provided in the certificate of incorporation, and except as provided in this section, the holders of voting shares of any class, in case of the proposed issuance by the corporation of, or the proposed granting by the corporation of rights or options to purchase, its voting shares of any class or any shares or other securities convertible into or carrying rights or options to purchase its voting shares of any class, shall, if the issuance of the voting shares proposed to be issued or issuable upon exercise of such rights or options or upon conversion of such other securities would adversely affect the voting rights of such holders, have the right during a reasonable time and on reasonable conditions, both to be fixed by the board, to purchase such shares or other securities in such proportions as shall be determined as provided in this section.

(d) The preemptive right provided for in paragraphs (b) and (c) shall entitle shareholders having such rights to purchase the shares or other securities to be offered or optioned for sale as nearly as practicable in such proportions as would, if such preemptive right were exercised, preserve the relative unlimited dividend rights and voting rights of such holders and at a price or prices not less favorable than the price or prices at which such shares or other securities are proposed to be offered for sale to others, without deduction of such reasonable expenses of and compensation for the sale, underwriting or purchase of such shares or other securities by underwriters or dealers as may lawfully be paid by the corporation. In case each of the shares entitling the holders thereof to preemptive rights does not confer the same unlimited dividend right or voting right, the board shall apportion the shares or other securities to be offered or optioned for sale among the shareholders having preemptive rights to purchase them in such proportions as in the opinion of the board shall preserve as far as practicable the relative unlimited dividend rights and voting rights of the holders at the time of such offering. The apportionment made by the board shall, in the absence of fraud or bad faith, be binding upon all shareholders.

(e) Unless otherwise provided in the certificate of incorporation, shares or other securities offered for sale or subjected to rights or options to purchase shall not be subject to preemptive rights if they:

(1) Are to be issued by the board to effect a merger or consolidation or offered or subjected to rights or options for consideration other than cash;

(2) Are to be issued or subjected to rights or options under paragraph (d) of section 505 (Rights and options to purchase shares; issue of rights and options to directors, officers and employees);

(3) Are to be issued to satisfy conversion or option rights theretofore granted by the corporation;

(4) Are treasury shares;

(5) Are part of the shares or other securities of the corporation authorized in its original certificate of incorporation and are issued, sold or optioned within two years from the date of filing such certificate; or

(6) Are to be issued under a plan of reorganization approved in a proceeding under any applicable act of congress relating to reorganization of corporations.

(f) Shareholders of record entitled to preemptive rights on the record date fixed by the board under section 604 (Fixing record date), or, if no record date is fixed, then on the record date determined under section 604, and no others shall be entitled to the right defined in this section.

(g) The board shall cause to be given to each shareholder entitled to purchase shares or other securities in accordance with this section, a notice directed to him in the manner provided in section 605 (Notice of meetings of shareholders) setting forth the time within which and the terms and conditions upon which the shareholder may purchase such shares or other securities and also the apportionment made of the right to purchase among the shareholders entitled to preemptive rights. Such notice shall be given personally or by mail at least fifteen days prior to the expiration of the period during which the shareholder shall have the right to purchase. All shareholders entitled to preemptive rights to whom notice shall have been given as aforesaid shall be deemed conclusively to have had a reasonable time in which to exercise their preemptive rights.

(h) Shares or other securities which have been offered to shareholders having preemptive rights to purchase and which have not been purchased by them within the time fixed by the board may thereafter, for a period of not exceeding one year following the expiration of the time during which shareholders might have exercised such preemptive rights, be issued, sold or subjected to rights or options to any other person or persons at a price, without deduction of such reasonable expenses of and compensation for the sale, underwriting or purchase of such shares by underwriters or dealers as may lawfully be paid by the corporation, not less than that at which they were offered to such shareholders. Any such shares or other securities not so issued, sold or subjected to rights or options to others during such one year period shall thereafter again be subject to the preemptive rights of shareholders.

(i) Except as otherwise provided in the certificate of incorporation and except as provided in this section, no holder of any shares of any class shall as such holder have any preemptive right to purchase any other shares or securities of any class which at any time may be sold or offered for sale by the corporation. Unless otherwise provided in the certificate of incorporation, holders of bonds on which voting rights are conferred under section 518 shall have no preemptive rights.

§ 623. Procedure to Enforce Shareholder's Right to Receive Payment for Shares

(a) A shareholder intending to enforce his right under a section of this chapter to receive payment for his shares if the proposed corporate action referred to therein is taken shall file with the corporation, before the meeting of shareholders at which the action is submitted to a vote, or at such meeting but before the vote, written objection to the action. ...

(c) Within twenty days after the giving of notice to him, any shareholder from whom written objection was not required and who elects to dissent shall file with the corporation a written notice of such election, stating his name and residence address, the number and classes of shares as to which he dissents and a demand for payment of the fair value of his shares. ...

(g) Within fifteen days after the expiration of the period within which shareholders may file their notices of election to dissent, or within fifteen days after the proposed corporate action is consummated, whichever is later (but in no case later than ninety days from the shareholders' authorization date), the corporation or, in the case of a merger or consolidation, the surviving or new corporation, shall make a written offer by registered mail to each shareholder who has filed such notice of election to pay for his shares at a specified price which the corporation considers to be their fair value. Such offer shall be accompanied by a statement setting forth the aggregate number of shares with respect to which notices of election to dissent have been received and the aggregate number of holders of such shares. If the corporate action has been consummated, such offer shall also be accompanied by (1) advance payment to each such shareholder who has submitted the certificates representing his shares to the corporation, as provided in paragraph (f), of an amount equal to eighty percent of the amount of such offer, or (2) as to each shareholder who has not yet submitted his certificates a statement that advance payment to him of an amount equal to eighty percent of the amount of such offer will be made by the corporation promptly upon submission of his certificates. If the corporate action has not been consummated at the time of the making of the offer, such advance payment or statement as to advance payment shall be sent to each shareholder entitled thereto forthwith upon consummation of the corporate action. Every advance payment or statement as to advance payment shall include advice to the shareholder to the effect that acceptance of such payment does not constitute a waiver of any dissenters' rights. ...

(h) The following procedure shall apply if the corporation fails to make such offer within such period of fifteen days, or if it makes the offer and any dissenting shareholder or shareholders fail to agree with it within the period of thirty days thereafter upon the price to be paid for their shares:

(1) The corporation shall, within twenty days after the expiration of whichever is applicable of the two periods last mentioned, institute a special proceeding in the supreme court in the judicial district in which the office of the corporation is located to determine the rights of dissenting shareholders and to fix the fair value of their shares. If, in the case of merger or consolidation, the surviving or new corporation is a foreign corporation without an office in this state, such proceeding shall be brought in the county where the office of the domestic corporation, whose shares are to be valued, was located.

(2) If the corporation fails to institute such proceeding within such period of twenty days, any dissenting shareholder may institute such proceeding for the same purpose not later than thirty days after the expiration of such twenty day period. If such proceeding is not instituted within such thirty day period, all dissenter's rights shall be lost unless the supreme court, for good cause shown, shall otherwise direct.

(3) All dissenting shareholders, excepting those who, as provided in paragraph (g), have agreed with the corporation upon the price to be paid for their shares, shall be made parties to such proceeding, which shall have the effect of an action quasi in rem against their shares. The corporation shall serve a copy of the petition in such proceeding upon each dissenting shareholder who is a resident of this state in the manner provided by law for the service of a summons, and upon each nonresident dissenting shareholder either by registered mail and publication, or in such other manner as is permitted by law. The jurisdiction of the court shall be plenary and exclusive.

(4) The court shall determine whether each dissenting shareholder, as to whom the corporation requests the court to make such determination, is entitled to receive payment for his shares. If the corporation does not request any such determination or if the court finds that any dissenting shareholder is so entitled, it shall proceed to fix the value of the shares, which, for the purposes of this section, shall be the fair value as of the close of business on the day prior to the shareholders'

authorization date. In fixing the fair value of the shares, the court shall consider the nature of the transaction giving rise to the shareholder's right to receive payment for shares and its effects on the corporation and its shareholders, the concepts and methods then customary in the relevant securities and financial markets for determining fair value of shares of a corporation engaging in a similar transaction under comparable circumstances and all other relevant factors. The court shall determine the fair value of the shares without a jury and without referral to an appraiser or referee. Upon application by the corporation or by any shareholder who is a party to the proceeding, the court may, in its discretion, permit pretrial disclosure, including, but not limited to, disclosure of any expert's reports relating to the fair value of the shares whether or not intended for use at the trial in the proceeding. . . .

§ 624. Books and Records; Right of Inspection, Prima Facie Evidence

(a) Each corporation shall keep correct and complete books and records of account and shall keep minutes of the proceedings of its shareholders, board and executive committee, if any, and shall keep at the office of the corporation in this state or at the office of its transfer agent or registrar in this state, a record containing the names and addresses of all shareholders, the number and class of shares held by each and the dates when they respectively became the owners of record thereof. Any of the foregoing books, minutes or records may be in written form or in any other form capable of being converted into written form within a reasonable time.

(b) Any person who shall have been a shareholder of record of a corporation for at least six months immediately preceding his demand, or any person holding, or thereunto authorized in writing by the holders of, at least five percent of any class of the outstanding shares, upon at least five days' written demand shall have the right to examine in person or by agent or attorney, during usual business hours, its minutes of the proceedings of its shareholders and record of shareholders and to make extracts therefrom. Holders of voting trust certificates representing shares of the corporation shall be regarded as shareholders for the purpose of this section. If the corporation has failed to pay wages as defined in paragraph (b) of section 630 (Liability of shareholders for wages due to laborers, servants or employees), any person to whom a shareholder may be liable thereunder upon at least five days written demand shall have the right to examine in person or by agent or attorney during usual business hours, the record of shareholders and to make extracts therefrom.

(c) An inspection authorized by paragraph (b) may be denied to such shareholder or other person upon his refusal to furnish to the corporation, its transfer agent or registrar an affidavit that such inspection is not desired for a purpose which is in the interest of a business or object other than the business of the corporation and that he has not within five years sold or offered for sale any list of shareholders of any corporation of any type or kind, whether or not formed under the laws of this state, or aided or abetted any person in procuring any such record of shareholders for any such purpose. The enforcement of liability under section 630 shall not be an object other than the business of the corporation.

(d) Upon refusal by the corporation or by an officer or agent of the corporation to permit an inspection of the minutes of the proceedings of its shareholders or of the record of shareholders as herein provided, the person making the demand for inspection may apply to the supreme court in the judicial district where the office of the corporation is located, upon such notice as the court may direct, for an order directing the corporation, its officer or agent to show cause why an order should not be granted permitting such inspection by the applicant. Upon the return day of the order to show cause, the court shall hear the parties summarily, by affidavit or otherwise, and if it appears that the applicant is qualified and entitled to such inspection, the court shall grant an order compelling such inspection and awarding such further relief as to the court may seem just and proper.

(e) Upon the written request of any person who shall have been a shareholder of record for at least six months immediately preceding his request, or of any person holding, or thereunto authorized in writing by the holders of, at least five percent of any class of the outstanding shares, the corporation shall give or mail to such shareholder an annual balance sheet and profit and loss statement for the preceding fiscal year, and, if any interim balance sheet or profit and loss statement has been distributed to its shareholders or otherwise made available to the public, the most recent such interim balance sheet or profit and loss statement. The corporation shall be allowed a reasonable time to prepare such annual balance sheet and profit and loss statement.

(f) Nothing herein contained shall impair the power of courts to compel the production for examination of the books and records of a corporation.

(g) The books and records specified in paragraph (a) shall be prima facie evidence of the facts therein stated in favor of the plaintiff in any action or special proceeding against such corporation or any of its officers, directors or shareholders.

§ 626. Shareholders' Derivative Action Brought in the Right of the Corporation to Procure a Judgment in Its Favor

(a) An action may be brought in the right of a domestic or foreign corporation to procure a judgment in its favor, by a holder of shares or of voting trust certificates of the corporation or of a beneficial interest in such shares or certificates.

(b) In any such action, it shall be made to appear that the plaintiff is such a holder at the time of bringing the action and that he was such a holder at the time of the transaction of which he complains, or that his shares or his interest therein devolved upon him by operation of law.

(c) In any such action, the complaint shall set forth with particularity the efforts of the plaintiff to secure the initiation of such action by the board or the reasons for not making such effort.

(d) Such action shall not be discontinued, compromised or settled, without the approval of the court having jurisdiction of the action. If the court shall determine that the interests of the shareholders or any class or classes thereof will be substantially affected by such discontinuance, compromise, or settlement, the court, in its discretion, may direct that notice, by publication or otherwise, shall be given to the shareholders or class or classes thereof whose interest it determines will be so affected; if notice is so directed to be given, the court may determine which one or more of the parties to the action shall bear the expense of giving the same, in such amount as the court shall determine and find to be reasonable in the circumstances, and the amount of such expense shall be awarded as special costs of the action and recoverable in the same manner as statutory taxable costs.

(e) If the action on behalf of the corporation was successful, in whole or in part, or if anything was received by the plaintiff or plaintiffs or a claimant or claimants as the result of a judgment, compromise or settlement of an action or claim, the court may award the plaintiff or plaintiffs, claimant or claimants, reasonable expenses, including reasonable attorney's fees, and shall direct him or them to account to the corporation for the remainder of the proceeds so received by him or them. This paragraph shall not apply to any judgment rendered for the benefit of injured shareholders only and limited to a recovery of the loss or damage sustained by them.

§ 627. Security for Expenses in Shareholders' Derivative Action Brought in the Right of the Corporation to Procure a Judgment in Its Favor

In any action specified in section 626 (Shareholders' derivative action brought in the right of the corporation to procure a judgment in its favor), unless the plaintiff or plaintiffs hold five percent or more of any class of the outstanding shares or hold voting trust certificates or a beneficial interest in shares representing five percent or more of any class of such shares, or the shares, voting trust certificates and beneficial interest of such plaintiff or plaintiffs have a fair value in excess of fifty thousand dollars, the corporation in whose right such action is brought shall be entitled at any stage of the proceedings before final judgment to require the plaintiff or plaintiffs to give security for the reasonable expenses, including attorney's fees, which may be incurred by it in connection with such action and by the other parties defendant in connection therewith for which the corporation may become liable under this chapter, under any contract or otherwise under law, to which the corporation shall have recourse in such amount as the court having jurisdiction of such action shall determine upon the termination of such action. The amount of such security may thereafter from time to time be increased or decreased in the discretion of the court having jurisdiction of such action upon showing that the security provided has or may become inadequate or excessive.

§ 630. Liability of Shareholders for Wages Due to Laborers, Servants or Employees

(a) The ten largest shareholders, as determined by the fair value of their beneficial interest as of the beginning of the period during which the unpaid services referred to in this section are performed, of every corporation (other than an investment company registered as such under an act of congress entitled "Investment Company Act of 1940"), no shares of which are listed on a national securities exchange or regularly quoted in an over-the-counter market by one or more members of a national or an affiliated securities association, shall jointly and severally be personally liable for all debts, wages or salaries due and owing to any of its laborers, servants or employees other than contractors, for services performed by them for such corporation. Before such laborer, servant or employee shall charge such shareholder for such services, he shall give notice in writing to such shareholder that he intends to hold him liable under this section. Such notice shall be given within one hundred and eighty days after termination of such services, except that if, within such period, the laborer, servant or employee demands an examination of the record of shareholders under paragraph (b) of section 624 (Books and records; right of inspection, prima facie evidence), such notice may be given within sixty days after he has been given the opportunity to examine the record of shareholders. An action to enforce such liability shall be commenced within ninety days after the return of an execution unsatisfied against the corporation upon a judgment recovered against it for such services.

(b) For the purposes of this section, wages or salaries shall mean all compensation and benefits payable by an employer to or for the account of the employee for personal services rendered by such employee. These shall specifically include but not be limited to salaries, overtime, vacation, holiday and severance pay; employer contributions to or payments of insurance or welfare benefits; employer contributions to pension or annuity funds; and any other moneys properly due or payable for services rendered by such employee.

(c) A shareholder who has paid more than his pro rata share under this section shall be entitled to contribution pro rata from the other shareholders liable under this section with respect to the excess so paid, over and above his pro rata share, and may sue them jointly or severally or any number of them to recover the amount due from them. Such recovery may be had in a separate action. As used in this paragraph, "pro rata" means in proportion to beneficial share interest. Before a shareholder may claim contribution from other shareholders under this paragraph, he shall, unless they have been given notice by a laborer, servant or employee under paragraph (a), give them notice in writing that he intends to hold them so liable to him. Such notice shall be given by him within twenty days after the date that notice was given to him by a laborer, servant or employee under paragraph (a).

ARTICLE 7

DIRECTORS AND OFFICERS

§ 701. Board of Directors

Subject to any provision in the certificate of incorporation authorized by paragraph (b) of section 620 (Agreements as to voting; provision in certificate of incorporation as to control of directors) or by paragraph (b) of section 715 (Officers), the business of a corporation shall be managed under the direction of its board of directors, each of whom shall be at least eighteen years of age. The certificate of incorporation or the by-laws may prescribe other qualifications for directors.

§ 705. Newly Created Directorships and Vacancies

(a) Newly created directorships resulting from an increase in the number of directors and vacancies occurring in the board for any reason except the removal of directors without cause may be filled by vote of the board. If the number of the directors then in office is less than a quorum, such newly created directorships and vacancies may be filled by vote of a majority of the directors then in office. Nothing in this paragraph shall affect any provision of the certificate of incorporation or the by-laws which provides that such newly created directorships or vacancies shall be filled by vote of the shareholders, or any provision of the certificate of incorporation specifying greater requirements as permitted under section 709 (Greater requirements as to quorum and vote of directors).

(b) Unless the certificate of incorporation or the specific provisions of a by-law adopted by the shareholders provide that the board may fill vacancies occurring in the board by reason of the removal of directors without cause, such vacancies may be filled only by vote of the shareholders.

(c) A director elected to fill a vacancy, unless elected by the shareholders, shall hold office until the next meeting of shareholders at which the election of directors is in the regular order of business, and until his successor has been elected and qualified.

§ 706. Removal of Directors

(a) Any or all of the directors may be removed for cause by vote of the shareholders. The certificate of incorporation or the specific provisions of a by-law adopted by the shareholders may provide for such removal by action of the board, except in the case of any director elected by cumulative voting, or by the holders of the shares of any class or series, or holders of bonds, voting as a class, when so entitled by the provisions of the certificate of incorporation.

(b) If the certificate of incorporation or the by-laws so provide, any or all of the directors may be removed without cause by vote of the shareholders.

(c) The removal of directors, with or without cause, as provided in paragraphs (a) and (b) is subject to the following:

(1) In the case of a corporation having cumulative voting, no director may be removed when the votes cast against his removal would be sufficient to elect him if voted cumulatively at an election at which the same total number of votes were cast and the entire board, or the entire class of directors of which he is a member, were then being elected; and

(2) When by the provisions of the certificate of incorporation the holders of the shares of any class or series, or holders of bonds, voting as a class, are entitled to elect one or more directors, any director so elected may be removed only by the applicable vote of the holders of the shares of that class or series, or the holders of such bonds, voting as a class.

(d) An action to procure a judgment removing a director for cause may be brought by the attorney-general or by the holders of ten percent of the outstanding shares, whether or not entitled to vote. The court may bar from re-election any director so removed for a period fixed by the court.

§ 707. Quorum of Directors

Unless a greater proportion is required by the certificate of incorporation, a majority of the entire board shall constitute a quorum for the transaction of business or of any specified item of business, except that the certificate of incorporation or the by-laws may fix the quorum at less than a majority of the entire board but not less than one-third thereof.

§ 709. Greater Requirement as to Quorum and Vote of Directors

(a) The certificate of incorporation may contain provisions specifying either or both of the following:

793

(1) That the proportion of directors that shall constitute a quorum for the transaction of business or of any specified item of business shall be greater than the proportion prescribed by this chapter in the absence of such provision.

(2) That the proportion of votes of directors that shall be necessary for the transaction of business or of any specified item of business shall be greater than the proportion prescribed by this chapter in the absence of such provision.

(b) An amendment of the certificate of incorporation which changes or strikes out a provision permitted by this section shall be authorized at a meeting of shareholders by vote of the holders of two-thirds of all outstanding shares entitled to vote thereon, or of such greater proportion of shares, or class or series of shares, as may be provided specifically in the certificate of incorporation for changing or striking out a provision permitted by this section.

(c) If the certificate of incorporation of any corporation contains a provision authorized by this section, the existence of such provision shall be noted conspicuously on the face or back of every certificate for shares issued by such corporation, except that this requirement shall not apply to any corporation having any class of any equity security registered pursuant to section twelve of the Securities Exchange Act of 1934, as amended.

§ 713. Interested Directors

(a) No contract or other transaction between a corporation and one or more of its directors, or between a corporation and any other corporation, firm, association or other entity in which one or more of its directors are directors or officers, or have a substantial financial interest, shall be either void or voidable for this reason alone or by reason alone that such director or directors are present at the meeting of the board, or of a committee thereof, which approves such contract or transaction, or that his or their votes are counted for such purpose:

(1) If the material facts as to such director's interest in such contract or transaction and as to any such common directorship, officership or financial interest are disclosed in good faith or known to the board or committee, and the board or committee approves such contract or transaction by a vote sufficient for such purpose without counting the vote of such interested director or, if the votes of the disinterested directors are insufficient to constitute an act of the board as defined in section 708 (Action by the board), by unanimous vote of the disinterested directors; or

(2) If the material facts as to such director's interest in such contract or transaction and as to any such common directorship, officership or financial interest are disclosed in good faith or known to the

shareholders entitled to vote thereon, and such contract or transaction is approved by vote of such shareholders.

(b) If such good faith disclosure of the material facts as to the director's interest in the contract or transaction and as to any such common directorship, officership or financial interest is made to the directors or shareholders, or known to the board or committee or shareholders approving such contract or transaction, as provided in paragraph (a), the contract or transaction may not be avoided by the corporation for the reasons set forth in paragraph (a). If there was no such disclosure or knowledge, or if the vote of such interested director was necessary for the approval of such contract or transaction at a meeting of the board or committee at which it was approved, the corporation may avoid the contract or transaction unless the party or parties thereto shall establish affirmatively that the contract or transaction was fair and reasonable as to the corporation at the time it was approved by the board, a committee or the shareholders.

(c) Common or interested directors may be counted in determining the presence of a quorum at a meeting of the board or of a committee which approves such contract or transaction.

(d) The certificate of incorporation may contain additional restrictions on contracts or transactions between a corporation and its directors and may provide that contracts or transactions in violation of such restrictions shall be void or voidable by the corporation.

(e) Unless otherwise provided in the certificate of incorporation or the by-laws, the board shall have authority to fix the compensation of directors for services in any capacity.

§ 715. Officers

(a) The board may elect or appoint a president, one or more vice-presidents, a secretary and a treasurer, and such other officers as it may determine, or as may be provided in the by-laws.

(b) The certificate of incorporation may provide that all officers or that specified officers shall be elected by the shareholders instead of by the board.

(c) Unless otherwise provided in the certificate of incorporation or the by-laws, all officers shall be elected or appointed to hold office until the meeting of the board following the next annual meeting of shareholders or, in the case of officers elected by the shareholders, until the next annual meeting of shareholders.

(d) Each officer shall hold office for the term for which he is elected or appointed, and until his successor has been elected or appointed and qualified.

(e) Any two or more offices may be held by the same person, except the offices of president and secretary. When all of the issued and outstanding stock of the corporation is owned by one person, such person may hold all or any combination of offices.

(f) The board may require any officer to give security for the faithful performance of his duties.

(g) All officers as between themselves and the corporation shall have such authority and perform such duties in the management of the corporation as may be provided in the by-laws or, to the extent not so provided, by the board.

(h) An officer shall perform his duties as an officer in good faith and with that degree of care which an ordinarily prudent person in a like position would use under similar circumstances. In performing his duties, an officer shall be entitled to rely on information, opinions, reports or statements including financial statements and other financial data, in each case prepared or presented by:

(1) one or more other officers or employees of the corporation or of any other corporation of which at least fifty percentum of the outstanding shares of stock entitling the holders thereof to vote for the election of directors is owned directly or indirectly by the corporation, whom the officer believes to be reliable and competent in the matters presented, or

(2) counsel, public accountants or other persons as to matters which the officer believes to be within such person's professional or expert competence, so long as in so relying he shall be acting in good faith and with such degree of care, but he shall not be considered to be acting in good faith if he has knowledge concerning the matter in question that would cause such reliance to be unwarranted. A person who so performs his duties shall have no liability by reason of being or having been an officer of the corporation.

§ 717. Duty of Directors

(a) A director shall perform his duties as a director, including his duties as a member of any committee of the board upon which he may serve, in good faith and with that degree of care which an ordinarily prudent person in a like position would use under similar circumstances. In performing his duties, a director shall be entitled to rely on information, opinions, reports or statements including financial statements and other financial data, in each case prepared or presented by:

(1) one or more officers or employees of the corporation or of any other corporation of which at least fifty percentum of the outstanding shares of stock entitling the holders thereof to vote for the election of directors is owned directly or indirectly by the corporation, whom the director believes to be reliable and competent in the matters presented,

(2) counsel, public accountants or other persons as to matters which the director believes to be within such person's professional or expert competence, or

(3) a committee of the board upon which he does not serve, duly designated in accordance with a provision of the certificate of incorporation or the by-laws, as to matters within its designated authority, which committee the director believes to merit confidence, so long as in so relying he shall be acting in good faith and with such degree of care, but he shall not be considered to be acting in good faith if he has knowledge concerning the matter in question that would cause such reliance to be unwarranted. A person who so performs his duties shall have no liability by reason of being or having been a director of the corporation.

(b) In taking action, including, without limitation, action which may involve or relate to a change or potential change in the control of the corporation, a director shall be entitled to consider, without limitation, (1) both the long-term and the short-term interests of the corporation and its shareholders and (2) the effects that the corporation's actions may have in the short-term or in the long-term upon any of the following:

(i) the prospects for potential growth, development, productivity and profitability of the corporation;

(ii) the corporation's current employees;

(iii) the corporation's retired employees and other beneficiaries receiving or entitled to receive retirement, welfare or similar benefits from or pursuant to any plan sponsored, or agreement entered into, by the corporation;

(iv) the corporation's customers and creditors; and

(v) the ability of the corporation to provide, as a going concern, goods, services, employment opportunities and employment benefits and otherwise to contribute to the communities in which it does business.

Nothing in this paragraph shall create any duties owed by any director to any person or entity to consider or afford any particular weight to any of the foregoing or abrogate any duty of the directors, either statutory or recognized by common law or court decisions.

For purposes of this paragraph, "control" shall mean the possession, directly or indirectly, of the power to direct or cause the direction of the management and policies of the corporation, whether through the ownership of voting stock, by contract, or otherwise.

§ 719. Liability of Directors in Certain Cases

(a) Directors of a corporation who vote for or concur in any of the following corporate actions shall be jointly and severally liable to the corporation for the benefit of its creditors or shareholders, to the extent of any injury suffered by such persons, respectively, as a result of such action:

(1) The declaration of any dividend or other distribution to the extent that it is contrary to the provisions of paragraphs (a) and (b) of section 510 (Dividends or other distributions in cash or property).

(2) The purchase of the shares of the corporation to the extent that it is contrary to the provisions of section 513 (Purchase or redemption by a corporation of its own shares).

(3) The distribution of assets to shareholders after dissolution of the corporation without paying or adequately providing for all known liabilities of the corporation, excluding any claims not filed by creditors within the time limit set in a notice given to creditors under articles 10 (Non-judicial dissolution) or 11 (Judicial dissolution).

(4) The making of any loan contrary to section 714 (Loans to directors).

(b) A director who is present at a meeting of the board, or any committee thereof, when action specified in paragraph (a) is taken shall be presumed to have concurred in the action unless his dissent thereto shall be entered in the minutes of the meeting, or unless he shall submit his written dissent to the person acting as the secretary of the meeting before the adjournment thereof, or shall deliver or send by registered mail such dissent to the secretary of the corporation promptly after the adjournment of the meeting. Such right to dissent shall not apply to a director who voted in favor of such action. A director who is absent from a meeting of the board, or any committee thereof, when such action is taken shall be presumed to have concurred in the action unless he shall deliver or send by registered mail his dissent thereto to the secretary of the corporation or shall cause such dissent to be filed with the minutes of the proceedings of the board or committee within a reasonable time after learning of such action.

(c) Any director against whom a claim is successfully asserted under this section shall be entitled to contribution from the other directors who voted for or concurred in the action upon which the claim is asserted.

(d) Directors against whom a claim is successfully asserted under this section shall be entitled, to the extent of the amounts paid by them to the corporation as a result of such claims:

(1) Upon payment to the corporation of any amount of an improper dividend or distribution, to be subrogated to the rights of the corporation against shareholders who received such dividend or distribution with knowledge of facts indicating that it was not authorized by section 510, in proportion to the amounts received by them respectively.

(2) Upon payment to the corporation of any amount of the purchase price of an improper purchase of shares, to have the corporation rescind such purchase of shares and recover for their benefit, but at their expense, the amount of such purchase price from any seller who sold

such shares with knowledge of facts indicating that such purchase of shares by the corporation was not authorized by section 513.

(3) Upon payment to the corporation of the claim of any creditor by reason of a violation of subparagraph (a)(3), to be subrogated to the rights of the corporation against shareholders who received an improper distribution of assets.

(4) Upon payment to the corporation of the amount of any loan made contrary to section 714, to be subrogated to the rights of the corporation against a director who received the improper loan.

(e) A director shall not be liable under this section if, in the circumstances, he performed his duty to the corporation under paragraph (a) of section 717.

(f) This section shall not affect any liability otherwise imposed by law upon any director.

§ 720. Action Against Directors and Officers for Misconduct

(a) An action may be brought against one or more directors or officers of a corporation to procure a judgment for the following relief:

(1) Subject to any provision of the certificate of incorporation authorized pursuant to paragraph (b) of section 402, to compel the defendant to account for his official conduct in the following cases:

(A) The neglect of, or failure to perform, or other violation of his duties in the management and disposition of corporate assets committed to his charge.

(B) The acquisition by himself, transfer to others, loss or waste of corporate assets due to any neglect of, or failure to perform, or other violation of his duties.

(2) To set aside an unlawful conveyance, assignment or transfer of corporate assets, where the transferee knew of its unlawfulness.

(3) To enjoin a proposed unlawful conveyance, assignment or transfer of corporate assets, where there is sufficient evidence that it will be made.

(b) An action may be brought for the relief provided in this section, and in paragraph (a) of section 719 (Liability of directors in certain cases) by a corporation, or a receiver, trustee in bankruptcy, officer, director or judgment creditor thereof, or, under section 626 (Shareholders' derivative action brought in the right of the corporation to procure a judgment in its favor), by a shareholder, voting trust certificate holder, or the owner of a beneficial interest in shares thereof.

(c) This section shall not affect any liability otherwise imposed by law upon any director or officer.

§ 721. Nonexclusivity of Statutory Provisions for Indemnification of Directors and Officers

The indemnification and advancement of expenses granted pursuant to, or provided by, this article shall not be deemed exclusive of any other rights to which a director or officer seeking indemnification or advancement of expenses may be entitled, whether contained in the certificate of incorporation or the by-laws or, when authorized by such certificate of incorporation or by-laws, (i) a resolution of shareholders, (ii) a resolution of directors, or (iii) an agreement providing for such indemnification, provided that no indemnification may be made to or on behalf of any director or officer if a judgment or other final adjudication adverse to the director or officer establishes that his acts were committed in bad faith or were the result of active and deliberate dishonesty and were material to the cause of action so adjudicated, or that he personally gained in fact a financial profit or other advantage to which he was not legally entitled. Nothing contained in this article shall affect any rights to indemnification to which corporate personnel other than directors and officers may be entitled by contract or otherwise under law.

§ 722. Authorization for Indemnification of Directors and Officers

(a) A corporation may indemnify any person made, or threatened to be made, a party to an action or proceeding (other than one by or in the right of the corporation to procure a judgment in its favor), whether civil or criminal, including an action by or in the right of any other corporation of any type or kind, domestic or foreign, or any partnership, joint venture, trust, employee benefit plan or other enterprise, which any director or officer of the corporation served in any capacity at the request of the corporation, by reason of the fact that he, his testator or intestate, was a director or officer of the corporation, or served such other corporation, partnership, joint venture, trust, employee benefit plan or other enterprise in any capacity, against judgments, fines, amounts paid in settlement and reasonable expenses, including attorneys' fees actually and necessarily incurred as a result of such action or proceeding, or any appeal therein, if such director or officer acted, in good faith, for a purpose which he reasonably believed to be in, or, in the case of service for any other corporation or any partnership, joint venture, trust, employee benefit plan or other enterprise, not opposed to, the best interests of the corporation and, in criminal actions or proceedings, in addition, had no reasonable cause to believe that his conduct was unlawful.

(b) The termination of any such civil or criminal action or proceeding by judgment, settlement, conviction or upon a plea of nolo contendere, or its equivalent, shall not in itself create a presumption that any such director or officer did not act, in good faith, for a purpose which he reasonably believed to be in, or, in the case of service for any other corporation or any partnership, joint venture, trust, employee benefit plan or other enterprise, not opposed to, the best interests of the corporation or that he had reasonable cause to believe that his conduct was unlawful.

(c) A corporation may indemnify any person made, or threatened to be made, a party to an action by or in the right of the corporation to procure a judgment in its favor by reason of the fact that he, his testator or intestate, is or was a director or officer of the corporation, or is or was serving at the request of the corporation as a director or officer of any other corporation of any type or kind, domestic or foreign, [or] of any partnership, joint venture, trust, employee benefit plan or other enterprise, against amounts paid in settlement and reasonable expenses, including attorneys' fees, actually and necessarily incurred by him in connection with the defense or settlement of such action, or in connection with an appeal therein, if such director or officer acted, in good faith, for a purpose which he reasonably believed to be in, or, in the case of service for any other corporation or any partnership, joint venture, trust, employee benefit plan or other enterprise, not opposed to, the best interests of the corporation, except that no indemnification under this paragraph shall be made in respect of (1) a threatened action, or a pending action which is settled or otherwise disposed of, or (2) any claim, issue or matter as to which such person shall have been adjudged to be liable to the corporation, unless and only to the extent that the court in which the action was brought, or, if no action was brought, any court of competent jurisdiction, determines upon application that, in view of all the circumstances of the case, the person is fairly and reasonably entitled to indemnity for such portion of the settlement amount and expenses as the court deems proper.

(d) For the purpose of this section, a corporation shall be deemed to have requested a person to serve an employee benefit plan where the performance by such person of his duties to the corporation also imposes duties on, or otherwise involves services by, such person to the plan or participants or beneficiaries of the plan; excise taxes assessed on a person with respect to an employee benefit plan pursuant to applicable law shall be considered fines; and action taken or omitted by a person with respect to an employee benefit plan in the performance of such person's duties for a purpose reasonably believed by such person to be in the interest of the participants and beneficiaries of the plan shall be deemed to be for a purpose which is not opposed to the best interests of the corporation.

§ 723. Payment of Indemnification Other Than by Court Award

(a) A person who has been successful, on the merits or otherwise, in the defense of a civil or criminal action or proceeding of the character described in section 722 shall be entitled to indemnification as authorized in such section.

(b) Except as provided in paragraph (a), any indemnification under section 722 or otherwise permitted by section 721, unless ordered by a court under section 724 (Indemnification of directors and officers by a court), shall be made by the corporation, only if authorized in the specific case:

(1) By the board acting by a quorum consisting of directors who are not parties to such action or proceeding upon a finding that the director or officer has met the standard of conduct set forth in section 722 or established pursuant to section 721, as the case may be, or,

(2) If a quorum under subparagraph (1) is not obtainable or, even if obtainable, a quorum of disinterested directors so directs;

(A) By the board upon the opinion in writing of independent legal counsel that indemnification is proper in the circumstances because the applicable standard of conduct set forth in such sections has been met by such director or officer, or

(B) By the shareholders upon a finding that the director or officer has met the applicable standard of conduct set forth in such sections.

(C) Expenses incurred in defending a civil or criminal action or proceeding may be paid by the corporation in advance of the final disposition of such action or proceeding upon receipt of an undertaking by or on behalf of such director or officer to repay such amount as, and to the extent, required by paragraph (a) of section 725.

§ 724. Indemnification of Directors and Officers by a Court

(a) Notwithstanding the failure of a corporation to provide indemnification, and despite any contrary resolution of the board or of the shareholders in the specific case under section 723 (Payment of indemnification other than by court award), indemnification shall be awarded by a court to the extent authorized under section 722 (Authorization for indemnification of directors and officers), and paragraph (a) of section 723. Application therefor may be made, in every case, either:

(1) In the civil action or proceeding in which the expenses were incurred or other amounts were paid, or

(2) To the supreme court in a separate proceeding, in which case the application shall set forth the disposition of any previous application made to any court for the same or similar relief and also reasonable cause for the failure to make application for such relief in the action or proceeding in which the expenses were incurred or other amounts were paid.

(b) The application shall be made in such manner and form as may be required by the applicable rules of court or, in the absence thereof, by direction of a court to which it is made. Such application shall be upon notice to the corporation. The court may also direct that notice be given at the expense of the corporation to the shareholders and such other persons as it may designate in such manner as it may require.

(c) Where indemnification is sought by judicial action, the court may allow a person such reasonable expenses, including attorneys' fees, during the pendency of the litigation as are necessary in connection with his defense therein, if the court shall find that the defendant has by his pleadings or during the course of the litigation raised genuine issues of fact or law.

§ 725. Other Provisions Affecting Indemnification of Directors and Officers

(a) All expenses incurred in defending a civil or criminal action or proceeding which are advanced by the corporation under paragraph (c) of section 723 (Payment of indemnification other than by court award) or allowed by a court under paragraph (c) of section 724 (Indemnification of directors and officers by a court) shall be repaid in case the person receiving such advancement or allowance is ultimately found, under the procedure set forth in this article, not to be entitled to indemnification or, where indemnification is granted, to the extent the expenses so advanced by the corporation or allowed by the court exceed the indemnification to which he is entitled.

(b) No indemnification, advancement or allowance shall be made under this article in any circumstance where it appears:

(1) That the indemnification would be inconsistent with the law of the jurisdiction of incorporation of a foreign corporation which prohibits or otherwise limits such indemnification;

(2) That the indemnification would be inconsistent with a provision of the certificate of incorporation, a by-law, a resolution of the board or of the shareholders, an agreement or other proper corporate action, in effect at the time of the accrual of the alleged cause of action asserted in the threatened or pending action or proceeding in which the expenses were incurred or other amounts were paid, which prohibits or otherwise limits indemnification; or

(3) If there has been a settlement approved by the court, that the indemnification would be inconsistent with any condition with respect to indemnification expressly imposed by the court in approving the settlement.

(c) If any expenses or other amounts are paid by way of indemnification, otherwise than by court order or action by the shareholders, the corporation shall, not later than the next annual meeting of shareholders unless such meeting is held within three months from the date of such payment, and, in any event, within fifteen months from the date of such payment, mail to its shareholders of record at the time entitled to vote for the election of directors a statement specifying the persons paid, the amounts paid, and the nature and status at the time of such payment of the litigation or threatened litigation.

(d) If any action with respect to indemnification of directors and officers is taken by way of amendment of the by-laws, resolution of directors, or by agreement, then the corporation shall, not later than the next annual meeting of shareholders, unless such meeting is held within three months from the date of such action, and, in any event, within fifteen months from the date of such action, mail to its shareholders of record at the time entitled to vote for the election of directors a statement specifying the action taken....

(f) The provisions of this article relating to indemnification of directors and officers and insurance therefor shall apply to domestic corporations and foreign corporations doing business in this state, except as provided in section 1320 (Exemption from certain provisions).

§ 726. Insurance for Indemnification of Directors and Officers

(a) Subject to paragraph (b), a corporation shall have power to purchase and maintain insurance:

(1) To indemnify the corporation for any obligation which it incurs as a result of the indemnification of directors and officers under the provisions of this article, and

(2) To indemnify directors and officers in instances in which they may be indemnified by the corporation under the provisions of this article, and

(3) To indemnify directors and officers in instances in which they may not otherwise be indemnified by the corporation under the provisions of this article provided the contract of insurance covering such directors and officers provides, in a manner acceptable to the superintendent of insurance, for a retention amount and for co-insurance.

(b) No insurance under paragraph (a) may provide for any payment, other than cost of defense, to or on behalf of any director or officer:

(1) if a judgment or other final adjudication adverse to the insured director or officer establishes that his acts of active and deliberate dishonesty were material to the cause of action so adjudicated, or that he personally gained in fact a financial profit or other advantage to which he was not legally entitled, or

(2) in relation to any risk the insurance of which is prohibited under the insurance law of this state.

(c) Insurance under any or all subparagraphs of paragraph (a) may be included in a single contract or supplement thereto. Retrospective rated contracts are prohibited.

(d) The corporation shall, within the time and to the persons provided in paragraph (c) of section 725 (Other provisions affecting indemnification of directors or officers), mail a statement in respect of any insurance it has purchased or renewed under this section, specifying the insurance carrier, date of the contract, cost of the insurance, corporate positions insured, and a statement explaining all sums, not previously reported in a statement to shareholders, paid under any indemnification insurance contract.

(e) This section is the public policy of this state to spread the risk of corporate management, notwithstanding any other general or special law of this state or of any other jurisdiction including the federal government.

ARTICLE 8

AMENDMENTS AND CHANGES

§ 802. Reduction of Stated Capital by Amendment

(a) A corporation may reduce its stated capital by an amendment of its certificate of incorporation under section 801 (Right to amend certificate of incorporation) which:

(1) Reduces the par value of any issued shares with par value.

(2) Changes issued shares under subparagraph (b)(11) of section 801 that results in a reduction of stated capital.

(3) Removes from authorized shares, shares that have been issued, reacquired and cancelled by the corporation.

(b) This section shall not prevent a corporation from reducing its stated capital in any other manner permitted by this chapter.

ARTICLE 9

MERGER OR CONSOLIDATION; GUARANTEE; DISPOSITION OF ASSETS

§ 912. Requirements Relating to Certain Business Combinations

(a) For the purposes of this section:

(1) "Affiliate" means a person that directly, or indirectly through one or more intermediaries, controls, or is controlled by, or is under common control with, a specified person.

(2) "Announcement date", when used in reference to any business combination, means the date of the first public announcement of the final, definitive proposal for such business combination.

(3) "Associate", when used to indicate a relationship with any person, means (A) any corporation or organization of which such person

is an officer or partner or is, directly or indirectly, the beneficial owner of ten percent or more of any class of voting stock, (B) any trust or other estate in which such person has a substantial beneficial interest or as to which such person serves as trustee or in a similar fiduciary capacity, and (C) any relative or spouse of such person, or any relative of such spouse, who has the same home as such person.

(4) "Beneficial owner", when used with respect to any stock, means a person:

(A) that, individually or with or through any of its affiliates or associates, beneficially owns such stock, directly or indirectly; or

(B) that, individually or with or through any of its affiliates or associates, has (i) the right to acquire such stock (whether such right is exercisable immediately or only after the passage of time), pursuant to any agreement, arrangement or understanding (whether or not in writing), or upon the exercise of conversion rights, exchange rights, warrants or options, or otherwise; provided, however, that a person shall not be deemed the beneficial owner of stock tendered pursuant to a tender or exchange offer made by such person or any of such person's affiliates or associates until such tendered stock is accepted for purchase or exchange; or (ii) the right to vote such stock pursuant to any agreement, arrangement or understanding (whether or not in writing); provided, however, that a person shall not be deemed the beneficial owner of any stock under this item if the agreement, arrangement or understanding to vote such stock (X) arises solely from a revocable proxy or consent given in response to a proxy or consent solicitation made in accordance with the applicable rules and regulations under the Exchange Act and (Y) is not then reportable on a Schedule 13D under the Exchange Act (or any comparable or successor report); or

(C) that has any agreement, arrangement or understanding (whether or not in writing), for the purpose of acquiring, holding, voting (except voting pursuant to a revocable proxy or consent as described in item (ii) of clause (B) of this subparagraph), or disposing of such stock with any other person that beneficially owns, or whose affiliates or associates beneficially own, directly or indirectly, such stock.

(5) "Business combination", when used in reference to any domestic corporation and any interested shareholder of such corporation, means:

(A) any merger or consolidation of such corporation or any subsidiary of such corporation with (i) such interested shareholder or (ii) any other corporation (whether or not itself an interested shareholder of such corporation) which is, or after such merger or consolidation would be, an affiliate or associate of such interested shareholder;

(B) any sale, lease, exchange, mortgage, pledge, transfer or other disposition (in one transaction or a series of transactions) to or with such interested shareholder or any affiliate or associate of such interested shareholder of assets of such corporation or any subsidiary of such corporation (i) having an aggregate market value equal to ten percent or more of the aggregate market value of all the assets, determined on a consolidated basis, of such corporation, (ii) having an aggregate market value equal to ten percent or more of the aggregate market value of all the outstanding stock of such corporation, or (iii) representing ten percent or more of the earning power or net income, determined on a consolidated basis, of such corporation;

(C) the issuance or transfer by such corporation or any subsidiary of such corporation (in one transaction or a series of transactions) of any stock of such corporation or any subsidiary of such corporation which has an aggregate market value equal to five percent or more of the aggregate market value of all the outstanding stock of such corporation to such interested shareholder or any affiliate or associate of such interested shareholder except pursuant to the exercise of warrants or rights to purchase stock offered, or a dividend or distribution paid or made, pro rata to all shareholders of such corporation;

(D) the adoption of any plan or proposal for the liquidation or dissolution of such corporation proposed by, or pursuant to any agreement, arrangement or understanding (whether or not in writing) with, such interested shareholder or any affiliate or associate of such interested shareholder;

(E) any reclassification of securities (including, without limitation, any stock split, stock dividend, or other distribution of stock in respect of stock, or any reverse stock split), or recapitalization of such corporation, or any merger or consolidation of such corporation with any subsidiary of such corporation, or any other transaction (whether or not with or into or otherwise involving such interested shareholder), proposed by, or pursuant to any agreement, arrangement or understanding (whether or not in writing) with, such interested shareholder or any affiliate or associate of such interested shareholder, which has the effect, directly or indirectly, of increasing the proportionate share of the outstanding shares of any class or series of voting stock or securities convertible into voting stock of such corporation or any subsidiary of such corporation which is directly or indirectly owned by such interested shareholder or any affiliate or associate of such interested shareholder, except as a result of immaterial changes due to fractional share adjustments; or

(F) any receipt by such interested shareholder or any affiliate or associate of such interested shareholder of the benefit, directly or indirectly (except proportionately as a shareholder of such corporation) of any loans, advances, guarantees, pledges or other financial assistance or any tax credits or other tax advantages provided by or through such corporation.

(6) "Common stock" means any stock other than preferred stock.

(7) "Consummation date", with respect to any business combination, means the date of consummation of such business combination, or, in the case of a business combination as to which a shareholder vote is taken, the later of the business day prior to the vote or twenty days prior to the date of consummation of such business combination.

(8) "Control", including the terms "controlling", "controlled by" and "under common control with", means the possession, directly or indirectly, of the power to direct or cause the direction of the management and policies of a person, whether through the ownership of voting stock, by contract, or otherwise. A person's beneficial ownership of ten percent or more of a corporation's outstanding voting stock shall create a presumption that such person has control of such corporation. Notwithstanding the foregoing, a person shall not be deemed to have control of a corporation if such person holds voting stock, in good faith and not for the purpose of circumventing this section, as an agent, bank, broker, nominee, custodian or trustee for one or more beneficial owners who do not individually or as a group have control of such corporation.

(9) "Exchange Act" means the Act of Congress known as the Securities Exchange Act of 1934, as the same has been or hereafter may be amended from time to time.

(10) "Interested shareholder", when used in reference to any domestic corporation, means any person (other than such corporation or any subsidiary of such corporation) that

(A)(i) is the beneficial owner, directly or indirectly, of twenty percent or more of the outstanding voting stock of such corporation; or

(ii) is an affiliate or associate of such corporation and at any time within the five-year period immediately prior to the date in question was the beneficial owner, directly or indirectly, of twenty percent or more of the then outstanding voting stock of such corporation; provided that

(B) for the purpose of determining whether a person is an interested shareholder, the number of shares of voting stock of such corporation deemed to be outstanding shall include shares deemed to be beneficially owned by the person through application of subparagraph four of this paragraph but shall not include any other unissued shares of voting stock of such corporation which may be issuable pursuant to any agreement, arrangement or understanding, or upon exercise of conversion rights, warrants or options, or otherwise.

(11) "Market value", when used in reference to stock or property of any domestic corporation, means:

(A) in the case of stock, the highest closing sale price during the thirty-day period immediately preceding the date in question of a share of such stock on the composite tape for New York stock exchange-listed stocks, or, if such stock is not quoted on such composite tape or if such stock is not listed on such exchange, on the principal United States securities exchange registered under the Exchange Act on which such stock is listed, or, if such stock is not listed on any such exchange, the highest closing bid quotation with respect to a share of such stock during the thirty-day period preceding the date in question on the National Association of Securities Dealers, Inc. Automated Quotations System or any system then in use, or if no such quotations are available, the fair market value on the date in question of a share of such stock as determined by the board of directors of such corporation in good faith; and

(B) in the case of property other than cash or stock, the fair market value of such property on the date in question as determined by the board of directors of such corporation in good faith.

(12) "Preferred stock" means any class or series of stock of a domestic corporation which under the by-laws or certificate of incorporation of such corporation is entitled to receive payment of dividends prior to any payment of dividends on some other class or series of stock, or is entitled in the event of any voluntary liquidation, dissolution or winding up of the corporation to receive payment or distribution of a preferential amount before any payments or distributions are received by some other class or series of stock.

(14) "Stock" means:

(A) any stock or similar security, any certificate of interest, any participation in any profit sharing agreement, any voting trust certificate, or any certificate of deposit for stock; and

(B) any security convertible, with or without consideration, into stock, or any warrant, call or other option or privilege of buying stock without being bound to do so, or any other security carrying any right to acquire, subscribe to or purchase stock.

(15) "Stock acquisition date", with respect to any person and any domestic corporation, means the date that such person first becomes an interested shareholder of such corporation.

(16) "Subsidiary" of any person means any other corporation of which a majority of the voting stock is owned, directly or indirectly, by such person.

(17) "Voting stock" means shares of capital stock of a corporation entitled to vote generally in the election of directors.

(b) Notwithstanding anything to the contrary contained in this chapter (except the provisions of paragraph (d) of this section), no domestic corporation shall engage in any business combination with any interested shareholder of such corporation for a period of five years following such interested shareholder's stock acquisition date unless such business combination or the purchase of stock made by such interested shareholder on such interested shareholder's stock acquisition date is approved by the board of directors of such corporation prior to such interested shareholder's stock acquisition date. If a good faith proposal is made in writing to the board of directors of such corporation regarding a business combination, the board of directors shall respond, in writing, within thirty days or such shorter period, if any, as may be required by the Exchange Act, setting forth its reasons for its decision regarding such proposal. If a good faith proposal to purchase stock is made in writing to the board of directors of such corporation, the board of directors, unless it responds affirmatively in writing within thirty days or such shorter period, if any, as may be required by the Exchange Act, shall be deemed to have disapproved such stock purchase.

(c) Notwithstanding anything to the contrary contained in this chapter (except the provisions of paragraphs (b) and (d) of this section), no domestic corporation shall engage at any time in any business combination with any interested shareholder of such corporation other than a business combination specified in any one of subparagraph (1), (2) or (3):

(1) A business combination approved by the board of directors of such corporation prior to such interested shareholder's stock acquisition date, or where the purchase of stock made by such interested shareholder on such interested shareholder's stock acquisition date had been approved by the board of directors of such corporation prior to such interested shareholder's stock acquisition date.

(2) A business combination approved by the affirmative vote of the holders of a majority of the outstanding voting stock not beneficially owned by such interested shareholder or any affiliate or associate of such interested shareholder at a meeting called for such purpose no earlier than five years after such interested shareholder's stock acquisition date.

(3) A business combination that meets all of the following conditions:

(A) The aggregate amount of the cash and the market value as of the consummation date of consideration other than cash to be received per share by holders of outstanding shares of common stock of such corporation in such business combination is [at] least equal to the higher of the following:

(i) the highest per share price paid by such interested shareholder at a time when he was the beneficial owner, directly or indirectly, of five percent or more of the outstanding voting stock of such corporation, for any shares of common stock of the same class or series acquired by it (X) within the five-year period immediately prior to the announcement date with respect to such business combination, or (Y) within the five-year period immediately prior to, or in, the transaction in which such interested shareholder became an interested shareholder, whichever is higher; plus, in either case, interest compounded annually from the earliest date on which such highest per share acquisition price was paid through the consummation date at the rate for one-year United States treasury obligations from time to time in effect; less the aggregate amount of any cash dividends paid, and the market value of any dividends paid other than in cash, per share of common stock since such earliest date, up to the amount of such interest; and

(ii) the market value per share of common stock on the announcement date with respect to such business combination or on such interested shareholder's stock acquisition date, whichever is higher; plus interest compounded annually from such date through the consummation date at the rate for one-year United States treasury obligations from time to time in effect; less the aggregate amount of any cash dividends paid, and the market value of any dividends paid other than in cash, per share of common stock since such date, up to the amount of such interest.

(B) The aggregate amount of the cash and the market value as of the consummation date of consideration other than cash to be received per share by holders of outstanding shares of any class or series of stock, other than common stock, of such corporation is at least equal to the highest of the following (whether or not such interested shareholder has previously acquired any shares of such class or series of stock):

(i) the highest per share price paid by such interested shareholder at a time when he was the beneficial owner, directly or indirectly, of five percent or more of the outstanding voting stock of such corporation, for any shares of such class or series of stock acquired by it (X) within the five-year period immediately prior to the announcement date with respect to such business combination, or (Y) within the five-year period immediately prior to, or in, the transaction in which such interested shareholder became an interested shareholder, whichever is higher; plus, in either case, interest compounded annually from the earliest date on which such highest per share acquisition price was paid through the consummation date at the rate for one-year United States treasury obligations from time to time in effect; less the aggregate amount of any cash dividends paid, and the market value of any dividends paid other than in cash, per share of such class or series of stock since such earliest date, up to the amount of such interest;

(ii) the highest preferential amount per share to which the holders of shares of such class or series of stock are entitled in the event of any voluntary liquidation, dissolution or winding up of such corporation, plus the aggregate amount of any dividends declared or due as to which such holders are entitled prior to payment of dividends on some other class or series of stock (unless the aggregate amount of such dividends is included in such preferential amount); and

(iii) the market value per share of such class or series of stock on the announcement date with respect to such business combination or on such interested shareholder's stock acquisition date, whichever is higher; plus interest compounded annually from such date through the consummation date at the rate for one-year United States treasury obligations from time to time in effect; less the aggregate amount of any cash dividends paid, and the market value of any dividends paid other than in cash, per share of such class or series of stock since such date, up to the amount of such interest.

(C) The consideration to be received by holders of a particular class or series of outstanding stock (including common stock) of such corporation in such business combination is in cash or in the same form as the interested shareholder has used to acquire the largest number of shares of such class or series of stock previously acquired by it, and such consideration shall be distributed promptly.

(D) The holders of all outstanding shares of stock of such corporation not beneficially owned by such interested shareholder immediately prior to the consummation of such business combination are entitled to receive in such business combination cash or other consideration for such shares in compliance with clauses (A), (B) and (C) of this subparagraph.

(E) After such interested shareholder's stock acquisition date and prior to the consummation date with respect to such business combination, such interested shareholder has not become the beneficial owner of any additional shares of voting stock of such corporation except:

(i) as part of the transaction which resulted in such interested shareholder becoming an interested shareholder;

(ii) by virtue of proportionate stock splits, stock dividends or other distributions of stock in respect of stock not constituting a business combination under clause (E) of subparagraph five of paragraph (a) of this section;

(iii) through a business combination meeting all of the conditions of paragraph (b) of this section and this paragraph; or

(iv) through purchase by such interested shareholder at any price which, if such price had been paid in an otherwise permissible business combination the announcement date and consummation date of which were the date of such purchase, would have satisfied the requirements of clauses (A), (B) and (C) of this subparagraph.

(d) The provisions of this section shall not apply:

(1) to any business combination of a domestic corporation that does not have a class of voting stock registered with the Securities and Exchange Commission pursuant to section twelve of the Exchange Act, unless the certificate of incorporation provides otherwise; or

(2) to any business combination of a domestic corporation whose certificate of incorporation has been amended to provide that such corporation shall be subject to the provisions of this section, which did not have a class of voting stock registered with the Securities and Exchange Commission pursuant to section twelve of the Exchange Act on the effective date of such amendment, and which is a business combination with an interested shareholder whose stock acquisition date is prior to the effective date of such amendment; or

(3) to any business combination of a domestic corporation (i) the original certificate of incorporation of which contains a provision expressly electing not to be governed by this section, or (ii) which adopts an amendment to such corporation's by-laws prior to March thirty-first, nineteen hundred eighty-six, expressly electing not to be governed by this section, or (iii) which adopts an amendment to such corporation's by-laws, approved by the affirmative vote of the holders, other than interested shareholders and their affiliates and associates, of a majority of the outstanding voting stock of such corporation, excluding the voting stock of interested shareholders and their affiliates and associates, expressly electing not to be governed by this section, provided that such amendment to the by-laws shall not be effective until eighteen months after such vote of such corporation's shareholders and shall not apply to any business combination of such corporation with an interested shareholder whose stock acquisition date is on or prior to the effective date of such amendment; or

(4) to any business combination of a domestic corporation with an interested shareholder of such corporation which became an interested shareholder inadvertently, if such interested shareholder (i) as soon as practicable, divests itself of a sufficient amount of the voting stock of such corporation so that it no longer is the beneficial owner, directly or indirectly, of twenty percent or more of the outstanding voting stock of such corporation, and (ii) would not at any time within the five-year period preceding the announcement date with respect to such business combination have been an interested shareholder but for such inadvertent acquisition; or

(5) to any business combination with an interested shareholder who was the beneficial owner, directly or indirectly, of five per cent or more of the outstanding voting stock of such corporation on October thirtieth, nineteen hundred eighty-five, and remained so to such interested shareholder's stock acquisition date.

ARTICLE 10

NON–JUDICIAL DISSOLUTION

§ 1001. Authorization of Dissolution

A corporation may be dissolved under this article. Such dissolution shall be authorized at a meeting of shareholders by the vote of the holders of two-thirds of all outstanding shares entitled to vote thereon, except as otherwise provided under section 1002 (Dissolution under provision in certificate of incorporation).

§ 1002. Dissolution Under Provision in Certificate of Incorporation

(a) The certificate of incorporation may contain a provision that any shareholder, or the holders of any specified number or proportion of shares, or of any specified number or proportion of shares of any class or series thereof, may require the dissolution of the corporation at will or upon the occurrence of a specified event. If the certificate of incorporation contains such a provision, a certificate of dissolution under section 1003 (Certificate of dissolution; contents) may be signed, verified and delivered to the department of state as provided in section 104 (Certificate; requirements, signing, filing, effectiveness) when authorized by a holder or holders of the number or proportion of shares specified in such provision, given in such manner as may be specified therein, or if no manner is specified therein, when authorized on written consent signed by such holder or holders; or such certificate may be signed, verified and delivered to the department by such holder or holders or by such of them as are designated by them.

(b) An amendment of the certificate of incorporation which adds a provision permitted by this section, or which changes or strikes out such a provision, shall be authorized at a meeting of shareholders by vote of all outstanding shares, whether or not otherwise entitled to vote on any amendment, or of such lesser proportion of shares and of such class or series of shares, but not less than a majority of all outstanding shares entitled to vote on any amendment, as may be provided specifically in the certificate of incorporation for adding, changing or striking out a provision permitted by this section.

(c) If the certificate of incorporation of any corporation contains a provision authorized by this section, the existence of such provision shall be noted conspicuously on the face or back of every certificate for shares issued by such corporation.

ARTICLE 11

JUDICIAL DISSOLUTION

§ 1101. Attorney–General's Action for Judicial Dissolution

(a) The attorney-general may bring an action for the dissolution of a corporation upon one or more of the following grounds:

(1) That the corporation procured its formation through fraudulent misrepresentation or concealment of a material fact.

(2) That the corporation has exceeded the authority conferred upon it by law, or has violated any provision of law whereby it has forfeited its

charter, or carried on, conducted or transacted its business in a persistently fraudulent or illegal manner, or by the abuse of its powers contrary to the public policy of the state has become liable to be dissolved. . . .

§ 1102. Directors' Petition for Judicial Dissolution

If a majority of the board adopts a resolution that finds that the assets of a corporation are not sufficient to discharge its liabilities or that a dissolution will be beneficial to the shareholders, it may present a petition for its dissolution.

§ 1103. Shareholders' Petition for Judicial Dissolution

(a) If the shareholders of a corporation adopt a resolution stating that they find that its assets are not sufficient to discharge its liabilities, or that they deem a dissolution to be beneficial to the shareholders, the shareholders or such of them as are designated for that purpose in such resolution may present a petition for its dissolution.

(b) A shareholders' meeting to consider such a resolution may be called, notwithstanding any provision in the certificate of incorporation, by the holders of ten percent of all outstanding shares entitled to vote thereon, or if the certificate of incorporation authorizes a lesser proportion of shares to call the meeting, by such lesser proportion. A meeting under this paragraph may not be called more often than once in any period of twelve consecutive months.

(c) Such a resolution may be adopted at a meeting of shareholders by vote of the holders of a majority of all outstanding shares entitled to vote thereon or if the certificate of incorporation requires a greater proportion of votes to adopt such a resolution, by such greater proportion.

§ 1104. Petition in Case of Deadlock Among Directors or Shareholders

(a) Except as otherwise provided in the certificate of incorporation under section 613 (Limitations on right to vote), the holders of one-half of all outstanding shares of a corporation entitled to vote in an election of directors may present a petition for dissolution on one or more of the following grounds:

(1) That the directors are so divided respecting the management of the corporation's affairs that the votes required for action by the board cannot be obtained.

(2) That the shareholders are so divided that the votes required for the election of directors cannot be obtained.

(3) That there is internal dissension and two or more factions of shareholders are so divided that dissolution would be beneficial to the shareholders.

(b) If the certificate of incorporation provides that the proportion of votes required for action by the board, or the proportion of votes of shareholders required for election of directors, shall be greater than that otherwise required by this chapter, such a petition may be presented by the holders of more than one-third of all outstanding shares entitled to vote on non-judicial dissolution under section 1001 (Authorization of dissolution).

(c) Notwithstanding any provision in the certificate of incorporation, any holder of shares entitled to vote at an election of directors of a corporation, may present a petition for its dissolution on the ground that the shareholders are so divided that they have failed, for a period which includes at least two consecutive annual meeting dates, to elect successors to directors whose terms have expired or would have expired upon the election and qualification of their successors.

§ 1104–a. Petition for Judicial Dissolution Under Special Circumstances

(a) The holders of twenty percent or more of all outstanding shares of a corporation, other than a corporation registered as an investment company under an act of congress entitled "Investment Company Act of 1940", no shares of which are listed on a national securities exchange or regularly quoted in an over-the-counter market by one or more members of a national or an affiliated securities association, who are entitled to vote in an election of directors may present a petition of dissolution on one or more of the following grounds:

(1) The directors or those in control of the corporation have been guilty of illegal, fraudulent or oppressive actions toward the complaining shareholders;

(2) The property or assets of the corporation are being looted, wasted, or diverted for non-corporate purposes by its directors, officers or those in control of the corporation.

(b) The court, in determining whether to proceed with involuntary dissolution pursuant to this section, shall take into account:

(1) Whether liquidation of the corporation is the only feasible means whereby the petitioners may reasonably expect to obtain a fair return on their investment; and

(2) Whether liquidation of the corporation is reasonably necessary for the protection of the rights and interests of any substantial number of shareholders or of the petitioners.

(c) In addition to all other disclosure requirements, the directors or those in control of the corporation, no later than thirty days after the filing of a petition hereunder, shall make available for inspection and copying to the petitioners under reasonable working conditions the corporate financial books and records for the three preceding years.

(d) The court may order stock valuations be adjusted and may provide for a surcharge upon the directors or those in control of the corporation upon a finding of wilful or reckless dissipation or transfer of assets or corporate property without just or adequate compensation therefor.

§ 1111. Judgment or Final Order of Dissolution

(a) In an action or special proceeding under this article if, in the court's discretion, it shall appear that the corporation should be dissolved, it shall make a judgment or final order dissolving the corporation.

(b) In making its decision, the court shall take into consideration the following criteria:

(1) In an action brought by the attorney-general, the interest of the public is of paramount importance.

(2) In a special proceeding brought by directors or shareholders, the benefit to the shareholders of a dissolution is of paramount importance.

(3) In a special proceeding brought under section 1104 (Petition in case of deadlock among directors or shareholders) or section 1104–a (Petition for judicial dissolution under special circumstances) dissolution is not to be denied merely because it is found that the corporate business has been or could be conducted at a profit.

(c) If the judgment or final order shall provide for a dissolution of the corporation, the court may, in its discretion, provide therein for the distribution of the property of the corporation to those entitled thereto according to their respective rights.

(d) The clerk of the court or such other person as the court may direct shall transmit certified copies of the judgment or final order of dissolution to the department of state and to the clerk of the county in which the office of the corporation was located at the date of the judgment or order. Upon filing by the department of state, the corporation shall be dissolved.

(e) The corporation shall promptly thereafter transmit a certified copy of the judgment or final order to the clerk of each other county in which its certificate of incorporation was filed.

§ 1118. Purchase of Petitioner's Shares; Valuation

(a) In any proceeding brought pursuant to section eleven hundred four-a of this chapter, any other shareholder or shareholders or the corporation may, at any time within ninety days after the filing of such petition or at such later time as the court in its discretion may allow, elect to purchase the shares owned by the petitioners at their fair value and upon such terms and conditions as may be approved by the court, including the conditions of paragraph (c) herein. An election pursuant to this section shall be irrevocable unless the court, in its discretion, for just and equitable considerations, determines that such election be revocable.

(b) If one or more shareholders or the corporation elect to purchase the shares owned by the petitioner but are unable to agree with the petitioner upon the fair value of such shares, the court, upon the application of such prospective purchaser or purchasers or the petitioner, may stay the proceedings brought pursuant to section 1104–a of this chapter and determine the fair value of the petitioner's shares as of the day prior to the date on which such petition was filed, exclusive of any element of value arising from such filing but giving effect to any adjustment or surcharge found to be appropriate in the proceeding under section 1104–a of this chapter. In determining the fair value of the petitioner's shares, the court, in its discretion, may award interest from the date the petition is filed to the date of payment for the petitioner's share at an equitable rate upon judicially determined fair value of his shares.

(c) In connection with any election to purchase pursuant to this section:

(1) If such election is made beyond ninety days after the filing of the petition, and the court allows such petition, the court, in its discretion, may award the petitioner his reasonable expenses incurred in the proceeding prior to such election, including reasonable attorneys' fees;

(2) The court, in its discretion, may require, at any time prior to the actual purchase of petitioner's shares, the posting of a bond or other acceptable security in an amount sufficient to secure petitioner for the fair value of his shares.

ARTICLE 13

FOREIGN CORPORATIONS

§ 1315. Record of Shareholders

(a) Any resident of this state who shall have been a shareholder of record, for at least six months immediately preceding his demand, of a foreign corporation doing business in this state, or any resident of this state holding, or thereunto authorized in writing by the holders of, at least five percent of any class of the outstanding shares, upon at least five days' written demand may require such foreign corporation to produce a record of its shareholders setting forth the names and addresses of all shareholders, the number and class of shares held by each and the dates when they respectively became the owners of record thereof and shall have the right to examine in person or by agent or attorney at the office of the foreign corporation in this state or at the office of its transfer agent or registrar in this state or at such other place in the county in this state in which the foreign corporation is doing business as may be designated by the foreign corporation, during the usual business hours, the record of shareholders or an exact copy thereof certified as correct by the corporate officer or agent responsible for keeping or producing such record and to make extracts therefrom. Resident holders of voting trust certificates representing shares of the foreign corporation shall for the purpose of this section be regarded as shareholders.

(b) An examination authorized by paragraph (a) may be denied to such shareholder or other person upon his refusal to furnish to the foreign corporation or its transfer agent or registrar an affidavit that such inspection is not desired for a purpose which is in the interest of a business or object other than the business of the foreign corporation and that such shareholder or other person has not within five years sold or offered for sale any list of shareholders of any corporation of any type or kind, whether or not formed under the laws of this state, or aided or abetted any person in procuring any such record of shareholders for any such purpose.

(c) Upon refusal by the foreign corporation or by an officer or agent of the foreign corporation to produce for examination or to permit an examination of the record of shareholders as herein provided, the person making the demand for production and examination may apply to the supreme court in the judicial district where the office of the foreign corporation within this state is located, upon such notice as the court may direct, for an order directing the foreign corporation, its officer or agent, to show cause why an order should not be granted directing such production and permitting such examination by the applicant. Upon the return day of the order to show cause, the court shall hear the parties summarily, by affidavit or otherwise, and if its appears that the applicant is qualified and entitled to such examination, the court shall grant an order compelling such production for examination and awarding such further relief as to the court may seem just and proper.

(d) Nothing herein contained shall impair the power of courts to compel the production for examination of the books of a foreign corporation. The record of shareholders specified in paragraph (a) shall be prima facie evidence of the facts therein stated in favor of the plaintiff in any action or special proceeding against such foreign corporation or any of its officers, directors or shareholders.

§ 1317. Liabilities of Directors and Officers of Foreign Corporations

(a) Except as otherwise provided in this chapter, the directors and officers of a foreign corporation doing business in this state are subject, to the same extent as directors and officers of a domestic corporation, to the provisions of:

(1) Section 719 (Liability of directors in certain cases) except subparagraph (a)(3) thereof, and

(2) Section 720 (Action against directors and officers for misconduct.)

(b) Any liability imposed by paragraph (a) may be enforced in, and such relief granted by, the courts in this state, in the same manner as in the case of a domestic corporation.

§ 1318. Liability of Foreign Corporations for Failure to Disclose Required Information

(a) A foreign corporation doing business in this state shall, in the same manner as a domestic corporation, disclose to its shareholders of record who are residents of this state the information required under paragraph (c) of section 510 (Dividends or other distributions in cash or property), . . . paragraph (d) of section 515 (Reacquired shares), paragraph (c) of section 516 (Reduction of stated capital in certain cases), [or] subparagraph (a)(4) of section 517 (Special provisions relative to surplus and reserves) . . . , and shall be liable as provided in section 520 (Liability for failure to disclose required information) for failure to comply in good faith with these requirements.

(b) For the purposes of this section, [a] foreign corporation [authorized to do business in New York] may by board action determine the amount of its earned surplus before the declaration of its first dividend after either (1) the effective date of this chapter or (2) the date of filing of its application for authority under this chapter, whichever is later; and such determination if made in good faith shall be conclusive. Thereafter such foreign corporation may determine the amount or availability of its earned surplus in the same manner as a domestic corporation.

§ 1319. Applicability of Other Provisions

(a) In addition to articles 1 (Short title; definitions; application; certificates; miscellaneous) and 3 (Corporate name and service of process) and the other sections of article 13, the following provisions, to the extent provided therein, shall apply to a foreign corporation doing business in this state, its directors, officers and shareholders:

(1) Section 623 (Procedure to enforce shareholder's right to receive payment for shares).

(2) Section 626 (Shareholders' derivative action brought in the right of the corporation to procure a judgment in its favor).

(3) Section 627 (Security for expenses in shareholders' derivative action brought in the right of the corporation to procure a judgment in its favor).

(4) Sections 721 (Exclusivity of statutory provisions for indemnification of directors and officers) through 727 (Insurance for indemnification of directors and officers), inclusive.

(5) Section 808 (Reorganization under act of congress).

(6) Section 907 (Merger or consolidation of domestic and foreign corporations).

§ 1320. Exemption From Certain Provisions

(a) Notwithstanding any other provision of this chapter, a foreign corporation doing business in this state which is authorized under this article, its directors, officers and shareholders, shall be exempt from the provisions of paragraph (e) of section 1316 (Voting trust records), subparagraph (a)(1) of section 1317 (Liabilities of directors and officers of foreign corporations), section 1318 (Liability of foreign corporations for failure to disclose required information) and subparagraph (a)(4) of section 1319 (Applicability of other provisions) if when such provision would otherwise apply:

(1) Shares of such corporation were listed on a national securities exchange, or

(2) Less than one-half of the total of its business income for the preceding three fiscal years, or such portion thereof as the foreign corporation was in existence, was allocable to this state for franchise tax purposes under the tax law.

PENNSYLVANIA CONSOL. STATS. ANN. TITLE 15

TITLE 15

CORPORATIONS AND UNINCORPORATED ASSOCIATIONS

PART II

CORPORATIONS

SUBPART B

BUSINESS CORPORATIONS

ARTICLE A

PRELIMINARY PROVISIONS

Chapter 11

GENERAL PROVISIONS

ARTICLE B

DOMESTIC CORPORATIONS GENERALLY

Chapter 17

OFFICERS, DIRECTORS, AND SHAREHOLDERS

Subchapter B

Fiduciary Duty

ARTICLE C

DOMESTIC CORPORATION ANCILLARIES

Chapter 25

REGISTERED CORPORATIONS

Subchapter A

Preliminary Provisions

Subchapter F

Business Combinations

Subchapter G

Control–Share Acquisitions

Subchapter H

Disgorgement by Certain Controlling Shareholders Following Attempts to Acquire Control

Subchapter I

Severance Compensation for Employees Terminated Following Certain Control–Share Acquisitions

Subchapter J

Business Combination Transactions—Labor Contracts

SUBPART B

BUSINESS CORPORATIONS

ARTICLE A

PRELIMINARY PROVISIONS

Chapter 11

GENERAL PROVISIONS

§ 1103. Definitions

"Exchange Act." The Securities Exchange Act of 1934 (48 Stat. 881, 15 U.S.C. § 78a et seq.)....

"Registered corporation." A corporation defined in section 2502 (relating to registered corporation status)....

ARTICLE B

DOMESTIC CORPORATIONS GENERALLY

Chapter 17

OFFICERS, DIRECTORS, AND SHAREHOLDERS

Subchapter B

Fiduciary Duty

§ 1711. Alternative provisions

(a) **General rule.**—Section 1716 (relating to alternative standard) shall not be applicable to any business corporation to which section 1715 (relating to exercise of powers generally) is applicable.

(b) **Exceptions.**—Section 1715 shall be applicable to:

(1) Any registered corporation described in section 2502(1)(i) (relating to registered corporation status), except a corporation:

    (i) the bylaws of which explicitly provide that section 1715 . . . shall not be applicable to the corporation by amendment adopted by the board of directors on or before July 26, 1990, in the case of a corporation that was a registered corporation described in section 2502(1)(i) on April 27, 1990; or

    (ii) in any other case, the articles of which explicitly provide that section 1715 . . . shall not be applicable to the corporation by a provision included in the original articles, or by an articles amendment adopted on or before 90 days after the corporation first becomes a registered corporation described in section 2502(1)(i).

(2) Any registered corporation described solely in section 2502(1)(ii), except a corporation:

    (i) the bylaws of which explicitly provide that section 1715 . . . shall not be applicable to the corporation by amendment adopted by the board of directors on or before April 27, 1991, in the case of a corporation that was a registered corporation described solely in section 2502(1)(ii) on April 27, 1990; or

    (ii) in any other case, the articles of which explicitly provide that section 1715 . . . shall not be applicable to the corporation by a provision included in the original articles, or by an articles amendment adopted on or before one year after the corporation first becomes a registered corporation described in section 2502(1)(ii).

(3) Any business corporation that is not a registered corporation described in section 2502(1), except a corporation:

    (i) the bylaws of which explicitly provide that section 1715 . . . shall not be applicable to the corporation by amendment adopted by the board of directors on or before April 27, 1991, in the case of a corporation that was a business corporation on April 27, 1990; or

    (ii) in any other case, the articles of which explicitly provide that section 1715 or corresponding provisions of prior law shall not be applicable to the corporation by a provision included in the original articles, or by an articles amendment adopted on or before one year after the corporation first becomes a business corporation. . . .

§ 1712. Standard of care and justifiable reliance

    (a) Directors.—A director of a business corporation shall stand in a fiduciary relation to the corporation and shall perform his duties as a director, including his duties as a member of any committee of the board upon which he may serve, in good faith, in a manner he reasonably believes to be in the best interests of the corporation and with such care, including reasonable inquiry, skill and diligence, as a person of ordinary prudence would use under similar circumstances. In performing his duties, a director shall be entitled to rely in good faith on information, opinions, reports or statements, including financial statements and other financial data, in each case prepared or presented by any of the following:

> (1) One or more officers or employees of the corporation whom the director reasonably believes to be reliable and competent in the matters presented.

> (2) Counsel, public accountants or other persons as to matters which the director reasonably believes to be within the professional or expert competence of such person.

> (3) A committee of the board upon which he does not serve, duly designated in accordance with law, as to matters within its designated authority, which committee the director reasonably believes to merit confidence.

(b) Effect of actual knowledge.—A director shall not be considered to be acting in good faith if he has knowledge concerning the matter in question that would cause his reliance to be unwarranted.

(c) Officers.—Except as otherwise provided in the bylaws, an officer shall perform his duties as an officer in good faith, in a manner he reasonably believes to be in the best interests of the corporation and with such care, including reasonable inquiry, skill and diligence, as a person of ordinary prudence would use under similar circumstances. A person who so performs his duties shall not be liable by reason of having been an officer of the corporation.

§ 1713. Personal liability of directors

(a) General rule.—If a bylaw adopted by the shareholders of a business corporation so provides, a director shall not be personally liable, as such, for monetary damages for any action taken unless:

> (1) the director has breached or failed to perform the duties of his office under this subchapter; and

> (2) the breach or failure to perform constitutes self-dealing, willful misconduct or recklessness.

(b) Exceptions.—

Subsection (a) shall not apply to:

> (1) the responsibility or liability of a director pursuant to any criminal statute; or

(2) the liability of a director for the payment of taxes pursuant to Federal, State or local law.

. . .

§ 1715. Exercise of powers generally

(a) General rule.—In discharging the duties of their respective positions, the board of directors, committees of the board and individual directors of a business corporation may, in considering the best interests of the corporation, consider to the extent they deem appropriate:

(1) The effects of any action upon any or all groups affected by such action, including shareholders, employees, suppliers, customers and creditors of the corporation, and upon communities in which offices or other establishments of the corporation are located.

(2) The short-term and long-term interests of the corporation, including benefits that may accrue to the corporation from its long-term plans and the possibility that these interests may be best served by the continued independence of the corporation.

(3) The resources, intent and conduct (past, stated and potential) of any person seeking to acquire control of the corporation.

(4) All other pertinent factors.

(b) Consideration of interests and factors.—The board of directors, committees of the board and individual directors shall not be required, in considering the best interests of the corporation or the effects of any action, to regard any corporate interest or the interests of any particular group affected by such action as a dominant or controlling interest or factor. The consideration of interests and factors in the manner described in this subsection and in subsection (a) shall not constitute a violation of section 1712 (relating to standard of care and justifiable reliance).

(c) Specific applications.—In exercising the powers vested in the corporation, including, without limitation, those powers pursuant to section 1502 (relating to general powers), and in no way limiting the discretion of the board of directors, committees of the board and individual directors pursuant to subsections (a) and (b), the fiduciary duty of directors shall not be deemed to require them:

(1) to redeem any rights under, or to modify or render inapplicable, any shareholder rights plan, including, but not limited to, a plan adopted pursuant or made subject to section 2513 (relating to disparate treatment of certain persons);

(2) to render inapplicable, or make determinations under, the provisions of Subchapter E (relating to control transactions), F (relating to business combinations), G (relating to control-share acquisitions) or H (relating to disgorgement by certain controlling

shareholders following attempts to acquire control) of Chapter 25 or under any other provision of this title relating to or affecting acquisitions or potential or proposed acquisitions of control; or

(3) to act as the board of directors, a committee of the board or an individual director solely because of the effect such action might have on an acquisition or potential or proposed acquisition of control of the corporation or the consideration that might be offered or paid to shareholders in such an acquisition.

(d) Presumption.—Absent breach of fiduciary duty, lack of good faith or self-dealing, any act as the board of directors, a committee of the board or an individual director shall be presumed to be in the best interests of the corporation. In assessing whether the standard set forth in section 1712 has been satisfied, there shall not be any greater obligation to justify, or higher burden of proof with respect to, any act as the board of directors, any committee of the board or any individual director relating to or affecting an acquisition or potential or proposed acquisition of control of the corporation than is applied to any other act as a board of directors, any committee of the board or any individual director. Notwithstanding the preceding provisions of this subsection, any act as the board of directors, a committee of the board or an individual director relating to or affecting an acquisition or potential or proposed acquisition of control to which a majority of the disinterested directors shall have assented shall be presumed to satisfy the standard set forth in section 1712, unless it is proven by clear and convincing evidence that the disinterested directors did not assent to such act in good faith after reasonable investigation.

(e) Definition.—The term "disinterested director" as used in subsection (d) and for no other purpose means:

(1) A director of the corporation other than:

(i) A director who has a direct or indirect financial or other interest in the person acquiring or seeking to acquire control of the corporation or who is an affiliate or associate, as defined in section 2552 (relating to definitions), of, or was nominated or designated as a director by, a person acquiring or seeking to acquire control of the corporation.

(ii) Depending on the specific facts surrounding the director and the act under consideration, an officer or employee or former officer or employee of the corporation.

(2) A person shall not be deemed to be other than a disinterested director solely by reason of any or all of the following:

(i) The ownership by the director of shares of the corporation.

(ii) The receipt as a holder of any class or series of any distribution made to all owners of shares of that class or series.

(iii) The receipt by the director of director's fees or other consideration as a director.

(iv) Any interest the director may have in retaining the status or position of director.

(v) The former business or employment relationship of the director with the corporation.

(vi) Receiving or having the right to receive retirement or deferred compensation from the corporation due to service as a director, officer or employee.

(f) Cross reference.—See section 1711 (relating to alternative provisions).

§ 1716. Alternative standard

(a) General rule.—In discharging the duties of their respective positions, the board of directors, committees of the board and individual directors of a business corporation may, in considering the best interests of the corporation, consider the effects of any action upon employees, upon suppliers and customers of the corporation and upon communities in which offices or other establishments of the corporation are located, and all other pertinent factors. The consideration of those factors shall not constitute a violation of section 1712 (relating to standard of care and justifiable reliance).

(b) Presumption.—Absent breach of fiduciary duty, lack of good faith or self-dealing, actions taken as a director shall be presumed to be in the best interests of the corporation.

(c) Cross reference.—See section 1711 (relating to alternative provisions).

§ 1717. Limitation on standing

The duty of the board of directors, committees of the board and individual directors under section 1712 (relating to standard of care and justifiable reliance) is solely to the business corporation and may be enforced directly by the corporation or may be enforced by a shareholder, as such, by an action in the right of the corporation, and may not be enforced directly by a shareholder or by any other person or group. Notwithstanding the preceding sentence, sections 1715(a) and (b) (relating to exercise of powers generally) and 1716(a) (relating to alternative standard) do not impose upon the board of directors, committees of the board and individual directors any legal or equitable duties, obligations or liabilities or create any right or cause of action against, or basis for standing to sue, the board of directors, committees of the board and individual directors.

ARTICLE C

DOMESTIC CORPORATION ANCILLARIES

Chapter 25

REGISTERED CORPORATIONS

Subchapter A

Preliminary Provisions

§ 2502. Registered corporation status

Subject to additional definitions contained in subsequent provisions of this chapter which are applicable to specific subchapters of this chapter, as used in this chapter, the term "registered corporation" shall mean:

    (1) A domestic business corporation:

        (i) that:

           (A) has a class or series of shares entitled to vote generally in the election of directors of the corporation registered under the [Exchange Act]; or . . .

        (ii) that is:

           (A) subject to the reporting obligations imposed by section 15(d) of the Exchange Act by reason of having filed a registration statement which has become effective under the Securities Act of 1933 relating to shares of a class or series of its equity securities entitled to vote generally in the election of directors . . . .

A corporation which satisfies both subparagraphs (i) and (ii) shall be deemed to be described solely in subparagraph (i) for the purposes of this chapter.

    (2) A domestic business corporation all of the shares of which are owned, directly or indirectly, by one or more registered corporations . . . .

Subchapter F

Business Combinations

§ 2552. Definitions

The following words and phrases when used in this subchapter shall have the meanings given to them in this section unless the context clearly indicates otherwise: . . .

"Beneficial owner." When used with respect to any shares, a person:

(1) that, individually or with or through any of its affiliates or associates, beneficially owns such shares, directly or indirectly;

(2) that, individually or with or through any of its affiliates or associates, has:

(i) the right to acquire such shares (whether the right is exercisable immediately or only after the passage of time), pursuant to any agreement, arrangement or understanding (whether or not in writing), or upon the exercise of conversion rights, exchange rights, warrants or options, or otherwise, except that a person shall not be deemed the beneficial owner of shares tendered pursuant to a tender or exchange offer made by such person or the affiliates or associates of any such person until the tendered shares are accepted for purchase or exchange; or

(ii) the right to vote such shares pursuant to any agreement, arrangement or understanding (whether or not in writing), except that a person shall not be deemed the beneficial owner of any shares under this subparagraph if the agreement, arrangement or understanding to vote such shares:

(A) arises solely from a revocable proxy or consent given in response to a proxy or consent solicitation made in accordance with the applicable rules and regulations under the Exchange Act; and

(B) is not then reportable on a Schedule 13D under the Exchange Act, (or any comparable or successor report); or

(3) that has any agreement, arrangement or understanding (whether or not in writing), for the purpose of acquiring, holding, voting (except voting pursuant to a revocable proxy or consent as described in paragraph (2)(ii)), or disposing of such shares with any other person that beneficially owns, or whose affiliates or associates beneficially own, directly or indirectly, such shares. . . .

"Voting shares." Shares of a corporation entitled to vote generally in the election of directors.

Subchapter G

Control–Share Acquisitions

§ 2562. Definitions

The following words and phrases when used in this subchapter shall have the meanings given to them in this section unless the context clearly indicates otherwise. . . .

"Publicly disclosed or caused to be disclosed." Includes, but is not limited to, any disclosure (whether or not required by law) that becomes public made by a person:

(1) with the intent or expectation that such disclosure become public; or

(2) to another where the disclosing person knows, or reasonably should have known, that the receiving person was not under an obligation to refrain from making such disclosure, directly or indirectly, to the public and such receiving person does make such disclosure, directly or indirectly, to the public. . . .

Subchapter H

Disgorgement by Certain Controlling Shareholders Following Attempts to Acquire Control

§ 2571.   Application and effect of subchapter

(a) *General rule.*—Except as otherwise provided in this section, this subchapter shall apply to every registered corporation.

(b) *Exceptions.*—This subchapter shall not apply to any transfer of an equity security:

(1) Of a registered corporation described in section 2502(1)(ii) or (2) (relating to registered corporation status).

(2) Of a corporation:

(i) the bylaws of which explicitly provide that this subchapter shall not be applicable to the corporation by amendment adopted by the board of directors on or before July 26, 1990, in the case of a corporation:

(A) which on April 27, 1990, was a registered corporation described in section 2502(1)(i); and

(B) did not on that date have outstanding one or more classes or series of preference shares entitled, upon the occurrence of a default in the payment of dividends or another similar contingency, to elect a majority of the members of the board of directors (a bylaw adopted on or before July 26, 1990, by a corporation excluded from the scope of this subparagraph by this clause shall be ineffective unless ratified under subparagraph (ii));

(ii) the bylaws of which explicitly provide that this sub-chapter shall not be applicable to the corporation by amendment ratified by the board of directors on or after December 19, 1990, and on or before March 19, 1991, in the case of a corporation:

(A) which on April 27, 1990, was a registered corporation described in section 2502(1)(i);

(B) which on that date had outstanding one or more classes or series of preference shares entitled, upon the occurrence of a default in the payment of dividends or another similar contingency, to elect a majority of the members of the board of directors; and

(C) the bylaws of which on that date contained a provision described in subparagraph (i); or

(iii) in any other case, the articles of which explicitly provide that this subchapter shall not be applicable to the corporation by a provision included in the original articles, or by an articles amendment adopted at any time while it is a corporation other than a registered corporation described in section 2502(1)(i) or on or before 90 days after the corporation first becomes a registered corporation described in section 2502(1)(i). . . .

(6) Consummated by:

(i) The corporation or any of its subsidiaries.

(ii) Any savings, stock ownership, stock option or other benefit plan of the corporation or any of its subsidiaries, or any fiduciary with respect to any such plan when acting in such capacity, or by any participant in any such plan with respect to any equity security acquired pursuant to any such plan or any equity security acquired as a result of the exercise or conversion of any equity security (specifically including any options, warrants or rights) issued to such participant by the corporation pursuant to any such plan. . . .

(7) (i) where the acquisition of the equity security has been approved by a resolution adopted prior to the acquisition of the equity security; or

(ii) where the disposition of the equity security has been approved by a resolution adopted prior to the disposition of the equity security if the equity security at the time of the adoption of the resolution is beneficially owned by a person or group that is or was a controlling person or group with respect to the corporation and is in control of the corporation if:

the resolution in either subparagraph (i) or (ii) is approved by the board of directors and ratified by the affirmative vote of the shareholders entitled to cast at least a majority of the votes which all shareholders are entitled to cast thereon and identifies the specific person or group that proposes such acquisition or disposition, the specific purpose of such acquisition or disposition and the specific number of equity securities that are proposed to be acquired or disposed of by such person or group.
. . .

(d) *Formation of group.*—For the purposes of this subchapter, if there is no change in the beneficial ownership of an equity security held by a person, then the formation of or participation in a group involving the person shall not be deemed to constitute an acquisition of the beneficial ownership of such equity security by the group.

§ 2572. Policy and purpose

(a) *General rule.*—The purpose of this subchapter is to protect certain registered corporations and legitimate interests of various groups related to such corporations from certain manipulative and coercive actions. Specifically, this subchapter seeks to:

(1) Protect registered corporations from being exposed to and paying "greenmail."

(2) Promote a stable relationship among the various parties involved in registered corporations, including the public whose confidence in the future of a corporation tends to be undermined when a corporation is put "in play."

(3) Ensure that speculators who put registered corporations "in play" do not misappropriate corporate values for themselves at the expense of the corporation and groups affected by corporate actions.

(4) Discourage such speculators from putting registered corporations "in play" through any means, including, but not limited to, offering to purchase at least 20% of the voting shares of the corporation or threatening to wage or waging a proxy contest in connection with or as a means toward or part of a plan to acquire control of the corporation, with the effect of reaping short-term speculative profits.

Moreover, this subchapter recognizes the right and obligation of the Commonwealth to regulate and protect the corporations it creates from abuses resulting from the application of its own laws affecting generally corporate governance and particularly director obligations, mergers and related matters. Such laws, and the obligations imposed on directors or others thereunder, should not be the vehicles by which registered corporations are manipulated in certain instances for the purpose of obtaining short-term profits.

(b) *Limitations.*—The purpose of this subchapter is not to affect legitimate shareholder activity that does not involve putting a corporation "in play" or involve seeking to acquire control of the corporation. Specifically, the purpose of this subchapter is not to:

(1) curtail proxy contests on matters properly submitted for shareholder action under applicable State or other law, including, but not limited to, certain elections of directors, corporate governance matters such as cumulative voting or staggered boards, or other corporate matters such as environmental issues or conducting business in a particular country if, in any such instance, such proxy contest is not utilized in connection with or as a means toward or part of a plan to put the corporation "in play" or to seek to acquire control of the corporation; or

(2) affect the solicitation of proxies or consents by or on behalf of the corporation in connection with shareholder meetings or actions of the corporation.

§ 2573. Definitions

The following words and phrases when used in this subchapter shall have the meanings given to them in this section unless the context clearly indicates otherwise:

"Beneficial owner." The term shall have the meaning specified in section 2552 (relating to definitions).

"Control." The power, whether or not exercised, to direct or cause the direction of the management and policies of a person, whether through the ownership of voting shares, by contract or otherwise.

"Controlling person or group."

(1)(i) A person or group who has acquired, offered to acquire or, directly or indirectly, publicly disclosed or caused to be disclosed (other than for the purpose of circumventing the intent of this subchapter) the intention of acquiring voting power over voting shares of a registered corporation that would entitle the holder thereof to cast at least 20% of the votes that all shareholders would be entitled to cast in an election of directors of the corporation; or

(ii) a person or group who has otherwise, directly or indirectly, publicly disclosed or caused to be disclosed (other than for the purpose of circumventing the intent of this subchapter) that it may seek to acquire control of a corporation through any means.

(2) Two or more persons acting in concert, whether or not pursuant to an express agreement, arrangement, relationship or understanding, including as a partnership, limited partnership, syndicate, or through any means of affiliation whether or not formally organized, for the purpose of acquiring, holding, voting or disposing of equity securities of a corporation shall be deemed a group for

purposes of this subchapter. Notwithstanding any other provision of this subchapter to the contrary, and regardless of whether a group has been deemed to acquire beneficial ownership of an equity security under this subchapter, each person who participates in a group, where such group is a controlling person or group as defined in this subchapter, shall also be deemed to be a controlling person or group for the purposes of this subchapter. . . .

"Equity security." Any security, including all shares, stock or similar security, and any security convertible into (with or without additional consideration) or exercisable for any such shares, stock or similar security, or carrying any warrant, right or option to subscribe to or purchase such shares, stock or similar security or any such warrant, right, option or similar instrument. . . .

"Profit." The positive value, if any, of the difference between:

(1) the consideration received from the disposition of equity securities less only the usual and customary broker's commissions actually paid in connection with such disposition; and

(2) the consideration actually paid for the acquisition of such equity securities plus only the usual and customary broker's commissions actually paid in connection with such acquisition.

"Proxy." Includes any proxy, consent or authorization.

"Proxy solicitation" or "solicitation of proxies." Includes any solicitation of a proxy, including a solicitation of a revocable proxy of the nature and under the circumstances described in section 2574(b)(3) (relating to controlling person or group safe harbor).

"Publicly disclosed or caused to be disclosed." The term shall have the meaning specified in section 2562 (relating to definitions).

"Transfer." Acquisition or disposition.

"Voting shares." The term shall have the meaning specified in section 2552 (relating to definitions).

§ 2574. Controlling person or group safe harbor

(a) *Nonparticipant.*—For the purpose of this subchapter, a person or group shall not be deemed a controlling person or group, absent significant other activities indicating that a person or group should be deemed a controlling person or group, by reason of voting or giving a proxy or consent as a shareholder of the corporation if the person or group is one who or which:

(1) did not acquire any voting shares of the corporation with the purpose of changing or influencing control of the corporation or seeking to acquire control of the corporation or in connection with or as a participant in any agreement, arrangement, relationship, understanding or otherwise having any such purpose;

(2) if control were acquired, would not be a person or group or a participant in a group that has control over the corporation and will not receive, directly or indirectly, any consideration from a person or group that has control over the corporation other than consideration offered proportionately to all holders of voting shares of the corporation; and

(3) if a proxy or consent is given, executes a revocable proxy or consent given without consideration in response to a proxy or consent solicitation made in accordance with the applicable rules and regulations under the Exchange Act under circumstances not then reportable on Schedule 13D under the Exchange Act (or any comparable or successor report) by the person or group who gave the proxy or consent.

(b) *Certain holders.*—For the purpose of this subchapter, a person or group shall not be deemed a controlling person or group under subparagraph (1)(i) of the definition of "controlling person or group" in section 2573 (relating to definitions) if such person or group holds voting power:

(1) in good faith and not for the purpose of circumventing this subchapter, as an agent, bank, broker, nominee or trustee for one or more beneficial owners who do not individually or, if they are a group acting in concert, as a group have the voting power specified in subparagraph (1)(i) of the definition of "controlling person or group" in section 2573;

(2) in connection with the solicitation of proxies or consents by or on behalf of the corporation in connection with shareholder meetings or actions of the corporation; or

(3) in the amount specified in subparagraph (1)(i) of the definition of "controlling person or group" in section 2573 as a result of the solicitation of revocable proxies or consents with respect to voting shares if such proxies or consents both:

(i) are given without consideration in response to a proxy or consent solicitation made in accordance with the applicable rules and regulations under the exchange act; and

(ii) do not empower the holder thereof, whether or not this power is shared with any other person, to vote such shares except on the specific matters described in such proxy or consent and in accordance with the instructions of the giver of such proxy or consent. . . .

§ 2575. Ownership by corporation of profits resulting from certain transactions

Any profit realized by any person or group who is or was a controlling person or group with respect to a registered corporation from the disposition of any equity security of the corporation to any person ... including, without limitation, to the corporation ... or to another member of the controlling person or group, shall belong to and be recoverable by the corporation where the profit is realized by such person or group:

(1) from the disposition of the equity security within 18 months after the person or group obtained the status of a controlling person or group; and

(2) the equity security had been acquired by the controlling person or group within 24 months prior to or 18 months subsequent to the obtaining by the person or group of the status of a controlling person or group.

Any transfer by a controlling person or group of the ownership of any equity security may be suspended on the books of the corporation, and certificates representing such securities may be duly legended, to enforce the rights of the corporation under this subchapter.

§ 2576. Enforcement actions

(a) *Venue.*—Actions to recover any profit due under this subchapter may be commenced in any court of competent jurisdiction by the registered corporation issuing the equity security or by any holder of any equity security of the corporation in the name and on behalf of the corporation if the corporation fails or refuses to bring the action within 60 days after written request by a holder or shall fail to prosecute the action diligently. If a judgment requiring the payment of any such profits is entered, the party bringing such action shall recover all costs, including reasonable attorney fees, incurred in connection with enforcement of this subchapter.

(b) *Jurisdiction.*—By engaging in the activities necessary to become a controlling person or group and thereby becoming a controlling person or group, the person or group and all persons participating in the group consent to personal jurisdiction in the courts of this Commonwealth for enforcement of this subchapter. Courts of this Commonwealth may exercise personal jurisdiction over any controlling person or group in actions to enforce this subchapter.... Service of process may be made upon such persons outside this Commonwealth in accordance with the procedures specified by 42 Pa.C.S. § 5323 (relating to service of process on persons outside this Commonwealth).

(c) *Limitation.*—Any action to enforce this subchapter shall be brought within two years from the date any profit recoverable by the corporation was realized.

Subchapter I

Severance Compensation for Employees Terminated Following Certain Control–Share Acquisitions

§ 2581. Definitions

The following words and phrases when used in this subchapter shall have the meanings given to them in this section unless the context clearly indicates otherwise:

"Acquiring person." The term shall have the meaning specified in section 2562 (relating to definitions).

"Control-share acquisition." The term shall have the meaning specified in section 2562.

"Control-share approval."

(1) The occurrence of both:

(i) a control-share acquisition to which Subchapter G (relating to control-share acquisitions) applies with respect to a registered corporation described in section 2502(1)(i) (relating to registered corporation status) by an acquiring person; and

(ii) the according by such registered corporation of voting rights pursuant to section 2564(a) (relating to voting rights of shares acquired in a control-share acquisition) in connection with such control-share acquisition to control shares of the acquiring person.

(2) The term shall also include a control-share acquisition effected by an acquiring person, other than a control-share acquisition described in section 2561(b)(3), (4) or (5) (other than subparagraph 2561(b)(5)(vii)) (relating to application and effect of subchapter) if the control-share acquisition:

(i)(A) occurs primarily in response to the actions of another acquiring person where Subchapter G (relating to control-share acquisitions) applies to a control-share acquisition or proposed control-share acquisition by such other acquiring person; and

(B) either:

(I) pursuant to an agreement or plan [of merger, consolidation, or share exchange] described in section 2561(b)(5)(vii);

839

(II) after adoption of an amendment to the articles of the registered corporation [which provide that Subchapter G shall not be applicable to the corporation] pursuant to section 2561(b)(2)(iii); or

(III) after reincorporation of the registered corporation in another jurisdiction;

if the agreement or plan is approved or the amendment or reincorporation is adopted by the board of directors of the corporation during the period commencing after the satisfaction by such other acquiring person of the requirements of section 2565(a) or (b) (relating to procedure for establishing voting rights of control shares) and ending 90 days after the date such issue is voted on by the shareholders, is withdrawn from consideration or becomes moot; or

(ii) is consummated in any manner by a person who satisfied, within two years prior to such acquisition, the requirements of section 2565(a) or (b).

"Control shares." The term shall have the meaning specified in section 2562.

"Eligible employee." Any employee of a registered corporation (or any subsidiary thereof) if:

(1) the registered corporation was the subject of a control-share approval;

(2) the employee was an employee of such corporation (or any subsidiary thereof) within 90 days before or on the day of the control-share approval and had been so employed for at least two years prior thereto; and

(3) the employment of the employee is in this Commonwealth.

"Employee." Any person lawfully employed by an employer.

"Employment in this Commonwealth."

(1) The entire service of an employee, performed inside and outside of this Commonwealth, if the service is localized in this Commonwealth.

(2) Service shall be deemed to be localized in this Commonwealth if:

(i) the service is performed entirely inside this Commonwealth; or

(ii) the service is performed both inside and outside of this Commonwealth but the service performed outside of this Commonwealth is incidental to the service of the employee inside this Commonwealth, as where such service is temporary or transitory in nature or consists of isolated transactions.

(3) Employment in this Commonwealth shall also include service of the employee, performed inside and outside of this Commonwealth, if the service is not localized in any state, but some of the service is performed in this Commonwealth, and:

(i) the base of operations of the employee is in this Commonwealth;

(ii) there is no base of operations, and the place from which such service is directed or controlled is in this Commonwealth; or

(iii) the base of operations of the employee or place from which such service is directed or controlled is not in any state in which some part of the service is performed, but the residence of the employee is in this Commonwealth.

"Minimum severance amount." With respect to an eligible employee, the weekly compensation of the employee multiplied by the number of the completed years of service of the employee, up to a maximum of 26 times the weekly compensation of the employee.

"Subsidiary." The term shall have the meaning specified in section 2552 (relating to definitions).

"Termination of employment." The layoff of at least six months, or the involuntary termination of an employee, except that any employee employed in a business operation who is continued or employed or offered employment (within 60 days) by the purchaser of such business operation, on substantially the same terms (including geographic location) as those pursuant to which the employee was employed in such business operation, shall not be deemed to have been laid off or involuntarily terminated for the purposes of this subchapter by such transfer of employment to the purchaser, but the purchaser shall make the lump-sum payment under this subchapter in the event of a layoff of at least six months or the involuntary termination of the employee within the period specified in section 2582 (relating to severance compensation).

"Weekly compensation." The average regular weekly compensation of an employee based on normal schedule of hours in effect for such employee over the last three months preceding the control-share approval.

"Year of service." Each full year during which the employee has been employed by the employer.

§ 2582. Severance compensation

(a) General rule.—Any eligible employee whose employment is terminated, other than for willful misconduct connected with the work of the employee, within 90 days before the control-share approval with respect to the registered corporation if such termination was pursuant to an agreement, arrangement or understanding, whether formal or informal, with the acquiring person whose control shares were accorded voting rights in connection with such control-share approval or within 24 calendar months after the control-share approval with respect to the registered corporation shall receive a one-time, lump-sum payment from the employer equal to:

> (1) the minimum severance amount with respect to the employee; less

> (2) any payments made to the employee by the employer due to termination of employment, whether pursuant to any contract, policy, plan or otherwise, but not including any final wage payments to the employee or payments to the employee under pension, savings, retirement or similar plans.

(b) Limitation.—If the amount specified in subsection (a)(2) is at least equal to the amount specified in subsection (a)(1), no payment shall be required to be made under this subchapter.

(c) Due date of payment.—Severance compensation under this subchapter to eligible employees shall be made within one regular pay period after the last day of work of the employee, in the case of a layoff known at such time to be at least six months or an involuntary termination and in all other cases within 30 days after the eligible employee first becomes entitled to compensation under this subchapter.

§ 2583. Enforcement and remedies

(a) Notice.—Within 30 days of the control-share approval, the employer shall provide written notice to each eligible employee and to the collective bargaining representative, if any, of the rights of eligible employees under this subchapter.

(b) Remedies.—In the event any eligible employee is denied a lump-sum payment in violation of this subchapter or the employer fails to provide the notice required by subsection (a), the employee on his or her own behalf or on behalf of other employees similarly situated, or the collective bargaining representative, if any, on the behalf of the employee, may, in addition to all other remedies available at law or in equity, bring an action to remedy such violation. In any such action, the court may order such equitable or legal relief as it deems just and proper.

(c) Civil penalty.—In the case of violations of subsection (a), the court may order the employer to pay to each employee who was subject to a termination of employment and entitled to severance compensation under this subchapter a civil penalty not to exceed $75 per day for each business day that notice was not provided to such employee.

(d) Successor liability.—The rights under this subchapter of any individual who was an eligible employee at the time of the control-share approval shall vest at that time, and, in any action based on a violation of this subchapter, recovery may be secured against:

(1) a merged, consolidated or resulting domestic or foreign corporation or other successor employer; or

(2) the corporation after its status as a registered corporation has terminated;

notwithstanding any provision of law to the contrary.

Subchapter J

Business Combination Transactions—Labor Contracts

§ 2585. Application and effect of subchapter

(a) General rule.—Except as otherwise provided in this section, this subchapter shall apply to every business combination transaction relating to a business operation if such business operation was owned by a registered corporation (or any subsidiary thereof) at the time of a control-share approval with respect to the corporation (regardless of the fact, if such be the case, that such operation after the control-share approval is owned by the registered corporation or any other person).

(b) Exceptions.—This subchapter shall not apply to:

(1) Any business combination transaction occurring more than five years after the control-share approval of the registered corporation.

(2) Any business operation located other than in this Commonwealth.

§ 2586. Definitions

The following words and phrases when used in this subchapter shall have the meanings given to them in this section unless the context clearly indicates otherwise:

"Business combination transaction." Any merger or consolidation, sale, lease, exchange or other disposition, in one transaction or a series of transactions, whether affecting all or substantially all the property and assets, including its good will, of the business operation that is the subject of the labor contract referred to in section 2587 (relating to labor contracts preserved in business combination transactions) or any transfer of a controlling interest in such business operation.

"Control-share approval." The term shall have the meaning specified in section 2581 (relating to definitions).

"Covered labor contract." Any labor contract if such contract:

(1) covers persons engaged in employment in this Commonwealth;

(2) was negotiated by a labor organization or by a collective bargaining agent or other representative;

(3) relates to a business operation that was owned by the registered corporation (or any subsidiary thereof) at the time of the control-share approval with respect to such corporation; and

(4) was in effect and covered such business operation and such employees at the time of such control-share approval.

"Employee" and **"employment in this Commonwealth."** The terms shall have the meanings specified in section 2581.

"Subsidiary." The term shall have the meaning specified in section 2552 (relating to definitions).

§ 2587. Labor contracts preserved in business combination transactions

No business combination transaction shall result in the termination or impairment of the provisions of any covered labor contract, and the contract shall continue in effect pursuant to its terms until it is terminated pursuant to any termination provision contained therein or until otherwise agreed upon by the parties to such contract or their successors.

§ 2588. Civil remedies

(a) General rule.—In the event that an employee is denied or fails to receive wages, benefits or wage supplements or suffers any contractual loss as a result of a violation of this subchapter, the employee on his or her own behalf or on behalf of other employees similarly situated, or the labor organization or collective bargaining agent party to the labor contract, may, in addition to all other remedies available at law or in equity, bring an action in any court of competent jurisdiction to recover such wages, benefits, wage supplements or contractual losses and to enjoin the violation of this subchapter.

(b) Successor liability.—The rights under this subchapter of any employee at the time of the control-share approval shall vest at that time, and, in any action based on a violation of this subchapter, recovery may be secured against:

(1) a merged, consolidated or resulting domestic or foreign corporation or other successor employer; or

(2) the corporation after its status as a registered corporation has terminated;

notwithstanding any provision of law to the contrary.

VIRGINIA CORPORATIONS
CODE § 13.1–690

§ 13.1–690 General standards of conduct for director

A. A director shall discharge his duties as a director, including his duties as a member of a committee, in accordance with his good faith business judgment of the best interests of the corporation. . . .

NEW YORK PROFESSIONAL SERVICE CORPORATION LAW

New York B.C.L. Article 15

ARTICLE 15—PROFESSIONAL SERVICE CORPORATIONS

ARTICLE 15—PROFESSIONAL SERVICE CORPORATIONS

1501 Definitions.—As used in this article, unless the context otherwise requires, the term:

(a) "licensing authority" means the regents of the university of the state of New York or the state education department, as the case may be, in the case of all professions licensed under title eight of the education law, and the appropriate appellate division of the supreme court in the case of the profession of law.

(b) "Profession" includes any practice as an attorney and counselor-at-law, or as a licensed physician, and those occupations designated in title eight of the education law.

(c) "Professional service" means any type of service to the public which may be lawfully rendered by a member of a profession within the purview of his profession.

(d) "Professional service corporation" means a corporation organized under this article.

(e) "Officer" does not include the secretary or an assistant secretary of a corporation having only one shareholder.

1502 Corporations Organized Under Other Provisions of Law.—The provisions of this article shall not apply to corporations heretofore or hereafter duly organized under any other provision of law.

1503 Organization.—(a) Notwithstanding any other provision of law, one or more individuals duly authorized by law to render the same professional service within the state may organize, or cause to be organized, a professional service corporation for pecuniary profit under this article for the purpose of rendering the same professional service, except that one or more individuals duly authorized by law to practice professional engineering, architecture, landscape architecture or land surveying within the state may organize, or cause to be organized, a professional service corporation for pecuniary profit under this article for the purpose of rendering such professional services as such individuals are authorized to practice.

(b) The certificate of incorporation of a professional service corporation shall meet the requirements of this chapter and (i) shall state the profession or professions to be practiced by such corporation and the names and residence addresses of all individuals who are to be the original shareholders, directors and officers of such corporation, and (ii) shall have attached thereto a certificate or certificates issued by the licensing authority certifying that each of the proposed shareholders, directors and officers is authorized by law to practice a profession which the corporation is being organized to practice and, if applicable, that one or more of such individuals is authorized to practice each profession which the corporation will be authorized to practice.

(c) A certified copy of the certificate of incorporation and of each amendment thereto shall be filed by the corporation with the licensing authority within thirty days after the filing of such certificate or amendment with the department of state.

(d) A professional service corporation, other than a corporation authorized to practice law, shall be under the supervision of the regents of the university of the state of New York and be subject to disciplinary proceedings and penalties, and its certificate of incorporation shall be subject to suspension, revocation or annulment for cause, in the same manner and to the same extent as is provided with respect to individuals and their licenses, certificates, and registrations in title eight of the education law relating to the applicable profession. Notwithstanding the provisions of this subdivision, a professional service corporation authorized to practice medicine shall be subject to the prehearing procedures and hearing procedures as is provided with respect to individual physicians and their licenses in Title II–A of article two of the public health law.

(e) A corporation authorized to practice law shall be subject to the regulation and control of, and its certificate of incorporation shall be subject to suspension, revocation or annulment for cause by, the appellate division of the supreme court and the court of appeals in the same manner and to the same extent provided in the judiciary law with respect to individual attorneys and counselors-at-law. Such corporation need not qualify for any certification under section four hundred sixty-four of the judiciary law [certification by state board of successful candidates], take an oath of office under section four hundred sixty-six of such law [attorney's oath of office] or register under section four hundred sixty-seven of such law [registration of attorneys].

(f) The order of suspension, revocation or annulment of the certificate of incorporation of a professional service corporation pursuant to subdivisions (e) and (f) of this section shall be effective upon the filing of such order with the department of state.

1504 Rendering of Professional Service.—(a) No professional service corporation may render professional services except through individuals authorized by law to render such professional services as individuals.

(b) Each final plan and report made or issued by a corporation practicing professional engineering, architecture, landscape architecture or land surveying shall bear the name and seal of one or more professional engineers, architects, landscape architects or land surveyors, respectively, who are in responsible charge of such plan or report.

(c) Each report, diagnosis, prognosis, and prescription made or issued by a corporation practicing medicine, dentistry, podiatry, optometry, ophthalmic dispensing, veterinary medicine, pharmacy, nursing, physiotherapy or chiropractic shall bear the signature of one or more physicians, dentists, podiatrists, optometrists, ophthalmic dispensers, veterinarians, pharmacists, nurses, physiotherapists, or chiropractors, respectively, who are in responsible charge of such report, diagnosis, prognosis, or prescription.

(d) Each record, transcript, report and hearing report prepared by a corporation practicing certified shorthand reporting shall bear the signature of one or more certified shorthand reporters who are in responsible charge of such record, transcript, report, or hearing report.

(e) Each corporation practicing public accounting or certified public accounting shall maintain records indicating the identity of each public accountant or certified public accountant, respectively, who was responsible for each report or statement which is issued prepared or examined by such corporation.

(f) Each opinion prepared by a corporation practicing law shall bear the signature of one more attorneys and counsellors-at-law who are in responsible charge of such opinion.

(g) In addition to the requirements in subdivisions (b) through (f), inclusive, each document prepared by a corporation which under the rules, regulations, laws or customs of the applicable profession is required to bear the signature of an individual in responsible charge of such document, shall be signed by one or more such individuals.

1505 Professional Relationships and Liabilities.—(a) Each shareholder, employee or agent of a professional service corporation shall be personally and fully liable and accountable for any negligent or wrongful act or misconduct committed by him or by any person under his direct supervision and control while rendering professional services on behalf of such corporation.

(b) The relationship of an individual to a professional service corporation with which such individual is associated, whether as shareholder, director, officer, employee or agent, shall not modify or diminish the jurisdiction over him of the licensing authority and in the case of an attorney and counsellor-at-law, the other courts of this state.

1506 Purposes of Incorporation.—No professional service corporation shall engage in any business other than the rendering of the professional services for which it was incorporated; provided that such corporation may invest its funds in real estate, mortgages, stocks, bonds or any other type of investments.

1507 Issuance of Shares.—A professional service corporation may issue shares only to individuals who are authorized by law to practice in this state a profession which such corporation is authorized to practice and who are or have been engaged in the practice of such profession in such corporation or a predecessor entity, or who will engage in the practice of such profession in such corporation within thirty days of the date such shares are issued. No shareholder of a professional service corporation shall enter into a voting trust agreement, proxy, or any other type agreement vesting in another person, other than another shareholder of the same corporation or a person who would be eligible to become a shareholder if employed by the corporation, the authority to exercise voting power of any or all of his shares. All shares issued, agreements made, or proxies granted in violation of this section shall be void.

1509 Disqualification of Shareholders, Directors, Officers and Employees.—If any shareholder, director, officer or employee of a professional service corporation who has been rendering professional service to the public becomes legally disqualified to practice his profession within this state, he shall sever all employment with, and financial interests (other than interests as a creditor) in, such corporation forthwith or as otherwise provided in section 1510. All provisions of law regulating the rendering of professional services by a person elected or appointed to a public office shall be applicable to a shareholder, director, officer and employee of such corporation in the same manner and to the same extent as if fully set forth herein. Such legal disqualification to practice his profession within this state shall be deemed to constitute an irrevocable offer by the disqualified shareholder to sell his shares to the corporation, pursuant to the provisions of section 1510 or of the certificate of incorporation, by-laws or agreement among the corporation and all shareholders, whichever is applicable. Compliance with the terms of such offer shall be specifically enforceable in the courts of this state. A professional service corporation's failure to enforce compliance with this provision shall constitute a ground for forfeiture of its certificate of incorporation and its dissolution.

1510 Death or Disqualification of Shareholders.—(a) A professional service corporation shall purchase or redeem the shares of a shareholder in case of his death or disqualification pursuant to the provisions of section 1509, within six months after the appointment of the executor or administrator or other legal representative of the estate of such deceased shareholder, or within six months after such disqualification, at the book value of such shares as of the end of the month immediately preceding the death or disqualification of the shareholder as determined from the books and records of the corporation in accordance with its regular method of accounting. The certificate of incorporation, the by-laws of the corporation or an agreement among the corporation and all shareholders may modify this section by providing for a shorter period of purchase or redemption, or an alternate method of determining the price to be paid for the shares, or both. If the corporation shall fail to purchase or redeem such shares within the required period, a successful plaintiff in an action to recover the purchase price of such shares shall also be awarded reasonable attorneys' fees and costs. Limitations on the purchase or redemption of shares set forth in section five hundred thirteen shall not apply to the purchase or redemption of shares pursuant to this section. Nothing herein contained shall prevent a corporation from paying pension benefits or other deferred compensation to or on behalf of a former or deceased officer, director or employee thereof as otherwise permitted by law. The provisions of this section shall not be deemed to require the purchase of the shares of a disqualified shareholder where the period of disqualification is for less than six months, and the shareholder again becomes eligible to practice his profession within six months from the date of disqualification.

(b) Notwithstanding the provisions of subdivision (a), the corporation shall not be required to purchase or redeem the shares of a deceased or disqualified shareholder if such shares, within the time limit prescribed by subdivision (a), are sold or transferred to another professional pursuant to the provisions of section 1511.

1511 Transfer of Shares.—No shareholder of a professional service corporation may sell or transfer his shares in such corporation except to another individual who is eligible to have shares issued to him by such corporation or except in trust to another individual who would be eligible to receive shares if he were employed by the corporation. Nothing herein contained shall be construed to prohibit the transfer of shares by operation of law or by court decree. No transferee of shares by operation of law or court decree may vote the shares for any purpose whatsoever except with respect to corporate action under section nine hundred nine [sale, lease, exchange or other disposition of assets] and section one thousand one [authorization of dissolution]. The restriction in the preceding sentence shall not apply, however, where such transferee would be eligible to have shares issued to him if he were an employee of the corporation and, if there are other shareholders, a majority of such other shareholders shall fail to redeem the shares so transferred, pursuant to section 1510, within sixty days of receiving written notice of such transfer. Any sale or transfer, except by operation of law or court decree or except for a corporation having only one shareholder, may be made only after the same shall have been approved by the board of directors, or at a shareholders' meeting specially called for such purpose by such proportion, not less than a majority, of the outstanding shares as may be provided in the certificate of incorporation or in the by-laws of such professional service corporation. At such shareholders' meeting the shares held by the shareholder proposing to sell or transfer his shares may not be voted or counted for any purpose, unless all shareholders consent that such shares be voted or counted. The certificate of incorporation or the by-laws of the professional service corporation, or the professional service corporation and the shareholders by private agreement, may provide, in lieu of or in addition to the foregoing provisions, for the alienation of shares and may require the redemption or purchase of such shares by such corporation at prices and in a manner specifically set forth therein. The existence of the restrictions on the sale or transfer of shares, as contained in this article and, if applicable, in the certificate of incorporation, by-laws, stock purchase or stock redemption agreement, shall be noted conspicuously on the face or back of every certificate for shares issued by a professional service corporation. Any sale or transfer in violation of such restrictions shall be void.

1512 Corporate Name.—(a) Notwithstanding any other provision of law, the name of a professional service corporation may contain any word which, at the time of incorporation, could be used in the name of a partnership practicing a profession which the corporation is authorized to practice, and may not contain any word which could not be used by such a partnership. Provided, however, the name of a professional service corporation may not contain the name of a deceased person unless

(1) such person's name was part of the corporate name at the time of such person's death; or

(2) such person's name was part of the name of an existing partnership and at least two-thirds of such partnership's partners become shareholders of the corporation.

(b) Such corporate name shall end with the words "Professional Corporation" or the abbreviation "P.C." The provisions of paragraph one of subdivision (a) of section three hundred one shall not apply to a professional service corporation.

1513 Business Corporation Law Applicable.—This chapter, except article thirteen [foreign corporations] and article fifteen–A [foreign professional service corporations], shall be applicable to a professional service corporation except to the extent that the provisions thereof conflict with this article. A professional service corporation may consolidate or merge only with another corporation organized under this article or authorized to do business in this state under article fifteen–A of this chapter or authorized and registered to practice the same profession pursuant to the applicable provisions of subdivision six of section seventy-two hundred nine of the education law or subdivision four of section seventy-three hundred seven of the education law, or may be a member of a professional service limited liability company, a foreign professional service limited liability company, a registered limited liability partnership or foreign limited liability partnership, and only if all of the professions practiced by such corporations, limited liability companies or limited liability partnerships could be practiced by a single corporation organized under this article.

1514 Triennial Statement.—Each professional service corporation shall, on or before the first day of July every three years, furnish a statement to the licensing authority listing the name and residence address of each shareholder, director and officer of such corporation and certifying that all such individuals are authorized by law in this state to practice a profession which such corporation is authorized to practice. The statement shall be signed by the president or any vice-president of the corporation and attested to by the secretary or any assistant secretary of the corporation.

1515 Regulation of Professions.—This article shall not repeal, modify or restrict any provision of the education law or the judiciary law regulating the professions referred to therein except to the extent in conflict herewith.

1516 Corporate Mergers, Consolidations and Other Reorganizations.—Notwithstanding any inconsistent provision of this article, a professional service corporation, pursuant to the provisions of article nine of this chapter [merger and consolidation], may be merged or consolidated with another corporation formed pursuant to the provisions of this chapter or with a corporation authorized and registered to practice the same profession pursuant to the applicable provisions of subdivision six of section seventy-two hundred nine of the education law (engineer or land surveyor) or subdivision four of section seventy-three hundred seven of the education law (architect) of article one hundred forty-five of the education law, or with a foreign corporation, or may be otherwise reorganized, provided that the corporation which survives or which is formed pursuant thereto is a professional service corporation or a foreign professional service corporation practicing the same profession or professions in this state or the state of incorporation or, if one of the original corporations is authorized to practice pursuant to the provisions of either subdivision six of section seven thousand two hundred nine or subdivision four of section seven thousand three hundred seven, a corporation authorized and registered to practice the same profession pursuant to the applicable provisions of subdivision six of section seventy-two hundred nine of the education law (engineer or land surveyor) or subdivision four of section seventy-three hundred seven of the education law (architect) of article one hundred forty-five of the education law. The restrictions on the issuance, transfer or sale of shares of a professional service corporation shall be suspended for a period not exceeding thirty days with respect to any issuance, transfer or sale of shares made pursuant to such merger, consolidation or reorganization, provided that (i) no person who would not be eligible to be a shareholder in the absence of this section shall vote the shares of or receive any distribution from such corporation; (ii) after such merger, consolidation or reorganization, any professional service corporation which survives or which is created thereby shall be subject to all of the provisions of this article, and (iii) shares thereafter only may be held by persons who are eligible to receive shares of such professional service corporation or such other corporation authorized and registered to practice the same profession pursuant to the applicable provisions of subdivision six of section seventy-two hundred nine of the education law (engineer or land surveyor) or subdivision four of section seventy-three hundred seven of the education law (architect) of article one hundred forty-five of the education law, which survives. Nothing herein contained shall be construed as permitting the practice of a profession in this state by a corporation which is not incorporated pursuant to the provisions of this article or authorized to do business in the state pursuant to the provisions of article fifteen-A of this chapter or authorized and registered to practice a profession pursuant to the applicable provisions of article one hundred forty-five of the education law. For the purposes of this section, other reorganizations shall be limited to those reorganizations defined in paragraph one of subsection (a) of section three hundred sixty-eight of the internal revenue code.

UNIFORM COMMERCIAL CODE

§ 8–204. Effect of Issuer's Restrictions on Transfer

A restriction on transfer of a security imposed by the issuer, even if otherwise lawful, is ineffective against any person without actual knowledge of it unless:

(a) the security is certificated and the restriction is noted conspicuously thereon; or

(b) the security is uncertificated and a notation of the restriction is contained in the initial transaction statement sent to the person or, if his interest is transferred to him other than by registration of transfer, pledge, or release, the initial transaction statement sent to the registered owner or the registered pledgee.

Official Comment....

1. Use of the words "noted" and "notation" is intended to make clear that the restriction need not be set forth in full text. See Allen v. Biltmore Tissue Corporation, 2 N.Y.2d 534, 141 N.E.2d 812 (1957).

2. Securities traded on financial markets are generally assumed to be free of adverse claims .... That assumption should not be lightly negated. Therefore, a strict rule as to notice of a restriction on transfer is here imposed. The issuer can protect itself by noting the restriction on the certificate or initial transaction statement. Refusal by an issuer to register a transfer on the basis of an unnoted restriction constitutes a conversion and the issuer can be compelled to register the transfer .... Conversely, the issuer to whom a certificated security with proper notation of a restriction is presented thereby receives timely notification of an adverse claim and is under a duty to inquire ....

A purchaser with actual knowledge of an unnoted restriction certainly has notice of an adverse claim ....

3. A transferee who purchases securities in organized financial markets often may neither take physical delivery of a certificated security nor have an uncertificated security registered in his name. ... Under those circumstances the transferee may have no occasion to examine the writing on the certificate or the initial transaction statement. Nonetheless the transferee is charged with notice of restrictions noted on the certificate or on the initial transaction statement sent to the registered owner or registered pledgee. ...

854

4. Most jurisdictions recognize the right of issuers to impose restrictions giving either the issuer itself or other stockholders the option to purchase the security at an ascertained price before it is offered to third parties. Vannucci v. Peduni, 217 Cal. 138, 17 P.2d 706 (1932); People ex rel. Rudaitis v. Galskis, 233 Ill.App. 414 (1924); Bloomingdale v. Bloomingdale, 107 Misc. 646, 177 N.Y.S. 873 (1919). This is the type of restriction contemplated by the present section. Mere notation on the certificate or initial transaction statement cannot, of course, validate an otherwise unlawful restriction. The present section in no way alters the prevailing case law which recognizes free alienability as an inherent attribute of securities and holds invalid unreasonable restraints on alienation such as those requiring consents of directors without establishing criteria for the granting or withholding of such consents and those giving the directors an option of purchase at a price to be fixed in their sole discretion. Howe v. Roberts, 209 Ala. 80, 95 So. 344 (1923); People ex rel. Malcom v. Lake Sand Corporation, 251 Ill.App. 499 (1929); Morris v. Hussong Dyeing Machine Co., 81 N.J.Eq. 256, 86 A. 1026 (1913); New England Trust Co. v. Abbott, 162 Mass. 148, 38 N.E. 432, 27 L.R.A. 271 (1894).

No interference is intended with the common practice of closing books for proper corporate purposes.

5. ...

Historically restrictions on transfer were most commonly imposed by so-called "closely-held" issuers (including cooperatives and the like) in an attempt to restrict control if not total membership to a homogeneous security holder group. They have been increasingly resorted to by issuers with publicly held securities seeking to police enforcement of the registration requirements of the Securities Act of 1933 against persons purchasing their securities in a transaction exempt from those requirements (e.g., one "not involving any public offering" [Securities Act of 1933, Section 4(2)]) or against persons in a "control" relationship to the issuer. [See Securities Act of 1933, Section 2(11) and Rule 405 of the Rules and Regulations of the Securities and Exchange Commission under that Act.] Particularly in the latter context in which notation of the restriction on all affected certificates or initial transaction statements may not be practical, the issuer enforces it by notifying the holders of such certificates and refusing requests to register transfer out of the name of the "controlling person" either for purposes of sale or for delivery after sale, relying on the stated exception as to a person "with actual knowledge" of the restriction.

6. This section deals only with restrictions imposed by the issuer and restrictions imposed by statute are not affected. See Quiner v. Marblehead Social Co., 10 Mass. 476 (1813); Madison Bank v. Price, 79 Kan. 289, 100 P. 280 (1909); Healey v. Steele Center Creamery Ass'n, 115 Minn. 451, 133 N.W. 69 (1911). Nor does it deal with private

agreements between stockholders containing restrictive covenants as to the sale of the security as in In re Consolidated Factors Corporation, 46 F.2d 561 (S.D.N.Y.1931)....

§ 8–408. Statements of Uncertificated Securities

(1) Within 2 business days after the transfer of an uncertificated security has been registered, the issuer shall send to the new registered owner and, if the security has been transferred subject to a registered pledge, to the registered pledgee a written statement containing:

    (a) a description of the issue of which the uncertificated security is a part;

    (b) the number of shares or units transferred;

    (c) the name and address and any taxpayer identification number of the new registered owner and, if the security has been transferred subject to a registered pledge, the name and address and any taxpayer identification number of the registered pledgee;

    (d) a notation of any liens and restrictions of the issuer and any adverse claims ... to which the uncertificated security is or may be subject at the time of registration or a statement that there are none of those liens, restrictions, or adverse claims; and

    (e) the date the transfer was registered....

(4) An "initial transaction statement" is the statement sent to:

    (a) the new registered owner and, if applicable, to the registered pledgee pursuant to subsection (1) ....

(6) At periodic intervals no less frequent than annually and at any time upon the reasonable written request of the registered owner, the issuer shall send to the registered owner of each uncertificated security a dated written statement containing:

    (a) a description of the issue of which the uncertificated security is a part;

    (b) the name and address and any taxpayer identification number of the registered owner;

    (c) the number of shares or units of the uncertificated security registered in the name of the registered owner on the date of the statement;

    (d) the name and address and any taxpayer identification number of any registered pledgee and the number of shares or units subject to the pledge; and

    (e) a notation of any liens and restrictions of the issuer and any adverse claims ... to which the uncertificated security is or may be subject or a statement that there are none of those liens, restrictions, or adverse claims....

FEDERAL RULES OF CIVIL PROCEDURE

RULES 11, 23, 23.1

Rule 11. Signing of Pleadings, Motions, and Other Papers; Representations to Court; Sanctions

(a) Signature. Every pleading, written motion, and other paper shall be signed by at least one attorney of record in the attorney's individual name, or, if the party is not represented by an attorney, shall be signed by the party. Each paper shall state the signer's address and telephone number, if any. Except when otherwise specifically provided by rule or statute, pleadings need not be verified or accompanied by affidavit. An unsigned paper omission of the signature is corrected promptly after being called to the attention of the attorney or party.

(b) Representations to Court. By presenting to the court (whether by signing, filing, submitting, or later advocating) a pleading, written motion, or other paper, an attorney or unrepresented party is certifying that to the best of the person's knowledge, information, and belief, formed after an inquiry reasonable under the circumstances,—

(1) it is not being presented for any improper purpose, such as to harass or to cause unnecessary delay or needless increase in the cost of litigation;

(2) the claims, defenses, and other legal contentions therein are warranted by existing law or by a nonfrivolous argument for the extension, modification, or reversal of existing law or the establishment of new law;

(3) the allegations and other factual contentions have evidentiary support or, if specifically so identified, are likely to have evidentiary support after a reasonable opportunity for further investigation or discovery; and

(4) the denials of factual contentions are warranted on the evidence or, if specifically so identified, are reasonably based on a lack of information or belief.

(c) Sanctions. If, after notice and a reasonable opportunity to respond, the court determines that subdivision (b) has been violated, the court may, subject to the conditions stated below, impose an appropriate sanction upon the attorneys, law firms, or parties that have violated subdivision (b) or are responsible for the violation.

(1) How Initiated.

(A) By Motion. A motion for sanctions under this rule shall be made separately from other motions or requests and shall describe the specific conduct alleged to violate subdivision (b). It shall be served as provided in Rule 5, but shall not be filed with or presented to the court unless, within 21 days after service of the motion (or such other period as the court may prescribe), the challenged paper, claim, defense, contention, allegation, or denial is not withdrawn or appropriately corrected. If warranted, the court may award to the party prevailing on the motion the reasonable expenses and attorney's fees incurred in presenting or opposing the motion. Absent exceptional circumstances, a law firm shall be held jointly responsible for violations committed by its partners, associates, and employees.

(B) On Court's Initiative. On its own initiative, the court may enter an order describing the specific conduct that appears to violate subdivision (b) and directing an attorney, law firm, or party to show cause why it has not violated subdivision (b) with respect thereto.

(2) Nature of Sanction; Limitations. A sanction imposed for violation of this rule shall be limited to what is sufficient to deter repetition of such conduct or comparable conduct by others similarly situated. Subject to the limitations in subparagraphs (A) and (B), the sanction may consist of, or include, directives of a nonmonetary nature, an order to pay a penalty into court, or, if imposed on motion and warranted for effective deterrence, an order directing payment to the movant of some or all of the reasonable attorneys' fees and other expenses incurred as a direct result of the violation.

(A) Monetary sanctions may not be awarded against a represented party for a violation of subdivision (b)(2).

(B) Monetary sanctions may not be awarded on the court's initiative unless the court issues its order to show cause before a voluntary dismissal or settlement of the claims made by or against the party which is, or whose attorneys are, to be sanctioned.

(3) Order. When imposing sanctions, the court shall describe the conduct determined to constitute a violation of this rule and explain the basis for the sanction imposed.

(d) Inapplicability to Discovery. Subdivisions (a) through (c) of this rule do not apply to disclosures and discovery requests, responses, objections, and motions that are subject to the provisions of Rules 26 through 37.

Rule 23.   Class Actions

(a) **Prerequisites to a Class Action.**   One or more members of a class may sue or be sued as representative parties on behalf of all only if (1) the class is so numerous that joinder of all members is impracticable, (2) there are questions of law or fact common to the class, (3) the claims or defenses of the representative parties are typical of the claims or defenses of the class, and (4) the representative parties will fairly and adequately protect the interests of the class.

(b) **Class Actions Maintainable.**   An action may be maintained as a class action if the prerequisites of subdivision (a) are satisfied, and in addition:

(1) the prosecution of separate actions by or against individual members of the class would create a risk of

(A) inconsistent or varying adjudications with respect to individual members of the class which would establish incompatible standards of conduct for the party opposing the class, or

(B) adjudications with respect to individual members of the class which would as a practical matter be dispositive of the interests of the other members not parties to the adjudications or substantially impair or impede their ability to protect their interests; or

(2) the party opposing the class has acted or refused to act on grounds generally applicable to the class, thereby making appropriate final injunctive relief or corresponding declaratory relief with respect to the class as a whole; or

(3) the court finds that the questions of law or fact common to the members of the class predominate over any questions affecting only individual members, and that a class action is superior to other available methods for the fair and efficient adjudication of the controversy.   The matters pertinent to the findings include: (A) the interest of members of the class in individually controlling the prosecution or defense of separate actions; (B) the extent and nature of any litigation concerning the controversy already commenced by or against members of the class; (C) the desirability or undesirability of concentrating the litigation of the claims in the particular forum; (D) the difficulties likely to be encountered in the management of a class action.

(c) **Determination by Order Whether Class Action to be Maintained; Notice; Judgment; Actions Conducted Partially as Class Actions.**

(1) As soon as practicable after the commencement of an action brought as a class action, the court shall determine by order whether it is to be so maintained.   An order under this subdivision may be conditional, and may be altered or amended before the decision on the merits.

(2) In any class action maintained under subdivision (b)(3), the court shall direct to the members of the class the best notice practicable under the circumstances, including individual notice to all members who can be identified through reasonable effort. The notice shall advise each member that (A) the court will exclude the member from the class if the member so requests by a specified date; (B) the judgment, whether favorable or not, will include all members who do not request exclusion; and (C) any member who does not request exclusion may, if the member desires, enter an appearance through counsel.

(3) The judgment in an action maintained as a class action under subdivision (b)(1) or (b)(2), whether or not favorable to the class, shall include and describe those whom the court finds to be members of the class. The judgment in an action maintained as a class action under subdivision (b)(3), whether or not favorable to the class, shall include and specify or describe those to whom the notice provided in subdivision (c)(2) was directed, and who have not requested exclusion, and whom the court finds to be members of the class.

(4) When appropriate (A) an action may be brought or maintained as a class action with respect to particular issues, or (B) a class may be divided into subclasses and each subclass treated as a class, and the provisions of this rule shall then be construed and applied accordingly.

(d) Orders in Conduct of Actions. In the conduct of actions to which this rule applies, the court may make appropriate orders: (1) determining the course of proceedings or prescribing measures to prevent undue repetition or complication in the presentation of evidence or argument; (2) requiring, for the protection of the members of the class or otherwise for the fair conduct of the action, that notice be given in such manner as the court may direct to some or all of the members of any step in the action, or of the proposed extent of the judgment, or of the opportunity of members to signify whether they consider the representation fair and adequate, to intervene and present claims or defenses, or otherwise to come into the action; (3) imposing conditions on the representative parties or on intervenors; (4) requiring that the pleadings be amended to eliminate therefrom allegations as to representation of absent persons, and that the action proceed accordingly; (5) dealing with similar procedural matters. The orders may be combined with an order under Rule 16 [Pre-Trial Procedure; Formulating Issues], and may be altered or amended as may be desirable from time to time.

(e) Dismissal or Compromise. A class action shall not be dismissed or compromised without the approval of the court, and notice of the proposed dismissal or compromise shall be given to all members of the class in such manner as the court directs.

Rule 23.1   Derivative Actions by Shareholders

In a derivative action brought by one or more shareholders or members to enforce a right of a corporation or of an unincorporated association, the corporation or association having failed to enforce a right which may properly be asserted by it, the complaint shall be verified and shall allege (1) that the plaintiff was a shareholder or member at the time of the transaction of which the plaintiff complains or that the plaintiff's share or membership thereafter devolved on the plaintiff by operation of law, and (2) that the action is not a collusive one to confer jurisdiction on a court of the United States which it would not otherwise have. The complaint shall also allege with particularity the efforts, if any, made by the plaintiff to obtain the action the plaintiff desires from the directors or comparable authority and, if necessary, from the shareholders or members, and the reasons for the plaintiff's failure to obtain the action or for not making the effort. The derivative action may not be maintained if it appears that the plaintiff does not fairly and adequately represent the interests of the shareholders or members similarly situated in enforcing the right of the corporation or association. The action shall not be dismissed or compromised without the approval of the court, and notice of the proposed dismissal or compromise shall be given to shareholders or members in such manner as the court directs.

UNIFORM FRAUDULENT TRANSFER ACT

§ 1. Definitions ....

As used in this [Act]:

(1) "Affiliate" means:

(i) a person who directly or indirectly owns, controls, or holds with power to vote, 20 percent or more of the outstanding voting securities of the debtor, other than a person who holds the securities,

(A) as a fiduciary or agent without sole discretionary power to vote the securities; or

(B) solely to secure a debt, if the person has not exercised the power to vote;

(ii) a corporation 20 percent or more of whose outstanding voting securities are directly or indirectly owned, controlled, or held with power to vote, by the debtor or a person who directly or indirectly owns, controls, or holds, with power to vote, 20 percent or more of the outstanding voting securities of the debtor, other than a person who holds the securities,

(A) as a fiduciary or agent without sole power to vote the securities; or

(B) solely to secure a debt, if the person has not in fact exercised the power to vote;

(iii) a person whose business is operated by the debtor under a lease or other agreement, or a person substantially all of whose assets are controlled by the debtor; or

(iv) a person who operates the debtor's business under a lease or other agreement or controls substantially all of the debtor's assets....

(7) "Insider" includes ...

(ii) if the debtor is a corporation,

(A) a director of the debtor;

(B) an officer of the debtor;

(C) a person in control of the debtor;

(D) a partnership in which the debtor is a general partner;

(E) a general partner in a partnership described in clause (D); or

(F) a relative of a general partner, director, officer, or person in control of the debtor;

(iii) if the debtor is a partnership,

(A) a general partner in the debtor;

(B) a relative of a general partner in, a general partner of, or a person in control of the debtor;

(C) another partnership in which the debtor is a general partner;

(D) a general partner in a partnership described in clause (C); or

(E) a person in control of the debtor;

(iv) an affiliate, or an insider of an affiliate as if the affiliate were the debtor; and

(v) a managing agent of the debtor . . . .

(12) "Transfer" means every mode, direct or indirect, absolute or conditional, voluntary or involuntary, of disposing of or parting with an asset or an interest in an asset, and includes payment of money, release, lease, and creation of a lien or other encumbrance.

§ 2. Insolvency

(a) A debtor is insolvent if the sum of the debtor's debts is greater than all of the debtor's assets at a fair valuation . . . .

(b) A debtor who is generally not paying his [or her] debts as they become due is presumed to be insolvent.

(c) A partnership is insolvent under subsection (a) if the sum of the partnership's debts is greater than the aggregate, at a fair valuation, of all of the partnership's assets and the sum of the excess of the value of each general partner's nonpartnership assets over the partner's nonpartnership debts . . . .

§ 4. Transfers Fraudulent as to Present and Future Creditors

(a) A transfer made or obligation incurred by a debtor is fraudulent as to a creditor, whether the creditor's claim arose before or after the transfer was made or the obligation was incurred, if the debtor made the transfer or incurred the obligation . . . .

(2) without receiving a reasonably equivalent value in exchange for the transfer or obligation, and the debtor:

(i) was engaged or was about to engage in a business or a transaction for which the remaining assets of the debtor were unreasonably small in relation to the business or transaction; or

(ii) intended to incur, or believed or reasonably should have believed that he [or she] would incur, debts beyond his [or her] ability to pay as they became due . . . .

(b) In determining actual intent under subsection (a)(1), consideration may be given, among other factors, to whether:

(1) the transfer or obligation was to an insider;

(2) the debtor retained possession or control of the property transferred after the transfer; . . .

(8) the value of the consideration received by the debtor was reasonably equivalent to the value of the asset transferred or the amount of the obligation incurred;

(9) the debtor was insolvent or became insolvent shortly after the transfer was made or the obligation was incurred;

(10) the transfer occurred shortly before or shortly after a substantial debt was incurred; and

(11) the debtor transferred the essential assets of the business to a lienor who transferred the assets to an insider of the debtor.

§ 5. Transfers Fraudulent as to Present Creditors

(a) A transfer made or obligation incurred by a debtor is fraudulent as to a creditor whose claim arose before the transfer was made or the obligation was incurred if the debtor made the transfer or incurred the obligation without receiving a reasonably equivalent value in exchange for the transfer or obligation and the debtor was insolvent at that time or the debtor became insolvent as a result of the transfer or obligation.

(b) A transfer made by a debtor is fraudulent as to a creditor whose claim arose before the transfer was made if the transfer was made to an insider for an antecedent debt, the debtor was insolvent at that time, and the insider had reasonable cause to believe that the debtor was insolvent.

§ 7. Remedies of Creditors

(a) In an action for relief against a transfer or obligation under this [Act], a creditor . . . may obtain:

(1) avoidance of the transfer or obligation to the extent necessary to satisfy the creditor's claim . . .

. . .

(3) subject to applicable principles of equity and in accordance with applicable rules of civil procedure,

(i) an injunction against further disposition by the debtor or a transferee, or both, of the asset transferred or of other property;

(ii) appointment of a receiver to take charge of the asset transferred or of other property of the transferee; or

(iii) any other relief the circumstances may require.

(b) If a creditor has obtained a judgment on a claim against the debtor, the creditor, if the court so orders, may levy execution on the asset transferred or its proceeds.

§ 8. Defenses, Liability, and Protection of Transferee

(a) A transfer or obligation is not voidable under Section 4(a)(1) against a person who took in good faith and for a reasonably equivalent value or against any subsequent transferee or obligee.

(b) Except as otherwise provided in this section, to the extent a transfer is voidable in an action by a creditor under Section 7(a)(1), the creditor may recover judgment for the value of the asset transferred [at the time of the transfer, subject to adjustment as the equities may require], or the amount necessary to satisfy the creditor's claim, whichever is less. The judgment may be entered against:

(1) the first transferee of the asset or the person for whose benefit the transfer was made; or

(2) any subsequent transferee other than a good faith transferee who took for value or from any subsequent transferee....

(d) Notwithstanding voidability of a transfer or an obligation under this [Act], a good-faith transferee or obligee is entitled, to the extent of the value given the debtor for the transfer or obligation, to

(1) a lien on or a right to retain any interest in the asset transferred;

(2) enforcement of any obligation incurred; or

(3) a reduction in the amount of the liability on the judgment....

§ 9. Extinguishment of [Claim for Relief] [Cause of Action]

A [claim for relief] [cause of action] with respect to a fraudulent transfer or obligation under this [Act] is extinguished unless action is brought....

(b) under Section 4(a)(2) or 5(a), within 4 years after the transfer was made or the obligation was incurred....

BANKRUPTCY ACT, 11 U.S.C.A.
§§ 101(31), 548(a)

§ 101. Definitions...

(32) "insolvent" means—

(A) with reference to an entity other than a partnership ... financial condition such that the sum of such entity's debts is greater than all of such entity's property, at a fair valuation....

Historical and Revision Notes

The definition of "insolvent" is ... the traditional bankruptcy balance sheet test of insolvency.

§ 548. Fraudulent Transfers and Obligations

(a) The trustee [in bankruptcy] may avoid any transfer of an interest of the debtor in property, or any obligation incurred by the debtor, that was made or incurred on or within one year before the date of the filing of the petition, if the debtor voluntarily or involuntarily ....

(2)(A) received less than a reasonably equivalent value in exchange for such transfer or obligation; and

(B)(i) was insolvent on the date that such transfer was made or such obligation was incurred, or became insolvent as a result of such transfer or obligation; [or]

(ii) was engaged in business or a transaction, or was about to engage in business or a transaction, for which any property remaining with the debtor was an unreasonably small capital ....

FEDERAL MAIL FRAUD ACT
18 U.S.C. §§ 1341 ET SEQ.

§ 1341. Frauds and swindles

Whoever, having devised or intending to devise any scheme or artifice to defraud, or for obtaining money or property by means of false or fraudulent pretenses, representations, or promises, or to sell, dispose of, loan, exchange, alter, give away, distribute, supply, or furnish or procure for unlawful use any counterfeit or spurious coin, obligation, security, or other article, or anything represented to be or intimated or held out to be such counterfeit or spurious article, for the purpose of executing such scheme or artifice or attempting so to do, places in any post office or authorized depository for mail matter, any matter or thing whatever to be sent or delivered by the Postal Service, or takes or receives therefrom, any such matter or thing, or knowingly causes to be delivered by mail according to the direction thereon, or at the place at which it is directed to be delivered by the person to whom it is addressed, any such matter or thing, shall be fined not more than $1,000 or imprisoned not more than five years, or both. If the violation affects a financial institution, such person shall be fined not more than $1,000,-000 or imprisoned not more than 30 years, or both.

§ 1343. Fraud by wire, radio, or television

Whoever, having devised or intending to devise any scheme or artifice to defraud, or for obtaining money or property by means of false or fraudulent pretenses, representations, or promises, transmits or causes to be transmitted by means of wire, radio, or television communication in interstate or foreign commerce, any writings, signs, signals, pictures, or sounds for the purpose of executing such scheme or artifice, shall be fined not more than $1,000 or imprisoned not more than five years, or both. If the violation affects a financial institution, such person shall be fined not more than $1,000,000 or imprisoned not more than 30 years, or both.

INTERNAL REVENUE CODE § 162(m)

§ 162. Trade or Business Expenses ...

(m) Certain Excessive Employee Remuneration.—

(1) In General.—In the case of any publicly held corporation, no deduction shall be allowed under this chapter for applicable employee remuneration with respect to any covered employee to the extent that the amount of such remuneration for the taxable year with respect to such employee exceeds $1,000,000.

(2) Publicly Held Corporation.—For purposes of this subsection, the term "publicly held corporation" means any corporation issuing any class of common equity securities required to be registered under section 12 of the Securities Exchange Act of 1934.

(3) Covered Employee.—For purposes of this subsection, the term "covered employee" means any employee of the taxpayer if—

(A) as of the close of the taxable year, such employee is the chief executive officer of the taxpayer or is an individual acting in such a capacity, or

(B) the total compensation of such employee for the taxable year is required to be reported to shareholders under the Securities Exchange Act of 1934 by reason of such employee being among the 4 highest compensated officers for the taxable year (other than the chief executive officer).

(4) Applicable Employee Remuneration.—For purposes of this subsection—

(A) In general.—Except as otherwise provided in this paragraph, the term "applicable employee remuneration" means, with respect to any covered employee for any taxable year, the aggregate amount allowable as a deduction under this chapter for such taxable year (determined without regard to this subsection) for remuneration for services performed by such employee (whether or not during the taxable year).

(B) Exception for remuneration payable on commission basis.—The term "applicable employee remuneration" shall not include any remuneration payable on a commission basis solely on account of income generated directly by the individual performance of the individual to whom such remuneration is payable.

(C) Other performance-based compensation.—The term "applicable employee remuneration" shall not include any remuneration payable solely on account of the attainment of one or more performance goals, but only if—

(i) the performance goals are determined by a compensation committee of the board of directors of the taxpayer which is comprised solely of 2 or more outside directors,

(ii) the material terms under which the remuneration is to be paid, including the performance goals, are disclosed to shareholders and approved by a majority of the vote in a separate shareholder vote before the payment of such remuneration, and

(iii) before any payment of such remuneration, the compensation committee referred to in clause (i) certifies that the performance goals and any other material terms were in fact satisfied.

(D) Exception for existing binding contracts.—The term "applicable employee remuneration" shall not include any remuneration payable under a written binding contract which was in effect on February 17, 1993, and which was not modified thereafter in any material respect before such remuneration is paid.

(E) Remuneration.—For purposes of this paragraph, the term "remuneration" includes any remuneration (including benefits) in any medium other than cash. . . .

REGULATIONS UNDER INTERNAL REVENUE CODE § 162(m) (26 C.F.R. § 1.162–27)

§ 1.162–27 Certain employee remuneration in excess of $1,000,-000

(b) *Limitation on deduction.* Section 162(m) precludes a deduction under chapter 1 of the Internal Revenue Code by any publicly held corporation for compensation paid to any covered employee to the extent that the compensation for the taxable year exceeds $1,000,000....

(e) *Exception for qualified performance-based compensation—*

(1) *In general.* The deduction limit in paragraph (b) of this section does not apply to qualified performance-based compensation. Qualified performance-based compensation is compensation that meets all of the requirements of paragraphs (e)(2) through (e)(5) of this section.

(2) *Performance goal requirement—*

(i) *Preestablished goal.* Qualified performance-based compensation must be paid solely on account of the attainment of one or more preestablished, objective performance goals. A performance goal is considered preestablished if it is established in writing by the compensation committee not later than 90 days after the commencement of the period of service to which the performance goal relates, provided that the outcome is substantially uncertain at the time the compensation committee actually establishes the goal. However, in no event will a performance goal be considered to be preestablished if it is established after 25 percent of the period of service (as scheduled in good faith at the time the goal is established) has elapsed. A performance goal is objective if a third party having knowledge of the relevant facts could determine whether the goal is met. Performance goals can be based on one or more business criteria that apply to the individual, a business unit, or the corporation as a whole. Such business criteria could include, for example, stock price, market share, sales, earnings per share, return on equity, or costs. A performance goal need not, however, be based upon an increase or positive result under a business criterion and could include, for example, maintaining the status quo or limiting economic losses (measured, in each case, by reference to a specific business criterion). A performance goal does not include the mere continued employment of the covered employee. Thus, a vesting provision based solely on continued employment would not constitute a performance goal. See paragraph (e)(2)(vi) of this section for rules on compensation that is based on an increase in the price of stock.

(ii) *Objective compensation formula.* A preestablished performance goal must state, in terms of an objective formula or standard, the method for computing the amount of compensation payable to the employee if the goal is attained. A formula or standard is objective if a third party having knowledge of the relevant performance results could calculate the amount to be paid to the employee. In addition, a formula or standard must specify the individual employees or class of employees to which it applies.

(iii) *Discretion.*

(A) The terms of an objective formula or standard must preclude discretion to increase the amount of compensation payable that would otherwise be due upon attainment of the goal. A performance goal is not discretionary for purposes of this paragraph (e)(2)(iii) merely because the compensation committee reduces or eliminates the compensation or other economic benefit that was due upon attainment of the goal. However, the exercise of negative discretion with respect to one employee is not permitted to result in an increase in the amount payable to another employee. Thus, for example, in the case of a bonus pool, if the amount payable to each employee is stated in terms of a percentage of the pool, the sum of these individual percentages of the pool is not permitted to exceed 100 percent. If the terms of an objective formula or standard fail to preclude discretion to increase the amount of compensation merely because the amount of compensation to be paid upon attainment of the performance goal is based, in whole or in part, on a percentage of salary or base pay and the dollar amount of the salary or base pay is not fixed at the time the performance goal is established, then the objective formula or standard will not be considered discretionary for purposes of this paragraph (e)(2)(iii) if the maximum dollar amount to be paid is fixed at that time....

(v) *Compensation contingent upon attainment of performance goal.* Compensation does not satisfy the requirements of this paragraph (e)(2) if the facts and circumstances indicate that the employee would receive all or part of the compensation regardless of whether the performance goal is attained. Thus, if the payment of compensation under a grant or award is only nominally or partially contingent on attaining a performance goal, none of the compensation payable under the grant or award will be considered performance-based. For example, if an employee is entitled to a bonus under either of two arrangements, where payment under a nonperformance-based arrangement is contingent upon the failure to attain the performance goals under an otherwise performance-based arrangement, then neither arrangement provides for compensation that satisfies the requirements of this paragraph (e)(2). Compensation does not fail to be qualified performance-based compensation merely because the plan allows the compensation to be payable upon death, disability, or change of ownership or control, although compensation actually paid on account of those events prior to the attainment of the performance goal would not satisfy the requirements of this paragraph (e)(2). . . .

(vi) *Application of requirements to stock options and stock appreciation rights*—

(A) *In general.*   Compensation attributable to a stock option or a stock appreciation right is deemed to satisfy the requirements of this paragraph (e)(2) if the grant or award is made by the compensation committee; the plan under which the option or right is granted states the maximum number of shares with respect to which options or rights may be granted during a specified period to any employee; and, under the terms of the option or right, the amount of compensation the employee could receive is based solely on an increase in the value of the stock after the date of the grant or award.   Conversely, if the amount of compensation the employee will receive under the grant or award is not based solely on an increase in the value of the stock after the date of grant or award (e.g., in the case of restricted stock, or an option that is granted with an exercise price that is less than the fair market value of the stock as of the date of grant), none of the compensation attributable to the grant or award is qualified performance-based compensation because it does not satisfy the requirement of this paragraph (e)(2)(vi)(A).   Whether a stock option grant is based solely on an increase in the value of the stock after the date of grant is determined without regard to any dividend equivalent that may be payable, provided that payment of the dividend equivalent is not made contingent on the exercise of the option.   The rule that the compensation attributable to a stock option or stock appreciation right must be based solely on an increase in the value of the stock after the date of grant or award does not apply if the grant or award is made on account of, or if the vesting or exercisability of the grant or award is contingent on, the attainment of a performance goal that satisfies the requirements of this paragraph (e)(2).

(B) *Cancellation and repricing.*   Compensation attributable to a stock option or stock appreciation right does not satisfy the requirements of this paragraph (e)(2) to the extent that the number of options granted exceeds the maximum number of shares for which options may be granted to the employee as specified in the plan.   If an option is canceled, the canceled option continues to be counted against the maximum number of shares for which options may be granted to the employee under the plan.   If, after grant, the exercise price of an option is reduced, the transaction is treated as a cancellation of the option and a grant of a new option.   In such case, both the option that is deemed to be canceled and the option that is deemed to be granted reduce the maximum number of shares for which options may be granted to the employee under the plan.   This paragraph (e)(2)(vi)(B) also applies in the case of a stock appreciation right where, after the award is made, the base amount on which stock appreciation is calculated is reduced to reflect a reduction in the fair market value of stock. . . .

(3) *Outside directors—*

(i) *General rule.* The performance goal under which compensation is paid must be established by a compensation committee comprised solely of two or more outside directors. A director is an outside director if the director—. . .

(B) Is not a former employee of the publicly held corporation who receives compensation for prior services (other than benefits under a tax-qualified retirement plan) during the taxable year;

(C) Has not been an officer of the publicly held corporation; and

(D) Does not receive remuneration from the publicly held corporation, either directly or indirectly, in any capacity other than as a director. For this purpose, remuneration includes any payment in exchange for goods or services.

(ii) *Remuneration received.* For purposes of this paragraph (e)(3), remuneration is received, directly or indirectly, by a director in each of the following circumstances:

(A) If remuneration is paid, directly or indirectly, to the director personally or to an entity in which the director has a beneficial ownership interest of greater than 50 percent. For this purpose, remuneration is considered paid when actually paid (and throughout the remainder of that taxable year of the corporation) and, if earlier, throughout the period when a contract or agreement to pay remuneration is outstanding.

(B) If remuneration, other than de minimis remuneration, was paid by the publicly held corporation in its preceding taxable year to an entity in which the director has a beneficial ownership interest of at least 5 percent but not more than 50 percent. For this purpose, remuneration is considered paid when actually paid or, if earlier, when the publicly held corporation becomes liable to pay it.

(C) If remuneration, other than de minimis remuneration, was paid by the publicly held corporation in its preceding taxable year to an entity by which the director is employed or self-employed other than as a director. For this purpose, remuneration is considered paid when actually paid or, if earlier, when the publicly held corporation becomes liable to pay it.

(iii) *De minimis remuneration—*

(A) *In general.* For purposes of paragraphs (e)(3)(ii)(B) and (C) of this section, remuneration that was paid by the publicly held corporation in its preceding taxable year to an entity is de minimis if payments to the entity did not exceed 5 percent of the gross revenue of the entity for its taxable year ending with or within that preceding taxable year of the publicly held corporation.

(B) *Remuneration for personal services and substantial owners.* Notwithstanding paragraph (e)(3)(iii)(A) of this section, remuneration in excess of $60,000 is not de minimis if the remuneration is paid to an entity described in paragraph (e)(3)(ii)(B) of this section, or is paid for personal services to an entity described in paragraph (e)(3)(ii)(C) of this section.

(iv) *Remuneration for personal services.* For purposes of paragraph (e)(3)(iii)(B) of this section, remuneration from a publicly held corporation is for personal services if—

(A) The remuneration is paid to an entity for personal or professional services, consisting of legal, accounting, investment banking, and management consulting services (and other similar services that may be specified by the Commissioner in revenue rulings, notices, or other guidance published in the Internal Revenue Bulletin), performed for the publicly held corporation, and the remuneration is not for services that are incidental to the purchase of goods or to the purchase of services that are not personal services; and

(B) The director performs significant services (whether or not as an employee) for the corporation, division, or similar organization (within the entity) that actually provides the services described in paragraph (e)(3)(iv)(A) of this section to the publicly held corporation, or more than 50 percent of the entity's gross revenues (for the entity's preceding taxable year) are derived from that corporation, subsidiary, or similar organization. . . .

(4) *Shareholder approval requirement—*

(i) *General rule.* The material terms of the performance goal under which the compensation is to be paid must be disclosed to and subsequently approved by the shareholders of the publicly held corporation before the compensation is paid. The requirements of this paragraph (e)(4) are not satisfied if the compensation would be paid regardless of whether the material terms are approved by shareholders. The material terms include the employees eligible to receive compensation; a description of the business criteria on which the performance goal is based; and either the maximum amount of compensation that could be paid to any employee or the formula used to calculate the amount of compensation to be paid to the employee if the performance goal is attained (except that, in the case of a formula that fails to preclude discretion to increase the amount of compensation (as described in paragraph (e)(2)(iii)(A) of this section) merely because the amount of compensation to be paid is based, in whole or in part, on a percentage of salary or base pay and the dollar amount of the salary or base pay is not fixed at the time the performance goal is established, the maximum dollar amount of compensation that could be paid to the employee must be disclosed) . . . .

(iii) *Description of business criteria—*

(A) *In general.* Disclosure of the business criteria on which the performance goal is based need not include the specific targets that must be satisfied under the performance goal. For example, if a bonus plan provides that a bonus will be paid if earnings per share increase by 10 percent, the 10–percent figure is a target that need not be disclosed to shareholders. However, in that case, disclosure must be made that the bonus plan is based on an earnings-per-share business criterion. In the case of a plan under which employees may be granted stock options or stock appreciation rights, no specific description of the business criteria is required if the grants or awards are based on a stock price that is no less than current fair market value.

(B) *Disclosure of confidential information.* The requirements of this paragraph (e)(4) may be satisfied even though information that otherwise would be a material term of a performance goal is not disclosed to shareholders, provided that the compensation committee determines that the information is confidential commercial or business information, the disclosure of which would have an adverse effect on the publicly held corporation. Whether disclosure would adversely affect the corporation is determined on the basis of the facts and circumstances. If the compensation committee makes such a determination, the disclosure to shareholders must state the compensation committee's belief that the information is confidential commercial or business information, the disclosure of which would adversely affect the company. In addition, the ability not to disclose confidential information does not eliminate the requirement that disclosure be made of the maximum amount of compensation that is payable to an individual under a performance goal. Confidential information does not include the identity of an executive or the class of executives to which a performance goal applies or the amount of compensation that is payable if the goal is satisfied.

(iv) *Description of compensation.* Disclosure as to the compensation payable under a performance goal must be specific enough so that shareholders can determine the maximum amount of compensation that could be paid to any employee during a specified period. If the terms of the performance goal do not provide for a maximum dollar amount, the disclosure must include the formula under which the compensation would be calculated. Thus, for example, if compensation attributable to the exercise of stock options is equal to the difference in the exercise price and the current value of the stock, disclosure would be required of the maximum number of shares for which grants may be made to any employee and the exercise price of those options (*e.g.,* fair market value on date of grant). In that case, shareholders could calculate the maximum amount of compensation that would be attributable to the exercise of options on the basis of their assumptions as to the future stock price.

(v) *Disclosure requirements of the Securities and Exchange Commission.* To the extent not otherwise specifically provided in this paragraph (e)(4), whether the material terms of a performance goal are adequately disclosed to shareholders is determined under the same standards as apply under the Exchange Act.

(vi) *Frequency of disclosure.* Once the material terms of a performance goal are disclosed to and approved by shareholders, no additional disclosure or approval is required unless the compensation committee changes the material terms of the performance goal. If, however, the compensation committee has authority to change the targets under a performance goal after shareholder approval of the goal, material terms of the performance goal must be disclosed to and reapproved by shareholders no later than the first shareholder meeting that occurs in the fifth year following the year in which shareholders previously approved the performance goal.

(vii) *Shareholder vote.* For purposes of this paragraph (e)(4), the material terms of a performance goal are approved by shareholders if, in a separate vote, a majority of the votes cast on the issue (including abstentions to the extent abstentions are counted as voting under applicable state law) are cast in favor of approval....

(5) *Compensation committee certification.* The compensation committee must certify in writing prior to payment of the compensation that the performance goals and any other material terms were in fact satisfied. For this purpose, approved minutes of the compensation committee meeting in which the certification is made are treated as a written certification. Certification by the compensation committee is not required for compensation that is attributable solely to the increase in the value of the stock of the publicly held corporation....

NEW YORK STOCK EXCHANGE LISTED COMPANY MANUAL PARAS. 202, 312, 313

202.01 Internal Handling of Confidential Corporate Matters

Unusual market activity or a substantial price change has on occasion occurred in a company's securities shortly before the announcement of an important corporate action or development. Such incidents are extremely embarrassing and damaging to both the company and the Exchange since the public may quickly conclude that someone acted on the basis of inside information.

Negotiations leading to mergers and acquisitions, stock splits, the making of arrangements preparatory to an exchange or tender offer, changes in dividend rates or earnings, calls for redemption, and new contracts, products, or discoveries are the type of developments where the risk of untimely and inadvertent disclosure of corporate plans are most likely to occur. Frequently, these matters require extensive discussion and study by corporate officials before final decisions can be made. Accordingly, extreme care must be used in order to keep the information on a confidential basis.

Where it is possible to confine formal or informal discussions to a small group of the top management of the company or companies involved, and their individual confidential advisors where adequate security can be maintained, premature public announcement may properly be avoided. In this regard, the market action of a company's securities should be closely watched at a time when consideration is being given to important corporate matters. If unusual market activity should arise, the company should be prepared to make an immediate public announcement of the matter.

At some point it usually becomes necessary to involve other persons to conduct preliminary studies or assist in other preparations for contemplated transactions, e.g., business appraisals, tentative financing arrangements, attitude of large outside holders, availability of major blocks of stock, engineering studies and market analyses and surveys.

Experience has shown that maintaining security at this point is virtually impossible. Accordingly, fairness requires that the company make an immediate public announcement as soon as disclosures relating to such important matters are made to outsiders.

The extent of the disclosures will depend upon the stage of discussions, studies, or negotiations. So far as possible, public statements should be definite as to price, ratio, timing and/or any other pertinent information necessary to permit a reasonable evaluation of the matter. As a minimum, they should include those disclosures made to outsiders. Where an initial announcement cannot be specific or complete, it will need to be supplemented from time to time as more definitive or different terms are discussed or determined.

Corporate employees, as well as directors and officers, should be regularly reminded as a matter of policy that they must not disclose confidential information they may receive in the course of their duties and must not attempt to take advantage of such information themselves.

In view of the importance of this matter and the potential difficulties involved, the Exchange suggests that a periodic review be made by each company of the manner in which confidential information is being handled within its own organization. A reminder notice of the company's policy to those in sensitive areas might also be helpful.

A sound corporate disclosure policy is essential to the maintenance of a fair and orderly securities market. It should minimize the occasions where the Exchange finds it necessary to temporarily halt trading in a security due to information leaks or rumors in connection with significant corporate transactions.

While the procedures are directed primarily at situations involving two or more companies, they are equally applicable to major corporate developments involving a single company.

202.02   Relationship Between Company Officials and Others

(A) Security Analysts, Institutional Investors, Etc.

Security analysts play an increasingly important role in the evaluation and interpretation of the financial affairs of listed companies. Annual reports, quarterly reports, and interim releases cannot by their nature provide all of the financial and statistical data that should be available to the investing public. The Exchange recommends that companies observe an "open door" policy in their relations with security analysts, financial writers, shareholders, and others who have legitimate investment interest in the company's affairs.

A company should not give information to one inquirer which it would not give to another, nor should it reveal information it would not willingly give or has not given to the press for publication. Thus, for companies to give advance earnings, dividend, stock split, merger, or tender information to analysts, whether representing an institution, brokerage house, investment advisor, large shareholder, or anyone else, would clearly violate Exchange policy. On the other hand, it should not withhold information in which analysts or other members of the investment public have a warrantable interest.

If during the course of a discussion with analysts substantive material not previously published is disclosed, that material should be simultaneously released to the public. The various security analysts societies usually have a regular procedure to be followed where formal presentations are made. The company should follow these same precautions when dealing with groups of industry analysts in small or closed meetings....

202.03 Dealing With Rumors or Unusual Market Activity

The market activity of a company's securities should be closely watched at a time when consideration is being given to significant corporate matters. If rumors or unusual market activity indicate that information on impending developments has leaked out, a frank and explicit announcement is clearly required. If rumors are in fact false or inaccurate, they should be promptly denied or clarified. A statement to the effect that the company knows of no corporate developments to account for the unusual market activity can have a salutary effect. It is obvious that if such a public statement is contemplated, management should be checked prior to any public comment so as to avoid any embarrassment or potential criticism. If rumors are correct or there are developments, an immediate candid statement to the public as to the state of negotiations or of development of corporate plans in the rumored area must be made directly and openly. Such statements are essential despite the business inconvenience which may be caused and even though the matter may not as yet have been presented to the company's Board of Directors for consideration.

The Exchange recommends that its listed companies contact their Exchange representative if they become aware of rumors circulating about their company. Exchange Rule 435 provides that no member, member organization or allied member shall circulate in any manner rumors of a sensational character which might reasonably be expected to affect market conditions on the Exchange. Information provided concerning rumors will be promptly investigated.

202.04 Exchange Market Surveillance

The Exchange maintains a continuous market surveillance program through its Market Surveillance and Evaluation Division. An "on-line" computer system has been developed which monitors the price movement of every listed stock—on a trade-to-trade basis—throughout the trading session. The program is designed to closely review the markets in those securities in which unusual price and volume changes occur or where there is a large unexplained influx of buy or sell orders. If the price movement of a stock exceeds a predetermined guideline, it is immediately "flagged" and review of the situation is immediately undertaken to seek the causes of the exceptional activity. Under these circumstances, the company may be called by its Exchange representative to inquire about any company developments which have not been publicly announced but which could be responsible for unusual market activity. Where the market appears to reflect undisclosed information, the company will normally be requested to make the information public immediately. Occasionally it may be necessary to carry out a review of the trading after the fact, and the Exchange may request such information from the company as may be necessary to complete the inquiry.

The Listing Agreement provides that a company must furnish the Exchange with such information concerning the company as the Exchange may reasonably require. . . .

202.05   Timely Disclosure of Material News Developments

A listed company is expected to release quickly to the public any news or information which might reasonably be expected to materially affect the market for its securities. This is one of the most important and fundamental purposes of the listing agreement which the company enters into with the Exchange.

A listed company should also act promptly to dispel unfounded rumors which result in unusual market activity or price variations.

202.06   Procedure for Public Release of Information

(A) Immediate Release Policy

The normal method of publication of important corporate data is by means of a press release. This may be either by telephone or in written form. Any release of information that could reasonably be expected to have an impact on the market for a company's securities should be given to the wire services and the press *"For Immediate Release."*

The spirit of the immediate release policy is not considered to be violated on weekends where a "Hold for Sunday or Monday A.M.'s" is used to obtain a broad public release of the news. This procedure facilitates the combination of a press release with a mailing to shareholders.

Annual and quarterly earnings, dividend announcements, mergers, acquisitions, tender offers, stock splits, major management changes, and any substantive items of unusual or non-recurrent nature are examples of news items that should be handled on an immediate release basis. News of major new products, contract awards, expansion plans, and discoveries very often fall into the same category. Unfavorable news should be reported as promptly and candidly as favorable news. Reluctance or unwillingness to release a negative story or an attempt to disguise unfavorable news endangers management's reputation for integrity. Changes in accounting methods to mask such occurrences can have a similar impact. . . .

312.00   Shareholder Approval Policy

312.01   Shareholders' interest and participation in corporate affairs has greatly increased. Management has responded by providing more extensive and frequent reports on matters of interest to investors. In addition, an increasing number of important corporate decisions are being referred to shareholders for their approval. This is especially true of transactions involving the issuance of additional securities.

Good business practice is frequently the controlling factor in the determination of management to submit a matter to shareholders for approval even though neither the law nor the company's charter makes such approvals necessary. The Exchange encourages this growth in corporate democracy.

312.02   Companies are urged to discuss questions relating to this subject with their Exchange representative sufficiently in advance of the time for the calling of a shareholders' meeting and the solicitation of proxies where shareholder approval may be involved. All relevant factors will be taken into consideration in applying the policy expressed in this Para. 312.00 and the Exchange will advise whether or not shareholder approval will be required in a particular case.

312.03   Shareholder approval of a plan or arrangement (under (a) below) or prior to the issuance of securities (under (b), (c) or (d) below) will be prerequisite to listing when:

(a) A stock option or purchase plan is to be established or other arrangements made pursuant to which stock may be acquired by officers or directors, except for warrants or rights issued generally to security holders of the company or broadly-based plans or arrangements including other employees (e.g., ESOPS). In a case where shares are issued to a person not previously employed by the company, as an inducement essential to his entering into an employment contract with the company, shareholder approval may not be required.

(b) A business, a company, tangible or intangible assets or property or securities representing any such interest are to be acquired, directly or indirectly, from a director, officer or substantial security holder of the company (including its subsidiaries, affiliates or other closely related persons) or from any company or party in which one of such persons has a substantial direct or indirect interest if the number of shares of common stock to be issued or the number of shares of common stock into which the securities may be convertible exceeds one percent of the number of shares of common stock or one percent of the voting power outstanding* before the issuance.

* "Voting power outstanding" refers to the aggregate number of votes which may be cast by holders of those securities outstanding which entitle the holders thereof

An interest consisting of less than either 5% of the number of shares of common stock or 5% of the voting power outstanding * of a company or party shall not be considered a substantial interest or cause the holder of such an interest to be regarded as a substantial security holder.

(c) Common stock or securities convertible into or exercisable for common stock are to be issued in any transaction or series of related transactions, other than a public offering for cash, (i) if the common stock has or will have upon issuance voting power equal to or in excess of 20% of the voting power outstanding* before the issuance of such stock or securities convertible into or exercisable for common stock, or (ii) the number of shares of common stock to be issued is or will be equal to or in excess of 20% of the number of shares of common stock outstanding before the issuance of the stock.

(d) The issuance will result in a change of control of the issuer.

(e) Only shares actually issued and outstanding (excluding treasury shares or shares held by a subsidiary) are to be used in making any calculation provided for in this paragraph. Unissued shares reserved for issuance upon conversion of securities or upon exercise of options or warrants will not be regarded as outstanding.

Exceptions may be made upon application to the Exchange when 1) the delay in securing stockholder approval would seriously jeopardize the financial viability of the enterprise and 2) reliance by the company on this exception is expressly approved by the Audit Committee of the Board.

A company relying on this exception must mail to all shareholders not later than ten days before issuance of the securities a letter alerting them to its omission to seek the shareholder approval that would otherwise be required under the policy of the Exchange and indicating that the Audit Committee of the Board has expressly approved the exception.

312.04   In the event that some or all of the shares to be issued in a transaction subject to shareholder approval under Para. 312.03 must be listed, Exchange procedures will ordinarily permit the filing of applicable listing applications and Exchange approval to precede the shareholder vote subject to notice to the Exchange of the results of the shareholder vote and the issuance of the shares to be listed.

312.05   Where shareholder approval is a prerequisite to the listing of any additional or new securities of a listed company, the minimum vote which will constitute shareholder approval for listing purposes is defined as approval by a majority of votes cast on a proposal in a proxy bearing on the particular matter, provided that the total vote cast on the

to vote generally on all matters submitted to the company's security holders for a vote. (Footnote by New York Stock Exchange.)

proposal represents over 50% in interest of all securities entitled to vote on the proposal.

313.00 Voting Rights

(A) Voting Rights Policy

Voting rights of existing shareholders of publicly traded common stock under Section 12 of the Exchange Act cannot be disparately reduced or restricted through any corporate action or issuance. Examples of such corporate action or issuance include, but are not limited to, the adoption of time phased voting plans, the adoption of capped voting rights plans, the issuance of super voting stock, or the issuance of stock with voting rights less than the per share voting rights of the existing common stock through an exchange offer.

Supplementary Material:

.10 Companies with Dual Class Structures—The restriction against the issuance of super voting stock is primarily intended to apply to the issuance of a new class of stock, and companies with existing dual class capital structures would generally be permitted to issue additional shares of the existing super voting stock without conflict with this Policy.

.20 Consultation with the Exchange—Violation of the Exchange's Voting Rights Policy could result in the loss of an Issuers's Exchange market or public trading market. The Policy can apply to a variety of corporate actions and securities issuances, not just super voting or so-called "time phase" voting common stock. While the Policy will continue to permit actions previously permitted under Rule 19c–4, it is extremely important that listed companies communicate their intentions to their Exchange representatives as early as possible before taking any action or committing to take any action that may be inconsistent with the Policy. The Exchange urges listed companies not to assume, without first discussing the matter with the Exchange staff, that a particular issuance of common or preferred stock or the taking of some other corporate action will necessarily be consistent with the Policy. It is suggested that copies of preliminary proxy or other material concerning matters subject to the Policy be furnished to the Exchange for review prior to formal filing.

.30 Review of Past Voting Rights Activities—In reviewing an application for initial listing on the Exchange, the Exchange will review the issuer's past corporate actions to determine whether another self-regulatory organization ("SRO") has found any of the issuer's actions to have been a violation or evasion of the SRO's voting rights policy. Based on such review, the Exchange may take any appropriate action, including the denial of the listing or the placing of restrictions on such listing. The Exchange will also review whether an issuer seeking initial listing on the Exchange has requested a ruling or interpretation from another SRO regarding the application of that SRO's voting rights policy with respect to a proposed transaction. If so, the Exchange will consider that fact in determining its response to any ruling or interpretation that the issuer may request on the same or similar transaction. . . .

(B) Non–Voting Common Stock

The Exchange's voting rights policy permits the listing of the voting common stock of a company which also has outstanding a non-voting common stock as well as the listing of non-voting common stock. However, certain safeguards must be provided to holders of a listed non-voting common stock:

> (1) Any class of non-voting common stock that is listed on the Exchange must meet all original listing standards. The rights of the holders of the non-voting common stock should, except for voting rights, be substantially the same as those of the holders of the company's voting common stock.

> (2) The requirement that listed companies publish at least once a year and submit to shareholders an annual report . . . applies equally to holders of voting common stock and to holders of listed non-voting common stock.

(3) In addition, although the holders of shares of listed non-voting common stock are not entitled to vote generally on matters submitted for shareholder action, holders of any listed non-voting common stock must receive all communications, including proxy material, sent generally to the holders of the voting securities of the listed company.

(C) Preferred Stock, Minimum Voting Rights Required

Preferred stock, voting as a class, should have the right to elect a minimum of two directors upon default of the equivalent of six quarterly dividends. The right to elect directors should accrue regardless of whether defaulted dividends occurred in consecutive periods.

The right to elect directors should remain in effect until cumulative dividends have been paid in full or until non-cumulative dividends have been paid regularly for at least a year. The preferred stock quorum should be low enough to ensure that the right to elect directors can be exercised as soon as it accrues. In no event should the quorum exceed the percentage required for a quorum of the common stock required for the election of directors. The Exchange prefers that no quorum requirement be fixed in respect of the right of a preferred stock, voting as a class, to elect directors when dividends are in default.

The Exchange recommends that preferred stock should have minimum voting rights even if the preferred stock is not listed.

Increase in Authorized Amount or Creation of a Pari Passu Issue—

- An increase in the authorized amount of a class of preferred stock or the creation of a pari passu issue should be approved by a majority of the holders of the outstanding shares of the class or classes to be affected. The Board of Directors may increase the authorized amount of a series or create an additional series ranking pari passu without a vote by the existing series if shareholders authorized such action by the Board of Directors at the time the class of preferred stock was created.

Creation of a Senior Issue—

- Creation of a senior equity security should require approval of at least two-thirds of the outstanding preferred shares. The Board of Directors may create a senior series without a vote by the existing series if shareholders authorized such action by the Board of Directors at the time of the existing series of preferred stock was created.

- A vote by an existing class of preferred stock is not required for the creation of a senior issue if the existing class has previously received adequate notice of redemption to occur within 90 days. However, the vote of the existing class should not be denied if all or part of the existing issue is being retired with proceeds from the sale of the new stock.

Alteration of Existing Provisions—

- Approval by the holders of at least two-thirds of the outstanding shares of a preferred stock should be required for adoption of any charter or by-law amendment that would materially affect existing terms of the preferred stock.

- If all series of a class of preferred stock are not equally affected by the proposed changes, there should be a two-thirds approval of the class and a two-thirds approval of the series that will have a diminished status.

- The charter should not hinder the shareholders' right to alter the terms of a preferred stock by limiting modification to specific items, e.g., interest rate, redemption price.

§ 712. Acquisitions

Approval of shareholders is required (pursuant to a proxy solicitation conforming to SEC proxy rules) as a prerequisite to approval of applications to list additional shares to be issued as sole or partial consideration for an acquisition of the stock or assets of another company in the following circumstances:

(a) if any individual director, officer or substantial shareholder of the listed company has a 5% or greater interest (or such persons collectively have a 10% or greater interest), directly or indirectly, in the company or assets to be acquired or in the consideration to be paid in the transaction and the present or potential issuance of common stock, or securities convertible into common stock, could result in an increase in outstanding common shares of 5% or more; or

(b) where the present or potential issuance of common stock, or securities convertible into common stock, could result in an increase in outstanding common shares of 20% or more.

NOTE: A series of closely related transactions may be regarded as one transaction for the purpose of this policy. Companies engaged in merger or acquisition discussions must be particularly mindful of the Exchange's timely disclosure policies. In view of possible market sensitivity and the importance of providing investors with sufficient information relative to an intended merger or acquisition, listed company representatives are strongly urged to consult with the Exchange in advance of such disclosure.

§ 713. Other Transactions

The Exchange will require shareholder approval (pursuant to a proxy solicitation conforming to SEC proxy rules) as a prerequisite to approval of applications to list additional shares to be issued in connection with:

(a) a transaction involving:

(i) the sale or issuance by the company of common stock (or securities convertible into common stock) at a price less than the greater of book or market value which together with sales by officers, directors or principal shareholders of the company equals 20% or more of presently outstanding common stock; or

(ii) the sale or issuance by the company of common stock (or securities convertible into common stock) equal to 20% or more of presently outstanding stock for less than the greater of book or market value of the stock....

NOTE: This section does not apply to public offerings.

ABA MODEL RULES OF PROFESSIONAL CONDUCT, RULE 1.13

Rule 1.13 Organization as the Client

[As Proposed by the ABA's Commission on
Evaluation of Professional Standards]

(a) A lawyer employed or retained to represent an organization represents the organization as distinct from its directors, officers, employees, members, shareholders or other constituents.

(b) If a lawyer for an organization knows that an officer, employee or other person associated with the organization is engaged in action, intends to act or refuses to act in a manner related to the representation that is a violation of a legal obligation to the organization, or a violation of law which reasonably might be imputed to the organization, and is likely to result in substantial injury to the organization, the lawyer shall proceed as is reasonably necessary in the best interest of the organization. In determining how to proceed, the lawyer shall give due consideration to the seriousness of the violation and its consequences, the scope and nature of the lawyer's representation, the responsibility in the organization and the apparent motivation of the person involved, the policies of the organization concerning such matters and any other relevant considerations. Any measures taken shall be designed to minimize disruption of the organization and the risk of revealing information relating to the representation to persons outside the organization. Such measures may include among others:

(1) asking reconsideration of the matter;

(2) advising that a separate legal opinion on the matter be sought for presentation to appropriate authority in the organization; and

(3) referring the matter to higher authority in the organization, including, if warranted by the seriousness of the matter, referral to the highest authority that can act on behalf of the organization as determined by applicable law.

(c) When the organization's highest authority insists upon action, or refuses to take action, that is clearly a violation of a legal obligation to the organization, or a violation of law which reasonably might be imputed to the organization, and is likely to result in substantial injury to the organization, the lawyer may take further remedial action that the lawyer reasonably believes to be in the best interest of the organization. Such action may include revealing information otherwise protected by Rule 1.6 [Confidentiality of Information] only if the lawyer reasonably believes that:

(1) the highest authority in the organization has acted to further the personal or financial interests of members of that authority which are in conflict with the interests of the organization; and

(2) revealing the information is necessary in the best interest of the organization.

(d) In dealing with an organization's directors, officers, employees, members, shareholders or other constituents, a lawyer shall explain the identity of the client when the lawyer believes that such explanation is necessary to avoid misunderstandings on their part.

(e) A lawyer representing an organization may also represent any of its directors, officers, employees, members, shareholders or other constituents, subject to the provisions of Rule 1.7 [Conflict of Interest: General Rule]. If the organization's consent to the dual representation is required by Rule 1.7, the consent shall be given by an appropriate official of the organization other than the individual who is to be represented or by the shareholders.

[As Adopted]

(a) A lawyer employed or retained by an organization represents the organization, through its constituents.

(b) (No change)

(c) If, despite the lawyer's efforts in accordance with paragraph (b), the highest authority that can act on behalf of the organization insists upon action, or a refusal to act, that is clearly a violation of law and is likely to result in substantial injury to the organization, the lawyer may resign....

(d) In dealing with an organization's directors, officers, employees, members, shareholders or other constituents, a lawyer shall explain the identity of the client when it is apparent that the organization's interests are adverse to those of the constituents with whom the lawyer is dealing.

(e) (No change)

Comment....

In an extreme case, it may be reasonably necessary for the lawyer to refer the matter to the organization's highest authority. Ordinarily, that is the Board of Directors or similar governing body. However, applicable law may prescribe that under certain conditions highest authority reposes elsewhere; for example, in the independent directors of a corporation....

AMERICAN LAW INSTITUTE PRINCIPLES OF CORPORATE GOVERNANCE: ANALYSIS AND RECOMMENDATIONS (1994) *

PART I

DEFINITIONS

* Most or all Sections of the Principles of Corporate Governance employ terms that are defined in Part I (Definitions). Normally, the first time a defined term is used in the text or Comment of each Section it is followed by a cross-reference, set in brackets, to the Section of Part I in which the term is defined. Usually, however, if the same term is used again in that Section, the term is not accompanied by further cross-references to Part I.

Italics. Italics are used in the text where a number recommended for a bright-line test is deemed preferable, but not clearly superior, to somewhat higher or lower numbers.

** Omitted.

PART V

DUTY OF FAIR DEALING

CHAPTER 1

GENERAL PRINCIPLE

CHAPTER 2

DUTY OF FAIR DEALING OF DIRECTORS AND SENIOR EXECUTIVES

CHAPTER 3

DUTY OF FAIR DEALING OF CONTROLLING SHAREHOLDERS

CHAPTER 4

TRANSFER OF CONTROL

* Omitted.

PART I

DEFINITIONS

§ 1.01   Effect of Definitions

The definitions in Part I apply for the purposes of Parts I–VII unless the context requires otherwise.

§ 1.02   Approved by the Shareholders

(a) "Approved by the shareholders" means approval by a majority of the voting shares, unless a greater percentage is required by the corporation's charter documents [§ 1.05] pursuant to Subsection (b).

(b) Any provision in a charter document (other than a fair-price provision) that increases the percentage of shares whose approval is required to more than a majority shall be approved by the same vote as is set forth in the provision.

(c) A change in the corporation's charter documents that affects shareholders' rights or control [§ 1.08] of the corporation that is made by the board of directors is to be considered as having been approved by the shareholders if the shareholders have clearly empowered the board of directors to adopt the change or provision.

§ 1.03 Associate

(a) "Associate" means:

(1)(A) The spouse (or a parent or sibling thereof) of a director [§ 1.13], senior executive [§ 1.33], or shareholder, or a child, grandchild, sibling, or parent (or the spouse of any thereof) of a director, senior executive, or shareholder, or an individual having the same home as a director, senior executive, or shareholder, or a trust or estate of which an individual specified in this Subsection (A) is a substantial beneficiary; or (B) a trust, estate, incompetent, conservatee, or minor of which a director, senior executive, or shareholder is a fiduciary; or

(2) A person [§ 1.28] with respect to whom a director, senior executive, or shareholder has a business, financial, or similar relationship that would reasonably be expected to affect the person's judgment with respect to the transaction or conduct in question in a manner adverse to the corporation.

(b) Notwithstanding § 1.03(a)(2), a business organization [§ 1.04] is not an associate of a director, senior executive, or shareholder solely because the director, senior executive, or shareholder is a director or principal manager [§ 1.29] of the business organization. A business organization in which a director, senior executive, or shareholder is the beneficial or record holder of not more than 10 percent of any class of equity interest [§ 1.19] is not presumed to be an associate of the holder by reason of the holding, unless the value of the interest to the holder would reasonably be expected to affect the holder's judgment with respect to the transaction in question in a manner adverse to the corporation. A business organization in which a director, senior executive, or shareholder is the beneficial or record holder (other than in a custodial capacity) of more than 10 percent of any class of equity interest is presumed to be an associate of the holder by reason of the holding, unless the value of the interest to the holder would not reasonably be expected to affect the holder's judgment with respect to the transaction or conduct in question in a manner adverse to the corporation.

§ 1.04 Business Organization

"Business organization" means an organization of any form (other than an agency or instrumentality of government) that is primarily engaged in business, including a corporation, a partnership or any other form of association, a sole proprietorship, or any form of trust or estate.

§ 1.05 Charter Documents

"Charter documents" means the articles or certificate of incorporation; documents supplementary thereto that set forth the rights, preferences, and privileges of equity securities [§ 1.20] and any limitations thereon; and the bylaws of the corporation.

§ 1.06 Closely Held Corporation

"Closely held corporation" means a corporation the equity securities [§ 1.20] of which are owned by a small number of persons, and for which securities no active trading market exists.

§ 1.07 Commercial Payment

"Commercial payment" means any payment except the following: a payment of interest on securities, a pro rata distribution to a class of shareholders, a payment to a corporation for its stock, a loan, a repayment of principal, a payment by an insurer on account of an insured loss, a payment to a public utility at a regulated rate, a director's fee, or a payment on behalf of a third party.

§ 1.08 Control

(a) "Control" means the power, directly or indirectly, either alone or pursuant to an arrangement or understanding with one or more other persons [§ 1.28], to exercise a controlling influence over the management or policies of a business organization [§ 1.04], through the ownership of or power to vote equity interests [§ 1.19], through one or more intermediary persons, by contract, or otherwise.

(b) A person who, either alone or pursuant to an arrangement or understanding with one or more other persons, owns or has the power to vote more than 25 percent of the equity interests in a business organization is presumed to be in control of the organization, unless some other person, either alone or pursuant to an arrangement or understanding with one or more other persons, owns or has the power to vote a greater percentage of equity interests. A person who does not, either alone or pursuant to an arrangement or understanding with one or more other persons, own or have the power to vote more than 25 percent of the equity interests in a business organization is not presumed to be in control of the business organization by virtue solely of ownership of or power to vote equity interests in that organization.

(c) A person is not in control of a business organization solely because the person is a director [§ 1.13] or principal manager [§ 1.29] of the organization.

§ 1.09 Control Group

"Control group" means a group of persons [§ 1.28] who act in concert to exercise a controlling influence over the management or policies of a business organization [§ 1.04] pursuant to an arrangement or understanding with each other.

§ 1.10 Controlling Shareholder

(a) A "controlling shareholder" means a person [§ 1.28] who, either alone or pursuant to an arrangement or understanding with one or more other persons:

(1) Owns and has the power to vote more than 50 percent of the outstanding voting equity securities [§ 1.40] of a corporation; or

(2) Otherwise exercises a controlling influence over the management or policies of the corporation or the transaction or conduct in question by virtue of the person's position as a shareholder.

(b) A person who, either alone or pursuant to an arrangement or understanding with one or more other persons, owns or has the power to vote more than 25 percent of the outstanding voting equity securities of a corporation is presumed to exercise a controlling influence over the management or policies of the corporation, unless some other person, either alone or pursuant to an arrangement or understanding with one or more other persons, owns or has the power to vote a greater percentage of the voting equity securities. A person who does not, either alone or pursuant to an arrangement with one or more other persons, own or have the power to vote more than 25 percent of the outstanding voting equity securities of a corporation is not presumed to be in control of the corporation by virtue solely of ownership of or power to vote voting equity securities.

§ 1.11 Corporate Decisionmaker

"Corporate decisionmaker" means that corporate official or body with the authority to make a particular decision for the corporation.

§ 1.12 Corporation

(a) A "corporation" means a corporation incorporated under a business corporation law or an analogue thereof.

(b) For purposes of the obligations imposed upon a corporation under § 7.23(c)–(e) (procedural standards for appraisal), including the obligation to pay fair value on the occurrence of the events specified in § 7.21 (Corporate Transactions Giving Rise to Appraisal Rights), "corporation" includes the surviving, successor, or acquiring entity in the case of a business combination that gives rise to appraisal rights under that section.

§ 1.13 Director

"Director" means an individual designated as a director by the corporation or an individual who acts in place of a director under applicable law or a standard of the corporation [§ 1.36].

§ 1.14 Disclosure

(a) *Disclosure Concerning a Conflict of Interest.* A director [§ 1.13], senior executive [§ 1.33], or controlling shareholder [§ 1.10] makes "disclosure concerning a conflict of interest" if the director, senior executive, or controlling shareholder discloses to the corporate decisionmaker [§ 1.11] who authorizes in advance or ratifies the transaction in question the material facts [§ 1.25] known to the director, senior executive, or controlling shareholder concerning the conflict of interest, or if the corporate decisionmaker knows of those facts at the time the transaction is authorized or ratified.

(b) *Disclosure Concerning a Transaction.* A director, senior executive, or controlling shareholder makes "disclosure concerning a transaction" if the director, senior executive, or controlling shareholder discloses to the corporate decisionmaker who authorizes in advance or ratifies the transaction in question the material facts known to the director, senior executive, or controlling shareholder concerning the transaction, or if the corporate decisionmaker knows of those facts at the time the transaction is authorized or ratified.

§ 1.15 Disinterested Directors

A provision that gives a specified effect to action by "disinterested directors" requires the affirmative vote of a majority, but not less than two, of the directors on the board or on an appropriate committee who are not interested [§ 1.23] in the transaction or conduct in question.

§ 1.16 Disinterested Shareholders

A provision that gives a specified effect to action by "disinterested shareholders" requires approval by a majority of the votes cast by shareholders who are not interested [§ 1.23] in the transaction or conduct in question. In the case of § 5.15 (Transfer of Control in Which a Director or Principal Senior Executive Is Interested), such approval shall be deemed to have been given when there has been a tender offer and it has been accepted by a majority of the shares for which the tender offer has been made.

§ 1.17 Eligible Holder

(a) "Eligible holder" means the holder [§ 1.22] of one or more shares, whether common or preferred, that (1) carry voting rights with respect to the election of directors, (2) are entitled to share in all or any portion of current or liquidating dividends after the payment of dividends on any shares entitled to a preference, or (3) are adversely affected by an amendment of the certificate of incorporation as described in § 7.21(d), in each case as of the date of the shareholder vote or other corporate action under § 7.21 (Corporate Transactions Giving Rise to Appraisal Rights).

(b) No person shall be deemed an eligible holder if (1) the shares owned by such person were voted in favor of the proposed transaction or provision, (2) the person fails to elect appraisal with respect to all shares of the class owned by the person, or (3) in the case of a beneficial owner who is not the record holder [§ 1.32] of the shares, the beneficial owner fails to submit to the corporation the record holder's written consent to the beneficial owner's dissent not later than 20 days after the date of the corporate action giving rise to appraisal rights (or such later date on which notice thereof is first given to shareholders).

§ 1.19 Equity Interest

"Equity interest" means an equity security [§ 1.20] in a corporation, or a beneficial interest in any other form of business organization [§ 1.04].

§ 1.20 Equity Security

"Equity security" means (a) a share in a corporation or similar security, or (b) a security convertible, with or without consideration, into such a security, or carrying a warrant or right to subscribe for or buy such a security, if the warrant or right or convertible security is issued by the issuer of that security.

§ 1.21 Family Group

"Family group" means a group of persons [§ 1.28], all of whom act in concert concerning the corporation's affairs and who are either individuals related by blood, marriage, or adoption, or trusts or other organizations created or acting primarily for the benefit of such individuals.

§ 1.22 Holder

A "holder" is a person [§ 1.28] having a legal or substantial beneficial interest in an equity security [§ 1.20].

§ 1.23 Interested

(a) A director [§ 1.13] or officer [§ 1.27] is "interested" in a transaction or conduct if either:

(1) The director or officer, or an associate [§ 1.03] of the director or officer, is a party to the transaction or conduct;

(2) The director or officer has a business, financial, or familial relationship with a party to the transaction or conduct, and that relationship would reasonably be expected to affect the director's or officer's judgment with respect to the transaction or conduct in a manner adverse to the corporation;

(3) The director or officer, an associate of the director or officer, or a person with whom the director or officer has a business, financial, or familial relationship, has a material pecuniary interest in the transaction or conduct (other than usual and customary directors' fees and benefits) and that interest and (if present) that

relationship would reasonably be expected to affect the director's or officer's judgment in a manner adverse to the corporation; or

(4) The director or officer is subject to a controlling influence by a party to the transaction or conduct or a person who has a material pecuniary interest in the transaction or conduct, and that controlling influence could reasonably be expected to affect the director's or officer's judgment with respect to the transaction or conduct in a manner adverse to the corporation.

(b) A shareholder is interested in a transaction or conduct if either the shareholder or, to the shareholder's knowledge, an associate of the shareholder is a party to the transaction or conduct, or the shareholder is also an interested director or officer with respect to the same transaction or conduct.

(c) A director is interested in an action within the meaning of Part VII, Chapter 1 (The Derivative Action), but not elsewhere in these Principles, if:

(1) The director is interested, within the meaning of Subsection (a), in the transaction or conduct that is the subject of the action, or

(2) The director is a defendant in the action, except that the fact a director is named as a defendant does not make the director interested under this section if the complaint against the director:

(A) is based only on the fact that the director approved of or acquiesced in the transaction or conduct that is the subject of the action, and

(B) does not otherwise allege with particularity facts that, if true, raise a significant prospect that the director would be adjudged liable to the corporation or its shareholders.

§ 1.24 Large Publicly Held Corporation

"Large publicly held corporation" means a corporation that as of the record date for its most recent annual shareholders' meeting had both 2,000 or more record holders [§ 1.32] of its equity securities [§ 1.20] and $100 million or more of total assets [§ 1.37]; but a corporation shall not cease to be a large publicly held corporation because its total assets fall below $100 million unless total assets remain below $100 million for *two* consecutive fiscal years.

§ 1.25 Material Fact

A fact is "material" if there is a substantial likelihood that a reasonable person would consider it important under the circumstances in determining the person's course of action.

§ 1.26 Member of the Immediate Family

"Member of the immediate family" of an individual means a spouse (or a parent or sibling thereof) of the individual, or a child, grandchild, sibling, parent (or spouse of any thereof) of the individual, or a natural person having the same home as the individual.

§ 1.27 Officer

"Officer" means (a) the chief executive, operating, financial, legal, and accounting officers of a corporation; (b) to the extent not encompassed by the foregoing, the chairman of the board of directors (unless the chairman neither performs a policymaking function other than as a director nor receives a material amount of compensation in excess of director's fees), president, treasurer, and secretary, and a vice-president or vice-chairman who is in charge of a principal business unit, division, or function (such as sales, administration, or finance) or performs a major policymaking function for the corporation; and (c) any other individual designated by the corporation as an officer.

§ 1.28 Person

"Person" means (a) an individual, (b) any form of organization, including a corporation, a partnership or any other form of association, any form of trust or estate, a government or any political subdivision, or an agency or instrumentality of government, or (c) any other legal or commercial entity.

§ 1.29 Principal Manager

"Principal manager" means a senior executive [§ 1.33] of a corporation, a general partner of a partnership, a person holding a comparable position in any other business organization [§ 1.04], or a trustee of a trust.

§ 1.30 Principal Senior Executive

"Principal senior executive" means an officer described in Subsection (a) of § 1.27 (Officer).

§ 1.31 Publicly Held Corporation

"Publicly held corporation" means a corporation that as of the record date for its most recent annual shareholders' meeting had both 500 or more record holders [§ 1.32] of its equity securities [§ 1.20] and $5 million or more of total assets [§ 1.37]; but a corporation shall not cease to be a publicly held corporation because its total assets fall below $5 million, unless total assets remain below $5 million for *two* consecutive fiscal years.

§ 1.32   Record Holder

A "record holder" of equity securities [§ 1.20] means a person [§ 1.28] identified as the owner of such securities on the record of security holders maintained by or on behalf of the corporation, except that: (a) a group of persons holding as co-owners or co-fiduciaries shall be treated as a single person; and (b) for purposes of §§ ..., 1.24 (Large Publicly Held Corporation), 1.31 (Publicly Held Corporation), and 1.35 (Small Publicly Held Corporation), there shall be included as record holders the number of beneficial owners of equity securities held in the name of a voting trustee, trustee of an employee stock ownership trust, stock depository, stockbroker, or nominee, and the number of owners of equity securities held in bearer form, that the corporation has a reasonable basis for estimating.

§ 1.33   Senior Executive

"Senior executive" means an officer described in Subsection (a) or (b) of § 1.27 (Officer).

§ 1.34   Significant Relationship

(a) Except as provided in § 1.34(b), a director has a "significant relationship" with the senior executives [§ 1.33] of a corporation if, as of the end of the corporation's last fiscal year, either:

(1) The director is employed by the corporation, or was so employed within the *two* preceding years;

(2) The director is a member of the immediate family [§ 1.26] of an individual who (A) is employed by the corporation as an officer [§ 1.27], or (B) was employed by the corporation as a senior executive within the *two* preceding years;

(3) The director has made to or received from the corporation during either of its *two* preceding years, commercial payments [§ 1.07] which exceeded *$200,000,* or the director owns or has power to vote an equity interest [§ 1.19] in a business organization [§ 1.04] to which the corporation made, or from which the corporation received, during either of its *two* preceding years, commercial payments that, when multiplied by the director's percentage equity interest in the organization, exceeded *$200,000;*

(4) The director is a principal manager [§ 1.29] of a business organization to which the corporation made, or from which the corporation received, during either of the organization's *two* preceding years, commercial payments that exceeded *five percent* of the organization's consolidated gross revenues for that year, or *$200,000,* whichever is more; or

(5) The director is affiliated in a professional capacity with a law firm that was the primary legal adviser to the corporation with

respect to general corporate or securities law matters, or with an investment banking firm that was retained by the corporation in an advisory capacity or acted as a managing underwriter in an issue of the corporation's securities, within the *two* preceding years, or was so affiliated with such a law or investment banking firm when it was so retained or so acted.

(b) A director shall not be deemed to have a significant relationship with the senior executives under § 1.34(a)(3)–(5) if, on the basis of countervailing or other special circumstances, it could not reasonably be believed that the judgment of a person in the director's position would be affected by the relationship under § 1.34(a)(3)–(5) in a manner adverse to the corporation.

(c) For purposes of § 1.34 (and § 1.27, to the extent it is incorporated in § 1.34 by reference) the term "the corporation" includes any corporation that controls [§ 1.08] the corporation, and any subsidiary or other business organization that is controlled by the corporation.

§ 1.35   Small Publicly Held Corporation

A "small publicly held corporation" is a publicly held corporation [§ 1.31] other than a large publicly held corporation [§ 1.24].

§ 1.36   Standard of the Corporation

"Standard of the corporation" means a valid certificate or bylaw provision or board of directors or shareholder resolution.

§ 1.37   Total Assets

A corporation's "total assets" means the total assets shown on the balance sheet for its most recent fiscal year-end.

§ 1.38   Transaction in Control

(a) Subject to Subsection (b), a "transaction in control" with respect to a corporation means:

(1) A business combination effected through (i) a merger, (ii) a consolidation, (iii) an issuance of voting equity securities [§ 1.40] to effect an acquisition of the assets of another corporation that would constitute a transaction in control under Subsection (a)(2) with respect to the other corporation, or (iv) an issuance of voting equity securities in exchange for at least a majority of the voting equity securities of another corporation, in each case whether effected directly or by means of a subsidiary;

(2) A sale of assets that would leave the corporation without a significant continuing business; or

(3) An issuance of securities or any other transaction by the corporation (other than pursuant to a transaction described in

Subsection (a)(1)) that, alone or in conjunction with other transactions or circumstances, would cause a change in control [§ 1.08] of the corporation;

(b) A transaction is not a transaction in control within § 1.38(a) if the transaction consists of:

(1) The issuance of voting equity securities (other than pursuant to a transaction described in Subsection (a)(1)) in a widely distributed offering;

(2) The issuance of debt or equity securities that would constitute a transaction in control only because the securities carry the right to approve transactions in control, and such right serves to protect dividend, interest, sinking fund, conversion, exchange, or other rights of the securities, or to protect against the issuance of additional securities that would be on a parity with or superior to the securities; or

(3) A transaction described in Subsection (a)(1) if those persons [§ 1.28] who were the holders of voting equity securities in the corporation immediately before the transaction would own immediately after the transaction at least 75 percent of the surviving corporation's voting equity securities, in substantially the same proportions in relation to other preexisting shareholders of the corporation.

§ 1.39   Unsolicited Tender Offer

"Unsolicited tender offer" means an offer to purchase or invitation to tender made to holders of voting equity securities [§ 1.40] of a corporation, without the approval of the corporation's board of directors, to effect a change in control [§ 1.08] of the corporation by purchasing the holders' securities for cash, securities, other consideration, or any combination thereof.

§ 1.40   Voting Equity Security

"Voting equity security" means an equity security [§ 1.20] that is a voting security [§ 1.41].

§ 1.41   Voting Security

(a) "Voting security" means a security that currently entitles its record holder [§ 1.32] to vote for the election of directors.

(b) A specified percentage of the voting securities of a corporation means whatever amount of its outstanding voting securities entitles the record holders to cast that specified percentage of the aggregate votes that the record holders of all the outstanding voting securities are entitled to cast in the election of directors.

§ 1.42 Waste of Corporate Assets

A transaction constitutes a "waste of corporate assets" if it involves an expenditure of corporate funds or a disposition of corporate assets for which no consideration is received in exchange and for which there is no rational business purpose, or, if consideration is received in exchange, the consideration the corporation receives is so inadequate in value that no person of ordinary sound business judgment would deem it worth that which the corporation has paid.

PART II

THE OBJECTIVE AND CONDUCT OF THE CORPORATION

§ 2.01 The Objective and Conduct of the Corporation

(a) Subject to the provisions of Subsection (b) and § 6.02 (Action of Directors That Has the Foreseeable Effect of Blocking Unsolicited Tender Offers), a corporation [§ 1.12] should have as its objective the conduct of business activities with a view to enhancing corporate profit and shareholder gain.

(b) Even if corporate profit and shareholder gain are not thereby enhanced, the corporation, in the conduct of its business:

(1) Is obliged, to the same extent as a natural person, to act within the boundaries set by law;

(2) May take into account ethical considerations that are reasonably regarded as appropriate to the responsible conduct of business; and

(3) May devote a reasonable amount of resources to public welfare, humanitarian, educational, and philanthropic purposes.

Comment . . .

f. The economic objective. In very general terms, Subsection (a) may be thought of as a broad injunction to enhance economic returns, while Subsection (b) makes clear that certain kinds of conduct must or may be pursued whether or not they enhance such returns (that is, even if the conduct either yields no economic return or entails a net economic loss). In most cases, however, the kinds of conduct described in Subsection (b) could be pursued even under the principle embodied in Subsection (a). Such conduct will usually be consistent with economic self-interest, because the principle embodied in Subsection (a)—that the objective of the corporation is to conduct business activities with a view to enhancing corporate profit and shareholder gain—does not mean that the objective of the corporation must be to realize corporate profit and shareholder gain in the short run. . . .

Illustrations:

1. Corporation A is a publicly held corporation with annual earnings in the range of $2–3 million. A has entered into a contract that is unenforceable against it under the Statute of Frauds. Performance of the contract will involve a loss of $70,000. A performs the contract, because the relevant corporate decisionmaker makes a judgment, in a manner that meets the standards of § 4.01 (Duty of Care of Directors and Officers; the Business Judgment Rule), that the loss is likely to be exceeded by long-run profits from preserving confidence in A's willingness to honor its commitments. A's action does not involve a departure from the economic objective stated in § 2.01(a).

2. B Corporation is a publicly held corporation with annual earnings in the range of $6–8 million. White, a long-time middle-manager of B, is forced to retire because of serious injuries sustained in an automobile accident. B has a pension plan covering White, but the plan was installed only recently, and White's benefits are only 30 percent vested. B purchases an annuity for White at a cost of $50,000 to bring White's retirement income up to a reasonable amount, because the relevant corporate decisionmaker makes a judgment, in a manner that meets the standards of § 4.01, that the cost of the annuity will be exceeded by long-run economic benefits from improving the morale of B's remaining employees. B's action does not involve a departure from the economic objective stated in § 2.01(a). . . .

g. Compliance with legal rules. Under § 2.01(b)(1), the corporation is obliged, to the same extent as a natural person, to act within the boundaries set by law. It is sometimes maintained that whether a corporation should adhere to a given legal rule may properly depend on a kind of cost-benefit analysis, in which probable corporate gains are weighed against either probable social costs, measured by the dollar liability imposed for engaging in such conduct, or probable corporate losses, measured by potential dollar liability discounted for likelihood of detection. Section 2.01 does not adopt this position. With few exceptions, dollar liability is not a "price" that can properly be paid for the privilege of engaging in legally wrongful conduct. Cost-benefit analysis may have a place in the state's determination whether a given type of conduct should be deemed legally wrongful. Once that determination has been made, however, the resulting legal rule normally represents a community decision that the conduct is wrongful as such, so that cost-benefit analysis whether to obey the rule is out of place. . . .

Illustrations:

7. F Corporation is a publicly held corporation with annual earnings in the range of $3–5 million. F hopes to be awarded a supply contract by P, a large publicly held corporation. The antici-

pated profits on the contract are $5 million over a two-year period. A vice-president of P has approached Brown, the relevant corporate decisionmaker of F, with the suggestion that if F pays the vice-president $20,000, F will be awarded the contract. Brown knows such a payment would be illegal, but correctly regards the risk of detection as extremely small. After carefully weighing that risk and the consequences of detection, Brown causes F to pay the $20,000. F's action involves a departure from the principle stated in § 2.01(b)(1).

8. G Corporation owns and operates 15 plants that were traditionally non-union. For the last several years, Union U has been attempting to organize G's workers, and has won elections at three of G's plants. Although G does not have a good faith belief that the elections were invalid, it adopts a strategy of refusing to bargain at these three plants and harassing members, adherents, and supporters of U at G's other 12 plants. The relevant corporate decisionmaker knows that the conduct violates the National Labor Relations Act, but believes that a long time will elapse before sanctions are imposed, and that the profit from this conduct will far exceed the cost of possible sanctions. G's action involves a departure from the principle stated in § 2.01(b)(1)....

h. Ethical considerations. Section 2.01(b)(2) provides that a corporation may take into account ethical considerations that are reasonably regarded as appropriate to the responsible conduct of business.... [O]bservation suggests that corporate decisions are not infrequently made on the basis of ethical considerations even when doing so would not enhance corporate profit or shareholder gain. Such behavior is not only appropriate, but desirable. Corporate officials are not less morally obliged than any other citizens to take ethical considerations into account, and it would be unwise social policy to preclude them from doing so.

This does not mean that corporate officials can properly take into account any ethical consideration, no matter how idiosyncratic. Because such officials are dealing with other people's money, they will act properly in taking ethical principles into account only where those considerations are reasonably regarded as appropriate to the responsible conduct of business. In this connection, however, it should be recognized that new principles may emerge over time. A corporate official therefore should be permitted to take into account emerging ethical principles, reasonably regarded as appropriate to the responsible conduct of business, that have significant support although less-than-universal acceptance....

Illustrations:

11. The facts being otherwise as stated in Illustration 1, A is about to be dissolved. A nevertheless honors the contract, because

907

ethical considerations that it reasonably regards as appropriate to the responsible conduct of business suggest that seriously made business promises should be kept even if there is a technical excuse for nonperformance. A's action can be justified under § 2.01(b)(2), and therefore does not involve a departure from the principles stated in § 2.01. . . .

i. Public welfare, humanitarian, educational, and philanthropic purposes. Section 2.01(b)(3) permits the corporation to devote a reasonable amount of resources to public welfare, humanitarian, educational, and philanthropic purposes, even if corporate profit and shareholder gain are not thereby enhanced. As in the case of ethical considerations, conduct that appears to be based on public welfare, humanitarian, educational, or philanthropic considerations may be intended to enhance corporate profit and shareholder gain. For example, a donation to public television may be made for reasons comparable to those for sponsoring a commercial, and a contribution to local Red Cross or Community Chest activities may be made for reasons of employee well-being and morale. . . .

Section 2.01(b)(3) goes beyond these justifications and allows corporate resources to be devoted to public welfare, humanitarian, educational, and philanthropic purposes even without a showing of expected profits or ethical norms. . . . Social policy . . . favors humane behavior by major social institutions. [Social policy also] favors the maintenance of diversity in educational and philanthropic activity, and this objective would be more difficult to achieve if corporations, which control a great share of national resources, were not allowed to devote a portion of those resources to those ends. However, corporate activity that is justified solely by social considerations should be subject to a limit of reasonableness. . . .

Illustrations:

13. The facts being otherwise as stated in Illustration 2, B is about to liquidate. Accordingly, it will have no remaining employees and therefore cannot justify the purchase of an annuity for White on the basis of long-term profitability. B's assets net of liabilities are $30 million. White is the only employee whom the liquidation will leave without retirement security. The relevant decisionmaker causes B to purchase an annuity, at a cost of $50,000, to bring White's retirement income up to a reasonable amount, partly for humanitarian reasons, and partly because ethical considerations that B reasonably regards as appropriate to the responsible conduct of business suggest that a business should make reasonable provision for a faithful long-term employee who has made a contribution to the business, and is forced by ill health to retire while in

the corporation's employ. B's action can be justified under both § 2.01(b)(2) and § 2.01(b)(3), and therefore does not involve a departure from the principles stated in § 2.01. . . .

19. O, a publicly held corporation, has assets of $100 million and annual earnings in the range of $13–15 million. O owns three aluminum plants, which are profitable, and one plastics plant, which is losing $4 million a year. The plastics plant shows no sign of ever becoming profitable, because of its very high operating costs, and there is no evidence that the plant and the underlying real estate will increase in value. O decides to sell the plastics plant. The only bidder for the plant is Gold, who intends to use the plant for a new purpose, introduce automation, and replace all existing employees. O turns down Gold's bid and keeps the plastics plant operating indefinitely for the purpose of preserving the employees' jobs. O's action involves a departure from the principles stated in § 2.01. The action is for a humanitarian purpose, but cannot be justified under § 2.01(b)(3), because the expenditures involved are unreasonable in amount in relation to earnings. It cannot be justified under § 2.01(b)(2), because a corporation is not ethically obliged to continue indefinitely the operation of a business that is losing large amounts of money, equal to more than one fourth of the corporation's earnings, for the purpose of keeping workers employed. The action cannot be justified under § 2.01(a), because the action is not motivated by profit considerations, and on the facts it would not be within the realm of business judgment to conclude that the action will result in short- or long-term profits exceeding the costs involved.

20. The facts being otherwise as stated in Illustration 19, the only person who bids on the plant is a real-estate developer who plans to close the plant and hold the land for investment. The developer is agreeable to leasing the plant back to O at a moderate rent for up to 12 months. O enters into a three-month lease, and continues to operate the plant during that period, at a loss of $500,000, so as to provide the employees at the plant a period of adjustment prior to its closing. This action is taken partly out of humanitarian considerations, and partly because ethical considerations that are reasonably regarded as appropriate to the responsible conduct of business suggest that an enterprise should make reasonable provision to cushion the transition of long-term employees who are about to be discharged. O's action can be justified under § 2.01(b)(2) and § 2.01(b)(3), and therefore does not involve a departure from the principles stated in § 2.01. . . .

PART III

CORPORATE STRUCTURE: FUNCTIONS AND POWERS OF DIRECTORS AND OFFICERS; AUDIT COMMITTEE IN LARGE PUBLICLY HELD CORPORATIONS

§ 3.01 Management of the Corporation's Business: Functions and Powers of Principal Senior Executives and Other Officers

The management of the business of a publicly held corporation [§ 1.31] should be conducted by or under the supervision of such principal senior executives [§ 1.30] as are designated by the board of directors, and by those other officers [§ 1.27] and employees to whom the management function is delegated by the board or those executives, subject to the functions and powers of the board under § 3.02.

§ 3.02 Functions and Powers of the Board of Directors

Except as otherwise provided by statute:

(a) The board of directors of a publicly held corporation [§ 1.31] should perform the following functions:

(1) Select, regularly evaluate, fix the compensation of, and, where appropriate, replace the principal senior executives [§ 1.30];

(2) Oversee the conduct of the corporation's business to evaluate whether the business is being properly managed;

(3) Review and, where appropriate, approve the corporation's financial objectives and major corporate plans and actions;

(4) Review and, where appropriate, approve major changes in, and determinations of other major questions of choice respecting, the appropriate auditing and accounting principles and practices to be used in the preparation of the corporation's financial statements;

(5) Perform such other functions as are prescribed by law, or assigned to the board under a standard of the corporation [§ 1.36].

(b) A board of directors also has power to:

(1) Initiate and adopt corporate plans, commitments, and actions;

(2) Initiate and adopt changes in accounting principles and practices;

(3) Provide advice and counsel to the principal senior executives;

(4) Instruct any committee, principal senior executive, or other officer [§ 1.27], and review the actions of any committee, principal senior executive, or other officer;

(5) Make recommendations to shareholders;

(6) Manage the business of the corporation;

(7) Act as to all other corporate matters not requiring shareholder approval.

(c) Subject to the board's ultimate responsibility for oversight under Subsection (a)(2), the board may delegate to its committees authority to perform any of its functions and exercise any of its powers.

Comment ...

d. The oversight function. In the publicly held corporation, the management function is normally vested in the principal senior executives. A basic function of the board is to select these executives and to oversee their performance (using the term "oversee" to refer to general observation and oversight, not active supervision or day-to-day scrutiny) to determine whether the business is being properly managed, having in mind the objective and conduct of the corporation under § 2.01. This oversight function is usually performed, not directly by actively supervising the principal senior executives, but indirectly by evaluating the performance of those executives and replacing any who are not meeting reasonable expectations concerning job performance. . . .

§ 3.03 Directors' Informational Rights

(a) Every director has the right, within the limits of § 3.03(b) (and subject to other applicable law), to inspect and copy all books, records, and documents of every kind, and to inspect the physical properties, of the corporation and of its subsidiaries, domestic or foreign, at any reasonable time, in person or by an attorney or other agent.

(b)(1) A judicial order to enforce such right should be granted unless the corporation establishes that the information to be obtained by the exercise of the right is not reasonably related to the performance of directorial functions and duties, or that the director or the director's agent is likely to use the information in a manner that would violate the director's fiduciary obligation to the corporation.

(2) An application for such an order should be decided expeditiously and may be decided on the basis of affidavits.

(3) Such an order may contain provisions protecting the corporation from undue burden or expense, and prohibiting the director from using the information in a manner that would violate the director's fiduciary obligation to the corporation.

(4) A director who makes an application for such an order after the corporation has denied a request should, if successful, be reim-

bursed by the corporation for expenses (including attorney's fees) reasonably incurred in connection with the application.

§ 3.04 Right of Directors Who Have No Significant Relationship With the Corporation's Senior Executives to Retain Outside Experts

The directors of a publicly held corporation [§ 1.31] who have no significant relationship [§ 1.34] with the corporation's senior executives [§ 1.33] should be entitled, acting as a body by the vote of a majority of such directors, to retain legal counsel, accountants, or other experts, at the corporation's expense, to advise them on problems arising in the exercise of their functions and powers (§ 3.02), if:

(a) Payment of such expense is authorized by the board; or

(b) A court approves an application for the payment of such expense upon a finding that the board had been requested to authorize the payment of such expense and had declined to do so, and the directors who have no relationship with the corporation's senior executives reasonably believed that (i) retention of an outside expert was required for the proper performance of the directors' functions and powers, (ii) the amount involved was reasonable in relation to both the importance of the problem and the corporation's assets and income, and (iii) assistance by corporate staff or corporate counsel was inappropriate or inadequate.

§ 3.05 Audit Committee in Large Publicly Held Corporations

Every large publicly held corporation [§ 1.24] should have an audit committee to implement and support the oversight function of the board (§ 3.02) by reviewing on a periodic basis the corporation's processes for producing financial data, its internal controls, and the independence of the corporation's external auditor.   The audit committee should consist of at least three members, and should be composed exclusively of directors who are neither employed by the corporation nor were so employed within the two preceding years, including at least a majority of members who have no significant relationship [§ 1.34] with the corporation's senior executives.

Comment:

a. Comparison with present law and practice.   An audit committee is not required as a matter of state law, except in Connecticut.   However, the New York Stock Exchange requires listed companies to establish and maintain an audit committee "comprised solely of directors independent of management and free from any relationship that, in the opinion of its Board of Directors, would interfere with the exercise of independent judgment as a committee member." ... The American Stock Exchange and NASDAQ also recommend or require audit committees, and the employment of such committees in publicly held corporations is now prevalent practice. . . .

PART III–A

RECOMMENDATIONS OF CORPORATE PRACTICE CONCERNING THE BOARD AND THE PRINCIPAL OVERSIGHT COMMITTEES

§ 3A.01 Composition of the Board in Publicly Held Corporations

It is recommended as a matter of corporate practice that:

(a) The board of every large publicly held corporation [§ 1.24] should have a majority of directors who are free of any significant relationship [§ 1.34] with the corporation's senior executives [§ 1.33], unless a majority of the corporation's voting securities [§ 1.41] are owned by a single person [§ 1.28], a family group [§ 1.21], or a control group [§ 1.09].

(b) The board of a publicly held corporation [§ 1.31] that does not fall within Subsection (a) should have at least three directors who are free of any significant relationship with the corporation's senior executives.

REPORTER'S NOTE. . . .

3. Data from various sources show that the concepts embodied in § 3A.01 have taken firm hold in practice. A 1991 study by Korn/Ferry reported that the boards of responding corporations had an average number of three inside and nine outside directors. Korn/Ferry, *Board of Directors* 5, 15 (1991). In 1985, Korn/Ferry had found that the comparable average was 10 outside directors and four inside directors; in 1975, the average had been eight outside directors and five inside directors. Id. at 3, 5. The 1990 Korn/Ferry study predicts that in the next decade, the number of insiders on the board will drop even further, from three to two, and that increasingly the only insiders on the board will be the chief executive officer and the chief operating officer. Id. at 3. Two studies by Heidrick & Struggles in the 1980s, using different samples, found that "independent" directors (defined as those who were neither management nor affiliated nonmanagement directors) made up 61 percent of the boards of responding companies in one sample, and 59 percent in the other. Heidrick & Struggles, *The Changing Board* 3 (1983); Heidrick & Struggles, *Director Data* 1.

§ 3A.02 Audit Committee in Small Publicly Held Corporations

It is recommended as a matter of corporate practice that every small publicly held corporation [§ 1.35] should have an audit committee to implement and support the oversight function of the board (§ 3.02) by reviewing on a periodic basis the corporation's processes for producing financial data, its internal controls, and the independence of the corporation's external auditor. The audit committee should consist of at least three members, and should be composed exclusively of directors who are neither employed by the corporation nor were so employed within the previous two years, including a majority of members who have no significant relationship [§ 1.34] with the corporation's senior executives.

§ 3A.03   Functions and Powers of Audit Committees

It is recommended as a matter of corporate practice that:

The audit committee of a publicly held corporation established under §§ 3.05 (Audit Committee in Large Publicly Held Corporations) or 3A.02 (Audit Committee in Small Publicly Held Corporations) should:

(a) Recommend the firm to be employed as the corporation's external auditor and review the proposed discharge of any such firm;

(b) Review the external auditor's compensation, the proposed terms of its engagement, and its independence;

(c) Review the appointment and replacement of the senior internal auditing executive, if any;

(d) Serve as a channel of communication between the external auditor and the board and between the senior internal auditing executive, if any, and the board;

(e) Review the results of each external audit of the corporation, the report of the audit, any related management letter, management's responses to recommendations made by the external auditor in connection with the audit, reports of the internal auditing department that are material to the corporation as a whole, and management's responses to those reports;

(f) Review the corporation's annual financial statements, any certification, report, opinion, or review rendered by the external auditor in connection with those financial statements, and any significant disputes between management and the external auditor that arose in connection with the preparation of those financial statements;

(g) Consider, in consultation with the external auditor and the senior internal auditing executive, if any, the adequacy of the corporation's internal controls;

(h) Consider major changes and other major questions of choice respecting the appropriate auditing and accounting principles and practices to be used in the preparation of the corporation's financial statements, when presented by the external auditor, a principal senior executive [§ 1.30], or otherwise.

§ 3A.04 Nominating Committee in Publicly Held Corporations: Composition, Powers, and Functions

It is recommended as a matter of corporate practice that:

(a) Every publicly held corporation [§ 1.31], except corporations a majority of whose voting securities are owned by a single person [§ 1.28], a family group [§ 1.21], or a control group [§ 1.09], should establish a nominating committee composed exclusively of directors who are not officers [§ 1.27] or employees of the corporation, including at least a majority of members who have no significant relationship [§ 1.34] with the corporation's senior executives [§ 1.33].

(b) The nominating committee should:

(1) Recommend to the board candidates for all directorships to be filled by the shareholders or the board.

(2) Consider, in making its recommendations, candidates for directorships proposed by the chief executive officer and, within the bounds of practicability, by any other senior executive or any director or shareholder.

(3) Recommend to the board directors to fill the seats on board committees.

Reporter's Note

... A 1990 study by Heidrick & Struggles, based on 1989 data, reported that 60 percent of the respondents had nominating committees.... A 1990 study by Korn/Ferry, based on 1989 data, reported that 57 percent of the respondents had nominating committees....

§ 3A.05 Compensation Committee in Large Publicly Held Corporations: Composition, Powers, and Functions

It is recommended as a matter of corporate practice that:

(a) Every large publicly held corporation [§ 1.24] should establish a compensation committee to implement and support the oversight function of the board in the area of compensation. The committee should be composed exclusively of directors who are not officers [§ 1.27] or employees of the corporation, including at least a majority of members who have no significant relationship [§ 1.34] with the corporation's senior executives [§ 1.33].

(b) The compensation committee should:

(1) Review and recommend to the board, or determine, the annual salary, bonus, stock options, and other benefits, direct and indirect, of the senior executives.

(2) Review new executive compensation programs; review on a periodic basis the operation of the corporation's executive

compensation programs to determine whether they are properly coordinated; establish and periodically review policies for the administration of executive compensation programs; and take steps to modify any executive compensation programs that yield payments and benefits that are not reasonably related to executive performance.

(3) Establish and periodically review policies in the area of management perquisites.

Reporter's Note

... A 1990 study by Heidrick & Struggles, based on 1989 data, reported that 93 percent of the respondents had compensation committees....   A 1990 study by Korn/Ferry, based on 1989 data, reported that 91 percent of the respondents had compensation committees....

PART IV

DUTY OF CARE AND THE BUSINESS JUDGMENT RULE

§ 4.01 Duty of Care of Directors and Officers; the Business Judgment Rule

(a) A director or officer has a duty to the corporation to perform the director's or officer's functions in good faith, in a manner that he or she reasonably believes to be in the best interests of the corporation, and with the care that an ordinarily prudent person would reasonably be expected to exercise in a like position and under similar circumstances. This Subsection (a) is subject to the provisions of Subsection (c) (the business judgment rule) where applicable.

(1) The duty in Subsection (a) includes the obligation to make, or cause to be made, an inquiry when, but only when, the circumstances would alert a reasonable director or officer to the need therefor. The extent of such inquiry shall be such as the director or officer reasonably believes to be necessary.

(2) In performing any of his or her functions (including oversight functions), a director or officer is entitled to rely on materials and persons in accordance with §§ 4.02 and 4.03 (reliance on directors, officers, employees, experts, other persons, and committees of the board).

(b) Except as otherwise provided by statute or by a standard of the corporation [§ 1.36] and subject to the board's ultimate responsibility for oversight, in performing its functions (including oversight functions), the board may delegate, formally or informally by course of conduct, any function (including the function of identifying matters requiring the attention of the board) to committees of the board or to directors, officers, employees, experts, or other persons; a director may rely on such committees and persons in fulfilling the duty under this Section with respect to any delegated function if the reliance is in accordance with §§ 4.02 and 4.03.

(c) A director or officer who makes a business judgment in good faith fulfills the duty under this Section if the director or officer:

(1) is not interested [§ 1.23] in the subject of the business judgment;

(2) is informed with respect to the subject of the business judgment to the extent the director or officer reasonably believes to be appropriate under the circumstances; and

(3) rationally believes that the business judgment is in the best interests of the corporation.

(d) A person challenging the conduct of a director or officer under this Section has the burden of proving a breach of the duty of care, including the inapplicability of the provisions as to the fulfillment of duty under Subsection (b) or (c), and, in a damage action, the burden of proving that the breach was the legal cause of damage suffered by the corporation.

Comment to § 4.01(a), first paragraph: ...

Illustrations:

6. C, who is rich and charming, has been a director of Y Corporation for several years. C's only significant contribution to Y has been a willingness to entertain important customers. C has said: "I do not have the capacity to oversee Y's business," and has made no attempt to oversee it. Y Corporation has gone into bankruptcy because of mismanagement. C, as a result of the failure to oversee the conduct of Y's business, has committed a breach of the duty of care. The fact that C may not have the capacity of an "ordinarily prudent person" is no defense. C will be held to an objective standard....

Comment to § 4.01(a)(1)–(a)(2):

Illustrations ...

1. Last year X Corporation, which had annual sales of $900,000,000 and a wide distribution system for its consumer products, was fined $1 million for horizontal price fixing, a criminal violation of the Sherman Act. It also had to settle a number of civil antitrust actions by paying an aggregate of $16.8 million. The directors of X Corporation have never been concerned with the existence of an antitrust compliance program, and X Corporation still has no company statement on

antitrust policy and no compliance program. A new horizontal price-fixing violation has just occurred. It is clear, however, that the directors of X Corporation had no knowledge of the new antitrust violation. The directors of X Corporation may well have violated their duty of care. The recent antitrust violations, the size of X Corporation, and its wide distribution system should have made compliance with the antitrust laws a particularly prominent concern. Unless other facts were present, such as the delegation of antitrust law compliance functions to the general counsel and proper reliance on the general counsel in accordance with § 4.01(b), the failure of the directors of X Corporation to be reasonably concerned with the existence of an antitrust compliance program would constitute a breach of the directors' duty of care.

2. The facts being otherwise as stated in Illustration 1, after the $1 million fine was paid, X Corporation did in fact install an antitrust compliance program which required X's local staff attorneys to refer all antitrust questions—and report all suspicious circumstances—to a designated staff attorney at company headquarters. An attorney in one regional office has, however, failed to report questionable conduct that may constitute a *per se* antitrust violation. X's directors have not failed to meet their duty of care due to an isolated breakdown in the compliance program. No violation of § 4.01(a) has occurred....

Comment to § 4.01(c) ...

c. *Prerequisite of a conscious exercise of judgment.* Section 4.01(c) affords protection only to a "business judgment." This means that to be afforded protection a decision must have been consciously made and judgment must, in fact, have been exercised. For efficiency reasons, corporate decisionmakers should be permitted to act decisively and with relative freedom from a judge's or jury's subsequent second-guessing. It is desirable to encourage directors and officers to enter new markets, develop new products, innovate, and take other business risks.

There is, however, no reason to provide special protection where no business decisionmaking is to be found. If, for example, directors have failed to oversee the conduct of the corporation's business (§ 3.02(a)(2)) by not even considering the need for an effective audit process, and this permits an executive to abscond with corporate funds, business judgment rule protection would be manifestly undesirable. The same would be true where a director received but did not read basic financial information, over a period of time, and thus allowed his corporation to be looted. Cf. Hoye v. Meek, 795 F.2d 893 (10th Cir.1986); DePinto v. Provident Security Life Insur. Co.,

374 F.2d 37 (9th Cir.1967), cert. denied 389 U.S. 822, 88 S.Ct. 48, 19 L.Ed.2d 74 (1967); Francis v. United Jersey Bank, 87 N.J. 15, 432 A.2d 814 (1981). In these and other "omission" situations, the director or officer would be judged under the reasonable care standards of § 4.01(a) and not protected by § 4.01(c). See, e.g., Aronson v. Lewis, 473 A.2d 805, 813 (Del.1984) ("the business judgment rule operates only in the context of director action.... [I]t has no role where directors have either abdicated their functions, or absent a conscious decision, failed to act."); Arsht, The Business Judgment Rule Revisited, 8 Hofstra L.Rev. 93, 112 (1979); Block & Prussin, The Business Judgment Rule and Shareholder Derivative Actions: Viva Zapata?, 37 Bus.Law. 27, 33 (1981) ("The [business judgment] rule does not apply where the director has in fact made no decision")....

e. Prerequisite of an informed decision. The great weight of case law and commentator authority supports the proposition that an informed decision (made, for example, on the basis of explanatory information presented to the board) is a prerequisite to the legal insulation afforded by the business judgment rule. In a much quoted statement, the court in Casey v. Woodruff, 49 N.Y.S.2d 625, 643 (1944), observed: "When courts say that they will not interfere in matters of business judgment, it is presupposed that judgment—reasonable diligence—has in fact been exercised." See ... Arsht, The Business Judgment Rule Revisited, 8 Hofstra L.Rev. 93, 111 (1979) (the business judgment rule should not be available to directors who do "not exercise due care to ascertain the relevant and available facts before voting")....

f. The "rationally believes" requirement. If the requirements of "good faith" and § 4.01(c)(1)–(c)(2) are met, § 4.01(c)(3) will protect a director or officer from liability for a business judgment if the director or officer "rationally believes that the business judgment is in the best interests of the corporation." The term "rationally believes" has both an objective and a subjective content. A director or officer must actually believe that the business judgment is in the best interests of the corporation and that belief must be rational....

There have been varying approaches taken in the cases and by commentators to the proper standard for judicial review of business judgments. Some courts have stated that a director's or officer's business judgment must be "reasonable" to be upheld.... On the other hand, a few cases have simply said that a director's or officer's judgment would be upheld if made with disinterest, in an informed manner, and in good faith....

Sound public policy dictates that directors and officers be given greater protection than courts and commentators using a "reasonableness" test would afford....

On the other hand, courts that have articulated only a "good faith" test may, depending on the court's meaning, provide too much legal insulation for directors and officers. A "good faith" test could be interpreted broadly to achieve the same result as the "rationally believes" standard. For example, in Sam Wong & Son v. New York Mercantile Exchange, 735 F.2d 653, 671, 678 n. 32 (2d Cir.1984), Judge Friendly held that the rationality of a decision by the Board of Governors of the Mercantile Exchange was relevant in determining whether the Board had acted in good faith, and concluded that "[a]bsent some basis in reason, action could hardly be in good faith even apart from ulterior motive.".... Serious problems arise, however, if the phrase "good faith" is interpreted narrowly to mean only the absence of subjective "bad motives." There is no reason to insulate an objectively irrational business decision—one so removed from the realm of reason that it should not be sustained—solely on the basis that it was made in subjective good faith....

§ 4.02   Reliance on Directors, Officers, Employees, Experts, and Other Persons

In performing his or her duties and functions, a director or officer who acts in good faith, and reasonably believes that reliance is warranted, is entitled to rely on information, opinions, reports, statements (including financial statements and other financial data), decisions, judgments, and performance (including decisions, judgments, and performance within the scope of § 4.01(b)) prepared, presented, made, or performed by:

(a) One or more directors, officers, or employees of the corporation, or of a business organization [§ 1.04] under joint control or common control [§ 1.08] with the corporation, who the director or officer reasonably believes merit confidence; or

(b) Legal counsel, public accountants, engineers, or other persons who the director or officer reasonably believes merit confidence.

§ 4.03   Reliance on a Committee of the Board

In performing his or her duties and functions, a director who acts in good faith, and reasonably believes that reliance is warranted, is entitled to rely on:

(a) The decisions, judgments, and performance (including decisions, judgments, and performance within the scope of § 4.01(b)), of a duly authorized committee of the board upon which the director does not serve, with respect to matters delegated to that committee, provided that the director reasonably believes the committee merits confidence.

(b) Information, opinions, reports, and statements (including financial statements and other financial data), prepared or presented by a duly authorized committee of the board upon which the director does not serve, provided that the director reasonably believes the committee merits confidence.

PART V

DUTY OF FAIR DEALING

Chapter 1

GENERAL PRINCIPLE

§ 5.01 Duty of Fair Dealing of Directors, Senior Executives, and Controlling Shareholders

Directors [§ 1.13], senior executives [§ 1.33], and controlling shareholders [§ 1.10], when interested [§ 1.23] in a matter affecting the corporation, are under a duty of fair dealing, which may be fulfilled as set forth in Chapters 2 and 3 of Part V. This duty includes the obligation to make appropriate disclosure as provided in such Chapters.

Chapter 2

DUTY OF FAIR DEALING OF DIRECTORS AND SENIOR EXECUTIVES

§ 5.02 Transactions With the Corporation

(a) *General Rule.* A director [§ 1.13] or senior executive [§ 1.33] who enters into a transaction with the corporation (other than a transaction involving the payment of compensation) fulfills the duty of fair dealing with respect to the transaction if:

(1) Disclosure concerning the conflict of interest [§ 1.14(a)] and the transaction [§ 1.14(b)] is made to the corporate decision-maker [§ 1.11] who authorizes in advance or ratifies the transaction; and

(2) either:

(A) The transaction is fair to the corporation when entered into;

(B) The transaction is authorized in advance, following disclosure concerning the conflict of interest and the transaction, by disinterested directors [§ 1.15], or in the case of a senior executive who is not a director by a disinterested superior, who could reasonably have concluded that the transaction was fair to the corporation at the time of such authorization;

(C) The transaction is ratified, following such disclosure, by disinterested directors who could reasonably have concluded that the transaction was fair to the corporation at the time it was entered into, provided (i) a corporate decisionmaker who is not interested [§ 1.23] in the transaction acted for the corporation in the transaction and could reasonably have concluded that the transaction was fair to the corporation; (ii) the interested director or senior executive made disclosure to such decisionmaker pursuant to Subsection (a)(1) to the extent he or she then knew of the material facts; (iii) the interested director or senior executive did not act unreasonably in failing to seek advance authorization of the transaction by disinterested directors or a disinterested superior; and (iv) the failure to obtain advance authorization of the transaction by disinterested directors or a disinterested superior did not adversely affect the interests of the corporation in a significant way; or

(D) the transaction is authorized in advance or ratified, following such disclosure, by disinterested shareholders [§ 1.16], and does not constitute a waste of corporate assets [§ 1.42] at the time of the shareholder action.

(b) *Burden of Proof.* A party who challenges a transaction between a director or senior executive and the corporation has the burden of proof, except that if such party establishes that none of Subsections (a)(2)(B), (a)(2)(C), or (a)(2)(D) is satisfied, the director or senior executive has the burden of proving that the transaction was fair to the corporation.

(c) *Ratification of Disclosure or Nondisclosure.* The disclosure requirements of § 5.02(a)(1) will be deemed to be satisfied if at any time (but no later than a reasonable time after suit is filed challenging the transaction) the transaction is ratified, following such disclosure, by the directors, the shareholders, or the corporate decisionmaker who initially approved the transaction or the decisionmaker's successor.

Comment to § 5.02(a)(1) ...

A director or senior executive may not deal with the corporation as a stranger at arm's length. Even where the conflict of interest is made known, there is a relationship of "trust and confidence" with the corporation, so as to require disclosure of "material matters," rather than the relationship of a stranger to the corporation with a much more limited duty of disclosure. Compare Restatement, Second, Torts § 551(2)(a) with Restatement, Second, Torts § 551(2)(e). See also Restatement, Second, Torts § 551, Comments *e, f* and *k.* The duty of one who occupies a relationship of trust and confidence to disclose material facts is widely recognized. See, e.g., Restatement, Second, Contracts § 161, Comment *f;* Restatement, Second, Agency § 390; Restatement of Restitution § 191, Comment on Clause (b). A director or senior executive owes a duty to the corporation not only to avoid misleading it by misstatements or omissions, but affirmatively to disclose the material facts known to the director or senior executive. The interested director or senior executive also has an obligation to explain the implications of a transaction, when he or she is in a position to realize those implications and the disinterested superior or director reviewing the transaction is not in a position to do so. See Globe Woolen Co. v. Utica Gas & Elec. Co., 224 N.Y. 483, 121 N.E. 378 (1918).

Section 1.14 sets forth the required elements of disclosure and § 1.25 sets forth the definition of material facts which are required to be disclosed. Under § 5.02, a director or senior executive who fails to make required disclosure has failed to fulfill the duty of fair dealing, even if the terms of the transaction are fair. A contract price might be fair in the sense that it corresponds to market price, and yet the corporation might have refused to make the contract if a given material fact had been disclosed. See, e.g., Illustrations 4 and 6. Furthermore, as pointed out in paragraph d of the Introductory Note, fairness is often a range, rather than a point, and disclosure of a material fact might have induced the corporation to bargain the price down lower in the range....

Illustrations ...

4. X Corporation is seeking a new headquarters building. D, a vice president of X Corporation, owns all the stock of R Corporation, which owns an office building. D causes a real estate agent to offer R Corporation's building to X Corporation, but does not disclose his ownership of R Corporation. X Corporation's board of directors agrees to purchase the building for a fair price. Two weeks later, X Corporation learns of D's interest in R Corporation. D has not fulfilled his duty to the corporation under [§] 5.02(a)(1)....

6. The facts being otherwise as stated in Illustration 4, D discloses to X Corporation, prior to the acquisition, his interest in R Corporation. D fails to disclose, however, that he has information, not publicly available, that the State Highway Department has formally decided to run a highway through the property on which R Corporation's building stands, and to condemn the building under its power of eminent domain. The price paid by X Corporation is fair, even taking the proposed condemnation into account, since the condemnation award is likely to equal or exceed the price. Two weeks after the acquisition, X Corporation learns of the Highway Department's decision. D has not fulfilled his duty to the corporation under § 5.02(a)(1)....

Illustrations [to Section 5.02(a)(2)(B)];

9. Corporation C is engaged in commercial agriculture. C's Board consists of L, its president, and N, O, and P, who own other types of agricultural businesses. C is potentially in the market for a new headquarters building. L recently inherited a commercial building that is somewhat rundown and only partially rented. Al-

though L has no experience in real estate, she is convinced that with a $1 million renovation the building will be worth $9 million. L offered the building to a number of sophisticated buyers, whose bids ranged between $3 and 5 million. Subsequently, L listed the building with a commercial real estate broker for six months at a price of $7.5 million, but received no offers. L then offered the building to C's board for $7.5 million, making full disclosure, but arguing that this was a bargain price. N, O, and P, who are disinterested within the meaning of § 1.15, consulted a real estate expert, who advised that the building might conceivably be worth $7.5 million, but this was an extremely high price, and the expert would not pay it. The board nevertheless accepted L's offer. N, O, and P did not act irrationally, since real estate cannot be precisely valued, and the value that will be added to a building by renovation is always somewhat problematic. However, the $7.5 million price could not reasonably be regarded as fair, considering that the building had been extensively marketed to sophisticated real estate investors who were aware of the possibility of renovation; that none of these investors was willing to pay more than $5 million; and that N, O, and P were not themselves experts in real estate. The transaction fails to meet the standard of § 5.02(a)(2)(B), and an action may be brought against L to rescind the transaction. However, N, O, and P are protected from liability as individuals since they meet the standard of the business judgment rule [§ 4.01(c)]....

§ 5.03 Compensation of Directors and Senior Executives

(a) *General Rule.* A director [§ 1.13] or senior executive [§ 1.33] who receives compensation from the corporation for services in that capacity fulfills the duty of fair dealing with respect to the compensation if either:

(1) The compensation is fair to the corporation when approved;

(2) The compensation is authorized in advance by disinterested directors [§ 1.15] or, in the case of a senior executive who is not a director, authorized in advance by a disinterested superior, in a manner that satisfies the standards of the business judgment rule [§ 4.01(c)];

(3) The compensation is ratified by disinterested directors [§ 1.15] who satisfy the requirements of the business judgment rule [§ 4.01(c)], provided (i) a corporate decisionmaker who was not interested [§ 1.23] in receipt of the compensation acted for the corporation in determining the compensation and satisfied the requirements of the business judgment rule; (ii) the interested director or senior executive did not act unreasonably in failing to seek advance authorization of the compensation by disinterested directors or a disinterested superior; and (iii) the failure to obtain

advance authorization of the compensation by disinterested directors or a disinterested superior did not adversely affect the interests of the corporation in a significant way; or

(4) The compensation is authorized in advance or ratified by disinterested shareholders [§ 1.16], and does not constitute a waste of corporate assets [§ 1.42] at the time of the shareholder action.

(b) *Burden of Proof.* A party who challenges a transaction involving the payment of compensation to a director or senior executive has the burden of proof, except that if such party establishes that the requirements of neither Subsections (a)(2), (a)(3), nor (a)(4) are met, the director or the senior executive has the burden of proving that the transaction was fair to the corporation.

§ 5.04 Use by a Director or Senior Executive of Corporate Property, Material Non-public Corporate Information, or Corporate Position

(a) *General Rule.* A director [§ 1.13] or senior executive [§ 1.33] may not use corporate property, material non-public corporate information, or corporate position to secure a pecuniary benefit, unless either:

(1) Value is given for the use and the transaction meets the standards of § 5.02 (Transactions with the Corporation);

(2) The use constitutes compensation and meets the standards of § 5.03 (Compensation of Directors and Senior Executives);

(3) The use is solely of corporate information, and is not in connection with trading of the corporation's securities, is not a use of proprietary information of the corporation, and does not harm the corporation;

(4) The use is subject neither to § 5.02 nor § 5.03 but is authorized in advance or ratified by disinterested directors [§ 1.15] or disinterested shareholders [§ 1.16], and meets the requirements and standards of disclosure and review set forth in § 5.02 as if that Section were applicable to the use; or

(5) The benefit is received as a shareholder and is made proportionately available to all other similarly situated shareholders,

and the use is not otherwise unlawful.

(b) *Burden of Proof.* A party who challenges the conduct of a director or senior executive under Subsection (a) has the burden of proof, except that if value was given for the benefit, the burden of proving whether the value was fair should be allocated as provided in § 5.02 in the case of a transaction with the corporation.

(c) *Special Rule on Remedies.* A director or senior executive is subject to liability under this Section only to the extent of any improper benefit received and retained, except to the extent that any foreseeable

925

harm caused by the conduct of the director or senior executive exceeds the value of the benefit received, and multiple liability based on receipt of the same benefit is not to be imposed.

§ 5.05 Taking of Corporate Opportunities by Directors or Senior Executives

(a) *General Rule.* A director [§ 1.13] or senior executive [§ 1.33] may not take advantage of a corporate opportunity unless:

(1) The director or senior executive first offers the corporate opportunity to the corporation and makes disclosure concerning the conflict of interest [§ 1.14(a)] and the corporate opportunity [§ 1.14(b)];

(2) The corporate opportunity is rejected by the corporation; and

(3) either:

(A) The rejection of the opportunity is fair to the corporation;

(B) The opportunity is rejected in advance, following such disclosure, by disinterested directors [§ 1.15], or, in the case of a senior executive who is not a director, by a disinterested superior, in a manner that satisfies the standards of the business judgment rule [§ 4.01(c)]; or

(C) The rejection is authorized in advance or ratified, following such disclosure, by disinterested shareholders [§ 1.16], and the rejection is not equivalent to a waste of corporate assets [§ 1.42].

(b) *Definition of a Corporate Opportunity.* For purposes of this Section, a corporate opportunity means:

(1) Any opportunity to engage in a business activity of which a director or senior executive becomes aware, either:

(A) In connection with the performance of functions as a director or senior executive, or under circumstances that should reasonably lead the director or senior executive to believe that the person offering the opportunity expects it to be offered to the corporation; or

(B) Through the use of corporate information or property, if the resulting opportunity is one that the director or senior executive should reasonably be expected to believe would be of interest to the corporation; or

(2) Any opportunity to engage in a business activity of which a senior executive becomes aware and knows is closely related to a business in which the corporation is engaged or expects to engage.

(c) *Burden of Proof.* A party who challenges the taking of a corporate opportunity has the burden of proof, except that if such party establishes that the requirements of Subsection (a)(3)(B) or (C) are not met, the director or the senior executive has the burden of proving that the rejection and the taking of the opportunity were fair to the corporation.

(d) *Ratification of Defective Disclosure.* A good faith but defective disclosure of the facts concerning the corporate opportunity may be cured if at any time (but no later than a reasonable time after suit is filed challenging the taking of the corporate opportunity) the original rejection of the corporate opportunity is ratified, following the required disclosure, by the board, the shareholders, or the corporate decisionmaker who initially approved the rejection of the corporate opportunity, or such decisionmaker's successor.

(e) *Special Rule Concerning Delayed Offering of Corporate Opportunities.* Relief based solely on failure to first offer an opportunity to the corporation under Subsection (a)(1) is not available if: (1) such failure resulted from a good faith belief that the business activity did not constitute a corporate opportunity, and (2) not later than a reasonable time after suit is filed challenging the taking of the corporate opportunity, the corporate opportunity is to the extent possible offered to the corporation and rejected in a manner that satisfies the standards of Subsection (a).

§ 5.06 Competition With the Corporation

(a) *General Rule.* Directors [§ 1.13] and senior executives [§ 1.33] may not advance their pecuniary interests by engaging in competition with the corporation unless either:

(1) Any reasonably foreseeable harm to the corporation from such competition is outweighed by the benefit that the corporation may reasonably be expected to derive from allowing the competition to take place, or there is no reasonably foreseeable harm to the corporation from such competition;

(2) The competition is authorized in advance or ratified, following disclosure concerning the conflict of interest [§ 1.14(a)] and the competition [§ 1.14(b)], by disinterested directors [§ 1.15], or in the case of a senior executive who is not a director, is authorized in advance by a disinterested superior, in a manner that satisfies the standards of the business judgment rule [§ 4.01(c)]; or

(3) The competition is authorized in advance or ratified, following such disclosure, by disinterested shareholders [§ 1.16], and the shareholders' action is not equivalent to a waste of corporate assets [§ 1.42].

(b) *Burden of Proof.* A party who challenges a director or senior executive for advancing the director's or senior executive's pecuniary interest by competing with the corporation has the burden of proof, except that if such party establishes that neither Subsection (a)(2) nor (3) is satisfied, the director or the senior executive has the burden of proving that any reasonably foreseeable harm to the corporation from such competition is outweighed by the benefit that the corporation may reasonably be expected to derive from allowing the competition to take place, or that there is no reasonably foreseeable harm to the corporation.

§ 5.07 Transactions Between Corporations With Common Directors or Senior Executives

(a) A transaction between two corporations is not to be treated as a transaction subject to the provisions of § 5.02 (Transactions With the Corporation) solely on the ground that the same person is a director [§ 1.13] or senior executive [§ 1.33] of both corporations unless:

(1) The director or senior executive participates personally and substantially in negotiating the transaction for either of the corporations; or

(2) The transaction is approved by the board of either corporation, and a director on that board who is also a director or senior executive of the other corporation casts a vote that is necessary to approve the transaction.

(b) If a transaction falls within Subsection (a)(1) or (a)(2), it will be reviewed under § 5.02.

§ 5.08 Conduct on Behalf of Associates of Directors or Senior Executives

A director [§ 1.13] or senior executive [§ 1.33] fails to fulfill the duty of fair dealing to the corporation if the director or senior executive knowingly advances the pecuniary interest of an associate [§ 1.03] in a manner that would fail to comply with the provisions of this Chapter 2 had the director or senior executive acted for himself or herself.

§ 5.09 Effect of a Standard of the Corporation

If a director [§ 1.13] or senior executive [§ 1.33] acts in reliance upon a standard of the corporation [§ 1.36] that authorizes a director or senior executive to either:

(a) Enter into a transaction with the corporation that is of a specified type and that could be expected to recur in the ordinary course of business of the corporation;

(b) Use corporate position or corporate property in a specified manner that is not unlawful and that could be expected to recur in the ordinary course of business of the corporation;

(c) Take advantage of a specified type of corporate opportunity of which the director or senior executive becomes aware other than (i) in connection with the performance of directorial or executive functions, or (ii) under circumstances that should reasonably lead the director or senior executive to believe that the person [§ 1.28] offering the opportunity expected it to be offered to the corporation, or (iii) through the use of corporate information or property; or

(d) Engage in competition of a specified type;

and the standard was authorized in advance by disinterested directors [§ 1.15] or disinterested shareholders [§ 1.16], following disclosure concerning the effect of the standard and of the type of transaction or conduct intended to be covered by the standard, then the standard is to be deemed equivalent to an authorization of the action in advance by disinterested directors or shareholders under §§ 5.02 (Transactions with the Corporation), 5.03 (Compensation of Directors and Senior Executives), 5.04 (Use by a Director or Senior Executive of Corporate Property, Material Non–Public Corporate Information, or Corporate Position), 5.05 (Taking of Corporate Opportunities by Directors or Senior Executives), or 5.06 (Competition with the Corporation), as the case may be.

Chapter 3

DUTY OF FAIR DEALING OF CONTROLLING SHAREHOLDERS

§ 5.10 Transactions by a Controlling Shareholder With the Corporation

(a) *General Rule.* A controlling shareholder [§ 1.10] who enters into a transaction with the corporation fulfills the duty of fair dealing to the corporation with respect to the transaction if:

(1) The transaction is fair to the corporation when entered into; or

(2) The transaction is authorized in advance or ratified by disinterested shareholders [§ 1.16], following disclosure concerning the conflict of interest [§ 1.14(a)] and the transaction [§ 1.14(b)], and does not constitute a waste of corporate assets [§ 1.42] at the time of the shareholder action.

(b) *Burden of Proof.* If the transaction was authorized in advance by disinterested directors [§ 1.15], or authorized in advance or ratified by disinterested shareholders, following such disclosure, the party challenging the transaction has the burden of proof. The party challenging the transaction also has the burden of proof if the transaction was ratified by disinterested directors and the failure to obtain advance authorization did not adversely affect the interests of the corporation in a significant way. If the transaction was not so authorized or ratified, the controlling shareholder has the burden of proof, except to the extent otherwise provided in Subsection (c).

(c) *Transactions in the Ordinary Course of Business.* In the case of a transaction between a controlling shareholder and the corporation that was in the ordinary course of the corporation's business, a party who challenges the transaction has the burden of coming forward with evidence that the transaction was unfair, whether or not the transaction was authorized in advance or ratified by disinterested directors or disinterested shareholders.

§ 5.11 Use by a Controlling Shareholder of Corporate Property, Material Non-public Corporate Information, or Corporate Position

(a) *General Rule.* A controlling shareholder may not use corporate property, its controlling position, or (when trading in the corporation's securities) material non-public corporate information to secure a pecuniary benefit, unless:

(1) Value is given for the use and the transaction meets the standards of § 5.10 (Transactions by a Controlling Shareholder with the Corporation), or

(2) Any resulting benefit to the controlling shareholder either is made proportionally available to the other similarly situated shareholders or is derived only from the use of controlling position and is not unfair to other shareholders,

and the use is not otherwise unlawful.

(b) *Burden of Proof.* A party who challenges the conduct of a controlling shareholder under Subsection (a) has the burden of proof, except that if value was given for the benefit, the burden of proving whether the value was fair should be determined as provided in § 5.10 in the case of a transaction with the corporation.

(c) *Special Rule on Remedies.* A controlling shareholder is subject to liability under this section only to the extent of any improper benefit received and retained, except to the extent that any foreseeable harm caused by the shareholder's conduct exceeds the value of the benefit received, and multiple liability based on receipt of the same benefit is not to be imposed.

§ 5.12 Taking of Corporate Opportunities by a Controlling Shareholder

(a) *General Rule.* A controlling shareholder [§ 1.10] may not take advantage of a corporate opportunity unless:

(1) The taking of the opportunity is fair to the corporation; or

(2) The taking of the opportunity is authorized in advance or ratified by disinterested shareholders [§ 1.16], following disclosure concerning the conflict of interest [§ 1.14(a)] and the corporate opportunity [§ 1.14(b)], and the taking of the opportunity is not equivalent to a waste of corporate assets [§ 1.42].

(b) *Definition of a Corporate Opportunity.* For purposes of this Section, a corporate opportunity means any opportunity to engage in a business activity that:

(1) Is developed or received by the corporation, or comes to the controlling shareholder primarily by virtue of its relationship to the corporation; or

(2) Is held out to shareholders of the corporation by the controlling shareholder, or by the corporation with the consent of the controlling shareholder, as being a type of business activity that will be within the scope of the business in which the corporation is engaged or expects to engage and will not be within the scope of the controlling shareholder's business.

(c) *Burden of Proof.* A party who challenges the taking of a corporate opportunity has the burden of proof, except that the controlling shareholder has the burden of proving that the taking of the opportunity is fair to the corporation if the taking of the opportunity was not authorized in advance or ratified by disinterested directors or disinterested shareholders, following the disclosure required by Subsection (a)(2).

§ 5.13 Conduct on Behalf of Associates of a Controlling Shareholder

A controlling shareholder [§ 1.10] fails to fulfill the duty of fair dealing to the corporation if it knowingly advances the pecuniary interest of an associate [§ 1.03] of the controlling shareholder in a manner that would fail to comply with the provisions of this Chapter 3 had the controlling shareholder acted for itself.

Chapter 4

TRANSFER OF CONTROL

§ 5.15 Transfer of Control in Which a Director or Principal Senior Executive Is Interested

(a) If directors or principal senior executives [§ 1.30] of a corporation are interested [§ 1.23] in a transaction in control [§ 1.38] or a tender offer that results in a transfer of control [§ 1.08] of the corporation to another person [§ 1.28], then those directors or principal senior executives have the burden of proving that the transaction was fair to the shareholders of the corporation unless (1) the transaction involves a transfer by a controlling shareholder [§ 1.10] or (2) the conditions of Subsection (b) are satisfied.

(b) If in connection with a transaction described in Subsection (a) involving a publicly held corporation [§ 1.31]:

(1) Public disclosure of the proposed transaction is made;

(2) Responsible persons who express an interest are provided relevant information concerning the corporation and given a reasonable opportunity to submit a competing proposal;

(3) The transaction is authorized in advance by disinterested directors [§ 1.15] after the procedures set forth in Subsections (1) and (2) have been complied with; and

(4) The transaction is authorized or ratified by disinterested shareholders [§ 1.16] (or, if the transaction is effected by a tender offer, the offer is accepted by disinterested shareholders), after disclosure concerning the conflict of interest [§ 1.14(a)] and the transaction [§ 1.14(b)] has been made;

then a party challenging the transaction has the burden of proving that the terms of the transaction are equivalent to a waste of corporate assets [§ 1.42].

(c) The fact that holders of equity securities are entitled to an appraisal remedy reflecting the general principles embodied in §§ 7.21–7.23 with respect to a transaction specified in Subsection (a) does not make an appraisal proceeding the exclusive remedy of a shareholder who proposes to challenge the transaction, unless the transaction falls within § 7.25 (Transactions in Control Involving Corporate Combinations to Which a Majority Shareholder Is a Party).

§ 5.16 Disposition of Voting Equity Securities by a Controlling Shareholder to Third Parties

A controlling shareholder [§ 1.10] has the same right to dispose of voting equity securities [§ 1.40] as any other shareholder, including the right to dispose of those securities for a price that is not made proportionally available to other shareholders, but the controlling shareholder does not satisfy the duty of fair dealing to the other shareholders if:

(a) The controlling shareholder does not make disclosure concerning the transaction [§ 1.14(b)] to other shareholders with whom the controlling shareholder deals in connection with the transaction; or

(b) It is apparent from the circumstances that the purchaser is likely to violate the duty of fair dealing under Part V in such a way as to obtain a significant financial benefit for the purchaser or an associate [§ 1.03].

PART VI

ROLE OF DIRECTORS AND SHAREHOLDERS IN TRANSACTIONS IN CONTROL AND TENDER OFFERS

§ 6.01 Role of Directors and Holders of Voting Equity Securities With Respect to Transactions in Control Proposed to the Corporation

(a) The board of directors, in the exercise of its business judgment [§ 4.01(c)], may approve, reject, or decline to consider a proposal to the corporation to engage in a transaction in control [§ 1.38].

(b) A transaction in control of the corporation to which the corporation is a party should require approval by the shareholders [§ 1.02].

§ 6.02 Action of Directors That Has the Foreseeable Effect of Blocking Unsolicited Tender Offers

(a) The board of directors may take an action that has the foreseeable effect of blocking an unsolicited tender offer [§ 1.39], if the action is a reasonable response to the offer.

(b) In considering whether its action is a reasonable response to the offer:

(1) The board may take into account all factors relevant to the best interests of the corporation and shareholders, including, among other things, questions of legality and whether the offer, if successful, would threaten the corporation's essential economic prospects; and

(2) The board may, in addition to the analysis under § 6.02(b)(1), have regard for interests or groups (other than shareholders) with respect to which the corporation has a legitimate concern if to do so would not significantly disfavor the long-term interests of shareholders.

(c) A person who challenges an action of the board on the ground that it fails to satisfy the standards of Subsection (a) has the burden of proof that the board's action is an unreasonable response to the offer.

(d) An action that does not meet the standards of Subsection (a) may be enjoined or set aside, but directors who authorize such an action are not subject to liability for damages if their conduct meets the standard of the business judgment rule [§ 4.01(c)].

PART VII

REMEDIES

INTRODUCTION ...

REPORTER'S NOTE

1. *The empirical evidence.* Critiques of the derivative action are not new. In the 1904s, the Chamber of Commerce of the State of New York sponsored a study by Franklin Wood that examined 1400 derivative actions filed between 1936 and 1942 in New York City. Wood reported a consistent pattern in which (1) the plaintiff's stockholdings were generally nominal, (2) the plaintiff seldom secured a litigated victory, and (3) private settlements (in which the corporation often received nothing) were common. F. Wood, Survey and Report Regarding Stockholders' Derivative Suits, 32 (1944) (the "Wood Report"). He concluded that the benefits of the action were outweighed by its costs. Partly as a result of the Wood Report and similar commentary, and partly because of the bar's uneasiness with an action in which the attorney was frequently the real party in interest, the derivative action was frequently derided as a "strike suit" that served no interests other than those of the plaintiff's attorney.

In response, legislative treatment of the action was generally skeptical and constraining: statutes requiring security for expenses' bonds were enacted, common law defenses were tightened, and an extraordinary procedural complexity developed around such questions as jurisdiction, alignment of the parties, demand on the board and shareholders, and settlement and dismissal. Later, other commentators re-analyzed Wood's data and, after excluding those cases that were still pending or in which the disposition was unknown, concluded that the overall rate of plaintiff's "success" (i.e., cases in which some recovery was secured) was about 44 percent, and thus compared favorably with the rate of plaintiff's success in similar forms of civil litigation. See Conard, A Behavioral Analysis of Directors' Liability for Negligence, 1972 Duke L.J. 895, 901 n.21; Hornstein, The Death Knell of Stockholders' Derivative Suits in New York, 32 Calif.L.Rev. 123, 127–28 (1944).

Important empirical work has been done in this area since the time of the original Wood study, but an overall evaluation of the derivative action remains difficult to reach. One such effort casts some partial light on the disputed benefits of the derivative action. An eight-year study followed 531 derivative and class action suits brought against the officers or directors of 205 publicly held corporations between 1971 and 1978. See Jones, An Empirical Examination of the Resolution of Shareholder Derivative and Class Action Lawsuits, 60 B.U.L.Rev. 542 (1980). The following results of that study seem salient:

(1) In roughly 75 percent of the cases, plaintiffs obtained some form of relief, typically by way of settlement (70%), but in less than one percent did plaintiffs win a litigated judgment. Although this study concluded that "the notion that shareholder plaintiffs rarely obtain relief is clearly a myth" (Id. at 545), it is uncertain at what price this relief came. Because data were not collected with respect to the size or adequacy of the settlement funds in these actions, and because direct and derivative actions were not carefully distinguished, it remains an open question whether these actions yielded a net compensatory benefit to their corporations.

(2) The incidence of "primary" shareholder litigation (i.e., litigation directed at corporate officials personally) did not significantly rise over the period from 1971 to 1978, and, if adjustment is made for a sudden spurt of "illegal payments" cases in the mid–1970s, probably fell slightly over this period.

(3) Derivative ligation tended to focus on self-dealing transactions and duty of loyalty issues and only infrequently involved challenges to arm's-length business decisions.

(4) Only a minority of publicly held corporations experienced such litigation. About 30 percent of the large publicly held corporations surveyed were involved in any form of shareholder litigation, direct or derivative, during the eight-year period. Once the impact of multiple suits arising out of the same event or transaction was adjusted for, the study concluded that the typical publicly held firm would be involved in such a suit only once every 17.6 years on average. See Jones, An Empirical Evaluation of the Incidence of Shareholder Derivative and Class Action Lawsuits, 1971–1978, 60 B.U.L.Rev. 306, 312–13 (1980).

Recently, social scientists have reanalyzed the data collected in the foregoing study. Although they found important information to be lacking from much of the sample, they still noted that, when the amount of the recovery was indicated, "one-third of the total reported settlements involved no monetary relief, and six of the fifteen cases in which attorney fees were reported involved only 'procedural changes,' but significant attorney fees." This pattern suggests the existence of a substantial conflict of interest may exist between the plaintiff's attorney and his nominal clients, the shareholders. See Garth, Nagel and Plager, The Role of Empirical Research in Assessing the Efficacy of the Shareholders' Derivative Suit: Promise and Potential, 48 Law and Contemp.Probs. 137, 146–47 (1985). See also Rosenfeld, An Empirical Test of Class Action Settlements, 5 J.Legal Stud. 113, 119 (1976); Coffee, The Unfaithful Champion: The Plaintiff as Monitor in Shareholder Litigation, 48 Law and Contemp.Probs. 5, 26–33 (1985).

The most recent study of shareholder litigation examined a random sample of 535 public corporations over a period extending from the late

1960s to 1987. See Romano, The Shareholder Suit: Litigation Without Foundation?, 7 J.Law, Econ., & Org. 55 (1991). Its findings underline the relative infrequency of derivative actions and the centrality of the settlement stage. Only 19 percent of the corporations in the sample experienced a derivative suit, but some corporations attracted recurrent litigation, and there was an increase in litigation frequency during the 1980s. Although very few judgments for plaintiffs were obtained, the most striking fact about derivative litigation in this study was the high rate of settlement. Eighty-three out of 128 actions resolved during this period (or roughly 65%) were settled. Id. at 60. Yet, only half of the settlements (46 out of 83) involved any monetary recovery; however, the vast majority (75 out of 83) involved fee awards to the plaintiffs' attorneys. In another 25 cases, the settlement afforded non-pecuniary structural relief (there was also a monetary recovery in four of the suits). In those cases where the settlement fund could be valued (39 out of 83), the average recovery was $9 million, but there was substantial variation within this class (as the median recovery was only $2 million). Interestingly, the average recovery in derivative actions was found to be about half that in class actions. Id. at 61. These results can be interpreted in various ways. Some would explain them on the hypothesis that a significant percentage of shareholder litigation is without merit; another hypothesis is that plaintiffs' attorneys in such actions have serious conflicts of interest that lead them not to maximize the possible recovery to their class. Yet, a paradox arises here: another recent study has found that securities class actions tend to settle at 25 percent of the asserted potential damages. See Alexander, Do the Merits Matter? A Study of Settlements in Securities Class Actions, 43 Stan.L.Rev. 497, 500 (1991). Although such findings can similarly be interpreted to show an excessive incentive to litigate and to settle, the puzzle is that the two contexts are closely related. Indeed, typically, the same plaintiffs' attorneys are suing similarly situated defendants in both types of actions. In this light, the difference in outcomes between class and derivative actions (and the greater recoveries in the former) may reflect the greater legal barriers surrounding the derivative action. Overbroad rules that deny standing to plaintiffs in derivative actions in which the underlying allegations have legal merit could explain the lesser apparent settlement value of legal claims in the derivative action context.

Some preliminary efforts have been made to use econometric techniques to study the impact of the termination of derivative actions on the stock prices of companies in whose name the action was brought. Early results have reported a marginally negative market reaction to the suit's termination, but one that was statistically insignificant. See Fischel and Bradley, The Role of Liability Rules and the Derivative Suit in Corporate Law: A Theoretical and Empirical Analysis, 71 Cornell L.Rev. 261, 277–83 (1986). However, both because the methodology underlying these studies makes questionable assumptions about the stock market's sensitivity to the prospect of relatively small recoveries and because there is no evidence that the market's expectation was frustrated by the suit's termination (i.e., the market may assume that most suits will be terminated, whatever their merit), little reliance is here placed on such data. Even if reliable data that showed an insignificant or negative trend in the wake of an action's filing were available, the interpretation that should be placed on such data would remain open to debate. Stock market indifference to derivative litigation could be explained as based on the expectation that such actions were likely to result in collusive or cosmetic settlements in which any recovery would be consumed by costly attorneys' fees and other expenses. In addition, if the principal benefit of such actions lies in their general deterrent effect on all corporate managements, the stock price reaction of any single corporation would not reveal this benefit.

The existing state of the empirical data does not answer many important questions. First, it does not tell us whether derivative actions yield on average a net compensatory benefit for the corporation (after appropriate deduction is made for the cost of attorneys' fees and indemnification). Second, although the data shows little evidence of any recent explosion in the rate of shareholder litigation and suggests that such litigation only infrequently concerns business decisions not complicated by an alleged conflict of interest, it is possible that directors' perception of such litigation may be very different, and it is the perceived threat that may shape their willingness to serve on boards. Finally, recent institutional changes—such as the decreased availability of liability insurance and the change in incidence of takeover contests—may not be reflected in historical data. Still, the empirical evidence does clearly highlight the centrality of the settlement stage and the possibility that the conflicts of interest attending this stage may weaken the ability of derivative litigation to serve shareholders' interests.

Chapter 1

THE DERIVATIVE ACTION

§ 7.01 Direct and Derivative Actions Distinguished

(a) A derivative action may be brought in the name or right of a corporation by a holder [§ 1.22], as provided in § 7.02 (Standing to Commence and Maintain a Derivative Action), to redress an injury sustained by, or enforce a duty owed to, a corporation. An action in which the holder can prevail only by showing an injury or breach of duty to the corporation should be treated as a derivative action.

(b) A direct action may be brought in the name and right of a holder to redress an injury sustained by, or enforce a duty owed to, the holder. An action in which the holder can prevail without showing an injury or breach of duty to the corporation should be treated as a direct action that may be maintained by the holder in an individual capacity.

(c) If a transaction gives rise to both direct and derivative claims, a holder may commence and maintain direct and derivative actions simultaneously, and any special restrictions or defenses pertaining to the maintenance, settlement, or dismissal of either action should not apply to the other.

(d) In the case of a closely held corporation [§ 1.06], the court in its discretion may treat an action raising derivative claims as a direct action, exempt it from those restrictions and defenses applicable only to derivative actions, and order an individual recovery, if it finds that to do so will not (i) unfairly expose the corporation or the defendants to a multiplicity of actions, (ii) materially prejudice the interests of creditors of the corporation, or (iii) interfere with a fair distribution of the recovery among all interested persons.

§ 7.02 Standing to Commence and Maintain a Derivative Action

(a) A holder [§ 1.22] of an equity security [§ 1.20] has standing to commence and maintain a derivative action if the holder:

(1) Acquired the equity security either (A) before the material facts relating to the alleged wrong were publicly disclosed or were known by, or specifically communicated to, the holder, or (B) by devolution of law, directly or indirectly, from a prior holder who acquired the security as described in the preceding Clause (A);

(2) Continues to hold the equity security until the time of judgment, unless the failure to do so is the result of corporate action in which the holder did not acquiesce, and either (A) the derivative action was commenced prior to the corporate action terminating the holder's status, or (B) the court finds that the holder is better able to represent the interests of the shareholders than any other holder who has brought suit;

(3) Has complied with the demand requirement of § 7.03 (Exhaustion of Intracorporate Remedies: The Demand Rule) or was excused by its terms; and

(4) Is able to represent fairly and adequately the interests of the shareholders.

(b) On a timely motion, a holder of an equity security should be permitted to intervene in a derivative action, unless the court finds that the interests to be represented by the intervenor are already fairly and adequately represented or that the intervenor is unable to represent fairly and adequately the interests of the shareholders.

(c) A director [§ 1.13] of a corporation has standing to commence and maintain a derivative action unless the court finds that the director is unable to represent fairly and adequately the interests of the shareholders.

§ 7.03 Exhaustion of Intracorporate Remedies: The Demand Rule

(a) Before commencing a derivative action, a holder [§ 1.22] or a director [§ 1.13] should be required to make a written demand upon the board of directors of the corporation, requesting it to prosecute the action or take suitable corrective measures, unless demand is excused under § 7.03(b). The demand should give notice to the board, with reasonable specificity, of the essential facts relied upon to support each of the claims made therein.

(b) Demand on the board should be excused only if the plaintiff makes a specific showing that irreparable injury to the corporation would otherwise result, and in such instances demand should be made promptly after commencement of the action.

(c) Demand on shareholders should not be required.

(d) Except as provided in § 7.03(b), the court should dismiss a derivative action that is commenced prior to the response of the board or a committee thereof to the demand required by § 7.03(a), unless the board or committee fails to respond within a reasonable time.

§ 7.04 Pleading, Demand Rejection, Procedure, and Costs in a Derivative Action

The legal standards applicable to a derivative action should provide that:

(a) *Particularity; Demand Rejection.*

(1) *In General.* The complaint shall plead with particularity facts that, if true, raise a significant prospect that the transaction or conduct complained of did not meet the applicable requirements of Parts IV (Duty of Care and the Business Judgment Rule), V (Duty of Fair Dealing), or VI (Role of Directors and Shareholders in Transactions in Control and Tender Offers), in light of any approvals of the transaction or conduct communicated to the plaintiff by the corporation.

(2) *Demand Rejection.* If a corporation rejects the demand made on the board pursuant to § 7.03, and if, at or following the rejection, the corporation delivers to the plaintiff a written reply to the demand which states that the demand was rejected by directors who were not interested [§ 1.23] in the transaction or conduct described in and forming the basis for the demand and that such directors constituted a majority of the entire board and were capable as a group of objective judgment in the circumstances, and provides specific reasons for those statements, then the complaint shall also

plead with particularity facts that, if true, raise a significant prospect that either:

(A) The statements in the reply are not correct;

(B) If Part IV, V, or VI provides that the underlying transaction or conduct would be reviewed under the standard of the business judgment rule, that the rejection did not satisfy the requirements of the business judgment rule as specified in § 4.01(c); or

(C) If Part IV, V, or VI provides that the underlying transaction or conduct would be reviewed under a standard other than the business judgment rule, either (i) that the disinterested directors who rejected the demand did not satisfy the good faith and informational requirements (§ 4.01(c)(2)) of the business judgment rule or (ii) that disinterested directors could not reasonably have determined that rejection of the demand was in the best interests of the corporation.

If the complaint fails to set forth sufficiently such particularized facts, defendants shall be entitled to dismissal of the complaint prior to discovery.

(b) *Attorney's Certification.* Each party's attorney of record shall sign every pleading, motion, and other paper filed on behalf of the party, and such signature shall constitute the attorney's certification that (i) to the best of the attorney's knowledge, information, and belief, formed after reasonable inquiry, the pleading, motion, or other paper is well grounded in fact and is warranted by existing law or by a good faith argument for the extension, modification, or reversal of existing law, and (ii) the pleading, motion, or other paper is not interposed for any improper purpose, such as to harass or to cause unnecessary delay or needless increase in the cost of litigation.

(c) *Security for Expenses.* Except as authorized by statute or judicial rule applicable to civil actions generally, no bond, undertaking, or other security for expenses shall be required.

(d) *Award of Costs.* The court may award applicable costs, including reasonable attorney's fees and expenses, against a party, or a party's counsel:

(1) At any time, if the court finds that any specific claim for relief or defense was asserted or any pleading, motion, request for discovery, or other action was made or taken in bad faith or without reasonable cause; or

(2) Upon final judgment, if the court finds, in light of all the evidence, and considering both the state and trend of the substantive law, that the action taken as a whole was brought, prosecuted, or defended in bad faith or in an unreasonable manner.

Comment ...

d. Section 7.04(a)(2) ...

Section 7.04(a)(1) and § 7.04(a)(2) state separate tests, so both are required to be met. There is nevertheless an interrelationship between the two tests. In applying § 7.04(a), a court should balance the strength and seriousness of the case set out by the particularized pleading of the plaintiff, as tested under § 7.04(a)(1), with that required under § 7.04(a)(2). The stronger and more serious the case set out by the plaintiff's particularized pleading, as tested under § 7.04(a)(1), the less the complaint must allege with particularity to establish under § 7.04(a)(2) that there is a significant prospect the directors could not have satisfied the business judgment rule under § 7.04(a)(2)(B), or could not reasonably have determined that rejection of the demand was in the best interests of the corporation under § 7.04(a)(2)(C).

§ 7.05 Board or Committee Authority in Regard to a Derivative Action

(a) The board of a corporation in whose name or right a derivative action is brought has standing on behalf of the corporation to:

(1) Move to dismiss the action on account of the plaintiff's lack of standing under § 7.02 (Standing to Commence and Maintain a Derivative Action) or the plaintiff's failure to comply with § 7.03 (Exhaustion of Intracorporate Remedies: The Demand Rule) or § 7.04(a) or (b) (Pleading, Demand Rejection, Procedure, and Costs in a Derivative Action) or move for dismissal of the complaint or for summary judgment;

(2) Move for a stay of the action, including discovery, as provided by § 7.06 (Authority of Court to Stay a Derivative Action);

(3) Move to dismiss the action as contrary to the best interests of the corporation, as provided in §§ 7.07–7.12 (dismissal of a derivative action based on a motion requesting dismissal by the board, a board committee, the shareholders, or a special panel);

(4) Oppose injunctive or other relief materially affecting the corporation's interests;

(5) Adopt or pursue the action in the corporation's right;

(6) Comment on, object to, or recommend any proposed settlement, discontinuance, compromise, or voluntary dismissal by agreement between the plaintiff and any defendant under § 7.14 (Settlement of a Derivative Action by Agreement Between the Plaintiff and a Defendant), or any award of attorney's fees and other expenses under § 7.17 (Plaintiff's Attorney's Fees and Expenses); and

(7) Seek to settle the action without agreement of the plaintiff under § 7.15 (Settlement of a Derivative Action Without the Agreement of the Plaintiff).

Except as provided above, the corporation may not otherwise defend the action in the place of, or raise defenses on behalf of, other defendants.

(b) The board of a corporation in whose name or right a derivative action is brought may:

(1) Delegate its authority to take any action specified in § 7.05(a) to a committee of directors; or

(2) Request the court to appoint a special panel in lieu of a committee of directors, or a special member of a committee, under § 7.12 (Special Panel or Special Committee Members).

§ 7.06 Authority of Court to Stay a Derivative Action

In the absence of special circumstances, the court should stay discovery and all further proceedings by the plaintiff in a derivative action on the motion of the corporation and upon such conditions as the court deems appropriate pending the court's determination of any motion made by the corporation under § 7.04(a)(2) and the completion within a reasonable period of any review and evaluation undertaken and diligently pursued pursuant to § 7.09 (Procedures for Requesting Dismissal of a Derivative Action). On the same basis, the court may stay discovery and further proceedings pending (a) the resolution of a related action or (b) such other event or development as the interests of justice may require.

§ 7.07 Dismissal of a Derivative Action Based on a Motion Requesting Dismissal by the Board or a Committee: General Statement

(a) The court having jurisdiction over a derivative action should dismiss the action as against one or more of the defendants based on a motion by the board or a properly delegated committee requesting dismissal of the action as in the best interests of the corporation, if:

(1) In the case of an action against a person [§ 1.28] other than a director [§ 1.13], senior executive [§ 1.33], or person in control [§ 1.08] of the corporation, or an associate [§ 1.03] of any such person, the determinations of the board or committee underlying the motion satisfy the requirements of the business judgment rule as specified in § 4.01;

(2) In the case of an action against a director, senior executive, or person in control of the corporation, or an associate of any such person, the conditions specified in § 7.08 (Dismissal of a Derivative Action Against Directors, Senior Executives, Controlling Persons, or

Associates Based on a Motion Requesting Dismissal by the Board or a Committee) are satisfied; or

(3) In any case, the shareholders approve a resolution requesting dismissal of the action in the manner provided in § 7.11 (Dismissal of a Derivative Action Based Upon Action by the Shareholders).

(b) Regardless of whether a corporation chooses to proceed under § 7.08 or § 7.11, it is free to make any other motion available to it under the law, including a motion to dismiss the complaint or for summary judgment.

§ 7.08 Dismissal of a Derivative Action Against Directors, Senior Executives, Controlling Persons, or Associates Based on a Motion Requesting Dismissal by the Board or a Committee

The court should, subject to the provisions of § 7.10(b) (retention of significant improper benefit), dismiss a derivative action against a defendant who is a director [§ 1.13], a senior executive [§ 1.33], or a person [§ 1.28] in control [§ 1.08] of the corporation, or an associate [§ 1.03] of any such person, if:

(a) The board of directors or a properly delegated committee thereof (either in response to a demand or following commencement of the action) has determined that the action is contrary to the best interests of the corporation and has requested dismissal of the action;

(b) The procedures specified in § 7.09 (Procedures for Requesting Dismissal of a Derivative Action) for the conduct of a review and evaluation of the action were substantially complied with (either in response to a demand or following commencement of the action), or any material departures therefrom were justified under the circumstances; and

(c) The determinations of the board or committee satisfy the applicable standard of review set forth in § 7.10(a) (Standard of Judicial Review with Regard to a Board or Committee Motion Requesting Dismissal of a Derivative Action Under § 7.08).

§ 7.09 Procedures for Requesting Dismissal of a Derivative Action

(a) The following procedural standards should apply to the review and evaluation of a derivative action by the board or committee under § 7.08 (Dismissal of a Derivative Action Against Directors, Senior Executives, Controlling Persons, or Associates Based on a Motion Requesting Dismissal by the Board or a Committee) or § 7.11 (Dismissal of a Derivative Action Based Upon Action by the Shareholders):

(1) The board or committee should be composed of two or more persons, no participating member of which was interested [§ 1.23] in the action, and should as a group be capable of objective judgment in the circumstances;

(2) The board or committee should be assisted by counsel of its choice and such other agents as it reasonably considers necessary;

(3) The determinations of the board or committee should be based upon a review and evaluation that was sufficiently informed to satisfy the standards applicable under § 7.10(a); and

(4) If the board or committee determines to request dismissal of the derivative action, it shall prepare and file with the court a report or other written submission setting forth its determinations in a manner sufficient to enable the court to conduct the review required under § 7.10 (Standard of Judicial Review with Regard to a Board or Committee Motion Requesting Dismissal of a Derivative Action Under § 7.08).

(b) If the court is unwilling to grant a motion to dismiss under § 7.08 or § 7.11 because the procedures followed by the board or committee departed materially from the standards specified in § 7.09(a), the court should permit the board or committee to supplement its procedures, and make such further reports or other written submissions, as will satisfy the standards specified in § 7.09(a), unless the court decides that (i) the board or committee did not act on the basis of a good faith belief that its procedures and report were justified in the circumstances; (ii) unreasonable delay or prejudice would result; or (iii) there is no reasonable prospect that such further steps would support dismissal of the action.

§ 7.10 Standard of Judicial Review With Regard to a Board or Committee Motion Requesting Dismissal of a Derivative Action Under § 7.08

(a) *Standard of Review.* In deciding whether an action should be dismissed under § 7.08 (Dismissal of a Derivative Action Against Directors, Senior Executives, Controlling Persons, or Associates Based on a Motion Requesting Dismissal by the Board or a Committee), the court should apply the following standards of review:

(1) If the gravamen of the claim is that the defendant violated a duty set forth in Part IV (Duty of Care and the Business Judgment Rule), other than by committing a knowing and culpable violation of law that is alleged with particularity, or if the underlying transaction or conduct would be reviewed under the business judgment rule under § 5.03, § 5.04, § 5.05, § 5.06, § 5.08, or § 6.02, the court should dismiss the claim unless it finds that the board's or committee's determinations fail to satisfy the requirements of the business judgment rule as specified in § 4.01(c).

944

(2) In other cases governed by Part V (Duty of Fair Dealing) or Part VI (Role of Directors and Shareholders in Transactions in Control and Tender Offers), or to which the business judgment rule is not applicable, including cases in which the gravamen of the claim is that defendant committed a knowing and culpable violation of law in breach of Part IV, the court should dismiss the action if the court finds, in light of the applicable standards under Part IV, V, or VI that the board or committee was adequately informed under the circumstances and reasonably determined that dismissal was in the best interests of the corporation, based on grounds that the court deems to warrant reliance.

(3) In cases arising under either Subsection (a)(1) or (a)(2), the court may substantively review and determine any issue of law.

(b) *Retention of Significant Improper Benefit.* The court shall not dismiss an action if the plaintiff establishes that dismissal would permit a defendant, or an associate [§ 1.03], to retain a significant improper benefit where:

(1) The defendant, either alone or collectively with others who are also found to have received a significant improper benefit arising out of the same transaction, possesses control [§ 1.08] of the corporation; or

(2) Such benefit was obtained:

(A) As the result of a knowing and material misrepresentation or omission or other fraudulent act; or

(B) Without advance authorization or the requisite ratification of such benefit by disinterested directors [§ 1.15] (or, in the case of a non-director senior executive, advance authorization by a disinterested superior), or authorization or ratification by disinterested shareholders [§ 1.16], and in breach of § 5.02 (Transactions with the Corporation) or § 5.04 (Use by a Director or Senior Executive of Corporate Property, Material Non–Public Corporate Information, or Corporate Position);

unless the court determines, in light of specific reasons advanced by the board or committee, that the likely injury to the corporation from continuation of the action convincingly outweighs any adverse impact on the public interest from dismissal of the action.

(c) *Subsequent Developments.* In determining whether the standards of § 7.10(a) are satisfied or whether § 7.10(b) or any of the exceptions set forth therein are applicable, the court may take into account considerations set forth by the board or committee (or otherwise brought to the court's attention) that reflect material developments subsequent to the time of the underlying transaction or conduct or to the time of the motion by the board or committee requesting dismissal.

§ 7.11 Dismissal of a Derivative Action Based Upon Action by the Shareholders

The court should dismiss a derivative action against any defendant upon approval by the shareholders of a resolution requesting dismissal of the action as in the best interests of the corporation if the court finds that:

(a) A resolution recommending such dismissal to the shareholders was adopted by the board of directors, or a properly delegated committee thereof, after a review and evaluation that substantially complied with the procedures specified in § 7.09(a)(1)–(3) (Procedures for Requesting Dismissal of a Derivative Action) or in which any material departures from those procedures were justified under the circumstances;

(b) Disclosure was made to the shareholders of all material facts [§ 1.25] concerning the derivative action and the board's resolution recommending its dismissal to the shareholders and, if requested by plaintiff, the disclosure statement included a brief statement by the plaintiff summarizing the plaintiff's views of the action and of the board's or committee's resolutions;

(c) The resolution was approved by a vote of disinterested shareholders [§ 1.16]; and

(d) Dismissal would not constitute a waste of corporate assets [§ 1.42].

§ 7.12 Special Panel or Special Committee Members

(a) On motion made by a corporation in whose name or right a derivative action is brought or upon which a demand has been made, the court may appoint one or more individuals to serve as a panel in lieu of a committee of directors for purposes of § 7.08 (Dismissal of a Derivative Action Against Directors, Senior Executives, Controlling Persons, or Associates Based on a Motion Requesting Dismissal by the Board or a Committee) or § 7.11 (Dismissal of a Derivative Action Based Upon Action by the Shareholders), none of whom should be interested [§ 1.23] in the action or have a significant relationship [§ 1.34] with a senior executive [§ 1.33] of the corporation or a similar relationship with any defendant or plaintiff. The panel so appointed should conduct a review and evaluation and prepare a report or other written submission as to the advisability of terminating the action, in compliance with the procedures specified in § 7.09 (Procedures for Requesting Dismissal of a Derivative Action). Any report or other written submission so prepared should have the same status under § 7.08, § 7.10, § 7.11, or § 7.13 (Judicial Procedures on Motions to Dismiss a Derivative Action Under § 7.08 or § 7.11) as a report or other written submission of the board or a properly delegated committee thereof. The costs of the inquiry and report or other written submission should be borne by the corporation, unless the court directs otherwise.

(b) In lieu of the appointment of a panel under § 7.12(a), the court on motion of a corporation may appoint one or more individuals who are not directors of the corporation and who meet the qualifications specified in § 7.12(a) to serve on a committee established by the corporation under § 7.05(b)(1).

§ 7.13 Judicial Procedures on Motions to Dismiss a Derivative Action Under § 7.08 or § 7.11

(a) *Filing of Report or Other Written Submission.* Upon a motion to dismiss an action under § 7.08 (Dismissal of a Derivative Action Against Directors, Senior Executives, Controlling Persons, or Associates Based on a Motion Requesting Dismissal by the Board or a Committee) or § 7.11 (Dismissal of a Derivative Action Based Upon Action by the Shareholders), the corporation shall file with the court a report or other written submission setting forth the procedures and determinations of the board or committee, or the resolution of the shareholders. A copy of the report or other written submission, including any supporting documentation filed by the corporation, shall be given to the plaintiff's counsel.

(b) *Protective Order.* The court may issue a protective order concerning such materials, where appropriate.

(c) *Discovery.* Subject to § 7.06 (Authority of Court to Stay a Derivative Action), if the plaintiff has demonstrated that a substantial issue exists whether the applicable standards of § 7.08, § 7.09, § 7.10, § 7.11, or § 7.12 have been satisfied and if the plaintiff is unable without undue hardship to obtain the information by other means, the court may order such limited discovery or limited evidentiary hearing, as to issues specified by the court, as the court finds to be (i) necessary to enable it to render a decision on the motion under the applicable standards of § 7.08, § 7.09, § 7.10, § 7.11, or § 7.12, and (ii) consistent with an expedited resolution of the motion. In the absence of special circumstances, the court should limit on a similar basis any discovery that is sought by the plaintiff in response to a motion for summary judgment by the corporation or any defendant to those facts likely to be in dispute. The results of any such discovery may be made subject to a protective order on the same basis as under § 7.13(b).

(d) *Burdens of Proof.* The plaintiff has the burden of proof in the case of a motion (1) under § 7.08 where the standard of judicial review is determined under § 7.10(a)(1) because the basis of the claim involves a breach of a duty set forth in Part IV (Duty of Care and the Business Judgment Rule) or because the underlying transaction would be reviewed under the business judgment rule, or (2) under § 7.07(a)(1) (suits against third parties and lesser corporate officials). The corporation has the burden of proof in the case of a motion under § 7.08 where the standard of judicial review is determined under § 7.10(a)(2) because the underlying transaction would be reviewed under a standard other than the business judgment rule, except that the plaintiff retains the burden of proof in all cases to show (i) that a defendant's conduct involved a knowing and culpable violation of law, (ii) that the board or committee as a group was not capable of objective judgment in the circumstances as required by § 7.09(a)(1), and (iii) that dismissal of the action would permit a defendant or an associate [§ 1.03] thereof to retain a significant improper benefit under § 7.10(b). The corporation shall also have the burden of proving under § 7.10(b) that the likely injury to the corporation from continuation of the action convincingly outweighs any adverse impact on the public interest from dismissal of the action. In the case of a motion under § 7.11 (Dismissal of a Derivative Action Based Upon Action by the Shareholders), the plaintiff has the burden of proof with respect to § 7.11(b), (c), and (d), and the corporation has the burden of proof with respect to § 7.11(a).

(e) *Privilege.* The plaintiff's counsel should be furnished a copy of related legal opinions received by the board or committee if any opinion is tendered to the court under § 7.13(a). Subject to that requirement, communications, both oral and written, between the board or committee and its counsel with respect to the subject matter of the action do not forfeit their privileged character, and documents, memoranda, or other material qualifying as attorney's work product do not become subject to discovery, on the grounds that the action is derivative or that the privilege was waived by the production to the plaintiff or the filing with the court of a report, other written submission, or supporting documents pursuant to § 7.13.

§ 7.14 Settlement of a Derivative Action by Agreement Between the Plaintiff and a Defendant

(a) A derivative action should not be settled, discontinued, compromised, or voluntarily dismissed by agreement between the plaintiff and a defendant, except with the approval of the court.

(b) The court should approve a proposed settlement or other disposition if the balance of corporate interests warrants approval and the settlement or other disposition is consistent with public policy. In evaluating a proposed settlement, the court should place special weight on the net benefit, including pecuniary and non-pecuniary elements, to the corporation.

(c) In the absence of circumstances leading the court to find that the interests of the shareholders will not be substantially affected by the settlement or other disposition, the court's approval should be preceded by notice (which should be on an individual basis to the extent practicable) to, and an opportunity of a hearing for, affected shareholders. At such a hearing, objecting shareholders should have a reasonable opportunity to contest a proposed settlement or other disposition, including an opportunity with the court's approval to present and to cross-examine witnesses, and the court may allow, upon good cause shown, reasonable discovery consistent with avoiding undue delay.

§ 7.15 Settlement of a Derivative Action Without the Agreement of the Plaintiff

(a) Once a derivative action is commenced, the board or a properly delegated committee, without the agreement of a plaintiff, may with the approval of the court enter into a settlement with, or grant a release to, a director [§ 1.13], a senior executive [§ 1.33], or a person [§ 1.28] in control [§ 1.08] of the corporation, or an associate [§ 1.03] of any such person, with respect to any claim raised on behalf of the corporation in the action. The court should approve the settlement or release if it finds, in response to a motion made on behalf of the corporation by its board of directors or a properly delegated committee, that the following conditions are satisfied:

(1) The board or a properly delegated committee, whose participating members in either case were not interested [§ 1.23] in the action, entered into the proposed settlement after conducting an adequately informed review and evaluation, and filed with the court a report or other written submission that was substantially in conformity with the requirements applicable to a motion requesting dismissal by the board or a committee under § 7.09 (Procedures for Requesting Dismissal of a Derivative Action), or any material departures from those procedures were justified in the circumstances.

(2) The provisions of § 7.14 (Settlement of a Derivative Action by Agreement Between the Plaintiff and a Defendant) applicable to notice and an opportunity for a hearing to affected shareholders in the case of a settlement between the plaintiff and a defendant were substantially complied with.

(3) On the basis of the entire record, the balance of corporate interests warrants approval and the settlement or release is consistent with public policy. In evaluating a proposed settlement, the court should place special weight on the net benefit, including pecuniary and nonpecuniary elements, to the corporation.

(b) Any settlement or release entered into in accordance with § 7.15(a) constitutes a valid affirmative defense with respect to the claims and liabilities covered to the same extent as a settlement entered into with the plaintiff and approved pursuant to § 7.14.

(c) In lieu of a report or other written submission from the board or a committee, the court may consider and rely upon the determinations and conclusions of a special panel appointed under procedures that were substantially in conformity with the procedures of § 7.12 (Special Panel or Special Committee Members) applicable to a panel appointed to consider whether a derivative action should be dismissed.

§ 7.16   Disposition of Recovery in a Derivative Action

Except in the special circumstances specified in § 7.18(e) (pro-rata recovery), the recovery in a derivative action should accrue exclusively to the corporation. Any plaintiff or attorney who brings (or threatens to bring) an action in the name or right of the corporation and who receives property or money (including reimbursement for expenses) from the corporation or any defendant, as a result of the settlement, compromise, discontinuance, or dismissal of an actual or threatened derivative action, should be required to account to the corporation therefor, unless such money or property was received pursuant to a judicial order or a judicially approved settlement.

§ 7.17   Plaintiff's Attorney's Fees and Expenses

A successful plaintiff in a derivative action should be entitled to recover reasonable attorney's fees and other reasonable litigation expenses from the corporation, as determined by the court having jurisdiction over the action, but in no event should the attorney's fee award exceed a reasonable proportion of the value of the relief (including nonpecuniary relief) obtained by the plaintiff for the corporation.

Comment ...

... Because individual shareholders would find it infeasible to organize and tax themselves the costs necessary for a successful action, the well-established rule that a successful plaintiff in a derivative action may look to the corporation for reimbursement of attorney's fees and expenses is a precondition to an effective litigation remedy. In effect, this rule represents the common law's efficient solution to the well-recognized "free rider" problem that arises whenever an individual must incur costs to benefit a group of which the individual is a member. Unless some mechanism exists by which to allocate these costs among the group in proportion to the respective benefits to be received, the individual (here, the plaintiff shareholder) has an inadequate incentive to proceed.

Although the foregoing logic is widely accepted, there is less agreement as to the appropriate formula by which to determine the amount of the fee. Two basic approaches exist. Under the traditional "salvage value" approach, courts have calculated counsel fees by awarding a percentage of the total recovery.... The alternative approach, recommended by the Manual for Complex Litigation, Second § 24.12 (1986), and prevalent among federal courts, focuses principally on the value of the attorney's time at the attorney's customary hourly rate, and then adjusts this "lodestar figure" upward (or downward) to reflect the risk assumed by the attorney and the quality of the work done.... Recently, there appears to have been a trend toward greater use of the percentage method, and in some Circuits a 30 percent fee award has now become presumptive.... Other courts have expressly used high multipliers under the lodestar formula in order to achieve the same desired percentage of the recovery....

Both the lodestar and the percentage-of-the-recovery approaches have well-recognized deficiencies if they are applied literally and without a sense of their impact upon the incentives held out to the plaintiff's attorney. Because a time-based formula, such as the "lodestar" method, compensates attorneys for the hours they expend, a number of commentators have suggested that such a formula gives rise to an incentive to expend unnecessary time and engage in dilatory tactics in order to maximize the attorney's recovery. Such an incentive is unfortunate not only because it delays the progress of the litigation, but also because it aggravates a latent conflict of interest between the attorney and the class he or she represents; the greater the fee, the smaller the net recovery will typically be for the shareholders. In addition, if the defendant strategically delays any settlement offer until just before the moment of trial or judgment, the defendant can further exacerbate this conflict, because at this point an inadequate settlement offer should produce nearly the same attorney's fee under a time-based formula as would a highly successful litigated victory. Thus, the plaintiff's attorney may have an incentive to accept an offer that is not in the best interests of the client in order to avoid the risk of trial and an adverse decision.

In contrast, a percentage-of-the-recovery formula avoids these problems (because the attorney's fee grows only in proportion to the recovery), but encounters others. First, a percentage formula may sometimes encourage premature settlements that are not in the best interests of the class.... Second, a percentage formula clearly does not work with respect to nonpecuniary recoveries, such as injunctive or equitable relief, where the value of the benefit conferred cannot be easily quantified. Finally, such a formula may produce windfall profits (such as where a case is settled immediately), which may evoke public criticism and erode respect for the law. Accordingly, § 7.17 proposes a compromise that attempts to retain the best of both formulas while avoiding their deficiencies. Section 7.17 permits the use of the percentage-of-the-recovery formula, but does not require it. Where it is not employed as the measure of the fee award, however, it should set a ceiling on the maximum fee allowable under any formula. The effect is to reduce the incentive to expend time needlessly, to minimize the danger of collusive settlements, and to align better the attorney's self-interest with that of the client; in addition, the danger of unjustified "windfall" profits is better avoided.

Chapter 2

RECOVERY FOR BREACH OF DUTY

§ 7.18 Recovery Resulting From a Breach of Duty: General Rules

(a) Except as otherwise provided in § 7.19 (Limitation on Damages for Certain Violations of the Duty of Care), a defendant who violates the standards of conduct set forth in Part IV (Duty of Care and the Business Judgment Rule), Part V (Duty of Fair Dealing), or Part VI (Role of Directors and Shareholders in Transactions in Control and Tender Offers) is subject to liability for the losses to the corporation (or, to the extent that a direct action lies under § 7.01 (Direct and Derivative Actions Distinguished), to its shareholders) of which the violation is a legal cause, and, in the case of a violation of the standards set forth in Part V, for any additional gains derived by the defendant or an associate [§ 1.03] to the extent necessary to make equitable restitution.

(b) A violation of the standards of conduct set forth in Part IV, Part V, or Part VI is the legal cause of loss if the plaintiff proves that (i) satisfaction of the applicable standard would have been a substantial factor in averting the loss, and (ii) the likelihood of injury would have been foreseeable to an ordinarily prudent person in like position to that of the defendant and in similar circumstances. It is not a defense to liability in such cases that damage to the corporation would not have resulted but for the acts or omissions of other individuals.

(c) A plaintiff bears the burden of proving causation and the amount of damages suffered by, or other recovery due to, the corporation or the shareholders as the result of a defendant's violation of a standard of conduct set forth in Part IV, Part V, or Part VI. The court may permit a defendant to offset against such liability any gains to the corporation that the defendant can establish arose out of the same transaction and whose recognition in this manner is not contrary to public policy.

(d) The losses deemed to be legally caused by a knowing violation of a standard of conduct set forth in Part V include the costs and expenses to which the corporation was subjected as a result of the violation, including the counsel fees and expenses of a successful plaintiff in a derivative action, except to the extent the court determines that inclusion of some or all of such costs and expenses would be inequitable in the circumstances.

(e) The court having jurisdiction over a derivative action may direct that all or a portion of the award be paid directly to individual shareholders, on a pro-rata basis, when such a payment is equitable in the circumstances and adequate provision has been made for the creditors of the corporation.

§ 7.19 Limitation on Damages for Certain Violations of the Duty of Care

Except as otherwise provided by statute, if a failure by a director [§ 1.13] or an officer [§ 1.27] to meet the standard of conduct specified in Part IV (Duty of Care and the Business Judgment Rule) did not either:

> (1) Involve a knowing and culpable violation of law by the director or officer;

> (2) Show a conscious disregard for the duty of the director or officer to the corporation under circumstances in which the director or officer was aware that the conduct or omission created an unjustified risk of serious injury to the corporation; or

> (3) Constitute a sustained and unexcused pattern of inattention that amounted to an abdication of the defendant's duty to the corporation;

and the director or officer, or an associate [§ 1.03], did not receive a benefit that was improper under Part V (Duty of Fair Dealing), then a provision in a certificate of incorporation that limits damages against an officer or a director for such failure to an amount not less than such person's annual compensation from the corporation should be given effect, if the provision is adopted by a vote of disinterested shareholders [§ 1.16] after disclosure [§ 1.14(b)] concerning the provision, may be repealed by the shareholders at any annual meeting without prior action by the board, and does not reduce liability with respect to pending actions or losses incurred prior to its adoption.

Chapter 3

INDEMNIFICATION AND INSURANCE

§ 7.20 Indemnification and Insurance

(a) *General Rule.* Subject to the limitations set forth in Subsection (b):

> (1) A corporation should have the power to indemnify a person who is or was a director [§ 1.13] or officer [§ 1.27] for liabilities and reasonable expenses incurred in connection with any threatened, pending, or completed action, suit, or other proceeding, formal or informal, whether civil, criminal, administrative, or investigative, to which the director or officer is or may be made a party or in connection with which the director or officer is or may be otherwise required to appear:

(A) Because such person was acting in his or her capacity as a director or officer of the corporation, or acting in some capacity on behalf of a third party at the request of the corporation, if such person was acting in good faith or otherwise engaged in good faith conduct in such capacity, or

(B) Solely because of the fact that such person is or was a director or officer.

(2) A corporation should have the power to pay expenses incurred by a person who is or was a director or officer in connection with a proceeding described in Subsection (a)(1) in advance of the final disposition of such proceeding, upon receipt of an undertaking by or on behalf of the director or officer to repay such expenses, if it is ultimately determined that the person is not entitled to be indemnified by the corporation.

(3) A corporation should be obligated to indemnify a person who is or was a director or officer for liabilities and reasonable expenses incurred in connection with a proceeding described in Subsection (a)(1) if:

(A) the director or officer was wholly successful, on the merits or otherwise, in the defense of such proceeding, or

(B) the corporation properly obligates itself to so indemnify the director or officer, to the extent permitted by this Section, by a provision in its charter documents or by contract.

(4) A corporation should have the power to purchase insurance on behalf of a person who is or was a director or officer against liability asserted against or expenses incurred by the person in connection with a proceeding described in Subsection (a)(1), whether or not the corporation would have the power to indemnify the person against the same liability or expenses.

(b) *Limitations on Indemnification and Insurance*

(1) A corporation should not have the power or be obligated to indemnify a director or officer for liabilities and reasonable expenses incurred in connection with a proceeding described in Subsection (a)(1):

(A) If the conduct for which indemnification is sought directly involved a knowing and culpable violation of law or a significant pecuniary benefit was obtained to which the director or officer was not legally entitled;

(B) To the extent that the indemnification would involve any amount paid in satisfaction of a fine, civil penalty, or similar judgment as a result of violation of statutory law, the policy of which clearly precludes indemnification;

(C) If the indemnification would involve any amount paid in settlement of the proceeding and the conduct directly involved a violation of statutory law, the policy of which clearly precludes indemnification; or

(D) To the extent that the indemnification would involve amounts paid (i) in satisfaction of a judgment or in settlement of an action that was brought by or in the right of the corporation, or (ii) for expenses incurred in any such proceeding in which the director or officer was adjudged liable to the corporation, except as provided in Subsection (c).

In the absence of a judicial determination, the applicability of Subsection (b)(1) may be determined by disinterested directors, disinterested shareholders, or independent counsel, but if a determination so made is adverse to the director or officer, the director or officer should have standing to seek a de novo court determination thereof.

(2) A corporation should not be entitled to purchase insurance pursuant to Subsection (a)(4), to the extent that the insurance would furnish protection against liability for conduct directly involving a knowing and culpable violation of law or involving a significant pecuniary benefit obtained by an insured person to which the person is not legally entitled.

(c) *Court–Ordered Indemnification*

(1) A court should order the payment of indemnification in the circumstances described in Subsection (a)(3) and should also order the corporation to pay the reasonable expenses incurred by the director or officer in successfully obtaining court-ordered indemnification.

(2) A court may order the indemnification of amounts paid in settlement of an action brought by or in the right of the corporation (other than amounts paid in settlement of an action in which the court determines that there was a substantial likelihood that the director or officer received a significant pecuniary benefit to which the director or officer was not legally entitled), or for expenses in any proceeding referred to in Subsection (b)(1)(A) or (D), if it determines that indemnification is fair and reasonable, in whole or in part, in view of all the circumstances.

(d) *Report to Shareholders Concerning Indemnification in Derivative Actions.* If a corporation indemnifies or advances expenses to a director or officer in connection with a proceeding by or in the right of the corporation, the corporation should report the indemnification or advance to the shareholders at or before the time notice of the next shareholders' meeting is sent.

(e) *Nonexclusivity of Indemnification Provisions.* Subject to the limitations set forth in Subsection (b): (1) a corporation should have the power to provide indemnification and the payment of expenses under a standard of the corporation [§ 1.36], agreement, or otherwise, and (2) this Section should not be deemed exclusive of any other rights to which a director or officer seeking indemnification or the payment of expenses may be entitled.

(f) *Legal Successors.* The power or obligation to indemnify or pay expenses under this section shall extend to executors, administrators, trustees, and other successors in interest of directors and officers against whom liabilities are threatened or asserted.

Chapter 4

THE APPRAISAL REMEDY

§ 7.21 Corporate Transactions Giving Rise to Appraisal Rights

An eligible holder [§ 1.17] of the corporation [§ 1.12(b)] should be entitled on demand to be paid in cash the fair value of the shares owned by the eligible holder as provided in §§ 7.22 (Standards for Determining Fair Value) and 7.23 (Procedural Standards) in the event of:

(a) A merger, a consolidation, a mandatory share exchange, or an exchange by the corporation of its stock for substantial assets or equity securities [§ 1.20] of another corporation (hereinafter collectively referred to as a "business combination"), whether effected directly or by means of a subsidiary, unless those persons who were shareholders of the corporation immediately before the combination own 60 percent or more of the total voting power of the surviving or issuing corporation immediately thereafter, in approximately the same proportions (in relation to the other preexisting shareholders) as before the combination;

(b) Any business combination, amendment of the corporation's charter documents [§ 1.05], or other corporate act or transaction that has the effect of involuntarily eliminating the eligible holder's equity interest [§ 1.19] (other than the elimination of less than a round lot in a publicly traded corporation or a similar elimination of a comparably insignificant interest in a non-publicly traded corporation);

(c) A sale, lease, exchange, or other disposition of substantial assets by the corporation that

(1) Falls within § 5.15(a) (Transfer of Control in Which a Director or Principal Senior Executive Is Interested) and the assets so disposed of would account for a majority of the corporation's earnings or total assets [§ 1.37] as of the end of its most recent fiscal year, unless (A) the procedures specified in § 5.15(b)(1)–(3) are complied with, and (B) at least one class of equity securities [§ 1.20]

of the corporation is listed on a national securities exchange or is included within NASDAQ's National Market System; or

(2) Leaves the corporation without a significant continuing business, unless the sale (A) is in the ordinary course of business, or (B) is for cash or for cash equivalents that are to be liquidated for cash or used to satisfy corporate obligations, and is pursuant to a plan of complete dissolution by which all or substantially all of the net assets will be distributed to the shareholders within one year after the date of such transaction;

(d) An amendment of the charter documents [§ 1.05], whether accomplished directly or through a merger or consolidation, whose effect is to (1) materially and adversely alter or abolish a preferential, preemptive, redemption, or conversion right applicable to the eligible holder's shares, (2) reduce the number of shares owned by the eligible holder (other than a holder of less than a round lot in a publicly traded corporation or a similar holder of a comparably insignificant interest in a non-publicly traded corporation) to a fraction of a share or less, (3) create a right to redeem the eligible holder's shares, or (4) exclude or limit the voting rights of shares with respect to any matter, other than simply through the authorization of new shares of an existing or new class or the elimination of cumulative voting rights; or

(e) Any corporate action as to which the charter documents, other than the bylaws, provide that eligible holders have applicable appraisal rights.

§ 7.22 Standards for Determining Fair Value

(a) The fair value of shares under § 7.21 (Corporate Transactions Giving Rise to Appraisal Rights) should be the value of the eligible holder's [§ 1.17] proportionate interest in the corporation, without any discount for minority status or, absent extraordinary circumstances, lack of marketability. Subject to Subsections (b) and (c), fair value should be determined using the customary valuation concepts and techniques generally employed in the relevant securities and financial markets for similar businesses in the context of the transaction giving rise to appraisal.

(b) In the case of a business combination that gives rise to appraisal rights, but does not fall within § 5.10 (Transactions by a Controlling Shareholder with the Corporation), § 5.15 (Transfer of Control in Which a Director or Principal Senior Executive Is Interested), or § 7.25 (Transactions in Control Involving Corporate Combinations to Which a Majority Shareholder Is a Party), the aggregate price accepted by the board of directors of the subject corporation should be presumed to represent the fair value of the corporation, or of the assets sold in the case of an asset sale, unless the plaintiff can prove otherwise by clear and convincing evidence.

(c) If the transaction giving rise to appraisal falls within § 5.10, § 5.15, or § 7.25, the court generally should give substantial weight to the highest realistic price that a willing, able, and fully informed buyer would pay for the corporation as an entirety. In determining what such a buyer would pay, the court may include a proportionate share of any gain reasonably to be expected to result from the combination, unless special circumstances would make such an allocation unreasonable.

§ 7.23 Procedural Standards

(a) *Notice.* A corporation that proposes to engage in a transaction giving rise to appraisal rights under § 7.21 (Corporate Transactions Giving Rise to Appraisal Rights) should:

(i) Notify each record holder [§ 1.32] as of the record date set for the shareholder vote, and attempt in good faith to notify each other beneficial holder [§ 1.22] of shares as of such date who is known to it, of the right to exercise appraisal reasonably in advance of the date on which the transaction is to be voted upon by the shareholders, or, if no shareholder vote is required, the date on which the corporate action giving rise to appraisal is to be taken;

(ii) Describe the method for exercising the right, including the procedures in § 7.23(f);

(iii) Disclose the material facts [§ 1.25] concerning the transaction or other action and furnish copies of the corporation's financial statements; and

(iv) Provide a reasonable means by which eligible holders [§ 1.17] can easily and effectively indicate their election to dissent.

(b) *Shareholder Response.* To perfect a right to dissent, an eligible holder should be required only to utilize the means provided for under § 7.23(a)(iv), or otherwise deliver a written instrument expressing an election to dissent, at or before the shareholders' meeting, or, if no shareholder vote is to be taken, on or before the day preceding the date on which the corporate action giving rise to the right to appraisal is to be taken; provided, however, that eligible holders should have a reasonable period in which to elect to dissent from the time notice is first sent by the corporation pursuant to § 7.23(a)(i). Any eligible holder who so responds should be deemed a "dissenting holder" for purposes of § 7.23. If notice is not given as required under § 7.23(a), any eligible holder may initiate an appraisal proceeding without taking any other action.

(c) *Mandatory Prepayment.* Promptly after the transaction that gives rise to appraisal under § 7.21 is consummated and upon the tender of the dissenting holder's shares to the corporation's transfer agent for the notation of an appropriate legend to reflect the payment required under this § 7.23(c), the corporation should pay to such dissenting holder the amount in cash that it reasonably estimates to be the fair value of the shares plus any interest due. Acceptance of such prepayment shall not constitute a waiver of the dissenting holder's rights under § 7.21.

(d) *Costs and Expenses.* If payment of the amount required under § 7.23(c) is not made within *30* days after the later of the date on which the transaction is consummated or the date on which shares are tendered under § 7.23(c), or if the amount so paid is materially less than the amount ultimately determined by the court to constitute fair value, the corporation should be required to pay all costs and expenses of the appraisal proceeding, including such dissenting holder's reasonable attorney's and experts' fees. In all other circumstances, the costs and expenses of the action shall be assessed or apportioned as the court deems equitable, except that the corporation's attorney's fees may be assessed or apportioned against a shareholder only where the court finds the shareholder's action to have been arbitrary, vexatious, or not in good faith.

(e) *Interest.* Interest on the amount awarded by the court (less the amount of prepayment) should be paid at the time of the payment of the award and should be computed from the time the relevant transaction is consummated at an appropriate market rate for the corporation.

(f) *Consolidation.* If there are any dissenting holders, the corporation should commence a consolidated proceeding in the state of incorporation under § 7.21 to fix fair value and determine eligibility to dissent. All dissenting holders should be made parties to the action. If such a consolidated action is not commenced by the corporation within a reasonable time after consummation of the transaction that gives rise to the appraisal right, it may be commenced by any dissenting holder. The court may appoint a lead counsel or steering committee to coordinate discovery and the trial of the proceeding and to represent any dissenting holders who have not secured other counsel. The court should also require the corporation to provide it with the names and addresses of all dissenting holders known to the corporation, and, subject to appropriate restrictions, such list should be available for inspection by dissenting holders or their agents.

§ 7.24 Transactions in Control Involving Corporate Combinations in Which Directors, Principal Senior Executives, and Controlling Shareholders Are Not Interested

(a) An appraisal proceeding is the exclusive remedy of an eligible holder [§ 1.17] to challenge a transaction in control [§ 1.38] involving a corporate combination that requires shareholder approval and is not subject to § 5.10 (Transactions by a Controlling Shareholder with the Corporation), § 5.15 (Transfer of Control in Which a Director or Principal Senior Executive Is Interested), or § 7.25 (Transactions in Control

Involving Corporate Combinations to Which a Majority Shareholder Is a Party), if:

(1) Disclosure concerning the transaction [§ 1.14(b)] is made to the shareholders who are entitled to authorize the transaction;

(2) The transaction is approved pursuant to, and is otherwise in accordance with, applicable provisions of law and the corporation's charter documents [§ 1.05]; and

(3) Eligible holders who are entitled to but do not vote to approve the transaction are entitled to an appraisal remedy reflecting the general principles embodied in §§ 7.22 (Standards for Determining Fair Value) and 7.23 (Procedural Standards).

(b) A party who challenges a transaction subject to this Section has the burden of proving failure to comply with Subsections (a)(1)–(3).

(c) If Subsections (a)(1) and (a)(2) are satisfied, but Subsection (a)(3) is not, the transaction may be challenged on the ground that it constituted a waste of corporate assets [§ 1.42].

(d) The availability of an appraisal remedy does not preclude a proceeding against a director, officer, controlling shareholder, or an associate of any of the foregoing, for a violation of Part V (Duty of Fair Dealing).

§ 7.25   Transactions in Control Involving Corporate Combinations to Which a Majority Shareholder Is a Party

(a) An appraisal proceeding is the exclusive remedy of an eligible holder [§ 1.17] to challenge a transaction in control [§ 1.38] involving a corporate combination to which a shareholder who holds sufficient voting shares of a corporation to approve the corporate combination under the law of the relevant jurisdiction, or its associate [§ 1.03], is a party if:

(1) The directors who approve the transaction on behalf of the corporation (or the directors of the shareholder if the directors of the corporation are not required by law to approve the transaction) have an adequate basis, grounded on substantial objective evidence, for believing that the consideration offered to the minority shareholders in the transaction constitutes fair value for their shares, as determined in accordance with the standards provided in § 7.22 (Standards for Determining Fair Value);

(2) Disclosure concerning the transaction [§ 1.14(b)] (including representations of the directors' belief with respect to the fair value of minority shares and the basis for such belief) and the conflict of interest [§ 1.14(a)] is made to the minority shareholders, as contemplated by § 7.23(a);

(3) The transaction is approved pursuant to, and is otherwise in accordance with, applicable provisions of law and the corporation's charter documents [§ 1.05]; and

(4) Holders of equity securities who do not vote to approve the transaction are entitled to an appraisal remedy reflecting the general principles embodied in §§ 7.22 (Standards for Determining Fair Value) and 7.23 (Procedural Standards).

(b) A party who challenges a transaction that is subject to this Section has the burden of proving a failure to comply with Subsections (a)(1)–(4) if the transaction was authorized in advance by disinterested directors [§ 1.15] and authorized in advance or ratified by disinterested shareholders [§ 1.16], following the disclosure set forth in Subsection (a)(2); otherwise, the burden is on the majority shareholder to prove compliance with Subsections (a)(1)–(4).

(c) If Subsections (a)(1)–(3) are satisfied but Subsection (a)(4) is not, then:

(1) If the transaction was approved by disinterested shareholders following the disclosure required by Subsection (a)(2), it may be challenged on the ground that it was not fair, with the burden on the challenging party to prove that the transaction was unfair to the minority shareholders; and

(2) If the transaction was not so approved, it may be challenged on the ground that it was not fair, with the burden on the majority shareholder to prove that the transaction was fair to the minority shareholders.

(d) The exclusivity provisions of this Section are not applicable to closely held corporations [§ 1.06].

CORPORATE FORMS

SIMPLE FORM OF CERTIFICATE OF INCORPORATION

[From 3 R. Balotti & J. Finkelstein, The Delaware Law of Corporations and Business Organizations, Form 1.5 (2d ed. 1990).]

CERTIFICATE OF INCORPORATION
OF

FIRST. The name of the corporation is _____.

SECOND. The address of the corporation's registered office in the State of Delaware is One Rodney Square, Tenth and King Streets, P.O. Box 551 in the City of Wilmington, County of New Castle 19801. The name of its registered agent at such address is _____.

THIRD. The purpose of the corporation is to engage in any lawful act or activity for which corporations may be organized under the General Corporation Law of Delaware.

FOURTH. The total number of shares which the corporation shall have authority to issue is 1,000 shares of capital stock, and the par value of each such share is $1.00 per share.

FIFTH. The name and mailing address of the incorporator is _____, Wilmington, Delaware 19899.

SIXTH. The Board of Directors of the corporation is expressly authorized to make, alter or repeal by-laws of the corporation, but the stockholders may make additional by-laws and may alter or repeal any by-law whether adopted by them or otherwise.

SEVENTH. Elections of directors need not be by written ballot except and to the extent provided in the by-laws of the corporation.

The undersigned incorporator hereby acknowledges that the foregoing certificate of incorporation is his act and deed and that the facts stated therein are true.

_____

FORM OF BY-LAWS

[From 3 R. Balotti & J. Finkelstein, The Delaware Law of
Corporations and Business Organizations,
Form 1.17 (2d ed. 1990).]

BY-LAWS
OF
_____ CORPORATION

ARTICLE I

Stockholders

Section 1.1. *Annual Meetings.* An annual meeting of stockholders
shall be held for the election of directors at such date, time and place,
either within or without the State of Delaware, as may be designated by
resolution of the Board of Directors from time to time. Any other
proper business may be transacted at the annual meeting.

Section 1.2. *Special Meetings.* Special meetings of stockholders for
any purpose or purposes may be called at any time by the Board of
Directors, or by a committee of the Board of Directors which has been
duly designated by the Board of Directors and whose powers and
authority, as expressly provided in a resolution of the Board of Directors,
include the power to call such meetings, but such special meetings may
not be called by any other person or persons.

Section 1.3. *Notice of Meetings.* Whenever stockholders are required or permitted to take any action at a meeting, a written notice of
the meeting shall be given which shall state the place, date and hour of
the meeting, and, in the case of a special meeting, the purpose or
purposes for which the meeting is called. Unless otherwise provided by
law, the certificate of incorporation or these by-laws, the written notice
of any meeting shall be given not less than ten nor more than sixty days
before the date of the meeting to each stockholder entitled to vote at
such meeting. If mailed, such notice shall be deemed to be given when
deposited in the mail, postage prepaid, directed to the stockholder at his
address as it appears on the records of the corporation.

Section 1.4. *Adjournments.* Any meeting of stockholders, annual
or special, may adjourn from time to time to reconvene at the same or
some other place, and notice need not be given of any such adjourned
meeting if the time and place thereof are announced at the meeting at
which the adjournment is taken. At the adjourned meeting the corporation may transact any business which might have been transacted at the
original meeting. If the adjournment is for more than thirty days, or if
after the adjournment a new record date is fixed for the adjourned

meeting, a notice of the adjourned meeting shall be given to each stockholder of record entitled to vote at the meeting.

Section 1.5. *Quorum.* Except as otherwise provided by law, the certificate of incorporation or these by-laws, at each meeting of stockholders the presence in person or by proxy of the holders of shares of stock having a majority of the votes which could be cast by the holders of all outstanding shares of stock entitled to vote at the meeting shall be necessary and sufficient to constitute a quorum. In the absence of a quorum, the stockholders so present may, by majority vote, adjourn the meeting from time to time in the manner provided in Section 1.4 of these by-laws until a quorum shall attend. Shares of its own stock belonging to the corporation or to another corporation, if a majority of the shares entitled to vote in the election of directors of such other corporation is held, directly or indirectly, by the corporation, shall neither be entitled to vote nor be counted for quorum purposes; provided, however, that the foregoing shall not limit the right of the corporation to vote stock, including but not limited to its own stock, held by it in a fiduciary capacity.

Section 1.6. *Organization.* Meetings of stockholders shall be presided over by the Chairman of the Board, if any, or in his absence by the Vice Chairman of the Board, if any, or in his absence by the President, or in his absence by a Vice President, or in the absence of the foregoing persons by a chairman designated by a chairman chosen at the meeting. The Secretary shall act as secretary of the meeting, but in his absence the chairman of the meeting may appoint any person to act as secretary of the meeting.

Section 1.7. *Voting: Proxies.* Except as otherwise provided by the certificate of incorporation, each stockholder entitled to vote at any meeting of stockholders shall be entitled to one vote for each share of stock held by him which has voting power upon the matter in question. Each stockholder entitled to vote at a meeting of stockholders may authorize another person or persons to act for him by proxy, but no such proxy shall be voted or acted upon after three years from its date, unless the proxy provides for a longer period. A duly executed proxy shall be irrevocable if it states that it is irrevocable and if, and only as long as, it is coupled with an interest sufficient in law to support an irrevocable power. A stockholder may revoke any proxy which is not irrevocable by attending the meeting and voting in person or by filing an instrument in writing revoking the proxy or another duly executed proxy bearing a later date with the Secretary of the corporation. Voting at meetings of stockholders need not be by written ballot and need not be conducted by inspectors of election unless so determined by the holders of shares of stock having a majority of the votes which could be cast by the holders of all outstanding shares of stock entitled to vote thereon which are present in person or by proxy at such meeting. At all meetings of stockholders for the election of directors a plurality of the votes cast shall be sufficient to elect. All other elections and questions shall, unless otherwise provided by law, the certificate of incorporation or these by-laws, be decided by the vote of the holders of shares of stock having a majority of the votes which could be cast by the holders of all shares of stock entitled to vote thereon which are present in person or represented by proxy at the meeting.

Section 1.8. *Fixing Date for Determination of Stockholders of Record.* In order that the corporation may determine the stockholders entitled to notice of or to vote at any meeting of stockholders or any adjournment thereof, or to express consent to corporate action in writing without a meeting, or entitled to receive payment of any dividend or other distribution or allotment of any rights, or entitled to exercise any rights in respect of any change, conversion or exchange of stock or for the purpose of any other lawful action, the Board of Directors may fix a record date, which record date shall not precede the date upon which the resolution fixing the record date is adopted by the Board of Directors and which record date: (1) in the case of determination of stockholders entitled to vote at any meeting of stockholders or adjournment thereof, shall, unless otherwise required by law, not be more than sixty nor less than ten days before the date of such meeting; (2) in the case of determination of stockholders entitled to express consent to corporate action in writing without a meeting, shall not be more than ten days from the date upon which the resolution fixing the record date is adopted by the Board of Directors; and (3) in the case of any other action, shall not be more than sixty days prior to such other action. If no record date is fixed: (1) the record date for determining stockholders entitled to notice of or to vote at a meeting of stockholders shall be at the close of business on the day next preceding the day on which notice is given, or, if notice is waived, at the close of business on the day next preceding the day on which the meeting is held; (2) the record date for determining stockholders entitled to express consent to corporate action in writing without a meeting when no prior action of the Board of Directors is required by law, shall be the first date on which a signed written consent setting forth the action taken or proposed to be taken is delivered to the corporation in accordance with applicable law, or, if prior action by the Board of Directors is required by law, shall be at the close of business on the day on which the Board of Directors adopts the resolution taking such prior action; and (3) the record date for determining stockholders for any other purpose shall be at the close of business on the day on which the Board of Directors adopts the resolution relating thereto. A determination of stockholders of record entitled to notice of or to vote at a meeting of stockholders shall apply to any adjournment of the meeting; provided, however, that the Board of Directors may fix a new record date for the adjourned meeting.

Section 1.9. *List of Stockholders Entitled to Vote.* The Secretary shall prepare and make, at least ten days before every meeting of

966

stockholders, a complete list of the stockholders entitled to vote at the meeting, arranged in alphabetical order, and showing the address of each stockholder and the number of shares registered in the name of each stockholder. Such list shall be open to the examination of any stockholder, for any purpose germane to the meeting, during ordinary business hours, for a period of at least ten days prior to the meeting, either at a place within the city where the meeting is to be held, which place shall be specified in the notice of the meeting, or, if not so specified, at the place where the meeting is to be held. The list shall also be produced and kept at the time and place of the meeting during the whole time thereof and may be inspected by any stockholder who is present. Upon the willful neglect or refusal of the directors to produce such a list at any meeting for the election of directors, they shall be ineligible for election to any office at such meeting. The stock ledger shall be the only evidence as to who are the stockholders entitled to examine the stock ledger, the list of stockholders or the books of the corporation, or to vote in person or by proxy at any meeting of stockholders.

Section 1.10. *Action By Consent of Stockholders.* Unless otherwise restricted by the certificate of incorporation, any action required or permitted to be taken at any annual or special meeting of the stockholders may be taken without a meeting, without prior notice and without a vote, if a consent in writing, setting forth the action so taken, shall be signed by the holders of outstanding stock having not less than the minimum number of votes that would be necessary to authorize or take such action at a meeting at which all shares entitled to vote thereon were present and voted. Prompt notice of the taking of the corporate action without a meeting by less than unanimous written consent shall be given to those stockholders who have not consented in writing.

ARTICLE II

Board of Directors

Section 2.1. *Number; Qualifications.* The Board of Directors shall consist of one or more members, the number thereof to be determined from time to time by resolution of the Board of Directors. Directors need not be stockholders.

Section 2.2. *Election; Resignation; Removal; Vacancies.* The Board of Directors shall initially consist of the persons named as directors in the certificate of incorporation, and each director so elected shall hold office until the first annual meeting of stockholders or until his successor is elected and qualified. At the first annual meeting of stockholders and at each annual meeting thereafter, the stockholders shall elect directors each of whom shall hold office for a term of one year or until his successor is elected and qualified. Any director may resign at any time upon written notice to the corporation. Any newly created directorship or any vacancy occurring in the Board of Directors for any cause may be filled by a majority of the remaining members of the Board of Directors, although such majority is less than a quorum, or by a plurality of the votes cast at a meeting of stockholders, and each director so elected shall hold office until the expiration of the term of office of the director whom he has replaced or until his successor is elected and qualified.

Section 2.3. *Regular Meetings.* Regular meetings of the Board of Directors may be held at such places within or without the State of Delaware and at such times as the Board of Directors may from time to time determine, and if so determined notices thereof need not be given.

Section 2.4. *Special Meetings.* Special meetings of the Board of Directors may be held at any time or place within or without the State of Delaware whenever called by the President, any Vice President, the Secretary, or by any member of the Board of Directors. Notice of a special meeting of the Board of Directors shall be given by the person or persons calling the meeting at least twenty-four hours before the special meeting.

Section 2.5. *Telephonic Meetings Permitted.* Members of the Board of Directors, or any committee designated by the Board of Directors, may participate in a meeting thereof by means of conference telephone or similar communications equipment by means of which all persons participating in the meeting can hear each other, and participation in a meeting pursuant to this by-law shall constitute presence in person at such meeting.

Section 2.6. *Quorum; Vote Required for Action.* At all meetings of the Board of Directors a majority of the whole Board of Directors shall constitute a quorum for the transaction of business. Except in cases in which the certificate of incorporation or these by-laws otherwise provide, the vote of a majority of the directors present at a meeting at which a quorum is present shall be the act of the Board of Directors.

Section 2.7. *Organization.* Meetings of the Board of Directors shall be presided over by the Chairman of the Board, if any, or in his absence by the Vice Chairman of the Board, if any, or in his absence by the President, or in their absence by a chairman chosen at the meeting. The Secretary shall act as secretary of the meeting, but in his absence the chairman of the meeting may appoint any person to act as secretary of the meeting.

Section 2.8. *Informal Action by Directors.* Unless otherwise restricted by the certificate of incorporation or these by-laws, any action required or permitted to be taken at any meeting of the Board of Directors, or of any committee thereof, may be taken without a meeting if all members of the Board of Directors or such committee, as the case may be, consent thereto in writing, and the writing or writings are filed with the minutes of proceedings of the Board of Directors or such committee.

ARTICLE III

Committees

Section 3.1. *Committees.* The Board of Directors may, by resolution passed by a majority of the whole Board of Directors, designate one or more committees, each committee to consist of one or more of the directors of the corporation. The Board of Directors may designate one or more directors as alternate members of any committee, who may replace any absent or disqualified member at any meeting of the committee. In the absence or disqualification of a member of the committee, the member or members thereof present at any meeting and not disqualified from voting, whether or not he or they constitute a quorum, may unanimously appoint another member of the Board of Directors to act at the meeting in place of any such absent or disqualified member. Any such committee, to the extent permitted by law and to the extent provided in the resolution of the Board of Directors, shall have and may exercise all the powers and authority of the Board of Directors in the management of the business and affairs of the corporation, and may authorize the seal of the corporation to be affixed to all papers which may require it.

Section 3.2. *Committee Rules.* Unless the Board of Directors otherwise provides, each committee designated by the Board of Directors may make, alter and repeal rules for the conduct of its business. In the absence of such rules each committee shall conduct its business in the same manner as the Board of Directors conducts its business pursuant to Article III of these by-laws.

ARTICLE IV

Officers

Section 4.1. *Executive Officers; Election; Qualifications; Term of Office; Resignation; Removal; Vacancies.* The Board of Directors shall elect a President and Secretary, and it may, if it so determines, choose a Chairman of the Board and a Vice Chairman of the Board from among its members. The Board of Directors may also choose one or more Vice Presidents, one or more Assistant Secretaries, a Treasurer and one or more Assistant Treasurers. Each such officer shall hold office until the first meeting of the Board of Directors after the annual meeting of stockholders next succeeding his election, and until his successor is elected and qualified or until his earlier resignation or removal. Any officer may resign at any time upon written notice to the corporation. The Board of Directors may remove any officer with or without cause at any time, but such removal shall be without prejudice to the contractual rights of such officer, if any, with the corporation. Any number of offices may be held by the same person. Any vacancy occurring in any office of the corporation by death, resignation, removal or otherwise may be filled for the unexpired portion of the term by the Board of Directors at any regular or special meeting.

Section 4.2. *Powers and Duties of Executive Officers.* The officers of the corporation shall have such powers and duties in the management of the corporation as may be prescribed by the Board of Directors and, to the extent not so provided, as generally pertain to their respective offices, subject to the control of the Board of Directors. The Board of Directors may require any officer, agent or employee to give security for the faithful performance of his duties.

ARTICLE V

Stock

Section 5.1. *Certificates.* Every holder of stock shall be entitled to have a certificate signed by or in the name of the corporation by the Chairman or Vice Chairman of the Board of Directors, if any, or the President or a Vice President, and by the Treasurer or an Assistant Treasurer, or the Secretary or an Assistant Secretary, of the corporation, certifying the number of shares owned by him in the corporation. Any of or all the signatures on the certificate may be a facsimile. In case any officer, transfer agent, or registrar who has signed or whose facsimile signature has been placed upon a certificate shall have ceased to be such officer, transfer agent, or registrar before such certificate is issued, it may be issued by the corporation with the same effect as if he were such officer, transfer agent, or registrar at the date of issue.

Section 5.2. *Lost, Stolen or Destroyed Stock Certificates; Issuance of New Certificates.* The corporation may issue a new certificate of stock in the place of any certificate theretofore issued by it, alleged to have been lost, stolen or destroyed, and the corporation may require the owner of the lost, stolen or destroyed certificate, or his legal representative, to give the corporation a bond sufficient to indemnify it against any claim that may be made against it on account of the alleged loss, theft or destruction of any such certificate or the issuance of such new certificate.

ARTICLE VI

Indemnification

Section 6.1. *Right to Indemnification.* The corporation shall indemnify and hold harmless, to the fullest extent permitted by applicable law as it presently exists or may hereafter be amended, any person who was or is made or is threatened to be made a party or is otherwise involved in any action, suit or proceeding, whether civil, criminal, administrative or investigative (a "proceeding") by reason of the fact that he, or a person for whom he is the legal representative, is or was a director, officer, employee or agent of the corporation or is or was serving at the request of the corporation as a director, officer, employee or agent of another corporation or of a partnership, joint venture, trust, enterprise or non-profit entity, including service with respect to employee benefit plans, against all liability and loss suffered and expenses reasonably incurred by such person. The corporation shall be required to indemnify a person in connection with a proceeding initiated by such person only if the proceeding was authorized by the Board of Directors of the corporation.

Section 6.2. *Prepayment of Expenses.* The corporation shall pay the expenses incurred in defending any proceeding in advance of its final disposition, *provided, however,* that the payment of expenses incurred by a director or officer in advance of the final disposition of the proceeding shall be made only upon receipt of an undertaking by the director or officer to repay all amounts advanced if it should be ultimately determined that the director or officer is not entitled to be indemnified under this Article or otherwise.

Section 6.3. *Claims.* If a claim for indemnification or payment of expenses under this Article is not paid in full within sixty days after a written claim therefor has been received by the corporation the claimant may file suit to recover the unpaid amount of such claim and, if successful in whole or in part, shall be entitled to be paid the expense of prosecuting such claim. In any such action the corporation shall have the burden of proving that the claimant was not entitled to the requested indemnification or payment of expenses under applicable law.

Section 6.4. *Non–Exclusivity of Rights.* The rights conferred on any person by this Article VI shall not be exclusive of any other rights which such person may have or hereafter acquire under any statute, provision of the certificate of incorporation, these by-laws, agreement, vote of stockholders or disinterested directors or otherwise.

Section 6.5. *Other Indemnification.* The corporation's obligation, if any, to indemnify any person who was or is serving at its request as a director, officer, employee or agent of another corporation, partnership, joint venture, trust, enterprise or non-profit entity shall be reduced by any amount such person may collect as indemnification from such other corporation, partnership, joint venture, trust, enterprise or non-profit enterprise.

Section 6.6. *Amendment or Repeal.* Any repeal or modification of the foregoing provisions of this Article VI shall not adversely affect any right or protection hereunder of any person in respect of any act or omission occurring prior to the time of such repeal or modification.

ARTICLE VII

Miscellaneous

Section 7.1. *Fiscal Year.* The fiscal year of the corporation shall be determined by resolution of the Board of Directors.

Section 7.2. *Seal.* The corporate seal shall have the name of the corporation inscribed thereon and shall be in such form as may be approved from time to time by the Board of Directors.

Section 7.3. *Waiver of Notice of Meetings of Stockholders, Directors and Committees.* Any written waiver of notice, signed by the person entitled to notice, whether before or after the time stated therein, shall be deemed equivalent to notice. Attendance of a person at a meeting shall constitute a waiver of notice of such meeting, except when the person attends a meeting for the express purpose of objecting, at the beginning of the meeting, to the transaction of any business because the meeting is not lawfully called or convened. Neither the business to be transacted at, nor the purpose of any regular or special meeting of the stockholders, directors, or members of a committee of directors need be specified in any written waiver of notice.

Section 7.4. *Interested Directors; Quorum.* No contract or transaction between the corporation and one or more of its directors or officers, or between the corporation and any other corporation, partnership, association, or other organization in which one or more of its directors or officers are directors or officers, or have a financial interest, shall be void or voidable solely for this reason, or solely because the director or officer is present at or participates in the meeting of the Board of Directors or committee thereof which authorizes the contract or transaction, or solely because his or their votes are counted for such purpose, if: (1) the material facts as to his relationship or interest and as to the contract or transaction are disclosed or are known to the Board of Directors or the committee, and the Board of Directors or committee in good faith authorizes the contract or transaction by the affirmative votes of a majority of the disinterested directors, even though the disinterested directors be less than a quorum; or (2) the material facts as to his relationship or interest and as to the contract or transaction are disclosed or are known to the stockholders entitled to vote thereon, and the contract or transaction is specifically approved in good faith by vote of the stockholders; or (3) the contract or transaction is fair as to the corporation as of the time it is authorized, approved or ratified, by the Board of Directors, a committee thereof, or the stockholders. Common or interested directors may be counted in determining the presence of a quorum at a meeting of the Board of Directors or of a committee which authorizes the contract or transaction.

Section 7.5. *Form of Records.* Any records maintained by the corporation in the regular course of its business, including its stock ledger, books of account, and minute books, may be kept on, or be in the form of, punch cards, magnetic tape, photographs, micro-photographs, or any other information storage device, provided that the records so kept can be converted into clearly legible form within a reasonable time. The corporation shall so convert any records so kept upon the request of any person entitled to inspect the same.

Section 7.6. *Amendment of By-Laws.* These by-laws may be altered or repealed, and new by-laws made, by the Board of Directors, but the stockholders may make additional by-laws and may alter and repeal any by-laws whether adopted by them or otherwise.

FORM OF MINUTES OF ORGANIZATION MEETING

[From 3 R. Balotti & J. Finkelstein, The Delaware Law of
Corporations and Business Organizations,
Form 1.24 (2d ed. 1990).]

MINUTES OF ORGANIZATION MEETING
OF THE BOARD OF DIRECTORS
OF
_____ CORPORATION

An organization meeting of the Board of Directors of _____
_____ Corporation was held at the offices of the Corporation, _____,
_____, on _____ __, 19__, pursuant to a written Waiver of Notice
signed by all of the Directors named in the Certificate of Incorporation
fixing the time and place aforesaid.

All the Directors were present in person, viz.:

_____

_____

_____

_____

Upon motion duly made and carried, _____ was elected temporary
Chairman and _____ was chosen Secretary of the meeting.

The Chairman reported that the original Certificate of Incorporation
was filed in the Office of the Secretary of State of the State of Delaware
on _____ __, 19__, that the state tax and other fees incident to the
filing thereof had been paid to the State of Delaware, and that a certified
copy of the Certificate of Incorporation has been filed for record on
_____ __, 19__, in the Office of the Recorder of Deeds in and for
_____ County.

The Secretary presented a copy of said certified copy of the Certificate of Incorporation and, on motion, it was ordered that said copy be
inserted in the Minute Book of the Corporation following the minutes of
this meeting.

The Secretary presented and read the Waiver of Notice of this
meeting, duly signed by all of the Directors as aforesaid, which waiver,
on motion, was ordered to be inserted in the Minute Book following the
minutes of this meeting.

The Secretary presented a form of By-Laws for the regulation of the
affairs of the Corporation, which was read article by article and unanimously adopted. Upon motion duly carried, it was ordered that the said

By–Laws as adopted be inserted in the Minute Book following the minutes of this meeting.

Upon motion made, seconded and unanimously carried, the following persons were elected to the offices set opposite their respective names, to hold such offices until their successors shall be duly elected and qualified:

President _____

Treasurer _____

Secretary _____

Upon motion duly made, seconded and unanimously carried, the following resolution was adopted, viz.:

RESOLVED, that the seal made in accordance with the By–Laws relating thereto, now presented to this meeting, an impression of which is directed to be made on the margin of these Minutes, be and the same hereby is, adopted as the seal of this corporation.

RESOLVED, that the proposed form of stock certificate presented to and examined by each of the undersigned is hereby adopted as the form of stock certificate for the common stock of this corporation, and a specimen of such stock certificate shall be inserted in the minute book of the corporation.

Upon motion duly made, seconded and unanimously carried, the following resolution was adopted, viz.:

RESOLVED, that the Treasurer be, and he hereby is, authorized to open a bank account in the name of the Corporation in the _____ Bank for the deposit of funds of the Corporation, and in this connection the resolution contained in the certificate of such bank attached hereto as Exhibit _____ is hereby adopted, and that (1) all checks, drafts, notes, bills of exchange, acceptances, undertakings, and other instruments or orders for payment, transfer, or withdrawal of money in the amount of One Thousand Dollars ($1,000.00) or less for whatever purpose and to whomever payable shall bear the signature of any one of the following:

_____

or

_____

and (2) all checks, drafts, notes, bills of exchange, acceptances, undertakings, and other instruments for payment, transfer, or withdrawal of money in excess of One Thousand Dollars ($1,000.00) for whatever reason and to whomever payable shall require the signature of any two of the following:

_____

_____

———————————————————

———————————————————

The Chairman then reported that the Corporation had received the offer of ———, to purchase ——— shares of the common stock of the Corporation for the purchase price of ——— Dollars ($———) per share. Thereupon, upon motion duly made, seconded and unanimously carried, the following resolution was adopted, viz.:

RESOLVED, that the appropriate officers of this Corporation be, and they are hereby, authorized and directed to accept the offer of ——— to purchase ——— (———) shares of the common stock of the Corporation for the price of ——— ($———), such consideration to be allocated $——— to the stated capital account on the books of the Corporation, and $——— to the surplus account on the books of the Corporation; and

FURTHER RESOLVED that the appropriate officers of this Corporation be, and they hereby are, authorized and directed to execute and deliver certificates evidencing such shares in exchange for the said purchase price.

There being no further business, on motion duly made, seconded and unanimously carried, the meeting was adjourned.

———————————————————
Secretary

FORM OF STOCK CERTIFICATE

[From 3 R. Balotti & J. Finkelstein, The Delaware Law of
Corporations and Business Organizations,
Form 5.1 (2d ed. 1990).]

COMMON STOCK CERTIFICATE

FORM OF STOCK CERTIFICATE

The corporation will furnish without charge to each stockholder who so requests the powers, designations, preferences and relative, participating, optional or other special rights of each class of stock or series thereof of the corporation, and the qualifications, limitations or restrictions of such preferences and/or rights. Such request may be made to the corporation or the transfer agent.

The following abbreviations, when used in the inscription on the face of this certificate, shall be construed as though they were written out in full according to applicable laws or regulations:

TEN COM — as tenants in common

TEN ENT — as tenants by the entireties

JT TEN — as joint tenants with right of survivorship and not as tenants in common

UNIF GIFT MIN ACT — _____ Custodian _____
(Cust) (Minor)

under Uniform Gifts to Minors Act

_____
(State)

Additional abbreviations may also be used though not in the above list.

For value received, _____ hereby sell, assign and transfer unto

Please insert social security or other
identifying number of assignee

_____

(Please print or typewrite name and address, including zip code, of assignee)

_____

_____

_____ Shares
of the capital stock represented by the within Certificate, and do hereby irrevocably constitute and appoint

_____ Attorney
to transfer the said stock on the books of the within named Corporation with full power of substitution in the premises.

Dated: _____

_____

Notice: The signature to this assignment must correspond with the name as written upon the face of the certificate in every particular, without alteration or enlargement or any change whatever.

FORM OF PROXY

[From Securities Exchange Act Release No. 16356 (1979)]

UB UNIVERSAL BUSINESS CORPORATION **Proxy**

270 Universal Center, Horizon, California 91770

This Proxy is Solicited on Behalf of the Board of Directors.

The undersigned hereby appoints John Red, Mary Blue, and Lee White as Proxies, each with the power to appoint his or her substitute, and hereby authorizes them to represent and to vote, as designated below, all the shares of common stock of Universal Business held on record by the undersigned on October 23, 1980, at the annual meeting of shareholders to be held on December 20, 1980 or any adjournment thereof.

1. ELECTION OF DIRECTORS

FOR all nominees listed below
(except as marked to the contrary below) ☐

WITHHOLD AUTHORITY
to vote for all nominees listed below ☐

(INSTRUCTION   To withhold authority to vote for any individual nominee strike a line through the nominees's name in the list below)

J. Allen, S. Brown, J. Doe, J. Green, G. Johansen, A. Jones, M. Roe, J. Smith and M. Stanton

2. PROPOSAL TO APPROVE THE APPOINTMENT OF DOLLAR AND CENTS as the independent public accountants of the corporation

☐ FOR   ☐ AGAINST   ☐ ABSTAIN

3. STOCKHOLDER PROPOSAL RELATING TO FORM AND CONTENT OF POST-MEETING REPORTS:

☐ FOR   ☐ AGAINST   ☐ ABSTAIN

[C6891]

---

4. In their discretion the Proxies are authorized to vote upon such other business as may properly come before the meeting

This proxy when properly executed will be voted in the manner directed herein by the undersigned stockholder.
If no direction is made, this proxy will be voted for Proposals 1, 2, and 3.

Please sign exactly as name appears below.   When shares are held by joint tenants, both should sign.   When signing as attorney, as executor, administrator, trustee or guardian, please give full title as such. If a corporation, please sign in full corporate name by President or other authorized officer. If a partnership please sign in partnership name by authorized person.

SAMPLE CARD A

DATED _____ 1980

PLEASE MARK SIGN DATE AND RETURN THE PROXY CARD PROMPTLY USING THE ENCLOSED ENVELOPE

Signature _____

Signature if held jointly _____

[C6892]

AMERICAN BAR FOUNDATION, COMMENTARIES ON DEBENTURES 410–411 (1971)

II. Discussion

Debenture indentures frequently contain a covenant of the Company to the effect that it will not make any distributions to its shareholders after a certain date (the "peg date") if, after giving effect thereto, the total of all such distributions would exceed the aggregate (or a stated percentage) of the net earnings accumulated since the peg date plus, in many cases, a specific amount representing a portion of earned surplus at the peg date and all or a portion of the proceeds received from the issuance of shares after the peg date. The peg date is usually the beginning of the fiscal year in which the debt is issued....

1. Net Income and the Proceeds of Stock Issues.

... [T]he covenant restricting distributions to shareholders is generally expressed in terms of limiting such distributions to an amount comprised of three items which are discussed below: *first,* all or part of the accumulated net earnings of the borrower after the peg date until the time of the declaration or payment, taken as one accounting period; *second,* the proceeds from the issuance or sale of stock after the peg date; and *third,* an additional dollar amount which in effect allows the borrower the flexibility of making distributions to shareholders out of a portion of the net earnings previously accumulated and existing as earned surplus at the peg date.[5]

(a) *Net Income.* One portion of the maximum amount of permitted distribution to shareholders under such a formula is all or some fraction of the net income of the Company after the peg date. Sometimes the peg date may be much earlier, even several years earlier, than the beginning of the current fiscal year in order to permit the Company to use a greater portion of the earnings accumulated before the negotiations for the new issue or to make the new restriction no more onerous than that under an outstanding debt issue.

For the purpose of considering allowable distributions to shareholders, the net income of the Company includes all net income from the peg date until a specified date at or close to the dividend, other distribution or purchase of shares. Many indentures provide that the specified date shall be the date of the declaration of the dividend or the date of the disbursement of any other distribution on or purchase of shares. Un-

---

5. The third item, permitting the use of a specified amount of existing earned surplus, is sometimes referred to as the "dip".

979

doubtedly exact figures for such entire period would not be available at the date of declaration or distribution, but could only be approximated. This will be sufficient unless the question of whether or not there is a violation of the covenant is a close one. To avoid such a problem, some indentures fix the end of the period as the end of a specified month or quarter prior to the dividend, distribution or acquisition.

Net income will be stated as either that of the Company or that of the Company and some or all of its subsidiaries on a consolidated basis. Net income may be defined for other covenants of the indenture, but, if not, some definition is frequently used in connection with the dividend covenant itself. Frequently the definition is that net income shall be that determined in accordance with generally accepted accounting principles. The parties may, however, desire to vary from generally accepted accounting principles in some respects, or may feel that the reference to such principles may leave questions as to certain items, and therefore will agree upon a more detailed definition of net income. . . .

4. Maintenance of Working Capital.

Dividends payable in cash necessarily reduce working capital as well as net worth and therefore indentures frequently include, as a condition to the declaration or payment of a dividend, that working capital be at least a specified amount.

As has been indicated, some indentures contain a separate covenant requiring the maintenance of working capital at a prescribed minimum level, and a decline below that level, whether because of a dividend payment, decline in sales, or for any other reason, is a default.

In other situations the parties may agree that declines in working capital should not create a default under the indenture unless they result from a voluntary distribution made while working capital is already at a low level. This is accomplished by including in the dividend covenant a condition that the working capital remaining after the distribution on stock will be in excess of a prescribed minimum.

Some indentures include both tests on the theory that the absolute maintenance test establishes a rock-bottom level and voluntary distributions ought to be restricted at a somewhat higher level.

Following are sample dividend covenants which illustrate some of the numerous variations which are common.

III. Sample Covenants ...

SAMPLE COVENANT 4

(Expanded Form Covering Practically All Types of Payments and Distributions to Shareholders)

To avoid a multiplicity of examples, which in any event could not cover the many combinations of elements which the parties might negotiate, the following Sample Covenant sets forth an expanded form covering practically all types of payments and distributions to shareholders.

§ 10–12. Limitations on Dividends and Other Stock Payments.

The Company will not declare any dividends on any class of its stock or make any payment on account of, or set apart money for a sinking or other analogous fund for, the purchase, redemption or other retirement of any shares of such stock, or make any distribution in respect thereof, either directly or indirectly, and whether in cash or property or in obligations of the Company (such dividends, payments and distributions being herein called *"Stock Payments"*), unless such dividends are declared to be payable not more than 60 days after the date of declaration, and unless, after giving effect to such proposed Stock Payment, all of the conditions set forth in the following *Subsections A to D,* inclusive, shall exist at the date of such declaration (in the case of a dividend) or at the date of such setting apart in the case of any such fund, or the date of such other payment or distribution in the case of any other Stock Payment (each such date being herein called a *"Computation Date"*):

A. no Event of Default [under the Indenture] has occurred which has not been cured.

B. the sum of

(1) $ [the dip];

(2) plus (or minus in the case of a deficit) [10] the Consolidated Net Income of the Company and its Consolidated Subsidiaries computed for the period beginning [the peg date] [11] to and including the Computation Date;

(3) plus the aggregate amount of all contributions to capital (including the fair value of property other than cash) received by the Company during such period;

(4) plus the aggregate net proceeds (including the fair value of property other than cash) received by the Company from the issue or sale of any class of its stock during such period;

shall be greater than all Stock Payments declared (in the case of dividends) or set apart (in the case of any such fund) or made (in the case of any other Stock Payment) during such period.

C. the Consolidated Working Capital [Consolidated Net Tangible Assets] [Consolidated Tangible Net Worth] of the Company and its Consolidated Subsidiaries shall be at least $_____.

10. If only a portion of such net income is to be included in the formula, there will be inserted at this point such words as "an amount equal to . . .% of".

11. Usually the peg date will be the same throughout the Section although special circumstances may dictate that different dates be used for different purposes.

D.   After deducting from both Consolidated Current Assets and Consolidated Current Liabilities of the Company and its Consolidated Subsidiaries an amount equal to the aggregate amount included in Consolidated Current Liabilities

> (1) as provision for taxes (to the extent not then due, or if due, payable without penalty) measured by income or profits or by salaries or wages, and

> (2) as liabilities to the federal or any state government, or to any subdivision or agency of any thereof, on account of amounts withheld or collected from salaries or wages of persons in its employ under any income tax law or any social security law applicable to such persons, or on account of amounts withheld or collected from employees for the purpose of purchasing obligations of the federal government, the remaining Consolidated Current Assets of the Company and its Consolidated Subsidiaries shall be at least ___% of the remaining Consolidated Current Liabilities of the Company and its Consolidated Subsidiaries.

Provided, however, that this Section shall not apply to, and the term "Stock Payment" shall not include, dividends payable solely in any class of stock of the Company, or the purchase, redemption or other retirement of any stock of any class of the Company by exchange for, or out of the proceeds of the substantially concurrent sale of, shares of any other class of stock of the Company, or the application to the redemption, purchase or other retirement of any such stock of any moneys previously and properly set apart for and then held in a sinking or other analogous fund established for such stock.

For the purposes of this Section, the amount of any Stock Payment declared or paid or distributed in property of the Company shall be deemed to be the book value of such property (after deducting related reserves for depreciation, depletion and amortization) at the Computation Date, and the amount of any Stock Payment declared or paid or distributed in obligations of the Company shall be deemed to be the value of such obligations as of the date of the adoption of the Board Resolution authorizing such Stock Payment, as determined by such Board Resolution.   The fair value of any obligations of the Company received by the Company as a contribution to capital or as the consideration for the issuance of stock of the Company (whether upon conversion of such obligations or otherwise) shall be the principal amount of such obligations.

Without regard to the foregoing restrictions of this Section, the Company may pay regular dividends upon shares of the _____ Preferred Stock of the Company outstanding on _____, and may set apart money and apply the same to the purchase or redemption of shares of said Preferred Stock through the operation of the sinking fund provided

for by the Company's Certificate of Incorporation as in effect on _____,
but all amounts so paid, set apart and/or applied shall be included in all
subsequent computations of Stock Payments for the purposes of this
Section.

The Company will not permit any Subsidiary to purchase any stock
of any class of the Company.

CHUBB EXECUTIVE PROTECTION POLICY

Executive Liability and Indemnification Coverage Section.
In consideration of payment of the premium and subject to the Declarations, General Terms and Conditions, and the limitations, conditions, provisions and other terms of this coverage section, the Company agrees as follows:

Insuring Clauses

1. ***Executive Liability Coverage—Insuring Clause 1.*** The Company shall pay on behalf of each of the **Insured Persons** all **Loss** for which the **Insured Person** is not indemnified by the **Insured Organization** and which the **Insured Person** becomes legally obligated to pay on account of any **Claim** first made against him, individually or otherwise, during the **Policy Period** or, if exercised, during the Extended Reporting Period, for a **Wrongful Act** committed, attempted, or allegedly committed or attempted by such **Insured Person** before or during the **Policy Period.**

2. ***Executive Indemnification Coverage—Insuring Clause 2.*** The Company shall pay on behalf of the **Insured Organization** all **Loss** for which the **Insured Organization** grants indemnification to each **Insured Person,** as permitted or required by law, which the **Insured Person** has become legally obligated to pay on account of any **Claim** first made against him, individually or otherwise, during the **Policy Period** or, if exercised, during the Extended Reporting Period, for a **Wrongful Act** committed, attempted, or allegedly committed or attempted by such **Insured Person** before or during the **Policy Period.** . . .

4. ***Extended Reporting Period.*** If the Company terminates or refuses to renew this coverage section other than for nonpayment of premium, the **Parent Organization** and the **Insured Persons** shall have the right, upon payment of the additional premium set forth in . . . the Declarations for this coverage section, to an extension of the coverage granted by this coverage section for the period set forth in . . . the Declarations for this coverage section (Extended Reporting Period) following the effective date of termination or nonrenewal, but only for any **Wrongful Act** committed, attempted, or allegedly committed or attempted, prior to the effective date of termination or nonrenewal. This right of extension shall lapse unless written notice of such election, together with payment of the additional premium due, is received by the Company within 30 days following the effective date of termination or nonrenewal. Any **Claim** made during the Extended Reporting Period shall be deemed to have been made during the immediately preceding **Policy Period.**

If the **Parent Organization** terminates or declines to accept renewal, the Company may, if requested, at its sole option, grant an Extended Reporting Period. The offer of renewal terms and conditions or premiums different from those in effect prior to renewal shall not constitute refusal to renew.

Exclusions

5. ***Exclusions Applicable to Insuring Clauses 1 and 2.*** The Company shall not be liable for **Loss** on account of any **Claim** made against any **Insured Person:**

(a) based upon, arising from, or in consequence of any circumstance if written notice of such circumstance has been given under any policy or coverage section of which this coverage section is a renewal or replacement and if such prior policy or coverage section affords coverage (or would afford such coverage except for the exhaustion of its limits of liability) for such **Loss,** in whole or in part, as a result of such notice;

(b) based upon, arising from, or in consequence of any demand, suit or other proceeding pending, or order, decree or judgment entered against any **Insured** on or prior to the Pending or Prior Date set forth in ... the Declarations for this coverage section, or the same or any substantially similar fact, circumstance or situation underlying or alleged therein;

(c) brought or maintained by or on behalf of any **Insured** except:

(i) a **Claim** that is a derivative action brought or maintained on behalf of an **Insured Organization** by one or more persons who are not **Insured Persons** and who bring and maintain the **Claim** without the solicitation, assistance or participation of any **Insured,**

(ii) a **Claim** brought or maintained by an **Insured Person** for the actual or alleged wrongful termination of the **Insured Person,** or

(iii) a **Claim** brought or maintained by an **Insured Person** for contribution or indemnity, if the **Claim** directly results from another **Claim** covered under this coverage section;

(d) for an actual or alleged violation of the responsibilities, obligations or duties imposed by the Employee Retirement Income Security Act of 1974 and amendments thereto or similar provisions of any federal, state or local statutory law or common law upon fiduciaries of any pension, profit sharing, health and welfare or other employee benefit plan or trust established or maintained for the purpose of providing benefits to employees of an **Insured Organization;**

(e) for bodily injury, mental or emotional distress, sickness, disease or death of any person or damage to or destruction of any tangible property including loss of use thereof; or

(f) based upon, arising from, or in consequence of (i) the actual, alleged or threatened discharge, release, escape or disposal of **Pollutants** into or on real or personal property, water or the atmosphere; or (ii) any direction or request that the **Insured** test for, monitor, clean up, remove, contain, treat, detoxify or neutralize **Pollutants,** or any voluntary decision to do so; including but not limited to any **Claim** for financial loss to the **Insured Organization,** its security holders or its creditors based upon, arising from, or in consequence of the matters described in (i) or (ii) of this exclusion.

6. *Exclusions Applicable to Insuring Clause 1 Only.* The Company shall not be liable under Insuring Clause 1 for **Loss** on account of any **Claim** made against any **Insured Person:**

(a) for an accounting of profits made from the purchase or sale by such **Insured Person** of securities of the **Insured Organization** within the meaning of Section 16(b) of the Securities Exchange Act of 1934 and amendments thereto or similar provisions of any federal, state or local statutory law or common law;

(b) based upon, arising from, or in consequence of any deliberately fraudulent act or omission or any willful violation of any statute or regulation by such **Insured Person,** if a judgement or other final adjudication adverse to the **Insured Person** establishes such a deliberately fraudulent act or omission or willful violation; or

(c) based upon, arising from, or in consequence of such **Insured Person** having gained in fact any personal profit, remuneration or advantage to which such **Insured Person** was not legally entitled.

7. *Severability of Exclusions.* With respect to the Exclusions in subsections 5 and 6 of this coverage section, no fact pertaining to or knowledge possessed by any **Insured Person** shall be imputed to any other **Insured Person** to determine if coverage is available.

Limit of Liability, Deductible and Coinsurance

8. For the purposes of this coverage section, all **Loss** arising out of the same **Wrongful Act** and all **Interrelated Wrongful Acts** of any **Insured Person** shall be deemed one **Loss,** and such **Loss** shall be deemed to have originated in the earliest **Policy Period** in which a **Claim** is first made against any **Insured Person** alleging any such **Wrongful Act** or **Interrelated Wrongful Acts.**

The Company's maximum liability for each **Loss,** whether covered under Insuring Clause 1 or Insuring Clause 2 or both, shall be the Limit of Liability for each **Loss** set forth in ... the Declarations for this coverage section. The Company's maximum aggregate liability for all **Loss** on account of all **Claims** first made during the same **Policy Period,** whether covered under Insuring Clause 1 or Insuring Clause 2 or both, shall be the Limit of Liability for each **Policy Period** set forth in ... the Declarations for this coverage section.

The Company's liability under Insuring Clause 2 shall apply only to that part of each **Loss** which is excess of the Deductible Amount set forth in ... the Declarations for this coverage section and such Deductible Amount shall be borne by the **Insureds** uninsured and at their own risk.

If a single **Loss** is covered in part under Insuring Clause 1 and in part under Insuring Clause 2, the Deductible Amount applicable to the **Loss** shall be the Insuring Clause 2 deductible set forth in ... the Declarations for this coverage section.

With respect to all **Loss** (excess of the applicable Deductible Amount) originating in any one **Policy Period,** the **Insureds** shall bear uninsured and at their own risk that percent of all such **Loss** specified as the Coinsurance Percent in ... the Declarations for this coverage section, and the Company's liability hereunder shall apply only to the remaining percent of all such **Loss.** ...

For purposes of this subsection 8 only, the Extended Reporting Period, if exercised, shall be part of and not in addition to the immediately preceding **Policy Period.**

Presumptive Indemnification

9.   If the **Insured Organization:**

(a) fails or refuses, other than for reason of **Financial Impairment,** to indemnify the **Insured Person** for **Loss;** and

(b) is permitted or required to indemnify the **Insured Person** for such **Loss** pursuant to:

(i) the by-laws or certificate of incorporation of the **Insured Organization** in effect at the inception of this coverage section, or

(ii) any subsequently amended or superseding by-laws or certificate of incorporation of the **Insured Organization** provided, however, that such amended or superseding by-laws or certificate of incorporation expand or broaden, and do not restrict or in any way limit, the **Insured Organization's** ability to indemnify the **Insured Person;**

then, notwithstanding any other conditions, provisions or terms of this coverage section to the contrary, any payment by the Company of such **Loss** shall be subject to (i) the Insuring Clause 2 Deductible Amount set forth in Item 4 of the Declarations for this coverage section, and (ii) all of the Exclusions set forth in subsections 5 and 6 of this coverage section.

For purposes of this subsection 9, the shareholder and board of director resolutions of the **Insured Organization** shall be deemed to provide indemnification for such **Loss** to the fullest extent permitted by such by-laws or certificate of incorporation.

Reporting and Notice

10. The **Insureds** shall, as a condition precedent to exercising their rights under this coverage section, give to the Company written notice as soon as practicable of any **Claim** made against any of them for a **Wrongful Act.**

If during the **Policy Period** or Extended Reporting Period (if exercised) an **Insured** becomes aware of circumstances which could give rise to a **Claim** and gives written notice of such circumstance(s) to the Company, then any **Claims** subsequently arising from such circumstances shall be considered to have been made during the **Policy Period** or the Extended Reporting Period in which the circumstances were first reported to the Company.

The **Insureds** shall, as a condition precedent to exercising their rights under this coverage section, give to the Company such information and cooperation as it may reasonably require, including but not limited to a description of the **Claim** or circumstances, the nature of the alleged **Wrongful Act,** the nature of the alleged or potential damage, the names of actual or potential claimants, and the manner in which the **Insured** first became aware of the **Claim** or circumstances.

Defense and Settlement

11. Subject to this subsection, it shall be the duty of the **Insured Persons** and not the duty of the Company to defend **Claims** made against the **Insured Persons.**

The **Insureds** agree not to settle any **Claim,** incur any **Defense Costs** or otherwise assume any contractual obligation or admit any liability with respect to any **Claim** without the Company's written consent, which shall not be unreasonably withheld. The Company shall not be liable for any settlement, **Defense Costs,** assumed obligation or admission to which it has not consented.

The Company shall have the right and shall be given the opportunity to effectively associate with the **Insureds** in the investigation, defense and settlement, including but not limited to the negotiation of a settlement, of any **Claim** that appears reasonably likely to be covered in whole or in part by this coverage section.

The **Insureds** agree to provide the Company with all information, assistance and cooperation which the Company reasonably requests and agree that in the event of a **Claim** the **Insureds** will do nothing that may prejudice the Company's position or its potential or actual rights of recovery.

Defense Costs are part of and not in addition to the Limits of Liability set forth in ... the Declarations for this coverage section, and the payment by the Company of **Defense Costs** reduces such Limits of Liability....

Definitions

18.   When used in this coverage section:

Claim means:

(i) a written demand for monetary damages,

(ii) a civil proceeding commenced by the service of a complaint or similar pleading,

(iii) a criminal proceeding commenced by a return of an indictment, or

(iv) a formal administrative or regulatory proceeding commenced by the filing of a notice of charges, formal investigative order or similar document,

against any **Insured Person** for a **Wrongful Act,** including any appeal therefrom.

Defense Costs means that part of **Loss** consisting of reasonable costs, charges, fees (including but not limited to attorneys' fees and experts' fees) and expenses (other than regular or overtime wages, salaries or fees of the directors, officers or employees of the **Insured Organization**) incurred in defending or investigating **Claims** and the premium for appeal, attachment or similar bonds.

Financial Impairment means the status of the **Insured Organization** resulting from (i) the appointment by any state or federal official, agency or court of any receiver, conservator, liquidator, trustee, rehabilitator or similar official to take control of, supervise, manage or liquidate the **Insured Organization,** or (ii) the **Insured Organization** becoming a debtor in possession.

Insured, either in the singular or plural, means the **Insured Organization** and any **Insured Person.**

Insured Capacity means the position or capacity designated in ... the Declarations for this coverage section held by any **Insured Person** but shall not include any position or capacity in any organization other than the **Insured Organization,** even if the **Insured Organization** directed or requested the **Insured Person** to serve in such other position or capacity.

Insured Organization means, collectively, those organizations designated in ... the Declarations for this coverage section.

Insured Person, either in the singular or plural, means any one or more of those persons designated in ... the Declarations for this coverage section.

Interrelated Wrongful Acts means all causally connected **Wrongful Acts.**

Loss means the total amount which any **Insured Person** becomes legally obligated to pay on account of each **Claim** and for all **Claims** in each **Policy Period** and the Extended Reporting Period, if exercised, made against them for **Wrongful Acts** for which coverage applies, including, but not limited to, damages, judgements, settlements, costs and **Defense Costs.** **Loss** does not include (i) any amount not indemnified by the **Insured Organization** for which the **Insured Person** is absolved from payment by reason of any covenant, agreement or court order, (ii) any amount incurred by the **Insured Organization** (including its board of directors or any committee of the board of directors) in connection with the investigation or evaluation of any **Claim** or potential **Claim** by or on behalf of the **Insured Organization,** (iii) fines or penalties imposed by law or the multiple portion of any multiplied damage award, or (iv) matters uninsurable under the law pursuant to which this coverage section is construed.

Pollutants means any substance located anywhere in the world exhibiting any hazardous characteristics as defined by, or identified on a list of hazardous substances issued by, the United States Environmental Protection Agency or a state, county, municipality or locality counterpart thereof. Such substances shall include, without limitation, solids, liquids, gaseous or thermal irritants, contaminants or smoke, vapor, soot, fumes, acids, alkalis, chemicals or waste materials. **Pollutants** shall also mean any other air emission, odor, waste water, oil or oil products, infectious or medical waste, asbestos or asbestos products and any noise.

Subsidiary, either in the singular or plural, means any organization in which more than 50% of the outstanding securities or voting rights representing the present right to vote for election of directors is owned or controlled, directly or indirectly, in any combination, by one or more **Insured Organizations.**

Wrongful Act means any error, misstatement, misleading statement, act, omission, neglect, or breach of duty committed, attempted, or allegedly committed or attempted, by an **Insured Person,** individually or otherwise, in his **Insured Capacity,** or any matter claimed against him solely by reason of his serving in such **Insured Capacity.**

SECURITIES ACT OF 1933

15 U.S.C. §§ 77a et seq.

§ 1. Short Title

This subchapter may be cited as the "Securities Act of 1933."

* Omitted.

§ 2. Definitions; Promotion of Efficiency, Competition, and Capital Formation

(a) Definitions

When used in this subchapter, unless the context otherwise requires—

(1) The term "security" means any note, stock, treasury stock, bond, debenture, evidence of indebtedness, certificate of interest or participation in any profit-sharing agreement, collateral-trust certificate, preorganization certificate or subscription, transferable share, investment contract, voting-trust certificate, certificate of deposit for a security, fractional undivided interest in oil, gas, or other mineral rights, any put, call, straddle, option, or privilege on any security, certificate of deposit, or group or index of securities (including any interest therein or based on the value thereof), or any put, call, straddle, option, or privilege entered into on a national securities exchange relating to foreign currency, or, in general, any interest or instrument commonly known as a "security", or any certificate of interest or participation in, temporary or interim certificate for, receipt for, guarantee of, or warrant or right to subscribe to or purchase, any of the foregoing.

(2) The term "person" means an individual, a corporation, a partnership, an association, a joint-stock company, a trust, any unincorporated organization, or a government or political subdivision thereof. As used in this paragraph the term "trust" shall include only a trust where the interest or interests of the beneficiary or beneficiaries are evidenced by a security.

(3) The term "sale" or "sell" shall include every contract of sale or disposition of a security or interest in a security, for value. The term "offer to sell", "offer for sale", or "offer" shall include every attempt or offer to dispose of, or solicitation of an offer to buy, a security or interest in a security, for value. The terms defined in this paragraph and the term "offer to buy" as used in subsection (c) of section 5 of this title shall not include preliminary negotiations or agreements between an issuer (or any person directly or indirectly controlling or controlled by an issuer, or under direct or indirect common control with an issuer) and any underwriter or among underwriters who are or are to be in privity of contract with an issuer (or any person directly or indirectly controlling or controlled by an issuer, or under direct or indirect common control with an issuer). Any security given or delivered with, or as a bonus on account of, any purchase of securities or any other thing, shall be conclusively presumed to constitute a part of the subject of such purchase and to have been offered and sold for value. The issue or transfer of a right or privilege, when originally issued or transferred with a security, giving the holder of such security the right to

convert such security into another security of the same issuer or of another person, or giving a right to subscribe to another security of the same issuer or of another person, which right cannot be exercised until some future date, shall not be deemed to be an offer or sale of such other security; but the issue or transfer of such other security upon the exercise of such right of conversion or subscription shall be deemed a sale of such other security.

(4) The term "issuer" means every person who issues or proposes to issue any security; except that with respect to certificates of deposit, voting-trust certificates, or collateral-trust certificates, or with respect to certificates of interest or shares in an unincorporated investment trust not having a board of directors (or persons performing similar functions) or of the fixed, restricted management, or unit type, the term "issuer" means the person or persons performing the acts and assuming the duties of depositor or manager pursuant to the provisions of the trust or other agreement or instrument under which such securities are issued; except that in the case of an unincorporated association which provides by its articles for limited liability of any or all of its members, or in the case of a trust, committee, or other legal entity, the trustees or members thereof shall not be individually liable as issuers of any security issued by the association, trust, committee, or other legal entity; except that with respect to equipment-trust certificates or like securities, the term "issuer" means the person by whom the equipment or property is or is to be used; and except that with respect to fractional undivided interests in oil, gas, or other mineral rights, the term "issuer" means the owner of any such right or of any interest in such right (whether whole or fractional) who creates fractional interests therein for the purpose of public offering.

(5) The term "Commission" means the Securities and Exchange Commission.

(6) The term "Territory" means Puerto Rico, Canal Zone, the Virgin Islands, and the insular possessions of the United States.

(7) The term "interstate commerce" means trade or commerce in securities or any transportation or communication relating thereto among the several States or between the District of Columbia or any Territory of the United States and any State or other Territory, or between any foreign country and any State, Territory, or the District of Columbia, or within the District of Columbia.

(8) The term "registration statement" means the statement provided for in section 6 of this title, and includes any amendment thereto and any report, document, or memorandum filed as part of such statement or incorporated therein by reference.

(9) The term "write" or "written" shall include printed, lithographed, or any means of graphic communication.

(10) The term "prospectus" means any prospectus, notice, circular, advertisement, letter, or communication, written or by radio or television, which offers any security for sale or confirms the sale of any security; except that (a) a communication sent or given after the effective date of the registration statement (other than a prospectus permitted under subsection (b) of section 10 of this title) shall not be deemed a prospectus if it is proved that prior to or at the same time with such communication a written prospectus meeting the requirements of subsection (a) of section 10 of this title at the time of such communication was sent or given to the person to whom the communication was made, and (b) a notice, circular, advertisement, letter, or communication in respect of a security shall not be deemed to be a prospectus if it states from whom a written prospectus meeting the requirements of section 10 of this title may be obtained and, in addition, does no more than identify the security, state the price thereof, state by whom orders will be executed, and contain such other information as the Commission, by rules or regulations deemed necessary or appropriate in the public interest and for the protection of investors, and subject to such terms and conditions as may be prescribed therein, may permit.

(11) The term "underwriter" means any person who has purchased from an issuer with a view to, or offers or sells for an issuer in connection with, the distribution of any security, or participates or has a direct or indirect participation in any such undertaking, or participates or has a participation in the direct or indirect underwriting of any such undertaking; but such term shall not include a person whose interest is limited to a commission from an underwriter or dealer not in excess of the usual and customary distributors' or sellers' commission. As used in this paragraph the term "issuer" shall include, in addition to an issuer, any person directly or indirectly controlling or controlled by the issuer, or any person under direct or indirect common control with the issuer.

(12) The term "dealer" means any person who engages either for all or part of his time, directly or indirectly, as agent, broker, or principal, in the business of offering, buying, selling, or otherwise dealing or trading in securities issued by another person.

(13) The term "insurance company" means a company which is organized as an insurance company, whose primary and predominant business activity is the writing of insurance or the reinsuring of risks underwritten by insurance companies, and which is subject to supervision by the insurance commissioner, or a similar official or agency, of a State or territory or the District of Columbia; or any receiver or similar official or any liquidating agent for such company, in his capacity as such.

(14) The term "separate account" means an account established and maintained by an insurance company pursuant to the laws of any State or territory of the United States, the District of Columbia, or of Canada or any province thereof, under which income, gains and losses, whether or not realized, from assets allocated to such account, are, in accordance with the applicable contract, credited to or charged against such account without regard to other income, gains, or losses of the insurance company.

(15) The term "accredited investor" shall mean—

(i) a bank as defined in section 3c(a)(2) of this title whether acting in its individual or fiduciary capacity; an insurance company as defined in paragraph (13); an investment company registered under the Investment Company Act of 1940 or a business development company as defined in section 2(a)(48) of that Act; a Small Business Investment Company licensed by the Small Business Administration; or an employee benefit plan, including an individual retirement account, which is subject to the provisions of the Employee Retirement Income Security Act of 1974, if the investment decision is made by a plan fiduciary, as defined in section 3(21) of such Act, which is either a bank, insurance company, or registered investment adviser; or

(ii) any person who, on the basis of such factors as financial sophistication, net worth, knowledge, and experience in financial matters, or amount of assets under management qualifies as an accredited investor under rules and regulations which the Commission shall prescribe.

(b) Consideration of promotion of efficiency, competition, and capital formation

Whenever pursuant to this subchapter the Commission is engaged in rulemaking and is required to consider or determine whether an action is necessary or appropriate in the public interest, the Commission shall also consider, in addition to the protection of investors, whether the action will promote efficiency, competition, and capital formation.

§ 3. Classes of Securities Under This Subchapter

(a) Exempted securities

Except as hereinafter expressly provided, the provisions of this subchapter shall not apply to any of the following classes of securities:

(1) Any security which, prior to or within sixty days after May 27, 1933, has been sold or disposed of by the issuer or bona fide offered to the public, but this exemption shall not apply to any new offering of any such security by an issuer or underwriter subsequent to such sixty days;

(2) Any security issued or guaranteed by the United States or any territory thereof, or by the District of Columbia, or by any State of the United States, or by any political subdivision of a State or territory, or by any public instrumentality of one or more States or territories, or by any person controlled or supervised by and acting as an instrumentality of the Government of the United States pursuant to authority granted by the Congress of the United States; or any certificate of deposit for any of the foregoing; or any security issued or guaranteed by any bank; or any security issued by or representing an interest in or a direct obligation of a Federal Reserve bank; or any interest or participation in any common trust fund or similar fund maintained by a bank exclusively for the collective investment and reinvestment of assets contributed thereto by such bank in its capacity as trustee, executor, administrator, or guardian . . . .

(3) Any note, draft, bill of exchange, or banker's acceptance which arises out of a current transaction or the proceeds of which have been or are to be used for current transactions, and which has a maturity at the time of issuance of not exceeding nine months, exclusive of days of grace, or any renewal thereof the maturity of which is likewise limited;

(4) Any security issued by a person organized and operated exclusively for religious, educational, benevolent, fraternal, charitable, or reformatory purposes and not for pecuniary profit, and no part of the net earnings of which inures to the benefit of any person, private stockholder, or individual . . . ;

(5) Any security issued . . . by a savings and loan association, building and loan association, cooperative bank, homestead association, or similar institution, which is supervised and examined by State or Federal authority having supervision over any such institution . . . ;

(6) Any interest in a railroad equipment trust. For purposes of this paragraph "interest in a railroad equipment trust" means any interest in an equipment trust, lease, conditional sales contract, or other similar arrangement entered into, issued, assumed, guaranteed by, or for the benefit of, a common carrier to finance the acquisition of rolling stock, including motive power;

(7) Certificates issued by a receiver or by a trustee or debtor in possession in a case under title 11, with the approval of the court;

(8) Any insurance or endowment policy or annuity contract or optional annuity contract, issued by a corporation subject to the supervision of the insurance commissioner, bank commissioner, or any agency or officer performing like functions, of any State or Territory of the United States or the District of Columbia;

(9) Except with respect to a security exchanged in a case under title 11, any security exchanged by the issuer with its existing security holders exclusively where no commission or other remuneration is paid or given directly or indirectly for soliciting such exchange;

(10) Except with respect to a security exchanged in a case under title 11, any security which is issued in exchange for one or more bona fide outstanding securities, claims or property interests, or partly in such exchange and partly for cash, where the terms and conditions of such issuance and exchange are approved, after a hearing upon the fairness of such terms and conditions at which all persons to whom it is proposed to issue securities in such exchange shall have the right to appear, by any court, or by any official or agency of the United States, or by any State or Territorial banking or insurance commission or other governmental authority expressly authorized by law to grant such approval;

(11) Any security which is a part of an issue offered and sold only to persons resident within a single State or Territory, where the issuer of such security is a person resident and doing business within or, if a corporation, incorporated by and doing business within, such State or Territory. . . .

(b) Additional exemptions

The Commission may from time to time by its rules and regulations, and subject to such terms and conditions as may be prescribed therein, add any class of securities to the securities exempted as provided in this section, if it finds that the enforcement of this subchapter with respect to such securities is not necessary in the public interest and for the protection of investors by reason of the small amount involved or the limited character of the public offering; but no issue of securities shall be exempted under this subsection where the aggregate amount at which such issue is offered to the public exceeds $5,000,000.

(c) Securities issued by small investment company

The Commission may from time to time by its rules and regulations and subject to such terms and conditions as may be prescribed therein, add to the securities exempted as provided in this section any class of securities issued by a small business investment company under the Small Business Investment Act of 1958 [15 U.S.C. 661 et seq.] if it finds, having regard to the purposes of that Act, that the enforcement of this subchapter with respect to such securities is not necessary in the public interest and for the protection of investors.

§ 4. Exempted Transactions

The provisions of section 5 of this title shall not apply to—

(1) transactions by any person other than an issuer, underwriter, or dealer.

(2) transactions by an issuer not involving any public offering.

(3) transactions by a dealer (including an underwriter no longer acting as an underwriter in respect of the security involved in such transaction), except—

    (A) transactions taking place prior to the expiration of forty days after the first date upon which the security was bona fide offered to the public by the issuer or by or through an underwriter,

    (B) transactions in a security as to which a registration statement has been filed taking place prior to the expiration of forty days after the effective date of such registration statement or prior to the expiration of forty days after the first date upon which the security was bona fide offered to the public by the issuer or by or through an underwriter after such effective date, whichever is later (excluding in the computation of such forty days any time during which a stop order issued under section 8 of this title is in effect as to the security), or such shorter period as the Commission may specify by rules and regulations or order, and

    (C) transactions as to securities constituting the whole or a part of an unsold allotment to or subscription by such dealer as a participant in the distribution of such securities by the issuer or by or through an underwriter.

With respect to transactions referred to in clause (B), if securities of the issuer have not previously been sold pursuant to an earlier effective registration statement the applicable period, instead of forty days, shall be ninety days, or such shorter period as the Commission may specify by rules and regulations or order.

    (4) brokers' transactions executed upon customers' orders on any exchange or in the over-the-counter market but not the solicitation of such orders. . . .

    (6) transactions involving offers or sales by an issuer solely to one or more accredited investors, if the aggregate offering price of an issue of securities offered in reliance on this paragraph does not exceed the amount allowed under section 3(b) of this title, if there is no advertising or public solicitation in connection with the transaction by the issuer or anyone acting on the issuer's behalf, and if the issuer files such notice with the Commission as the Commission shall prescribe.

§ 5. Prohibitions Relating to Interstate Commerce and the Mails

(a) Sale or delivery after sale of unregistered securities

Unless a registration statement is in effect as to a security, it shall be unlawful for any person, directly or indirectly—

(1) to make use of any means or instruments of transportation or communication in interstate commerce or of the mails to sell such security through the use or medium of any prospectus or otherwise; or

(2) to carry or cause to be carried through the mails or in interstate commerce, by any means or instruments of transportation, any such security for the purpose of sale or for delivery after sale.

(b) Necessity of prospectus meeting requirements of section 10 of this title

It shall be unlawful for any person, directly or indirectly—

(1) to make use of any means or instruments of transportation or communication in interstate commerce or of the mails to carry or transmit any prospectus relating to any security with respect to which a registration statement has been filed under this subchapter, unless such prospectus meets the requirements of section 10 of this title; or

(2) to carry or cause to be carried through the mails or in interstate commerce any such security for the purpose of sale or for delivery after sale, unless accompanied or preceded by a prospectus that meets the requirements of subsection (a) of section 10 of this title.

(c) Necessity of filing registration statement

It shall be unlawful for any person, directly or indirectly, to make use of any means or instruments of transportation or communication in interstate commerce or of the mails to offer to sell or offer to buy through the use or medium of any prospectus or otherwise any security, unless a registration statement has been filed as to such security, or while the registration statement is the subject of a refusal order or stop order or (prior to the effective date of the registration statement) any public proceeding or examination under section 8 of this title.

§ 6. Registration of Securities

(a) Method of registration

Any security may be registered with the Commission under the terms and conditions hereinafter provided, by filing a registration statement in triplicate, at least one of which shall be signed by each issuer, its principal executive officer or officers, its principal financial officer, its comptroller or principal accounting officer, and the majority of its board of directors or persons performing similar functions (or, if there is no board of directors or persons performing similar functions, by the majority of the persons or board having the power of management of the issuer), and in case the issuer is a foreign or Territorial person by its duly authorized representative in the United States; except that when such registration statement relates to a security issued by a foreign government, or political subdivision thereof, it need be signed only by the underwriter of such security. Signatures of all such persons when written on the said registration statements shall be presumed to have been so written by authority of the person whose signature is so affixed and the burden of proof, in the event such authority shall be denied, shall be upon the party denying the same. The affixing of any signature without the authority of the purported signer shall constitute a violation of this subchapter. A registration statement shall be deemed effective only as to the securities specified therein as proposed to be offered....

§ 7. Information Required in Registration Statement

(a) The registration statement, when relating to a security other than a security issued by a foreign government, or political subdivision thereof, shall contain the information, and be accompanied by the documents, specified in Schedule A of section 27 of this title, and when relating to a security issued by a foreign government, or political subdivision thereof, shall contain the information, and be accompanied by the documents, specified in Schedule B of section 27 of this title; except that the Commission may by rules or regulations provide that any such information or document need not be included in respect of any class of issuers or securities if it finds that the requirement of such information or document is inapplicable to such class and that disclosure fully adequate for the protection of investors is otherwise required to be included within the registration statement. If any accountant, engineer, or appraiser, or any person whose profession gives authority to a statement made by him, is named as having prepared or certified any part of the registration statement, or is named as having prepared or certified a report or valuation for use in connection with the registration statement, the written consent of such person shall be filed with the registration statement. If any such person is named as having prepared or certified a report or valuation (other than a public official document or statement) which is used in connection with the registration statement, but is not named as having prepared or certified such report or valuation for use in connection with the registration statement, the written consent of such person shall be filed with the registration statement unless the Commission dispenses with such filing as impracticable or as involving undue hardship on the person filing the registration statement. Any such registration statement shall contain such other information, and be accompanied by such other documents, as the Commission may by rules or regulations require as being necessary or appropriate in the public interest or for the protection of investors.

(b)(1) The Commission shall prescribe special rules with respect to registration statements filed by any issuer that is a blank check company. Such rules may, as the Commission determines necessary or appropriate in the public interest or for the protection of investors—

(A) require such issuers to provide timely disclosure, prior to or after such statement becomes effective under section 8, of (i) information regarding the company to be acquired and the specific application of the proceeds of the offering, or (ii) additional information necessary to prevent such statement from being misleading;

(B) place limitations on the use of such proceeds and the distribution of securities by such issuer until the disclosures required under subparagraph (A) have been made; and

(C) provide a right of rescission to shareholders of such securities.

(2) The Commission may, as it determines consistent with the public interest and the protection of investors, by rule or order exempt any issuer or class of issuers from the rules prescribed under paragraph (1).

(3) For purposes of paragraph (1) of this subsection, the term "blank check company" means any development stage company that is issuing a penny stock (within the meaning of section 3(a)(51) of the Securities Exchange Act of 1934) and that—

(A) has no specific business plan or purpose; or

(B) has indicated that its business plan is to merge with an unidentified company or companies.

§ 8. Taking Effect of Registration Statements and Amendments Thereto

(a) Effective date of registration statement

Except as hereinafter provided, the effective date of a registration statement shall be the twentieth day after the filing thereof or such earlier date as the Commission may determine, having due regard to the adequacy of the information respecting the issuer theretofore available to the public, to the facility with which the nature of the securities to be registered, their relationship to the capital structure of the issuer and the rights of holders thereof can be understood, and to the public interest and the protection of investors. If any amendment to any such statement is filed prior to the effective date of such statement, the registration statement shall be deemed to have been filed when such amendment was filed; except that an amendment filed with the consent of the Commission, prior to the effective date of the registration statement, or filed pursuant to an order of the Commission, shall be treated as a part of the registration statement.

(b) Incomplete or inaccurate registration statement

If it appears to the Commission that a registration statement is on its face incomplete or inaccurate in any material respect, the Commission may, after notice by personal service or the sending of confirmed telegraphic notice not later than ten days after the filing of the registration statement, and opportunity for hearing (at a time fixed by the Commission) within ten days after such notice by personal service or the sending of such telegraphic notice, issue an order prior to the effective date of registration refusing to permit such statement to become effective until it has been amended in accordance with such order. When such statement has been amended in accordance with such order the Commission shall so declare and the registration shall become effective at the time provided in subsection (a) of this section or upon the date of such declaration, whichever date is the later.

(c) Effective Date of Amendment to Registration Statement

An amendment filed after the effective date of the registration statement, if such amendment, upon its face, appears to the Commission not to be incomplete or inaccurate in any material respect, shall become effective on such date as the Commission may determine, having due regard to the public interest and the protection of investors.

(d) Untrue statements or omissions in registration statement

If it appears to the Commission at any time that the registration statement includes any untrue statement of a material fact or omits to state any material fact required to be stated therein or necessary to make the statements therein not misleading, the Commission may, after notice by personal service or the sending of confirmed telegraphic notice, and after opportunity for hearing (at a time fixed by the Commission) within fifteen days after such notice by personal service or the sending of such telegraphic notice, issue a stop order suspending the effectiveness of the registration statement. When such statement has been amended in accordance with such stop order, the Commission shall so declare and thereupon the stop order shall cease to be effective.

(e) Examination for issuance of stop order

The Commission is empowered to make an examination in any case in order to determine whether a stop order should issue under subsection (d) of this section. In making such examination the Commission or any officer or officers designated by it shall have access to and may demand the production of any books and papers of, and may administer oaths and affirmations to and examine, the issuer, underwriter, or any other person, in respect of any matter relevant to the examination, and may, in its discretion, require the production of a balance sheet exhibiting the assets and liabilities of the issuer, or its income statement, or both, to be certified to by a public or certified accountant approved by the Commission. If the issuer or underwriter shall fail to cooperate, or shall obstruct or refuse to permit the making of an examination, such conduct shall be proper ground for the issuance of a stop order.

(f) Notice requirements

Any notice required under this section shall be sent to or served on the issuer, or, in case of a foreign government or political subdivision thereof, to or on the underwriter, or, in the case of a foreign or Territorial person, to or on its duly authorized representative in the United States named in the registration statement, properly directed in each case of telegraphic notice to the address given in such statement.

§ 8A. Cease-and-Desist Proceedings

(a) Authority of the Commission

If the Commission finds, after notice and opportunity for hearing, that any person is violating, has violated, or is about to violate any provision of this title, or any rule or regulation thereunder, the Commission may publish its findings and enter an order requiring such person, and any other person that is, was, or would be a cause of the violation, due to an act or omission the person knew or should have known would contribute to such violation, to cease and desist from committing or causing such violation and any future violation of the same provision, rule, or regulation. Such order may, in addition to requiring a person to cease and desist from committing or causing a violation, require such person to comply, or to take steps to effect compliance, with such provision, rule, or regulation, upon such terms and conditions and within such time as the Commission may specify in such order. Any such order may, as the Commission deems appropriate, require future compliance or steps to effect future compliance, either permanently or for such period of time as the Commission may specify, with such provision, rule, or regulation with respect to any security, any issuer, or any other person. . . .

(e) Authority to enter an order requiring an accounting and disgorgement

In any cease-and-desist proceeding under subsection (a), the Commission may enter an order requiring accounting and disgorgement, including reasonable interest. The Commission is authorized to adopt rules, regulations, and orders concerning payments to investors, rates of interest, periods of accrual, and such other matters as it deems appropriate to implement this subsection.

§ 9. Court Review of Orders

(a) Any person aggrieved by an order of the Commission may obtain a review of such order in the Court of Appeals of the United States, within any circuit wherein such person resides or has his principal place of business, or in the United States Court of Appeals for the District of Columbia, by filing in such court, within sixty days after the entry of such order, a written petition praying that the order of the Commission be modified or be set aside in whole or in part. A copy of such petition shall be forthwith transmitted by the clerk of the court to the Commission, and thereupon the Commission shall file in the court the record upon which the order complained of was entered, as provided in section 2112 of title 28. No objection to the order of the Commission shall be considered by the court unless such objection shall have been urged before the Commission. The finding of the Commission as to the facts, if supported by evidence, shall be conclusive. If either party shall apply to the court for leave to adduce additional evidence, and shall show to the satisfaction of the court that such additional evidence is material and that there were reasonable grounds for failure to adduce such evidence in the hearing before the Commission, the court may order such additional evidence to be taken before the Commission and to be adduced upon the hearing in such manner and upon such terms and conditions as to the court may seem proper. The Commission may modify its findings as to the facts, by reason of the additional evidence so taken, and it shall file such modified or new findings, which, if supported by evidence, shall be conclusive, and its recommendation, if any, for the modification or setting aside of the original order. The jurisdiction of the court shall be exclusive and its judgment and decree, affirming, modifying, or setting aside, in whole or in part, any order of the Commission, shall be final, subject to review by the Supreme Court of the United States upon certiorari or certification as provided in section 1254 of title 28.

(b) The commencement of proceedings under subsection (a) of this section shall not, unless specifically ordered by the court, operate as a stay of the Commission's order.

§ 10. Information Required in Prospectus

(a) Information in registration statement; documents not required

Except to the extent otherwise permitted or required pursuant to this subsection or subsections (c), (d), or (e) of this section—

(1) a prospectus relating to a security other than a security issued by a foreign government or political subdivision thereof, shall contain the information contained in the registration statement . . . .

(3) notwithstanding the provisions of paragraphs (1) and (2) of this subsection when a prospectus is used more than nine months after the effective date of the registration statement, the informa-

tion contained therein shall be as of a date not more than sixteen months prior to such use, so far as such information is known to the user of such prospectus or can be furnished by such user without unreasonable effort or expense;

(4) there may be omitted from any prospectus any of the information required under this subsection which the Commission may by rules or regulations designate as not being necessary or appropriate in the public interest or for the protection of investors.

(b) Summarizations and omissions allowed by rules and regulations

In addition to the prospectus permitted or required in subsection (a) of this section, the Commission shall by rules or regulations deemed necessary or appropriate in the public interest or for the protection of investors permit the use of a prospectus for the purposes of subsection (b)(1) of section 5 of this title which omits in part or summarizes information in the prospectus specified in subsection (a) of this section. A prospectus permitted under this subsection shall, except to the extent the Commission by rules or regulations deemed necessary or appropriate in the public interest or for the protection of investors otherwise provides, be filed as part of the registration statement but shall not be deemed a part of such registration statement for the purposes of section 11 of this title. The Commission may at any time issue an order preventing or suspending the use of a prospectus permitted under this subsection, if it has reason to believe that such prospectus has not been filed (if required to be filed as part of the registration statement) or includes any untrue statement of a material fact or omits to state any material fact required to be stated therein or necessary to make the statements therein, in the light of the circumstances under which such prospectus is or is to be used, not misleading. Upon issuance of an order under this subsection, the Commission shall give notice of the issuance of such order and opportunity for hearing by personal service or the sending of confirmed telegraphic notice. The Commission shall vacate or modify the order at any time for good cause or if such prospectus has been filed or amended in accordance with such order.

(c) Additional information required by rules and regulations

Any prospectus shall contain such other information as the Commission may by rules or regulations require as being necessary or appropriate in the public interest or for the protection of investors.

(d) Classification of prospectuses

In the exercise of its powers under subsections (a), (b), or (c) of this section, the Commission shall have authority to classify prospectuses according to the nature and circumstances of their use or the nature of the security, issue, issuer, or otherwise, and, by rules and regulations and subject to such terms and conditions as it shall specify therein, to prescribe as to each class the form and contents which it may find appropriate and consistent with the public interest and the protection of investors.

(e) Information in conspicuous part of prospectus

The statements or information required to be included in a prospectus by or under authority of subsections (a), (b), (c), or (d) of this section, when written, shall be placed in a conspicuous part of the prospectus and, except as otherwise permitted by rules or regulations, in type as large as that used generally in the body of the prospectus.

(f) Prospectus consisting of radio or television broadcast

In any case where a prospectus consists of a radio or television broadcast, copies thereof shall be filed with the Commission under such rules and regulations as it shall prescribe. The Commission may by rules and regulations require the filing with it of forms and prospectuses used in connection with the offer or sale of securities registered under this subchapter.

§ 11. Civil Liabilities on Account of False Registration Statement

(a) Persons possessing cause of action; persons liable

In case any part of the registration statement, when such part became effective, contained an untrue statement of a material fact or omitted to state a material fact required to be stated therein or necessary to make the statements therein not misleading, any person acquiring such security (unless it is proved that at the time of such acquisition he knew of such untruth or omission) may, either at law or in equity, in any court of competent jurisdiction, sue—

(1) every person who signed the registration statement;

(2) every person who was a director of (or person performing similar functions) or partner in the issuer at the time of the filing of the part of the registration statement with respect to which his liability is asserted;

(3) every person who, with his consent, is named in the registration statement as being or about to become a director, person performing similar functions, or partner;

(4) every accountant, engineer, or appraiser, or any person whose profession gives authority to a statement made by him, who has with his consent been named as having prepared or certified any part of the registration statement, or as having prepared or certified any report or valuation which is used in connection with the registration statement, with respect to the statement in such regis-

tration statement, report, or valuation, which purports to have been prepared or certified by him;

(5) every underwriter with respect to such security.

If such person acquired the security after the issuer has made generally available to its security holders an earning statement covering a period of at least twelve months beginning after the effective date of the registration statement, then the right of recovery under this subsection shall be conditioned on proof that such person acquired the security relying upon such untrue statement in the registration statement or relying upon the registration statement and not knowing of such omission, but such reliance may be established without proof of the reading of the registration statement by such person.

(b) Persons exempt from liability upon proof of issues

Notwithstanding the provisions of subsection (a) of this section no person, other than the issuer, shall be liable as provided therein who shall sustain the burden of proof—

(1) that before the effective date of the part of the registration statement with respect to which his liability is asserted (A) he had resigned from or had taken such steps as are permitted by law to resign from, or ceased or refused to act in, every office, capacity, or relationship in which he was described in the registration statement as acting or agreeing to act, and (B) he had advised the Commission and the issuer in writing that he had taken such action and that he would not be responsible for such part of the registration statement; or

(2) that if such part of the registration statement became effective without his knowledge, upon becoming aware of such fact he forthwith acted and advised the Commission, in accordance with paragraph (1) of this subsection, and, in addition, gave reasonable public notice that such part of the registration statement had become effective without his knowledge; or

(3) that (A) as regards any part of the registration statement not purporting to be made on the authority of an expert, and not purporting to be a copy of or extract from a report or valuation of an expert, and not purporting to be made on the authority of a public official document or statement, he had, after reasonable investigation, reasonable ground to believe and did believe, at the time such part of the registration statement became effective, that the statements therein were true and that there was no omission to state a material fact required to be stated therein or necessary to make the statements therein not misleading; and (B) as regards any part of the registration statement purporting to be made upon his authority as an expert or purporting to be a copy of or extract from a report or valuation of himself as an expert, (i) he had, after reasonable

investigation, reasonable ground to believe and did believe, at the time such part of the registration statement became effective, that the statements therein were true and that there was no omission to state a material fact required to be stated therein or necessary to make the statements therein not misleading, or (ii) such part of the registration statement did not fairly represent his statement as an expert or was not a fair copy of or extract from his report or valuation as an expert; and (C) as regards any part of the registration statement purporting to be made on the authority of an expert (other than himself) or purporting to be a copy of or extract from a report or valuation of an expert (other than himself), he had no reasonable ground to believe and did not believe, at the time such part of the registration statement became effective, that the statements therein were untrue or that there was an omission to state a material fact required to be stated therein or necessary to make the statements therein not misleading, or that such part of the registration statement did not fairly represent the statement of the expert or was not a fair copy of or extract from the report or valuation of the expert; and (D) as regards any part of the registration statement purporting to be a statement made by an official person or purporting to be a copy of or extract from a public official document, he had no reasonable ground to believe and did not believe, at the time such part of the registration statement became effective, that the statements therein were untrue, or that there was an omission to state a material fact required to be stated therein or necessary to make the statements therein not misleading, or that such part of the registration statement did not fairly represent the statement made by the official person or was not a fair copy of or extract from the public official document.

(c)   Standard of reasonableness

In determining, for the purpose of paragraph (3) of subsection (b) of this section, what constitutes reasonable investigation and reasonable ground for belief, the standard of reasonableness shall be that required of a prudent man in the management of his own property.

(d)   Effective date of registration statement with regard to underwriters

If any person becomes an underwriter with respect to the security after the part of the registration statement with respect to which his liability is asserted has become effective, then for the purposes of paragraph (3) of subsection (b) of this section such part of the registration statement shall be considered as having become effective with respect to such person as of the time when he became an underwriter.

(e) Measure of damages; undertaking for payment of costs

The suit authorized under subsection (a) of this section may be to recover such damages as shall represent the difference between the amount paid for the security (not exceeding the price at which the security was offered to the public) and (1) the value thereof as of the time such suit was brought, or (2) the price at which such security shall have been disposed of in the market before suit, or (3) the price at which such security shall have been disposed of after suit but before judgment if such damages shall be less than the damages representing the difference between the amount paid for the security (not exceeding the price at which the security was offered to the public) and the value thereof as of the time such suit was brought: *Provided,* That if the defendant proves that any portion or all of such damages represents other than the depreciation in value of such security resulting from such part of the registration statement, with respect to which his liability is asserted, not being true or omitting to state a material fact required to be stated therein or necessary to make the statements therein not misleading, such portion of or all such damages shall not be recoverable. In no event shall any underwriter (unless such underwriter shall have knowingly received from the issuer for acting as an underwriter some benefit, directly or indirectly, in which all other underwriters similarly situated did not share in proportion to their respective interests in the underwriting) be liable in any suit or as a consequence of suits authorized under subsection (a) of this section for damages in excess of the total price at which the securities underwritten by him and distributed to the public were offered to the public. In any suit under this or any other section of this subchapter the court may, in its discretion, require an undertaking for the payment of the costs of such suit, including reasonable attorney's fees, and if judgment shall be rendered against a party litigant, upon the motion of the other party litigant, such costs may be assessed in favor of such party litigant (whether or not such undertaking has been required) if the court believes the suit or the defense to have been without merit, in an amount sufficient to reimburse him for the reasonable expenses incurred by him, in connection with such suit, such costs to be taxed in the manner usually provided for taxing of costs in the court in which the suit was heard.

(f) Joint and several liability

(1) Except as provided in paragraph (2), all or any one or more of the persons specified in subsection (a) of this section shall be jointly and severally liable, and every person who becomes liable to make any payment under this section may recover contribution as in cases of contract from any person who, if sued separately, would have been liable to make the same payment, unless the person who has become liable was, and the other was not, guilty of fraudulent misrepresentation.

(2)(A) The liability of an outside director under subsection (e) of this section shall be determined in accordance with section [21D(g)] of the Securities Exchange Act of 1934.

(B) For purposes of this paragraph, the term "outside director" shall have the meaning given such term by rule or regulation of the Commission.

(g) Offering price to public as maximum amount recoverable

In no case shall the amount recoverable under this section exceed the price at which the security was offered to the public.

§ 12. Civil Liabilities Arising in Connection With Prospectuses and Communications

(a) In General

Any person who—

(1) offers or sells a security in violation of section 5 of this title, or

(2) offers or sells a security (whether or not exempted by the provisions of section 3 of this title, other than paragraph (2) of subsection (a) of said section), by the use of any means or instruments of transportation or communication in interstate commerce or of the mails, by means of a prospectus or oral communication, which includes an untrue statement of a material fact or omits to state a material fact necessary in order to make the statements, in the light of the circumstances under which they were made, not misleading (the purchaser not knowing of such untruth or omission), and who shall not sustain the burden of proof that he did not know, and in the exercise of reasonable care could not have known, of such untruth or omission,

shall be liable, subject to subsection (b), to the person purchasing such security from him, who may sue either at law or in equity in any court of competent jurisdiction, to recover the consideration paid for such security with interest thereon, less the amount of any income received thereon, upon the tender of such security, or for damages if he no longer owns the security.

(b) Loss Causation

In an action described in subsection (a)(2), if the person who offered or sold such security proves that any portion or all of the amount recoverable under subsection (a)(2) represents other than the depreciation in value of the subject security resulting from such part of the prospectus or oral communication, with respect to which the liability of that person is asserted, not being true or omitting to state a material fact required to be stated therein or necessary to make the statement not misleading, then such portion or amount, as the case may be, shall not be recoverable.

§ 13. Limitation of Actions

No action shall be maintained to enforce any liability created under section 11 or 12(2) of this title unless brought within one year after the discovery of the untrue statement or the omission, or after such discovery should have been made by the exercise of reasonable diligence, or, if the action is to enforce a liability created under section 12(1) of this title, unless brought within one year after the violation upon which it is based. In no event shall any such action be brought to enforce a liability created under section 11 or 12(1) of this title more than three years after the security was bona fide offered to the public, or under section 12(2) of this title more than three years after the sale.

§ 14. Contrary Stipulations Void

Any condition, stipulation, or provision binding any person acquiring any security to waive compliance with any provision of this subchapter or of the rules and regulations of the Commission shall be void.

§ 15. Liability of Controlling Persons

Every person who, by or through stock ownership, agency, or otherwise, or who, pursuant to or in connection with an agreement or understanding with one or more other persons by or through stock ownership, agency, or otherwise, controls any person liable under sections 11 or 12 of this title, shall also be liable jointly and severally with and to the same extent as such controlled person to any person to whom such controlled person is liable, unless the controlling person had no knowledge of or reasonable ground to believe in the existence of the facts by reason of which the liability of the controlled person is alleged to exist.

§ 16. Additional Remedies

The rights and remedies provided by this subchapter shall be in addition to any and all other rights and remedies that may exist at law or in equity.

§ 17. Fraudulent Interstate Transactions

(a) Use of interstate commerce for purpose of fraud or deceit

It shall be unlawful for any person in the offer or sale of any securities by the use of any means or instruments of transportation or communication in interstate commerce or by the use of the mails, directly or indirectly—

> (1) to employ any device, scheme, or artifice to defraud, or

(2) to obtain money or property by means of any untrue statement of a material fact or any omission to state a material fact necessary in order to make the statements made, in the light of the circumstances under which they were made, not misleading, or

(3) to engage in any transaction, practice, or course of business which operates or would operate as a fraud or deceit upon the purchaser.

(b) Use of interstate commerce for purpose of offering for sale

It shall be unlawful for any person, by the use of any means or instruments of transportation or communication in interstate commerce or by the use of the mails, to publish, give publicity to, or circulate any notice, circular, advertisement, newspaper, article, letter, investment service, or communication which, though not purporting to offer a security for sale, describes such security for a consideration received or to be received, directly or indirectly, from an issuer, underwriter, or dealer, without fully disclosing the receipt, whether past or prospective, of such consideration and the amount thereof.

(c) Exemptions of section 3 not applicable to this section

The exemptions provided in section 3 of this title shall not apply to the provisions of this section.

§ 18   Exemption From State Regulation of Securities Offerings

(a) Scope of exemption

Except as otherwise provided in this section, no law, rule, regulation, or order, or other administrative action of any State or any political subdivision thereof—

(1) requiring, or with respect to, registration or qualification of securities, or registration or qualification of securities transactions, shall directly or indirectly apply to a security that—

(A) is a covered security; or

(B) will be a covered security upon completion of the transaction;

(2) shall directly or indirectly prohibit, limit, or impose any conditions upon the use of—

(A) with respect to a covered security described in subsection (b) of this section, any offering document that is prepared by or on behalf of the issuer; or

(B) any proxy statement, report to shareholders, or other disclosure document relating to a covered security or the issuer thereof that is required to be and is filed with the Commission or any national securities organization registered under section

15A of the Securities Exchange Act, except that this subparagraph does not apply to the laws, rules, regulations, or orders, or other administrative actions of the State of incorporation of the issuer; or

(3) shall directly or indirectly prohibit, limit, or impose conditions, based on the merits of such offering or issuer, upon the offer or sale of any security described in paragraph (1).

(b) Covered securities

For purposes of this section, the following are covered securities:

(1) *Exclusive Federal registration of nationally traded securities*

A security is a covered security if such security is—

(A) listed, or authorized for listing, on the New York Stock Exchange or the American Stock Exchange, or listed on the National Market System of the Nasdaq Stock Market (or any successor to such entities);

(B) listed, or authorized for listing, on a national securities exchange (or tier or segment thereof) that has listing standards that the Commission determines by rule (on its own initiative or on the basis of a petition) are substantially similar to the listing standards applicable to securities described in subparagraph (A); or

(C) is a security of the same issuer that is equal in seniority or that is a senior security to a security described in subparagraph (A) or (B).

(2) *Exclusive Federal registration of investment companies*

A security is a covered security if such security is a security issued by an investment company that is registered, or that has filed a registration statement, under the Investment Company Act of 1940.

(3) *Sales to qualified purchasers*

A security is a covered security with respect to the offer or sale of the security to qualified purchasers, as defined by the Commission by rule. In prescribing such rule, the Commission may define the term "qualified purchaser" differently with respect to different categories of securities, consistent with the public interest and the protection of investors.

(4) *Exemption in connection with certain exempt offerings*

A security is a covered security with respect to a transaction that is exempt from registration under this subchapter pursuant to—

(A) paragraph (1) or (3) of section 4, and the issuer of such security files reports with the Commission pursuant to section 13 or 15(d) of the Securities Exchange Act;

(B) section 4(4);

(C) section 3(a), other than the offer or sale of a security that is exempt from such registration pursuant to paragraph (4) or (11) of such section, except that a municipal security that is exempt from such registration pursuant to paragraph (2) of such section is not a covered security with respect to the offer or sale of such security in the State in which the issuer of such security is located; or

(D) Commission rules or regulations issued under section 4(2), except that this subparagraph does not prohibit a State from imposing notice filing requirements that are substantially similar to those required by rule or regulation under section 4(2) that are in effect on September 1, 1996.

(c) Preservation of authority

(1) *Fraud authority*

Consistent with this section, the securities commission (or any agency or officer performing like functions) of any State shall retain jurisdiction under the laws of such State to investigate and bring enforcement actions with respect to fraud or deceit, or unlawful conduct by a broker or dealer, in connection with securities or securities transactions.

(2) *Preservation of filing requirements*

(A) *Notice filings permitted*

Nothing in this section prohibits the securities commission (or any agency or office performing like functions) of any State from requiring the filing of any document filed with the Commission pursuant to this subchapter, together with annual or periodic reports of the value of securities sold or offered to be sold to persons located in the State (if such sales data is not included in documents filed with the Commission), solely for notice purposes and the assessment of any fee, together with a consent to service of process and any required fee.

(B) *Preservation of fees*

(i) *In general*

Until otherwise provided by law, rule, regulation, or order, or other administrative action of any State, or any political subdivision thereof, adopted after October 11, 1996, filing or registration fees with respect to securities or securities transactions shall continue to be collected in amounts determined pursuant to State law as in effect on the day before such date.

(ii) *Schedule*

The fees required by this subparagraph shall be paid, and all necessary supporting data on sales or offers for sales required under subparagraph (A), shall be reported on the same schedule as would have been applicable had the issuer not relied on the exemption provided in subsection (a) of this section.

(C) *Availability of preemption contingent on payment of fees*

(i) *In general*

During the period beginning on October 11, 1996, and ending 3 years after October 11, 1996, the securities commission (or any agency or office performing like functions) of any State may require the registration of securities issued by any issuer who refuses to pay the fees required by subparagraph (B).

(ii) *Delays*

For purposes of this subparagraph, delays in payment of fees or underpayments of fees that are promptly remedied shall not constitute a refusal to pay fees.

(D) *Fees not permitted on listed securities*

Notwithstanding subparagraphs (A), (B), and (C), no filing or fee may be required with respect to any security that is a covered security pursuant to subsection (b)(1) of this section, or will be such a covered security upon completion of the transaction, or is a security of the same issuer that is equal in seniority or that is a senior security to a security that is a covered security pursuant to subsection (b)(1) of this section.

(3) *Enforcement of requirements*

Nothing in this section shall prohibit the securities commission (or any agency or office performing like functions) of any State from suspending the offer or sale of securities within such State as a result of the failure to submit any filing or fee required under law and permitted under this section.

(d) Definitions

For purposes of this section, the following definitions shall apply:

(1) *Offering document*

The term "offering document"—

(A) has the meaning given the term "prospectus" in section 2(10) of this title, but without regard to the provisions of subparagraphs (A) and (B) of that section; and

(B) includes a communication that is not deemed to offer a security pursuant to a rule of the Commission.

(2) *Prepared by or on behalf of the issuer*

Not later than 6 months after the date of enactment of the Securities Amendments Act of 1996, the Commission shall, by rule, define the term "prepared by or on behalf of the issuer" for purposes of this section.

(3) *State*

The term "State" has the same meaning as in section 3.

(4) *Senior security*

For purposes of this paragraph, the term "senior security" means any bond, debenture, note, or similar obligation or instrument constituting a security and evidencing indebtedness, and any stock of a class having priority over any other class as to distribution of assets or payment of dividends.

§ 19. Special Powers of Commission

(a) The Commission shall have authority from time to time to make, amend, and rescind such rules and regulations as may be necessary to carry out the provisions of this subchapter, including rules and regulations governing registration statements and prospectuses for various classes of securities and issuers, and defining accounting, technical, and trade terms used in this subchapter. Among other things, the Commission shall have authority, for the purposes of this subchapter, to prescribe the form or forms in which required information shall be set forth, the items or details to be shown in the balance sheet and earning statement, and the methods to be followed in the preparation of accounts, in the appraisal or valuation of assets and liabilities, in the determination of depreciation and depletion, in the differentiation of recurring and nonrecurring income, in the differentiation of investment and operating income, and in the preparation, where the Commission deems it necessary or desirable, of consolidated balance sheets or income accounts of any person directly or indirectly controlling or controlled by the issuer, or any person under direct or indirect common control with the issuer. The rules and regulations of the Commission shall be effective upon publication in the manner which the Commission shall prescribe. No provision of this subchapter imposing any liability shall apply to any act done or omitted in good faith in conformity with any rule or regulation of the Commission, notwithstanding that such rule or regulation may, after such act or omission, be amended or rescinded or be determined by judicial or other authority to be invalid for any reason.

(b) For the purpose of all investigations which, in the opinion of the Commission, are necessary and proper for the enforcement of this subchapter, any member of the Commission or any officer or officers designated by it are empowered to administer oaths and affirmations, subpoena witnesses, take evidence, and require the production of any books, papers, or other documents which the Commission deems relevant or material to the inquiry. Such attendance of witnesses and the production of such documentary evidence may be required from any place in the United States or any Territory at any designated place of hearing....

§ 20. Injunctions and Prosecution of Offenses ....

(b) Action for injunction or criminal prosecution in district court

Whenever it shall appear to the Commission that any person is engaged or about to engage in any acts or practices which constitute or will constitute a violation of the provisions of this subchapter, or of any rule or regulation prescribed under authority thereof, it may in its discretion, bring an action in any district court of the United States or United States court of any Territory, to enjoin such acts or practices, and upon a proper showing a permanent or temporary injunction or restraining order shall be granted without bond. The Commission may transmit such evidence as may be available concerning such acts or practices to the Attorney General who may, in his discretion, institute the necessary criminal proceedings under this subchapter. Any such criminal proceeding may be brought either in the district wherein the transmittal of the prospectus or security complained of begins, or in the district wherein such prospectus or security is received....

(d) Money penalties in civil actions

(1) *Authority of commission.* Whenever it shall appear to the Commission that any person has violated any provision of this title, the rules or regulations thereunder, or a cease-and-desist order entered by the Commission pursuant to section 8A of this title, other than by committing a violation subject to a penalty pursuant to section 21A of the Securities Exchange Act of 1934, the Commission may bring an action in a United States district court to seek, and the court shall have jurisdiction to impose, upon a proper showing, a civil penalty to be paid by the person who committed such violation.

(2) *Amount of penalty.*

(A) *First tier.* The amount of the penalty shall be determined by the court in light of the facts and circumstances. For each violation, the amount of the penalty shall not exceed the greater of (i) [$5,500]* for a natural person or [$55,000] for any other person, or (ii) the gross amount of pecuniary gain to such defendant as a result of the violation.

(B) *Second tier.* Notwithstanding subparagraph (A), the amount of penalty for each such violation shall not exceed the greater of (i) [$55,000] for a natural person or [$275,000] for any other person, or (ii) the gross amount of pecuniary gain to such defendant as a result of the violation, if the violation described in paragraph (1) involved fraud, deceit, manipulation, or deliberate or reckless disregard of a regulatory requirement.

(C) *Third tier.* Notwithstanding subparagraphs (A) and (B), the amount of penalty for each such violation shall not exceed the greater of (i) [$110,000] for a natural person or [$550,000] for any other person, or (ii) the gross amount of pecuniary gain to such defendant as a result of the violation, if—

(I) the violation described in paragraph (1) involved fraud, deceit, manipulation, or deliberate or reckless disregard of a regulatory requirement; and

(II) such violation directly or indirectly resulted in substantial losses or created a significant risk of substantial losses to other persons.

(3) *Procedures for collection.*

(A) *Payment of penalty to treasury.* A penalty imposed under this section shall be payable into the Treasury of the United States.

(B) *Collection of penalties.* If a person upon whom such a penalty is imposed shall fail to pay such penalty within the time prescribed in the court's order, the Commission may refer the matter to the Attorney General who shall recover such penalty by action in the appropriate United States district court.

(C) *Remedy not exclusive.* The actions authorized by this subsection may be brought in addition to any other action that the Commission or the Attorney General is entitled to bring.

(D) *Jurisdiction and venue.* For purposes of section 22 of this title, actions under this section shall be actions to enforce a liability or a duty created by this title.

(4) *Special provisions relating to a violation of a cease-and-desist order.* In an action to enforce a cease-and-desist order entered by the Commission pursuant to section 8A, each separate

* The bracketed figures in this section have been adjusted for inflation by the SEC under the Debt Collection Act of 1996, which requires the Commission to make inflationary adjustments to civil penalties in the Securities Act, the Exchange Act, and other Acts that the Commission administers. (Footnote by ed.)

violation of such order shall be a separate offense, except that in the case of a violation through a continuing failure to comply with such an order, each day of the failure to comply with the order shall be deemed a separate offense.

(e) Authority of a court to prohibit persons from serving as Officers and Directors

In any proceeding under subsection (b), the court may prohibit, conditionally or unconditionally, and permanently or for such period of time as it shall determine, any person who violated section 17(a)(1) of this title from acting as an officer or director of any issuer that has a class of securities registered pursuant to section 12 of the Securities Exchange Act of 1934 or that is required to file reports pursuant to section 15(d) of such Act if the person's conduct demonstrates substantial unfitness to serve as an officer or director of any such issuer.

(f) Prohibition of Attorneys' Fees Paid From Commission Disgorgement Funds

Except as otherwise ordered by the court upon motion by the Commission, or, in the case of an administrative action, as otherwise ordered by the Commission, funds disgorged as the result of an action brought by the Commission in Federal court, or as a result of any Commission administrative action, shall not be distributed as payment for attorneys' fees or expenses incurred by private parties seeking distribution of the disgorged funds.

§ 22. Jurisdiction of Offenses and Suits

(a) Federal and State courts; venue; service of process; review; removal; costs

The district courts of the United States, and the United States courts of any Territory, shall have jurisdiction of offenses and violations under this subchapter and under the rules and regulations promulgated by the Commission in respect thereto, and, concurrent with State and Territorial courts, of all suits in equity and actions at law brought to enforce any liability or duty created by this subchapter. Any such suit or action may be brought in the district wherein the defendant is found or is an inhabitant or transacts business, or in the district where the offer or sale took place, if the defendant participated therein, and process in such cases may be served in any other district of which the defendant is an inhabitant or wherever the defendant may be found. Judgments and decrees so rendered shall be subject to review as provided in sections 1254, 1291, and 1292 of title 28. No case arising under this subchapter and brought in any State court of competent jurisdiction shall be removed to any court of the United States. No costs shall be assessed for or against the Commission in any proceeding under this subchapter brought by or against it in the Supreme Court or such other courts.

(b) Contumacy or refusal to obey subpoena: contempt

In case of contumacy or refusal to obey a subpoena issued to any person, any of the said United States courts, within the jurisdiction of which said person guilty of contumacy or refusal to obey is found or resides, upon application by the Commission may issue to such person an order requiring such person to appear before the Commission, or one of its examiners designated by it, there to produce documentary evidence if so ordered, or there to give evidence touching the matter in question; and any failure to obey such order of the court may be punished by said court as a contempt thereof.

§ 23. Unlawful Representations

Neither the fact that the registration statement for a security has been filed or is in effect nor the fact that a stop order is not in effect with respect thereto shall be deemed a finding by the Commission that the registration statement is true and accurate on its face or that it does not contain an untrue statement of fact or omit to state a material fact, or be held to mean that the Commission has in any way passed upon the merits of, or given approval to, such security. It shall be unlawful to make, or cause to be made to any prospective purchaser any representation contrary to the foregoing provisions of this section.

§ 24. Penalties

Any person who willfully violates any of the provisions of this subchapter, or the rules and regulations promulgated by the Commission under authority thereof, or any person who willfully, in a registration statement filed under this subchapter, makes any untrue statement of a material fact or omits to state any material fact required to be stated therein or necessary to make the statements therein not misleading, shall upon conviction be fined not more than $10,000 or imprisoned not more than five years, or both. . . .

§ 27. Private Securities Litigation

(a) Private Class Actions

(1) *In general.*—The provisions of this subsection shall apply to each private action arising under this title that is brought as a plaintiff class action pursuant to the Federal Rules of Civil Procedure.

(2) *Certification filed with complaint.—*

(A) In general.—Each plaintiff seeking to serve as a representative party on behalf of a class shall provide a sworn certification, which shall be personally signed by such plaintiff and filed with the complaint, that—

(i) states that the plaintiff has reviewed the complaint and authorized its filing;

(ii) states that the plaintiff did not purchase the security that is the subject of the complaint at the direction of plaintiff's counsel or in order to participate in any private action arising under this title;

(iii) states that the plaintiff is willing to serve as a representative party on behalf of a class, including providing testimony at deposition and trial, if necessary;

(iv) sets forth all of the transactions of the plaintiff in the security that is the subject of the complaint during the class period specified in the complaint;

(v) identifies any other action under this title, filed during the 3–year period preceding the date on which the certification is signed by the plaintiff, in which the plaintiff has sought to serve, or served, as a representative party on behalf of a class; and

(vi) states that the plaintiff will not accept any payment for serving as a representative party on behalf of a class beyond the plaintiff's pro rata share of any recovery, except as ordered or approved by the court in accordance with paragraph (4).

(B) Nonwaiver of attorney-client privilege.—The certification filed pursuant to subparagraph (A) shall not be construed to be a waiver of the attorney-client privilege.

(3) *Appointment of lead plaintiff.*—

(A) Early notice to class members.—

(i) In general.—Not later than 20 days after the date on which the complaint is filed, the plaintiff or plaintiffs shall cause to be published, in a widely circulated national business-oriented publication or wire service, a notice advising members of the purported plaintiff class—

(I) of the pendency of the action, the claims asserted therein, and the purported class period; and

(II) that, not later than 60 days after the date on which the notice is published, any member of the purported class may move the court to serve as lead plaintiff of the purported class.

(ii) Multiple actions.—If more than one action on behalf of a class asserting substantially the same claim or claims arising under this title is filed, only the plaintiff or plaintiffs in the first filed action shall be required to cause notice to be published in accordance with clause (i).

(iii) Additional notices may be required under federal rules.—Notice required under clause (i) shall be in addition to any notice required pursuant to the Federal Rules of Civil Procedure.

(B) Appointment of lead plaintiff.—

(i) In general.—Not later than 90 days after the date on which a notice is published under subparagraph (A)(i), the court shall consider any motion made by a purported class member in response to the notice, including any motion by a class member who is not individually named as a plaintiff in the complaint or complaints, and shall appoint as lead plaintiff the member or members of the purported plaintiff class that the court determines to be most capable of adequately representing the interests of class members (hereafter in this paragraph referred to as the "most adequate plaintiff") in accordance with this subparagraph.

(ii) Consolidated actions.—If more than one action on behalf of a class asserting substantially the same claim or claims arising under this title has been filed, and any party has sought to consolidate those actions for pretrial purposes or for trial, the court shall not make the determination required by clause (i) until after the decision on the motion to consolidate is rendered. As soon as practicable after such decision is rendered, the court shall appoint the most adequate plaintiff as lead plaintiff for the consolidated actions in accordance with this subparagraph.

(iii) Rebuttable presumption.—

(I) In general.—Subject to subclause (II), for purposes of clause (i), the court shall adopt a presumption that the most adequate plaintiff in any private action arising under this title is the person or group of persons that—

(aa) has either filed the complaint or made a motion in response to a notice under subparagraph (A)(i);

(bb) in the determination of the court, has the largest financial interest in the relief sought by the class; and

(cc) otherwise satisfies the requirements of Rule 23 of the Federal Rules of Civil Procedure.

(II) Rebuttal evidence.—The presumption described in subclause (I) may be rebutted only upon proof by a member of the purported plaintiff class that the presumptively most adequate plaintiff—

(aa) will not fairly and adequately protect the interests of the class; or

(bb) is subject to unique defenses that render such plaintiff incapable of adequately representing the class.

(iv) *Discovery.*—For purposes of this subparagraph, discovery relating to whether a member or members of the purported plaintiff class is the most adequate plaintiff may be conducted by a plaintiff only if the plaintiff first demonstrates a reasonable basis for a finding that the presumptively most adequate plaintiff is incapable of adequately representing the class.

(v) *Selection of lead counsel.*—The most adequate plaintiff shall, subject to the approval of the court, select and retain counsel to represent the class.

(vi) *Restrictions on professional plaintiffs.*—Except as the court may otherwise permit, consistent with the purposes of this section, a person may be a lead plaintiff, or an officer, director, or fiduciary of a lead plaintiff, in no more than 5 securities class actions brought as plaintiff class actions pursuant to the Federal Rules of Civil Procedure during any 3-year period.

(4) *Recovery by plaintiffs.*—The share of any final judgment or of any settlement that is awarded to a representative party serving on behalf of a class shall be equal, on a per share basis, to the portion of the final judgment or settlement awarded to all other members of the class. Nothing in this paragraph shall be construed to limit the award of reasonable costs and expenses (including lost wages) directly relating to the representation of the class to any representative party serving on behalf of the class.

(5) *Restrictions on settlements under seal.*—The terms and provisions of any settlement agreement of a class action shall not be filed under seal, except that on motion of any party to the settlement, the court may order filing under seal for those portions of a settlement agreement as to which good cause is shown for such filing under seal. For purposes of this paragraph, good cause shall exist only if publication of a term or provision of a settlement agreement would cause direct and substantial harm to any party.

(6) *Restrictions on payment of attorneys' fees and expenses.*— Total attorneys' fees and expenses awarded by the court to counsel for the plaintiff class shall not exceed a reasonable percentage of the amount of any damages and prejudgment interest actually paid to the class.

(7) *Disclosure of settlement terms to class members.*—Any proposed or final settlement agreement that is published or otherwise

disseminated to the class shall include each of the following statements, along with a cover page summarizing the information contained in such statements:

(A) Statement of plaintiff recovery.—The amount of the settlement proposed to be distributed to the parties to the action, determined in the aggregate and on an average per share basis.

(B) Statement of potential outcome of case.—

(i) Agreement on amount of damages.—If the settling parties agree on the average amount of damages per share that would be recoverable if the plaintiff prevailed on each claim alleged under this title, a statement concerning the average amount of such potential damages per share.

(ii) Disagreement on amount of damages.—If the parties do not agree on the average amount of damages per share that would be recoverable if the plaintiff prevailed on each claim alleged under this title, a statement from each settling party concerning the issue or issues on which the parties disagree.

(iii) Inadmissibility for certain purposes.—A statement made in accordance with clause (i) or (ii) concerning the amount of damages shall not be admissible in any Federal or State judicial action or administrative proceeding, other than an action or proceeding arising out of such statement.

(C) Statement of attorneys' fees or costs sought.—If any of the settling parties or their counsel intend to apply to the court for an award of attorneys' fees or costs from any fund established as part of the settlement, a statement indicating which parties or counsel intend to make such an application, the amount of fees and costs that will be sought (including the amount of such fees and costs determined on an average per share basis), and a brief explanation supporting the fees and costs sought.

(D) Identification of lawyers' representatives.—The name, telephone number, and address of one or more representatives of counsel for the plaintiff class who will be reasonably available to answer questions from class members concerning any matter contained in any notice of settlement published or otherwise disseminated to the class.

(E) Reasons for settlement.—A brief statement explaining the reasons why the parties are proposing the settlement.

(F) Other information.—Such other information as may be required by the court.

(8) *Attorney conflict of interest.*—If a plaintiff class is represented by an attorney who directly owns or otherwise has a beneficial interest in the securities that are the subject of the litigation, the court shall make a determination of whether such ownership or other interest constitutes a conflict of interest sufficient to disqualify the attorney from representing the plaintiff class.

(b) Stay of Discovery; Preservation of Evidence

(1) *In general.*—In any private action arising under this title, all discovery and other proceedings shall be stayed during the pendency of any motion to dismiss, unless the court finds, upon the motion of any party, that particularized discovery is necessary to preserve evidence or to prevent undue prejudice to that party.

(2) *Preservation of evidence.*—During the pendency of any stay of discovery pursuant to this subsection, unless otherwise ordered by the court, any party to the action with actual notice of the allegations contained in the complaint shall treat all documents, data compilations (including electronically recorded or stored data), and tangible objects that are in the custody or control of such person and that are relevant to the allegations, as if they were the subject of a continuing request for production of documents from an opposing party under the Federal Rules of Civil Procedure.

(3) *Sanction for willful violation.*—A party aggrieved by the willful failure of an opposing party to comply with paragraph (2) may apply to the court for an order awarding appropriate sanctions.

(c) Sanctions for Abusive Litigation

(1) *Mandatory review by court.*—In any private action arising under this title, upon final adjudication of the action, the court shall include in the record specific findings regarding compliance by each party and each attorney representing any party with each requirement of Rule 11(b) of the Federal Rules of Civil Procedure as to any complaint, responsive pleading, or dispositive motion.

(2) *Mandatory sanctions.*—If the court makes a finding under paragraph (1) that a party or attorney violated any requirement of Rule 11(b) of the Federal Rules of Civil Procedure as to any complaint, responsive pleading, or dispositive motion, the court shall impose sanctions on such party or attorney in accordance with Rule 11 of the Federal Rules of Civil Procedure. Prior to making a finding that any party or attorney has violated Rule 11 of the Federal Rules of Civil Procedure, the court shall give such party or attorney notice and an opportunity to respond.

(3) *Presumption in favor of attorneys' fees and costs.*—

(A) In general.—Subject to subparagraphs (B) and (C), for purposes of paragraph (2), the court shall adopt a presumption that the appropriate sanction—

(i) for failure of any responsive pleading or dispositive motion to comply with any requirement of Rule 11(b) of the Federal Rules of Civil Procedure is an award to the opposing party of the reasonable attorneys' fees and other expenses incurred as a direct result of the violation; and

(ii) for substantial failure of any complaint to comply with any requirement of Rule 11(b) of the Federal Rules of Civil Procedure is an award to the opposing party of the reasonable attorneys' fees and other expenses incurred in the action.

(B) Rebuttal evidence.—The presumption described in subparagraph (A) may be rebutted only upon proof by the party or attorney against whom sanctions are to be imposed that—

(i) the award of attorneys' fees and other expenses will impose an unreasonable burden on that party or attorney and would be unjust, and the failure to make such an award would not impose a greater burden on the party in whose favor sanctions are to be imposed; or

(ii) the violation of Rule 11(b) of the Federal Rules of Civil Procedure was de minimis.

(C) Sanctions.—If the party or attorney against whom sanctions are to be imposed meets its burden under subparagraph (B), the court shall award the sanctions that the court deems appropriate pursuant to Rule 11 of the Federal Rules of Civil Procedure.

(d) Defendant's Right to Written Interrogatories

In any private action arising under this title in which the plaintiff may recover money damages only on proof that a defendant acted with a particular state of mind, the court shall, when requested by a defendant, submit to the jury a written interrogatory on the issue of each such defendant's state of mind at the time the alleged violation occurred.

§ 27A. Application of Safe Harbor for Forward–Looking Statements

(a) Applicability

This section shall apply only to a forward-looking statement made by—

(1) an issuer that, at the time that the statement is made, is subject to the reporting requirements of section 13(a) or section 15(d) of the Securities Exchange Act of 1934;

(2) a person acting on behalf of such issuer;

(3) an outside reviewer retained by such issuer making a statement on behalf of such issuer; or

(4) an underwriter, with respect to information provided by such issuer or information derived from information provided by the issuer.

(b) Exclusions

Except to the extent otherwise specifically provided by rule, regulation, or order of the Commission, this section shall not apply to a forward-looking statement—

(1) that is made with respect to the business or operations of the issuer, if the issuer—

(A) during the 3–year period preceding the date on which the statement was first made—

(i) was convicted of any felony or misdemeanor described in clauses (i) through (iv) of section 15(b)(4)(B) of the Securities Exchange Act of 1934; or

(ii) has been made the subject of a judicial or administrative decree or order arising out of a governmental action that—

(I) prohibits future violations of the antifraud provisions of the securities laws;

(II) requires that the issuer cease and desist from violating the antifraud provisions of the securities laws; or

(III) determines that the issuer violated the antifraud provisions of the securities laws;

(B) makes the forward-looking statement in connection with an offering of securities by a blank check company;

(C) issues penny stock;

(D) makes the forward-looking statement in connection with a rollup transaction; or

(E) makes the forward-looking statement in connection with a going private transaction; or

(2) that is—

(A) included in a financial statement prepared in accordance with generally accepted accounting principles;

(B) contained in a registration statement of, or otherwise issued by, an investment company;

(C) made in connection with a tender offer;

(D) made in connection with an initial public offering;

(E) made in connection with an offering by, or relating to the operations of, a partnership, limited liability company, or a direct participation investment program; or

(F) made in a disclosure of beneficial ownership in a report required to be filed with the Commission pursuant to section 13(d) of the Securities Exchange Act of 1934.

(c) Safe Harbor

(1) *In general.*—Except as provided in subsection (b), in any private action arising under this title that is based on an untrue statement of a material fact or omission of a material fact necessary to make the statement not misleading, a person referred to in subsection (a) shall not be liable with respect to any forward-looking statement, whether written or oral, if and to the extent that—

(A) the forward-looking statement is—

(i) identified as a forward-looking statement, and is accompanied by meaningful cautionary statements identifying important factors that could cause actual results to differ materially from those in the forward-looking statement; or

(ii) immaterial; or

(B) the plaintiff fails to prove that the forward-looking statement—

(i) if made by a natural person, was made with actual knowledge by that person that the statement was false or misleading; or

(ii) if made by a business entity; was—

(I) made by or with the approval of an executive officer of that entity, and

(II) made or approved by such officer with actual knowledge by that officer that the statement was false or misleading.

(2) *Oral forward-looking statements.*—In the case of an oral forward-looking statement made by an issuer that is subject to the reporting requirements of section 13(a) or section 15(d) of the Securities Exchange Act of 1934, or by a person acting on behalf of such issuer, the requirement set forth in paragraph (1)(A) shall be deemed to be satisfied—

(A) if the oral forward-looking statement is accompanied by a cautionary statement—

(i) that the particular oral statement is a forward-looking statement; and

(ii) that the actual results could differ materially from those projected in the forward-looking statement; and

(B) if—

(i) the oral forward-looking statement is accompanied by an oral statement that additional information concerning factors that could cause actual results to differ materially from those in the forward-looking statement is contained in a readily available written document, or portion thereof;

(ii) the accompanying oral statement referred to in clause (i) identifies the document, or portion thereof, that contains the additional information about those factors relating to the forward-looking statement; and

(iii) the information contained in that written document is a cautionary statement that satisfies the standard established in paragraph (1)(A).

(3) *Availability.*—Any document filed with the Commission or generally disseminated shall be deemed to be readily available for purposes of paragraph (2).

(4) *Effect on other safe harbors.*—The exemption provided for in paragraph (1) shall be in addition to any exemption that the Commission may establish by rule or regulation under subsection (g).

(d) Duty To Update

Nothing in this section shall impose upon any person a duty to update a forward-looking statement.

(e) Dispositive Motion

On any motion to dismiss based upon subsection (c)(1), the court shall consider any statement cited in the complaint and cautionary statement accompanying the forward-looking statement, which are not subject to material dispute, cited by the defendant.

(f) Stay Pending Decision on Motion

In any private action arising under this title, the court shall stay discovery (other than discovery that is specifically directed to the applicability of the exemption provided for in this section) during the pendency of any motion by a defendant for summary judgment that is based on the grounds that—

(1) the statement or omission upon which the complaint is based is a forward-looking statement within the meaning of this section; and

(2) the exemption provided for in this section precludes a claim for relief.

(g) Exemption Authority

In addition to the exemptions provided for in this section, the Commission may, by rule or regulation, provide exemptions from or under any provision of this title, including with respect to liability that is based on a statement or that is based on projections or other forward-looking information, if and to the extent that any such exemption is consistent with the public interest and the protection of investors, as determined by the Commission.

(h) Effect on Other Authority of Commission

Nothing in this section limits, either expressly or by implication, the authority of the Commission to exercise similar authority or to adopt similar rules and regulations with respect to forward-looking statements under any other statute under which the Commission exercises rulemaking authority.

(i) Definitions

For purposes of this section, the following definitions shall apply:

(1) *Forward-looking statement.*—The term "forward-looking statement" means—

(A) a statement containing a projection of revenues, income (including income loss), earnings (including earnings loss) per share, capital expenditures, dividends, capital structure, or other financial items;

(B) a statement of the plans and objectives of management for future operations, including plans or objectives relating to the products or services of the issuer;

(C) a statement of future economic performance, including any such statement contained in a discussion and analysis of financial condition by the management or in the results of operations included pursuant to the rules and regulations of the Commission;

(D) any statement of the assumptions underlying or relating to any statement described in subparagraph (A), (B), or (C);

(E) any report issued by an outside reviewer retained by an issuer, to the extent that the report assesses a forward-looking statement made by the issuer; or

(F) a statement containing a projection or estimate of such other items as may be specified by rule or regulation of the Commission.

(2) *Investment company.*—The term "investment company" has the same meaning as in section 3(a) of the Investment Company Act of 1940.

(3) *Penny stock.*—The term "penny stock" has the same meaning as in section 3(a)(51) of the Securities Exchange Act of 1934, and the rules and regulations, or orders issued pursuant to that section.

(4) *Going private transaction.*—The term "going private transaction" has the meaning given that term under the rules or regulations of the Commission issued pursuant to section 13(e) of the Securities Exchange Act of 1934.

(5) *Securities laws.*—The term "securities laws" has the same meaning as in section 3 of the Securities Exchange Act of 1934.

(6) *Person acting on behalf of an issuer.*—The term "person acting on behalf of an issuer" means an officer, director, or employee of the issuer.

(7) *Other terms.*—The terms "blank check company", "roll-up transaction", "partnership", "limited liability company", "executive officer of an entity" and "direct participation investment program", have the meanings given those terms by rule or regulation of the Commission.

§ 28. General Exemptive Authority

The Commission, by rule or regulation, may conditionally or unconditionally exempt any person, security, or transaction, or any class or classes of persons, securities, or transactions, from any provision or provisions of this subchapter or of any rule or regulation issued under subchapter, to the extent that such exemption is necessary or appropriate in the public interest, and is consistent with the protection of investors.

RULES AND FORMS UNDER THE SECURITIES ACT OF 1933 (SELECTED PROVISIONS)

17 C.F.R. §§ 230.100 et seq.

GENERAL

REGULATION A—CONDITIONAL SMALL ISSUES EXEMPTION

GENERAL

Rule 134.   Communications Not Deemed a Prospectus

The term "prospectus" as defined in section 2(10) of the Act shall not include a notice, circular, advertisement, letter, or other communication published or transmitted to any person after a registration statement has been filed if it contains only the statements required or permitted to be included therein by the following provisions of this section:

(a) Such communication may include any one or more of the following items of information, which need not follow the numerical sequence of this paragraph:

* Omitted.

(1) The name of the issuer of the security;

(2) The full title of the security and the amount being offered;

(3) A brief indication of the general type of business of the issuer, limited to the following:

(i) In the case of a manufacturing company, the general type of manufacturing and the principal products or classes of products manufactured;

(ii) In the case of a public utility company, the general type of services rendered and a brief indication of the area served;

(iii) In the case of an investment company registered under the Investment Company Act of 1940, the company's classification and subclassification under the Act, whether it is a balanced, specialized, bond, preferred stock or common stock fund and whether in the selection of investments emphasis is placed upon income or growth characteristics, and a general description of an investment company including its general attributes, methods of operation and services offered provided that such description is not inconsistent with the operation of the particular investment company for which more specific information is being given, identification of the company's investment adviser, any logo, corporate symbol or trademark of the company or its investment adviser and any graphic design or device or an attention-getting headline, not involving performance figures, designed to direct the reader's attention to textual material included in the communication pursuant to other provisions of this rule . . . . ;

(iv) In the case of any other type of company, a corresponding statement;

(4) The price of the security, or if the price is not known, the method of its determination or the probable price range as specified by the issuer or the managing underwriter;

(5) In the case of a debt security with a fixed (non-contingent) interest provision, the yield or, if the yield is not known, the probable yield range, as specified by the issuer or the managing underwriter;

(6) The name and address of the sender of the communication and the fact that he is participating, or expects to participate, in the distribution of the security;

(7) The names of the managing underwriters;

(8) The approximate date upon which it is anticipated the proposed sale to the public will commence;

(9) Whether, in the opinion of counsel, the security is a legal investment for savings banks, fiduciaries, insurance companies, or similar investors under the laws of any State or Territory or the District of Columbia;

(10) Whether, in the opinion of counsel, the security is exempt from specified taxes, or the extent to which the issuer has agreed to pay any tax with respect to the security or measured by the income therefrom;

(11) Whether the security is being offered through rights issued to security holders, and, if so, the class of securities the holders of which will be entitled to subscribe, the subscription ratio, the actual or proposed record date, the date upon which the rights were issued or are expected to be issued, the actual or anticipated date upon which they will expire, and the approximate subscription price, or any of the foregoing;

(12) Any statement or legend required by any state law or administrative authority . . . . ;

(14)(i) With respect to any class of debt securities, any class of convertible debt securities or any class of preferred stock, the security rating or ratings assigned to the class of securities by any nationally recognized statistical rating organization and the name or names of the nationally recognized statistical rating organization(s) which assigned such rating(s) . . . .

(b) Except as provided in paragraph (c) of this section, every communication used pursuant to this section shall contain the following:

(1) If the registration statement has not yet become effective, the following statement:

> A registration statement relating to these securities has been filed with the Securities and Exchange Commission but has not yet become effective. These securities may not be sold nor may offers to buy be accepted prior to the time the registration statement becomes effective. This (communication) shall not constitute an offer to sell or the solicitation of an offer to buy nor shall there be any sale of these securities in any State in which such offer, solicitation or sale would be unlawful prior to registration or qualification under the securities laws of any such State.

(2) A statement whether the security is being offered in connection with a distribution by the issuer or by a security holder, or both, and whether the issue represents new financing or refunding or both; and

(3) The name and address of a person or persons from whom a written prospectus meeting the requirements of section 10 of the Act may be obtained.

(c) Any of the statements or information specified in paragraph (b) of this section may, but need not, be contained in a communication: (i) Which does no more than state from whom a written prospectus meeting the requirements of section 10 of the Act may be obtained, identify the security, state the price thereof and state by whom orders will be executed; or (ii) which is accompanied or preceded by a prospectus or a summary prospectus which meets the requirements of section 10 of the act at the date of such preliminary communication.

(d) A communication sent or delivered to any person pursuant to this rule which is accompanied or preceded by a prospectus which meets the requirements of section 10 of the Act at the date of such communication, may solicit from the recipient of the communication an offer to buy the security or request the recipient to indicate, upon an enclosed or attached coupon or card, or in some other manner, whether he might be interested in the security, if the communication contains substantially the following statement:

> No offer to buy the securities can be accepted and no part of the purchase price can be received until the registration statement has become effective, and any such offer may be withdrawn or revoked, without obligation or commitment of any kind, at any time prior to notice of its acceptance given after the effective date. An indication of interest in response to this advertisement will involve no obligation or commitment of any kind.

Provided, That such statement need not be included in such a communication to a dealer if the communication refers to a prior communication to the dealer, with respect to the same security, in which the statement was included.

Rule 135. Notice of Certain Proposed Offerings

(a) For the purpose only of section 5 of the Act, a notice given by an issuer that it proposes to make a public offering of securities to be registered under the Act shall not be deemed to offer any securities for sale if such notice states that the offering will be made only by means of a prospectus and contains no more than the following additional information:

(1) The name of the issuer;

(2) The title, amount, and basic terms of the securities proposed to be offered, the amount of the offering, if any, to be made by selling security holders, the anticipated time of the offering and a brief statement of the manner and purpose of the offering without naming the underwriters;

(3) In the case of a rights offering to security holders of the issuer, the class of securities the holders of which will be entitled to subscribe to the securities proposed to be offered, the subscription ratio, the proposed record date, the approximate date upon which the rights are proposed to be issued, the proposed term or expiration date of the rights and the approximate subscription price, or any of the foregoing;

(4) In the case of an offering of securities in exchange for other securities of the issuer or of another issuer, the name of the issuer and the title of the securities to be surrendered in exchange for the securities to be offered, the basis upon which the exchange may be made, or any of the foregoing;

(5) In the case of an offering to employees of the issuer or to employees of any affiliate of the issuer, the name of the employer and class or classes of employees to whom the securities are proposed to be offered, the offering price or basis of the offering and the period during which the offering is to be made, or any of the foregoing; and

(6) Any statement or legend required by State law or foreign or administrative authority.

(b) Any notice contemplated by this section may take the form of a news release or a written communication directed to security holders or employees, as the case may be, or other published statement.

(c) Notwithstanding the provisions of paragraphs (a) and (b) of this section, in the case of a rights offering of a security listed or subject to unlisted trading privileges on a national securities exchange or quoted on the NASDAQ inter-dealer quotation system information with respect to the interest rate, conversion ratio and subscription price may be disseminated through the facilities of the exchange, the consolidated transaction reporting system, the NASDAQ system or the Dow Jones broad tape, provided such information is already disclosed in a registration statement on file with the Commission.

Rule 135c. Notice of Certain Proposed Unregistered Offerings

(a) For the purposes only of Section 5 of the Act, a notice given by an issuer required to file reports pursuant to Section 13 or 15(d) of the Securities Exchange Act of 1934 or a foreign issuer that is exempt from registration under the Securities Exchange Act of 1934 pursuant to Rule 12g3–2(b) that it proposes to make, is making or has made an offering of securities not registered or required to be registered under the Act shall not be deemed to offer any securities for sale if:

(1) Such notice is not used for the purpose of conditioning the market in the United States for any of the securities offered;

(2) Such notice states that the securities offered will not be or have not been registered under the Act and may not be offered or sold in the United States absent registration or an applicable exemption from registration requirements; and

(3) Such notice contains no more than the following additional information:

(i) The name of the issuer;

(ii) The title, amount and basic terms of the securities offered, the amount of the offering, if any, made by selling security holders, the time of the offering and a brief statement of the manner and purpose of the offering without naming the underwriters;

(iii) In the case of a rights offering to security holders of the issuer, the class of securities the holders of which will be or were entitled to subscribe to the securities offered, the subscription ratio, the record date, the date upon which the rights are proposed to be or were issued, the term or expiration date of the rights and the subscription price, or any of the foregoing;

(iv) In the case of an offering of securities in exchange for other securities of the issuer or of another issuer, the name of the issuer and the title of the securities to be surrendered in exchange for the securities offered, the basis upon which the exchange may be made, or any of the foregoing;

(v) In the case of an offering to employees of the issuer or to employees of any affiliate of the issuer, the name of the employer and class or classes of employees to whom the securities are offered, the offering price or basis of the offering and the period during which the offering is to be or was made or any of the foregoing; and

(vi) Any statement or legend required by State or foreign law or administrative authority.

(b) Any notice contemplated by this section may take the form of a news release or a written communication directed to security holders or employees, as the case may be, or other published statements.

(c) Notwithstanding the provisions of paragraphs (a) and (b) of this section, in the case of a rights offering of a security listed or subject to unlisted trading privileges on a national securities exchange or quoted on the NASDAQ inter-dealer quotation system information with respect to the interest rate, conversion ratio and subscription price may be disseminated through the facilities of the exchange, the consolidated transaction reporting system, the NASDAQ system or the Dow Jones broad tape, provided such information is already disclosed in a Form 8–K on file with the Commission, in a Form 6–K furnished to the Commission or, in the case of an issuer relying on Rule 12g3–2(b), in a submission made pursuant to that Rule to the Commission.

(d) The issuer shall file any notice contemplated by this section with the Commission under cover of Form 8–K or furnish such notice under Form 6–K, as applicable, and, if relying on Rule 12g3–2(b), shall furnish such notice to the Commission in accordance with the provisions of that exemptive Section.

Rule 137. Definition of "Offers", "Participates", or "Participation" in Section 2(11) in Relation to Certain Publications by Persons Independent of Participants in a Distribution

The terms "offers", "participates", or "participation" in section 2(11) of the Act shall not be deemed to apply to the publication or distribution of information, opinions or recommendations with respect to the securities of a registrant which is required to file reports pursuant to section 13 or 15(d) of the Securities Exchange Act of 1934 and proposes to file, has filed or has an effective registration statement under the Securities Act of 1933 if—

(a) Such information, opinions, and recommendations are published and distributed in the regular course of its business by a broker or dealer which is not and does not propose to be a participant in the distribution of the security to which the registration statement relates; and

(b) Such broker or dealer receives no consideration, directly or indirectly, in connection with the publication and distribution of such information, opinions or recommendations from the registrant, a selling security holder or any participant in the distribution or any other person interested in the securities to which the registration statement relates, and such information, opinions or recommendations are not published or distributed pursuant to any arrangement or understanding, direct or indirect, with such registrant, underwriter, dealer, or selling security holder; *Provided, however,* That nothing herein shall forbid payment of the regular subscription or purchase price of the document or other written communication in which such information, opinions or recommendations appear.

Rule 139. Definition of "Offer for Sale" and "Offer to Sell" in Sections 2(10) and 5(c) in Relation to Certain Publications

Where a registrant which is required to file reports pursuant to section 13 or 15(d) of the Securities Exchange Act of 1934 ... proposes to file, has filed or has an effective registration statement under the Securities Act of 1933 relating to its securities, the publication or distribution by a broker or dealer of information, an opinion or a recommendation with respect to the registrant or any class of its securities shall not be deemed to constitute an offer for sale or offer to sell the securities registered or proposed to be registered for purposes of sections 2(10) and 5(c) of the Act, even though such broker or dealer is or will be a participant in the distribution of such securities, if the conditions of paragraph (a) or (b) of this section have been met:

(a)(1) The registrant meets the registrant requirements of Form S-3 ... or Form F-3 ... and the minimum float or investment grade securities provisions of either paragraph (B)(1) or (2) of General Instruction I of the respective form and such information, opinion or recommendation is contained in a publication which is distributed with reasonable regularity in the normal course of business....

(b)(1) Such information, opinion or recommendation is contained in a publication which:

(i) Is distributed with reasonable regularity in the normal course of business and

(ii) Includes similar information, opinions or recommendations with respect to a substantial number of companies in the registrant's industry, or sub-industry, or contains a comprehensive list of securities currently recommended by such broker or dealer.

(2) Such information, opinion or recommendation is given no materially greater space or prominence in such publication than that given to other securities or registrants; and

(3) An opinion or recommendation as favorable or more favorable as to the registrant or any class of its securities was published by the broker or dealer in the last publication of such broker or dealer addressing the registrant or its securities prior to the commencement of participation in the distribution.

Rule 144. Persons Deemed Not to Be Engaged in a Distribution and Therefore Not Underwriters

Preliminary Note

Rule 144 is designed to implement the fundamental purposes of the Act, as expressed in its preamble, "To provide full and fair disclosure of the character of the securities sold in interstate commerce and through the mails, and to prevent fraud in the sale thereof ..." The rule is designed to prohibit the creation of public markets in securities of issuers concerning which adequate current information is not available to the public. At the same time, where adequate current information concerning the issuer is available to the public, the rule permits the public sale in ordinary trading transactions of limited amounts of securities owned by persons controlling, controlled by or under common control with the issuer and by persons who have acquired restricted securities of the issuer.

Certain basic principles are essential to an understanding of the requirement of registration in the Act:

1. If any person utilizes the jurisdictional means to sell any nonexempt security to any other person, the security must be registered unless a statutory exemption can be found for the transaction.

2. In addition to the exemptions found in section 3, four exemptions applicable to transactions in securities are contained in section 4. Three of these section 4 exemptions are clearly not available to anyone acting as an "underwriter" of securities. (The fourth, found in section 4(4), is available only to those who act as brokers under certain limited circumstances.) An understanding of the term "underwriter" is therefore important to anyone who wishes to determine whether or not an exemption from registration is available for his sale of securities.

The term underwriter is broadly defined in section 2(11) of the Act to mean any person who has purchased from an issuer with a view to, or offers or sells for an issuer in connection with, the distribution of any security, or participates, or has a direct or indirect participation in any such undertaking, or participates or has a participation in the direct or indirect underwriting of any such undertaking. The interpretation of this definition has traditionally focused on the words "with a view to" in the phrase "purchased from an issuer with a view to ... distribution." Thus, an investment banking firm which arranges with an issuer for the public sale of its securities is clearly an "underwriter" under that section. Individual investors who are not professionals in the securities business may also be "underwriters" within the meaning of that term as used in the Act if they act as links in a chain of transactions through which securities move from an issuer to the public. Since it is difficult to ascertain the mental state of the purchaser at the time of his acquisition, subsequent acts and circumstances have been considered to determine whether such person took with a view to distribution at the time of his acquisition. Emphasis has been placed on factors such as the length of time the person has held the securities and whether there has been an unforeseeable change in circumstances of the holder. Experience has shown, however, that reliance upon such factors as the above has not assured adequate protection of investors through the maintenance of informed trading markets and has led to uncertainty in the application of the registration provisions of the Act.

It should be noted that the statutory language of section 2(11) is in the disjunctive. Thus, it is insufficient to conclude that a person is not an underwriter solely because he did not purchase securities from an issuer with a view to their distribution. It must also be established that the person is not offering or selling for an issuer in connection with the distribution of the securities, does not participate or have a direct or indirect participation in any such undertaking, and does not participate or have a participation in the direct or indirect underwriting of such an undertaking.

In determining when a person is deemed not to be engaged in a distribution several factors must be considered.

First, the purpose and underlying policy of the Act to protect investors requires that there be adequate current information concerning the issuer, whether the resales of securities by persons result in a distribution or are effected in trading transactions. Accordingly, the availability of the rule is conditioned on the existence of adequate current public information.

Secondly, a holding period prior to resale is essential, among other reasons, to assure that those persons who buy under a claim of a section 4(2) exemption have assumed the economic risks of investment, and therefore are not acting as conduits for sale to the public of unregistered securities, directly or indirectly, on behalf of an issuer. It should be noted that there is nothing in section 2(11) which places a time limit on a person's status as an underwriter. The public has the same need for protection afforded by registration whether the securities are distributed shortly after their purchase or after a considerable length of time.

A third factor, which must be considered in determining what is deemed not to constitute a "distribution", is the impact of the particular transaction or transactions on the trading markets. Section 4(1) was intended to exempt only routine trading transactions between individual investors with respect to securities already issued and not to exempt distributions by issuers or acts of other individuals who engage in steps necessary to such distributions. Therefore, a person reselling securities under section 4(1) of the Act must sell the securities in such limited quantities and in such a manner as not to disrupt the trading markets. The larger the amount of securities involved, the more likely it is that such resales may involve methods of offering and amounts of compensation usually associated with a distribution rather than routine trading transactions. Thus, solicitation of buy orders or the payment of extra compensation are not permitted by the rule.

In summary, if the sale in question is made in accordance with all of the provisions of the section as set forth below, any person who sells restricted securities shall be deemed not to be engaged in a distribution of such securities and therefore not an underwriter thereof. The rule also provides that any person who sells restricted or other securities on behalf of a person in a control relationship with the issuer shall be deemed not to be engaged in a distribution of such securities and therefore not to be an underwriter thereof, if the sale is made in accordance with all the conditions of the section.

(a) *Definitions.* The following definitions shall apply for the purposes of this section.

(1) An "affiliate" of an issuer is a person that directly, or indirectly through one or more intermediaries, controls, or is controlled by, or is under common control with, such issuer. ...

(3) The term "restricted securities" means:

(i) securities that are acquired directly or indirectly from the issuer, or from an affiliate of the issuer, in a transaction or chain of transactions not involving any public offering; or

(ii) securities acquired from the issuer that are subject to the resale limitations of Regulation D ... under the Act; or

(iii) securities that are subject to the resale limitations of Regulation D and acquired in a transaction or chain of transactions not involving any public offering; or

(iv) securities that are acquired in a transaction or chain of transactions meeting the requirements of Rule 144A.

(b) *Conditions to be met.* Any affiliate or other person who sells restricted securities of an issuer for his own account, or any person who sells restricted or any other securities for the account of an affiliate of the issuer of such securities, shall be deemed not to be engaged in a distribution of such securities and therefore not to be an underwriter thereof within the meaning of section 2(11) of the Act if all of the conditions of this section are met.

(c) *Current public information.* There shall be available adequate current public information with respect to the issuer of the securities. Such information shall be deemed to be available only if either of the following conditions is met:

(1) *Filing of reports.* The issuer has securities registered pursuant to section 12 of the Securities Exchange Act of 1934, has been subject to the reporting requirements of section 13 of that Act for a period of at least 90 days immediately preceding the sale of the securities and has filed all the reports required to be filed thereunder during the 12 months preceding such sale (or for such shorter period that the issuer was required to file such reports); or has securities registered pursuant to the Securities Act of 1933, has been subject to the reporting require- ments of section 15(d) of the Securities Exchange Act of 1934 for a period of at least 90 days immediately preceding the sale of the securities and has filed all the reports required to be filed thereunder during the 12 months preceding such sale (or for such shorter period that the issuer was required to file such reports). The person for whose account the securities are to be sold shall be entitled to rely upon a statement in whichever is the most recent report, quarterly or annual, required to be filed and filed by the issuer that such issuer has filed all reports required to be filed by section 13 or 15(d) of the Securities Exchange Act of 1934 during the preceding 12 months (or for such shorter period that the issuer was required to file such reports) and has been subject to such filing requirements for the past 90 days, unless he knows or has reason to believe that the issuer has not complied with such requirements. Such person shall also be entitled to rely upon a written statement from the issuer that it has complied with such reporting requirements unless he knows or has reasons to believe that the issuer has not complied with such requirements.

(2) *Other public information.* If the issuer is not subject to section 13 or 15(d) of the Securities Exchange Act of 1934, there is publicly available the information concerning the issuer specified in paragraph (a)(5)(i) to (xiv), inclusive, and paragraph (a)(5)(xvi) of Rule 15c2–11 [under the 1934 Act] or, if the issuer is an insurance company, the information specified in section 12(g)(2)(G)(i) of that Act.

(d) *Holding period for restricted securities.* If the securities sold are restricted securities, the following provisions apply:

(1) *General rule.* A minimum of one year must elapse between the later of the date of the acquisition of the securities from the issuer or from an affiliate of the issuer, and any resale of such securities in reliance on this section for the account of either the acquiror or any subsequent holder of those securities. If the acquiror takes the securi- ties by purchase, the one-year period shall not begin until the full

purchase price or other consideration is paid or given by the person acquiring the securities from the issuer or from an affiliate of the issuer. . . .

(e) *Limitation on amount of securities sold.* Except as hereinafter provided, the amount of securities which may be sold in reliance upon this rule shall be determined as follows:

(1) *Sales by affiliates.* If restricted or other securities are sold for the account of an affiliate of the issuer, the amount of securities sold, together with all sales of restricted and other securities of the same class for the account of such person within the preceding three months, shall not exceed the greater of

(i) One percent of the shares or other units of the class outstanding as shown by the most recent report or statement published by the issuer, or

(ii) The average weekly reported volume of trading in such securities on all national securities exchanges and/or reported through the automated quotation system of a registered securities association during the four calendar weeks preceding the filing of notice required by paragraph (h), or if no such notice is required the date of receipt of the order to execute the transaction by the broker or the date of execution of the transaction directly with a market maker, or

(iii) The average weekly volume of trading in such securities reported through the consolidated transaction reporting system contemplated by Rule 11Aa3–1 under the Securities Exchange Act of 1934 ... during the four-week period specified in paragraph (e)(1)(ii) of this section.

(2) *Sales by persons other than affiliates.* The amount of restricted securities sold for the account of any person other than an affiliate of the issuer, together with all other sales of restricted securities of the same class for the account of such person within the preceding three months, shall not exceed the amount specified in paragraphs (e)(1)(i), (ii) or (iii) of this section, whichever is applicable, unless the conditions of paragraph (k) of this rule are satisfied. . . .

(f) *Manner of sale.* The securities shall be sold in "brokers' transactions" within the meaning of section 4(4) of the Act or in transactions directly with a "market maker," as that term is defined in section 3(a)(38) of the Securities Exchange Act of 1934, and the person selling the securities shall not (1) solicit or arrange for the solicitation of orders to buy the securities in anticipation of or in connection with such transaction, or (2) make any payment in connection with the offer or sale of the securities to any person other than the broker who executes an order to sell the securities. . . .

(g) *Brokers' transactions.* The term "brokers' transactions" in section 4(4) of the Act shall for the purposes of this rule be deemed to include transactions by a broker in which such broker:

(1) Does no more than execute the order or orders to sell the securities as agent for the person for whose account the securities are sold; and receives no more than the usual and customary broker's commission;

(2) Neither solicits nor arranges for the solicitation of customers' orders to buy the securities in anticipation of or in connection with the transaction . . . .

(h) *Notice of proposed sale.* If the amount of securities to be sold in reliance upon the rule during any period of three months exceeds 500 shares or other units or has an aggregate sale price in excess of $10,000, three copies of a notice on Form 144 shall be filed with the Commission at its principal office in Washington, D.C.; and if such securities are admitted to trading on any national securities exchange, one copy of such notice shall also be transmitted to the principal exchange on which such securities are so admitted. The Form 144 shall be signed by the person for whose account the securities are to be sold and shall be transmitted for filing concurrently with either the placing with a broker of an order to execute a sale of securities in reliance upon this rule or the execution directly with a market maker of such a sale. Neither the filing of such notice nor the failure of the Commission to comment thereon shall be deemed to preclude the Commission from taking any action it deems necessary or appropriate with respect to the sale of the securities referred to in such notice. The requirements of this paragraph, however, shall not apply to securities sold for the account of any person other than an affiliate of the issuer, provided the conditions of paragraph (k) of this rule are satisfied.

(i) *Bona fide intention to sell.* The person filing the notice required by paragraph (h) of this section shall have a bona fide intention to sell the securities referred to therein within a reasonable time after the filing of such notice.

(j) *Non-exclusive rule.* Although this rule provides a means for reselling restricted securities and securities held by affiliates without registration, it is not the exclusive means for reselling such securities in that manner. Therefore, it does not eliminate or otherwise affect the availability of any exemption for resales under the Securities Act that a person or entity may be able to rely upon.

(k) *Termination of certain restrictions on sales of restricted securities by persons other than affiliates.* The requirements of paragraphs (c), (e), (f) and (h) of this rule shall not apply to restricted securities sold for the account of a person who is not an affiliate of the issuer at the time of the sale and has not been an affiliate during the preceding three months, provided a period of at least two years has elapsed since the later of the date the securities were acquired from the issuer or from an affiliate of the issuer. The two-year period shall be calculated as described in paragraph (d) of this rule. . . .

Rule 144A.   Private Resales of Securities to Institutions

Preliminary Notes

1. This section relates solely to the application of Section 5 of the Act and not to antifraud or other provisions of the federal securities laws.

2. Attempted compliance with this section does not act as an exclusive election; any seller hereunder may also claim the availability of any other applicable exemption from the registration requirements of the Act.

3. In view of the objective of this section and the policies underlying the Act, this section is not available with respect to any transaction or series of transactions that, although in technical compliance with this section, is part of a plan or scheme to evade the registration provisions of the Act. In such cases, registration under the Act is required.

4. Nothing in this section obviates the need for any issuer or any other person to comply with the securities registration or broker-dealer registration requirements of the Securities Exchange Act of 1934 (the "Exchange Act"), whenever such requirements are applicable.

5. Nothing in this section obviates the need for any person to comply with any applicable state law relating to the offer or sale of securities.

6. Securities acquired in a transaction made pursuant to the provisions of this section are deemed to be "restricted securities" within the meaning of Rule 144(a)(3).

7. The fact that purchasers of securities from the issuer thereof may purchase such securities with a view to reselling such securities pursuant to this section will not affect the availability to such issuer of an exemption under Section 4(2) of the Act, or Regulation D under the Act, from the registration requirements of the Act.

(a) *Definitions*

(1) For purposes of this section, "qualified institutional buyer" shall mean:

(i) Any of the following entities, acting for its own account or the accounts of other qualified institutional buyers, that in the aggregate owns and invests on a discretionary basis at least $100 million in securities of issuers that are not affiliated with the entity:

(A) Any *insurance company* as defined in Section 2(13) of the Act;

> *NOTE:* A purchase by an insurance company for one or more of its separate accounts, as defined by section 2(a)(37) of the Investment Company Act of 1940 (the "Investment Company Act"), which are neither registered under section 8 of the

Investment Company Act nor required to be so registered, shall be deemed to be a purchase for the account of such insurance company.

(B) Any *investment company* registered under the Investment Company Act or any *business development company* as defined in Section 2(a)(48) of that Act;

(C) Any *Small Business Investment Company* licensed by the U.S. Small Business Administration under Section 301(c) or (d) of the Small Business Investment Act of 1958;

(D) Any *plan* established and maintained by a state, its political subdivisions, or any agency or instrumentality of a state or its political subdivisions, for the benefit of its employees;

(E) Any *employee benefit plan* within the meaning of Title I of the Employee Retirement Income Security Act of 1974;

(F) Any *trust fund* whose trustee is a bank or trust company and whose participants are exclusively plans of the types identified in paragraph (a)(1)(i)(D) or (E) of this section, except trust funds that include as participants individual retirement accounts or H.R. 10 plans.

(G) Any *business development company* as defined in Section 202(a)(22) of the Investment Advisers Act of 1940;

(H) Any *organization described in Section 501(c)(3)* of the Internal Revenue Code, corporation (other than a bank as defined in Section 3(a)(2) of the Act or a savings and loan association or other institution referenced in Section 3(a)(5)(A) of the Act or a foreign bank or savings and loan association or equivalent institution), partnership, or Massachusetts or similar business trust; and

(I) Any *investment adviser* registered under the Investment Advisers Act.

(ii) Any *dealer* registered pursuant to Section 15 of the Exchange Act, acting for its own account or the accounts of other qualified institutional buyers, that in the aggregate owns and invests on a discretionary basis at least $10 million of securities of issuers that are not affiliated with the dealer, *provided that* securities constituting the whole or a part of an unsold allotment to or subscription by a dealer as a participant in a public offering shall not be deemed to be owned by such dealer;

(iii) Any *dealer* registered pursuant to Section 15 of the Exchange Act acting in a riskless principal transaction on behalf of a qualified institutional buyer . . . ;

(iv) Any investment company registered under the Investment Company Act, acting for its own account or for the accounts of other qualified institutional buyers, that is part of a *family of investment companies* which own in the aggregate at least $100 million in securities of issuers, other than issuers that are affiliated with the investment company or are part of such family of investment companies. "Family of investment companies" means any two or more investment companies registered under the Investment Company Act, except for a unit investment trust whose assets consist solely of shares of one or more registered investment companies, that have the same investment adviser (or, in the case of unit investment trusts, the same depositor)...;

(v) Any entity, all of the equity owners of which are qualified institutional buyers, acting for its own account or the accounts of other qualified institutional buyers; and

(vi) Any *bank* as defined in Section 3(a)(2) of the Act, any *savings and loan association* or other institution as referenced in Section 3(a)(5)(A) of the Act, *or any foreign bank or savings and loan association or equivalent institution,* acting for its own account or the accounts of other qualified institutional buyers, that in the aggregate owns and invests on a discretionary basis at least $100 million in securities of issuers that are not affiliated with it and that has an audited net worth of at least $25 million as demonstrated in its latest annual financial statements, as of a date not more than 16 months preceding the date of sale ... in the case of a U.S. bank or savings and loan association, and not more than 18 months preceding such date of sale for a foreign bank or savings and loan association or equivalent institution.

(2) In determining the aggregate amount of securities owned and invested on a discretionary basis by an entity, the following instruments and interests shall be excluded: bank deposit notes and certificates of deposit; loan participations; repurchase agreements; securities owned but subject to a repurchase agreement; and currency, interest rate and commodity swaps.

(3) The aggregate value of securities owned and invested on a discretionary basis by an entity shall be the cost of such securities, except where the entity reports its securities holdings in its financial statements on the basis of their market value, and no current information with respect to the cost of those securities has been published. In the latter event, the securities may be valued at market for purposes of this section....

(5) For purposes of this section, "riskless principal transaction" means a transaction in which a dealer buys a security from any person and makes a simultaneous offsetting sale of such security to a qualified institutional buyer, including another dealer acting as riskless principal for a qualified institutional buyer....

(b) *Sales by Persons Other Than Issuers or Dealers.* Any person, other than the issuer or a dealer, who offers or sells securities in compliance with the conditions set forth in paragraph (d) of this section shall be deemed not to be engaged in a distribution of such securities and therefore not to be an underwriter of such securities within the meaning of Sections 2(11) and 4(1) of the Act.

(c) *Sales by Dealers.* Any dealer who offers or sells securities in compliance with the conditions set forth in paragraph (d) of this section shall be deemed not to be a participant in a distribution of such securities within the meaning of Section 4(3)(C) of the Act and not to be an underwriter of such securities within the meaning of Section 2(11) of the Act, and such securities shall be deemed not to have been offered to the public within the meaning of Section 4(3)(A) of the Act.

(d) *Conditions to Be Met.* To qualify for exemption under this section, an offer or sale must meet the following conditions:

(1) The securities are offered or sold only to a qualified institutional buyer or to an offeree or purchaser that the seller and any person acting on behalf of the seller reasonably believe is a qualified institutional buyer . . . . ;

(2) The seller and any person acting on its behalf takes reasonable steps to ensure that the purchaser is aware that the seller may rely on the exemption from the provisions of Section 5 of the Act provided by this section;

(3) The securities offered or sold:

(i) Were not, when issued, of the same class as securities listed on a national securities exchange registered under Section 6 of the Exchange Act or quoted in a U.S. automated inter-dealer quotation system . . . ; and

(ii) Are not securities of an open-end investment company, unit investment trust or face-amount certificate company that is or is required to be registered under Section 8 of the Investment Company Act; and

(4)(i) In the case of securities of an issuer that is neither subject to Section 13 or 15(d) of the Exchange Act, nor exempt from reporting pursuant to Rule 12g3–2(b) under the Exchange Act, nor a foreign government as defined in Rule 405 eligible to register securities under Schedule B of the Act, the holder and a prospective purchaser designated by the holder have the right to obtain from the issuer, upon request of the holder, and the prospective purchaser has received from the issuer, the seller, or a person acting on either of their behalf, at or prior to the time of sale, upon such prospective purchaser's request to the holder or the issuer, the following information (which shall be reasonably current in relation to the date of resale under this section): a very brief statement of the nature of the business of the issuer and the products and services it offers; and the issuer's most recent balance sheet and profit and loss and retained earnings statements, and similar financial statements for such part of the two preceding fiscal years as the issuer has been in operation (the financial statements should be audited to the extent reasonably available).

(ii) The requirement that the information be "reasonably current" will be presumed to be satisfied if:

(A) the balance sheet is as of a date less than 16 months before the date of resale, the statements of profit and loss and retained earnings are for the 12 months preceding the date of such balance sheet, and if such balance sheet is not as of a date less than 6 months before the date of resale, it shall be accompanied by additional statements of profit and loss and retained earnings for the period from the date of such balance sheet to a date less than 6 months before the date of resale; and

(B) the statement of the nature of the issuer's business and its products and services offered is as of a date within 12 months prior to the date of resale; or

(C) with regard to foreign private issuers, the required information meets the timing requirements of the issuer's home country or principal trading markets.

(e) Offers and sales of securities pursuant to this section shall be deemed not to affect the availability of any exemption or safe harbor relating to any previous or subsequent offer or sale of such securities by the issuer or any prior or subsequent holder thereof.

Rule 145. Reclassification of Securities, Mergers, Consolidations and Acquisitions of Assets

Preliminary Note

Rule 145 ... is designed to make available the protection provided by registration under the Securities Act of 1933, as amended (Act), to persons who are offered securities in a business combination of the type described in paragraphs (a)(1), (2) and (3) of the rule. The thrust of the rule is that an "offer," "offer to sell," "offer for sale," or "sale" occurs when there is submitted to security holders a plan or agreement pursuant to which such holders are required to elect, on the basis of what is in substance a new investment decision, whether to accept a new or different security in exchange for their existing security. Rule 145 embodies the Commission's determination that such transactions are subject to the registration requirements of the Act . . . .

Transactions for which statutory exemptions under the Act, including those contained in sections 3(a)(9), (10), (11) and 4(2), are otherwise available are not affected by Rule 145. . . .

Note 2: A reclassification of securities covered by Rule 145 would be exempt from registration pursuant to section 3(a)(9) or (11) of the Act if the conditions of either of these sections are satisfied.

(a) *Transactions within this section.* An "offer," "offer to sell," "offer for sale," or "sale" shall be deemed to be involved, within the meaning of section 2(3) of the Act, so far as the security holders of a corporation or other person are concerned where, pursuant to statutory provisions of the jurisdiction under which such corporation or other person is organized, or pursuant to provisions contained in its certificate of incorporation or similar controlling instruments, or otherwise, there is submitted for the vote or consent of such security holders a plan or agreement for:

(1) *Reclassifications.* A reclassification of securities of such corporation or other person, other than a stock split, reverse stock split, or change in par value, which involves the substitution of a security for another security;

(2) *Mergers of Consolidations.* A statutory merger or consolidation or similar plan or acquisition in which securities of such corporation or other person held by such security holders will become or be exchanged for securities of any person, unless the sole purpose of the transaction is to change an issuer's domicile solely within the United States; or

(3) *Transfers of assets.* A transfer of assets of such corporation or other person, to another person in consideration of the issuance of securities of such other person or any of its affiliates, if:

(i) Such plan or agreement provides for dissolution of the corporation or other person whose security holders are voting or consenting; or

(ii) Such plan or agreement provides for a pro rata or similar distribution of such securities to the security holders voting or consenting; or

(iii) The board of directors or similar representatives of such corporation or other person, adopts resolutions relative to paragraph (a)(3)(i) or (ii) of this section within 1 year after the taking of such vote or consent; or

(iv) The transfer of assets is a part of a preexisting plan for distribution of such securities, notwithstanding paragraph (a)(3)(i), (ii), or (iii) of this section.

(b) *Communications not deemed to be a "Prospectus" or "Offer to Sell".* For the purpose of this section, the term "prospectus" as defined in section 2(10) of the Act and the term "offer to sell" in section 5 of the Act shall not be deemed to include the following:

(1) Any written communication or other published statement which contains no more than the following information: The name of the issuer of the securities to be offered, or the person whose assets are to be sold in exchange for the securities to be offered, and the names of other parties to any transaction specified in paragraph (a) of this section; a brief description of the business of parties to such transaction; the date, time, and place of the meeting of security holders to vote on or consent

to any such transaction specified in paragraph (a) of this section; a brief description of the transaction to be acted upon and the basis upon which such transaction will be made; and any legend or similar statement required by State or Federal law or administrative authority.

(2) Any written communication subject to and meeting the requirements of paragraph (a) of Rule 14a–12 [under the 1934 Act] and filed in accordance with paragraph (b) of that section.

(c) *Persons and parties deemed to be underwriters.* For purposes of this section, any party to any transaction specified in paragraph (a) of this section, other than the issuer, or any person who is an affiliate of such party at the time any such transaction is submitted for vote or consent, who publicly offers or sells securities of the issuer acquired in connection with any such transaction, shall be deemed to be engaged in a distribution and therefore to be an underwriter thereof within the meaning of section 2(11) of the Act. The term "party" as used in this paragraph (c) shall mean the corporations, business entities, or other persons, other than the issuer, whose assets or capital structure are affected by the transactions specified in paragraph (a) of this section.

(d) *Resale provisions for persons and parties deemed underwriters.* Notwithstanding the provisions of paragraph (c), a person or party specified therein shall not be deemed to be engaged in a distribution and therefore not to be an underwriter of registered securities acquired in a transaction specified in paragraph (a) of this section if:

(1) such securities are sold by such person or party in accordance with the provisions of paragraphs (c), (e), (f) and (g) of Rule 144;

(2) such person or party is not an affiliate of the issuer and a period of at least one year, as determined in accordance with paragraph (d) of Rule 144, has elapsed since the date the securities were acquired from the issuer in such transaction, and the issuer meets the requirements of paragraph (c) of Rule 144; or

(3) such person or party is not, and has not been for at least three months, an affiliate of the issuer, and a period of at least two years, as determined in accordance with paragraph (d) of Rule 144, has elapsed since the date the securities were acquired from the issuer in such transaction....

Rule 147. "Part of an Issue," "Person Resident," and "Doing Business Within" for Purposes of Section 3(a)(11)

Preliminary Notes

1. This rule shall not raise any presumption that the exemption provided by section 3(a)(11) of the Act is not available for transactions by an issuer which do not satisfy all of the provisions of the rule.

2. Nothing in this rule obviates the need for compliance with any state law relating to the offer and sale of the securities.

3. Section 5 of the Act requires that all securities offered by the use of the mails or by any means or instruments of transportation or communication in interstate commerce be registered with the Commission. Congress, however, provided certain exemptions in the Act from such registration provisions where there was no practical need for registration or where the benefits of registration were too remote. Among those exemptions is that provided by section 3(a)(11) of the Act for transactions in "any security which is a part of an issue offered and sold only to persons resident within a single State or Territory, where the issuer of such security is a person resident and doing business within . . . such State or Territory." The legislative history of that Section suggests that the exemption was intended to apply only to issues genuinely local in character, which in reality represent local financing by local industries, carried out through local investment. Rule 147 is intended to provide more objective standards upon which responsible local businessmen intending to raise capital from local sources may rely in claiming the section 3(a)(11) exemption.

All of the terms and conditions of the rule must be satisfied in order for the rule to be available. These are: (i) That the issuer be a resident of and doing business within the state or territory in which all offers and sales are made; and (ii) that no part of the issue be offered or sold to non-residents within the period of time specified in the rule. For purposes of the rule the definition of "issuer" in section 2(4) of the Act shall apply.

All offers, offers to sell, offers for sale, and sales which are part of the same issue must meet all of the conditions of Rule 147 for the rule to be available. The determination whether offers, offers to sell, offers for sale and sales of securities are part of the same issue (i.e., are deemed to be "integrated") will continue to be a question of fact and will depend on the particular circumstances. See Securities Act of 1933 Release No. 4434 (December 6, 1961) (26 FR 9158). Securities Act Release No. 4434 indicated that in determining whether offers and sales should be regarded as part of the same issue and thus should be integrated any one or more of the following factors may be determinative:

(i) Are the offerings part of a single plan of financing;

(ii) Do the offerings involve issuance of the same class of securities;

(iii) Are the offerings made at or about the same time;

(iv) Is the same type of consideration to be received; and

(v) Are the offerings made for the same general purpose.

Subparagraph (b)(2) of the rule, however, is designed to provide certainty to the extent feasible by identifying certain types of offers and sales of securities which will be deemed not part of an issue, for purposes of the rule only.

Persons claiming the availability of the rule have the burden of proving that they have satisfied all of its provisions. However, the rule does not establish exclusive standards for complying with the section 3(a)(11) exemption. The exemption would also be available if the issuer satisfied the standards set forth in relevant administrative and judicial interpretations at the time of the offering but the issuer would have the burden of proving the availability of the exemption. Rule 147 relates to transactions exempted from the registration requirements of section 5 of the Act by section 3(a)(11). Neither the rule nor section 3(a)(11) provides an exemption from the registration requirements of section 12(g) of the Securities Exchange Act of 1934, the anti-fraud provisions of the federal securities laws, the civil liability provisions of section 12(2) of the Act or other provisions of the federal securities laws.

Finally, in view of the objectives of the rule and the purposes and policies underlying the Act, the rule shall not be available to any person with respect to any offering which, although in technical compliance with the rule, is part of a plan or scheme by such person to make interstate offers or sales of securities. In such cases registration pursuant to the Act is required.

4. The rule provides an exemption for offers and sales by the issuer only. It is not available for offers or sales of securities by other persons. Section 3(a)(11) of the Act has been interpreted to permit offers and sales by persons controlling the issuer, if the exemption provided by that section would have been available to the issuer at the time of the offering. See Securities Act Release No. 4434. Controlling persons who want to offer or sell securities pursuant to section 3(a)(11) may continue to do so in accordance with applicable judicial and administrative interpretations.

(a) *Transactions covered.* Offers, offers to sell, offers for sale and sales by an issuer of its securities made in accordance with all of the terms and conditions of this rule shall be deemed to be part of an issue offered and sold only to persons resident within a single state or territory where the issuer is a person resident and doing business within such state or territory, within the meaning of section 3(a)(11) of the Act.

(b) *Part of an issue.* (1) For purposes of this rule, all securities of the issuer which are part of an issue shall be offered, offered for sale or sold in accordance with all of the terms and conditions of this rule.

(2) For purposes of this rule only, an issue shall be deemed not to include offers, offers to sell, offers for sale or sales of securities of the issuer pursuant to the exemption provided by section 3 or section 4(2) of the Act or pursuant to a registration statement filed under the Act, that take place prior to the six month period immediately preceding or after the six month period immediately following any offers, offers for sale or sales pursuant to this rule, *Provided,* That, there are during either of said six month periods no offers, offers for sale or sales of securities by or

for the issuer of the same or similar class as those offered, offered for sale or sold pursuant to the rule.

(c) *Nature of the issuer.* The issuer of the securities shall at the time of any offers and the sales be a person resident and doing business within the state or territory in which all of the offers, offers to sell, offers for sale and sales are made.

(1) The issuer shall be deemed to be a resident of the state or territory in which:

(i) It is incorporated or organized, if a corporation, limited partnership, trust or other form of business organization that is organized under state or territorial law;

(ii) Its principal office is located, if a general partnership or other form of business organization that is not organized under any state or territorial law;

(iii) His principal residence is located if an individual.

(2) The issuer shall be deemed to be doing business within a state or territory if:

(i) The issuer derived at least 80 percent of its gross revenues and those of its subsidiaries on a consolidated basis

(A) For its most recent fiscal year, if the first offer of any part of the issue is made during the first six months of the issuer's current fiscal year; or

(B) For the first six months of its current fiscal year or during the twelve-month fiscal period ending with such six-month period, if the first offer of any part of the issue is made during the last six months of the issuer's current fiscal year

from the operation of a business or of real property located in or from the rendering of services within such state or territory; provided, however, that this provision does not apply to any issuer which has not had gross revenues in excess of $5,000 from the sale of products or services or other conduct of its business for its most recent twelve-month fiscal period;

(ii) The issuer had at the end of its most recent semi-annual fiscal period prior to the first offer of any part of the issue, at least 80 percent of its assets and those of its subsidiaries on a consolidated basis located within such state or territory;

(iii) The issuer intends to use and uses at least 80 percent of the net proceeds to the issuer from sales made pursuant to this rule in connection with the operation of a business or of real property, the purchase of real property located in, or the rendering of services within such state or territory; and

(iv) The principal office of the issuer is located within such state or territory.

(d) *Offerees and purchasers: Person Resident.* Offers, offers to sell, offers for sale and sales of securities that are part of an issue shall be made only to persons resident within the state or territory of which the issuer is a resident. For purposes of determining the residence of offerees and purchasers:

(1) A corporation, partnership, trust or other form of business organization shall be deemed to be a resident of a state or territory if, at the time of the offer and sale to it, it has its principal office within such state or territory.

(2) An individual shall be deemed to be a resident of a state or territory if such individual has, at the time of the offer and sale to him, his principal residence in the state or territory.

(3) A corporation, partnership, trust or other form of business organization which is organized for the specific purpose of acquiring part of an issue offered pursuant to this rule shall be deemed not to be a resident of a state or territory unless all of the beneficial owners of such organization are residents of such state or territory.

(e) *Limitation of resales.* During the period in which securities that are part of an issue are being offered and sold by the issuer, and for a period of nine months from the date of the last sale by the issuer of such securities, all resales of any part of the issue, by any person, shall be made only to persons resident within such state or territory.

(f) *Precautions against interstate offers and sales.* (1) The issuer shall, in connection with any securities sold by it pursuant to this rule:

(i) Place a legend on the certificate or other document evidencing the security stating that the securities have not been registered under the Act and setting forth the limitations on resale contained in paragraph (e) of this section;

(ii) Issue stop transfer instructions to the issuer's transfer agent, if any, with respect to the securities, or, if the issuer transfers its own securities make a notation in the appropriate records of the issuer; and

(iii) Obtain a written representation from each purchaser as to his residence.

(2) The issuer shall, in connection with the issuance of new certificates for any of the securities that are part of the same issue that are presented for transfer during the time period specified in paragraph (e), take the steps required by paragraphs (f)(1)(i) and (ii) of this section.

(3) The issuer shall, in connection with any offers, offers to sell, offers for sale or sales by it pursuant to this rule, disclose, in writing, the limitations on resale contained in paragraph (e) and the provisions of paragraphs (f)(1)(i) and (ii) and paragraph (f)(2) of this section.

Rule 153. Definition of "Preceded by a Prospectus", as Used in Section 5(b)(2), in Relation to Certain Transactions

(a) The term "preceded by a prospectus," as used in section 5(b)(2) of the Securities Act of 1933 . . . in respect of any requirement of delivery of a prospectus to a member of a national securities exchange, on account of a transaction in a security effected on such exchange, shall mean delivery, prior to such transaction, of copies of a prospectus descriptive of such security and meeting the requirements of section 10(a) . . . to such exchange by the issuer or any underwriter, for the purpose of redelivery to members of such exchange upon their request: *Provided,* That as to any transaction occurring prior to the expiration of forty days after the effective date of the registration statement or the expiration of forty days after the first date upon which the security was bona fide offered to the public by the issuer or by or through an underwriter after such effective date, whichever is later (exclusive of the time during which a stop order issued under section 8 is in effect as to such security):

(1) Such exchange shall theretofore have requested of the issuer or, if such requests shall not have been complied with, of a "principal underwriter" (as that term is defined in Rule 405), from time to time, such number of copies of such prospectus as may have appeared reasonably necessary to comply with the requests of its members, and shall have delivered from its supply on hand a copy to any member theretofore making a written request therefor, and

(2) The issuer or any underwriter shall theretofore have furnished such exchange with such reasonable number of copies of such prospectus as may have been requested by the exchange for the purpose stated above.

(b) The term "national securities exchange", as used herein shall mean a securities exchange registered as a national securities exchange under the Securities Exchange Act of 1934 . . . .

Rule 174. Delivery of Prospectus by Dealers: Exemptions Under Section 4(3) of the Act

The obligations of a dealer (including an underwriter no longer acting as an underwriter in respect of the security involved in such transactions) to deliver a prospectus in transactions in a security as to which a registration statement has been filed taking place prior to the expiration of the 40– or 90–day period specified in section 4(3) of the Act after the effective date of such registration statement or prior to the expiration of such period after the first date upon which the security was bona fide offered to the public by the issuer or by or through an underwriter after such effective date, whichever is later, shall be subject to the following provisions . . .

(b) No prospectus need be delivered if the issuer is subject, immediately prior to the time of filing the registration statement, to the reporting requirements of section 13 or 15(d) of the Securities Exchange Act of 1934.

(c) Where a registration statement relates to offerings to be made from time to time no prospectus need be delivered after the expiration of the initial prospectus delivery period specified in section 4(3) of the Act following the first bona fide offering of securities under such registration statement.

(d) If (1) the registration statement relates to the security of an issuer that is not subject, immediately prior to the time of filing the registration statement, to the reporting requirements of Section 13 or 15(d) of the Securities Exchange Act of 1934, and (2) as of the offering date, the security is listed on a registered national securities exchange or authorized for inclusion in an electronic interdealer quotation system sponsored and governed by the rules of a registered securities association, no prospectus need be delivered after the expiration of twenty-five calendar days after the offering date. For purposes of this provision, the term "offering date" refers to the later of the effective date of the registration statement or the first date on which the security was bona fide offered to the public.

(e) Notwithstanding the foregoing, the period during which a prospectus must be delivered by a dealer shall be:

(1) As specified in section 4(3) of the Act if the registration statement was the subject of a stop order issued under section 8 of the Act; or

(2) As the Commission may provide upon application or on its own motion in a particular case.

(f) Nothing in this section shall affect the obligation to deliver a prospectus pursuant to the provisions of section 5 of the Act by a dealer who is acting as an underwriter with respect to the securities involved or who is engaged in a transaction as to securities constituting the whole or a part of an unsold allotment to or subscription by such dealer as a participant in the distribution of such securities by the issuer or by or through an underwriter.

Rule 175. Liability for Certain Statements by Issuers

(a) A statement within the coverage of paragraph (b) of this section which is made by or on behalf of an issuer or by an outside reviewer retained by the issuer shall be deemed not to be a fraudulent statement (as defined in paragraph (d) of this section), unless it is shown that such statement was made or reaffirmed without a reasonable basis or was disclosed other than in good faith.

(b) This rule applies to the following statements:

(1) A forward-looking statement (as defined in paragraph (c) of this section) made in a document filed with the Commission, in Part I of a quarterly report on Form 10–Q . . ., or in an annual report to shareholders meeting the requirements of Rules 14a–3(b) and (c) or 14c–3(a) and (b) under the Securities Exchange Act of 1934, a statement reaffirming such forward-looking statement subsequent to the date the document was filed or the annual report was made publicly available, or a forward-looking statement made prior to the date the document was filed or the date the annual report was publicly available if such statement is reaffirmed in a filed document, in Part I of a quarterly report on Form 10–Q, or in an annual report made publicly available within a reasonable time after the making of such forward-looking statement; *Provided,* That

(i) At the time such statements are made or reaffirmed, either the issuer is subject to the reporting requirements of section 13(a) or 15(d) of the Securities Exchange Act of 1934 and has complied with the requirements of Rule 13a–1 or 15d–1 thereunder, if applicable, to file its most recent annual report on Form 10–K . . .; or if the issuer is not subject to the reporting requirements of section 13(a) or 15(d) of the Securities Exchange Act of 1934, the statements are made in a registration statement filed under [the Securities Act of 1933], offering statement or solicitation of interest written document or broadcast script under Regulation A or pursuant to section 12(b) or (g) of the Securities Exchange Act of 1934, and

(ii) The statements are not made by or on behalf of an issuer that is an investment company registered under the Investment Company Act of 1940; and

(2) Information which is disclosed in a document filed with the Commission, in Part I of a quarterly report on Form 10–Q . . . or in an annual report to shareholders meeting the requirements of Rules 14a–3(b) and (c) or 14c–3(a) and (b) under the Securities Exchange Act of 1934 . . . and which relates to (i) the effects of changing prices on the business enterprise, . . . or (ii) the value of proved oil and gas reserves . . . .

(c) For the purpose of this rule, the term "forward-looking statement" shall mean and shall be limited to:

(1) A statement containing a projection of revenues, income (loss), earnings (loss) per share, capital expenditures, dividends, capital structure or other financial items;

(2) A statement of management's plans and objectives for future operations;

(3) A statement of future economic performance contained in management's discussion and analysis of financial condition and results of operations included pursuant to Item 303 of Regulation S–K . . . or

(4) Disclosed statements of the assumptions underlying or relating to any of the statements described in paragraphs (c)(1), (2), or (3) of this section.

(d) For the purpose of this rule the term "fraudulent statement" shall mean a statement which is an untrue statement of a material fact, a statement false or misleading with respect to any material fact, an omission to state a material fact necessary to make a statement not misleading, or which constitutes the employment of a manipulative, deceptive, or fraudulent device, contrivance, scheme, transaction, act, practice, course of business, or an artifice to defraud, as those terms are used in the Securities Act of 1933 or the rules or regulations promulgated thereunder.

Rule 176. Circumstances Affecting the Determination of What Constitutes Reasonable Investigation and Reasonable Grounds for Belief Under Section 11 of the Securities Act

In determining whether or not the conduct of a person constitutes a reasonable investigation or a reasonable ground for belief meeting the standard set forth in section 11(c), relevant circumstances include, with respect to a person other than the issuer.

(a) The type of issuer;

(b) The type of security;

(c) The type of person;

(d) The office held when the person is an officer;

(e) The presence or absence of another relationship to the issuer when the person is a director or proposed director;

(f) Reasonable reliance on officers, employees, and others whose duties should have given them knowledge of the particular facts (in the light of the functions and responsibilities of the particular person with respect to the issuer and the filing);

(g) When the person is an underwriter, the type of underwriting arrangement, the role of the particular person as an underwriter and the availability of information with respect to the registrant; and

(h) Whether, with respect to a fact or document incorporated by reference, the particular person had any responsibility for the fact or document at the time of the filing from which it was incorporated. . . .

Rule 215. Accredited Investor

The term "accredited investor" as used in section 2(15)(ii) of the Securities Act of 1933 . . . shall include the following persons:

(a) Any savings and loan association or other institution specified in section 3(a)(5)(A) of the Act whether acting in its individual or fiduciary capacity; any broker or dealer registered pursuant to section 15 of the Securities Exchange Act of 1934; any plan established and maintained by a state, its political subdivisions, or any agency or instrumentality of a state or its political subdivisions, for the benefit of its employees, if such plan has total assets in excess of $5,000,000; any employee benefit plan within the meaning of Title I of the Employee Retirement Income Security Act of 1974, if the investment decision is made by a plan fiduciary, as defined in section 3(21) of such Act, which is a savings and loan association, or if the employee benefit plan has total assets in excess of $5,000,000 or, if a self-directed plan, with investment decisions made solely by persons that are accredited investors;

(b) Any private business development company as defined in section 202(a)(22) of the Investment Advisers Act of 1940;

(c) Any organization described in section 501(c)(3) of the Internal Revenue Code, corporation, Massachusetts or similar business trust, or partnership, not formed for the specific purpose of acquiring the securities offered, with total assets in excess of $5,000,000;

(d) Any director, executive officer, or general partner of the issuer of the securities being offered or sold, or any director, executive officer, or general partner of a general partner of that issuer;

(e) Any natural person whose individual net worth, or joint net worth with that person's spouse, at the time of his purchase exceeds $1,000,000;

(f) Any natural person who had an individual income in excess of $200,000 in each of the two most recent years or joint income with that person's spouse in excess of $300,000 in each of those years and has a reasonable expectation of reaching the same income level in the current year;

(g) Any trust, with total assets in excess of $5,000,000, not formed for the specific purpose of acquiring the securities offered, whose purchase is directed by a sophisticated person as described in Rule 506(b)(2)(ii); and

(h) Any entity in which all of the equity owners are accredited investors.

―――――

REGULATION A—CONDITIONAL
SMALL ISSUES EXEMPTION

Rule 251. Scope of Exemption

A public offer or sale of securities that meets the following terms and conditions shall be exempt under section 3(b) from the registration requirements of the Securities Act of 1933 (the "Securities Act"):

(a) *Issuer.* The issuer of the securities:

(1) is an entity organized under the laws of the United States or Canada, or any State, Province, Territory or possession thereof, or the District of Columbia, with its principal place of business in the United States or Canada;

(2) is not subject to section 13 or 15(d) of the Securities Exchange Act of 1934 (the "Exchange Act") immediately before the offering;

(3) is not a development stage company that either has no specific business plan or purpose, or has indicated that its business plan is to merge with an unidentified company or companies;

(4) is not an investment company registered or required to be registered under the Investment Company Act of 1940;

(5) is not issuing fractional undivided interests in oil or gas rights . . ., or a similar interest in other mineral rights; and

(6) is not disqualified because of Rule 262.

(b) *Aggregate Offering Price.* The sum of all cash and other consideration to be received for the securities ("aggregate offering price") shall not exceed $5,000,000, including no more than $1,500,000 offered by all selling security holders, less the aggregate offering price for all securities sold within the twelve months before the start of and during the offering of securities in reliance upon Regulation A. No affiliate resales are permitted if the issuer has not had net income from continuing operations in at least one of its last two fiscal years. . . .

(c) *Integration With Other Offerings.* Offers and sales made in reliance on this Regulation A will not be integrated with:

(1) prior offers or sales of securities; or

(2) subsequent offers or sales of securities that are:

(i) registered under the Securities Act, except as provided in Rule 254(d);

(ii) made in reliance on Rule 701;

(iii) made pursuant to an employee benefit plan;

(iv) made in reliance on Regulation S; or

(v) made more than six months after the completion of the Regulation A offering.

> *NOTE:* If the issuer offers or sells securities for which the safe harbor rules are unavailable, such offers and sales still may not be integrated with the Regulation A offering, depending on the particular facts and circumstances. . . .

(d) *Offering Conditions.*

(1) *Offers.*

(i) Except as allowed by Rule 254, no offer of securities shall be made unless a Form 1–A offering statement has been filed with the Commission.

(ii) After the Form 1–A offering statement has been filed:

(A) oral offers may be made;

(B) written offers under Rule 255 may be made;

(C) printed advertisements may be published or radio or television broadcasts made, if they state from whom a Preliminary Offering Circular or Final Offering Circular may be obtained, and contain no more than the following information:

(*1*) The name of the issuer of the security;

(*2*) the title of the security, the amount being offered and the per unit offering price to the public;

(*3*) the general type of the issuer's business; and

(*4*) a brief statement as to the general character and location of its property.

(iii) after the Form 1–A offering statement has been qualified, other written offers may be made, but only if accompanied with or preceded by a Final Offering Circular.

(2) *Sales.*

(i) No sale of securities shall be made until:

(A) the Form 1–A offering statement has been qualified;

(B) a Preliminary Offering Circular or Final Offering Circular is furnished to the prospective purchaser at least 48 hours prior to the mailing of the confirmation of sale to that person; and

(C) a Final Offering Circular is delivered to the purchaser with the confirmation of sale, unless it has been delivered to that person at an earlier time.

(ii) Sales by a dealer (including an underwriter no longer acting in that capacity for the security involved in such transaction) that take place within 90 days after the qualification of the Regulation A offering statement may be made only if the dealer delivers a copy of the current offering circular to the purchaser before or with the confirmation of sale. The issuer or underwriter of the offering shall provide requesting dealers with reasonable quantities of the offering circular for this purpose.

(3) *Continuous or delayed offerings.* Continuous or delayed offerings may be made under this Regulation A if permitted by Rule 415.

Rule 252. Offering Statement

(a) *Documents to Be Included.* The offering statement consists of the facing sheet of Form 1–A, the contents required by the form and any other material information necessary to make the required statements, in the light of the circumstances under which they are made, not misleading. . . .

(e) *Number of Copies and Where to File.* Seven copies of the offering statement, at least one of which is manually signed, shall be filed with the Commission's main office in Washington, D.C. . . .

(g) *Qualification.* (1) If there is no delaying notation as permitted by paragraph (g)(2) of this section or suspension proceeding under Rule 258, an offering statement is qualified without Commission action on the 20th calendar day after its filing.

(2) An offering statement containing the following notation can be qualified only by order of the Commission, unless such notation is removed prior to Commission action as described in paragraph (g)(3) of this section:

This offering statement shall only be qualified upon order of the Commission, unless a subsequent amendment is filed indicating the intention to become qualified by operation of the terms of Regulation A.

(3) The delaying notation specified in paragraph (g)(2) of this section can be removed only by an amendment to the offering statement that contains the following language:

This offering statement shall become qualified on the 20th calendar day following the filing of this amendment.

(h) *Amendments.*

(1) If any information in the offering statement is amended, an amendment, signed in the same manner as the initial filing, shall be filed. Seven copies of every amendment shall be filed with the Commission's main office in Washington, D.C.

(2) An amendment to include a delaying notation pursuant to paragraph (g)(2) or to remove one pursuant to paragraph (g)(3) of this section after the initial filing of an offering statement may be made by telegram, letter or facsimile transmission. Each such telegraphic amendment shall be confirmed in writing within a reasonable time by filing a signed copy. Such confirmation shall not be deemed an amendment.

Rule 253. Offering Circular

(a) *Contents.* An offering circular shall include the narrative and financial information required by Form 1–A.

(b) *Presentation of Information.* Information in the offering circular shall be presented in a clear, concise and understandable manner and in a type size that is easily readable. Repetition of information should be avoided; cross-referencing of information within the document is permitted.

(c) *Date.* An offering circular shall be dated approximately as of the date of the qualification of the offering statement of which it is a part.

(d) *Cover Page Legend.* The cover page of every offering circular shall display the following statement in capital letters printed in bold-faced type at least as large as that used generally in the body of such offering circular:

THE UNITED STATES SECURITIES AND EXCHANGE COMMISSION DOES NOT PASS UPON THE MERITS OF OR GIVE ITS APPROVAL TO ANY SECURITIES OFFERED OR THE TERMS OF THE OFFERING, NOR DOES IT PASS UPON THE ACCURACY OR COMPLETENESS OF ANY OFFERING CIRCULAR OR OTHER SELLING LITERATURE. THESE SECURITIES ARE OFFERED PURSUANT TO AN EXEMPTION FROM REGISTRATION WITH THE COMMISSION; HOWEVER, THE COMMISSION HAS NOT MADE AN INDEPENDENT DETERMINATION THAT THE SECURITIES OFFERED HEREUNDER ARE EXEMPT FROM REGISTRATION.

(e) *Revisions.* (1) An offering circular shall be revised during the course of an offering whenever the information it contains has become false or misleading in light of existing circumstances, material developments have occurred, or there has been a fundamental change in the information initially presented.

(2) An offering circular for a continuous offering shall be updated to include, among other things, updated financial statements, 12 months after the date the offering statement was qualified.

(3) Every revised or updated offering circular shall be filed as an amendment to the offering statement and requalified in accordance with Rule 252.

Rule 254. Solicitation of Interest Document for Use Prior to an Offering Statement

(a) An issuer may publish or deliver to prospective purchasers a written document or make scripted radio or television broadcasts to determine whether there is any interest in a contemplated securities offering. Following submission of the written document or script of the broadcast to the Commission, as required by paragraph (b) of this section, oral communications with prospective investors and other broadcasts are permitted. The written documents, broadcasts and oral communications are each subject to the antifraud provisions of the federal securities laws. No solicitation or acceptance of money or other consideration, nor of any commitment, binding or otherwise, from any prospective investor is permitted. No sale may be made until qualification of the offering statement.

(b) While not a condition to any exemption pursuant to this section:

(1) On or before the date of its first use, the issuer shall submit a copy of any written document or the script of any broadcast with the Commission's main office in Washington, D.C. (*Attention:* Office of Small Business Review). The document or broadcast script shall either contain or be accompanied by the name and telephone number of a person able to answer questions about the document or the broadcast.

NOTE: Only solicitation of interest material that contains substantive changes from or additions to previously submitted material needs to be submitted.

(2) The written document or script of the broadcast shall:

(i) state that no money or other consideration is being solicited, and if sent in response, will not be accepted;

(ii) state that no sales of the securities will be made or commitment to purchase accepted until delivery of an offering circular that includes complete information about the issuer and the offering;

(iii) state that an indication of interest made by a prospective investor involves no obligation or commitment of any kind; and

(iv) identify the chief executive officer of the issuer and briefly and in general its business and products.

(3) Solicitations of interest pursuant to this provision may not be made after the filing of an offering statement.

(4) Sales may not be made until 20 calendar days after the last publication or delivery of the document or radio or television broadcast.

(c) Any written document under this section may include a coupon, returnable to the issuer indicating interest in a potential offering, revealing the name, address and telephone number of the prospective investor.

(d) Where an issuer has a bona fide change of intention and decides to register an offering after using the process permitted by this section without having filed the offering statement prescribed by Rule 252, the Regulation A exemption for offers made in reliance upon this section will not be subject to integration with the registered offering, if at least 30 calendar days have elapsed between the last solicitation of interest and the filing of the registration statement with the Commission, and all solicitation of interest documents have been submitted to the Commission. With respect to integration with other offerings, see Rule 251(c).

(e) Written solicitation of interest materials submitted to the Commission and otherwise in compliance with this section shall not be deemed to be a prospectus as defined in Section 2(10) of the Securities Act.

Rule 255. Preliminary Offering Circulars

(a) Prior to qualification of the required offering statement, but after its filing, a written offer of securities may be made if it meets the following requirements:

(1) The outside front cover page of the material bears the caption "Preliminary Offering Circular," the date of issuance, and the following statement, which shall run along the left hand margin of the page and be printed perpendicular to the text, in boldfaced type at least as large as that used generally in the body of such offering circular:

An offering statement pursuant to Regulation A relating to these securities has been filed with the Securities and Exchange Commission.

Information contained in this Preliminary Offering Circular is subject to completion or amendment. These securities may not be sold nor may offers to buy be accepted prior to the time an offering circular which is not designated as a Preliminary Offering Circular is delivered and the offering statement filed with the Commission becomes qualified. This Preliminary Offering Circular shall not constitute an offer to sell or the solicitation of an offer to buy nor shall there be any sales of these securities in any state in which such offer, solicitation or sale would be unlawful prior to registration or qualification under the laws of any such state.

(2) The Preliminary Offering Circular contains substantially the information required in an offering circular by Form 1–A, except that information with respect to offering price, underwriting discounts or commissions, discounts or commissions to dealers, amount of proceeds, conversions rates, call prices, or other matters dependent upon the offering price may be omitted. The outside front cover page of the Preliminary Offering Circular shall include a bona fide estimate of the range of the maximum offering price and maximum number of shares or other units of securities to be offered or a bona fide estimate of the principal amount of debt securities to be offered.

(3) The material is filed as a part of the offering statement.

(b) If a Preliminary Offering Circular is inaccurate or inadequate in any material respect, a revised Preliminary Offering Circular or a complete Offering Circular shall be furnished to all persons to whom securities are to be sold at least 48 hours prior to the mailing of any confirmation of sale to such persons, or shall be sent to such persons under such circumstances that it would normally be received by them 48 hours prior to receipt of confirmation of the sale.

Rule 256.   Filing of Sales Material

While not a condition to an exemption pursuant to this provision, seven copies of any advertisement or written communication, or the script of any radio or television broadcast, shall be filed with the main office of the Commission in Washington, D.C.

> *NOTE:* Only sales material that contains substantive changes from or additions from previously filed material needs to be filed.

Rule 257.   Reports of Sales and Use of Proceeds

While not a condition to an exemption pursuant to this provision, the issuer and/or each selling security holder shall file seven copies of a report concerning sales and use of proceeds on Form 2–A, or other prescribed form with the main office of the Commission in Washington, D.C. This report shall be filed at the following times:

(a) every six months after the qualification of the offering statement or any amendment until substantially all the proceeds have been applied; and

(b) within 30 calendar days after the termination, completion or final sale of securities in the offering, or the application of the proceeds from the offering, whichever is the latest event. This report should be labelled the final report. For purposes of this section, the temporary investment of proceeds pending final application shall not constitute application of the proceeds.

Rule 258.   Suspension of the Exemption

(a) The Commission may at any time enter an order temporarily suspending a Regulation A exemption if it has reason to believe that:

(1) no exemption is available or any of the terms, conditions or requirements of the Regulation have not been complied with, including failures to provide the Commission a copy of the document or broadcast script under Rule 254, to file any sales material as required by Rule 256 or report as required by Rule 257;

(2) the offering statement [or] any sales or solicitation of interest material contains any untrue statement of a material fact or omits to state a material fact necessary in order to make the statements made, in light of the circumstances under which they are made, not misleading;

(3) the offering is being made or would be made in violation of section 17 of the Securities Act;

(4) an event has occurred after the filing of the offering statement which would have rendered the exemption hereunder unavailable if it had occurred prior to such filing;

(5) any person specified in paragraph (a) of Rule 262 has been indicted for any crime or offense of the character specified in paragraph

(a)(3) of Rule 262, or any proceeding has been initiated for the purpose of enjoining any such person from engaging in or continuing any conduct or practice of the character specified in paragraph (a)(4) of Rule 262;

(6) any person specified in paragraph (b) of Rule 262 has been indicted for any crime or offense of the character specified in paragraph (b)(1) of Rule 262, or any proceeding has been initiated for the purpose of enjoining any such person from engaging in or continuing any conduct or practice of the character specified in paragraph (b)(2) of Rule 262; or

(7) the issuer or any promoter, officer, director or underwriter has failed to cooperate, or has obstructed or refused to permit the making of an investigation by the Commission in connection with any offering made or proposed to be made in reliance on Regulation A.

(b) Upon the entry of an order under paragraph (a) of this section, the Commission will promptly give notice to the issuer, any underwriter and any selling security holder:

(1) that such order has been entered, together with a brief statement of the reasons for the entry of the order; and

(2) that the Commission upon receipt of a written request within 30 calendar days after the entry of the order, will within 20 calendar days after receiving the request, order a hearing at a place to be designated by the Commission.

(c) If no hearing is requested and none is ordered by the Commission, an order entered under paragraph (a) of this section shall become permanent on the 30th calendar day after its entry and shall remain in effect unless or until it is modified or vacated by the Commission. Where a hearing is requested or is ordered by the Commission, the Commission will, after notice of and opportunity for such hearing, either vacate the order or enter an order permanently suspending the exemption.

(d) The Commission may, at any time after notice of and opportunity for hearing, enter an order permanently suspending the exemption for any reason upon which it could have entered a temporary suspension order under paragraph (a) of this section. Any such order shall remain in effect until vacated by the Commission.

(e) All notices required by this section shall be given by personal service, registered or certified mail to the addresses given by the issuer, any underwriter and any selling security holder in the offering statement.

Rule 259. Withdrawal or Abandonment of Offering Statements

(a) If none of the securities which are the subject of an offering statement have been sold and such offering statement is not the subject of a proceeding under Rule 258, the offering statement may be withdrawn with the Commission's consent. The application for withdrawal shall state the reason the offering statement is to be withdrawn, shall be signed by an authorized representative of the issuer and shall be provided to the main office of the Commission in Washington, D.C.

(b) When an offering statement has been on file with the Commission for nine months without amendment and has not become qualified, the Commission may, in its discretion, proceed in the following manner to determine whether such offering statement has been abandoned by the issuer. If the offering statement has been amended, the 9–month period shall be computed from the date of the latest amendment.

(1) Notice will be sent to the issuer, and to any counsel for the issuer named in the offering statement, by registered or certified mail, return receipt requested, addressed to the most recent addresses for the issuer and issuer's counsel as reflected in the offering statement. Such notice will inform the issuer and issuer's counsel that the offering statement or amendments thereto is out of date and must be either amended to comply with applicable requirements of Regulation A or be withdrawn within 30 calendar days after the notice.

(2) If the issuer or issuer's counsel fail to respond to such notice by filing a substantive amendment or withdrawing the offering statement or does not furnish a satisfactory explanation as to why the issuer has not done so within 30 calendar days, the Commission may declare the offering statement abandoned.

Rule 260. Insignificant Deviations From a Term, Condition or Requirement of Regulation A

(a) A failure to comply with a term, condition or requirement of Regulation A will not result in the loss of the exemption from the requirements of section 5 of the Securities Act for any offer or sale to a particular individual or entity, if the person relying on the exemption establishes:

(1) the failure to comply did not pertain to a term, condition or requirement directly intended to protect that particular individual or entity;

(2) the failure to comply was insignificant with respect to the offering as a whole, provided that any failure to comply with paragraphs (a), (b), (d)(1) and (3) of Rule 251 shall be deemed to be significant to the offering as a whole; and

(3) a good faith and reasonable attempt was made to comply with all applicable terms, conditions and requirements of Regulation A.

(b) A transaction made in reliance upon Regulation A shall comply with all applicable terms, conditions and requirements of the regulation. Where an exemption is established only through reliance upon paragraph (a) of this section, the failure to comply shall nonetheless be actionable by the Commission under section 20 of the Act.

(c) This provision provides no relief or protection from a proceeding under Rule 258.

Rule 261. Definitions

As used in this Regulation A, all terms have the same meanings as in Rule 405, except that all references to "registrant" in those definitions shall refer to the issuer of the securities to be offered and sold under Regulation A. In addition, these terms have the following meanings:

(a) Final Offering Circular—The current offering circular contained in a qualified offering statement;

(b) Preliminary Offering Circular—The offering circular described in Rule 255(a).

Rule 262. Disqualification Provisions

Unless, upon a showing of good cause and without prejudice to any other action by the Commission, the Commission determines that it is not necessary under the circumstances that the exemption provided by this Regulation A be denied, the exemption shall not be available for the offer or sale of securities, if:

(a) the issuer, any of its predecessors or any affiliated issuer:

(1) has filed a registration statement which is the subject of any pending proceeding or examination under section 8 of the Act, or has been the subject of any refusal order or stop order thereunder within 5 years prior to the filing of the offering statement required by Rule 252;

(2) is subject to any pending proceeding under Rule 258 or any similar section adopted under section 3(b) of the Securities Act, or to an order entered thereunder within 5 years prior to the filing of such offering statement;

(3) has been convicted within 5 years prior to the filing of such offering statement of any felony or misdemeanor in connection with the purchase or sale of any security or involving the making of any false filing with the Commission;

(4) is subject to any order, judgment, or decree of any court of competent jurisdiction temporarily or preliminarily restraining or enjoining, or is subject to any order, judgment or decree of any court of competent jurisdiction, entered within 5 years prior to the filing of such offering statement, permanently restraining or enjoining, such person from engaging in or continuing any conduct or practice in connection with the purchase or sale of any security or involving the making of any false filing with the Commission; or

(5) is subject to a United States Postal Service false representation order entered under 39 U.S.C. § 3005 within 5 years prior to the filing of the offering statement, or is subject to a temporary restraining order or

preliminary injunction entered under 39 U.S.C. § 3007 with respect to conduct alleged to have violated 39 U.S.C. § 3005. The entry of an order, judgment or decree against any affiliated entity before the affiliation with the issuer arose, if the affiliated entity is not in control of the issuer and if the affiliated entity and the issuer are not under the common control of a third party who was in control of the affiliated entity at the time of such entry does not come within the purview of this paragraph (a) of this section.

(b) any director, officer or general partner of the issuer, beneficial owner of 10 percent or more of any class of its equity securities, any promoter of the issuer presently connected with it in any capacity, any underwriter of the securities to be offered, or any partner, director or officer of any such underwriter:

(1) has been convicted within 10 years prior to the filing of the offering statement required by Rule 252 of any felony or misdemeanor in connection with the purchase or sale of any security, involving the making of a false filing with the Commission, or arising out of the conduct of the business of an underwriter, broker, dealer, municipal securities dealer, or investment adviser;

(2) is subject to any order, judgment, or decree of any court of competent jurisdiction temporarily or preliminarily enjoining or restraining, or is subject to any order, judgment, or decree of any court of competent jurisdiction, entered within 5 years prior to the filing of such offering statement, permanently enjoining or restraining such person from engaging in or continuing any conduct or practice in connection with the purchase or sale of any security, involving the making of a false filing with the Commission, or arising out of the conduct of the business of an underwriter, broker, dealer, municipal securities dealer, or investment adviser;

(3) is subject to an order of the Commission entered pursuant to section 15(b), 15B(a), or 15B(c) of the Exchange Act, or section 203(e) or (f) of the Investment Advisers Act of 1940;

(4) is suspended or expelled from membership in, or suspended or barred from association with a member of, a national securities exchange registered under section 6 of the Exchange Act or a national securities association registered under section 15A of the Exchange Act for any act or omission to act constituting conduct inconsistent with just and equitable principles of trade; or

(5) is subject to a United States Postal Service false representation order entered under 39 U.S.C. § 3005 within 5 years prior to the filing of the offering statement required by Rule 252, or is subject to a restraining order or preliminary injunction entered under 39 U.S.C. § 3007 with respect to conduct alleged to have violated 39 U.S.C. § 3005.

(c) any underwriter of such securities was an underwriter or was named as an underwriter of any securities:

(1) covered by any registration statement which is the subject of any pending proceeding or examination under section 8 of the Act, or is the subject of any refusal order or stop order entered thereunder within 5 years prior to the filing of the offering statement required by Rule 252; or

(2) covered by any filing which is subject to any pending proceeding under Rule 258 or any similar rule adopted under section 3(b) of the Securities Act, or to an order entered thereunder within 5 years prior to the filing of such offering statement.

———

FORM 1–A—REGULATION A OFFERING STATEMENT

SECURITIES AND EXCHANGE COMMISSION

FORM 1–A

REGULATION A OFFERING STATEMENT UNDER THE SECURITIES ACT OF 1933

———

(Exact name of issuer as specified in its charter)

———

(State or other jurisdiction of incorporation or organization)

———

(Address, including zip code, and telephone number, including area code of issuer's principal executive offices)

———

(Name, address, including zip code, and telephone number, including area code, of agent for service)

———

(Primary Standard Industrial Classification Code Number)   (I.R.S. Employer Identification Number)

. . .

GENERAL INSTRUCTIONS

1. Eligibility Requirements for Use of Form 1–A.

This form is to be used for securities offerings made pursuant to Regulation A . . . . Careful attention should be directed to the terms, conditions and requirements of the regulation, especially Rule 251, inasmuch as the exemption is not available to all issuers or to every type of securities transaction. Further, the aggregate offering amount of securities which may be sold in any 12 month period is strictly limited to $5 million.

II. Preparation and Filing of the Offering Statement.

An offering statement shall be prepared by all persons seeking exemption pursuant to the provisions of Regulation A. Parts I, II and III shall be addressed by all issuers. Part II of the form which relates to the content of the required offering circular provides several alternate formats depending upon the nature and/or business of the issuer; only one format needs to be followed and provided in the offering statement. General information regarding the preparation, format, content of, and where to file the offering statement is contained in Rule 252. Requirements relating to the offering circular are contained in Rules 253 and 255. The offering statement may be printed, mimeographed, lithographed, or typewritten or prepared by any similar process which will result in clearly legible copies.

III. Supplemental Information.

The following information shall be furnished to the Commission as supplemental information:

(1) A statement as to whether or not the amount of compensation to be allowed or paid to the underwriter has been cleared with the NASD.

(2) Any engineering, management or similar report referenced in the offering circular.

(3) Such other information as requested by the staff in support of statements, representations and other assertions contained in the offering statement.

[The balance of Form 1–A is omitted.]

———

REGULATION C—REGISTRATION . . . .

GENERAL REQUIREMENTS . . . .

Rule 405. Definitions of Terms

Unless the context otherwise requires, all terms used in 400 to 494, inclusive, or in the forms for registration have the same meanings as in the Act and in the general rules and regulations. In addition, the following definitions apply, unless the context otherwise requires:

Affiliate. An "affiliate" of, or person "affiliated" with, a specified person, is a person that directly, or indirectly through one or more intermediaries, controls or is controlled by, or is under common control with, the person specified. . . .

Associate. The term "associate," when used to indicate a relationship with any person, means (1) a corporation or organization (other than the registrant or a majority-owned subsidiary of the registrant) of which such person is an officer or partner or is, directly or indirectly, the beneficial owner of 10 percent or more of any class of equity securities, (2) any trust or other estate in which such person has a substantial beneficial interest or as to which such person serves as trustee or in a similar capacity, and (3) any relative or spouse of such person, or any relative of such spouse, who has the same home as such person or who is a director or officer of the registrant or any of its parents or subsidiaries. . . .

Control. The term "control" (including the terms "controlling," "controlled by" and "under common control with") means the possession, direct or indirect, of the power to direct or cause the direction of the management and policies of a person, whether through the ownership of voting securities, by contract, or otherwise. . . .

Equity security. The term "equity security" means any stock or similar security, certificate of interest or participation in any profit sharing agreement, preorganization certificate or subscription, transferable share, voting trust certificate or certificate of deposit for an equity security, limited partnership interest, interest in a joint venture, or certificate of interest in a business trust; or any security convertible, with or without consideration into such a security, or carrying any warrant or right to subscribe to or purchase such a security; or any such warrant or right; or any put, call, straddle, or other option or privilege of buying such a security from or selling such a security to another without being bound to do so.

Executive officer. The term "executive officer," when used with reference to a registrant, means its president, any vice president of the registrant in charge of a principal business unit, division or function (such as sales, administration or finance), any other officer who performs a policy making function or any other person who performs similar policy making functions for the registrant. Executive officers of subsidiaries may be deemed executive officers of the registrant if they perform such policy making functions for the registrant. . . .

Material. The term "material," when used to qualify a requirement for the furnishing of information as to any subject, limits the information required to those matters to which there is a substantial likelihood that a reasonable investor would attach importance in determining whether to purchase the security registered.

Officer. The term "officer" means a president, vice president, secretary, treasurer or principal financial officer, comptroller or principal accounting officer, and any person routinely performing corresponding functions with respect to any organization whether incorporated or unincorporated.

Parent. A "parent" of a specified person is an affiliate controlling such person directly, or indirectly through one or more intermediaries. . . .

Principal underwriter. The term "principal underwriter" means an underwriter in privity of contract with the issuer of the securities as to which he is underwriter, the term "issuer" having the meaning given in sections 2(4) and 2(11) of the Act.

Promoter. (1) The term "promoter" includes:

(i) Any person who, acting alone or in conjunction with one or more other persons, directly or indirectly takes initiative in founding and organizing the business or enterprise of an issuer; or

(ii) Any person who, in connection with the founding and organizing of the business or enterprise of an issuer, directly or indirectly receives in consideration of services or property, or both services and property, 10 percent or more of any class of securities of the issuer or 10 percent or more of the proceeds from the sale of any class of such securities. However, a person who receives such securities or proceeds either solely as underwriting commissions or solely in consideration of property shall not be deemed a promoter within the meaning of this paragraph if such person does not otherwise take part in founding and organizing the enterprise.

(2) All persons coming within the definition of "promoter" in paragraph (1) of this definition may be referred to as "founders" or "organizers" or by another term provided that such term is reasonably descriptive of those persons' activities with respect to the issuer....

Small Business Issuer. The term "small business issuer" means an entity that meets the following criteria:

(1) has revenues of less than $25,000,000;

(2) is a U.S. or Canadian issuer;

(3) is not an investment company; and

(4) if a majority owned subsidiary, the parent corporation is also a small business issuer.

Provided however, that an entity is not a small business issuer if it has a public float (the aggregate market value of the outstanding securities held by nonaffiliates) of $25,000,000 or more. ...

Subsidiary. A "subsidiary" of a specified person is an affiliate controlled by such person directly, or indirectly through one or more intermediaries. ...

Voting securities. The term "voting securities" means securities the holders of which are presently entitled to vote for the election of directors....

Rule 415. Delayed or Continuous Offering and Sale of Securities

(a) Securities may be registered for an offering to be made on a continuous or delayed basis in the future, *Provided,* That:

(1) The registration statement pertains only to:

(i) Securities which are to be offered or sold solely by or on behalf of a person or persons other than the registrant, a subsidiary of the registrant or a person of which the registrant is a subsidiary;

(ii) Securities which are to be offered and sold pursuant to a dividend or interest reinvestment plan or an employee benefit plan of the registrant;

(iii) Securities which are to be issued upon the exercise of outstanding options, warrants or rights;

(iv) Securities which are to be issued upon conversion of other outstanding securities;

(v) Securities which are pledged as collateral . . . ;

(vii) Mortgage related securities, including such securities as mortgage backed debt and mortgage participation or pass through certificates;

(viii) Securities which are to be issued in connection with business combination transactions;

(ix) Securities the offering of which will be commenced promptly, will be made on a continuous basis and may continue for a period in excess of 30 days from the date of initial effectiveness;

(x) Securities registered (or qualified to be registered) on Form S–3 or Form F–3 . . . which are to be offered and sold on a continuous or delayed basis by or on behalf of the registrant, a subsidiary of the registrant or a person of which the registrant is a subsidiary. . . .

(2) Securities in paragraphs (a)(1)(viii) through (x) may only be registered in an amount which, at the time the registration statement becomes effective, is reasonably expected to be offered and sold within two years from the initial effective date of the registration.

(3) The registrant furnishes the undertakings required by Item 512(a) of Regulation S–K. . . .

(4) In the case of a registration statement pertaining to an at the market offering of equity securities by or on behalf of the registrant:

(i) The offering comes within paragraph (a)(1)(x); (ii) where voting stock is registered, the amount of securities registered for such purposes must not exceed 10% of the aggregate market value of the registrant's outstanding voting stock held by non-affiliates of the registrant (calculated as of a date within 60 days prior to the date of filing); (iii) the securities must be sold through an underwriter or underwriters, acting as principal(s) or as agent(s) for the registrant; and (iv) the underwriter or underwriters must be named in the prospectus which is part of the registration statement. As used in this paragraph, the term "at the market offering" means an offering of securities into an existing trading market for outstanding shares of the same class at other than a fixed price on or through the facilities of a national securities exchange or to or through a market maker otherwise than on an exchange. ...

Rule 427. Contents of Prospectus Used After Nine Months

There may be omitted from any prospectus used more than 9 months after the effective date of the registration statement any information previously required to be contained in the prospectus insofar as later information covering the same subjects, including the latest available certified financial statement, as of a date not more than 16 months prior to the use of the prospectus is contained therein.

Rule 430. Prospectus for Use Prior to Effective Date

A form of prospectus filed as a part of the registration statement shall be deemed to meet the requirements of section 10 of the Act for the purpose of section 5(b)(1) thereof prior to the effective date of the registration statement, provided such form of prospectus contains substantially the information required by the Act and the rules and regulations thereunder to be included in a prospectus meeting the requirements of section 10(a) of the Act for the securities being registered, or contains substantially that information except for the omission of information with respect to the offering price, underwriting discounts or commissions, discounts or commissions to dealers, amount of proceeds, conversion rates, call prices, or other matters dependent upon the offering price. Every such form of prospectus shall be deemed to have been filed as a part of the registration statement for the purpose of section 7 of the Act.

Rule 431. Summary Prospectuses

(a) A summary prospectus prepared and filed as a part of a registration statement in accordance with this rule shall be deemed to be a prospectus permitted under section 10(b) of the Act for the purpose of section 5(b)(1) of the Act if the form used for registration of the securities to be offered provides for the use of a summary prospectus and, if the issuer is not a registered open-end investment company, the following conditions are met:

(1)(i) The registrant is organized under the laws of the United States or any State or Territory or the District of Columbia and has its principal business operations in the United States or its territories; or

(ii) The registrant is a foreign private issuer eligible to use Form F-2...;

(2) The registrant has a class of securities registered pursuant to section 12(b) of the Securities Exchange Act of 1934 or has a class of equity securities registered pursuant to section 12(g) of that Act or is required to file reports pursuant to section 15(d) of that Act;

(3) The registrant: (i) Has been subject to the requirements of section 12 or 15(d) of the Securities Exchange Act of 1934 and has filed all the material required to be filed pursuant to sections 13, 14 or 15(d) of that Act for a period of at least thirty-six calendar months immediately preceding the filing of the registration statement; and (ii) has filed in a timely manner all reports required to be filed during the twelve calendar months and any portion of a month immediately preceding the filing of the registration statement and . . .

(4) Neither the registrant nor any of its consolidated or unconsolidated subsidiaries has, since the end of its last fiscal year for which certified financial statements of the registrant and its consolidated subsidiaries were included in a report filed pursuant to section 13(a) or 15(d) of the Securities Exchange Act of 1934: (i) failed to pay any dividend or sinking fund installment on preferred stock; or (ii) defaulted on any installment or installments on indebtedness for borrowed money, or on any rental on one or more long term leases, which defaults in the aggregate are material to the financial position of the registrant and its consolidated and unconsolidated subsidiaries, taken as a whole.

(b) A summary prospectus shall contain the information specified in the instructions as to summary prospectuses in the form used for registration of the securities to be offered. Such prospectus may include any other information the substance of which is contained in the registration statement except as otherwise specifically provided in the instructions as to summary prospectuses in the form used for registration. It shall not include any information the substance of which is not contained in the registration statement except that a summary prospectus may contain any information specified in Rule 134(a). . . .

(c) All information included in a summary prospectus, other than the statement required by paragraph (e) of this section, may be expressed in such condensed or summarized form as may be appropriate in the light of the circumstances under which the prospectus is to be used. The information need not follow the numerical sequence of the items of the form used for registration. Every summary prospectus shall be dated approximately as of the date of its first use.

(d) When used prior to the effective date of the registration statement, a summary prospectus shall be captioned a "Preliminary Summary Prospectus" and shall comply with the applicable requirements relating to a preliminary prospectus.

(e) A statement to the following effect shall be prominently set forth in conspicuous print at the beginning or at the end of every summary prospectus:

"Copies of a more complete prospectus may be obtained from" (Insert name(s), address(es) and telephone number(s)).

Copies of a summary prospectus filed with the Commission pursuant to paragraph (g) of this section may omit the names of persons from whom the complete prospectus may be obtained.

(f) Any summary prospectus published in a newspaper, magazine or other periodical need only be set in type at least as large as 7 point modern type. Nothing in this rule shall prevent the use of reprints of a summary prospectus published in a newspaper, magazine, or other periodical, if such reprints are clearly legible.

(g) Eight copies of every proposed summary prospectus shall be filed as a part of the registration statement, or as an amendment thereto, at least 5 days (exclusive of Saturdays, Sundays and holidays) prior to the use thereof, or prior to the release for publication by any newspaper, magazine or other person, whichever is earlier. The Commission may, however, in its discretion, authorize such use or publication prior to the expiration of the 5–day period upon a written request for such authorization. Within 7 days after the first use or publication thereof, 5 additional copies shall be filed in the exact form in which it was used or published. . . .

Rule 460. Distribution of Preliminary Prospectus

(a) Pursuant to the statutory requirement that the Commission in ruling upon requests for acceleration of the effective date of a registration statement shall have due regard to the adequacy of the information respecting the issuer theretofore available to the public, the Commission may consider whether the persons making the offering have taken reasonable steps to make the information contained in the registration statement conveniently available to underwriters and dealers who it is reasonably anticipated will be invited to participate in the distribution of the security to be offered or sold.

(b) As a minimum, reasonable steps to make the information conveniently available would involve the distribution, to each underwriter and dealer who it is reasonably anticipated will be invited to participate in the distribution of the security, a reasonable time in advance of the anticipated effective date of the registration statement, of as many copies of the proposed form of preliminary prospectus permitted by Rule 430 . . . as appears to be reasonable to secure adequate distribution of the preliminary prospectus. . . .

REGULATION D—RULES GOVERNING THE LIMITED OFFER AND SALE OF SECURITIES WITHOUT REGISTRATION UNDER THE SECURITIES ACT OF 1933

Preliminary Notes

1. The following rules relate to transactions exempted from the registration requirements of section 5 of the Securities Act of 1933 (the

"Act") .... Such transactions are not exempt from the antifraud, civil liability, or other provisions of the federal securities laws. Issuers are reminded of their obligation to provide such further material information, if any, as may be necessary to make the information required under this regulation, in light of the circumstances under which it is furnished, not misleading. . . .

3. Attempted compliance with any rule in Regulation D does not act as an exclusive election; the issuer can also claim the availability of any other applicable exemption. For instance, an issuer's failure to satisfy all the terms and conditions of Rule 506 shall not raise any presumption that the exemption provided by section 4(2) of the Act is not available. . . .

5. These rules may be used for business combinations that involve sales by virtue of Rule 145(a) . . . or otherwise.

6. In view of the objectives of these rules and the policies underlying the Act, Regulation D is not available to any issuer for any transaction or chain of transactions that, although in technical compliance with these rules, is part of a plan or scheme to evade the registration provisions of the Act. In such cases, registration under the Act is required. . . .

Rule 501. Definitions and Terms Used in Regulation D

As used in Regulation D (Rules 501–506), the following terms shall have the meaning indicated:

(a) *Accredited investor.* "Accredited investor" shall mean any person who comes within any of the following categories, or who the issuer reasonably believes comes within any of the following categories, at the time of the sale of the securities to that person:

(1) Any bank as defined in section 3(a)(2) of the Act, or any savings and loan association or other institution as defined in section 3(a)(5)(A) of the Act whether acting in its individual or fiduciary capacity; any broker or dealer registered pursuant to section 15 of the Securities Exchange Act of 1934; any insurance company as defined in section 2(13) of the Act; any investment company registered under the Investment Company Act of 1940 or a business development company as defined in section 2(a)(48) of that Act; any Small Business Investment Company licensed by the U.S. Small Business Administration under section 301(c) or (d) of the Small Business Investment Act of 1958; any plan established and maintained by a state, its political subdivisions, or any agency or instrumentality of a state or its political subdivisions, for the benefit of its employees, if such plan has total assets in excess of $5,000,000; any employee benefit plan within the meaning of the Employee Retirement Income Security Act of 1974 if the investment decision is made by a plan fiduciary, as defined in section 3(21) of such Act, which is either a bank, savings and loan association, insurance company,

or registered investment adviser, or if the employee benefit plan has total assets in excess of $5,000,000 or, if a self-directed plan, with investment decisions made solely by persons that are accredited investors;

(2) Any private business development company as defined in section 202(a)(22) of the Investment Advisers Act of 1940;

(3) Any organization described in section 501(c)(3) of the Internal Revenue Code, corporation, Massachusetts or similar business trust, or partnership, not formed for the specific purpose of acquiring the securities offered, with total assets in excess of $5,000,000;

(4) Any director, executive officer, or general partner of the issuer of the securities being offered or sold, or any director, executive officer, or general partner of a general partner of that issuer;

(5) Any natural person whose individual net worth, or joint net worth with that person's spouse, at the time of his purchase exceeds $1,000,000;

(6) Any natural person who had an individual income in excess of $200,000 in each of the two most recent years or joint income with that person's spouse in excess of $300,000 in each of those years and has a reasonable expectation of reaching the same income level in the current year;

(7) Any trust, with total assets in excess of $5,000,000, not formed for the specific purpose of acquiring the securities offered, whose purchase is directed by a sophisticated person as described in Rule 506(b)(2)(ii); and

(8) Any entity in which all of the equity owners are accredited investors.

(b) *Affiliate.* An "affiliate" of, or person "affiliated" with, a specified person shall mean a person that directly, or indirectly through one or more intermediaries, controls or is controlled by, or is under common control with, the person specified.

(c) *Aggregate offering price.* "Aggregate offering price" shall mean the sum of all cash, services, property, notes, cancellation of debt, or other consideration to be received by an issuer for issuance of its securities. ...

(d) *Business combination.* "Business combination" shall mean any transaction of the type specified in paragraph (a) of Rule 145 under the Act ... and any transaction involving the acquisition by one issuer, in exchange for all or a part of its own or its parent's stock, of stock of another issuer if, immediately after the acquisition, the acquiring issuer has control of the other issuer (whether or not it had control before the acquisition).

(e) *Calculation of number of purchasers.* For purposes of calculating the number of purchasers under Rules 505(b) and 506(b) only, the following shall apply:

(1) The following purchasers shall be excluded:

(i) Any relative, spouse or relative of the spouse of a purchaser who has the same principal residence as the purchaser;

(ii) Any trust or estate in which a purchaser and any of the persons related to him as specified in paragraph (e)(1)(i) or (e)(1)(iii) of this Rule 501 collectively have more than 50 percent of the beneficial interest (excluding contingent interests);

(iii) Any corporation or other organization of which a purchaser and any of the persons related to him as specified in paragraph (e)(1)(i) or (e)(1)(ii) of this section collectively are beneficial owners of more than 50 percent of the equity securities (excluding directors' qualifying shares) or equity interests; and

(iv) Any accredited investor....

(f) *Executive officer.* "Executive officer" shall mean the president, any vice president in charge of a principal business unit, division or function (such as sales, administration or finance), any other officer who performs a policy making function, or any other person who performs similar policy making functions for the issuer. Executive officers of subsidiaries may be deemed executive officers of the issuer if they perform such policy making functions for the issuer. ...

(h) *Purchaser representative.* "Purchaser representative" shall mean any person who satisfies all of the following conditions or who the issuer reasonably believes satisfies all of the following conditions:

(1) Is not an affiliate, director, officer or other employee of the issuer, or beneficial owner of 10 percent or more of any class of the equity securities or 10 percent or more of the equity interest in the issuer ...;

(2) Has such knowledge and experience in financial and business matters that he is capable of evaluating, alone, or together with other purchaser representatives of the purchaser, or together with the purchaser, the merits and risks of the prospective investment;

(3) Is acknowledged by the purchaser in writing, during the course of the transaction, to be his purchaser representative in connection with evaluating the merits and risks of the prospective investment; and

(4) Discloses to the purchaser in writing a reasonable time prior to the sale of securities to that purchaser any material relationship between himself or his affiliates and the issuer or its affiliates that then exists, that is mutually understood to be contemplated, or that has existed at any time during the previous two years, and any compensation received or to be received as a result of such relationship.

Rule 502. General Conditions to Be Met

The following conditions shall be applicable to offers and sales made under Regulation D (Rules 501–506):

(a) *Integration.* All sales that are part of the same Regulation D offering must meet all of the terms and conditions of Regulation D. Offers and sales that are made more than six months before the start of a Regulation D offering or are made more than six months after completion of a Regulation D offering will not be considered part of that Regulation D offering, so long as during those six month periods there are no offers or sales of securities by or for the issuer that are of the same or a similar class as those offered or sold under Regulation D, other than those offers or sales of securities under an employee benefit plan . . . .

> NOTE: The term "offering" is not defined in the Act or in Regulation D. If the issuer offers or sells securities for which the safe harbor rule in paragraph (a) of this Rule 502 is unavailable, the determination as to whether separate sales of securities are part of the same offering (i.e. are considered "integrated") depends on the particular facts and circumstances. . . .

> The following factors should be considered in determining whether offers and sales should be integrated for purposes of the exemptions under Regulation D:

>   (a) whether the sales are part of a single plan of financing;

>   (b) whether the sales involve issuance of the same class of securities;

>   (c) whether the sales have been made at or about the same time;

>   (d) whether the same type of consideration is received; and

>   (e) whether the sales are made for the same general purpose. . . .

(b) *Information requirements* —(1) *When information must be furnished.* If the issuer sells securities under Rule 505 or Rule 506 to any purchaser that is not an accredited investor, the issuer shall furnish the information specified in paragraph (b)(2) of this section to such purchaser a reasonable time prior to sale. The issuer is not required to furnish the specified information to purchasers when it sells securities under Rule 504, or to any accredited investor.

> NOTE: When an issuer provides information to investors pursuant to paragraph (b)(1), it should consider providing such information to accredited investors as well, in view of the anti-fraud provisions of the federal securities laws.

(2) *Type of information to be furnished.*

(i) If the issuer is not subject to the reporting requirements of section 13 or 15(d) of the Exchange Act, at a reasonable time prior to the sale of securities the issuer shall furnish to the purchaser, to the extent material to an understanding of the issuer, its business and the securities being offered:

(A) *Non-financial statement information.* If the issuer is eligible to use Regulation A, the same kind of information as would be required in Part II of Form 1–A. If the issuer is not eligible to use Regulation A, the same kind of information as required in Part I of a registration statement filed under the Securities Act on the form that the issuer would be entitled to use.

(B) *Financial statement information. (1) Offering up to $2,000,000.* The information required in Item 310 of Regulation S–B, except that only the issuer's balance sheet, which shall be dated within 120 days of the start of the offering, must be audited.

(2) Offerings up to $7,500,000. The financial statement information required in Form SB–2. If an issuer, other than a limited partnership, cannot obtain audited financial statements without unreasonable effort or expense, then only the issuer's balance sheet, which shall be dated within 120 days of the start of the offering, must be audited. If the issuer is a limited partnership and cannot obtain the required financial statements without unreasonable effort or expense, it may furnish financial statements that have been prepared on the basis of Federal income tax requirements and examined and reported on in accordance with generally accepted auditing standards by an independent public or certified accountant.

(3) Offerings over $7,500,000. The financial statement as would be required in a registration statement filed under the Act on the form that the issuer would be entitled to use. If an issuer, other than a limited partnership, cannot obtain audited financial statements without unreasonable effort or expense, then only the issuer's balance sheet, which shall be dated within 120 days of the start of the offering, must be audited. If the issuer is a limited partnership and cannot obtain the required financial statements without unreasonable effort or expense, it may furnish financial statements that have been prepared on the basis of Federal income tax requirements and examined and reported on in accordance with generally accepted auditing standards by an independent public or certified accountant. . . .

(ii) If the issuer is subject to the reporting requirements of section 13 or 15(d) of the Exchange Act, at a reasonable time prior to the sale of securities the issuer shall furnish to the purchaser the information specified in paragraph (b)(2)(ii)(A) or (B) of this section, and in either event the information specified in paragraph (b)(2)(ii)(C) of this section:

(A) The issuer's annual report to shareholders for the most recent fiscal year, if such annual report meets the requirements of Rule 14a–3 or 14c–3 under the Exchange Act, the definitive proxy statement filed in connection with that annual report, and, if requested by the purchaser in writing, a copy of the issuer's most recent Form 10–K ... under the Exchange Act.

(B) The information contained in an annual report on Form 10–K ... under the Exchange Act or in a registration statement on Form S–1, Form S–11, or Form S–18 ..., under the Act or on Form 10 under the Exchange Act, whichever filing is the most recent required to be filed.

(C) The information contained in any reports or documents required to be filed by the issuer under sections 13(a), 14(a), 14(c), and 15(d) of the Exchange Act since the distribution or filing of the report or registration statement specified in paragraphs (b)(2)(ii)(A) or (B), and a brief description of the securities being offered, the use of the proceeds from the offering, and any material changes in the issuer's affairs that are not disclosed in the documents furnished. ...

(iii) Exhibits required to be filed with the Commission as part of a registration statement or report, other than an annual report to shareholders or parts of that report incorporated by reference in a Form 10–K ... report, need not be furnished to each purchaser that is not an accredited investor if the contents of material exhibits are identified and such exhibits are made available to the purchaser, upon his written request, a reasonable time prior to his purchase.

(iv) At a reasonable time prior to the sale of securities to any purchaser that is not an accredited investor in a transaction under Rule 505 or Rule 506, the issuer shall furnish to the purchaser a brief description in writing of any material written information concerning the offering that has been provided by the issuer to any accredited investor but not previously delivered to such unaccredited purchaser. The issuer shall furnish any portion or all of this information to the purchaser, upon his written request a reasonable time prior to his purchase.

(v) The issuer shall also make available to each purchaser at a reasonable time prior to his purchase of securities in a transaction under Rule 505 or 506 the opportunity to ask questions and receive answers concerning the terms and conditions of the offering and to obtain any additional information which the issuer possesses or can acquire without unreasonable effort or expense that is necessary to verify the accuracy of information furnished under paragraph (b)(2)(i) or (ii) of this Rule 502.

(vi) For business combinations or exchange offers, in addition to information required by Form S–4, the issuer shall provide to each purchaser at the time the plan is submitted to security holders, or, with an exchange, during the course of the transaction and prior to sale, written information about any terms or arrangements of the proposed transactions that are materially different from those for all other security holders. ...

(vii) At a reasonable time prior to the sale of securities to any purchaser that is not an accredited investor in a transaction under Rules 505 or 506, the issuer shall advise the purchaser of the limitations on resale in the manner contained in paragraph (d)(2) of this Rule. Such disclosure may be contained in other materials required to be provided by this paragraph.

(c) *Limitation on manner of offering.* Except as provided in Rule 504(b)(1), neither the issuer nor any person acting on its behalf shall offer or sell the securities by any form of general solicitation or general advertising, including, but not limited to, the following:

(1) Any advertisement, article, notice or other communication published in any newspaper, magazine, or similar media or broadcast over television or radio; and

(2) Any seminar or meeting whose attendees have been invited by any general solicitation or general advertising;

Provided, however, that publication by an issuer of a notice in accordance with Rule 135c shall not be deemed to constitute general solicitation or general advertising for purposes of this section.

(d) *Limitations on resale.* Except as provided in Rule 504(b)(1), securities acquired in a transaction under Regulation D shall have the status of securities acquired in a transaction under section 4(2) of the Act and cannot be resold without registration under the Act or an exemption therefrom. The issuer shall exercise reasonable care to assure that the purchasers of the securities are not underwriters within the meaning of section 2(11) of the Act, which reasonable care may be demonstrated by the following:

(1) Reasonable inquiry to determine if the purchaser is acquiring the securities for himself or for other persons;

(2) Written disclosure to each purchaser prior to sale that the securities have not been registered under the Act and, therefore, cannot be resold unless they are registered under the Act or unless an exemption from registration is available; and

(3) Placement of a legend on the certificate or other document that evidences the securities stating that the securities have not been registered under the Act and setting forth or referring to the restrictions on transferability and sale of the securities.

While taking these actions will establish the requisite reasonable care, it is not the exclusive method to demonstrate such care. Other actions by the issuer may satisfy this provision. In addition, Rule 502(b)(2)(vii) requires the delivery of written disclosure of the limitations on resale to investors in certain instances.

Rule 503. Filing of Notice of Sales

(a) An issuer offering or selling securities in reliance on Rule 504, Rule 505 or Rule 506 shall file with the Commission five copies of a notice on Form D no later than 15 days after the first sale of securities.

(b) One copy of every notice on Form D shall be manually signed by a person duly authorized by the issuer.

(c) If sales are made under Rule 505, the notice shall contain an undertaking by the issuer to furnish to the Commission, upon the written request of its staff, the information furnished by the issuer under Rule 502(b)(2) to any purchaser that is not an accredited investor.

. . .

Rule 504. Exemption for Limited Offerings and Sales of Securities Not Exceeding $1,000,000

(a) *Exemption.* Offers and sales of securities that satisfy the conditions in paragraph (b) of this Rule 504 by an issuer that is not:

(1) subject to the reporting requirements of section 13 or 15(d) of the Exchange Act;

(2) an investment company; or

(3) a development stage company that either has no specific business plan or purpose or has indicated that its business plan is to engage in a merger or acquisition with an unidentified company or companies, or other entity or person, shall be exempt from the provision of section 5 of the Act under section 3(b) of the Act.

(b) *Conditions to be met.* (1) To qualify for exemption under this Rule 504, offers and sales must satisfy the terms and conditions of Rules 501 and 502(a).

(2) The aggregate offering price for an offering of securities under this Rule 504, as defined in Rule 501(c), shall not exceed $1,000,000, less the aggregate offering price for all securities sold within the twelve months before the start of and during the offering of securities under this Rule 504, in reliance on any exemption under section 3(b), or in violation of section 5(a) of the Securities Act.

NOTE 1: The calculation of the aggregate offering price is illustrated as follows:

If an issuer sold $900,000 on June 1, 1987 under this Rule 504 and an additional $4,100,000 on December 1, 1987 under Rule 505, the issuer could not sell any of its securities under this Rule 504 until December 1, 1988. Until then the issuer must count the December 1, 1987 sale towards the $1,000,000 limit within the preceding twelve months.

NOTE 2: If a transaction under Rule 504 fails to meet the limitation on the aggregate offering price, it does not affect the availability of this Rule 504 for the other transactions considered in applying such limitation. For example, if an issuer sold $1,000,000 worth of its securities on January 1, 1988 under this Rule 504 and an additional $500,000 worth on July 1, 1988, this Rule 504 would not be available for the later sale, but would still be applicable to the January 1, 1988 sale.

Rule 505. Exemption for Limited Offers and Sales of Securities Not Exceeding $5,000,000

(a) *Exemption.* Offers and sales of securities that satisfy the conditions in paragraph (b) of this Rule 505 by an issuer that is not an investment company shall be exempt from the provisions of section 5 of the Act under section 3(b) of the Act.

(b) *Conditions to be met* —(1) *General conditions.* To qualify for exemption under this section, offers and sales must satisfy the terms and conditions of Rules 501 and 502.

(2) *Specific conditions* —(i) *Limitation on aggregate offering price.* The aggregate offering price for an offering of securities under this Rule 505, as defined in Rule 501(c), shall not exceed $5,000,000, less the aggregate offering price for all securities sold within the twelve months before the start of and during the offering of securities under this section in reliance on any exemption under section 3(b) of the Act or in violation of section 5(a) of the Act.

(ii) *Limitation on number of purchasers.* There are no more than or the issuer reasonably believes that there are no more than 35 purchasers of securities from the issuer in any offering under this section.

(iii) *Disqualifications.* No exemption under this section shall be available for the securities of any issuer described in Rule 262 of Regulation A, except that for purposes of this section only:

(A) The term "filing of the offering statement required by Rule 252" as used in Rule 262(a), (b) and (c) shall mean the first sale of securities under this Rule 505;

(B) The term "underwriter" as used in Rule 262(b) and (c) shall mean a person that has been or will be paid directly or indirectly remuneration for solicitation of purchasers in connection with sales of securities under this Rule 505; and

(C) Paragraph (b)(2)(iii) of this Rule 505 shall not apply to any issuer if the Commission determines, upon a showing of good cause, that it is not necessary under the circumstances that the exemption be denied. Any such determination shall be without prejudice to any other action by the Commission in any other proceeding or matter with respect to the issuer or any other person.

Rule 506. Exemption for Limited Offers and Sales Without Regard to Dollar Amount of Offering

(a) *Exemption.* Offers and sales of securities by an issuer that satisfy the conditions in paragraph (b) of this section shall be deemed to be transactions not involving any public offering within the meaning of section 4(2) of the Act.

(b) *Conditions to be met*—(1) *General conditions.* To qualify for an exemption under this Rule 506, offers and sales must satisfy all the terms and conditions of Rules 501 and 502.

(2) *Specific conditions*—(i) *Limitation on number of purchasers.* There are no more than or the issuer reasonably believes that there are no more than 35 purchasers of securities from the issuer in any offering under this section.

(ii) *Nature of purchasers.* Each purchaser who is not an accredited investor either alone or with his purchaser representative(s) has such knowledge and experience in financial and business matters that he is capable of evaluating the merits and risks of the prospective investment, or the issuer reasonably believes immediately prior to making any sale that such purchaser comes within this description.

Rule 507. Disqualifying Provision Relating to Exemptions Under Rule 504, Rule 505 and Rule 506

(a) No exemption under Rule 504, Rule 505 or Rule 506 shall be available for an issuer if such issuer, any of its predecessors or affiliates have been subject to any order, judgment, or decree of any court of competent jurisdiction temporarily, preliminarily or permanently enjoining such person for failure to comply with Rule 503.

(b) Paragraph (a) of this section shall not apply if the Commission determines, upon a showing of good cause, that it is not necessary under the circumstances that the exemption be denied.

Rule 508. Insignificant Deviations From a Term, Condition or Requirement of Regulation D

(a) A failure to comply with a term, condition or requirement of Rule 504, Rule 505 or Rule 506 will not result in the loss of the exemption from the requirements of section 5 of the Act for any offer or sale to a particular individual or entity, if the person relying on the exemption shows:

(1) the failure to comply did not pertain to a term, condition or requirement directly intended to protect that particular individual or entity; and

(2) The failure to comply was insignificant with respect to the offering as a whole, provided that any failure to comply with paragraph (c) of Rule 502, paragraph (b)(2) of Rule 504, paragraphs (b)(2)(i) and (ii)

of Rule 505 and paragraph (b)(2)(i) of Rule 506 shall be deemed to be significant to the offering as a whole; and

(3) a good faith and reasonable attempt was made to comply with all applicable terms, conditions and requirements of Rule 504, Rule 505 or Rule 506.

(b) A transaction made in reliance on Rule 504, Rule 505 or Rule 506 shall comply with all applicable terms, conditions and requirements of Regulation D. Where an exemption is established only through reliance upon paragraph (a) of this section, the failure to comply shall nonetheless be actionable by the Commission under section 20 of the Act.

FORM S–1

SECURITIES AND EXCHANGE COMMISSION

REGISTRATION STATEMENT UNDER THE SECURITIES ACT OF 1933

_____

(Exact name of registrant as specified in its charter)

_____

(State or other jurisdiction of incorporation or organization)

_____

(Primary Standard Industrial Classification Code Number)

_____

(I.R.S. Employer Identification No.)

_____

(Address, including zip code, and telephone number, including area code, of registrant's principal executive offices)

_____

(Name, address, including zip code, and telephone number, including area code, of agent for service)

Approximate date of commencement of proposed sale to the public _____. . . .

GENERAL INSTRUCTIONS

I. Eligibility Requirements for Use of Form S–1

This Form shall be used for the registration under the Securities Act of 1933 ("Securities Act") of securities of all registrants for which no other form is authorized or prescribed, except that this Form shall not be used for securities of foreign governments or political subdivisions thereof....

PART I—INFORMATION REQUIRED IN PROSPECTUS ....

Item 3.   Summary Information, Risk Factors and Ratio of Earnings to Fixed Charges....

Item 4.   Use of Proceeds....

Item 5.   Determination of Offering Price....

Item 6.   Dilution....

Item 7.   Selling Security Holders....

Item 8.   Plan of Distribution....

Item 9.   Description of Securities to Be Registered....

Item 10.   Interests of Named Experts and Counsel....

Item 11.   Information With Respect to the Registrant. Furnish the following information with respect to the registrant:

(a) Information required by Item 101 of Regulation S–K ... [concerning] description of business;

(b) Information required by Item 102 of Regulation S–K ... [concerning] description of property;

(c) Information required by Item 103 of Regulation S–K ... [concerning] legal proceedings;

(d) Where common equity securities are being offered, information required by Item 201 of Regulation S–K ... [concerning] market price of and dividends on the registrant's common equity and related stockholder matters;

(e) Financial statements meeting the requirements of Regulation S–X ...

(f) Information required by Item 301 of Regulation S–K ... [concerning] selected financial data;

(g) Information required by Item 302 of Regulation S–K ... [concerning] supplementary financial information;

(h) Information required by Item 303 of Regulation S–K ... [concerning] management's discussion and analysis of financial condition and results of operations;

(i) Information required by Item 304 of Regulation S–K ... [concerning] changes in and disagreements with accountants on accounting and financial disclosure;

(j) Information required by Item 401 of Regulation S–K ... [concerning] directors and executive officers;

(k) Information required by Item 402 of Regulation S–K ... [concerning] executive compensation;

(*l*) Information required by Item 403 of Regulation S–K ... [concerning] security ownership of certain beneficial owners and management;

(m) Information required by Item 404 of Regulation S–K ... [concerning] certain relationships and related transactions. ...

PART II—INFORMATION NOT REQUIRED IN PROSPECTUS

Item 13.   Other Expenses of Issuance and Distribution....

Item 14.   Indemnification of Directors and Officers....

Item 15.   Recent Sales of Unregistered Securities....

Item 16.   Exhibits and Financial Statement Schedules....

Item 17.   Undertakings....

FORM S–2

SECURITIES AND EXCHANGE COMMISSION

REGISTRATION STATEMENT UNDER
THE SECURITIES ACT OF 1933

(Exact name of registrant as specified in its charter)

(State or other jurisdiction of incorporation or
organization)

(I.R.S. Employer Identification No.)

(Address, including zip code, and telephone number,
including area code, of registrant's principal
executive offices)

(Name, address, including zip code, and telephone
number, including area code, of agent for service)

Approximate date of commencement of proposed sale to the public

————. ...

GENERAL INSTRUCTIONS

I.   Eligibility Requirements for Use of Form S–2

Any registrant which meets the following conditions may use this Form for registration of securities under the Securities Act of 1933

("Securities Act") which are offered or to be offered in any transaction other than an exchange offer for securities of another person:

A. The registrant is organized under the laws of the United States or any State or Territory or the District of Columbia and has its principal business operations in the United States or its territories.

B. The registrant has a class of securities registered pursuant to Section 12(b) of the Securities Exchange Act of 1934 ("Exchange Act") or has a class of equity securities registered pursuant to Section 12(g) of the Exchange Act or is required to file reports pursuant to Section 15(d) of the Exchange Act.

C. The registrant: (1) has been subject to the requirements of Section 12 or 15(d) of the Exchange Act and has filed all the material required to be filed pursuant to Sections 13, 14 or 15(d) for a period of at least thirty-six calendar months immediately preceding the filing of the registration statement on this Form; and (2) has filed in a timely manner all reports required to be filed during the twelve calendar months and any portion of a month immediately preceding the filing of the registration statement . . . .

D. Neither the registrant nor any of its consolidated or unconsolidated subsidiaries have, since the end of their last fiscal year for which certified financial statements of the registrant and its consolidated subsidiaries were included in a report filed pursuant to Section 13(a) or 15(d) of the Exchange Act: (a) failed to pay any dividend or sinking fund installment on preferred stock; or (b) defaulted (i) on any installment or installments on indebtedness for borrowed money, or (ii) on any rental on one or more long term leases, which defaults in the aggregate are material to the financial position of the registrant and its consolidated and unconsolidated subsidiaries, taken as a whole. . . .

II. Application of General Rules and Regulations. . .

C. A "small business issuer," defined in Rule 405, that is eligible to use Form S-2, shall refer to the disclosure items in Regulation S-B and not Regulation S-K. For example, while Item 1 of Form S-2 requires the information required by Item 501 of Regulation S-K, a small business issuer shall provide the information in Item 501 of Regulation S-B. Where Regulation S-B does not contain a comparable Item, for example there is no Item "301" in Regulation S-B, then a small business issuer may omit the Item. A small business issuer shall provide the financial information in Item 310 of Regulation S-B in lieu of the financial information called for by Item 11 of Form S-2. . . .

PART I—INFORMATION REQUIRED IN PROSPECTUS . . . .

Item 3. Summary Information, Risk Factors and Ratio of Earnings to Fixed Charges. . . .

Item 4. Use of Proceeds. . . .

Item 5. Determination of Offering Price....

Item 6. Dilution....

Item 7. Selling Security Holders....

Item 8. Plan of Distribution....

Item 9. Description of Securities to be Registered....

Item 10. Interests of Named Experts and Counsel....

Item 11. Information with Respect to the Registrant.

Furnish the information required by either paragraph (a) or paragraph (b) of this Item. The information required by paragraph (b) shall be furnished if the registrant satisfies the conditions of paragraph (c) of this Item.

(a) If the registrant elects to deliver this prospectus together with a copy of ... its latest Form 10–K ... filed pursuant to Sections 13(a) or 15(d) of the Exchange Act or its latest annual report to security holders, which at the time of original preparation met the requirements of either Rule 14a–3 or Rule 14c–3:

(1) Indicate that the prospectus is accompanied by ... a copy of the registrant's latest Form 10–K ... or a copy of its latest annual report to security holders, whichever the registrant elects to deliver pursuant to paragraph (a) of this Item.

(2) Provide financial and other information with respect to the registrant in the form required by Part I of Form 10–Q ... as of the end of the most recent fiscal quarter which ended after the end of the latest fiscal year for which certified financial statements were included in the latest Form 10–K ... or the latest report to security holders (whichever the registrant elects to deliver pursuant to paragraph (a) of this Item), and more than forty-five days prior to the effective date of this registration statement (or as of a more recent date) by one of the following means:

(i) Including such information in the prospectus; or

(ii) Providing without charge to each person to whom a prospectus is delivered a copy of the registrant's latest Form 10–Q ...; or

(iii) Providing without charge to each person to whom a prospectus is delivered a copy of the registrant's latest quarterly report which was delivered to its shareholders and which included the required financial information....

(4) Describe any and all material changes in the registrant's affairs which have occurred since the end of the latest fiscal year for which certified financial statements were included in the latest Form 10–K ... or the latest annual report to security holders (whichever the registrant elects to deliver pursuant to paragraph (a) of this Item) and which were

not described in a Form 10–Q ... or delivered with the prospectus in accordance with paragraph (a)(2)(ii) or (iii) of this Item....

Item 12. Incorporation of Certain Information by Reference. (a) The documents listed in (1), (2), and, if applicable, the portions of the documents listed in (3) and (4) below, shall be specifically incorporated by reference into the prospectus, by means of a statement to that effect in the prospectus listing all such documents. In lieu of incorporating portions of the documents listed in (3) and (4) below, the registrant may incorporate by reference its entire annual or quarterly report to security holders.

(1) The registrant's latest Form 10–K ... filed pursuant to Section 13(a) or 15(d) of the Exchange Act which contains certified financial statements for the registrant's latest fiscal year for which a Form 10–K ... was required to have been filed.

(2) All other reports filed pursuant to Section 13(a) or 15(d) of the Exchange Act since the end of the fiscal year covered by the annual report referred to in (1) above.

(3) If the registrant elects to deliver its latest annual report to security holders, pursuant to Item 11(a)(1) of this Form:

(i) description of business furnished in accordance with the provisions of Rule 14a–3(b)(6) under the Exchange Act....

(ii) financial statements and information furnished in accordance with the provisions of Rule 14a–3(b)(1);

(iii) information relating to industry segments, classes of similar products or services, foreign and domestic operations, and export sales furnished as required by paragraphs (b), (c)(1)(i) and (d) of Item 101 of Regulation S–K ... ;

(iv) where common equity securities are being offered, market price and dividends on the registrant's common equity and related stockholder matters furnished as required by Item 201 of Regulation S–K ... ;

(v) selected financial data furnished as required by Item 301 of Regulation S–K ... ;

(vi) supplementary financial information furnished as required by Item 302 of Regulation S–K ... ;

(vii) management's discussion and analysis of financial condition and results of operations furnished as required by Item 303 of Regulation S–K ...; and

(viii) information concerning disagreements with accountants on accounting and financial disclosure furnished as required by Item 304 of Regulation S–K ....

(4) If the registrant elects, pursuant to Item 11(a)(2)(iii) of this Form, to provide a copy of its latest quarterly report which was delivered

to shareholders, the financial information equivalent to that required to be presented in Part I of Form 10–Q.

(b) The registrant may also state, if it so chooses, that specifically described portions of its annual or quarterly report to security holders, other than those portions required to be incorporated by reference pursuant to paragraphs (a)(3) and (4) above, are not part of the registration statement. In such case, the description of portions which are not incorporated by reference or which are excluded shall be made with clarity and in reasonable detail. . . .

PART II—INFORMATION NOT REQUIRED IN PROSPECTUS

Item 14.   **Other Expenses of Issuance and Distribution**. . . .

Item 15.   **Indemnification of Directors and Officers**. . . .

Item 16.   **Exhibits**. . . .

Item 17.   **Undertakings**. . . .

FORM S-3

SECURITIES AND EXCHANGE COMMISSION

REGISTRATION STATEMENT UNDER THE SECURITIES ACT OF 1933

(Exact name of registrant as specified in its charter)

(State or other jurisdiction of incorporation or organization)

(I.R.S. Employer Identification No.)

(Address, including zip code, and telephone number,
including area code, of registrant's principal
executive offices)

(Name, address, including zip code, and telephone
number, including area code, of agent for service)

Approximate date of commencement of proposed sale to the public

————. . . .

GENERAL INSTRUCTIONS

I. Eligibility Requirements for Use of Form S-3

This instruction sets forth registrant requirements and transaction requirements for the use of Form S-3. Any registrant which meets the requirements of I.A. below ("Registrant Requirements") may use this Form for the registration of securities under the Securities Act of 1933 ("Securities Act") which are offered in any transaction specified in I.B. below ("Transaction Requirement") provided that the requirements applicable to the specified transaction are met. . . .

A. *Registrant Requirements.* Registrants must meet the following conditions in order to use this Form for registration under the Securities Act of securities offered in the transactions specified in I.B. below:

1. The registrant is organized under the laws of the United States or any State or Territory or the District of Columbia and has its principal business operations in the United States or its territories.

2. The registrant has a class of securities registered pursuant to Section 12(b) of the Securities Exchange Act of 1934 ("Exchange Act") or a class of equity securities registered pursuant to Section 12(g) of the Exchange Act or is required to file reports pursuant to Section 15(d) of the Exchange Act.

3. The registrant: (a) has been subject to the requirements of Section 12 or 15(d) of the Exchange Act and has filed all the material required to be filed pursuant to Sections 13, 14 or 15(d) for a period of at least twelve calendar months immediately preceding the filing of the registration statement on this Form; and (b) has filed in a timely manner all reports required to be filed during the twelve calendar months and any portion of a month immediately preceding the filing of the registration statement. . . .

5. Neither the registrant nor any of its consolidated or unconsolidated subsidiaries have, since the end of the last fiscal year for which certified financial statements of the registrant and its consolidated subsidiaries were included in a report filed pursuant to Section 13(a) or 15(d) of the Exchange Act: (a) failed to pay any dividend or sinking fund installment on preferred stock; or (b) defaulted (i) on any installment or installments on indebtedness for borrowed money, or (ii) on any rental on one or more long term leases, which defaults in the aggregate are material to the financial position of the registrant and its consolidated and unconsolidated subsidiaries, taken as a whole. . . .

B. *Transaction Requirements.* Security offerings meeting any of the following conditions and made by a registrant meeting the Registrant Requirements specified in I.A. above may be registered on this Form:

1. *Primary Offerings by Certain Registrants.* Securities to be offered for cash by or on behalf of a registrant, or outstanding securities to be offered for cash for the account of any person other than the registrant, including securities acquired by standby underwriters in connection with the call or redemption by the registrant of warrants or a class of convertible securities; *provided* that the aggregate market value

of the voting stock held by non-affiliates of the registrant is $75 million or more. . . .

2. *Primary Offerings of Non-convertible Investment Grade Securities.* Non-convertible securities to be offered for cash by or on behalf of a registrant, provided such securities at the time of sale are "investment grade securities," as defined below. A non-convertible security is an "investment grade security" if, at the time of sale, at least one nationally recognized statistical rating organization . . . has rated the security in one of its generic rating categories which signifies investment grade; typically, the four highest rating categories (within which there may be sub-categories or gradations indicating relative standing) signify investment grade.

3. *Transactions Involving Secondary Offerings.* Outstanding securities to be offered for the account of any person other than the issuer . . . if securities of the same class are listed and registered on a national securities exchange or are quoted on the automated quotation system of a national securities association. . . .

5. *Offerings of Investment Grade Asset-backed Securities.* Asset-backed securities to be offered for cash, provided the securities are "investment grade securities," as defined in I.B.2. above (Primary Offerings of Non-convertible Investment Grade Securities). For purposes of this Form, the term "asset-backed security" means a security that is primarily serviced by the cashflows of a discrete pool of receivables or other financial assets, either fixed or revolving, that by their terms convert into cash within a finite time period plus any rights or other assets designed to assure the servicing or timely distribution of proceeds to the securityholders. . . .

II. Application of General Rules and Regulations

. . .

C. A "small business issuer," defined in Rule 405, that is eligible to use Form S–3 shall refer to the disclosure items in Regulation S–B and not Regulation S–K. For example, while Item 1 of Form S–3 requires the information required by Item 501 of Regulation S–K, small business issuers shall provide the information in Item 501 of Regulation S–B. Where Regulation S–B does not contain a comparable Item, for example there is no Item "301" in Regulation S–B, then small business issuers may omit the Item. Small business issuers shall provide the financial information called for by Item 310 of Regulation S–B in lieu of the financial information called for by Item 11. . . .

PART I—INFORMATION REQUIRED IN PROSPECTUS

Item 3. Summary Information, Risk Factors and Ratio of Earnings to Fixed Charges. . . .

Item 4.   Use of Proceeds....

Item 5.   Determination of Offering Price....

Item 6.   Dilution....

Item 7.   Selling Security Holders....

Item 8.   Plan of Distribution....

Item 9.   Description of Securities to be Registered....

Item 10.   Interests of Named Experts and Counsel....

Item 11.   Material Changes.   (a) Describe any and all material changes in the registrant's affairs which have occurred since the end of the latest fiscal year for which certified financial statements were included in the latest annual report to security holders and which have not been described in a report on Form 10–Q ... or Form 8–K ... filed under the Exchange Act....

Item 12.   Incorporation of Certain Information by Reference.   (a) The documents listed in (1) and (2) below shall be specifically incorporated by reference into the prospectus, by means of a statement to that effect in the prospectus listing all such documents ...

(1) the registrant's latest annual report on Form 10–K ... filed pursuant to Section 13(a) or 15(d) of the Exchange Act which contains financial statements for the registrant's latest fiscal year for which a Form 10–K ... was required to have been filed; and

(2) all other reports filed pursuant to Section 13(a) or 15(d) of the Exchange Act since the end of the fiscal year covered by the annual report referred to in (1) above; and

(3) if capital stock is to be registered and securities of the same class are registered under Section 12 of the Exchange Act, the description of such class of securities which is contained in a registration statement filed under the Exchange Act, including any amendment or reports filed for the purpose of updating such description.

(b) The prospectus shall also state that all documents subsequently filed by the registrant pursuant to Sections 13(a), 13(c), 14 or 15(d) of the Exchange Act, prior to the termination of the offering shall be deemed to be incorporated by reference into the prospectus....

PART II—INFORMATION NOT REQUIRED IN PROSPECTUS

Item 14.   Other Expenses of Issuance and Distribution....

Item 15.   Indemnification of Directors and Officers....

Item 16.   Exhibits....

Item 17.   Undertakings....

FORM SB–2

REGISTRATION STATEMENT UNDER THE SECURITIES ACT OF 1933 . . .

_____

(Name of small business issuer in its charter)

_____

| (State or jurisdiction of incorporation or organization) | (Primary Standard Industrial Classification Code Number) | (I.R.S. Employer Identification No.) |

_____

(Address and telephone number of principal executive offices)

_____

(Address of principal place of business or intended principal place of business)

_____

(Name, address and telephone number of agent for service)

Approximate date of proposed sale to the public _____ . . .

GENERAL INSTRUCTIONS

A. *Use of Form and Place of Filing.*

1. A "small business issuer," defined in Rule 405 of the Securities Act of 1933 (the "Securities Act") may use this form to register securities to be sold for cash. See also Item 10(a) of Regulation S–B . . .

PART I—INFORMATION REQUIRED IN PROSPECTUS

Item 1. Front of Registration Statement and Outside Front Cover of Prospectus.

Furnish the information required by Item 501 of Regulation S–B.

Item 2. Inside Front and Outside Back Cover Pages of Prospectus.

Furnish the information required by Item 502 of Regulation S–B.

Item 3. Summary Information and Risk Factors.

Furnish the information required by Item 503 of Regulation S–B.

Item 4. Use of Proceeds.

Furnish the information required by Item 504 of Regulation S–B.

Item 5. Determination of Offering Price.

Furnish the information required by Item 505 of Regulation S–B.

Item 6. Dilution.

Furnish the information required by Item 506 of Regulation S–B.

Item 7. Selling Security Holders.

Furnish the information required by Item 507 of Regulation S–B.

Item 8. Plan of Distribution.

Furnish the information required by Item 508 of Regulation S–B.

Item 9. Legal Proceedings.

Furnish the information required by Item 103 of Regulation S–B.

Item 10. Directors, Executive Officers, Promoters and Control Persons.

Furnish the information required by Item 401 of Regulation S–B.

Item 11. Security Ownership of Certain Beneficial Owners and Management.

Furnish the information required by Item 403 of Regulation S–B.

Item 12. Description of Securities.

Furnish the information required by Item 202 of Regulation S–B.

Item 13. Interest of Named Experts and Counsel.

Furnish the information required by Item 509 of Regulation S–B.

Item 14. Disclosure of Commission Position on Indemnification for Securities Act Liabilities.

Furnish the information required by Item 510 of Regulation S–B.

Item 15. Organization Within Last Five Years.

Furnish the information required by Item 404 of Regulation S–B.

Item 16. Description of Business.

Furnish the information required by Item 101 of Regulation S–B.

Item 17. Management's Discussion and Analysis or Plan of Operation.

Furnish the information required by Item 303 of Regulation S–B.

Item 18. Description of Property.

Furnish the information required by Item 102 of Regulation S–B.

Item 19. Certain Relationships and Related Transactions.

Furnish the information required by Item 404 of Regulation S–B.

Item 20. Market for Common Equity and Related Stockholder Matters.

Furnish the information required by Item 201 of Regulation S–B.

Item 21. Executive Compensation.

Furnish the information required by Item 402 of Regulation S–B.

Item 22. Financial Statements.

Furnish the information required by Item 310 of Regulation S–B.

Item 23.   Changes In and Disagreements With Accountants on Accounting and Financial Disclosure.

Furnish the information required by Item 304 of Regulation S–B.

PART II—INFORMATION NOT REQUIRED IN PROSPECTUS

Item 24.   Indemnification of Directors and Officers.

Furnish the information required by Item 702 of Regulation S–B.

Item 25.   Other Expenses of Issuance and Distribution.

Furnish the information required by Item 511 of Regulation S–B.

Item 26.   Recent Sales of Unregistered Securities.

Furnish the information required by Item 701 of Regulation S–B.

Item 27.   Exhibits.

Furnish the exhibits required by Item 601 of Regulation S–B.

Item 28.   Undertakings.

Furnish the undertakings required by Item 512 of Regulation S–B. . . .

[The balance of Form SB–2 is omitted.]

———

REGULATION S–B—INTEGRATED DISCLOSURE SYSTEM FOR SMALL BUSINESS ISSUERS (EXCERPTS)

17 C.F.R. §§ 228.10 et seq.

Item 10. General

(a) *Application of Regulation S–B.* Regulation S–B is the source of disclosure requirements for "small business issuer" filings under the

* Omitted.

Securities Act of 1933 (the "Securities Act") and the Securities Exchange Act of 1934 (the "Exchange Act").

(1) *Definition of small business issuer.* A small business issuer is defined as a company that meets all of the following criteria:

(i) has revenues of less than $25,000,000;

(ii) is a U.S. or Canadian issuer;

(iii) is not an investment company; and

(iv) if a majority owned subsidiary, the parent corporation is also a small business issuer.

Provided however, that an entity is not a small business issuer if it has a public float (the aggregate market value of the issuer's outstanding securities held by non-affiliates) of $25,000,000 or more. . . .

(2) *Entering and Exiting the Small Business Disclosure System.* (i) A company that meets the definition of small business issuer may use Form SB–2 for registration of its securities under the Securities Act; Form 10–SB for registration of its securities under the Exchange Act; and Forms 10–KSB and 10–QSB for its annual and quarterly reports.

(ii) For a non-reporting company entering the disclosure system for the first time either by filing a registration statement under the Securities Act on Form SB–2 or a registration statement under the Exchange Act on Form 10–SB, the determination as to whether a company is a small business issuer is made with reference to its revenues during its last fiscal year and public float as of a date within 60 days of the date the registration statement is filed. . . .

(iii) Once a small business issuer becomes a reporting company it will remain a small business issuer until it exceeds the revenue limit or the public float limit at the end of two consecutive years. For example, if a company exceeds the revenue limit for two consecutive years, it will no longer be considered a small business. However, if it exceeds the revenue limit in one year and the next year exceeds the public float limit, but not the revenue limit, it will still be considered a small business. . . .

(iv) A reporting company that is not a small business company must meet the definition of a small business issuer at the end of two consecutive fiscal years before it will be considered a small business issuer for purposes of using Form SB–2, Form 10–SB, Form 10–KSB and Form 10–QSB.

(v) The determination as to the reporting category (small business issuer or other issuer) made for a non-reporting company at the time it enters the disclosure system governs all reports relating to the remainder of the fiscal year. The determination made for a reporting company at the end of its fiscal year governs all reports relating to the next fiscal year. An issuer may not change from one category to another with respect to its reports under the Exchange Act for a single fiscal year. A company may, however, choose not to use a Form SB–2 for a registration under the Securities Act.

(b) *Definitions of terms.*

(1) *Common equity*—means the small business issuer's common stock. If the small business issuer is a limited partnership, the term refers to the equity interests in the partnership.

(2) *Public market*—no public market shall be deemed to exist unless, within the past 60 business days, both bid and asked quotations at fixed prices (excluding "bid wanted" or "offer wanted" quotations) have appeared regularly in any established quotation system on at least half of such business days. Transactions arranged without the participation of a broker or dealer functioning as such are not indicative of a "public market."

(3) *Reporting company*—means a company that is obligated to file periodic reports with the Securities and Exchange Commission under section 15(d) or 13(a) of the Exchange Act.

(4) *Small business issuer*—refers to the issuer and all of its consolidated subsidiaries.

(c) *Preparing the disclosure document.* (1) The purpose of a disclosure document is to inform investors. Hence, information should be presented in a clear, concise and understandable fashion. Avoid unnecessary details, repetition or the use of technical language. The responses to the items of this Regulation should be brief and to the point.

(2) Small business issuers should consult the General Rules and Regulations under the Securities Act and Exchange Act for requirements concerning the preparation and filing of documents. Small business issuers should be aware that there are special rules concerning such matters as the kind and size of paper that is allowed and how filings should be bound. These special rules are located in Regulation C of the Securities Act and in Regulation 12B of the Exchange Act.

(d) *Commission policy on projections.* The Commission encourages the use of management's projections of future economic performance that have a reasonable basis and are presented in an appropriate format. The guidelines below set forth the Commission's views on important factors to be considered in preparing and disclosing such projections. (*See also* Rule 175 . . .).

(1) *Basis for projections.* Management has the option to present in Commission filings its good faith assessment of a small business issuer's future performance. Management, however, must have a reasonable basis for such an assessment. An outside review of management's projections may furnish additional support in this regard. If management decides to include a report of such a review in a Commission filing, it should also disclose the qualifications of the reviewer, the extent of the review, the relationship between the reviewer and the registrant, and

other material factors concerning the process by which any outside review was sought or obtained. Moreover, in the case of a registration statement under the Securities Act, the reviewer would be deemed an expert and an appropriate consent must be filed with the registration statement.

(2) *Format for projections.* Traditionally, projections have been given for three financial items generally considered to be of primary importance to investors (revenues, net income (loss) and earnings (loss) per share) ... [P]rojection information need not necessarily be limited to these three items. However, management should take care to assure that the choice of items projected is not susceptible to misleading inferences through selective projection of only favorable items. It generally would be misleading to present sales or revenue projections without one of the foregoing measures of income. The period that appropriately may be covered by a projection depends to a large extent on the particular circumstances of the company involved. For certain companies in certain industries, a projection covering a two or three year period may be entirely reasonable. Other companies may not have a reasonable basis for projections beyond the current year.

(3) *Investor understanding.* Disclosures accompanying the projections should facilitate investor understanding of the basis for and limitations of projections. The Commission believes that investor understanding would be enhanced by disclosure of the assumptions which in management's opinion are most significant to the projections or are the key factors upon which the financial results of the enterprise depend and encourages disclosure of assumptions in a manner that will provide a frame-work for analysis of the projection. Management also should consider whether disclosure of the accuracy or inaccuracy of previous projections would provide investors with important insights into the limitations of projections.

(e) *Commission policy on security ratings.* In view of the importance of security ratings ("ratings") to investors and the marketplace, the Commission permits small business issuers to disclose ratings assigned by rating organizations to classes of debt securities, convertible debt securities and preferred stock in registration statements and periodic reports. In addition, the Commission permits, disclosure of ratings assigned by any nationally recognized statistical rating organizations ("NRSROs") in certain communications deemed not to be a prospectus ("tombstone advertisements"). Below are the Commission's views on important matters to be considered in disclosing security ratings.

(1)(i) If a small business issuer includes in a filing any rating(s) assigned to a class of securities, it should consider including any other rating assigned by a different NRSRO that is materially different. A statement that a security rating is not a recommendation to buy, sell or hold securities and that it may be subject to revision or withdrawal at any time by the assigning rating organization should also be included.

(ii)(A) If the rating is included in a filing under the Securities Act, the written consent of any rating organization that is not a NRSRO whose rating is included should be filed. The consent of any NRSRO is not required. ...

(B) If a change in a rating already included is available before effectiveness of the registration statement, the small business issuer should consider including such rating change in the prospectus. If the rating change is material, consideration should be given to recirculating the preliminary prospectus.

(C) If a materially different additional NRSRO rating or a material change in a rating already included becomes available during any period in which offers or sales are being made, the small business issuer should consider disclosing this information in a sticker to the prospectus.

(iii) If there is a material change in the rating(s) assigned by any NRSRO(s) to any outstanding class(es) of securities of a reporting company, the registrant should consider filing a report on Form 8–K ... or other appropriate report under the Exchange Act disclosing such rating change. ...

REGULATION S–K—STANDARD INSTRUCTIONS FOR FILING FORMS UNDER SECURITIES ACT OF 1933 [AND] SECURITIES EXCHANGE ACT OF 1934 (SELECTED PROVISIONS)

17 C.F.R. §§ 229.10 et seq.

SUBPART 300—FINANCIAL INFORMATION

Subpart 300—Financial Information

Item 301. Selected Financial Data

Furnish in comparative columnar form the selected financial data for the registrant referred to below, for

(a) Each of the last five fiscal years of the registrant (or for the life of the registrant and its predecessors, if less), and

(b) Any additional fiscal years necessary to keep the information from being misleading.

Instructions to Item 301.

1. The purpose of the selected financial data shall be to supply in a convenient and readable format selected financial data which highlight certain significant trends in the registrant's financial condition and results of operations.

2. Subject to appropriate variation to conform to the nature of the registrant's business, the following items shall be included in the table of financial data: net sales or operating revenues; income (loss) from continuing operations; income (loss) from continuing operations per common share; total assets; long-term obligations and redeemable preferred stock . . . .

Briefly describe, or cross-reference to a discussion thereof, factors such as accounting changes, business combinations or dispositions of business operations, that materially affect the comparability of the information reflected in selected financial data. Discussion of, or reference to, any material uncertainties should also be included where such matters might cause the data reflected herein not to be indicative of the registrant's future financial condition or results of operations. . . .

Item 303. Management's Discussion and Analysis of Financial Condition and Results of Operations

(a) *Full fiscal years.* Discuss registrant's financial condition, changes in financial condition and results of operations. The discussion shall provide information as specified in paragraphs (a)(1), (2) and (3) with respect to liquidity, capital resources and results of operations and also shall provide such other information that the registrant believes to be necessary to an understanding of its financial condition, changes in financial condition and results of operations. Discussions of liquidity and capital resources may be combined whenever the two topics are interrelated. Where in the registrant's judgment a discussion of segment information or of other subdivisions of the registrant's business would be appropriate to an understanding of such business, the discussion shall focus on each relevant, reportable segment or other subdivision of the business and on the registrant as a whole.

(1) *Liquidity.* Identify any known trends or any known demands, commitments, events or uncertainties that will result in or that are reasonably likely to result in the registrant's liquidity increasing or decreasing in any material way. If a material deficiency is identified, indicate the course of action that the registrant has taken or proposes to take to remedy the deficiency. Also identify and separately describe internal and external sources of liquidity, and briefly discuss any material unused sources of liquid assets.

(2) *Capital resources.* (i) Describe the registrant's material commitments for capital expenditures as of the end of the latest fiscal period,

and indicate the general purpose of such commitments and the anticipated source of funds needed to fulfill such commitments.

(ii) Describe any known material trends, favorable or unfavorable, in the registrant's capital resources. Indicate any expected material changes in the mix and relative cost of such resources. The discussion shall consider changes between equity, debt and any off-balance sheet financing arrangements.

(3) *Results of operations.* (i) Describe any unusual or infrequent events or transactions or any significant economic changes that materially affected the amount of reported income from continuing operations and, in each case, indicate the extent to which income was so affected. In addition, describe any other significant components of revenues or expenses that, in the registrant's judgment, should be described in order to understand the registrant's results of operations.

(ii) Describe any known trends or uncertainties that have had or that the registrant reasonably expects will have a material favorable or unfavorable impact on net sales or revenues or income from continuing operations. If the registrant knows of events that will cause a material change in the relationship between costs and revenues (such as known future increases in costs of labor or materials or price increases or inventory adjustments), the change in the relationship shall be disclosed.

(iii) To the extent that the financial statements disclose material increases in net sales or revenues, provide a narrative discussion of the extent to which such increases are attributable to increases in prices or to increases in the volume or amount of goods or services being sold or to the introduction of new products or services.

(iv) For the three most recent fiscal years of the registrant ... or for those fiscal years in which the registrant has been engaged in business, whichever period is shortest, discuss the impact of inflation and changing prices on the registrant's net sales and revenues and on income from continuing operations.

Instructions to Paragraph 303(a). ...

3. The discussion and analysis shall focus specifically on material events and uncertainties known to management that would cause reported financial information not to be necessarily indicative of future operating results or of future financial condition. This would include descriptions and amounts of (A) matters that would have an impact on future operations and have not had an impact in the past, and (B) matters that have had an impact on reported operations and are not expected to have an impact upon future operations.

4. Where the consolidated financial statements reveal material changes from year to year in one or more line items, the causes for

the changes shall be described to the extent necessary to an understanding of the registrant's businesses as a whole. . . .

7. Registrants are encouraged, but not required, to supply forward-looking information. This is to be distinguished from presently known data which will impact upon future operating results, such as known future increases in costs of labor or materials. This latter data may be required to be disclosed. Any forward-looking information supplied is expressly covered by the safe harbor rule for projections. See Rule 175 under the Securities Act. . . .

(b) *Interim periods*. If interim period financial statements are included or are required to be included by Article 3 of Regulation S–X . . ., a management's discussion and analysis of the financial condition and results of operations shall be provided so as to enable the reader to assess material changes in financial condition and results of operations. . . .

Item 304. Changes in and Disagreements With Accountants on Accounting and Financial Disclosure

(a)(1) If during the registrant's two most recent fiscal years or any subsequent interim period, an independent accountant who was previously engaged as the principal accountant to audit the registrant's financial statements, or an independent accountant who was previously engaged to audit a significant subsidiary and on whom the principal accountant expressed reliance in its reports, has resigned (or indicated it has declined to stand for re-election after the completion of the current audit) or was dismissed, then the registrant shall:

(i) State whether the former accountant resigned, declined to stand for re-election or was dismissed and the date thereof.

(ii) State whether the principal accountant's report on the financial statements for either of the past two years contained an adverse opinion or a disclaimer of opinion, or was qualified or modified as to uncertainty, audit scope, or accounting principles; and also describe the nature of each such adverse opinion, disclaimer of opinion, modification, or qualification.

(iii) State whether the decision to change accountants was recommended or approved by:

(A) any audit or similar committee of the board of directors, if the issuer has such a committee; or

(B) the board of directors, if the issuer has no such committee.

(iv) State whether during the registrant's two most recent fiscal years and any subsequent interim period preceding such resignation, declination or dismissal there were any disagreements with the former accountant on any matter of accounting principles or practices, financial statement disclosure, or auditing scope or procedure, which disagreement(s), if not resolved to the satisfaction of the former accountant, would have caused it to make reference to the subject matter of the disagreement(s) in connection with its report. Also, (A) describe each such disagreement; (B) state whether any audit or similar committee of the board of directors, or the board of directors, discussed the subject matter of each of such disagreements with the former accountant; and (C) state whether the registrant has authorized the former accountant to respond fully to the inquiries of the successor accountant concerning the subject matter of each of such disagreements and, if not, describe the nature of any limitation thereon and the reason therefore. The disagreements required to be reported in response to this Item include both those resolved to the former accountant's satisfaction and those not resolved to the former accountant's satisfaction. Disagreements contemplated by this Item are those that occur at the decision-making level, i.e., between personnel of the registrant responsible for presentation of its financial statements and personnel of the accounting firm responsible for rendering its report.

(v) Provide the information required by paragraph (a)(1)(iv) of this Item for each of the kinds of events (even though the registrant and the former accountant did not express a difference of opinion regarding the event) listed in paragraphs (A) through (D) below, that occurred within the registrant's two most recent fiscal years and any subsequent interim period preceding the former accountant's resignation, declination to stand for re-election, or dismissal ("reportable events"). If the event led to a disagreement or difference of opinion, then the event should be reported as a disagreement under paragraph (a)(1)(iv) and need not be repeated under this paragraph.

(A) [t]he accountant's having advised the registrant that the internal controls necessary for the registrant to develop reliable financial statements do not exist;

(B) the accountant's having advised the registrant that information has come to the accountant's attention that has led it to no longer be able to rely on management's representations, or that has made it unwilling to be associated with the financial statements prepared by management;

(C)*(1)* the accountant's having advised the registrant of the need to expand significantly the scope of its audit, or that information has come to the accountant's attention during the time period covered by Item 304(a)(1)(iv), that if further investigated may *(i)* materially impact the fairness or reliability of either: a previously issued audit report or the underlying financial statements; or the financial statements issued or to be issued covering the fiscal period(s) subsequent to the date of the most recent financial statements covered by an audit report (including information that may prevent it from rendering an unqualified audit report on those financial statements), or *(ii)* cause it to be unwilling to rely on management's representations or be associated with the registrant's financial statements, and *(2)* due to the accountant's resignation (due to audit scope limitations or otherwise) or dismissal, or for any other reason, the accountant did not so expand the scope of its audit or conduct such further investigation; or

(D)*(1)* the accountant's having advised the registrant that information has come to the accountant's attention that it has concluded materially impacts the fairness or reliability of either *(i)* a previously issued audit report or the underlying financial statements, or *(ii)* the financial statements issued or to be issued covering the fiscal period(s) subsequent to the date of the most recent financial statements covered by an audit report (including information that, unless resolved to the accountant's satisfaction, would prevent it from rendering an unqualified audit report on those financial statements), and *(2)* due to the accountant's resignation, dismissal or declination to stand for re-election, or for any other reason, the issue has not been resolved to the accountant's satisfaction prior to its resignation, dismissal or declination to stand for re-election.

(2) If during the registrant's two most recent fiscal years or any subsequent interim period, a new independent accountant has been engaged as either the principal accountant to audit the registrant's financial statements, or as an independent accountant to audit a significant subsidiary and on whom the principal accountant is expected to express reliance in its report, then the registrant shall identify the newly engaged accountant and indicate the date of such accountant's engagement. In addition, if during the registrant's two most recent fiscal years, and any subsequent interim period prior to engaging that accountant, the registrant (or someone on its behalf) consulted the newly engaged accountant regarding (i) either: the application of accounting principles to a specified transaction, either completed or proposed; or the type of audit opinion that might be rendered on the registrant's financial statements, and either a written report was provided to the registrant or oral advice was provided that the new accountant concluded was an important factor considered by the registrant in reaching a decision as to the accounting, auditing or financial reporting issue; or (ii) any matter that was either the subject of a disagreement (as defined in paragraph 304(a)(1)(iv) and the related instructions to this item) or a reportable event (as described in paragraph 304(a)(1)(v)), then the registrant shall:

(A) so state and identify the issues that were the subjects of those consultations;

(B) briefly describe the views of the newly engaged accountant as expressed orally or in writing to the registrant on each such issue and, if written views were received by the registrant, file them as an exhibit to the report or registration statement requiring compliance with this Item 304(a);

(C) state whether the former accountant was consulted by the registrant regarding any such issues, and if so, provide a summary of the former accountant's views; and

(D) request the newly engaged accountant to review the disclosure required by this Item 304(a) before it is filed with the Commission and provide the new accountant the opportunity to furnish the registrant with a letter addressed to the Commission containing any new information, clarification of the registrant's expression of its views, or the respects in which it does not agree with the statements made by the registrant in response to Item 304(a). The registrant shall file any such letter as an exhibit to the report or registration statement containing the disclosure required by this Item.

(3) The registrant shall provide the former accountant with a copy of the disclosures it is making in response to this Item 304(a) that the former accountant shall receive no later than the day that the disclosures are filed with the Commission. The registrant shall request the former accountant to furnish the registrant with a letter addressed to the Commission stating whether it agrees with the statements made by the registrant in response to this Item 304(a) and, if not, stating the respects in which it does not agree. The registrant shall file the former accountant's letter as an exhibit to the report or registration statement containing this disclosure. If the former accountant's letter is unavailable at the time of filing such report or registration statement, then the registrant shall request the former accountant to provide the letter as promptly as possible so that the registrant can file the letter with the Commission within ten business days after the filing of the report or registration statement. Notwithstanding the ten business day period, the registrant shall file the letter by amendment within two business days of receipt; if the letter is received on a Saturday, Sunday or holiday on which the Commission is not open for business, then the two business day period shall begin to run on and shall include the first business day thereafter. The former accountant may provide the registrant with an interim letter highlighting specific areas of concern and indicating that a more detailed letter will be forthcoming within the ten business day period noted above. If not filed with the report or registration statement containing the registrant's disclosure under this Item 304(a), then the interim letter, if any, shall be filed by the registrant by amendment within two business days of receipt.

(b) If, (1) in connection with a change in accountants subject to paragraph (a) of this Item 304, there was any disagreement of the type described in paragraph (a)(1)(iv) or any reportable event as described in paragraph (a)(1)(v) of this Item; (2) during the fiscal year in which the change in accountants took place or during the subsequent fiscal year, there have been any transactions or events similar to those which involved such disagreement or reportable event and (3) such transactions or events were material and were accounted for or disclosed in a manner different from that which the former accountants apparently would have concluded was required, the registrant shall state the existence and nature of the disagreement or reportable event and also state the effect on the financial statements if the method had been followed which the former accountants apparently would have concluded was required. These disclosures need not be made if the method asserted by the former accountants ceases to be generally accepted because of authoritative standards or interpretations subsequently issued.

Instructions to Item 304 . . . .

4. The term "disagreements" as used in this Item shall be interpreted broadly, to include any difference of opinion concerning any matter of accounting principles or practices, financial statement disclosure, or auditing scope or procedure which (if not resolved to the satisfaction of the former accountant) would have caused it to make reference to the subject matter of the disagreement in connection with its report. It is not necessary for there to have been an argument to have had a disagreement, merely a difference of opinion. For purposes of this Item, however, the term disagreements does not include initial differences of opinion based on incomplete facts or preliminary information that were later resolved to the former accountant's satisfaction by, and providing the registrant and the accountant do not continue to have a difference of opinion upon, obtaining additional relevant facts or information.

5. In determining whether any disagreement or reportable event has occurred, an oral communication from the engagement partner or another person responsible for rendering the accounting firm's opinion (or their designee) will generally suffice as the accountant advising the registrant of a reportable event or as a statement of a disagreement at the "decision-making level" within the accounting firm and require disclosure under this Item.

Subpart 400—Management and Certain Security Holders

Item 401. Directors, Executive Officers, Promoters and Control Persons

(a) *Identification of directors.* List the names and ages of all directors of the registrant and all persons nominated or chosen to become directors; indicate all positions and offices with the registrant held by each such person; state his term of office as director and any period(s) during which he has served as such; describe briefly any arrangement or understanding between him and any other person(s) (naming such person(s)) pursuant to which he was or is to be selected as a director or nominee. . . .

(b) *Identification of executive officers.* List the names and ages of all executive officers of the registrant and all persons chosen to become executive officers; indicate all positions and offices with the registrant held by each such person; state his term of office as officer and the period during which he has served as such and describe briefly any arrangement or understanding between him and any other person(s) (naming such person) pursuant to which he was or is to be selected as an officer.

(c) *Identification of certain significant employees.* Where the registrant employs persons such as production managers, sales managers, or research scientists who are not executive officers but who make or are expected to make significant contributions to the business of the registrant, such persons shall be identified and their background disclosed to the same extent as in the case of executive officers. Such disclosure need not be made if the registrant was subject to section 13(a) or 15(d) of the Exchange Act or was exempt from section 13(a) by section 12(g)(2)(G) of such Act immediately prior to the filing of the registration statement, report, or statement to which this Item is applicable.

(d) *Family relationships.* State the nature of any family relationship between any director, executive officer, or person nominated or chosen by the registrant to become a director or executive officer.

Instruction to Paragraph 401(d).

The term "family relationship" means any relationship by blood, marriage, or adoption, not more remote than first cousin.

(e) *Business experience* —(1) *Background.* Briefly describe the business experience during the past five years of each director, executive officer, person nominated or chosen to become a director or executive officer, and each person named in answer to paragraph (c) of Item 401, including: Each person's principal occupations and employment during the past five years; the name and principal business of any corporation or other organization in which such occupations and employment were carried on; and whether such corporation or organization is a parent, subsidiary or other affiliate of the registrant. When an executive officer or person named in response to paragraph (c) of Item 401 has been employed by the registrant or a subsidiary of the registrant for less than five years, a brief explanation shall be included as to the nature of the responsibility undertaken by the individual in prior positions to provide adequate disclosure of his prior business experience. What is required is information relating to the level of his professional competence, which may include, depending upon the circumstances, such specific information as the size of the operation supervised.

(2) *Directorships.* Indicate any other directorships held by each director or person nominated or chosen to become a director in any company with a class of securities registered pursuant to section 12 of the Exchange Act or subject to the requirements of section 15(d) of such Act....

(f) *Involvement in certain legal proceedings.* Describe any of the following events that occurred during the past five years and that are material to an evaluation of the ability or integrity of any director, person nominated to become a director or executive officer of the registrant:

(1) A petition under the Federal bankruptcy laws or any state insolvency law was filed by or against, or a receiver, fiscal agent or similar officer was appointed by a court for the business or property of such person, or any partnership in which he was a general partner at or within two years before the time of such filing, or any corporation or business association of which he was an executive officer at or within two years before the time of such filing;

(2) Such person was convicted in a criminal proceeding or is a named subject of a pending criminal proceeding (excluding traffic violations and other minor offenses);

(3) Such person was the subject of any order, judgment, or decree, not subsequently reversed, suspended or vacated, of any court of competent jurisdiction, permanently or temporarily enjoining him from, or otherwise limiting, the following activities:

(i) Acting as a futures commission merchant, introducing broker, commodity trading advisor, commodity pool operator, floor broker, leverage transaction merchant, any other person regulated by the Commodity Futures Trading Commission, or an associated person of any of the foregoing, or as an investment adviser, underwriter, broker or dealer in securities, or as an affiliated person, director or employee of any investment company, bank, savings and loan association or insurance company, or engaging in or continuing any conduct or practice in connection with such activity;

(ii) Engaging in any type of business practice; or

(iii) Engaging in any activity in connection with the purchase or sale of any security or commodity or in connection with any violation of Federal or State securities laws or Federal commodities laws ....

(g) *Promoters and control persons.* (1) Registrants, which have not been subject to the reporting requirements of section 13(a) or 15(d) of the Exchange Act for the twelve months immediately prior to the filing of the registration statement, report, or statement to which this Item is applicable, and which were organized within the last five years, shall describe with respect to any promoter, any of the events enumerated in [paragraph (f)] that occurred during the past five years and that are material to a voting or investment decision.

(2) Registrants, which have not been subject to the reporting requirements of section 13(a) or 15(d) of the Exchange Act for the twelve months immediately prior to the filing of the registration statement, report, or statement to which this Item is applicable, shall describe with respect to any control person, any of the events enumerated in [paragraph (f)] that occurred during the past five years and that are material to a voting or investment decision. . . .

Item 402. Executive Compensation

(a) *General*. . . .

(3) *Persons Covered.* Disclosure shall be provided pursuant to this item for each of the following (the "named executive officers"):

(i) all individuals serving as the registrant's chief executive officer or acting in a similar capacity during the last completed fiscal year ("CEO"), regardless of compensation level;

(ii) the registrant's four most highly compensated executive officers other than the CEO who were serving as executive officers at the end of the last completed fiscal year; and

(iii) up to two additional individuals for whom disclosure would have been provided pursuant to paragraph (a)(3)(ii) of this item but for the fact that the individual was not serving as an executive officer of the registrant at the end of the last completed fiscal year.

Instructions to Item 402(a)(3).

1. *Determination of Most Highly Compensated Executive Officers.* The determination as to which executive officers are most highly compensated shall be made by reference to total annual salary and bonus for the last completed fiscal year (as required to be disclosed pursuant to paragraph (b) . . . of this item), . . . *provided, however,* that no disclosure need be provided for any executive officer, other than the CEO, whose total annual salary and bonus . . . does not exceed $100,000.

2. *Inclusion of Executive Officer of Subsidiary.* It may be appropriate in certain circumstances for a registrant to include an executive officer of a subsidiary in the disclosure required by this item. *See* Rule 3b–7 under the Exchange Act. . . .

(7) *Definitions.* For purposes of this item:

(i) The term "stock appreciation rights" ("SARs") refers to SARs payable in cash or stock, including SARs payable in cash or stock at the election of the registrant or a named executive officer.

(ii) The term "plan" includes, but is not limited to, the following: any plan, contract, authorization or arrangement, whether or not set forth in any formal documents, pursuant to which the following may be received: cash, stock, restricted stock or restricted stock units, phantom stock, stock options, SARs, stock options in tandem with SARs, warrants, convertible securities, performance units and performance shares, and similar instruments. A plan may be applicable to one person. Registrants may omit information regarding group life, health, hospitalization, medical reimbursement or relocation plans that do not discriminate in scope, terms or operation, in favor of executive officers or directors of the registrant and that are available generally to all salaried employees.

(iii) The term "long-term incentive plan" means any plan providing compensation intended to serve as incentive for performance to occur over a period longer than one fiscal year, whether such performance is measured by reference to financial performance of the registrant or an affiliate, the registrant's stock price, or any other measure, but excluding restricted stock, stock option and SAR plans.

(8) *Location of Specified Information.* The information required by paragraphs (i), (k) and (*l*) of this item need not be provided in any filings other than a registrant proxy or information statement relating to an annual meeting of security holders at which directors are to be elected (or special meeting or written consents in lieu of such meeting). Such information will not be deemed to be incorporated by reference into any filing under the Securities Act or the Exchange Act, except to the extent that the registrant specifically incorporates it by reference.

(9) *Liability for Specified Information.* The information required by paragraphs (k) and (*l*) of this item shall not be deemed to be "soliciting material" or to be "filed" with the Commission or subject to Regulations 14A or 14C, other than as provided in this item, or to the liabilities of Section 18 of the Exchange Act, except to the extent that the registrant specifically requests that such information be treated as soliciting material or specifically incorporates it by reference into a filing under the Securities Act or the Exchange Act.

(b) *Summary Compensation Table.* *(1) General.* The information specified in paragraph (b)(2) of this item, concerning the compensation of the named executive officers for each of the registrant's last three completed fiscal years shall be provided in a Summary Compensation Table, in the tabular format specified below.

SUMMARY COMPENSATION TABLE

(a) Name and Principal Position	(b) Year	Annual Compensation			Long Term Compensation			(i) All Other Compensation ($)
		(c) Salary ($)	(d) Bonus ($)	(e) Other Annual Compensation ($)	Awards		Payouts	
					(f) Restricted Stock Award(s) ($)	(g) Securities Underlying Options/ SARs (#)	(h) LTIP Payouts ($)	
CEO	——							
	——							
A	——							
	——							
B	——							
	——							
C	——							
	——							
D	——							
	——							

(2) The Table shall include ...

(iii) Annual compensation ... including....

(C) The dollar value of other annual compensation not properly categorized as salary or bonus, as follows (column (e)):

(1) Perquisites and other personal benefits, securities or property, unless the aggregate amount of such compensation is the lesser of either $50,000 or 10% of the total of annual salary and bonus reported for the named executive officer in columns (c) and (d) ...; and

(5) The dollar value of the difference between the price paid by a named executive officer for any security of the registrant or its subsidiaries purchased from the registrant or its subsidiaries (through deferral of salary or bonus, or otherwise), and the fair market value of such security at the date of purchase, unless that discount is available generally, either to all security holders or to all salaried employees of the registrant.

Instructions to Item 402(b)(2)(iii)(C).

1. Each perquisite or other personal benefit exceeding 25% of the total perquisites and other personal benefits reported for a named executive officer must be identified by type and amount in a footnote or accompanying narrative discussion to column (e).

2. Perquisites and other personal benefits shall be valued on the basis of the aggregate incremental cost to the registrant and its subsidiaries....

(iv) Long-term compensation (columns (f), (g) and (h)), including:

(A) The dollar value (net of any consideration paid by the named executive officer) of any award of restricted stock, including share units (calculated by multiplying the closing market price of the registrant's unrestricted stock on the date of grant by the number of shares awarded) (column (f));

(B) The sum of the number of securities underlying stock options granted, with or without tandem SARs, and the number of freestanding SARs (column (g)): and

(C) The dollar value of all payouts pursuant to long-term incentive plans ("LTIPs") as defined in paragraph (a)(7)(iii) of this item (column (h)).

(c) *Option/SAR Grants Table.*

(1) The [following] information ... concerning individual grants of stock options (whether or not in tandem with SARs), and freestanding SARs made during the last completed fiscal year to each of the named executive officers shall be provided in the tabular format specified below:

Option/SAR Grants in Last Fiscal Year

		Individual Grants			Potential Realizable Value at Assumed Annual Rates of Stock Price Appreciation for Option Term		Alternative to (f) and (g): Grant Date Value
(a)	(b)	(c)	(d)	(e)	(f)	(g)	(f)
	Number of Securities Underlying Options/ SARs Granted	% of Total Options/ SARs Granted to Employees in Fiscal					Grant Date Present
Name	(#)	Year	Exercise or Base Price ($/Sh)	Expiration Date	5% ($)	10% ($)	Value $
CEO							
A							
B							
C							
D							

(2) The Table shall include, with respect to each grant ...

(ii) The number of securities underlying option SARs granted (column (b))....

(vi) Either (A) the potential realizable value of each grant of options or freestanding SARs or (B) the present value of each grant, as follows:

(A) The potential realizable value of each grant of options or freestanding SARs, assuming that the market price of the underlying security appreciates in value from the date of grant to the end of the option or SAR term, at the following annualized rates:

(1) 5% (column (f));

(2) 10% (column (g)); and

(3) If the exercise or base price was below the market price of the underlying security at the date of grant, provide an additional column labeled 0%, to show the value at grant-date market price; or

(B) The present value of the grant at the date of grant, under any option pricing model (alternative column (f)).

Instructions to Item 402(c)....

7. The potential realizable dollar value of a grant (columns (f) and (g)) shall be the product of: (a) the difference between: (i) the product of the per-share market price at the time of the grant and the sum of 1 plus the adjusted stock price appreciation rate (the assumed rate of appreciation compounded annually over the term of the option or SAR); and (ii) the per-share exercise price of the option or SAR; and (b) the number of securities underlying the grant at fiscal year end. ...

9. Where the registrant chooses to use the grant-date valuation alternative specified in paragraph (c)(2)(vi)(B) of this item, the valuation shall be footnoted to describe the valuation method used. Where the registrant has used a variation of the Black–Scholes or binomial option pricing model, the description shall identify the use of such pricing model and describe the assumptions used relating to the expected volatility, risk-free rate of return, dividend yield and time of exercise. Any adjustments for non-transferability or risk of forfeiture also shall be disclosed. In the event another valuation method is used, the registrant is required to describe the methodology as well as any material assumption.

(d) *Aggregated Option/SAR Exercises and Fiscal Year–End Option/SAR Value Table.*

(1) The [following] information ... concerning each exercise of stock options (or tandem SARs) and freestanding SARs during the last completed fiscal year by each of the named executive officers and the fiscal year-end value of unexercised options and SARs, shall be provided on an aggregated basis in the tabular format specified below:

Aggregated Option/SAR Exercises in Last Fiscal Year and FY–End Option/SAR Values				
(a)	(b)	(c)	(d)	(e)
			Number of Securities Underlying Unexercised Options/SARs at FY–End (#)	Value of Unexercised In-the-Money Options/SARs at FY–End ($)
Name	Shares Acquired on Exercise (#)	Value Realized ($)	Exercisable/ Unexercisable	Exercisable/ Unexercisable
CEO				
A				
B				
C				
D				

. . .

(e) *Long–Term Incentive Plan ("LTIP") Awards Table.*

(1) The [following] information ... regarding each award made to a named executive officer in the last completed fiscal year under any LTIP, shall be provided in the tabular format specified below:

Long–Term Incentive Plans—Awards in Last Fiscal Year

| (a) | (b) | (c) | Estimated Future Payouts under Non–Stock Price–Based Plans | | |
| | | | (d) | (e) | (f) |
Name	Number of Shares, Units or Other Rights (#)	Performances or Other Period Until Maturation or Payout	Threshold ($ or #)	Target ($ or #)	Maximum ($ or #)
CEO					
A					
B					
C					
D					

. . .

Instructions to Item 402(e).

1. For purposes of this paragraph, the term "long-term incentive plan" or "LTIP" shall be defined in accordance with paragraph (a)(7)(iii) of this item.

2. Describe in a footnote or in narrative text accompanying this table the material terms of any award, including a general description of the formula or criteria to be applied in determining the amounts payable. Registrants are not required to disclose any factor, criterion or performance-related or other condition to payout or maturation of a particular award that involves confidential commercial or business information, disclosure of which would adversely affect the registrant's competitive position. . . .

4. For column (d), "threshold" refers to the minimum amount payable for a certain level of performance under the plan. For column (e), "target" refers to the amount payable if the specified performance target(s) are reached. For column (f), "maximum" refers to the maximum payout possible under the plan. . . .

(f) *Defined Benefit or Actuarial Plan Disclosure.*

(1) *Pension Plan Table.*

(i) For any defined benefit or actuarial plan under which benefits are determined primarily by final compensation (or average final compensation) and years of service, provide a separate Pension Plan Table showing estimated annual benefits payable upon retirement (including amounts attributable to any defined benefit supplementary or excess pension award plans) in specified compensation and years of service classifications in the format specified below.

PENSION PLAN TABLE

| Remuneration | Years of Service | | | | |
	15	20	25	30	35
125,000					
150,000					
175,000					

PENSION PLAN TABLE Years of Service				
Remuneration	15	20	25	30	35
200,000					
225,000					
250,000					
300,000					
400,000					
450,000					
500,000					

(ii) Immediately following the Table, the registrant shall disclose:

. . .

(B) The estimated credited years of service for each of the named executive officers; and

(C) A statement as to the basis upon which benefits are computed (e.g., straight-life annuity amounts), and whether or not the benefits listed in the Pension Plan Table are subject to any deduction for Social Security or other offset amounts.

(2) *Alternative Pension Plan Disclosure.* For any defined benefit or actuarial plan under which benefits are not determined primarily by final compensation (or average final compensation) and years of service, the registrant shall state in narrative form:

(i) The formula by which benefits are determined; and

(ii) The estimated annual benefits payable upon retirement at normal retirement age for each of the named executive officers.

Instructions to Item 402(f).

1. *Pension Levels.* Compensation set forth in the Pension Plan Table pursuant to paragraph (f)(1)(i) of this item shall allow for reasonable increases in existing compensation levels; alternatively, registrants may present as the highest compensation level in the Pension Plan Table an amount equal to 120% of the amount of covered compensation of the most highly compensated individual named in the Summary Compensation Table required by paragraph (b)(2) of this item . . . .

(g) *Compensation of Directors.*

(1) *Standard Arrangements.* Describe any standard arrangements, stating amounts, pursuant to which directors of the registrant are compensated for any services provided as a director, including any additional amounts payable for committee participation or special assignments.

(2) *Other Arrangements.* Describe any other arrangements pursuant to which any director of the registrant was compensated during the registrant's last completed fiscal year for any service provided as a director, stating the amount paid and the name of the director.

Instruction to Item 402(g)(2).

The information required by paragraph (g)(2) of this item shall include any arrangement, including consulting contracts, entered into in consideration of the director's service on the board. The material terms of any such arrangement shall be included.

(h) *Employment Contracts and Termination of Employment and Change-in-Control Arrangements.* Describe the terms and conditions of each of the following contracts or arrangements:

(1) Any employment contract between the registrant and a named executive officer; and

(2) Any compensatory plan or arrangement, including payments to be received from the registrant, with respect to a named executive officer, if such plan or arrangement results or will result from the resignation, retirement or any other termination of such executive officer's employment with the registrant and its subsidiaries or from a change-in-control of the registrant or a change in the named executive officer's responsibilities following a change-in-control and the amount involved, including all periodic payments or installments, exceeds $100,-000.

(i) *Report on Repricing of Options/SARs.* (1) If at any time during the last completed fiscal year, the registrant, while a reporting company pursuant to Section 13(a) or 15(d) of the Exchange Act, has adjusted or amended the exercise price of stock options or SARs previously awarded to any of the named executive officers, whether through amendment, cancellation or replacement grants, or any other means ("repriced"), the registrant shall provide the information specified in paragraphs (i)(2) and (i)(3) of this item.

(2) The compensation committee (or other board committee performing equivalent functions or, in the absence of any such committee, the entire board of directors) shall explain in reasonable detail any such repricing of options and/or SARs held by a named executive officer in the last completed fiscal year, as well as the basis for each such repricing.

(3)(i) The [following] information ... concerning all such repricings of options and SARs held by *any* executive officer during the last ten completed fiscal years, shall be provided in the tabular format specified below:

Ten–Year Option/SAR Repricings

(a)	(b)	(c)	(d)	(e)	(f)	(g)
		Number of Securities Underlying Options/ SARs Repriced or	Market Price of Stock at Time of Repricing or Amendment	Exercise Price At Time of Repricing or Amendment	New Exercise	Length of Original Option Term Remaining at Date of Repricing or
Name	Date	Amended (#)	($)	($)	Price ($)	Amendment

Instructions to Item 402(i).

1. The required report shall be made over the name of each member of the registrant's compensation committee, or other board committee performing equivalent functions or, in the absence of any such committee, the entire board of directors. . . .

(j) *Additional Information with Respect to Compensation Committee Interlocks and Insider Participation in Compensation Decisions.* Under the caption "Compensation Committee Interlocks and Insider Participation,"

(1) The registrant shall identify each person who served as a member of the compensation committee of the registrant's board of directors (or board committee performing equivalent functions) during the last completed fiscal year, indicating each committee member who:

(i) was, during the fiscal year, an officer or employee of the registrant or any of its subsidiaries;

(ii) was formerly an officer of the registrant or any of its subsidiaries; or

(iii) had any relationship requiring disclosure by the registrant under any paragraph of Item 404 of Regulation S–K. In this event, the disclosure required by Item 404 shall accompany such identification.

(2) If the registrant has no compensation committee (or other board committee performing equivalent functions), the registrant shall identify each officer and employee of the registrant or any of its subsidiaries, and any former officer of the registrant or any of its subsidiaries, who, during the last completed fiscal year, participated in deliberations of the registrant's board of directors concerning executive officer compensation.

(3) The registrant shall describe any of the following relationships that existed during the last completed fiscal year:

(i) an executive officer of the registrant served as a member of the compensation committee (or other board committee performing equivalent functions or, in the absence of any such committee, the entire board of directors) of another entity, one of whose executive officers served on the compensation committee (or other board committee performing equivalent functions or, in the absence of any such committee, the entire board of directors) of the registrant;

(ii) an executive officer of the registrant served as a director of another entity, one of whose executive officers served on the compensation committee (or other board committee performing equivalent functions or, in the absence of any such committee, the entire board of directors) of the registrant; and

(iii) an executive officer of the registrant served as a member of the compensation committee (or other board committee performing equivalent functions or, in the absence of any such committee, the entire board of directors) of another entity, one of whose executive officers served as a director of the registrant.

(4) Disclosure required under paragraph (j)(3) of this item regarding any compensation committee member or other director of the registrant who also served as an executive officer of another entity shall be accompanied by the disclosure called for by Item 404 with respect to that person. . . .

(k) *Board Compensation Committee Report on Executive Compensation.*

(1) Disclosure of the compensation committee's compensation policies applicable to the registrant's executive officers (including the named executive officers), including the specific relationship of corporate performance to executive compensation, is required with respect to compensation reported for the last completed fiscal year.

(2) Discussion is required of the compensation committee's bases for the CEO's compensation reported for the last completed fiscal year, including the factors and criteria upon which the CEO's compensation was based. The committee shall include a specific discussion of the relationship of the registrant's performance to the CEO's compensation for the last completed fiscal year, describing each measure of the registrant's performance, whether qualitative or quantitative, on which the CEO's compensation was based.

(3) The required disclosure shall be made over the name of each member of the registrant's compensation committee (or other board committee performing equivalent functions or, in the absence of any such committee, the entire board of directors). If the board of directors modified or rejected in any material way any action or recommendation by such committee with respect to such decisions in the last completed fiscal year, the disclosure must so indicate and explain the reasons for the board's actions, and be made over the names of all members of the board. . . .

(l) *Performance Graph.*

(1) Provide a line graph comparing the yearly percentage change in the registrant's cumulative total shareholder return on a class of common stock registered under Section 12 of the Exchange Act (as measured by dividing (i) the sum of (A) the cumulative amount of dividends for the measurement period, assuming dividend reinvestment, and (B) the difference between the registrant's share price at the end and the beginning of the measurement period; by (ii) the share price at the beginning of the measurement period) with

(i) the cumulative total return of a broad equity market index assuming reinvestment of dividends, that includes companies whose equity securities are traded on the same exchange or NASDAQ market or are of comparable market capitalization; *provided, however,* that if the registrant is a company within the Standard & Poor's 500 Stock Index, the registrant must use that index; and

(ii) the cumulative total return, assuming reinvestment of dividends, of:

(A) a published industry or line-of-business index;

(B) peer issuer(s) selected in good faith. If the registrant does not select its peer issuer(s) on an industry or line-of-business basis, the registrant shall disclose the basis for its selection; or

(C) [i]ssuer(s) with similar market capitalization(s), but only if the registrant does not use a published industry or line-of-business index and does not believe it can reasonably identify a peer group. If the registrant uses this alternative, the graph shall be accompanied by a statement of the reasons for this selection.

(2) For purposes of paragraph $(l)(1)$ of this item, the term "measurement period" shall be the period beginning at the "measurement point" established by the market close on the last trading day before the beginning of the registrant's fifth preceding fiscal year, through and including the end of the registrant's last completed fiscal year. If the class of securities has been registered under section 12 of the Exchange Act for a shorter period of time, the period covered by the comparison may correspond to that time period.

(3) For purposes of paragraph $(l)(1)(ii)(A)$ of this item, the term "published industry or line-of-business index" means any index that is prepared by a party other than the registrant or an affiliate and is accessible to the registrant's security holders; provided, however, that registrants may use an index prepared by the registrant or affiliate if such index is widely recognized and used.

(4) If the registrant selects a different index from an index used for the immediately preceding fiscal year, explain the reason(s) for this change and also compare the registrant's total return with that of both the newly selected index and the index used in the immediately preceding fiscal year.

Instructions to Item 402(l)....

4. Registrants may include comparisons using performance measures in addition to total return, such as return on average common shareholders' equity, so long as the registrant's compensation committee (or other board committee performing equivalent functions or, in the absence of any such committee, the entire board of directors) describes the link between that measure and the level of executive compensation in the statement required by paragraph (k) of this Item.

Item 403. Security Ownership of Certain Beneficial Owners and Management

(a) *Security ownership of certain beneficial owners.* Furnish the following information, as of the most recent practicable date, substantially in the tabular form indicated, with respect to any person (including any "group" as that term is used in section 13(d)(3) of the Exchange Act) who is known to the registrant to be the beneficial owner of more than five percent of any class of the registrant's voting securities. The address given in column (2) may be a business, mailing or residence address. Show in column (3) the total number of shares beneficially owned and in column (4) the percentage of class so owned. Of the number of shares shown in column (3), indicate by footnote or otherwise the amount known to be shares with respect to which such listed beneficial owner has the right to acquire beneficial ownership, as specified in Rule 13d–3(d)(1) under the Exchange Act....

(1) Title of class	(2) Name and address of beneficial owner	(3) Amount and nature of beneficial ownership	(4) Percent of class

(b) *Security ownership of management.* Furnish the following information, as of the most recent practicable date, in substantially the tabular form indicated, as to each class of equity securities of the registrant or any of its parents or subsidiaries other than directors' qualifying shares, beneficially owned by all directors and nominees, naming them, each of the named executive officers as defined in Item 402(a)(3), and directors and executive officers of the registrant as a group, without naming them. Show in column (3) the total number of shares beneficially owned and in column (4) the percent of class so owned. Of the number of shares shown in column (3), indicate, by footnote or otherwise, the amount of shares with respect to which such persons have the right to acquire beneficial ownership as specified in Rule 13d–3(d)(1) [under the Exchange Act].

(1) Title of class	(2) Name of beneficial owner	(3) Amount and Nature of beneficial ownership	(4) Percent of class

(c) *Changes in control.* Describe any arrangements, known to the registrant, including any pledge by any person of securities of the registrant or any of its parents, the operation of which may at a subsequent date result in a change in control of the registrant.

Item 404. Certain Relationships and Related Transactions

(a) *Transactions with management and others.* Describe briefly any transaction, or series of similar transactions, since the beginning of the registrant's last fiscal year, or any currently proposed transaction, or series of similar transactions, to which the registrant or any of its subsidiaries was or is to be a party, in which the amount involved exceeds $60,000 and in which any of the following persons had, or will have, a direct or indirect material interest, naming such person and indicating the person's relationship to the registrant, the nature of such person's interest in the transaction(s), the amount of such transaction(s) and, where practicable, the amount of such person's interest in the transaction(s):

(1) Any director or executive officer of the registrant;

(2) Any nominee for election as a director;

(3) Any security holder who is known to the registrant to own of record or beneficially more than five percent of any class of the registrant's voting securities; and

(4) Any member of the immediate family of any of the foregoing persons.

Instructions to Paragraph (a) of Item 404.

1. The materiality of any interest is to be determined on the basis of the significance of the information to investors in light of all the circumstances of the particular case. The importance of the interest to the person having the interest, the relationship of the parties to the transaction with each other and the amount involved in the transactions are among the factors to be considered in determining the significance of the information to investors.

2. For purposes of paragraph (a), a person's immediate family shall include such person's spouse; parents; children; siblings; mothers and fathers-in-law; sons and daughters-in-law; and brothers and sisters-in-law.

3. In computing the amount involved in the transaction or series of similar transactions, include all periodic installments in the case of any lease or other agreement providing for periodic payments or installments.

4. The amount of the interest of any person specified in paragraphs (a)(1) through (4) shall be computed without regard to the amount of the profit or loss involved in the transaction(s).

5. In describing any transaction involving the purchase or sale of assets by or to the registrant or any of its subsidiaries, otherwise than in the ordinary course of business, state the cost of the assets to the purchaser and, if acquired by the seller within two years prior to the transaction, the cost thereof to the seller. Indicate the principle followed in determining the registrant's purchase or sale price and the name of the person making such determination.

6. Information shall be furnished in answer to paragraph (a) with respect to transactions that involve remuneration from the registrant or its subsidiaries, directly or indirectly, to any of the persons specified in paragraphs (a)(1) through (4) for services in any capacity unless the interest of such person arises solely from the ownership individually and in the aggregate of less than ten percent of any class of equity securities of another corporation furnishing the services to the registrant or its subsidiaries.

7. No information need be given in answer to paragraph (a) as to any transactions where:

A. The rates or charges involved in the transaction are determined by competitive bids, or the transaction involves the rendering of services as a common or contract carrier, or public utility, at rates or charges fixed in conformity with law or governmental authority;

B. The transaction involves services as a bank depositary of funds, transfer agent, registrar, trustee under a trust indenture, or similar services; or

C. The interest of the person specified in paragraphs (a)(1) through (4) arises solely from the ownership of securities of the registrant and such person receives no extra or special benefit not shared on a pro rata basis.

8. Paragraph (a) requires disclosure of indirect, as well as direct, material interests in transactions. A person who has a position or relationship with a firm, corporation, or other entity that engages in a transaction with the registrant or its subsidiaries may have an indirect interest in such transaction by reason of such position or relationship. Such an interest, however, shall not be deemed "material" within the meaning of paragraph (a) where:

A. The interest arises only: (i) From such person's position as a director of another corporation or organization which is a party to the transaction; or (ii) from the direct or indirect ownership by such person and all other persons specified in paragraphs (a)(1) through (4), in the aggregate, of less than a ten percent equity interest in another person (other than a partnership) which is a party to the transaction; or (iii) from both such position and ownership;

B. The interest arises only from such person's position as a limited partner in a partnership in which the person and all other persons specified in paragraphs (a)(1) through (4) have an interest of less than ten percent; or

C. The interest of such person arises solely from the holding of an equity interest (including a limited partnership interest, but excluding a general partnership interest) or a creditor interest in another person that is a party to the transaction with the registrant or any of its subsidiaries, and the transaction is not material to such other person.

9. There may be situations where, although these instructions do not expressly authorize nondisclosure, the interest of a person specified in paragraphs (a)(1) through (4) in a particular transaction or series of transactions is not a direct or indirect material interest. In that case, information regarding such interest and transaction is not required to be disclosed in response to this paragraph.

(b) *Certain business relationships.* Describe any of the following relationships regarding directors or nominees for director that exist, or have existed during the registrant's last fiscal year, indicating the identity of the entity with which the registrant has such a relationship, the name of the nominee or director affiliated with such entity and the nature of such nominee's or director's affiliation, the relationship between such entity and the registrant and the amount of the business done between the registrant and the entity during the registrant's last full fiscal year or proposed to be done during the registrant's current fiscal year:

(1) If the nominee or director is, or during the last fiscal year has been, an executive officer of, or owns, or during the last fiscal year has owned, of record or beneficially in excess of ten percent equity interest in, any business or professional entity that has made during the registrant's last full fiscal year, or proposes to make during the registrant's current fiscal year, payments to the registrant or its subsidiaries for property or services in excess of five percent of (i) the registrant's consolidated gross revenues for its last full fiscal year, or (ii) the other entity's consolidated gross revenues for its last full fiscal year;

(2) If the nominee or director is, or during the last fiscal year has been, an executive officer of, or owns, or during the last fiscal year has owned, of record or beneficially in excess of ten percent equity interest in, any business or professional entity to which the registrant or its subsidiaries has made during the registrant's last full fiscal year, or proposes to make during the registrant's current fiscal year, payments for property or services in excess of five percent of (i) the registrant's consolidated gross revenues for its last full fiscal year, or (ii) the other entity's consolidated gross revenues for its last full fiscal year;

(3) If the nominee or director is, or during the last fiscal year has been, an executive officer of, or owns, or during the last fiscal year has owned, of record or beneficially in excess of ten percent equity interest in, any business or professional entity to which the registrant or its subsidiaries was indebted at the end of the registrant's last full fiscal year in an aggregate amount in excess of five percent of the registrant's total consolidated assets at the end of such fiscal year;

(4) If the nominee or director is, or during the last fiscal year has been, a member of, or of counsel to, a law firm that the issuer has retained during the last fiscal year or proposes to retain during the current fiscal year; *Provided, however,* that the dollar amount of fees paid to a law firm by the registrant need not be disclosed if such amount does not exceed five percent of the law firm's gross revenues for that firm's last full fiscal year;

(5) If the nominee or director is, or during the last fiscal year has been, a partner or executive officer of any investment banking firm that has performed services for the registrant, other than as a participating underwriter in a syndicate, during the last fiscal year or that the registrant proposes to have perform services during the current year; *Provided, however,* That the dollar amount of compensation received by an investment banking firm need not be disclosed if such amount does not exceed five percent of the investment banking firm's consolidated gross revenues for that firm's last full fiscal year; or

(6) Any other relationships that the registrant is aware of between the nominee or director and the registrant that are substantially similar in nature and scope to those relationships listed in paragraphs (b)(1) through (5).

Instructions to Paragraph (b) of Item 404. ...

2. In calculating payments for property and services the following may be excluded:

A. Payments where the rates or charges involved in the transaction are determined by competitive bids, or the transaction involves the rendering of services as a common contract carrier, or public utility, at rates or charges fixed in conformity with law or governmental authority;

B. Payments that arise solely from the ownership of securities of the registrant and no extra or special benefit not shared on a pro rata basis by all holders of the class of securities is received. . . .

3. In calculating indebtedness the following may be excluded:

A. Debt securities that have been publicly offered, admitted to trading on a national securities exchange, or quoted on the automated quotation system of a registered securities association;

B. Amounts due for purchases subject to the usual trade terms. . . .

(c) *Indebtedness of management.* If any of the following persons has been indebted to the registrant or its subsidiaries at any time since the beginning of the registrant's last fiscal year in an amount in excess of $60,000, indicate the name of such person, the nature of the person's relationship by reason of which such person's indebtedness is required to be described, the largest aggregate amount of indebtedness outstanding at any time during such period, the nature of the indebtedness and of the transaction in which it was incurred, the amount thereof outstanding as of the latest practicable date and the rate of interest paid or charged thereon:

(1) Any director or executive officer of the registrant;

(2) Any nominee for election as a director;

(3) Any member of the immediate family of any of the persons specified in paragraph (c)(1) or (2);

(4) Any corporation or organization (other than the registrant or a majority-owned subsidiary of the registrant) of which any of the persons specified in paragraph (c)(1) or (2) is an executive officer or partner or is, directly or indirectly, the beneficial owner of ten percent or more of any class of equity securities; and

(5) Any trust or other estate in which any of the persons specified in paragraph (c)(1) or (2) has a substantial beneficial interest or as to which such person serves as a trustee or in a similar capacity.

Instructions to Paragraph (c) of Item 404.

1. For purposes of paragraph (c), the members of a person's immediate family are those persons specified in Instruction 2 to Item 404(a).

2. Exclude from the determination of the amount of indebtedness all amounts due from the particular person for purchases subject to usual trade terms, for ordinary travel and expense payments and for other transactions in the ordinary course of business.

3. If the lender is a bank, savings and loan association, or broker-dealer extending credit under Federal Reserve Regulation T ... and the loans are not disclosed as nonaccrual, past due, restructured or potential problems ... disclosure may consist of a statement, if such is the case, that the loans to such persons (A) were made in the ordinary course of business, (B) were made on substantially the same terms, including interest rates and collateral, as those prevailing at the time for comparable transactions with other persons, and (C) did not involve more than the normal risk of collectibility or present other unfavorable features.

4. If any indebtedness required to be described arose under section 16(b) of the Exchange Act and has not been discharged by payment, state the amount of any profit realized, that such profit will inure to the benefit of the registrant or its subsidiaries and whether suit will be brought or other steps taken to recover such profit. If, in the opinion of counsel, a question reasonably exists as to the recoverability of such profit, it will suffice to state all facts necessary to describe the transactions, including the prices and number of shares involved.

(d) *Transactions with promoters.* Registrants that have been organized within the past five years and that are filing a registration statement on Form S–1 under the Securities Act . . . or on Form 10 under the Exchange Act . . . shall:

(1) State the names of the promoters, the nature and amount of anything of value (including money, property, contracts, options or rights of any kind) received or to be received by each promoter, directly or indirectly, from the registrant and the nature and amount of any assets, services or other consideration therefore received or to be received by the registrant; and

(2) As to any assets acquired or to be acquired by the registrant from a promoter, state the amount at which the assets were acquired or are to be acquired and the principle followed or to be followed in determining such amount and identify the persons making the determination and their relationship, if any, with the registrant or any promoter. If the assets were acquired by the promoter within two years prior to their transfer to the registrant, also state the cost thereof to the promoter.

Item 405. Compliance With Section 16(a) of the Exchange Act

Every registrant having a class of equity securities registered pursuant to Section 12 of the Exchange Act . . . shall:

(a) Based solely upon a review of Forms 3 and 4 and amendments thereto furnished to the registrant pursuant to Rule 16a–3(e) during its most recent fiscal year and Forms 5 and amendments thereto furnished to the registrant with respect to its most recent fiscal year, and any written representation referred to in (b)(2)(i) below:

(1) Under the caption "Section 16(a) Beneficial Ownership Reporting Compliance," identify each person who, at any time during the fiscal year, was a director, officer, [or] beneficial owner of more than ten percent of any class of equity securities of the registrant registered pursuant to Section 12 of the Exchange Act . . . ("reporting person") that failed to file on a timely basis, as disclosed in the above Forms, reports required by Section 16(a) of the Exchange Act during the most recent fiscal year or prior fiscal years.

(2) For each such person, set forth the number of late reports, the number of transactions that were not reported on a timely basis, and any known failure to file a required Form. A known failure to file would include, but not be limited to, a failure to file a Form 3, which is required of all reporting persons, and a failure to file a Form 5 in the absence of the written representation referred to in paragraph (b)(2)(i) of this section, unless the registrant otherwise knows that no Form 5 is required.

(b) With respect to the disclosure required by paragraph (a) of this Item:

(1) A form received by the registrant within three calendar days of the required filing date may be presumed to have been filed with the Commission by the required filing date.

(2) If the registrant (i) receives a written representation from the reporting person that no Form 5 is required; and (ii) maintains the representation for two years, making a copy available to the Commission or its staff upon request, the registrant need not identify such reporting person pursuant to paragraph (a) as having failed to file a Form 5 with respect to that fiscal year.

Subpart 500—Registration Statement and Prospectus Provisions....

Item 512. Undertakings

Include each of the following undertakings that is applicable to the offering being registered.

(a) *Rule 415 Offering*. Include the following if the securities are registered pursuant to Rule 415 under the Securities Act ... :

The undersigned registrant hereby undertakes:

(1) To file, during any period in which offers or sales are being made, a post-effective amendment to this registration statement:

(i) To include any prospectus required by section 10(a)(3) of the Securities Act of 1933;

(ii) To reflect in the prospectus any facts or events arising after the effective date of the registration statement (or the most recent post-effective amendment thereof) which, individually or in the aggregate, represent a fundamental change in the information set forth in the registration statement. Notwithstanding the foregoing, any increase or decrease in volume of securities offered (if the total dollar value of securities offered would not exceed that which was registered) and any deviation from the low or high end of the estimated maximum offering range may be reflected in the form of prospectus filed with the Commission pursuant to Rule 424(b) ... if, in the aggregate, the changes in volume and price represent no more than a 20% change in the maximum aggregate offering price set forth in the "Calculation of Registration Fee" table in the effective registration statement.

(iii) To include any material information with respect to the plan of distribution not previously disclosed in the registration statement or any material change to such information in the registration statement;

Provided, however, That paragraphs (a)(1)(i) and (a)(1)(ii) of this section do not apply if the registration statement is on Form S–3, Form S–8 or Form F–3, and the information required to be included in a post-effective amendment by those paragraphs is contained in periodic reports filed with or furnished to the Commission by the registrant pursuant to section 13 or section 15(d) of the Securities Exchange Act of 1934 that are incorporated by reference in the registration statement.

(2) That, for the purpose of determining any liability under the Securities Act of 1933, each such post-effective amendment shall be deemed to be a new registration statement relating to the securities offered therein, and the offering of such securities at that time shall be deemed to be the initial bona fide offering thereof.

(3) To remove from registration by means of a post-effective amendment any of the securities being registered which remain unsold at the termination of the offering. ...

(b) *Filings incorporating subsequent Exchange Act documents by reference.* Include the following if the registration statement incorporates by reference any Exchange Act document filed subsequent to the effective date of the registration statement:

> The undersigned registrant hereby undertakes that, for purposes of determining any liability under the Securities Act of 1933, each filing of the registrant's annual report pursuant to section 13(a) or section 15(d) of the Securities Exchange Act of 1934 (and, where applicable, each filing of an employee benefit plan's annual report pursuant to section 15(d) of the Securities Exchange Act of 1934) that is incorporated by reference in the registration statement shall be deemed to be a new registration statement relating to the securities offered therein, and the offering of such securities at that time shall be deemed to be the initial bona fide offering thereof....

Subpart 900—Roll-Up Transactions

Item 901.   [Definitions] ...

(b)(1) *Partnership* means any:

(i) Finite-life limited partnership; or

(ii) Other finite-life entity.

(2)(i) Except as provided in paragraph (b)(2)(ii) of this Item ..., a limited partnership or other entity is "finite-life" if:

(A) It operates as a conduit vehicle for investors to participate in the ownership of assets for a limited period of time; and

(B) It has as a policy or purpose distributing to investors proceeds from the sale, financing or refinancing of assets or cash from operations, rather than reinvesting such proceeds or cash in the business (whether for the term of the entity or after an initial period of time following commencement of operations).

(ii) A real estate investment trust as defined in I.R.C. section 856 is not *finite-life* solely because of the distribution to investors of net income as provided by the I.R.C. if its policies or purposes do not include the distribution to investors of proceeds from the sale, financing or refinancing of assets, rather than the reinvestment of such proceeds in the business. . . .

(c)(1) Except as provided in paragraph (c)(2) or (c)(3) of this Item, *roll-up transaction* means a transaction involving the combination or reorganization of one or more partnerships, directly or indirectly, in which some or all of the investors in any of such partnerships will receive new securities, or securities in another entity.

(2) Notwithstanding paragraph (c)(1) of this Item, *roll-up transaction* shall not include:

(i) A transaction wherein the interests of all of the investors in each of the partnerships are repurchased, recalled, or exchanged in accordance with the terms of the preexisting partnership agreement for securities in an operating company specifically identified at the time of the formation of the original partnership;

(ii) A transaction in which the securities to be issued or exchanged are not required to be and are not registered under the Securities Act of 1933 . . . ;

(iii) A transaction that involves only issuers that are not required to register or report under Section 12 of the Securities Exchange Act of 1934, . . . both before and after the transaction;

(iv) A transaction that involves the combination or reorganization of one or more partnerships in which a non-affiliated party succeeds to the interests of a general partner or sponsor, if:

(A) Such action is approved by not less than 66⅔% of the outstanding units of each of the participating partnerships; and

(B) As a result of the transaction, the existing general partners will receive only compensation to which they are entitled as expressly provided for in the preexisting partnership agreements; . . .

. . .

(C) For purposes of paragraph (c)(2)(v) of this item . . . , a *regularly traded* security means any security with a minimum closing price of $2.00 or more for a majority of the business days during the preceding three-month period and a six-month minimum average daily trading volume of 1,000 shares . . . ;

(vii) A transaction in which the investors in any of the partnerships involved in the transaction are not subject to a significant adverse change with respect to voting rights, the terms of existence of the entity, management compensation or investment objectives; or

(viii) A transaction in which all investors are provided an option to receive or retain a security under substantially the same terms and conditions as the original issue. . . .

Item 908. Reasons for and Alternatives to the Roll–Up Transaction

(a) Describe the reason(s) for the roll-up transaction.

(b)(1) If the general partner or sponsor considered alternatives to the roll-up transaction being proposed, describe such alternative(s) and state the reason(s) for their rejection.

(2) Whether or not described in response to paragraph (b)(1) of this Item, describe in reasonable detail the potential alternative of continuation of the partnerships in accordance with their existing business plans, including the effects of such continuation and the material risks and benefits that likely would arise in connection therewith, and, if applicable, the general partner's reasons for not considering such alternative.

(3) Whether or not described in response to paragraph (b)(1) of this Item, describe in reasonable detail the potential alternative of liquidation of the partnerships, the procedures required to accomplish liquidation, the effects of liquidation, the material risks and benefits that likely would arise in connection with liquidation, and, if applicable, the general partner's reasons for not considering such alternative.

(c) State the reasons for the structure of the roll-up transaction and for undertaking such transaction at this time.

(d) State whether the general partner initiated the roll-up transaction and, if not, whether the general partner participated in the structuring of the transaction.

(e) State whether the general partner recommends the roll-up transaction and briefly describe the reasons for such recommendation.

Item 909. Conflicts of Interest

(a) Briefly describe the general partner's fiduciary duties to each partnership subject to the roll-up transaction and each actual or potential material conflict of interest between the general partner and the investors relating to the roll-up transaction.

(b)(1) State whether or not the general partner has retained an unaffiliated representative to act on behalf of investors for purposes of negotiating the terms of the roll-up transaction. If no such representative has been retained, describe the reasons therefor and the risks arising from the absence of separate representation. . . .

Item 910. Fairness of the Transaction

(a) State whether the general partner reasonably believes that the roll-up transaction is fair or unfair to investors and the reasons for such belief. Such discussion must address the fairness of the roll-up transaction to investors in each of the partnerships and as a whole. If the roll-up transaction may be completed with a combination of partnerships consisting of less than all partnerships, or with portions of partnerships, the belief stated must address each possible combination.

(b) Discuss in reasonable detail the material factors upon which the belief stated in paragraph (a) of this Item is based and, to the extent practicable, the weight assigned to each such factor. Such discussion should include an analysis of the extent, if any, to which such belief is based on the factors set forth in Instructions (2) and (3) to this Item, paragraph (b)(1) of Item 909 ... and Item 911.... This discussion also must:

(1) Compare the value of the consideration to be received in the roll-up transaction to the value of the consideration that would be received pursuant to each of the alternatives discussed in response to Item 908(b) ...; and

(2) Describe any material differences among the partnerships (e.g., different types of assets or different investment objectives) relating to the fairness of the transaction.

(c) If any offer of the type described in Instruction (2)(viii) to this Item has been received, describe such offer and state the reason(s) for its rejection.

(d) Describe any factors known to the general partner that may affect materially the value of the consideration to be received by investors in the roll-up transaction, the values assigned to the partnerships for purposes of the comparisons to alternatives required by paragraph (b) of this Item and the fairness of the transaction to investors.

(e) State whether the general partner's statements in response to paragraphs (a) and (b) of this Item are based, in whole or in part, on any report, opinion or appraisal described in response to Item 911 of this subpart. If so, describe any material uncertainties known to the general partner that relate to the conclusions in any such report, opinion or appraisal including, but not limited to, developments or trends that have affected or are reasonably likely to affect materially such conclusions.

Instructions to Item 910. (1) A statement that the general partner has no reasonable belief as to the fairness of the roll-up transaction to investors will not be considered sufficient disclosure in response to paragraph (a) of this Item.

(2) The factors which are important in determining the fairness of a roll-up transaction to investors and the weight, if any, which should be given to them in a particular context will vary. Normally such factors will include, among others, those referred to in paragraph (b)(1) of Item 909 and whether the consideration offered to investors constitutes fair value in relation to:

(i) Current market prices, if any;

(ii) Historic market prices, if any;

(iii) Net book value;

(iv) Going concern value;

(v) Liquidation value;

(vi) Purchases of limited partnership interests by the general partner or sponsor or their affiliates since the commencement of the partnership's second full fiscal year preceding the date of filing of the disclosure document for the roll-up transaction;

(vii) Any report, opinion, or appraisal described in Item 911; and

(viii) Offers of which the general partner or sponsor is aware made during the preceding eighteen months for a merger, consolidation, or combination of any of the partnerships; an acquisition of any of the partnerships or a material amount of their assets; a tender offer for or other acquisition of securities of any class issued by any of the partnerships; or a change in control of any of the partnerships.

(3) The discussion concerning fairness should specifically address material terms of the transaction including whether the consideration offered to investors constitutes fair value in relation to:

(i) The form and amount of consideration to be received by investors and the sponsor in the roll-up transaction;

(ii) The methods used to determine such consideration; and

(iii) The compensation to be paid to the sponsor in the future.

(4) Conclusory statements, such as "The roll-up transaction is fair to investors in relation to net book value, going concern value, liquidation value and future prospects of the partnership," will not be considered sufficient disclosure in response to paragraph (b) of this Item. . . .

Item 911. Reports, Opinions and Appraisals

(a)(1) *All material reports, opinions or appraisals.* State whether or not the general partner or sponsor has received any report, opinion (other than an opinion of counsel) or appraisal from an outside party which is materially related to the roll-up transaction including, but not limited to, any such report, opinion or appraisal relating to the consideration or the fairness of the consideration to be offered to investors in connection with the roll-up transaction or the fairness of such transaction to the general partner or investors. . . .

(b) *Fairness Opinions:* (1) If any report, opinion or appraisal relates to the fairness of the roll-up transaction to investors in the partnerships, state whether or not the report, opinion or appraisal addresses the fairness of:

(i) The roll-up transaction as a whole and to investors in each partnership; and

(ii) All possible combinations of partnerships in the roll-up transaction (including portions of partnerships if the transaction is structured to permit portions of partnerships to participate). If all possible combinations are not addressed:

(A) Identify the combinations that are addressed;

(B) Identify the person(s) that determined which combinations would be addressed and state the reasons for the selection of the combinations; and

(C) State that if the roll-up transaction is completed with a combination of partnerships not addressed, no report, opinion or appraisal concerning the fairness of the roll-up transaction will have been obtained.

(2) If the sponsor or the general partner has not obtained any opinion on the fairness of the proposed roll-up transaction to investors in each of the affected partnerships, state the sponsor's or general partner's reasons for concluding that such an opinion is not necessary in order to permit the limited partners or shareholders to make an informed decision on the proposed transaction....

SECURITIES EXCHANGE ACT OF 1934

15 U.S.C. §§ 78a et seq.

§ 1. Short Title

This chapter may be cited as the "Securities Exchange Act of 1934."

. . .

§ 3. Definitions and Application

(a) Definitions

When used in this chapter, unless the context otherwise requires

. . . .

(4) The term "broker" means any person engaged in the business of effecting transactions in securities for the account of others, but does not include a bank.

(5) The term "dealer" means any person engaged in the business of buying and selling securities for his own account, through a broker or otherwise, but does not include a bank, or any person insofar as he buys or sells securities for his own account, either individually or in some fiduciary capacity, but not as a part of a regular business. . . .

(8) The term "issuer" means any person who issues or proposes to issue any security . . . .

(10) The term "security" means any note, stock, treasury stock, bond, debenture, certificate of interest or participation in any profit-sharing agreement or in any oil, gas, or other mineral royalty or lease, any collateral-trust certificate, preorganization certificate or subscription, transferable share, investment contract, voting-trust certificate, certificate of deposit, for a security, any put, call, straddle, option, or privilege on any security, certificate of deposit, or group or index of securities (including any interest therein or based on the value thereof),

* Omitted.

or any put, call, straddle, option, or privilege entered into on a national securities exchange relating to foreign currency, or in general, any instrument commonly known as a "security"; or any certificate of interest or participation in, temporary or interim certificate for, receipt for, or warrant or right to subscribe to or purchase, any of the foregoing; but shall not include currency or any note, draft, bill of exchange, or banker's acceptance which has a maturity at the time of issuance of not exceeding nine months, exclusive of days of grace, or any renewal thereof the maturity of which is likewise limited.

(11) The term "equity security" means any stock or similar security; or any security convertible, with or without consideration, into such a security, or carrying any warrant or right to subscribe to or purchase such a security; or any such warrant or right; or any other security which the Commission shall deem to be of similar nature and consider necessary or appropriate, by such rules and regulations as it may prescribe in the public interest or for the protection of investors, to treat as an equity security.

(12)(A) The term "exempted security" or "exempted securities" includes—

(i) government securities, as defined in paragraph (42) of this subsection;

(ii) municipal securities, as defined in paragraph (29) of this subsection;

(iii) any interest or participation in any common trust fund or similar fund maintained by a bank exclusively for the collective investment and reinvestment of assets contributed thereto by such bank in its capacity as trustee, executor, administrator, or guardian;

(iv) any interest or participation in a single trust fund, or a collective trust fund maintained by a bank, or any security arising out of a contract issued by an insurance company, which interest, participation, or security is issued in connection with a qualified plan as defined in subparagraph (C) of this paragraph;

(v) any security issued by or any interest or participation in any pooled income fund, collective trust fund, collective investment fund, or similar fund that is excluded from the definition of an investment company under section 3(c)(10)(B) of the Investment Company Act of 1940; ...

(vii) such other securities (which may include, among others, unregistered securities, the market in which is predominantly intrastate) as the Commission may, by such rules and regulations as it deems consistent with the public interest and the protection of investors, either unconditionally or upon specified terms and conditions or for stated periods, exempt from the operation of any one or more provisions of this chapter which by their terms do not apply to an "exempted security" or to "exempted securities". . . .

(13) The terms "buy" and "purchase" each include any contract to buy, purchase, or otherwise acquire.

(14) The terms "sale" and "sell" each include any contract to sell or otherwise dispose of. . . .

(26) The term "self-regulatory organization" means any national securities exchange, registered securities association, or registered clearing agency . . . .

(27) The term "rules of an exchange", "rules of an association", or "rules of a clearing agency" means the constitution, articles of incorporation, bylaws, and rules, or instruments corresponding to the foregoing, of an exchange, association of brokers and dealers, or clearing agency, respectively, and such of the stated policies, practices, and interpretations of such exchange, association, or clearing agency as the Commission, by rule, may determine to be necessary or appropriate in the public interest or for the protection of investors to be deemed to be rules of such exchange, association, or clearing agency.

(28) The term "rules of a self-regulatory organization" means the rules of an exchange which is a national securities exchange, the rules of an association of brokers and dealers which is a registered securities association, the rules of a clearing agency which is a registered clearing agency or the rules of the Municipal Securities Rulemaking Board. . . .

(29) The term "municipal securities" means securities which are direct obligations of, or obligations guaranteed as to principal or interest by, a State or any political subdivision thereof, or any agency or instrumentality of a State or any political subdivision thereof, or any municipal corporate instrumentality of one or more States. . . .

(42) The term "government securities" means—

(A) securities which are direct obligations of, or obligations guaranteed as to principal or interest by, the United States;

(B) securities which are issued or guaranteed by corporations in which the United States has a direct or indirect interest and which are designated by the Secretary of the Treasury for exemption as necessary or appropriate in the public interest or for the protection of investors;

(C) securities issued or guaranteed as to principal or interest by any corporation the securities of which are designated, by statute specifically naming such corporation, to constitute exempt securities within the meaning of the laws administered by the Commission. . . .

(51)(A) The term "penny stock" means any equity security other than a security that is—

(i) registered or approved for registration and traded on a national securities exchange that meets such criteria as the Commission shall prescribe by rule or regulation for purposes of this paragraph;

(ii) authorized for quotation on an automated quotation system sponsored by a registered securities association, if such system (I) was established and in operation before January 1, 1990, and (II) meets such criteria as the Commission shall prescribe by rule or regulation for purposes of this paragraph;

(iii) issued by an investment company registered under the Investment Company Act of 1940;

(iv) excluded, on the basis of exceeding a minimum price, net tangible assets of the issuer, or other relevant criteria, from the definition of such term by rule or regulation which the Commission shall prescribe for purposes of this paragraph; or

(v) exempted, in whole or in part, conditionally or unconditionally, from the definition of such term by rule, regulation, or order prescribed by the Commission.

(B) The Commission may, by rule, regulation, or order, designate any equity security or class of equity securities described in clause (i) or (ii) of subparagraph (A) as within the meaning of the term "penny stock" if such security or class of securities is traded other than on a national securities exchange or through an automated quotation system described in clause (ii) of subparagraph (A).

(C) In exercising its authority under this paragraph to prescribe rules, regulations, and orders, the Commission shall determine that such rule, regulation, or order is consistent with the public interest and the protection of investors. . . .

(f) Consideration of promotion of efficiency, competition, and capital formation

Whenever pursuant to this chapter the Commission is engaged in rulemaking, or in the review of a rule of a self-regulatory organization, and is required to consider or determine whether an action is necessary or appropriate in the public interest, the Commission shall also consider, in addition to the protection of investors, whether the action will promote efficiency, competition, and capital formation. . . .

§ 4.   Securities and Exchange Commission

(a)   Establishment; composition; limitations on commissioners; terms of office

There is hereby established a Securities and Exchange Commission (hereinafter referred to as the "Commission") to be composed of five commissioners to be appointed by the President by and with the advice and consent of the Senate. Not more than three of such commissioners shall be members of the same political party, and in making appointments members of different political parties shall be appointed alternately as nearly as may be practicable. . . .

§ 5. Transactions on Unregistered Exchanges

It shall be unlawful for any broker, dealer, or exchange, directly or indirectly, to make use of the mails or any means or instrumentality of interstate commerce for the purpose of using any facility of an exchange within or subject to the jurisdiction of the United States to effect any transaction in a security, or to report any such transaction, unless such exchange (1) is registered as a national securities exchange under section 6 of this title, or (2) is exempted from such registration upon application by the exchange because, in the opinion of the Commission, by reason of the limited volume of transactions effected on such exchange, it is not practicable and not necessary or appropriate in the public interest or for the protection of investors to require such registration.

§ 6. National Securities Exchanges

(a) Registration; Application

An exchange may be registered as a national securities exchange under the terms and conditions hereinafter provided in this section and in accordance with the provisions of section 19(a) of this title, by filing with the Commission an application for registration in such form as the Commission, by rule, may prescribe containing the rules of the exchange and such other information and documents as the Commission, by rule, may prescribe as necessary or appropriate in the public interest or for the protection of investors. . . .

(b) Determination by Commission requisite to registration of applicant as national securities exchange. . . . *

An exchange shall not be registered as a national securities exchange unless the Commission determines that . . .

(9) The rules of the exchange prohibit the listing of any security issued in a limited partnership rollup transaction (as such term is defined in paragraphs (4) and (5) of section 14(h)), unless such transaction was conducted in accordance with procedures designed to protect the rights of limited partners, including—

(A) the right of dissenting limited partners to one of the following:

(i) an appraisal and compensation;

(ii) retention of a security under substantially the same terms and conditions as the original issue;

* Section 6(b)(9) is effective December 17, 1994. (Footnote by ed.)

(iii) approval of the limited partnership rollup transaction by not less than 75 percent of the outstanding securities of each of the participating limited partnerships;

(iv) the use of a committee of limited partners that is independent, as determined in accordance with rules prescribed by the exchange, of the general partner or sponsor, that has been approved by a majority of the outstanding units of each of the participating limited partnerships, and that has such authority as is necessary to protect the interest of limited partners, including the authority to hire independent advisors, to negotiate with the general partner or sponsor on behalf of the limited partners, and to make a recommendation to the limited partners with respect to the proposed transaction; or

(v) other comparable rights that are prescribed by rule by the exchange and that are designed to protect dissenting limited partners;

(B) the right not to have their voting power unfairly reduced or abridged;

(C) the right not to bear an unfair portion of the costs of a proposed limited partnership rollup transaction that is rejected; and

(D) restrictions on the conversion of contingent interests or fees into non-contingent interests or fees and restrictions on the receipt of a non-contingent equity interest in exchange for fees for services which have not yet been provided.

As used in this paragraph, the term "dissenting limited partner" means a person who, on the date on which soliciting material is mailed to investors, is a holder of a beneficial interest in a limited partnership that is the subject of a limited partnership rollup transaction, and who casts a vote against the transaction and complies with procedures established by the exchange, except that for purposes of an exchange or tender offer, such person shall file an objection in writing under the rules of the exchange during the period during which the offer is outstanding.

§ 9. Manipulation of Security Prices

(a) Transactions relating to purchase or sale of security

It shall be unlawful for any person, directly or indirectly, by the use of the mails or any means or instrumentality of interstate commerce, or of any facility of any national securities exchange, or for any member of a national securities exchange—

(1) For the purpose of creating a false or misleading appearance of active trading in any security registered on a national securities exchange, or a false or misleading appearance with respect to the market for any such security, (A) to effect any transaction in such security which involves no change in the beneficial ownership there-

of, or (B) to enter an order or orders for the purchase of such security with the knowledge that an order or orders of substantially the same size, at substantially the same time, and at substantially the same price, for the sale of any such security, has been or will be entered by or for the same or different parties, or (C) to enter any order or orders for the sale of any such security with the knowledge that an order or orders of substantially the same size, at substantially the same time, and at substantially the same price, for the purchase of such security, has been or will be entered by or for the same or different parties.

(2) To effect, alone or with one or more other persons, a series of transactions in any security registered on a national securities exchange creating actual or apparent active trading in such security or raising or depressing the price of such security, for the purpose of inducing the purchase or sale of such security by others.

(3) If a dealer or broker, or other person selling or offering for sale or purchasing or offering to purchase the security, to induce the purchase or sale of any security registered on a national securities exchange by the circulation or dissemination in the ordinary course of business of information to the effect that the price of any such security will or is likely to rise or fall because of market operations of any one or more persons conducted for the purpose of raising or depressing the prices of such security.

(4) If a dealer or broker, or other person selling or offering for sale or purchasing or offering to purchase the security, to make, regarding any security registered on a national securities exchange, for the purpose of inducing the purchase or sale of such security, any statement which was at the time and in the light of the circumstances under which it was made, false or misleading with respect to any material fact, and which he knew or had reasonable ground to believe was so false or misleading.

(5) For a consideration, received directly or indirectly from a dealer or broker, or other person selling or offering for sale or purchasing or offering to purchase the security, to induce the purchase or sale of any security registered on a national securities exchange by the circulation or dissemination of information to the effect that the price of any such security will or is likely to rise or fall because of the market operations of any one or more persons conducted for the purpose of raising or depressing the price of such security.

(6) To effect either alone or with one or more other persons any series of transactions for the purchase and/or sale of any security registered on a national securities exchange for the purpose of pegging, fixing, or stabilizing the price of such security in contravention of such rules and regulations as the Commission may prescribe

as necessary or appropriate in the public interest or for the protection of investors.

(b) Transactions relating to puts, calls, straddles, or options

It shall be unlawful for any person to effect, by use of any facility of a national securities exchange, in contravention of such rules and regulations as the Commission may prescribe as necessary or appropriate in the public interest or for the protection of investors—

(1) any transaction in connection with any security whereby any party to such transaction acquires any put, call, straddle, or other option or privilege of buying the security from or selling the security to another without being bound to do so; or

(2) any transaction in connection with any security with relation to which he has, directly or indirectly, any interest in any such put, call, straddle, option, or privilege; or

(3) any transaction in any security for the account of any person who he has reason to believe has, and who actually has, directly or indirectly, any interest in any such put, call, straddle, option, or privilege with relation to such security....

(e) Persons liable; suits at law or in equity

Any person who willfully participates in any act or transaction in violation of subsections (a), (b), or (c) of this section, shall be liable to any person who shall purchase or sell any security at a price which was affected by such act or transaction, and the person so injured may sue in law or in equity in any court of competent jurisdiction to recover the damages sustained as a result of any such act or transaction. In any such suit the court may, in its discretion, require an undertaking for the payment of the costs of such suit, and assess reasonable costs, including reasonable attorneys' fees, against either party litigant. Every person who becomes liable to make any payment under this subsection may recover contribution as in cases of contract from any person who, if joined in the original suit, would have been liable to make the same payment. No action shall be maintained to enforce any liability created under this section, unless brought within one year after the discovery of the facts constituting the violation and within three years after such violation.

(f) Subsection (a) not applicable to exempted securities

The provisions of subsection (a) of this section shall not apply to an exempted security....

(h) Limitations on practices that affect market volatility

It shall be unlawful for any person, by the use of the mails or any means or instrumentality of interstate commerce or of any facility of any national securities exchange, to use or employ any act or practice in connection with the purchase or sale of any equity security in contravention of such rules or regulations as the Commission may adopt, consistent with the public interest, the protection of investors, and the maintenance of fair and orderly markets—

> (1) to prescribe means reasonably designed to prevent manipulation of price levels of the equity securities market or a substantial segment thereof; and

> (2) to prohibit or constrain, during periods of extraordinary market volatility, any trading practice in connection with the purchase or sale of equity securities that the Commission determines (A) has previously contributed significantly to extraordinary levels of volatility that have threatened the maintenance of fair and orderly markets; and (B) is reasonably certain to engender such levels of volatility if not prohibited or constrained.

In adopting rules under paragraph (2), the Commission shall, consistent with the purposes of this subsection, minimize the impact on the normal operations of the market and a natural person's freedom to buy or sell any equity security.

§ 10. Manipulative and Deceptive Devices

It shall be unlawful for any person, directly or indirectly, by the use of any means or instrumentality of interstate commerce or of the mails, or of any facility of any national securities exchange—

(a) To effect a short sale, or to use or employ any stop-loss order in connection with the purchase or sale, of any security registered on a national securities exchange, in contravention of such rules and regulations as the Commission may prescribe as necessary or appropriate in the public interest or for the protection of investors.

(b) To use or employ, in connection with the purchase or sale of any security registered on a national securities exchange or any security not so registered, any manipulative or deceptive device or contrivance in contravention of such rules and regulations as the Commission may prescribe as necessary or appropriate in the public interest or for the protection of investors.

§ 10A. Audit Requirements

(a) In General.

Each audit required pursuant to this title of the financial statements of an issuer by an independent public accountant shall include, in accordance with generally accepted auditing standards, as may be modified or supplemented from time to time by the Commission—

(1) procedures designed to provide reasonable assurance of detecting illegal acts that would have a direct and material effect on the determination of financial statement amounts;

(2) procedures designed to identify related party transactions that are material to the financial statements or otherwise require disclosure therein; and

(3) an evaluation of whether there is substantial doubt about the ability of the issuer to continue as a going concern during the ensuing fiscal year.

(b) Required Response to Audit Discoveries

(1) *Investigation and report to management.*—If, in the course of conducting an audit pursuant to this title to which subsection (a) applies, the independent public accountant detects or otherwise becomes aware of information indicating that an illegal act (whether or not perceived to have a material effect on the financial statements of the issuer) has or may have occurred, the accountant shall, in accordance with generally accepted auditing standards, as may be modified or supplemented from time to time by the Commission—

(A)

(i) determine whether it is likely that an illegal act has occurred; and

(ii) if so, determine and consider the possible effect of the illegal act on the financial statements of the issuer, including any contingent monetary effects, such as fines, penalties, and damages; and

(B) as soon as practicable, inform the appropriate level of the management of the issuer and assure that the audit committee of the issuer, or the board of directors of the issuer in the absence of such a committee, is adequately informed with respect to illegal acts that have been detected or have otherwise come to the attention of such accountant in the course of the audit, unless the illegal act is clearly inconsequential.

(2) *Response to failure to take remedial action.*—If, after determining that the audit committee of the board of directors of the issuer, or the board of directors of the issuer in the absence of an audit committee, is adequately informed with respect to illegal acts that have been detected or have otherwise come to the attention of the accountant in the course of the audit of such accountant, the independent public accountant concludes that—

(A) the illegal act has a material effect on the financial statements of the issuer;

(B) the senior management has not taken, and the board of directors has not caused senior management to take, timely and appropriate remedial actions with respect to the illegal act; and

(C) the failure to take remedial action is reasonably expected to warrant departure from a standard report of the auditor, when made, or warrant resignation from the audit engagement;

the independent public accountant shall, as soon as practicable, directly report its conclusions to the board of directors.

(3) *Notice to commission; response to failure to notify.*—An issuer whose board of directors receives a report under paragraph (2) shall inform the Commission by notice not later than 1 business day after the receipt of such report and shall furnish the independent public accountant making such report with a copy of the notice furnished to the Commission. If the independent public accountant fails to receive a copy of the notice before the expiration of the required 1–business–day period, the independent public accountant shall—

(A) resign from the engagement; or

(B) furnish to the Commission a copy of its report (or the documentation of any oral report given) not later than 1 business day following such failure to receive notice.

(4) *Report after resignation.*—If an independent public accountant resigns from an engagement under paragraph (3)(A), the accountant shall, not later than 1 business day following the failure by the issuer to notify the Commission under paragraph (3), furnish to the Commission a copy of the accountant's report (or the documentation of any oral report given).

(c) Auditor Liability Limitation

No independent public accountant shall be liable in a private action for any finding, conclusion, or statement expressed in a report made pursuant to paragraph (3) or (4) of subsection (b), including any rule promulgated pursuant thereto.

(d) Civil Penalties in Cease-and-Desist Proceedings

If the Commission finds, after notice and opportunity for hearing in a proceeding instituted pursuant to section 21C, that an independent public accountant has willfully violated paragraph (3) or (4) of subsection (b), the Commission may, in addition to entering an order under section 21C, impose a civil penalty against the independent public accountant and any other person that the Commission finds was a cause of such violation. The determination to impose a civil penalty and the amount of the penalty shall be governed by the standards set forth in section 21B.

(e) Preservation of Existing Authority

Except as provided in subsection (d), nothing in this section shall be held to limit or otherwise affect the authority of the Commission under this title.

(f) Definition

As used in this section, the term "illegal act" means an act or omission that violates any law, or any rule or regulation having the force of law.

§ 12. Registration Requirements for Securities

(a) General requirement of registration

It shall be unlawful for any member, broker, or dealer to effect any transaction in any security (other than an exempted security) on a national securities exchange unless a registration is effective as to such security for such exchange in accordance with the provisions of this chapter and the rules and regulations thereunder.

(b) Procedure for registration; information

A security may be registered on a national securities exchange by the issuer filing an application with the exchange (and filing with the Commission such duplicate originals thereof as the Commission may require), which application shall contain—

(1) Such information, in such detail, as to the issuer and any person directly or indirectly controlling or controlled by, or under direct or indirect common control with, the issuer, and any guarantor of the security as to principal or interest or both, as the Commission may by rules and regulations require, as necessary or appropriate in the public interest or for the protection of investors, in respect of the following:

(A) the organization, financial structure, and nature of the business;

(B) the terms, position, rights, and privileges of the different classes of securities outstanding;

(C) the terms on which their securities are to be, and during the preceding three years have been, offered to the public or otherwise;

(D) the directors, officers, and underwriters, and each security holder of record holding more than 10 per centum of any class of any equity security of the issuer (other than an exempted security), their remuneration and their interests in the securities of, and their material contracts with, the issuer and any person directly or indirectly controlling or controlled by, or under direct or indirect common control with, the issuer;

(E) remuneration to others than directors and officers exceeding $20,000 per annum;

(F) bonus and profit-sharing arrangements;

(G) management and service contracts;

(H) options existing or to be created in respect of their securities;

(I) material contracts, not made in the ordinary course of business, which are to be executed in whole or in part at or after the filing of the application or which were made not more than two years before such filing, and every material patent or contract for a material patent right shall be deemed a material contract;

(J) balance sheets for not more than the three preceding fiscal years, certified if required by the rules and regulations of the Commission by independent public accountants;

(K) profit and loss statements for not more than the three preceding fiscal years, certified if required by the rules and regulations of the Commission by independent public accountants; and

(L) any further financial statements which the Commission may deem necessary or appropriate for the protection of investors.

(2) Such copies of articles of incorporation, bylaws, trust indentures, or corresponding documents by whatever name known, underwriting arrangements, and other similar documents of, and voting trust agreements with respect to, the issuer and any person directly or indirectly controlling or controlled by, or under direct or indirect common control with, the issuer as the Commission may require as necessary or appropriate for the proper protection of investors and to insure fair dealing in the security.

(3) Such copies of material contracts, referred to in paragraph (1)(I) above, as the Commission may require as necessary or appropriate for the proper protection of investors and to insure fair dealing in the security. . . .

(g) Registration of securities by issuer; exemptions

(1) Every issuer which is engaged in interstate commerce, or in a business affecting interstate commerce, or whose securities are traded by use of the mails or any means or instrumentality of interstate commerce shall— . . .

(B) within one hundred and twenty days after the last day of its first fiscal year . . . on which the issuer has total assets exceeding

$1,000,000 and a class of equity security (other than an exempted security) held of record by five hundred or more ... persons, register such security by filing with the Commission a registration statement (and such copies thereof as the Commission may require) with respect to such security containing such information and documents as the Commission may specify comparable to that which is required in an application to register a security pursuant to subsection (b) of this section. Each such registration statement shall become effective sixty days after filing with the Commission or within such shorter period as the Commission may direct. Until such registration statement becomes effective it shall not be deemed filed for the purposes of section 18 of this title. Any issuer may register any class of equity security not required to be registered by filing a registration statement pursuant to the provisions of this paragraph. The Commission is authorized to extend the date upon which any issuer or class of issuers is required to register a security pursuant to the provisions of this paragraph.

(2) The provisions of this subsection shall not apply in respect of—

(A) any security listed and registered on a national securities exchange.

(B) any security issued by an investment company registered pursuant to section 80a–8 of this title. . . .

(G) any security issued by an insurance company if all of the following conditions are met:

(i) Such insurance company is required to and does file an annual statement with the Commissioner of Insurance (or other officer or agency performing a similar function) of its domiciliary State, and such annual statement conforms to that prescribed by the National Association of Insurance Commissioners or in the determination of such State commissioner, officer or agency substantially conforms to that so prescribed.

(ii) Such insurance company is subject to regulation by its domiciliary State of proxies, consents, or authorizations in respect of securities issued by such company and such regulation conforms to that prescribed by the National Association of Insurance Commissioners.

(iii) ... [T]he purchase and sales of securities issued by such insurance company by beneficial owners, directors, or officers of such company are subject to regulation (including reporting) by its domiciliary State substantially in the manner provided in section 16 of this title. . . .

(3) The Commission may by rules or regulations or, on its own motion, after notice and opportunity for hearing, by order, exempt from this subsection any security of a foreign issuer, including any certificate of deposit for such a security, if the Commission finds that such

exemption is in the public interest and is consistent with the protection of investors.

(4) Registration of any class of security pursuant to this subsection shall be terminated ninety days, or such shorter period as the Commission may determine, after the issuer files a certification with the Commission that the number of holders of record of such class of security is reduced to less than three hundred persons. The Commission shall after notice and opportunity for hearing deny termination of registration if it finds that the certification is untrue. Termination of registration shall be deferred pending final determination on the question of denial.

(5) For the purposes of this subsection the term "class" shall include all securities of an issuer which are of substantially similar character and the holders of which enjoy substantially similar rights and privileges. The Commission may for the purpose of this subsection define by rules and regulations the terms "total assets" and "held of record" as it deems necessary or appropriate in the public interest or for the protection of investors in order to prevent circumvention of the provisions of this subsection.

(h) Exemption by rules and regulations from certain provisions of section

The Commission may by rules and regulations, or upon application of an interested person, by order, after notice and opportunity for hearing, exempt in whole or in part any issuer or class of issuers from the provisions of subsection (g) of this section or from section 13, 14, or 15(d) of this title or may exempt from section 16 of this title any officer, director, or beneficial owner of securities of any issuer, any security of which is required to be registered pursuant to subsection (g) hereof, upon such terms and conditions and for such period as it deems necessary or appropriate, if the Commission finds, by reason of the number of public investors, amount of trading interest in the securities, the nature and extent of the activities of the issuer, income or assets of the issuer, or otherwise, that such action is not inconsistent with the public interest or the protection of investors. The Commission may, for the purposes of any of the above-mentioned sections or subsections of this chapter, classify issuers and prescribe requirements appropriate for each such class. . . .

(j) Denial, suspension, or revocation of registration; notice and hearing

The Commission is authorized, by order, as it deems necessary or appropriate for the protection of investors to deny, to suspend the effective date of, to suspend for a period not exceeding twelve months, or to revoke the registration of a security, if the Commission finds, on the record after notice and opportunity for hearing, that the issuer of such security has failed to comply with any provision of this chapter or the rules and regulations thereunder. No member of a national securities exchange, broker, or dealer shall make use of the mails or any means or instrumentality of interstate commerce to effect any transaction in, or to induce the purchase or sale of, any security the registration of which has been and is suspended or revoked pursuant to the preceding sentence.

(k) Trading suspensions; emergency authority

(1) *Trading Suspensions.* If in its opinion the public interest and the protection of investors so require, the Commission is authorized by order—

(A) summarily to suspend trading in any security (other than an exempted security) for a period not exceeding 10 business days, and

(B) summarily to suspend all trading on any national securities exchange or otherwise, in securities other than exempted securities, for a period not exceeding 90 calendar days.

The action described in subparagraph (B) shall not take effect unless the Commission notifies the President of its decision and the President notifies the Commission that the President does not disapprove of such decision.

(2) *Emergency orders.* (A) The Commission, in an emergency, may by order summarily take such action to alter, supplement, suspend, or impose requirements or restrictions with respect to any matter or action subject to regulation by the Commission or a self-regulatory organization under this title, as the Commission determines is necessary in the public interest and for the protection of investors—

(i) to maintain or restore fair and orderly securities markets (other than markets in exempted securities); or

(ii) to ensure prompt, accurate, and safe clearance and settlement of transactions in securities (other than exempted securities).

(B) An order of the Commission under this paragraph (2) shall continue in effect for the period specified by the Commission, and may be extended, except that in no event shall the Commission's action continue in effect for more than 10 business days, including extensions. . . .

(3) *Termination of Emergency Actions by president.* The President may direct that action taken by the Commission under paragraph (1)(B) or paragraph (2) of this subsection shall not continue in effect. . . .

. . .

(6) *Definition of emergency.* For purposes of this subsection, the term "emergency" means a major market disturbance characterized by or constituting—

(A) sudden and excessive fluctuations of securities prices generally, or a substantial threat thereof, that threaten fair and orderly markets, or

(B) a substantial disruption of the safe or efficient operation of the national system for clearance and settlement of securities, or a substantial threat thereof.

(l) **Issuance of any security in contravention of rules and regulations; application to annuity contracts and variable life policies**

It shall be unlawful for an issuer, any class of whose securities is registered pursuant to this section or would be required to be so registered except for the exemption from registration provided by subsection (g)(2)(B) or (g)(2)(G) of this section, by the use of any means or instrumentality of interstate commerce, or of the mails, to issue, either originally or upon transfer, any of such securities in a form or with a format which contravenes such rules and regulations as the Commission may prescribe as necessary or appropriate for the prompt and accurate clearance and settlement of transactions in securities. The provisions of this subsection shall not apply to variable annuity contracts or variable life policies issued by an insurance company or its separate accounts....

§ 13. Periodical and Other Reports

(a) Reports by issuer of security; contents

Every issuer of a security registered pursuant to section 12 of this title shall file with the Commission, in accordance with such rules and regulations as the Commission may prescribe as necessary or appropriate for the proper protection of investors and to insure fair dealing in the security—

(1) such information and documents (and such copies thereof) as the Commission shall require to keep reasonably current the information and documents required to be included in or filed with an application or registration statement filed pursuant to section 12 of this title....

(2) such annual reports (and such copies thereof), certified if required by the rules and regulations of the Commission by independent public accountants, and such quarterly reports (and such copies thereof), as the Commission may prescribe.

Every issuer of a security registered on a national securities exchange shall also file a duplicate original of such information, documents, and reports with the exchange.

(b) Form of report; books, records, and internal accounting; directives

(1) The Commission may prescribe, in regard to reports made pursuant to this chapter, the form or forms in which the required information shall be set forth, the items or details to be shown in the balance sheet and the earning statement, and the methods to be followed in the preparation of reports, in the appraisal or valuation of assets and liabilities, in the determination of depreciation and depletion, in the differentiation of recurring and nonrecurring income, in the differentiation of investment and operating income, and in the preparation, where the Commission deems it necessary or desirable, of separate and/or consolidated balance sheets or income accounts of any person directly or indirectly controlling or controlled by the issuer, or any person under direct or indirect common control with the issuer . . . .

(2) Every issuer which has a class of securities registered pursuant to section 12 of this title and every issuer which is required to file reports pursuant to section 15(d) of this title shall—

(A) make and keep books, records, and accounts, which, in reasonable detail, accurately and fairly reflect the transactions and dispositions of the assets of the issuer; and

(B) devise and maintain a system of internal accounting controls sufficient to provide reasonable assurances that—

(i) transactions are executed in accordance with management's general or specific authorization;

(ii) transactions are recorded as necessary (I) to permit preparation of financial statements in conformity with generally accepted accounting principles or any other criteria applicable to such statements, and (II) to maintain accountability for assets;

(iii) access to assets is permitted only in accordance with management's general or specific authorization; and

(iv) the recorded accountability for assets is compared with the existing assets at reasonable intervals and appropriate action is taken with respect to any differences. . . .

(d) Reports by persons acquiring more than five per centum of certain classes of securities

(1) Any person who, after acquiring directly or indirectly the beneficial ownership of any equity security of a class which is registered pursuant to section 12 of this title, or any equity security of an insurance company which would have been required to be so registered except for the exemption contained in section 12(g)(2)(G) of this title, or any equity security issued by a closed-end investment company registered under the Investment Company Act of 1940, is directly or indirectly the beneficial owner of more than 5 per centum of such class shall, within ten days

after such acquisition, send to the issuer of the security at its principal executive office, by registered or certified mail, send to each exchange where the security is traded, and file with the Commission, a statement containing such of the following information, and such additional information, as the Commission may by rules and regulations, prescribe as necessary or appropriate in the public interest or for the protection of investors—

(A) the background, and identity, residence, and citizenship of, and the nature of such beneficial ownership by, such person and all other persons by whom or on whose behalf the purchases have been or are to be effected;

(B) the source and amount of the funds or other consideration used or to be used in making the purchases, and if any part of the purchase price is represented or is to be represented by funds or other consideration borrowed or otherwise obtained for the purpose of acquiring, holding, or trading such security, a description of the transaction and the names of the parties thereto, except that where a source of funds is a loan made in the ordinary course of business by a bank, ... if the person filing such statement so requests, the name of the bank shall not be made available to the public;

(C) if the purpose of the purchases or prospective purchases is to acquire control of the business of the issuer of the securities, any plans or proposals which such persons may have to liquidate such issuer, to sell its assets to or merge it with any other persons, or to make any other major change in its business or corporate structure;

(D) the number of shares of such security which are beneficially owned, and the number of shares concerning which there is a right to acquire, directly or indirectly, by (i) such person, and (ii) by each associate of such person, giving the background, identity, residence, and citizenship of each such associate; and

(E) information as to any contracts, arrangements, or understandings with any person with respect to any securities of the issuer, including but not limited to transfer of any of the securities, joint ventures, loan or option arrangements, puts or calls, guaranties of loans, guaranties against loss or guaranties of profits, division of losses or profits, or the giving or withholding of proxies, naming the persons with whom such contracts, arrangements, or understandings have been entered into, and giving the details thereof.

(2) If any material change occurs in the facts set forth in the statements to the issuer and the exchange, and in the statement filed with the Commission, an amendment shall be transmitted to the issuer and the exchange and shall be filed with the Commission, in accordance with such rules and regulations as the Commission may prescribe as necessary or appropriate in the public interest or for the protection of investors.

(3) When two or more persons act as a partnership, limited partnership, syndicate, or other group for the purpose of acquiring, holding, or disposing of securities of an issuer, such syndicate or group shall be deemed a "person" for the purposes of this subsection.

(4) In determining, for purposes of this subsection, any percentage of a class of any security, such class shall be deemed to consist of the amount of the outstanding securities of such class, exclusive of any securities of such class held by or for the account of the issuer or a subsidiary of the issuer.

(5) The Commission, by rule or regulation or by order, may permit any person to file in lieu of the statement required by paragraph (1) of this subsection or the rules and regulations thereunder, a notice stating the name of such person, the number of shares of any equity securities subject to paragraph (1) which are owned by him, the date of their acquisition and such other information as the Commission may specify, if it appears to the Commission that such securities were acquired by such person in the ordinary course of his business and were not acquired for the purpose of and do not have the effect of changing or influencing the control of the issuer nor in connection with or as a participant in any transaction having such purpose or effect.

(6) The provisions of this subsection shall not apply to—

(A) any acquisition or offer to acquire securities made or proposed to be made by means of a registration statement under the Securities Act of 1933;

(B) any acquisition of the beneficial ownership of a security which, together with all other acquisitions by the same person of securities of the same class during the preceding twelve months, does not exceed 2 per centum of that class;

(C) any acquisition of an equity security by the issuer of such security;

(D) any acquisition or proposed acquisition of a security which the Commission, by rules or regulations or by order, shall exempt from the provisions of this subsection as not entered into for the purpose of, and not having the effect of, changing or influencing the control of the issuer or otherwise as not comprehended within the purposes of this subsection.

(e)   Purchase of securities by issuer

(1) It shall be unlawful for an issuer which has a class of equity securities registered pursuant to section 12 of this title, or which is a closed-end investment company registered under the Investment Company Act of 1940, to purchase any equity security issued by it if such purchase is in contravention of such rules and regulations as the Commission, in the public interest or for the protection of investors, may

adopt (A) to define acts and practices which are fraudulent, deceptive, or manipulative, and (B) to prescribe means reasonably designed to prevent such acts and practices. Such rules and regulations may require such issuer to provide holders of equity securities of such class with such information relating to the reasons for such purchase, the source of funds, the number of shares to be purchased, the price to be paid for such securities, the method of purchase, and such additional information, as the Commission deems necessary or appropriate in the public interest or for the protection of investors, or which the Commission deems to be material to a determination whether such security should be sold.

(2) For the purpose of this subsection, a purchase by or for the issuer or any person controlling, controlled by, or under common control with the issuer, or a purchase subject to control of the issuer or any such person, shall be deemed to be a purchase by the issuer. The Commission shall have power to make rules and regulations implementing this paragraph in the public interest and for the protection of investors, including exemptive rules and regulations covering situations in which the Commission deems it unnecessary or inappropriate that a purchase of the type described in this paragraph shall be deemed to be a purchase by the issuer for purposes of some or all of the provisions of paragraph (1) of this subsection. . . .

(g) Statement of equity security ownership

(1) Any person who is directly or indirectly the beneficial owner of more than 5 per centum of any security of a class described in subsection (d)(1) of this section shall send to the issuer of the security and shall file with the Commission a statement setting forth, in such form and at such time as the Commission may, by rule, prescribe—

(A) such person's identity, residence, and citizenship; and

(B) the number and description of the shares in which such person has an interest and the nature of such interest.

(2) If any material change occurs in the facts set forth in the statement sent to the issuer and filed with the Commission, an amendment shall be transmitted to the issuer and shall be filed with the Commission, in accordance with such rules and regulations as the Commission may prescribe as necessary or appropriate in the public interest or for the protection of investors.

(3) When two or more persons act as a partnership, limited partnership, syndicate, or other group for the purpose of acquiring, holding, or disposing of securities of an issuer, such syndicate or group shall be deemed a "person" for the purposes of this subsection.

(4) In determining, for purposes of this subsection, any percentage of a class of any security, such class shall be deemed to consist of the amount of the outstanding securities of such class, exclusive of any

securities of such class held by or for the account of the issuer or a subsidiary of the issuer.

(5) In exercising its authority under this subsection, the Commission shall take such steps as it deems necessary or appropriate in the public interest or for the protection of investors (A) to achieve centralized reporting of information regarding ownership, (B) to avoid unnecessarily duplicative reporting by and minimize the compliance burden on persons required to report, and (C) to tabulate and promptly make available the information contained in any report filed pursuant to this subsection in a manner which will, in the view of the Commission, maximize the usefulness of the information to other Federal and State agencies and the public.

(6) The Commission may, by rule or order, exempt, in whole or in part, any person or class of persons from any or all of the reporting requirements of this subsection as it deems necessary or appropriate in the public interest or for the protection of investors....

(h) Large trader reporting

(1) Identification requirements for large traders.

For the purpose of monitoring the impact on the securities markets of securities transactions involving a substantial volume or a large fair market value or exercise value and for the purpose of otherwise assisting the Commission in the enforcement of this title, each large trader shall—

(A) provide such information to the Commission as the Commission may by rule or regulation prescribe as necessary or appropriate, identifying such large trader and all accounts in or through which such large trader effects such transactions; and

(B) identify, in accordance with such rules or regulations as the Commission may prescribe as necessary or appropriate, to any registered broker or dealer by or through whom such large trader directly or indirectly effects securities transactions, such large trader and all accounts directly or indirectly maintained with such broker or dealer by such large trader in or through which such transactions are effected.

(2) Recordkeeping and reporting requirements for brokers and dealers. Every registered broker or dealer shall make and keep for prescribed periods such records as the Commission by rule or regulation prescribes as necessary or appropriate in the public interest, for the protection of investors, or otherwise in furtherance of the purposes of this title, with respect to securities transactions that equal or exceed the reporting activity level effected directly or indirectly by or through such registered broker or dealer of or for any person that such broker or dealer knows is a large trader, or any person that such broker or dealer has reason to know is a large

trader on the basis of transactions in securities effected by or through such broker or dealer. Such records shall be available for reporting to the Commission, or any self-regulatory organization that the Commission shall designate to receive such reports, on the morning of the day following the day the transactions were effected, and shall be reported to the Commission or a self-regulatory organization designated by the Commission immediately upon request by the Commission or such a self-regulatory organization. Such records and reports shall be in a format and transmitted in a manner prescribed by the Commission (including, but not limited to, machine readable form)....

(8) Definitions. For purposes of this subsection—

(A) the term "large trader" means every person who, for his own account or an account for which he exercises investment discretion, effects transactions for the purchase or sale of any publicly traded security or securities by use of any means or instrumentality of interstate commerce or of the mails, or of any facility of a national securities exchange, directly or indirectly by or through a registered broker or dealer in an aggregate amount equal to or in excess of the identifying activity level;

(B) the term "publicly traded security" means any equity security (including an option on individual equity securities, and an option on a group or index of such securities) listed, or admitted to unlisted trading privileges, on a national securities exchange, or quoted in an automated interdealer quotation system;

(C) the term "identifying activity level" means transactions in publicly traded securities at or above a level of volume, fair market value, or exercise value as shall be fixed from time to time by the Commission by rule or regulation, specifying the time interval during which such transactions shall be aggregated;

(D) the term "reporting activity level" means transactions in publicly traded securities at or above a level of volume, fair market value, or exercise value as shall be fixed from time to time by the Commission by rule, regulation, or order, specifying the time interval during which such transactions shall be aggregated; and

(E) the term "person" has the meaning given in section 3(a)(9) of this title and also includes two or more persons acting as a partnership, limited partnership, syndicate, or other group, but does not include a foreign central bank.

§ 14. Proxies

(a) Solicitation of proxies in violation of rules and regulations

It shall be unlawful for any person, by the use of the mails or by any means or instrumentality of interstate commerce or of any facility of a national securities exchange or otherwise, in contravention of such rules and regulations as the Commission may prescribe as necessary or appropriate in the public interest or for the protection of investors, to solicit or to permit the use of his name to solicit any proxy or consent or authorization in respect of any security (other than an exempted security) registered pursuant to section 12 of this title....

(b) Giving or refraining from giving proxy in respect of any security carried for account of customer; disclosure of beneficial owners

(1) It shall be unlawful for any member of a national securities exchange, or any broker or dealer registered under this chapter, or any bank, association, or other entity that exercises fiduciary powers, in contravention of such rules and regulations as the Commission may prescribe as necessary or appropriate in the public interest or for the protection of investors, to give, or to refrain from giving a proxy, consent, authorization, or information statement in respect of any security registered pursuant to section 12 of this title, or any security issued by an investment company registered under the Investment Company Act of 1940, and carried for the account of a customer....

(c) Information to holders of record prior to annual or other meeting

Unless proxies, consents, or authorizations in respect of a security registered pursuant to section 12 of this title, or a security issued by an investment company registered under the Investment Company Act of 1940, are solicited by or on behalf of the management of the issuer from the holders of record of such security in accordance with the rules and regulations prescribed under subsection (a) of this section, prior to any annual or other meeting of the holders of such security, such issuer shall, in accordance with rules and regulations prescribed by the Commission, file with the Commission and transmit to all holders of record of such security information substantially equivalent to the information which would be required to be transmitted if a solicitation were made....

(d) Tender offer by owner of more than five per centum of class of securities; exceptions

(1) It shall be unlawful for any person, directly or indirectly, by use of the mails or by any means or instrumentality of interstate commerce or of any facility of a national securities exchange or otherwise, to make

a tender offer for, or a request or invitation for tenders of, any class of any equity security which is registered pursuant to section 12 of this title, or any equity security of an insurance company which would have been required to be so registered except for the exemption contained in section 12(g)(2)(G) of this title, or any equity security issued by a closed-end investment company registered under the Investment Company Act of 1940, if, after consummation thereof, such person would, directly or indirectly, be the beneficial owner of more than 5 per centum of such class, unless at the time copies of the offer or request or invitation are first published or sent or given to security holders such person has filed with the Commission a statement containing such of the information specified in section 13(d) of this title, and such additional information as the Commission may by rules and regulations prescribe as necessary or appropriate in the public interest or for the protection of investors. All requests or invitations for tenders or advertisements making a tender offer or requesting or inviting tenders of such a security shall be filed as a part of such statement and shall contain such of the information contained in such statement as the Commission may by rules and regulations prescribe. Copies of any additional material soliciting or requesting such tender offers subsequent to the initial solicitation or request shall contain such information as the Commission may by rules and regulations prescribe as necessary or appropriate in the public interest or for the protection of investors, and shall be filed with the Commission not later than the time copies of such material are first published or sent or given to security holders. Copies of all statements, in the form in which such material is furnished to security holders and the Commission, shall be sent to the issuer not later than the date such material is first published or sent or given to any security holders.

(2) When two or more persons act as a partnership, limited partnership, syndicate, or other group for the purpose of acquiring, holding, or disposing of securities of an issuer, such syndicate or group shall be deemed a "person" for purposes of this subsection.

(3) In determining, for purposes of this subsection, any percentage of a class of any security, such class shall be deemed to consist of the amount of the outstanding securities of such class, exclusive of any securities of such class held by or for the account of the issuer or a subsidiary of the issuer.

(4) Any solicitation or recommendation to the holders of such a security to accept or reject a tender offer or request or invitation for tenders shall be made in accordance with such rules and regulations as the Commission may prescribe as necessary or appropriate in the public interest or for the protection of investors.

(5) Securities deposited pursuant to a tender offer or request or invitation for tenders may be withdrawn by or on behalf of the depositor at any time until the expiration of seven days after the time definitive

copies of the offer or request or invitation are first published or sent or given to security holders, and at any time after sixty days from the date of the original tender offer or request or invitation, except as the Commission may otherwise prescribe by rules, regulations, or order as necessary or appropriate in the public interest or for the protection of investors.

(6) Where any person makes a tender offer, or request or invitation for tenders, for less than all the outstanding equity securities of a class, and where a greater number of securities is deposited pursuant thereto within ten days after copies of the offer or request or invitation are first published or sent or given to security holders than such person is bound or willing to take up and pay for, the securities taken up shall be taken up as nearly as may be pro rata, disregarding fractions, according to the number of securities deposited by each depositor. The provisions of this subsection shall also apply to securities deposited within ten days after notice of an increase in the consideration offered to security holders, as described in paragraph (7), is first published or sent or given to security holders.

(7) Where any person varies the terms of a tender offer or request or invitation for tenders before the expiration thereof by increasing the consideration offered to holders of such securities, such person shall pay the increased consideration to each security holder whose securities are taken up and paid for pursuant to the tender offer or request or invitation for tenders whether or not such securities have been taken up by such person before the variation of the tender offer or request or invitation.

(8) The provisions of this subsection shall not apply to any offer for, or request or invitation for tenders of, any security—

(A) if the acquisition of such security, together with all other acquisitions by the same person of securities of the same class during the preceding twelve months, would not exceed 2 per centum of that class;

(B) by the issuer of such security; or

(C) which the Commission, by rules or regulations or by order, shall exempt from the provisions of this subsection as not entered into for the purpose of, and not having the effect of, changing or influencing the control of the issuer or otherwise as not comprehended within the purposes of this subsection.

(e) Untrue statement of material fact or omission of fact with respect to tender offer

It shall be unlawful for any person to make any untrue statement of a material fact or omit to state any material fact necessary in order to make the statements made, in the light of the circumstances under which they are made, not misleading, or to engage in any fraudulent, deceptive, or manipulative acts or practices, in connection with any tender offer or request or invitation for tenders, or any solicitation of security holders in opposition to or in favor of any such offer, request, or invitation. The Commission shall, for the purposes of this subsection, by rules and regulations define, and prescribe means reasonably designed to prevent, such acts and practices as are fraudulent, deceptive, or manipulative.

(f) Election or designation of majority of directors of issuer by owner of more than five per centum of class of securities at other than meeting of security holders

If, pursuant to any arrangement or understanding with the person or persons acquiring securities in a transaction subject to subsection (d) of this section or subsection (d) of section 13 of this title, any persons are to be elected or designated as directors of the issuer, otherwise than at a meeting of security holders, and the persons so elected or designated will constitute a majority of the directors of the issuer, then, prior to the time any such person takes office as a director, and in accordance with rules and regulations prescribed by the Commission, the issuer shall file with the Commission, and transmit to all holders of record of securities of the issuer who would be entitled to vote at a meeting for election of directors, information substantially equivalent to the information which would be required by subsection (a) or (c) of this section to be transmitted if such person or persons were nominees for election as directors at a meeting of such security holders. . . .

(h) Proxy solicitations and tender offers in connection with limited partnership rollup transactions

(1) Proxy rules to contain special provisions

It shall be unlawful for any person to solicit any proxy, consent, or authorization concerning a limited partnership rollup transaction, or to make any tender offer in furtherance of a limited partnership rollup transaction, unless such transaction is conducted in accordance with rules prescribed by the Commission under subsections (a) and (d) of this section as required by this subsection. Such rules shall—

(A) permit any holder of a security that is the subject of the proposed limited partnership rollup transaction to engage in preliminary communications for the purpose of determining whether to solicit proxies, consents, or authorizations in opposition to the proposed limited partnership rollup transaction, without regard to whether any such communication would otherwise be considered a solicitation of proxies, and without being required to file soliciting material with the Commission prior to making that determination, except that—

(i) nothing in this subparagraph shall be construed to limit the application of any provision of this chapter prohibiting, or reasonably designed to prevent, fraudulent, deceptive, or manipulative acts or practices under this chapter; and

(ii) any holder of not less than 5 percent of the outstanding securities that are the subject of the proposed limited partnership rollup transaction who engages in the business of buying and selling limited partnership interests in the secondary market shall be required to disclose such ownership interests and any potential conflicts of interests in such preliminary communications;

(B) require the issuer to provide to holders of the securities that are the subject of the limited partnership rollup transaction such list of the holders of the issuer's securities as the Commission may determine in such form and subject to such terms and conditions as the Commission may specify;

(C) prohibit compensating any person soliciting proxies, consents, or authorizations directly from security holders concerning such a limited partnership rollup transaction—

(i) on the basis of whether the solicited proxy, consent, or authorization either approves or disapproves the proposed limited partnership rollup transaction; or

(ii) contingent on the approval, disapproval, or completion of the limited partnership rollup transaction;

(D) set forth disclosure requirements for soliciting material distributed in connection with a limited partnership rollup transaction, including requirements for clear, concise, and comprehensible disclosure with respect to—

(i) any changes in the business plan, voting rights, form of ownership interest, or the compensation of the general partner in the proposed limited partnership rollup transaction from each of the original limited partnerships;

(ii) the conflicts of interest, if any, of the general partner;

(iii) whether it is expected that there will be a significant difference between the exchange values of the limited partnerships and the trading price of the securities to be issued in the limited partnership rollup transaction;

(iv) the valuation of the limited partnerships and the method used to determine the value of the interests of the limited partners to be exchanged for the securities in the limited partnership rollup transaction;

(v) the differing risks and effects of the limited partnership rollup transaction for investors in different limited partnerships proposed to be included, and the risks and effects of completing the limited partnership rollup transaction with less than all limited partnerships;

(vi) the statement by the general partner required under subparagraph (E);

(vii) such other matters deemed necessary or appropriate by the Commission;

(E) require a statement by the general partner as to whether the proposed limited partnership rollup transaction is fair or unfair to investors in each limited partnership, a discussion of the basis for that conclusion, and an evaluation and a description by the general partner of alternatives to the limited partnership rollup transaction, such as liquidation;

(F) provide that, if the general partner or sponsor has obtained any opinion (other than an opinion of counsel), appraisal, or report that is prepared by an outside party and that is materially related to the limited partnership rollup transaction, such soliciting materials shall contain or be accompanied by clear, concise, and comprehensible disclosure with respect to—

(i) the analysis of the transaction, scope of review, preparation of the opinion, and basis for and methods of arriving at conclusions, and any representations and undertakings with respect thereto;

(ii) the identity and qualifications of the person who prepared the opinion, the method of selection of such person, and any material past, existing, or contemplated relationships between the person or any of its affiliates and the general partner, sponsor, successor, or any other affiliate;

(iii) any compensation of the preparer of such opinion, appraisal, or report that is contingent on the transaction's approval or completion; and

(iv) any limitations imposed by the issuer on the access afforded to such preparer to the issuer's personnel, premises, and relevant books and records;

(G) provide that, if the general partner or sponsor has obtained any opinion, appraisal, or report as described in subparagraph (F) from any person whose compensation is contingent on the transaction's approval or completion or who has not been given access by the issuer to its personnel and premises and relevant books and records, the general partner or sponsor shall state the reasons therefor;

(H) provide that, if the general partner or sponsor has not obtained any opinion on the fairness of the proposed limited partnership rollup transaction to investors in each of the affected partnerships, such soliciting materials shall contain or be accompanied by a statement of such partner's or sponsor's reasons for concluding that such an opinion is not necessary in order to permit the limited partners to make an informed decision on the proposed transaction;

(I) require that the soliciting material include a clear, concise, and comprehensible summary of the limited partnership rollup transaction (including a summary of the matters referred to in clauses (i) through (vii) of subparagraph (D) and a summary of the matter referred to in subparagraphs (F), (G), and (H)), with the risks of the limited partnership rollup transaction set forth prominently in the fore part thereof;

(J) provide that any solicitation or offering period with respect to any proxy solicitation, tender offer, or information statement in a limited partnership rollup transaction shall be for not less than the lesser of 60 calendar days or the maximum number of days permitted under applicable State law; and

(K) contain such other provisions as the Commission determines to be necessary or appropriate for the protection of investors in limited partnership rollup transactions.

(2) Exemptions

The Commission may, consistent with the public interest, the protection of investors, and the purposes of this chapter, exempt by rule or order any security or class of securities, any transaction or class of transactions, or any person or class of persons, in whole or in part, conditionally or unconditionally, from the requirements imposed pursuant to paragraph (1) or from the definition contained in paragraph (4).

(3) Effect on Commission authority

Nothing in this subsection limits the authority of the Commission under subsection (a) or (d) of this section or any other provision of this chapter or precludes the Commission from imposing, under subsection (a) or (d) of this section or any other provision of this chapter, a remedy or procedure required to be imposed under this subsection.

(4) Definition of limited partnership rollup transaction

Except as provided in paragraph (5), as used in this subsection, the term "limited partnership rollup transaction" means a transaction involving the combination or reorganization of one or more limited partnerships, directly or indirectly, in which—

(A) some or all of the investors in any of such limited partnerships will receive new securities, or securities in another entity, that will be reported under a transaction reporting plan declared effective before December 17, 1993, by the Commission under section 11A of this title;

(B) any of the investors' limited partnership securities are not, as of the date of filing, reported under a transaction reporting plan declared effective before December 17, 1993, by the Commission under section 11A of this title;

(C) investors in any of the limited partnerships involved in the transaction are subject to a significant adverse change with respect to voting rights, the term of existence of the entity, management compensation, or investment objectives; and

(D) any of such investors are not provided an option to receive or retain a security under substantially the same terms and conditions as the original issue.

(5) Exclusions from definition

Notwithstanding paragraph (4), the term "limited partnership roll-up transaction" does not include—

(A) a transaction that involves only a limited partnership or partnerships having an operating policy or practice of retaining cash available for distribution and reinvesting proceeds from the sale, financing, or refinancing of assets in accordance with such criteria as the Commission determines appropriate;

(B) a transaction involving only limited partnerships wherein the interests of the limited partners are repurchased, recalled, or exchanged in accordance with the terms of the preexisting limited partnership agreements for securities in an operating company specifically identified at the time of the formation of the original limited partnership;

(C) a transaction in which the securities to be issued or exchanged are not required to be and are not registered under the Securities Act of 1933;

(D) a transaction that involves only issuers that are not required to register or report under section 12 of this title, both before and after the transaction;

(E) a transaction, except as the Commission may otherwise provide by rule for the protection of investors, involving the combination or reorganization of one or more limited partnerships in which a non-affiliated party succeeds to the interests of a general partner or sponsor, if—

(i) such action is approved by not less than 66⅔ percent of the outstanding units of each of the participating limited partnerships; and

(ii) as a result of the transaction, the existing general partners will receive only compensation to which they are entitled as expressly provided for in the preexisting limited partnership agreements; or

(F) a transaction, except as the Commission may otherwise provide by rule for the protection of investors, in which the securities offered to investors are securities of another entity that are reported under a transaction reporting plan declared effective before December 17, 1993, by the Commission under section 11A of this title, if—

    (i) such other entity was formed, and such class of securities was reported and regularly traded, not less than 12 months before the date on which soliciting material is mailed to investors; and

    (ii) the securities of that entity issued to investors in the transaction do not exceed 20 percent of the total outstanding securities of the entity, exclusive of any securities of such class held by or for the account of the entity or a subsidiary of the entity.

§ 15. Registration and Regulation of Brokers and Dealers

(a) Registration of all persons utilizing exchange facilities to effect transactions; exemptions

(1) It shall be unlawful for any broker or dealer which is either a person other than a natural person or a natural person not associated with a broker or dealer which is a person other than a natural person (other than such a broker or dealer whose business is exclusively intrastate and who does not make use of any facility of a national securities exchange) to make use of the mails or any means or instrumentality of interstate commerce to effect any transactions in, or to induce or attempt to induce the purchase or sale of, any security (other than an exempted security or commercial paper, bankers' acceptances, or commercial bills) unless such broker or dealer is registered in accordance with subsection (b) of this section. . . .

(d) Filing of supplementary and periodic information

Each issuer which has filed a registration statement containing an undertaking which is or becomes operative under this subsection as in effect prior to August 20, 1964, and each issuer which shall after such date file a registration statement which has become effective pursuant to the Securities Act of 1933 ... shall file with the Commission, in accordance with such rules and regulations as the Commission may prescribe as necessary or appropriate in the public interest or for the protection of investors, such supplementary and periodic information, documents, and reports as may be required pursuant to section 13 of this title in respect of a security registered pursuant to section 12 of this title. The duty to file under this subsection shall be automatically suspended if and so long as any issue of securities of such issuer is registered pursuant to section 12 of this title. The duty to file under this subsection shall also be automatically suspended as to any fiscal year, other than the fiscal year within which such registration statement became effective, if, at the beginning of such fiscal year, the securities of each class to which the registration statement relates are held of record by less than three hundred persons. For the purposes of this subsection, the term "class" shall be construed to include all securities of an issuer which are of substantially similar character and the holders of which enjoy substantially similar rights and privileges. The Commission may, for the purpose of this subsection, define by rules and regulations the term "held of record" as it deems necessary or appropriate in the public interest or for the protection of investors in order to prevent circumvention of the provisions of this subsection....

(f) Prevention of misuse of nonpublic information

Every registered broker or dealer shall establish, maintain, and enforce written policies and procedures reasonably designed, taking into consideration the nature of such broker's or dealer's business, to prevent the misuse in violation of this title, or the rules or regulations thereunder, of material, nonpublic information by such broker or dealer or any person associated with such broker or dealer. The Commission, as it deems necessary or appropriate in the public interest or for the protection of investors, shall adopt rules or regulations to require specific policies or procedures reasonably designed to prevent misuse in violation of this title (or the rules or regulations thereunder) of material, nonpublic information.

(g) Requirements for transactions in penny stocks

(1) *In general.* No broker or dealer shall make use of the mails or any means or instrumentality of interstate commerce to effect any transaction in, or to induce or attempt to induce the purchase or sale of, any penny stock by any customer except in accordance with the requirements of this subsection and the rules and regulations prescribed under this subsection.

(2) *Risk disclosure with respect to penny stocks.* Prior to effecting any transaction in any penny stock, a broker or dealer shall give the customer a risk disclosure document that—

(A) contains a description of the nature and level of risk in the market for penny stocks in both public offerings and secondary trading;

(B) contains a description of the broker's or dealer's duties to the customer and of the rights and remedies available to the customer with respect to violations of such duties or other requirements of Federal securities laws;

(C) contains a brief, clear, narrative description of a dealer market, including "bid" and "ask" prices for penny stocks and the significance of the spread between the bid and ask prices . . . .

(3) *Commission rules relating to disclosure.* The Commission shall adopt rules setting forth additional standards for the disclosure by brokers and dealers to customers of information concerning transactions in penny stocks. Such rules—

(A) shall require brokers and dealers to disclose to each customer, prior to effecting any transaction in, and at the time of confirming any transaction with respect to any penny stock, in accordance with such procedures and methods as the Commission may require consistent with the public interest and the protection of investors—

(i) the bid and ask prices for penny stock, or such other information as the Commission may, by rule, require to provide customers with more useful and reliable information relating to the price of such stock;

(ii) the number of shares to which such bid and ask prices apply, or other comparable information relating to the depth and liquidity of the market for such stock; and

(iii) the amount and a description of any compensation that the broker or dealer and the associated person thereof will receive or has received in connection with such transaction . . . .

(5) *Regulations.* It shall be unlawful for any person to violate such rules and regulations as the Commission shall prescribe in the public interest or for the protection of investors or to maintain fair and orderly markets—

(A) as necessary or appropriate to carry out this subsection; or

(B) as reasonably designed to prevent fraudulent, deceptive, or manipulative acts and practices with respect to penny stocks. . . .

§ 16.   Directors, Officers, and Principal Stockholders

(a)   Filing of statement of all ownership of securities of issuer by owner of more than ten per centum of any class of security

Every person who is directly or indirectly the beneficial owner of more than 10 per centum of any class of any equity security (other than an exempted security) which is registered pursuant to section 12 of this title, or who is a director or an officer of the issuer of such security, shall file, at the time of the registration of such security on a national securities exchange or by the effective date of a registration statement filed pursuant to section 12(g) of this title, or within ten days after he becomes such beneficial owner, director, or officer, a statement with the Commission (and, if such security is registered on a national securities exchange, also with the exchange) of the amount of all equity securities of such issuer of which he is the beneficial owner, and within ten days after the close of each calendar month thereafter, if there has been a change in such ownership during such month, shall file with the Commission (and if such security is registered on a national securities exchange, shall also file with the exchange), a statement indicating his ownership at the close of the calendar month and such changes in his ownership as have occurred during such calendar month.

(b) Profits from purchase and sale of security within six months

For the purpose of preventing the unfair use of information which may have been obtained by such beneficial owner, director, or officer by reason of his relationship to the issuer, any profit realized by him from any purchase and sale, or any sale and purchase, of any equity security of such issuer (other than an exempted security) within any period of less than six months, unless such security was acquired in good faith in connection with a debt previously contracted, shall inure to and be recoverable by the issuer, irrespective of any intention on the part of such beneficial owner, director, or officer in entering into such transaction of holding the security purchased or of not repurchasing the security sold for a period exceeding six months. Suit to recover such profit may be instituted at law or in equity in any court of competent jurisdiction by the issuer, or by the owner of any security of the issuer in the name and in behalf of the issuer if the issuer shall fail or refuse to bring such suit within sixty days after request or shall fail diligently to prosecute the same thereafter; but no such suit shall be brought more than two years after the date such profit was realized. This subsection shall not be construed to cover any transaction where such beneficial owner was not such both at the time of the purchase and sale, or the sale and purchase, of the security involved, or any transaction or transactions which the Commission by rules and regulations may exempt as not comprehended within the purpose of this subsection.

(c) Conditions for sale of security by beneficial owner, director, or officer

It shall be unlawful for any such beneficial owner, director, or officer, directly or indirectly, to sell any equity security of such issuer (other than an exempted security), if the person selling the security or his principal (1) does not own the security sold, or (2) if owning the security, does not deliver it against such sale within twenty days thereafter, or does not within five days after such sale deposit it in the mails or other usual channels of transportation; but no person shall be deemed to have violated this subsection if he proves that notwithstanding the exercise of good faith he was unable to make such delivery or deposit within such time, or that to do so would cause undue inconvenience or expense. . . .

§ 18.   Liability for Misleading Statements

(a)   Persons liable; persons entitled to recover; defense of good faith; suit at law or in equity; costs, etc.

Any person who shall make or cause to be made any statement in any application, report, or document filed pursuant to this chapter or any rule or regulation thereunder or any undertaking contained in a registration statement as provided in subsection (d) of section 15 of this title, which statement was at the time and in the light of the circumstances under which it was made false or misleading with respect to any material fact, shall be liable to any person (not knowing that such statement was false or misleading) who, in reliance upon such statement, shall have purchased or sold a security at a price which was affected by such statement, for damages caused by such reliance, unless the person sued shall prove that he acted in good faith and had no knowledge that such statement was false or misleading. A person seeking to enforce such liability may sue at law or in equity in any court of competent jurisdiction. In any such suit the court may, in its discretion, require an undertaking for the payment of the costs of such suit, and assess reasonable costs, including reasonable attorneys' fees, against either party litigant.

(b)   Contribution

Every person who becomes liable to make payment under this section may recover contribution as in cases of contract from any person who, if joined in the original suit, would have been liable to make the same payment.

(c)   Period of limitations

No action shall be maintained to enforce any liability created under this section unless brought within one year after the discovery of the facts constituting the cause of action and within three years after such cause of action accrued.

§ 19.   Registration, Responsibilities, and Oversight of Self–Regulatory Organizations. . . .

(b)   Proposed rule changes; notice; proceedings

(1) Each self-regulatory organization shall file with the Commission, in accordance with such rules as the Commission may prescribe, copies

of any proposed rule or any proposed change in, addition to, or deletion from the rules of such self-regulatory organization (hereinafter in this subsection collectively referred to as a "proposed rule change") accompanied by a concise general statement of the basis and purpose of such proposed rule change. The Commission shall, upon the filing of any proposed rule change, publish notice thereof together with the terms of substance of the proposed rule change or a description of the subjects and issues involved. The Commission shall give interested persons an opportunity to submit written data, views, and arguments concerning such proposed rule change. No proposed rule change shall take effect unless approved by the Commission or otherwise permitted in accordance with the provisions of this subsection.

(2) Within thirty-five days of the date of publication of notice of the filing of a proposed rule change in accordance with paragraph (1) of this subsection, or within such longer period as the Commission may designate up to ninety days of such date if it finds such longer period to be appropriate and publishes its reasons for so finding or as to which the self-regulatory organization consents, the Commission shall—

(A) by order approve such proposed rule change, or

(B) institute proceedings to determine whether the proposed rule change should be disapproved. Such proceedings shall include notice of the grounds for disapproval under consideration and opportunity for hearing and be concluded within one hundred eighty days of the date of publication of notice of the filing of the proposed rule change. At the conclusion of such proceedings the Commission, by order, shall approve or disapprove such proposed rule change. The Commission may extend the time for conclusion of such proceedings for up to sixty days if it finds good cause for such extension and publishes its reasons for so finding or for such longer period as to which the self-regulatory organization consents.

The Commission shall approve a proposed rule change of a self-regulatory organization if it finds that such proposed rule change is consistent with the requirements of this chapter and the rules and regulations thereunder applicable to such organization. The Commission shall disapprove a proposed rule change of a self-regulatory organization if it does not make such finding. The Commission shall not approve any proposed rule change prior to the thirtieth day after the date of publication of notice of the filing thereof, unless the Commission finds good cause for so doing and publishes its reasons for so finding. . . .

(c) Amendment by Commission of rules of self-regulatory organizations

The Commission, by rule, may abrogate, add to, and delete from (hereinafter in this subsection collectively referred to as "amend") the rules of a self-regulatory organization (other than a registered clearing agency) as the Commission deems necessary or appropriate to insure the fair administration of the self-regulatory organization, to conform its rules to requirements of this chapter and the rules and regulations thereunder applicable to such organization, or otherwise in furtherance of the purposes of this chapter, in the following manner:

(1) The Commission shall notify the self-regulatory organization and publish notice of the proposed rulemaking in the Federal Register. The notice shall include the text of the proposed amendment to the rules of the self-regulatory organization and a statement of the Commission's reasons, including any pertinent facts, for commencing such proposed rulemaking.

(2) The Commission shall give interested persons an opportunity for the oral presentation of data, views, and arguments, in addition to an opportunity to make written submissions. A transcript shall be kept of any oral presentation.

(3) A rule adopted pursuant to this subsection shall incorporate the text of the amendment to the rules of the self-regulatory organization and a statement of the Commission's basis for and purpose in so amending such rules. This statement shall include an identification of any facts on which the Commission considers its determination so to amend the rules of the self-regulatory agency to be based, including the reasons for the Commission's conclusions as to any of such facts which were disputed in the rulemaking.

(4)(A) Except as provided in paragraphs (1) through (3) of this subsection, rulemaking under this subsection shall be in accordance with the procedures specified in section 553 of title 5 for rulemaking not on the record.

(B) Nothing in this subsection shall be construed to impair or limit the Commission's power to make, or to modify or alter the procedures the Commission may follow in making, rules and regulations pursuant to any other authority under this chapter.

(C) Any amendment to the rules of a self-regulatory organization made by the Commission pursuant to this subsection shall be considered for all purposes of this chapter to be part of the rules of such self-regulatory organization and shall not be considered to be a rule of the Commission....

§ 20. Liability of Controlling Persons and Persons Who Aid and Abet Violations

(a) Joint and several liability; good faith defense

Every person who, directly or indirectly, controls any person liable under any provision of this chapter or of any rule or regulation thereunder shall also be liable jointly and severally with and to the same extent as such controlled person to any person to whom such controlled person is liable, unless the controlling person acted in good faith and did not directly or indirectly induce the act or acts constituting the violation or cause of action.

(b) Unlawful activity through or by means of any other person

It shall be unlawful for any person, directly or indirectly, to do any act or thing which it would be unlawful for such person to do under the provisions of this chapter or any rule or regulation thereunder through or by means of any other person.

(c) Hindering, delaying, or obstructing the making or filing of any document, report, or information

It shall be unlawful for any director or officer of, or any owner of any securities issued by, any issuer required to file any document, report, or information under this chapter or any rule or regulation thereunder without just cause to hinder, delay, or obstruct the making or filing of any such document, report, or information. . . .

(d) Liability for trading in securities while in possession of material nonpublic information

Wherever communicating, or purchasing or selling a security while in possession of, material nonpublic information would violate, or result in liability to any purchaser or seller of the security under any provision of this chapter, or any rule or regulation thereunder, such conduct in connection with a purchase or sale of a put, call, straddle, option, or privilege with respect to such security or with respect to a group or index of securities including such security, shall also violate and result in comparable liability to any purchaser or seller of that security under such provision, rule, or regulation. . . .

(f) Prosecution of Persons Who Aid and Abet Violations.

For purposes of any action brought by the Commission under paragraph (1) or (3) of section 21(d), any person that knowingly provides substantial assistance to another person in violation of a provision of this title, or of any rule or regulation issued under this title, shall be deemed to be in violation of such provision to the same extent as the person to whom such assistance is provided.

§ 20A. Liability to Contemporaneous Traders for Insider Trading

(a) Private rights of action based on contemporaneous trading

Any person who violates any provision of this title or the rules or regulations thereunder by purchasing or selling a security while in possession of material, nonpublic information shall be liable in an action in any court of competent jurisdiction to any person who, contemporaneously with the purchase or sale of securities that is the subject of such violation, has purchased (where such violation is based on a sale of securities) or sold (where such violation is based on a purchase of securities) securities of the same class.

(b)   Limitations on liability

(1) *Contemporaneous trading actions limited to profit gained or loss avoided.* The total amount of damages imposed under subsection (a) shall not exceed the profit gained or loss avoided in the transaction or transactions that are the subject of the violation.

(2) *Offsetting disgorgements against liability.* The total amount of damages imposed against any person under subsection (a) shall be diminished by the amounts, if any, that such person may be required to disgorge, pursuant to a court order obtained at the instance of the Commission, in a proceeding brought under section 21(d) of this title [Investigations; Injunctions and Prosecution of Offenses] relating to the same transaction or transactions.

(3) *Controlling person liability.* No person shall be liable under this section solely by reason of employing another person who is liable under this section, but the liability of a controlling person under this section shall be subject to section 20(a) of this title.

(4) *Statute of limitations.* No action may be brought under this section more than 5 years after the date of the last transaction that is the subject of the violation.

(c)   Joint and several liability for communicating

Any person who violates any provision of this title or the rules or regulations thereunder by communicating material, nonpublic information shall be jointly and severally liable under subsection (a) with, and to the same extent as, any person or persons liable under subsection (a) to whom the communication was directed.

(d)   Authority not to restrict other express or implied rights of action

Nothing in this section shall be construed to limit or condition the right of any person to bring an action to enforce a requirement of this title or the availability of any cause of action implied from a provision of this title.

(e)   Provisions not to affect public prosecutions

This section shall not be construed to bar or limit in any manner any action by the Commission or the Attorney General under any other provision of this title, nor shall it bar or limit in any manner any action to recover penalties, or to seek any other order regarding penalties.

§ 21.   Investigations and Actions . . .

(d)(1) Wherever it shall appear to the Commission that any person is engaged or is about to engage in acts or practices constituting a violation of any provision of this chapter, the rules or regulations thereunder, the rules of a national securities exchange or registered securities association of which such person is a member or a person associated with a member, the rules of a registered clearing agency in which such person is a participant, or the rules of the Municipal Securities Rulemaking Board, it may in its discretion bring an action in the proper district court of the United States, the United States District Court for the District of Columbia, or the United States courts of any territory or other place subject to the jurisdiction of the United States, to enjoin such acts or practices, and upon a proper showing a permanent or temporary injunction or restraining order shall be granted without bond.   The Commission may transmit such evidence as may be available concerning such acts or practices as may constitute a violation of any provision of this chapter or the rules or regulations thereunder to the Attorney General, who may, in his discretion, institute the necessary criminal proceedings under this chapter.

(2) *Authority of a court to prohibit persons from serving as officers and directors.*   In any proceeding under paragraph (1) of this subsection, the court may prohibit, conditionally or unconditionally, and permanently or for such period of time as it shall determine, any person who violated section 10(b) of this title or the rules or regulations thereunder from acting as an officer or director of any issuer that has a class of securities registered pursuant to section 12 of this title or that is required to file reports pursuant to section 15(d) of this title if the person's conduct demonstrates substantial unfitness to serve as an officer or director of any such issuer.

(3) *Money penalties in civil actions.*

(A) *Authority of commission.*   Whenever it shall appear to the Commission that any person has violated any provision of this title, the rules or regulations thereunder, or a cease-and-desist order entered by the Commission pursuant to section 21C of this title, other than by committing a violation subject to a penalty pursuant to section 21A, the Commission may bring an action in a United States district court to seek, and the court shall have jurisdiction to impose, upon a proper showing, a civil penalty to be paid by the person who committed such violation.

(B) *Amount of penalty.*

(i) *First tier.*   The amount of the penalty shall be determined by the court in light of the facts and circumstances.   For each violation, the amount of the penalty shall not exceed the greater of (I) [$5,500]* for a natural person or [$55,000] for any other person, or (II) the gross amount of pecuniary gain to such defendant as a result of the violation.

(ii) *Second tier.* Notwithstanding clause (i), the amount of penalty for each such violation shall not exceed the greater of (I) [$55,000] for a natural person or [$275,-000] for any other person, or (II) the gross amount of pecuniary gain to such defendant as a result of the violation, if the violation described in subparagraph (A) involved fraud, deceit, manipulation, or deliberate or reckless disregard of a regulatory requirement.

(iii) *Third tier.* Notwithstanding clauses (i) and (ii), the amount of penalty for each such violation shall not exceed the greater of (I) [$110,000] for a natural person or [$550,000] for any other person, or (II) the gross amount of pecuniary gain to such defendant as a result of the violation, if—

(aa) the violation described in subparagraph (A) involved fraud, deceit, manipulation, or deliberate or reckless disregard of a regulatory requirement; and

(bb) such violation directly or indirectly resulted in substantial losses or created a significant risk of substantial losses to other persons. . . .

(4) *Prohibition of attorneys' fees paid from commission disgorgement funds*—Except as otherwise ordered by the court upon motion by the Commission, or, in the case of an administrative action, as otherwise ordered by the Commission, funds disgorged as the result of an action brought by the Commission in Federal court, or as a result of any Commission administrative action, shall not be distributed as payment for attorneys' fees or expenses incurred by private parties seeking distribution of the disgorged funds.

§ 21A.   Civil Penalties for Insider Trading

(a)   Authority to impose civil penalties

(1) *Judicial actions by commission authorized.* Whenever it shall appear to the Commission that any person has violated any provision of this title or the rules or regulations thereunder by purchasing or selling a security while in possession of material, nonpublic information in, or has violated any such provision by

---

* The bracketed figures in this section have been adjusted for inflation by the SEC under the Debt Collection Act of 1996, which requires the Commission to make inflationary adjustments to civil penalties in the Securities Act, the Exchange Act, and other Acts that the Commission administers. (Footnote by ed.)

communicating such information in connection with, a transaction on or through the facilities of a national securities exchange or from or through a broker or dealer, and which is not part of a public offering by an issuer of securities other than standardized options, the Commission—

(A) may bring an action in a United States district court to seek, and the court shall have jurisdiction to impose, a civil penalty to be paid by the person who committed such violation; and

(B) may, subject to subsection (b)(1), bring an action in a United States district court to seek, and the court shall have jurisdiction to impose, a civil penalty to be paid by a person who, at the time of the violation, directly or indirectly controlled the person who committed such violation.

(2) *Amount of penalty for person who committed violation.* The amount of the penalty which may be imposed on the person who committed such violation shall be determined by the court in light of the facts and circumstances, but shall not exceed three times the profit gained or loss avoided as a result of such unlawful purchase, sale, or communication.

(3) *Amount of penalty for controlling person.* The amount of the penalty which may be imposed on any person who, at the time of the violation, directly or indirectly controlled the person who committed such violation, shall be determined by the court in light of the facts and circumstances, but shall not exceed the greater of [$1,100,000],* or three times the amount of the profit gained or loss avoided as a result of such controlled person's violation. If such controlled person's violation was a violation by communication, the profit gained or loss avoided as a result of the violation shall, for purposes of this paragraph only, be deemed to be limited to the profit gained or loss avoided by the person or persons to whom the controlled person directed such communication.

(b) Limitations on liability

(1) *Liability of controlling persons.* No controlling person shall be subject to a penalty under subsection (a)(1)(B) unless the Commission establishes that—

(A) such controlling person knew or recklessly disregarded the fact that such controlled person was likely to engage in the act or acts constituting the violation and failed to take appropriate steps to prevent such act or acts before they occurred; or

---

* The bracketed figure in this section has been adjusted for inflation by the SEC under the Debt Collection Act of 1996, which requires the Commission to make inflationary adjustments to civil penalties in the Securities Act, the Exchange Act, and other Acts that the Commission administers. (Footnote by ed.)

(B) such controlling person knowingly or recklessly failed to establish, maintain, or enforce any policy or procedure required under section 15(f) of this title or section 204A of the Investment Advisers Act of 1940 and such failure substantially contributed to or permitted the occurrence of the act or acts constituting the violation.

(2) *Additional restrictions on liability.* No person shall be subject to a penalty under subsection (a) solely by reason of employing another person who is subject to a penalty under such subsection, unless such employing person is liable as a controlling person under paragraph (1) of this subsection. Section 20(a) of this title shall not apply to actions under subsection (a) of this section....

(e) Authority to award bounties to informants

Notwithstanding the provisions of subsection (d)(1), there shall be paid from amounts imposed as a penalty under this section and recovered by the Commission or the Attorney General, such sums, not to exceed 10 percent of such amounts, as the Commission deems appropriate, to the person or persons who provide information leading to the imposition of such penalty. Any determinations under this subsection, including whether, to whom, or in what amount to make payments, shall be in the sole discretion of the Commission, except that no such payment shall be made to any member, officer, or employee of any appropriate regulatory agency, the Department of Justice, or a self-regulatory organization. Any such determination shall be final and not subject to judicial review.

(f) Definition

For purposes of this section, "profit gained" or "loss avoided" is the difference between the purchase or sale price of the security and the value of that security as measured by the trading price of the security a reasonable period after public dissemination of the nonpublic information.

§ 21B. Civil Remedies in Administrative Proceedings

(a) Commission authority to assess money penalties

In any proceeding instituted pursuant to sections 15(b)(4), 15(b)(6), 15B, 15C, or 17A of this title against any person, the Commission or the appropriate regulatory agency may impose a civil penalty if it finds, on the record after notice and opportunity for hearing, that such person—

(1) has willfully violated any provision of the Securities Act of 1933, the Investment Company Act of 1940, the Investment Advisers Act of 1940, or this title, or the rules or regulations thereunder, or the rules of the Municipal Securities Rulemaking Board;

(2) has willfully aided, abetted, counseled, commanded, induced, or procured such a violation by any other person;

(3) has willfully made or caused to be made in any application for registration or report required to be filed with the Commission or with any other appropriate regulatory agency under this title, or in any proceeding before the Commission with respect to registration, any statement which was, at the time and in the light of the circumstances under which it was made, false or misleading with respect to any material fact, or has omitted to state in any such application or report any material fact which is required to be stated therein; or

(4) has failed reasonably to supervise, within the meaning of section 15(b)(4)(E) of this title, with a view to preventing violations of the provisions of such statutes, rules and regulations, another person who commits such a violation, if such other person is subject to his supervision;

and that such penalty is in the public interest.

(b) Maximum amount of penalty

(1) *First tier.*—The maximum amount of penalty for each act or omission described in subsection (a) shall be [$5,500]* for a natural person or [$55,000] for any other person.

(2) *Second tier.*—Notwithstanding paragraph (1), the maximum amount of penalty for each such act or omission shall be [$55,000] for a natural person or [$275,000] for any other person if the act or omission described in subsection (a) involved fraud, deceit, manipulation, or deliberate or reckless disregard of a regulatory requirement.

(3) *Third tier.*—Notwithstanding paragraphs (1) and (2), the maximum amount of penalty for each such act or omission shall be [$110,000] for a natural person or [$550,000] for any other person if—

(A) The act or omission described in subsection (a) involved fraud, deceit, manipulation, or deliberate or reckless disregard of a regulatory requirement; and

(B) such act or omission directly or indirectly resulted in substantial losses or created a significant risk of substantial losses to other persons or resulted in substantial pecuniary gain to the person who committed the act or omission.

* The bracketed figures in this section have been adjusted for inflation by the SEC under the Debt Collection Act of 1996, which requires the Commission to make inflationary adjustments to civil penalties in the Securities Act, the Exchange Act, and other Acts that the Commission administers. (Footnote by ed.)

(c) Determination of public interest

In considering under this section whether a penalty is in the public interest, the Commission or the appropriate regulatory agency may consider—

(1) whether the act or omission for which such penalty is assessed involved fraud, deceit, manipulation, or deliberate or reckless disregard of a regulatory requirement;

(2) the harm to other persons resulting either directly or indirectly from such act or omission;

(3) the extent to which any person was unjustly enriched, taking into account any restitution made to persons injured by such behavior;

(4) whether such person previously has been found by the Commission, another appropriate regulatory agency, or a self-regulatory organization to have violated the Federal securities laws, State securities laws, or the rules of a self-regulatory organization, has been enjoined by a court of competent jurisdiction from violations of such laws or rules, or has been convicted by a court of competent jurisdiction of violations of such laws or of any felony or misdemeanor described in section 15(b)(4)(B) of this title;

(5) the need to deter such person and other persons from committing such acts or omissions; and

(6) such other matters as justice may require.

(d) Evidence concerning ability to pay

In any proceeding in which the Commission or the appropriate regulatory agency may impose a penalty under this section, a respondent may present evidence of the respondent's ability to pay such penalty. The Commission or the appropriate regulatory agency may, in its discretion, consider such evidence in determining whether such penalty is in the public interest. Such evidence may relate to the extent of such person's ability to continue in business and the collectability of a penalty, taking into account any other claims of the United States or third parties upon such person's assets and the amount of such person's assets.

(e) Authority to enter an order requiring an accounting and disgorgement

In any proceeding in which the Commission or the appropriate regulatory agency may impose a penalty under this section, the Commission or the appropriate regulatory agency may enter an order requiring accounting and disgorgement, including reasonable interest. The Commission is authorized to adopt rules, regulations, and orders concerning payments to investors, rates of interest, periods of accrual, and such other matters as it deems appropriate to implement this subsection.

§ 21C. Cease–and–Desist Proceedings

(a) Authority of the Commission

If the Commission finds, after notice and opportunity for hearing, that any person is violating, has violated, or is about to violate any provision of this title, or any rule or regulation thereunder, the Commission may publish its findings and enter an order requiring such person, and any other person that is, was, or would be a cause of the violation, due to an act or omission the person knew or should have known would contribute to such violation, to cease and desist from committing or causing such violation and any future violation of the same provision, rule, or regulation. Such order may, in addition to requiring a person to cease and desist from committing or causing a violation, require such person to comply, or to take steps to effect compliance, with such provision, rule, or regulation, upon such terms and conditions and within such time as the Commission may specify in such order. Any such order may, as the Commission deems appropriate, require future compliance or steps to effect future compliance, either permanently or for such period of time as the Commission may specify, with such provision, rule, or regulation with respect to any security, any issuer, or any other person. . . .

(e) Authority to enter an order requiring an accounting and disgorgement

In any cease-and-desist proceeding under subsection (a), the Commission may enter an order requiring accounting and disgorgement, including reasonable interest. The Commission is authorized to adopt rules, regulations, and orders concerning payments to investors, rates of interest, periods of accrual, and such other matters as it deems appropriate to implement this subsection.

§ 21D. Private Securities Litigation

(a) Private Class Actions

(1) *In general.*—The provisions of this subsection shall apply in each private action arising under this title that is brought as a plaintiff class action pursuant to the Federal Rules of Civil Procedure.

(2) *Certification filed with complaint.*—

(A) In General.—Each plaintiff seeking to serve as a representative party on behalf of a class shall provide a sworn certification, which shall be personally signed by such plaintiff and filed with the complaint, that—

(i) states that the plaintiff has reviewed the complaint and authorized its filing;

(ii) states that the plaintiff did not purchase the security that is the subject of the complaint at the direction of plaintiff's counsel or in order to participate in any private action arising under this title;

(iii) states that the plaintiff is willing to serve as a representative party on behalf of a class, including providing testimony at deposition and trial, if necessary;

(iv) sets forth all of the transactions of the plaintiff in the security that is the subject of the complaint during the class period specified in the complaint;

(v) identifies any other action under this title, filed during the 3–year period preceding the date on which the certification is signed by the plaintiff, in which the plaintiff has sought to serve as a representative party on behalf of a class; and

(vi) states that the plaintiff will not accept any payment for serving as a representative party on behalf of a class beyond the plaintiff's pro rata share of any recovery, except as ordered or approved by the court in accordance with paragraph (4).

(B) Nonwaiver of attorney-client privilege.—The certification filed pursuant to subparagraph (A) shall not be construed to be a waiver of the attorney-client privilege.

(3) *Appointment of lead plaintiff.*

(A) Early notice to class members.—

(i) In General.—Not later than 20 days after the date on which the complaint is filed, the plaintiff or plaintiffs shall cause to be published, in a widely circulated national business-oriented publication or wire service, a notice advising members of the purported plaintiff class—

(I) of the pendency of the action, the claims asserted therein, and the purported class period; and

(II) that, not later than 60 days after the date on which the notice is published, any member of the purported class may move the court to serve as lead plaintiff of the purported class.

(ii) Multiple actions.—If more than one action on behalf of a class asserting substantially the same claim or claims arising under this title is filed, only the plaintiff or plaintiffs in the first filed action shall be required to cause notice to be published in accordance with clause (i).

(iii) Additional notices may be required under federal rules.—Notice required under clause (i) shall be in addition to any notice required pursuant to the Federal Rules of Civil Procedure.

(B) Appointment of lead plaintiff.—

(i) In general.—Not later than 90 days after the date on which a notice is published under subparagraph (A)(i), the court shall consider any motion made by a purported class member in response to the notice, including any motion by a class member who is not individually named as a plaintiff in the complaint or complaints, and shall appoint as lead plaintiff the member or members of the purported plaintiff class that the court determines to be most capable of adequately representing the interests of class members (hereafter in this paragraph referred to as the "most adequate plaintiff") in accordance with this subparagraph.

(ii) Consolidated actions.—If more than one action on behalf of a class asserting substantially the same claim or claims arising under this title has been filed, and any party has sought to consolidate those actions for pretrial purposes or for trial, the court shall not make the determination required by clause (i) until after the decision on the motion to consolidate is rendered. As soon as practicable after such decision is rendered, the court shall appoint the most adequate plaintiff as lead plaintiff for the consolidated actions in accordance with this paragraph.

(iii) Rebuttable presumption.—

(I) In general.—Subject to subclause (II), for purposes of clause (i), the court shall adopt a presumption that the most adequate plaintiff in any private action arising under this title is the person or group of persons that—

(aa) has either filed the complaint or made a motion in response to a notice under subparagraph (A)(i);

(bb) in the determination of the court, has the largest financial interest in the relief sought by the class; and

(cc) otherwise satisfies the requirements of Rule 23 of the Federal Rules of Civil Procedure.

(II) Rebuttal evidence.—The presumption described in subclause (I) may be rebutted only upon proof by a member of the purported plaintiff class that the presumptively most adequate plaintiff—

(aa) will not fairly and adequately protect the interests of the class; or

(bb) is subject to unique defenses that render such plaintiff incapable of adequately representing the class.

(iv) Discovery.—For purposes of this subparagraph, discovery relating to whether a member or members of the purported plaintiff class is the most adequate plaintiff may be conducted by a plaintiff only if the plaintiff first demonstrates a reasonable basis for a finding that the presumptively most adequate plaintiff is incapable of adequately representing the class.

(v) Selection of lead counsel.—The most adequate plaintiff shall, subject to the approval of the court, select and retain counsel to represent the class.

(vi) Restrictions on professional plaintiffs.—Except as the court may otherwise permit, consistent with the purposes of this section, a person may be a lead plaintiff, or an officer, director, or fiduciary of a lead plaintiff, in no more than 5 securities class actions brought as plaintiff class actions pursuant to the Federal Rules of Civil Procedure during any 3-year period.

(4) *Recovery by plaintiffs.*—The share of any final judgment or of any settlement that is awarded to a representative party serving on behalf of a class shall be equal, on a per share basis, to the portion of the final judgment or settlement awarded to all other members of the class. Nothing in this paragraph shall be construed to limit the award of reasonable costs and expenses (including lost wages) directly relating to the representation of the class to any representative party serving on behalf of a class.

(5) *Restrictions on settlements under seal.*—The terms and provisions of any settlement agreement of a class action shall not be filed under seal, except that on motion of any party to the settlement, the court may order filing under seal for those portions of a settlement agreement as to which good cause is shown for such filing under seal. For purposes of this paragraph, good cause shall exist only if publication of a term or provision of a settlement agreement would cause direct and substantial harm to any party.

(6) *Restrictions on payment of attorneys' fees and expenses.*—Total attorneys' fees and expenses awarded by the court to counsel for the plaintiff class shall not exceed a reasonable percentage of the amount of any damages and prejudgment interest actually paid to the class.

(7) *Disclosure of settlement terms to class members.*—Any proposed or final settlement agreement that is published or otherwise

disseminated to the class shall include each of the following statements, along with a cover page summarizing the information contained in such statements:

(A) Statement of plaintiff recovery.—The amount of the settlement proposed to be distributed to the parties to the action, determined in the aggregate and on an average per share basis.

(B) Statement of potential outcome of case.—

(i) Agreement on amount of damages.—If the settling parties agree on the average amount of damages per share that would be recoverable if the plaintiff prevailed on each claim alleged under this title, a statement concerning the average amount of such potential damages per share.

(ii) Disagreement on amount of damages.—If the parties do not agree on the average amount of damages per share that would be recoverable if the plaintiff prevailed on each claim alleged under this title, a statement from each settling party concerning the issue or issues on which the parties disagree.

(iii) Inadmissibility for certain purposes.—A statement made in accordance with clause (i) or (ii) concerning the amount of damages shall not be admissible in any Federal or State judicial action or administrative proceeding, other than an action or proceeding arising out of such statement.

(C) Statement of attorneys' fees or costs sought.—If any of the settling parties or their counsel intend to apply to the court for an award of attorneys' fees or costs from any fund established as part of the settlement, a statement indicating which parties or counsel intend to make such an application, the amount of fees and costs that will be sought (including the amount of such fees and costs determined on an average per share basis), and a brief explanation supporting the fees and costs sought. Such information shall be clearly summarized on the cover page of any notice to a party of any proposed or final settlement agreement.

(D) Identification of lawyers' representatives.—The name, telephone number, and address of one or more representatives of counsel for the plaintiff class who will be reasonably available to answer questions from class members concerning any matter contained in any notice of settlement published or otherwise disseminated to the class.

(E) Reasons for settlement.—A brief statement explaining the reasons why the parties are proposing the settlement.

(F) Other information.—Such other information as may be required by the court.

(8) *Security for payment of costs in class actions.*—In any private action arising under this title that is certified as a class action pursuant to the Federal Rules of Civil Procedure, the court may require an undertaking from the attorneys for the plaintiff class, the plaintiff class, or both, or from the attorneys for the defendant, the defendant, or both, in such proportions and at such times as the court determines are just and equitable, for the payment of fees and expenses that may be awarded under this subsection.

(9) *Attorney conflict of interest.*—If a plaintiff class is represented by an attorney who directly owns or otherwise has a beneficial interest in the securities that are the subject of the litigation, the court shall make a determination of whether such ownership or other interest constitutes a conflict of interest sufficient to disqualify the attorney from representing the plaintiff class.

(b) Requirements for Securities Fraud Actions

(1) *Misleading statements and omissions.*—In any private action arising under this title in which the plaintiff alleges that the defendant—

    (A) made an untrue statement of a material fact; or

    (B) omitted to state a material fact necessary in order to make the statements made, in the light of the circumstances in which they were made, not misleading;

the complaint shall specify each statement alleged to have been misleading, the reason or reasons why the statement is misleading, and, if an allegation regarding the statement or omission is made on information and belief, the complaint shall state with particularity all facts on which that belief is formed.

(2) *Required state of mind.*—In any private action arising under this title in which the plaintiff may recover money damages only on proof that the defendant acted with a particular state of mind, the complaint shall, with respect to each act or omission alleged to violate this title, state with particularity facts giving rise to a strong inference that the defendant acted with the required state of mind.

(3) *Motion to dismiss; stay of discovery.—*

    (A) Dismissal for failure to meet pleading requirements.—In any private action arising under this title, the court shall, on the motion of any defendant, dismiss the complaint if the requirements of paragraphs (1) and (2) are not met.

    (B) Stay of discovery.—In any private action arising under this title, all discovery and other proceedings shall be stayed during the pendency of any motion to dismiss, unless the court finds upon the motion of any party that particularized discovery is necessary to preserve evidence or to prevent undue prejudice to that party.

(C) Preservation of evidence.—

(i) In general.—During the pendency of any stay of discovery pursuant to this paragraph, unless otherwise ordered by the court, any party to the action with actual notice of the allegations contained in the complaint shall treat all documents, data compilations (including electronically recorded or stored data), and tangible objects that are in the custody or control of such person and that are relevant to the allegations, as if they were the subject of a continuing request for production of documents from an opposing party under the Federal Rules of Civil Procedure.

(ii) Sanction for willful violation.—A party aggrieved by the willful failure of an opposing party to comply with clause (i) may apply to the court for an order awarding appropriate sanctions.

(4) *Loss causation.*—In any private action arising under this title, the plaintiff shall have the burden of proving that the act or omission of the defendant alleged to violate this title caused the loss for which the plaintiff seeks to recover damages.

(c) Sanctions for Abusive Litigation

(1) *Mandatory review by court.*—In any private action arising under this title, upon final adjudication of the action, the court shall include in the record specific findings regarding compliance by each party and each attorney representing any party with each requirement of Rule 11(b) of the Federal Rules of Civil Procedure as to any complaint, responsive pleading, or dispositive motion.

(2) *Mandatory sanctions.*—If the court makes a finding under paragraph (1) that a party or attorney violated any requirement of Rule 11(b) of the Federal Rules of Civil Procedure as to any complaint, responsive pleading, or dispositive motion, the court shall impose sanctions on such party or attorney in accordance with Rule 11 of the Federal Rules of Civil Procedure. Prior to making a finding that any party or attorney has violated Rule 11 of the Federal Rules of Civil Procedure, the court shall give such party or attorney notice and an opportunity to respond.

(3) *Presumption in favor of attorneys' fees and costs.*—

(A) In general.—Subject to subparagraphs (B) and (C), for purposes of paragraph (2), the court shall adopt a presumption that the appropriate sanction—

(i) for failure of any responsive pleading or dispositive motion to comply with any requirement of Rule 11(b) of the Federal Rules of Civil Procedure is an award to the opposing party of the reasonable attorneys' fees and other expenses incurred as a direct result of the violation; and

(ii) for substantial failure of any complaint to comply with any requirement of Rule 11(b) of the Federal Rules of Civil Procedure is an award to the opposing party of the reasonable attorneys' fees and other expenses incurred in the action.

(B) Rebuttal evidence.—The presumption described in subparagraph (A) may be rebutted only upon proof by the party or attorney against whom sanctions are to be imposed that—

(i) the award of attorneys' fees and other expenses will impose an unreasonable burden on that party or attorney and would be unjust, and the failure to make such an award would not impose a greater burden on the party in whose favor sanctions are to be imposed; or

(ii) the violation of Rule 11(b) of the Federal Rules of Civil Procedure was de minimis.

(C) Sanctions.—If the party or attorney against whom sanctions are to be imposed meets its burden under subparagraph (B), the court shall award the sanctions that the court deems appropriate pursuant to Rule 11 of the Federal Rules of Civil Procedure.

(d) Defendant's Right to Written Interrogatories

In any private action arising under this title in which the plaintiff may recover money damages, the court shall, when requested by a defendant, submit to the jury a written interrogatory on the issue of each such defendant's state of mind at the time the alleged violation occurred.

(e) Limitation on Damages

(1) *In general.*—Except as provided in paragraph (2), in any private action arising under this title in which the plaintiff seeks to establish damages by reference to the market price of a security, the award of damages to the plaintiff shall not exceed the difference between the purchase or sale price paid or received, as appropriate, by the plaintiff for the subject security and the mean trading price of that security during the 90–day period beginning on the date on which the information correcting the misstatement or omission that is the basis for the action is disseminated to the market.

(2) *Exception.*—In any private action arising under this title in which the plaintiff seeks to establish damages by reference to the market price of a security, if the plaintiff sells or repurchases the subject security prior to the expiration of the 90–day period described in paragraph (1), the plaintiff's damages shall not exceed the difference between the purchase or sale price paid or received, as appropriate, by the plaintiff for the security and the mean trading price of the security during the period beginning immediately after dissemination of information correcting the misstatement or omission and ending on the date on which the plaintiff sells or repurchases the security.

(3) *Definition.*—For purposes of this subsection, the "mean trading price" of a security shall be an average of the daily trading price of that security, determined as of the close of the market each day during the 90–day period referred to in paragraph (1).*

(g) Proportionate Liability

(1) *Applicability.*—Nothing in this subsection shall be construed to create, affect, or in any manner modify, the standard for liability associated with any action arising under the securities laws.

(2) *Liability for damages.*—

(A) Joint and several liability.—Any covered person against whom a final judgment is entered in a private action shall be liable for damages jointly and severally only if the trier of fact specifically determines that such covered person knowingly committed a violation of the securities laws.

(B) Proportionate liability.—

(i) In general.—Except as provided in paragraph (1), a covered person against whom a final judgment is entered in a private action shall be liable solely for the portion of the judgment that corresponds to the percentage of responsibility of that covered person, as determined under paragraph (3).

(ii) Recovery by and costs of covered person.—In any case in which a contractual relationship permits, a covered person that prevails in any private action may recover the attorney's fees and costs of that covered person in connection with the action.

(3) *Determination of responsibility.*—

(A) In general.—In any private action, the court shall instruct the jury to answer special interrogatories, or if there is no

* The Private Securities Litigation Reform Act of 1995 added Sections 21D(a)–(e), (g).

jury, shall make findings, with respect to each covered person and each of the other persons claimed by any of the parties to have caused or contributed to the loss incurred by the plaintiff, including persons who have entered into settlements with the plaintiff or plaintiffs, concerning—

(i) whether such person violated the securities laws;

(ii) the percentage of responsibility of such person, measured as a percentage of the total fault of all persons who caused or contributed to the loss incurred by the plaintiff; and

(iii) whether such person knowingly committed a violation of the securities laws.

(B) Contents of special interrogatories or findings.—The responses to interrogatories, or findings, as appropriate, under subparagraph (A) shall specify the total amount of damages that the plaintiff is entitled to recover and the percentage of responsibility of each covered person found to have caused or contributed to the loss incurred by the plaintiff or plaintiffs.

(C) Factors for consideration.—In determining the percentage of responsibility under this paragraph, the trier of fact shall consider—

(i) the nature of the conduct of each covered person found to have caused or contributed to the loss incurred by the plaintiff or plaintiffs; and

(ii) the nature and extent of the causal relationship between the conduct of each such person and the damages incurred by the plaintiff or plaintiffs.

(4) *Uncollectible share.*—

(A) In general.—Notwithstanding paragraph (2)(B), [if] upon motion made not later than 6 months after a final judgment is entered in any private action, the court determines that all or part of the share of the judgment of the covered person is not collectible against that covered person, and is also not collectible against a covered person described in paragraph (2)(A), each covered person described in paragraph (2)(B) shall be liable for the uncollectible share as follows:

(i) Percentage of net worth.—Each covered person shall be jointly and severally liable for the uncollectible share if the plaintiff establishes that—

(I) the plaintiff is an individual whose recoverable damages under the final judgment are equal to more than 10 percent of the net worth of the plaintiff; and

(II) the net worth of the plaintiff is equal to less than $200,000.

(ii) Other plaintiffs.—With respect to any plaintiff not described in subclauses (I) and (II) of clause (i), each covered person shall be liable for the uncollectible share in proportion to the percentage of responsibility of that covered person, except that the total liability of a covered person under this clause may not exceed 50 percent of the proportionate share of that covered person, as determined under paragraph (3)(B).

(iii) Net worth.—For purposes of this subparagraph, net worth shall be determined as of the date immediately preceding the date of the purchase or sale (as applicable) by the plaintiff of the security that is the subject of the action, and shall be equal to the fair market value of assets, minus liabilities, including the net value of the investments of the plaintiff in real and personal property (including personal residences).

(B) Overall limit.—In no case shall the total payments required pursuant to subparagraph (A) exceed the amount of the uncollectible share.

(C) Covered persons subject to contribution.—A covered person against whom judgment is not collectible shall be subject to contribution and to any continuing liability to the plaintiff on the judgment.

(5) *Right of contribution.*—To the extent that a covered person is required to make an additional payment pursuant to paragraph (4), that covered person may recover contribution—

(A) from the covered person originally liable to make the payment;

(B) from any covered person liable jointly and severally pursuant to paragraph (2)(A);

(C) from any covered person held proportionately liable pursuant to this paragraph who is liable to make the same payment and has paid less than his or her proportionate share of that payment; or

(D) from any other person responsible for the conduct giving rise to the payment that would have been liable to make the same payment.

(6) *Nondisclosure to jury.*—The standard for allocation of damages under paragraphs (2) and (3) and the procedure for reallocation of uncollectible shares under paragraph (4) shall not be disclosed to members of the jury.

(7) *Settlement discharge.*—

(A) In general.—A covered person who settles any private action at any time before final verdict or judgment shall be discharged from all claims for contribution brought by other persons. Upon entry of the settlement by the court, the court shall enter a bar order constituting the final discharge of all obligations to the plaintiff of the settling covered person arising out of the action. The order shall bar all future claims for contribution arising out of the action—

(i) by any person against the settling covered person; and

(ii) by the settling covered person against any person, other than a person whose liability has been extinguished by the settlement of the settling covered person.

(B) Reduction.—If a covered person enters into a settlement with the plaintiff prior to final verdict or judgment, the verdict or judgment shall be reduced by the greater of—

(i) an amount that corresponds to the percentage of responsibility of that covered person; or

(ii) the amount paid to the plaintiff by that covered person.

(8) *Contribution.*—A covered person who becomes jointly and severally liable for damages in any private action may recover contribution from any other person who, if joined in the original action, would have been liable for the same damages. A claim for contribution shall be determined based on the percentage of responsibility of the claimant and of each person against whom a claim for contribution is made.

(9) *Statute of limitations for contribution.*—In any private action determining liability, an action for contribution shall be brought not later than 6 months after the entry of a final, nonappealable judgment in the action, except that an action for contribution brought by a covered person who was required to make an additional payment pursuant to paragraph (4) may be brought not later than 6 months after the date on which such payment was made.

(10) *Definitions.*—For purposes of this subsection—

(A) a covered person "knowingly commits a violation of the securities laws"—

(i) with respect to an action that is based on an untrue statement of material fact or omission of a material fact necessary to make the statement not misleading, if—

(I) that covered person makes an untrue statement of a material fact, with actual knowledge that the representation is false, or omits to state a fact necessary in order to make the statement made not misleading, with actual knowledge that, as a result of the omission, one of the material representations of the covered person is false; and

(II) persons are likely to reasonably rely on that misrepresentation or omission; and

(ii) with respect to an action that is based on any conduct that is not described in clause (i), if that covered person engages in that conduct with actual knowledge of the facts and circumstances that make the conduct of that covered person a violation of the securities laws;

(B) reckless conduct by a covered person shall not be construed to constitute a knowing commission of a violation of the securities laws by that covered person;

(C) the term "covered person" means—

(i) a defendant in any private action arising under this title; or

(ii) a defendant in any private action arising under section 11 of the Securities Act of 1933, who is an outside director of the issuer of the securities that are the subject of the action; and

(D) the term "outside director" shall have the meaning given such term by rule or regulation of the Commission.

§ 21E. Application of Safe Harbor for Forward–Looking Statements

(a) Applicability

This section shall apply only to a forward-looking statement made by—

(1) an issuer that, at the time that the statement is made, is subject to the reporting requirements of section 13(a) or section 15(d);

(2) a person acting on behalf of such issuer;

(3) an outside reviewer retained by such issuer making a statement on behalf of such issuer; or

(4) an underwriter, with respect to information provided by such issuer or information derived from information provided by such issuer.

(b) Exclusions

Except to the extent otherwise specifically provided by rule, regulation, or order of the Commission, this section shall not apply to a forward-looking statement—

(1) that is made with respect to the business or operations of the issuer, if the issuer—

(A) during the 3-year period preceding the date on which the statement was first made—

(i) was convicted of any felony or misdemeanor described in clauses (i) through (iv) of section 15(b)(4)(B); or

(ii) has been made the subject of a judicial or administrative decree or order arising out of a governmental action that—

(I) prohibits future violations of the antifraud provisions of the securities laws;

(II) requires that the issuer cease and desist from violating the antifraud provisions of the securities laws; or

(III) determines that the issuer violated the antifraud provisions of the securities laws;

(B) makes the forward-looking statement in connection with an offering of securities by a blank check company;

(C) issues penny stock;

(D) makes the forward-looking statement in connection with a rollup transaction; or

(E) makes the forward-looking statement in connection with a going private transaction; or

(2) that is—

(A) included in a financial statement prepared in accordance with generally accepted accounting principles;

(B) contained in a registration statement of, or otherwise issued by, an investment company;

(C) made in connection with a tender offer;

(D) made in connection with an initial public offering;

(E) made in connection with an offering by, or relating to the operations of, a partnership, limited liability company, or a direct participation investment program; or

(F) made in a disclosure of beneficial ownership in a report required to be filed with the Commission pursuant to section 13(d).

(c) Safe Harbor

(1) *In general.*—Except as provided in subsection (b), in any private action arising under this title that is based on an untrue statement of a material fact or omission of a material fact necessary to make the statement not misleading, a person referred to in subsection (a) shall not be liable with respect to any forward-looking statement, whether written or oral, if and to the extent that—

(A) the forward-looking statement is—

(i) identified as a forward-looking statement, and is accompanied by meaningful cautionary statements identifying important factors that could cause actual results to differ materially from those in the forward-looking statement; or

(ii) immaterial; or

(B) the plaintiff fails to prove that the forward-looking statement—

(i) if made by a natural person, was made with actual knowledge by that person that the statement was false or misleading; or

(ii) if made by a business entity; was—

(I) made by or with the approval of an executive officer of that entity; and

(II) made or approved by such officer with actual knowledge by that officer that the statement was false or misleading.

(2) *Oral forward-looking statements.*—In the case of an oral forward-looking statement made by an issuer that is subject to the reporting requirements of section 13(a) or section 15(d), or by a person acting on behalf of such issuer, the requirement set forth in paragraph (1)(A) shall be deemed to be satisfied—

(A) if the oral forward-looking statement is accompanied by a cautionary statement—

(i) that the particular oral statement is a forward-looking statement; and

(ii) that the actual results might differ materially from those projected in the forward-looking statement; and

(B) if—

(i) the oral forward-looking statement is accompanied by an oral statement that additional information concerning factors that could cause actual results to materially differ from those in the forward-looking statement is contained in a readily available written document, or portion thereof;

(ii) the accompanying oral statement referred to in clause (i) identifies the document, or portion thereof, that contains the additional information about those factors relating to the forward-looking statement; and

(iii) the information contained in that written document is a cautionary statement that satisfies the standard established in paragraph (1)(A).

(3) *Availability.*—Any document filed with the Commission or generally disseminated shall be deemed to be readily available for purposes of paragraph (2).

(4) *Effect on other safe harbors.*—The exemption provided for in paragraph (1) shall be in addition to any exemption that the Commission may establish by rule or regulation under subsection (g).

(d) Duty to Update

Nothing in this section shall impose upon any person a duty to update a forward-looking statement.

(e) Dispositive Motion

On any motion to dismiss based upon subsection (c)(1), the court shall consider any statement cited in the complaint and any cautionary statement accompanying the forward-looking statement, which are not subject to material dispute, cited by the defendant.

(f) Stay Pending Decision on Motion

In any private action arising under this title, the court shall stay discovery (other than discovery that is specifically directed to the applicability of the exemption provided for in this section) during the pendency of any motion by a defendant for summary judgment that is based on the grounds that—

(1) the statement or omission upon which the complaint is based is a forward-looking statement within the meaning of this section; and

(2) the exemption provided for in this section precludes a claim for relief.

(g) Exemption Authority

In addition to the exemptions provided for in this section, the Commission may, by rule or regulation, provide exemptions from or under any provision of this title, including with respect to liability that is based on a statement or that is based on projections or other forward-looking information, if and to the extent that any such exemption is consistent with the public interest and the protection of investors, as determined by the Commission.

(h) Effect on Other Authority of Commission

Nothing in this section limits, either expressly or by implication, the authority of the Commission to exercise similar authority or to adopt similar rules and regulations with respect to forward-looking statements under any other statute under which the Commission exercises rulemaking authority.

(i) Definitions

For purposes of this section, the following definitions shall apply:

(1) *Forward-looking statement.*—The term "forward-looking statement" means—

(A) a statement containing a projection of revenues, income (including income loss), earnings (including earnings loss) per share, capital expenditures, dividends, capital structure, or other financial items;

(B) a statement of the plans and objectives of management for future operations, including plans or objectives relating to the products or services of the issuer;

(C) a statement of future economic performance, including any such statement contained in a discussion and analysis of financial condition by the management or in the results of operations included pursuant to the rules and regulations of the Commission;

(D) any statement of the assumptions underlying or relating to any statement described in subparagraph (A), (B), or (C);

(E) any report issued by an outside reviewer retained by an issuer, to the extent that the report assesses a forward-looking statement made by the issuer; or

(F) a statement containing a projection or estimate of such other items as may be specified by rule or regulation of the Commission.

(2) *Investment Company.*—The term "investment company" has the same meaning as in section 3(a) of the Investment Company Act of 1940.

(3) *Going Private Transaction.*—The term "going private transaction" has the meaning given that term under the rules or regulations of the Commission issued pursuant to section 13(e).

(4) *Person acting on behalf of an issuer.*—The term "person acting on behalf of an issuer" means any officer, director, or employee of such issuer.

(5) *Other terms.*—The terms "blank check company", "rollup transaction", "partnership", "limited liability company", "executive officer of an entity" and "direct participation investment program", have the meanings given those terms by rule or regulation of the Commission.

§ 27. Jurisdiction of Offenses and Suits

The district courts of the United States, and the United States courts of any Territory or other place subject to the jurisdiction of the United States shall have exclusive jurisdiction of violations of this chapter or the rules and regulations thereunder, and of all suits in equity and actions at law brought to enforce any liability or duty created by this chapter or the rules and regulations thereunder. Any criminal proceeding may be brought in the district wherein any act or transaction constituting the violation occurred. Any suit or action to enforce any liability or duty created by this chapter or rules and regulations thereunder, or to enjoin any violation of such chapter or rules and regulations, may be brought in any such district or in the district wherein the defendant is found or is an inhabitant or transacts business, and process in such cases may be served in any other district of which the defendant is an inhabitant or wherever the defendant may be found. . . .

§ 27A. Special Provision Relating to Statute of Limitations on Private Causes of Action

(a) Effect on Pending Causes of Action

The limitation period for any private civil action implied under section 10(b) of this Act that was commenced on or before June 19, 1991, shall be the limitation period provided by the laws applicable in the jurisdiction, including principles of retroactivity, as such laws existed on June 19, 1991.

(b) Effect on Dismissed Causes of Action

Any private civil action implied under section 10(b) of this Act that was commenced on or before June 19, 1991—

(1) which was dismissed as time barred subsequent to June 19, 1991, and

(2) which would have been timely filed under the limitation period provided by the laws applicable in the jurisdiction, including principles of retroactivity, as such laws existed on June 19, 1991,

shall be reinstated on motion by the plaintiff not later than 60 days after the date of enactment of this section.

§ 28. Effect on Existing Law

(a) Addition of rights and remedies; recovery of actual damages; State Securities Commissions

The rights and remedies provided by this chapter shall be in addition to any and all other rights and remedies that may exist at law or in equity; but no person permitted to maintain a suit for damages under the provisions of this chapter shall recover, through satisfaction of judgment in one or more actions, a total amount in excess of his actual damages on account of the act complained of. Except as otherwise specifically provided in this title, nothing in this chapter shall affect the jurisdiction of the securities commission (or any agency or officer performing like functions) of any State over any security or any person insofar as it does not conflict with the provisions of this chapter or the rules and regulations thereunder. No State law which prohibits or regulates the making or promoting of wagering or gaming contracts, or the operation of "bucket shops" or other similar or related activities, shall invalidate any put, call, straddle, option, privilege, or other security, or apply to any activity which is incidental or related to the offer, purchase, sale, exercise, settlement, or closeout of any such instrument, if such instrument is traded pursuant to rules and regulations of a self-regulatory organization that are filed with the Commission pursuant to section 19(b) of this title....

§ 29. Validity of Contracts

(a) Waiver provisions

Any condition, stipulation, or provision binding any person to waive compliance with any provision of this chapter or of any rule or regulation thereunder, or of any rule of an exchange required thereby shall be void.

(b) Contract provisions in violation of chapter

Every contract made in violation of any provision of this chapter or of any rule or regulation thereunder, and every contract (including any contract for listing a security on an exchange) heretofore or hereafter made, the performance of which involves the violation of, or the continuance of any relationship or practice in violation of, any provision of this chapter or any rule or regulation thereunder, shall be void (1) as regards the rights of any person who, in violation of any such provision, rule, or regulation, shall have made or engaged in the performance of any such contract, and (2) as regards the rights of any person who, not being a party to such contract, shall have acquired any right thereunder with actual knowledge of the facts by reason of which the making or performance of such contract was in violation of any such provision, rule, or regulation....

§ 30A. Prohibited Foreign Trade Practices by Issuers

(a) Prohibition

It shall be unlawful for any issuer which has a class of securities registered pursuant to section 12 of this title or which is required to file reports under section 15(d) of this title, or for any officer, director, employee, or agent of such issuer or any stockholder thereof acting on behalf of such issuer, to make use of the mails or any means or instrumentality of interstate commerce corruptly in furtherance of an offer, payment, promise to pay, or authorization of the payment of any money, or offer, gift, promise to give, or authorization of the giving of anything of value to—

(1) any foreign official for purposes of—

(A)(i) influencing any act or decision of such foreign official in his official capacity, or (ii) inducing such foreign official to do or omit to do any act in violation of the lawful duty of such official, or

(B) inducing such foreign official to use his influence with a foreign government or instrumentality thereof to affect or influence any act or decision of such government or instrumentality,

in order to assist such issuer in obtaining or retaining business for or with, or directing business to, any person;

(2) any foreign political party or official thereof or any candidate for foreign political office for purposes of—

(A)(i) influencing any act or decision of such party, official, or candidate in its or his official capacity, or (ii) inducing such party, official, or candidate to do or omit to do an act in violation of the lawful duty of such party, official, or candidate[, or]

(B) inducing such party, official, or candidate to use its or his influence with a foreign government or instrumentality thereof to affect or influence any act or decision of such government or instrumentality

in order to assist such issuer in obtaining or retaining business for or with, or directing business to, any person; or

(3) any person, while knowing that all or a portion of such money or thing of value will be offered, given, or promised, directly or indirectly, to any foreign official, to any foreign political party or official thereof, or to any candidate for foreign political office, for purposes of—

(A)(i) influencing any act or decision of such foreign official, political party, party official, or candidate in his or its official capacity, or (ii) inducing such foreign official, political party, party official, or candidate to do or omit to do any act in violation of the lawful duty of such foreign official, political party, party official, or candidate, or

(B) inducing such foreign official, political party, party official, or candidate to use his or its influence with a foreign government or instrumentality thereof to affect or influence any act or decision of such government or instrumentality

in order to assist such issuer in obtaining or retaining business for or with, or directing business to, any person.

(b) Exception for routine governmental action

Subsection (a) of this section shall not apply to any facilitating or expediting payment to a foreign official, political party, or party official the purpose of which is to expedite or to secure the performance of a routine governmental action by a foreign official, political party, or party official.

(c) Affirmative defenses

It shall be an affirmative defense to actions under subsection (a) of this section that—

(1) the payment, gift, offer, or promise of anything of value that was made, was lawful under the written laws and regulations of the foreign official's, political party's, party official's, or candidate's country; or

(2) the payment, gift, offer, or promise of anything of value that was made, was a reasonable and bona fide expenditure, such as travel and lodging expenses, incurred by or on behalf of a foreign official, party, party official, or candidate and was directly related to—

(A) the promotion, demonstration, or explanation of products or services; or

(B) the execution or performance of a contract with a foreign government or agency thereof. . . .

§ 32. Penalties

(a) Willful violations; false and misleading statements

Any person who willfully violates any provision of this chapter (other than section 30A of this title), or any rule or regulation thereunder the violation of which is made unlawful or the observance of which is required under the terms of this chapter, or any person who willfully and knowingly makes, or causes to be made, any statement in any application, report, or document required to be filed under this chapter or any rule or regulation thereunder or any undertaking contained in a registration statement as provided in subsection (d) of section 15 of this title, or by any self-regulatory organization in connection with an application for membership or participation therein or to become associated with a member thereof, which statement was false or misleading with respect to any material fact, shall upon conviction be fined not more than $1,000,000, or imprisoned not more than 10 years, or both, except that when such person is a person other than a natural person, a fine not exceeding $2,500,000 may be imposed; but no person shall be subject to imprisonment under this section for the violation of any rule or regulation if he proves that he had no knowledge of such rule or regulation.

(b) Failure to file information, documents, or reports

Any issuer which fails to file information, documents, or reports required to be filed under subsection (d) of section 15 of this title or any rule or regulation thereunder shall forfeit to the United States the sum of [$110]* for each and every day such failure to file shall continue. Such forfeiture, which shall be in lieu of any criminal penalty for such failure to file which might be deemed to arise under subsection (a) of this section, shall be payable into the Treasury of the United States and shall be recoverable in a civil suit in the name of the United States.

(c) Violations by issuers, officers, directors, stockholders, employees, or agents of issuers

(1)(A) Any issuer that violates section 30A(a) of this title shall be fined no more than $2,000,000.

(B) Any issuer that violates section 30A(a) of this title shall be subject to a civil penalty of not more than [$11,000] imposed in an action brought by the Commission.

(2)(A) Any officer or director of an issuer, or stockholder acting on behalf of such issuer, who willfully violates section 30A(a) of this title shall be fined not more than $100,000, or imprisoned not more than 5 years, or both.

(B) Any employee or agent of an issuer who is a United States citizen, national, or resident or is otherwise subject to the jurisdiction of the United States (other than an officer, director, or stockholder acting on behalf of such issuer), and who willfully violates section 30A(a) of this title, shall be fined not more than $100,000, or imprisoned not more than 5 years, or both.

(C) Any officer, director, employee, or agent of an issuer, or stockholder acting on behalf of such issuer, who violates section 30A(a) of this title shall be subject to a civil penalty of not more than [$11,000] imposed in an action brought by the Commission.

* The bracketed figures in this section have been adjusted for inflation by the SEC under the Debt Collection Act of 1996, which requires the Commission to make inflationary adjustments to civil penalties in the Securities Act, the Exchange Act, and other Acts that the Commission administers. (Footnote by ed.)

(3) Whenever a fine is imposed under paragraph (2) upon any officer, director, employee, agent, or stockholder of an issuer, such fine may not be paid, directly or indirectly, by such issuer.

§ 36. General Exemptive Authority

(a) Authority

(1) *In general*

Except as provided in subsection (b) of this section, but notwithstanding any other provision of this chapter, the Commission, by rule, regulation, or order, may conditionally or unconditionally exempt any person, security, or transaction, or any class or classes of persons, securities, or transactions, from any provision or provisions of this chapter or of any rule or regulation thereunder, to the extent that such exemption is necessary or appropriate in the public interest, and is consistent with the protection of investors.

(2) *Procedures*

The Commission shall, by rule or regulation, determine the procedures under which an exemptive order under this section shall be granted and may, in its sole discretion, decline to entertain any application for an order of exemption under this section.

(b) Limitation

The Commission may not, under this section, exempt any person, security, or transaction, or any class or classes of persons, securities, or transactions from section 15C [Government Securities Brokers and Dealers] or the rules or regulations issued thereunder . . . .

RULES AND FORMS UNDER THE SECURITIES EXCHANGE ACT OF 1934 (SELECTED PROVISIONS)

17 C.F.R. §§ 240.0–1 et seq.

DEFINITIONS

MANIPULATIVE AND DECEPTIVE DEVICES AND CONTRIVANCES

REGULATION 12B: REGISTRATION AND REPORTING

EXTENSIONS AND TEMPORARY EXEMPTIONS; DEFINITIONS

REGULATION 13A: REPORTS OF ISSUERS OF SECURITIES REGISTERED PURSUANT TO SECTION 12

REGULATION 13D

DEFINITIONS ...

Rule 3a11–1. Definition of the Term "Equity Security"

The term "equity security" is hereby defined to include any stock or similar security, certificate of interest or participation in any profit sharing agreement, preorganization certificate or subscription, transferable share, voting trust certificate or certificate of deposit for an equity security, limited partnership interest, interest in a joint venture, or certificate of interest in a business trust; or any security convertible, with or without consideration into such a security, or carrying any warrant or right to subscribe to or purchase such a security; or any such warrant or right; or any put, call, straddle, or other option or privilege of buying such a security from or selling such a security to another without being bound to do so....

Rule 3b–2. Definition of "Officer"

The term "officer" means a president, vice president, secretary, treasurer or principal financial officer, comptroller or principal accounting officer, and any person routinely performing corresponding functions with respect to any organization whether incorporated or unincorporated.

Rule 3b–6. Liability for Certain Statements by Issuers

(a) A statement within the coverage of paragraph (b) of this section which is made by or on behalf of an issuer or by an outside reviewer retained by the issuer shall be deemed not to be a fraudulent statement (as defined in paragraph (d) of this section), unless it is shown that such statement was made or reaffirmed without a reasonable basis or was disclosed other than in good faith.

(b) This rule applies to the following statements:

(1) A forward-looking statement (as defined in paragraph (c) of this section) made in a document filed with the Commission, in Part I of a quarterly report on Form 10–Q ... or in an annual report to shareholders meeting the requirements of Rules 14a–3(b) and (c) or 14c–3(a) and (b) under the Securities Exchange Act of 1934, a statement reaffirming such forward-looking statement subsequent

to the date the document was filed or the annual report was made publicly available, or a forward-looking statement made prior to the date the document was filed or the date the annual report was made publicly available if such statement is reaffirmed in a filed document, in Part I of a quarterly report on Form 10–Q ... or in an annual report made publicly available within a reasonable time after the making of such forward-looking statement; *Provided,* That:

(i) At the time such statements are made or reaffirmed, either the issuer is subject to the reporting requirements of section 13(a) or 15(d) of the Securities Exchange Act of 1934 and has complied with the requirements of Rule 13a–1 or 15d–1 thereunder, if applicable, to file its most recent annual report on Form 10–K ..., or if the issuer is not subject to the reporting requirements of section 13(a) or 15(d) of the Securities Exchange Act of 1934, the statements are made in a registration statement filed under the Securities Act of 1933 offering statement or solicitation of interest[,] written document or broadcast script under Regulation A or pursuant to section 12(b) or (g) of the Securities Exchange Act of 1934, and ...

(2) Information which is disclosed in a document filed with the Commission in Part I of a quarterly report on Form 10–Q....

(c) For the purpose of this rule, the term *forward-looking statement* shall mean and shall be limited to:

(1) A statement containing a projection of revenues, income (loss), earnings (loss) per share, capital expenditures, dividends, capital structure or other financial items;

(2) A statement of management's plans and objectives for future operations;

(3) A statement of future economic performance contained in management's discussion and analysis of financial condition and results of operations included pursuant to Item 303 of Regulation S–K ...

(4) Disclosed statements of the assumptions underlying or relating to any of the statements described in paragraphs (c)(1), (2), or (3) of this section.

(d) For the purpose of this rule the term *fraudulent statement* shall mean a statement which is an untrue statement of a material fact, a statement false or misleading with respect to any material fact, an omission to state a material fact necessary to make a statement not misleading, or which constitutes the employment of a manipulative, deceptive, or fraudulent device, contrivance, scheme, transaction, act, practice, course of business, or an artifice to defraud, as those terms are used in the Securities Exchange Act of 1934 or the rules or regulations promulgated thereunder.

Rule 3b–7. Definition of "Executive Officer"

The term "executive officer," when used with reference to a registrant, means its president, any vice president of the registrant in charge of a principal business unit, division or function (such as sales, administration, or finance), any other officer who performs a policy making function or any other person who performs similar policy making functions for the registrant. Executive officers of subsidiaries may be deemed executive officers of the registrant if they perform such policy making functions for the registrant.

Rule 3b–11. Definitions Relating to Limited Partnership Roll–Up Transactions for Purposes of Sections 6(b)(9), 14(h) and 15A(b)(12)–(13)

For purposes of Sections 6(b)(9), 14(h) and 15A(b)(12)–(13) of the Act . . .;

(a) The term *limited partnership roll-up transaction* does not include a transaction involving only entities that are not "finite-life" as defined in Item 901(b)(2) of Regulation S–K. . . .

(c) The term "regularly traded" shall be defined as in Item 901(c)(2)(v)(C) of Regulation S–K.

MANIPULATIVE AND DECEPTIVE DEVICES AND CONTRIVANCES . . . .

Rule 10b–5. Employment of Manipulative and Deceptive Devices

It shall be unlawful for any person, directly or indirectly, by the use of any means or instrumentality of interstate commerce, or of the mails or of any facility of any national securities exchange,

(a) To employ any device, scheme, or artifice to defraud,

(b) To make any untrue statement of a material fact or to omit to state a material fact necessary in order to make the statements made, in the light of the circumstances under which they were made, not misleading, or

(c) To engage in any act, practice, or course of business which operates or would operate as a fraud or deceit upon any person,

in connection with the purchase or sale of any security.

Rule 10b–13. Prohibiting Other Purchases During Tender Offer or Exchange Offer

(a) No person who makes a cash tender offer or exchange offer for any equity security shall, directly or indirectly, purchase, or make any arrangement to purchase, any such security (or any other security which is immediately convertible into or exchangeable for such security), otherwise than pursuant to such tender offer or exchange offer, from the time such tender offer or exchange offer is publicly announced or otherwise made known by such person to holders of the security to be acquired until the expiration of the period, including any extensions thereof, during which securities tendered pursuant to such tender offer or exchange offer may by the terms of such offer be accepted or rejected: *Provided, however,* That if such person is the owner of another security which is immediately convertible into or exchangeable for the security which is the subject of the offer, his subsequent exercise of his right of conversion or exchange with respect to such other security shall not be prohibited by this section.

(b) The term "exchange offer" as used in this section shall include a tender offer for, or request or invitation for tenders of, any security in exchange for any consideration other than for all cash. . . .

REGULATION 12B: REGISTRATION AND REPORTING

GENERAL

Rule 12b–2. Definitions

Unless the context otherwise requires, the following terms, when used in the rules contained in this regulation or in Regulation 13A or 15D or in the forms for statements and reports filed pursuant to sections 12, 13 or 15(d) of the act, shall have the respective meanings indicated in this rule:

Affiliate. An "affiliate" of, or a person "affiliated" with, a specified person, is a person that directly, or indirectly through one or more intermediaries, controls, or is controlled by, or is under common control with, the person specified. . . .

Associate. The term "associate" used to indicate a relationship with any person, means (1) any corporation or organization (other than the registrant or a majority-owned subsidiary of the registrant) of which such person is an officer or partner or is, directly or indirectly, the beneficial owner of 10 percent or more of any class of equity securities, (2) any trust or other estate in which such person has a substantial beneficial interest or as to which such person serves as trustee or in a similar fiduciary capacity, and (3) any relative or spouse of such person, or any relative of such spouse, who has the same home as such person or who is a director or officer of the registrant or any of its parents or subsidiaries. . . .

Control. The term "control" (including the terms "controlling," "controlled by" and "under common control with") means the possession, direct or indirect, of the power to direct or cause the direction of the management and policies of a person, whether through the ownership of voting securities, by contract, or otherwise....

Small Business Issuer. The term "small business issuer" means an entity that meets the following criteria:

(1) has revenues of less than $25,000,000;

(2) is a U.S. or Canadian issuer;

(3) is not an investment company; and

(4) if a majority owned subsidiary, the parent corporation is also a small business issuer.

Provided however, that an entity is not a small business issuer if it has a public float (the aggregate market value of the issuer's outstanding securities held by non-affiliates) of $25,000,000 or more.

> *NOTE:* The public float of a reporting company shall be computed by use of the price at which the stock was last sold, or the average of the bid and asked prices of such stock, on a date within 60 days prior to the end of its most recent fiscal year. The public float of a company filing an initial registration statement under the Exchange Act shall be determined as of a date within 60 days of the date the registration statement is filed. In the case of an initial public offering of securities, public float shall be computed on the basis of the number of shares outstanding prior to the offering and the estimated public offering price of the securities.

Subsidiary. A "subsidiary" of a specified person is an affiliate controlled by such person directly, or indirectly through one or more intermediaries....

EXTENSIONS AND TEMPORARY EXEMPTIONS: DEFINITIONS

Rule 12g–1. Exemption From Section 12(g)

An issuer shall be exempt from the requirement to register any class of equity securities pursuant to section 12(g)(1) if on the last day of its most recent fiscal year the issuer had total assets not exceeding $10 million and, with respect to a foreign private issuer, such securities were not quoted in an automated inter-dealer quotation system.

Rule 12g3–2. Exemptions for ... Certain Foreign Securities....

(b)(1) Securities of any foreign private issuer shall be exempt from section 12(g) of the Act if the issuer, or a government official or agency of the country of the issuer's domicile or in which it is incorporated or organized:

(i) Shall furnish to the Commission whatever information in each of the following categories the issuer since the beginning of its last fiscal year (A) has made or is required to make public pursuant to the law of the country of its domicile or in which it is incorporated or organized, (B) has filed or is required to file with a stock exchange on which its securities are traded and which was made public by such exchange, or (C) has distributed or is required to distribute to its security holders. . . .

(3) The information required to be furnished under this paragraph (b) is information material to an investment decision such as: the financial condition or results of operations; changes in business; acquisitions or dispositions of assets; issuance, redemption or acquisitions of their securities; changes in management or control; the granting of options or the payment of other remuneration to directors or officers; and transactions with directors, officers or principal security holders. . . .

REGULATION 13A: REPORTS OF ISSUERS OF SECURITIES REGISTERED PURSUANT TO SECTION 12

Rule 13a–1. Requirements of Annual Reports

Every issuer having securities registered pursuant to section 12 of the Act shall file an annual report on the appropriate form authorized or prescribed therefor for each fiscal year after the last full fiscal year for which financial statements were filed in its registration statement. . . .

Rule 13a–11. Current Reports on Form 8–K

(a) Except as provided in paragraph (b) of this section, every registrant subject to Rule 13a–1 shall file a current report on Form 8–K within the period specified in that form. . . .

Rule 13a–13. Quarterly Reports on Form 10–Q . . .

(a) Except as provided in paragraphs (b) and (c) of this section, every issuer that has securities registered pursuant to section 12 of the Act and which is required to file annual reports pursuant to section 13 of the Act on Form 10–K . . . shall file a quarterly report on Form 10–Q . . . for each of the first three fiscal quarters of each fiscal year of the issuer. . . .

FORM 8–K

CURRENT REPORT

Pursuant to Section 13 or 15(d) of the Securities Exchange Act of 1934

Date of Report (Date of earliest event reported) _____

(Exact name of registrant as specified in its charter)

| (State or other jurisdiction of incorporation) | (Commission File Number) | (IRS Employer Identification No.) |

(Address of principal executive offices)   (Zip Code)

Registrant's telephone number, including area code _____

(Former name or former address, if changed since last report.)

GENERAL INSTRUCTIONS....

B.   Events to be Reported and Time for Filing of Reports

1.   A report on this form is required to be filed upon the occurrence of any one or more of the events specified in Items 1–4 and 6 of this form.   A report of an event specified in Items 1–3 is to be filed within 15 calendar days after the occurrence of the event.   A report of an event specified in Item 4 or 6 is to be filed within 5 business days after the occurrence of the event....

3.   A "small business issuer," defined under Rule 12b–2 of the Exchange Act, shall refer to the disclosure items in Regulation S–B and not Regulation S–K.   If there is no comparable disclosure item in Regulation S–B, a small business issuer need not provide the information requested.   A small business issuer shall provide the information required by Item 310(a) of Regulation S–B in lieu of the financial information required by Item 7 of this Form....

INFORMATION TO BE INCLUDED IN THE REPORT

Item 1.   Changes in Control of Registrant.

(a) If, to the knowledge of management, a change in control of the registrant has occurred, state the name of the person(s) who acquired such control;   the amount and the source of the consideration used by such person(s);   the basis of the control;   the date and a description of the transaction(s) which resulted in the change in control;   the percentage of voting securities of the registrant now beneficially owned directly or indirectly by the person(s) who acquired control;   and the identity of the person(s) from whom control was assumed.   If the source of all or any part of the consideration used is a loan made in the ordinary course of business by a bank ..., the identity of such bank shall be omitted provided a request for confidentiality has been made ... by the person(s) who acquired control.   In lieu thereof, the material shall indicate that disclosure of the identity of the bank has been so omitted and filed separately with the Commission.

Instruction 1. State the terms of any loans or pledges obtained by the new control group for the purpose of acquiring control, and the names of the lenders or pledgees.

2. Any arrangements or understandings among members of both the former and new control groups and their associates with respect to election of directors or other matters should be described.

(b) Furnish the information required by Item 403(c) of Regulation S–K.

Item 2. Acquisition or Disposition of Assets.

If the registrant or any of its majority-owned subsidiaries has acquired or disposed of a significant amount of assets, otherwise than in the ordinary course of business, furnish the following information:

(a) The date and manner of the acquisition or disposition and a brief description of the assets involved, the nature and amount of consideration given or received therefor, the principle followed in determining the amount of such consideration, the identity of the person(s) from whom the assets were acquired or to whom they were sold and the nature of any material relationship between such person(s) and the registrant or any of its affiliates, any director or officer of the registrant, or any associate of any such director or officer. If the transaction being reported is an acquisition, identify the source(s) of the funds used unless all or any part of the consideration used is a loan made in the ordinary course of business by a bank ... in which case the identity of such bank shall be omitted provided a request for confidentiality has been made.... In lieu thereof, the material shall indicate that the identity of the bank has been so omitted and filed separately with the Commission.

(b) If any assets so acquired by the registrant or its subsidiaries constituted plant, equipment or other physical property, state the nature of the business in which the assets were used by the persons from whom acquired and whether the registrant intends to continue such use or intends to devote the assets to other purposes, indicating such other purposes....

GENERAL INSTRUCTIONS ....

4. An acquisition or disposition shall be deemed to involve a significant amount of assets (i) if the registrant's and its other subsidiaries' equity in the net book value of such assets or the amount paid or received therefor upon such acquisition or disposition exceeded 10 percent of the total assets of the registrant and its consolidated subsidiaries, or (ii) if it involved a business (see 17 C.F.R. § 210.11–01(d)) which is

significant (see 17 C.F.R. § 210.11.01(b)).* Acquisitions of individually insignificant businesses are not required to be reported pursuant to this item unless they are related businesses ... and are, in the aggregate, significant.

Item 3.   *Bankruptcy or Receivership.*

(a) If a receiver, fiscal agent or similar officer has been appointed for a registrant or its parent, in a proceeding under the Bankruptcy Act or in any other proceeding under State or Federal law in which a court or governmental agency has assumed jurisdiction over substantially all of the assets or business of the registrant or its parent, or if such

* 17 C.F.R. §§ 210.11–01(b), (d), provide:

(b) A business combination or disposition of a business shall be considered significant if:

(1) A comparison of the most recent annual financial statements of the business acquired or to be acquired and the registrant's most recent annual consolidated financial statements filed at or prior to the date of acquisition indicates that the business would be a significant subsidiary pursuant to the conditions specified in § 210.1–02, or

(2) The business to be disposed of meets the conditions of a significant subsidiary in § 210.1–02. . . .

(d) For purposes of this rule, the term business should be evaluated in light of the facts and circumstances involved and whether there is sufficient continuity of the acquired entity's operations prior to and after the transactions so that disclosure of prior financial information is material to an understanding of future operations. A presumption exists that a separate entity, a subsidiary, or a division is a business. However, a lesser component of an entity may also constitute a business. Among the facts and circumstances which should be considered in evaluating whether an acquisition of a lesser component of an entity constitutes a business are the following:

(1) Whether the nature of the revenue-producing activity of the component will remain generally the same as before the transaction; or

(2) Whether any of the following attributes remain with the component after the transaction:

(i) Physical facilities,

(ii) Employee base,

(iii) Market distribution system,

(iv) Sales force,

(v) Customer base,

(vi) Operating rights,

(vii) Production techniques, or

(viii) Trade names.

17 C.F.R. § 210.1–02, which is referred to in 17 C.F.R. § 210–11.01(b), (d), provides:

(w) Significant subsidiary. The term significant subsidiary means a subsidiary, including its subsidiaries, which meets any of the following conditions:

(1) The registrant's and its other subsidiaries' investments in and advances to the subsidiary exceed 10 percent of the total assets of the registrant and its subsidiaries consolidated as of the end of the most recently completed fiscal year (for a proposed business combination to be accounted for as a pooling of interests, this condition is also met when the number of common shares exchanged or to be exchanged by the registrant exceeds 10 percent of its total common shares outstanding at the date the combination is initiated); or

(2) The registrant's and its other subsidiaries' proportionate share of the total assets (after intercompany eliminations) of the subsidiary exceeds 10 percent of the total assets of the registrants and its subsidiaries consolidated as of the end of the most recently completed fiscal year; or

(3) The registrant's and its other subsidiaries' equity in the income from continuing operations before income taxes, extraordinary items and cumulative effect of a change in accounting principle of the subsidiary exceeds 10 percent of such income of the registrant and its subsidiaries consolidated for the most recently completed fiscal year. (Footnote by ed.)

jurisdiction has been assumed by leaving the existing directors and officers in possession but subject to the supervision and orders of a court or governmental body, identify the proceeding, the court or governmental body, the date jurisdiction was assumed, the identity of the receiver, fiscal agent or similar officer and the date of his appointment....

Item 4. *Changes in Registrant's Certifying Accountant.*

(a) If an independent accountant who was previously engaged as the principal accountant to audit the registrant's financial statements, or an independent accountant upon whom the principal accountant expressed reliance in its report regarding a significant subsidiary, resigns (or indicates it declines to stand for re-election after the completion of the current audit) or is dismissed, then provide the information required by Item 304(a)(1), including compliance with Item 304(a)(3), of Regulation S–K ....

(b) If a new independent accountant has been engaged as either the principal accountant to audit the registrant's financial statements or as an independent accountant on whom the principal accountant has expressed, or is expected to express, reliance in its report regarding a significant subsidiary, then provide the information required by Item 304(a)(2), of Regulation S–K ....

Item 5. *Other Events.*

The registrant may, at its option, report under this item any events, with respect to which information is not otherwise called for by this form, that the registrant deems of importance to security holders.

Item 6. *Resignations of Registrant's Directors.*

(a) If a director has resigned or declined to stand for re-election to the board of directors since the date of the last annual meeting of shareholders because of a disagreement with the registrant on any matter relating to the registrant's operations, policies or practices, and if the director has furnished the registrant with a letter describing such disagreement and requesting that the matter be disclosed, the registrant shall state the date of such resignation or declination to stand for re-election and summarize the director's description of the disagreement.

(b) If the registrant believes that the description provided by the director is incorrect or incomplete, it may include a brief statement presenting its views of the disagreement.

(c) The registrant shall file a copy of the director's letter as an exhibit ....

FORM 10–Q

GENERAL INSTRUCTIONS

... A quarterly report on this form ... shall be filed within 45 days after the end of the first three fiscal quarters of each fiscal year, but no quarterly report need be filed for the fourth quarter of any fiscal year....

Quarterly Report Under Section 13 or 15(d) of the Securities Exchange Act of 1934

For Quarter Ended _____

Commission file number _____

_____

(Exact name of registrant as specified in its charter)

_____

(State or other jurisdiction of incorporation   (I.R.S. Employer
or organization)   Identification No.)

_____

(Address of principal executive offices) (Zip Code)

_____

(Registrant's telephone number, including area code)

_____

(Former name, former address and former fiscal year, if changed since last report.)

. . .

PART 1—FINANCIAL INFORMATION

Item 1. Financial Statements.

Provide the information required by Rule 10–01 of Regulation S–X [Interim Financial Statements]....

Item 2. Management's Discussion and Analysis of Financial Condition and Results of Operations.

Furnish the information required by Item 303 of Regulation S–K ...

PART II—OTHER INFORMATION....

Item 1. Legal Proceedings.

Furnish the information required by Item 103 of Regulation S–K [Legal Proceedings]. As to such proceedings which have been terminated during the period covered by the report, provide similar information, including the date of termination and a description of the disposition thereof with respect to the registrant and its subsidiaries.

Item 2. Changes in Securities.

(a) If the constituent instruments defining the rights of the holders of any class of registered securities have been materially modified, give the title of the class of securities involved and state briefly the general effect of such modification upon the rights of holders of such securities.

(b) If the rights evidenced by any class of registered securities have been materially limited or qualified by the issuance or modification of any other class of securities, state briefly the general effect of the issuance or modification of such other class of securities upon the rights of the holders of the registered securities....

Item 3.   Defaults Upon Senior Securities.

(a) If there has been any material default in the payment of principal, interest, a sinking or purchase fund installment, or any other material default not cured within 30 days, with respect to any indebtedness of the registrant or any of its significant subsidiaries exceeding 5 percent of the total assets of the registrant and its consolidated subsidiaries, identify the indebtedness and state the nature of the default. In the case of such a default in the payment of principal, interest, or a sinking or purchase fund installment, state the amount of the default and the total arrearage on the date of filing this report.

(b) If any material arrearage in the payment of dividends has occurred or if there has been any other material delinquency not cured within 30 days, with respect to any class of preferred stock of the registrant which is registered or which ranks prior to any class of registered securities, or with respect to any class of preferred stock of any significant subsidiary of the registrant, give the title of the class and state the nature of the arrearage or delinquency. In the case of an arrearage in the payment of dividends, state the amount and the total arrearage on the date of filing this report....

Item 4.   Submission of Matters to a Vote of Security Holders.

If any matter has been submitted to a vote of security holders during the period covered by this report, through the solicitation of proxies or otherwise, furnish the following information:

(a) The date of the meeting and whether it was an annual or special meeting.

(b) If the meeting involved the election of directors, the name of each director elected at the meeting and the name of each other director whose term of office as a director continued after the meeting.

(c) A brief description of each matter voted upon at the meeting and state the number of votes cast for, against or withheld, as well as the number of abstentions and broker non-votes, as to each such matter, including a separate tabulation with respect to each nominee for office.

(d) A description of the terms of any settlement between the registrant and any other participant (as defined in Rule 14a–11 ... of

Regulation 14A under the Act) terminating any solicitation subject to Rule 14a–11, including the cost or anticipated cost to the registrant....

———

FORM 10-K

Annual Report Pursuant to Section 13 or 15(d) of The Securities Exchange Act of 1934

GENERAL INSTRUCTIONS ....

This Form shall be used for annual reports pursuant to section 13 or 15(d) of the Securities Exchange Act of 1934 (the "Act") for which no other form is prescribed. Annual reports on this form shall be filed within 90 days after the end of the fiscal year covered by the report....

For the fiscal year ended _____ Commission file number _____

_____
(Exact name of registrant as specified in its charter)

_____   _____
(State or other jurisdiction of incorporation or organization)   (I.R.S. Employer Identification No.)

_____   _____
(Address of principal executive offices)   (Zip Code)

Registrant's telephone number, including area code _____

Securities registered pursuant to Section 12(b) of the Act:

Title of each class	Name of each exchange on which registered
_____	_____
_____	_____

Securities registered pursuant to section 12(g) of the Act:

_____
(Title of class)

. . .

PART I ...

Item 1. Business....

Item 2. Properties....

Item 3. Legal Proceedings....

Item 4. Submission of Matters to a Vote of Security Holders.

If any matter was submitted during the fourth quarter of the fiscal year covered by this report to a vote of security holders, through the solicitation of proxies or otherwise, furnish the following information:

(a) The date of the meeting and whether it was an annual or special meeting.

(b) If the meeting involved the election of directors, the name of each director elected at the meeting and the name of each other director whose term of office as a director continued after the meeting.

(c) A brief description of each matter voted upon at the meeting and state the number of votes cast for, against or withheld, as well as the number of abstentions and broker non-votes as to each such matter, including a separate tabulation with respect to each nominee for office.

PART II ...

Item 5. Market for Registrant's Common Equity and Related Stockholder Matters....

Item 6. Selected Financial Data.

Furnish the information required by Item 301 of Regulation S–K....

Item 7. Management's Discussion and Analysis of Financial Condition and Results of Operation.

Furnish the information required by Item 303 of Regulation S–K....

Item 8. Financial Statements and Supplementary Data....

Furnish financial statements meeting the requirements of Regulation S–X....

Item 9. Changes in and Disagreements With Accountants on Accounting and Financial Disclosure.

Furnish the information required by Item 304 of Regulation S–K....

PART III ...

Item 10. Directors and Executive Officers of the Registrant.

Furnish the information required by Items 401 and 405 of Regulation S–K....

Item 11. Executive Compensation.

Furnish the information required by Item 402 Regulation S–K....

Item 12. Security Ownership of Certain Beneficial Owners and Management.

Furnish the information required by Item 403 of Regulation S–K....

Item 13. Certain Relationships and Related Transactions.

Furnish the information required by Item 404 of Regulation S–K. . . .

REGULATION 13D

Rule 13d–1. Filing of Schedules 13D and 13G

(a) Any person who, after acquiring directly or indirectly the beneficial ownership of any equity security of a class which is specified in paragraph (d) of this section, is directly or indirectly the beneficial owner of more than 5 percent of such class shall, within 10 days after such acquisition, send to the issuer of the security at its principal executive office, by registered or certified mail, and to each exchange where the security is traded, and file with the Commission, a statement containing the information required by Schedule 13D. . . . Six copies of the statement, including all exhibits, shall be filed with the Commission. . . .

(d) For the purpose of this regulation, the term "equity security" means any equity security of a class which is registered pursuant to section 12 of that Act, or any equity security of any insurance company which would have been required to be so registered except for the exemption contained in section 12(g)(2)(G) of the Act, or any equity security issued by a closed-end investment company registered under the Investment Company Act of 1940; *Provided,* Such term shall not include securities of a class of non-voting securities. . . .

Rule 13d–2. Filing of Amendments to Schedules 13D or 13G

(a) *Schedule 13D.* If any material change occurs in the facts set forth in the statement required by Rule 13d–1(a), including, but not limited to, any material increase or decrease in the percentage of the class beneficially owned, the person or persons who were required to file such statement shall promptly file or cause to be filed with the Commission and send or cause to be sent to the issuer at its principal executive office, by registered or certified mail, and to each exchange on which the security is traded an amendment disclosing such change. An acquisition or disposition of beneficial ownership of securities in an amount equal to one percent or more of the class of securities shall be deemed "material" for purposes of this rule; acquisitions or dispositions of less than such amounts may be material, depending upon the facts and circumstances. Six copies of each such amendment shall be filed with the Commission. . . .

Rule 13d–3. Determination of Beneficial Owner

(a) For the purposes of sections 13(d) and 13(g) of the Act a beneficial owner of a security includes any person who, directly or indirectly, through any contract, arrangement, understanding, relationship, or otherwise has or shares:

(1) Voting power which includes the power to vote, or to direct the voting of, such security; and/or,

(2) Investment power which includes the power to dispose, or to direct the disposition of, such security.

(b) Any person who, directly or indirectly, creates or uses a trust, proxy, power of attorney, pooling arrangement or any other contract, arrangement, or device with the purpose or effect of divesting such person of beneficial ownership of a security or preventing the vesting of such beneficial ownership as part of a plan or scheme to evade the reporting requirements of section 13(d) or (g) of the Act shall be deemed for purposes of such sections to be the beneficial owner of such security.

(c) All securities of the same class beneficially owned by a person, regardless of the form which such beneficial ownership takes, shall be aggregated in calculating the number of shares beneficially owned by such person.

(d) Notwithstanding the provisions of paragraphs (a) and (c) of this rule:

(1)(i) A person shall be deemed to be the beneficial owner of a security, subject to the provisions of paragraph (b) of this rule, if that person has the right to acquire beneficial ownership of such security, as defined in Rule 13d–3(a) ... within sixty days, including but not limited to any right to acquire: (A) Through the exercise of any option, warrant or right; (B) through the conversion of a security; (C) pursuant to the power to revoke a trust, discretionary account, or similar arrangement; or (D) pursuant to the automatic termination of a trust, discretionary account or similar arrangement; provided, however, any person who acquires a security or power specified in paragraphs (d)(1)(i)(A), (B) or (C), of this section, with the purpose or effect of changing or influencing the control of the issuer, or in connection with or as a participant in any transaction having such purpose or effect, immediately upon such acquisition shall be deemed to be the beneficial owner of the securities which may be acquired through the exercise or conversion of such security or power. Any securities not outstanding which are subject to such options, warrants, rights or conversion privileges shall be deemed to be outstanding for the purpose of computing the percentage of outstanding securities of the class owned by such person but shall not be deemed to be outstanding for the purpose of computing the percentage of the class [owned] by any other person.

(ii) Paragraph (i) remains applicable for the purpose of determining the obligation to file with respect to the underlying security even though the option, warrant, right or convertible security is of a class of equity security, as defined in Rule 13d–1(c), and may therefore give rise to a separate obligation to file....

Rule 13d–5. Acquisition of Securities

(a) A person who becomes a beneficial owner of securities shall be deemed to have acquired such securities for purposes of section 13(d)(1) of the Act, whether such acquisition was through purchase or otherwise....

(b)(1) When two or more persons agree to act together for the purpose of acquiring, holding, voting or disposing of equity securities of an issuer, the group formed thereby shall be deemed to have acquired beneficial ownership, for purposes of sections 13(d) and (g) of the Act, as of the date of such agreement, of all equity securities of that issuer beneficially owned by any such persons....

SCHEDULE 13D. INFORMATION TO BE INCLUDED IN STATEMENTS FILED PURSUANT TO RULE 13d–1(a) and ... RULE 13d–2(a)

(Name of Issuer)

(Title of Class of Securities)

(CUSIP Number)

(Name, Address and Telephone Number of Person Authorized
to Receive Notices and Communications)

(Date of Event Which Requires Filing of This Statement)....

SPECIAL INSTRUCTIONS FOR COMPLYING WITH SCHEDULE 13D ...

Item 1. Security and Issuer. State the title of the class of equity securities to which this statement relates and the name and address of the principal executive offices of the issuer of such securities.

Item 2. Identity and Background. If the person filing this statement ... is a corporation, general partnership, limited partnership, syndicate or other group of persons, state its name, the state or other place of its organization, its principal business, the address of its principal office and the information required by (d) and (e) of this Item. If the person filing this statement or any person enumerated in Instruction C is a natural person, provide the information specified in (a) through (f) of this Item with respect to such person(s).

(a) Name;

(b) Residence or business address;

(c) Present principal occupation or employment and the name, principal business and address of any corporation or other organization in which such employment is conducted;

(d) Whether or not, during the last five years, such person has been convicted in a criminal proceeding (excluding traffic violations or similar misdemeanors) and, if so, give the dates, nature of conviction, name and location of court, any penalty imposed, or other disposition of the case;

(e) Whether or not, during the last five years, such person was a party to a civil proceeding of a judicial or administrative body of competent jurisdiction and as a result of such proceeding was or is subject to a judgment, decree or final order enjoining future violations of, or prohibiting or mandating activities subject to, federal or state securities laws or finding any violation with respect to such laws; and, if so, identify and describe such proceedings and summarize the terms of such judgment, decree or final order; and

(f) Citizenship.

Item 3. Source and Amount of Funds or Other Consideration. State the source and the amount of funds or other consideration used or to be used in making the purchases, and if any part of the purchase price is or will be represented by funds or other consideration borrowed or otherwise obtained for the purpose of acquiring, holding, trading or voting the securities, a description of the transaction and the names of the parties thereto. Where material, such information should also be provided with respect to prior acquisitions not previously reported pursuant to this regulation. If the source of all or any part of the funds is a loan made in the ordinary course of business by a bank ..., the name of the bank shall not be made available to the public if the person at the time of filing the statement so requests in writing and files such request, naming such bank, with the Secretary of the Commission. If the securities were acquired other than by purchase, describe the method of acquisition.

Item 4. Purpose of Transaction. State the purpose or purposes of the acquisition of securities of the issuer. Describe any plans or proposals which the reporting persons may have which relate to or would result in:

(a) The acquisition by any person of additional securities of the issuer, or the disposition of securities of the issuer;

(b) An extraordinary corporate transaction, such as a merger, reorganization or liquidation, involving the issuer or any of its subsidiaries;

(c) A sale or transfer of a material amount of assets of the issuer or any of its subsidiaries;

(d) Any change in the present board of directors or management of the issuer, including any plans or proposals to change the number or term of directors or to fill any existing vacancies on the board;

(e) Any material change in the present capitalization or dividend policy of the issuer;

(f) Any other material change in the issuer's business or corporate structure . . . ;

(g) Changes in the issuer's charter, bylaws or instruments corresponding thereto or other actions which may impede the acquisition of control of the issuer by any person;

(h) Causing a class of securities of the issuer to be delisted from a national securities exchange or to cease to be authorized to be quoted in an inter-dealer quotation system of a registered national securities association;

(i) A class of equity securities of the issuer becoming eligible for termination of registration pursuant to section 12(g)(4) of the Act; or

(j) Any action similar to any of those enumerated above.

Item 5. Interest in Securities of the Issuer. (a) State the aggregate number and percentage of the class of securities identified pursuant to Item 1 . . . beneficially owned (identifying those shares which there is a right to acquire) by each person named in Item 2. The above mentioned information should also be furnished with respect to persons who, together with any of the persons named in Item 2, comprise a group within the meaning of section 13(d)(3) of the Act;

(b) For each person named in response to paragraph (a), indicate the number of shares as to which there is sole power to vote or to direct the vote, sole power to dispose or to direct the disposition, or shared power to dispose or to direct the disposition. Provide the applicable information required by Item 2 with respect to each person with whom the power to vote or to direct the vote or to dispose or direct the disposition is shared;

(c) Describe any transactions in the class of securities reported on that were effected during the past sixty days or since the most recent filing of Schedule 13D . . . whichever is less, by the persons named in response to paragraph (a). . . .

Item 6. Contracts, Arrangements, Understandings or Relationships With Respect to Securities of the Issuer. Describe any contracts, arrangements, understandings or relationships (legal or otherwise) among the persons named in Item 2 and between such persons and any person with respect to any securities of the issuer, including but not limited to transfer or voting of any of the securities, finder's fees, joint ventures, loan or option arrangements, puts or calls, guarantees of profits, division of profits or loss, or the giving or withholding of proxies, naming the persons with whom such contracts, arrangements, understandings or relationships have been entered into. Include such information for any of the securities that are pledged or otherwise subject to a contingency the occurrence of which would give another person voting power or investment power over such securities except that disclosure of standard default and similar provisions contained in loan agreements need not be included. . . .

Rule 13e–1.   Purchase of Securities by Issuer Thereof

When a person other than the issuer makes a tender offer for, or request or invitation for tenders of, any class of equity securities of an issuer subject to section 13(e) of the Act, and such person has filed a statement with the Commission pursuant to Rule 14d–1 and the issuer has received notice thereof, such issuer shall not thereafter, during the period such tender offer, request or invitation continues, purchase any equity securities of which it is the issuer unless . . .

(a) The issuer has filed with the Commission eight copies of a statement containing the information specified below with respect to the proposed purchases:

(1) The title and amount of securities to be purchased, the names of the persons or classes of persons from whom, and the market in which, the securities are to be purchased, including the name of any exchange on which the purchase is to be made;

(2) The purpose for which the purchase is to be made and whether the securities are to be retired, held in the treasury of the issuer or otherwise disposed of, indicating such disposition; and

(3) The source and amount of funds or other consideration used or to be used in making the purchases, and if any part of the purchase price or proposed purchase price is represented by funds or other consideration borrowed or otherwise obtained for the purpose of acquiring, holding, or trading the securities, a description of the transaction and the names of the parties thereto. . . .

(c) The issuer has at any time within the past 6 months sent or given to its equity security holders the substance of the information contained in the statement required by paragraph (a) of this section. . . .

Rule 13e–3.   Going Private Transactions by Certain Issuers or Their Affiliates

(a) *Definitions.* Unless indicated otherwise or the context otherwise requires, all terms used in this section and in Schedule 13E–3 . . . shall have the same meaning as in the Act or elsewhere in the General Rules and Regulations thereunder. In addition, the following definitions apply:

(1) An "affiliate" of an issuer is a person that directly or indirectly through one or more intermediaries controls, is controlled by, or is under common control with such issuer. For the purposes of this section only, a person who is not an affiliate of an issuer at the commencement of such person's tender offer for a class of equity securities of such issuer will not be deemed an affiliate of such issuer prior to the stated termination of such tender offer and any extensions thereof;

(2) The term "purchase" means any acquisition for value including, but not limited to, (i) any acquisition pursuant to the dissolution of an issuer subsequent to the sale or other disposition of substantially all the assets of such issuer to its affiliate, (ii) any acquisition pursuant to a merger, (iii) any acquisition of fractional interests in connection with a reverse stock split, and (iv) any acquisition subject to the control of an issuer or an affiliate of such issuer;

(3) A "Rule 13e–3 transaction" is any transaction or series of transactions involving one or more of the transactions described in paragraph (a)(3)(i) of this section which has either a reasonable likelihood or a purpose of producing, either directly or indirectly, any of the effects described in paragraph (a)(3)(ii) of this section;

(i) The transactions referred to in paragraph (a)(3) of this section are:

(A) A purchase of any equity security by the issuer of such security or by an affiliate of such issuer;

(B) A tender offer for or request or invitation for tenders of any equity security made by the issuer of such class of securities or by an affiliate of such issuer; or

(C) A solicitation subject to Regulation 14A ... of any proxy, consent or authorization of, or a distribution subject to Regulation 14C ... of information statements to, any equity security holder by the issuer of the class of securities or by an affiliate of such issuer, in connection with: a merger, consolidation, reclassification, recapitalization, reorganization or similar corporate transaction of an issuer or between an issuer (or its subsidiaries) and its affiliate; a sale of substantially all the assets of an issuer to its affiliate or group of affiliates; or a reverse stock split of any class of equity securities of the issuer involving the purchase of fractional interests.

(ii) The effects referred to in paragraph (a)(3) of this section are:

(A) Causing any class of equity securities of the issuer which is subject to section 12(g) or section 15(d) of the Act to be held of record by less than 300 persons; or

(B) Causing any class of equity securities of the issuer which is either listed on a national securities exchange or authorized to be quoted in an inter-dealer quotation system of a registered national securities association to be neither listed on any national securities exchange nor authorized to be quoted on an inter-dealer quotation system of any registered national securities association. . . .

(b) *Application of section to an issuer (or an affiliate of such issuer) subject to section 12 of the Act.* (1) It shall be a fraudulent, deceptive or manipulative act or practice, in connection with a Rule 13e–3 transaction, for an issuer which has a class of equity securities registered pursuant to section 12 of the Act or which is a closed-end investment company registered under the Investment Company Act of 1940, or an affiliate of such issuer, directly or indirectly

(i) To employ any device, scheme or artifice to defraud any person;

(ii) To make any untrue statement of a material fact or to omit to state a material fact necessary in order to make the statements made, in light of the circumstances under which they were made, not misleading; or

(iii) To engage in any act, practice or course of business which operates or would operate as a fraud or deceit upon any person.

(2) As a means reasonably designed to prevent fraudulent, deceptive or manipulative acts or practices in connection with any Rule 13e–3 transaction, it shall be unlawful for an issuer which has a class of equity securities registered pursuant to section 12 of the Act, or an affiliate of such issuer, to engage, directly or indirectly, in a Rule 13e–3 transaction unless:

(i) Such issuer or affiliate complies with the requirements of paragraphs (d), (e) and (f) of this section; and

(ii) The Rule 13e–3 transaction is not in violation of paragraph (b)(1) of this section. . . .

(d) *Material required to be filed.* The issuer or affiliate engaging in a Rule 13e–3 transaction shall, in accordance with the General Instructions to the Rule 13e–3 Transaction Statement on Schedule 13E–3 . . . :

(1) File with the Commission eight copies of such schedule, including all exhibits thereto. . . .

(e) *Disclosure of certain information.* (1) The issuer or affiliate engaging in the Rule 13e–3 transaction, in addition to any other information required to be disclosed pursuant to any other applicable rule or regulation under the federal securities laws, shall disclose to security holders of the class of equity securities which is the subject of the transaction, in the manner prescribed by paragraph (f) of this section, the information required by . . . Schedule 13e–3. . . . If the Rule 13e–3 transaction involves (i) a transaction subject to Regulation 14A . . . or 14C . . . of the Act, (ii) the registration of securities pursuant to the Securities Act of 1933 and the General Rules and Regulations promulgated thereunder, or (iii) a tender offer subject to Regulation 14D . . . or Rule 13e–4 . . . , such information shall be included in the proxy statement, the information statement, the registration statement or the tender offer for or request or invitation for tenders of securities published, sent or given to security holders, respectively. . . .

Rule 13e–4. Tender Offers by Issuers

(a) *Definitions.* Unless the context otherwise requires, all terms used in this section and in Schedule 13E–4 . . . shall have the same meaning as in the Act or elsewhere in the General Rules and Regulations thereunder. In addition, the following definitions shall apply:

(1) The term "issuer" means any issuer which has a class of equity security registered pursuant to section 12 of the Act, or which is required to file periodic reports pursuant to section 15(d) of the Act, or which is a closed-end investment company registered under the Investment Company Act of 1940.

(2) The term "issuer tender offer" refers to a tender offer for, or a request or invitation for tenders of, any class of equity security, made by the issuer of such class of equity security or by an affiliate of such issuer. . . .

(b)(1) It shall be a fraudulent, deceptive or manipulative act or practice, in connection with an issuer tender offer, for an issuer or an affiliate of such issuer, in connection with an issuer tender offer:

(i) To employ any device, scheme or artifice to defraud any person;

(ii) To make any untrue statement of a material fact or to omit to state a material fact necessary in order to make the statements made, in the light of the circumstances under which they were made, not misleading; or

(iii) To engage in any act, practice or course of business which operates or would operate as a fraud or deceit upon any person.

(2) As a means reasonably designed to prevent fraudulent, deceptive or manipulative acts or practices in connection with any issuer tender offer, it shall be unlawful for an issuer or an affiliate of such issuer to make an issuer tender offer unless:

(i) Such issuer or affiliate complies with the requirements of paragraphs (c), (d), (e) and (f) of this section; and

(ii) The issuer tender offer is not in violation of paragraph (b)(1) of this section.

(c) *Material required to be filed.* The issuer or affiliate making the issuer tender offer shall, in accordance with the General Instructions to the Issuer Tender Offer Statement on Schedule 13E–4 . . . :

(1) File with the Commission ten copies of such schedule, including all exhibits thereto, prior to or as soon as practicable on the date of commencement of the issuer tender offer. . . .

(d) *Disclosure of certain information.*   (1) The issuer or affiliate making the issuer tender offer shall publish, send or give to security holders in the manner prescribed in paragraph (e)(1) of this section a statement containing the following information:

(i) The scheduled termination date of the issuer tender offer and whether it may be extended;

(ii) The specified dates prior to which, and after which, persons who tender securities pursuant to the issuer tender offer may withdraw their securities pursuant to paragraph (f)(2) of this section;

(iii) If the issuer tender offer is for less than all the securities of a class, the exact dates of the period during which securities will be accepted on a pro rata basis pursuant to paragraph (f)(3) of this section and the manner in which securities will be accepted for payment and in which securities may be withdrawn; and

(iv) The information required by Items 1 through 8 of Schedule 13E–4 . . . or a fair and adequate summary thereof. . . .

(e) *Dissemination of tender offers.*

(1) The issuer or affiliate making the issuer tender offer will be deemed to have published, sent or given the issuer tender offer to security holders if such issuer or affiliate complies fully with one or more of the following methods of dissemination. Depending on the facts and circumstances involved, and for purposes of paragraphs (e)(1)(i) and (iii) of this section, adequate publication of the issuer tender offer may require publication in a newspaper with a national circulation or may require only publication in newspaper with metropolitan or regional circulation or may require publication in a combination thereof.

(i) *Dissemination of cash issuer tender offers by long-form publication:* By making adequate publication in a newspaper or newspapers, on the date of commencement of the issuer tender offer, of the statement required by paragraph (d)(1) of this section.

(ii) *Dissemination of any issuer tender offer by use of shareholder and other lists:* (A) By mailing the statement required by paragraph (d)(1) of this section to each security holder whose name appears on the most recent shareholder list of the issuer;

(B) By contracting each participant named on the most recent security position listing of any clearing agency within the possession or access of the issuer or affiliate making the tender offer, and making inquiry of each such participant as to the approximate number of beneficial owners of the securities for which the issuer tender offer is made which are held by such participant;

(C) By furnishing to each such participant a sufficient number of copies of the statement required by paragraph (d)(1) of this section for transmittal to the beneficial owners; and

(D) By agreeing to reimburse promptly each such participant for reasonable expenses incurred by it in forwarding such statement to the beneficial owners. . . .

(f) *Manner of making tender offer.* (1) The issuer tender offer, unless withdrawn, shall remain open until the expiration of:

(i) At least twenty business days from its commencement; and

(ii) At least ten business days from the date that notice of an increase or decrease in the percentage of the class of securities being sought or the consideration offered or the dealer's soliciting fee to be given is first published, sent or given to security holders.

Provided, however, That, for purposes of this paragraph, the acceptance for payment by the issuer or affiliate of an additional amount of securities not to exceed two percent of the class of securities that is the subject of the tender offer shall not be deemed to be an increase. For purposes of this paragraph, the percentage of a class of securities shall be calculated in accordance with section 14(d)(3) of the Act.

(2) The issuer or affiliate making the issuer tender offer shall permit securities tendered pursuant to the issuer tender offer to be withdrawn:

(i) At any time during the period such issuer tender offer remains open; and

(ii) If not yet accepted for payment, after the expiration of forty business days from the commencement of the issuer tender offer.

(3) If the issuer or affiliate makes a tender offer for less than all of the outstanding equity securities of a class, and if a greater number of securities is tendered pursuant thereto than the issuer or affiliate is bound or willing to take up and pay for, the securities taken up and paid for shall be taken up and paid for as nearly as may be pro rata, disregarding fractions, according to the number of securities tendered by each security holder during the period such offer remains open; *Provided, however,* That this provision shall not prohibit the issuer or affiliate making the issuer tender offer from:

(i) Accepting all securities tendered by persons who own, beneficially or of record, an aggregate of not more than a specified number which is less than one hundred shares of such security and who tender all their securities, before prorating securities tendered by others; or

(ii) Accepting by lot securities tendered by security holders who tender all securities held by them and who, when tendering their securities, elect to have either all or none or at least a minimum amount or none accepted, if the issuer or affiliate first accepts all securities tendered by security holders who do not so elect;

(4) In the event the issuer or affiliate making the issuer tender increases the consideration offered after the issuer tender offer has

commenced, such issuer or affiliate shall pay such increased consideration to all security holders whose tendered securities are accepted for payment by such issuer or affiliate.

(5) The issuer or affiliate making the tender offer shall either pay the consideration offered, or return the tendered securities, promptly after the termination or withdrawal of the tender offer.

(6) Until the expiration of at least ten business days after the date of termination of the issuer tender offer, neither the issuer nor any affiliate shall make any purchases, otherwise than pursuant to the tender offer, of:

(i) Any security which is the subject of the issuer tender offer, or any security of the same class and series, or any right to purchase any such securities; and

(ii) In the case of an issuer tender offer which is an exchange offer, any security being offered pursuant to such exchange offer, or any security of the same class and series, or any right to purchase any such security.

(7) The time periods for the minimum offering periods pursuant to this section shall be computed on a concurrent as opposed to a consecutive basis.

(8) No issuer or affiliate shall make a tender offer unless:

(i) The tender offer is open to all security holders of the class of securities subject to the tender offer; and

(ii) The consideration paid to any security holder pursuant to the tender offer is the highest consideration paid to any other security holder during such tender offer....

SCHEDULE 13E–3.   RULE 13E–3 TRANSACTION STATEMENT ....

_____
(Name of the Issuer)

_____
(Name of Person(s) Filing Statement)

_____
(Title of Class of Securities)

_____
(CUSIP Number of Class of Securities)

_____
(Name, address and telephone number of person authorized to receive notices and communications on behalf of person(s) filing statement) ...

Item 1.   Issuer and Class of Security Subject to the Transaction. (a) State the name of the issuer of the class of equity security which is the subject of the Rule 13e–3 transaction and the address of its principal executive offices.

(b) State the exact title, the amount of securities outstanding of the class of security which is the subject of the Rule 13e–3 transaction as of the most recent practicable date and the approximate number of holders of record of such class as of the most recent practicable date.

(c) Identify the principal market in which such securities are being traded and, if the principal market is an exchange, state the high and low sales prices for such securities as reported in the consolidated transaction reporting system or, if not so reported, on such principal exchange for each quarterly period during the past two years. If the principal market is not an exchange, state the range of high and low bid quotations for each quarterly period during the past two years, the source of such quotations and, if there is currently no established trading market for such securities (excluding limited or sporadic quotations), furnish a statement to that effect.

(d) State the frequency and amount of any dividends paid during the past two years with respect to such class of securities and briefly describe any restriction on the issuer's present or future ability to pay such dividends. . . .

(e) If the issuer and/or affiliate filing this statement has made an underwritten public offering of such securities for cash during the past three years which was registered under the Securities Act of 1933 or exempt from registration thereunder pursuant to Regulation A, state the date of such offering, the amount of securities offered, the offering price per share (which should be appropriately adjusted for stock splits, stock dividends, etc.) and the aggregate proceeds received by such issuer and/or such affiliate.

(f) With respect to any purchases of such securities made by the issuer or affiliate since the commencement of the issuer's second full fiscal year preceding the date of this schedule, state the amount of such securities purchased, the range of prices paid for such securities and the average purchase price for each quarterly period of the issuer during such period. . . .

Item 2. Identity and Background. . . .

Item 3. Past Contacts, Transactions or Negotiations. . . .

Item 4. Terms of the Transaction. (a) State the material terms of the Rule 13e–3 transaction.

(b) Describe any term or arrangement concerning the Rule 13e–3 transaction relating to any security holder of the issuer which is not identical to that relating to other security holders of the same class of securities of the issuer.

Item 5. Plans or Proposals of the Issuer or Affiliate. Describe any plan or proposal of the issuer or affiliate regarding activities or transactions which are to occur after the Rule 13e–3 transaction which relate to or would result in: (a) An extraordinary corporate transaction, such as a merger, reorganization or liquidation, involving the issuer or any of its subsidiaries;

(b) A sale or transfer of a material amount of assets of the issuer or any of its subsidiaries;

(c) Any change in the present board of directors or management of the issuer including, but not limited to, any plan or proposal to change the number or term of directors, to fill any existing vacancy on the board or to change any material term of the employment contract of any executive officer;

(d) Any material change in the present dividend rate or policy or indebtedness or capitalization of the issuer;

(e) Any other material change in the issuer's corporate structure or business;

(f) A class of equity securities of the issuer becoming eligible for termination of registration pursuant to section 12(g)(4) of the Act; or

(g) The suspension of the issuer's obligation to file reports pursuant to section 15(d) of the Act.

Item 6. Source and Amounts of Funds or Other Consideration. . . .

Item 7. Purpose(s), Alternatives, Reasons and Effects. (a) State the purpose(s) for the Rule 13e–3 transaction.

(b) If the issuer or affiliate considered alternative means to accomplish such purpose(s), briefly describe such alternative(s) and state the reason(s) for their rejection.

(c) State the reasons for the structure of the Rule 13e–3 transaction and for undertaking such transaction at this time.

(d) Describe the effects of the Rule 13e–3 transaction on the issuer, its affiliates and unaffiliated security holders, including the federal tax consequences.

Instructions. (1) Conclusory statements will not be considered sufficient disclosure in response to Item 7.

(2) The description required by Item 7(d) should include a reasonably detailed discussion of the benefits and detriments of the Rule 13e–3 transaction to the issuer, its affiliates and unaffiliated security holders. The benefits and detriments of the Rule 13e–3 transaction should be quantified to the extent practicable.

(3) If this statement is filed by an affiliate of the issuer, the description required by Item 7(d) should include but not be limited to, the effect of the Rule 13e–3 transaction on the affiliate's interest

in the net book value and net earnings of the issuer in terms of both dollar amounts and percentages.

Item 8. Fairness of the Transaction. (a) State whether the issuer or affiliate filing this schedule reasonably believes that the Rule 13e–3 transaction is fair or unfair to unaffiliated security holders. If any director dissented to or abstained from voting on the Rule 13e–3 transaction, identify each such director, and indicate, if known, after making reasonable inquiry, the reasons for each dissent or abstention.

Instruction. A statement that the issuer or affiliate has no reasonable belief as to the fairness of the Rule 13e–3 transaction to unaffiliated security holders will not be considered sufficient disclosure in response to Item 8(a).

(b) Discuss in reasonable detail the material factors upon which the belief stated in Item 8(a) is based and, to the extent practicable, the weight assigned to each such factor. Such discussion should include an analysis of the extent, if any, to which such belief is based on the factors set forth in instruction (1) to paragraph (b) of this Item, paragraphs (c), (d), and (e) of this Item, and Item 9.

Instructions. (1) The factors which are important in determining the fairness of a transaction to unaffiliated security holders and the weight, if any, which should be given to them in a particular context will vary. Normally such factors will include, among others, those referred to in paragraphs (c), (d) and (e) of this Item and whether the consideration offered to unaffiliated security holders constitutes fair value in relation to:

(i) Current market prices,

(ii) Historical market prices,

(iii) Net book value,

(iv) Going concern value,

(v) Liquidation value,

(vi) The purchase price paid in previous purchases disclosed in Item 1(f) of Schedule 13e–3,

(vii) Any report, opinion, or appraisal described in Item 9 and

(viii) Firm offers of which the issuer or affiliate is aware made by any unaffiliated person, other than the person filing this statement, during the preceding eighteen months for:

(A) The merger or consolidation of the issuer into or with such person or of such person into or with the issuer,

(B) The sale or other transfer of all or any substantial part of the assets of the issuer or

(C) Securities of the issuer which would enable the holder thereof to exercise control of the issuer.

(2) Conclusory statements, such as "The Rule 13e–3 transaction is fair to unaffiliated security holders in relation to net book value, going concern value and future prospects of the issuer" will not be considered sufficient disclosure in response to Item 8(b).

(c) State whether the transaction is structured so that approval of at least a majority of unaffiliated security holders is required.

(d) State whether a majority of directors who are not employees of the issuer has retained an unaffiliated representative to act solely on behalf of unaffiliated security holders for the purposes of negotiating the terms of the Rule 13e–3 transaction and/or preparing a report concerning the fairness of such transaction.

(e) State whether the Rule 13e–3 transaction was approved by a majority of the directors of the issuer who are not employees of the issuer.

(f) If any offer of the type described in instruction (vii) to Item 8(b) has been received, describe such offer and state the reason(s) for its rejection.

Item 9. Reports, Opinions, Appraisals and Certain Negotiations. (a) State whether or not the issuer or affiliate has received any report, opinion (other than an opinion of counsel) or appraisal from an outside party which is materially related to the Rule 13e–3 transaction including, but not limited to, any such report, opinion or appraisal relating to the consideration or the fairness of the consideration to be offered to security holders of the class of securities which is the subject of the Rule 13e–3 transaction or the fairness of such transaction to the issuer or affiliate or to security holders who are not affiliates.

(b) With respect to any report, opinion or appraisal described in Item 9(a) or with respect to any negotiation or report described in Item 8(d) concerning the terms of the Rule 13e–3 transaction:

(1) Identify such outside party and/or unaffiliated representative;

(2) Briefly describe the qualifications of such outside party and/or unaffiliated representative;

(3) Describe the method of selection of such outside party and/or unaffiliated representative;

(4) Describe any material relationship between (i) the outside party, its affiliates, and/or unaffiliated representative, and (ii) the issuer or its affiliates, which existed during the past two years or is mutually understood to be contemplated and any compensation received or to be received as a result of such relationship;

(5) If such report, opinion or appraisal relates to the fairness of the consideration, state whether the issuer or affiliate determined the

amount of consideration to be paid or whether the outside party recommended the amount of consideration to be paid.

(6) Furnish a summary concerning such negotiation report, opinion or appraisal which shall include, but not be limited to, the procedures followed; the findings and recommendations; the bases for and methods of arriving at such findings and recommendations; instructions received from the issuer or affiliate; and any limitation imposed by the issuer or affiliate on the scope of the investigation.

(c) Furnish a statement to the effect that such report, opinion or appraisal shall be made available for inspection and copying at the principal executive offices of the issuer or affiliate during its regular business hours by any interested equity security holder of the issuer or his representative who has been so designated in writing. This statement may also provide that a copy of such report, opinion or appraisal will be transmitted by the issuer or affiliate to any interested equity security holder of the issuer or his representative who has been so designated in writing upon written request and at the expense of the requesting security holder.

Item 10. Interest in Securities of the Issuer. (a) With respect to the class of equity security to which the Rule 13e–3 transaction relates, state the aggregate amount and percentage of securities beneficially owned (identifying those securities for which there is a right to acquire) as of the most recent practicable date by the person filing this statement (unless such person is the issuer), by any pension, profit sharing or similar plan of the issuer or affiliate, by [each general partner, and each member of a group, filing this Form] or by any associate or majority owned subsidiary of the issuer or affiliate giving the name and address of any such associate or subsidiary....

Item 11. Contracts, Arrangements or Understandings with Respect to the Issuer's Securities....

Item 12. Present Intention and Recommendation of Certain Persons with Regard to the Transaction. (a) To the extent known by the person filing this statement after making reasonable inquiry, furnish a statement of present intention with regard to the Rule 13e–3 transaction indicating whether or not any executive officer, director or affiliate of the issuer or any person enumerated in Instruction C of this statement will tender or sell securities of the issuer owned or held by such person and/or how such securities, and securities with respect to which such person holds proxies, will be voted and the reasons therefor....

Item 13. Other Provisions of the Transaction. (a) State whether or not appraisal rights are provided under applicable state law or under the issuer's articles of incorporation or will be voluntarily accorded by the issuer or affiliate to security holders in connection with the Rule 13e–3 transaction and, if so, summarize such appraisal rights. If appraisal rights will not be available under the applicable state law, to security holders who object to the transaction, briefly outline the rights which may be available to such security holders under such law.

(b) If any provision has been made by the issuer or affiliate in connection with the Rule 13e–3 transaction to allow unaffiliated security holders to obtain access to the corporate files of the issuer or affiliate or to obtain counsel or appraisal services at the expense of the issuer or affiliate, describe such provision.

(c) If the Rule 13e–3 transaction involves the exchange of debt securities of the issuer or affiliate for the equity securities held by security holders of the issuer who are not affiliates, describe whether or not the issuer or affiliate will take steps to provide or assure that such securities are or will be eligible for trading on any national securities exchange or an automated inter-dealer quotation system.

Item 14. Financial Information....

———

SCHEDULE 13E–4. TENDER OFFER STATEMENT PURSUANT TO SECTION 13(E)(1) OF THE SECURITIES EXCHANGE ACT OF 1934 AND RULE 13E–4 THEREUNDER ....

Name of Issuer _____

Name of person(s) filing statement _____

Title of class of securities _____

CUSIP number of class of securities _____

Name, address and telephone number of person authorized to receive notices and communications on behalf of the person(s) filing statement

_____

Date tender offer first published, sent or given to security holders

_____

. . .

Item 1. Security and Issuer. (a) State the name of the issuer and the address of its principal executive office;

(b) State the exact title and the amount of securities outstanding of the class of security being sought as of the most recent practicable date; the exact amount of such securities being sought and the consideration being offered therefor; whether any such securities are to be purchased from any officer, director or affiliate of the issuer, and the details of each such transaction; and

(c) Identify the principal market in which such securities are being traded and, if the principal market is an exchange, state the high and low sales prices for such securities as reported in the consolidated transaction reporting system or, if not so reported, on such principal exchange for each quarterly period during the past two years. If the principal market is not an exchange, state the range of high and low bid quotations for each quarterly period during the past two years, the source of such quotations, and if there is currently no established trading market for such securities (excluding limited or sporadic) furnish a statement to that effect.

(d) State the name and address of the person filing this statement, if other than the issuer, and the nature of the affiliation between such person and the issuer.

Item 2. Source and Amount of Funds or Other Consideration....

Item 3. Purpose of the Tender Offer and Plans or Proposals of the Issuer or Affiliate. State the purpose or purposes of the tender offer, and whether the securities are to be retired, held in the treasury of the issuer, or otherwise disposed of, indicating such disposition, and any plans or proposals which relate to or would result in:

(a) The acquisition by any person of additional securities of the issuer, or the disposition of securities of the issuer;

(b) An extraordinary corporate transaction, such as a merger, reorganization or liquidation, involving the issuer or any of its subsidiaries;

(c) A sale or transfer of a material amount of assets of the issuer or any of its subsidiaries;

(d) Any change in the present board of directors or management of the issuer including, but not limited to, any plans or proposals to change the number or the term of directors, to fill any existing vacancy on the board or to change any material term of the employment contract of any executive officer;

(e) Any material change in the present dividend rate or policy, or indebtedness or capitalization of the issuer;

(f) Any other material change in the issuer's corporate structure or business, including if the issuer is a registered closed-end investment company, any plans or proposals to make any changes in its investment policy for which a vote would be required by section 13 of the Investment Company Act of 1940;

(g) Changes in the issuer's charter, bylaws or instruments corresponding thereto or other actions which may impede the acquisition of control of the issuer by any person;

(h) Causing a class of equity security of the issuer to be delisted from a national securities exchange or to cease to be authorized to be quoted in an inter-dealer quotation system of a registered national securities association;

(i) A class of equity security of the issuer becoming eligible for termination of registration pursuant to section 12(g)(4) of the Act; or

(j) The suspension of the issuer's obligation to file reports pursuant to section 15(d) of the Act.

Item 4. Interest in Securities of the Issuer....

Item 5. Contracts, Arrangements, Understandings or Relationships With Respect to the Issuer's Securities....

Item 6. Persons Retained, Employed or to be Compensated....

Item 7. Financial Information. (a) If material, furnish the following financial data of the issuer:

(1) Audited financial statements for the two fiscal years required to be filed with the issuer's most recent annual report under Sections 13 and 15(d) of the Act;

(2) Unaudited balance sheets and comparative year-to-date income statements and statements of cash flows and related earnings per share amounts required to be included in the issuer's most recent quarterly report filed pursuant to the Act;

(3) Ratio of earnings to fixed charges for the two most recent fiscal years and the interim periods provided under Item 7(a)(2); and

(4) Book value per share as of the most recent fiscal year end and as of the date of the latest interim balance sheet provided under Item 7(a)(2)....

REGULATION 14A: SOLICITATION OF PROXIES

Rule 14a–1. Definitions

Unless the context otherwise requires, all terms used in this regulation have the same meanings as in the Act or elsewhere in the general rules and regulations thereunder. In addition, the following definitions apply unless the context otherwise requires:

(a) *Associate.* The term "associate," used to indicate a relationship with any person, means:

(1) Any corporation or organization (other than the registrant or a majority owned subsidiary of the registrant) of which such person is an officer or partner or is, directly or indirectly, the beneficial owner of 10 percent or more of any class of equity securities;

(2) Any trust or other estate in which such person has a substantial beneficial interest or as to which such person serves as trustee or in a similar fiduciary capacity; and

(3) Any relative or spouse of such person, or any relative of such spouse, who has the same home as such person or who is a director or officer of the registrant or any of its parents or subsidiaries....

(f) *Proxy.* The term "proxy" includes every proxy, consent or authorization within the meaning of section 14(a) of the Act. The consent or authorization may take the form of failure to object or to dissent.

(g) *Proxy statement.* The term "proxy statement" means the statement required by Rule 14a–3(a) whether or not contained in a single document....

(j) *Registrant.* The term "registrant" means the issuer of the securities in respect of which proxies are to be solicited....

(k) *Respondent bank.* For purposes of Rules 14a–13, 14b–1 and 14b–2, the term "respondent bank" means any bank, association or other entity that exercises fiduciary powers which holds securities on behalf of beneficial owners and deposits such securities for safekeeping with another bank, association or other entity that exercises fiduciary powers.

(*l*) *Solicitation.* (1) The terms "solicit" and "solicitation" include:

(i) Any request for a proxy whether or not accompanied by or included in a form of proxy;

(ii) Any request to execute or not to execute, or to revoke, a proxy; or

(iii) The furnishing of a form of proxy or other communication to security holders under circumstances reasonably calculated to result in the procurement, withholding or revocation of a proxy.

(2) The terms do not apply, however, to:

(i) The furnishing of a form of proxy to a security holder upon the unsolicited request of such security holder;

(ii) The performance by the registrant of acts required by Rule 14a–7;

(iii) The performance by any person of ministerial acts on behalf of a person soliciting a proxy; or

(iv) A communication by a security holder who does not otherwise engage in a proxy solicitation (other than a solicitation exempt under Rule 14a–2) stating how the security holder intends to vote and the reasons therefor, provided that the communication:

(A) is made by means of speeches in public forums, press releases, published or broadcast opinions, statements, or advertisements appearing in a broadcast media, or newspaper, magazine or other bona fide publication disseminated on a regular basis,

(B) is directed to persons to whom the security holder owes a fiduciary duty in connection with the voting of securities of a registrant held by the security holder, or

(C) is made in response to unsolicited requests for additional information with respect to a prior communication by the security holder made pursuant to this paragraph (*l*)(2)(iv).

Rule 14a–2.   Solicitations to Which Rule 14a–3 to Rule 14a–15 Apply

Rules 14a–3 to 14a–15, except as specified below, apply to every solicitation of a proxy with respect to securities registered pursuant to Section 12 of the Act whether or not trading in such securities has been suspended.   To the extent specified below, certain of these sections also apply to roll-up transactions that do not involve an entity with securities registered pursuant to Section 12 of the Act.

(a) Rules 14a–3 to 14a–15 do not apply to the following:

(1) Any solicitation by a person in respect to securities carried in his name or in the name of his nominee (otherwise than as voting trustee) or held in his custody, if such person—

(i) Receives no commission or remuneration for such solicitation, directly or indirectly, other than reimbursement of reasonable expenses,

(ii) Furnishes promptly to the person solicited a copy of all soliciting material with respect to the same subject matter or meeting received from all persons who shall furnish copies thereof for such purpose and who shall, if requested, defray the reasonable expenses to be incurred in forwarding such material, and

(iii) In addition, does no more than impartially instruct the person solicited to forward a proxy to the person, if any, to whom the person solicited desires to give a proxy, or impartially request from the person solicited instructions as to the authority to be conferred by the proxy and state that a proxy will be given if no instructions are received by a certain date.

(2) Any solicitation by a person in respect of securities of which he is the beneficial owner . . . .

(6) Any solicitation through the medium of a newspaper advertisement which informs security holders of a source from which they may obtain copies of a proxy statement, form of proxy and any other soliciting material and does no more than:

(i) Name the registrant,

(ii) State the reason for the advertisement, and

(iii) Identify the proposal or proposals to be acted upon by security holders.

(b) Rules 14a–3 to 14a–6 (other than Rules 14a–6(g)), 14a–8, and 14a–10 to 14a–15 do not apply to the following:

(1) Any solicitation by or on behalf of any person who does not, at any time during such solicitation, seek directly or indirectly, either on its own or another's behalf, the power to act as proxy for a security holder and does not furnish or otherwise request, or act on behalf of a person who furnishes or requests, a form of revocation, abstention, consent or authorization. *Provided, however,* that the exemption set forth in this paragraph shall not apply to:

(i) the registrant or an affiliate or associate of the registrant (other than an officer or director or any person serving in a similar capacity);

(ii) an officer or director of the registrant or any person serving in a similar capacity engaging in a solicitation financed directly or indirectly by the registrant;

(iii) an officer, director, affiliate or associate of a person that is ineligible to rely on the exemption set forth in this paragraph (other than persons specified in paragraph (b)(1)(i) of this section), or any person serving in a similar capacity;

(iv) any nominee for whose election as a director proxies are solicited;

(v) any person soliciting in opposition to a merger, recapitalization, reorganization, sale of assets or other extraordinary transaction recommended or approved by the board of directors of the registrant who is proposing or intends to propose an alternative transaction to which such person or one of its affiliates is a party;

(vi) any person who is required to report beneficial ownership of the registrant's equity securities on a Schedule 13D, unless such person has filed a Schedule 13D and has not disclosed pursuant to Item 4 thereto an intent, or reserved the right, to engage in a control transaction, or any contested solicitation for the election of directors;

(vii) Any person who received compensation from an ineligible person directly related to the solicitation of proxies, other than pursuant to Rule 14a–13; . . .

(ix) any person who, because of a substantial interest in the subject matter of the solicitation, is likely to receive a benefit from a successful solicitation that would not be shared pro rata by all other holders of the same class of securities, other than a benefit arising from the person's employment with the registrant; and

(x) any person acting on behalf of any of the foregoing.

(2) Any solicitation made otherwise than on behalf of the registrant where the total number of persons solicited is not more than ten; and

(3) The furnishing of proxy voting advice by any person (the "advisor") to any other person with whom the advisor has a business relationship, if:

(i) The advisor renders financial advice in the ordinary course of his business;

(ii) The advisor discloses to the recipient of the advice any significant relationship with the registrant or any of its affiliates, or a security holder proponent of the matter on which advice is given, as well as any material interests of the advisor in such matter;

(iii) The advisor receives no special commission or remuneration for furnishing the proxy voting advice from any person other than a recipient of the advice and other persons who receive similar advice under this subsection; and

(iv) The proxy voting advice is not furnished on behalf of any person soliciting proxies or on behalf of a participant in an election subject to the provisions of Rule 14a–11.

(4) Any solicitation in connection with a roll-up transaction as defined in Item 901(c) of Regulation S–K ... in which the holder of a security that is the subject of a proposed roll-up transaction engages in preliminary communications with other holders of securities that are the subject of the same limited partnership roll-up transaction for the purpose of determining whether to solicit proxies, consents, or authorizations in opposition to the proposed limited partnership roll-up transaction; *provided, however,* that:

(i) This exemption shall not apply to a security holder who is an affiliate of the registrant or general partner or sponsor; and

(ii) This exemption shall not apply to a holder of five percent (5%) or more of the outstanding securities of a class that is the subject of the proposed roll-up transaction who engages in the business of buying and selling limited partnership interests in the secondary market unless that holder discloses to the persons to whom the communications are made such ownership interest and any relations of the holder to the parties [to] the transaction or to the transaction itself, as required by Rule 14a–6(n)(1) and specified in the Notice of Exempt Preliminary Roll-up Communication (Rule 14a–104). If the communication is oral, this disclosure may be provided to the security holder orally. Whether the communication is written or oral, the notice required by Rule 14a–6(n) and Rule 14a–104 shall be furnished to the Commission.

Rule 14a–3.   Information to Be Furnished to Security Holders

(a) No solicitation subject to this regulation shall be made unless each person solicited is concurrently furnished or has previously been furnished with a publicly filed preliminary or definitive written proxy statement containing the information specified in Schedule 14A....

(b) If the solicitation is made on behalf of the registrant and relates to an annual (or special meeting in lieu of the annual) meeting of security holders, or written consent in lieu of such meeting, at which directors are to be elected, each proxy statement furnished pursuant to paragraph (a) of this section shall be accompanied or preceded by an annual report to security holders as follows:

> *Note to Small Business Issuers.* A "small business issuer," defined under Rule 12b–2 of the Exchange Act, shall refer to the disclosure items in Regulation S–B rather than Regulation S–K. If there is no comparable disclosure item in Regulation S–B, a small business issuer need not provide the information requested. A small business issuers shall provide the information in Item 310(a) of Regulation S–B in lieu of the financial information required by Rule 14a–3(b)(1). . . .

(1) The report shall include, for the registrant and its subsidiaries[,] consolidated, audited balance sheets as of the end of each of the two most recent fiscal years and audited statements of income and cash flows for each of the three most recent fiscal years prepared in accordance with Regulation S–X. . . .

(3) The report shall contain the supplementary financial information required by Item 302 of Regulation S–K. . . .

(4) The report shall contain information concerning changes in and disagreements with accountants on accounting and financial disclosure required by Item 304 of Regulation S–K. . . .

(5)(i) The report shall contain the selected financial data required by Item 301 of Regulation S–K. . . .

(ii) The report shall contain management's discussion and analysis of financial condition and results of operations required by Item 303 of Regulation S–K. . . .

(6) The report shall contain a brief description of the business done by the registrant and its subsidiaries during the most recent fiscal year which will, in the opinion of management, indicate the general nature and scope of the business of the registrant and its subsidiaries.

(7) The report shall contain information relating to the registrant's industry segments, classes of similar products or services, foreign and domestic operations and exports sales required by paragraphs (b), (c)(1)(i) and (d) of Item 101 of Regulation S–K [Description of Business] . . . .

(8) The report shall identify each of the registrant's directors and executive officers, and shall indicate the principal occupation or employment of each such person and the name and principal business of any organization by which such person is employed.

(9) The report shall contain the market price of and dividends on the registrant's common equity and related security holder matters required by Item 201 of Regulation S–K [Market Price of and Dividends on the Registrant's Common Equity and Related Stockholder Matters] . . . .

(10) The registrant's proxy statement, or the report, shall contain an undertaking in bold face or otherwise reasonably prominent type to provide without charge to each person solicited upon the written request of any such person, a copy of the registrant's annual report on Form 10–K, . . . including the financial statements and the financial statement schedules, required to be filed with the Commission pursuant to Rule 13a–1 under the Act for the registrant's most recent fiscal year, and shall indicate the name and address (including title or department) of the person to whom such a written request is to be directed. . . . If the registrant's annual report to security holders complies with all of the disclosure requirements of Form 10–K . . . and is filed with the Commission in satisfaction of its Form 10–K . . . filing requirements, such registrant need not furnish a separate Form 10–K . . . to security holders who receive a copy of such annual report. . . .

(c) Seven copies of the report sent to security holders pursuant to this rule shall be mailed to the Commission, solely for its information, not later than the date on which such report is first sent or given to security holders or the date on which preliminary copies, or definitive copies, if preliminary filing was not required, of solicitation material are filed with the Commission pursuant to Rule 14a–6, whichever date is later. The report is not deemed to be "soliciting material" or to be "filed" with the Commission or subject to this regulation otherwise than as provided in this Rule, or to the liabilities of section 18 of the Act, except to the extent that the registrant specifically requests that it be treated as a part of the proxy soliciting material or incorporates it in the proxy statement or other filed report by reference. . . .

(f) The provisions of paragraph (a) of this section shall not apply to a communication made by means of speeches in public forums, press releases, published or broadcast opinions, statements, or advertisements appearing in a broadcast media, newspaper, magazine or other bona fide publication disseminated on a regular basis, provided that:

(1) no form of proxy, consent or authorization or means to execute the same is provided to a security holder in connection with the communication; and

(2) at the time the communication is made, a definitive proxy statement is on file with the Commission pursuant to Rule 14a–6(b).

Rule 14a-4. Requirements as to Proxy

(a) The form of proxy (1) shall indicate in bold-face type whether or not the proxy is solicited on behalf of the registrant's board of directors or, if provided other than by a majority of the board of directors, shall indicate in bold-face type on whose behalf the solicitation is made;

(2) Shall provide a specifically designated blank space for dating the proxy card; and

(3) Shall identify clearly and impartially each separate matter intended to be acted upon, whether or not related to or conditioned on the approval of other matters, and whether proposed by the registrant or by security holders. No reference need be made, however, to proposals as to which discretionary authority is conferred pursuant to paragraph (c) of this section.

(b)(1) Means shall be provided in the form of proxy whereby the person solicited is afforded an opportunity to specify by boxes a choice between approval or disapproval of, or abstention with respect to each separate matter referred to therein as intended to be acted upon, other than elections to office. A proxy may confer discretionary authority with respect to matters as to which a choice is not specified by the security holder provided that the form of proxy states in bold-face type how it is intended to vote the shares represented by the proxy in each such case.

(2) A form of proxy which provides for the election of directors shall set forth the names of persons nominated for election as directors. Such form of proxy shall clearly provide any of the following means for security holders to withhold authority to vote for each nominee:

(i) A box opposite the name of each nominee which may be marked to indicate that authority to vote for such nominee is withheld; or

(ii) An instruction in bold-face type which indicates that the security holder may withhold authority to vote for any nominee by lining through or otherwise striking out the name of any nominee; or

(iii) Designated blank spaces in which the security holder may enter the names of nominees with respect to whom the security holder chooses to withhold authority to vote; or

(iv) Any other similar means, provided that clear instructions are furnished indicating how the security holder may withhold authority to vote for any nominee.

Such form of proxy also may provide a means for the security holder to grant authority to vote for the nominees set forth, as a group, provided that there is a similar means for the security holder to withhold authority to vote for such group of nominees. Any such form of proxy which is executed by the security holder in such manner as not to withhold authority to vote for the election of any nominee shall be deemed to grant such authority, provided that the form of proxy so states in bold-face type.

Instructions. 1. Paragraph (2) does not apply in the case of a merger, consolidation or other plan if the election of directors is an integral part of the plan.

2. If applicable state law gives legal effect to votes cast against a nominee, then in lieu of, or in addition to, providing a means for security holders to withhold authority to vote, the registrant should provide a similar means for security holders to vote against each nominee.

(c) A proxy may confer discretionary authority to vote with respect to any of the following matters:

(1) Matters which the persons making the solicitation do not know, a reasonable time before the solicitation, are to be presented at the meeting, if a specific statement to that effect is made in the proxy statement or form of proxy;

(2) Approval of the minutes of the prior meeting if such approval does not amount to ratification of the action taken at that meeting;

(3) The election of any person to any office for which a bona fide nominee is named in the proxy statement and such nominee is unable to serve or for good cause will not serve.

(4) Any proposal omitted from the proxy statement and form of proxy pursuant to Rule 14a–8 or 14a–9 of this chapter.

(5) Matters incident to the conduct of the meeting.

(d) No proxy shall confer authority:

(1) To vote for the election of any person to any office for which a bona fide nominee is not named in the proxy statement,

(2) To vote at any annual meeting other than the next annual meeting (or any adjournment thereof) to be held after the date on which the proxy statement and form of proxy are first sent or given to security holders,

(3) To vote with respect to more than one meeting (and any adjournment thereof) or more than one consent solicitation or

(4) To consent to or authorize any action other than the action proposed to be taken in the proxy statement, or matters referred to in paragraph (c) of this rule. A person shall not be deemed to be a bona fide nominee and he shall not be named as such unless he has consented to being named in the proxy statement and to serve if elected.

Provided, however, that nothing in this Rule 4a–4 shall prevent any person soliciting in support of nominees who, if elected, would constitute a minority of the board of directors, from seeking authority to vote for nominees named in the registrant's proxy statement, so long as the soliciting party:

(i) seeks authority to vote in the aggregate for the number of director positions then subject to election;

(ii) represents that it will vote for all the registrant nominees, other than those registrant nominees specified by the soliciting party;

(iii) provides the security holder an opportunity to withhold authority with respect to any other registrant nominee by writing the name of that nominee on the form of proxy; and

(iv) states on the form of proxy and in the proxy statement that there is no assurance that the registrant's nominees will serve if elected with any of the soliciting party's nominees.

(e) The proxy statement or form of proxy shall provide, subject to reasonable specified conditions, that the shares represented by the proxy will be voted and that where the person solicited specifies by means of a ballot provided pursuant to paragraph (b) of this section a choice with respect to any matter to be acted upon, the shares will be voted in accordance with the specifications so made.

(f) No person conducting a solicitation subject to this regulation shall deliver a form of proxy, consent or authorization to any security holder unless the security holder concurrently receives, or has previously received, a definitive proxy statement that has been filed with, or mailed for filing to, the Commission pursuant to Rule 14a–6(b).

Rule 14a–5. Presentation of Information in Proxy Statement

(a) The information included in the proxy statement shall be clearly presented and the statements made shall be divided into groups according to subject matter and the various groups of statements shall be preceded by appropriate headings. The order of items and sub-items in the schedule need not be followed. Where practicable and appropriate, the information shall be presented in tabular form. All amounts shall be stated in figures. Information required by more than one applicable item need not be repeated. No statement need be made in response to any item or sub-item which is inapplicable.

(b) Any information required to be included in the proxy statement as to terms of securities or other subject matter which from a standpoint of practical necessity must be determined in the future may be stated in terms of present knowledge and intention. To the extent practicable, the authority to be conferred concerning each such matter shall be confined within limits reasonably related to the need for discretionary authority. Subject to the foregoing, information which is not known to the persons on whose behalf the solicitation is to be made and which it is not reasonably within the power of such persons to ascertain or procure may be omitted, if a brief statement of the circumstances rendering such information unavailable is made.

(c) Any information contained in any other proxy soliciting material which has been furnished to each person solicited in connection with the same meeting or subject matter may be omitted from the proxy statement, if a clear reference is made to the particular document containing such information.

(d) All printed proxy statements shall be in roman type at least as large and as legible as 10–point modern type, except that to the extent necessary for convenient presentation financial statements and other tabular data, but not the notes thereto, may be in roman type at least as large and as legible as 8–point modern type. All such type shall be leaded at least 2 points.

(e) All proxy statements shall disclose, under an appropriate caption, the date by which proposals of security holders intended to be presented at the next annual meeting must be received by the registrant for inclusion in the registrant's proxy statement and form of proxy relating to that meeting, such date to be calculated in accordance with the provisions of Rule 14a–8(a)(3)(i). If the date of the next annual meeting is subsequently advanced by more than 30 calendar days or delayed by more than 90 calendar days from the date of the annual meeting to which the proxy statement relates, the registrant shall, in a timely manner, inform security holders of such change, and the date by which proposals of security holders must be received, by any means reasonably calculated to so inform them.

Rule 14a–6.   Filing Requirements

(a) *Preliminary proxy statement.* Five preliminary copies of the proxy statement and form of proxy shall be filed with the Commission at least 10 calendar days prior to the date definitive copies of such material are first sent or given to security holders, or such shorter period prior to that date as the Commission may authorize upon a showing of good cause thereunder. A registrant, however, shall not file with the Commission a preliminary proxy statement, form of proxy or other soliciting material to be furnished to security holders concurrently therewith if the solicitation relates to an annual (or special meeting in lieu of the annual) meeting, ... if the solicitation relates to any meeting of security holders at which the only matters to be acted upon are: (1) the election of directors; (2) the election, approval or ratification of accountant(s); [or] (3) a security holder proposal included pursuant to Rule 14a–8 .... This exclusion from filing preliminary proxy material does not apply if the registrant comments upon or refers to a solicitation in opposition in connection with the meeting in its proxy material.

(b) *Definitive proxy statement and other soliciting materials.* Eight definitive copies of the proxy statement, form of proxy and all other soliciting material, in the form in which such material is furnished to security holders, shall be filed with, or mailed for filing to, the Commission not later than the date such material is first sent or given to any security holders. Three copies of such material shall at the same time be filed with, or mailed for filing to, each national securities exchange upon which any class of securities of the registrant is listed and registered.

(c) *Personal Solicitation Materials.* If the solicitation is to be made in whole or in part by personal solicitation, eight copies of all written instructions or other material which discusses or reviews, or comments upon the merits of, any matter to be acted upon and which is furnished to the persons making the actual solicitation for their use directly or indirectly in connection with the solicitation shall be filed with, or mailed for filing to, the Commission by the person on whose behalf the solicitation is made not later than the date any such material is first sent or given to such individuals.

(d) *Release dates.* All preliminary proxy statements and forms of proxy filed pursuant to paragraph (a) of this section shall be accompanied by a statement of the date on which definitive copies thereof filed pursuant to paragraph (b) of this section are intended to be released to security holders. All definitive material filed pursuant to paragraph (b) of this section shall be accompanied by a statement of the date on which copies of such material were released to security holders, or, if not released, the date on which copies thereof are intended to be released. All material filed pursuant to paragraph (c) of this section shall be accompanied by a statement of the date on which copies thereof were released to the individual who will make the actual solicitation or if not released, the date on which copies thereof are intended to be released.

(e)(1) *Public Availability of Information.* All copies of preliminary proxy statements and forms of proxy filed pursuant to paragraph (a) of this section shall be clearly marked "Preliminary Copies," and shall be deemed immediately available for public inspection unless confidential treatment is obtained pursuant to paragraph (e)(2) of this section.

(2) *Confidential Treatment.* If action is to be taken with respect to any matter specified in Item 14 of Schedule 14A, all copies of the preliminary proxy statement and form of proxy filed pursuant to paragraph (a) of this section shall be for the information of the Commission only and shall not be deemed available for public inspection until filed with the Commission in definitive form, provided that:

(i) the proxy statement does not relate to a matter or proposal subject to Rule 13e–3 or a roll-up transaction as defined in Item 901(c) of Regulation S–K; and

(ii) the filed material is marked "Confidential, For Use of the Commission Only." In any and all cases, such material may be disclosed to any department or agency of the United States Government and to the Congress, and the Commission may make such inquiries or investigation in regard to the material as may be necessary for an adequate review thereof by the Commission. . . .

(g) *Solicitations subject to Rule 14a–2(b)(1).*

(1) Any person who:

(i) engages in a solicitation pursuant to Rule 14a–2(b)(1), and

(ii) at the commencement of that solicitation owns beneficially securities of the class which is the subject of the solicitation with a market value of over $5 million, shall furnish or mail to the Commission, not later than three days after the date the written solicitation is first sent or given to any security holder, five copies of a statement containing the information specified in the [Form of] Notice of Exempt Solicitation which statement shall attach as an exhibit all written soliciting materials. Five copies of an amendment to such statement shall be furnished or mailed to the Commission, in connection with dissemination of any additional communications, not later than three days after the date the additional material is first sent or given to any security holder. Three copies of the Notice of Exempt Solicitation and amendments thereto shall, at the same time the materials are furnished or mailed to the Commission, be furnished or mailed to each national securities exchange upon which any class of securities of the registrant is listed and registered.

(2) Notwithstanding paragraph (g)(1) of this section, no such submission need be made with respect to oral solicitations (other than with respect to scripts used in connection with such oral solicitations), speeches delivered in a public forum, press releases, published or broadcast opinions, statements, and advertisements appearing in a broadcast media, or a newspaper, magazine or other bona fide publication disseminated on a regular basis. . . .

(n) *Solicitations subject to Rule 14a–2(b)(4).* Any person who:

(1) Engages in a solicitation pursuant to Rule 14a–2(b)(4), and

(2) At the commencement of that solicitation both owns five percent (5%) or more of the outstanding securities of a class that is the subject of the proposed roll-up transaction, and engages in the business of buying and selling limited partnership interests in the secondary market, shall furnish or mail to the Commission, not later than three days after the date an oral or written solicitation by that person is first made, sent or provided to any security holder, five copies of a statement containing the information specified in the Notice of Exempt Preliminary Roll-up Communication (Rule 14a–104). Five copies of any amendment to such statement shall be furnished or mailed to the Commission not later than three days after a communication containing revised material is first made, sent or provided to any security holder.

Rule 14a–7. Obligations of Registrants to Provide a List of, or Mail Soliciting Material to, Security Holders

(a) If the registrant has made or intends to make a proxy solicitation in connection with a security holder meeting or action by consent or authorization, upon the written request by any record or beneficial holder of securities of the class entitled to vote at the meeting, or to execute a consent or authorization to provide a list of security holders or to mail the requesting security holder's materials, regardless of whether the request references this section, the registrant shall:

(1) deliver to the requesting security holder within five business days after receipt of the request:

(i) notification as to whether the registrant has elected to mail the security holder's soliciting materials or provide a security holder list if the election under paragraph (b) of this section is to be made by the registrant;

(ii) a statement of the approximate number of record holders and beneficial holders, separated by type of holder and class, owning securities in the same class or classes as holders which have been or are to be solicited on management's behalf, or any more limited group of such holders designated by the security holder if available or retrievable under the registrant's or its transfer agent's security holder data systems; and

(iii) the estimated cost of mailing a proxy statement, form of proxy or other communication to such holders, including to the extent known or reasonably available, the estimated costs of any bank, broker, and similar person through whom the registrant has solicited or intends to solicit beneficial owners in connection with the security holder meeting or action;

(2) perform the acts set forth in either paragraphs (a)(2)(i) or (a)(2)(ii) of this section, at the registrant's or requesting security holder's option, as specified in paragraph (b) of this section:

(i) Mail copies of any proxy statement, form of proxy or other soliciting material furnished by the security holder to the record holders, including banks, brokers, and similar entities, designated by the security holder. A sufficient number of copies must be mailed to the banks, brokers and similar entities for distribution to all beneficial owners designated by the security holder. The registrant shall mail the security holder material with reasonable promptness after tender of the material to be mailed, envelopes or other containers therefor, postage or payment for postage and other reasonable expenses of effecting such mailing. The registrant shall not be responsible for the content of the material; or

(ii) Deliver the following information to the requesting security holder within five business days of receipt of the request: a reasonably current list of the names, addresses and security positions of the record holders, including banks, brokers and similar entities, holding securities in the same class or classes as holders which have been or are to be solicited on management's behalf, or any more limited group of such holders designated by the security holder if available or retrievable under the registrant's or its transfer agent's security holder data systems; the most recent list of names, addresses and security positions of beneficial owners as specified in Rule 14a–13(b), in the possession, or which subsequently comes into the possession, of the registrant. All security holder list information shall be in the form requested by the security holder to the extent that such form is available to the registrant without undue burden or expense. The registrant shall furnish the security holder with updated record holder information on a daily basis or, if not available on a daily basis, at the shortest reasonable intervals, *provided, however,* the registrant need not provide beneficial or record holder information more current than the record date for the meeting or action.

(b)(1) The requesting security holder shall have the options set forth in paragraph (a)(2) of this section, and the registrant shall have corresponding obligations, if the registrant or general partner or sponsor is soliciting or intends to solicit with respect to:

(i) A proposal that is subject to Rule 13e–3;

(ii) A roll-up transaction as defined in Item 901(c) of Regulation S–K that involves an entity with securities registered pursuant to Section 12 of the Act;

(iii) A roll-up transaction as defined in Item 901(c) of Regulation S–K that involves a limited partnership....

(2) With respect to all other requests pursuant to this section, the registrant shall have the option to either mail the security holder's material or furnish the security holder list as set forth in this section.

(c) At the time of a list request, the security holder making the request shall:

(1) if holding the registrant's securities through a nominee, provide the registrant with a statement by the nominee or other independent third party, or a copy of a current filing made with the Commission and furnished to the registrant, confirming such holder's beneficial ownership; and

(2) provide the registrant with an affidavit, declaration, affirmation or other similar document provided for under applicable state law identifying the proposal or other corporate action that will be the subject of the security holder's solicitation or communication and attesting that:

(i) the security holder will not use the list information for any purpose other than to solicit security holders with respect to the same meeting or action by consent or authorization for which the registrant is soliciting or intends to solicit or to communicate with security holders with respect to a solicitation commenced by the registrant; and

(ii) the security holder will not disclose such information to any person other than a beneficial owner for whom the request was made and an employee or agent to the extent necessary to effectuate the communication or solicitation.

(d) The security holder shall not use the information furnished by the registrant pursuant to paragraph (a)(2)(ii) of this section for any purpose other than to solicit security holders with respect to the same meeting or action by consent or authorization for which the registrant is soliciting or intends to solicit or to communicate with security holders with respect to a solicitation commenced by the registrant; or disclose such information to any person other than an employee, agent, or beneficial owner for whom a request was made to the extent necessary to effectuate the communication or solicitation. The security holder shall return the information provided pursuant to paragraph (a)(2)(ii) of this section and shall not retain any copies thereof or of any information derived from such information after the termination of the solicitation.

(e) The security holder shall reimburse the reasonable expenses incurred by the registrant in performing the acts requested pursuant to paragraph (a) of this section.

Rule 14a–8. Proposals of Security Holders

(a) If any security holder of a registrant notifies the registrant of his intention to present a proposal for action at a forthcoming meeting of the registrant's security holders, the registrant shall set forth the proposal in its proxy statement and identify it in its form of proxy and provide means by which security holders can make the specification required by Rule 14a–4(b).... Notwithstanding the foregoing, the registrant shall not be required to include the proposal in its proxy statement or form of proxy unless the security holder (hereinafter, the "proponent") has complied with the requirements of this paragraph and paragraphs (b) and (c) of this section:

(1) *Eligibility.* (1) At the time he submits the proposal, the proponent shall be a record or beneficial owner of at least 1% or $1000 in market value of securities entitled to be voted on the proposal at the meeting and have held such securities for at least one year, and he shall continue to own such securities through the date on which the meeting is held. If the registrant requests documentary support for a proponent's claim that he is the beneficial owner of at least 1% or $1000 in market value of such voting securities of the registrant or that he has been a beneficial owner of the securities for one or more years, the registrant shall make such request within 14 calendar days after receiving the security holder proposal and the proponent shall furnish appropriate documentation within 21 calendar days after receiving the request.... In the event the registrant includes the proponent's proposal in its proxy soliciting material for the meeting and the proponent fails to comply with the requirement that he continuously hold such securities

through the meeting date, the registrant shall not be required to include any proposals submitted by the proponent in its proxy material for any meeting held in the following two calendar years.

(2) *Notice and Attendance at the Meeting.* At the time he submits a proposal, a proponent shall provide the registrant in writing with his name, address, the number of the registrant's voting securities that he holds of record or beneficially, the dates upon which he acquired such securities, and documentary support for a claim of beneficial ownership. A proposal may be presented at the meeting either by the proponent or his representative who is qualified under state law to present the proposal on the proponent's behalf at the meeting. In the event that the proponent or his representative fails, without good cause, to present the proposal for action at the meeting, the registrant shall not be required to include any proposals submitted by the proponent in its proxy soliciting material for any meeting held in the following two calendar years.

(3) *Timeliness.* The proponent shall submit his proposal sufficiently far in advance of the meeting so that it is received by the registrant within the following time periods:

(i) *Annual Meetings.* A proposal to be presented at an annual meeting shall be received at the registrant's principal executive offices not less than 120 calendar days in advance of the date of the registrant's proxy statement released to security holders in connection with the previous year's annual meeting of security holders except that if no annual meeting was held in the previous year or the date of the annual meeting has been changed by more than 30 calendar days from the date contemplated at the time of the previous year's proxy statement, a proposal shall be received by the registrant a reasonable time before the solicitation is made.

(ii) *Other Meetings.* A proposal to be presented at any meeting other than an annual meeting specified in paragraph (a)(3)(i) of this section shall be received a reasonable time before the solicitation is made. . . .

(4) *Number of Proposals.* The proponent may submit no more than one proposal and an accompanying supporting statement for inclusion in the registrant's proxy materials for a meeting of security holders. If the proponent submits more than one proposal, or if he fails to comply with the 500 word limit mentioned in paragraph (b)(1) of this section, he shall be provided the opportunity to reduce the items submitted by him to the limits required by this rule, within 14 calendar days of notification of such limitations by the registrant.

(b)(1) *Supporting Statement.* The registrant, at the request of the proponent, shall include in its proxy statement a statement of the proponent in support of the proposal, which statement shall not include the name and address of the proponent. A proposal and its supporting statement in the aggregate shall not exceed 500 words. The supporting statement shall be furnished to the registrant at the time that the proposal is furnished, and the registrant shall not be responsible for such statement and the proposal to which it relates.

(2) *Identification of Proponent.* The proxy statement shall also include either the name and address of the proponent and the number of shares of the voting security held by the proponent or a statement that such information will be furnished by the registrant to any person, orally or in writing as requested, promptly upon the receipt of any oral or written request therefor.

(c) The registrant may omit a proposal and any statement in support thereof from its proxy statement and form of proxy under any of the following circumstances:

(1) If the proposal is, under the laws of the registrant's domicile, not a proper subject for action by security holders.

Note: Whether a proposal is a proper subject for action by security holders will depend on the applicable state law. Under certain states' laws, a proposal that mandates certain action by the registrant's board of directors may not be a proper subject matter for shareholder action, while a proposal recommending or requesting such action of the board may be proper under such state laws.

(2) If the proposal, if implemented, would require the registrant to violate any state law or federal law of the United States, or any law of any foreign jurisdiction to which the registrant is subject, except that this provision shall not apply with respect to any foreign law compliance with which would be violative of any state law or Federal law of the United States.

(3) If the proposal or the supporting statement is contrary to any of the Commission's proxy rules and regulations, including Rule 14a–9, which prohibits false or misleading statements in proxy soliciting materials;

(4) If the proposal relates to the redress of a personal claim or grievance against the registrant or any other person, or if it is designed to result in a benefit to the proponent or to further a personal interest, which benefit or interest is not shared with the other security holders at large;

(5) If the proposal relates to operations which account for less than 5 percent of the registrant's total assets at the end of its most recent fiscal year, and for less than 5 percent of its net earnings and gross sales for its most recent fiscal year, and is not otherwise significantly related to the registrant's business;

(6) If the proposal deals with a matter beyond the registrant's power to effectuate;

(7) If the proposal deals with a matter relating to the conduct of the ordinary business operations of the registrant;

(8) If the proposal relates to an election to office;

(9) If the proposal is counter to a proposal to be submitted by the registrant at the meeting;

(10) If the proposal has been rendered moot;

(11) If the proposal is substantially duplicative of a proposal previously submitted to the registrant by another proponent, which proposal will be included in the registrant's proxy material for the meeting;

(12) If the proposal deals with substantially the same subject matter as a prior proposal submitted to security holders in the registrant's proxy statement and form of proxy relating to any annual or special meeting of security holders held within the preceding five calendar years, it may be omitted from the registrant's proxy materials relating to any meeting of security holders held within three calendar years after the latest such previous submission: *Provided,* That—

(i) If the proposal was submitted at only one meeting during such preceding period, it received less than three percent of the total number of votes cast in regard thereto; or

(ii) If the proposal was submitted at only two meetings during such preceding period, it received at the time of its second submission less than six percent of the total number of votes cast in regard thereto; or

(iii) If the prior proposal was submitted at three or more meetings during such preceding period, it received at the time of its latest submission less than 10 percent of the total number of votes cast in regard thereto; or

(13) If the proposal relates to specific amounts of cash or stock dividends.

(d) Whenever the registrant asserts, for any reason, that a proposal and any statement in support thereof received from a proponent may properly be omitted from its proxy statement and form of proxy, it shall file with the Commission, not later than 80 calendar days prior to the date the definitive copies of the proxy statement and form of proxy are filed pursuant to Rule 14a–6, or such shorter period prior to such date as the Commission or its staff may permit, six copies of the following items:

(1) The proposal;

(2) Any statement in support thereof as received from the proponent;

(3) A statement of the reasons why the registrant deems such omission to be proper in the particular case; and

(4) Where such reasons are based on matters of law, a supporting opinion of counsel. The registrant shall at the same time, if it has not

already done so, notify the proponent of its intention to omit the proposal from its proxy statement and form of proxy and shall forward to him a copy of the statement of reasons why the registrant deems the omission of the proposal to be proper and a copy of such supporting opinion of counsel.

(e) If the registrant intends to include in the proxy statement a statement in opposition to a proposal received from a proponent, it shall, not later than 30 calendar days prior to the date the definitive copies of the proxy statement and form of proxy are filed pursuant to Rule 14a-6, or, in the event that the proposal must be revised to be includable, not later than five calendar days after receipt by the registrant of the revised proposal, promptly forward to the proponent a copy of the statement in opposition to the proposal.

In the event the proponent believes that the statement in opposition contains materially false or misleading statements within the meaning of Rule 14a-9 and the proponent wishes to bring this matter to the attention of the Commission, the proponent promptly should provide the staff with a letter setting forth the reasons for this view and at the same time promptly provide the registrant with a copy of his letter.

Rule 14a-9. False or Misleading Statements

(a) No solicitation subject to this regulation shall be made by means of any proxy statement, form of proxy, notice of meeting or other communication, written or oral, containing any statement which, at the time and in the light of the circumstances under which it is made, is false or misleading with respect to any material fact, or which omits to state any material fact necessary in order to make the statements therein not false or misleading or necessary to correct any statement in any earlier communication with respect to the solicitation of a proxy for the same meeting or subject matter which has become false or misleading.

(b) The fact that a proxy statement, form of proxy or other soliciting material has been filed with or examined by the Commission shall not be deemed a finding by the Commission that such material is accurate or complete or not false or misleading, or that the Commission has passed upon the merits of or approved any statement contained therein or any matter to be acted upon by security holders. No representation contrary to the foregoing shall be made....

Rule 14a-10. Prohibition of Certain Solicitations

No person making a solicitation which is subject to Rules 14a-1 to 14a-10 shall solicit:

(a) Any undated or postdated proxy; or

(b) Any proxy which provides that it shall be deemed to be dated as of any date subsequent to the date on which it is signed by the security holder.

Rule 14a–11. Special Provisions Applicable to Election Contests

(a) *Solicitations to which this section applies.* This section applies to any solicitation subject to Rules 14a–1 to 14a–11 by any person or group of persons for the purpose of opposing a solicitation subject to Rules 14a–1 to 14a–11 by any other person or group of persons with respect to the election or removal of directors at any annual or special meeting of security holders.

(b) *Solicitations prior to furnishing required written proxy statement.* Notwithstanding the provisions of Rule 14a–3(a) ... , a solicitation subject to this section may be made prior to furnishing security holders a written proxy statement containing the information specified in Schedule 14A ... with respect to such solicitation: *Provided,* That—

(1) No form of proxy is furnished to security holders prior to the time the written proxy statement required by Rule 14a–3(a) ... is furnished to security holders: *Provided, however,* That this paragraph (b)(1) shall not apply where a proxy statement then meeting the requirements of Schedule 14A ... has been furnished to security holders by or on behalf of the person making the solicitation.

(2) The identity of the participants in the solicitation (as defined in Instruction 3 of Item 4 of Schedule 14A) and a description of their interests, direct or indirect, by security holdings or otherwise, are set forth in each communication published, sent or given to security holders in connection with the solicitation.

(3) A written proxy statement meeting the requirements of this regulation is sent or given to security holders solicited pursuant to this paragraph (b) at the earliest practicable date.

(c) *Solicitation prior to furnishing required written proxy statement; filing requirements.* Eight copies of any soliciting material published, sent or given to security holders prior to the furnishing of the written proxy statement required by Rule 14a–3(a) shall be filed with, or mailed for filing to, the Commission no later than the date such material is published, sent or given to any security holder. Three copies of such material shall at the same time be filed with, or mailed for filing to, each national securities exchange upon which any class of securities of the registrant is listed and registered. ...

(e) *Application of Rule 14a–6.* The provisions of paragraphs (b), (c), (d), and (e) of Rule 14a–6 shall apply, to the extent pertinent, to soliciting material subject to paragraphs (c) and (d) of this section.

Rule 14a–12. Solicitation Prior to Furnishing Required Proxy Statement

(a) Notwithstanding the provisions of Rule 14a–3(a), a solicitation (other than one subject to Rule 14a–11) may be made prior to furnishing security holders a written proxy statement meeting the requirements of Rule 14a–3(a) if—

(1) The solicitation is made in opposition to a prior solicitation or an invitation for tenders or other publicized activity, which if successful, could reasonably have the effect of defeating the action proposed to be taken at the meeting;

(2) No form of proxy is furnished to security holders prior to the time the written proxy statement required by Rule 14a–3(a) is furnished to security holders: *Provided, however,* That this subparagraph (2) shall not apply where a proxy statement then meeting the requirements of Rule 14a–3(a) has been furnished to security holders by or on behalf of the person making the solicitation.

(3) The identity of the participants in the solicitation (as defined in Instruction 3 to Item 4 of Schedule 14A) and a description of their interests direct or indirect, by security holdings or otherwise, are set forth in each communication published, sent or given to security holders in connection with the solicitation; and

(4) A written proxy statement meeting the requirements of this regulation is sent or given to security holders solicited pursuant to this section at the earliest practicable date.

(b) Eight copies of any soliciting material published, sent or given to security holders prior to the furnishing of a written proxy statement required by Rule 14a–3(a) shall be filed with, or mailed for filing to, the Commission no later than the date such material is published, sent or given to any security holders. Three copies of such material shall at the same time be filed with, or mailed for filing to, each national securities exchange upon which any class of securities of the registrant is listed and registered....

Rule 14a–15. Differential and Contingent Compensation in Connection With Roll–Up Transactions

(a) It shall be unlawful for any person to receive compensation for soliciting proxies, consents, or authorizations directly from security holders in connection with a roll-up transaction as provided in paragraph (b) of this section, if the compensation is:

(1) Based on whether the solicited proxy, consent, or authorization either approves or disapproves the proposed roll-up transaction; or

(2) Contingent on the approval, disapproval, or completion of the roll-up transaction.

(b) This section is applicable to a roll-up transaction as defined in Item 901(c) of Regulation S–K, except for a transaction involving only:

(1) Finite-life entities that are not limited partnerships. . . .

SCHEDULE 14A.   INFORMATION REQUIRED IN PROXY STATEMENT. . . .

Item 1. Date, time and place information. (a) State the date, time and place of the meeting of security holders, and the complete mailing address, including ZIP Code, of the principal executive offices of the registrant, unless such information is otherwise disclosed in material furnished to security holders with or preceding the proxy statement. If action is to be taken by written consent, state the date by which consents are to be submitted if state law requires that such a date be specified or if the person soliciting intends to set a date.

(b) On the first page of the proxy statement, as delivered to security holders, state the approximate date on which the proxy statement and form of proxy are first sent or given to security holders.

(c) Furnish the information required to be in the proxy statement by Rule 14a–5(e). . . .

Item 2. Revocability of proxy. State whether or not the person giving the proxy has the power to revoke it. If the right of revocation before the proxy is exercised is limited or is subject to compliance with any formal procedure, briefly describe such limitation or procedure.

Item 3. Dissenters' right of appraisal. Outline briefly the rights of appraisal or similar rights of dissenters with respect to any matter to be acted upon and indicate any statutory procedure required to be followed by dissenting security holders in order to perfect such rights. Where such rights may be exercised only within a limited time after the date of adoption of a proposal, the filing of a charter amendment or other similar act, state whether the persons solicited will be notified of such date.

> *Instruction.* Indicate whether a security holder's failure to vote against a proposal will constitute a waiver of his appraisal or similar rights and whether a vote against a proposal will be deemed to satisfy any notice requirements under State law with respect to appraisal rights. If the State law is unclear, state what position will be taken in regard to these matters.

Item 4. Persons Making the Solicitation —(a) *Solicitations not subject to Rule 14a–11*. . . .   (1) If the solicitation is made by the registrant, so state. Give the name of any director of the registrant who has informed the registrant in writing that he intends to oppose any action intended to be taken by the registrant and indicate the action which he intends to oppose.

(2) If the solicitation is made otherwise than by the registrant, so state and give the names of the participants in the solicitation, as defined in paragraphs (a)(iii), (iv), (v) and (vi) of Instruction 3 to this Item.

(3) If the solicitation is to be made otherwise than by the use of the mails, describe the methods to be employed. If the solicitation is to be made by specially engaged employees or paid solicitors, state (i) the material features of any contract or arrangement for such solicitation and identify the parties, and (ii) the cost or anticipated cost thereof.

(4) State the names of the persons by whom the cost of solicitation has been or will be borne, directly or indirectly.

(b) *Solicitations subject to Rule 14a–11*.... (1) State by whom the solicitation is made and describe the methods employed and to be employed to solicit security holders.

(2) If regular employees of the registrant or any other participant in a solicitation have been or are to be employed to solicit security holders, describe the class or classes of employees to be so employed, and the manner and nature of their employment for such purpose.

(3) If specially engaged employees, representatives or other persons have been or are to be employed to solicit security holders, state (i) the material features of any contract or arrangement for such solicitation and the identity of the parties, (ii) the cost or anticipated cost thereof and (iii) the approximate number of such employees or employees of any other person (naming such other person) who will solicit security holders.

(4) State the total amount estimated to be spent and the total expenditures to date for, in furtherance of, or in connection with the solicitation of security holders.

(5) State by whom the cost of the solicitation will be borne. If such cost is to be borne initially by any person other than the registrant, state whether reimbursement will be sought from the registrant, and, if so, whether the question of such reimbursement will be submitted to a vote of security holders.

(6) If any such solicitation is terminated pursuant to a settlement between the registrant and any other participant in such solicitation, describe the terms of such settlement, including the cost or anticipated cost thereof to the registrant....

Instructions. ...

3. For purposes of this Item 4 and Item 5 of this Schedule 14A:

(a) The terms "participant" and "participant in a solicitation" include the following:

(i) the registrant;

(ii) any director of the registrant, and any nominee for whose election as a director proxies are solicited;

(iii) any committee or group which solicits proxies, any member of such committee or group, and any person whether or not named as a member who, acting alone or with one or more other persons, directly or indirectly takes the initiative, or engages, in organizing, directing, or arranging for the financing of any such committee or group;

(iv) any person who finances or joins with another to finance the solicitation of proxies, except persons who contribute not more than $500 and who are not otherwise participants;

(v) any person who lends money or furnishes credit or enters into any other arrangements, pursuant to any contract or understanding with a participant, for the purpose of financing or otherwise inducing the purchase, sale, holding or voting of securities of the registrant by any participant or other persons, in support of or in opposition to a participant; except that such terms do not include a bank, broker or dealer who, in the ordinary course of business, lends money or executes orders for the purchase or sale of securities and who is not otherwise a participant; and

(vi) any person who solicits proxies.

(b) The terms "participant" and "participant in a solicitation" do not include:

(i) any person or organization retained or employed by a participant to solicit security holders and whose activities are limited to the duties required to be performed in the course of such employment;

(ii) any person who merely transmits proxy soliciting material or performs other ministerial or clerical duties;

(iii) any person employed by a participant in the capacity of attorney, accountant, or advertising, public relations or financial adviser, and whose activities are limited to the duties required to be performed in the course of such employment;

(iv) any person regularly employed as an officer or employee of the registrant or any of its subsidiaries who is not otherwise a participant; or

(v) any officer or director of, or any person regularly employed by, any other participant, if such officer, director or employee is not otherwise a participant.

Item 5. Interest of certain persons in matters to be acted upon—(a) *Solicitations not subject to Rule 14a–11* .... Describe briefly any substantial interest, direct or indirect, by security holdings or otherwise, of each of the following persons in any matter to be acted upon, other than elections to office:

(1) If the solicitation is made on behalf of the registrant, each person who has been a director or executive officer of the registrant at any time since the beginning of the last fiscal year.

(2) If the solicitation is made otherwise than on behalf of the registrant, each participant in the solicitation, as defined in paragraphs (a)(iii), (iv), (v), and (vi) of Instruction 3 to Item 4 of this Schedule 14A.

(3) Each nominee for election as a director of the registrant.

(4) Each associate of any of the foregoing persons. . . .

(b) *Solicitation subject to Rule 14a–11.* With respect to any solicitation subject to Rule 14a–11:

(1) Describe briefly any substantial interest, direct or indirect, by security holdings or otherwise, of each participant as defined in paragraphs (a)(ii), (iii), (iv), (v) and (vi) of Instruction 3 to Item 4 of this Schedule 14A, in any matter to be acted upon at the meeting, and include with respect to each participant the following information, or a fair and accurate summary thereof:

(i) Name and business address of the participant.

(ii) The participant's present principal occupation or employment and the name, principal business and address of any corporation or other organization in which such employment is carried on.

(iii) State whether or not, during the past ten years, the participant has been convicted in a criminal proceeding (excluding traffic violations or similar misdemeanors) and, if so, give dates, nature of conviction, name and location of court, and penalty imposed or other disposition of the case. A negative answer need not be included in the proxy statement or other soliciting material.

(iv) State the amount of each class of securities of the registrant which the participant owns beneficially, directly or indirectly.

(v) State the amount of each class of securities of the registrant which the participant owns of record but not beneficially.

(vi) State with respect to all securities of the registrant purchased or sold within the past two years, the dates on which they were purchased or sold and the amount purchased or sold on each such date.

(vii) If any part of the purchase price or market value of any of the shares specified in paragraph (b)(1)(vi) of this Item is represented by funds borrowed or otherwise obtained for the purpose of acquiring or holding such securities, so state and indicate the amount of the indebtedness as of the latest practicable date. If such funds were borrowed or obtained otherwise than pursuant to a margin account or bank loan in the regular course of business of a bank, broker or dealer, briefly describe the transaction, and state the names of the parties.

(viii) State whether or not the participant is, or was within the past year, a party to any contract, arrangements or understandings with any person with respect to any securities of the registrant, including, but not limited to joint ventures, loan or option arrangements, puts or calls, guarantees against loss or guarantees of profit, division of losses or profits, or the giving or withholding of proxies. If so, name the parties to such contracts, arrangements or understandings and give the details thereof.

(ix) State the amount of securities of the registrant owned beneficially, directly or indirectly, by each of the participant's associates and the name and address of each such associate.

(x) State the amount of each class of securities of any parent or subsidiary of the registrant which the participant owns beneficially, directly or indirectly.

(xi) Furnish for the participant and associates of the participant the information required by Item 404(a) of Regulation S–K.

(xii) State whether or not the participant or any associates of the participant have any arrangement or understanding with any person—

(A) with respect to any future employment by the registrant or its affiliates; or

(B) with respect to any future transactions to which the registrant or any of its affiliates will or may be a party.

If so, describe such arrangement or understanding and state the names of the parties thereto.

(2) With respect to any person, other than a director or executive officer of the registrant acting solely in that capacity, who is a party to an arrangement or understanding pursuant to which a nominee for election as director is proposed to be elected, describe any substantial interest, direct or indirect, by security holdings or otherwise, that such person has in any matter to be acted upon at the meeting, and furnish the information called for by paragraphs (b)(1)(xi) and (xii) of this Item.
. . .

Item 6. Voting securities and principal holders thereof. (a) As to each class of voting securities of the registrant entitled to be voted at the meeting (or by written consents or authorizations if no meeting is held), state the number of shares outstanding and the number of votes to which each class is entitled.

(b) State the record date, if any, with respect to this solicitation. If the right to vote or give consent is not to be determined, in whole or in part, by reference to a record date, indicate the criteria for the determination of security holders entitled to vote or give consent.

(c) If action is to be taken with respect to the election of directors and if the persons solicited have cumulative voting rights: (1) Make a statement that they have such rights, (2) briefly describe such rights, (3) state briefly the conditions precedent to the exercise thereof, and (4) if discretionary authority to cumulate votes is solicited, so indicate.

(d) Furnish the information required by Item 403 of Regulation S–K . . . to the extent known by the persons on whose behalf the solicitation is made.

(e) If, to the knowledge of the persons on whose behalf the solicitation is made, a change in control of the registrant has occurred since the beginning of its last fiscal year, state the name of the person(s) who acquired such control, the amount and the source of the consideration used by such person or persons; the basis of the control, the date and a description of the transaction(s) which resulted in the change of control and the percentage of voting securities of the registrant now beneficially owned directly or indirectly by the person(s) who acquired control; and the identity of the person(s) from whom control was assumed. If the source of all or any part of the consideration used is a loan made in the ordinary course of business by a bank . . ., the identity of such bank shall be omitted provided a request for confidentiality has been made . . . by the person(s) who acquired control. In lieu thereof, the material shall indicate that the identity of the bank has been so omitted and filed separately with the Commission.

> *Instruction.* 1. State the terms of any loans or pledges obtained by the new control group for the purpose of acquiring control, and the names of the lenders or pledgees.
>
> 2. Any arrangements or understandings among members of both the former and new control groups and their associates with respect to election of directors or other matters should be described.

Item 7. Directors and executive officers. If action is to be taken with respect to the election of directors, furnish the following information in tabular form to the extent practicable. If, however, the solicitation is made on behalf of persons other than the registrant, the information required need be furnished only as to nominees of the persons making the solicitation.

(a) The information required by instruction 4 to Item 103 of Regulation S–K [Legal Proceedings] . . . with respect to directors and executive officers.

(b) The information required by Items 401, 404(a) and (c), and 405 of Regulation S–K . . . .

(c) With respect to registrants other than investment companies registered under the Investment Company Act of 1940, furnish the information required by Item 404(b) of Regulation S–K. . . .

(e)(1) State whether or not the registrant has standing audit, nominating and compensation committees of the Board of Directors, or committees performing similar functions. If the registrant has such committees, however designated, identify each committee member, state the number of committee meetings held by each such committee during the last fiscal year and describe briefly the functions performed by such committees. . . .

(2) If the registrant has a nominating or similar committee, state whether the committee will consider nominees recommended by security holders and, if so, describe the procedures to be followed by security holders in submitting such recommendations.

(f) State the total number of meetings of the board of directors (including regularly scheduled and special meetings) which were held during the last full fiscal year. Name each incumbent director who during the last full fiscal year attended fewer than 75 percent of the aggregate of (1) the total number of meetings of the board of directors (held during the period for which he has been a director) and (2) the total number of meetings held by all committees of the board on which he served (during the periods that he served).

(g) If a director has resigned or declined to stand for re-election to the board of directors since the date of the last annual meeting of security holders because of a disagreement with the registrant on any matter relating to the registrant's operations, policies or practices, and if the director has furnished the registrant with a letter describing such disagreement and requesting that the matter be disclosed, the registrant shall state the date of resignation or declination to stand for re-election and summarize the director's description of the disagreement.

If the registrant believes that the description provided by the director is incorrect or incomplete, it may include a brief statement presenting its view of the disagreement.

Item 8. Compensation of directors and executive officers. Furnish the information required by Item 402 of Regulation S–K if action is to be taken with regard to:

(a) the election of directors;

(b) any bonus, profit sharing or other compensation plan, contract or arrangement in which any director, nominee for election as a director, or executive officer of the registrant will participate;

(c) any pension or retirement plan in which any such person will participate; or

(d) the granting or extension to any such person of any options, warrants or rights to purchase any securities, other than warrants or rights issued to security holders as such, on a pro rata basis. However, if the solicitation is made on behalf of persons other than the registrant, the information required need be furnished only as to nominees of the persons making the solicitation and associates of such nominees....

Item 9.   Independent public accountants.   If the solicitation is made on behalf of the registrant and relates to: (1) The annual (or special meeting in lieu of annual) meeting of security holders at which directors are to be elected, or a solicitation of consents or authorizations in lieu of such meeting or (2) the election, approval or ratification of the registrant's accountant, furnish the following information describing the registrant's relationship with its independent public accountant:

(a) The name of the principal accountant selected or being recommended to security holders for election, approval or ratification for the current year.   If no accountant has been selected or recommended, so state and briefly describe the reasons therefor.

(b) The name of the principal accountant for the fiscal year most recently completed if different from the accountant selected or recommended for the current year or if no accountant has yet been selected or recommended for the current year.

(c) The proxy statement shall indicate: (1) Whether or not representatives of the principal accountant for the current year and for the most recently completed fiscal year are expected to be present at the security holders' meeting, (2) whether or not they will have the opportunity to make a statement if they desire to do so, and (3) whether or not such representatives are expected to be available to respond to appropriate questions.

(d) If during the registrant's two most recent fiscal years or any subsequent interim period, (1) an independent accountant who was previously engaged as the principal accountant to audit the registrant's financial statements, or an independent accountant on whom the principal accountant expressed reliance in its report regarding a significant subsidiary, has resigned (or indicated it has declined to stand for reelection after the completion of the current audit) or was dismissed, or (2) a new independent accountant has been engaged as either the principal accountant to audit the registrant's financial statements or as an independent accountant on whom the principal accountant has expressed or is expected to express reliance in its report regarding a significant subsidiary, then, notwithstanding any previous disclosure, provide the information required by Item 304(a) of Regulation S–K.

Item 10.   Compensation Plans.   If action is to be taken with respect to any plan pursuant to which cash or noncash compensation may be paid or distributed, furnish the following information:

(a) *Plans Subject to Security Holder Action.*

(1) Describe briefly the material features of the plan being acted upon, identify each class of persons who will be eligible to participate

therein, indicate the approximate number of persons in each such class, and state the basis of such participation.

(2)(i) In the tabular format specified below, disclose the benefits or amounts that will be received by or allocated to each of the following under the plan being acted upon, if such benefits or amounts are determinable:

NEW PLAN BENEFITS		
	Plan Name	
Name and Position	Dollar Value ($)	Number of Units
CEO		
A		
B		
C		
D		
Executive Group		
Non–Executive Director Group		
Non–Executive Officer Employee Group		

(ii) The table required by paragraph (a)(2)(i) of this Item shall provide information as to the following persons:

(A) Each person (stating name and position) specified in paragraph (a)(3) of Item 402 of Regulation S–K;

(B) All current executive officers as a group;

(C) All current directors who are not executive officers as a group; and

(D) All employees, including all current officers who are not executive officers, as a group....

(b)(1) *Additional Information Regarding Specified Plans Subject to Security Holder Action.* With respect to any pension or retirement plan submitted for security holder action, state:

(i) The approximate total amount necessary to fund the plan with respect to past services, the period over which such amount is to be paid and the estimated annual payments necessary to pay the total amount over such period; and

(ii) The estimated annual payment to be made with respect to current services. In the case of a pension or retirement plan, information called for by paragraph (a)(2) of this Item may be furnished in the format specified by paragraph (f)(1) of Item 402 of Regulation S–K.

(2)(i) With respect to any specific grant of or any plan containing options, warrants or rights submitted for security holder action, state:

(A) The title and amount of securities underlying such options, warrants or rights;

(B) The prices, expiration dates and other material conditions upon which the options, warrants or rights may be exercised;

(C) The consideration received or to be received by the registrant or subsidiary for the granting or extension of the options, warrants or rights;

(D) The market value of the securities underlying the option, warrants, or rights as of the latest practicable date; and

(E) In the case of options, the federal income tax consequences of the issuance and exercise of such options to the recipient and the registrant; and

(ii) State separately the amount of such options received or to be received by the following persons if such benefits or amounts are determinable:

(A) Each person (stating name and position) specified in paragraph (a)(3) of Item 402 of Regulation S–K;

(B) All current executive officers as a group;

(C) All current directors who are not executive officers as a group;

(D) Each nominee for election as a director;

(E) Each associate of any of such directors, executive officers or nominees;

(F) Each other person who received or is to receive 5 percent of such options, warrants or rights; and

(G) All employees, including all current officers who are not executive officers, as a group. . . .

Item 18. Matters not required to be submitted. If action is to be taken with respect to any matter which is not required to be submitted to a vote of security holders, state the nature of such matter, the reasons for submitting it to a vote of security holders and what action is intended to be taken by the registrant in the event of a negative vote on the matter by the security holders. . . .

Item 21. Voting Procedures. As to each matter which is to be submitted to a vote of security holders, furnish the following information:

(a) State the vote required for approval or election, other than for the approval of auditors.

(b) Disclose the method by which votes will be counted, including the treatment and effect of abstentions and broker non-votes under applicable state law as well as registrant charter and by-law provisions. . . .

[FORM OF] NOTICE OF EXEMPT SOLICITATION— INFORMATION TO BE INCLUDED IN STATEMENTS SUBMITTED BY OR ON BEHALF OF A PERSON PURSUANT TO RULE 6(g)

Notice of Exempt Solicitation

1. Name of the Registrant:

_____

2. Name of person relying on exemption:

_____

3. Address of person relying on exemption:

_____

4. Written materials. Attach written material required to be submitted pursuant to Rule 14a–6(g)(1).

Rule 14b–1. Obligation of Registered Brokers and Dealers in Connection With the Prompt Forwarding of Certain Communications to Beneficial Owners

(a) *Definitions.* Unless the context otherwise requires, all terms used in this section shall have the same meanings as in the Act and, with respect to proxy soliciting material, as in Rule 14a–1 thereunder and, with respect to information statements, as in Rule 14c–1 thereunder. In addition, as used in this section, the term "registrant" means:

(1) The issuer of a class of securities registered pursuant to Section 12 of the Act....

(2) An investment company registered under the Investment Company Act of 1940.

(b) *Dissemination and beneficial owner information requirements.* A broker or dealer registered under Section 15 of the Act shall comply with the following requirements for disseminating certain communications to beneficial owners and providing beneficial owner information to registrants.

(1) The broker or dealer shall respond, by first class mail or other equally prompt means, directly to the registrant no later than seven business days after the date it receives an inquiry ... by indicating, by means of a search card or otherwise:

(i) The approximate number of customers of the broker or dealer who are beneficial owners of the registrant's securities that are held of record by the broker, dealer, or its nominee;

(ii) The number of customers of the broker or dealer who are beneficial owners of the registrant's securities who have objected to disclosure of their names, addresses, and securities positions if the registrant has indicated ... that it will distribute the annual report to security holders to beneficial owners of its securities whose names, addresses and securities positions are disclosed pursuant to paragraph (b)(3) of this section; ...

(2) The broker or dealer shall, upon receipt of the proxy, other proxy soliciting material, information statement, and/or annual reports to security holders, forward such materials to its customers who are beneficial owners of the registrant's securities no later than five business days after receipt of the proxy material, information statement or annual reports.

(3) The broker or dealer shall, through its agent or directly:

(i) Provide the registrant, upon the registrant's request, with the names, addresses, and securities positions, compiled as of a date specified in the registrant's request which is no earlier than five business days after the date the registrant's request is received, of its customers who are beneficial owners of the registrant's securities and who have not objected to disclosure of such information ...; and

(ii) Transmit the data specified in paragraph (b)(3)(i) of this section to the registrant no later than five business days after the record date or other date specified by the registrant....

(c) *Exceptions to dissemination and beneficial owner information requirements*....

(2) A broker or dealer need not satisfy:

(i) Its obligations under paragraphs (b)(2) and (b)(3) of this section if a registrant does not provide assurance of reimbursement of the broker's or dealer's reasonable expenses, both direct and indirect, incurred in connection with performing the obligations imposed by paragraphs (b)(2) and (b)(3) of this section....

Rule 14b–2. Obligation of Banks, Associations and Other Entities That Exercise Fiduciary Powers in Connection With the Prompt Forwarding of Certain Communications to Beneficial Owners

(a) *Definitions.* Unless the context otherwise requires, all terms used in this section shall have the same meanings as in the Act and, with respect to proxy soliciting material, as in Rule 14a–1 thereunder and, with respect to information statements, as in Rule 14c–1 thereunder. In addition, as used in this section, the following terms shall apply:

(1) The term "bank" means a bank, association, or other entity that exercises fiduciary powers.

(2) The term "beneficial owner" includes any person who has or shares, pursuant to an instrument, agreement, or otherwise, the power to vote, or to direct the voting of a security. . . .

(3) The term "registrant" means:

(i) The issuer of a class of securities registered pursuant to Section 12 of the Act.

(ii) . . . .

(b) *Dissemination and beneficial owner information requirements.* A bank shall comply with the following requirements for disseminating certain communications to beneficial owners and providing beneficial owner information to registrants.

(1) The bank shall:

(i) Respond, by first class mail or other equally prompt means, directly to the registrant, no later than one business day after the date it receives an inquiry . . . by indicating the name and address of each of its respondent banks that holds the registrant's securities on behalf of beneficial owners, if any; and

(ii) Respond, by first class mail or other equally prompt means, directly to the registrant no later than seven business days after the date it receives an inquiry . . . by indicating, by means of a search card or otherwise:

(A) The approximate number of customers of the bank who are beneficial owners of the registrant's securities that are held of record by the bank or its nominee;

(B) If the registrant has indicated . . . that it will distribute the annual report to security holders to beneficial owners of its securities, whose names, addresses, and securities positions are disclosed pursuant to paragraphs (b)(4)(ii) and (iii) of this section:

(1) With respect to customer accounts opened on or before December 28, 1986, the number of beneficial owners of the registrant's securities who have affirmatively consented to disclosure of their names, addresses, and securities positions; and

(2) With respect to customer accounts opened after December 28, 1986, the number of beneficial owners of the registrant's securities who have not objected to disclosure of their names, addresses, and securities positions; and

(C) The identity of its designated agent, if any, acting on its behalf in fulfilling its obligations under paragraphs (b)(4)(ii) and (iii) of this section; . . .

(2) Where proxies are solicited, the bank shall, within five business days after the record date:

(i) Execute an omnibus proxy, including a power of substitution, in favor of its respondent banks and forward such proxy to the registrant; and

(ii) Furnish a notice to each respondent bank in whose favor an omnibus proxy has been executed that it has executed such a proxy, including a power of substitution, in its favor pursuant to paragraph (b)(2)(i) of this section.

(3) Upon receipt of the proxy, other proxy soliciting material, information statement, and/or annual reports to security holders, the bank shall forward such materials to each beneficial owner on whose behalf it holds securities, no later than five business days after the date it receives such material and, where a proxy is solicited, the bank shall forward, with the other proxy soliciting material and/or the annual report, either:

(i) A properly executed proxy:

(A) indicating the number of securities held for such beneficial owner;

(B) bearing the beneficial owner's account number or other form of identification, together with instructions as to the procedures to vote the securities;

(C) briefly stating which other proxies, if any, are required to permit securities to be voted under the terms of the instrument creating that voting power or applicable state law; and

(D) being accompanied by an envelope addressed to the registrant or its agent, if not provided by the registrant; or

(ii) A request for voting instructions (for which registrant's form of proxy may be used and which shall be voted by the record holder bank or respondent bank in accordance with the instructions received), together with an envelope addressed to the record holder bank or respondent bank.

(4) The bank shall:

(i) Respond, by first class mail or other equally prompt means, directly to the registrant no later than one business day after the date it receives an inquiry made in accordance with Rule 14a–13(b)(1) or Rule 14c–7(b)(1) by indicating the name and address of each of its respondent banks that holds the registrant's securities on behalf of beneficial owners, if any;

(ii) Through its agent or directly, provide the registrant, upon the registrant's request, and within the time specified in paragraph (b)(4)(iii) of this section, with the names, addresses, and securities position, compiled as of a date specified in the registrant's request which is no earlier than five business days after the date the registrant's request is received, of:

(A) With respect to customer accounts opened on or before December 28, 1986, beneficial owners of the registrant's securities on whose behalf it holds securities who have consented affirmatively to disclosure of such information, subject to paragraph (b)(5) of this section; and

(B) With respect to customer accounts opened after December 28, 1986, beneficial owners of the registrant's securities on whose behalf it holds securities who have not objected to disclosure of such information;
. . .

(iii) Through its agent or directly, transmit the data specified in paragraph (b)(4)(ii) of this section to the registrant no later than five business days after the date specified by the registrant. . . .

(5) For customer accounts opened on or before December 28, 1986, unless the bank has made a good faith effort to obtain affirmative consent to disclosure of beneficial owner information pursuant to paragraph (b)(4)(ii) of this section, the bank shall provide such information as to beneficial owners who do not object to disclosure of such information. A good faith effort to obtain affirmative consent to disclosure of beneficial owner information shall include, but shall not be limited to, making an inquiry:

(i) Phrased in neutral language, explaining the purpose of the disclosure and the limitations on the registrant's use thereof:

(ii) Either in at least one mailing separate from other account mailings or in repeated mailings; and

(iii) In a mailing that includes a return card, postage paid enclosure.

(c) *Exceptions to dissemination and beneficial owner information requirements*. . . .

(2) The bank need not satisfy:

(i) Its obligations under paragraphs (b)(2), (b)(3), and (b)(4) of this section if a registrant does not provide assurance of reimbursement of its reasonable expenses, both direct and indirect, incurred in connection with performing the obligations imposed by paragraphs (b)(2), (b)(3), and (b)(4) of this section. . . .

REGULATION 14C: DISTRIBUTION OF INFORMATION PURSUANT TO SECTION 14(c) . . .

Rule 14c–2. Distribution of Information Statement

(a) In connection with every annual or other meeting of the holders of the class of securities registered pursuant to section 12 of the Act . . . , including the taking of corporate action by the written authorization or consent of security holders, the registrant shall transmit a written information statement containing the information specified in Schedule 14C ..., and containing the information specified in such form, to every security holder of the class that is entitled to vote or give an authorization or consent in regard to any matter to be acted upon and from whom proxy authorization or consent is not solicited on behalf of the registrant pursuant to Section 14(a) of the Act....

Rule 14c–3. Annual Report to Be Furnished Security Holders

(a) If the information statement relates to an annual (or special meeting in lieu of the annual) meeting, or written consent in lieu of such meeting, of security holders at which directors are to be elected, it shall be accompanied or preceded by an annual report to such security holders....

(1) The annual report shall contain the information specified in paragraphs (b)(1) through (b)(11) of Rule 14a–3....

SCHEDULE 14C. INFORMATION REQUIRED IN INFORMATION STATEMENT ...

Note: Where any item, other than Item 4, calls for information with respect to any matter to be acted upon at the meeting or, if no meeting is being held, by written authorization or consent, such item need be answered only with respect to proposals to be made by the registrant....

Item 1. Information required by Items of Schedule 14A.... Furnish the information called for by all of the items of Schedule 14A of Regulation 14A (other than Items 1(c), 2, 4 and 5 thereof) which would be applicable to any matter to be acted upon at the meeting if proxies were to be solicited in connection with the meeting....

Item 2. Statement that proxies are not solicited. The following statement shall be set forth on the first page of the information statement in bold-face type:

WE ARE NOT ASKING YOU FOR A PROXY AND YOU ARE REQUESTED NOT TO SEND US A PROXY

Item 3. Interest of certain persons in or opposition to matters to be acted upon. (a) Describe briefly any substantial interest, direct or indirect, by security holdings or otherwise, of each of the following persons in any matter to be acted upon, other than elections to office:

(1) Each person who has been a director or officer of the registrant at any time since the beginning of the last fiscal year;

(2) Each nominee for election as a director of the registrant;

(3) Each associate of any of the foregoing persons.

(b) Give the name of any director of the registrant who has informed the registrant in writing that he intends to oppose any action to be taken by the registrant at the meeting and indicate the action which he intends to oppose.

Item 4. Proposals by security holders. If any security holder entitled to vote at the meeting or by written authorization or consent has submitted to the registrant a reasonable time before the information statement is to be transmitted to security holders a proposal, other than elections to office, which is accompanied by notice of his intention to present the proposal for action at the meeting the registrant shall, if a meeting is held, make a statement to that effect, identify the proposal and indicate the disposition proposed to be made of the proposal by the registrant at the meeting....

REGULATION 14D

Rule 14d–1. Scope of and Definitions Applicable to Regulations 14D and 14E

(a) *Scope.* Regulation 14D (Rules 14d–1 through Schedule 14D) shall apply to any tender offer which is subject to section 14(d)(1) of the Act, including, but not limited to, any tender offer for securities of a class described in that section which is made by an affiliate of the issuer of such class. Regulation 14E (Rules 14e–1 and 14e–2) shall apply to any tender offer for securities (other than exempted securities) unless otherwise noted therein....

(c) *Definitions.* Unless the context otherwise requires, all terms used in Regulation 14D and Regulation 14E have the same meaning as in the Act and in Rule 12b–2 ... promulgated thereunder. In addition, for purposes of sections 14(d) and 14(e) of the Act and Regulations 14D and 14E, the following definitions apply:

(1) The term "bidder" means any person who makes a tender offer or on whose behalf a tender offer is made: *Provided, however,* That the term does not include an issuer which makes a tender offer for securities of any class of which it is the issuer;

(2) The term "subject company" means any issuer of securities which are sought by a bidder pursuant to a tender offer;

(3) The term "security holders" means holders of record and beneficial owners of securities which are the subject of a tender offer; ...

(5) The term "tender offer material" means:

(i) The bidder's formal offer, including all the material terms and conditions of the tender offer and all amendments thereto;

(ii) The related transmittal letter (whereby securities of the subject company which are sought in the tender offer may be transmitted to the bidder or its depositary) and all amendments thereto; and

(iii) Press releases, advertisements, letters and other documents published by the bidder or sent or given by the bidder to security holders which, directly or indirectly, solicit, invite or request tenders of the securities being sought in the tender offer;

(6) The term "business day" means any day, other than Saturday, Sunday or a federal holiday....

Rule 14d–2. Date of Commencement of a Tender Offer

(a) *Commencement.* A tender offer shall commence for the purposes of section 14(d) of the Act and the rules promulgated thereunder at 12:01 a.m. on the date when the first of the following events occurs:

(1) The long form publication of the tender offer is first published by the bidder pursuant to Rule 14d–4(a)(1) ...;

(2) The summary advertisement of the tender offer is first published by the bidder pursuant to Rule 14d–4(a)(2) ...;

(4) Definitive copies of a tender offer, in which the consideration offered by the bidder consists of securities registered pursuant to the Securities Act of 1933, are first published or sent or given by the bidder to security holders; or

(5) The tender offer is first published or sent or given to security holders by the bidder by any means not otherwise referred to in paragraphs (a)(1) through (4) of this section.

(b) *Public announcement.* A public announcement by a bidder through a press release, newspaper advertisement or public statement which includes the information in paragraph (c) of this section with respect to a tender offer in which the consideration consists solely of cash and/or securities exempt from registration under section 3 of the Securities Act of 1933 shall be deemed to constitute the commencement of a tender offer under paragraph (a)(5) of this section *Except,* That such tender offer shall not be deemed to be first published or sent or given to security holders by the bidder under paragraph (a)(5) of this section on the date of such public announcement if within five business days of such public announcement, the bidder either:

(1) Makes a subsequent public announcement stating that the bidder has determined not to continue with such tender offer, in which event paragraph (a)(5) of this section shall not apply to the initial public announcement; or

(2) Complies with Rule 14d-3(a) and contemporaneously disseminates the disclosure required by Rule 14d-6 to security holders pursuant to Rule 14d-4 or otherwise in which event:

(i) The date of commencement of such tender offer under paragraph (a) of this section will be determined by the date the information required by Rule 14d-6 is first published or sent or given to security holders pursuant to Rule 14d-4 or otherwise; and

(ii) Notwithstanding paragraph (b)(2)(i) of this section, section 14(d)(7) of the Act shall be deemed to apply to such tender offer from the date of such public announcement.

(c) *Information.* The information referred to in paragraph (b) of this section is as follows:

(1) The identity of the bidder;

(2) The identity of the subject company; and

(3) The amount and class of securities being sought and the price or range of prices being offered therefor.

(d) *Announcements not resulting in commencement.* A public announcement by a bidder through a press release, newspaper advertisement or public statement which only discloses the information in paragraphs (d)(1) through (3) of this section concerning a tender offer in which the consideration consists solely of cash and/or securities exempt from registration under section 3 of the Securities Act of 1933 shall not be deemed to constitute the commencement of a tender offer under paragraph (a)(5) of this section.

(1) The identity of the bidder;

(2) The identity of the subject company; and

(3) A statement that the bidder intends to make a tender offer in the future for a class of equity securities of the subject company which statement does not specify the amount of securities of such class to be sought or the consideration to be offered therefor....

Rule 14d-3. Filing and Transmission of Tender Offer Statement

(a) *Filing and transmittal.* No bidder shall make a tender offer if, after consummation thereof, such bidder would be the beneficial owner of more than 5 percent of the class of the subject company's securities for which the tender offer is made, unless as soon as practicable on the date of the commencement of the tender offer such bidder:

(1) Files with the Commission ten copies of a Tender Offer Statement on Schedule 14D-1 ..., including all exhibits thereto;

(2) Hand delivers a copy of such Schedule 14D-1, including all exhibits thereto:

(i) To the subject company at its principal executive office; and

(ii) To any other bidder, which has filed a Schedule 14D–1 with the Commission relating to a tender offer which has not yet terminated for the same class of securities of the subject company, at such bidder's principal executive office or at the address of the person authorized to receive notices and communications (which is disclosed on the cover sheet of such other bidder's Schedule 14D–1);

(3) Gives telephonic notice of the information required by Rule 14d–6(e)(2)(i) and (ii) and mails by means of first class mail a copy of such Schedule 14D–1, including all exhibits thereto:

(i) To each national securities exchange where such class of the subject company's securities is registered and listed for trading ... which telephonic notice shall be made when practicable prior to the opening of each such exchange; and

(ii) To the National Association of Securities Dealers, Inc. ("NASD") if such class of the subject company's securities is authorized for quotation in the NASDAQ interdealer quotation system....

Rule 14d–4. **Dissemination of Certain Tender Offers**

(a) *Materials deemed published or sent or given.* A tender offer in which the consideration consists solely of cash and/or securities exempt from registration under section 3 of the Securities Act of 1933 shall be deemed "published or sent or given to security holders" within the meaning of section 14(d)(1) of the Act if the bidder complies with all of the requirements of any one of the following sub-paragraphs: *Provided, however,* That any such tender offers may be published or sent or given to security holders by other methods, but with respect to summary publication ... [paragraph (a)(2) of this section is] exclusive.

(1) *Long-form publication.* The bidder makes adequate publication in a newspaper or newspapers of long-form publication of the tender offer.

(2) *Summary publication.* (i) If the tender offer is not subject to Rule 13e–3 ... , the bidder makes adequate publication in a newspaper or newspapers of a summary advertisement of the tender offer; and

(ii) Mails by first class mail or otherwise furnishes with reasonable promptness the bidder's tender offer materials to any security holder who requests such tender offer materials pursuant to the summary advertisement or otherwise....

(b) *Adequate publication.* Depending on the facts and circumstances involved, adequate publication of a tender offer pursuant to this section may require publication in a newspaper with a national circulation or may only require publication in a newspaper with metropolitan or regional circulation or may require publication in a combination thereof: *Provided, however,* That publication in all editions of a daily newspaper with a national circulation shall be deemed to constitute adequate publication....

Rule 14d–6.   Disclosure Requirements With Respect to Tender Offers

(a) *Information required on date of commencement* —(1) *Long-form publication.* If a tender offer is published or sent or given to security holders on the date of commencement by means of long-form publication pursuant to Rule 14d–4(a)(1) ... such long-form publication shall include the information required by paragraph (e)(1) of this section.

(2) *Summary publication.* If a tender offer is published or sent or given to security holders on the date of commencement by means of summary publication pursuant to Rule 14d–4(a)(2) ...

(i) The summary advertisement shall contain and shall be limited to, the information required by paragraph (e)(2) of this section; and

(ii) The tender offer materials furnished by the bidder upon the request of any security holder shall include the information required by paragraph (e)(1) of this section....

(e) *Information to be included*—(1) *Long-form publication and tender offer materials.* The information required to be disclosed by paragraphs (a)(1), (2)(ii) ... of this section shall include the following:

(i) The identity of the bidder;

(ii) The identity of the subject company;

(iii) The amount and class of securities being sought and the type and amount of consideration being offered therefor;

(iv) The scheduled expiration date of the tender offer, whether the tender offer may be extended and, if so, the procedures for extension of the tender offer;

(v) The exact dates prior to which, and after which, security holders who deposit their securities will have the right to withdraw their securities pursuant to section 14(d)(5) of the Act and Rule 14d–7 ... and the manner in which shares will be accepted for payment and in which withdrawal may be effected;

(vi) If the tender offer is for less than all the outstanding securities of a class of equity securities and the bidder is not obligated to purchase all of the securities tendered, the period or periods, and in the case of the period from the commencement of the offer, the date of the expiration of such period during which the securities will be taken up pro rata pursuant to section 14(d)(6) of the Act or Rule 14d–8 ... , and the present intention or plan of the bidder with respect to the tender offer in the event of an oversubscription by security holders;

(vii) The disclosure required by Items 1(c); 2 (with respect to persons other than the bidder, excluding sub-items (b) and (d)); 3; 4; 5;

6; 7; 8; and 10 of Schedule 14D-1 ... or a fair and adequate summary thereof. . . .

(viii) The disclosure required by Item 9 of Schedule 14D-1 or a fair and adequate summary thereof. . . .

(2) *Summary publication.* The information required to be disclosed by [paragraph (a)(2)(i)] ... of this section in a summary advertisement is as follows:

(i) The information required by paragraphs (e)(1)(i) through (vi) of this section;

(ii) If the tender offer is for less than all the outstanding securities of a class of equity securities, a statement as to whether the purpose or one of the purposes of the tender offer is to acquire or influence control of the business of the subject company;

(iii) A statement that the information required by paragraph (e)(1)(vii) of this section is incorporated by reference into the summary advertisement;

(iv) Appropriate instructions as to how security holders may obtain promptly, at the bidder's expense, the bidder's tender offer materials. . . .

Rule 14d-7. Additional Withdrawal Rights

(a) *Rights.* In addition to the provisions of section 14(d)(5) of the Act, any person who has deposited securities pursuant to a tender offer has the right to withdraw any such securities during the period such offer, request or invitation remains open.

(b) *Notice of withdrawal.* Notice of withdrawal pursuant to this section shall be deemed to be timely upon the receipt by the bidder's depositary of a written notice of withdrawal specifying the name(s) of the tendering stockholder(s), the number or amount of the securities to be withdrawn and the name(s) in which the certificate(s) is (are) registered, if different from that of the tendering security holder(s). A bidder may impose other reasonable requirements, including certificate numbers and a signed request for withdrawal accompanied by a signature guarantee, as conditions precedent to the physical release of withdrawn securities.

Rule 14d-8. Exemption From Statutory Pro Rata Requirements

Notwithstanding the pro rata provisions of section 14(d)(6) of the Act, if any person makes a tender offer or request or invitation for tenders, for less than all of the outstanding equity securities of a class, and if a greater number of securities are deposited pursuant thereto than such person is bound or willing to take up and pay for, the securities taken up and paid for shall be taken up and paid for as nearly as may be pro rata, disregarding fractions, according to the number of securities deposited by each depositor during the period such offer, request or invitation remains open.

Rule 14d–9. Solicitation/Recommendation Statements With Respect to Certain Tender Offers

(a) *Filing and transmittal of recommendation statement.* No solicitation or recommendation to security holders shall be made by any person described in paragraph (d) of this section with respect to a tender offer for such securities unless as soon as practicable on the date such solicitation or recommendation is first published or sent or given to security holders such person complies with the following subparagraphs.

(1) Such person shall file with the Commission eight copies of a Tender Offer Solicitation/Recommendation Statement on Schedule 14D–9 . . . and

(2) If such person is either the subject company or an affiliate of the subject company,

(i) Such person shall hand deliver a copy of the Schedule 14D–9 to the bidder at its principal office . . . ; and

(ii) Such person shall give telephonic notice (which notice to the extent possible shall be given prior to the opening of the market) of the information required by Items 2 and 4(a) of Schedule 14D–9 and shall mail a copy of the Schedule to each national securities exchange where the class of securities is registered and listed for trading and, if the class is authorized for quotation in the NASDAQ interdealer quotation system, to the National Association of Securities Dealers, Inc. ("NASD").

(3) If such person is neither the subject company nor an affiliate of the subject company,

(i) Such person shall mail a copy of the schedule to the bidder at its principal office . . . ; and

(ii) Such person shall mail a copy of the Schedule to the subject company at its principal office. . . .

(c) *Information required in solicitation or recommendation.* Any solicitation or recommendation to holders of a class of securities referred to in section 14(d)(1) of the Act with respect to a tender offer for such securities shall include the name of the person making such solicitation or recommendation and the information required by Items 1, 2, 3(b), 4, 6, 7 and 8 of Schedule 14D–9 . . . or a fair and adequate summary thereof: *Provided, however,* That such solicitation or recommendation may omit any of such information previously furnished to security holders of such class of securities by such person with respect to such tender offer.

(d) *Applicability.* (1) Except as is provided in paragraphs (d)(2) and (e) of this section, this section shall only apply to the following persons:

(i) The subject company, any director, officer, employee, affiliate or subsidiary of the subject company;

(ii) Any record holder or beneficial owner of any security issued by the subject company, by the bidder, or by any affiliate of either the subject company or the bidder; and

(iii) Any person who makes a solicitation or recommendation to security holders on behalf of any of the foregoing or on behalf of the bidder other than by means of a solicitation or recommendation to security holders which has been filed with the Commission pursuant to this section or Rule 14d–3....

(2) Notwithstanding paragraph (d)(1) of this section, this section shall not apply to the following persons:

(i) A bidder who has filed a Schedule 14D–1 ... pursuant to Rule 14d–3 ...;

(ii) Attorneys, banks, brokers, fiduciaries or investment advisers who are not participating in a tender offer in more than a ministerial capacity and who furnish information and/or advice regarding such tender offer to their customers or clients on the unsolicited request of such customers or clients or solely pursuant to a contract or a relationship providing for advice to the customer or client to whom the information and/or advice is given.

(e) *Stop-look-and-listen communication.* This section shall not apply to the subject company with respect to a communication by the subject company to its security holders which only:

(1) Identifies the tender offer by the bidder;

(2) States that such tender offer is under consideration by the subject company's board of directors and/or management;

(3) States that on or before a specified date (which shall be no later than 10 business days from the date of commencement of such tender offer) the subject company will advise such security holders of (i) whether the subject company recommends acceptance or rejection of such tender offer; expresses no opinion and remains neutral toward such tender offer; or is unable to take a position with respect to such tender offer and (ii) the reason(s) for the position taken by the subject company with respect to the tender offer (including the inability to take a position); and

(4) Requests such security holders to defer making a determination whether to accept or reject such tender offer until they have been advised of the subject company's position with respect thereto pursuant to paragraph (e)(3) of this section.

(f) *Statement of management's position.* A statement by the subject company of its position with respect to a tender offer which is required to be published or sent or given to security holders pursuant to Rule 14e–2 shall be deemed to constitute a solicitation or recommendation within the meaning of this section and section 14(d)(4) of the Act.

Rule 14d–10.   Equal Treatment of Security Holders

(a) No bidder shall make a tender offer unless:

(1) The tender offer is open to all security holders of the class of securities subject to the tender offer; and

(2) The consideration paid to any security holder pursuant to the tender offer is the highest consideration paid to any other security holder during such tender offer. . . .

SCHEDULE 14D–1.   TENDER OFFER STATEMENT PURSUANT TO SECTION 14(d)(1) OF THE SECURITIES EXCHANGE ACT OF 1934. . . .

Name of Subject Company [Issuer]
(Bidder)
(Title of Class of Securities)
(CUSIP Number of Class of Securities)
(Name, Address, and Telephone Numbers of Person Authorized to Receive Notices and Communications on Behalf of Bidder) . . .

Item 1.   Security and Subject Company.   (a) State the name of the subject company and the address of its principal executive offices;

(b) State the exact title and the number of shares outstanding of the class of equity securities being sought . . . , the exact amount of such securities being sought and the consideration being offered therefor; and

(c) Identify the principal market in which such securities are traded and state the high and low sales prices for such securities in such principal market (or, in the absence thereof, the range of high and low bid quotations) for each quarterly period during the past two years.

Item 2.   Identity and Background [*of Persons Filing the Schedule*]. . . .

Item 3.   Past Contacts, Transactions or Negotiations with the Subject Company. . . .

Item 4.   Source and Amount of Funds or other Consideration.   (a) State the source and the total amount of funds or other consideration for the purchase of the maximum number of securities for which the tender offer is being made.

(b) If all or any part of such funds or other consideration are or are expected to be, directly or indirectly, borrowed for the purpose of the tender offer:

(1) Provide a summary of each loan agreement or arrangement containing the identity of the parties, the term, the collateral, the stated and effective interest rates, and other material terms or conditions relative to such loan agreement; and

(2) Briefly describe any plans or arrangements to finance or repay such borrowings, or if no such plans or arrangements have been made, make a statement to that effect.

(c) If the source of all or any part of the funds to be used in the tender offer is a loan made in the ordinary course of business by a bank ..., the name of such bank shall not be made available to the public if the person filing the statement so requests in writing and files such request, naming such bank, with the Secretary of the Commission.

Item 5. Purpose of the Tender Offer and Plans or Proposals of the Bidder. State the purpose or purposes of the tender offer for the subject company's securities. Describe any plans or proposals which relate to or would result in:

(a) An extraordinary corporate transaction, such as a merger, reorganization or liquidation, involving the subject company or any of its subsidiaries;

(b) A sale or transfer of a material amount of assets of the subject company or any of its subsidiaries;

(c) Any change in the present board of directors or management of the subject company including, but not limited to, any plans or proposals to change the number or the term of directors or to fill any existing vacancies on the board;

(d) Any material change in the present capitalization or dividend policy of the subject company;

(e) Any other material change in the subject company's corporate structure or business. . . .

(f) Causing a class of securities of the subject company to be delisted from a national securities exchange or to cease to be authorized to be quoted in an inter-dealer quotation system of a registered national securities association; or

(g) A class of equity securities of the subject company becoming eligible for termination of registration pursuant to section 12(g)(4) of the Act.

Item 6. Interest in Securities of the Subject Company. (a) State the aggregate number and percentage of the class represented by such shares ... beneficially owned ... by each person named in Item 2 of this schedule and by each associate and majority-owned subsidiary of such person giving the name and address of any such associate or subsidiary.

(b) Describe any transaction in the class of securities reported on that was effected during the past 60 days by the persons named in response to paragraph (a) of this item or by any executive officer, director or subsidiary of such person....

Item 7. Contracts, Arrangements, Understandings or Relationships with Respect to the Subject Company's Securities. Describe any contract, arrangement, understanding or relationship (whether or not legally enforceable) between the bidder ... and any person with respect to any securities of the subject company (including, but not limited to, any contract, arrangement, understanding or relationship concerning the transfer or the voting of any of such securities, joint ventures, loan or option arrangements, puts or calls, guarantees of loans, guarantees against loss, or the giving or withholding of proxies), naming the persons with whom such contracts, arrangements, understandings or relationships have been entered into and giving the material provisions thereof....

Item 8. Persons Retained, Employed or to be Compensated. Identify all persons and classes of persons employed, retained or to be compensated by the bidder, or by any person on the bidder's behalf, to make solicitations or recommendations in connection with the tender offer and describe briefly the terms of such employment, retainer or arrangement for compensation.

Item 9. Financial Statements of Certain Bidders. Where the bidder is other than a natural person and the bidder's financial condition is material to a decision by a security holder of the subject company whether to sell, tender or hold securities being sought in the tender offer, furnish current, adequate financial information concerning the bidder....

Item 10. Additional Information. If material to a decision by a security holder whether to sell, tender or hold securities being sought in the tender offer, furnish information as to the following:

(a) Any present or proposed material contracts, arrangements, understandings or relationships between the bidder or any of its executive officers, directors, controlling persons or subsidiaries and the subject company or any of its executive officers, directors, controlling persons or subsidiaries (other than any contract, arrangement or understanding required to be disclosed pursuant to Items 3 or 7 of this schedule);

(b) To the extent known by the bidder after reasonable investigation, the applicable regulatory requirements which must be complied with or approvals which must be obtained in connection with the tender offer;

(c) The applicability of anti-trust laws;

(d) The applicability of the margin requirements of section 7 of the Act and the regulations promulgated thereunder;

(e) Any material pending legal proceedings relating to the tender offer including the name and location of the court or agency in which the proceedings are pending, the date instituted, the principal parties thereto and a brief summary of the proceedings; and . . .

(f) Such additional material information, if any, as may be necessary to make the required statements, in light of the circumstances under which they are made, not materially misleading. . . .

———

SCHEDULE 14D–9. SOLICITATION/RECOMMENDATION STATEMENT PURSUANT TO SECTION 14(d)(4) OF THE SECURITIES EXCHANGE ACT OF 1934

(Name of Subject Company)

(Name of Person(s) Filing Statement)

(Title of Class of Securities)

(CUSIP Number of Class of Securities)

(Name, address and telephone number of person authorized to receive notice and communications on behalf of the person(s) filing statement) . . .

Item 1. Security and Subject Company. State the title of the class of equity securities to which this statement relates and the name and the address of the principal executive offices of the subject company.

Item 2. Tender Offer of the Bidder. Identify the tender offer to which this statement relates, the name of the bidder and the address of its principal executive offices or, if the bidder is a natural person, the bidder's residence or business address (which may be based on the bidder's Schedule 14D–1 . . . filed with the Commission).

Item 3. Identity and Background [*of the Person Filing the Statement*] . . . .

Item 4. The Solicitation or Recommendation. (a) State the nature of the solicitation or the recommendation. If this statement relates to a recommendation, state whether the person filing this statement is advising security holders of the securities being sought by the bidder to accept or reject the tender offer or to take other action with respect to the tender offer and, if so, furnish a description of such other action being recommended. If the person filing this statement is the subject company and a recommendation is not being made, state whether the subject company is either expressing no opinion and is remaining neutral toward the tender offer or is unable to take a position with respect to the tender offer.

(b) State the reason(s) for the position (including the inability to take a position) stated in (a) of this Item.

Instruction: Conclusory statements such as "The tender offer is in the best interest of shareholders," will not be considered sufficient disclosure in response to Item 4(b).

Item 5. Persons Retained, Employed or To Be Compensated. Identify any person or class of persons employed, retained or to be compensated by the person filing this statement or by any person on its behalf, to make solicitations or recommendations to security holders and describe briefly the terms of such employment, retainer or arrangement for compensation.

Item 6. Recent Transactions and Intent With Respect to Securities. (a) Describe any transaction in the securities referred to in Item 1 which was effected during the past 60 days by the person(s) named in response to Item 3(a) and by any executive officer, director, affiliate or subsidiary of such person(s).

(b) To the extent known by the person filing this statement, state whether the persons referred to in Item 6(a) presently intend to tender to the bidder, sell or hold securities of the class of securities being sought by the bidder which are held of record or beneficially owned by such persons.

Item 7. Certain Negotiations and Transactions by the Subject Company. (a) If the person filing this statement is the subject company, state whether or not any negotiation is being undertaken or is underway by the subject company in response to the tender offer which relates to or would result in:

(1) An extraordinary transaction such as a merger or reorganization, involving the subject company or any subsidiary of the subject company;

(2) A purchase, sale or transfer of a material amount of assets by the subject company or any subsidiary of the subject company;

(3) A tender offer for or other acquisition of securities by or of the subject company; or

(4) Any material change in the present capitalization or dividend policy of the subject company.

Instruction: If no agreement in principle has yet been reached, the possible terms of any transaction or the parties thereto need not be disclosed if in the opinion of the Board of Directors of the subject company such disclosure would jeopardize continuation of such negotiations. In such event, disclosure that negotiations are being undertaken or are underway and are in the preliminary stages will be sufficient.

(b) Describe any transaction, board resolution, agreement in principle, or a signed contract in response to the tender offer ... which relates to or would result in one or more of the matters referred to in Item 7(a)(1), (2), (3) or (4).

Item 8. Additional Information To Be Furnished. Furnish such additional information, if any, as may be necessary to make the required statements, in light of the circumstances under which they are made, not materially misleading....

REGULATION 14E

Rule 14e–1. Unlawful Tender Offer Practices

As a means reasonably designed to prevent fraudulent, deceptive or manipulative acts or practices within the meaning of section 14(e) of the Act, no person who makes a tender offer shall:

(a) Hold such tender offer open for less than twenty business days from the date such tender offer is first published or sent or given to security holders ...;

(b) Increase or decrease the percentage of the class of securities being sought or the consideration offered or the dealer's soliciting fee to be given in a tender offer unless such tender offer remains open for at least ten business days from the date that notice of such increase or decrease is first published or sent or given to security holders....

Rule 14e–2. Position of Subject Company With Respect to a Tender Offer

(a) *Position of subject company.* As a means reasonably designed to prevent fraudulent, deceptive or manipulative acts or practices within the meaning of section 14(e) of the Act, the subject company, no later than 10 business days from the date the tender offer is first published or sent or given, shall publish, send or give to security holders a statement disclosing that the subject company:

(1) Recommends acceptance or rejection of the bidder's tender offer;

(2) Expresses no opinion and is remaining neutral toward the bidder's tender offer; or

(3) Is unable to take a position with respect to the bidder's tender offer. Such statement shall also include the reason(s) for the position (including the inability to take a position) disclosed therein.

(b) *Material change.* If any material change occurs in the disclosure required by paragraph (a) of this section, the subject company shall promptly publish or send or give a statement disclosing such material change to security holders. ...

Rule 14e–3. Transactions in Securities on the Basis of Material, Nonpublic Information in the Context of Tender Offers

(a) If any person has taken a substantial step or steps to commence, or has commenced, a tender offer (the "offering person"), it shall constitute a fraudulent, deceptive or manipulative act or practice within the meaning of section 14(e) of the Act for any other person who is in possession of material information relating to such tender offer which information he knows or has reason to know is nonpublic and which he knows or has reason to know has been acquired directly or indirectly from:

(1) The offering person,

(2) The issuer of the securities sought or to be sought by such tender offer, or

(3) Any officer, director, partner or employee or any other person acting on behalf of the offering person or such issuer,

to purchase or sell or cause to be purchased or sold any of such securities or any securities convertible into or exchangeable for any such securities or any option or right to obtain or to dispose of any of the foregoing securities, unless within a reasonable time prior to any purchase or sale such information and its source are publicly disclosed by press release or otherwise.

(b) A person other than a natural person shall not violate paragraph (a) of this section if such person shows that:

(1) The individual(s) making the investment decision on behalf of such person to purchase or sell any security described in paragraph (a) of this section or to cause any such security to be purchased or sold by or on behalf of others did not know the material, nonpublic information; and

(2) Such person had implemented one or a combination of policies and procedures, reasonable under the circumstances, taking into consideration the nature of the person's business, to ensure that individual(s) making investment decision(s) would not violate paragraph (a) of this section, which policies and procedures may include, but are not limited to, (i) those which restrict any purchase, sale and causing any purchase and sale of any such security or (ii) those which prevent such individual(s) from knowing such information.

(c) Notwithstanding anything in paragraph (a) of this section to the contrary, the following transactions shall not be violations of paragraph (a) of this section:

(1) Purchase(s) of any security described in paragraph (a) of this section by a broker or by another agent on behalf of an offering person; or

(2) Sale(s) by any person of any security described in paragraph (a) of this section to the offering person.

(d)(1) As a means reasonably designed to prevent fraudulent, deceptive or manipulative acts or practices within the meaning of section 14(e) of the Act, it shall be unlawful for any person described in paragraph (d)(2) of this section to communicate material, nonpublic information relating to a tender offer to any other person under circumstances in which it is reasonably foreseeable that such communication is likely to result in a violation of this section *except* that this paragraph shall not apply to a communication made in good faith.

(i) To the officers, directors, partners or employees of the offering person, to its advisors or to other persons, involved in the planning, financing, preparation or execution of such tender offer;

(ii) To the issuer whose securities are sought or to be sought by such tender offer, to its officers, directors, partners, employees or advisors or to other persons, involved in the planning, financing, preparation or execution of the activities of the issuer with respect to such tender offer; or

(iii) To any person pursuant to a requirement of any statute or rule or regulation promulgated thereunder.

(2) The persons referred to in paragraph (d)(1) of this section are:

(i) The offering person or its officers, directors, partners, employees or advisors;

(ii) The issuer of the securities sought or to be sought by such tender offer or its officers, directors, partners, employees or advisors;

(iii) Anyone acting on behalf of the persons in paragraph (d)(2)(i) of this section or the issuer or persons in paragraph (d)(2)(ii) of this section; and

(iv) Any person in possession of material information relating to a tender offer which information he knows or has reason to know is nonpublic and which he knows or has reason to know has been acquired directly or indirectly from any of the above.

Rule 14e–4. Prohibited Transactions in Connection With Partial Tender Offers

(a) *Definitions.* For purposes of this section:

(1) The amount of a person's "net long position" in a subject security shall equal the excess, if any, of such person's "long position" over such person's "short position." For the purposes of

determining the net long position as of the end of the proration period and for tendering concurrently to two or more partial tender offers, securities that have been tendered in accordance with the Rule and not withdrawn are deemed to be part of the person's long position.

(i) Such person's "long position," is the amount of subject securities that such person:

(A) or his agent has title to or would have title to but for having lent such securities; or

(B) has purchased, or has entered into an unconditional contract, binding on both parties thereto, to purchase but has not yet received; or

(C) has exercised a standardized call option for; or

(D) has converted, exchanged, or exercised an equivalent security for; or

(E) is entitled to receive upon conversion, exchange, or exercise of an equivalent security.

(ii) Such person's "short position," is the amount of subject securities or subject securities underlying equivalent securities that such person:

(A) has sold, or has entered into an unconditional contract, binding on both parties thereto, to sell; or

(B) has borrowed; or

(C) has written a non-standardized call option, or granted any other right pursuant to which his shares may be tendered by another person; or

(D) is obligated to deliver upon exercise of a standardized call option sold on or after the date that a tender offer is first publicly announced or otherwise made known by the bidder to holders of the security to be acquired, if the exercise price of such option is lower than the highest tender offer price or stated amount of the consideration offered for the subject security. For the purpose of this paragraph, if one or more tender offers for the same security are ongoing on such date, the announcement date shall be that of the first announced offer.

(2) The term "equivalent security" means:

(i) Any security (including any option, warrant, or other right to purchase the subject security), issued by the person whose securities are the subject of the offer, that is immediately convertible into, or exchangeable or exercisable for, a subject security, or

(ii) Any other right or option (other than a standardized call option) that entitles the holder thereof to acquire a subject security, but only if the holder thereof reasonably believes that the maker or writer of the right or option has title to and possession of the subject security and upon exercise will promptly deliver the subject security.

(3) The term "subject security" means a security that is the subject of any tender offer or request or invitation for tenders.

(4) For purposes of this rule, a person shall be deemed to "tender" a security if he:

(i) Delivers a subject security pursuant to an offer,

(ii) Causes such delivery to be made,

(iii) Guarantees delivery of a subject security pursuant to a tender offer,

(iv) Causes a guarantee of such delivery to be given by another person, or

(v) Uses any other method by which acceptance of a tender offer may be made.

(5) The term "partial tender offer" means a tender offer or request or invitation for tenders for less than all of the outstanding securities subject to the offer in which tenders are accepted either by lot or on a *pro rata* basis for a specified period, or a tender offer for all of the outstanding shares that offers a choice of consideration in which tenders for different forms of consideration may be accepted either by lot or on a *pro rata* basis for a specified period.

(6) The term "standardized call option" means any call option that is traded on an exchange, or for which quotation information is disseminated in an electronic interdealer quotation system of a registered national securities association.

(b) It shall be unlawful for any person acting alone or in concert with others, directly or indirectly, to tender any subject security in a partial tender offer:

(1) For his own account unless at the time of tender, and at the end of the proration period or period during which securities are accepted by lot (including any extensions thereof), he has a net long position equal to or greater than the amount tendered in:

(i) the subject security and will deliver or cause to be delivered such security for the purpose of tender to the person making the offer within the period specified in the offer; or

(ii) an equivalent security and, upon the acceptance of his tender will acquire the subject security by conversion, exchange, or exercise of such equivalent security to the extent required by the terms of the offer, and will deliver or cause to be delivered the subject security so acquired for the purpose of tender to the person making the offer within the period specified in the offer; or

(2) For the account of another person unless the person making the tender:

(i) Possesses the subject security or an equivalent security, or

(ii) Has a reasonable belief that, upon information furnished by the person on whose behalf the tender is made, such person owns the subject security or an equivalent security and will promptly deliver the subject security or such equivalent security for the purpose of tender to the person making the tender.

(c) This rule shall not prohibit any transaction or transactions which the Commission, upon written request or upon its own motion, exempts, either unconditionally or on specified terms and conditions.

Rule 14e–7. Unlawful Tender Offer Practices in Connection With Roll–Ups

In order to implement Section 14(h) of the Act:

(a)(1) It shall be unlawful for any person to receive compensation for soliciting tenders directly from security holders in connection with a roll-up transaction as provided in paragraph (a)(2) of this section, if the compensation is:

(i) Based on whether the solicited person participates in the tender offer; or

(ii) Contingent on the success of the tender offer.

(2) Paragraph (a)(1) of this section is applicable to a roll-up transaction as defined in Item 901(c) of Regulation S–K, structured as a tender offer, except for a transaction involving only:

(i) Finite-life entities that are not limited partnerships....

(b)(1) It shall be unlawful for any finite-life entity that is the subject of a roll-up transaction as provided in paragraph (b)(2) of this section to fail to provide a security holder list or mail communications related to a tender offer that is in furtherance of the roll-up transaction, at the option of a requesting security holder, pursuant to the procedures set forth in Rule 14a–7.

(2) Paragraph (b)(1) of this section is applicable to a roll-up transaction as defined in Item 901(c) of Regulation S–K, structured as a tender offer, that involves:

(i) An entity with securities registered pursuant to Section 12 of the Act; or

(ii) A limited partnership....

Rule 14f–1. Change in Majority of Directors

If, pursuant to any arrangement or understanding with the person or persons acquiring securities in a transaction subject to section 13(d) or 14(d) of the Act, any persons are to be elected or designated as directors of the issuer, otherwise than at a meeting of security holders, and the persons so elected or designated will constitute a majority of the directors of the issuer, then, not less than 10 days prior to the date any such person take office as a director, or such shorter period prior to that date as the Commission may authorize upon a showing of good cause therefor, the issuer shall file with the Commission and transmit to all holders of record of securities of the issuer who would be entitled to vote at a meeting for election of directors, information substantially equivalent to the information which would be required by Items 6(a), (d) and (e), 7 and 8 of Schedule 14A of Regulation 14A ... to be transmitted if such person or persons were nominees for election as directors at a meeting of such security holders. Eight copies of such information shall be filed with the Commission.

REGULATION 15D: REPORTS OF REGISTRANTS UNDER THE SECURITIES ACT OF 1933

Rule 15d–1. Requirement of Annual Reports

Every registrant under the Securities Act of 1933 shall file an annual report, on the appropriate form authorized or prescribed therefor, for the fiscal year in which the registration statement under the Securities Act of 1933 became effective and for each fiscal year thereafter, unless the registrant is exempt from such filing by section 15(d) of the Act or rules thereunder....

Rule 15d–11. Current Reports on Form 8–K ...

(a) Except as provided in paragraph (b) of this section, every registrant subject to Rule 15d–1 shall file a current report on Form 8–K within the period specified in that form unless substantially the same information as that required by Form 8–K has been previously reported by the registrant....

Rule 15d–13. Quarterly Reports on Form 10–Q ...

(a) Except as provided in paragraphs (b) and (c) of this section, every issuer that has securities registered pursuant to the Securities Act of 1933 and which is required to file annual reports pursuant to section 15(d) of the Securities Exchange Act of 1934 on Form 10–K ... shall file a quarterly report on Form 10–Q ... for each of the first three fiscal quarters of each fiscal year of the issuer ....

REPORTS OF DIRECTORS, OFFICERS, AND PRINCIPAL SHAREHOLDERS

Rule 16a–1.   Definition of Terms

Terms defined in this Rule shall apply solely to Section 16 of the Act and the rules thereunder. These terms shall not be limited to Section 16(a) of the Act but also shall apply to all other subsections under Section 16 of the Act.

(a) The term "beneficial owner" shall have the following applications:

(1) Solely for purposes of determining whether a person is a beneficial owner of more than ten percent of any class of equity securities registered pursuant to Section 12 of the Act, the term "beneficial owner" shall mean any person who is deemed a beneficial owner pursuant to Section 13(d) of the Act and the rules thereunder; *provided, however,* that the following institutions or persons shall not be deemed the beneficial owner of securities of such class held for the benefit of third parties or in customer or fiduciary accounts in the ordinary course of business ... as long as such shares are acquired by such institutions or persons without the purpose or effect of changing or influencing control of the issuer or engaging in any arrangement subject to Rule 13d–3(b):

(i) A broker or dealer ...;

(ii) A bank ...;

(iii) An insurance company ...;

(iv) An investment company ...;

(v) An investment adviser ...;

(vi) An employee benefit plan or a pension fund ... or an endowment fund; ...

Note to paragraph (a). Pursuant to this section, a person deemed a beneficial owner of more than ten percent of any class of equity securities registered under Section 12 of the Act would file a Form 3, but the securities holdings disclosed on Form 3, and changes in beneficial ownership reported on subsequent Forms 4 or 5, would be determined by the definition of "beneficial owner" in paragraph (a)(2) of this section.

(2) Other than for purposes of determining whether a person is a beneficial owner of more than ten percent of any class of equity securities registered under Section 12 of the Act, the term "beneficial owner" shall mean any person who, directly or indirectly,

through any contract, arrangement, understanding, relationship or otherwise, has or shares a direct or indirect pecuniary interest in the equity securities, subject to the following:

(i) The term "pecuniary interest" in any class of equity securities shall mean the opportunity, directly or indirectly, to profit or share in any profit derived from a transaction in the subject securities.

(ii) The term "indirect pecuniary interest" in any class of equity securities shall include, but not be limited to:

(A) securities held by members of a person's immediate family sharing the same household; *provided, however,* that the presumption of such beneficial ownership may be rebutted . . . ,

(B) a general partner's proportionate interest in the portfolio securities held by a general or limited partnership. . . .

(E) A person's interest in securities held by a trust . . . ; and

(F) A person's right to acquire equity securities through the exercise or conversion of any derivative security, whether or not presently exercisable.

(iii) A shareholder shall not be deemed to have a pecuniary interest in the portfolio securities held by a corporation or similar entity in which the person owns securities if the shareholder is not a controlling shareholder of the entity and does not have or share investment control over the entity's portfolio. . . .

(b) The term "call equivalent position" shall mean a derivative security position that increases in value as the value of the underlying equity increases, including, but not limited to, a long convertible security, a long call option, and a short put option position.

(c) The term "derivative securities" shall mean any option, warrant, convertible security, stock appreciation right, or similar right with an exercise or conversion privilege at a price related to an equity security, or similar securities with a value derived from the value of an equity security . . . .

(d) The term "equity security of such issuer" shall mean any equity security or derivative security relating to an issuer, whether or not issued by that issuer.

(e) The term "immediate family" shall mean any child, stepchild, grandchild, parent, stepparent, grandparent, spouse, sibling, mother-in-law, father-in-law, son-in-law, daughter-in-law, brother-in-law, or sister-in-law, and shall include adoptive relationships.

(f) The term "officer" shall mean an issuer's president, principal financial officer, principal accounting officer (or, if there is no such accounting officer, the controller), any vice-president of the issuer in charge of a principal business unit, division or function (such as sales, administration or finance), any other officer who performs a policy-making function, or any other person who performs similar policy-making functions for the issuer. Officers of the issuer's parent(s) or subsidiaries shall be deemed officers of the issuer if they perform such policy-making functions for the issuer. . . .

(g) The term "portfolio securities" shall mean all securities owned by an entity, other than securities issued by the entity.

(h) The term "put equivalent position" shall mean a derivative security position that increases in value as the value of the underlying equity decreases, including, but not limited to, a long put option and a short call option position.

Rule 16a–2. Persons and Transactions Subject to Section 16

Any person who is the beneficial owner, directly or indirectly, of more than ten percent of any class of equity securities ("ten percent beneficial owner") registered pursuant to Section 12 of the Act, any director or officer of the issuer of such securities, and any person specified in Section 17(a) of the Public Utility Holding Company Act of 1935 or Section 30(f) of the Investment Company Act of 1940, . . . shall be subject to the provisions of Section 16 of the Act. The rules under Section 16 of the Act apply to any class of equity securities of an issuer whether or not registered under Section 12 of the Act. . . . With respect to transactions by persons subject to Section 16 of the Act:

(a) A transaction(s) carried out by a director or officer in the six months prior to the director or officer becoming subject to Section 16 of the Act shall be subject to Section 16 of the Act and reported on the first required Form 4 only if the transaction(s) occurred within six months of the transaction giving rise to the Form 4 filing obligation and the director or officer became subject to Section 16 of the Act solely as a result of the issuer registering a class of equity securities pursuant to Section 12 of the Act.

(b) A transaction(s) following the cessation of director or officer status shall be subject to section 16 of the Act only if:

(1) Executed within a period of less than six months of an opposite transaction subject to section 16(b) of the Act that occurred while that person was a director or officer; and

(2) Not otherwise exempted from section 16(b) of the Act pursuant to the provisions of this chapter.

Note to Paragraph (b): For purposes of this paragraph, an acquisition and a disposition each shall be an opposite transaction with respect to the other.

(c) The transaction that results in a person becoming a ten percent beneficial owner is not subject to Section 16 of the Act unless the person otherwise is subject to Section 16 of the Act. A ten percent beneficial owner not otherwise subject to Section 16 of the Act must report only those transactions conducted while the beneficial owner of more than ten percent of a class of equity securities of the issuer registered pursuant to Section 12 of the Act....

Rule 16a–3. Reporting Transactions and Holdings

(a) Initial statements of beneficial ownership of equity securities required by Section 16(a) of the Act shall be filed on Form 3. Statements of changes in beneficial ownership required by that Section shall be filed on Form 4. Annual statements shall be filed on Form 5. At the election of the reporting person, any transaction required to be reported on Form 5 may be reported on an earlier filed Form 4. All such statements shall be prepared and filed in accordance with the requirements of the applicable form....

(e) Any person required to file a statement under Section 16(a) of the Act shall, not later than the time the statement is transmitted for filing with the Commission, send or deliver a duplicate to the person designated by the issuer to receive such statements, or, in the absence of such a designation, to the issuer's corporate secretary or person performing equivalent functions.

(f)(1) A Form 5 shall be filed by every person who at any time during the issuer's fiscal year was subject to Section 16 of the Act with respect to such issuer, except as provided in paragraph (2) below. The Form shall be filed within 45 days after the issuer's fiscal year end, and shall disclose the following holdings and transactions not reported previously on Forms 3, 4 or 5:

(i) All transactions during the most recent fiscal year that were exempt from section 16(b) of the Act, except:

(A) Exercises and conversions of derivative securities exempt under either Rule 16b–3 or Rule 16b–6(b) (these are required to be reported on Form 4);

(B) Transactions exempt from section 16(b) of the Act pursuant to Rule 16b–3(c), which shall be exempt from section 16(a) of the Act; and

(C) Transactions exempt from section 16(a) of the Act pursuant to another rule;

(ii) Transactions that constituted small acquisitions pursuant to Rule 16a–6(a);

(iii) all holdings and transactions that should have been reported during the most recent fiscal year, but were not; and

(iv) with respect to the first Form 5 requirement for a reporting person, all holdings and transactions that should have been reported in each of the issuer's last two fiscal years but were not, based on the reporting person's reasonable belief in good faith in the completeness and accuracy of the information.

(2) Notwithstanding the above, no Form 5 shall be required where all transactions otherwise required to be reported on the Form 5 have been reported before the due date of the Form 5.

Note: Persons no longer subject to Section 16 of the Act, but who were subject to the Section at any time during the issuer's fiscal year, must file a Form 5 unless paragraph (f)(2) is satisfied. See also Rule 16a–2(b) regarding the reporting obligations of persons ceasing to be officers or directors.

(g)(1) A Form 4 shall be filed to report all transactions not exempt from section 16(b) of the Act and all exercises and conversions of derivative securities, regardless of whether exempt from section 16(b) of the Act. . . .

(3) Transactions that are exempted by operation of any rule pursuant to Section 16(b) of the Act, other than exercises and conversions of derivative securities exempted pursuant to Rule 16b–6(b), shall be reported on either Form 5, or, at the option of the reporting person, Form 4, but in no event later than the due date of the Form 5 with respect to the fiscal year in which the transaction occurred. . . .

Rule 16a–4.   Derivative Securities

(a) For purposes of Section 16 of the Act, both derivative securities and the underlying securities to which they relate shall be deemed to be the same class of equity securities, *except that* the acquisition or disposition of any derivative security shall be separately reported. . . .

Rule 16a–6.   Small Acquisitions

(a) Any acquisition of an equity security not exceeding $10,000 in market value, or of the right to acquire such securities, shall be reported on Form 5, subject to the following conditions:

(1) Such acquisition, when aggregated with other acquisitions of securities of the same class (including securities underlying derivative securities, but excluding acquisitions exempted by rule from section 16(b) or previously reported on Form 4 or Form 5) within the prior six months, does not exceed a total of $10,000 in market value; and

(2) The person making the acquisition does not within six months thereafter make any disposition, other than by a transaction exempt from section 16(b) of the Act.

(b) Should an acquisition no longer qualify for the reporting deferral in paragraph (a) of this section, all such acquisitions that have not yet been reported shall be reported on a Form 4 within ten days after the close of the calendar month in which the conditions of paragraph (a) are no longer met. . . .

Rule 16a–8. Trusts

(a) *Persons Subject to Section 16.*

(1) *Trusts.* A trust shall be subject to section 16 of the Act with respect to securities of the issuer if the trust is a beneficial owner, pursuant to Rule 16a–1(a)(1), of more than ten percent of any class of equity securities of the issuer registered pursuant to section 12 of the Act ("ten percent beneficial owner").

(2) *Trustees, Beneficiaries, and Settlors.* In determining whether a trustee, beneficiary, or settlor is a ten percent beneficial owner with respect to the issuer:

(i) such persons shall be deemed the beneficial owner of the issuer's securities held by the trust, to the extent specified by Rule 16a–1(a)(1); and

(ii) settlors shall be deemed the beneficial owner of the issuer's securities held by the trust where they have the power to revoke the trust without the consent of another person. . . .

Rule 16a–9. Stock Splits, Stock Dividends, and Pro Rata Rights

The following shall be exempt from Section 16 of the Act:

(a) The increase or decrease in the number of securities held as a result of a stock split or stock dividend applying equally to all securities of a class, including a stock dividend in which equity securities of a different issuer are distributed; and

(b) the acquisition of rights, such as shareholder or preemptive rights, pursuant to a pro rata grant to all holders of the same class of equity securities registered under Section 12 of the Act. . . .

Rule 16a–10. Exemptions Under Section 16(a)

Except as provided in Rule 16a–6, any transaction exempted from the requirements of Section 16(a) of the Act, insofar as it is otherwise subject to the provisions of Section 16(b), shall be likewise exempt from Section 16(b) of the Act.

Rule 16a–12 Domestic Relations Orders

The acquisition or disposition of equity securities pursuant to a domestic relations order, as defined in the Internal Revenue Code or Title I of the Employee Retirement Income Security Act, or the rules thereunder, shall be exempt from section 16 of the Act.

Rule 16a–13 Change in Form of Beneficial Ownership

A transaction, other than the exercise or conversion of a derivative security or deposit into or withdrawal from a voting trust, that effects only a change in the form of beneficial ownership without changing a person's pecuniary interest in the subject equity securities shall be exempt from section 16 of the Act.

EXEMPTION OF CERTAIN TRANSACTIONS FROM SECTION 16(b) ...

Rule 16b–3 Transactions Between an Issuer and Its Officers or Directors

(a) *General.* A transaction between the issuer (including an employee benefit plan sponsored by the issuer) and an officer or director of the issuer that involves issuer equity securities shall be exempt from section 16(b) of the Act if the transaction satisfies the applicable conditions set forth in this section.

(b) *Definitions.*

(1) A *Discretionary Transaction* shall mean a transaction pursuant to an employee benefit plan that:

(i) Is at the volition of a plan participant;

(ii) Is not made in connection with the participant's death, disability, retirement or termination of employment;

(iii) Is not required to be made available to a plan participant pursuant to a provision of the Internal Revenue Code; and

(iv) Results in either an intra-plan transfer involving an issuer equity securities fund, or a cash distribution funded by a volitional disposition of an issuer equity security.

(2) An *Excess Benefit Plan* shall mean an employee benefit plan that is operated in conjunction with a Qualified Plan, and provides only the benefits or contributions that would be provided under a Qualified Plan but for any benefit or contribution limitations set forth in the Internal Revenue Code of 1986, or any successor provisions thereof.

(3)(i) A *Non–Employee Director* shall mean a director who:

(A) Is not currently an officer (as defined in Rule 16a–1(f)) of the issuer or a parent or subsidiary of the issuer, or otherwise currently employed by the issuer or a parent or subsidiary of the issuer;

(B) Does not receive compensation, either directly or indirectly, from the issuer or a parent or subsidiary of the issuer, for services rendered as a consultant or in any capacity other than as a director, except for an amount that does not exceed the dollar amount for which disclosure would be required pursuant to Item 404(a) [under Regulation S–U];

(C) Does not possess an interest in any other transaction for which disclosure would be required pursuant to Item 404(a) [under Regulation S–K]; and

(D) Is not engaged in a business relationship for which disclosure would be required pursuant to Item 404(b)....

(4) A *Qualified Plan* shall mean an employee benefit plan that satisfies the coverage and participation requirements of sections 410 and 401(a)(26) of the Internal Revenue Code of 1986, or any successor provisions thereof.

(5) A *Stock Purchase Plan* shall mean an employee benefit plan that satisfies the coverage and participation requirements of sections 423(b)(3) and 423(b)(5), or section 410, of the Internal Revenue Code of 1986, or any successor provisions thereof.

(c) *Tax-conditioned plans.* Any transaction (other than a Discretionary Transaction) pursuant to a Qualified Plan, an Excess Benefit Plan, or a Stock Purchase Plan shall be exempt without condition.

(d) *Grants, awards and other acquisitions from the issuer.* Any transaction involving a grant, award or other acquisition from the issuer (other than a Discretionary Transaction) shall be exempt if:

(1) The transaction is approved by the board of directors of the issuer, or a committee of the board of directors that is composed solely of two or more Non–Employee Directors;

(2) The transaction is approved or ratified, in compliance with section 14 of the Act, by either: the affirmative votes of the holders of a majority of the securities of the issuer present, or represented, and entitled to vote at a meeting duly held in accordance with the applicable laws of the state or other jurisdiction in which the issuer is incorporated; or the written consent of the holders of a majority of the securities of the issuer entitled to vote; *provided that* such ratification occurs no later than the date of the next annual meeting of shareholders; or

(3) The issuer equity securities so acquired are held by the officer or director for a period of six months following the date of such acquisition, *provided that* this condition shall be satisfied with

respect to a derivative security if at least six months elapse from the date of acquisition of the derivative security to the date of disposition of the derivative security (other than upon exercise or conversion) or its underlying equity security.

(e) *Dispositions to the issuer.* Any transaction involving the disposition to the issuer of issuer equity securities (other than a Discretionary Transaction) shall be exempt, *provided that* the terms of such disposition are approved in advance in the manner prescribed by either paragraph (d)(1) or paragraph (d)(2) of this section.

(f) *Discretionary Transactions.* A Discretionary Transaction shall be exempt only if effected pursuant to an election made at least six months following the date of the most recent election, with respect to any plan of the issuer, that effected a Discretionary Transaction that was:

(1) An acquisition, if the transaction to be exempted would be a disposition; or

(2) A disposition, if the transaction to be exempted would be an acquisition.

Notes to Rule 16b–3:

Note (1): The exercise or conversion of a derivative security that does not satisfy the conditions of this section is eligible for exemption from section 16(b) of the Act to the extent that the conditions of Rule 16b–6(b) are satisfied.

Note (2): Section 16(a) reporting requirements applicable to transactions exempt pursuant to this section are set forth in Rule 16a–3(f) and (g) and Rule 16a–4.

Note (3): The approval conditions of paragraphs (d)(1), (d)(2) and (e) of this section require the approval of each specific transaction, and are not satisfied by approval of a plan in its entirety except for the approval of a plan pursuant to which the terms and conditions of each transaction are fixed in advance, such as a formula plan. Where the terms of a subsequent transaction (such as the exercise price of an option, or the provision of an exercise or tax withholding right) are provided for in a transaction as initially approved pursuant to paragraphs (d)(1), (d)(2) or (e), such subsequent transaction shall not require further specific approval.

Rule 16b–5.   Bona Fide Gifts and Inheritance

Both the acquisition and the disposition of equity securities shall be exempt from the operation of Section 16(b) of the Act if they are: (a) bona fide gifts; or (b) transfers of securities by will or the laws of descent and distribution.

Rule 16b–6.   Derivative Securities

(a) The establishment of or increase in a call equivalent position or liquidation of or decrease in a put equivalent position shall be deemed a purchase of the underlying security for purposes of Section 16(b) of the Act, and the establishment of or increase in a put equivalent position or liquidation of or decrease in a call equivalent position shall be deemed a sale of the underlying securities for purposes of Section 16(b) of the Act . . . .

(b) The closing of a derivative security position as a result of its exercise or conversion shall be exempt from the operation of Section 16(b) of the Act, and the acquisition of underlying securities at a fixed exercise price due to the exercise or conversion of a call equivalent position or the disposition of underlying securities at a fixed exercise price due to the exercise of a put equivalent position shall be exempt from the operation of Section 16(b) of the Act. . . .

(c) In determining the short-swing profit recoverable pursuant to Section 16(b) of the Act from transactions involving the purchase and sale or sale and purchase of derivative and other securities, the following rules apply:

(1) Short-swing profits in transactions involving the purchase and sale or sale and purchase of derivative securities that have identical characteristics (*e.g.,* purchases and sales of call options of the same strike price and expiration date, or purchases and sales of the same series of convertible debentures) shall be measured by the actual prices paid or received in the short-swing transactions.

(2) Short-swing profits in transactions involving the purchase and sale or sale and purchase of derivative securities having different characteristics but related to the same underlying security (*e.g.,* the purchase of a call option and the sale of a convertible debenture) or derivative securities and underlying securities shall not exceed the difference in price of the underlying security on the date of purchase or sale and the date of sale or purchase. . . .

Rule 16b–7.   Mergers, Reclassifications, and Consolidations

(a) The following transactions shall be exempt from the provisions of Section 16(b) of the Act:

(1) The acquisition of a security of a company, pursuant to a merger or consolidation, in exchange for a security of a company which, prior to the merger or consolidation, owned 85 percent or more of either

(i) the equity securities of all other companies involved in the merger or consolidation, or in the case of a consolidation, the resulting company; or

(ii) the combined assets of all the companies involved in the merger or consolidation, computed according to their book values prior to the merger or consolidation as determined by reference to their most recent available financial statements for a 12 month period prior to the merger or consolidation, or such shorter time as the company has been in existence.

(2) The disposition of a security, pursuant to a merger or consolidation, of a company which, prior to the merger or consolidation, owned 85 percent or more of either

(i) the equity securities of all other companies involved in the merger or consolidation or, in the case of a consolidation, the resulting company; or

(ii) the combined assets of all the companies undergoing merger or consolidation, computed according to their book values prior to the merger or consolidation as determined by reference to their most recent available financial statements for a 12 month period prior to the merger or consolidation.

(b) A merger within the meaning of this section shall include the sale or purchase of substantially all the assets of one company by another in exchange for equity securities which are then distributed to the security holders of the company that sold its assets.

(c) Notwithstanding the foregoing, if a person subject to Section 16 of the Act makes any non-exempt purchase of a security in any company involved in the merger or consolidation and any non-exempt sale of a security in any company involved in the merger or consolidation within any period of less than six months during which the merger or consolidation took place, the exemption provided by this Rule shall be unavailable to the extent of such purchase and sale.

FORM 3

UNITED STATES SECURITIES AND EXCHANGE COMMISSION
Washington, D.C. 20549

FORM 3
INITIAL STATEMENT OF BENEFICIAL OWNERSHIP OF SECURITIES . . .

GENERAL INSTRUCTIONS

1. Who Must File

(a) This Form must be filed by the following persons ("reporting person"):

(i) any director or officer of an issuer with a class of equity securities registered pursuant to Section 12 of the Securities Exchange Act of 1934 ("Exchange Act"); (*Note:* Title is not determinative for purposes of determining "officer" status. See Rule 16a–1(f) for the definition of "officer");

(ii) any beneficial owner of greater than 10% of a class of equity securities registered under Section 12 of the Exchange Act, as determined by voting or investment control over the securities pursuant to Rule 16a–1(a)(1) ("ten percent holder"); ...

(v) any trust, trustee, beneficiary or settlor required to report pursuant to Rule 16a–8. ...

(c) If a person described above does not beneficially own any securities required to be reported (*see* Rule 16a–1 and Instruction 5), the person is required to file this Form and state that no securities are beneficially owned.

2. When Form Must Be Filed

... This Form must be filed within 10 days after the event by which the person becomes a reporting person (*i.e.*, officer, director, ten percent holder or other person). ...

3. Where Form Must Be Filed

(a) File three copies of this Form or any amendment, at least one of which is manually signed, with the Securities and Exchange Commission, 450 5th Street, N.W., Washington, D.C., 20549. Alternatively, this Form is permitted to be submitted to the Commission in electronic format at the option of the reporting person.

(b) At the time this Form or any amendment is filed with the Commission, file one copy with each Exchange on which any class of securities of the issuer is registered. ...

4. Class of Securities Reported

... Persons reporting pursuant to Section 16(a) of the Exchange Act shall include information as to their beneficial ownership of any class of equity securities of the issuer, even though one or more of such classes may not be registered pursuant to Section 12 of the Exchange Act. ...

5. Holdings Required to Be Reported

(a) *General Requirements*

Report holdings of each class of securities of the issuer beneficially owned as of the date of the event requiring the filing of this Form. See Instruction 4 as to securities required to be reported.

(b) *Beneficial Ownership Reported (Pecuniary Interest)*

(i) Although, for purposes of determining status as a ten percent holder, a person is deemed to beneficially own securities over which that person has voting or investment control (*see* Rule 16a–1(a)(1)), for reporting purposes, a person is deemed to be the beneficial owner of securities if that person has or shares the opportunity, directly or indirectly, to profit or share in any profit derived from a transaction in the securities ("pecuniary interest"). *See* Rule 16a–1(a)(2)....

(ii) Both direct and indirect beneficial ownership of securities shall be reported. Securities beneficially owned directly are those held in the reporting person's name or in the name of a bank, broker or nominee for the account of the reporting person. In addition, securities held as joint tenants, tenants in common, tenants by the entirety, or as community property are to be reported as held directly. If a person has a pecuniary interest, by reason of any contract, understanding or relationship (including a family relationship or arrangement), in securities held in the name of another person, that person is an indirect beneficial owner of those securities. *See* Rule 16a–1(a)(2)(ii) for certain indirect beneficial ownerships.

(iii) Report securities beneficially owned directly on a separate line from those beneficially owned indirectly. Report different forms of indirect ownership on separate lines. The nature of indirect ownership shall be stated as specifically as possible; for example, "By Self as Trustee for X," "By Spouse," "By X Trust," "By Y Corporation," etc.

(iv) In stating the amount of securities owned indirectly through a partnership, corporation, trust, or other entity, report the number of securities representing the reporting person's proportionate interest in securities beneficially owned by that entity....

FORM 3

U.S. SECURITIES AND EXCHANGE COMMISSION

Washington, D.C. 20549

INITIAL STATEMENT OF BENEFICIAL OWNERSHIP OF SECURITIES

Filed pursuant to Section 16(a) of the Securities Exchange Act of 1934, Section 17(a) of the Public Utility Holding Company Act of 1935 or Section 30(f) of the Investment Company Act of 1940

1. Name and Address of Reporting Person*	2. Date of Event Requiring Statement (Month/Day/Year)	4. Issuer Name and Ticker or Trading Symbol			
(Last) (First) (Middle)	3. IRS or Social Security Number of Reporting Person (Voluntary)	5. Relationship of Reporting Person to Issuer (Check all applicable) ___Director ___10% Owner ___Officer (give title below) ___Other (specify below)	6. If Amendment, Date of Original (Month/Day/Year)	7. Individual or Joint/Group Filing (Check applicable line) ___Form filed by One Reporting Person ___Form filed by More than One Reporting Person	
(Street)					
(City) (State) (Zip)					

Table 1 - Non-Derivative Securities Beneficially Owned

1. Title of Security	2. Amount of Securities Beneficially Owned Instr. 4	3. Ownership Form: Direct (D) or Indirect (I) (Instr. 5)	4. Nature of Indirect Beneficial Ownership (Instr. 5)

* If the Form is filed by more than one Reporting Person, see instruction 5(b)(v).

Reminder: Report on a separate line for each class of securities beneficially owned directly or indirectly.

(Print or Type Responses)

1321

FORM 3 (continued)   Table II—Derivative Securities Beneficially Owned (e.g., puts, calls, warrants, options, convertible securities)

1. Title of Derivative Security (Instr. 4)	2. Date Exercisable and Expiration Date (Month/Day/Year)		3. Title and Amount of Securities Underlying Derivative Security (Instr. 4)		4. Conversion or Exercise Price of Derivative Security	5. Ownership Form of Derivative Security: Direct (D) or Indirect (I) (Instr. 5)	6. Nature of Indirect Beneficial Ownership (Instr. 5)
	Date Exercisable	Expiration Date	Title	Amount or Number of Shares			

Explanation of Responses:

_____   _____
** Signature of Reporting Person   Date

** Intentional misstatements or omissions of facts constitute Federal Criminal Violations
See 18 U.S.C. 1001 and 15 U.S.C. 78ff(a).

Note: File three copies of this Form, one of which must be manually signed. If space provided is insufficient,
See Instruction 6 for procedure.

FORM 4

UNITED STATES SECURITIES AND EXCHANGE COMMISSION
Washington, D.C. 20549

FORM 4
STATEMENT OF CHANGES OF BENEFICIAL OWNERSHIP OF SECURITIES ...

GENERAL INSTRUCTIONS

1. When Form Must Be Filed

(a) This Form must be filed on or before the tenth day after the end of the month in which a change in beneficial ownership has occurred (the term "beneficial owner" is defined in Rule 16a–1(a)(2) and discussed in Instruction 4)....

(b) A reporting person no longer subject to Section 16 of the Securities Exchange Act of 1934 ("Exchange Act") must check the exit box appearing on this Form. However, Form 4 and Form 5 obligations may continue to be applicable. *See* Rules 16a–3(f) and 16a–2(b)....

2. Where Form Must Be Filed ...*

3. Class of Securities Reported ...

4. Transactions and Holdings Required to be Reported

(a) *General Requirements*

(i) Report, in accordance with Rule 16a–3(g), all transactions not exempt from section 16(b) of the Act and all exercises and conversions of derivative securities, regardless of whether exempt from section 16(b) of the Act, resulting in a change of beneficial ownership in the issuer's securities. Every transaction shall be reported even though acquisitions and dispositions during the month are equal. Report total beneficial ownership as of the end of the month for each class of securities in which a transaction was reported....

---

* Instructions 2, 3, and 4(b) parallel in-   (Footnote by ed.)
structions 3, 4, and 5(b) for Form 3, supra.

Form 4

SECURITIES EXCHANGE ACT OF 1934

FORM 4

☐ Check this box if no longer subject to Section 16.
Form 4 or Form 5 obligations may continue. See
Instructions 1(b).

U.S. SECURITIES AND EXCHANGE COMMISSION
Washington, D.C. 20549

STATEMENT OF CHANGES IN BENEFICIAL OWNERSHIP

Filed pursuant to Section 16(a) of the Securities Exchange Act of 1934, Section 17(a) of the Public Utility Holding Company Act of 1935 or Section 30(f) of the Investment Company Act of 1940

1. Name and Address of Reporting Person*	2. Issuer Name and Ticker or Trading Symbol		6. Relationship of Reporting Person to Issuer (Check all applicable)
(Last) (First) (Middle) (Street) (City) (State) (Zip)	3. IRS or Social Security Number of Reporting Person (Voluntary)	4. Statement for Month/Year 5. If Amendment, Date of Original (Month/Year)	___Director ___10% Owner ___Officer (give title below) ___Other (specify below) 7. Individual or Joint/Group Filing (Check applicable line) ___Form filed by One Reporting Person ___Form filed by More than One Reporting Person

Table 1—Non-Derivative Securities Acquired, Disposed of, or Beneficially Owned

1. Title of Security (Instr. 3)	2. Transaction Date (Month/Day/Year)	3. Transaction Code (Instr. 8)		4. Securities Acquired (A) or Disposed of (D) (Instr. 3, 4 and 5)			5. Amount of Securities Beneficially Owned at End of Month (Instr. 3 and 4)	6. Ownership Form: Direct (D) or Indirect (I) (Instr. 4)	7. Nature of Indirect Beneficial Ownership (Instr. 4)
		Code	V	Amount	(A) or (D)	Price			

* If the Form is filed by more than one Reporting Person see Instruction 4(b)(v).
Reminder: Report on a separate line for each class of securities beneficially owned directly or indirectly.
(Print or Type Responses)

1324

FORM 4 (continued)

Table II—Derivative Securities Acquired, Disposed of, or Beneficially Owned
(e.g., puts, calls, warrants, options, convertible securities)

1. Title of Derivative Security (Instr. 3)	2. Conversion or Exercise Price of Derivative Security	3. Transaction Date (Month/Day/Year)	4. Transaction Code (Instr. 8)		5. Number of Derivative Securities Acquired (A) or Disposed of (D) (Instr. 3, 4, and 5)		6. Date Exercisable and Expiration Date (Month/Day/Year)		7. Title and Amount of Underlying Securities (Instr. 3 and 4)		8. Price of Derivative Security (Instr. 5)	9. Number of Derivative Securities Beneficially Owned at End of Month (Instr. 4)	10. Ownership Form of Derivative Security: Direct (D) or Indirect (I) (Instr. 4)	11. Nature of Indirect Beneficial Ownership (Instr. 4)
			Code	V	(A)	(D)	Date Exercisable	Expiration Date	Title	Amount or Number of Shares				

Explanation of Responses:

_____   _____
** Signature of Reporting Person   Date

** Intentional misstatements or omissions of facts constitute Federal Criminal Violations.
See 18 U.S.C. 1001 and 15 U.S.C. 78ff(a).

Note: File three copies of this Form, one of which must be manually signed.
If space provided is insufficient, see Instruction 6 for procedure.

[The next page is 22,631.]

FORM 5

UNITED STATES SECURITIES AND EXCHANGE COMMISSION

Washington, D.C. 20549

FORM 5

ANNUAL STATEMENT OF BENEFICIAL OWNERSHIP OF SECURITIES ...

GENERAL INSTRUCTIONS

1. When Form Must Be Filed

(a) This Form must be filed on or before the 45th day after the end of the issuer's fiscal year in accordance with Rule 16a–3(f)....

(b) A reporting person no longer subject to Section 16 of the Securities Exchange Act of 1934 ("Exchange Act") must check the exit box appearing on this Form. Transactions and holdings previously reported are not required to be included on this Form. Form 4 or Form 5 obligations may continue to be applicable. *See* Rules 16a–3(f) and 16a–2(b)....

2. Where Form Must Be Filed ...*

3. Class of Securities Reported ...

4. Transactions and Holdings Required to Be Reported

(a) *General Requirements*

(i) Pursuant to Rule 16a–3(f), if not previously reported, the following transactions, and total beneficial ownership as of the end of the issuer's fiscal year (or the earlier date applicable to a person ceasing to be an insider during the fiscal year) for any class of securities for which a transaction is reported, shall be reported:

(A) any transaction during the issuer's fiscal year that was exempt by operation of any rule under Section 16(b);

(B) any small acquisition or series of acquisitions in a six month period during the issuer's fiscal year not exceeding $10,000 in market value (*see* Rule 16a–6); and

(C) any transactions or holdings that should have been reported during the issuer's fiscal year on a Form 3 or Form 4, but were not reported. The first Form 5 filing obligation shall include all holdings and transactions that should have been reported in each of the issuer's last two fiscal years but were not.....

---

* Instructions 2, 3, and 4(b) generally parallel the corresponding instructions 3, 4, and 5(b) for Form 3, supra. (Footnote by ed.)

FORM 5

☐ Check box if no longer subject to Section 16
Form 4 or Form 5 obligations may continue. *See*
Instruction 1(b).

☐ Form 3 Holdings Reported

☐ Form 4 Transactions Reported

U.S. SECURITIES AND EXCHANGE COMMISSION
Washington, D.C. 20549

ANNUAL STATEMENT OF CHANGES IN BENEFICIAL OWNERSHIP

Filed pursuant to Section 16(a) of the Securities Exchange Act of 1934, Section 17(a) of the Public Utility Holding Company Act of 1935 or Section 30(f)
of the Investment Company Act of 1940

1. Name and Address of Reporting Person*	2. Issuer Name and Ticker or Trading Symbol	5. Relationship of Reporting Person to Issuer (Check all applicable)
(Last) (First) (Middle)	3. IRS or Social Security Number of Reporting Person (Voluntary)	___ Director ___ 10% Owner ___ Officer (give title below) ___ Other (specify below)
(Street)	4. Statement for Month/Year	7. Individual or Joint/Group Filing (Check applicable line) ___ Form filed by One Reporting Person ___ Form filed by More than One Reporting Person
(City) (State) (Zip)	5. If Amendment, Date of Original (Month/Year)	

Table 1—Non-Derivative Securities Acquired, Disposed of, or Beneficially Owned

1. Title of Security (Instr. 3)	2. Transaction Date (Month/Day/Year)	3. Transaction Code (Instr. 8)	4. Securities Acquired (A) or Disposed of (D) (Instr. 3, 4 and 5)			5. Amount of Securities Beneficially Owned at End of Issuer's Fiscal Year (Instr. 3 and 4)	6. Ownership Form: Direct (D) or Indirect (I) (Instr. 4)	7. Nature of Indirect Beneficial Ownership (Instr. 4)
			Amount	(A) or (D)	Price			

* If the Form is filed by more than one Reporting Person, see Instruction 4(b)(v).

Reminder: Report on a separate line for each class of securities beneficially owned directly or indirectly.
(Print or Type Responses)

FORM 5 (continued)

Table II—Derivative Securities Acquired, Disposed of, or Beneficially Owned
(e.g., puts, calls, warrants, options, convertible securities)

1. Title of Derivative Security (Instr. 3)	2. Conversion or Exercise Price of Derivative Security	3. Transaction Date (Month/Day/Year)	4. Transaction Code (Instr. 8)	5. Number of Derivative Securities Acquired (A) or Disposed of (D) (Instr. 3, 4, and 5)		6. Date Exercisable and Expiration Date (Month/Day/Year)		7. Title and Amount of Underlying Securities (Instr. 3 and 4)		8. Price of Derivative Security (Instr. 5)	9. Number of Derivative Securities Beneficially Owned at End of Year (Instr. 4)	10. Ownership of Derivative Security: Direct (D) or Indirect (I) (Instr. 4)	11. Nature of Indirect Beneficial Ownership (Instr. 4)
				(A)	(D)	Date Exercisable	Expiration Date	Title	Amount or Number of Shares				

Explanation of Responses:

_____ _____
** Signature of Reporting Person Date

Note: File three copies of this Form, one of which must be manually signed.
If space provided is insufficient, see Instruction 6 for procedure.

RACKETEER INFLUENCED AND CORRUPT ORGANIZATIONS (RICO)

18 U.S.C. § 1961 et seq.

§ 1961. Definitions

As used in this chapter—

(1) "racketeering activity" means (A) any act or threat involving murder, kidnaping, gambling, arson, robbery, bribery, extortion, dealing in obscene matter, or dealing in narcotic or other dangerous drugs, which is chargeable under State law and punishable by imprisonment for more than one year; ... (D) any offense involving fraud connected with a case under title 11, fraud in the sale of securities, or the felonious manufacture, importation, receiving, concealment, buying, selling, or otherwise dealing in narcotic or other dangerous drugs, punishable under any law of the United States, or (E) any act which is indictable under the Currency and Foreign Transactions Reporting Act; ...

(4) "enterprise" includes any individual, partnership, corporation, association, or other legal entity, and any union or group of individuals associated in fact although not a legal entity;

(5) "pattern of racketeering activity" requires at least two acts of racketeering activity, one of which occurred after the effective date of this chapter and the last of which occurred within ten years (excluding any period of imprisonment) after the commission of a prior act of racketeering activity ....

§ 1962. Prohibited Activities

(a) It shall be unlawful for any person who has received any income derived, directly or indirectly, from a pattern of racketeering activity ... to use or invest, directly or indirectly, any part of such income, or the proceeds of such income, in [the] acquisition of any interest in, or the establishment or operation of, any enterprise which is engaged in, or the

* Omitted.

activities of which affect, interstate or foreign commerce. A purchase of securities on the open market for purposes of investment, and without the intention of controlling or participating in the control of the issuer, or of assisting another to do so, shall not be unlawful under this subsection if the securities of the issuer held by the purchaser, the members of his immediate family, and his or their accomplices in any pattern or racketeering activity ... do not amount in the aggregate to one percent of the outstanding securities of any one class, and do not confer, either in law or in fact, the power to elect one or more directors of the issuer.

(b) It shall be unlawful for any person through a pattern of racketeering activity ... to acquire or maintain, directly or indirectly, any interest in or control of any enterprise which is engaged in, or the activities of which affect, interstate or foreign commerce.

(c) It shall be unlawful for any person employed by or associated with any enterprise engaged in, or the activities of which affect, interstate or foreign commerce, to conduct or participate, directly or indirectly, in the conduct of such enterprise's affairs through a pattern of racketeering activity....

(d) It shall be unlawful for any person to conspire to violate any of the provisions of subsection (a), (b), or (c) of this section.

§ 1963. Criminal Penalties

(a) Whoever violates any provision of section 1962 of this chapter shall be fined under this title or imprisoned not more than 20 years (or for life if the violation is based on a racketeering activity for which the maximum penalty includes life imprisonment), or both, and shall forfeit to the United States, irrespective of any provision of State law—

(1) any interest the person has acquired or maintained in violation of section 1962;

(2) any—

(A) interest in;

(B) security of;

(C) claim against; or

(D) property or contractual right of any kind affording a source of influence over;

any enterprise which the person has established, operated, controlled, conducted, or participated in the conduct of in violation of section 1962; and

(3) any property constituting, or derived from, any proceeds which the person obtained, directly or indirectly, from racketeering activity ... in violation of section 1962....

§ 1964. Civil Remedies

(a) The district courts of the United States shall have jurisdiction to prevent and restrain violations of section 1962 of this chapter by issuing appropriate orders, including, but not limited to: ordering any person to divest himself of any interest, direct or indirect, in any enterprise; imposing reasonable restrictions on the future activities or investments of any person, including, but not limited to, prohibiting any person from engaging in the same type of endeavor as the enterprise engaged in, the activities of which affect interstate or foreign commerce; or ordering dissolution or reorganization of any enterprise, making due provision for the rights of innocent persons.

(b) The Attorney General may institute proceedings under this section. Pending final determination thereof, the court may at any time enter such restraining orders or prohibitions, or take such other actions, including the acceptance of satisfactory performance bonds, as it shall deem proper.

(c) Any person injured in his business or property by reason of a violation of section 1962 of this chapter may sue therefor in any appropriate United States district court and shall recover threefold the damages he sustains and the cost of the suit, including a reasonable attorney's fee except that no person may rely upon any conduct that would have been actionable as fraud in the purchase or sale of securities to establish a violation of section 1962. The exception contained in the preceding sentence does not apply to an action against any person that is criminally convicted in connection with the fraud, in which case the statute of limitations shall start to run on the date on which the conviction becomes final.

(d) A final judgment or decree rendered in favor of the United States in any criminal proceeding brought by the United States under this chapter shall estop the defendant from denying the essential allegations of the criminal offense in any subsequent civil proceeding brought by the United States....

HART–SCOTT–RODINO ANTITRUST IMPROVEMENTS ACT

15 U.S.C. § 18a, Clayton Act § 7A

§ 18a. Premerger Notification and Waiting Period

(a) Filing

Except as exempted pursuant to subsection (c) of this section, no person shall acquire, directly or indirectly, any voting securities or assets of any other person, unless both persons (or in the case of a tender offer, the acquiring person) file notification pursuant to rules under subsection (d)(1) of this section and the waiting period described in subsection (b)(1) of this section has expired, if—

> (1) the acquiring person, or the person whose voting securities or assets are being acquired, is engaged in commerce or in any activity affecting commerce;

> (2) (A) any voting securities or assets of a person engaged in manufacturing which has annual net sales or total assets of $10,-000,000 or more are being acquired by any person which has total assets or annual net sales of $100,000,000 or more;

> (B) any voting securities or assets of a person not engaged in manufacturing which has total assets of $10,000,000 or more are being acquired by any person which has total assets or annual net sales of $100,000,000 or more; or

> (C) any voting securities or assets of a person with annual net sales or total assets of $100,000,000 or more are being acquired by any person with total assets or annual net sales of $10,000,000 or more; and

> (3) as a result of such acquisition, the acquiring person would hold—

>> (A) 15 per centum or more of the voting securities or assets of the acquired person, or

>> (B) an aggregate total amount of the voting securities and assets of the acquired person in excess of $15,000,000.

In the case of a tender offer, the person whose voting securities are sought to be acquired by a person required to file notification under this subsection shall file notification pursuant to rules under subsection (d) of this section.

(b) Waiting period; publication; voting securities

(1) The waiting period required under subsection (a) of this section shall—

(A) begin on the date of the receipt by the Federal Trade Commission and the Assistant Attorney General in charge of the Antitrust Division of the Department of Justice (hereinafter referred to in this section as the "Assistant Attorney General") of—

(i) the completed notification required under subsection (a) of this section, or

(ii) if such notification is not completed, the notification to the extent completed and a statement of the reasons for such noncompliance,

from both persons, or, in the case of a tender offer, the acquiring person; and

(B) end on the thirtieth day after the date of such receipt (or in the case of a cash tender offer, the fifteenth day), or on such later date as may be set under subsection (e)(2) or (g)(2) of this section.

(2) The Federal Trade Commission and the Assistant Attorney General may, in individual cases, terminate the waiting period specified in paragraph (1) and allow any person to proceed with any acquisition subject to this section, and promptly shall cause to be published in the Federal Register a notice that neither intends to take any action within such period with respect to such acquisition.

(3) As used in this section—

(A) The term "voting securities" means any securities which at present or upon conversion entitle the owner or holder thereof to vote for the election of directors of the issuer or, with respect to unincorporated issuers, persons exercising similar functions.

(B) The amount or percentage of voting securities or assets of a person which are acquired or held by another person shall be determined by aggregating the amount or percentage of such voting securities or assets held or acquired by such other person and each affiliate thereof.

(c) Exempt transactions

The following classes of transactions are exempt from the requirements of this section—

(1) acquisitions of goods or realty transferred in the ordinary course of business;

(2) acquisitions of bonds, mortgages, deeds of trust, or other obligations which are not voting securities;

(3) acquisitions of voting securities of an issuer at least 50 per centum of the voting securities of which are owned by the acquiring person prior to such acquisition;

(4) transfers to or from a Federal agency or a State or political subdivision thereof;

(5) transactions specifically exempted from the antitrust laws by Federal statute;

(6) transactions specifically exempted from the antitrust laws by Federal statute if approved by a Federal agency, if copies of all information and documentary material filed with such agency are contemporaneously filed with the Federal Trade Commission and the Assistant Attorney General; ...

(9) acquisitions, solely for the purpose of investment, of voting securities, if, as a result of such acquisition, the securities acquired or held do not exceed 10 per centum of the outstanding voting securities of the issuer;

(10) acquisitions of voting securities, if, as a result of such acquisition, the voting securities acquired do not increase, directly or indirectly, the acquiring person's per centum share of outstanding voting securities of the issuer; ...

(12) such other acquisitions, transfers, or transactions, as may be exempted under subsection (d)(2)(B) of this section.

(d) Commission rules

The Federal Trade Commission, with the concurrence of the Assistant Attorney General ... consistent with the purposes of this section—

(1) shall require that the notification required under subsection (a) of this section be in such form and contain such documentary material and information relevant to a proposed acquisition as is necessary and appropriate to enable the Federal Trade Commission and the Assistant Attorney General to determine whether such acquisition may, if consummated, violate the antitrust laws; and

(2) may—

(A) define the terms used in this section;

(B) exempt, from the requirements of this section, classes of persons, acquisitions, transfers, or transactions which are not likely to violate the antitrust laws; and

(C) prescribe such other rules as may be necessary and appropriate to carry out the purposes of this section.

(e) Additional information; waiting period extensions

(1) The Federal Trade Commission or the Assistant Attorney General may, prior to the expiration of the 30-day waiting period (or in the

case of a cash tender offer, the 15-day waiting period) specified in subsection (b)(1) of this section, require the submission of additional information or documentary material relevant to the proposed acquisition, from a person required to file notification with respect to such acquisition under subsection (a) of this section prior to the expiration of the waiting period specified in subsection (b)(1) of this section, or from any officer, director, partner, agent, or employee of such person.

(2) The Federal Trade Commission or the Assistant Attorney General, in its or his discretion, may extend the 30-day waiting period (or in the case of a cash tender offer, the 15-day waiting period) specified in subsection (b)(1) of this section for an additional period of not more than 20 days (or in the case of a cash tender offer, 10 days) after the date on which the Federal Trade Commission or the Assistant Attorney General, as the case may be, receives from any person to whom a request is made under paragraph (1), or in the case of tender offers, the acquiring person, (A) all the information and documentary material required to be submitted pursuant to such a request, or (B) if such request is not fully complied with, the information and documentary material submitted and a statement of the reasons for such noncompliance. . . .

(g) Civil penalty; compliance; power of court

(1) Any person, or any officer, director, or partner thereof, who fails to comply with any provision of this section shall be liable to the United States for a civil penalty of not more than $10,000 for each day during which such person is in violation of this section. Such penalty may be recovered in a civil action brought by the United States. . . .

REGULATIONS UNDER THE HART–SCOTT–RODINO ANTITRUST IMPROVEMENTS ACT

16 C.F.R. § 800.1 et seq.

§ 801.1 Definitions

When used in the act and these rules . . .

(h) *Notification threshold.* The term "notification threshold" means:

(1) Fifteen percent of the outstanding voting securities of an issuer, or an aggregate total amount of voting securities and assets of the acquired person valued in excess of $15 million;

(2) Fifteen percent of the outstanding voting securities of an issuer, if valued in excess of $15 million;

(3) Twenty-five percent of the outstanding voting securities of an issuer; or

(4) Fifty percent of the outstanding voting securities of an issuer.

(i)(1) *Solely for the purpose of investment.* Voting securities are held or acquired "solely for the purpose of investment" if the person holding or acquiring such voting securities has no intention of participating in the formulation, determination, or direction of the basic business decisions of the issuer. . . .

§ 801.13 Voting Securities or Assets to Be Held as a Result of Acquisition

(a) *Voting securities.* (1) Subject to the provisions of § 801.15, and paragraph (a)(3) of this section, all voting securities of the issuer which will be held by the acquiring person after the consummation of an acquisition shall be deemed voting securities held as a result of the acquisition. The value of such voting securities shall be the sum of the value of the voting securities to be acquired . . . and the value of the voting securities held by the acquiring person prior to the acquisition, determined in accordance with paragraph (a)(2) of this section. . . .

Examples: 1. Assume that acquiring person "A" holds $19 million of the voting securities of X, and is to acquire another $1 million of the same voting securities. Since under paragraph (a) of this rule all voting securities "A" will hold after the acquisition are held "as a result of" the acquisition, "A" will hold $20 million of the voting securities of X as a result of the acquisition. "A" must therefore observe the requirements of the act before making the acquisition, unless the present acquisition is exempt under section 7A(c), § 802.21 or any other rule....

(3) Voting securities held by the acquiring person prior to an acquisition shall not be deemed voting securities held as a result of that subsequent acquisition if:

(i) The acquiring person is, in the subsequent acquisition, acquiring only assets; and

(ii) The acquisition of the previously acquired voting securities was subject to the filing and waiting requirements of the act (and such requirements were observed) or was exempt pursuant to § 802.21....

§ 802.20   Minimum Dollar Value

An acquisition which would be subject to the requirements of the act and which satisfies section 7A(a)(3)(A), but which does not satisfy section 7A(a)(3)(B), shall be exempt from the requirements of the act if as a result of the acquisition the acquiring person would not hold:

(a) Assets of the acquired person valued at more than $15 million; or

(b) Voting securities which confer control of an issuer which, together with all entities which it controls, has annual net sales or total assets of $25 million or more.

§ 802.21   Acquisitions of Voting Securities Not Meeting or Exceeding Greater Notification Threshold

An acquisition of voting securities shall be exempt from the requirements of the act if:

(a) The acquiring person and all other persons required by the act and these rules to file notification filed notification with respect to an earlier acquisition of voting securities of the same issuer;

(b) The waiting period with respect to the earlier acquisition has expired, or been terminated pursuant to § 803.11, and the acquisition will be consummated within 5 years of such expiration or termination; and

(c) The acquisition will not increase the holdings of the acquiring person to meet or exceed a notification threshold greater than the greatest notification threshold met or exceeded in the earlier acquisition.

Examples: 1.   Corporation A acquires 15 percent of the voting securities of corporation B and both "A" and "B" file notification as required.   Within five years of the expiration of the original waiting period, "A" acquires additional voting securities of B but not in an amount sufficient to meet or exceed 25 percent of the voting securities of B.   No additional notification is required.

2.   In example 1, "A" continues to acquire B's securities.   Before "A's" holdings meet or exceed 25 percent of B's outstanding voting securities, "A" and "B" must file notification and wait the prescribed period, regardless of whether the acquisition occurs within five years after the expiration of the earlier waiting period.

3.   In example 2, suppose that "A" and "B" file notification at the 25 percent level and that, within 5 years after expiration of the waiting period, "A" continues to acquire voting securities of B.   No further notification is required until "A" plans to make the acquisition that will give it 50 percent ownership of B.   (Once "A" holds 50 percent, further acquisitions of voting securities are exempt under section 7A(c)(3).)   ...

†